CONTENTS

III. SEXUALITIES   145

Sexual Relations, Intimacy, Power

Sexuality and Identity

IV. IDENTITIES   233

V. FAMILIES   269

Motherhood, Fatherhood

*Denotes a reading new to this edition

PREFACE

O ver the past 40 years, texts and readers intended for use in women's studies and gender studies courses have changed and developed in important ways. In the 1970s and into the early 1980s, many courses and texts focused almost exclusively on women as a relatively undifferentiated category. Two developments have broadened the study of women. First, in response to criticisms by women of color and by lesbians that heterosexual, white, middle-class feminists had tended to "falsely universalize" their own experiences and issues, courses and texts on gender began in the 1980s to systematically incorporate race and class diversity. And simultaneously, as a result of feminist scholars' insistence that gender be studied as a relational construct, more concrete studies of men and masculinity began to emerge in the 1980s.

This book reflects this belief that race, class, and sexual diversity among women and men should be central to the study of gender. But this collection adds an important new dimension that will broaden the frame of gender studies. By including some articles that are based on research in nations connected to the United States through globalization, tourism, and labor migrations, we hope that *Gender Through the Prism of Difference* will contribute to a transcendence of the often myopic, U.S.-based, and Eurocentric focus in the study of sex and gender. The inclusion of these perspectives is not simply useful for illuminating our own cultural blind spots: It also begins to demonstrate how, early in the twenty-first century, gender relations are increasingly centrally implicated in current processes of globalization.

Because the amount of high-quality research on gender has expanded so dramatically in the past decade, the most difficult task in assembling this collection was deciding *what* to include. The fourth edition, while retaining the structure of the previous edition, is different and improved. This edition includes 26 new articles, and discusses material on gender issues relevant to the college-age generation, including gender and popular culture. We have also included articles on Hurricane Katrina, the Iraq War, and the 2008 election, the intersection of gender and immigration, and terrorism.

We thank faculty and staff colleagues in the Department of Sociology and the Gender Studies program at the University of Southern California and in the Department of Sociology at Michigan State University for their generous support and assistance. Other people contributed their labor to the development of this book. We are grateful to our research assistants, particularly Paula Miller of Michigan State University, who contributed invaluable groundwork.

We acknowledge the helpful criticism and suggestions made by the following reviewers: Arlene Avakian, University of Massachusetts-Amherst; Shannon K. Carter, University of Central Florida; Susannah Chewning, Union County College; Rachel Joffe Falmagne, Clark University; Janice McCabe, Florida State University; Esther Rothblum, San Diego State

University; and Elena Windsong, University of New Mexico. We would also like to thank our editor at Oxford University Press, Sherith Pankratz, who has been encouraging, helpful, and patient and Marianne Paul and Jaimee Biggins. We also thank Rich Beck and Taylor Pilkington for their editorial assistance as the book moved into production.

Finally, we thank our families for their love and support as we worked on this book. Alan Zinn, Prentice Zinn, Gabrielle Cobbs, and Edan Zinn provide inspiration through their work for progressive social change. Miles Hondagneu-Messner and Sasha Hondagneu-Messner continually challenge the neatness of Mike and Pierrette's image of social life. We do hope, though, that the kind of work that is collected in this book will eventually help them and their generation make sense of the world and move that world into more peaceful, humane, and just directions.

Introduction

Sex and Gender Through the Prism of Difference

"Men can't cry." "Women are victims of patriarchal oppression." "After divorces, single mothers are downwardly mobile, often moving into poverty." "Men don't do their share of housework and child care." "Professional women face barriers such as sexual harassment and a 'glass ceiling' that prevent them from competing equally with men for high-status positions and high salaries." "Heterosexual intercourse is an expression of men's power over women." Sometimes, the students in our sociology and gender studies courses balk at these kinds of generalizations. And they are right to do so. After all, some men are more emotionally expressive than some women, some women have more power and success than some men, some men do their share—or more—of housework and child care, and some women experience sex with men as both pleasurable and empowering. Indeed, contemporary gender relations are complex and changing in various directions, and as such, we need to be wary of simplistic, if handy, slogans that seem to sum up the essence of relations between women and men.

On the other hand, we think it is a tremendous mistake to conclude that "all individuals are totally unique and different," and that therefore all generalizations about social groups are impossible or inherently oppressive. In fact, we are convinced that it is this very complexity, this multifaceted nature of contemporary gender relations, that fairly begs for a sociological analysis of gender. In the title of this book, we use the image of "the prism of difference" to illustrate our approach to developing this sociological perspective on contemporary gender relations. The *American Heritage Dictionary* defines "prism," in part, as "a homogeneous transparent solid, usually with triangular bases and rectangular sides, used to produce or analyze a continuous spectrum." Imagine a ray of light—which to the naked eye appears to be only one color—refracted through a prism onto a white wall. To the eye, the result is not an infinite, disorganized scatter of individual colors. Rather, the refracted light displays an order, a structure of relationships among the different colors—a rainbow. Similarly, we propose to use the "prism of difference" in this book to analyze a continuous spectrum of people, in order to show how gender is organized and experienced differently when refracted through the prism of sexual, racial/ethnic, social class, physical abilities, age, and national citizenship differences.

1

EARLY WOMEN'S STUDIES: CATEGORICAL VIEWS OF "WOMEN" AND "MEN"

Taken together, the articles in this book make the case that it is possible to make good generalizations about women and men. But these generalizations should be drawn carefully, by always asking the questions *"which* women?" and *"which* men?" Scholars of sex and gender have not always done this. In the 1960s and 1970s, women's studies focused on the differences *between* women and men rather than *among* women and men. The very concept of gender, women's studies scholars demonstrated, is based on socially defined difference between women and men. From the macro level of social institutions such as the economy, politics, and religion, to the micro level of interpersonal relations, distinctions between women and men structure social relations. Making men and women *different* from one another is the essence of gender. It is also the basis of men's power and domination. Understanding this was profoundly illuminating. Knowing that difference produced domination enabled women to name, analyze, and set about changing their victimization.

In the 1970s, riding the wave of a resurgent feminist movement, colleges and universities began to develop women's studies courses that aimed first and foremost to make women's lives visible. The texts that were developed for these courses tended to stress the things that women shared under patriarchy—having the responsibility for housework and child care, the experience or fear of men's sexual violence, a lack of formal or informal access to education, and exclusion from high-status professional and managerial jobs, political office, and religious leadership positions (Brownmiller, 1975; Kanter, 1977).

The study of women in society offered new ways of seeing the world. But the 1970s approach was limited in several ways. Thinking of gender primarily in terms of differences *between* women and men led scholars to overgeneralize about both. The concept of patriarchy led to a dualistic perspective of male privilege and female subordination. Women and men were cast as opposites. Each was treated as a homogeneous category with common characteristics and experiences. This approach *essentialized* women and men. Essentialism, simply put, is the notion that women's and men's attributes and indeed women and men themselves are categorically different. From this perspective, male control and coercion of women produced conflict between the sexes. The feminist insight originally introduced by Simone De Beauvoir in 1953—that women, as a group, had been socially defined as the "other" and that men had constructed themselves as the subjects of history, while constructing women as their objects—fueled an energizing sense of togetherness among many women. As college students read books such as *Sisterhood Is Powerful* (Morgan, 1970), many of them joined organizations that fought—with some success—for equality and justice for women.

THE VOICES OF "OTHER" WOMEN

Although this view of women as an oppressed "other" was empowering for certain groups of women, some women began to claim that the feminist view of universal sisterhood ignored and marginalized their major concerns. It soon became apparent that treating women as a group united in its victimization by patriarchy was biased by too narrow a focus on the experiences and perspectives of women from more privileged social groups. "Gender" was treated as a generic category, uncritically applied to women. Ironically, this analysis, which was meant to unify women, instead produced divisions between and among them. The concerns projected as "universal" were removed from the realities of many women's lives. For example, it became a matter of faith in second-wave feminism that women's liberation would be accomplished by breaking down the "gendered public-domestic split." Indeed, the feminist call for women to move out of the kitchen and into the workplace resonated in the experiences of many of the college-educated white women who were inspired by Betty Friedan's 1963 book, *The Feminine Mystique.* But the idea that women's movement into workplaces was itself empowering or liberating seemed absurd or irrelevant to many working-class women and women of color. They were already working for wages, as had many of their mothers and grandmothers, and did not consider access to jobs and public life "liberating." For many of these women, liberation had more to do with organizing in communities and workplaces—often alongside men—for better schools, better pay, decent benefits, and other policies to benefit their neighborhoods, jobs, and families. The feminism of the 1970s did not seem to address these issues.

As more and more women analyzed their own experiences, they began to address the power relations that created differences among women and the part that privileged women played in the oppression of others. For many women of color, working-class women, lesbians, and women in contexts outside the United States (especially women in non-Western societies), the focus on male domination was a distraction from other oppressions. Their lived experiences could support neither a unitary theory of gender nor an ideology of universal sisterhood. As a result, finding common ground in a universal female victimization was never a priority for many groups of women.

Challenges to gender stereotypes soon emerged. Women of varied races, classes, national origins, and sexualities insisted that the concept of gender be broadened to take their differences into account (Baca Zinn et al., 1986; Hartmann, 1976; Rich, 1980; Smith, 1977). Many women began to argue that their lives were affected by their location in a number of different hierarchies: as African Americans, Latinas, Native Americans, or Asian Americans in the race hierarchy; as young or old in the age hierarchy; as heterosexual, lesbian, or bisexual in the sexual orientation hierarchy; and as women outside the Western industrialized nations, in subordinated geopolitical contexts. These arguments made it clear that women were not victimized by gender alone but by the historical and systematic denial of rights and privileges based on other differences as well.

MEN AS GENDERED BEINGS

As the voices of "other" women in the mid- to late 1970s began to challenge and expand the parameters of women's studies, a new area of scholarly inquiry was beginning to stir—a critical examination of men and masculinity. To be sure, in those early years of gender studies, the major task was to conduct studies and develop courses about the lives of women in order to begin to correct centuries of scholarship that rendered invisible women's lives, problems, and accomplishments. But the core idea of feminism—that "femininity" and women's subordination is a social construction—logically led to an examination of the social construction of "masculinity" and men's power. Many of the first scholars to take on this task were psychologists who were concerned with looking at the social construction of "the male sex role" (e.g., Pleck,

1981). By the late 1980s, there was a growing interdisciplinary collection of studies of men and masculinity, much of it by social scientists (Brod, 1987; Kaufman, 1987; Kimmel, 1987; Kimmel & Messner, 1989).

Reflecting developments in women's studies, the scholarship on men's lives tended to develop three themes: First, what we think of as "masculinity" is not a fixed, biological essence of men, but rather is a social construction that shifts and changes over time as well as between and among various national and cultural contexts. Second, power is central to understanding gender as a relational construct, and the dominant definition of masculinity is largely about expressing difference from—and superiority over—anything considered "feminine." And third, there is no singular "male sex role." Rather, at any given time there are various masculinities. R. W. Connell (1987, 1995, 2002) has been among the most articulate advocates of this perspective. Connell argues that hegemonic masculinity (the dominant form of masculinity at any given moment) is constructed in relation to femininities *as well as* in relation to various subordinated or marginalized masculinities. For example, in the United States, various racialized masculinities (e.g., as represented by African American men, Latino immigrant men, etc.) have been central to the construction of hegemonic (white middle-class) masculinity. This "othering" of racialized masculinities helps to shore up the privileges that have been historically connected to hegemonic masculinity. When viewed this way, we can better understand hegemonic masculinity as part of a system that includes gender as well as racial, class, sexual, and other relations of power.

The new literature on men and masculinities also begins to move us beyond the simplistic, falsely categorical, and pessimistic view of men simply as a privileged sex class. When race, social class, sexual orientation, physical abilities, immigrant, or national status are taken into account, we can see that in some circumstances, "male privilege" is partly—sometimes substantially—muted (Kimmel & Messner, 2010). Although it is unlikely that we will soon see a "men's movement" that aims to undermine the power and privileges that are connected with hegemonic masculinity, when we begin to look at "masculinities" through the prism of difference, we can begin to see similarities and possible points of coalition between and among certain groups of women and men (Messner, 1998). Certain kinds of changes in gender relations— for instance, a national family leave policy for working parents—might serve as a means of uniting particular groups of women and men.

GENDER IN GLOBAL CONTEXTS

It is an increasingly accepted truism that late twentieth-century increases in transnational trade, international migration, and global systems of production and communication have diminished both the power of nation-states and the significance of national borders. A much more ignored issue is the extent to which gender relations—in the United States and elsewhere in the world— are increasingly linked to patterns of global economic restructuring. Decisions made in corporate headquarters located in Los Angeles, Tokyo, or London may have immediate repercussions on how women and men thousands of miles away organize their work, community, and family lives (Sassen, 1991). It is no longer possible to study gender relations without giving attention to global processes and inequalities. Scholarship on women in third world contexts has moved from liberal concerns for the impact of development policies on women (Boserup, 1970), to more critical perspectives that acknowledge how international labor and capital mobility are transforming gender and family relations (Hondagneu-Sotelo & Avila, this volume), to theoretical debates on third world feminisms (Mohanty, 1991). The transformation of international relations from a

1990s "post–cold war" environment to an expansion of militarism and warfare in recent years has realigned international gender relations in key ways that call for new examinations of gender, violence, militarism, and culture (Enloe, 1993, 2000; Okin, 1999). The now extended U.S. military presence in Iraq has brought with it increasing deployments of female troops, and with that, new social constructions of racialized gender and sexuality (Nagel & Feitz, this volume).

Around the world, women's paid and unpaid labor is key to global development strategies. Yet it would be a mistake to conclude that gender is molded from the "top down." What happens on a daily basis in families and workplaces simultaneously constitutes and is constrained by structural transnational institutions. For instance, in the second half of the twentieth century young, single women, many of them from poor rural areas, were (and continue to be) recruited for work in export assembly plants along the U.S.-Mexico border, in East and Southeast Asia, in Silicon Valley, in the Caribbean, and in Central America. While the profitability of these multinational factories depends, in part, on management's ability to manipulate the young women's ideologies of gender, the women do not respond passively or uniformly, but actively resist, challenge, and accommodate. At the same time, the global dispersion of the assembly line has concentrated corporate facilities in many U.S. cities, making available myriad managerial, administrative, and clerical jobs for college educated women. Women's paid labor is used at various points along this international system of production. Not only employment but also consumption embodies global interdependencies. There is a high probability that the clothing you are wearing and the computer you use originated in multinational corporate headquarters and in assembly plants scattered around third world nations. And if these items were actually manufactured in the United States, they were probably assembled by Latin American and Asian-born women.

Worldwide, international labor migration and refugee movements are creating new types of multiracial societies. While these developments are often discussed and analyzed with respect to racial differences, gender typically remains absent. As several commentators have noted, the white feminist movement in the United States has not addressed issues of immigration and nationality. Gender, however, has been fundamental in shaping immigration policies (Chang, 1994; Hondagneu-Sotelo, 1994). Direct labor recruitment programs generally solicit either male or female labor (e.g., Filipina nurses and Mexican male farm workers), national disenfranchisement has particular repercussions for women and men, and current immigrant laws are based on very gendered notions of what constitutes "family unification." As Chandra Mohanty suggests, "analytically these issues are the contemporary metropolitan counterpart of women's struggles against colonial occupation in the geographical third world" (1991:23). Moreover, immigrant and refugee women's daily lives often challenge familiar feminist paradigms. The occupations in which immigrant and refugee women concentrate—paid domestic work, informal sector street vending, assembly or industrial piecework performed in the home—often blur the ideological distinction between work and family and between public and private spheres (Hondagneu-Sotelo, 2001; Parrenas, 2001). And as Gloria Gonzalez-Lopez (this volume) shows, immigrant women creatively respond to changes in work and family brought about through migration, innovating changes in what were once thought to be stable, fixed sexuality practices and mores.

FROM PATCHWORK QUILT TO PRISM

All of these developments—the voices of "other" women, the study of men and masculinities, and the examination of gender in transnational contexts—have helped redefine the study of gender. By working to develop knowledge that is inclusive of the experiences of all groups, new insights about gender have begun to emerge. Examining gender in the context of other differences makes it clear that nobody experiences themselves as solely gendered. Instead, gender is configured through cross-cutting forms of difference that carry deep social and economic consequences.

By the mid-1980s, thinking about gender had entered a new stage, which was more carefully grounded in the experiences of diverse groups of women and men. This perspective is a general way of looking at women and men and understanding their relationships to the structure of society. Gender is no longer viewed simply as a matter of two opposite categories of people, males and females, but a range of social relations among differently situated people. Because centering on difference is a radical challenge to the conventional gender framework, it raises several concerns. If we think of all the systems that converge to simultaneously influence the lives of women and men, we can imagine an infinite number of effects these interconnected systems have on different women and men. Does the recognition that gender can be understood only contextually (meaning that there is no singular "gender" per se) make women's studies and men's studies newly vulnerable to critics in the academy? Does the immersion in difference throw us into a whirlwind of "spiraling diversity" (Hewitt, 1992:316) whereby multiple identities and locations shatter the categories "women" and "men"?

Throughout the book, we take a position directly opposed to an empty pluralism. Although the categories "woman" and "man" have multiple meanings, this does not reduce gender to a "postmodern kaleidoscope of lifestyles. Rather, it points to the *relational* character of gender" (Connell, 1992:736). Not only are masculinity and femininity relational, but different *masculinities* and *femininities* are interconnected through other social structures such as race, class, and nation. The concept of relationality suggests that "the lives of different groups are interconnected even without face-to-face relations (Glenn, 2002:14). The meaning of "woman" is defined by the existence of women of different races and classes. Being a white woman in the United States is meaningful only insofar as it is set apart from and in contradistinction to women of color.

Just as masculinity and femininity each depend on the definition of the other to produce domination, differences *among* women and *among* men are also created in the context of structured relations between dominant and subordinate groups. Situating women's lives in the context of other forms of inequality makes it clear that the privileges of some groups are directly tied to the oppression of others. "Powerful groups gain and maintain power by exploiting the labor and lives of others" (Weber, 2010:6). They may even use their race and class advantage to minimize some of the consequences of patriarchy and/or to oppose other women. Similarly, one can become a man in opposition to other men. For example, "the relation between heterosexual and homosexual men is central, carrying heavy symbolic freight. To many people, homosexuality is the *negation* of masculinity. . . . Given that assumption, antagonism toward homosexual men may be used to define masculinity" (Connell, 1992:736).

In the past two decades, viewing gender through the prism of difference has profoundly reoriented the field (Acker, 1999; Acker, 2006; Andersen, 2005; Glenn, 1999, 2002; Messner, 1996; West & Fenstermaker, 1995). Yet analyzing the multiple constructions of gender does not just mean studying groups of women and groups of men as different. It is clearly time to go beyond what we call the "patchwork quilt" phase in the study of women and men—that is, the phase in which we have acknowledged the importance of examining differences within constructions of gender, but do so largely by collecting together a study here on African American women, a study there on gay men, a study on working-class Chicanas, and so on. This patchwork quilt approach too often amounts to no more than "adding difference and stirring." The result may be a lovely mosaic, but like a patchwork quilt, it still tends to overemphasize boundaries rather than to highlight bridges of interdependency. In addition, this approach too often does not explore the ways that social constructions of femininities and masculinities are based on and reproduce relations of power. In short, we think that the substantial quantity of research that has now been done on various groups and subgroups needs to be analyzed within a framework that emphasizes differences and inequalities not as discrete areas of separation, but as interrelated bands of color that together make up a spectrum.

A recent spate of sophisticated sociological theorizing along these lines has introduced some useful ways to think about difference in relational terms. Patricia Hill Collins (1990, 1998, 2004) has suggested that we think of race, class, and gender as a socially structured "matrix of domination"; Raewyn Connell has pressed us to think of multiple differences not in simple additive ways, but rather as they "abrade, inflame, amplify, twist, negate, dampen, and complicate each other" (Kessler et al., 1985). Similarly, Maxine Baca Zinn and Bonnie Thornton Dill (in this volume) have suggested that we consider a body of theory and practice they call "multiracial feminism" as a means of coming to grips with the relations between various systems of inequality. Scholarship linking the interactive effects of race, class, gender, and sexuality has emerged into a new feminist paradigm (Andersen, 2005:443). Today, "intersectional" frameworks foster a more complete view of the different experiences of women and men across and within varied groups.

These are the kinds of concerns that we had in mind in putting together this collection. We sought individual articles that explored intersections or axes in the matrix of domination by comparing different groups. We brought together articles that explored the lives of people who experience the daily challenges of multiple marginality (e.g., black lesbians, immigrant women, etc.) or the often paradoxical realities of those who may identify simultaneously with a socially marginalized or subordinated identity (e.g., gay, poor, physically disabled, Latino, etc.) along with a socially dominant identity (e.g., man, white, professional class, etc.). When we could not find articles that directly compared or juxtaposed categories or groups, we attempted to juxtapose two or three articles that, together, explored differences and similarities between groups. To this end, we added a fifth dimension to the now commonly accepted "race/class/gender/sexuality" matrix: national origin. Reflecting a tendency in U.S. sociology in general, courses on sex and gender have been far too U.S.-focused and Eurocentric. Focusing on the construction of gender in industrializing societies or the shifting relations of gender among transnational immigrant groups challenges and broadens our otherwise narrow assumptions about the constraints and possibilities facing contemporary women and men. But it is not enough to remain within the patchwork quilt framework, to simply focus on women and men in other nations as though they were somehow separate from processes occurring in the United States. Again, the metaphor of the prism better illustrates the dual challenges we face in integrating analyses of national inequalities. A central challenge facing scholars today is to understand how constructions of masculinities and feminities move across national borders. In this regard, we need to acknowledge two distinct but interrelated outcomes. In the process of moving across national boundaries—through media images, immigration, or global systems of production—gender inequalities are reconstructed and take new shape. At the same time, global movements of gender transform the gendered institutions with which they come into contact. While it may seem ironic to focus on the nation in this era that some commentators have termed "postnational," we believe that we need to focus more on national difference precisely because of the increasing number and intensity of global connections and interdependencies.

The fourth edition of this book continues with all of these themes but adds attention to three arenas of gender to which previous editions of the book did not give sufficient attention: differences of generation, the images of gender promulgated by mass media and popular culture and new challenges to binary thinking. In recent years, pundits have employed the term *Generation X* to refer to the vast and diverse group of the "twenty-something" (and by now "thirty-something") population. While celebrated by some as a new market for new products and condemned as spoiled slackers by others, Generation X is, in fact, more heterogeneous than the pundits would allow. In addition, boys, girls, and young women and men tend to relate to gender and sexuality issues in somewhat different ways than did the older generation of writers and activists who made up the "second wave" of feminism. "Third-wave" feminism is a generational sensibility that is beginning to have an impact on college campuses and in popular culture in recent years (Snyder, 2008). The articles we have assembled on youth culture and generational differences are sprinkled throughout the various sections of this volume. The gendered character of these generational communities is, in many instances, defined by differences of race, class, sexuality, and nation. Yet these constituencies are also deliberately constructed by young people in ways that underline their distinctiveness, and sometimes oppositional stances, to other groups and older generations. The structuring of youth culture—and the agency of youth groups—can be seen in various contexts. The fourth edition also includes an expanded focus on popular culture and ideology. In recent years, the flourishing scholarship in cultural studies has shown that our experiences of gender are strongly shaped by mass media, advertisements, consumption, and leisure activities. Music, sports, and the marketing of difference through consumer goods, to cite a few examples, convey particular embodiments of gender. And yet, as much of the new scholarship on consumption suggests, people situated differently in a matrix of difference and inequality tend to interpret, use, and respond to popular culture and marketing messages in quite different ways. In recent years, an emergent trend in gender studies questions the limits of simplistic binary thinking: male-female; masculinity-femininity; gay-straight, etc. As many of today's college students point out to their professors, people do not neatly fit into these binary boxes. Instead, people's gender and sexual performances and identities vary across a wide-ranging spectrum. In this fourth edition of the book, we more clearly reflect this refracting prism of sexual and gender differences with articles that touch on intersexed infants and children, transgender adults, and women whose gender displays lead them sometimes to be misattributed as men.

We hope this book contributes to a new generation of scholarship in the study of sex and gender—one that moves beyond the patchwork quilt approach, which lists or catalogs difference, to an approach that takes up the challenge to explore the relations of power that structure these differences. The late Gloria Anzaldúa (1990), a Chicana lesbian and feminist, used the border as a metaphor to capture the spatial, ethnic, class, and sexual transitions traversed in one's lifetime. She states in a poem that "To survive the borderlands you must live *sin fronteras*" (without borders). Breaking down, reassessing, and crossing the borders that divide the patches on the quilt—both experientially and analytically—is key to the difficult task of transforming knowledge about gender. Looking at the various prisms that organize gender relations, we think, will contribute to the kind of bridge-building that will be needed for constructing broad-based coalitions to push for equality and social justice in the twenty-first century.

REFERENCES

Acker, Joan. 1999. "Rewriting Class, Race and Gender: Problems in Feminist Rethinking." Pp. 44–69 in Myra Marx Ferree, Judith Lorber, and Beth B. Hess (eds.), *Revisioning Gender.* Thousand Oaks, CA: Sage Publications.

Acker, Joan. 2006. "Inequality Regimes, Gender, Class, and Race in Organizations," *Gender & Society 20*: (4): 441–464.

Anzaldúa, Gloria. 1990. "To Live in the Borderlands Means You." Pp. 194–195 in Gloria Anzaldúa, *Borderlands La Frontera: The New Mestiza.* San Francisco, CA: Spinsters/Aunt Lute.

Andersen, Margaret L. 2005. "Thinking About Women: A Quarter Century's View," *Gender & Society 19*: (4): 437–455.

Baca Zinn, M., L. Weber Cannon, E. Higginbotham, & B. Thornton Dill. 1986. "The Costs of Exclusionary Practices in Women's Studies," *Signs: Journal of Women in Culture and Society 11*: 290–303.

Boserup, Ester. 1970. *Woman's Role in Economic Development.* London: George Allen & Unwin.

Brod, Harry (ed.). 1987. *The Making of Masculinities: The New Men's Studies.* Boston: Allen & Unwin.

Brownmiller, Susan. 1975. *Against Our Will: Men, Women, and Rape.* New York: Simon & Schuster.

Chang, Grace. 1994. "Undocumented Latinas: The New 'Employable Mothers.'" Pp. 259–285 in Evelyn Nakano Glenn, Grace Chang, and Linda Rennie Forcey (eds.), *Mothering, Ideology, Experience, and Agency.* New York and London: Routledge.

Collins, Patricia Hill. 1990. *Black Feminist Thought: Knowledge, Consciousness, and the Politics of Empowerment.* Boston: Unwin Hyman.

Collins, Patricia Hill. 1998. *Fighting Words: Black Women and the Search for Justice.* Minneapolis: University of Minnesota Press.

Collins, Patricia Hill. 2004. *Black Sexual Politics: African Americans, Gender and the New Racism.* New York and London: Routledge.

Connell, Raewyn 1987. *Gender and Power.* Stanford, CA: Stanford University Press.

Connell, Raewyn 1992. "A Very Straight Gay: Masculinity, Homosexual Experience, and the Dynamics of Gender," *American Sociological Review 57*: 735–751.

Connell, Raewyn 1995. *Masculinities.* Berkeley: University of California Press.

Connell, Raewyn 2002. *Gender.* Cambridge: Polity.

De Beauvoir, Simone. 1953. *The Second Sex.* New York: Knopf.

Enloe, Cynthia. 1993. *The Morning After: Sexual Politics at the End of the Cold War.* Berkeley: University of California Press.

Enloe, Cynthia. 2000. *Maneuvers: The International Politics of Militarizing Women's Lives.* Berkeley: University of California Press

Glenn, Evelyn Nakano. 1999. "The Social Construction and Institutionalization of Gender and Race: An Integrative Framework." Pp. 3–43 in Myra Marx Ferree, Judith Lorber, and Beth B. Hess (eds.), *Revisioning Gender.* Thousand Oaks, CA: Sage Publications.

Glenn, Evelyn Nakano. 2002. *Unequal Freedom: How Race and Gender Shaped American Citizenship and Labor.* Cambridge, MA: Harvard University Press.

Hartmann, Heidi. 1976. "Capitalism, Patriarchy, and Job Segregation by Sex," *Signs: Journal of Women in Culture and Society 1*: (3), part 2, spring: 137–167.

Hewitt, Nancy A. 1992. "Compounding Differences," *Feminist Studies 18*: 313–326.

Heywood, L. & J. Drake (eds.). 1997. *Third Wave Agenda: Being Feminist, Doing Feminism.* Minneapolis: University of Minnesota Press.

Hondagneu-Sotelo, Pierrette. 1994. *Gendered Transitions: Mexican Experiences of Immigration.* Berkeley: University of California Press.

Hondagneu-Sotelo, Pierrette. 2001. *Domestica: Immigrant Workers Cleaning and Caring in the Shadows of Affluence.* Berkeley: University of California Press.

Kanter, Rosabeth Moss. 1977. *Men and Women of the Corporation.* New York: Basic Books.

Kaufman, Michael. 1987. *Beyond Patriarchy: Essays by Men on Pleasure, Power, and Change.* Toronto and New York: Oxford University Press.

Kessler, Sandra, Dean J. Ashendon, R. W. Connell, & Gary W. Dowsett. 1985. "Gender Relations in Secondary Schooling," *Sociology of Education 58:* 34–48.

Kimmel, Michael S. (ed.). 1987. *Changing Men: New Directions in Research on Men and Masculinity.* Newbury Park, CA: Sage.

Kimmel, Michael S. & Michael A. Messner (eds.). 1989. *Men's Lives.* New York: Macmillan.

Kimmel, Michael S. & Michael A. Messner (eds.). 2004. *Men's Lives,* 6th ed. Boston: Pearson Allyn & Bacon.

Messner, Michael A. 1996. "Studying Up on Sex," *Sociology of Sport Journal 13:* 221–237.

Messner, Michael A. 1998. *Politics of Masculinities: Men in Movements.* Thousand Oaks, CA: Sage Publications.

Mohanty, Chandra Talpade. 1991. "Cartographies of Struggle: Third World Women and the Politics of Feminism." Pp. 51–80 in Chandra Talpade Mohanty, Ann Russo, and Lourdes Torres (eds.), *Third World Women and the Politics of Feminism.* Bloomington: Indiana University Press.

Morgan, Robin. 1970. *Sisterhood Is Powerful: An Anthology of Writing from the Women's Liberation Movement.* New York: Vintage Books.

Okin, Susan Moller. 1999. *Is Multiculturalism Bad for Women?* Princeton: Princeton University Press.

Parrenas, Rhacel Salazar. 2001. *Servants of Globalization: Women, Migration and Domestic Work.* Stanford: Stanford University Press.

Pleck, J. H. 1976. "The Male Sex Role: Definitions, Problems, and Sources of Change," *Journal of Social Issues 32:* 155–164.

Rich, Adrienne. 1980. "Compulsory Heterosexuality and the Lesbian Experience," *Signs: Journal of Women in Culture and Society 5:* 631–660.

Sassen, Saskia. 1991. *The Global City: New York, London, Tokyo.* Princeton: Princeton University Press.

Smith, Barbara. 1977. *Toward a Black Feminist Criticism.* Freedom, CA: Crossing Press.

Snyder, R. Claire. 2008. "What is Third-Wave Feminism? A New Directions Essay," *Signs: Journal of Women in Culture and Society 34*: (1): 175–196.

Weber, Lynn. 2010. *Understanding Race, Class, Gender, and Sexuality: A Conceptual Framework*, 2nd ed. New York: Oxford University Press.

West, Candace, & Sarah Fenstermaker. 1995. "Doing Difference," *Gender & Society 9:* 8–37.

PART I

PERSPECTIVES ON SEX, GENDER, AND DIFFERENCE

Are women and men or boys and girls really different, or do we just think and act as though they are different? In other words, are gender differences and inequalities rooted in biology, or are they socially constructed? Today, these questions are rarely answered with simplistic, pat answers. And the questions that gender scholars are asking have also grown more complex. Are these differences constant over time, historically invariant? If women and men are different, then are women—as a group—similar to one another? Do white women share similar experiences to those of women of color? Do women in various parts of the world share commonalities, or are their differences more important? The chapters in this opening section reflect a sampling of gender scholarship on the remarkable variability of gender. They tackle tricky questions of difference between women and men, as well as issues of difference among groups of women and among groups of men.

Difference has always preoccupied feminist thought. Not long ago, difference *between* women and men was a primary concern. "Difference feminism" rested on the notion that women's distinctive characteristics required a special approach to overcome discrimination. Unlike feminist demands that women and men receive "the same" treatment, difference feminists sought women's equality by appealing to the logic of a gender dichotomy. By acknowledging and sometimes even underscoring biological, emotional, and social differences between women and men, they argued that women should not rely on men's strategies to achieve equality.

Perspectives on difference have been transformed. Today, it is clear that although women and men everywhere are constructed in opposition to each other, the categories "women" and "men" have wide-ranging meanings. Gender is always complicated by complex stratification of intersecting power systems. More important, gender operates with and through other systems of opportunity and oppression, which give rise to vastly different gender experiences among women and among men. The chapters in this section move beyond dichotomous simplifications of women and men and show how gender is contingent on other dimensions of difference. Collectively, the chapters provide a foundation for seeing gender through a prism of difference.

In the first reading, Ann Fausto-Sterling takes up a subject of much current debate—the relationship between sex and gender. By deconstructing the "making" of dichotomous sexual identities of masculine and feminine, she disputes the division of the world into only two genders based simply on genital differences. This raises provocative questions about gender and

11

about sex, and whether the relationship between them is a given. Our conceptions of gender begin to look very different if the human sexes are multiple. In the following reading, Maxine Baca Zinn and Bonnie Thornton Dill argue that a focus on race and class makes it clear that there can be no unitary analysis of women as a category. They analyze the development of multiracial feminism, noting both the tensions and the benefits, as they explore the theories and concepts in the growing body of scholarship on the intersections of race, class, and gender. A key insight here is recognition of the ways in which the differences among women are historically and socially constructed and grounded in diverse locations and interconnected inequalities.

The next article expands this perspective by addressing how age relations intersect with other inequalities. Toni Calasanti, Kathleen Slevin, and Neal King argue that not only are old people oppressed, but age relations represent a political location that should be addressed in its own right. They show how shifting the focus to old people would change feminist theories and activism. The next three readings consider issues of gender and difference in relation to globalization. Exactly how is global restructuring affecting gender, and how is gender affecting global restructuring? In contrast to the common image of a homogenizing process sweeping the globe to make gender more uniform, global forces are, in fact, creating new gender hierarchies. R. W. Connell untangles the key strands in "the world gender order" to reveal how masculinities are being reconfigured by transnational power relations. Barbara Ehrenreich and Arlie Hochschild expose some of the contradictory demands globalization places on women in different parts of the world. They describe a global labor market in which much of the work associated with women's traditional roles—child care, homemaking, and sex—is being transferred from poor countries to rich ones. Much "care work" in the United States is becoming the domain of immigrant women of color who are driven from their countries, only to remain disenfranchised. This global transfer of services benefits many professional women and their careers, yet it rests on both global and intimate relations of dominance and subordination. As we broaden the lens through which we view gender relations and global diversity, we must guard against essentialist images of "local" women in different parts of the world. In the final reading, Chandra Mohanty reviews three strategies currently used to internationalize the women's studies curriculum. She calls for a comparative model that bridges the histories, experiences, and struggles of women in local communities and the effects of globalization on their differences, commonalities, and interconnections.

1

The Five Sexes, Revisited

ANNE FAUSTO-STERLING

As Cheryl Chase stepped to the front of the packed meeting room in the Sheraton Boston Hotel, nervous coughs made the tension audible. Chase, an activist for intersexual rights, had been invited to address the May 2000 meeting of the Lawson Wilkins Pediatric Endocrine Society (LWPES), the largest organization in the United States for specialists in children's hormones. Her talk would be the grand finale to a four-hour symposium on the treatment of genital ambiguity in newborns, infants born with a mixture of both male and female anatomy, or genitals that appear to differ from their chromosomal sex. The topic was hardly a novel one to the assembled physicians.

Yet Chase's appearance before the group was remarkable. Three and a half years earlier, the American Academy of Pediatrics had refused her request for a chance to present the patients' viewpoint on the treatment of genital ambiguity, dismissing Chase and her supporters as "zealots." About two dozen intersex people had responded by throwing up a picket line. The Intersex Society of North America (ISNA) even issued a press release: "Hermaphrodites Target Kiddie Docs."

It had done my 1960s street-activist heart good. In the short run, I said to Chase at the time, the picketing would make people angry. But eventually, I assured her, the doors then closed would open. Now, as Chase

began to address the physicians at their own convention, that prediction was coming true. Her talk, titled "Sexual Ambiguity: The Patient-Centered Approach," was a measured critique of the near-universal practice of performing immediate, "corrective" surgery on thousands of infants born each year with ambiguous genitalia. Chase herself lives with the consequences of such surgery. Yet her audience, the very endocrinologists and surgeons Chase was accusing of reacting with "surgery and shame," received her with respect. Even more remarkably, many of the speakers who preceded her at the session had already spoken of the need to scrap current practices in favor of treatments more centered on psychological counseling.

What led to such a dramatic reversal of fortune? Certainly, Chase's talk at the LWPES symposium was a vindication of her persistence in seeking attention for her cause. But her invitation to speak was also a watershed in the evolving discussion about how to treat children with ambiguous genitalia. And that discussion, in turn, is the tip of a biocultural iceberg—the gender iceberg—that continues to rock both medicine and our culture at large.

Chase made her first national appearance in 1993, in these very pages, announcing the formation of ISNA in a letter responding to an essay I had written for *The*

Ann Fausto-Sterling, "The Five Sexes, Revisited," from *The Sciences,* July/August, 2000, Volume 40, Issue 4, pp. 18–24.

Sciences, titled "The Five Sexes" [March/April 1993]. In that article I argued that the two-sex system embedded in our society is not adequate to encompass the full spectrum of human sexuality. In its place, I suggested a five-sex system. In addition to males and females, I included "herms" (named after true hermaphrodites, people born with both a testis and an ovary); "merms" (male pseudohermaphrodites, who are born with testes and some aspect of female genitalia); and "ferms" (female pseudohermaphrodites, who have ovaries combined with some aspect of male genitalia).

I had intended to be provocative, but I had also written with tongue firmly in cheek. So I was surprised by the extent of the controversy the article unleashed. Right-wing Christians were outraged, and connected my idea of five sexes with the United Nations–sponsored Fourth World Conference on Women, held in Beijing in September 1995. At the same time, the article delighted others who felt constrained by the current sex and gender system.

Clearly, I had struck a nerve. The fact that so many people could get riled up by my proposal to revamp our sex and gender system suggested that change—as well as resistance to it—might be in the offing. Indeed, a lot has changed since 1993, and I like to think that my article was an important stimulus. As if from nowhere, intersexuals are materializing before our very eyes. Like Chase, many have become political organizers, who lobby physicians and politicians to change current treatment practices. But more generally, though perhaps no less provocatively, the boundaries separating masculine and feminine seem harder than ever to define.

Some find the changes underway deeply disturbing. Others find them liberating.

Who is an intersexual—and how many intersexuals are there? The concept of intersexuality is rooted in the very ideas of male and female. In the idealized, Platonic, biological world, human beings are divided into two kinds: a perfectly dimorphic species. Males have an X and a Y chromosome, testes, a penis and all of the appropriate internal plumbing for delivering urine and semen to the outside world. They also have well-known secondary sexual characteristics including a muscular build and facial hair. Women have two X chromosomes, ovaries, all of the internal plumbing to transport urine and ova to the outside world, a system to support pregnancy and fetal development, as well as a variety of recognizable secondary sexual characteristics.

That idealized story papers over many obvious caveats: some women have facial hair, some men have none; some women speak with deep voices, some men veritably squeak. Less well known is the fact that, on close inspection, absolute dimorphism disintegrates even at the level of basic biology. Chromosomes, hormones, the internal sex structures, the gonads and the external genitalia all vary more than most people realize. Those born outside of the Platonic dimorphic mold are called intersexuals.

In "The Five Sexes" I reported an estimate by a psychologist expert in the treatment of intersexuals, suggesting that some 4 percent of all live births are intersexual. Then, together with a group of Brown University undergraduates, I set out to conduct the first systematic assessment of the available data on intersexual birthrates. We scoured the medical literature for estimates of the frequency of various categories of intersexuality, from additional chromosomes to mixed gonads, hormones and genitalia. For some conditions we could find only anecdotal evidence; for most, however numbers exist. On the basis of that evidence, we calculated that for every 1,000 children born, seventeen are intersexual in some form. That number—1.7 percent—is a ballpark estimate, not a precise count, though we believe it is more accurate than the 4 percent I reported.

Our figure represents all chromosomal, anatomical and hormonal exceptions to the dimorphic ideal; the number of intersexuals who might, potentially, be subject to surgery as infants is smaller—probably between one in 1,000 and one in 2,000 live births. Furthermore, because some populations possess the relevant genes at high frequency, the intersexual birthrate is not uniform throughout the world.

Consider, for instance, the gene for congenital adrenal hyperplasia (CAH). When the CAH gene is inherited from both parents, it leads to a baby with masculinized external genitalia who possesses two X chromosomes and the internal reproductive organs of a potentially fertile woman. The frequency of the gene varies widely around the world: in New Zealand it occurs in only forty-three children per million; among the Yupik Eskimos of southwestern Alaska, its frequency is 3,500 per million.

Intersexuality has always been to some extent a matter of definition. And in the past century physicians have been the ones who defined children as intersexual—and provided the remedies. When only the chromosomes are unusual, but the external genitalia and gonads clearly indicate either a male or a female, physicians do not advocate intervention. Indeed, it is not clear what kind of intervention could be advocated in such cases. But the story is quite different when infants are born with mixed genitalia, or with external genitals that seem at odds with the baby's gonads.

Most clinics now specializing in the treatment of intersex babies rely on case-management principles developed in the 1950s by the psychologist John Money and the psychiatrists Joan G. Hampson and John L. Hampson, all of Johns Hopkins University in Baltimore, Maryland. Money believed that gender identity is completely malleable for about eighteen months after birth. Thus, he argued, when a treatment team is presented with an infant who has ambiguous genitalia, the team could make a gender assignment solely on the basis of what made the best surgical sense. The physicians could then simply encourage the parents to raise the child according to the surgically assigned gender. Following that course, most physicians maintained, would eliminate psychological distress for both the patient and the parents. Indeed, treatment teams were never to use such words as "intersex" or "hermaphrodite"; instead, they were to tell parents that nature intended the baby to be the boy or the girl that the physicians had determined it was. Through surgery, the physicians were merely completing nature's intention.

Although Money and the Hampsons published detailed case studies of intersex children who they said had adjusted well to their gender assignments, Money thought one case in particular proved his theory. It was a dramatic example, inasmuch as it did not involve intersexuality at all: one of a pair of identical twin boys lost his penis as a result of a circumcision accident. Money recommended that "John" (as he came to be known in a later case study) be surgically turned into "Joan" and raised as a girl. In time, Joan grew to love wearing dresses and having her hair done. Money proudly proclaimed the sex reassignment a success.

But as recently chronicled by John Colapinto, in his book *As Nature Made Him,* Joan—now known to be an adult male named David Reimer—eventually rejected his female assignment. Even without a functioning penis and testes (which had been removed as part of the reassignment) John/Joan sought masculinizing medication, and married a woman with children (whom he adopted).

Since the full conclusion to the John/Joan story came to light, other individuals who were reassigned as males or females shortly after birth but who later rejected their early assignments have come forward. So, too, have cases in which the reassignment has worked—at least into the subject's mid-twenties. But even then the aftermath of the surgery can be problematic. Genital surgery often leaves scars that reduce sexual sensitivity. Chase herself had a complete clitoridectomy, a procedure that is less frequently performed on intersexuals today. But the newer surgeries, which reduce the size of the clitoral shaft, still greatly reduce sensitivity.

The revelation of cases of failed reassignments and the emergence of intersex activism have led an increasing number of pediatric endocrinologists, urologists and psychologists to reexamine the wisdom of early genital surgery. For example, in a talk that preceded Chase's at the LWPES meeting, the medical ethicist Laurence B. McCullough of the Center for Medical Ethics and Health Policy at Baylor College of Medicine in Houston, Texas, introduced an ethical framework for the treatment of children with ambiguous genitalia. Because sex phenotype (the manifestation of genetically and embryologically determined sexual characteristics) and gender presentation (the sex role projected by the individual in society) are highly variable, McCullough argues, the various forms of intersexuality should be defined as normal. All of them fall within the statistically expected variability of sex and gender. Furthermore, though certain disease states may accompany some forms of intersexuality, and may require medical intervention, intersexual conditions are not themselves diseases.

McCullough also contends that in the process of assigning gender, physicians should minimize what he calls irreversible assignments: taking steps such as the surgical removal or modification of gonads or genitalia that the patient may one day want to have reversed. Finally, McCullough urges physicians to abandon their practice of treating the birth of a child with genital ambiguity as a medical or social emergency. Instead, they should take the time to perform a thorough medical workup and should disclose everything to the parents, including the uncertainties about the final outcome. The treatment mantra, in other words, should be therapy, not surgery.

I believe a new treatment protocol for intersex infants, similar to the one outlined by McCullough, is close at hand. Treatment should combine some basic medical and ethical principles with a practical but less drastic approach to the birth of a mixed-sex child. As a first step, surgery on infants should be performed only to save the child's life or to substantially improve the child's physical well-being. Physicians may assign a sex—male or female—to an intersex infant on the basis of the probability that the child's particular condition will lead to the formation of a particular gender identity. At the same time, though, practitioners ought to be humble enough to recognize that as the child grows, he or she may reject the assignment—and they should be wise enough to listen to what the child has to say. Most important, parents should have access to the full range of information and options available to them.

Sex assignments made shortly after birth are only the beginning of a long journey. Consider, for instance, the life of Max Beck: Born intersexual, Max was surgically assigned as a female and consistently raised as such. Had her medical team followed her into her early twenties, they would have deemed her assignment a success because she was married to a man. (It should be noted that success in gender assignment has traditionally been defined as living in that gender as a heterosexual.) Within a few years, however, Beck had come out as a butch lesbian; now in her mid-thirties, Beck has become a man and married his lesbian partner, who (through the miracles of modern reproductive technology) recently gave birth to a girl.

Transsexuals, people who have an emotional gender at odds with their physical sex, once described themselves in terms of dimorphic absolutes—males trapped in female bodies, or vice versa. As such, they sought psychological relief through surgery. Although many still do, some so-called transgendered people today are content to inhabit a more ambiguous zone. A male-to-female transsexual, for instance, may come out as a lesbian. Jane, born a physiological male, is now in her late thirties and living with her wife, whom she married when her name was still John. Jane takes hormones to feminize herself, but they have not yet interfered with her ability to engage in intercourse as a man. In her mind Jane has a lesbian relationship with her wife, though she views their intimate moments as a cross between lesbian and heterosexual sex.

It might seem natural to regard intersexuals and transgendered people as living midway between the poles of male and female. But male and female, masculine and feminine, cannot be parsed as some kind of continuum. Rather, sex and gender are best conceptualized as points in a multidimensional space. For some time, experts on gender development have distinguished between sex at the genetic level and at the cellular level (sex-specific gene expression, X and Y chromosomes); at the hormonal level (in the fetus, during childhood and after puberty); and at the anatomical level (genitals and secondary sexual characteristics). Gender identity presumably emerges from all of those corporeal aspects via some poorly understood interaction with environment and experience. What has become increasingly clear is that one can find levels of masculinity and femininity in almost every possible permutation. A chromosomal, hormonal and genital male (or female) may emerge with a female (or male) gender identity. Or a chromosomal female with male fetal hormones and masculinized genitalia—but with female pubertal hormones—may develop a female gender identity.

The medical and scientific communities have yet to adopt a language that is capable of describing such diversity. In her book *Hermaphrodites and the Medical Invention of Sex,* the historian and medical ethicist Alice Domurat Dreger of Michigan State University in East Lansing documents the emergence of current medical systems for classifying gender ambiguity. The current usage remains rooted in the Victorian approach to sex. The logical structure of the commonly used terms "true hermaphrodite," "male pseudohermaphrodite" and "female pseudohermaphrodite" indicates that only the so-called true hermaphrodite is a genuine mix of male and female. The others, no matter how confusing their body parts, are really hidden males or females. Because true hermaphodites are rare—possibly only one in 100,000—such a classification system supports the idea that human beings are an absolutely dimorphic species.

At the dawn of the twenty-first century, when the variability of gender seems so visible, such a position is hard to maintain. And here, too, the old medical consensus has begun to crumble. Last fall the pediatric urologist Ian A. Aaronson of the Medical University of South Carolina in Charleston organized the North American Task Force on Intersexuality (NATFI) to review the clinical responses to genital ambiguity in infants. Key medical associations, such as the American Academy of Pediatrics, have endorsed NATFI. Specialists in surgery, endocrinology, psychology, ethics, psychiatry, genetics and public health, as well as intersex patient-advocate groups, have joined its ranks.

One of the goals of NATFI is to establish a new sex nomenclature. One proposal under consideration replaces the current system with emotionally neutral terminology that emphasizes developmental processes rather than preconceived gender categories. For example, Type I intersexes develop out of anomalous virilizing influences; Type II result from some interruption of virilization; and in Type III intersexes the gonads themselves may not have developed in the expected fashion.

What is clear is that since 1993, modern society has moved beyond five sexes to a recognition that gender variation is normal and, for some people, an arena for playful exploration. Discussing my "five sexes" proposal in her book *Lessons from the Intersexed,* the psychologist Suzanne J. Kessler of the State University of New York at Purchase drives this point home with great effect:

> The limitation with Fausto-Sterling's proposal is that . . . [it] still gives genitals . . . primary signifying status and ignores the fact that in the everyday world

gender attributions are made without access to genital inspection. . . . What has primacy in everyday life is the gender that is performed, regardless of the flesh's configuration under the clothes.

I now agree with Kessler's assessment. It would be better for intersexuals and their supporters to turn everyone's focus away from genitals. Instead, as she suggests, one should acknowledge that people come in an even wider assortment of sexual identities and characteristics than mere genitals can distinguish. Some women may have "large clitorises or fused labia," whereas some men may have "small penises or misshapen scrota," as Kessler puts it, "phenotypes with no particular clinical or identity meaning."

As clearheaded as Kessler's program is—and despite the progress made in the 1990s—our society is still far from that ideal. The intersexual or transgendered person who projects a social gender—what Kessler calls "cultural genitals"—that conflicts with his or her physical genitals still may die for the transgression. Hence legal protection for people whose cultural and physical genitals do not match is needed during the current transition to a more gender-diverse world. One easy step would be to eliminate the category of "gender" from official documents, such as driver's licenses and passports. Surely attributes both more visible (such as height, build and eye color) and less visible (fingerprints and genetic profiles) would be more expedient.

A more far-ranging agenda is presented in the International Bill of Gender Rights, adopted in 1995 at the fourth annual International Conference on Transgender Law and Employment Policy in Houston, Texas. It lists ten "gender rights," including the right to define one's own gender, the right to change one's physical gender if one so chooses and the right to marry whomever one wishes. The legal bases for such rights are being hammered out in the courts as I write and, most recently, through the establishment, in the state of Vermont, of legal same-sex domestic partnerships.

No one could have foreseen such changes in 1993. And the idea that I played some role, however small, in reducing the pressure—from the medical community as well as from society at large—to flatten the diversity of human sexes into two diametrically opposed camps gives me pleasure.

Sometimes people suggest to me, with not a little horror, that I am arguing for a pastel world in which androgyny reigns and men and women are boringly the same. In my vision, however, strong colors coexist with pastels. There are and will continue to be highly masculine people out there; it's just that some of them are women. And some of the most feminine people I know happen to be men.

2

Theorizing Difference from Multiracial Feminism

Maxine Baca Zinn

Bonnie Thornton Dill

Women of color have long challenged the hegemony of feminisms constructed primarily around the lives of white middle-class women. Since the late 1960s, U.S. women of color have taken issue with unitary theories of gender. Our critiques grew out of the widespread concern about the exclusion of women of color from feminist scholarship and the misinterpretation of our experiences,[1] and ultimately "out of the very discourses, denying, permitting, and producing difference."[2] Speaking simultaneously from "within and against" *both* women's liberation and antiracist movements, we have insisted on the need to challenge systems of domination,[3] not merely as gendered subjects but as women whose lives are affected by our location in multiple hierarchies.

Recently, and largely in response to these challenges, work that links gender to other forms of domination is increasing. In this article, we examine this connection further as well as the ways in which difference and diversity infuse contemporary feminist studies. Our analysis draws on a conceptual framework that we refer to as "multiracial feminism."[4] This perspective is an attempt to go beyond a mere recognition of diversity and difference among women to examine structures of domination, specifically the importance of race in understanding the social construction of gender. Despite the varied concerns and multiple intellectual stances which characterize the feminisms of women of color, they share an emphasis on race as a primary force situating genders differently. It is the centrality of race, of institutionalized racism, and of struggles against racial oppression that link the various feminist perspectives within this framework. Together, they demonstrate that racial meanings offer new theoretical directions for feminist thought.

TENSIONS IN CONTEMPORARY DIFFERENCE FEMINISM

Objections to the false universalism embedded in the concept "woman" emerged within other discourses as well as those of women of color.[5] Lesbian feminists and postmodern feminists put forth their own versions of what Susan Bordo has called "gender skepticism."[6]

Many thinkers within mainstream feminism have responded to these critiques with efforts to contextualize gender. The search for women's "universal" or "essential" characteristics is being abandoned. By examining gender in the context of other social divisions and

This article is reprinted from *Feminist Studies,* Volume 22, Number 2 (Summer 1996), pp. 321–331, by permission of the publisher, Feminist Studies, Inc.

perspectives, difference has gradually become important—even problematizing the universal categories, "women" and "men." Sandra G. Harding expresses the shift best in her claim that "there are no gender relations *per se,* but only gender relations as constructed by and between classes, races, and cultures."[7]

Many feminists now contend that difference occupies center stage as *the* project of women studies today.[8] According to one scholar, "difference has replaced equality as the central concern of feminist theory."[9] Many have welcomed the change, hailing it as a major revitalizing force in U.S. feminist theory.[10] But if *some* priorities within mainstream feminist thought have been refocused by attention to difference, there remains an "uneasy alliance"[11] between women of color and other feminists.

If difference has helped revitalize academic feminisms, it has also "upset the apple cart," and introduced new conflicts into feminist studies.[12] For example, in a recent and widely discussed essay, Jane Rowland Martin argues that the current preoccupation with difference is leading feminism into dangerous traps. She fears that in giving privileged status to a predetermined set of analytic categories (race, ethnicity, and class), "we affirm the existence of nothing but difference." She asks, "How do we know that for us, difference does not turn on being fat, or religious, or in an abusive relationship?"[13]

We, too, see pitfalls in some strands of the difference project. However, our perspectives take their bearings from social relations. Race and class difference are crucial, we argue, not as individual characteristics (such as being fat) but insofar as they are primary organizing principles of a society which locates and positions groups within that society's opportunity structures.

Despite the much-heralded diversity trend within feminist studies, difference is often reduced to mere pluralism; a "live and let live" approach where principles of relativism generate a long list of diversities which begin with gender, class, and race and continue through a range of social structural as well as personal characteristics.[14] Another disturbing pattern, which bell hooks refers to as "the commodification of difference," is the representation of diversity as a form of exotica, "a spice, seasoning that livens up the dull dish

that is mainstream white culture."[15] The major limitation of these approaches is the failure to attend to the power relations that accompany difference. Moreover, these approaches ignore the inequalities that cause some characteristics to be seen as "normal" while others are seen as "different" and thus, deviant.

Maria C. Lugones expresses irritation at those feminists who see only the *problem* of difference without recognizing *difference.*[16] Increasingly, we find that difference *is* recognized. But this in no way means that difference occupies a "privileged" theoretical status. Instead of using difference to rethink the category of women, difference is often a euphemism for women who differ from the traditional norm. Even in purporting to accept difference, feminist pluralism often creates a social reality that reverts to universalizing women:

> So much feminist scholarship assumes that when we cut through all of the diversity among women created by differences of racial classification, ethnicity, social class, and sexual orientation, a "universal truth" concerning women and gender lies buried underneath. But if we can face the scary possibility that no such certainty exists and that persisting in such a search will always distort or omit someone's experiences, with what do we replace this old way of thinking? Gender differences and gender politics begin to look very different if there is no essential woman at the core.[17]

WHAT IS MULTIRACIAL FEMINISM?

A new set of feminist theories have emerged from the challenges put forth by women of color. Multiracial feminism is an evolving body of theory and practice informed by wide-ranging intellectual traditions. This framework does not offer a singular or unified feminism but a body of knowledge situating women and men in multiple systems of domination. U.S. multiracial feminism encompasses several emergent perspectives developed primarily by women of color: African Americans, Latinas, Asian Americans, and Native Americans, women whose analyses are shaped by their unique perspectives as "outsiders within"— marginal intellectuals whose social locations provide them a particular perspective on self and society.[18] Although U.S. women of color represent many races and ethnic backgrounds—with different histories and cultures—our feminisms cohere in their treatment of race as a basic social division, a structure of power, a focus of political struggle and hence a fundamental force in shaping women's and men's lives.

This evolving intellectual and political perspective uses several terms. While we adopt the label "multiracial," other terms have been used to describe this broad framework. For example, Chela Sandoval refers to "U.S. Third World feminisms,"[19] while other scholars refer to "indigenous feminisms." In their theory text-reader, Alison M. Jagger and Paula M. Rothenberg adopt the label "multicultural feminism."[20]

We use "multiracial" rather than "multicultural" as a way of underscoring race as a power system that interacts with other structured inequalities to shape genders. Within the U.S. context, race, and the system of meanings and ideologies which accompany it, is a fundamental organizing principle of social relationships.[21] Race affects all women and men, although in different ways. Even cultural and group differences among women are produced through interaction within a racially stratified social order. Therefore, although we do not discount the importance of culture, we caution that cultural analytic frameworks that ignore race tend to view women's differences as the product of group-specific values and practices that often result in the marginalization of cultural groups which are then perceived as exotic expressions of a normative center. Our focus on race stresses the social construction of differently situated social groups and their varying degrees of advantage and power. Additionally, this emphasis on race takes on increasing political importance in an era where discourse about race is governed by color-evasive language[22] and a preference for individual rather than group remedies for social inequalities. Our analyses insist upon the primary and pervasive nature of race in contemporary U.S. society while at the same time acknowledging how race both shapes and is shaped by a variety of other social relations.

In the social sciences, multiracial feminism grew out of socialist feminist thinking. Theories about how political economic forces shape women's lives were influential as we began to uncover the social causes of racial ethnic women's subordination. But socialist feminism's concept of capitalist patriarchy, with its focus on women's unpaid (reproductive) labor in the home failed to address racial differences in the organization of reproductive labor. As feminists of color have argued, "reproductive labor has divided along racial as well as gender lines, and the specific characteristics have varied regionally and changed over time as capitalism has reorganized."[23] Despite the limitations of socialist feminism, this body of literature has been especially useful in pursuing questions about the interconnections among systems of domination.[24]

Race and ethnic studies was the other major social scientific source of multiracial feminism. It provided a basis for comparative analyses of groups that are socially and legally subordinated and remain culturally distinct within U.S. society. This includes the systematic discrimination of socially constructed racial groups and their distinctive cultural arrangements. Historically, the categories of African American, Latino, Asian American, and Native American were constructed as both racially and culturally distinct. Each group has a distinctive culture, shares a common heritage, and has developed a common identity within a larger society that subordinates them.[25]

We recognize, of course, certain pitfalls inherent in an uncritical use of the multiracial label. First, the perspective can be hampered by a biracial model in which only African Americans and whites are seen as racial categories and all other groups are viewed through the prism of cultural differences. Latinos and Asians have always occupied distinctive places within the racial hierarchy, and current shifts in the composition of the U.S. population are racializing these groups anew.[26]

A second problem lies in treating multiracial feminism as a single analytical framework, and its principle architects, women of color, as an undifferentiated category. The concepts "multiracial feminism," "racial ethnic women," and "women of color" homogenize quite different experiences and can falsely universalize experiences across race, ethnicity, sexual orientation, and age.[27] The feminisms created by women of color exhibit a plurality of intellectual and political positions. We speak in many voices, with inconsistencies that are born of our different social locations. Multiracial feminism embodies this plurality and richness. Our intent is not to falsely universalize women of color. Nor do we wish to promote a new racial essentialism in place of the old gender essentialism. Instead, we use these concepts to examine the structures and experiences produced by intersecting forms of race and gender.

It is also essential to acknowledge that race itself is a shifting and contested category whose meanings construct definitions of all aspects of social life.[28] In the United States it helped define citizenship by excluding everyone who was not a white, male property owner. It defined labor as slave or free, coolie or contract, and family as available only to those men whose marriages were recognized or whose wives could immigrate with them. Additionally, racial meanings are contested both within groups and between them.[29]

Although definitions of race are at once historically and geographically specific, they are also transnational, encompassing diasporic groups and crossing traditional geographic boundaries. Thus, while U.S. multiracial feminism calls attention to the fundamental importance of race, it must also locate the meaning of race within specific national traditions.

THE DISTINGUISHING FEATURES OF MULTIRACIAL FEMINISM

By attending to these problems, multiracial feminism offers a set of analytic premises for thinking about and theorizing gender. The following themes distinguish this branch of feminist inquiry.

First, multiracial feminism asserts that gender is constructed by a range of interlocking inequalities, what Patricia Hill Collins calls a "matrix of domination."[30] The idea of a matrix is that several fundamental systems work with and through each other. People experience race, class, gender, and sexuality differently depending upon their social location in the structures of race, class, gender, and sexuality. For example, people of the same race will experience race differently depending upon their location in the class structure as working class, professional managerial class, or unemployed; in the gender structure as female or male; and in structures of sexuality as heterosexual, homosexual, or bisexual.

Multiracial feminism also examines the simultaneity of systems in shaping women's experience and identity. Race, class, gender, and sexuality are not reducible to individual attributes to be measured and assessed for their separate contribution in explaining given social outcomes, an approach that Elizabeth Spelman calls "pop-bead metaphysics," where a woman's identity consists of the sum of parts neatly divisible from one another.[31] The matrix of domination seeks to account for the multiple ways that women experience themselves as gendered, raced, classed, and sexualized.

Second, multiracial feminism emphasizes the intersectional nature of hierarchies at all levels of social life. Class, race, gender, and sexuality are components of both social structure and social interaction. Women and men are differently embedded in locations created by these cross-cutting hierarchies. As a result, women and men throughout the social order experience different forms of privilege and subordination, depending on their race, class, gender, and sexuality. In other words, intersecting forms of domination produce *both* oppression *and* opportunity. At the same time that structures of race, class, and gender create disadvantages for women of color, they provide unacknowledged benefits for those who are at the top of these hierarchies—whites, members of the upper classes, and males. Therefore, multiracial feminism applies not only to racial ethnic women but also to women and men of all races, classes, and genders.

Third, multiracial feminism highlights the relational nature of dominance and subordination. Power is the cornerstone of women's differences.[32] This means that women's differences are *connected* in systematic ways.[33] Race is a vital element in the pattern of relations among minority and white women. As Linda Gordon argues, the very meanings of being a white woman in the United States have been affected by the existence of subordinated women of color; "They intersect in conflict and in occasional cooperation, but always in mutual influence."[34]

Fourth, multiracial feminism explores the interplay of social structure and women's agency. Within the constraints of race, class, and gender oppression, women create viable lives for themselves, their families, and their communities. Women of color have resisted and often undermined the forces of power that control them. From acts of quiet dignity and steadfast determination to involvement in revolt and rebellion, women struggle to shape their own lives. Racial oppression has been a common focus of the "dynamic of oppositional agency" of women of color. As Chandra Talpade Mohanty points out, it is the nature and organization of women's opposition which mediates and differentiates the impact of structures of domination.[35]

Fifth, multiracial feminism encompasses wide-ranging methodological approaches, and like other branches of feminist thought, relies on varied theoretical tools as well. Ruth Frankenberg and Lata Mani identify three guiding principles of inclusive feminist inquiry: "building complex analyses, avoiding erasure, specifying location."[36] In the last decade, the opening up of academic feminism has focused attention on social location in the production of knowledge. Most basically, research by and about marginalized women has destabilized what used to be universal categories of gender. Marginalized locations are well-suited for grasping social relations that remained obscure from more privileged vantage points. Lived experience, in other words, creates alternative ways of understanding the social world and the experience of different groups of women within it. Racially informed standpoint epistemologies have provided new topics, fresh questions, and new understandings of women and men. Women of color have, as Norma Alarcon argues, asserted ourselves as subjects, using our voices to challenge dominant conceptions of truth.[37]

Sixth, multiracial feminism brings together understandings drawn from the lived experiences of diverse and continuously changing groups of women. Among Asian Americans, Native Americans, Latinas, and blacks are many different national cultural and ethnic groups. Each one is engaged in the process of testing, refining, and reshaping these broader categories in its own image. Such internal differences heighten awareness of and sensitivity to both commonalities and differences, serving as a constant reminder of the importance of comparative study and maintaining a creative tension between diversity and universalization.

DIFFERENCE AND TRANSFORMATION

Efforts to make women's studies less partial and less distorted have produced important changes in aca-demic feminism. Inclusive thinking has provided a way to build multiplicity and difference into our analyses. This has lead to the discovery that race matters for everyone. White women, too, must be reconceptualized as a category that is multiple defined by race, class, and other differences. As Ruth Frankenberg demonstrates in a study of whiteness among contemporary women, all kinds of social relations, even those that appear neutral, are, in fact, racialized. Frankenberg further complicates the very notion of a unified white identity by introducing issues of Jewish identity.[38] Therefore, the lives of women of color cannot be seen as a *variation* on a more general model of white American womanhood. The model of womanhood that feminist social science once held as "universal" is also a product of race and class.

When we analyze the power relations constituting all social arrangements and shaping women's lives in distinctive ways, we can begin to grapple with core feminist issues about how genders are socially constructed and constructed differently. Women's difference is built into our study of gender. Yet this perspective is quite far removed from the atheoretical pluralism implied in much contemporary thinking about gender.

Multiracial feminism, in our view, focuses not just on differences but also on the way in which differences and domination intersect and are historically and socially constituted. It challenges feminist scholars to go beyond the mere recognition and inclusion of difference to reshape the basic concepts and theories of our disciplines. By attending to women's social location based on race, class, and gender, multiracial feminism seeks to clarify the structural sources of diversity. Ultimately, multiracial feminism forces us to see privilege and subordination as interrelated and to pose such questions as, How do the existences and experiences of all people—women and men, different racial-ethnic groups, and different classes—shape the experiences of each other? How are those relationships defined and enforced through social institutions that are the primary sites for negotiating power within society? How do these differences contribute to the construction of both individual and group identity? Once we acknowledge that all women are affected by the racial order of society, then it becomes clear that the insights of multiracial feminism provide an analytical framework, not solely for understanding the experiences of women of color but for understanding *all* women, and men, as well.

NOTES

1. Maxine Baca Zinn, Lynn Weber Cannon, Elizabeth Higginbotham, and Bonnie Thornton Dill, "The Costs of Exclusionary Practices in Women's Studies," *Signs* 11 (winter, 1986): 290–303.

2. Chela Sandoval, "U.S. Third World Feminism: The Theory and Method of Oppositional Consciousness in the Postmodern World," *Genders* (spring, 1991): 1–24.

3. Ruth Frankenberg and Lata Mani, "Cross Currents, Crosstalk: Race, 'Postcoloniality' and the Politics of Location," *Cultural Studies* 7 (May, 1993): 292–310.

4. We use the term "multiracial feminism" to convey the multiplicity of racial groups and feminist perspectives.

5. A growing body of works on difference in feminist thought now exists. Although we cannot cite all of the current work, the following are representative: Michèle Barrett, "The Concept of Difference," *Feminist Review* 26 (July, 1987): 29–42; Christina Crosby, "Dealing With Difference," in *Feminists Theorize the Political,* ed. Judith Butler and Joan W. Scott (New York: Routledge, 1992): 130–43; Elizabeth Fox-Genovese, "Difference, Diversity, and Divisions in an Agenda for the Women's Movement" in *Color, Class, and Country: Experiences of Gender,* ed. Gay Young and Bette J. Dickerson (London: Zed Books, 1994): 232–48; Nancy A. Hewitt, "Compounding Differences," *Feminist Studies* 18 (summer, 1992): 313–26; Maria C. Lugones, "On the Logic of Feminist Pluralism," in *Feminist Ethics*, ed. Claudia Card (Lawrence: University of Kansas Press, 1991), 35–44; Rita S. Gallin and Anne Ferguson, "The Plurality of Feminism: Rethinking 'Difference,'" in *The Woman and International Development Annual* (Boulder: Westview Press, 1993), 3: 1–16; and Linda Gordon, "On Difference," *Genders* 10 (spring, 1991): 91–111.

6. Susan Bordo, "Feminism, Postmodernism, and Gender Skepticism," in *Feminism/Postmodernism,* ed. Linda J. Nicholson (London: Routledge, 1990), 133–56.

7. Sandra G. Harding, *Whose Science? Whose Knowledge? Thinking from Women's Lives* (Ithaca: Cornell University Press, 1991), 179.

8. Crosby, 131.

9. Fox-Genovese, 232.

10. Faye Ginsberg and Anna Lowenhaupt Tsing, Introduction to *Uncertain Terms, Negotiating Gender in American Culture,* ed. Faye Ginsberg and Anna Lowenhaupt Tsing (Boston: Beacon Press, 1990), 3.

11. Sandoval, 2.

12. Sandra G. Morgan, "Making Connections: Socialist-Feminist Challenges to Marxist Scholarship," in *Women and a New Academy: Gender and Cultural Contexts,* ed. Jean F. O'Barr (Madison: University of Wisconsin Press, 1989), 149.

13. Jane Rowland Martin, "Methodological Essentialism, False Difference, and Other Dangerous Traps," *Signs* 19 (spring, 1994): 647.

14. Barrett, 32.

15. bell hooks, *Black Looks: Race and Representation* (Boston: South End Press, 1992), 21.

16. Lugones, 35–44.

17. Patricia Hill Collins, Foreword to *Women of Color in U.S. Society,* ed. Maxine Baca Zinn and Bonnie Thornton Dill (Philadelphia: Temple University Press, 1994), xv.

18. Patricia Hill Collins, "Learning from the Outsider Within: The Sociological Significance of Black Feminist Thought," *Social Problems* 33 (December, 1986): 514–32.

19. Sandoval, 1.

20. Alison M. Jagger and Paula S. Rothenberg, *Feminist Frameworks: Alternative Theoretical Accounts of the Relations between Women and Men.* 3d ed. (New York: McGraw Hill, 1993).

21. Michael Omi and Howard Winant, *Racial Formation in United States: From the 1960s to the 1980s,* 2d ed. (New York: Routledge, 1994).

22. Ruth Frankenberg, *The Social Construction of Whiteness: White Women, Race Matters* (Minneapolis: University of Minnesota Press, 1993).

23. Evelyn Nakano Glenn, "From Servitude to Service Work: Historical Continuities in the Racial Division of Paid Reproductive Labor," *Signs* 18 (autumn, 1992): 3. See also Bonnie Thornton Dill, "Our Mothers' Grief: Racial-Ethnic Women and the Maintenance of Families," *Journal of Family History* 13, no. 4 (1988): 415–31.

24. Morgan, 146.

25. Maxine Baca Zinn and Bonnie Thornton Dill, "Difference and Domination," in *Women of Color in U.S. Society,* 11–12.

26. See Omi and Winant, 53–76, for a discussion of racial formation.

27. Margaret L. Andersen and Patricia Hill Collins, *Race, Class, and Gender: An Anthology* (Belmont, Calif.: Wadsworth, 1992), xvi.

28. Omi and Winant.

29. Nazli Kibria, "Migration and Vietnamese American Women: Remaking Ethnicity," in *Women of Color in U.S. Society,* 247–61.

30. Patricia Hill Collins, *Black Feminist Thought: Knowledge, Consciousness, and the Politics of Empowerment* (Boston: Unwin Hyman, 1990).

31. Elizabeth Spelman, *Inessential Women: Problems of Exclusion in Feminist Thought* (Boston: Beacon Press, 1988).

32. Several discussions of difference make this point. See Baca Zinn and Dill, 10; Gordon, 106; and Lynn Weber, in the "Sym-

posium on West and Fenstermaker's 'Doing Difference,'" *Gender & Society* 9 (August, 1995): 515–19.

33. Glenn, 10.

34. Gordon, 106.

35. Chandra Talpade Mohanty, "Cartographies of Struggle: Third World Women and the Politics of Feminism," in *Third World Women and the Politics of Feminism,* ed. Chandra Talpade Mohanty, Ann Russo, and Lourdes Torres (Bloomington: Indiana University Press, 1991), 13.

36. Frankenberg and Mani, 307.

37. Norma Alarcon, "The Theoretical Subject(s) of *This Bridge Called My Back* and Anglo American Feminism," in *Making Face, Making Soul, Haciendo Caras: Creative and Critical Perspectives by Women of Color,* ed. Gloria Anzaldua, (San Francisco: Aunt Lute, 1990), 356.

38. Frankenberg. See also Evelyn Torton Beck, "The Politics of Jewish Invisibility," *NWSA Journal* (fall, 1988): 93–102.

3

Ageism and Feminism

From "Et Cetera" to Center

Toni Calasanti

Kathleen F. Slevin

Neal King

Although women's studies scholars and activists do not deny the reality of ageism, they have relegated it to secondary status, neglecting to theorize age relations or place old age at the center of analysis. After explaining what we mean by age relations and their intersections with other inequalities, we discuss the ways in which old people are oppressed, and why age relations represent a political location that needs to be addressed in its own right. We then demonstrate ways in which feminist theories and activism might change if the focus shifted to old people.

An inadvertent but pernicious ageism burdens much of women's studies scholarship and activism. It stems from failing to study old people on their own terms and from failing to theorize age relations—the system of inequality, based on age, which privileges the not-old at the expense of the old (Calasanti 2003). Some feminists mention age-based oppression but treat it as a given—an "et cetera" on a list of oppressions, as if to indicate that we already know what it is. As a re-sult, feminist work suffers, and we engage in our own oppression. Using scholarship on the body and care-work as illustrative, this article explores both the absence of attention to the old and age relations, and how feminist scholarship can be transformed by the presence of such attention.

NEGLECTING OLD AGE

Feminist scholars have given little attention either to old women or to aging (Arber and Ginn 1991), despite Barbara Macdonald's work in the women's movement in the 1980s and her plea that old age be recognized (Macdonald and Rich 1983); despite the increases in absolute and relative numbers of those over age 65, and the skewed sex ratio among old people in the United States; and despite the shifting age ratios in nations worldwide. In her NWSA presidential address at the turn of the century, Berenice Carroll showed where

Women's Studies had been and where it will head in the new millennium. She discussed the challenges of women of color and lauds the more recent inclusion of lesbian studies. Nowhere, however, did she mention aging issues (2001). The number of women's studies scholars engaged in work on later life is still so small that those with any interest in aging can count them; the rest (probably the majority) may know their names (such as Woodward 1999; Gullette 2004; and Cruikshank 2003) but not their work. The issues go ignored by most scholars, and one must ask why.

THE BIAS OF MIDDLE AGE

Feminists consider age but neither old people nor age relations. They focus on young adult or middle-aged women and on girls. For instance, in the (mostly British) *Feminist Perspective Series,* the editors argue that the works therein reflect "the current interest in feminist issues and in women's studies in a wide range of fields" (Wallace and Abbott 1999, vii) but exclude aging and old age. Some attend to Sontag's notion of the "double standard of aging," by which women suffer scorn and exclusion as they grow old—"a humiliating process of gradual sexual disqualification" (Sontag 1972, 102). But even studies of women "of a certain age" (Sontag 1972, 99) focus on middle age—a time when physical markers such as menopause, wrinkles, and the like emerge, and carework for old people begins to occupy women's time. Even though feminists have contributed to the literature on bodies, discussion of old bodies is sorely lacking (Laz 2003). As Twigg notes, a handful of scholars in their 50s or 60s have done important work on age oppression. However, such literature "primarily refers not to deep old age but to the late middle years, roughly equating to fifties to seventies, and to the processes and experiences of aging rather than old age itself" (2004, 62). That is, she contends that feminist scholarship on aging bodies has generally not been concerned with the "Fourth Age"—a time qualitatively different from the "Third Age" in that it is marked by serious infirmity. Carework research tends not to examine *old* women who give or *receive* care. Brook's scholarship on feminist perspectives on the body—part of the feminist series mentioned earlier—illustrates the neglect of old women by ending its

attention to women's bodies at menopause (1999). Old age, as a political location, has been ignored.

Women's studies scholars recently have expressed more concern about *aging* (perhaps because more feminists are aging); but rarely do they study the *old.* Not even the few exceptions to this rule examine age relations critically.[1] The scant scholarship on old age differs markedly from the passionate work on late middle age; it is "Written from the outside, it is about *them—* the old—not us" (Twigg 2004, 64). Scholars employ others' data to document the disadvantages that women face in old age, such as low income, widowhood, and physical disability. But these accounts of the "problems of old women" (Gibson 1996) do not analyze age relations. For the most part, feminists have not talked to old women to explore their daily experiences; they have not attuned to the *advantages* old women also might have in relation to old men, such as stronger support networks (see Barker, Morrow, and Mitteness 1998). They have not considered the intersections of inequalities with old age such that, for example, old black men are more likely to be poor than are old white women (Calasanti and Slevin 2001).

Feminists exclude old people in their choice of research questions but also in their theoretical approaches when they do study the old. They often write or say "older" rather than "old," to avoid the negativity of the latter. They may see old age as a social construction, and take it as a sign of women's inequality that they are denigrated as "old" before men are; but we do not often question the stigma affixed to old age. We don't ask why it seems denigrating to label someone old. Rather than accept this subordination of old people, we should ask what is so unmentionable about this stage of life. Feminists have analyzed how terms related to girls and women, such as "sissy" and "girly," are used to put men and boys down and reinforce women's inferiority. Yet we have not considered the *age* relations that use these terms to keep old and young groups in their respective places. For instance, we have been mostly silent about the divisive effects of the so-called "age war" in which the media fuel animosity between generations, especially around matters of employment (Gullette 2004).

Only via a critique of age relations can feminists intervene in the oppression that old people face, especially those marginalized at the intersections of multiple hierarchies. For example, by accepting the cultural dictate to "age successfully" (see Friedan 1993) that underlies the "new gerontology" (Holstein and Minkler 2003), feminists reinforce ageism. Developed by Rowe and Kahn (1998), the notion of successful aging was meant to displace the view of old age as a time of disease and decline with a "vigorous emphasis on the potential for and indeed the likelihood of a healthy and engaged old age" (Holstein and Minkler 2003, 787). Successful aging requires maintenance of the activities popular among the middle-aged privileged with money and leisure time. Thus, staying fit, or at least appearing fit, is highly valued social capital. In this sense, successful aging means not aging, not being "old" or, at the very least, not looking old. The body has become central to identity and to aging, and the maintenance of its youthful appearance has become a lifelong project that requires increasing levels of work.

Many of the age-resisting cultural practices are the purview of women. Successful aging assumes a "feminine" aspect in the ideal that the good, elderly woman be healthy, slim, discreetly sexy, and independent (Ruddick 1999). Suffice it to say, our standard constructions of old age contain little that is positive. Fear of and disgust with growing old are widespread; people stigmatize it and associate it with personal failure, with "letting yourself go." Furthermore, class, gender, and racial biases embedded in these middle-aged standards emphasize control over and choice about aging. We see advertising images of old people playing golf or tennis, traveling, sipping wine in front of sunsets, and strolling (or jogging) on the beaches of upscale resorts. Such pursuits, and the consumption depicted in ads for posh retirement communities, assume a sort of active lifestyle available only to a select group (McHugh 2000): men, whose race and class make them most likely to be able to afford it, and their spouses.

Cruikshank notes the "almost inescapable" judgment that old women's bodies are unattractive; but we know little about how old women endure this rejection (Cruikshank 2003, 147). Thus, though reporting on women who have aged "successfully" (Friedan 1993) might help negate ageist stereotypes of old women as useless or unhappy, it remains ageist in that it reinforces these middle-aged standards. In light of the physical changes that occur as they age, then, many old people must develop strategies to preserve their "youthfulness" so that they will not be seen as old. As a result, old people and their bodies have become subject to a kind of discipline to activity. Those who are chronically impaired, or who prefer to be contemplative are considered to be "problem" old people (Katz 2000; Holstein 1999; Holstein and Minkler 2003). Those who remain active are "not old"; those who are less active are "old" and thus, less valuable.

This study of age relations also complicates theories of gender privilege. For instance, consumer capitalists can profit by the degradation of the status of men as they age. Katz (2001/2002) argues that the advertisements of the anti-aging industry present old men as potentially manly but in need of consumer regimens to remain so. Even old men who are white and rich are also generally retired and weakening, thus losing their institutional grips on the hegemonic ideals of manhood. Once out of the labor market and the realm of those considered sexually desirable by the young, old men find themselves second-class citizens. The men pictured in the anti-aging advertisements drive themselves into expensive and strenuous fun, translating the achievement orientations of the labor market into those of recreational consumption. Banned from the competition for salaries and promotions, they struggle for status by spending the wealth and strength they have to play as young men do, desperate to appear as vigorous as possible.

Proponents of "agelessness" argue that being old is *all* a social construction (Andrews 1999)—all in how one thinks and acts and ought therefore to be defined away, solving the problem of old age by cultural fiat. To be sure, age categories are subjective, and all stages are constructions. Nevertheless, as Andrews observes, "there is not much serious discussion about eliminating infancy, adolescence, or adulthood from the developmental landscape. It is only old age which comes under the scalpel" (302). Whether our quest is to age successfully or to be ageless, this need to deny old age lies at the heart of ageism. We deny that we are aging, and when forced to confront the process, treat it as ugly and tragic.

Age categories have real consequences, and bodies—old bodies—matter. They have a material reality along with their social interpretation (Laz 2003). Old people are *not*, in fact, just like middle-aged persons but only older. They are different. As is the case with other forms of oppression, we must acknowledge and accept these differences, and even see them as valuable. We must distinguish between age resistance and age denial (Twigg 2004, 63); and to do so, we must theorize the age relations that underlie the devaluation of old age.

AGE RELATIONS

Scholars, including gerontologists, have scarcely theorized age relations beyond Laws's (1995) important work on age as one of a complex of social relations.[2] As a result, our discussion here represents an early stage in this endeavor. Our notion of age relations comprises three dimensions. First, age serves a social *organizing principle*; second, different age groups gain *identities and power* in relation to one another; and third, age relations *intersect with other power relations*. Together, these have consequences for life chances—for people's abilities to enjoy economic security and good health. The focus on age relations enables us to learn more about how all of our positions and experiences rest upon power relations based on age.

The first assertion, that societies are organized on the basis of age, is widely documented by scholars in aging studies. Age is a master status characteristic that defines individuals as well as groups (Hendricks 2003). Societies proscribe appropriate behaviors and obligations based on age. The second and third aspects of age relations speak more directly to issues of power, and how and why such age-based organization matters for life chances. Old age does not just exacerbate other inequalities but is a social location in its own right, conferring a loss of power for all those designated as "old" regardless of their advantages in other hierarchies.

When feminists explore power relations such as those based on gender, we point to systematic differences between women and men (recognizing that other power relations come into play). In theorizing age relations, then, we also posit systematic differences between being, for instance, an *old* woman and a *young* woman. This position does not deny the importance of life course and aging processes but instead posits discrimination and exclusion based on age—across lines of such inequalities as race, ethnicity, sexuality, class, or gender. The point at which one becomes "old" varies with these other inequalities. Once reached, old age brings losses of authority and status. Old age is a unique time of life and not simply an additive result of events occurring over the life course. Those who are perceived to be old are marginalized and lose power, they are subjected to violence (such as elder abuse) and to exploitation and cultural imperialism (Laws 1995). They suffer inequalities in distributions of authority, status, and money, and these inequalities are seen to be natural, and thus beyond dispute. Below, we briefly discuss how old people experience these inequalities.

Loss of Power

Old people lose authority and autonomy. For instance, doctors treat old patients differently than younger clients, more often withholding information, services, and treatment of medical problems (Robb, Chen, and Haley 2002). On the one hand, doctors often take the complaints of old people less seriously than younger clients, attributing them to "old age" (Quadagno 1999). On the other hand, old age has been biomedicalized—a process whereby the outcomes of social factors are defined as medical or personal problems to be alleviated by medical intervention. Old people lose their ability to make decisions about their bodies and undergo drug therapies rather than other curative treatments (Wilson 2000; Estes and Binney 1991).

Workplace Issues and Marginalization

Ageism costs old people in the labor market both status and money. Although the attitudes and beliefs of employers are certainly implicated (see Encel 1999), often ageism is more subtly incorporated into staffing and recruitment policies, career structures, and retirement policies (Bytheway 1995). The inability to earn money in later life means that most old people must rely on others—family members or the state. And when we consider the economic dependence and security of old people, the oppressive nature of age relations becomes apparent. The fiscal policies and welfare retrenchment in many Western countries provide one lens on the discrimination faced by old people as they increasingly face cutbacks. As Wilson notes, "Economic policies are often presented as rational and inevitable but, given the power structure of society, these so-called inevitable choices usually end up protecting younger age groups and resulting in unpleasant outcomes for those in later life (cuts in pensions or charges for health care)" (2000, 9). Demographic projections about aging populations are often used to justify such changes, even though relevant evidence is often lacking. Further, neither the public nor decision makers seem willing to consider counterevidence, such as cross-cultural comparisons that reveal little relationship between the percentage of social spending on old persons and their percentage within the overall population (2000). Predictions of dire consequences attendant upon an aging population are similarly unrelated. Indeed, with only 12.4 percent of its population age 65 and over, the United States ranks 37th among countries with at least 10 percent of their population age 65 and over, well below the almost 19 percent of the top three countries, Italy, Japan, and Greece (Federal Interagency Forum on Aging Related Statistics 2004).

Decreases in income, erosion of pensions, and proposals to "reform" Social Security are not the only ways old people are marginalized when they leave the labor market. Laws suggest that labor market participation shapes identity—such that participation in waged labor "is a crucial element of citizenship, in the definition of social worthiness, and in the development of a subject's self-esteem" (1995, 115). In conjunction with the sort of cultural denigration we describe next, the lack of labor market participation encourages young people to see old people as "other" and not fully deserving of citizenship rights (Wilson 2000, 161). Such disenfranchisement may be informal (rather than based in laws), but it is real nonetheless as seen in the previous policy discussion (Laws 1995).

Wealth and Income

In the contemporary United States, many people believe that many old people hold vast economic resources—an assertion that is certainly counter to

claims that old people lose status or money in later life. However, the greatest inequalities in terms of income and wealth exist among old people, such, that many are quite poor (Pampel 1998). The vast majority that relies on Social Security to stay above the poverty line offsets the small number of old people with tremendous wealth. In concrete terms, Social Security—with monthly payments that averaged $1,013 for men and $764 for women in 2003—provides more than half of all income received for two-thirds of old people in the United States; indeed, it amounts to almost half of all income for four-fifths. Even more, it comprises 90 percent or more of all income for a full one-third of elderly people, and 100 percent of all income for more than one-fifth (22 percent). Reliance on these payments is high for all but the richest quintile of old people, whose earnings and pensions add more income than does Social Security. Overall economic dependence of old people on this state-administered program is thus quite high, and higher still when we realize that, even with Social Security, about one-fifth of old minority men and more than a fourth of old minority women fall below the age-adjusted poverty line (Social Security Administration 2004; Federal Interagency Forum on Aging Related Statistics 2004).

The poverty line itself provides an example of the differential treatment of old people. The poverty threshold is lower for old people. In 2003, an old person's income had to be below $8,825—compared to $9,573 for those under 65—in order to be officially designated "poor" (DeNavas-Walt, Proctor, and Mills 2004). It's worth noting that most of the public is unaware of this. Poverty thresholds are calculated based on estimates of costs for nutritionally adequate diets, and because of slower metabolism, old people need fewer calories than younger people. Thus, old people are assumed to need less money than those under 65, despite their high medical expenses. As a result, official statistics greatly underestimate the number of old people who are poor.

Cultural Devaluation

Finally, old people are subject to a "cultural imperialism" exemplified by "the emphasis on youth and vitality that undermines the positive contributions of older people" (Laws 1995, 113). The reality that being old, in and of itself, is a position of low status is apparent in the burgeoning anti-aging industry (including the new field of "longevity medicine"), which is estimated to gross between 27 and 43 billion dollars a year (with the expectation of a rise to $64 billion by 2007), depending on how expansive a definition one uses (Mehlman et al. 2004; U.S. Senate, Special Committee on Aging 2001; *Dateline NBC,* March 6, 2001). Besides ingesting nutritional supplements and testosterone or human growth hormones, increasing numbers of people spend hours at the gym, undergo cosmetic surgery, and use lotions, creams, and hair dyes to erase the physical markers of age. The equation of old age with disease and physical and mental decline is so prevalent that visible signs of aging serve to justify the limitation of the rights and authority of old people. Many view old age as a "natural" part of life with unavoidable decrements—an equation apparent in the medical doctors' treatment of symptoms as "just old age" rather than as signs of illness or injury that merit care. The equation of aging with a natural order justifies ageism.

Old people internalize these notions of old age in early life and carry them as they age. Indeed, they may come to see old age as "a social contagion" that compels them to avoid other old people and to seek the company of those younger than themselves (Slevin 2006/in press). Further, to protest ageism would mean acknowledging one's own old age and stigma (Levy 2001; Minichiello, Browne, and Kendig 2000). As a result, and contrary to common belief that old people vote as a bloc, ageism makes it less likely that old people would band together politically to promote age-based power and rights.[3]

Age relations differ from other power relations in that one's group membership shifts over time. As a result, one can experience both aspects of age relations—advantage and disadvantage—over the course of a lifetime. Although other social locations can be malleable, such dramatic shifts in status remain uncommon. Few change racial or gender identities, but we all grow old or die first. Intersecting inequalities affect when this (becoming old) occurs, but the fact remains, where individuals stand in relation to old age *must* change (Calasanti and Slevin 2001).

Next, we explore how placing old age and age relations at the center of our analysis might transform feminist theories and practices. We look at issues of the body and carework as illustrative of how this deliberate shift of focus creates a more inclusive feminist lens—one that can be applied to multiple issues.

CENTERING ON OLD AGE: THE CHALLENGE TO FEMINISMS

Aging Bodies

Because women's studies scholars begin with the experiences of young adults and middle-aged women, much of their argument against cosmetic surgery and the skin-care industry centers on women's relationship to the "male gaze." In this theory, women are styled in visual media to function as erotic spectacle for the pleasure of men (Mulvey 1990, 33). Thus, these critiques concentrate on the *male-defined* nature of both cosmetic surgery and the skin-care industry. However, when we recognize that an old woman's attractiveness is judged by the disciplining "gaze of youth," then age is revealed as an intersecting axis of inequality (Twigg 2004, 65). Each "gaze" freezes a person as an object defined by subordinate status; and such judgments may he internalized or rejected as foreign by their objects. Yet, the judgments implicit in the male and youthful gazes differ sharply. Twigg describes the power relations between the old care receivers and the younger women who typically bathe them. The naked old people are subjected to the judgmental, always potentially disgusted gaze of youth, indicative of the more subtle stigma attached to old bodies.

Figures of ignorance or scorn, women grow invisible as sexual beings through the aging process—not only in terms of the disappearance of the desirous male gaze, for instance, but also in terms of neglect by younger members of the women's movement and lesbian communities (Holstein 1999; Copper 1986; Macdonald and Rich 1983). Such invisibility calls forth a different set of responses and generates a different form of dependence than those experienced by younger women. In addition, we might ask how putting old women's sexuality at the center of theorizing might change feminist theories. What if we explore the lives of old, heterosexual women who still see themselves as sexual, but feel *cast aside* rather than *objectified*? Neither circumstance amounts to privilege, but they are worth exploring separately. Would the expropriation of women's reproductive labor or exploitation of their bodies still seem like defining moments of women's oppression if we took age relations seriously? And how would our judgments be affected by intersecting inequalities? For instance, many black, retired, professional women express an appreciation for themselves as sexual beings, in contrast to similar white women who feel less desirous or desired (Slevin and Wingrove 1998; Wingrove and Slevin 1991).

Hurtado argues that white, heterosexual women can gain power by aligning as (potential) mates with white men, a possibility from which women of color are typically excluded (1989). White women thus profit from the subordination of racial and ethnic minority women. Furthering Hurtado's argument about relational privilege, we might point to the ways in which younger women benefit from old women's de/sexualization. That old women are cast aside as sexual partners enhances the abilities of younger women to gain power by partnering with privileged men.

In addition, when we put old women who are lesbian at the center of our analysis, we uncover the ways old age intersects with other social locations in shaping responses to aging and old age. For example, old lesbians may openly reproduce the ageism and age inequality that burdens them in the first place by consciously avoiding other old lesbians and electing to spend time only with younger lesbians (Slevin 2006/in press). Exploring the challenges of being an old lesbian in an ageist and homophobic society enhances a focus on what it means to he a woman in the years when reproduction and heterosexual desirability are no longer privileged.

Carework mid Dependence

Centering on old people also would transform our study of carework. Although many feminists have contributed to this research, they have attended to elder care only in relation to the younger women who must balance it with their paid work (and perhaps other forms of care), Research on and interest in old care re-

ceivers or spousal caregivers is nonexistent. Yet, spousal caregivers are both preferred and far more like one another than not, exhibiting few gender differences. Spouses engaged in primary care tend to spend similar amounts of time in carework and perform similar tasks, including personal care (Thompson 2000).[4] Understanding how and why spouses provide similar care gives us a different lens on carework, such as men's abilities and structural inducements to give care (Risman 1987). Focusing on caregiving relationships among the old also can point to ways in which gender shapes the meanings of the carework experience and how people negotiate identities in its context. For instance, most people believe that women are natural caregivers. As a result, white, middle-class wives who give care may experience more stress than husbands, despite the fact that husbands are often less prepared to engage in these tasks at the outset. At the same time, men may describe their stress in different terms, or keep it to themselves and use alcohol to cope (Calderon and Tennstedt 1998; Calasanti 2006/in press). Such study can reveal problems for caregivers that result from their being men or being old, or ways in which frail elders can receive care without feeling dependent (Gibson 1998).

Centering on old careworkers and receivers reveals the power relations embedded in the gaze of youth and the relatively high status given to the care of children. Feminists have long noted that some forms of care work are undervalued, particularly the care of old people (Diamond 1992; Hooyman and Gonyea 1999; Milne and Hazidimitriadou 2002). This is not simply due to the greater value accorded care performed by men. In part, this is so because care for children is more highly valued. To be sure, the carework that men perform for the young is recognized and often lauded, as we see in the esteem accorded the "stay-at-home father" or fathers who share child care. But the carework that old husbands perform for their wives is virtually invisible—from the public eye and from feminist concern.

These discrepant values also should prompt feminists to rethink issues of dependence. Feminists have exposed the gender and race relations underlying "dependence" on the welfare state (see Fraser and Gordon 1994; Estes 2004); but age relations also are implicated. For instance, we noted that projections of age-skewed dependency ratios have been used to promote fiscal retrenchment and cutbacks in old-age policies and programs, including the present call for Social Security "reform" (Estes 2004). Yet, when such skewed ratios reflect a large young population, they do not create the same sort of public outcry, despite the reality that young children are more likely to need care than those, say, ages 65–70 (Gee 2000; Calasanti and Slevin 2001).

Those who are economically active—be they family members or the state—hold economic power over those who are not; and the latter are thus dependent upon them (Bytheway 1995). Women largely depend upon men or the state (Gibson 1998), but in old age, men also become dependents of the state, relying upon the redistribution of economic resources through such policies as public pensions. Although many men are cushioned by multiple privileges when old, they still end up in a position regarded as unmanly (Calasanti and Slevin 2001).

Feminists have demonstrated women's productivity by pointing to their engagement in economic but unpaid activities, such as domestic labor. And gerontologists have followed suit in relation to old people. Still, an unchallenged middle-aged bias guides much of this work, so that arguments assume that "productive" is better than "unproductive." As a result, old people feel compelled to stay active in order to be of worth. Making age-blind arguments to demonstrate that old people also are productive, and hence valuable, can result in a sort of tyranny to prove one's productive value, one that is also shaped by gender relations. For example, grandmothers may be pressed into service caring for grandchildren so that their mothers can pursue paid labor or other activities that carry greater status. In this way, younger women exploit their elders. Grandmothers may enjoy caring for grandchildren, but the role confines them as well, limiting the freedom old women might otherwise enjoy (Browne 1998; Facio 1996). It reinforces women's status as domestic laborers and servers of others, and it exploits women based on their age in that their unpaid labor benefits other family members (Laws 1995, 116).

The feminist silence on policy issues related to old persons, particularly those disadvantaged by other inequalities, is striking. For instance, little discussion

among women's studies scholars ensued before or after Medicare "reform," despite old women's greater reliance on this program and the fact that they are further disadvantaged by its focus on acute illnesses (Hendricks, Hatch, and Cutler 1999), More surprising still, given the women's movement's concern for equal economic opportunities, is the quiet surrounding proposals to "reform" Social Security. The multiple relations of oppression embedded in the debates over privatization and concrete proposals have received attention only from those few feminists within aging studies. It seems likely that age relations not only shape Social Security debates but also the lack of concern of the majority of feminist scholars, intentionally or not. This situation may be analogous to the advantages younger women may have in terms of sexual attractiveness such that they do not question this privilege until it is lost. In like manner, it may be that younger women, who have more job opportunities, pension plans, and the like at their disposal, may well favor privatization at the expense of older women. Thus, the fact that schemes touted by politicians will benefit few younger women does not come to light as such plans are not held up to close scrutiny. Cloaked as the debates are in the sort of "voodoo demographics" (Gee 2000) concerning dependence that we discussed above, much of the public, perhaps including feminist scholars, appear to believe that reform must occur. The ageism and other relations of inequality underlying the privatization movement are palpable. But because feminists focus so closely on earlier ages when they explore dependence, the potentially devastating impact of Social Security reform on disadvantaged groups goes unexplored.

DISCUSSION

In the 1970s, feminists who argued for the inclusion of women were often ignored or treated with hostility. To overcome the apathy of other scholars and activists, they emphasized gender and relationality. They demonstrated that the inclusion of women would broaden understanding and improve the quality of life for both sexes. Likewise, scholars and activists whose work focuses on aging and ageism have been ignored by the mainstream, including those in Women's Studies. They too must argue for inclusion and must demonstrate that old age is a political location, one related to lives of other age groups. But feminists also had other women scholars and advocates with whom they could work, a handful of women in positions of power, and a smattering of pro-feminist men with whom to ally. Where are the old women in Women's Studies, or their advocates? The age relations that push old women from our professions leave us ignorant of their perspectives as we do our collective work. Perhaps because privilege is often invisible, most women's studies scholars and activists have been blind to age relations and deaf to age studies advocates. As with other systems of oppression, people tend not to see the importance or contours of age relations when they are privileged by youth, even if they are disadvantaged in other ways. Are we to wait, then, until we are old before we will take seriously age relations?

To leave age relations unexplored reinforces the inequality old people face, an inequality that shapes other relations of oppression, and one that we reproduce for ourselves. Unlike other hierarchies, in which the privileged rarely become the oppressed, we all face age oppression if we live long enough. We can envision feminists striving to be empowered and to "age successfully" while overlooking the contradictory nature of this endeavor, embedded as it is in the denial of age. Yet, we hope that this specter will prompt women's studies scholars and activists to bring age relations to the center of their analyses.

As feminists and people growing old, we need to be smarter about this. We need to recognize that just as gender, race, class, and sexual orientation serve as organizing principles of power, so too does age. We should no longer assume, rather than theorize, these age relations. We cannot continue to write of gender, or generalize about "women," for instance, as if they were all middle aged or younger any more than we can assume they are all white, middle class, or heterosexual. Further, "adding old people in" to theories developed on the basis of younger groups' experiences is just as fraught as was adding women to male models. It renders old people deviant, telling us little beyond the extent to which they conform to middle-aged norms. We learn little of how their daily lives are shaped by broader social currents as well as their own actions, or how age relations privilege their younger counterparts.

As with other systems of inequality, an exploration of age relations must begin by listening to those disadvantaged by them. However, this process can present complications not encountered with the study of other groups. Because old age is a social location into which people grow, admitting that we are "old" is to admit to loss of privilege and membership in a devalued group—a transition that many people will resist (Minichiello, Browne, and Kendig 2000). In theorizing age relations, then, we would worry less about affixing the chronological age at which middle age or old age occur than about the tensions surrounding the designation of age categories, particularly old age. For instance, if an employer or co-workers see a worker as "old," what is the consequence for the individual? How does this vary by gender, race, or other inequalities? Does it matter that women in the workplace are viewed as "old" sooner than men are (Rodeheaver 1990), and if so, how?

Women's studies scholars can explore the process by which old people (and other age groups) "accomplish age" (Laz 2003), an analogous endeavor to doing gender or doing difference (Fenstermaker and West 2002). Of course, our premise is that these are not accomplished alone, but simultaneously. Feminists have given little thought to how age might influence the ways that women and men might do gender. The dubious claim that men and women become more androgynous with age has not been challenged, nor the related claim that they become less sexual. Certainly the way in which 80-year-old women accomplish gender is different from a 20-year-old female; and her race, ethnicity, class, and sexual orientation would shape this process.

Finally, we hope that once women's studies scholars and activists take old age into account, they will work to imbue old age with positive content—a content that reflects the diversity of old people, their lives, and their varied contributions. Rather than having to deny old age, or to strive to look young, old people should be able to be flabby, contemplative, or sexual, or not. In short, the goal of women's studies scholars and activists should be to enhance old people's freedom to choose lifestyles and ways of being old that are suited to them.

NOTES

1. This holds regardless of whether the focus is on men or women. Even in those few instances where men's studies scholars adopt a life course view, "the theoretical discourse on masculinities has concentrated on social practices of young to middle-aged men and, by default, marginalized the masculinities of elderly men" (Thompson 1994, 9).

2. For further discussion of some of the issues involved in theorizing age relations, see Calasanti (2003).

3. The Association for the Advancement of Retired People's successful campaign and the subsequent repeal of the Catastrophic Care Act, which would have provided old people with coverage in cases of catastrophic illnesses, is but one example of old people promoting diverse political agendas.

4. This also appears true of non-married partners, though research has rarely focused on this group.

REFERENCES

Andrews, M. 1999. "The Seductiveness of Agelessness." *Ageing and Society* 19:301–18.

Arber, Sara, and Jay Ginn. 1991. *Gender and Later Life.* Thousand Oaks, CA: Sage Publications.

Barker, Judith C., Joelle Morrow, and Linda S. Mitteness. 1998. "Gender, Informal Social Support Networks, and Elderly Urban African Americans." *Journal of Aging Studies* 12(2):199–222.

Brook, Barbara. 1999. *Feminist Perspectives on the Body.* London: Longman.

Browne, Colette V. 1998. *Women Feminism, and Aging.* New York: Springer Publishing Company.

Bytheway, Bill. 1995. *Ageism.* Buckingham, UK: Open University Press.

Calasanti, Toni M. 2006/in press. "Gender and Old Age: Lessons from Spousal Caregivers." In *Age Matters: Re-Aligning Feminist Thinking.* New York: Routledge.

———. 2003. "Theorizing Age Relations." In *The Need for Theory: Critical Approaches to Social Gerontology,* eds. Simon Biggs, Ariela Lowenstein, and Jon Hendricks, 199–218. New York: Baywood Press.

Calasanti, Toni M., and Kathleen F. Selvin. 2001. *Gender, Social Inequalities, and Aging,* Walnut Creek, CA: Alta Mira Press.

Calderon, V., and S. L. Tennstedt, 1998. "Ethnic Differences in the Expression of Caregiver Burden: Results of a Qualitative Study." *Journal of Gerontological Social Work* 30(1–2):162–75.

Carroll, Berenice A. 2001. "Reflections on '2000 Subversions: Women's Studies and the 21st Century.'" *NWSA Journal* 13(1): 139–49.

Copper, Baba. 1986. "Voices: On Becoming Old Women." In *Woman and Aging:An Anthology by Women*, eds. Jo Alexander, Debi Berrow, and Lisa Domitrovich, 46–57. Corvallis, OR: Calyx Books.

Cruikshank, Margaret. 2003. *Learning to Be Old.* New York: Rowman and Littlefield.

Dateline NBC. 2001. 6 March.

DeNavas-Walt, Carmen, Bernadette D. Proctor, and Robert J. Mills. 2004. "Income, Poverty, and Health Insurance Coverage in the United States: 2003." *Current Population Reports, P60–226.* U.S. Census Bureau. Washington, D.C.: U.S. Government Printing Office.

Diamond, Timothy. 1992. *Making Gray Gold: Narratives of Nursing Home Care.* Chicago: University of Chicago Press.

Encel, Sol. 1999. "Age Discrimination in Employment in Australia." *Ageing International* 25:69–84.

Estes, Carroll L. 2004. "Social Security Privatization and Older Women: A Feminist Political Economy Perspective." *Journal of Aging Studies* 18(1):9–26.

Estes, Carroll L., and E. A. Binney. 1991. "The Biomedicalization of Aging: Dangers and Dilemmas." In *Critical Perspectives on Aging: The Political and Moral Economy of Growing Old,* eds. Meredith Minkler and Carroll L. Estes, 117–34. New York: Baywood.

Facio, Elisa. 1996. *Understanding Older Chicanas: Sociological and Policy Perspectives.* Thousand Oaks, CA: Sage Publications.

Federal Interagency Forum on Aging Related Statistics. 2004. *Older Americans 2004: Key Indicators of Well-Being.* Washington, D.C.: U.S. Government Printing Office.

Fenstermaker, Sarah, and Candace West, eds. 2002. *Doing Gender, Doing Difference: Inequality, Power, and Institutional Change.* New York: Routledge.

Fraser, Nancy, and Linda Gordon. 1994. "A Genealogy of Dependency: Tracing a Keyword of the U.S. Welfare State." *Signs* 19:309–36.

Friedan, Betty. 1993. *The Fountain of Age.* New York: Simon and Schuster.

Gee, E. M. 2000. "Population Politics: Voodoo Demography, Population Aging, and Social Policy." In *The Overselling of Population Aging,* eds. Ellen Margaret Gee and Gloria Gutman, 5–25. New York: Oxford University Press.

Gibson, Diane. 1998, *Aged Care: Old Policies, New Problems.* New York: Cambridge University Press.

———. 1996. "Broken Down by Age and Gender: 'The Problem of Old Women' Redefined." *Gender & Society* 10:433–48.

Gullette, Margaret M. 2004. *Aged by Culture.* Chicago: University of Chicago Press.

Hendricks, Jon. 2003. "Structure and Identity—Mind the Gap: Toward a Personal Resource Model of Successful Aging." In *The Need for Theory; Critical Approaches to Social Gerontology,* eds. Simon Biggs, Ariela Lowenstein, and Jon Hendricks, 63–87. New York: Baywood Press.

Hendricks, Jon, Laurie Russell Hatch, and Stephen J. Cutler. 1999. "Entitlement, Social Compact, and the Trend toward Retrenchment in U.S. Old-Age Programs." *Hallym International Journal of Aging* 1(1):14–32.

Holstein, Martha B. 1999. "Women and Productive Aging: Troubling Implications." In *Critical Gerontology: Perspectives from Political and Moral Economy,* eds. Meredith Minkler and Carroll L. Estes, 359–73. Amityville, NY: Baywood Press.

Holstein, Martha B., and Meredith Minkler. 2003. "Self, Society, and the 'New Gerontology.'" *The Gerontologist* 43(6):787–96.

Hooyman, N. R., and Gonyea, J. G. 1999. "A. Feminist Model of Family Care: Practice and Policy Directions." *Journal of Women & Aging* 11(2/3):149–69.

Hurtado, Aida. 1989. "Relating to Privilege: Seduction and Rejection in the Subordination of White Women and Women of Color." *Signs* 14:833–55.

Katz, Stephen. 2000. "Busy Bodies: Activity, Aging, and the Management of Everyday Life." *Journal of Aging Studies* 14:135–52.

———. 2001/2002. "Growing Older Without Aging? Positive Aging, Anti-Ageism, and Anti-Aging." *Generations* 25(4):27–32.

Laws, Glenda. 1995. "Understanding Ageism: Lessons From Feminism and Postmodernism." *The Gerontologist* 35(1):112–8.

Laz, Cheryl. 2003. "Age Embodied." *Journal of Aging Studies* 17:503–19.

Levy, Becca R. 2001. "Eradication of Ageism Requires Addressing the Enemy Within." *The Gerontologist* 41(5):578–9.

Macdonald, Barbara, and Cynthia Rich. 1983. *Look Me in the Eye: Old Women, Aging and Ageism.* San Francisco: Spinsters Ink.

McHugh, K. 2000. "The 'Ageless Self'? Emplacement of Identities in Sun-Belt Retirement Communities." *Journal of Aging Studies* 14:103–15.

Mehlman, Maxwell J., Robert H. Binstock, Eric T. Juengst, Roseel S. Ponsaran, and Peter J. Whitehouse. 2004. "Anti-Aging Medicine: Can Consumers Be Better Protected?" *The Gerontologist* 44(3):304–10.

Milne, A., and E. Hatzidimitriadou. 2002. "Isn't He Wonderful? Exploring the Contribution and Conceptualisation of Older Husbands as Carers." Paper presented at the Reconceptualising Gender and Ageing Conference, University of Surrey, UK, June 2002:25–7.

Minichiello, Victor, Jan Browne, and Hal Kendig. 2000. "Perceptions and Consequences of Ageism: Views of Older People." *Ageing and Society* 20(3): 253–78.

Mulvey, Laura. 1990. "Visual Pleasure and Narrative Cinema." In *Issues in Feminist Film Criticism,* ed, Paula Erens, 28–40. Bloomington: Indiana University Press.

Pampel, Fred C. 1998. *Aging, Social Inequality, and Public Policy.* Thousand Oaks, CA: Pine Forge Press.

Quadagno, Jill S. 1999. *Aging, and the Life Course.* Boston: McGraw-Hill.

Risman, B. J. 1987. "Intimate Relationships from a Microstructural Perspective: Men Who Mother." *Gender & Society* 1(1): 6–32.

Robb, Claire, Hongbin Chen, and William E. Haley. 2002. "Ageism in Mental Health Care: A Critical Review." *Journal of Clinical Geropsychology* 8(1):1–2.

Rodeheaver, Dean. 1990. "Labor Market Progeria." *Generations* 14(3):53–8.

Rowe, John W., and Robert L. Kahn. 1998. *Successful Aging.* New York: Pantheon Books.

Ruddick, Sara. 1999. "Virtues and Age." In *Mother Time Women, Aging and Ethics,* ed. Margaret U. Walker, 45–60. Lanham, MD: Rowman and Littlefield.

Slevin, Kathleen F. 2006/in press. "Lesbians Inhabiting Ageing Bodies." In *Age Matters: Re-Aligning Feminist Thinking,* eds. Toni Calasanti and Kathleen F. Slevin. New York: Routledge.

Slevin, Kathleen F., and C. Ray Wingrove. 1998. *From Stumbling Blocks to Stepping Stones: The Life Experiences of Fifty Professional African American Women.* New York: New York University Press.

Social Security Administration. 2004. *Fast Facts & Figures about Social Security, 2004.* Washington, D.C.: U.S. Government Printing Office.

Sontag, Susan. 1972. "The Double Standard of Aging." In *Saturday Review of the Society* 55: 29–38. Rpt. in *On the Contrary: Essays by Men and Women,* eds. Martha Rainbolt and Janet Fleetwood, 1983, 99–112. Albany: State University of New York Press.

Thompson, Edward H., Jr. 2000. "Gendered Caregiving of Husbands and Sons." In *Intersections of Aging: Read-*

ings in Social Gerontology, eds. Elisabeth W. Markson and Lisa A. Hollis-Sawyer, 333–4. Los Angeles: Roxbury Publishing Company.

———. 1994. "Older Men as Invisible in Contemporary Society." In *Older Men's Lives,* ed. Edward H. Thompson, Jr., 197–219. Thousand Oaks, CA: Sage Publications.

Twigg, Julia. 2004. "The Body, Gender, and Age: Feminist Insights in Social Gerontology." *Journal of Aging Studies* 18(1):59–73.

U.S. Senate, Special Committee on Aging. 2001. *Swindlers, Hucksters and Snake Oil Salesman: Hype and Hope Marketing Anti-Aging Products to Seniors.* (Serial No. 107–14), Washington, DC: U.S. Government Printing Office.

Wallace, Claire, and Pamela Abbott. 1999. "Series Editors' Preface." In *Feminist Perspectives on the Body,* ed. Barbara Brook, vii. London: Longman.

Wilson, Gail. 2000. *Understanding Old Age.* Thousand Oaks, CA: Sage Publications.

Wingrove, C. Ray, and Kathleen F. Slevin. 1991. "A Sample of Professional and Managerial Women's Success in Work and Retirement." *Journal of Women & Aging* 3:95–117.

Woodward, Kathleen, ed. 1999. *Figuring Age: Women, Bodies, Generations.* Bloomington: Indiana University Press.

4

Masculinities and Globalization

RAEWYN W. CONNELL

The current wave of research and debate on masculinity stems from the impact of the women's liberation movement on men, but it has taken time for this impact to produce a new intellectual agenda. Most discussions of men's gender in the 1970s and early 1980s centered on an established concept, the male sex role, and an established problem: how men and boys were socialized into this role. There was not much new empirical research. What there was tended to use the more abstracted methods of social psychology (e.g., paper-and-pencil masculinity/femininity scales) to measure generalized attitudes and expectations in ill-defined populations. The largest body of empirical research was the continuing stream of quantitative studies of sex differences—which continued to be disappointingly slight (Carrigan, Connell, and Lee 1985).

The concept of a unitary male sex role, however, came under increasing criticism for its multiple oversimplifications and its incapacity to handle issues about power (Kimmel 1987; Connell 1987). New conceptual frameworks were proposed that linked feminist work on institutionalized patriarchy, gay theoretical work on homophobia, and psychoanalytic ideas about the person (Carrigan, Connell, and Lee 1985; Hearn 1987). Increasing attention was given to certain studies that located issues about masculinity in a fully described local context, whether a British printing shop (Cockburn 1983) or a Papuan mountain community (Herdt 1981). By the late 1980s, a genre of empirical research based on these ideas was developing, most clearly in sociology but also in anthropology, history, organization studies, and cultural studies. This has borne fruit in the 1990s in what is now widely recognized as a new generation of social research on masculinity and men in gender relations (Connell 1995; *Widersprueche* 1995; Segal 1997).

Although the recent research has been diverse in subject matter and social location, its characteristic focus is the construction of masculinity in a particular milieu or moment—a clergyman's family (Tosh 1991), a professional sports career (Messner 1992), a small group of gay men (Connell 1992), a bodybuilding gym (Klein 1993), a group of colonial schools (Morrell 1994), an urban police force (McElhinny 1994), drinking groups in bars (Tomsen 1997), a corporate office on the verge of a decision (Messerschmidt 1997). Accordingly, we might think of this as the "ethnographic moment" in masculinity research, in which the specific and the local are in focus. (This is not to deny that this work *deploys* broader structural concepts simply to note the characteristic focus of the empirical work and its analysis.)

The ethnographic moment brought a much-needed gust of realism to debates on men and masculinity, a corrective to the simplifications of role theory. It also provided a corrective to the trend in popular culture where vague discussions of men's sex roles were giving way to the mystical generalities of the mythopoetic movement and the extreme simplifications of religious revivalism.

Although the rich detail of the historical and field studies defies easy summary, certain conclusions emerge from this body of research as a whole. In short form, they are the following.

Plural Masculinities   A theme of theoretical work in the 1980s, the multiplicity of masculinities has now been very fully documented by descriptive research. Different cultures and different periods of history construct gender differently. Striking differences exist, for instance, in the relationship of homosexual practice to dominant forms of masculinity (Herdt 1984). In multicultural societies, there are varying definitions and enactments of masculinity, for instance, between Anglo and Latino communities in the United States (Hondagneu-Sotelo and Messner 1994). Equally important, more than one kind of masculinity can be found within a given cultural setting or institution. This is particularly well documented in school studies (Foley 1990) but can also be observed in workplaces (Messerschmidt 1997) and the military (Barrett 1996).

Hierarchy and Hegemony   These plural masculinities exist in definite social relations, often relations of hierarchy and exclusion. This was recognized early, in gay theorists' discussions of homophobia; it has become clear that the implications are far-reaching. There is generally a hegemonic form of masculinity, the most honored or desired in a particular context. For Western popular culture, this is extensively documented in research on media representations of masculinity (McKay and Huber 1992). The hegemonic form need not be the most common form of masculinity. Many men live in a state of some tension with, or distance from, hegemonic masculinity; others (such as sporting heroes) are taken as exemplars of hegemonic masculinity and are required to live up to it strenuously (Connell 1990a). The dominance of hegemonic masculinity over other forms may be quiet and implicit, but it may also be vehement and violent, as in the important case of homophobic violence.

Collective Masculinities   Masculinities, as patterns of gender practice, are sustained and enacted not only by individuals but also by groups and institutions. This fact was visible in Cockburn's (1983) pioneering research on informal workplace culture, and it has been confirmed over and over: in workplaces (Donaldson 1991), in organized sport (Whitson 1990; Messner 1992), in schools (Connell 1996), and so on. This point must be taken with the previous two: institutions may construct multiple masculinities and define relationships between them. Barrett's (1996) illuminating study of hegemonic masculinity in the U.S. Navy shows how this takes different forms in the different subbranches of the one military organization.

Bodies as Arenas   Men's bodies do not determine the patterns of masculinity, but they are still of great importance in masculinity. Men's bodies are addressed, defined, and disciplined (as in sport; see Theberge 1991), and given outlets and pleasures by the gender order of society. But men's bodies are not blank slates. The enactment of masculinity reaches certain limits, for instance, in the destruction of the industrial worker's body (Donaldson 1991). Masculine conduct with a female body is felt to be anomalous or transgressive, like feminine conduct with a male body; research on gender crossing (Bolin 1988) shows the work that must be done to sustain an anomalous gender.

Active Construction   Masculinities do not exist prior to social interaction, but come into existence as people act. They are actively produced, using the resources and strategies available in a given milieu. Thus the exemplary masculinities of sports professionals are not a product of passive disciplining, but as Messner (1992) shows, result from a sustained, active engagement with the demands of the institutional setting, even to the point of serious bodily damage from "playing hurt" and accumulated stress. With boys learning masculinities, much of what was previously taken as socialization appears, in close-focus studies of schools

(Walker 1988; Thorne 1993), as the outcome of intricate and intense maneuvering in peer groups, classes, and adult-child relationships.

Contradiction   Masculinities are not homogeneous, simple states of being. Close-focus research on masculinities commonly identifies contradictory desires and conduct; for instance, in Klein's (1993) study of bodybuilders, the contradiction between the heterosexual definition of hegemonic masculinity and the homosexual practice by which some of the bodybuilders finance the making of an exemplary body. Psychoanalysis provides the classic evidence of conflicts within personality, and recent psychoanalytic writing (Chodorow 1994; Lewes 1988) has laid some emphasis on the conflicts and emotional compromises within both hegemonic and subordinated forms of masculinity. Life-history research influenced by existential psychoanalysis (Connell 1995) has similarly traced contradictory projects and commitments within particular forms of masculinity.

Dynamics   Masculinities created in specific historical circumstances are liable to reconstruction, and any pattern of hegemony is subject to contestation, in which a dominant masculinity may be displaced. Heward (1988) shows the changing gender regime of a boys' school responding to the changed strategies of the families in its clientele. Roper (1991) shows the displacement of a production-oriented masculinity among engineering managers by new financially oriented generic managers. Since the 1970s, the reconstruction of masculinities has been pursued as a conscious politics. Schwalbe's (1996) close examination of one mythopoetic group shows the complexity of the practice and the limits of the reconstruction.

If we compare this picture of masculinity with earlier understandings of the male sex role, it is clear that the ethnographic moment in research has already had important intellectual fruits.

Nevertheless, it has always been recognized that some issues go beyond the local. For instance, mythopoetic movements such as the highly visible Promise Keepers are part of a spectrum of masculinity politics; Messner (1997) shows for the United States that this

spectrum involves at least eight conflicting agendas for the remaking of masculinity. Historical studies such as Phillips (1987) on New Zealand and Kimmel (1996) on the United States have traced the changing public constructions of masculinity for whole countries over long periods; ultimately, such historical reconstructions are essential for understanding the meaning of ethnographic details.

I consider that this logic must now be taken a step further, and in taking this step, we will move toward a new agenda for the whole field. What happens in localities is affected by the history of whole countries, but what happens in countries is affected by the history of the world. Locally situated lives are now (indeed, have long been) powerfully influenced by geopolitical struggles, global markets, multinational corporations, labor migration, transnational media. It is time for this fundamental fact to be built into our analysis of men and masculinities.

To understand local masculinities, we must think in global terms. But how? That is the problem pursued in this article. I will offer a framework for thinking about masculinities as a feature of world society and for thinking about men's gender practices in terms of the global structure and dynamics of gender. This is by no means to reject the ethnographic moment in masculinity research. It is, rather, to think how we can use its findings more adequately.

THE WORLD GENDER ORDER

Masculinities do not first exist and then come into contact with femininities; they are produced together, in the process that constitutes a gender order. Accordingly, to understand the masculinities on a world scale, we must first have a concept of the globalization of gender.

This is one of the most difficult points in current gender analysis because the very conception is counterintuitive. We are so accustomed to thinking of gender as the attribute of an individual, even as an unusually intimate attribute, that it requires a considerable wrench to think of gender on the vast scale of global society. Most relevant discussions, such as the literature on women and development, fudge the issue.

They treat the entities that extend internationally (markets, corporations, intergovernmental programs, etc.) as ungendered in principle—but affecting unequally gendered recipients of aid in practice, because of bad policies. Such conceptions reproduce the familiar liberal-feminist view of the state as in principle gender-neutral, though empirically dominated by men.

But if we recognize that very large scale institutions such as the state are themselves gendered, in quite precise and specifiable ways (Connell 1990b), and if we recognize that international relations, international trade, and global markets are inherently an arena of gender formation and gender politics (Enloe 1990), then we can recognize the existence of a world gender order. The term can be defined as the structure of relationships that interconnect the gender regimes of institutions, and the gender orders of local society, on a world scale. That is, however, only a definition. The substantive questions remain: what is the shape of that structure, how tightly are its elements linked, how has it arisen historically, what is its trajectory into the future?

Current business and media talk about globalization pictures a homogenizing process sweeping across the world, driven by new technologies, producing vast unfettered global markets in which all participate on equal terms. This is a misleading image. As Hirst and Thompson (1996) show, the global economy is highly unequal and the current degree of homogenization is often overestimated. Multinational corporations based in the three major economic powers (the United States, European Union, and Japan) are the major economic actors worldwide.

The structure bears the marks of its history. Modern global society was historically produced as Wallerstein (1974) argued, by the economic and political expansion of European states from the fifteenth century on and by the creation of colonial empires. It is in this process that we find the roots of the modern world gender order. Imperialism was, from the start, a gendered process. Its first phase, colonial conquest and settlement, was carried out by gender-segregated forces, and it resulted in massive disruption of indigenous gender orders. In its second phase, the stabilization of colonial societies, new gender divisions of labor were produced in plantation economies and colonial cities, while gender ideologies were linked with racial hierarchies and the cultural defense of empire. The third phase, marked by political decolonization, economic neocolonialism, and the current growth of world markets and structures of financial control, has seen gender divisions of labor remade on a massive scale in the "global factory" (Fuentes and Ehrenreich 1983), as well as the spread of gendered violence alongside Western military technology.

The result of this history is a partially integrated, highly unequal, and turbulent world society, in which gender relations are partly but unevenly linked on a global scale. The unevenness becomes clear when different substructures of gender (Connell 1987; Walby 1990) are examined separately.

The Division of Labor   A characteristic feature of colonial and neocolonial economies was the restructuring of local production systems to produce a male wage worker–female domestic worker couple (Mies 1986). This need not produce a "housewife" in the Western suburban sense, for instance, where the wage work involved migration to plantations or mines (Moodie 1994). But it has generally produced the identification of masculinity with the public realm and the money economy and of femininity with domesticity, which is a core feature of the modern European gender system (Holter 1997).

Power Relations   The colonial and postcolonial world has tended to break down purdah systems of patriarchy in the name of modernization, if not of women's emancipation (Kandiyoti 1994). At the same time, the creation of a westernized public realm has seen the growth of large-scale organizations in the form of the state and corporations, which in the great majority of cases are culturally masculinized and controlled by men. In *comprador* capitalism, however, the power of local elites depends on their relations with the metropolitan powers, so the hegemonic masculinities of neocolonial societies are uneasily poised between local and global cultures.

Emotional Relations   Both religious and cultural missionary activity has corroded indigenous homosexual and cross-gender practice, such as the native American *berdache* and the Chinese "passion of the cut sleeve" (Hinsch 1990). Recently developed Western models of romantic heterosexual love as the basis for marriage and of gay identity as the main alternative have now circulated globally—though as Altman (1996) observes, they do not simply displace indigenous models, but interact with them in extremely complex ways.

Symbolization Mass media, especially electronic media, in most parts of the world follow North American and European models and relay a great deal of metropolitan content; gender imagery is an important part of what is circulated. A striking example is the reproduction of a North American imagery of femininity by Xuxa, the blonde television superstar in Brazil (Simpson 1993). In counterpoint, exotic gender imagery has been used in the marketing strategies of newly industrializing countries (e.g., airline advertising from Southeast Asia)—a tactic based on the longstanding combination of the exotic and the erotic in the colonial imagination (Jolly 1997).

Clearly, the world gender order is not simply an extension of a traditional European-American gender order. That gender order was changed by colonialism, and elements from other cultures now circulate globally. Yet in no sense do they mix on equal terms, to produce a United Colours of Benetton gender order. The culture and institutions of the North Atlantic countries are hegemonic within the emergent world system. This is crucial for understanding the kinds of masculinities produced within it.

THE REPOSITIONING OF MEN AND THE RECONSTITUTION OF MASCULINITIES

The positioning of men and the constitution of masculinities may be analyzed at any of the levels at which gender practice is configured: in relation to the body, in personal life, and in collective social practice. At each level, we need to consider how the processes of globalization influence configurations of gender.

Men's bodies are positioned in the gender order, and enter the gender process, through body-reflexive

practices in which bodies are both objects and agents (Connell 1995)—including sexuality, violence, and labor. The conditions of such practice include where one is and who is available for interaction. So it is a fact of considerable importance for gender relations that the global social order distributes and redistributes bodies, through migration, and through political controls over movement and interaction.

The creation of empire was the original "elite migration," though in certain cases mass migration followed. Through settler colonialism, something close to the gender order of Western Europe was reassembled in North America and in Australia. Labor migration within the colonial systems was a means by which gender practices were spread, but also a means by which they were reconstructed, since labor migration was itself a gendered process—as we have seen in relation to the gender division of labor. Migration from the colonized world to the metropole became (except for Japan) a mass process in the decades after World War II. There is also migration within the periphery, such as the creation of a very large immigrant labor force, mostly from other Muslim countries, in the oil-producing Gulf states.

These relocations of bodies create the possibility of hybridization in gender imagery, sexuality, and other forms of practice. The movement is not always toward synthesis, however, as the race/ethnic hierarchies of colonialism have been recreated in new contexts, including the politics of the metropole. Ethnic and racial conflict has been growing in importance in recent years, and as Klein (1997) and Tillner (1997) argue, this is a fruitful context for the production of masculinities oriented toward domination and violence. Even without the context of violence, there can be an intimate interweaving of the formation of masculinity with the formation of ethnic identity, as seen in the study by Poynting, Noble, and Tabar (1997) of Lebanese youths in the Anglo-dominant culture of Australia.

At the level of personal life as well as in relation to bodies, the making of masculinities is shaped by global forces. In some cases, the link is indirect, such as the working-class Australian men caught in a situation of structural unemployment (Connell 1995), which arises from Australia's changing position in the global economy. In other cases, the link is obvious, such as the executives of multinational corporations and the financial sector servicing international trade. The requirements of a career in international business set up strong pressures on domestic life: almost all multinational executives are men, and the assumption in business magazines and advertising directed toward them is that they will have dependent wives running their homes and bringing up their children.

At the level of collective practice, masculinities are reconstituted by the remaking of gender meanings and the reshaping of the institutional contexts of practice. Let us consider each in turn.

The growth of global mass media, especially electronic media, is an obvious "vector" for the globalization of gender. Popular entertainment circulates stereotyped gender images, deliberately made attractive for marketing purposes. The example of Xuxa in Brazil has already been mentioned. International news media are also controlled or strongly influenced from the metropole and circulate Western definitions of authoritative masculinity, criminality, desirable femininity, and so on. But there are limits to the power of global mass communications. Some local centers of mass entertainment differ from the Hollywood model, such as the Indian popular film industry centered in Bombay. Further, media research emphasizes that audiences are highly selective in their reception of media messages, and we must allow for popular recognition of the fantasy in mass entertainment. Just as economic globalization can be exaggerated, the creation of a global culture is a more turbulent and uneven process than is often assumed (Featherstone 1995).

More important, I would argue, is a process that began long before electronic media existed, the export of institutions. Gendered institutions not only circulate definitions of masculinity (and femininity), as sex role theory notes. The functioning of gendered institutions, creating specific conditions for social practice, calls into existence specific patterns of practice. Thus, certain patterns of collective violence are embedded in the organization and culture of a Western-style army, which are different from the patterns of precolonial violence. Certain patterns of calculative egocentrism are embedded in the working of a stock market; certain patterns of rule following and domination are embedded in a bureaucracy.

Now, the colonial and postcolonial world saw the installation in the periphery, on a very large scale, of a range of institutions on the North Atlantic model: armies, states, bureaucracies, corporations, capital markets, labor markets, schools, law courts, transport systems. These are gendered institutions and their functioning has directly reconstituted masculinities in the periphery. This has not necessarily meant photocopies of European masculinities. Rather, pressures for change are set up that are inherent in the institutional form.

To the extent that particular institutions become dominant in world society, the patterns of masculinity embedded in them may become global standards. Masculine dress is an interesting indicator: almost every political leader in the world now wears the uniform of the Western business executive. The more common pattern, however, is not the complete displacement of local patterns but the articulation of the local gender order with the gender regime of global-model institutions. Case studies such as Hollway's (1994) account of bureaucracy in Tanzania illustrate the point; there, domestic patriarchy articulated with masculine authority in the state in ways that subverted the government's formal commitment to equal opportunity for women.

We should not expect the overall structure of gender relations on a world scale simply to mirror patterns known on the smaller scale. In the most vital of respects, there is continuity. The world gender order is unquestionably patriarchal, in the sense that it privileges men over women. There is a patriarchal dividend for men arising from unequal wages, unequal labor force participation, and a highly unequal structure of ownership, as well as cultural and sexual privileging. This has been extensively documented by feminist work on women's situation globally (e.g., Taylor 1985), though its implications for masculinity have mostly been ignored. The conditions thus exist for the production of a hegemonic masculinity on a world scale, that is to say, a dominant form of masculinity that embodies, organizes, and legitimates men's domination in the gender order as a whole.

The conditions of globalization, which involve the interaction of many local gender orders, certainly multiply the forms of masculinity in the global gender order. At the same time, the specific shape of globalization, concentrating economic and cultural power on an unprecedented scale, provides new resources for dominance by particular groups of men. This dominance may become institutionalized in a pattern of masculinity that becomes, to some degree, standardized across localities. I will call such patterns *globalizing masculinities,* and it is among them, rather than narrowly within the metropole, that we are likely to find candidates for hegemony in the world gender order.

GLOBALIZING MASCULINITIES

In this section, I will offer a sketch of major forms of globalizing masculinity in the three historical phases identified above in the discussion of globalization.

Masculinities of Conquest and Settlement

The creation of the imperial social order involved peculiar conditions for the gender practices of men. Colonial conquest itself was mainly carried out by segregated groups of men—soldiers, sailors, traders, administrators, and a good many who were all these by turn (such as the Rum Corps in early New South Wales, Australia). They were drawn from the more segregated occupations and milieu in the metropole, and it is likely that the men drawn into colonization tended to be the more rootless. Certainly the process of conquest could produce frontier masculinities that combined the occupational culture of these groups with an unusual level of violence and egocentric individualism. The vehement contemporary debate about the genocidal violence of the Spanish conquistadors— who in fifty years completely exterminated the population of Hispaniola—points to this pattern (Bitterli 1989).

The political history of empire is full of evidence of the tenuous control over the frontier exercised by the state—the Spanish monarchs unable to rein in the conquistadors, the governors in Sydney unable to hold back the squatters and in Capetown unable to hold back the Boers, gold rushes breaking boundaries every-

where, even an independent republic set up by escaped slaves in Brazil. The point probably applies to other forms of social control too, such as customary controls on men's sexuality. Extensive sexual exploitation of indigenous women was a common feature of conquest. In certain circumstances, frontier masculinities might be reproduced as a local cultural tradition long after the frontier had passed, such as the gauchos of southern South America and the cowboys of the western United States.

In other circumstances, however, the frontier of conquest and exploitation was replaced by a frontier of settlement. Sex ratios in the colonizing population changed, as women arrived and locally born generations succeeded. A shift back toward the family patterns of the metropole was likely. As Cain and Hopkins (1993) have shown for the British empire, the ruling group in the colonial world as a whole was an extension of the dominant class in the metropole, the landed gentry, and tended to reproduce its social customs and ideology. The creation of a settler masculinity might be the goal of state policy, as it seems to have been in late-nineteenth-century New Zealand, as part of a general process of pacification and the creation of an agricultural social order (Phillips 1987). Or it might be undertaken through institutions created by settler groups, such as the elite schools in Natal studied by Morrell (1994).

The impact of colonialism on the construction of masculinity among the colonized is much less documented, but there is every reason to think it was severe. Conquest and settlement disrupted all the structures of indigenous society, whether or not this was intended by the colonizing powers (Bitierli 1989). Indigenous gender orders were no exception. Their disruption could result from the pulverization of indigenous communities (as in the seizure of land in eastern North America and southeastern Australia), through gendered labor migration (as in gold mining with Black labor in South Africa; see Moodie 1994), to ideological attacks on local gender arrangements (as in the missionary assault on the *berdache* tradition in North America; see Williams 1986). The varied course of resistance to colonization is also likely to have affected the making of masculinities. This is clear in the region of Natal in South Africa, where sustained resistance to colonization by the Zulu kingdom was a key to the mobilization of ethnic-national masculine identities in the twentieth century (Morrell 1996).

Masculinities of Empire

The imperial social order created a hierarchy of masculinities, as it created a hierarchy of communities and races. The colonizers distinguished "more manly" from "less manly" groups among their subjects. In British India, for instance, Bengali men were supposed effeminate while Pathans and Sikhs were regarded as strong and warlike. Similar distinctions were made in South Africa between Hottentots and Zulus, in North America between Iroquois, Sioux, and Cheyenne on one side, and southern and southwestern tribes on the other.

At the same time, the emerging imagery of gender difference in European culture provided general symbols of superiority and inferiority. Within the imperial "poetics of war" (MacDonald 1994), the conqueror was virile, while the colonized were dirty, sexualized, and effeminate or childlike. In many colonial situations, indigenous men were called "boys" by the colonizers (e.g., in Zimbabwe; see Shire 1994). Sinha's (1995) interesting study of the language of political controversy in India in the 1880s and 1890s shows how the images of "manly Englishman" and "effeminate Bengali" were deployed to uphold colonial privilege and contain movements for change. In the late nineteenth century, racial barriers in colonial societies were hardening rather than weakening, and gender ideology tended to fuse with racism in forms that the twentieth century has never untangled.

The power relations of empire meant that indigenous gender orders were generally under pressure from the colonizers, rather than the other way around. But the colonizers too might change. The barriers of late colonial racism were not only to prevent pollution from below but also to forestall "going native," a well-recognized possibility—the starting point, for instance, of Kipling's famous novel *Kim* ([1901] 1987). The pressures, opportunities, and profits of empire might also work changes in gender arrangements among the colonizers, for instance, the division of labor in households with a large supply of indigenous workers as domestic servants (Bulbeck 1992). Empire

might also affect the gender order of the metropole itself by changing gender ideologies, divisions of labor, and the nature of the metropolitan state. For instance, empire figured prominently as a source of masculine imagery in Britain, in the Boy Scouts, and in the cult of Lawrence of Arabia (Dawson 1991). Here we see examples of an important principle: the interplay of gender dynamics between different parts of the world order.

The world of empire created two very different settings for the modernization of masculinities. In the periphery, the forcible restructuring of economics and workforces tended to individualize, on one hand, and rationalize, on the other. A widespread result was masculinities in which the rational calculation of self-interest was the key to action, emphasizing the European gender contrast of rational man/irrational woman. The specific form might be local—for instance, the Japanese "salaryman," a type first recognized in the 1910s, was specific to the Japanese context of large, stable industrial conglomerates (Kinmonth 1981). But the result generally was masculinities defined around economic action, with both workers and entrepreneurs increasingly adapted to emerging market economies.

In the metropole, the accumulation of wealth made possible a specialization of leadership in the dominant classes, and struggles for hegemony in which masculinities organized around domination or violence were split from masculinities organized around expertise. The class compromises that allowed the development of the welfare state in Europe and North America were paralleled by gender compromises—gender reform movements (most notably the women's suffrage movement) contesting the legal privileges of men and forcing concessions from the state. In this context, agendas of reform in masculinity emerged: the temperance movement, compassionate marriage, homosexual rights movements, leading eventually to the pursuit of androgyny in "men's liberation" in the 1970s (Kimmel and Mosmiller 1992). Not all reconstructions of masculinity, however, emphasized tolerance or moved toward androgyny. The vehement masculinity politics of fascism, for instance, emphasized dominance and difference and glorified violence, a pattern still found in contemporary racist movements (Tillner 1997).

Masculinities of Postcolonialism and Neoliberalism

The process of decolonization disrupted the gender hierarchies of the colonial order and, where armed struggle was involved, might have involved a deliberate cultivation of masculine hardness and violence (as in South Africa; see Xaba 1997). Some activists and theorists of liberation struggles celebrated this, as a necessary response to colonial violence and emasculation; women in liberation struggles were perhaps less impressed. However one evaluates the process, one of the consequences of decolonization was another round of disruptions of community-based gender orders and another step in the reorientation of masculinities toward national and international contexts.

Nearly half a century after the main wave of decolonization, the old hierarchies persist in new shapes. With the collapse of Soviet communism, the decline of postcolonial socialism, and the ascendancy of the new right in Europe and North America, world politics is more and more organized around the needs of transnational capital and the creation of global markets.

The neoliberal agenda has little to say, explicitly, about gender: it speaks a gender-neutral language of "markets," "individuals," and "choice." But the world in which neoliberalism is ascendant is still a gendered world, and neoliberalism has an implicit gender politics. The "individual" of neoliberal theory has in general the attributes and interests of a male entrepreneur, the attack on the welfare state generally weakens the position of women, while the increasingly unregulated power of transnational corporations places strategic power in the hands of particular groups of men. It is not surprising, then, that the installation of capitalism in Eastern Europe and the former Soviet Union has been accompanied by a reassertion of dominating masculinities and, in some situations, a sharp worsening in the social position of women.

We might propose, then, that the hegemonic form of masculinity in the current world gender order is the masculinity associated with those who control its dominant institutions: the business executives who operate in global markets, and the political executives who interact (and in many contexts, merge) with them. I will call this *trans-national business masculinity.* This is

not readily available for ethnographic study, but we can get some clues to its character from its reflections in management literature, business journalism, and corporate self-promotion, and from studies of local business elites (e.g., Donaldson 1997).

As a first approximation, I would suggest this is a masculinity marked by increasing egocentrism, very conditional loyalties (even to the corporation), and a declining sense of responsibility for others (except for purposes of image making). Gee, Hall, and Lankshear (1996), studying recent management textbooks, note the peculiar construction of the executive in "fast capitalism" as a person with no permanent commitments, except (in effect) to the idea of accumulation itself. Transnational business masculinity is characterized by a limited technical rationality (management theory), which is increasingly separate from science.

Transnational business masculinity differs from traditional bourgeois masculinity by its increasingly libertarian sexuality, with a growing tendency to commodify relations with women. Hotels catering to businessmen in most parts of the world now routinely offer pornographic videos, and in some parts of the world, there is a well-developed prostitution industry catering for international businessmen. Transnational business masculinity does not require bodily force, since the patriarchal dividend on which it rests is accumulated by impersonal, institutional means. But corporations increasingly use the exemplary bodies of elite sportsmen as a marketing tool (note the phenomenal growth of corporate "sponsorship" of sport in the last generation) and indirectly as a means of legitimation for the whole gender order.

MASCULINITY POLITICS ON A WORLD SCALE

Recognizing global society as an arena of masculinity formation allows us to pose new questions about masculinity politics. What social dynamics in the global arena give rise to masculinity politics, and what shape does global masculinity politics take?

The gradual creation of a world gender order has meant many local instabilities of gender. Gender instability is a familiar theme of poststructuralist theory, but this school of thought takes as a universal condition a situation that is historically specific. Instabilities range from the disruption of men's local cultural dominance as women move into the public realm and higher education, through the disruption of sexual identities that produced "queer" politics in the metropole, to the shifts in the urban intelligentsia that produced "the new sensitive man" and other images of gender change.

One response to such instabilities, on the part of groups whose power is challenged but still dominant, is to reaffirm *local* gender orthodoxies and hierarchies. A masculine fundamentalism is, accordingly, a common response in gender politics at present. A soft version, searching for an essential masculinity among myths and symbols, is offered by the mythopoetic men's movement in the United States and by the religious revivalists of the Promise Keepers (Messner 1997). A much harder version is found, in that country, in the right-wing militia movement brought to world attention by the Oklahoma City bombing (Gibson 1994), and in contemporary Afghanistan, if we can trust Western media reports, in the militant misogyny of the Taliban. It is no coincidence that in the two latter cases, hardline masculine fundamentalism goes together with a marked anti-internationalism. The world system—rightly enough—is seen as the source of pollution and disruption.

Not that the emerging global order is a hotbed of gender progressivism. Indeed, the neoliberal agenda for the reform of national and international economics involves closing down historic possibilities for gender reform. I have noted how it subverts the gender compromise represented by the metropolitan welfare state. It has also undermined the progressive-liberal agendas of sex role reform represented by affirmative action programs, anti-discrimination provisions, child care services, and the like. Right-wing parties and governments have been persistently cutting such programs, in the name of either individual liberties or global competitiveness. Through these means, the patriarchal dividend to men is defended or restored, without an *explicit* masculinity politics in the form of a mobilization of men.

Within the arenas of international relations, the international state, multinational corporations, and global markets, there is nevertheless a deployment of masculinities and a reasonably clear hegemony. The transnational business masculinity described above has had only one major competitor for hegemony in recent decades, the rigid, control-oriented masculinity of the military, and the military-style bureaucratic dictatorships of Stalinism. With the collapse of Stalinism and the end of the cold war, Big Brother (Orwell's famous parody of this form of masculinity) is a fading threat, and the more flexible, calculative, egocentric masculinity of the fast capitalist entrepreneur holds the world stage.

We must, however, recall two important conclusions of the ethnographic moment in masculinity research: that different forms of masculinity exist together and that hegemony is constantly subject to challenge. These are possibilities in the global arena too. Transnational business masculinity is not completely homogeneous; variations of it are embedded in different parts of the world system, which may not be completely compatible. We may distinguish a Confucian variant, based in East Asia, with a stronger commitment to hierarchy and social consensus, from a secularized Christian variant, based in North America, with more hedonism and individualism and greater tolerance for social conflict. In certain arenas, there is already conflict between the business and political leaderships embodying these forms of masculinity: initially over human rights versus Asian values, and more recently over the extent of trade and investment liberalization.

If these are contenders for hegemony, there is also the possibility of opposition to hegemony. The global circulation of "gay" identity (Altman 1996) is an important indication that nonhegemonic masculinities may operate in global arenas, and may even find a certain political articulation, in this case around human rights and AIDS prevention.

REFERENCES

Altman, Dennis. 1996. Rupture or continuity? The internationalisation of gay identities. *Social Text* 48 (3): 77–94.

Barrett, Frank J. 1996. The organizational construction of hegemonic masculinity: The case of the U.S. Navy. *Gender Work and Organization* 3 (3): 129–42.

BauSteineMaenner, ed. 1996. *Kritische Maennerforschung* [Critical research on men]. Berlin: Argument.

Bitterli, Urs. 1989. *Cultures in conflict: Encounters between European and non-European cultures, 1492–1800,* Stanford, CA: Stanford University Press.

Bolin, Anne. 1988. *In search of Eve: Transsexual rites of passage.* Westport, CT: Bergin & Garvey.

Bulbeck, Chilla. 1992. *Australian women in Papua New Guinea: Colonial passages 1920–1960.* Cambridge, U.K.: Cambridge University Press.

Cain, P. J., and A. G. Hopkins. 1993. *British Imperialism: Innovation and expansion, 1688–1914.* New York: Longman.

Carrigan, Tim, Bob Connell, and John Lee. 1985. Toward a new sociology of masculinity. *Theory and Society* 14 (5): 551–604.

Chodorow, Nancy. 1994. *Femininities, masculinities, sexualities: Freud and beyond.* Lexington: University Press of Kentucky.

Cockburn, Cynthia. 1983. *Brothers: Male dominance and technological change.* London: Pluto.

Cohen, Jon. 1991. NOMAS: Challenging male supremacy. *Changing Men* (Winter/Spring): 45–46.

Connell, R. W. 1987. *Gender and power.* Cambridge, MA: Polity.

———. 1990a. An iron man: The body and some contradictions of hegemonic masculinity. In *Sport, men and the gender order: Critical feminist perspectives,* edited by Michael A. Messner and Donald F. Sabo, 83–95. Champaign. IL: Human Kinetics Books.

———. 1990b. The state, gender and sexual politics: Theory and appraisal. *Theory and Society* 19: 507–44.

———. 1992. A very straight gay: Masculinity, homosexual experience and the dynamics of gender. *American Sociological Review* 57 (6): 735–51.

———. 1995. *Masculinities.* Cambridge, MA: Polity.

———. 1996. Teaching the boys: New research on masculinity, and gender strategies for schools. *Teachers College Record* 98 (2): 206–35.

Cornwall, Andrea, and Nancy Lindisfarne, eds. 1994. *Dislocating masculinity: Comparative ethnographies.* London: Routledge.

Dawson, Graham. 1991. The blond Bedouin: Lawrence of Arabia, imperial adventure and the imagining of English-British masculinity. In *Manful assertions: Masculinities in Britain since 1800,* edited by Michael Roper and John Tosh, 113–44. London: Routledge.

Donaldson, Mike. 1991. *Time of our lives: Labour and love in the working class.* Sydney: Allen & Unwin.

———. 1997. Growing up very rich: The masculinity of the hegemonic. Paper presented at the conference Masculinities: Renegotiating Genders, June, University of Wollongong, Australia.

Enloe, Cynthia. 1990. *Bananas, beaches and bases: Making feminist sense of international politics.* Berkeley: University of California Press.

Featherstone, Mike. 1995. *Undoing culture: Globalization, postmodernism and identity.* London: Sage.

Foley, Douglas E. 1990. *Learning capitalist culture: Deep in the heart of Tejas.* Philadelphia: University of Pennsylvania Press.

Fuentes, Annette, and Barbara Ehrenreich. 1983. *Women in the global factory.* Boston: South End.

Gee, James Paul, Glynda Hall, and Colin Lankshear. 1996. *The new work order: Behind the language of the new capitalism.* Sydney: Allen & Unwin.

Gender Equality Ombudsman. 1997. *The father's quota.* Information sheet on parental leave entitlements, Oslo.

Gibson, J. William. 1994. *Warrior dreams: Paramilitary culture in post-Vietnam America.* New York: Hill and Wang.

Hagemann-White, Carol, and Maria S. Rerrich, eds. 1988. *FrauenMaennerBilder* (Women, Imaging, Men). Bielefeld: AJZ-Verlag.

Hearn, Jeff. 1987. *The gender of oppression: Men, masculinity and the critique of Marxism.* Brighton, U.K.: Wheatsheaf.

Herdt, Gilbert H. 1981. *Guardians of the flutes: Idioms of masculinity.* New York: McGraw-Hill.

———. ed. 1984. *Ritualized homosexuality in Melanesia.* Berkeley: University of California Press.

Heward, Christine. 1988. *Making a man of him: Parents and their sons' education at an English public school 1929–1950.* London: Routledge.

Hinsch, Bret. 1990. *Passions of the cut sleeve: The male homosexual tradition in China.* Berkeley: University of California Press.

Hirst, Paul, and Grahame Thompson. 1996. *Globalization in question: The international economy and the possibilities of governance.* Cambridge, MA: Polity.

Hollstein, Walter. 1992. *Machen Sie Platz, mein Herr! Teilen statt Herrschen* [Sharing instead of dominating]. Hamburg: Rowohlt.

Hollway, Wendy. 1994. Separation, integration and difference: Contradictions in a gender regime. In *Power/gender: Social relations in theory and practice,* edited by H. Lorraine Radtke and Henderikus Stam, 247–69. London: Sage.

Holter, Oystein Gullvag. 1997. Gender, patriarchy and capitalism: A social forms analysis. Ph.D. diss., University of Oslo, Faculty of Social Science.

Hondagneu-Sotelo, Pierrette, and Michael A. Messner. 1994. Gender displays and men's power: The "new man" and the Mexican immigrant man. In *Theorizing masculini-*

ties, edited by Harry Brod and Michael Kaufman, 200–218. Twin Oaks, CA: Sage.

Ito Kimio. 1993. *Otokorashisa-no-yukue* [Directions for masculinities]. Tokyo: Shinyo-sha.

Jolly, Margaret. 1997. From point Venus to Bali Ha'i: Eroticism and exoticism in representations of the Pacific. In *Sites of desire, economies of pleasure: Sexualities in Asia and the Pacific,* edited by Lenore Manderson and Margaret Jolly, 99–122. Chicago: University of Chicago Press.

Kandiyoti, Deniz. 1994. The paradoxes of masculinity: Some thoughts on segregated societies. In *Dislocating masculinity: Comparative ethnographies,* edited by Andrea Cornwall and Nancy Lindisfarne, 197–213. London: Routledge.

Kaufman, Michael. 1997. Working with men and boys to challenge sexism and end men's violence. Paper presented at UNESCO expert group meeting on Male Roles and Masculinities in the Perspective of a Culture of Peace, September, Oslo.

Kimmel, Michael S. 1987. Rethinking "masculinity": New directions in research. In *Changing men: New directions in research on men and masculinity,* edited by Michael S. Kimmel, 9–24. Newbury Park, CA: Sage.

———. 1996. *Manhood in America: A cultural history.* New York: Free Press.

Kimmel, Michael S., and Thomas P. Mosmiller, eds. 1992. *Against the tide: Pro-feminist men in the United States, 1776–1990, a documentary history.* Boston: Beacon.

Kindler, Heinz. 1993. *Maske(r)ade: Jungen- und Maennerarbeit fuer die Pratis* [Work with youth and men]. Neuling: Schwaebisch Gmuend und Tuebingen.

Kinmonth, Earl H. 1981. *The self-made man in Meiji Japanese thought: From Samurai to salary man.* Berkeley: University of California Press.

Kipling, Rudyard. [1901] 1987. *Kim.* London: Penguin.

Klein, Alan M. 1993. *Little big men: Bodybuilding subculture and gender construction.* Albany: State University of New York Press.

Klein, Uta. 1997. Our best boys: The making of masculinity in Israeli society. Paper presented at UNESCO expert group meeting on Male Roles and Masculinities in the Perspectives of a Culture of Peace, September, Oslo.

Lewes, Kenneth. 1988. *The psychoanalytic theory of male homosexuality.* New York: Simon & Schuster.

MacDonald, Robert H. 1994. *The language of empire: Myths and metaphors of popular imperialism, 1880–1918.* Manchester, U.K.: Manchester University Press.

McElhinny, Bonnie. 1994. An economy of affect: Objectivity, masculinity and the gendering of police work. In *Dislocating masculinity: Comparative ethnographies,* edited by Andrea Cornwall and Nancy Lindisfarne, 159–71. London: Routledge.

McKay, Jim, and Debbie Huber. 1992. Anchoring media images of technology and sport. *Women's Studies International Forum* 15 (2): 205–18.

Messerschmidt, James W. 1997. *Crime as structured action: Gender, race, class, and crime in the making.* Thousand Oaks, CA: Sage.

Messner, Michael A. 1992. *Power at play: Sports and the problem of masculinity.* Boston: Beacon.

———. 1997. *The politics of masculinities: Men in movements.* Thousand Oaks, CA: Sage.

Metz-Goeckel, Sigrid, and Ursula Mueller. 1986. *Der Mann: Die Brigitte-Studie* [The male]. Beltz: Weinheim & Basel.

Mies, Maria. 1986. *Patriarchy and accumulation on a world scale: Women in the international division of labour.* London: Zed.

Moodie, T. Dunbar. 1994. *Going for gold: Men, mines, and migration.* Johannesburg: Witwatersand University Press.

Morrell, Robert. 1994. Boys, gangs, and the making of masculinity in the White secondary schools of Natal, 1880–1930. *Masculinities* 2 (2): 56–82.

———. ed. 1996. *Political economy and identities in KwaZulu-Natal: Historical and social perspectives.* Durban, Natal: Indicator Press.

Nakamura, Akira. 1994. *Watashi-no Danseigaku* [My men's studies]. Tokyo: Kindaibugei-sha.

Oftung, Knut, ed. 1994. *Menns bilder og bilder av menn* [Images of men]. Oslo: Likestillingsradet.

Phillips, Jock. 1987. *A man's country? The image of the Pakeha male, a history.* Auckland: Penguin.

Poynting, S., G. Noble, and P. Tabar. 1997. "Intersections" of masculinity and ethnicity: A study of male Lebanese immigrant youth in Western Sydney. Paper presented at the conference Masculinities: Renegotiating Genders, June, University of Wollongong, Australia.

Roper, Michael. 1991. Yesterday's model: Product fetishism and the British company man, 1945–85. In *Manful assertions: Masculinities in Britain since 1800,* edited by Michael Roper and John Tosh, 190–211. London: Routledge.

Schwalbe, Michael. 1996. *Unlocking the iron cage: The men's movement gender politics, and the American culture.* New York: Oxford University Press.

Segal, Lynne. 1997. *Slow motion: Changing masculinities, changing men.* 2d ed. London: Virago.

Seidler, Victor J. 1991. *Achilles heel reader: Men, sexual politics and socialism.* London: Routledge.

Shire, Chenjerai. 1994. Men don't go to the moon: Language, space and masculinities in Zimbabwe. In *Dislocating masculinity: Comparative ethnographies,* edited by Andrea Cornwall and Nancy Lindisfarne, 147–58. London: Routledge.

Simpson, Amelia. 1993. *Xuxa: The mega-marketing of a gender, race and modernity.* Philadelphia: Temple University Press.

Sinha, Mrinalini. 1995. *Colonial masculinity: The manly Englishman and the effeminate Bengali in the late nineteenth century.* Manchester, U.K.: Manchester University Press.

Taylor, Debbie. 1985. Women: An analysis. In *Women: A world report,* 1–98. London: Methuen.

Theberge, Nancy. 1991. Reflections on the body in the sociology of sport. *Quest* 43:123–34.

Thorne, Barrie. 1993. *Gender play: Girls and boys in school.* New Brunswick. NJ: Rutgers University Press.

Tillner, Georg. 1997. Masculinity and xenophobia. Paper presented at UNESCO meeting on Male Roles and Masculinities in the Perspective of a Culture of Peace, September, Oslo.

Tomsen, Stephen. 1997. A top night: Social protest, masculinity and the culture of drinking violence. *British Journal of Criminology* 37 (1): 90–103.

Tosh, John. 1991. Domesticity and manliness in the Victorian middle class: The family of Edward White Benson. In *Manful assertions: Masculinities in Britain since 1800,* edited by Michael Roper and John Tosh, 44–73. London: Routledge.

United Nations Educational, Scientific and Cultural Organization (UNESCO). 1997. *Male roles and masculinities in the perspective of a culture of peace: Report of expert group meeting, Oslo, 24–28 September 1997.* Paris: Women and a Culture of Peace Programme, Culture of Peace Unit, UNESCO.

Walby, Sylvia. 1990. *Theorizing patriarchy.* Oxford, U.K.: Blackwell.

Walker, James C. 1988. *Louts and legends: Male youth culture in an inner-city school.* Sydney: Allen & Unwin.

Wallerstein, Immanuel. 1974. *The modern world-system: Capitalist agriculture and the origins of the European world-economy in the sixteenth century.* New York: Academic Press.

Whitson, David. 1990. Sport in the social construction of masculinity. In *Sport, men, and the gender order: Critical feminist perspectives,* edited by Michael A. Messner and Donald F. Sabo, 19–29. Champaign, IL: Human Kinetics Books.

Widersprueche. 1995. Special Issue: Maennlichkeiten. Vol. 56/57.

Williams, Walter L. 1986. *The spirit and the flesh: Sexual diversity in American Indian culture.* Boston: Beacon.

Xaba, Thokozani. 1997. Masculinity in a transitional society: The rise and fall of the "young lions." Paper presented at the conference Masculinities in Southern Africa, June, University of Natal-Durban, Durban.

5

Global Woman

BARBARA EHRENREICH

ARLIE RUSSELL HOCHSCHILD

"Whose baby are you?" Josephine Perera, a nanny from Sri Lanka, asks Isadora, her pudgy two-year-old charge in Athens, Greece.

Thoughtful for a moment, the child glances toward the closed door of the next room, in which her mother is working, as if to say, "That's my mother in there."

"No, you're *my* baby," Josephine teases, tickling Isadora lightly. Then, to settle the issue, Isadora answers, "Together!" She has two mommies—her mother and Josephine. And surely a child loved by many adults is richly blessed.

In some ways, Josephine's story—which unfolds in an extraordinary documentary film, *When Mother Comes Home for Christmas,* directed by Nilita Vachani—describes an unparalleled success. Josephine has ventured around the world, achieving a degree of independence her mother could not have imagined, and amply supporting her three children with no help from her ex-husband, their father. Each month she mails a remittance check from Athens to Hatton, Sri Lanka, to pay the children's living expenses and school fees. On her Christmas visit home, she bears gifts of pots, pans, and dishes. While she makes payments on a new bus that Suresh, her oldest son, now drives for a living, she is also saving for a modest dowry for her

daughter, Norma. She dreams of buying a new house in which the whole family can live. In the meantime, her work as a nanny enables Isadora's parents to devote themselves to their careers and avocations.

But Josephine's story is also one of wrenching global inequality. While Isadora enjoys the attention of three adults, Josephine's three children in Sri Lanka have been far less lucky. According to Vachani, Josephine's youngest child, Suminda, was two—Isadora's age—when his mother first left home to work in Saudi Arabia. Her middle child, Norma, was nine; her oldest son, Suresh, thirteen. From Saudi Arabia, Josephine found her way first to Kuwait, then to Greece. Except for one two-month trip home, she has lived apart from her children for ten years. She writes them weekly letters, seeking news of relatives, asking about school, and complaining that Norma doesn't write back.

Although Josephine left the children under her sister's supervision, the two youngest have shown signs of real distress. Norma has attempted suicide three times. Suminda, who was twelve when the film was made, boards in a grim, Dickensian orphanage that forbids talk during meals and showers. He visits his aunt on holidays. Although the oldest, Suresh, seems to be

---

on good terms with his mother, Norma is tearful and sullen, and Suminda does poorly in school, picks quarrels, and otherwise seems withdrawn from the world. Still, at the end of the film, we see Josephine once again leave her three children in Sri Lanka to return to Isadora in Athens. For Josephine can either live with her children in desperate poverty or make money by living apart from them. Unlike her affluent First World employers, she cannot both live with her family and support it.

Thanks to the process we loosely call "globalization," women are on the move as never before in history. In images familiar to the West from television commercials for credit cards, cell phones, and airlines, female executives jet about the world, phoning home from luxury hotels and reuniting with eager children in airports. But we hear much less about a far more prodigious flow of female labor and energy: the increasing migration of millions of women from poor countries to rich ones, where they serve as nannies, maids, and sometimes sex workers. In the absence of help from male partners, many women have succeeded in tough "male world" careers only by turning over the care of their children, elderly parents, and homes to women from the Third World. This is the female underside of globalization, whereby millions of Josephines from poor countries in the south migrate to do the "women's work" of the north—work that affluent women are no longer able or willing to do. These migrant workers often leave their own children in the care of grandmothers, sisters, and sisters-in-law. Sometimes a young daughter is drawn out of school to care for her younger siblings.

This pattern of female migration reflects what could be called a world-wide gender revolution. In both rich and poor countries, fewer families can rely solely on a male breadwinner. In the United States, the earning power of most men has declined since 1970, and many women have gone out to "make up the difference." By one recent estimate, women were the sole, primary, or coequal earners in more than half of American families (Gallinsky and Friedman 1995). So the question arises: Who will take care of the children, the sick, the elderly? Who will make dinner and clean house?

While the European or American woman commutes to work an average twenty-eight minutes a day, many nannies from the Philippines, Sri Lanka, and India cross the globe to get to their jobs. Some female migrants from the Third World do find something like "liberation," or at least the chance to become independent breadwinners and to improve their children's material lives. Other, less fortunate migrant women end up in the control of criminal employers—their passports stolen, their mobility blocked, forced to work without pay in brothels or to provide sex along with cleaning and child-care services in affluent homes. But even in more typical cases, where benign employers pay wages on time, Third World migrant women achieve their success only by assuming the cast-off domestic roles of middle- and high-income women in the First World—roles that have been previously rejected, of course, by men. And their "commute" entails a cost we have yet to fully comprehend.

The migration of women from the Third World to do "women's work" in affluent countries has so far received little scholarly or media attention—for reasons that are easy enough to guess. First, many, though by no means all, of the new female migrant workers are women of color, and therefore subject to the racial "discounting" routinely experienced by, say, Algerians in France, Mexicans in the United States, and Asians in the United Kingdom. Add to racism the private "indoor" nature of so much of the new migrants' work. Unlike factory workers, who congregate in large numbers, or taxi drivers, who are visible on the street, nannies and maids are often hidden away, one or two at a time, behind closed doors in private homes. Because of the illegal nature of their work, most sex workers are even further concealed from public view.

At least in the case of nannies and maids, another factor contributes to the invisibility of migrant women and their work—one that, for their affluent employers, touches closer to home. The Western culture of individualism, which finds extreme expression in the United States, militates against acknowledging help or human interdependency of nearly any kind. Thus, in the time-pressed upper middle class, servants are no longer displayed as status symbols, decked out in white caps and aprons, but often remain in the background, or disappear when company comes. Furthermore, affluent careerwomen increasingly earn their status not through leisure, as they might have a century ago, but by apparently "doing it all"—producing a fulltime career, thriving children, a contented spouse, and a well-managed home. In order to preserve this illusion, domestic workers and nannies make the house hotel-room perfect, feed and bathe the children, cook and clean up—and then magically fade from sight.

The lifestyles of the First World are made possible by a global transfer of the services associated with a wife's traditional role—child care, home-making, and sex—from poor countries to rich ones. To generalize and perhaps oversimplify: in an earlier phase of imperialism, northern countries extracted natural resources and agricultural products—rubber, metals, and sugar, for example—from lands they conquered and colonized. Today, while still relying on Third World countries for agricultural and industrial labor, the wealthy countries also seek to extract something harder to measure and quantify, something that can look very much like love. Nannies like Josephine bring the distant families that employ them real maternal affection, no doubt enhanced by the heartbreaking absence of their own children in the poor countries they leave behind. Similarly, women who migrate from country to country to work as maids bring not only their muscle power but an attentiveness to detail and to the human relationships in the household that might otherwise have been invested in their own families. Sex workers offer the simulation of sexual and romantic love, or at least transient sexual companionship. It is as if the wealthy parts of the world are running short on precious emotional and sexual resources and have had to turn to poorer regions for fresh supplies.

There are plenty of historical precedents for this globalization of traditional female services. In the ancient Middle East, the women of populations defeated in war were routinely enslaved and hauled off to serve as household workers and concubines for the victors. Among the Africans brought to North America as slaves in the sixteenth through nineteenth centuries, about a third were women and children, and many of those women were pressed to be concubines, domestic servants, or both. Nineteenth-century Irishwomen—along with many rural Englishwomen—migrated to English towns and cities to work as domestics in the homes of the growing upper middle class. Services

thought to be innately feminine—child care, housework, and sex—often win little recognition or pay. But they have always been sufficiently in demand to transport over long distances if necessary. What is new today is the sheer number of female migrants and the very long distances they travel. Immigration statistics show huge numbers of women in motion, typically from poor countries to rich. Although the gross statistics give little clue as to the jobs women eventually take, there are reasons to infer that much of their work is "caring work," performed either in private homes or in institutional settings such as hospitals, hospices, child-care centers, and nursing homes.

The statistics are, in many ways, frustrating. We have information on legal migrants but not on illegal migrants, who, experts tell us, travel in equal if not greater numbers. Furthermore, many Third World countries lack data for past years, which makes it hard to trace trends over time; or they use varying methods of gathering information, which makes it hard to compare one country with another. Nevertheless, the trend is clear enough for some scholars . . . to speak of a "feminization of migration." From 1950 to 1970, for example, men predominated in labor migration to northern Europe from Turkey, Greece, and North Africa. Since then, women have been replacing men. In 1946, women were fewer than 3 percent of the Algerians and Moroccans living in France; by 1990, they were more than 40 percent. Overall, half of the world's 120 million legal and illegal migrants are now believed to be women.

Patterns of international migration vary from region to region, but women migrants from a surprising number of sending countries actually outnumber men, sometimes by a wide margin. For example, in the 1990s, women make up over half of Filipino migrants to all countries and 84 percent of Sri Lankan migrants to the Middle East. Indeed, by 1993 statistics, Sri Lankan women such as Josephine vastly outnumbered Sri Lankan men as migrant workers who'd left for Saudi Arabia, Kuwait, Lebanon, Oman, Bahrain, Jordan, and Qatar, as well as to all countries of the Far East, Africa, and Asia. About half of the migrants leaving Mexico, India, Korea, Malaysia, Cyprus, and Swaziland to work elsewhere are also women. Throughout the 1990s women outnumbered men among migrants to the United States, Canada, Sweden, the United Kingdom, Argentina, and Israel.

Most women, like men, migrate from the south to the north and from poor countries to rich ones. Typically, migrants go to the nearest comparatively rich country, preferably one whose language they speak or whose religion and culture they share. There are also local migratory flows: from northern to southern Thailand, for instance, or from East Germany to West. But of the regional or cross-regional flows, four stand out. One goes from Southeast Asia to the oil-rich Middle and Far East—from Bangladesh, Indonesia, the Philippines, and Sri Lanka to Bahrain, Oman, Kuwait, Saudi Arabia, Hong Kong, Malaysia, and Singapore. Another stream of migration goes from the former Soviet bloc to western Europe—from Russia, Romania, Bulgaria, and Albania to Scandinavia, Germany, France, Spain, Portugal, and England. A third goes from south to north in the Americas, including the stream from Mexico to the United States, which scholars say is the longest-running labor migration in the world. A fourth stream moves from Africa to various parts of Europe. France receives many female migrants from Morocco, Tunisia, and Algeria. Italy receives female workers from Ethiopia, Eritrea, and Cape Verde.

Female migrants overwhelmingly take up work as maids or domestics. As women have become an ever greater proportion of migrant workers, receiving countries reflect a dramatic influx of foreign-born domestics. In the United States, African-American women, who accounted for 60 percent of domestics in the 1940s, have been largely replaced by Latinas, many of them recent migrants from Mexico and Central America. In England, Asian migrant women have displaced the Irish and Portuguese domestics of the past. In French cities, North African women have replaced rural French girls. In western Germany, Turks and women from the former East Germany have replaced rural native-born women. Foreign females from countries outside the European Union made up only 6 percent of all domestic workers in 1984. By 1987, the percentage had jumped to 52, with most coming from the Philippines, Sri Lanka, Thailand, Argentina, Colombia, Brazil, El Salvador, and Peru.

The governments of some sending countries actively encourage women to migrate in search of domestic jobs, reasoning that migrant women are more likely than their male counterparts to send their hard-earned wages to their families rather than spending the money on themselves. In general, women send home anywhere from half to nearly all of what they earn. These remittances have a significant impact on the lives of children, parents, siblings, and wider networks of kin—as well as on cash-strapped Third World governments. Thus, before Josephine left for Athens, a program sponsored by the Sri Lankan government taught her how to use a microwave oven, a vacuum cleaner, and an electric mixer. As she awaited her flight, a song piped into the airport departure lounge extolled the opportunity to earn money abroad. The songwriter was in the pay of the Sri Lanka Bureau of Foreign Employment, an office devised to encourage women to migrate. The lyrics say:

> *After much hardship, such difficult times*
> *How lucky I am to work in a foreign land.*
> *As the gold gathers so do many greedy flies.*
> *But our good government protects us from them.*
> *After much hardship, such difficult times,*
> *How lucky I am to work in a foreign land.*
> *I promise to return home with treasures for everyone.*

Why this transfer of women's traditional services from poor to rich parts of the world? The reasons are, in a crude way, easy to guess. Women in Western countries have increasingly taken on paid work, and hence need others—paid domestics and caretakers for children and elderly people—to replace them. For their part, women in poor countries have an obvious incentive to migrate: relative and absolute poverty. The "care deficit" that has emerged in the wealthier countries as women enter the workforce *pulls* migrants from the Third World and postcommunist nations; poverty *pushes* them.

In broad outline, this explanation holds true. Throughout western Europe, Taiwan, and Japan, but above all in the United States, England, and Sweden, women's employment has increased dramatically since the 1970s. In the United States, for example, the proportion of women in paid work rose from 15 percent of mothers of children six and under in 1950 to 65 percent today. Women now make up 46 percent of the U.S. labor force. Three-quarters of mothers of children eighteen and under and nearly two-thirds of mothers of children age one and younger now work for pay. Furthermore, according to a recent International Labor Organization study, working Americans averaged longer hours at work in the late 1990s than they did in the 1970s. By some measures, the number of hours spent at work have increased more for women than for men, and especially for women in managerial and professional jobs.

Meanwhile, over the last thirty years, as the rich countries have grown much richer, the poor countries have become—in both absolute and relative terms—poorer. Global inequalities in wages are particularly striking. In Hong Kong, for instance, the wages of a Filipina domestic are about fifteen times the amount she could make as a schoolteacher back in the Philippines. In addition, poor countries turning to the IMF or World Bank for loans are often forced to undertake measures of so-called structural adjustment, with disastrous results for the poor and especially for poor women and children. To qualify for loans, governments are usually required to devalue their currencies, which turns the hard currencies of rich countries into gold and the soft currencies of poor countries into straw. Structural adjustment programs also call for cuts in support for "noncompetitive industries," and for the reduction of public services such as health care and food subsidies for the poor. Citizens of poor countries, women as well as men, thus have a strong incentive to seek work in more fortunate parts of the world.

But it would be a mistake to attribute the globalization of women's work to a simple synergy of needs among women—one group, in the affluent countries, needing help and the other, in poor countries, needing jobs. For one thing, this formulation fails to account for the marked failure of First World governments to meet the needs created by its women's entry into the workforce. The downsized American—and to a lesser degree, western European—welfare state has become a "deadbeat dad." Unlike the rest of the industrialized world, the United States does not offer public child care for working mothers, nor does it ensure paid family and medical leave. Moreover, a series of state tax revolts in the 1980s reduced the number of hours public libraries were open and slashed school-enrichment

and after-school programs. Europe did not experience anything comparable. Still, tens of millions of western European women are in the workforce who were not before—and there has been no proportionate expansion in public services.

Secondly, any view of the globalization of domestic work as simply an arrangement among women completely omits the role of men. Numerous studies, including some of our own, have shown that as American women took on paid employment, the men in their families did little to increase their contribution to the work of the home. For example, only one out of every five men among the working couples whom Hochschild interviewed for *The Second Shift* (Hochschild 1989), in the 1980s shared the work at home, and later studies suggest that while working mothers are doing somewhat less housework than their counterparts twenty years ago, most men are doing only a little more. With divorce, men frequently abdicate their child-care responsibilities to their ex-wives. In most cultures of the First World outside the United States, powerful traditions even more firmly discourage husbands from doing "women's work." So, strictly speaking, the presence of immigrant nannies does not enable affluent women to enter the workforce; it enables affluent *men* to continue avoiding the second shift.

The men in wealthier countries are also, of course, directly responsible for the demand for immigrant sex workers—as well as for the sexual abuse of many migrant women who work as domestics. Why, we wondered, is there a particular demand for "imported" sexual partners? Part of the answer may lie in the fact that new immigrants often take up the least desirable work, and, thanks to the AIDS epidemic, prostitution has become a job that ever fewer women deliberately choose. But perhaps some of this demand grows out of the erotic lure of the "exotic." Immigrant women may seem desirable sexual partners for the same reason that First World employers believe them to be especially gifted as caregivers: they are thought to embody the traditional feminine qualities of nurturance, docility, and eagerness to please. Some men feel nostalgic for these qualities, which they associate with a bygone way of life. Even as many wage-earning Western women assimilate to the competitive culture of "male" work and ask respect for making it in a man's world, some men seek in the "exotic Orient" or "hot-blooded tropics" a woman from the imagined past.

Of course, not all sex workers migrate voluntarily. An alarming number of women and girls are trafficked by smugglers and sold into bondage. Because trafficking is illegal and secret, the numbers are hard to know with any certainty. Kevin Bales estimates that in Thailand alone, a country of 60 million, half a million to a million women are prostitutes, and one out of every twenty of these is enslaved (Bales 1999). Many of these women are daughters whom northern hill-tribe families have sold to brothels in the cities of the South. Believing the promises of jobs and money, some begin the voyage willingly, only to discover days later that the "arrangers" are traffickers who steal their passports, define them as debtors, and enslave them as prostitutes. Other women and girls are kidnapped, or sold by their impoverished families, and then trafficked to brothels. Even worse fates befall women from neighboring Laos and Burma, who flee crushing poverty and repression at home only to fall into the hands of Thai slave traders.

If the factors that pull migrant women workers to affluent countries are not as simple as they at first appear, neither are the factors that push them. Certainly relative poverty plays a major role, but, interestingly, migrant women often do not come from the poorest classes of their societies. In fact, they are typically more affluent and better educated than male migrants. Many female migrants from the Philippines and Mexico, for example, have high school or college diplomas and have held middle-class—albeit low-paid—jobs back home. One study of Mexican migrants suggests that the trend is toward increasingly better-educated female migrants. Thirty years ago, most Mexican-born maids in the United States had been poorly educated maids in Mexico. Now a majority have high school degrees and have held clerical, retail, or professional jobs before leaving for the United States. Such women are likely to be enterprising and adventurous enough to resist the social pressures to stay home and accept their lot in life.

Noneconomic factors—or at least factors that are not immediately and directly economic—also influence a woman's decision to emigrate. By migrating, a woman may escape the expectation that she care for elderly family members, relinquish her paycheck to a husband or father, or defer to an abusive husband. Migration may also be a practical response to a failed marriage and the need to provide for children without male help. In the Philippines, Rhacel Salazar Parreñas (2002) tells us, migration is sometimes called a "Philippine divorce." And there are forces at work that may be making the men of poor countries less desirable as husbands. Male unemployment runs high in the countries that supply female domestics to the First World. Unable to make a living, these men often grow demoralized and cease contributing to their families in other ways. Many female migrants, tell of unemployed husbands who drink or gamble their remittances away. Notes one study of Sri Lankan women working as maids in the Persian Gulf: "It is not unusual . . . for the women to find upon their return that their Gulf wages by and large have been squandered on alcohol, gambling and other dubious undertakings while they were away" (Gamburd, 2002).

To an extent then, the globalization of child care and housework brings the ambitious and independent women of the world together: the career-oriented upper-middle-class woman of an affluent nation and the striving woman from a crumbling Third World or postcommunist economy. Only it does not bring them together in the way that second-wave feminists in affluent countries once liked to imagine—as sisters and allies struggling to achieve common goals. Instead, they come together as mistress and maid, employer and employee, across a great divide of privilege and opportunity.

This trend toward global redivision of women's traditional work throws new light on the entire process of globalization. Conventionally, it is the poorer countries that are thought to be dependent on the richer ones—a dependency symbolized by the huge debt they owe to global financial institutions. What we explore, however, is a dependency that works in the other direction, and it is a dependency of a particularly intimate kind. Increasingly often, as affluent and middle-class families in the First World come to depend on migrants from poorer regions to provide child care, homemaking, and sexual services, a global relationship arises that in some ways mirrors the traditional relationship between the sexes. The First World takes on a role like that of the old-fashioned male in the family—pampered, entitled, unable to cook, clean, or find his socks. Poor countries take on a role like that of the traditional woman within the family—patient, nurturing, and self-denying. A division of labor feminists critiqued when it was "local" has now, metaphorically speaking, gone global.

To press this metaphor a bit further, the resulting relationship is by no means a "marriage," in the sense of being openly acknowledged. In fact, it is striking how invisible the globalization of women's work remains, how little it is noted or discussed in the First World. Trend spotters have had almost nothing to say about the fact that increasing numbers of affluent First World children and elderly persons are tended by immigrant care workers or live in homes cleaned by immigrant maids. Even the political groups we might expect to be concerned about this trend—antiglobalization and feminist activists—often seem to have noticed only the most extravagant abuses, such as trafficking and female enslavement. So if a metaphorically gendered relationship has developed between rich and poor countries, it is less like a marriage and more like a secret affair.

But it is a "secret affair" conducted in plain view of the children. Little Isadora and the other children of the First World raised by "two mommies" may be learning more than their ABC's from a loving surrogate parent. In their own living rooms, they are learning a vast and tragic global politics. Children see. But they also learn how to disregard what they see. They learn how adults make the visible invisible. That is their "early childhood education." . . .

The globalization of women's traditional role poses important challenges to anyone concerned about gender and economic inequity. How can we improve the lives and opportunities of migrant women engaged in legal occupations such as nannies and maids? How can we prevent trafficking and enslavement? More basically, can we find a way to counterbalance the systematic transfer of caring work from poor countries to rich, and the inevitable trauma of the children left behind? . . . Before we can hope to find activist solutions, we need to see these women as full human beings. They are strivers as well as victims, wives and mothers as well as workers—sisters, in other words, with whom we in the First World may someday define a common agenda.

REFERENCES

Bales, Kevin. 1999. *Disposable People: New Slavery in the Global Economy.* Berkeley: University of California Press.

Hochschild, Arlie Russell with Anne Machung. 1989. *The Second Shift.* New York: Viking Penguin.

Gallinsky, Ellen, and Dana Friedman. 1995. *Woman: The New Providers.* Whirlpool Foundation Study, Part 1. New York: Families and Work Institute.

Gamburd, Michele. 2002. "Breadwinner No More," In *Global Woman.* Barbara Ehrenreich and Arlie Russell Hochschild (eds.), 190–206. New York: Metropolitan Books.

Parrenas, Rhacel Salazar. 2002. "The Care Crisis in The Philippines: Children and Transnational Families in the New Global Economy," In *Global Woman.* Barbara Ehrenreich and Arlie Russell Hochschild (eds.), 39–54. New York: Metropolitan Books.

6

Antiglobalization Pedagogies and Feminism

CHANDRA TALPADE MOHANTY

ANTIGLOBALIZATION STRUGGLES

. . . What does it mean to make antiglobalization a key factor for feminist theorizing and struggle? To illustrate my thinking about antiglobalization, let me focus on two specific sites where knowledge about globalization is produced. The first site is a pedagogical one and involves an analysis of the various strategies being used to internationalize (or globalize) the women's studies curriculum in U.S. colleges and universities. I argue that this move to internationalize women's studies curricula and the attendant pedagogies that flow from this is one of the main ways we can track a discourse of global feminism in the United States. Other ways of tracking global feminist discourses include analyzing the documents and discussions flowing out of the Beijing United Nations conference on women, and of course popular television and globalization scholarship I focus on is the emerging, notably ungendered and deracialized discourse on activism against globalization.

Antiglobalization Pedagogies

Let me turn to the struggles over the dissemination of a feminist cross-cultural knowledge base through pedagogical strategies "internationalizing" the women's studies curriculum. The problem of "the (gendered) color line" remains, but is more easily seen today as developments of transnational and global capital. While I choose to focus on women's studies curricula, my arguments hold for curricula in any discipline or academic field that seeks to internationalize or globalize its curriculum. I argue that the challenge for "internationalizing" women's studies is no different from the one involved in "racializing" women's studies in the 1980s, for very similar politics of knowledge come into play here.

So the question I want to foreground is the politics of knowledge in bridging the "local" and the "global" in women's studies. How we teach the "new" scholarship in women's studies is at least as important as the scholarship itself in the struggles over knowledge and citizenship in the U.S. academy. . . .

Drawing on my own work with U.S. feminist academic communities, I describe three pedagogical models used in "internationalizing" the women's studies curriculum and analyze the politics of knowledge at work. Each of these perspectives is grounded in particular conceptions of the local and the global, of women's agency, and of national identity, and each curricular model presents different stories and ways of crossing borders and building bridges. I suggest that a "comparative feminist studies" or "feminist solidarity" model is the most useful and productive pedagogical strategy for feminist cross-cultural work. It is this particular model that provides a way to theorize a complex relational understanding of experience, location, and history such that feminist cross-cultural work moves through the specific context to construct a real notion of universal and of democratization rather than colonization. It is through this model that we can put into practice the idea of "common differences" as the basis for deeper solidarity across differences and unequal power relations.

Feminist-as-Tourist Model This curricular perspective could also be called the "feminist as international consumer" or, in less charitable terms, the "white women's burden or colonial discourse" model. It involves a pedagogical strategy in which brief forays are made into non–Euro-American cultures, and particular sexist cultural practices addressed from an otherwise Eurocentric women's studies gaze. In other words, the "add women as global victims or powerful women and stir" perspective. This is a perspective in which the primary Euro-American narrative of the syllabus remains untouched, and examples from non-Western or Third World/South cultures are used to supplement and "add" to this narrative. The story here is quite old. The effects of this strategy are that students and teachers are left with a clear sense of the difference and distance between the local (defined as self, nation, and Western) and the global (defined as other, non-Western, and transnational). Thus the local is always grounded in nationalist assumptions—the United States or Western European nation-state provides a normative context. This strategy leaves power relations and hierarchies untouched since ideas about center and margin are reproduced along Eurocentric lines.

For example, in an introductory feminist studies course, one could include the obligatory day or week on dowry deaths in India, women workers in Nike factories in Indonesia, or precolonial matriarchies in West Africa, while leaving the fundamental identity of the Euro-American feminist on her way to liberation untouched. Thus Indonesian workers in Nike factories or dowry deaths in India stand in for the totality of women in these cultures. These women are not seen in their everyday lives (as Euro-American women are)— just in these stereotypical terms. Difference in the case of non–Euro-American women is thus congealed, not seen contextually with all of its contradictions. This pedagogical strategy for crossing cultural and geographical borders is based on a modernist paradigm, and the bridge between the local and the global becomes in fact a predominantly self-interested chasm. This perspective confirms the sense of the "evolved U.S./Euro feminist." While there is now more consciousness about not using an "add and stir" method in teaching about race and U.S. women of color, this does not appear to be the case in "internationalizing" women's studies. Experience in this context is assumed to be static and frozen into U.S.- or Euro-centered categories. Since in this paradigm feminism is always/already constructed as Euro-American in origin and development, women's lives and struggles outside this geographical context only serve to confirm or contradict this originary feminist (master) narrative. This model is the pedagogical counterpart of the orientalizing and colonizing Western feminist scholarship of the past decades. In fact it may remain the predominant model at this time. Thus implicit in this pedagogical strategy is the crafting of the "Third World difference," the creation of monolithic images of Third World/South women. This contrasts with images of Euro-American women who are vital, changing, complex, and central subjects within such a curricular perspective.

Feminist-as-Explorer Model This particular pedagogical perspective originates in area studies, where the "foreign" woman is the object and subject of knowledge and the larger intellectual project is entirely about countries other than the United States. Thus, here the local and the global are both defined as non–Euro-American. The focus on the international implies that it exists outside the U.S. nation-state. Women's, gender, and feminist issues are based on spatial/geographical and temporal/historical categories located elsewhere. Distance from "home" is fundamental to the definition of international in this framework. This strategy can result in students and teachers being left with a notion of difference and separateness, a sort of "us and them" attitude, but unlike the tourist model, the explorer perspective can provide a deeper, more contextual understanding of feminist issues in discretely defined geographical and cultural spaces. However, unless these discrete spaces are taught in relation to one another, the story told is usually a cultural relativist one, meaning that differences between cultures are discrete and relative with no real connection or common basis for evaluation. The local and the global are here collapsed into the international that by definition excludes the United States. If the dominant discourse is the discourse of cultural relativism, questions of power, agency, justice, and common criteria for critique and evaluation are silenced.

In women's studies curricula this pedagogical strategy is often seen as the most culturally sensitive way to "internationalize" the curriculum. For instance, entire courses on "Women in Latin America" or "Third World Women's Literature" or "Postcolonial Feminism" are added on to the predominantly U.S.-based curriculum as a way to "globalize" the feminist knowledge base. These courses can be quite sophisticated and complex studies, but they are viewed as entirely separate from the intellectual project of U.S. race and ethnic studies. The United States is not seen as part of "area studies," as white is not a color when one speaks of people of color. This is probably related to the particular history of institutionalization of area studies in the U.S. academy and its ties to U.S. imperialism. Thus areas to be studied/conquered "out there," never within the United States. The fact that area studies in U.S. academic settings were federally funded and conceived as having a political project in the service of U.S. geopolitical interests suggests the need examine the contemporary interests of these fields, especially as they relate to the logic of global capitalism. In addition, as Ella Shohat argues, it is to "reimagine the study of regions and cultures in a way that transcends the conceptual borders inherent in the global cartography of the cold war" (2001, 1271). The field of American studies is an interesting location to examine here, especially since its more recent focus on U.S. imperialism. However, American studies rarely falls under the purview of "area studies."

The problem with the feminist-as-explorer strategy is that globalization is an economic, political, and ideological phenomenon that actively brings the world and its various communities under connected and interdependent discursive and material regimes. The lives of women are connected and interdependent, albeit not the same, no matter which geographical area we happen to live in.

Separating area studies from race and ethnic studies thus leads to understanding or teaching about the global as a way of not addressing internal racism, capitalist hegemony, colonialism, and heterosexualization as central to processes of global domination, exploitation, and resistance. Global or international is thus understood apart from racism—as if racism were not central to processes of globalization and relations of rule at this time. An example of this pedagogical strategy in the context of the larger curriculum is the usual separation of "world cultures" courses from race and ethnic studies courses. Thus identifying the kinds of representations of (non–Euro-American) women mobilized by this pedagogical strategy, and the relation of these representations to implicit images of First World/North women are important foci for analysis. What kind of power is being exercised in this strategy? What kinds of ideas of agency and struggle are being consolidated? What are the potential effects of a kind of cultural relativism on our understandings of the differences and commonalities among communities of women around the world? Thus the feminist-as-explorer model has its own problems, and I believe this is an inadequate way of building a feminist cross-cultural knowledge base because in the context of an interwoven world with clear directionalities of power and domination, cultural relativism serves as an apology for the exercise of power.

The Feminist Solidarity or Comparative Feminist Studies Model This curricular strategy is based on the premise that the local and the global are not defined in terms of physical geography or territory but exist simultaneously and constitute each other. It is then the links, the relationships, between the local and the global that are foregrounded, and these links are conceptual, material, temporal, contextual, and so on. This framework assumes a comparative focus and analysis of the directionality of power no matter what the subject of the women's studies course is—and it assumes both distance and proximity (specific/universal) as its analytic strategy.

Differences and commonalities thus exist in relation and tension with each other in all contexts. What is emphasized are relations of mutuality, co-responsibility, and common interests, anchoring the idea of feminist solidarity. For example, within this model, one would not teach a U.S. women of color course with additions on Third World/South or white women, but a comparative course that shows the interconnectedness of the histories, experiences, and struggles of U.S. women of color, white women, and women from the Third World/South. By doing this kind of comparative teaching that is attentive to power, each historical experience illuminates the experiences of the others. Thus, the focus is not just on the intersections of race, class, gender, nation, and sexuality in different communities of women but on mutuality and coimplication, which suggests attentiveness to the interweaving of the histories of these communities. In addition the focus is simultaneously on individual and collective experiences of oppression and exploitation and of struggle and resistance.

Students potentially move away from the "add and stir" and the relativist "separate but equal" (or different) perspective to the coimplication/solidarity one. This solidarity perspective requires understanding the historical and experiential specificities and differences of women's lives as well as the historical and experiential connections between women from different national, racial, and cultural communities. Thus it suggests organizing syllabi around social and economic processes and histories of various communities of women in particular substantive areas like sex work, militarization, environmental justice, the prison/industrial complex, and human rights, and looking for points of contact and connection as well as disjunctures. It is important to always foreground not just the connections of domination but those of struggle and resistance as well.

In the feminist solidarity model the One-Third/Two-Thirds paradigm makes sense. Rather than Western/Third World, or North/South, or local/global seen as oppositional and incommensurate categories, the One-Third/Two-Thirds differentiation allows for teaching and learning about points of connection and distance among and between communities of women marginalized and privileged along numerous local and global dimensions. Thus the very notion of inside/outside necessary to the distance between local/global is transformed through the use of a One-Third/Two-Thirds paradigm, as both categories must be understood as containing difference/similarities, inside/outside, and distance/proximity. Thus sex work, militarization, human rights, and so on can be framed in their multiple local and global dimensions using the One-Third/Two-Thirds, social minority/social majority paradigm. I am suggesting then that we look at the women's studies curriculum in its entirety and that we attempt to use a comparative feminist studies model wherever possible.

I refer to this model as the feminist solidarity model because, besides its focus on mutuality and common interests, it requires one to formulate questions about connection and disconnection between activist women's movements around the world. Rather than formulating activism and agency in terms of discrete and disconnected cultures and nations, it allows us to frame agency and resistance across the borders of nation and culture. I think feminist pedagogy should not simply expose students to a particularized academic scholarship but that it should also envision the possibility of activism and struggle outside the academy. Political education through feminist pedagogy should teach active citizenship in such struggles for justice.

My recurring question is how pedagogies can supplement, consolidate, or resist the dominant logic of globalization. How do students learn about the inequities among women and men around the world? . . .

After almost two decades of teaching feminist studies in U.S. classrooms, it is clear to me that the way we theorize experience, culture, and subjectivity in relation to histories, institutional practice, and collective struggles determines the kind of stories we tell in the classroom. If these varied stories are to be taught such that students learn to democratize rather than colonize the experiences of different spatially and temporally located communities of women, neither a Eurocentric nor a cultural pluralist curricular practice will do. In fact narratives of historical experience are crucial to political thinking not because they present an unmediated version of the "truth" but because they can destabilize received truths and locate debate in the complexities and contradictions of historical life. . . . These are the kinds of stories we need to weave into a feminist solidarity pedagogical model.

Antiglobalization Scholarship and Movements

Women's and girls' bodies determine democracy: free from violence and sexual abuse, free from malnutrition and environmental degradation, free to plan their families, free to not have families, free to choose their sexual lives and preferences
—*Zillah Eisenstein*, Global Obscenities, *1998*

There is now an increasing and useful feminist scholarship critical of the practices and effects of globalization. Instead of attempting a comprehensive review of this scholarship, I want to draw attention to some of the most useful kinds of issues it raises. Let me turn, then, to a feminist reading of antiglobalization movements and argue for a more intimate, closer alliance between women's movements, feminist pedagogy, cross-cultural feminist theorizing, and these ongoing anticapitalist movements.

I return to an earlier question: What are the concrete effects of global restructuring on the "real" raced, classed, national, sexual bodies of women in the academy, in workplaces, streets, households, cyberspaces, neighborhoods, prisons, and in social movements? And how do we recognize these gendered effects in movements against globalization? Some of the most complex analyses of the centrality of gender in understanding economic globalization attempt to link questions of subjectivity, agency, and identity with those of political economy and the state. This scholarship argues persuasively for a need to rethink patriarchies and hegemonic masculinities in relation to present-day

globalization and nationalisms, and it also attempts to retheorize the gendered aspects of the refigured relations of the state, the market, and civil society by focusing on unexpected and unpredictable sites of resistance to the often devastating effects of global restructuring on women. And it draws on a number of disciplinary paradigms and political perspectives in making the case for the centrality of gender in processes of global restructuring, arguing that the reorganization of gender is part of the global strategy of capitalism.

Women workers of particular caste/class, race, and economic status are necessary to the operation of the capitalist global economy. Women are not only the preferred candidates for particular jobs, but particular kinds of women—poor, Third and Two-Thirds World, working-class, and immigrant/migrant women—are the preferred workers in these global, "flexible" temporary job markets. The documented increase in the migration of poor, One-Third/Two-Thirds World women in search of labor across national borders has led to a rise in the international "maid trade" (Parrenas 2001) and in international sex trafficking and tourism. Many global cities now require and completely depend on the service and domestic labor of immigrant and migrant women. The proliferation of structural adjustment policies around the world has reprivatized women's labor by shifting the responsibility for social welfare from the state to the household and to women located there. The rise of religious fundamentalisms in conjunction with conservative nationalisms, which are also in part reactions to global capital and its cultural demands, has led to the policing of women's bodies in the streets and in the workplaces.

Global capital also reaffirms the color line in its newly articulated class structure evident in the prisons in the One-Third World. The effects of globalization and deindustrialization on the prison industry in the One-Third World leads to a related policing of the bodies of poor, One-Third/Two-Thirds World, immigrant and migrant women behind the concrete spaces and bars of privatized prisons. Angela Davis and Gina Dent (2001) argue that the political economy of U.S. prisons, and the punishment industry in the West/ North, brings the intersection of gender, race, colonialism, and capitalism into sharp focus. Just as the factories and workplaces of global corporations seek and discipline the labor of poor, Third World/South, immigrant/migrant women, the prisons of Europe and the United States incarcerate disproportionately large numbers of women of color, immigrants, and noncitizens of African, Asian, and Latin American descent.

Making gender and power visible in the processes of global restructuring demands looking at, naming, and seeing the particular raced, and classed communities of women from poor countries as they are constituted as workers in sexual, domestic, and service industries; as prisoners; and as household managers and nurturers. . . .

While feminist scholarship is moving in important and useful directions in terms of a critique of global restructuring and the culture of globalization, I want to ask some of the same questions I posed in 1986 once again. In spite of the occasional exception, I think that much of present-day scholarship tends to reproduce particular "globalized" representations of women. Just as there is an Anglo-American masculinity produced in and by discourses of globalization, it is important to ask what the corresponding femininities being produced are. Clearly there is the ubiquitous global teenage girl factory worker, the domestic worker, and the sex worker. There is also the migrant/immigrant service worker, the refugee, the victim of war crimes, the woman-of-color prisoner who happens to be a mother and drug user, the consumer-housewife, and so on. There is also the mother-of-the-nation/religious bearer of traditional culture and morality.

Although these representations of women correspond to real people, they also often stand in for the contradictions and complexities of women's lives and roles. Certain images, such as that of the factory or sex worker, are often geographically located in the Third World/South, but many of the representations identified above are dispersed throughout the globe. Most refer to women of the Two-Thirds World, and some to women of the One-Third World. And a woman from the Two-Thirds World can live in the One-Third World. The point I am making here is that women are workers, mothers, or consumers in the global economy, but we are also all those things simultaneously. Singular and monolithic categorizations of women in discourses of globalization circumscribe ideas about experience,

agency, and struggle. While there are other, relatively new images of women that also emerge in this discourse—the human rights worker or the NGO advocate, the revolutionary militant and the corporate bureaucrat—there is also a divide between false, overstated images of victimized and empowered womanhood, and they negate each other. We need to further explore how this divide plays itself out in terms of a social majority/minority, One-Third/Two-Thirds World characterization. The concern here is with whose agency is being colonized and who is privileged in these pedagogies and scholarship. These then are my new queries for the twenty-first century.

Because social movements are crucial sites for the construction of knowledge, communities, and identities, it is very important for feminists to direct themselves toward them. The antiglobalization movements of the last five years have proven that one does not have to be a multinational corporation, controller of financial capital, or transnational governing institution to cross national borders. These movements form an important site for examining the construction of transborder democratic citizenship. But first a brief characterization of antiglobalization movements is in order.

Unlike the territorial anchors of the anticolonial movements of the early twentieth century, antiglobalization movements have numerous spatial and social origins. These include anticorporate environmental movements such as the Narmada Bachao Andolan in central India and movements against environmental racism in the U.S. Southwest, as well as the antiagribusiness small-farmer movements around the world. The 1960s consumer movements, people's movements against the IMF and World Bank for debt cancelation and against structural adjustment programs, and the antisweatshop student movements in Japan, Europe, and the United States are also a part of the origins of the antiglobalization movements. In addition, the identity-based social movements of the late twentieth century (feminist, civil rights, indigenous rights, etc.) and the transformed U.S. labor movement of the 1990s also play a significant part in terms of the history of antiglobalization movements.

While women are present as leaders and participants in most of these antiglobalization movements, a feminist agenda only emerges in the post-Beijing "women's rights as human rights" movement and in some peace and environmental justice movements. In other words, while girls and women are central to the labor of global capital, antiglobalization work does not seem to draw on feminist analysis or strategies. Thus, while I have argued that feminists need to be anticapitalists, I would now argue that antiglobalization activists and theorists also need to be feminists. Gender is ignored as a category of analysis and a basis for organizing in most of the antiglobalization movements, and antiglobalization (and anticapitalist critique) does not appear to be central to feminist organizing projects, especially in the First World/North. In terms of women's movements, the earlier "sisterhood is global" form of internationalization of the women's movement has now shifted into the "human rights" arena. This shift in language from "feminism" to "women's rights" has been called the mainstreaming of the feminist movement—a successful attempt to raise the issue of violence against women on to the world stage.

If we look carefully at the focus of the antiglobalization movements, it is the bodies and labor of women and girls that constitute the heart of these struggles. For instance, in the environmental and ecological movements such as Chipko in India and indigenous movements against uranium mining and breast-milk contamination in the United States, women are not only among the leadership: their gendered and racialized bodies are the key to demystifying and combating the processes of recolonization put in place by corporate control of the environment. . . .

Women have been in leadership roles in some of the cross-border alliances against corporate injustice. Thus, making gender, and women's bodies and labor visible, and theorizing this visibility as a process of articulating a more inclusive politics are crucial aspects of feminist anticapitalist critique. Beginning from the social location of poor women of color of the Two-Thirds World is an important, even crucial, place for feminist analysis. . . .

A transnational feminist practice depends on building feminist solidarities across the divisions of place, identity, class, work, belief, and so on. In these very fragmented times it is both very difficult to build these alliances and also never more important to do so. Global capitalism both destroys the possibilities and also offers up new ones. . . .

REFERENCES

Davis, Angela, and Gina Dent. 2001. "Prison as a Border: A Conversation on Gender, Globalization, and Punishment." *Signs* 26, no. 4 (summer): 1235–42.

Elsenstein, Zillah R. 1998. *Global Obscenities: Patriarchy, Capitalism, and the Lure of Cyberfantasy.* New York: New York University Press.

Parrenas, Rachel Salazar. 2001. "Transgressing the Nation-State: The Partial Citizenship and 'Imagined (Global) Community' of Migrant Filipina Domestic Workers." *Signs* 26, no. 4 (summer): 1129–54.

Shohat, Ella. 2001. "Area Studies, Transnationalism, and the Feminist Production of Knowledge." *Signs* 26, no. 4 (summer): 1269–72.

PART II

BODIES

What are we to make of the old Freudian dictim that "biology is destiny?" Are women's and men's different *social* positions and practices simply reflections of their *natural* differences between the sexes? The articles in this section show that this belief does not stand up to critical scrutiny. First, even when we acknowledge the feet that there are some average differences between women's and men's bodies (for instance, on average, men are taller than women), average differences are not categorical differences (e.g., some women are taller than some men). Second, average bodily differences between women and men do not necessarily translate into particular social structures or practices. In fact, recent research in the sociology of the body shows a dynamic, reciprocal relationship between bodies and their social environments. For example, boys and men have been encouraged and rewarded for "building" muscular bodies, while girls and women have been discouraged or punished for this. Even among today's fitness-conscious young women, most feel that "too much muscle" is antithetical to feminine attractiveness. All kinds of food products and dietary supplements, from high protein "muscle milk" to low-calorie diet foods are marketed in gendered ways. These social beliefs, practices and products result in more muscular male bodies, and "slimmed and toned" female bodies that, together, appear to reflect "natural" differences.

As the articles in the first section of Part II demonstrate, bodies can be used for both control and resistance. Moreover, the articles complicate the idea of women as disempowered body-objects and men as empowered body-subjects. The reality is more complicated and nuanced. In the first article, Nomy Lamm offers a powerfully personal statement of resistance to the culture of thinness. Lamm discloses how her youthful "punk grrrl" feminism has provided her with a means of resisting the narrow mainstream media constructions of beauty. She shifts the discussion from thinness obsession, to fat oppression, and in doing so, lays the groundwork for the revolutionary reclaiming of the fat body as beautiful. The next chapter stays on the topic of cultural norms and expectations for preferred female bodies, as author Betsy Lucal offers us a fascinating glimpse into her lived experiences with "gender bending." What is it like, Lucal asks, to be a person whose physical appearance does not neatly "fit" into one of U.S. culture's two acceptable sex categories? Lucal is a woman who is regularly mistaken as a man, yet she chooses nonparticipation in the accoutrements of femininity, in part as an act towards dismantling patriarchal culture. Next, Don Sabo draws on his experience as an instructor in a maximum security men's prison to reflect on how, for survival reasons, male inmates tend to value and display a "hard" muscular masculinity and suppress any signs of softness. But masculine body projects are not always about muscles and in the following chapter, Kristen Barber analyzes a group of white, middle-class and affluent heterosexual men who favor getting their hair cut at women's beauty salons rather than barbershops. While these men resist feminization, they also appear to be seeking status differentiation from other men. They deliberately groom and perform a particular kind of class-based masculinity. The final chapter in this section by Evelyn Nakano Glenn shifts the focus to skin bleaching and beauty. Around the globe, but particularly in the global South, the consumption of skin lightening products is growing among young, urban and educated women. Rather than focusing only on individual consciousness, Nakano Glenn shows the role of transnational pharmaceutical and cosmetics companies in fueling the desire for lighter skin, and the association of light skin with feminine beauty.

Men's violence against other men in wars has historically been seen through the lens of patriotism and heroism, but it is not usually analyzed through a gendered prism of difference, and women's participation in military violence has received scant attention. In the first article in the section on violence, Joanne Nagel and Lindsey Feitz provide a corrective by examining the implications of the unprecedented numbers of women in the U.S. military efforts in Iraq. They argue that early in the war, some white U.S. military women were portrayed as "damsels in distress" in order to dramatize U.S. military men's courage, and Iraqi men's cowardice. Particular configurations of race, class, gender and sexuality were deployed to achieve both public relations and combat goals. Government inflicted violence extends beyond wars to government inaction in providing relief to the victims of Karrina, and as Barbara Ransby suggests in the next article, it was poor black women who suffered most in this event. Political discourse that indicts black women's poverty and family forms set the stage for this scenario, and as Ransby shows, black women activists in New Orleans have responded with resilience and creativity. In recent years, the media has amplified a relatively new form of violence, that of Palestinean and Muslim female suicide bombers. The article by Naaman underscores the ways in which "women" and 'terrorist" have traditionally been seen as antithetical and dichotonomous terms, and she argues that when women operate as suicide bombers, they are not only transgressing the old dichotomies, but they are also enacting a performative aspect of violence. Media representations, however, continue to frame them in ways that reassert old gender dichotomies and negate female agency, with Western media positioning the women as victims of patriarchy, and Arab media framing them as "brides of Palestine."

7

It's a Big Fat Revolution

NOMY LAMM

I am going to write an essay describing my experiences with fat oppression and the ways in which feminism and punk have affected my work. It will be clear, concise and well thought-out, and will be laid out in the basic thesis paper, college essay format. I will deal with these issues in a mature and intellectual manner. I will cash in on as many fifty-cent words as possible.

I lied. (You probably already picked up on that, huh?) I can't do that. This is my life, and my words are the most effective tool I have for challenging Whiteboyworld (that's my punk-rock cutesy but oh-so-revolutionary way of saying "patriarchy"). If there's one thing that feminism has taught me, it's that the revolution is gonna be on my terms. The revolution will be incited through my voice, my words, not the words of the universe of male intellect that already exists. And I know that a hell of a lot of what I say is totally contradictory. My contradictions can coexist, cuz they exist inside of me, and I'm not gonna simplify them so that they fit into the linear, analytical pattern that I know they're supposed to. I think it's important to recognize that all this stuff does contribute to the

revolution, for real. The fact that I write like this cuz it's the way I want to write makes this world just that much safer for me.

I wanna explain what I mean when I say "the revolution," but I'm not sure whether I'll be able to. Cuz at the same time that I'm being totally serious, I also see my use of the term as a mockery of itself. Part of the reason for this is that I'm fully aware that I still fit into dominant culture in many ways. The revolution could very well be enacted against me, instead of for me. I don't want to make myself sound like I think I'm the most oppressed, most punk-rock, most revolutionary person in the world. But at the same time I do think that revolution is a word I should use as often as I can, because it's a concept that we need to be aware of. And I don't just mean it in an abstract, intellectualized way, either. I really do think that the revolution has begun. Maybe that's not apparent to mainstream culture yet, but I see that as a good sign. As soon as mainstream culture picks up on it, they'll try to co-opt it.

For now the revolution takes place when I stay up all night talking with my best friends about feminism and marginalization and privilege and oppression and power and sex and money and real-life rebellion. For now the revolution takes place when I watch a girl stand up in front of a crowd of people and talk about her sexual abuse. For now the revolution takes place when I get a letter from a girl I've never met who says that the zine I wrote changed her life. For now the revolution takes place when the homeless people in my town camp out for a week in the middle of downtown. For now the revolution takes place when I am confronted by a friend about something racist that I have said. For now the revolution takes place in my head when I know how fucking brilliant my girlfriends and I are.

And I'm living the revolution through my memories and through my pain and through my triumphs. When I think about all the marks I have against me in this society, I am amazed that I haven't turned into some worthless lump of shit. Fatkikecripplecuntqueer. In a nutshell. But then I have to take into account the fact that I'm an articulate, white, middle-class college kid, and that provides me with a hell of a lot of privilege and opportunity for dealing with my oppression that may not be available to other oppressed people. And since my personality/being isn't divided up into a privileged part and an oppressed part, I have to deal with the ways that these things interact, counterbalance and sometimes even overshadow each other. For example, I was born with one leg. I guess it's a big deal, but it's never worked into my body image in the same way that being fat has. And what does it mean to be a white woman as opposed to a woman of color? A middle-class fat girl as opposed to a poor fat girl? What does it mean to be fat, physically disabled and bisexual? (Or fat, disabled and *sexual at all?*)

See, of course, I'm still a real person, and I don't always feel up to playing the role of the revolutionary. Sometimes it's hard enough for me to just get out of bed in the morning. Sometimes it's hard enough to just talk to people at all, without having to deal with the political nuances of everything that comes out of their mouths. Despite the fact that I do tons of work that deals with fat oppression, and that I've been working so so hard on my own body image, there are times when I really hate my body and don't want to deal with being strong all the time. Because I am strong and have thought all of this through in so many different ways,

and I do have naturally high self-esteem, I've come to a place where I can honestly say that I love my body and I'm happy with being fat. But occasionally, when I look in the mirror and I see this body that is so different from my friends', so different from what I'm told it should be, I just want to hide away and not deal with it anymore. At these times it doesn't seem fair to me that I have to always be fighting to be happy. Would it be easier for me to just give in and go on another diet so that I can stop this perpetual struggle? Then I could still support the fat grrrl revolution without having it affect me personally in every way. And I know I know I know that's not the answer and I could never do that to myself, but I can't say that the thought never crosses my mind.

And it doesn't help much when my friends and family, who all know how I feel about this, continue to make anti-fat statements and bitch about how fat they feel and mention new diets they've heard about and are just dying to try. "I'm shaped like a watermelon." "Wow, I'm so happy, I now wear a size seven instead of a size nine." "I like this mirror because it makes me look thinner."

I can't understand how they could still think these things when I'm constantly talking about these issues, and I can't believe that they would think that these are okay things to talk about in front of me. And it's not like I want them to censor their conversation around me. . . . I just want them to not think it. I know that most of this is just a reflection of how they feel about themselves and isn't intended as an attack on me or an invalidation of my work, but it makes it that much harder for me. It puts all those thoughts inside me. Today I was standing outside of work and I caught a glimpse of myself in the window and thought, "Hey, I don't look that fat!" And I immediately realized how fucked up that was, but that didn't stop me from feeling more attractive because of it.

I want this out of me. This is not a part of me, and theoretically I can separate it all out and throw away the shit, but it's never really gone. When will this finally be over? When can I move on to other issues? It will never be over, and that's really fucking hard to accept.

I am living out this system of oppression through my memories, and even when I'm not thinking about them they are there, affecting everything I do. Five years old, my first diet. Seven years old, being declared officially "overweight" because I weigh ten pounds over what a "normal" seven-year-old should weigh. Ten years old, learning to starve myself and be happy feeling constantly dizzy. Thirteen years old, crossing the border from being bigger than my friends to actually being "fat." Fifteen years old, hearing the boys in the next room talk about how fat (and hence unattractive) I am. Whenever I perform, I remember the time when my dad said he didn't like the dance I choreographed because I looked fat while I was doing it. Every time I dye my hair I remember when my mom wouldn't let me dye my hair in seventh grade because seeing fat people with dyed hair made her think they were just trying to cover up the fact that they're fat, trying to look attractive despite it (when of course it's obvious what they should really do if they want to look attractive, right?). And these are big memorable occurrences that I can put my finger on and say, "This hurt me." But what about the lifetime of media I've been exposed to that tells me that only thin people are lovable, healthy, beautiful, talented, fun? I know that those messages are all packed in there with the rest of my memories, but I just can't label them and their effects on my psyche. They are elusive and don't necessarily feel painful at the time. They are well disguised and often even appear alluring and romantic. (I will never fall in love because I cannot be picked up and swung around in circles. . . .)

All my life the media and everyone around me have told me that fat is ugly. Which of course is just a cultural standard that has many, many medical lies to fall back upon. Studies have shown that fat people are unhealthy and have short life expectancies. Studies have also shown that starving people have these same peculiarities. These health risks to fat people have been proven to be a result of continuous starvation—dieting—and not of fat itself. I am not fat due to lack of willpower. I've been a vegetarian since I was ten years old. Controlling what I eat is easy for me. Starving myself is not (though for most of my life I wished it was). My body is supposed to be like this, and I've been on plenty of diets where I've kept off some weight for a period of several months and then gained it all back. Two years ago I finally ended the cycle. I am not dieting anymore because I know that this is how my body

is supposed to be, and this is how I want it to be. Being fat does not make me less healthy or less active. Being fat does not make me less attractive.

On TV I see a thin woman dancing with a fabulously handsome man, and over that I hear, "I was never happy until I went on [fill in the blank] diet program, but now I'm getting attention from men, and I feel so good! I don't have to worry about what people are saying about me behind my back, because I know I look good. You owe it to yourself to give yourself the life you deserve. Call [fill in the blank] diet program today, and start taking off the pounds right away!" TV shows me a close-up of a teary-eyed fat girl who says, "I've tried everything, but nothing works. I lose twenty pounds, and I gain back twenty-five. I feel so ashamed. What can I do?" The first time I saw that commercial I started crying and memorized the number on the screen. I know that feeling of shame. I know that feeling of having nowhere left to turn, of feeling like I'm useless because I can't lose all that "unwanted fat." But I know that the unhappiness is not a result of my fat. It's a result of a society that tells me I'm bad.

Where's the revolution? My body is fucking beautiful, and every time I look in the mirror and acknowledge that, I am contributing to the revolution.

I feel like at this point I'm expected to try to prove to you that fat can be beautiful by going into descriptions of "rippling thighs and full smooth buttocks." I won't. It's not up to me to convince you that fat can be attractive. I refuse to be the self-appointed full-figured porno queen. Figure it out on your own.

It's not good enough for you to tell me that you "don't judge by appearances"—so fat doesn't bother you. Ignoring our bodies and "judging only by what's on the inside" is not the answer. This seems to be along the same line of thinking as that brilliant school of thought called "humanism": "We are all just people, so let's ignore trivialities such as race, class, gender, sexual preference, body type and so on." Bullshit! The more we ignore these aspects of ourselves, the more shameful they become and the more we are expected to be what is generally implied when these qualifiers are not given—white, straight, thin, rich, male. It's unrealistic to try to overlook these exterior (and hence meaningless, right?) differences, because we're still being brainwashed with the same shit as everyone else. This way we're just not talking about it. And I don't want to be told, "Yes you're fat, but you're beautiful on the inside." That's just another way of telling me that I'm ugly, that there's no way that I'm beautiful on the outside. Fat does not equal ugly, don't give me that. My body *is* me. I want you to see my body, acknowledge my body. True revolution comes not when we learn to ignore our fat and pretend we're no different, but when we learn to use it to our advantage, when we learn to deconstruct all the myths that propagate fat-hate.

My thin friends are constantly being validated by mainstream feminism, while I am ignored. The most widespread mentality regarding body image at this point is something along these lines: Women look in the mirror and think, "I'm fat," but really they're not. Really they're thin.

Really they're thin. But really I'm fat. According to mainstream feminist theory, I don't even exist. I know that women do often look in the mirror and think that they are fatter than they are. And yes, this is a problem. But the analysis can't stop there. There are women who *are* fat, and that needs to be dealt with. Rather than just reassuring people, "No, you're not fat, you're just curvy," maybe we should be demystifying fat and dealing with fat politics as a whole. And I don't mean maybe, I mean it's a necessity. Once we realize that fat is not "inherently bad" (and I can't even believe I'm writing that—"inherently bad"—it sounds so ridiculous), then we can work out the problem as a whole instead of dealing only with this very minute part of it. All forms of oppression work together, and so they have to be fought together.

I think that a lot of the mainstream feminist authors who claim to be dealing with this issue are doing it in a very wrong way. Susie Orbach, for example, with *Fat Is a Feminist Issue.* She tells us: Don't diet, don't try to lose weight, don't feed the diet industry. But she then goes on to say: But if you eat right and exercise, you will lose weight! And I feel like, great, nice, it's so very wonderful that that worked for her, but she's totally missing the point. She is trying to help women, but really she is hurting us. She is hurting us because she's saying that there's still only one body that's okay for us (and she's the one to help us get it!). It's almost like that *Stop the Insanity* woman, Susan Powter. One of

my friends read her book and said that the first half of it is all about fat oppression and talks about how hard it is to be fat in our society, but then it says: So use my great new diet plan! This kind of thing totally plays on our emotions so that we think, Wow, this person really understands me. They know where I'm coming from, so they must know what's best for me.

And there are so many "liberal" reasons for perpetuating fat-hate. Yes, we're finally figuring out that dieting never works. How, then, shall we explain this horrible monstrosity? And how can we get rid of it? The new "liberal" view on fat is that it is caused by deep psychological disturbances. Her childhood was bad, she was sexually abused, so she eats and gets fat in order to hide herself away. She uses her fat as a security blanket. Or maybe when she was young her parents caused her to associate food with comfort and love, so she eats to console herself. Or maybe, like with me, her parents were always on diets and always nagging her about what she was eating, so food became something shameful that must be hoarded and kept secret. And for a long, long time I really believed that if my parents hadn't instilled in me all these fucked-up attitudes about food, I wouldn't be fat. But then I realized that my brother and sister both grew up in exactly the same environment, and they are both thin. Obviously this is not the reason that I am fat. Therapy won't help, because there's nothing to cure. When will we stop grasping for reasons to hate fat people and start realizing that fat is a totally normal and natural thing that cannot and should not be gotten rid of?

Despite what I said earlier about my friends saying things that are really hurtful to me, I realize that they are actually pretty exceptional. I don't want to make them seem like uncaring, ignorant people. I'm constantly talking about these issues, and I feel like I'm usually able to confront my friends when they're being insensitive, and they'll understand or at least try to. Sometimes when I leave my insular circle of friends I'm shocked at what the "real world" is like. Hearing boys on the bus refer to their girlfriends as their "bitches," seeing fat women being targeted for harassment on the street, watching TV and seeing how every fat person is depicted as a food-obsessed slob, seeing women treated as property by men who see masculinity as a right to power. . . . I leave these situations feeling like the punk scene, within which most of my interactions take place, is so sheltered. I cannot imagine living in a community where I had nowhere to go for support. I cannot imagine living in the "real world."

But then I have to remember that it's still there in my community—these same fucked-up attitudes are perpetuated within the punk scene as well; they just take on more subtle forms. I feel like these issues are finally starting to be recognized and dealt with, but fat hating is still pretty standard. Of course everyone agrees that we shouldn't diet and that eating disorders are a result of our oppressive society, but it's not usually taken much further than that. It seems like people have this idea that punk is disconnected from the media. That because we are this cool underground subculture, we are immune to systems of oppression. But the punkest, coolest kids are still the skinny kids. And the same cool kids who are so into defying mainstream capitalist "Amerika" are the ones who say that fat is a symbol of capitalist wealth and greed. Yeah, that's a really new and different way of thinking: Blame the victim. Perpetuate institutionalized oppression. Fat people are not the ones who are oppressing these poor, skinny emo boys.

This essay is supposed to be about fat oppression. I feel like that's all I ever talk about. Sometimes I feel my whole identity is wrapped up in my fat. When I am fully conscious of my fat, it can't be used against me. Outside my secluded group of friends, in hostile situations, I am constantly aware that at any moment I could be harassed. Any slight altercation with another person could lead to a barrage of insults thrown at my body. I am always ready for it. I've found it doesn't happen nearly as often as I expect it, but still I always remain aware of the possibility. I am "the Fat Girl." I am "the Girl Who Talks About Fat Oppression." Within the punk scene, that's my security blanket. People know about me and know about my work, so I assume that they're not gonna be laughing behind my back about my fat. And if they are, then I know I have support from other people around me. The punk scene gives me tons of support that I know I wouldn't get elsewhere. Within the punk scene, I am able to put out zines, play music, do spoken-word performances that are intensely personal to me. I feel really strongly about keeping nothing secret. I can go back to the old cliché about the personal being political, and no matter how trite it may sound, it's true. I went for so long never talking about being fat, never talking about how that affects my self-esteem, never talking about the ways that I'm oppressed by this society. Now I'm talking. Now I'm talking. I'm talking all the time, and people listen to me. I have support.

And at the same time I know that I have to be wary of the support that I receive. Because I think to some people this is just seen as the cool thing, that by supporting me they're somehow receiving a certain amount of validation from the punk scene. Even though I am totally open and don't keep secrets, I have to protect myself.

This is the revolution. I don't understand the revolution. I can't lay it all out in black and white and tell you what is revolutionary and what is not. The punk scene is a revolution, but not in and of itself. Feminism is a revolution; it is solidarity as well as critique and confrontation. This is the fat grrrl revolution. It's mine, but it doesn't belong to me. Fuckin' yeah.

8

What It Means to Be Gendered Me

Life on the Boundaries of a Dichotomous Gender System

BETSY LUCAL

I understood the concept of "doing gender" (West and Zimmerman 1987) long before I became a sociologist. I have been living with the consequences of inappropriate "gender display" (Goffman 1976; West and Zimmerman 1987) for as long as I can remember.

My daily experiences are a testament to the rigidity of gender in our society, to the real implications of "two and only two" when it comes to sex and gender categories (Garfinkel 1967; Kessler and McKenna 1978). Each day, I experience the consequences that our gender system has for my identity and interactions. I am a woman who has been called "Sir" so many times that I no longer even hesitate to assume that it is being directed at me. I am a woman whose use of public rest rooms regularly causes reactions ranging from confused stares to confrontations over what a man is doing in the women's room. I regularly enact a variety of practices either to minimize the need for others to know my gender or to deal with their misattributions.

I am the embodiment of Lorber's (1994) ostensibly paradoxical assertion that the "gender bending" I engage in actually might serve to preserve and per-petuate gender categories. As a feminist who sees gender rebellion as a significant part of her contribution to the dismantling of sexism, I find this possibility disheartening.

In this article, I examine how my experiences both support and contradict Lorber's (1994) argument using my own experiences to illustrate and reflect on the social construction of gender. My analysis offers a discussion of the consequences of gender for people who do not follow the rules as well as an examination of the possible implications of the existence of people like me for the gender system itself. Ultimately, I show how life on the boundaries of gender affects me and how my life, and the lives of others who make similar decisions about their participation in the gender system, has the potential to subvert gender.

Because this article analyzes my experiences as a woman who often is mistaken for a man, my focus is on the social construction of gender for women. My assumption is that, given the gendered nature of the gendering process itself, men's experiences of this phenomenon might well be different from women's.

THE SOCIAL CONSTRUCTION OF GENDER

. . . We apply gender labels for a variety of reasons; for example, an individual's gender cues our interactions with her or him. Successful social relations require all participants to present, monitor, and interpret gender displays (Martin 1998; West and Zimmerman 1987). We have, according to Lorber, "no social place for a person who is neither woman nor man" (1994, 96); that is, we do not know how to interact with such a person. There is, for example, no way of addressing such a person that does not rely on making an assumption about the person's gender ("Sir" or "Ma'am"). In this context, gender is "omnirelevant" (West and Zimmerman 1987). Also, given the sometimes fractious nature of interactions between men and women, it might be particularly important for women to know the gender of the strangers they encounter, do the women need to be wary, or can they relax (Devor 1989)?

According to Kessler and McKenna (1978), each time we encounter a new person, we make a gender attribution. In most cases, this is not difficult. We learn how to read people's genders by learning which traits culturally signify each gender and by learning rules that enable us to classify individuals with a wide range of gender presentations into two and only two gender categories. As Weston observed, "Gendered traits are called attributes for a reason: People attribute traits to others. No one possesses them. Traits are the product of evaluation" (1996, 21). The fact that most people use the same traits and rules in presenting genders makes it easier for us to attribute genders to them.

We also assume that we can place each individual into one of two mutually exclusive categories in this binary system. As Bem (1993) notes, we have a polarized view of gender; there are two groups that are seen as polar opposites. Although there is "no rule for deciding 'male' or 'female' that will always work" and no attributes "that always and without exception are true of only one gender" (Kessler and McKenna 1978, 158), we operate under the assumption that there are such rules and attributes. . . .

Not only do we rely on our social skills in attributing genders to others, but we also use our skills to present our own genders to them. The roots of this understanding of how gender operates lie in Goffman's (1959) analysis of the "presentation of self in everyday life," elaborated later in his work on "gender display" (Goffman 1976). From this perspective, gender is a performance, "a stylized repetition of acts" (Butler 1990, 140, emphasis removed). Gender display refers to "conventionalized portrayals" of social correlates of gender (Goffman 1976). These displays are culturally established sets of behaviors, appearances, mannerisms, and other cues that we have learned to associate with members of a particular gender. . . .

A person who fails to establish a gendered appearance that corresponds to the person's gender faces challenges to her or his identity and status. First, the gender nonconformist must find a way in which to construct an identity in a society that denies her or him any legitimacy (Bem 1993). A person is likely to want to define herself or himself as "normal" in the face of cultural evidence to the contrary. Second, the individual also must deal with other people's challenges to identity and status—deciding how to respond, what such reactions to their appearance mean, and so forth.

Because our appearances, mannerisms, and so forth constantly are being read as part of our gender display, we do gender whether we intend to or not. For example, a woman athlete, particularly one participating in a nonfeminine sport such as basketball, might deliberately keep her hair long to show that, despite actions that suggest otherwise, she is a "real" (i.e., feminine) woman. But we also do gender in less conscious ways such as when a man takes up more space when sitting than a woman does. In fact, in a society so clearly organized around gender, as ours is, there is no way in which to not do gender (Lorber 1994).

Given our cultural rules for identifying gender (i.e., that there are only two and that masculinity is assumed in the absence of evidence to the contrary), a person who does not do gender appropriately is placed not into a third category but rather into the one with which her or his gender display seems most closely to fit; that is, if a man appears to be a woman, then he will be categorized as "woman," not as something else. Even if a person does not want to do gender or would like to do a gender other than the two recognized by our society, other people will, in effect, do gender for that person by placing her or him in one and only one of the two available categories. We cannot escape doing gender or, more specifically, doing one of two genders. (There are exceptions in limited contexts such as people doing "drag" [Butler 1990; Lorber 1994].)

People who follow the norms of gender can take their genders for granted. Kessler and McKenna asserted, "Few people besides transsexuals think of their gender as anything other than 'naturally' obvious"; they believe that the risks of not being taken for the gender intended "are minimal for nontranssexuals" (1978, 126). However, such an assertion overlooks the experiences of people such as those women Devor (1989) calls "gender blenders" and those people Lorber (1994) refers to as "gender benders." As West and Zimmerman (1987) pointed out, we all are held accountable for, and might be called on to account for, our genders.

People who, for whatever reasons, do not adhere to the rules, risk gender misattribution and any interactional consequences that might result from this misidentification. What are the consequences of misattribution for social interaction? When must misattribution be minimized? What will one do to minimize such mistakes? In this article, I explore these and related questions using my biography.

For me, the social processes and structures of gender mean that, in the context of our culture, my appearance will be read as masculine. Given the common conflation of sex and gender, I will be assumed to be a male. Because of the two-and-only-two genders rule, I will be classified, perhaps more often than not, as a man—not as an atypical woman, not as a genderless person. I must be one gender or the other; I cannot be neither, nor can I be both. This norm has a variety of mundane and serious consequences for my everyday existence. Like Myhre (1995), I have found that the choice not to participate in femininity is not one made frivolously.

My experiences as a woman who does not do femininity illustrate a paradox of our two-and-only-two gender system. Lorber argued that "bending gender rules and passing between genders does not erode but rather preserves gender boundaries" (1994, 21). Although people who engage in these behaviors and appearances do "demonstrate the social constructedness of sex, sexuality, and gender" (Lorber 1994, 96), they do not actually disrupt gender. Devor made a similar point: "When gender blending females refused to mark

themselves by publicly displaying sufficient femininity to be recognized as women, they were in no way challenging patriarchal gender assumptions" (1989, 142). As the following discussion shows, I have found that my own experiences both support and challenge this argument. . . .

GENDERED ME

Each day, I negotiate the boundaries of gender. Each day, I face the possibility that someone will attribute the "wrong" gender to me based on my physical appearance.

I am six feet tall and large-boned. I have had short hair for most of my life. For the past several years, I have worn a crew cut or flat top. I do not shave or otherwise remove hair from my body (e.g., no eyebrow plucking). I do not wear dresses, skirts, high heels, or makeup. My only jewelry is a class ring, a "men's" watch (my wrists are too large for a "women's" watch), two small earrings (gold hoops, both in my left ear), and (occasionally) a necklace. I wear jeans or shorts, T-shirts, sweaters, polo/golf shirts, button-down collar shirts, and tennis shoes or boots. The jeans are "women's" (I do have hips) but do not look particularly "feminine." The rest of the outer garments are from men's departments. I prefer baggy clothes, so the fact that I have "womanly" breasts often is not obvious (I do not wear a bra). Sometimes, I wear a baseball cap or some other type of hat. I also am white and relatively young (30 years old).[1]

My gender display—what others interpret as my presented identity—regularly leads to the misattribution of my gender. An incongruity exists between my gender self-identity and the gender that others perceive. In my encounters with people I do not know, I sometimes conclude, based on our interactions, that they think I am a man. This does not mean that other people do not think I am a man, just that I have no way of knowing what they think without interacting with them.

Living with It

I have no illusions or delusions about my appearance. I know that my appearance is likely to be read as "masculine" (and male) and that how I see myself is socially irrelevant. Given our two-and-only-two gender structure, I must live with the consequences of my appearance. These consequences fall into two categories: issues of identity and issues of interaction.

My most common experience is being called "Sir" or being referred to by some other masculine linguistic marker (e.g., "he," "man"). This has happened for years for as long as I can remember, when having encounters with people I do not know.[2] Once, in fact, the same worker at a fast-food restaurant called me "Ma'am" when she took my order and "Sir" when she gave it to me.

Using my credit cards sometimes is a challenge. Some clerks subtly indicate their disbelief, looking from the card to me and back at the card and checking my signature carefully. Others challenge my use of the card, asking whose it is or demanding identification. One cashier asked to see my driver's license and then asked me whether I was the son of the cardholder. Another clerk told me that my signature on the receipt "had better match" the one on the card. Presumably, this was her way of letting me know that she was not convinced it was my credit card.

My identity as a woman also is called into question when I try to use women-only spaces. Encounters in public rest rooms are an adventure. I have been told countless times that "This is the ladies' room." Other women say nothing to me, but their stares and conversations with others let me know what they think. I will hear them say, for example, "There was a man in there." I also get stares when I enter a locker room. However, it seems that women are less concerned about my presence there, perhaps because, given that it is a space for changing clothes, showering, and so forth, they will be able to make sure that I am really a woman. Dressing rooms in department stores also are problematic spaces. I remember shopping with my sister once and being offered a chair outside the room when I began to accompany her into the dressing room.

Women who believe that I am a man do not want me in women-only spaces. For example, one woman would not enter the rest room until I came out, and others have told me that I am in the wrong place. They also might not want to encounter me while they are alone. For example, seeing me walking at night when they are alone might be scary.[3]

I, on the other hand, am not afraid to walk alone, day or night. I do not worry that I will be subjected to the public harassment that many women endure (Gardner 1995). I am not a clear target for a potential rapist. I rely on the fact that a potential attacker would not want to attack a big man by mistake. This is not to say that men never are attacked, just that they are not viewed, and often do not view themselves, as being vulnerable to attack.

Being perceived as a man has made me privy to male-male interactional styles of which most women are not aware. I found out, quite by accident, that many men greet, or acknowledge, people (mostly other men) who make eye contact with them with a single nod. For example, I found that when I walked down the halls of my brother's all-male dormitory making eye contact, men nodded their greetings at me. Oddly enough, these same men did not greet my brother; I had to tell him about making eye contact and nodding as a greeting ritual. Apparently, in this case I was doing masculinity better than he was!

I also believe that I am treated differently, for example, in auto parts stores (staffed almost exclusively by men in most cases) because of the assumption that I am a man. Workers there assume that I know what I need and that my questions are legitimate requests for information. I suspect that I am treated more fairly than a feminine-appearing woman would be. I have not been able to test this proposition. However, Devor's participants did report "being treated more respectfully" (1989, 132) in such situations.

There is, however, a negative side to being assumed to be a man by other men. Once, a friend and I were driving in her car when a man failed to stop at an intersection and nearly crashed into us. As we drove away, I mouthed "stop sign" to him. When we both stopped our cars at the next intersection, he got out of his car and came up to the passenger side of the car, where I was sitting. He yelled obscenities at us and pounded and spit on the car window. Luckily, the windows were closed. I do not think he would have done that if he thought I was a woman. This was the first time I realized that one of the implications of being seen as a man was that I might be called on to defend myself from physical aggression from other men who felt challenged by me. This was a sobering and somewhat frightening thought.

Recently, I was verbally accosted by an older man who did not like where I had parked my car. As I walked down the street to work, he shouted that I should park at the university rather than on a side street nearby. I responded that it was a public street and that I could park there if I chose. He continued to yell, but the only thing I caught was the last part of what he said: "Your tires are going to get cut!" Based on my appearance that day—I was dressed casually and carrying a backpack, and I had my hat on backward—I believe he thought that I was a young male student rather than a female professor. I do not think he would have yelled at a person he thought to be a woman—and perhaps especially not a woman professor.

Given the presumption of heterosexuality that is part of our system of gender, my interactions with women who assume that I am a man also can be viewed from that perspective. For example, once my brother and I were shopping when we were "hit on" by two young women. The encounter ended before I realized what had happened. It was only when we walked away that I told him that I was pretty certain that they had thought both of us were men. A more common experience is realizing that when I am seen in public with one of my women friends, we are likely to be read as a heterosexual dyad. It is likely that if I were to walk through a shopping mall holding hands with a woman, no one would look twice, not because of their openmindedness toward lesbian couples but rather because of their assumption that I was the male half of a straight couple. Recently, when walking through a mall with a friend and her infant, my observations of others' responses to us led me to believe that many of them assumed that we were a family on an outing, that is, that I was her partner and the father of the child.

Dealing with It

Although I now accept that being mistaken for a man will be a part of my life so long as I choose not to participate in femininity, there have been times when I consciously have tried to appear more feminine. I did this for a while when I was an undergraduate and again recently when I was on the academic job market. The first time, I let my hair grow nearly down to my shoulders and had it permed. I also grew long fingernails and wore nail polish. Much to my chagrin, even then one of my professors, who did not know my name, insistently referred to me in his kinship examples as "the son." Perhaps my first act on the way to my current stance was to point out to this man, politely and after class, that I was a woman.

More recently, I again let my hair grow out for several months, although I did not alter other aspects of my appearance. Once my hair was about two and a half inches long (from its original quarter inch), I realized, based on my encounters with strangers, that I had more or less passed back into the category of "woman." Then, when I returned to wearing a flat top, people again responded to me as if I were a man.

Because of my appearance, much of my negotiation of interactions with strangers involves attempts to anticipate their reactions to me. I need to assess whether they will be likely to assume that I am a man and whether that actually matters in the context of our encounters. Many times, my gender really is irrelevant, and it is just annoying to be misidentified. Other times, particularly when my appearance is coupled with something that identifies me by name (e.g., a check or credit card) without a photo, I might need to do something to ensure that my identity is not questioned. As a result of my experiences, I have developed some techniques to deal with gender misattribution.

In general, in unfamiliar public places, I avoid using the rest room because I know that it is a place where there is a high likelihood of misattribution and where misattribution is socially important. If I must use a public rest room, I try to make myself look as nonthreatening as possible. I do not wear a hat, and I try to rearrange my clothing to make my breasts more obvious. Here, I am trying to use my secondary sex characteristics to make my gender more obvious rather than the usual use of gender to make sex obvious. While in the rest room, I never make eye contact, and I get in and out as quickly as possible. Going in with a woman friend also is helpful; her presence legitimizes my own. People are less likely to think I am entering a space where I do not belong when I am with someone who looks like she does belong.[4]

To those women who verbally challenge my presence in the rest room, I reply, "I know," usually in an annoyed tone. When they stare or talk about me to the women they are with, I simply get out as quickly as possible. In general, I do not wait for someone I am with because there is too much chance of an unpleasant encounter.

I stopped trying on clothes before purchasing them a few years ago because my presence in the changing areas was met with stares and whispers. Exceptions are stores where the dressing rooms are completely private, where there are individual stalls rather than a room with stalls separated by curtains, or where business is slow and no one else is trying on clothes. If I am trying on a garment clearly intended for a woman, then I usually can do so without hassle. I guess the attendants assume that I must be a woman if I have, for example, a women's bathing suit in my hand. But usually, I think it is easier for me to try the clothes on at home and return them, if necessary, rather than risk creating a scene. Similarly, when I am with another woman who is trying on clothes, I just wait outside.

My strategy with credit cards and checks is to anticipate wariness on a clerk's part. When I sense that there is some doubt or when they challenge me, I say, "It's my card." I generally respond courteously to requests for photo ID, realizing that these might be routine checks because of concerns about increasingly widespread fraud. But for the clerk who asked for ID and still did not think it was my card, I had a stronger reaction. When she said that she was sorry for embarrassing me, I told her that I was not embarrassed but that she should be. I also am particularly careful to make sure that my signature is consistent with the back of the card. Faced with such situations, I feel somewhat nervous about signing my name—which, of course, makes me worry that my signature will look different from how it should.

Another strategy I have been experimenting with is wearing nail polish in the dark bright colors currently fashionable. I try to do this when I travel by plane. Given more stringent travel regulations, one always must present a photo ID. But my experiences have shown that my driver's license is not necessarily convincing. Nail polish might be. I also flash my polished nails when I enter airport rest rooms, hoping that they will provide a clue that I am indeed in the right place.

There are other cases in which the issues are less those of identity than of all the norms of interaction that, in our society, are gendered. My most common response to misattribution actually is to appear to ignore it, that is, to go on with the interaction as if nothing out of the ordinary has happened. Unless I feel that there is a good reason to establish my correct gender, I assume the identity others impose on me for the sake of smooth interaction. For example, if someone is selling me a movie ticket, then there is no reason to make sure that the person has accurately discerned my gender. Similarly, if it is clear that the person using "Sir" is talking to me, then I simply respond as appropriate. I accept the designation because it is irrelevant to the situation. It takes enough effort to be alert for misattributions and to decide which of them matter; responding to each one would take more energy than it is worth.

Sometimes, if our interaction involves conversation, my first verbal response is enough to let the other person know that I am actually a woman and not a man. My voice apparently is "feminine" enough to shift people's attributions to the other category. I know when this has happened by the apologies that usually accompany the mistake. I usually respond to the apologies by saying something like "No problem" and/or "It happens all the time." Sometimes, a misattributor will offer an account for the mistake, for example, saying that it was my hair or that they were not being very observant.

These experiences with gender and misattribution provide some theoretical insights into contemporary Western understandings of gender and into the social structure of gender in contemporary society. Although there are a number of ways in which my experiences confirm the work of others, there also are some ways in which my experiences suggest other interpretations and conclusions.

WHAT DOES IT MEAN?

Gender is pervasive in our society. I cannot choose not to participate in it. Even if I try not to do gender, other people will do it for me. That is, given our two-and-only-two rule, they must attribute one of two genders to me. Still, although I cannot choose not to participate in gender, I can choose not to participate in femininity (as I have), at least with respect to physical appearance.

That is where the problems begin. Without the decorations of femininity, I do not look like a woman. That is, I do not look like what many people's commonsense understanding of gender tells them a woman looks like. How I see myself, even how I might wish others would see me, is socially irrelevant. It is the gender that I *appear* to be (my "perceived gender") that is most relevant to my social identity and interactions with others. The major consequence of this fact is that I must be continually aware of which gender I "give off" as well as which gender I "give" (Goffman 1959).

Because my gender self-identity is "not displayed obviously, immediately, and consistently" (Devor 1989, 58), I am somewhat of a failure in social terms with respect to gender. Causing people to be uncertain or wrong about one's gender is a violation of taken-for-granted rules that leads to embarrassment and discomfort; it means that something has gone wrong with the interaction (Garfinkel 1967; Kessler and McKenna 1978). This means that my nonresponse to misattribution is the more socially appropriate response; I am allowing others to maintain face (Goffman 1959, 1967). By not calling attention to their mistakes, I uphold their images of themselves as competent social actors. I also maintain my own image as competent by letting them assume that I am the gender I appear to them to be.

But I still have discreditable status; I carry a stigma (Goffman 1963). Because I have failed to participate appropriately in the creation of meaning with respect to gender (Devor 1989), I can be called on to account for my appearance. If discredited, I show myself to be an incompetent social actor. I am the one not following the rules, and I will pay the price for not providing people with the appropriate cues for placing me in the gender category to which I really belong.

I do think that it is, in many cases, safer to be read as a man than as some sort of deviant woman. "Man" is an acceptable category; it fits properly into people's

gender worldview. Passing as a man often is the "path of least resistance" (Devor 1989; Johnson 1997). For example, in situations where gender does not matter, letting people take me as a man is easier than correcting them.

Conversely, as Butler noted, "We regularly punish those who fail to do their gender right" (1990, 140). Feinberg maintained, "Masculine girls and women face terrible condemnation and brutality—including sexual violence—for crossing the boundary of what is 'acceptable' female expression" (1996, 114). People are more likely to harass me when they perceive me to be a woman who looks like a man. For example, when a group of teenagers realized that I was not a man because one of their mothers identified me correctly, they began to make derogatory comments when I passed them. One asked, for example, "Does she have a penis?"

Because of the assumption that a "masculine" woman is a lesbian, there is the risk of homophobic reactions (Gardner 1995; Lucal 1997). Perhaps surprisingly, I find that I am much more likely to be taken for a man than for a lesbian, at least based on my interactions with people and their reactions to me. This might be because people are less likely to reveal that they have taken me for a lesbian because it is less relevant to an encounter or because they believe this would be unacceptable. But I think it is more likely a product of the strength of our two-and-only-two system. I give enough masculine cues that I am seen not as a deviant woman but rather as a man, at least in most cases. The problem seems not to be that people are uncertain about my gender, which might lead them to conclude that I was a lesbian once they realized I was a woman. Rather, I seem to fit easily into a gender category—just not the one with which I identify.

In fact, because men represent the dominant gender in our society, being mistaken for a man can protect me from other types of gendered harassment. Because men can move around in public spaces safely (at least relative to women), a "masculine" woman also can enjoy this freedom (Devor 1989).

On the other hand, my use of particular spaces—those designated as for women only—may be challenged. Feinberg provided an intriguing analysis of the public restroom experience. She characterized women's reactions to a masculine person in a public rest-room as "an example of genderphobia" (1996, 117), viewing such women as policing gender boundaries rather than believing that there really is a man in the women's restroom. She argued that women who truly believed that there was a man in their midst would react differently. Although this is an interesting per-spective on her experiences, my experiences do not lead to the same conclusion.[5] Enough people have said to me that "This is the ladies' room" or have said to their companions that "There was a man in there" that I take their reactions at face value.

Still, if the two-and-only-two gender system is to be maintained, participants must be involved in policing the categories and their attendant identities and spaces. Even if policing boundaries is not explicitly intended, boundary maintenance is the effect of such responses to people's gender displays.

Boundaries and margins are an important compo-nent of both my experiences of gender and our theo-retical understanding of gendering processes. I am, in effect, both woman and not-woman. As a woman who often is a social man but who also is a woman living in a patriarchal society, I am in a unique position to see and act. I sometimes receive privileges usually lim-ited to men, and I sometimes am oppressed by my status as a deviant woman. I am, in a sense, an outsider-within (Collins 1991). Positioned on the boundaries of gender categories, I have developed a consciousness that I hope will prove transformative (Anzaldua 1987).

In fact, one of the reasons why I decided to continue my nonparticipation in femininity was that my so-ciological training suggested that this could be one of my contributions to the eventual dismantling of patri-archal gender constructs. It would be my way of mak-ing the personal political. I accepted being taken for a man as the price I would pay to help subvert patriarchy. I believed that all of the inconveniences I was enduring meant that I actually was doing something to bring down the gender structures that entangled all of us.

Then, I read Lorber's (1994) *Paradoxes of Gender* and found out, much to my dismay, that I might not ac-tually be challenging gender after all. Because of the way in which doing gender works in our two-and-

only-two system, gender displays are simply read as evidence of one of the two categories. Therefore, gen-der bending, blending, and passing between the cate-gories do not question the categories themselves. If one's social gender and personal (true) gender do not correspond, then this is irrelevant unless someone no-tices the lack of congruence.

This reality brings me to a paradox of my experi-ences. First, not only do others assume that I am one gender or the other, but I also insist that I *really am* a member of one of the two gender categories. That is, I am female; I self-identify as a woman. I do not claim to be some other gender or to have no gender at all. I simply place myself in the wrong category according to stereotypes and cultural standards; the gender I pre-sent, or that some people perceive me to be presenting, is inconsistent with the gender with which I identify myself as well as with the gender I could be "proven" to be. Socially, I display the wrong gender; personally, I identify as the proper gender.

Second, although I ultimately would like to see the destruction of our current gender structure, I am not to the point of personally abandoning gender. Right now, I do not want people to see me as genderless as much as I want them to see me as a woman. That is, I would like to expand the category of "woman" to include people like me. I, too, am deeply embedded in our gen-der system, even though I do not play by many of its rules. For me, as for most people in our society, gender is a substantial part of my personal identity (Howard and Hollander 1997). Socially, the problem is that I do not present a gender display that is consistently read as feminine. In fact, I consciously do not participate in the trappings of femininity. However, I do identify my-self as a woman, not as a man or as someone outside of the two-and-only-two categories.

Yet, I do believe, as Lorber (1994) does, that the purpose of gender, as it currently is constructed, is to oppress women. Lorber analyzed gender as a "process of creating distinguishable social statuses for the as-signment of rights and responsibilities" that ends up putting women in a devalued and oppressed position (1994, 32). As Martin put it, "Bodies that clearly de-lineate gender status facilitate the maintenance of the gender hierarchy" (1998, 495).

For society, gender means difference (Lorber 1994). The erosion of the boundaries would problematize that structure. Therefore, for gender to operate as it currently does, the category "woman" *cannot* be expanded to include people like me. The maintenance of the gender structure is dependent on the creation of a few categories that are mutually exclusive, the members of which are as different as possible (Lorber 1994). It is the clarity of the boundaries between the categories that allows gender to be used to assign rights and responsibilities as well as resources and rewards.

It is that part of gender—what it is used for—that is most problematic. Indeed, is it not *patriarchal*—or, even more specifically, *heteropatriarchal*—constructions of gender that are actually the problem? It is not the differences between men and women, or the categories themselves, so much as the meanings ascribed to the categories and, even more important, the hierarchical nature of gender under patriarchy that is the problem (Johnson 1997). Therefore, I am rebelling not against my femaleness or even my womanhood; instead, I am protesting contemporary constructions of femininity and, at least indirectly, masculinity under patriarchy. We do not, in fact, know what gender would look like if it were not constructed around heterosexuality in the context of patriarchy.

Although it is possible that the end of patriarchy would mean the end of gender, it is at least conceivable that something like what we now call gender could exist in a postpatriarchal future. The two-and-only-two categorization might well disappear, there being no hierarchy for it to justify. But I do not think that we should make the assumption that gender and patriarchy are synonymous. . . .

. . . In a recent book, *The Gender Knot,* Johnson (1997) argued that when it comes to gender and patriarchy, most of us follow the paths of least resistance; we "go along to get along," allowing our actions to be shaped by the gender system. Collectively, our actions help patriarchy maintain and perpetuate a system of oppression and privilege. Thus, by withdrawing our support from this system by choosing paths of greater resistance, we can start to chip away at it. Many people participate in gender because they cannot imagine any alternatives. In my classroom, and in my interactions and encounters with strangers, my presence can make it difficult for people not to see that there *are* other paths. In other words, following from West and Zimmerman (1987), I can subvert gender by doing it differently. . . .

NOTES

1. I obviously have left much out by not examining my gendered experiences in the context of race, age, class, sexuality, region, and so forth. Such a project clearly is more complex. As Weston pointed out, gender presentations are complicated by other statuses of their presenters: "What it takes to kick a person over into another gendered category can differ with race, class, religion, and time" (1996, 168). Furthermore, I am well aware that my whiteness allows me to assume that my experiences are simply a product of gender. For now, suffice it to say that it is my privileged position on some of these axes and my more disadvantaged position on others that combine to delineate my overall experience.

2. In fact, such experiences are not always limited to encounters with strangers. My grandmother, who does not see me often, twice has mistaken me for either my brother-in-law or some unknown man.

3. My experiences in rest rooms and other public spaces might be very different if I were, say, African American rather than white. Given the stereotypes of African American men, I think that white women would react very differently to encountering me.

4. I also have noticed that there are certain types of rest rooms in which I will not be verbally challenged; the higher the social status of the place, the less likely I will be harassed. For example, when I go to the theater, I might get stared at, but my presence never has been challenged.

5. An anonymous reviewer offered one possible explanation for this. Women see women's rest rooms as their space; they feel safe, and even empowered, there. Instead of fearing men in such space, they might instead pose a threat to any man who might intrude. Their invulnerability in this situation is, of course, not physically based but rather socially constructed. I thank the reviewer for this suggestion.

REFERENCES

Anzaldua, G. 1987. *Borderlands/La Frontera.* San Francisco: Aunt Lute Books.

Bem, S. L. 1993. *The lenses of gender.* New Haven, CT: Yale University Press.

Butler, J. 1990. *Gender trouble.* New York: Routledge.

Collins, P. H. 1991. *Black feminist thought.* New York: Routledge.

Devor, H. 1989. *Gender blending: Confronting the limits of duality.* Bloomington: Indiana University Press.

Feinberg, L. 1996. *Transgender warriors.* Boston: Beacon.

Gardner, C. B. 1995. *Passing by: Gender and public harassment.* Berkeley: University of California.

Garfinkel, H. 1967. *Studies in ethnomethodology.* Englewood Cliffs, NJ: Prentice Hall.

Goffman, E. 1959. *The presentation of self in everyday life.* Garden City, NY: Doubleday.

———. 1963. *Stigma.* Englewood Cliffs, NJ: Prentice Hall.

———. 1967. *Interaction ritual.* New York: Anchor/Doubleday.

———. 1976. Gender display. *Studies in the Anthropology of Visual Communication* 3:69–77.

Howard, J. A., and J. Hollander. 1997. *Gendered situations, gendered selves.* Thousand Oaks, CA: Sage.

Kessler, S. J., and W. McKenna. 1978. *Gender: An ethnomethodological approach.* New York: John Wiley.

Johnson, A. G. 1997. *The gender knot: Unraveling our patriarchal legacy.* Philadelphia: Temple University Press.

Lorber, J. 1996. Beyond the binaries: Depolarizing the categories of sex, sexuality, and gender. *Sociological Inquiry* 66:143–59.

Lucal, B. 1997. "Hey, this is the ladies' room!": Gender misattribution and public harassment. *Perspectives on Social Problems* 9:43–57.

Martin, K. A. 1998. Becoming a gendered body: Practices of preschools. *American Sociological Review* 63:494–511.

Myhre, J. R. M. 1995. One bad hair day too many, or the hairstory of an androgynous young feminist. In *Listen up: Voices from the next feminist generation,* edited by B. Findlen. Seattle, WA: Seal Press.

West, C., and D. H. Zimmerman. 1987. Doing gender. *Gender & Society* 1:125–51.

Weston, K. 1996. *Render me, gender me.* New York: Columbia University Press.

9

Doing Time, Doing Masculinity

Sports and Prison

DON SABO

I am a white, male college professor in my forties, hunched over a table in Attica Correctional Facility. My heart is pounding, my upper body is locked taut and shaking, and I am gazing into the eyes of an African American prisoner who, like so many of the men in this New York State prison, comes from what sociologists call the "underclass." We are different in most respects, but right now we are alike. Like me, he's puffing and straining, trying not to show it, sometimes cursing, and returning my gaze. We are arm wrestling, and in this case he puts me down in about two minutes, which in arm wrestling can be a long, long time.

I started arm wrestling in the joint about five years ago. I enjoy the physical connection that the contest brings. The participants initially stalk one another over a period of days or weeks, keeping their distance, evaluating each other's strengths and weaknesses. There may be some playful bad-mouthing or boasting that leads up to a bout. Eventually, they make the necessary moves that bring each to the table hand-in-hand, eye-to-eye. Even though arm wrestling is overtly combative, it can breed a closer connection with another man

than is allowed for in most aspects of men's lives. It allows me to climb outside the bourgeois husk of my life and join with somebody in a way that temporarily suspends the hierarchical distinctions between free man and inmate, white and black, privileged and underprivileged, and teacher and student.

Arm wrestling also lets me pull my athletic past into the present, to enjoin youthful masculine spirits and facades. At the same time that these manly juices are resurrected, though, I try to tell myself and others that I don't take the competition so seriously. I want to learn the lesson that it is OK to be vulnerable to defeat.

Sometimes I win; sometimes I lose. It still matters to me whether I win or lose. I try hard to win, but, when I lose, I get over it quickly, accept it, and even welcome it as inevitable. Part of me is happy for the man who beat me. When I win, I savor the victories for a few days, bragging to myself, sometimes others, soothing my middle-aging ego with transparently masculine rationalizations that I am still strong, not over the bloody hill yet. Arm wrestlers understand that nobody wins all the time. Beneath the grit and show, we know there is more to it than winning or losing. We also know that part of what makes arm wrestling more than just a contest or pastime is that it somehow speaks to our beliefs and feelings about being a man.

I have taught in prisons for fourteen years. My experiences, observations, and discussions with inmates have revealed that prison sports have different meanings for different men. I have learned that a great many motives, messages, and contradictions are crammed into the muscles and athletic pastimes of men in prison. Like men outside the walls, however, prisoners use sports as vehicles for creating and maintaining masculine identity.

DOING TIME, DOING SPORTS

Perhaps the most striking aspect of prison sports is their visibility. The yard is often a hub of athletic activity. Weight lifters huddle in small groups around barbells and bench press racks. Runners circle the periphery, while hoopsters spin and shoot on the basketball courts. There is the occasional volleyball game and bocce tournament. Depending on the facility and time of year, there may be football practices or games, replete with equipment and fans along the sidelines. Some prisons maintain softball leagues and facilities.

Inside the buildings, you will find a gym, basketball courts, and weight rooms. Power lifters struggle against gravity and insanity. Feats of strength produce heroes in the joint, sometimes even legends, or at least local legends. I have been told stories about Jihad Al-Sibbar, a man past his forties who weighs about 155 pounds. He is believed to be the strongest man in the New York State prison system, and I have heard it said more than once that, if given the opportunity, he could have competed at the Olympic level. I want and need to believe in these stories, not so much because they are tales of a strong man but because his triumphs say something about the potential of athletics to sustain sanity in an insane place.

Sports and fitness activities spill into the prison environment in other ways. An inmate may do daily calisthenics while in solitary. For example, Martin Sostre was an African American black power activist and inner-city bookstore owner who was framed by the police in 1967 and imprisoned for nine years. Sostre used physical exercise and yoga to survive long stints of solitary and to bolster his political struggles against prison and legal authorities (Copeland, 1970).

In almost any sector of the prison, fans may jabber about who will win the Super Bowl, the NBA finals, or the next heavyweight boxing match. The taunting, teasing, and betting that typify sports fans outside the walls are also rife among inmates and guards and other personnel. Some men gather in groups around television sets to watch the Final Four or "Monday Night Football," while others sit alone in their cells jabbing with George Foreman or soaring with Michael Jordan.

In short, sports and fitness activities in prison engage men's minds and bodies to varying degrees and, in the process, help them do their time. For some men, especially the young ones, athletics are no more than a fleeting pastime, a simple form of physical play, something to do to get to the end of another day. For others, sports and fitness activities are a crucial survival strategy, a life practice that is intended to create and maintain physical and mental health in a hostile, unhealthy place. For still others, working out or participating in sports helps them to displace anger and frustration, to get the rage out of their bodies and psyches before it explodes or turns in on them. And for some, the goal is to get big to be bad, to manufacture muscle and a jock presence in order to intimidate and dominate.

DOING MASCULINITY

The prison environment triggers a masculine awareness in me. I go on masculine alert. I don't walk around with biceps flexed and chest expanded, pretending to be a tough guy in front of anybody looking my way. That kind of suck-in-your-belly-and-lower-your-voice stuff faded away with my twenties. The masculinity that surfaces in the prison is more an attitude, a hazy cluster of concerns and expectations that get translated into emotion and physical movement in ways that never quite come clear. Though there are a few women around (for example, an occasional female guard, some women teachers), I see and smell the prison as an all-male domain. I sense a greater potential for danger and a heightened need to protect myself. I could get caught in a bad situation. I have been told not to trust anybody—prisoners, guards, or bureaucrats. Nobody. It sounds crazy, but the tinges of distrust and paranoia almost feel good. Indeed, there are parts of me, call them "threads" or "echoes" of a masculine identity, that embrace the distrust and welcome the presumed danger and potential for violence.

These masculine prompts are seldom uppermost in my mind. They do not emanate from inside of me; they are more like visitors that come and go, moving in and out of me like tap water gushing through an overfilled glass. Arm wrestling allows me to play out masculinity in tune with other elements of jailhouse jock culture. At the same time, the wrestling breeds familiarity with prisoners, pushes toward closeness and trust, and subverts hierarchical distinctions based on class, race, and professional status.

Like me, many men in prison deploy sports and fitness activities as resources to do masculinity—that is, to spin masculine identities, to build reputations, to achieve or dissolve status. For the men in prison, as elsewhere, masculine identity is earned, enacted, rehearsed, refined, and relived through each day's activities and choices. I'm not saying that the gender scripts that men follow in prison are reinvented each day, from moment to moment, man to man. Masculinity does not unfold inside us as much as it flows through us. It is not a strictly individual or psychological process. In doing gender, each individual participates in the larger prison culture, which scripts masculinity by supplying direction, role models, props, motivations, rewards, and values (Messerschmidt, 1993; West and Zimmerman, 1987). For many men, sports are a part of the formula for shaping gender identity.

SOFTNESS AND HARDNESS

In prison, the manly injunction to be strong is evident not only in the bulk or bearing of many men's bodies but in everyday speech as well. I have often heard prisoners describe other men as "hard" or "soft." Over the years, I have learned that there are many guises of hardness, which, inside and outside the prison culture, illustrate a variety of masculine expressions that stretch between the honorable and the perverse.

Being hard can mean that the individual is toned, strong, conditioned, or fit, rather than weak, flabby, or out of shape. A hard man cares for and respects his body. Life in prison is extremely oppressive, and it is extraordinarily difficult to eke out a healthy lifestyle. Cigarette smoke is everywhere. The noise on the blocks can jam the senses. Most inmates will tell you that the chow stinks, and, for those who think about such matters, a nutritionally sound diet is impossible to scrape together from the available cafeteria fare. For some men, then, the pursuit of sports and fitness activity is a personal quest to create a healthy body in an unhealthy environment. Those who succeed build a sense of accomplishment and garner the respect of others. Some men strive to be hard in order to build self-esteem. Being in prison is a colossal reminder of personal failure. A regular fitness regimen helps some men center mind and identity in the undeniably tangible locus of the body. For others, getting good at basketball or being recognized as a leading athlete earns the respect of peers. Damaged egos and healing psyches drink in the recognition and repair themselves.

Being hard can also be a defense against prison violence. The hard man sends the message that he is somebody to contend with, not a pushover, not somebody to "fuck with." The sexual connotations of this last phrase take on particular significance in the prison subculture, where man-on-man rape is part of life. The act of prison rape is tied to maintaining the status order among a maze of male groups. Blacks may rape whites or vice versa in order to establish dominant status. Older prisoners may use rape to enslave newcomers. Guards or prison administrators have been known to threaten to expose prisoners to greater threat of rape in order to evoke good behavior, to punish, or to squeeze out information. As Tom Cahill, himself a victim of prison rape, observed, "Once 'turned out'—prison parlance for raped—a survivor is caught in a bind. If an inmate reports a sexual assault, even without naming the assailant, he will be labeled a 'snitch,' a contract will automatically be placed on him, and his life expectancy will be measured in minutes from then" (1990:32).

Men's efforts to weave webs of domination through rape and physical intimidation *in prison* also reflect and reproduce men's domination of women in the social world beyond the walls. In the muscled, violent, and tattooed world of prison rape, woman is symbolically ever present. She resides in the pulpy, supple, and muted linguistic folds of the hardness/softness dichotomy. The prison phrase "make a woman out of you" means that you will be raped. Rape-based relationships between prisoners are often described as relationships between "men" and "girls" who are, in effect, thought of as "master" and "slave," victor and vanquished.

The hardness/softness split also echoes and fortifies stereotypes of masculinity and femininity (Bordo, 1999). To be "hard" means to be more manly than the next guy, who is said to be "soft" and more feminine. It is better to be hard than soft in prison. To be called hard is a compliment. To be labeled soft can be a playful rebuke or a serious put-down. The meanings around hardness and softness also flow from and feed homophobia, which is rampant in prison. The stigma of being labeled a homosexual can make a man more vulnerable to ridicule, attack, ostracism, or victimization.

CONCLUSION

Prison somehow magnifies the contradictions in men's lives, making them palpable, visible. For many prisoners, the pursuit of manhood was closely linked to their efforts to define masculine identity and worth—for example, robbing in order to be a good provider or husband, joining a gang in hopes of becoming a "big man" on the street, being a "badass" or "gangster" as a way of getting respect from peers, braving the violence of the drug trade, raping or beating on women in order prove manly superiority, or embezzling to achieve financial success and masculine adequacy. The irony here is that these scripted quests for manly power led, in part, to incarceration and loss of freedom and dignity. For lots of prisoners, and countless men on the outside, adherence to the traditional pathways to masculinity turned out to be a trap.

Men's participation in prison sports is fused with yet another contradiction. On one hand, sports and exercise provide prisoners with vehicles for self-expression and physical freedom. On the other hand, prison officials know that involvement in sports and exercise activities helps make inmates more tractable and compliant. Therefore, the cultivation of the body through sports and fitness activities is simultaneously a source of personal liberation and social control.

It is easy for men in prison or on the outside to get trapped by the cultural mandate of hardness. The image of the male athlete as a muscled, aggressive, competitive, and emotionally controlled individual dovetails the prevailing definition of masculinity in sexist culture. Conformity to this model for manliness can be socially and emotionally destructive. Muscles may remain "*the* sign of masculinity" (Glassner, 1988:192) in the male-dominated culture and the gender hierarchies that constitute the North American prison system. And yet my observations tell me that prisoners' relationships to muscle and masculinity are not simple or one-sided. Men cultivate their bodies in order to send a variety of messages about the meaning of masculinity to themselves and others. Whereas conformity to the credo of hardness for some men feeds the forces of domination and subordination, for others athletics and fitness are forms of self-care. Whereas many prison jocks are literally playing out the masculine scripts they learned in their youth, others are attempting to attach new meanings to sports and exercise that affirm health, sanity, and alternative modes of masculinity.

Perhaps the greatest contradiction pervading prison sports is that, despite the diversity of gendered meanings and practices that prisoners attach to their bodies through sports and exercise, the cultural mandate for hardness and toughness prevails. Men's soft sides remain hidden, suppressed, and underground. The punitive and often violent structures of prison hierarchies persist, breathing aggression and fear into men's bodies and minds. The same tragic contradiction informs men's lives in sports outside the prison walls, where structured gender inequality and sexism constrain efforts to reform gender relationships toward equity and healthful affirmation of the body.

Arm wrestling teaches me that the cages in men's lives can be made of iron bars, muscles, or myths. The harder I wrestle, the more I dream of escape.

REFERENCES

Bordo, S. 1999. *The Male Body: A New Look at Men in Public and in Private.* New York: Farrar, Straus and Giroux.

Cahill, T. 1990. "Prison Rape: Torture in the American Gulag." In *Men and Intimacy: Personal Accounts Exploring the Dilemmas of Modern Male Sexuality,* ed. Franklin Abbott. Freedom, Calif.: Crossing Press.

Copeland, V. 1970. *The Crime of Martin Sostre.* New York: McGraw Hill.

Glassner, B. 1988. *Bodies: Why We Look the Way We Do (and How We Feel about It).* New York: Putnam.

Messerschmidt, James W. 1993. *Masculinities and Crime: Critique and Reconceptualization of Theory.* Lanham, Md.: Rowman and Littlefield.

West, Candace, and Don H. Zimmerman. 1987. "Doing Gender." *Gender and Society* 1 (2):125–51.

10

The Well-Coiffed Man

Class, Race, and Heterosexual Masculinity in the Hair Salon

Kristen Barber

"With all the money modern man has begun to spend on pampering and coining himself . . . we might be forgiven for thinking that traditional masculinity has entirely given way."

—*Salzman, Matathia, and O'Reilly 2005, 38*

Few people know what exactly to make of the metrosexual, a man who turns himself into a project (Brumberg 1997) in the seeming pursuit of the body beautiful. Traditionally associated with women and with gay men, the body beautiful has been tightly linked to the concept of femininity. In her book on *The Male Body,* Bordo (1999) suggests that the media now positions men as sexualized objects of the gaze, just as it has done for women. She claims that women, for the first time in recent history, are now encouraged to consume the beautified male bodily form. As a result, Bordo and others (e.g., Salzman, Matathia, and O'Reilly 2005) contend that the sexualization of men in the media and their participation in appearance-enhancing practices destabilize traditional gender dichotomies. This seeming subversion leads Bordo to exclaim, "I never dreamed that 'equality' would move in the direction of men worrying *more* about their looks rather than women worrying less" (1999, 217).

Scholars who study the meaning of *women's* body work help us understand that participation in beauty culture is not rooted solely in gendered relationships, it is tied up with interlocking systems of race, class, gender, sexuality, and age (Battle-Walters 2004; Bordo 1993; Candelario 2000; Clark and Griffin 2007; Cogan 1999; Craig 2006; Furman 1997; Gimlin 1996; Jacobs-Huey 2006; Taub 1999). That is, for women beauty work is often about more than beauty, it is about appropriating and expressing a particular social status by grooming the body in a particular way. Few scholars have examined the meaning of men's participation in beauty culture, however.

In this article, I use a case study of Shear Style,[1] a small hair salon in a Southern California suburb, to explore how men hair salon clients make sense of their participation in beauty work. I find that men at Shear Style empty beauty work of its association with feminized aesthetics and instead construct it as a practice necessary for them to embody a class-based masculinity. But as the quote that opens this article suggests, not all men are able to participate in the beauty industry. Rather, it is men with enough disposable income, "all the money," who are able to purchase beauty work and beauty products—or "grooming products" as they are often called for men—that

Kristen Barber, Gender & Society (Vol. 22, Issue 4) 22 pp. Copyright © 2008 Sage Publications. Reprinted by permission of Sage Publications.

promise to deliver aesthetics compatible with social standards. For the men at Shear Style, preference for "stylish" and "superior" hair embodies expectations of white professional-class masculinity. These men use beauty work to "do difference" (West and Fenstermaker 1995) in a way that distinguishes themselves from white working-class men, while at the same time distancing themselves from the feminizing character of the "women's" hair salon.

LITERATURE REVIEW

Race, Class, Gender, and the Body

In West and Fenstermaker's (1995) work on "doing difference," they describe difference as a methodical, ongoing, and interactional accomplishment. That is, differences along the lines of race, class, and gender are simultaneously experienced and rendered as "normal" and "natural" ways of organizing social life. The body is often a central mechanism through which people appropriate, perform, and negotiate difference. The clothes we wear, the way we style our hair, how we walk, talk, and gesture are all tied up with doing difference. For example, the Mexican-American girls in Bettie's study "wore makeup and tight-fitting clothing" (2003, 58) to emphasize the difference between themselves and their white, "preppy," middle-class counterparts. Similarly, in her study on exotic dancers, Trautner (2005) found that the body was a central tool with which the women dancers were able to accomplish classed expectations of feminine sexuality. Dancers dressed and groomed their bodies in ways that expressed either working- or middle-class expectations of beauty. The women, mostly white, who worked in clubs that catered to middle-class men, emphasized a body type that was tan and thin, with long blonde hair and breast implants; they covered their bodies and accentuated their eyes. The women of color and white women in working-class clubs often had more robust figures, wore less clothing, and used makeup to accentuate their lips. In these clubs, "beauty" was defined in terms relative to the expectations of the men customers. As a result, the women came to embody raced and classed femininities evoking "different amounts of cultural and educational capital" (Trautner 2005, 774).

The beauty industry generates services and products with which women groom their bodies according to social expectations of raced, classed, and sexualized femininities. The hair salon is a key space in the perpetuation of women's body projects. Hair is a social symbol that allows people to associate themselves with others along the lines of race, class, gender, sexuality, and age. Women cut, shape, and dye their hair in ways that express social location (Weitz 2004), and talk about their hair in ways that define their relationships with other women (Gimlin 1996; Jacobs-Huey 2006).

The Hair Salon as a Gendered Space for Women

Feminist scholars who study the hair salon are often interested in shifting the analytic focus away from masculine representations of the world and refocusing on the everyday experiences of women. The hair salon is understood by these scholars as part of a larger "women's culture" in which women shape their perceptions of self and body, as well as form relationships and social networks (Black 2004; Furman 1997), participate in informal therapy (Black 2004; Sharma and Black 2001; see Kang 2003 on emotional labor in the nail salon), create entrepreneurial opportunities, resist dominant racist frames (Harvey 2005; Harvey-Wingfield 2007), and produce representations of femininity mediated through class (Gimlin 1996), race (Battle-Walters 2004; Candelario 2000; Craig 2006; Jacobs-Huey 2006), and age (Furman 1997). Purchasing beauty work in the salon is one way women accomplish difference and participate in the "naturalizing" of social arrangements.

One of the ways women in the hair salon negotiate their relationships with one another is by expressing or denying a sense of beauty expertise. For example, in Jacobs-Huey's (2006) look at the Black beauty shop, she finds that some women customers share their knowledge of straightening and styling techniques with their stylists, who also sometimes enlist the clients as co-experts in hair care. In a study on women in a predominantly white beauty shop, Gimlin (1996) finds that customers often refuse to take the beauty advice of the "beautician," and instead direct their stylists to produce appropriate hair styles for women of their social class. In both examples, women negotiate their status and relationships with their stylists by situating themselves as experts on raced and classed expectations of beauty. Still, other research (Battle-Walters 2004; Furman 1997) shows that some women deny a sense of expertise in beauty, and instead rely on their women stylists for an appropriate cut and style.

The hair salon is a space in which women create bonds and form friendships with each other. These relationships emerge out of "women's talk" (Alexander 2003) and touch (Furman 1997), which are both implicated in the care work performed by women beauty workers. This emotional labor is often not interpreted by customers as work, however. This is because people feel relationships are less legitimate if mediated by economic exchange (Zelizer 2005) and since this labor is already gendered, it comes to be understood as an essential aspect of women's characters—as something they *are* rather than something they *do* (Hochschild 1983; Tancred 1995).

Feminist scholars interested in women, beauty, and the body find that women's participation in beauty work is about relationships, pleasure, and "achiev[ing] a look, and sometimes also a feeling, which is regarded as 'appropriate' in relation to categories of gender, age, sexuality, class and ethnicity" (Black 2004, 11). The hair salon is one space in which women shape their bodies and relationships with others in ways that mark them as members of particular social groups. Since we have long associated beauty work and the hair salon with "women's culture," the hair salon is a space in which men do not venture, or do so infrequently. In this way, "the salon both reflects and reinforces divisions along gender, [as well as] ethnicity and class lines" (Black 2004, 11). Hair salons are for women, barbershops are for men (Lawson 1999). Under this ideological regime, a heterosexual man in a hair salon is an anomaly who transgresses gender boundaries by moving into a women's space and by participating in a beauty practice traditionally associated with women.

Men: From the Laboring Body to the Flannel Suit to the Well-Coiffed Man

During the Fordist-era of industrial production, definitions of masculinity were attached to men's ability to perform laborious tasks. We continue to see this today

as "scarred and weathered men are seen as more 'manly' and thus socially valuable in many working-class settings and venues" (Paap 2008, 101; see also Paap 2006). For the working class, the literal sweat and blood of men are outward signs of the appropriate performance of masculinity. However, postwar America between 1945 and 1960 saw rapid economic growth, and with it came the corporation and an exponential increase in white-collar jobs. While men's identities continued to be bound up with their jobs, opportunities for intellectual work grew. Many middle-class white men flooded into corporations, trading in their denim work-jumpers for grey flannel suits. As it became necessary for the corporate man to interact with customers and clients, interpersonal skills, personality, and appearance became essential hiring and firing criteria (Luciano 2001).

Luciano (2001) describes how the emphasis on the appearance of middle-class white men emerged from capitalist notions of who a successful professional-class man is. Corporations encouraged these men to package their bodies and personalities for success. Employers correlated softness with Communism, fatness with laziness, and saw baldness as a detriment to sales. Marketers quickly produced sales gimmicks that attached the accomplishment of "professional success" to products such as toupees and pomade, products that had long been considered symbols of vanity, narcissism, and, thus, femininity.

It is no longer enough for some men to work hard, they must also look good. In their discussion of the metrosexual man, Salzman, Matathia, and O'Reilly note the way occupation is tied up with appearance: "In a 2003 poll of American men, 89 percent agreed that grooming is *essential* to the *business world*" (2005, 36; emphasis added). Despite this reported need for businessmen to groom their bodies and to "look good," there remains little empirical work on men's beauty practices (though for a discussion of Japanese men and beauty, see Miller 2006).

Thus far, most research on men and hair care has focused on the Black barbershop. This research reveals Black barbershops as spaces for community and the socialization of Black boys into Black men (Alexander 2003; Williams 1993; Wright 1998). In a society that marginalizes Black masculinity, the Black barbershop acts as a safe place for men to congregate, socialize, and reject oppressive stereotyped notions of masculinity. In the Black barbershop, appearance and the cutting of hair are often secondary to the conversations that are important in perpetuating culture and community (Alexander 2003). Research on the Black barbershop and the women's hair salon shows us how race, class, and gender are constructed differently in different spaces.

Unlike the barbershop, the hair salon is not an obvious place in which men participate in the reproduction of masculinity. Certainly it is not a space in which men could create community with other men. Hence, for those men who choose the salon, it is their participation in feminized beauty work that becomes salient. In this article, I seek to address three questions. First, how might men's participation in beauty work be wrapped up with their social locations? Second, how are the men at Shear Style hair salon involved in appropriating an identity that is simultaneously raced, classed, and gendered? And finally, how is their participation in salon hair care tied up with distinction and the doing of difference?

THE STUDY

In this study, I employed both ethnographic methods and in-depth interviews to explore the roles of class, gender, race, and heterosexuality in the purchase of beauty work by men in a small Southern California hair salon, Shear Style. From October 2006 through February 2007, I conducted 40 hours of observations, 15 formal in-depth interviews with men salon clients, and a group interview with three of the four salon stylists.[2] The small size of the salon, with only four work stations in close proximity to each other, made it an ideal space for me to observe client/stylist interaction, talk with men patrons, and recruit interview respondents. I had a number of informal conversations with men as they waited for their appointments or exited the salon. These conversations allowed me to quickly probe men about why they were at the salon and what it was about the salon that retained them as clients. These informal conversations also helped me to structure and refine my questions for the formal interviews.

Of the 15 men I formally interviewed, 14 are white and one is Mexican. Over the course of the study, I saw only one Asian man and two Latino men with appointments for haircuts. Thirteen of the men identify as heterosexual, while two did not disclose their sexual orientation or marital status. Of the heterosexual men, 10 are married, two are single, and one is divorced. Their ages range from 30 to 63, with the average being 49. While one of the men I formally interviewed is a stay-at-home father, the rest are professional white-collar workers (see Table 1).

The salon's services are priced as follows: A woman's haircut costs $65, dye costs $65 per color, and a man's haircut costs $45. This price for a man's haircut is more than three times as much as the cost at the Supercuts and the barbershop which are located right across the street from the salon. While women often purchase a cut and a color, which can take several hours to complete, men's haircuts usually take half an hour. I observed only one man have his hair colored; he declined to be interviewed for this study.[3]

The interview questions revolved around the men's opinions of the salon and their perspectives on why they and other men choose salon hair care. I asked the men to describe the salon, talk about why they came to the salon, and tell me about other places they had gone for a haircut. I transcribed each interview before coding. To analyze the interviews, I first used open-coding to look for emerging themes on why the men said they patronize the salon and how they made sense of their purchase of beauty work. As solid themes emerged, I turned to more focused coding to see how the men agreed and diverged on their perceptions and experiences.

THE SALON

The context of Shear Style is important to an understanding of what it means for men to enter the gendered space of the "women's" hair salon. Shear Style is a feminized space marked by pink walls, fresh flowers, and regular cookie samplers. The men at the salon transgress gender boundaries and risk feminization (Kimmel 2001 [1994]) to enter the salon and get their hair cut there. Eleven of the 15 men I interviewed had

Table 1 Interview Participant Demographic Data

Pseudonym	Age	Race	Income	Occupation*	Sexual Orientation**
Tom	58	White	60/70,000	Educational consultant	Divorced/heterosexual
Steve	40	White	—	Professor	—
Don	50	White	150,000	Animator	Married/heterosexual
Evan	37	White	—	Stay-at-home father	Married/heterosexual
Robert	57	White	85,000	High school administrator	Married/heterosexual
Neil	43	White	—	Engineer	Married/heterosexual
Patrick	61	White	500,000	Corporate official	—
John	58	White	500,000	Lawyer	Married/heterosexual
Andy	36	White	—	Orthodontist	Married/heterosexual
Coby	30	Mexican	120,000	Realtor	Single/heterosexual
Hamilton	57	White	78,250	Investment manager	Married/heterosexual
Sam	53	White	100,000	Architect	Married/heterosexual
Kerry	50	White	157,000	Marketer	Single/heterosexual
Mack	39	White	125,000	Art director	Married/heterosexual
Dan	63	White	250,000	PR consultant	Married/heterosexual

*Three of the men were not comfortable reporting their annual incomes. The forth, Evan, is a stay-at-home-father and, therefore, had no income to report. However, he did report his family income to be approximately $100,000.

**This data is indicative of men's reported marital status and sexual orientation. Two of the men, Steve and Patrick, did not report their sexual orientation or their marital status.

followed their hairstylists from a prior salon to Shear Style. With its white walls and clean lines, the atmosphere of the previous salon is much more androgynous and, in contrast, Shear Style is understood by the men as "feminine."

Inside the salon, long thin lights snake down from the ceiling. The floors are a dark glossy wood and the walls are painted a dusty pink. On the back wall are old kitchen cabinets that display products for sale such as mousse, hairspray, and hair-wax, as well as jewelry, purses, and Suzanne Somers self-help books. Below these shelves are drawers that store curling-irons and blow-dryers. On Saturdays, the salon is usually at maximum capacity with women everywhere: sitting on the waiting bench, having their hair cut, and working. The salon rings out with the laughter of women as they talk about what is going on in their lives and which celebrity is wearing what.

The men are keenly aware that they are outnumbered in this gendered space, reporting that they rarely see other men in the salon. Hamilton, a 57-year-old white investment manager, points to the women around him as he describes his aversion to the salon, "It's jammed full of housewives . . . and there are bimbos walking around chatting." Hamilton trivializes the salon and the practice of beauty work in the salon by associating it with "bimbos" and "housewives." His privileged position as a white upper-middle-class man likely allows him to feel he has the authority to make such disparaging remarks. Many of my respondents recommended steps the salon could take to better serve its men clients. For example, two men proposed that flat screen televisions be affixed to the walls and tuned to the sports and the news channels. Also, many of the men would like to see available reading material other than "gossip" and bridal magazines. Evan, a 37-year-old white stay-at-home-father, says that men's magazines would be "kind of nice to see . . . Maybe I'll suggest that next time I see her [his stylist]." He laughs, "Where's my *GQ*? Where's my *Esquire*?" Evan's laugh implies that asking for "men's magazines" is not appropriate since the salon mainly belongs to women. By recommending magazines such as *GQ* and *Esquire* (magazines targeted to middle- and upper-middle-class white men), instead of *Ebony* or *JET* (which are aimed at Black audiences), Evan suggests that he and the other men at the salon are interested in appropriating a particular kind of professional-class whiteness.

The pink walls, throw pillows on the waiting bench, fresh weekly flowers, and cookie samplers further feminize the salon in the eyes of the men. Neil, a 43-year-old white engineer, describes the salon as a "fairly feminine atmosphere." When I asked him what it is about the salon that makes it "feminine," he told me that you have to "perch" on a cushioned bench while waiting, "and men don't perch." He then gestured toward the maroon, purple, and gold tasseled throw pillows that decorated the bench on which we sat and exclaimed that the "the pillows, food, [and] décor" make him feel he is in a "woman's space." Relying on my assumed reading of him as a man, this description allowed Neil to situate himself in contrast to the feminized character of the salon.

The gender composition of the salon's clientele, the lack of amenities for men, and the décor of the salon provides clues to the men that they are in a "women's" space. By articulating an understanding of the space as feminine (see Craig and Liberti 2007), the men set themselves against and create distance from the potentially contaminating "feminine" character of the salon. They contend the salon is not an appropriate space for *them*, as men, despite their regular visits. While the men enter the salon to purchase beauty work from the stylists, they simultaneously maintain a sense of masculinity by distancing themselves from the "feminine" salon and by situating themselves as anomalies in this space.

MEN'S MOTIVATIONS FOR GOING TO THE HAIR SALON

Three themes emerge from this study that help us to understand why the men at Shear Style purchase beauty work in a "women's" hair salon: (1) Because they enjoy the salon as a place of leisure, luxury, and pampering; (2) For the personalized relationships they feel they form with their women stylists; and (3) To obtain a stylish haircut they conflate with white professional-class aesthetics. As I discuss these themes in turn, what emerges is a picture of how the men at Shear Style understand the salon as a place important to the appropriation of a white professional-class embodiment, how they contrast the salon and the barbershop

to differentiate themselves from white working-class masculinity, and how they resist feminization while transgressing gender boundaries.

The Pampered Heterosexual Man: Leisure, Luxury, and Touch in the Hair Salon

Bodily pampering, which includes attention to appearance and which takes place within a traditionally feminized space, could be considered a feminized form of leisure. However, the class and race privilege of the men at Shear Style allow them to access this leisure and pleasure without marginalization. The men also maintain a sense of masculinity by marking the salon services as *less* feminine than those offered by nail salons and spas. While they can afford to pay for stylish hair, they would not pay for nail care, for example. Finally, by heterosexualizing the touch that accompanies this pampering the men resist feminization and instead position themselves as heterosexually masculine.

Many of my respondents described the salon as a place of leisure, where they go to relax and pause from their hectic daily lives. The men at Shear Style are professionals who live in a speeded-up metropolis where work and family life collide and compete, and where people's social lives often lose out to the occupational expectations of white-collar "success." The 45 minutes they spend at the salon, waiting and getting their hair cut, is time for themselves, and time to relax and enjoy the services the salon provides. For example, Coby, a 30-year-old Mexican realtor, says,

> You know, I don't have a lot of time; I'm really busy during the week. I have a son, I have a five-year old, [and] so I don't have a lot of time to do things for myself. So this is cool. I like to just come out and get some coffee or something . . . It's kind of relaxing; it's something I do for myself.

While Coby is pleased with the haircut he receives at the salon, it is the wait for the haircut he seems to enjoy most. As work becomes increasingly demanding, the salon serves an important function in the lives of the men at Shear Style; they pay for space in which they can escape from their busy lives. This is despite the feminized décor of the salon and the "girly" pillows which decorate the waiting bench.

While many of the men described the salon as a place of leisure, there are any number of places they could go to find time for themselves. So, why do these men choose the gendered space of the "woman's" hair salon? Shear Style provides the men with services that are unique to the salon experience, services that make many of the men feel "pampered" and taken care of. Sharma and Black's interviews with women beauty workers show that "'pampering' was seen as a service which the stressed and hardworking (female) client deserved and needed" (2001, 918). This pampering comes in the form of paid touch, which is a key aspect of the hair salon experience (Furman 1997). As I observed,

> When Rosa was done cutting Evan's thick brown hair, she took him to the other room to wash and rinse off the fine bits of hair that had fallen around his neck and were nestled in his hair. When she was done washing his hair, she brought him back to the seat and toweled off his head and neck. She proceeded to blow-dry his hair while ruffling her fingers through it. (Fieldnote: 10/21/2006)

In addition to this more mundane touch, the men especially enjoy the pampering aspect of the "scalp massage" which is included in the shampoo. They describe this massage as "nice" and "lovely." Don says, "They're going to wash your hair. That's really nice; they put you in a chair, flip you back, [and] wash your hair . . . It's just a lovely experience." Mack, a 39-year-old white art director, echoes this sentiment:

> You know, there's nothing like putting your head back and getting a little head massage while you're getting your hair washed, it feels good. Sal's [a hypothetical barber] not going to do that . . . That more than anything, it's one of those things where it just feels good. You get a little pampered; you get detail.

Mack notes that it is in the hair salon where beauty services include physical pleasure. He suggests that the men's barbershop does not include touch that can be described as pleasurable or pampering. In his work on the Black barbershop, Alexander (2003) describes being touched by the barber as *secretly* pleasurable. That is, while he enjoys having the barber touch his

scalp, this touch could never be discussed openly as pleasurable since doing so might be interpreted by other men as homoerotic. Comparatively, the heterosocial interactions the men have with their women salon stylists allow the men to access paid touch without their presumed heterosexuality falling under suspicion.

By couching paid touch in heterosexuality, the men position themselves as heterosexual and resist the potential feminization of pampering in a hair salon. They clearly receive pleasure from the scalp massages and shampooing; but state that they enjoy this aspect of pampering solely because they are being touched by a woman. "It's like when you go to get a massage [and] they want to know if you want a man or a woman [masseuse]; I'm like, 'a woman sounds nice,' " Don told me. Sam, a 53-year-old white architect, agrees, "I would say I prefer women. It's kind of like a massage too. They ask, 'do you want a man or a woman?' I always prefer a woman." Don and Sam suggest that a massage from a man would be uncomfortable for them, presumably because it does not fit with their sense of themselves as heterosexual. Therefore, touch in the salon is possible and pleasurable for the men because it is done within the context of a heterosexual interaction. If the men were shampooed by another man, such as a barber, they might not enjoy, or at least discuss, the pampering aspect of paid touch because it could compromise their association with privileged heterosexuality.

Although some of the men classed their hair salon experience by describing it as akin to a "mini spa day," they had not, and declared that they would not, enter a spa. These men define the spa as a place where people (presumably women) purchase services such as pedicures, manicures, facials, massages, body-wraps, and mud-baths. They counterpose their more utilitarian haircut to spa and nail services, which they describe as not a "priority" for them. As one man notes, "I think it's one of those things where I value my spare time so much that it's like when I look at my priorities and things I want to do in my time, [the] spa isn't there." I briefly spoke with a man who was leaving the salon after his haircut; he said that the salon is a nice way to "sneak pampering in while doing something you would have to do anyway." He elaborated by telling me that for professional-class men, paying $45 for a haircut is more acceptable than spending money in a spa or a nail salon because it can be veiled as a necessity. Many of the men admitted that it would probably feel good to get a pedicure, for example, but said such services do not serve a utilitarian purpose and, therefore, cannot be adequately disguised as masculine.

Personalized Relationships and Gendered Care Work

The relationships the men have with their stylists involve both touch and the exchange of personal information. Many of the men at Shear Style have grown attached and loyal to their stylists partially because of relationships they believe they share. For example, Don describes his relationship with his stylist,

> It's like totally a relationship . . . It's a person you talk to on a regular basis, and they're really good listeners . . . Rosa always says, "So where are you going this weekend?" . . . It's like this is Rosa, this is my friend; I'll tell her what I'm doing this weekend. It's like another kind of relationship that's really important.

While I often observed friendly familiar bantering between the clients and their stylists, many of the men also shared intimate details of what was going on in their lives; they talked about spouses, children, and traveling. The men pride themselves on their familiar relationships with their stylists, a relationship that they say makes them feel genuinely cared for.

Building relationships with clients is an integral part of the workers' tasks in many body service occupations. Sharma and Black (2001) show that when "beauty therapists" draw customers into a conversation, they often ask questions regarding the customer's family and recent events in the customer's life. The men perceive their stylists' interest in their families as sincere and mutual. Patrick, a 61-year-old white corporate official, reports that he and his stylist have "become kind of friends . . . She tells me about [her daughter] and stuff, and I tell her about my sons and daughter." This personalized relationship motivates the men to come back to get their hair cut by the same stylist time and time again. For example, I asked one man why he comes back to Rosa for his haircuts and he said, "She's very friendly and she knows my kid's, my

son's name. We keep kind of going on what happened last time, if something happened in my personal life, we talk about it." Another man said that he patronizes the salon because, "You know my daughters have come here, my wife has come here; so we [my stylist and I] can talk about *our* families."

The men appreciate their stylists' seemingly genuine interest in their lives. During my observations, I witnessed the pleasure many of the men receive when their stylists ask them to share what is going on in their personal lives. For example, during my fieldwork, I noted that,

> [A man] was already in the chair when I arrived at the salon. Rosa was cutting his hair and they were chatting away. He seemed comfortable as she talked about her husband and daughter. She asked him about his new baby boy, who was only two months old. I spoke with this man briefly after his haircut. He described the salon as a space in which he felt authentically cared for. He said that it is "fun" to talk with his hairstylist and that they "talk about life." "At the barbershop, they don't care about you," he said. When he left the salon, Rosa pleaded with him to bring his baby with him the next time he came to the salon. He beamed with pride and assured her he would. (Fieldnote: 2/16/2007)

This client reinforces the notion that care work is gendered by claiming that the men in the barbershop "don't care about you." A barber is assumed to not provide care work or emotional labor; instead the men make a distinction whereby the women salon stylists are sincerely interested in the clients' families and want to talk with the men "about life."

Unlike the men, the stylists perceive their relationships with their clients as simply part of the job. They confided that they are not always interested in their clients' lives or families. This demonstrates the way in which beauty work involves the physical labor of cutting and styling hair as well as emotional labor (Black 2004; Sharma and Black 2001). The stylists recognize the care work they perform, as well as the fact that it is not valued as such, claiming that their men clients come to them for a haircut because "it's cheaper than a psychiatrist." The men clients, however, do not see their relationships with their stylists as one-sided; nor do they understand their stylists as paid informal therapists. This is because emotional labor is often taken for granted and naturalized as part of women's essential character (Hochschild 1983; Tancred 1995). This is analogous to domestic employers who see their nannies and housekeepers as part of the family rather than as employees (Hondagneu-Sotelo 2001). Furthermore, the men believe their relationships with their stylists are genuine, not "marred" by economic exchange (Zelizer 2005). By personalizing these relationships, they make invisible the fact that they are paying for *body labor:* both the physical and emotional labor of women beauty workers (Kang 2003).

In the men's discussions of their relationships with their stylists, they not only appropriate women's body work, they also establish themselves as members of a particular class. The men position themselves as "classy" by comparing "salon talk" to barbershop talk and by describing the barbershop as a place for the expression of working-class masculinity in which men talk about "beer and pussy," sports and cars. While the men explicitly class the barbershop and the hair salon, they also implicitly racialize these settings. Though these men do not discuss race, by setting up the barbershop as a place for the expression of a masculinity that differs from their own, they define the barbershop as a space for a *white* working-class masculinity. One man describes the difference between the salon and the barbershop as "night and day" and explains that, "You have garage talk [read as barbershop talk] and you have salon talk." By describing the conversation in the barbershop as "garage talk," the man genders the two spaces and suggests that traditionally "masculine" topics, which do not include feelings and family, are the only things discussed at the barbershop. Many of the men I spoke with contend that the gendered difference between the barbershop and the hair salon lies in conversation. "[T]he masculine view is that you're supposed to go to a barbershop and get a standard haircut from a man, talk about football, locker rooms, [and] sex," Mack reported. The men prefer the more personal and intimate conversations they have with their stylists to those that take place in the barbershop.

While the men at Shear Style have the option of getting their hair cut in a men's barbershop, they describe the barbershop as a place that does not provide them

with *caring* relationships. The value the men place on women as sincere care workers is not surprising given the expectation that women perform emotional labor while providing services. However, by comparing the salon to the barbershop, the men indicate that the barbershop acts to uphold "traditional" notions of masculinity by informally discouraging the sharing of intimate information (Bird 1996). Consequently, they differentiate themselves from what they describe as the white working-class masculinity of barbershop men, whom they say prefer to talk about "beer and pussy," to successfully situate themselves as progressive, professional-class white men.

A Stylish and Classed Haircut

The men at Shear Style also set themselves apart as members of a particular class by describing salon hair care as important to the accomplishment of a "stylish" white professional-class embodiment. They conflate salon hair care with "stylish" customized, and contemporary haircuts. For example, Mack notes, "[If I] want something a little more stylish, I'll come to the salon because the salon develops more current styles [and] different techniques [that are] more relevant." The men understand the salon as a space in which they are able to purchase current trends in hair, and they attribute the ability to deliver this style to the women hairstylists whom they suggest have a "high taste level" and are highly skilled. The men trust their stylists and take comfort in knowing they will get a "good" haircut each and every time they come to the salon. "I know that I'm going to have a consistently good haircut every time I go [to the salon]," one man told me. This consistency gives the men "peace of mind," and alleviates the worry and the stress they feel when they have their hair cut elsewhere.

The men's desires for aesthetic enhancement are potentially threatening to their masculinity since, as men, their sense of self-worth is not supposed to be tied to how they look. To counteract this potential threat, the men claim they do not *want* to look stylish for themselves; rather they *need to* look good to succeed professionally. They construct their purchase of beauty work in the salon as a practice that helps them to compete in the workplace and to persuade their clients that they are professional, responsible, and will do the job well. Tom says,

> I mean, you know, I have clients. That means before they become clients, I have to win them over. Now who are they going to go with? The person who has . . . this great appearance package [pointing to himself] including grooming, style, professionalism, mannerism . . . Who are they going to go with, that person, or are they going to go with somebody who looks like they came in and dressed by accident or [that they are] indifferent about their hair?

Tom equates appearance with professionalism, explaining that he has to look a particular way, which includes "grooming [and] style," to be successful with his business clients. Hamilton also feels pressured because he works with "wealthy clients" "When you walk in a room and there are billionaires sitting there, you need to uphold the same appearance," he told me.

These men suggest that there are unwritten appearance rules in the workplace for men as well as women (Dellinger and Williams 1997) and that these rules require them to purchase beauty work in the hair salon. This resonates with Luciano's (2001) study, which links men's appearance standards to the work that they do and describes professional men as likely to invest in appearance-enhancing practices because of their interactions with clients and customers. Like the women in Gimlin's (1996) research, the men at Shear Style embed the meaning of their beauty work in professionalism. That is, their purchase of beauty services in the hair salon becomes about fulfilling what they interpret as expectations of white professional-class masculinity.

Few of these clients directly acknowledge the role class and occupation play in both their desire for and ability to purchase beauty work and "style" in the hair salon. Kerry, a 50-year-old white marketer, first describes the typical male client in the salon as "somebody who has more money than somebody who can only afford 10 dollars." However, he quickly reassesses his answer and decides, "It doesn't matter how rich or how poor you are, you have budgets and you have allocations. And some people who make less money will spend more on entertainment than people who make a lot of money. What's your priority[?]" In this way, Kerry marks himself, and the other men at

Shear Style, as distinct in "priority," not privilege. This works to erase class privilege, although the purchase of salon hair care is made possible by the men's income and is rooted in the ability to succeed in a professional white-collar occupation.

The men also solidify their class status by again distancing themselves from the masculinity they associate with the "old school" barbershop. They reject the barbershop as a place where men purchase mass produced hairstyles by an out-of-date barber. For example, one man told me, "I think there is a difference; I think she [his stylist] cuts hair a little bit better [than a barber]." A good, stylish haircut is one that is current and modern, and is in contrast with the haircut the men feel they would receive from "old barber[s]." "The male barber is just bad," Hamilton exclaims, "80-year-old barbers who can't see just chop your hair." These men believe that white professional-class men do not need to get their hair cut at the barbershop since they can afford the "superior" and "customized" work of a salon stylist. Rather, they claim that working-class men purchase what they consider the inferior haircuts of the barbershop. As Evan says, "I can't see a mechanic working at, or a grease-monkey working at a Jiffy-Lube, or something like that, going to a shop that charges 65 bucks for a haircut." Evan differentiates the clients of the salon and barbershop in terms of class, and also sets the men salon clients up as superior by derogatorily referring to white working-class men as "grease-monkeys."

The men clients at Shear Style contrast the salon with the barbershop to justify their presence in a "women's" space. They refer to the barbershop as "old" and out of date, allowing them to position themselves in contrast as contemporary stylish men who rightfully seek the beauty work of women. Both the haircuts and the space of the barbershop are associated with an out-of-date style. For example, in justifying his preference for the salon, Mack again connects the barbershop with a passé aggressive and misogynist masculinity,

> [The barbershop's] got the owner's old boxing gloves up on the wall, black and white photos from being in the war, the naugahyde seats, [and] the pile of *Playboys* in the corner . . . I guess it just depends on how machismo I was feeling at the time, if I wanted to go

"Grrr" [pretending to be "machismo" as he furrows his brow, grunts, and shakes his head from side to side] and go old school [to the barbershop] or you know, if I wanted to come here [to the salon].

Mack genders the barbershop and describes it is a place of the past with its "black and white photos from the war" and "old school" haircuts. He classes the barbershop by associating it with the cheap material of "naugahyde seats" and with a working-class masculinity that is involved in the physical aspect of war and the aggressive sport of boxing. Neil also classed the barbershop and its customers by describing it as having "no music, vinyl flooring, and *Auto Week* magazines." By contrasting themselves with the traditional "machismo" barbershop which they say does not deliver its supposed working-class customers with "style," the men at Shear Style construct themselves as a class of "new men": progressive, stylish, and professional.

DISCUSSION

In this article, I investigate how men at Shear Style make sense of their participation in salon hair care and how they reinforce a class-based sense of masculinity while within a space defined as feminine. By situating salon hair care as necessary for the appropriation of a professional-class whiteness, the men "do difference" in a way that distinguishes them from the white working-class masculinity they associate with the barbershop. The concept of "doing difference" helps us to understand how the men at Shear Style are involved in "naturalizing" the social order along the lines of race and class, and how their purchase of beauty work is tied up with status maintenance. The men at Shear Style "naturalize" the social order by suggesting that working-class men are misogynist and do not value or prioritize style. The men at the salon contrast themselves with this supposed barbershop masculinity to reinforce their status as white middle-class men, and use the hair salon to mark themselves as progressive and stylish men.

In talking about the salon, the men create a binary that pits professional-class white men against working-class white men. They report that they *must* purchase the beauty work of salon hairstylists to appropriately embody and "do" a particular classed-whiteness.

As a result, the men's participation in salon hair care does not compromise their masculinity; instead, their stylish hair becomes an outward sign of professional status which sets them apart from white working-class men. The men use "taste" and "priorities" to describe themselves as different from the "mechanic" and the "grease-monkey" whom they claim are the typical clients of the barbershop. The men disdain the barbershop and the class status it represents. They describe the barbershop as "old school," traditionally and conservatively masculine, situating salon hair care as for the "new" progressive man. The men create a contemporary, white, professional-class masculinity by transferring traditional masculine characteristics onto, and thus othering, white working-class men (Hondagneu-Sotelo and Messner 1994).

The exchange of personal family information with their women stylists makes the men feel their relationships with their stylists are more intimate and "caring" than those they would form with barbers. The men enjoy a particular kind of bonding that exists most often within women's spaces, not men's (Bird 1996). By differentiating the "beer and pussy" talk which they presume takes place in the working-class white barbershop with that which takes place in the "women's" hair salon, the men both set themselves up as progressive modern men and consumers of gender care work. Like the customers of luxury hotels (Sherman 2007), the men at Shear Style ignore the fact that their seemingly intimate and personal relationships are mediated by economic exchange and are made possible through the emotional labor of the stylists.

Pampering which involves attention to appearance and takes place within a "women's" space is a feminized experience. The salon serves as a place for men to indulge in pampering services while at the same time veiling this indulgence and marking it as *more* masculine than other forms of beauty work. The men heterosexualize the touch that accompanies this pampering and situate salon hair care as utilitarian; one *has to* have a haircut after all. The men construct salon hair care as necessary for professional success and thus are able to enjoy the pleasures involved in practices that are considered feminine and have been traditionally "off-limits" to men. The necessity of a haircut, its professionalizing character, and the rejection of the feminine allow the men to enter the "women's" salon and purchase beauty work. The men at Shear Style suggest that as long as feminized beauty routines serve a utilitarian purpose, and reinforce race and class privilege, they can be folded into meanings of white professional-class masculinity.

Like the women in Bettie (2003) and Trautner's (2005) research, the men at Shear Style—through the purchase and consumption of beauty work—appropriate embodied symbols of educational and cultural capital that distinguish them as raced, classed, sexualized, and gendered. While within a space defined as feminine, the men maintain a sense of masculinity by situating themselves as anomalies in a "women's" salon and by heterosexualizing their interactions with the women hairstylists. This research allows us to see how race and especially class privilege are reproduced by men through the consumption of beauty work, and how this privilege both allows men a "pass" to enter into a "women's" space while protecting them from the powerless aspects associated with the feminine culture of beauty.

NOTES

1. The names of the salon, the stylists, and the clients have been changed to protect the privacy of those involved in the study.

2. The fourth stylist did not cut men's hair.

3. A number of men declined to be formally interviewed because of family and work engagements.

REFERENCES

Alexander, Bryant Keith. 2003. Fading, twisting, and weaving: An interpretive ethnography of the Black barbershop as cultural space. *Qualitative Inquiry* 9 (1): 105–28.

Battle-Walters, Kimberly. 2004. *Sheila's shop: Working-class African American women talk about life, love, race, and hair.* New York: Rowman and Littlefield Publishers, Inc.

Bettie, Julie. 2003. *Women without class: Girls, race, and identity.* Berkeley: University of California Press.

Bird, Sharon R. 1996. Welcome to the men's club: Homosociality and the maintenance of hegemonic masculinity. *Gender & Society* 10(2):120–32.

Black, Paula. 2004. *The beauty industry: Gender, culture, pleasure.* New York: Routledge.

Bordo, Susan. 1993. *Unbearable weight: Feminism, western culture, and the body.* Berkeley: University of California Press.

———. 1999. *The male body: A new look at men in public and in private.* New York: Farrar, Straus and Giroux.

Brumberg, Joan Jacobs. 1997. *The body project: An intimate history of American girls.* New York: Random House.

Candelario, Ginetta. 2000. Hair race-ing: Dominican beauty culture and identity production. *Meridians: Feminism, Race, and Transnationalism* 1 (1): 128–56.

Clark, Laura Hurd, and Meridith Griffin. 2007. The body natural and the body unnatural: Beauty work and aging. *Journal of Aging Studies* 21: 187–201.

Cogan, Jeanine C. 1999. Lesbians walk the tightrope of beauty: Thin is in but femme is out. *Journal of Lesbian Studies* 3 (4): 77–89.

Craig, Maxine Leeds. 2006. Race, beauty, and the tangled knot of guilty pleasure. *Feminist Theory* 7 (2): 159–77.

Craig, Maxine Leeds, and Rita Liberti. 2007. "Cause that's what girls do": The making of a feminized gym. *Gender & Society* 21 (5): 676–99.

Dellinger, Kirsten, and Christine L. Williams. 1997. Makeup at work: Negotiating appearance rules in the workplace. *Gender & Society* 11 (2): 151–77.

Furman, Frida Kerner. 1997. *Facing the mirror: Older women and beauty shop culture.* New York: Routledge.

Gimlin, Debra. 1996. Pamela's place: Power and negotiation in the hair salon. *Gender & Society* 10 (5): 505–26.

Harvey, Adia M. 2005. Becoming entrepreneurs: Intersections of race, class, and gender at the Black beauty salon. *Gender & Society* 19 (6): 789–808.

Harvey-Wingfield, Adia. 2007. *Doing business with beauty: Black women, hair salons, and the racial enclave economy.* New York: Rowman and Littlefield Publishers, Inc.

Hochschild, Arlie Russell. 1983. *The managed heart: Commercialization of human feeling.* Berkeley: University of California Press.

Hondagneu-Sotelo, Pierrette. 2001. *Domestica: Immigrant workers cleaning and caring in the shadows of affluence.* Berkeley: University of California Press.

Hondagneu-Sotelo, Pierrette, and Michael A. Messner. 1994. Gender displays and men's power: The "new man" and the Mexican immigrant man. In *Theorizing masculinities,* edited by H. Brod and M. Kaufman. London: Sage Publications.

Jacobs-Huey, Lanita. 2006. *From the kitchen to the parlor: Language and becoming in African American women's hair care.* New York: Oxford University Press.

Kang, Miliann. 2003. The managed hand: The commereialization of bodies and emotions in Korean immigrant-owned nail salons. *Gender & Society* 17 (6): 820–39.

Kimmel, Michael S. 2001 [1994]. Masculinity as homophobia: Fear, shame, and the silence in the construction of gender identity. In *Gender: A sociological reader,* edited by S. Jackson and S. Scott. New York: Routledge.

Lawson, Helene M. 1999. Working on hair. *Qualitative Sociology* 22 (3): 235–57.

Luciano, Lynne. 2001. *Looking good: Male body image in modern America.* New York: Hill and Wang.

Miller, Laura. 2006. *Beauty up: Exploring contemporary Japanese body aesthetics.* Berkeley: University of California Press.

Paap, Kris. 2006. *Working construction: Why white working-class men put themselves, and the labor movement, in harm's way.* Ithaca, NY: Cornell University Press.

———. 2008. Power and embodiment: Comment on Anderson. *Gender & Society* 22 (1): 99–103.

Salzman, Marian, Ira Matathia, and Ann O'Reilly. 2005. *The future of men.* New York: Palgrave MacMillan.

Sharma, Ursula, and Paula Black. 2001. Look good, feel better: Beauty therapy as emotional labor. *Sociology* 35 (4): 913–31.

Sherman, Rachel. 2007. *Class acts: Service and inequality in luxury hotels.* Berkeley: University of California Press.

Tancred, Peta E. 1995. Women's work: A challenge to the sociology of work. *Gender, Work and Organization* 2 (1): 11–20.

Taub, Jennifer. 1999. Bisexual women and beauty norms: A qualitative examination. *Journal of Lesbian Studies* 3 (4): 27–36.

Trautner, Mary Nell. 2005. Doing gender, doing class: The performance of sexuality in exotic dance clubs. *Gender & Society* 19 (6): 771–88.

Weitz, Rose. 2004. *Rapunzel's daughters: What women's hair tells us about women's lives.* New York: Farrar, Straus and Giroux.

West, Candace, and Sarah Fenstermaker. 1995. Doing difference. *Gender & Society* 9 (1): 8–37.

Williams, Louis. 1993. The relationship between a Black barbershop and the community that supports it. *Human Mosaic* 27: 29–33.

Wright, Earl II. 1998. More than just a haircut: Sociability within the urban African American barbershop. *Challenge: A Journal of Research on African American Men* 9: 1–13.

Zelizer, Vivian. 2005. *The purchase of intimacy.* Princeton, NJ: Princeton University Press.

11

Yearning For Lightness

Transnational Circuits in the Marketing and Consumption of Skin Lighteners

Evelyn Nakano Glenn

With the breakdown of traditional racial categories in many areas of the world, colorism, by which I mean the preference for and privileging of lighter skin and discrimination against those with darker skin, remains a persisting frontier of intergroup and intragroup relations in the twenty-first century. Sociologists and anthropologists have documented discrimination against darker-skinned persons and correlations between skin tone and socioeconomic status and achievement in Brazil and the United States (Hunter 2005; Sheriff 2001; Telles 2004). Other researchers have revealed that people's judgments about other people are literally colored by skin tone, so that darker-skinned individuals are viewed as less intelligent, trustworthy, and attractive than their lighter-skinned counterparts (Herring, Keith, and Horton 2003; Hunter 2005; Maddox 2004).

One way of conceptualizing skin color, then, is as a form of symbolic capital that affects, if not determines, one's life chances. The relation between skin color and judgments about attractiveness affect women most acutely, since women's worth is judged heavily on the basis of appearance. For example, men who have wealth, education, and other forms of human capital are considered "good catches," while women who are physically attractive may be considered desirable despite the lack of other capital. Although skin tone is usually seen as a form of fixed or unchangeable capital, in fact, men and women may attempt to acquire light-skinned privilege. Sometimes this search takes the form of seeking light-skinned marital partners to raise one's status and to achieve intergenerational mobility by increasing the likelihood of having light-skinned children. Often, especially for women, this search takes the form of using cosmetics or other treatments to change the appearance of one's skin to make it look lighter.

This article focuses on the practice of skin lightening, the marketing of skin lighteners in various societies around the world, and the multinational corporations that are involved in the global skin-lightening trade. An analysis of this complex topic calls for a multilevel approach. First, we need to place the production, marketing, and consumption of skin lighteners into a global political-economic context. I ask, How is skin lightening interwoven into the world economic system and its transnational circuits of products, capital, culture, and people? Second, we need to examine the mediating entities and processes by which skin lighteners reach specific national/ethnic/racial/class consumers. I ask,

---

Evelyn Nakano Glenn, *Gender & Society* (Vol. 22, Issue 3) 22 pp. Copyright © 2008 Sage Publications. Reprinted by permission of Sage Publications.

What are the media and messages, cultural themes and symbols, used to create the desire for skin-lightening products among particular groups? Finally, we need to examine the meaning and significance of skin color for consumers of skin lighteners. I ask, How do consumers learn about, test, and compare skin-lightening products, and what do they seek to achieve through their use?

The issue of skin lightening may seem trivial at first glance. However, it is my contention that a close examination of the global circuits of skin lightening provides a unique lens through which to view the workings of the Western-dominated global system as it simultaneously promulgates a "white is right" ideology while also promoting the desire for and consumption of Western culture and products.

SKIN LIGHTENING AND GLOBAL CAPITAL

Skin lightening has long been practiced in many parts of the world. Women concocted their own treatments or purchased products from self-styled beauty experts offering special creams, soaps, or lotions, which were either ineffective sham products or else effective but containing highly toxic materials such as mercury or lead. From the perspective of the supposedly enlightened present, skin lightening might be viewed as a form of vanity or a misguided and dangerous relic of the past.

However, at the beginning of the twenty-first century, the search for light skin, free of imperfections such as freckles and age spots, has actually accelerated, and the market for skin-lightening products has mushroomed in all parts of the world. The production and marketing of products that offer the prospect of lighter, brighter, whiter skin has become a multi-billion-dollar global industry. Skin lightening has been incorporated into transnational flows of capital, goods, people, and culture. It is implicated in both the formal global economy and various informal economies. It is integrated into both legal and extralegal transnational circuits of goods. Certain large multinational corporations have become major players, spending vast sums on research and development and on advertising and marketing to reach both mass and specialized markets. Simultaneously, actors in informal or underground economies, including smugglers, transnational migrants, and petty traders, are finding unprecedented opportunities in producing, transporting, and selling unregulated lightening products.

One reason for this complex multifaceted structure is that the market for skin lighteners, although global in scope, is also highly decentralized and segmented along socioeconomic, age, national, ethnic, racial, and cultural lines. Whether the manufacturers are multi-billion-dollar corporations or small entrepreneurs, they make separate product lines and use distinct marketing strategies to reach specific segments of consumers. Ethnic companies and entrepreneurs may be best positioned to draw on local cultural themes, but large multinationals can draw on local experts to tailor advertising images and messages to appeal to particular audiences.

The Internet has become a major tool/highway/engine for the globalized, segmented, lightening market. It is the site where all of the players in the global lightening market meet. Large multinationals, small local firms, individual entrepreneurs, skin doctors, direct sales merchants, and even eBay sellers use the Internet to disseminate the ideal of light skin and to advertise and sell their products. Consumers go on the Internet to do research on products and shop. Some also participate in Internet message boards and forums to seek advice and to discuss, debate, and rate skin lighteners. There are many such forums, often as part of transnational ethnic Web sites. For example, IndiaParenting.com and sukhdukh.com, designed for South Asians in India and other parts of the world, have chat rooms on skin care and lightening, and Rexinteractive.com, a Filipino site, and Candymag.com, a site sponsored by a magazine for Filipina teens, have extensive forums on skin lightening. The discussions on these forums provide a window through which to view the meaning of skin color to consumers, their desires and anxieties, doubts and aspirations. The Internet is thus an important site from which one can gain a multilevel perspective on skin lightening.

CONSUMER GROUPS AND MARKET NICHES

Africa and African Diaspora

In Southern Africa, colorism is just one of the negative inheritances of European colonialism. The ideology of white supremacy that European colonists brought included the association of Blackness with primitive-ness, lack of civilization, unrestrained sexuality, pollution, and dirt. The association of Blackness with dirt can be seen in a 1930 French advertising poster for Dirtoff. The poster shows a drawing of a dark African man washing his hands, which have become white, as he declares, "Le Savon Dirtoff me blanchit!" The soap was designed not for use by Africans but, as the poster notes, *pour mechanciens automobilises et menagers*—French auto mechanics and housewives. Such images showing Black people "dramatically losing their pigmentation as a result of the cleansing process," were common in late nineteenth- and early twentieth-century soap advertisements, according to art historian Jean Michel Massing (1995, 180).

Some historians and anthropologists have argued that precolonial African conceptions of female beauty favored women with light brown, yellow, or reddish tints. If so, the racial hierarchies established in areas colonized by Europeans cemented and generalized the privilege attached to light skin (Burke 1996; Ribane 2006, 12). In both South Africa and Rhodesia/Zimbabwe, an intermediate category of those considered to be racially mixed was classified as "coloured" and subjected to fewer legislative restrictions than those classified as "native." Assignment to the coloured category was based on ill-defined criteria, and on arrival in urban areas, people found themselves classified as native or coloured on the basis of skin tone and other phenotypic characteristics. Indians arriving in Rhodesia from Goa, for example, were variously classified as "Portuguese Mulatto" or coloured. The multiplication of discriminatory laws targeting natives led to a growing number of Blacks claiming to be coloured in both societies (Muzondidya 2005, 23–24).

The use of skin lighteners has a long history in Southern Africa, which is described by Lynn Thomas and which I will not recount here (in press). Rather, I will discuss the current picture, which shows both a rise in the consumption of skin-lightening products and concerted efforts to curtail the trade of such products. Despite bans on the importation of skin lighteners, the widespread use of these products currently constitutes a serious health issue in Southern Africa because the products often contain mercury, corticosteroids, or high doses of hydroquinone. Mercury of course is highly toxic, and sustained exposure can lead to neurological damage and kidney disease. Hydroquinone (originally an industrial chemical) is effective in suppressing melanin production, but exposure to the sun—hard to avoid in Africa—damages skin that has been treated. Furthermore, in dark-skinned people, long-term hydroquinone use can lead to ochronosis, a disfiguring condition involving gray and blue-black discoloration of the skin (Mahe, Ly, and Dangou 2003). The overuse of topical steroids can lead to contact eczema, bacterial and fungal infection, Cushing's syndrome, and skin atrophy (Margulies n.d.; Ntambwe 2004).

Perhaps the most disturbing fact is that mercury soaps used by Africans are manufactured in the European Union (EU), with Ireland and Italy leading in the production of mercury soap. One company that has been the target of activists is Killarney Enterprises, Ltd., in County Wicklow, Ireland. Formerly known as W&E Products and located in Lancashire, England, the company was forced to close following out-of-court settlements of suits filed by two former employers who had given birth to stillborn or severely malformed infants due to exposure to mercury. However, W&E Products then secured a 750,000-pound grant from the Irish Industrial Development Authority to relocate to Ireland, where it changed its name to Killarney Enterprises, Ltd. The company remained in business until April 17, 2007, producing soaps under the popular names Tura, Arut, Swan, Sukisa Bango, Meriko, and Jeraboo (which contained up to 3 percent mercuric iodide). Distribution of mercury soap has been illegal in the EU since 1989, but its manufacture has remained legal as long as the product is exported (Chadwick 2001; Earth Summit 2002, 13–14). These soaps are labeled for use as antiseptics and to prevent body odor; however, they are understood to be and are used as skin bleaches. To complete the circuit, EU-manufactured mercury soaps are smuggled back into the EU to sell in shops catering to African immigrant communities. An Irish journalist noted that the very same brands made by Killarney Enterprises, including Meriko and Tura (banned in both the EU and South Africa) could easily be found in African shops in Dublin (De Faoite 2001; O'Farrell 2002).

As a result of the serious health effects, medical researchers have conducted interview studies to determine how prevalent the practice of skin lightening is among African women. They estimate that 25 percent of women in Bamaki, Mali; 35 percent in Pretoria, South Africa; and 52 percent in Dakar, Senegal, use skin lighteners, as do an astonishing 77 percent of women traders in Lagos, Nigeria (Adebajo 2002; del Guidice and Yves 2002; Mahe, Ly, and Dangou 2003; Malangu and Ogubanjo 2006).

There have been local and transnational campaigns to stop the manufacture of products containing mercury in the EU and efforts to inform African consumers of the dangers of their use and to foster the idea of Black pride. Governments in South Africa, Zimbabwe, Nigeria, and Kenya have banned the import and sale of mercury and hydroquinone products, but they continue to be smuggled in from other African nations (Dooley 2001; Thomas 2004).

Despite these efforts, the use of skin lighteners has been increasing among modernized and cosmopolitan African women. A South African newspaper reported that whereas in the 1970s, typical skin lightener users in South Africa were rural and poor, currently, it is upwardly mobile Black women, those with technical diplomas or university degrees and well-paid jobs, who are driving the market in skin lighteners. A recent study by Mictert Marketing Research found that 1 in 13 upwardly mobile Black women aged 25 to 35 used skin lighteners. It is possible that this is an underestimation, since there is some shame attached to admitting to using skin lighteners (Ntshingila 2005).

These upwardly mobile women turn to expensive imported products from India and Europe rather than cheaper, locally made products. They also go to doctors to get prescriptions for imported lighteners containing corticosteroids, which are intended for short-term use to treat blemishes. They continue using them for long periods beyond the prescribed duration, thus risking damage (Ntshingila 2005). This recent rise in the use of skin lighteners cannot be seen as simply a legacy of colonialism but rather is a consequence of the penetration of multinational capital and Western consumer culture. The practice therefore is likely to continue to increase as the influence of these forces grows.

African America

Color consciousness in the African American community has generally been viewed as a legacy of slavery, under which mulattos, the offspring of white men and slave women, were accorded better treatment than "pure" Africans. While slave owners considered dark-skinned Africans suited to fieldwork, lighter-skinned mulattos were thought to be more intelligent and better suited for indoor work as servants and artisans. Mulattos were also more likely to receive at least rudimentary education and to be manumitted. They went on to form the nucleus of many nineteenth-century free Black communities. After the civil war, light-skinned mulattos tried to distance themselves from their darker-skinned brothers and sisters, forming exclusive civic and cultural organizations, fraternities, sororities, schools, and universities (Russell, Wilson, and Hall 1992, 24–40). According to Audrey Elisa Kerr, common folklore in the African American community holds that elite African Americans used a "paper bag" test to screen guests at social events and to determine eligibility for membership in their organizations: anyone whose skin was darker than the color of the bag was excluded. Although perhaps apocryphal, the widespread acceptance of the story as historical fact is significant. It has been credible to African Americans because it was consonant with their observations of the skin tone of elite African American society (Kerr 2005).

The preference and desire for light skin can also be detected in the longtime practice of skin lightening. References to African American women using powders and skin bleaches appeared in the Black press as early as the 1850s, according to historian Kathy Peiss. She notes that *American Magazine* criticized African Americans who tried to emulate white beauty standards: "Beautiful black and brown faces by application of rouge and lily white are made to assume unnatural tints, like the vivid hue of painted corpses" (Peiss 1998, 41). How common such practices were is unknown. However, by the 1880s and 1890s, dealers in skin bleaches were widely advertising their wares in the African American press. A Crane and Company ad in the *Colored American Magazine* (1903) promised that use of the company's "wonderful Face Bleach" would result in a "peach-like complexion" and "turn the skin of a black or brown person five or six shades lighter and of a mulatto person perfectly white" (Peiss 1998, 41, 42).

Throughout the twentieth century, many African American leaders spoke out against skin bleaching, as well as hair straightening, and the African American press published articles decrying these practices. However, such articles were far outnumbered by advertisements for skin bleaches in prominent outlets such as the *Crusader, Negro World,* and the *Chicago Defender.* An estimated 30 to 40 percent of advertisements in these outlets were for cosmetics and toiletries including skin bleaches. Many of the advertised lighteners were produced by white manufacturers; for example, Black and White Cream was made by Plough Chemicals (which later became Plough-Shearing), and Nadolina was made by the National Toilet Company. A chemical analysis of Nadolina Bleach conducted in 1930 found it contained 10 percent ammoniated mercury, a concentration high enough to pose a serious health risk. Both brands are still marketed in African American outlets, although with changed ingredients (Peiss 1998, 210, 212).[1]

The manufacture and marketing of Black beauty products, including skin lighteners, provided opportunities for Black entrepreneurs. Annie Turnbo Malone, who founded the Poro brand, and Sara Breedlove, later known as Madam C. J. Walker, who formulated and marketed the Wonder Hair Grower, were two of the most successful Black entrepreneurs of the late nineteenth and early twentieth centuries. Malone and Walker championed African American causes and were benefactors of various institutions (Peiss 1998, 67–70; see also Bundles 2001). Significantly, both refused to sell skin bleaches or to describe their hair care products as hair straighteners. After Walker died in 1919, her successor, F. B. Ransom, introduced Tan-Off, which became one of the company's best sellers in the 1920s and 1930s. Other Black-owned companies, such as Kashmir (which produced Nile Queen), Poro, Overton, and Dr. Palmer, advertised and sold skin lighteners. Unlike some white-produced products, they did not contain mercury but relied on such ingredients as borax and hydrogen peroxide (Peiss 1998, 205, 212, 213).

Currently, a plethora of brands is marketed especially to African Americans, including Black and White Cream, Nadolina (sans mercury), Ambi, Palmer's, DR Daggett and Remsdell (fade cream and facial brightening cream), Swiss Whitening Pills, Ultra Glow, Skin Success, Avre (which produces the Pallid Skin Lightening System and B-Lite Fade Cream), and Clear Essence (which targets women of color more generally). Some of these products contain hydroquinone, while others claim to use natural ingredients.

Discussions of skin lightening on African American Internet forums indicate that the participants seek not white skin but "light" skin like that of African American celebrities such as film actress Halle Berry and singer Beyonce Knowles. Most women say they want to be two or three shades lighter or to get rid of dark spots and freckles to even out their skin tones, something that many skin lighteners claim to do. Some of the writers believe that Halle Berry and other African American celebrities have achieved their luminescent appearance through skin bleaching, skillful use of cosmetics, and artful lighting. Thus, some skin-lightening products, such as the Pallid Skin Lightening System, purport to offer the "secret" of the stars. A Web site for Swiss Lightening Pills claims that "for many years Hollywood has been keeping the secret of whitening pills" and asks, rhetorically, "Have you wondered why early childhood photos of many top celebs show a much darker skin colour than they have now?"[2]

India and Indian Diaspora

As in the case of Africa, the origins of colorism in India are obscure, and the issue of whether there was a privileging of light skin in precolonial Indian societies is far from settled. Colonial-era and postcolonial Indian writings on the issue may themselves have been influenced by European notions of caste, culture, and race. Many of these writings expound on a racial distinction between lighter-skinned Aryans, who migrated into India from the North and darker-skinned "indigenous" Dravidians of the South. The wide range of skin color from North to South and the variation in skin tone within castes make it hard to correlate light skin with high caste. The most direct connection between skin color and social status could be found in the paler hue of those whose position and wealth enabled them to spend their lives sheltered indoors, compared to the darker hue of those who toiled outdoors in the sun (Khan 2008).

British racial concepts evolved over the course of its colonial history as colonial administrators and settlers attempted to make sense of the variety of cultural and language groups and to justify British rule in India. British observers attributed group differences variously to culture, language, climate, or biological race. However, they viewed the English as representing the highest culture and embodying the optimum physical type; they made invidious comparisons between lighter-skinned groups, whose men they viewed as more intelligent and marital and whose women they considered more attractive, and darker-skinned groups, whose men they viewed as lacking intelligence and masculinity, and whose women they considered to be lacking in beauty (Arnold 2004).

Regardless of the origins of color consciousness in India, the preference for light skin seems almost universal today, and in terms of sheer numbers, India and Indian diasporic communities around the world constitute the largest market for skin lighteners. The major consumers of these products in South Asian communities are women between the ages of 16 and 35. On transnational South Asian blog sites, women describing themselves as "dark" or "wheatish" in color state a desire to be "fair." Somewhat older women seek to reclaim their youthful skin color, describing themselves as having gotten darker over time. Younger women tend to be concerned about looking light to make a good marital match or to appear lighter for large family events, including their own weddings. These women recognize the reality that light skin constitutes valuable symbolic capital in the marriage market (Views on Article n.d.).

Contemporary notions of feminine beauty are shaped by the Indian mass media. Since the 1970s, beauty pageants such as Miss World–India have been exceedingly popular viewer spectacles; they are a source of nationalist pride since India has been highly successful in international pageants such as Miss World. As might be expected, the competitors, although varying in skin tone, tend to be lighter than average. The other main avatars of feminine allure are

Bollywood actresses, such as Isha Koopikari and Aiswarya Rai, who also tend to be light skinned or, if slightly darker, green eyed (see http://www.indianindustry.com/herbalcosmetics/10275.htm).

Many Indian women use traditional homemade preparations made of plant and fruit products. On various blog sites for Indians both in South Asia and diasporic communities in North America, the Caribbean, and the United Kingdom, women seek advice about "natural" preparations and trade recipes. Many commercial products are made by Indian companies and marketed to Indians around the globe under such names as "fairness cream," "herbal bleach cream," "whitening cream," and "fairness cold cream." Many of these products claim to be based on ayurvedic medicine and contain herbal and fruit extracts such as saffron, papaya, almonds, and lentils (Runkle 2004).

With economic liberalization in 1991, the number of products available on the Indian market, including cosmetics and skin care products, has mushroomed. Whereas prior to 1991, Indian consumers had the choice of two brands of cold cream and moisturizers, today, they have scores of products from which to select. With deregulation of imports, the rise of the Indian economy, and growth of the urban middle class, multinational companies see India as a prime target for expansion, especially in the area of personal care products. The multinationals, through regional subsidiaries, have developed many whitening product lines in various price ranges that target markets ranging from rural villagers to white-collar urban dwellers and affluent professionals and managers (Runkle 2005).

Southeast Asia: the Philippines

Because of its history as a colonial dependency first of Spain and then of the United States, the Philippines has been particularly affected by Western ideology and culture, both of which valorize whiteness. Moreover, frequent intermarriage among indigenous populations, Spanish colonists, and Chinese settlers has resulted in a substantially mestizo population that ranges widely on the skin color spectrum. The business and political elites have tended to be disproportionately light skinned with visible Hispanic and/or Chinese appearance. In the contemporary period, economic integration has led to the collapse of traditional means of livelihood, resulting in large-scale emigration by both working-class and middle-class Filipinos to seek better-paying jobs in the Middle East, Asia, Europe, and North America. An estimated 10 million Filipinos were working abroad as of 2004, with more than a million departing each year. Because of the demand for domestic workers, nannies, and care workers in the global North, women make up more than half of those working abroad (Tabbada 2006). Many, if not most, of these migrants remit money and send Western consumer goods to their families in the Philippines. They also maintain transnational ties with their families at home and across the diaspora through print media, phone, and the Internet. All of these factors contribute to an interest in and fascination with Western consumer culture, including fashion and cosmetics in the Philippines and in Filipino diasporic communities (Parrenas 2001).

Perhaps not surprising, interest in skin lightening seems to be huge and growing in the Philippines, especially among younger urban women. Synovate, a market research firm, reported that in 2004, 50 percent of respondents in the Philippines reported currently using skin lightener (Synovate 2004). Young Filipinas participate in several Internet sites seeking advice on lightening products. They seek not only to lighten their skin overall but also to deal with dark underarms, elbows, and knees. Judging by their entries in Internet discussion sites, many teens are quite obsessed with finding "the secret" to lighter skin and have purchased and tried scores of different brands of creams and pills. They are disappointed to find that these products may have some temporary effects but do not lead to permanent change. They discuss products made in the Philippines but are most interested in products made by large European and American multinational cosmetic firms and Japanese and Korean companies. Clearly, these young Filipinas associate light skin with modernity and social mobility. Interesting to note, the young Filipinas do not refer to Americans or Europeans as having the most desirable skin color. They are more apt to look to Japanese and Koreans or to Spanish- or Chinese-appearing (and light-skinned) Filipina

celebrities, such Michelle Reis, Sharon Kuneta, or Claudine Baretto, as their ideals.[3]

The notion that Japanese and Korean women represent ideal Asian beauty has fostered a brisk market in skin lighteners that are formulated by Korean and Japanese companies. Asian White Skin and its sister company Yumei Misei, headquartered in Korea, sell Japanese and Korean skin care products in the Philippines both in retail outlets and online. Products include Asianwhiteskin Underarm Whitening Kit, Japanese Whitening Cream Enzyme Q-10, Japan Whitening Fruit Cream, Kang Tian Sheep Placenta Whitening Capsules, and Kyusoku Bhaku Lightening Pills (see http://yumeimise.com/store/index).

East Asia: Japan, China, and Korea

East Asian societies have historically idealized light or even white skin for women. Intage (2001), a market research firm in Japan, puts it, "Japan has long idolized ivory-like skin that is 'like a boiled egg'—soft, white and smooth on the surface." Indeed, prior to the Meiji Period (starting in the 1860s), men and women of the higher classes wore white-lead powder makeup (along with blackened teeth and shaved eyebrows). With modernization, according to Mikiko Ashikari, men completely abandoned makeup, but middle- and upper-class women continued to wear traditional white-lead powder when dressed in formal kimonos for ceremonial occasions, such as marriages, and adopted light-colored modern face powder to wear with Western clothes. Ashikari finds through observations of 777 women at several sites in Osaka during 1996-1997 that 97.4 percent of women in public wore what she calls "white face," that is, makeup that "makes their faces look whiter than they really are" (2003, 3).

Intage (2001) reports that skin care products, moisturizers, face masks, and skin lighteners account for 66 percent of the cosmetics market in Japan. A perusal of displays of Japanese cosmetics and skin care products shows that most, even those not explicitly stated to be whitening products, carry names that contain the word "white," for example, facial masks labeled "Clear Turn White" or "Pure White." In addition, numerous products are marketed specifically as whiteners. All of the leading Japanese firms in the cosmetics field, Shiseido, Kosa, Kanebo, and Pola, offer multiproduct skin-whitening lines, with names such as "White Lucent" and "Whitissimo." Fytokem, a Canadian company that produces ingredients used in skin-whitening products, reports that Japan's market in skin lighteners topped $5 billion in 1999 (Saskatchewan Business Unlimited 2005). With deregulation of imports, leading multinational firms, such as L'Oreal, have also made large inroads in the Japanese market. French products have a special cachet (Exhibitor Info 2006).

While the Japanese market has been the largest, its growth rate is much lower than those of Korea and China. Korea's cosmetic market has been growing at a 10 percent rate per year while that of China has been growing by 20 percent. Fytokem estimates that the market for skin whiteners in China was worth $1 billion in 2002 and was projected to grow tremendously. A 2007 Nielsen global survey found that 46 percent of Chinese, 47 percent of people in Hong Kong, 46 percent of Taiwanese, 29 percent of Koreans, and 24 percent of Japanese had used a skin lightener in the past year. As to regular users, 30 percent of Chinese, 20 percent of Taiwanese, 18 percent of Japanese and Hong Kongers, and 8 percent of Koreans used them weekly or daily. However, if money were no object, 52 percent of Koreans said they would spend more on skin lightening, compared to 26 percent of Chinese, 23 percent of Hong Kongers and Taiwanese, and 21 percent of Japanese (Nielsen 2007).

Latin America: Mexico and the Mexican Diaspora

Throughout Latin America, skin tone is a major marker of status and a form of symbolic capital, despite national ideologies of racial democracy. In some countries, such as Brazil, where there was African chattel slavery and extensive miscegenation, there is considerable color consciousness along with an elaborate vocabulary to refer to varying shades of skin. In other countries, such as Mexico, the main intermixture was between Spanish colonists and indigenous peoples, along with an unacknowledged admixture with African slaves. *Mestizaje* is the official national ideal. The Mexican concept of mestizaje meant that through racial and ethnic mixture, Mexico would gradually be peopled by a whiter "cosmic race" that surpassed its initial ingredients. Nonetheless, skin tone, along with other phenotypical traits, is a significant marker of social status, with lightness signifying purity and beauty and darkness signifying contamination and ugliness (Stepan 1991, 135). The elite has remained overwhelmingly light skinned and European appearing while rural poor are predominantly dark skinned and Indigenous appearing.

Ethnographic studies of Mexican communities in Mexico City and Michoacan found residents to be highly color conscious, with darker-skinned family members likely to be ridiculed or teased. The first question that a relative often poses about a newborn is about his or her color (Farr 2006, chap. 5; Guttman 1996, 40; Martinez 2001). Thus, it should not be a surprise that individuals pursue various strategies to attain light-skinned identity and privileges. Migration from rural areas to the city or to the United States has been one route to transformation from an Indian to a mestizo identity or from a mestizo to a more cosmopolitan urban identity; another strategy has been lightening one's family line through marriage with a lighter-skinned partner. A third strategy has been to use lighteners to change the appearance of one's skin (Winders, Jones, and Higgins 2005, 77–78).

In one of the few references to skin whitening in Mexico, Alan Knight claims that it was "an ancient practice . . . reinforced by film, television, and advertising stereotypes" (1990, 100). As in Africa, consumers seeking low-cost lighteners can easily purchase mercury-laden creams that are still manufactured and used in parts of Latin America (e.g., Recetas de la Farmacia–Crema Blanqueadora, manufactured in the Dominican Republic, contains 6000 ppm of mercury) (NYC Health Dept. 2005). The use of these products has come to public attention because of their use by Latino immigrants in the United States. Outbreaks of mercury poisoning have been reported in Texas, New Mexico, Arizona, and California among immigrants who used Mexican-manufactured creams such as Crema de Belleza–Manning. The cream is manufactured in Mexico by Laboratories Vide Natural SA de CV., Tampico, Tamaulipas, and is distributed primarily in Mexico. However, it has been found for sale in shops and flea markets in the United States in areas located along the U.S.-Mexican border in Arizona, California, New Mexico, and Texas. The label lists the ingredient calomel, which is mercurous chloride (a salt of mercury). Product samples have been found to contain 6 to 10 percent mercury by weight (Centers for Disease Control 1996; U.S. Food and Drug Administration 1996).

For high-end products, hydroquinone is the chemical of choice. White Secret is one of the most visible products since it is advertised in a 30-minute, late-night television infomercial that is broadcast nationally almost nightly.[4] Jamie Winders and colleagues (2005), who analyze the commercial, note that the commercial continually stresses that White Secret is "una formula Americana." According to Winders, Jones, and Higgins, the American pedigree and English-language name endow White Secret with a cosmopolitan cachet and "a first worldliness." The infomercial follows the daily lives of several young urban women, one of whom narrates and explains how White Secret cream forms a barrier against the darkening rays of the sun while a sister product transforms the color of the skin itself. The infomercial conjures the power of science, showing cross sections of skin cells. By showing women applying White Secret in modern, well-lit bathrooms, relaxing in well-appointed apartments, and protected from damaging effects of the sun while walking around the city, the program connects skin lightening with cleanliness, modernity, and mobility (Winders, Jones, and Higgins 2005, 80–84).

Large multinational firms are expanding the marketing of skin care products, including skin lighteners, in Mexico and other parts of Latin America. For example, Stiefel Laboratories, the world's largest privately held pharmaceutical company, which specializes in dermatology products, targets Latin America for skin-lightening products. Six of its 28 wholly owned subsidiaries are located in Latin America. It offers Clariderm, an over-the-counter hydroquinone cream and gel (2 percent), in Brazil, as well as Clasifel,

a prescription-strength hydroquinone cream (4 percent), in Mexico, Peru, Bolivia, Venezuela, and other Latin American countries. It also sells Claripel, a 4 percent hydroquinone cream, in the United States.[5]

Middle-Aged and Older White Women in North America and Europe

Historically, at least in the United States, the vast majority of skin lightener users have been so-called white women. Throughout the nineteenth and early twentieth centuries, European American women, especially those of Southern and Eastern European origins, sought to achieve whiter and brighter skin through use of the many whitening powders and bleaches on the market. In 1930, J. Walter Thomson conducted a survey and found 232 brands of skin lighteners and bleaches for sale. Advertisements for these products appealed to the association of white skin with gentility, social mobility, Anglo-Saxon superiority, and youth. In large cities, such as New York and Chicago, some Jewish women used skin lighteners and hair straighteners produced by Black companies and frequented Black beauty parlors (Peiss 1998, 85, 149, 224).

By the mid-1920s, tanning became acceptable for white women, and in the 1930s and 1940s, it became a craze. A year-round tan came to symbolize high social status since it indicated that a person could afford to travel and spend time at tropical resorts and beaches. In addition, there was a fad for "exotic" Mediterranean and Latin types, with cosmetics designed to enhance "olive" complexions and brunette hair (Peiss 1998, 150–51, 148–49).

However, in the 1980s, as the damaging effects of overexposure to sun rays became known, skin lightening among whites reemerged as a major growth market. Part of this growth was fueled by the aging baby boom generation determined to stave off signs of aging. Many sought not only toned bodies and uplifted faces but also youthful skin—that is, smooth, unblemished, glowing skin without telltale age spots. Age spots are a form of hyperpigmentation that results from exposure to the sun over many years. The treatment is the same as that for overall dark skin: hydroquinone, along with skin peeling, exfoliants, and sunscreen.[6]

MULTINATIONAL COSMETIC AND PHARMACEUTICAL FIRMS AND THEIR TARGETING STRATEGIES

Although there are many small local manufacturers and merchants involved in the skin-lightening game, I want to focus on the giant multinationals, which are fueling the desire for light skin through their advertisement and marketing strategies. The accounts of the skin-lightening markets have shown that the desire for lighter skin and the use of skin bleaches is accelerating in places where modernization and the influence of Western capitalism and culture are most prominent. Multinational biotechnology, cosmetic, and pharmaceutical corporations have coalesced through mergers and acquisitions to create and market personal care products that blur the lines between cosmetics and pharmaceuticals. They have jumped into the field of skin lighteners and correctors, developing many product lines to advertise and sell in Europe, North America, South Asia, East and Southeast Asia, and the Middle East (Wong 2004).

Three of the largest corporations involved in developing the skin-lightening market are L'Oreal, Shiseido, and Unilever. The French-based L'Oreal, with €15.8 billion in sales in 2006, is the largest cosmetics company in the world. It consists of 21 major subsidiaries including Lancome; Vichy Laboratories; La Roche-Posay Laboratoire Pharmaceutique; Biotherm; Garnier; Giorgio Armani Perfumes; Maybelline, New York; Ralph Lauren Fragrances; Skinceuticals, Shu Uemura; Matrix; Redken; and SoftSheen Carlson. L'Oreal is also a 20 percent shareholder of Sanofi-Synthelabo, a major France-based pharmaceutical firm. Three L'Oreal subsidiaries produce the best-known skin-lightening lines marketed around the world (which are especially big in Asia): Lancome Blanc Expert with Melo-No Complex, LaRoche-Posay Mela-D White skin lightening daily lotion with a triple-action formula, and Vichy Biwhite, containing procystein and vitamin C.

A second major player in the skin-lightening market is Shiseido, the largest and best-known Japanese cosmetics firm, with net sales of $5.7 billion. Shiseido cosmetics are marketed in 65 countries and regions, and it operates factories in Europe, the Americas, and other Asian countries. The Shiseido Group, including affiliates, employs approximately 25,200 people around the globe. Its two main luxury lightening lines are White Lucent (for whitening) and White Lucency (for spots/aging). Each product line consists of seven or eight components, which the consumer is supposed to use as part of a complicated regimen involving applications of specific products several times a day.[7]

The third multinational corporation is Unilever, a diversified Anglo-Dutch company with an annual turnover of more than €40 billion and net profits of €5 billion in 2006 (Unilever 2006). It specializes in so-called fast-moving consumer goods in three areas: food (many familiar brands, including Hellman's Mayonnaise and Lipton Tea), home care (laundry detergents, etc.), and personal care, including deodorants, hair care, oral care, and skin care. Its most famous brand in the skin care line is Ponds, which sells cold creams in Europe and North America and whitening creams in Asia, the Middle East, and Latin America.

Through its Indian subsidiary, Hindustan Lever Limited, Unilever patented Fair & Lovely in 1971 following the patenting of niacinamide, a melanin suppressor, which is its main active ingredient. Test marketed in South India in 1975, it became available throughout India in 1978. Fair & Lovely has become the largest-selling skin cream in India, accounting for 80 percent of the fairness cream market. According to anthropologist Susan Runkle (2005), "Fair and Lovely has an estimated sixty million consumers throughout the Indian subcontinent and exports to thirty four countries in Southeast and Central Asia as well as the Middle East."

Fair & Lovely ads claim that "with regular daily use, you will be able to unveil your natural radiant fairness in just 6 weeks!" As with other successful brands, Fair & Lovely has periodically added new lines to appeal to special markets. In 2003, it introduced Fair & Lovely, Ayurvedic, which claims to be formulated according to a 4,500-year-old Indian medical system. In 2004, it introduced Fair & Lovely Oil-Control Gel and Fair & Lovely Anti-Marks. In 2004, Fair & Lovely also announced the "unveiling" of a premium line, Perfect

Radiance, "a complete range of 12 premium skin care solutions" containing "international formulations from Unilever's Global Skin Technology Center, combined with ingredients best suited for Indian skin types and climates." Its ads say "Experience Perfect Radiance from Fair & Lovely. Unveil Perfect Skin." Intended to compete with expensive European brands, Perfect Radiance is sold only in select stores in major cities, including Delhi, Mumbai, Chennai, and Bangalore.[8]

Unilever is known for promoting its brands by being active and visible in the locales where they are marketed. In India, Ponds sponsors the Femina Miss India pageant, in which aspiring contestants are urged to "be as beautiful as you can be." Judging by photos of past winners, being as beautiful as you can be means being as light as you can be. In 2003, partly in response to criticism by the All India Democratic Women's Association of "racist" advertisement of fairness products, Hindustani Lever launched the Fair and Lovely Foundation, whose mission is to "encourage economic empowerment of women across India" through educational and guidance programs, training courses, and scholarships.[9]

Unilever heavily promotes both Ponds and Fair & Lovely with television and print ads tailored to local cultures. In one commercial shown in India, a young, dark-skinned woman's father laments that he has no son to provide for him and his daughter's salary is not high enough. The suggestion is that she could neither get a better job nor marry because of her dark skin. The young woman then uses Fair & Lovely, becomes fairer, and lands a job as an airline hostess, making her father happy. A Malaysian television spot shows a college student who is dejected because she cannot get the attention of a classmate at the next desk. After using Pond's lightening moisturizer, she appears in class brightly lit and several shades lighter, and the boy says, "Why didn't I notice her before?" (BBC 2003).

Such advertisements can be seen as not simply responding to a preexisting need but actually creating a need by depicting having dark skin as a painful and depressing experience. Before "unveiling" their fairness, dark-skinned women are shown as unhappy, suffering from low self-esteem, ignored by young men, and denigrated by their parents. By using Fair & Lovely or Ponds, a woman undergoes a transformation of not only her complexion but also her personality and her fate. In short, dark skin becomes a burden and handicap that can be overcome only by using the product being advertised.

CONCLUSION

The yearning for lightness evident in the widespread and growing use of skin bleaching around the globe can rightfully be seen as a legacy of colonialism, a manifestation of "false consciousness," and the internalization of "white is right" values by people of color, especially women. Thus, one often-proposed solution to the problem is reeducation that stresses the diversity of types of beauty and desirability and that valorizes darker skin shades, so that lightness/whiteness is dislodged as the dominant standard.

While such efforts are needed, focusing only on individual consciousness and motives distracts attention from the very powerful economic forces that help to create the yearning for lightness and that offer to fulfill the yearning at a steep price. The manufacturing, advertising, and selling of skin lightening is no longer a marginal, underground economic activity. It has become a major growth market for giant multinational corporations with their sophisticated means of creating and manipulating needs.

The multinationals produce separate product lines that appeal to different target audiences. For some lines of products, the corporations harness the prestige of science by showing cross-sectional diagrams of skin cells and by displaying images of doctors in white coats. Dark skin or dark spots become a disease for which skin lighteners offer a cure. For other lines, designed to appeal to those who respond to appeals to naturalness, corporations call up nature by emphasizing the use of plant extracts and by displaying images of light-skinned women against a background of blue skies and fields of flowers. Dark skin becomes a veil that hides one's natural luminescence, which natural skin lighteners will uncover. For all products, dark skin is associated with pain, rejection, and limited options; achieving light skin is seen as necessary to being youthful, attractive, modern, and affluent—in short, to being "all that you can be."

NOTES

1. Under pressure from African American critics, Nadolina reduced the concentration to 6 percent in 1937 and 1.5 percent in 1941.

2. Discussions on Bright Skin Forum, Skin Lightening Board, are at http://excoboard.com/exco/forum.php?forumid=65288. Pallid Skin Lightening system information is at http://www.avreskincare.com/skin/pallid/index.html. Advertisement for Swiss Whitening Pills is at http://www.skinbleaching.net.

3. Skin whitening forums are at http://www.candymag.com/teentalk/index.php/topic,131753.0.html and http://www.rexinteractive.com/forum/topic.asp?TOPIC_ ID=41.

4. Discussion of the ingredients in White Secret is found at http://www.vsantivirus.com/hoax-white-secret.htm.

5. I say that Stiefel targets Latin America because it markets other dermatology products, but not skin lighteners, in the competitive Asian, Middle Eastern, African, and European countries. Information about Stiefel products is at its corporate Web site, http://www.stiefel.com/why/about.aspx (accessed May 1, 2007).

6. Many of the products used by older white and Asian women to deal with age spots are physician-prescribed pharmaceuticals, including prescription-strength hydroquinone formulas. See information on one widely used system, Obagi, at http://www.obagi.com/article/homepage.html (accessed December 13, 2006).

7. *Shiseido Annual Report 2006,* 34, was downloaded from http://www.shiseido.co.jp/e/annual/html/index.htm. Data on European, American, and Japanese markets are at http://www.shiseido.co.jp/e/story/html/sto40200.htm. World employment figures are at http://www.shiseido.co.jp/e/story/html/sto40200.htm. White Lucent information is at http://www.shiseido.co.jp/e/whitelucent_us/products/product5.htm. White Lucency information is at http://www.shiseido.co.jp/e/whitelucency/ (all accesseld May 6, 2007).

8. "Fair & Lovely Launches Oil-Control Fairness Gel" (Press Release, April 27, 2004) is found at http://www.hll.com/mediacentre/release.asp?fl=2004/PR_HLL_042704.htm (accessed May 6, 2007). "Fair & Lovely Unveils Premium Range" (Press Release, May 25, 2004) is available at http://www.hll.com/mediacentre/release.asp?fl=2004/PR_HLL_052104_2.htm (accessed on May 6, 2007).

9. The Pond's Femina Miss World site is http://feminamissindia.indiatimes.com/ articleshow/1375041.cms. The All India Democratic Women's Association objects to skin lightening ad is at http://www.aidwa.org/content/issues_of_concern/women_and_media.php. Reference to Fair & Lovely campaign is at http://www.aidwa.org/content/issues_of_concern/women_and_media.php. "Fair & Lovely Launches Foundation to Promote Economic Empowerment of Women" (Press Release, March 11, 2003) is found at http://www.hll.com/mediacentre/release.asp?fl=2003/PR_HLL_031103.htm (all accessed December 2, 2006).

REFERENCES

Adebajo, S. B. 2002. An epidemiological survey of the use of cosmetic skin lightening cosmetics among traders in Lagos, Nigeria. *West African Journal of Medicine* 21 (1): 51–55.

Arnold, David. 2004. Race, place and bodily difference in early nineteenth century India. *Historical Research* 77:162.

Ashikari, Makiko. 2003. Urban middle-class Japanese women and their white faces: Gender, ideology, and representation. *Ethos* 31 (1): 3, 3–4, 9–11.

BBC. 2003. India debates "racist" skin cream ads. *BBC News World Edition,* July 24. http://news.bbc.co.uk/1/hi/world/south_asia/3089495.stm (accessed May 8, 2007).

Bundles, A'Lelia. 2001. *On her own ground: The life and times of Madam C. J. Walker.* New York: Scribner.

Burke, Timothy. 1996. *Lifebuoy men, lux women: Commodification, consumption, and cleanliness in modern Zimbabwe.* Durham, NC: Duke University Press.

Centers for Disease Control and Prevention. 1996. *FDA warns consumers not to use Crema De Belleza.* FDA statement. Rockville, MD: U.S. Food and Drug Administration.

Chadwick, Julia. 2001. Arklow's toxic soap factory. *Wicklow Today,* June. http://www.wicklowtoday.com/features/mercurysoap.htm (accessed April 18, 2007).

De Faoite, Dara. 2001. Investigation into the sale of dangerous mercury soaps in ethnic shops. *The Observer,* May 27. http://observer.guardian.co.uk/uk_news/story/0,6903,497227,00.html (accessed May 1, 2007).

del Guidice, P., and P. Yves. 2002. The widespread use of skin lightening creams in Senegal: A persistent public health problem in West Africa. *International Journal of Dermatology* 41:69–72.

Dooley, Erin. 2001. Sickening soap trade. *Environmental Health Perspectives,* October.

Earth Summit. 2002. *Telling it like it is: 10 years of unsustainable development in Ireland.* Dublin, Ireland: Earth Summit.

Exhibitor info. 2006. http://www.beautyworldjapan.com/en/efirst.html (accessed May 8, 2007).

Farr, Marcia. 2006. *Rancheros in Chicagocan: Language and identity in a transnational community.* Austin: University of Texas Press.

Guttman, Matthew C. 1996. *The meanings of macho: Being a man in Mexico City.* Berkeley: University of California Press.

Herring, Cedric, Verna M. Keith, and Hayward Derrick Horton, eds. 2003. *Skin deep: How race and complexion matter in the "color blind" era.* Chicago: Institute for Research on Race and Public Policy.

Hunter, Margaret. 2005. *Race, gender, and the politics of skin tone.* New York: Routledge.

Intage. 2001. Intelligence on the cosmetic market in Japan. http://www.intage.co.jp/express/01_08/market/index1.html (accessed November 2005).

Kerr, Audrey Elisa. 2005. The paper bag principle: The myth and the motion of colorism. *Journal of American Folklore* 118:271–89.

Khan, Aisha. 2008. "Caucasian," "coolie," "Black," or "white"? Color and race in the Indo-Caribbean Diaspora. Unpublished paper.

Knight, Alan. 1990. Racism, revolution, and indigenismo: Mexico, 1910–1940. In *The idea of race in Latin America, 1870-1940,* edited by Richard Graham. Austin: University of Texas Press.

Maddox, Keith B. 2004. Perspectives on racial phenotypicality bias. *Personality and Social Psychology Review* 8:383–401.

Mahe, Antoine, Fatimata Ly, and Jean-Marie Dangou. 2003. Skin diseases associated with the cosmetic use of bleaching products in women from Dakar, Senegal. *British Journal of Dermatology* 148 (3): 493–500.

Malangu, N., and G. A. Ogubanjo. 2006. Predictors of tropical steroid misuse among patrons of pharmacies in Pretoria. *South African Family Practices* 48 (1): 14.

Margulies, Paul. n.d. Cushing's syndrome: The facts you need to know. http://www.nadf.us/diseases/cushingsmedhelp.org/www/nadf4.htm (accessed May 1, 2007).

Martinez, Ruben. 2001. *Crossing over: A Mexican family on the migrant trail.* New York: Henry Holt.

Massing, Jean Michel. 1995. From Greek proverb to soap advert: Washing the Ethiopian. *Journal of the Warburg and Courtauld Institutes* 58:180.

Muzondidya, James. 2005. *Walking a tightrope, towards a social history of the coloured community of Zimbabwe.* Trenton, NJ: Africa World Press.

Nielsen. 2007. Prairie plants take root. In *Health, beauty & personal grooming: A global Nielsen consumer report.* http://www.acnielsen.co.in/news/20070402.shtml (accessed May 3, 2007).

Ntambwe, Malangu. 2004. Mirror mirror on the wall, who is the fairest of them all? *Science in Africa, Africa's First On-Line Science Magazine,* March. http://www.scienceinafrica.co.za/2004/march/skinlightening.htm (accessed May 1, 2007).

Ntshingila, Futhi. 2005. Female buppies using harmful skin lighteners. *Sunday Times, South Africa,* November 27.

http://www.sundaytimes.co.za (accessed January 25, 2006).

NYC Health Dept. 2005. NYC Health Dept. warns against use of "skin lightening" creams containing mercury or similar products which do not list ingredients. http://www.nyc.gov/html/doh/html/pr/pr008-05.shtml (accessed May 7, 2007).

O'Farrell, Michael. 2002. Pressure mounts to have soap plant shut down. *Irish Examiner,* August 26. http://archives.tcm.ie/irishexaminer/2002/08/26/story510455503.asp (accessed May 1, 2007).

Parrenas, Rhacel. 2001. *Servants of globalization: Women, migration, and domestic work.* Palo Alto, CA: Stanford University Press.

Peiss, Kathy. 1998. *Hope in a jar: The making of America's beauty culture.* New York: Metropolitan Books.

Ribane, Nakedi. 2006. *Beauty: A Black perspective.* Durban, South Africa: University of KwaZulu-Natal Press.

Runkle, Susan. 2004. Making "Miss India": Constructing gender, power and nation. *South Asian Popular Culture* 2 (2): 145–59.

———. 2005. The beauty obsession. *Manushi* 145 (February). http://www.indiatogether.org/manushi/issue145/lovely.htm (accessed May 5, 2007).

Russell, Kathy, Midge Wilson, and Ronald Hall. 1992. *The color complex: The politics of skin color among African Americans.* New York: Harcourt Brace Jankovich.

Saskatchewan Business Unlimited. 2005. Prairie plants take root in cosmetics industry. *Saskatchewan Business Unlimited* 10 (1): 1–2.

Sheriff, Robin E. 2001. *Dreaming equality: Color, race and racism in urban Brazil.* New Brunswick, NJ: Rutgers University Press.

Stepan, Nancy Ley. 1991. *The hour of eugenics: Race, gender, and nation in Latin America.* Ithaca, NY: Cornell University Press.

Synovate. 2004. In:fact. http://www.synovate.com/knowledge/infact/issues/200406 (accessed March 21, 2007).

Tabbada, Reyna Mae L. 2006. Trouble in paradise. Press release, September 20. http://www.bulatlat.com/news/6-33/6-33-trouble.htm (accessed May 5, 2007).

Telles, Edward E. 2004. *Race in another America: The significance of skin color in Brazil.* Princeton, NJ: Princeton University Press.

Thomas, Iyamide. 2004. "Yellow fever": The disease that is skin bleaching. *Mano Vision* 33 (October): 32-33. http://www.manovision.com/ISSUES/ISSUE33/33skin.pdf (accessed May 7, 2007).

Thomas, Lynn M. (in press.) Skin lighteners in South Africa: Transnational entanglements and technologies of the self. In *Shades of difference: Why skin color matters,* edited by Evelyn Nakano Glenn. Stanford, CA: Stanford University Press.

Unilever. 2006. Annual report. http://www.unilever.com/ourcompany/investorcentre/annual_reports/archives.asp (accessed May 6, 2007).

U.S. Food and Drug Administration. 1996. *FDA warns consumers not to use Crema De Belleza*. FDA statement, July 23. Rockville, MD: U.S. Food and Drug Administration.

Views on article—Complextion. n.d. http://www.indiaparenting.com/beauty/beauty041book.shtml (accessed November 2005).

Winders, Jamie, John Paul Jones III, and Michael James Higgins. 2005. Making gueras: Selling white identities on late-night Mexican television. *Gender, Place and Culture* 12 (1): 71–93.

Wong, Stephanie. 2004. Whitening cream sales soar as Asia's skin-deep beauties shun Western suntans. *Manila Bulletin.* http://www.mb.com.ph/issues/2004/08/24/SCTY2004082416969.html# (accessed March 24, 2007).

12

Deploying Race, Gender, Class, and Sexuality in the Iraq War[1]

JOANE NAGEL

LINDSEY FEITZ

At about 0700 hours (local time) on 23 March 2003, while moving through the outskirts of the city of An Nasiriyah in southeastern Iraq, an element of the 507th Maintenance Company was attacked by Iraqi forces and irregulars. There were 33 U.S. Soldiers in the 18-vehicle convoy . . . The Iraqi forces in An Nasiriyah conducted fierce attacks against the convoy. Of the 22 Soldiers who survived, nine were wounded in action. Although all details of the battle could not be determined with certainty, it is clear that every U.S. Soldier did their duty.

—*U.S. Army, 2003*

There were three women soldiers serving with the 507th who were taken prisoner by the Iraqis:

Private First Class Jessica Lynch of Palestine, West Virginia, was born in April, 1983. When the Humvee she was riding in crashed, this 19-year-old supply clerk suffered lacerations, a broken arm, broken leg, and head and back injuries. She was taken by Iraqis to a hospital, treated for her injuries, and rescued on April 1 by U.S. forces. Jessica's rescue was filmed by the U.S. military and was widely circulated in the U.S. media. Seven months later 500,000 copies of her biography, *I Am a Soldier. Too: The Jessica Lynch Story*, were released; during the next week she was interviewed by Diane Sawyer on ABC's *20–20*, by Katie Couric on NBC's *Today* show, by David Letterman on CBS's *Late Night Show*, and by Larry King on CNN's *Larry King Live*. On August 23, 2003, Jessica Lynch received a medical honorable discharge from the Army and an 80 percent disability benefit.

Army Specialist Shoshana Johnson of El Paso, Texas, was born in January, 1973. During her capture outside Nasiriyah the 31-year-old cook was shot in the ankle and injured in both legs. She was held by the Iraqis until she and six others were rescued on April 13 by U.S. forces. Johnson was the first African American woman POW. During the next few months Shoshana received awards and invitations to speak from a number of organizations including *Essence* magazine, the NAACP, the Rainbow Push Coalition, the Congressional Hispanic and Black Caucuses, the Olender Foundation, and the historically black institution of higher education, Fayetteville State University. On December 12, 2003, Shoshana Johnson retired from the Army with a temporary disability honorable discharge and a 30 percent disability benefit.

Private First Class Lori Piestewa of Tuba City, Arizona, and member of the Hopi Nation, was born in December, 1979. The 23-year-old supply clerk was driving the same Humvee carrying Jessica Lynch when they were attacked by Iraqi forces near Nasiriyah. According to eye witness accounts (including that of Jessica Lynch) Piestewa maneuvered the Humvee around firing Iraqi troops and debris, circling around crippled vehicles in an effort to give aid to her fellow soldiers until her vehicle was struck by a rocket-propelled grenade and crashed (Shaffer, 2003). She was wounded in the head and died a few hours later in captivity. Lori was the first Native American woman to die in combat while serving with the U.S. military. She was posthumously promoted to Specialist by the Army, the Arizona state government renamed "Squaw Peak" in the Phoenix Mountains, "Piestewa Peak, the Grand Canyon Games organizers instituted annual Lori Piestewa National Native American Games, an Arizona freeway has been named for her, and a plaque bearing her names is located at the White Sands Missile Range in New Mexico.

RACE, GENDER, CLASS, AND SEXUALITY IN THE IRAQ WAR NARRATIVE

We expect that readers will be much more familiar, as we were when we started this research, with the story and image of Jessica Lynch than with those of Shoshana Johnson or Lori Piestewa. It certainly can be argued that the bravery and actions under fire of Johnson and Piestewa were more newsworthy than the passive role played by Lynch who reported she was knocked unconscious when her Humvee crashed. The fame and treatment of the three women constitute a kind of natural ex-

periment for examining how race, gender, class, and sexuality operate in the U.S. military and in the larger society. Gender and class are "controlled for" in this experiment, but race and sexuality are variables. All three soldiers were from working class backgrounds, were of similar rank, and all three were women. They differed by race: Lynch was white; Johnson was black; Piestewa was native. They also differed in terms of their sexual backgrounds: Lynch was unmarried with no children; Johnson was a single mother with one child; Piestewa was divorced with two children. What also differed were the circumstances of their rescue and, more important, their treatment by the military and the media after their ordeals. Investigations in the months following the women's capture and release have revealed that Jessica Lynch's rescue was dramatized, if not entirely staged, by the U.S. military, that it was filmed and promoted for media and public consumption, and that the U.S. military did not attempt to correct the record when the excesses and distortions of the media were pointed out to them, including by Lynch herself. The discovery of Shoshana Johnson and her six co-POWs during a search of houses in Nasiriyah three weeks after their capture was much less made-for-prime time, in fact it was somewhat accidental; it was not filmed, nor has it been the subject of made-for-TV movies, books, or extensive television interviews. There was virtually no national news coverage of Lori Piestewa's capture and death.

Before moving to our analysis of the ways in which racial and sexual depictions of these three service women were deployed by the U.S. military and media to narrate the Iraq war, we would like to locate the Jessica Lynch story in the larger media landscape of embedded reporting, military censorship, official secrecy, and news media collaboration with the U.S. government's "official story" about the war in Iraq (see Smith, 2003). The U.S. military has learned well the media lessons of Vietnam, in particular, how to control the visual images coming out of a war. Although the Iraq war is approaching its sixth year with thousands of military and civilian deaths and casualties, we see virtually no body bags, no rows of flag-draped coffins, no helicopters medevacing dying and wounded GIs, no Americans gunning down Iraqis, no blood, no suffering. We are struck by how very few images of death and mayhem in Iraq haunt the evening news. Those few pictures from Abu Ghraib circulated in late 2003, all of which have yet to be released officially, were all the more shocking not only because of their content, but also because of their rarity. Embedded reporters seem to have forgotten their cameras and misplaced their keyboards. Michael Weisskopf (2006), a reporter with *Time* magazine, was imbedded with the First Armored Division in Iraq in 2003, when he lost his hand tossing a bomb out of his armored vehicle; he identifies that as the moment when the line between reporter and soldier began to blur for him. Critics of the embedding process argue that even when such drastic injuries do not occur, it is inevitable that reporters will come to identify with the troops who protect them. This dependency has led Hess and Kalb (2003) to ask whether war reporting is distorted by a "Stockholm syndrome" in which the journalists start to "identify with the soldiers and lose their professional detachment?"

News releases from the U.S. military and government control the message and camouflage the violence associated with the Iraq war. We hear about the daily deaths but we see almost nothing despite the fact that nearly 4000 service personnel and an estimated 80,625 to 88,048 civilians had been killed in Iraq by the end of January, 2008 (U.S. Defense Department, 2007a; Iraq Body Count, 2007). There are very few pictures to replace the thousands of words. We are, instead, treated to optimistic appraisals: we are told that we are witnessing the "last throes of the insurgency," the "evildoers" are losing, and "mission accomplished." And we are regaled with tales of the heroic rescue of damsels in distress—brave American men saving white American women from sexual ravishment and murder by brown Iraqis. As we noted above, the hyperdramatized story of saving Private Jessica Lynch was the U.S. military's, American government's, and U.S. news media's story, and it went unchallenged for several weeks after its initial release.

The first major assault on the veracity of the Lynch rescue account was aired on BBC television on May 18, 2003 in a documentary entitled, "War Spin," in which correspondent John Kampmer referred to the story of saving Jessica Lynch as "one of the most stunning pieces of news management ever conceived." In the broadcast he questioned the entire "rescue"—from the storming of the Iraqi hospital by U.S. Special Operations forces to the filming of the operation on a night vision camera. Kampfher (2003) reported:

witnesses told U.S. that the special forces knew the Iraqi military had fled a day before they swooped on the hospital . . . Dr. Anmar Uday [reported]: "There were no [Iraqi] soldiers in the hospital . . . It was like a Hollywood film. They cried, "go, go, go," with guns and blanks without bullets . . . and the sound of explosions. They made a show for the American attack on the hospital-action movies like Sylvester Stallone or Jackie Chan."

In fact, according to Kampfner (2003),

Two days before the snatch squad arrived, [Dr.] Harith [a-Houssona] had arranged to deliver Jessica to the Americans in an ambulance. But as the ambulance, with Private Lynch inside, approached a checkpoint American troops opened fire, forcing it to flee back to the hospital . . . When footage of the rescue was released, General Vincent Brooks, U.S. spokesman in Doha, said, "Some brave souls put their lives on the line to make this happen, loyal to a creed that they know that they'll never leave a fallen comrade."

Kampfher's recounting of Iraqis' efforts to return Lynch to the Americans was confirmed by Jessica Lynch herself in her April 25, 2007 testimony before the U.S. Congress: "We were fired upon at a checkpoint, and the driver of the ambulance had to turn around and brought me back to the hospital" (U.S. House of Representatives, 2007).

There was no dramatized or even particularly well-documented rescue of Shoshana Johnson and her six fellow male POWs, and no saga of the brave death of Lori Piestewa. Only the rescue of pretty young Jessica Lynch made it to the front pages of American newspapers and opening stories of news broadcasts. Although *Glamour* magazine named both Jessica Lynch and Shoshana Johnson as its 2003 Women of the Year (Lori Piestewa apparently was not on their radar), critics have pointed out a number of disparities in the treatment, coverage, and rewards given to the two women: Lynch became a poster girl for the U.S. military and her rescue not only was planned and filmed, it was reenacted on network television as a dramatized spectacle of U.S. Special Operations derring-do; she received a one million dollar advance on the first book published about her (Bragg, 2003). Johnson has become neither a poster girl nor a millionaire; there were no instant book deals, movie contracts, or prime time interviews for Shoshana.[2] Lynch and Johnson also differed in how the U.S. Army assessed their injuries. Although both women have lingering physical problems from the incident and both have difficulty walking, the Army has classified Johnson as 30 percent disabled and Lynch as 80 percent disabled. This is a difference worth several hundred dollars more a month for Lynch—one that has not been lost on many observers (see Grundy, 2003; Douglas, 2003; Wise, 2003).

Both Jessica Lynch and Shoshana Johnson have been modest about their actions during their capture. Lynch has disavowed initial government and media reports that she attempted to shoot her way out of captivity testifying that she blamed "the military for not setting the record straight and the media for spreading it and not seeking the true facts . . . My weapon had jammed, and I didn't even get a shot off. I'm still confused as to why they chose to lie and try to make me a legend" (U.S. House of Representatives, 2007); she says she does not recall being raped as the book written right after her release reported (Bragg, 2003). Johnson has not confirmed reports that she violently attempted to resist her capture: "I got off one round and then my gun jammed . . . All of our weapons jammed because of the sand, so we had no way to return fire'; she credits the bravery of her fellow servicemen who rescued her: "I'm a survivor, not a hero . . . The heroes are the soldiers who paid the ultimate price and the Marines who risked their lives to rescue us. Who knows what they could have walked into? It could have been a trap. But just the thought of getting us out was enough. They took a chance, and because they did, I'm here" (Byrd, 2004). The national media have remained mute on the subject of Piestewa's bravery under fire, although to her credit, Lynch has told the story of her friend's heroism and efforts to help her fellow soldiers, stating that Piestewa fought to her death (CNN, 2003; Kirkpatrick, 2003; U.S. House of Representatives, 2007).

As a point of reference, the men who were killed and captured on March 23, 2003, remain largely unnamed—they were not photographed, dramatized, or even reported about. So, gender matters—women appear to be more valuable media commodities than men where dramatic rescues are concerned. And as the treatment of the three women above indicates, race also matters. William Smith, a Vietnam veteran and media advisor for the National Association for Black Veterans laid the race card squarely on the table in his comparison of the treatment of Johnson and Lynch: "There before you is the American dilemma: We are unfair in treatment and view when it comes to people of color" (Douglas, 2003). Robert Thompson, a professor of television and popular culture at Syracuse University, isn't so sure. He doubts "that race was the reason Lynch became a media celebrity", instead he attributes her celebrity to the tastes of those presumably colorblind casting executives in Hollywood: "with her good looks and compelling story, Lynch looked like a figure from Central Casting at a time when the Pentagon, under heavy criticism over its war plan, desperately needed one" (Douglas, 2003). Consistent with this analysis is the conclusion that the American Indian woman who died trying to aid her comrades, Lori Piestewa, also simply was not as visible or attractive to Central Casting as the pretty white girl who, in her own words, "was just there in that spot, you know, the wrong place, the wrong time" (CNN, 2003).

Sexuality also matters in the comparative publicity and outcomes of the capture and release of these three servicewomen. Both Shoshana Johnson and Lori Piestewa were single mothers. Jessica Lynch had no such history: no children, no marriages, no divorces. Sexual purity is an important qualifier for the successful deployment of even déclassé female whiteness in the war of words that accompanies military operations. Not only Lynch's race, but her youth and presumed innocence made her an attractive candidate for the role of damsel in distress. Her sexual and moral worth were easy to market, especially since her story reproduced familiar images from U.S. history and reflected longstanding popular media accounts of other damsels in distress. McAlister (2003) describes Lynch's rescue as an updated version of seventeenth century captivity narratives which featured white women in peril, captured by savage Indians, rescued by heroic American men. She argues that foregrounding Lynch's physical and sexual vulnerability provided America with a historically comfortable moral justification for the war in Iraq because now one of our brave, sexually chaste, and virtuous American women needed rescuing from their dangerous, sexually alien, evil-doing foreign men. McAllister notes that this mediated script could only be enacted by a white woman because captivity narratives (and in this case, Special

Operations rescue missions) do not exist for women of color like Johnson and Piestewa. The lesson here: not all gender is equally deployable to pique the national interest; race matters and sex is the most valuable commodity in political and media markets.

The importance of Lynch's persona as a "girl next door" is emphasized by Howard and Prividera (2004:92) who find that the majority of media reports following Lynch's rescue focused primarily on her femininity rather than her soldier identity. They note that little was said about the duties Lynch performed in the military and instead the authors report that she was repeatedly described as "cute," "young," "attractive," "blonde," and a winner of "Miss Congeniality" who loved her hairbrush. In addition to her physical appearance, they found that Lynch's sexuality also was widely discussed, especially ruminations about reports of her being sexually assaulted while held captive. Together, the military and the media represented Jessica Lynch as a hero of circumstance rather than a war hero honored for her military skill and prowess. Howard and Prividera (2004:96) also argue that the rhetorical significance of Lynch's rescue and her public transformation from a brave warrior to a female victim/captive in need of male rescuers perpetuates dangerous dichotomous gender stereotypes within the military and the media and illustrates the exploitive power of patriarchy "as the identities of and relationships between 'Jessica' and her rescuers were constructed for the media public."

MASCULINITY, FEMININITY, AND WAR

The Iraq war constitutes an important case study of the deployment of gender, race, class, and sexuality in military conflicts. The militarization of race and class illustrated by these three women soldiers draws on familiar themes in U.S. culture and history. In their images and biographies we can see evidence of the military's reliance on and reproduction of class and race relations in the larger society: the recruitment of working class individuals for low-level, low-status, dangerous military work, the valorization of whiteness, and the devaluation of the contributions and sacrifices of soldiers of color. What is new in these pictures and the stories behind them is the militarization of gender and sexuality. We argue that these women's images and the

circumstances by which they came to our attention reveal disturbing new implications of increasing enlistments of women in the U.S. armed forces.

Although we focus here on the "damsels in distress" narrative, we note and have written elsewhere that this story represents only one episode in the saga of deploying of gender and sexuality in the Iraq war (Feitz, 2005; Feitz & Nagel, 2008). Other installments include what we title "chicks with guns"—the use of female sexuality as an instrument of torture at Abu Ghraib and Guantanamo prisons, "comrades in arms"—the recurrent scandals involving women's sexual abuse at the hands of their fellow servicemen, and "fall gals"—the strategy of blaming servicewoman, especially female officers, and protecting servicemen, especially male officers, when problems become public.[3] These cases provide evidence of the military's assignment of women soldiers to various special duties-as propaganda tools (e.g., the rescue of women soldiers to showcase masculine military bravery), as instruments of torture (e.g., the use of female sexuality to assault and humiliate the enemy), as emotional and sexual workers (e.g., women soldiers expected to service the servicemen), and as scapegoats (e.g., women officers blamed for military failures).

In order to understand what these representations of women in uniform tell us, and in order to identify what is new and what is important about the experiences of these and other women serving in the U.S. military and in the Iraq war, we look first to scholarship on masculinity and the military. Studies of masculinity and war provide some insight into the contemporary deployment of femininity in war. This research emphasizes masculinism and its cultural fit with militarism, nationalism, and patriotism, with male codes of honor, with warrior ideologies, with hierarchical military organization, with officially sanctioned and unofficially enacted aggression in conflicts (e.g., rape, torture, other rituals of manliness), and with manly posturing in national politics and international relations (see Mosse, 1996; Nagel, 1998, 2003; Enloe, 2000; 2004; Connell, 2005; Hutchings, 2007). Scholars note that war is intimately linked to 4t nationalism, patriotism, and masculinity, and as Enloe (1990:45) comments, "nationalism [and nationalist conflicts have] typically sprung up from masculinized memory, masculinized humiliation, and masculinized hope."

Given this emphasis on men and masculinity in matters of patriotism, nationalism, and militarism, it is no surprise that sexuality also is central to understanding both women and men at war. In her work on "gendering war talk," Cohn (1993) has documented the use of sexual insults, threats, and homophobia in national "defense" and war discourse. Men use homosexual jokes and banter and misogynistic humor and insults, such as calling one another "faggots," or "ladies" or "girls," to foster solidarity and enforce moral boundaries (see also Goldstein, 2003; Winslow, 1999). During the first war with Iraq—the Gulf war in 1990/91—for instance, a commonly reported phrase alleged to have been written on U.S. missiles targeted on Iraqi positions was, "Bend over, Saddam" (Cohn, 1993:236).

This scholarship, with its emphasis on the masculinist aspects of war, has tended to depict women in historically passive rather than active roles: as the objects of national defense—what Enloe (1993:165) calls the "womenandchildren" category; as support staff on home fronts and in the military itself for the real work undertaken by men; as sources or emotional, physical, and sexual comfort for men at war. Women have been shown historically to be central to the justification for war—as the source of the warm and fuzzy feelings and moral mobilization of warriors defending home and hearth. Women also are recognized as important contributors to war efforts as workers in industry and in service sectors such as medicine, sex work, domestic work, and childcare, and until recently, only occasionally as actual combatants (see Apeles, 2004; Fenner & DeYoung, 2001; Zimbabwe Women Writers, 2001).

The military may be a man's world ruled by masculine codes of honor with women cast primarily in historical roles as objects of defense, but women's place in the U.S. military is changing (Stiehm, 1989; 1996; Herbert, 1998; Skaine, 1999; Solaro, 2006). These changes are reflected in growing numbers of women in uniform, expansion of women's military roles, and ambiguities associated with defining combat and locating battlefronts in contemporary peacekeeping duty and military conflicts such as the Iraq war.[4] Since the early 1970s the U.S. armed forces have adopted two policies that increased the recruitment of women: the elimination of a 2 percent cap on women's enlistment

and the adoption of gender-neutral recruiting policies.[5] The result has been a steady increase in the proportion of women serving in the U.S. military (Segal & Segal, 2004). In 1970, before the new policies were adopted, there were 27,948 women in the four armed services (Army, Navy, Marine Corps, Air Force); they comprised 1.1 percent of active service personnel. In the two decades after the 1973 lifting of the 2 percent cap, but before gender-neutral recruiting was instituted, women's representation in the armed forces grew tenfold, rising to 8.5 percent in 1980 and 10.9 percent in 1990. After the implementation of gender-neutral recruitment in the early 1990s, women's representation in the military increased again to 14.7 percent in 2000. In 2006, there were 197,622 women serving in the four U.S. military services comprising 14.5 percent of active service personnel (U.S. Defense Department, 2002; 2006). Women constituted 7 percent of the troops deployed in the 1991 Gulf war (Quester & Gilroy, 2002) and 14 percent of the troops deployed in Iraq in 2003 (Curphey, 2003). Women's duties and rank have expanded as their numbers have grown. In 1973 women constituted 4.2 percent of the officers in the four military services; in the past three decades that proportion has more than tripled: in 2002, 15.6 percent of officers were women (U.S. Defense Department, 2002). Although women are still officially restricted to non-combat roles, they serve in virtually all areas of the military, including as pilots of combat aircraft (Hurrell et al., 2002).[6]

Women are not only a growing presence in the military because of their sheer numbers and responsibilities associated with rank. Despite prohibitions against combat duty for women, most military observers report that women are involved in military violence and combat situations on a daily basis in Iraq (see Skiba, 2005; Williams & Staub, 2005; Jervis, 2005; Walters, 2005). This is partly because there is no clear "front line" in the Iraq occupation since urban warfare and guerrilla tactics defy conventional notions of battle zones. It is also the case that women's expanded police and guard roles bring them into close contact with Iraqi combatants and prisoners, further blurring the line between combat and non-combat duty. Despite its continued insistence in women's official exclusion from combat, the military has been quick to capitalize on the presence of women soldiers in a variety of military settings in Iraq—as police and security workers searching women and men Iraqi civilians, as prison guards, as pilots, and as wives and lovers of servicemen (Scarborough, 2005).

It remains to be seen what are the implications of the increased number and role of women in the U.S. military. Do women who join the military become "men?" Or if enough women join the military, will they "feminize" it? Is there a critical mass—a point at which women cease to become masculinized in male-dominated institutions and begin to transform the institutions according to the feminine interests and culture they bring with them? in other words, do women who participate in masculine organizations or situations "feminize" those institutions and settings, or do they conform to manly codes of conduct or to masculinist definitions of women's proper places? What does the increased number of servicewomen mean for the experiences of women soldiers in Iraq?

The answer to the question of women becoming masculinized or masculine institutions becoming feminized is an important one not only for understanding the place of women in the Iraq war, but also for making sense of national and international politics. As women enter the political realm in greater numbers around the world, will we see a shifting of state agendas and a decoupling of nationalism and militarism from masculinity—will state politics emphasize guns or butter? Enloe (1990) is skeptical about the prospects of butter rising to the top of national politics any time soon. She notes the limited change that has resulted from the many nationalist independence movements around the world, and observes that in most post–World War II states it is "business as usual" with indigenous masculinities replacing colonial masculinities at the helms of states and employing local and global patriarchal and masculinist logics in governance and international relations:

Given the scores of nationalist movements which have managed to topple empires and create new ones, it is surprising that the international political system hasn't been more radically altered than it has. But a nationalist movement informed by masculinist pride and holding a patriarchal vision of the new nation-state is likely to produce just one more actor in the international arena. A dozen new patriarchal nation-states

may make the international bargaining table a bit more crowded, but it won't change the international game being played at that table (Enloe 1990:64).

If the Iraq war is any indication of the shape of military things to come, we are seeing support for Enloe's observations about the entrenched institutionalization of patriarchy and masculinism—not only in the international system, but in the way the U.S. interacts with that system. Critics long have complained about the militarization of U.S. politics in the post–Second World War period. Mills (1956) referred to the mentality of perpetual conflict that characterized the Cold War as "military metaphysics." Despite the end of the Cold War and the anticipated "peace dividend," the speed and magnitude of U.S. militarization in the post-Soviet era, especially during the unending "War on Terror," has alarmed scholars and policy analysts on the political Left and Right. Johnson (2004) argues that the shift in the locus of U.S. foreign policy from the State Department to the Defense Department threatens to destroy both the American republic and the U.S. economy. The rush to military "solutions" to a variety of problems marks what Bacevich (2005) refers to as "the new American militarism" and leads Andreas (2004) to conclude that the U.S. is "addicted to war."

The end of the military draft in 1973 necessitated the often difficult recruitment of young Americans disaffected by the dangers of military service. In order to meet its staffing needs, the military has shown an elastic institutional capacity to stretch its boundaries to include women in a broad array of roles. What is ironic, but predictable from Enloe's analysis, is that as have women entered deeper and higher into the military's ranks, the patriarchal, gendered institutional character of the military as a male cultural and political space has remained intact (for a discussion of gendered institutions, see Wharton, 2002). Instead of being feminized, the military has found new ways to take advantage of femininity and of women's symbolic and material presence.

CONCLUSION

We have argued here that all war is raced, gendered, classed, and sexualized and that wars are primarily masculinist undertakings defined by manly codes of honor and justified by appeals to men to protect home, hearth, and the women and children waiting there. We have noted the growing numbers and roles of women in the U.S. military, and we recognize that the expanded opportunities for servicewomen are greater than at any time in U.S. history. Despite these changes, we have concluded that the war in Iraq is no exception to the historical masculinist rules of war. We find that the U.S. military has deployed women and femininity to achieve public relations and combat goals, and we conclude that, despite much official rhetoric about the limitations of women in combat, the deployment of women's gender and sexuality has been integrated into the U.S. military's structure and operations.

Women who choose military service are paying their dues and then some. Not only are they entering male domains, working at men's jobs, and facing serious injury and death just like their male comrades, they also are serving a military second shift, deployed as symbolic and service workers in propaganda campaigns, prison abuse programs, and the military-sexual complex. We find that when women enter longstanding, entrenched masculinist spaces like military organizations, even when their numbers grow and they are promoted to positions of authority, the racial, gender, class, and sexual politics of the U.S. military and American society shape the policies and realities of day-today operations in war zones. The deployment of race, gender, class, and sexuality in the Iraq war suggests strongly that racial and gender integration are not guarantees of racial and gender equality. The recent experiences of servicewomen in the Iraq war illustrate the capacity of U.S. military organization to incorporate difference and maintain established power relations even in the face of demographic changes in its personnel.

NOTES

1. We would like to thank the Institute for Policy & Social Research at the University of Kansas for its support and Monique Laney and Erik Nielsen for their help in researching this paper.

2. Johnson signed a contract with Kensington Publishing for her story in 2006, but the contract was cancelled; she has a new contract with Simon & Schuster for a book slated for publication in 2008 (Pride, 2007).

3. Servicewomen's post-traumatic stress associated with their sexual harassment and assault by their mostly male comrades has been labeled officially, "military sexual trauma" or "MST" and the U.S. Veterans Affairs Administration has instituted special treatment programs at VA hospitals (U.S. Veterans Administration, 2007); for a list of major U.S. Defense Department investigations into sexual abuse scandals, see U.S. Department of Defense (2003, 2004, 2005, 2007b). One of the most egregious examples of scapegoating women is the case of former Brigadier General Janis Karpinski, who had no prior experience in the field of corrections, was put in charge of 15 military prisons in Iraq; she was blamed for the Abu Ghraib scandal, lost her command, and was demoted to Colonel. We compare Karpinski's treatment to the lack of disciplinary action against Major General Geoffrey Miller, who commanded the U.S. detention facility at Guantanamo Bay, traveled to Iraq in 2003 to help "Gitmo-ize" operations at Abu Ghraib, and received a Distinguished Service Medal from the Army when he retired in 2005 (White, 2005; see also Karpinski, 2006).

4. For a discussion of the ambiguities of women's role in combat zones, see Nantaisand Lee (1999); Miller and Moskos (1995); for a discussion of women in peacekeeping see DeGroot (2001); for a discussion of the problems of locating battlefronts and, some argue, impossibility of keeping women out of combat situations, see Jervis (2005); Agostini (2005); CNN (2005).

5. In 1973 the 2 percent cap was eliminated and in the 1990s the various services adopted gender-neutral recruit policies; the Navy later rescinded its gender-neutral policy because of constrained berthing policies on Navy vessels—as a result here was a 6 percent drop in women's recruitment from 20 percent in 1995 to 14 percent in 1997, though that percentage of women recruited increased to between 17 and 20 percent after 1997 (U.S. Department of Defense, 2002).

6. The U.S. Air Force began training women as fighter pilots in 1993; in 2005 4.1 percent of USAF pilots were women (Wilson, 2005).

REFERENCES

Agostini, L. (2005). Women's combat support role could end in Iraq. http://www.marines.miymarinelink/mcn2000.nsf/0/BEBFFC30B3A4917A85257006005AF8E8?opendocument (accessed 7/20/05).

Andreas, J. (2004). *Addicted to war: Why the U.S. can't kick militarism*. Oakland, CA: AK Press.

Apeles, T. (2004). *Women warriors: Adventures from history's greatest female fighters*. Emoryville, CA: Seal Press.

Bacevich, A. (2005). *The new American militarism: How Americans are seduced by war*. New York: Oxford University Press.

Bragg, R. (2003). *I am a soldier, too: The Jessica Lynch story*. New York: Knopf.

Byrd, V. (2004). Shoshana Johnson's "to hell and back." *Essence* (March). http://www.essence.eom/essence/prin/0,14882,590888,00.html (accessed 11/29/07).

CNN. (2003, November 7). Lynch: Military played up rescue too much. CNN.com. http://www.cnn.eom/2003/US/11/07/lynch.interview/ (accessed 7/18/05).

———. (2005, June 28). Female troops in Iraq exposed to combat. CNN.com http://www.cnn.com/2005/WORLD/meast06/25/women.comba/ (accessed 7/21/05).

Cohn, C. (1993). Wars, wimps, and women: Talking gender and thinking war. In M. Cooke & A. Woollacott (eds.), *Gendering war talk*, pp. 227–246. Princeton, NJ: Princeton University Press.

Connell, R.W. (2005). *Masculinities*. 2nd edition. Berkeley: University of California Press.

Curphey, S. (2003). 1 in 7 U.S. military personnel in Iraq is female. Women's E-News. http://www.womensenews.org/article.cfm/dyn/aid/1265/contex/cover/ (accessed 7/21/05).

DeGroot, G. (2001). A few good women: Gender stereotypes, the military and peacekeeping. *International Peacekeeping*, 8:23–38.

Douglas, W. (2003, November 9). A case of race? One POW acclaimed, another ignored. *Seattle Times*. http.//seattletimes.nwsource.com/html/nationworld/2001786800_shoshana09.html (accessed 7/12/05).

Enloe, C. (1990). *Bananas, beaches, and bases: Making feminist sense of international politics*. Berkeley: University of California Press.

———. (1993). *The morning after: Sexual politics at the end of the cold war*. Berkeley: University of California Press.

———. (2000). *Maneuvers: The International politics of militarizing women's lives*. Berkeley: University of California Press.

———. (2004). *The curious feminist: Searching for women in a new age of empire*. Berkeley: University of California Press.

Feitz, L. (2005). The U.S. military's deployment of female sexuality as an instrument of torture at Abu Ghraib. Paper presented at the Hall Center for the Humanities, University of Kansas, Lawrence, Kansas, March 3.

Feitz, L. & Nagel, J. (2008). The militarization of gender and sexuality in the Iraq War. In C.H. Carreiras & G. Kümmel (eds.), *Women, violence and the military*. Wiesbaden, Germany: VS Verlag.

Fenner, L.M. & De Young, M. (2001). *Women in combat: Civic duty or military liability?* Washington, DC: Georgetown University Press.

Goldstein, J. (2003). *War and gender: How gender shapes the war system and vice versa*. NY: Cambridge University Press.

Grundy, G. (2003, November 6). Three-fifths of a heroine. The record (Harvard Law School), http://www.hhecord.org/media/paper609/news/2003/11/06/Opinion/ThreeFifths.Of.A.Heroine-551069.shtml (accessed 6/28/05).

Herbert, M.S. (1998). *Camouflage isn't only for combat: Gender, sexuality, and women in the military*. New York: New York University Press.

Hess, S. & Kalb, M. (2003). *The media and the war on terrorism*. Washington, DC: Brookings Institution Press.

Howard, J.W. III & Prividera, L.C. (2004). Rescuing patriarchy or saving 'Jessica Lynch': The rhetorical construction of the American woman soldier. *Women and Language*, 27:89–97.

Hurrell, M.C., Beckett, M.K., Chien, C.S., & Sollinger, J.M. (2002). *The status of gender integration in the military: Analysis of selected occupations*. Santa Monica, CA: The Rand Corporation.

Hutchings, K. (2007). Making sense of masculinity and war. *Men and Masculinities Online*. First (10):1–16. http://jmm.sagepub.com.www2.lib.ku.edu:2048/cgi/rapidpdf/1097184X07306740vl (accessed 11/29/07).

Iraq Body Count. (2007). Documented civilian deaths from violence. http://www.iraqbodycount.net (accessed 1/25/08).

Jervis, R. (2005, June 27), Despite rule, U.S. women on front line in Iraq war. USAToday.com. http://www.marines.mil/marinelink/mcn2000.nsf/0/BEBFFC30B3A4917A85257006005AF8E8?opendocument (accessed 7/5/05).

Johnson, C. (2004). *Blowback: The costs and consequences of American empire*. New York: Henry Holt.

Kampfher, J. (2003, May 18). Saving private Lynch story 'flawed'. BBC. Afewihttp://news.bbc.co.uk/2/hi/programmes/correspondent/3028585.stm (accessed 7/19/05).

Karpinski, J. (2006). *One woman's army: The commanding general of Abu Ghraib tells her story*. New York; Miramax Books.

Kirkpatrick, D. (2003, November 7). Jessica Lynch criticizes U.S. accounts of her ordeal. *New York Times*, http://query.nytimes.com/gst/fullpage.html7res=9D02E4DB1539F934A35752ClA9659C8B63 (accessed 7/705).

McAlister, M. (2003, April 6), Saving private Lynch. *New York Times*, pp. 4, 14.

Miller, L. & Moskos, C. (1995). Humanitarians or warriors? Race, gender and combat status in operation restore hope. *Armed Forces and Society*, 21:615–635.

Mills. C.W. (1956). *The power elite*. New York: Oxford University Press.

Mosse. G.L. (1996). *The image of man: The creation of modern masculinity*. New York: Oxford University Press.

Nagel, J. (1998). *Masculinity and nationalism: Gender and sexuality in the making of nations*. Ethnic and Racial Studies, 21:242–269.

———. (2003). *Race, ethnicity, and sexuality: Intimate intersections, forbidden frontiers*. New York: Oxford University Press.

Nantals, C & Lee, M.F. (1999). Woman in the United States military: Protectors or protected? The case of prisoner of war Melissa Rathbun-Nealy. *Journal of Gender Studies*, 8:181–191.

New York Times. (2005, July 15), The woman of Gitmo. New York Times.com. http://www.nytimes.com/2005/07/15/opinion/15fri1.html (accessed 7/15/05).

Pride, F. (2007, June 18). Shoshana Johnson title lands at S&S. *Publishers Weekly*. http://www.publishersweekly.com/article/CA6452847.html (accessed 11/24/07).

Quester, A.O. & Gilroy, C.L. (2002). Women and minorities in America's volunteer military. *Contemporary Economic Policy*, 20:111–121. http://www.dtic.mll/dacowlts/research/Women_Minorities_in_Amer_Vol_Military.pdf (accessed 7/21/05).

Scarborough, R. (2005, July 11). Iraq lacks women trained in security. *Washington Times*, http://washingtontimes.com/national/20050711-122346-9856r.htm (accessed 7/11/05).

Segal, D. & Segal. M. (2004). America's military population. *Population Bulletin*, 59(4). http://www.pro.org/Source/ACF1396.pdf (accessed 11/25/407).

Shaffer, M. (2003, November 12). Piestewa went to war for Lynch, book says. *Arizona Republic*, http://www.azcentral.com/news/special/veterans/articles/piestewa-3.html (accessed 7/5/05).

Skaine, R. (1999). *Women at war: Gender issues of Americans in combat*. Jefferson, NC; McFarland Publishers.

Skiba, K.M. (2005). *Sister in the band of brothers: Embedded with the 101st airborne in Iraq*. Lawrence: University Press of Kansas.

Smith, T. (2003, June 3). Saving private Lynch. On-line Newshour. http://www.pbs.org/newshour/bb/media/jan-june03/lynch_06-10.html (accessed 7/20/05).

Solaro, E. (2006). *Women in the line of fire: What you should know about women in the military*. Emeryville, CA: Seal Press.

Stiehm, Judith H. 1989. *Arms and the enlisted woman*. Philadelphia: Temple University Press.

———. 1996. *It's our military too! Woman in the U.S. military*. Philadelphia: Temple University Press.

U.S. Army. 2003. Special Report: Attack on the 507th Maintenance Company. http://www.army.mil/features/507thMaintCmpy/AttackOnThe507Maint Cmpy.pdf (accessed 7/13/05).

———. (2005). Army sexual assault prevention and response program. http://www.sexualassault.army.mil/ (accessed 7/22/05).

U.S. Department of Defense. (2002). Population representation in the military services. http://www.dod.mil/prhome/poprep2002/index.htm (accessed 7/21/05).

———. (2003). Defense task force report on domestic violence. http://www.dtic.mil/domesticviolence/reports/DV_RPT3.PDF (accessed 7/18/05).

———. (2004). Task force report on sexual assault policies. http://www.asmra.army.mil/eo/eo_docs/Army%20Report%20 (May%2027%202004).pdf (accessed 778/05).

———. (2005). Confidentiality policy for victims of sexual assault (March 31). http://www.defenselink.mil.proxy2.cl.msu.edu/news/Mar2005/d20050318dsd.pdf (accessed 7/22/05).

———. (2006). Statistics on women in the military: Women serving today. Women in Military Service for America Memorial Foundation. http://www.womensmemorial.org/Press/stats.html (accessed 11/26/07).

———. (2007a). Operation Iraqi freedom U.S. casualty status and fatalities as of November 29, 2007. http://www.defenselink.mil.proxy2.cl.msu.edu/news/casualty.pdf (accessed 11/29/07).

———. (2007b). Annual report on military services sexual assault for CY2006" (March 15). http://www.sapr.mil/contents/references/2006%20Annual%20Report.pdf (accessed 11/26/07).

U.S. House of Representatives. (2007). Testimony before house oversight and government reform committee (April 25). http://oversight.house.gov/documemnt/20070424110022.pdf (accessed 11/25/07).

U.S. Veterans Administration. (2007). Military sexual trauma program. http://www1.va.gov/wvhp/page.cfm?pg=20 (accessed 11/26/07).

Walters, J. (2005, April 30). As casualties soar, America's women face reality of front line. The Guardian. http://www.buzzle.com/editorials/4-30-2005-69348.asp (accessed 7/11/05).

Weisskopf, M. (2006). *Blood brothers: Among the soldiers of ward 57*, New York: Henry Holt & Company.

Wharton, A. (2002). Gender, institutions, and difference: The continuing importance of social structure in understanding gender inequality in organizations. In S.C. Chew & J.D. Knottnerus (eds.), *Structure, culture, and history: Recent issues in social theory*, pp. 257–270. New York: Rowman and Littlefield.

White, J. (2005, July 14). Abu Ghraib tactics were first used at Guantanamo. *Washington Post*, A1.

Williams, K. & Staub, M. E. (2005). *Love my rifle more than you: Young and female in the U.S. Army*. New York: W.W. Norton.

Wilson, Capt., B. A. (1996). Military women pilots. http://user pages.aug.com/captbarb/pilots.html (accessed 7/21/05).

Winslow, D. (1999). Rites of passage and group bonding in the Canadian airborne. *Armed Forces and Society*, 25:429–457.

Wise, B.S. (2003, October 28). On Shoshana Johnson, Jessica Lynch and disability. Dissent, http://www.intellectual-conservative.com/article2798.html (accessed 7/5/05).

Zimbabwe Women Writers. (2001). *Women of resilience: The voices of women combatants*. London & Harare: African Books Collective.

13

Katrina, Black Women, and the Deadly Discourse on Black Poverty in America

BARBARA RANSBY

Most observers, even some of the most conservative and purportedly color-blind observers, have conceded the overwhelmingly racial character of the social disaster that followed in Hurricane Katrina's wake. Journalists covering the story could not help but acknowledge that those left behind to endure nature's wrath, and for whom little help and few resources were provided in the critical days following the hurricane, were disproportionately poor and Black. What does not often get added is that by most accounts those hardest hit and least able to rebound from it were also women: poor Black women who waded through chest-high water with sick and elderly parents, with young children on their hips and meager belongings in tow. This should not be surprising given the correlation between gender, race, and poverty. Black single mothers are more likely to be poor than any other demographic group, and New Orleans was no exception to the rule. In fact, a study by the Institute for Women's Policy Research points out that the percentage of women in poverty in New Orleans before the storm was considerably *higher* than in other parts of the country: more than half of the poor families of the city were headed by single mothers, and the median income for African American women workers in New Orleans before the storm was a paltry $19,951 a year (DeWeever 2005).

The effect of the hurricane on African American women was not merely a consequence of demographics; it was also fueled and framed by the rabid anti-poor discourse that has cast Black single mothers as unworthy of public aid or sympathy. In this paper, I will discuss several aspects of the gendered nature of the disaster: the effect of government inaction on Black women in New Orleans after the hurricane, the pre-Katrina discourse on Black female poverty that set the stage for that inaction, and how Black women activists have responded. Even though this was clearly a regional crisis, the various contradictions came together with particular vividness in New Orleans, so I will focus my observations on that city alone.

WOMEN IN KATRINA'S WAKE

When Katrina slapped New Orleans, she slapped everyone hard, but she slapped women especially hard.

The impact is not simply measured in the number of injuries, deaths, and the amount of property loss, but in the kind of human currency that is difficult to measure. Women were more encumbered and less mobile. One gets a window into how women's lives were turned upside down by this crisis by looking at what women did and where women were situated in the community in ordinary times. As a number of commentators and experts have pointed out, there was a social crisis in New Orleans that had been fueled by the widespread prevalence of poverty and the absence of resources long before meteorologists sighted a category five hurricane bearing down on the Gulf Coast. There was already a 40% poverty rate among single mothers in the city. A state-by-state breakdown of poverty statistics ranked Louisiana number forty-seven out of fifty-one, and forty-third in terms of health-care insurance coverage. And 13% of Louisiana's children live in extreme poverty, which is defined as a family of four surviving on less than $10,000 a year.[1] A large percentage of New Orleans' poor single mothers also lived in the historic Ninth Ward, the low-lying area of the city most vulnerable to flooding. So, as in any crisis, those with few assets, little money, and even less maneuverability were hard-pressed to get out of the path of the storm and further compromised in their ability to recover after the blow.

ORAL HISTORIES

The impact of Katrina on women of African descent in New Orleans is best reflected in the stories and anecdotes that emerged from the storm. Our understanding of this tragedy and its aftermath is aided by the plethora of oral history projects that have emerged in response to the situation.[2] Some of them are an extension of preexisting archival or public history projects, and some are grassroots interventions by students, artists, historians, and activists determined to document what actually happened and provide an outlet for those who want to tell their stories. The narratives, testimonies, and profiles of real flesh and blood people are the best rebuttal to one-dimensional stereotypes. One very powerful story, collected by *Alive in Truth: The New Orleans Disaster Oral History and Memory*

Project, tells of the experience of a woman named Clarice B. (later identified as Clarice Butler), who describes her life before and after Katrina. "I worked all my life," she explains:

> I worked all my life for Metropolitan Homecare for 28 years: homecare, nurse's assistant. I took care of a lot of people in my life, a lot of people. I was good at my job, oh, yeah. It's not a clean job and it's not no dirty, dirty job. But no job is clean all the time, but it's a job. And I did good. I had to go to school: I went to school and wound up working in a nursing home.

Here is how she describes her ordeal after the levee broke and she found herself stranded on the interstate highway with thousands of others:

> And you want me to tell you the truth, my version of it? They tried to kill us. "When you keep somebody on top of the Interstate for five days, with no food and water, that's killing people. And there ain't no ands, ifs, or buts about it, that was NOPD [New Orleans Police Department] killing people. Four people died around me. Four. Diabetes. I am a diabetic and I survived it, by the grace of God, but I survived it. . . . Look, I was on top of the Interstate. Five days, okay? Helicopters at night shining a light down on us. They know we was there. Policemen, the army, the whole nine yards, ambulance passing us up like we wasn't nothing. Drove by and by all day. At night when they got ready to pull out, they pulled out and left us in darkness. We was treated worse than an animal. People do leave a dog in a house, but they do leave him food and water. They didn't do that . . .

Clarice goes on to recall the trauma of leaving her home:

> And of course I had to leave my birds and my dog. Of course I didn't want to. But I didn't have no other choice. Didn't have a choice. So I brought my dogs and my bird to as far as I could bring them. And I left them there upstairs. And I'm hoping I can retrieve them. I'm hoping. I have to call the SPCA [Society for the Prevention of Cruelty to Animals] or somebody. I left them upstairs on the deck, and I think if they was captured I should get them back. I'm hoping, anyway. I had a little Chihuahua. He was 9 months old. I had five birds. Two parakeets and two cockatiels. And my

cockatiels just had a baby bird which was five weeks old. So you know I'm heartbroken. But again, my life was more important at that moment.

Finally, she wonders aloud;

Now why our Mayor and government did this I'll never understand it. I never would understand what happened to New Orleans. That is really a disaster. Nobody would never believe it until you get into that situation. I go to bed one night with everything that I needed, and wake up the next morning with nothing.[3]

There was another woman's story that made a powerful impression on me, and which I could not get out of my mind for weeks after I saw it on CNN. The scene was of a middle-aged Black woman, dirty, desperate, and crying. She looked into the camera and said to the viewers, "We do not live like this."[4] She repeated it over and over again. Contradicting the image of slovenly, hapless, poor folk this woman's face reflected not simply fatigue and hunger, but humiliation as well. Most poor people spend a lot of time and attention making sure their homes and their children are as neat and clean as possible so that they will not be straightjacketed into the stereotypes associated with poverty. And here this seemingly hard-working woman was left with nothing, not even her dignity.

Whatever circumstances led to poor Black women's lives being battered and devastated by this storm, as Clarice's story *so* painfully recounts, the real unforgivable disaster is the fact that they were abandoned by those whose job it was to intervene and help in such situations. The local government was paralyzed, and the federal government looked the other way. Despite the tens of millions of dollars spent on the various apparatuses of the Office of Homeland Security (OHS), no one seemed to have spent much time worrying about the widely predicted hurricane that terrorized the Gulf Coast region or the security of those who were its victims. There was no plan to help those who could not help themselves, and even after the failure of FEMA and the OHS to aid and coordinate relief efforts, the president's silence, and the federal government's inaction for days after the crisis occurred left tough veteran journalists dumbfounded, angry, and sometimes even in tears. Initially, President Bush seemed not to take the crisis and human suffering seriously. Perhaps his mother spoke for the family when she visited displaced families forced to flee to Houston. During that visit she made the following disturbing comment: "so many of the people in the area here, you know, were underprivileged anyway, so this, this is working very well for them."[5] In her mind, those poor families really didn't need to have real homes or familiar communities; instead, like animals, they just needed basic shelter and food, no matter under what conditions.

On one level, many of us could not help but be surprised by the level of disregard for the collective well-being of New Orleans' Black poor, White poor, its elderly and infirm. However, when we zero in on the plight of Black women, again, the stage was set long before the scandalous treatment they received after Katrina. The dismantling of welfare for the poor in 1996, which climaxed with President Clinton's Personal Responsibility Act, was surrounded by a public discourse that dehumanized and denigrated the Black poor, charging them as the main culprits in their own misfortune. Black women were implicitly deemed lazy, promiscuous, and irresponsible; hence the withdrawal of public aid was ostensibly designed to jolt them into the labor force and into more responsible sexual behavior. Never mind that there were shrinking jobs for applicants with few skills and little education, and never mind that the president himself was breaking the very same sexual moral code that he was so mightily imposing on single mothers. Still, the problem was defined as that of Black women having babies out of the confines of heterosexual marriages, rather than the low pay and lack of jobs and affordable housing that marked their condition and compromised the future of their children.

Post-Katrina pundits continued the "blame the Black poor" rhetoric even as the blame clearly lay elsewhere. Six weeks after Katrina wreaked havoc on the Gulf Coast region, Mona Charen, columnist and former staffer for President Ronald Reagan, wrote: "Still it is true as the aftermath of Katrina underlined that parts of the Black community remain poor and dysfunctional" (Charen 2005). The word *dysfunctional* is usually offered to modify *family,* and the association Charen is making is clear. The rest of her article goes on to make the case that the biggest problem facing the

Black poor before and after Katrina is that of single-mother families. But Charen was just one of many making this argument. Conservative pundit Rich Lowry of the *National Review* argued that "If people are stripped of the most basic social support—the two parent family . . . they will be more vulnerable in countless ways" in times of crisis. He went on to propose government programs that "include greater attention to out of wedlock births" (Lowry 2005). Liberals such as *New York Times* columnist Nicholas Kristof even jumped on the bandwagon, giving a positive nod to Lowry's proposal.

BLACK CONSERVATIVES WEIGH IN

The attack on Black mothers did not stop with journalists such as Lowry. Black conservatives weighed in with a vengeance.

Syndicated columnist George Will (2005) was one of the most outrageous in his slander of the Black women of New Orleans. He first contended that there was too much obsession about race. In his words: "America's always fast-flowing river of race-obsessing has overflowed its banks," in discussions about Katrina. Those who are poor are poor because they don't follow the rules, Will insists, and those rules mean conforming to his code of sexual and social behavior. He offered "three not-at-all recondite rules for avoiding poverty: Graduate from high school, don't have a baby until you are married, don't marry while you are a teenager. Among people who obey those rules, poverty is minimal." If only things were so simple. Will drives the ill-conceived argument home, however, by making an even more explicit point:

> . . . it is a safe surmise that more than 80 percent of African American births in inner-city New Orleans—as in some other inner cities—were to women without husbands. That translates into a large and constantly renewed cohort of lightly parented adolescent males, and that translates into chaos in neighborhoods and schools, come rain or come shine. (Will 2005)

So, in Will's view, the chaos of Katrina was an extension of the self-inflicted chaos created by homes without strong father figures. These are the distorted realities that conservatives have to craft for themselves in order to sleep at night, I suppose. The reality on the ground is of course quite different, as the stories of Clarice B. and others illustrate so compellingly.

A powerful hurricane ravaged the lives of poor Black women and their families and neighbors, not because the women did not have wedding bands on their fingers, nor because their sons lacked strong paternal figures in the home to enforce curfew. To suggest as much is another way of devaluing the suffering and strivings of these families. Putting the issue in an international context, writer and activist Ritu Sharma, who works with the Washington-based advocacy group *Woman's Edge* (the Coalition for Women's Economic Development and Global Equity), writes that "women are the vast majority of the world's poor and money is the great protector" (Sharma 2006). Those who have little or none are more vulnerable than others to hurricanes, tsunamis, and all other forms of natural disasters that quickly escalate into human and social disasters.

WOMEN TAKE ACTION AFTER THE STORM

While they may have little else, poor Black women are creative and resilient. They have to be in order to survive in such difficult and challenging times. So, if one part of this story is what happened to African American women after Katrina hit, the other half of the story is how they responded. And if part one is depressing and disturbing, part two is uplifting and encouraging. African American women have responded to the crisis as individuals and in groups. One individual response was that of long-time New Orleans resident and organizer Diane "Momma D." Frenchcoat, an older resident who became a self-appointed relief worker after the storm. In the weeks following the hurricane, each day she would collect food, pile it in her cart, and navigate the flooded and filthy streets to deliver meals to hungry and isolated neighbors. She eventually recruited others to help in her efforts, dubbing them the "Soul Patrol." When asked by a newspaper reporter why she did not evacuate the city for safer ground, she replied: "Why would I leave now? Why would I leave my people when so many of them are still here and suffering?" The reporter described her in this way: "Graying dreadlocks flowed down the nape of her neck, spilling over her sturdy, sloping shoulders as she spoke of a city she hopes will be reborn" (Lee 2005).

Another inspiring story of determination against the odds is that of Beverly Wright, initiator of the volunteer-driven *A Safe Way Back Home* project. A professor of Environmental Studies at Dillard University and a lifelong New Orleans resident, Dr. Wright's project has educated New Orleans residents about the toxins still prevalent in the soil and in their homes. She was particularly concerned about the lawns of contaminated homes. With advice from the Environmental Protection Agency (EPA) and donations from several foundations, *A Safe Way Back Home* has provided equipment, information, and protective gear for dozens of residents to skim off toxic topsoil and replace it with healthy sod. The coalitions that Wright was able to forge were an interesting and important aspect of the project. Based on her past research and consulting for national labor unions about environmental dangers in the workplace, she was able to enlist the United Steelworkers Union to help train volunteers and to provide tools and equipment for the project. College students were recruited, and the National Black Environmental Justice Network, to which Wright belongs, lent its support and resources as well. A creative team effort of some unlikely allies is making a difference in the lives of dozens of families.

On the surface, a very masculine and muscular image of relief workers dominates popular images. Men are pictured lifting boxes, operating heavy equipment, and toting guns, ostensibly to keep the peace. However, women are working tirelessly and courageously in the trenches, as has so often been the case. Even within the larger coalitions and community-based organizations such as the People's Hurricane Relief Fund and Oversight Coalition (PHRFOC), women are important actors, leaders, and contributors. The PHRFOC even has a women's caucus to highlight and make visible the work of women, providing a forum where women can support one another within the larger effort. The work of Diane Frenchcoat, Beverly Wright, and the women of the PHRFOC are but three examples of African American women taking initiative, being

imaginative, and acting boldly. These real stories stand in stark contrast to what the George Wills and Rich Lowrys of the world would have us believe.

A sober read of the situation in New Orleans . . . is still worrisome. Some biased and shortsighted city builders are trying to push Black women and children out of the picture altogether, to reconfigure a city without what must be perceived as the burden of the Black poor. PHRFOC and others have fought this scheme by demanding the right to return and by insisting upon voting rights for displaced citizens. A number of scholars and activists have referred to this period of rebuilding and remapping of this southern subregion as another "Reconstruction." At stake today, as they were in the years following the Civil War, are land rights, voting rights, control of the military, accountability, jobs, and the reconstitution of families and communities. Wherever New Orleans is headed in the future, hardworking Black women with big hearts and steel-willed determination will be a part of the picture. They have needs and problems to be sure, but their presence adds to rather than detracts from the strength and vitality of a remarkable American city.[6]

NOTES

1. Statistics taken from DeWeever. Avis Jones (2005). *The Women of New Orleans and the Gulf Coast: Multiple Disadvantages and Key Assets for Recovery, Part I.* Published by the Institute for Women's Policy Research Washington, DC, October 11, 2005. www.iwpr.org/pdf/D464.pdf (accessed May 25, 2006).

2. A few of the projects that are attempting to document the stories of hurricane survivors include: the 1–10 Witness Project (www.i10witness.com), which emerged out of a group of artists, teachers, and activists; the Story Corps radio project; projects hosted by the Center for Cultural Resources in Baton Rouge (www.himicanestories.org); and projects initiated by the University of Southwestern Mississippi and the Mississippi Humanities Council.

3. Oral history collected by AliveinTruth.org, and posted at www.Alternet.org on October 29, 2005.

4. Claudette Paul was also quoted in the *New York Times* as saying that "We need help. We don't live like this in America" (Appleborne et al. 2005).

5. Barbara Bush interviewed on Marketplace, National Public Radio (NPR), September 5, 2005.

6. Thanks to Joseph Lipari for his assistance with the research for this essay.

REFERENCES

Alive in Truth: The New Orleans Disaster Oral History and Memory Project. www.aliveintruth.org/index.html (accessed May 25, 2006).

Appleborne, Peter, Christopher Drew, Jere Longman, and Andrew Revkin (2005). A Delicate Balance Is Undone in a Flash. *New York Times,* September 4, A25.

Bonavoglia, Angela (2005). Hurricane Pundits Blow Hot Air on Single Mothers. Women' Enews, September 14. (http://www.womensenews.org/article.cmi/dyn/aid/24 49) (accessed May 25, 2006).

Charen, Mona (2005), No More Marches, Townhall.com, October 14. www.townhall.com (accessed May 25, 2006).

DeWeever, Avis Jones (2005). *The Women of New Orleans and the Gulf Coast: Multiple Disadvantages and Key Assets for Recovery, Part I, October 11.* Washington, DC: Institute for Women's Policy Research. www.iwpr.org/pdf/D464.pdf (accessed May 25, 2006).

Lee, Tymaine D. (2005). Momma's Mission. *Times-Picayune,* September 18, Metro Section, available at www.nola.com (accessed May 25, 2006).

Lowry, Rich (2005). The Coming Battle Over New Orleans. National Review Online, September 2. www.national-review.com (accessed September 4, 2005).

Peterson, Jesse Lee (2005a). Moral poverty costs Blacks in New Orleans. Worldnetdaily.com, September 21. (http://www.worldnetdaily.com) (accessed May 25, 2006).

Peterson, Jesse Lee (2005b). Truth: solution to Black America's moral poverty. Worldnetdaily.com, October 7. (http://www.worldnetdaily.com) (accessed May 25, 2006).

Rosen, Ruth (2005). Get Hitched, Young Woman. Tonipaine.com, September 26. (http://www.tompaine.com) (accessed May 25, 2006).

Sharma, Ritu (2006). Disasters Dramatize How Women's Poverty Is Lethal. Women's eNews, January 5. www.womensenews.org (accessed May 25, 2006).

Will, George (2005). Poverty of Thought. *Washington Post,* September 14, A27.

14

Brides of Palestine/Angels of Death

Media, Gender, and Performance in the Case of the Palestinian Female Suicide Bombers

DORIT NAAMAN

In January 2002, Wafa Idris, a twenty-seven-year-old Palestinian woman, strapped ten kilograms of explosives to her body and killed herself and two Israelis on a crowded Jerusalem street. Idris was the first Palestinian female suicide bomber, to be followed by nine others and several dozen failed attempts. The female suicide bomber is a social phenomenon that has left Israel and the West shocked, signaling (in both Arab and Western views) an escalation in the conflict. Idris was not the first Palestinian woman to be recruited for the fight for national liberation, as women have taken part in the Palestinian struggle from its onset, with some, including Leila Khaled and Dalai el Moughrabi, having partaken in highly publicized hijacking operations. Idris was not the first female suicide bomber either, with Hezbollah and the Tamil Tigers utilizing female suicide bombers since the 1980s. The reactions to Idris's actions vary widely, as labels such as *martyr, hero, monster,* and *terrorist* indicate. But reactions in the Arab world, in Israel, and in the West cannot be reduced to simple labels. Instead, the reactions all highlight junctures of ideological crises in the perceived

roles of women in armed struggles, religion, and traditional gendered settings. Particularly in the Arab world these actions were not simply hailed but actually debated—pragmatically, morally, and, most notably, religiously. For instance, Sheikh Ahmed Yassin, spiritual leader of Hamas until his assassination by Israel in March 2004, objected to the inclusion of women initially, then altered his principled position, and in 2004 Hamas sent its first female suicide bomber, Reem el Riyashi.[1] The debates in the Arab world around Western-style feminism, religion, and the roles women should take in armed struggles are complex and, I would argue, push the already highly charged gender debate to its logical limits.

In this article I focus on the issue of terrorism—especially its performative aspect—and how media representations deal with the loaded image of the Palestinian female suicide bomber and her message. With regard to Western media, my aim is to show the constructed nature of the label *terrorist,* especially as it stands in stark contrast to the highly coded and constructed label *woman.* My claim is that both terms rep-

Dorit Naaman, "Bridges of Palestine/Angels of Death: Media Gender, and Performance in the Case of Palestinian female suicide bombers," in *Signs: Journal of Women and Culture in Society* (2007). Copyright © 2007 University of Chicago Press. Reprinted by permission.

resent ideological expectations of performance rather than reflect actual actions or natural (maybe even essential) states of being in the world. In the case of the Arab media, the term *shaheeda* (martyr) enables people to bypass the loaded deviation from traditional gendered roles and as such mythicizes actions taken rather than engaging with their gender politics. In contrast to news media, filmic representations from Israel and Palestine provide a much more nuanced and complex view of terrorism and the place of women in it. Those images sometimes challenge media stereotypes and sometimes employ them to diverse political ends.[2]

GENDER AND WAR

War generally brings with it images that fall into normative gender categories: men are fighters, women the victims. Images of women and children as widows and orphans fleeing war zones to become refugees, or media focus on rape as a war tactic in Rwanda and the former Yugoslavia, figure women as fragile, vulnerable, and in need of defense by men. Rape and forced pregnancies in particular bring forth issues of ethnic purity and position women as vehicles for the production of the next generation of ethnically pure fighters but as defenseless in and of themselves.[3] Furthermore, one aspect of any occupation (and colonization) is the perceived feminization of the occupied men. Men who were used to being sovereign agents are now subject to the rules, regulations, and whims of the occupier. As the economic situation in the occupied Palestinian territories deteriorated and as the limitations on freedom of movement increased, men were stripped of their stereotypically masculine qualities—independence, courage, ability to provide economically, and protection of the weak (women and children in particular). A video art piece titled *Chic Point* (2003) addresses this feminization by designing men's clothes for the checkpoints. In a fashion show setup, men model shirts with zippers, fishnet, clear material, or patterned holes, all meant to simplify the crossing of the checkpoints. The models all conform to so-called metrosexual ideals (straight men dressing like gay men), and together the catwalk setup, the flirtatious gaze at the camera, and the clothes themselves intentionally blur the categories of masculine and feminine. The video then cuts into documentary black-and-white still photographs of men stripping for soldiers' inspection in the middle of checkpoints, often in front of their entire families. The piece at once exposes the humiliation inherent in the situation while at the same time calling attention to the negative gendered attributes of associating men's humiliation and lack of sovereignty with femininity and submissiveness.

When women opt to fight alongside men, they challenge the dichotomy of woman as victim/man as defender. Women fighters are physically strong, are active (therefore agents), and, most important, are willing to kill (hence, they are violent). They challenge not only the images of women as victims of war but also the traditional patriarchal binary opposition that postulates women as physically and emotionally weak and incapable of determining and defending the course of their own lives. As a result, women fighters have often been represented—especially in mass media—as deviant from prescribed forms of femininity, forms that emphasize a woman's delicacy and fragility but also her generosity, caring nature, motherliness, and sensitivity to others' needs.[4]

Suicide operations complicate these stereotypical dynamics further—not only does the woman willingly sacrifice herself, but her actions also carry a performative aspect typical of terrorist actions by substate groups. Since these groups do not have large and well-equipped armies, they organize their political violence as spectacles that attract media and public attention. When women partake in such operations, their performance of violence and political agency—so drastically different from that of typical female roles in both news and entertainment media—enhances the sense of perplexity, fear, and aversion to the perpetrators of the acts. For instance, in response to Ayat Akhras's suicide operation, Anne Applebaum writes, "Not only was she not male, she was not overtly religious, not estranged from her family, not openly associated with any radical groups. She can hardly be described as a woman without a nature. She was young, she was a good student, and she was engaged to be married" (2002).

Relying on the stereotypical gap between traditional feminine qualities (i.e., engaged to be married, good student) and political, violent, and supposedly masculine actions, journalists and analysts alike could not explain the phenomenon. The solution was to search for a personal explanation. For instance, after Idris's suicide attack, Western media focused on the fact that Idris was infertile and had allowed her husband to marry another woman, watching him live nearby as he became a father. It was claimed that she was unhappy and, as she could not bear children, that her life was unworthy to her.[5] This explanation is typical, but in many of the cases that followed, the logic of such explanations is unfounded. Some of the women were happy, engaged to be married (Ayat Akhras), good students (Dareen Abu Aisheh), professionals (Hanadi Jaridat), and mothers (Reem el Riyashi). What this attempt at explanation exposes is how gendered the discussion around the female suicide bombers is. While the dozens of male suicide bombers' identities and life stories are hardly ever delved into, their reasons are assumed to be clear and grounded in both political and religious ideology. In contrast, a woman as a suicide bomber seems so oxymoronic that an individualized psychological explanation for the deviation must be found.

However, this sort of psychological explanation fails time and again. The image of woman as the symbolic nurturer, healer, and spiritual mother of the nation is challenged beyond repair, a rupture that is dealt with in the Arab world quite differently than it is in the West. Idris in particular highlights this symbolic contradiction; in her spare time Idris volunteered as a medic on an ambulance, caring for the wounded of the intifada. How did the "angel of mercy" become an "angel of death," asked one headline (Beaumont 2002a). Indeed, the idea that a woman who heals people could turn around and kill others seemed so improbable that it could indicate to Western media and society only that something was wrong with this particular individual or else that there is something monstrous about the society that produces such a person.[6] In the Arab press the discourse generally focuses on the harshness of the occupation, which drives women to defend the land and the people. Although suicide bombing is met with ambivalence in the Arab world, it is nevertheless understood as an extreme means derived from an extreme situation.[7]

In his feature films, Palestinian director Elia Suleiman bluntly addresses the ways in which the Palestinian woman has become a kind of political femme fatale. In *Divine Intervention* (2002), Suleiman shows the narrator's girlfriend, as she crosses the checkpoint, refusing to stop for the soldiers' inspection. The woman is wearing a short, tight, pink dress and is not carrying anything, so she clearly is not a risk of being a suicide bomber, yet the soldiers point their guns at her. In an extended slow sequence, the woman walks through the checkpoint seductively and assertively while the soldiers objectify her through their guns' viewfinders, but at the same time they fear her. This sequence is particularly poignant since the woman's appearance, hairstyle, and dress are all Western in style; in this way she mocks the idea that (potential) terrorists are Muslim fundamentalists.[8] But even more important, the woman can easily pass as an Israeli, and therefore the danger that Suleiman's mute female protagonist poses clearly is not in political violence but in her challenge to the concept of ethnic purity and the risk of miscegenation, an issue Israeli cinema has been obsessed with for years.[9]

Toward the end of the film, the still-nameless female protagonist, dressed in the traditional Palestinian checkered kaffiyeh, is left standing as the target in an Israeli shooting range where a dozen Israeli security men are practicing. In a sequence that combines ninja-style aesthetics with a musical's choreography, the woman eliminates all the men. The surreal scene represents the best of Suleiman's style; its political poignancy and depth are not minimized by the supernatural aesthetics. Although the film's shooting preceded the first Palestinian female suicide operation, the film clearly points to the loaded potential of women partaking in combative roles. In order to fully comprehend the genius of this scene, we need to look very briefly at the discourse about terrorism.

TERRORISM OR POLITICAL VIOLENCE

Terrorism is a term that emerged during the French Revolution, when the Jacobins instigated seventeen hundred civilian deaths, in what is now called the Reign of Terror. It is generally agreed that terrorism includes violence (and fear and intimidation) that is directed at civilians, in hopes of obtaining political goals. Terrorism also needs to be regarded as a communication process whereby the terrorists send a message via the act of violence to a target audience or audiences that are usually not the actual victims of the violence.[10] In this way, terrorism is rhetorical and a media event, and mass media become tools of persuasion and propaganda.[11] Since substate groups have limited access to the public sphere (both media and state institutions), terrorism becomes not only a form of communication but also a form of performance, orchestrated to garner as much media and public attention as possible.

Naturally, most of those called terrorists do not see themselves as such; that is, they believe they have legitimate and unheard grievances against a state, and their attacks are directed at voicing those grievances. War rhetoric acknowledges both the positionality of the speaker vis-à-vis the enemy (if you are my enemy, I understand that I am your enemy) and the historical reasons that lead to a particular conflict. In contrast, the discourse on terrorism is generally devoid of historical perspectives ("terrorists are pure evil" is one popular trope) and lacks any positionality because, it is assumed, terrorists simply live outside of morality and social norms. But such ahistorical and essentialist attitudes came to haunt this discourse when a former terrorist, Nelson Mandela, became a Nobel Peace Prize winner, or, more recently, when Osama bin Laden, a former American ally, "turned" terrorist. The discourse on terrorism also does not account for state terrorism, whereby state institutions such as the army or police inflict violence on civilian populations, as was the case in Nicaragua and Chechnya (and by the United States via the Contras and Russian forces, respectively). This last point is particularly missing from the discourse on the Palestinian-Israeli conflict.[12] All attacks on Israelis, whether inside the 1967 border or outside, whether targeting soldiers or civilians, are dubbed terrorist attacks. But dropping a one-ton bomb from an Israeli airplane on a five-story Palestinian house, in which a militant may be present, knowing full well that dozens of civilians will be killed, is hardly ever described in Western media as terrorism. One example can be seen in the case of Ayat Akhras, the third female suicide bomber, who killed herself and two others in a supermarket in Jerusalem. One of her victims was seventeen-year-old Rachel

Levy, who was buying fish for Shabbat. The two girls looked alike, and the media repeatedly showed their pictures together, juxtaposed as the victim and the perpetrator, the innocent and the monster (see Wente 2003). But in the media discourse it was never mentioned that Levy was just months away from her mandatory army service, which would have directly or indirectly put her in a position that would have endangered the lives of Palestinian civilians. It is, of course, unlikely that Levy would have been in a position to kill (very few women in the Israeli army are in combat positions), but being a soldier is hardly the same as being an innocent civilian. These configurations also fail to account for asymmetric conflicts, in which one side has an army and can play by the rules of war while the other does not have airplanes, tanks, or the privilege of borders (French 2003, 36). Recent theorizing of suicidal terrorism addresses cycles of violence between states and sub-state groups, but such a discourse is still largely missing from the press (Kapitan 2004, 182–86; Bloom 2005, 37–41). The discourse on terrorism then effaces the root causes of political violence and prevents a sober discussion that explains (but does not necessarily justify) the historical and political reasons for such violence.

One Israeli film that addresses the mutual nature of political violence in Palestine and Israel is Ra'anan Alexandrowicz's documentary *The Inner Tour* (2001). In the film, Alexandrowicz takes a group of Palestinians on a three-day tour of Israel prior to the beginning of the second intifada. Two women befriend each other and have a conversation:

"Imagine as if the person who killed your husband was here," says Jihad Salah. "What would you do?"

Siham al Ouq, an impoverished widow whose husband was accidentally shot dead by Israeli Defense Forces at his own doorstep, replies, "If he was here, and no one was paying attention, and I wasn't to be held accountable . . . me and my kids would have eaten him alive."

"My husband took part in a mission in which a soldier was killed," says Jihad. "This soldier has a mother too. Imagine as if his mother was here right now. How would she feel about me if she met me here?"

The film then cuts to shots of the bus traveling at night, which allows time for contemplation. The discourse is progressive in that it draws equivalences between the violence, loss, and pain on both sides of the conflict and does not demean or label either one but rather historicizes the situation. But in the film Alexandrowicz never acknowledges the power imbalance between Israel and Palestine, not only as it manifests itself in the reality of both women but also in the power structure of the film.[13] Still, the film is innovative, since unlike most Israeli and Western media coverage, it does not simply demonize the enemy, and it never slides into the simplistic and problematic language of terrorism but employs the more nuanced and historicized language of political violence.

Suicidal terrorism presents a special case in the destructive (rather than demonstrative) category of terrorism, and to a large extent it alienates the enemy target audience (as well as neutral communities) completely but serves the purposes of coercing the terrorists' own communities (Pape 2005, 9–10). Robert Pape shows that suicidal terrorism campaigns are neither erratic nor religious but primarily nationalistic and that they operate at strategic social and individual levels that need to be accounted for as a complex set (Pape 2005, 21–22). As will be clear from examples used in this article, both Israeli and Western media (as well as some academic research) often focus on one target audience—that of the enemy—and its alienation by such acts and on the individual reasons for the suicidal terror attack. But since such an approach ignores the internal social structures and lacks in historical narratives as they are perceived by the terrorists' communities, Western media generally fail in providing a comprehensive overview of suicidal terrorizing.[14]

SUICIDE OPERATIONS IN THE CONTEXT OF GENDER AND MEDIA

The phenomenon of Palestinian female suicide bombers ignited the cultural imagination in Western societies, which have produced a Suicide Bomber Barbie, a recent American independent film about a would-be female suicide bomber, and artworks, to name just a few responses.[15] This response highlights the gender discrepancies in reporting, editing, and exposure in mass media coverage. It is a common practice for Palestinian suicide bombers to leave videotapes of themselves, filmed against the Palestinian flag or the Dome of the Rock, holding a rifle.[16] The text is somewhat scripted and incorporates a medley of religious and nationalistic language. In Arab media the tapes are aired repeatedly, and the suicide bomber is culturally classified as a *shaheed*.[17] But in the West we rarely see the videos of the men, and even their names are often not disclosed. The case with the women is quite different, as their names are publicly emphasized and the videos aired; furthermore, they are contrasted with photos of the women from their previous lives, photos that emphasize the tact that they were young women engaged in traditional teenage habits and activities. In particular, pictures of Idris and Akhras in ordinary and secular settings were publicized and compared to pictures taken just before they headed out on their missions. Although the verbal text tries to explain the reasoning in psychological terms (revenge or sense of worthlessness, for example), the contrast of the images creates an unbridgeable gap whereby the Western viewer cannot reconcile the image of the young beautiful woman with her fundamentalist, terrorist dark side.[18] The result is a demonization not only of these particular women but also of the society that could produce such monsters. In the context of mass media (especially but not only television outlets), the need for shows to sell advertisements (and ultimately products) make women a major target audience. However, as Dawn Heinecken points out, "it is crucial to note that television producers are less interested in creating shows that appeal to women than they are in building (or reinforcing) an identity for women that is favorable to what advertisers hope to sell" (2003, 15). The notion of an aggressive, violent, and discontented woman is contrary to advertisers' desire to see a docile female becoming active only in the practice of consumption. In addition, what media are selling are not just physical products but a worldview that carries with it ideological ramifications: "Clearly, the media are the contemporary mediators of hegemony, the question being how, and to whose avail, particular ideological constructs of femininity are produced in media content" (van Zoonen 1994, 24). As a result of such media dynamics, the hegemonic Western position cannot tolerate Palestinian female suicide bombers in the context either of Islamic terrorism or of their deviation from desired feminine behavior.

Furthermore, Western media tend to focus on the mothers of both men and women suicide bombers, showing them ululating and celebrating their children's actions. These images are used as supporting evidence for the ills of Palestinian society at large. But Maha Abu-Dayyeh Shamas claims that "compounding their private pain, women are subjected to extreme social pressure to behave in a certain way in public. Their private pain has to be denied for the sake of the public. Some women who have not been able to meet such societal demands (i.e. suppressing their grief in public) have actually been tranquilized by local doctors" (2003, 9). Mothers, then, are expected to perform the loss of their children in certain cultural codes that deny them their own expression of grief and that are used in Western media to mark them as uncaring mothers. This performance masks their personal pain and robs them of a genuine expression of political position, both gender-wise and via the conflict.

The most common way that Western media grapple with the deviation from traditional womanly roles is by adopting a thesis that female suicide bombers are victims of patriarchy. In a *Guardian* article (with the suggestive title "Death and the Maidens"), Giles Foden writes:

> Are men in fact to blame for women in terrorism? Litvak certainly believes the role of women in Muslim suicide bombing is a function of patriarchal control: "Those who send these women do not really care for women's rights," he says. "They are exploiting the personal frustrations and grievances of these women for their own political goals, while they continue to limit the role of women in other aspects of life." He also thinks that the use of women in terrorism has a simple practical application for their leaders. "They believe that women can evade security checks more easily than men, since they arouse fewer suspicions." (2003)

Journalist Barbara Victor utilizes her entire book, *Army of Roses,* to look at the stories of the first four successful Palestinian female suicide bombers, as well as to present interviews with some women whose suicide-bombing attempts failed. Victor finds personal problems among all of the women, mostly emanating from their status as women in a patriarchal society: Idris was unable to bear children, Andaleeb Taktakeh did not want to get married, and Akhras was protecting family honor (her father was accused of collaborating with Israel). In the introduction Victor employs an outdated Western feminist perspective on the matter and claims, "This book tells the story of four women who died for reasons that go beyond the liberation of Palestine. If nothing else, let it serve as an example of the exploitation of women taken to a cynical and lethal extreme" (2003, 8). Throughout the book, Victor claims that all these women were manipulated by men who convinced them that a suicide operation was the only way to redeem themselves and their family name (2003, 7).

Academic feminist discourse in the West is equally problematic. Although Victor refuses to see the potential agency of individual women and paints them instead as mindless, naive, and manipulable creatures, Andrea Dworkin goes further, blaming gender oppression entirely for the situation: "It is better, easier, and more logical to blame the Israelis for women's suffering than to blame the men who both sexually abuse and then kill them according to honor society rules" (Dworkin 2002). Dworkin applies a universalist feminist framework whereby gender oppression should be considered primary to other forms of oppression or injustice. And Mia Bloom notes that seventeen organizations around the world currently use suicidal terrorism as a tactic, and about half of them employ women in their missions. Her answer to the question of why women carry out suicide bombings is, "So many of these women have been raped or sexually abused in the previous conflict either by representatives of the state or by the insurgents themselves" (Bloom 2005, 143). Elsewhere in her work Bloom makes similar assertions about the Tamil Tigresses and the Black Widows of Chechnya. But nowhere in the book does she provide sources affirming such claims.

Israeli criminologist Anat Berko interviewed would-be suicide bombers in Israeli prison, and she too concludes that "unlike the men, the women had been pushed to suicide by despair at their problematic family situations, such as not being allowed to decide their future, and/or by family members in order to restore the family honour after an illicit relationship" (2004). But in similar interviews Yoram Schweitzer finds that a more nuanced picture emerges from the conversations, whereby nationalist zeal and personal problems (only some of which are gender based) are considered in tandem as motivational reasons (Schweitzer 2006, 40).

Feminist academics in both Israel and North America choose to see the oppression of women in a patriarchal structure as the chief reason for their decision to volunteer for a suicide mission. But in fact, Palestinian feminists have recognized the need to fight simultaneously for national liberation and gender equality. Zahira Kamal, former minister of women's affairs in the Palestinian National Authority, claims that the first intifada "not only challenged the Israelis for the first time in a way that did not provoke negative world reaction, but it changed the second-class status of women within the Palestinian community" (in Victor 2003, 10–11). Over the last twenty years Palestinian feminist organizations have flourished, and their research accounts for our understanding of the complex interaction among nationalism, religion, gender, and the occupation. These researchers remind us to look at multiple axes of victimization, agency, activism, and empowerment that exist within Palestinian society (see Abdo 2002; Jamal 2004). That is, as with other third-world feminist issues, a comprehensive approach to the Palestinian female suicide bomber cannot reduce or even prioritize gender oppression over other (national, economic) circumstances but rather needs to be accounted for in the complex web of power and social relations in Palestinian society and in the particular political predicament of that society. But until now, the representation of the issue in both Western media and academe is mostly limited to problematic approaches such as those of Dworkin, Bloom, Berko, and Victor.

Meanwhile, in Arab media, the female suicide bombers take on a special role as the symbolic brides of Palestine. For instance, Hanadi Jaradat, who killed herself and twenty-one others, including some Palestinians, in a restaurant in Haifa, is often called "the bride of Haifa."[19] Similarly, in a few cases, men would come to the mourning house and perform symbolic weddings to the *shaheeda*, the mourning scenes transformed into brideless wedding scenes. Taking this feminine symbolism even further, Mufid Fawzie writes, "She bore in her belly the fetus of a rare heroism, and gave birth by blowing herself up!" (quoted in Bennet 2002, A8).

That is, while female suicide bombers are hailed as heroes and martyrs, they are also elevated to mythic realms that solve the problem of dealing with nontraditional gender behavior in their own society. Since women have always been accepted in national liberation struggles as the symbol of the mother nation, the designation of the title *bride* suggests a comfortable place in the patriarchal nationalist project (Abdo 2002, 592).[20] Interestingly, Frances Hasso shows that the application of the title *bride* (implying also "feminine beauty, female weakness and womanly sacrifice" [Hasso 2005, 42]) is selective and does not apply to all female suicide bombers. Particularly telling is the lack of attention in the Arab media to the second female suicide bomber, Dareen Abu Aisheh. Abu Aisheh was a brilliant student of English at Al Najah University in Nablus, an outspoken feminist, and a devout Muslim. She was also a militant and was the first to leave a videotape recording indicating her intentions and implicating Arab leaders as weak in their response to the Palestinian situation. Hasso argues that Arab media ignored Abu Aisheh "because she can be constructed in no other way but as a militant *woman* and a devout Muslim. The words, images, and known history of Abu Aisheh were not conducive to deployments of heterosexual romance, desire, frailty, and feminized beauty" (2005, 42).[21] Regardless of the narratives the women tried to communicate in their actions and videos, the dominant narrative in the Arab public sphere (political, media, and local) tied these women into heteronormative narratives as mothers and brides, narratives that affirmed the gender status quo. Whether discussing mythic brides or monsters, the discourse in both the Arab world and the West generally avoids uncomfortable questions of subjectivity, agency, and aggression, all qualities that are not befitting women according to patriarchal norms.

SUICIDE IN THE CONTEXT OF THE ISRAELI-PALESTINIAN CONFLICT

So far, I have looked at suicide bombing mostly in relation to the discourse on political violence. But it is also important to examine it in the context of suicides and gender. The majority of Palestinian and Arab writers on the topic try to separate suicide from suicide operations. First, Islam (especially in the hadith, or interpretation of the Qu'ran [Dabbagh 2005, 26]) bans suicide altogether and deems the person who commits suicide as weak, despairing, and selfish. In contrast, suicide bombers are referred to as *shaheeds* and are considered brave and selfless warriors in a holy war (jihad). The word suicide (*al-intihar*) is hardly ever mentioned in Arabic-language discussions about suicide operations (Dabbagh 2005, 83). Some Islamist clerics have provided religious justification for such operations by claiming that it is not the person who chooses to die, that it is God who decides when a person dies; martyrdom then is merely "a Muslim's choice of the manner in which he seeks to die" (Sheikh Naim Qassem, quoted in Reuter 2004, 64). In addition, secularist and nationalist discourses praise suicide operations as a sign of a strong spirit of resistance, a contradiction to the idea of depression leading to suicide. Ghassan Hage writes, for instance, "In this unequal struggle, the Palestinians are always imagined on the verge of being squashed and with them all the Arab masses' aspirations of a dignified life. The suicide bombers become a sign that Palestinians have not been broken" (2003, 74).

But the reality of suicide operations is more complex, as data shows that since 1996 and the Palestinian realization of the failures of the Oslo Accords, the rates of suicide cases in Palestinian society have increased dramatically (although they are still much lower than those in industrialized societies) (Dabbagh 2005, chap. 4). Most psychological research with Palestinian youth shows deep levels of hopelessness and a sense of defeat. Rita Giacaman, who studies youth suicide in Palestine, claims, "Our students generally have an inability to dream, an inability to visualize a better future than their hopelessly miserable life offers" (in Hage 2003, 79). And Hage adds, "Nothing symbolizes social death like this inability to dream a future" (2003, 79). Furthermore, in a study of nine male suicide bombers from the Gaza Strip, it was found that all of the men experienced personal humiliation and physical violence under occupation and/or watched a relative experience such abuses; thus all exhibited signs of being terrorized, some with clear posttraumatic stress disorder symptoms (Fields, Elbedour, and Hein 2002).

For ideological reasons, neither Arab nor Western narratives of suicidal violence explore or emphasize these psychological issues. But two recent films explore the links between the political and the psychological. Golden Globe winner and Academy Award nominee *Paradise Now* (2005) is a Palestinian fiction film discussing the last twenty-four hours in the lives of two male would-be suicide bombers. Said and Khaled live in Nablus, with little or no employment, no possibility of leaving the city (the Israeli authorities hardly ever give permits to young men), and no future prospects in sight. As the two debate the action they are about to take, we find out that the father of one collaborated with the Israelis and was eventually killed, while the father of the other submitted to the occupier's abuse and humiliations to the point of choosing which of his two legs would be shot by an Israeli soldier. As Salman Elbedour argues, exposure to political violence, humiliation, and economic devastation leads to high levels of psychological distress and low levels of self-esteem (1998, 539).[22] Both characters in *Paradise Now* see absolutely no future for themselves, and in tact, when Said falls in love with Suha, he cannot fathom a life where the two could be together because he cannot sustain himself economically or in any other way and he cannot imagine the situation changing. These Palestinian youth can see no personal future but instead see a respectable, even celebrated, way to die.

The situation for women in a patriarchal society poses additional sets of restrictions leading to further humiliation and victimization based on gender. Abu-Dayyeh Shamas claims:

At present, [women] are victimised by the political violence, living in perpetual fear for their safety and that of their families, while bearing the additional burdens imposed on them under harrowing conditions, such as the destruction of homes, the razing of agricultural property, the uprooting of trees and rampant unemployment. Additionally, they are victims of heightened violence within the home, but are unable to express any of their suffering or anxiety, as they are forced into silence for fear of being blamed at the public level for being selfish and inconsiderate given the national emergency the whole society is undergoing, and at the private level from being blamed for their own victimisation—a vicious circle. (2003, 2)

Breaking out of this vicious cycle is not a simple feat, and depression is a likely and common outcome of the circumstances, even—maybe especially—when the society rarely acknowledges depression in its midst. While personal depression may not be the primal cause of suicidal terrorism, societal depression certainly takes its toll on individuals. In that respect, suicide in the context of a conflict should be examined as a marker not only of depression but also of martyrdom. The Israeli documentary *Avenge but One of My Two Eyes* (2005) investigates the culture of Israeli martyrdom as it is manifested in two foundational myths: the myth of Massada and the tale of the biblical Samson. Samson was the first suicide operator recorded in history, using his immense physical prowess to pull down the roof on himself and hundreds of Philistines after they blinded him. He has been celebrated in Israel as Samson the hero, and there is a cult around his act and choice. Massada was the last fortress held by Jews in the rebellion against the Romans, which ended in AD 73. On Massada—once surrounded and devoid of all hope—a thousand Jews allegedly committed suicide rather than become slaves to the Romans. The site, on the shores of the Dead Sea, was discovered by an archeologist in the early 1940s and quickly became a symbol for proud Zionists who saw themselves as diametrically opposed to the perceived weakness of the European Jewry during the Holocaust. Avi Mograbi follows dozens of tours of Massada, as well as celebrations of Samson, and he intercuts those sequences with footage from the West Bank: shots of the apartheid wall that Israel is erecting, checkpoints, economic devastation, and daily humiliations. As these images of hopeless Palestinians are contrasted with the story of the hopeless Jews at Massada and with the celebrated decision of Samson to take his own life while hurting as many of his enemies as possible, a complex view of martyrdom and suicide emerges. Both Judaism and Islam forbid suicide and consider anyone who takes his or her life to be weak. But both Israeli and Palestinian societies celebrate forms of self-sacrifice that are considered to be serving the better good of the society, even if it emanates from deep desperation and hopelessness. Mograbi's film also shows that martyrdom is not inherent to one monstrous society but is a product of circumstances—sociopolitical as well as interpersonal.

NARRATIVES OF MARTYRDOM

In suicide a subject declares "my life is not worth living." But in suicide bombing the subject declares "my life is not worth living, but in my death I will produce a myth that is worth dying for." That is, the subject turns her or his own body into an instrument, a bomb that will not only define her or his life and death but also contribute to a larger national story of heroism and sacrifice (Bilsky 2004). While this account applies for both male and female suicide bombers, I would argue that it reflects women's predicament in patriarchal society rather well. In psychoanalytic terms, since women have no access to the symbolic realms of power, they are relegated to the imaginary, to the realm of the body, emotions, and the irrational. It is therefore not completely surprising that in a society lacking gender equality few women actually make it into fighting forces but dozens are accepted as potential suicide bombers. As suicide bombers they are disposable, one-time instruments and objects in a project designed and controlled by men.[23] Hasso shows that the videotape narratives of the female suicide bombers often use their gendered position to mount a critique of the Arab leadership (Hasso 2005, 29–35). Akhras, for instance, says in her video, "I say to the Arab leaders, stop sleeping. Stop failing to fulfill your duty. Shame on the Arab armies who are sitting and watching the girls of Palestine fighting while they are asleep" (quoted in Hasso 2005, 29).

Hasso shows that Arab women, feminists and others, take great inspiration from the women's messages and acts, while Arab men often minimize the loaded gender critique by focusing on nationalist issues instead. One Arab commentator writes in the Jordanian daily *At Dustour,* "Wafa Idrees, like the rest of the young women of her generation, never dreamed of owning a BMW or of having a cellular phone. Wafa did not carry makeup in her suitcase, but enough explosives to fill the enemy with horror. Wasn't it the west that kept demanding that eastern woman become equal to the man? Well, this is how we understand equality—this is how the martyr Wafa understood equality" (quoted in Chancellor 2002). Similarly, an editorial in a Palestinian paper suggests that "he who marries a good girl will not be asked for a high bride price—girl marries a warrior and asks for a rifle in place of a dowry" (quoted in Marcus 2002). Thus many Arab men bypass the gender critique and reinscribe a narrative that fits into a more traditional patriarchal structure.

Female suicide bombers use their bodies as weapons, thus circumventing the patriarchal system and entering the symbolic order as (dead) symbols or as myths. Most feminist critics agree that national movements, particularly in the postcolonial context, have for the most part betrayed women's struggle for gender equality and blocked their participation in the newly established nation-state (see, e.g., Abdo and Lentin 2002; Giles et al. 2003). The phenomenon of female suicide bombers highlights some of the problematic relations of gender to the nationalist project of liberation, but at the same time, female suicide bombers get more attention than women combatants because of their ahistorical (either mythic or terrorist) classification. I believe the reason for this discrepancy is that women fighters challenge the patriarchal army order in more profound ways than suicide bombers, ways that are harder to dismiss or subvert. Khaled, perhaps the best-known Palestinian woman fighter, has commented about the reception of the Palestinian female suicide bombers by religious leaders: "When the religious leaders say that women who make those actions are finally equal to men, I have a problem. Everyone is equal in deaths—rich, poor, Arab, Jew, Christian, we are all equal. I would rather see women equal to men in life" (quoted in Victor 2003, 63–64). Like Khaled and Kamila Shamise, other feminists call for nuanced attention to the way that gender plays into the already complex medley of politics, nationalism, religion, patriarchy, economy, tradition, honor, and social norms in the Palestinian-Israeli conflict.

CONCLUSION

I close this article with a short detour. In the Hollywood vehicle *So Proudly We Hail* (1943), a group of American nurses are posted to the Pacific front in the Second World War. One of the nurses is the surly Olivia, played by Veronica Lake. She refuses to min-

gle, party, or socialize and eventually breaks down and tells the others that her fiancé was killed in Pearl Harbor just days before their wedding. She says passionately, "I know what I am doing. I know why I am here. I know what I am going to do. I'm going to kill Japs, every blood-stained one I can get my hands on." Later in the film she requests to be posted in a hospital ward where wounded Japanese prisoners are kept, but ultimately she cannot kill them, as the nurturing nurse in her wins over the vindictive widow. Eventually the women are trapped behind enemy lines, and Olivia saves her friends by taking off her helmet, loosening her blonde long hair, and attracting the Japanese soldiers closer so that she can detonate a hand grenade (hidden in her breast pocket), killing herself and the soldiers. This suicide bombing, interestingly, takes place in the frame's dark background, and the film does not linger on this climax but instead cuts immediately to the escape of the others, and Olivia is rarely even mentioned thereafter. But in the narrative of the film, and in the logic of the Western viewer, it is impossible to label Olivia a terrorist. Nor do we think of the Christian-American nurse Kitty from *Exodus* (1960), last seen armed and ready to fight for Israel's independence, as anything but a freedom fighter.

Now let us return to Idris, the medic and first Palestinian female suicide bomber. Is she a monster? A terrorist? A freedom fighter? A martyr? A victim? The answer clearly lies not in her action or even in her choice of how to represent herself but in the diverse and often competing narratives of politicians and media alike. The politicians' narratives tend to frame the actions of women suicide bombers in ways that minimize and subvert the overt confrontation of gender politics present in the women's own narratives and actions. Ultimately, this co-optation renders the affront on gender politics ineffective, or effective only insofar as it serves the nationalist and patriarchal project. The media treatment of the phenomenon both in the Arab world and in the West relies on convenient stereotypes and conventional narrative frames. Those representations deny women agency and instead represent them as monsters or brides in a hegemonic framework that enables readers and viewers to maintain both the comfortable gender status quo and their preconceived notions about the

Palestinian-Israeli conflict.[24] In this respect, the case of the female suicide bomber is not that different from other news events as they are covered by media. That is, while the phenomenon of female suicide bombers is relatively new, its media coverage is organized as news stories packaged to reassert old beliefs. As such, news coverage of the phenomenon is in the end rather old news insofar as gender, terrorism, and the Palestinian-Israeli conflict go.

NOTES

1. For Yassin's and others' positions on the matter, see MEMRI (2002).

2. Although the purpose of this study is to look at news media in general, space limitations guided me to limit the scope of the news sources for this article to print media. My selection focuses on leading English-language newspapers from Israel, the United States, Canada, and Britain, which I generally call Western media (although I am aware that reports in German and French might provide a different picture). This article does not attempt a comprehensive media review but uses the examples chosen to substantiate a theoretical argument.

3. For an extended discussion, see Coomaraswamy (2003). There are also reports of women joining the Liberation Tamil Tiger Eelam in Sri Lanka as a way to defend themselves against the danger of rape by Indian soldiers of the Indian Peacekeeping Force units. I thank Neloufer De Mel for pointing this out.

4. A good feminist analysis of those stereotypes can be found in Heinecken (2003).

5. Fawzia Sheikh (2006) writes; "In Idris' case, Israeli security forces at the time had noted her husband rejected her for being unable to conceive, and as a result she was alienated by a conservative society in which marriage and children are the norm." Peter Beaumont (2002b) writes: "We rationalised that as a woman whose marriage had broken up in a Traditional society that somehow she was an outsider, and vulnerable to the persuasion of those who send the bombers out."

6. For instance, Olivia Ward of the *Toronto Star* writes: "The participation of women and, sometimes, teenage girls in an increasing number of deadly acts has horrified the international public, and a wave of revulsion has rolled through the media at female violence in its most ruthless form. Yet, the extent and causes of women's violence arc uncertain and remain unpredictable in a world in which aggression has been the province of men, and violent women considered mentally unbalanced or possessed by unimaginable evil" (2004, A6).

7. For a good overview of the discourse in Arab media surrounding suicide operations and martyrdom, see Hasso (2005). In the conclusion to the article, Frances S. Hasso writes: "My analysis and understanding of suicide/martyrdom attacks takes for granted that Palestinians in the West Bank and Gaza Strip undertake them to resist settler-colonial domination at a historical point of Zionism's almost complete (ideological, economic, diplomatic and military) 'triumph' over the native population" (2005, 43).

8. Interestingly, in an interview, Zarema Muzhakhoeva, a Chechen who botched a suicide attack, describes how she first dressed in *hijab* (head scarf) and a black dress for the purposes of recording the suicide video, while later being dressed "like a Muscovite—fashionably. Blue Jeans, cross-shoes, T shirt. . . . Also they gave me beautiful dark glasses and a baseball cap" (Muzhakhoeva 2004). It is clear that Muzhakhoeva is dressed to fit in and not draw suspicion, but it is also interesting to note that she sees herself as in costume; she describes her acts (videotaping and suicide operation) almost like performative acts, not necessarily natural.

9. For an excellent discussion of sexuality and interethnic romance in Israeli cinema, see Loshitzky (2001).

10. For a good overview of terrorism as a communication process, see Tuman (2003). Interestingly, Joseph Tuman accounts for diverse audiences (state, media, other nations) but does not discuss the primary duality of addressing at once the enemy and one's own society.

11. In some cases the media are not just transmission tools but actually determinate political agents (Gupta 2002, 19).

12. Research about suicide bombings indicates that this tactic is chosen only when other means, both diplomatic and less extreme measures of violence, have failed in providing independence. (All conflicts where suicide operations are used are conflicts over the independence of an ethnically occupied or colonized minority.) (See Bloom 2005, chap. 2; Pape 2005, 42–44.)

13. The film acknowledges neither the cinematic device nor the fact that the director is Israeli. This masking is problematic, as it is difficult to imagine a Palestinian filmmaker presenting this sequence without acknowledging the power asymmetry in the conflict. Furthermore, the film is in Arabic, but in large sections music overrides the dialogue, so the audience is forced to read subtitles. This is evidence that the film was made for Israeli and Western audiences and not for Palestinian and Arab audiences.

14. A comprehensive and concise review of this problem in the Palestinian-Israeli conflict can be found in Kapitan (2004). For a problematic account of the same set of issues, see Bloom (2005). Mia Bloom relies almost entirely on Israeli sources; when she uses Palestinian and Arabic sources, they are always secondary sources cited in the English press. As a result, there are numerous blind spots in historicizing and explaining Palestinian suicidal terror.

15. For the Suicide Bomber Barbie, see http://www.theculrure.net/barbie/index.html. *Day Night Day Night* (2006) describes the last forty-eight hours in the life of a would-be female suicide bomber in New York City. The film never explains her personal motivation, her social background, or even the goals of those who sent her on the mission, and as such is vacuous at hest. Dror Felier, an Israeli-born Swedish citizen, created an art installation in which Hanadi Jaradat's picture floats in a pool of blood. The work inspired

a diplomatic incident whereby the Israeli ambassador to Sweden tried to destroy it during a gala opening. Tamil Tiger female suicide operations in Sri Lanka have already inspired an Indian film, *The Terrorist* (1999).

16. There are also posters produced in the local towns and villages that are collages of an image of the person with the Dome of the Rock, the flag, and other nationalist symbols as well as accompanying text. These posters produce a narrative of the act of martyrdom that conforms to a script. For a good discussion of the role of the posters, see Abu Hashhash (2006).

17. It is important to note that anyone who dies from Israeli fire is considered a *shaheed,* regardless of whether she or he has been violent or involved in fighting.

18. The layout of Margaret Wente's (2003) article presents an image of Ayat Akhras's grieving mother on the left; in the middle are two pictures of Akhras, one as a teenager, the other wrapped in the kaffiyeh and holding a rifle; and on the right a picture of one of her victims, Rachel Levy. The caption under Akhras's image reads: "The two faces of Ayat Akhras." See also the cover page for *Newsweek* from April 15, 2002. The title reads "War in the Middle East." The accompanying image places side by side Akhras and Levy, and the caption reads: "A Human Bomb and Her Victim: How Two Teens Lived and Died."

19. "The military wing of Islamic Jihad . . . termed Hanadi Jaradat the 'bride of Haifa' and declared, 'The wedding in Haifa will teach the Zionists an unforgettable lesson'" (Levy-Barzilai 2003).

20. For a fuller discussion of the mother nation, see Naaman (2000).

21. I would also like to point out that while testimonies from Abu Aisheh's friends and family account for diverse reasons for her action, Victor's own selective narrative concludes that "Darine Abu Aisheh is . . . a woman who killed herself because she couldn't face the prospect of an arranged marriage when her goal in life was to continue her education and work in academia" (Victor 2003, 196). Nowhere in the friends' interviews is it suggested that if Abu Aisheh did marry she would be barred from an academic career. Such a reading is not only reductive, but it also conforms to and reaffirms stereotypes about the gender backwardness of Muslim society. Hasso's own (2005) reading—while critical of the manipulation of women in the patriarchal structure of Palestinian society—accounts for the complexity of the situation.

22. Similar results are found with Tamil youth who volunteer for suicide missions. Neloufer De Mel (2004) writes: "It [willingness to go on a suicide mission] mirrors the sense of desperation in Tamil youth lacking an alternative meaningful life with opportunities of education, employment and career advancement outside of the armed struggle" (78).

23. Kamila Shamise (2002) calls the Palestinian suicide bombers Charlie's Angels, with Yassir Arafat in Charlie's seat: "Men are considered more suited to training recruits, so it's just more efficient to have women kill themselves. No surprise to find men keeping themselves at the centre of things, relegating women to positions of service rather than strategy."

24. For a discussion of news narratives and how they reiterate social and cultural narratives, see Johnson-Cartee (2005). For discussions of the media coverage of war, see Hoskins (2004) and also Allan and Zelizer (2004).

REFERENCES

Abdo, Nahla. 2002. "Women, War and Peace: Reflection from the Intifada." *Women's Studies International Forum* 25(5):585–93.

Abdo, Nahla, and Ronit Lentin, eds. 2002. *Women and the Politics of Military Confrontation: Palestinian and Israeli Gendered Narratives of Dislocation.* New York: Berghahn.

Abu-Dayyeh Shamas, Maha. 2003. "Women in Situations of Organized Violence: A Case of Double Jeopardy." Report, Women's Centre for Legal Aid and Counseling. http://www.wclac.org/reports/violence.pdf.

Abu Hashhash, Mahmoud. 2006. "On the Visual Representation of Martyrdom in Palestine." *Third Text* 20(3/4):391–404.

Allan, Stuart, and Barbie Zelizer, eds. 2004. *Reporting War: Journalism in Wartime.* London: Routledge.

Applebaum, Anne. 2002. "Girl Suicide Bombers." *Slate,* April 2. http://slate.msn.com/?id=2063954.

Avenge but One of My Two Eyes. 2005. Directed by Avi Mograbi. Paris: MograbiFilms.

Beaumont, Peter. 2002a. "From an Angel of Mercy to Angel of Death." *Guardian,* January 31. http://www.guardian.co.uk/Archive/Article/0,4273,4346503,00.html.

———. 2002b. "'Suicide Notes." *Observer,* December 22. http://observer.guardian.co.uk/2002review/story/0,,862850,00.html.

Bennet, James. 2002. "Arab Press Glorifies Bomber as Heroine." *New York Times,* February 11, A8.

Berko, Anat. 2004. *In the Path to the Garden of Eden.* Tel Aviv: Miscal. English excerpt available at http://web.amnesty.org/library/Index/ENGMDE150162005?open&of=ENG-ISR.

Bilsky, Leora. 2004. "Suicidal Terror, Radical Evil, and the Distortion of Politics and Law." *Theoretical Inquiries in Law* 5(1). http://www.bepress.com/til/default/vol5/iss1/art5/.

Bloom, Mia. 2005. *Dying to Kill: The Allure of Suicide Terror.* New York: Columbia University Press.

Chancellor, Alexander. 2002. "The Ultimate Equaliser." *Guardian,* February 23. http://www.guardian.co.uk/Archive/Article/0,4273,4360317,00.html.

Chic Point. 2003. Directed by Sharif Waked. Independently produced.

Coomaraswamy, Radhika. 2003. "A Question of Honour: Women, Ethnicity, and Armed Conflict." In Giles et al. 2003, 91–102.

Dabbagh, Nadia Tyasir. 2005. *Suicide in Palestine: Narratives of Despair.* Northampton, MA: Interlink.

Day Night Day Night. 2006. Directed by Julia Loktev. Brooklyn, NY: FaceFilm.

De Mel, Neloufer. 2004. "Body Politics: (Re)Cognising the Female Suicide Bomber in Sri Lanka." *Indian Journal of Gender Studies* 11(1):75–92.

Divine Intervention. 2002. Directed by Elia Suleiman. New York: Avatar Films.

Dworkin, Andrea. 2002. "The Women Suicide Bombers." *Feminista!* 5(1). http://www.feminista.com/archives /v5nl/dworkin.html.

Elbedour, Salman. 1998. "Youth in Crisis: The Well-Being of Middle Eastern Youth and Adolescents during War and Peace." *Journal of Youth and Adolescence* 27(5):539–56.

Exodus. 1960. Directed by Otto Preminger. Culver City, CA: Metro-Goldwyn-Mayer.

Fields, Rona M., Salman Elbedour, and Fadel Abu Hein. 2002. "The Palestinian Suicide Bomber." In *The Psychology of Terrorism,* vol. 2, *Clinical Aspects and Responses,* ed. Chris E. Stout, 193–223. Westport, CT: Praeger.

Foden, Giles. 2003. "Death and the Maidens." *Guardian,* July 18. http://www.guardian.co.uk/women/story /0,,1000647,00.html.

French, Shannon E. 2003. "Murderers, Not Warriors: The Moral Distinction between Terrorists and Legitimate Fighters in Asymmetric Conflicts." In *Terrorism and International Justice,* ed. James P. Sterba, 31–46. Oxford: Oxford University Press.

Giles, Wenona, Malathi de Alwis, Edith Klein, and Nekula Silva, eds. 2003. *Feminists under Fire: Exchanges across War Zones.* Toronto: Between the Lines.

Gupta, Suman. 2002. *The Replication of Violence: Thoughts on International Terrorism after September 11th, 2001.* London: Pluto.

Hage, Ghassan. 2003. "'Comes a Time We Are All Enthusiasm': Understanding Palestinian Suicide Bombers in Times of Exighophobia." *Public Culture* 15(1): 65–89.

Hasso, Frances S. 2005. "Discursive and Political Deployments by/of the 2002 Palestinian Women Suicide Bombers/Martyrs." *Feminist Review* 81:23–51.

Heinecken, Dawn. 2003. *The Warrior Women of Television: A Feminist Cultural Analysis of the New Female Body in Popular Media.* New York: Peter Lang.

Hoskins, Andrew. 2004. *Televising War: From Vietnam to Iraq.* London: Continuum.

The Inner Tour. 2001. Directed by Ra'anan Alexandrowicz. Tel Aviv: Belfilms.

Jamal, Amal. 2004. "Feminist Media Discourse in Palestine and the Predicament of Politics." *Feminist Media Studies* 4(2): 129–46.

Johnson-Cartee, Karen S. 2005. *News Narratives and News Framing: Constructing Political Reality.* Lanham, MD: Rowman & Littlefield.

Kapitan, Tomis. 2004. "Terrorism in the Arab Israeli Conflict." In *Terrorism: The Philosophical Issues,* ed. Igor Primoratz, 175–91. New York: Palgrave.

Levy-Barzilai, Vered. 2003. "Ticking Bomb." *Ha'aretz,* November 16. http://www.haaretz.com/hasen/pages/ShArt .jhtml?itemNo=350272.

Loshitzky, Yosefa. 2001. *Identity Politics on the Israeli Screen.* Austin: University of Texas Press.

Marcus, Itamar. 2002. "PMW Encouraging Woman Terrorists." *Independent Media Review Analysis,* March 19. http://www.imra.org.il/story.php3?id=10761.

MEMRI (Middle East Media Research Institute). 2002. "The Celebration of the First Palestinian Female Suicide Bomber, Part 1." *Al-Sharq Al-Awsat,* February 12. http://www.imra.org.il/story.php3Md=10155.

Muzhakhoeva, Zarema. 2004. "'1 Suspected I Had to Commit a Suicide Attack': A Surviving Suicide Bomber Answers Questions of *Izvestia* from a 'Lefortovo' Cell." *Izvestia* 18(5): 1–13.

Naaman, Dorit. 2000. "Woman/Nation: A Postcolonial Look at Female Subjectivity." *Quarterly Review of Film and Video* 17(4):333–42.

Pape, Robert. 2005. *Dying to Win: The Strategic Logic of Suicide Terrorism.* New York: Random House.

Paradise Now. 2005. Directed by Hany Abu Assad. Burbank, CA: Warner Independent Pictures.

Reuter, Christoph. 2004. *My Life Is a Weapon: A Modern History of Suicide Bombing.* Trans. Helena Ragg-Kirkby. Princeton, NJ: Princeton University Press.

Schweitzer, Yoram. 2006. "Palestinian Female Suicide Bombers: Reality vs. Myth." In his *Female Suicide Bombers: Dying for Equality?* 25–41. Tel Aviv: Jaffe Center for Strategic Studies.

Shamise, Kamila. 2002. "Exploding the Myths." *Guardian,* April 27. http://www.guardian.co.uk/Archive/Article /0,4273,4401137,00.html.

Sheikh, Fawzia. 2006. "Mideast: Occupation, Conflict Hold Back Palestinian Women." *Inter Press Service,* March 7, Article no. 42424. http://www.globalinfo.org/eng /reader.asp?ArticleId=42424.

So Proudly We Hail. 1943. Directed by Mark Sandrich. Universal City, CA: Universal Studios.

The Terrorist. 1999. Directed by Santosh Sivan. Port Washington, NY: Fox Lorber.

Tuman, Joseph. 2003. *Communicating Terror: The Rhetorical Dimensions of Terrorism.* Thousand Oaks, CA: Sage.

van Zoonen, Liesbet. 1994. *Feminist Media Studies.* London: Sage.

Victor, Barbara. 2003. *Army of Roses: Inside the World of Palestinian Women Suicide Bombers.* Emmaus, PA: Rodale.

Ward, Olivia. 2004. "The Changing Face of Violence." *Toronto Star*, October 10, A6.

Wente, Margaret. 2003. "How to Make a Martyr." *Globe and Mail,* February 8, F6–F7.

PART III

SEXUALITIES

re sexual relations a realm of pleasure, empowerment, danger or oppression? Why is gender violence so often associated with sex? The women's movement reawakened during the late 1960s and 1970s during a sexual revolution that told youth, "It if feels good, do it!" In this context, an initial impulse of second wave feminism began to argue that "sexual liberation" had simply freed men to objectify and exploit women more. As studies began to illuminate the widespread realities of rape, sexual harassment in workplaces, and sexual exploitation of women in sex work, it beame clear that for women, sexuality was too often a realm of danger rather than pleasure. As a result, by the mid- to late 1970s, feminist activism focused more and more on anti-rape and anti-pornography efforts.

By the mid-1980s other feminists—often younger women, women of color, lesbian and bisexual women—began to criticize radical feminists' preoccupation with the centrality of male heterosexuality and pornography in women's oppression. By the 1990s, many younger feminists sought to reclaim sexual pleasure as a realm of empowerment for women. Today, feminists tend to see sexuality in complicated ways—as a potential source of both pleasure *and* danger, both empowerment *and* oppression. Moreover, research now indicates that the experience of sexuality is not simply determined by gender; rather, race, age, sexual orientation, religion and culture and nationality also shape sexual experiences and attitudes. In the first article in this section, Rashawn Ray and Jason A. Rosow analyze the distinctive approaches to sexuality exhibited by white and black fraternity men. Relying on data from interviews and focus groups, they argue that normative institutional arrangements on college campuses shape sexuality in ways that encourage black Greeks to be more gender egalitarian than their white peers. The black men are held more accountable, and the black Greek system promotes more consciousness of the dangers of objectifying women than does the white Greek system. The next two articles examine commodified sex in non-U. S. contexts. Kevin Bales analyzes prostitution and sex slavery of girls and young women in Thailand. He offers a close up look at the experience of Siri, a fifteen-year-old sex worker, while illustrating how the economy of Thailand, positioned in an increasingly tightly networked world economy, creates the context for the growth of the sex trade in Thailand and across national borders. In the next chapter, Julie O'Connell Davidson examines the "demand side" of international sex tourism. "Sexpatriots" in the Dominican Republic, Davidson observes, are mostly middle-aged, white heterosexual Euro-American men whose activities simultaneously endanger the health and safety of Dominican women, and serve to shore up the fragile identities of these privileged men.

Are gay men and lesbians clearly and categorically distinguishable from heterosexual men and women? Are Filipina and Mexican immigrant women and girls always objects of the sexual gaze of others, and if not, how do they negotiate their own sexual identities? The articles in the second part of this section explore the area of sexual identity. It is widely accepted among scholars today that the idea that there are distinct sexual 'types" of people such as "the homosexual" and "the heterosexual" is a very recent modern construction. But it is also recognized that social constructions have real consequences. Modern medical and scientific discourse may have created "the homosexual" with the goal of controlling "deviant" character types and normalizing "the heterosexual," but starting mostly in the 1970s, men and women who identified as "gay" and "lesbian" drew strength from their shared identities. And from this strength, they challenged prevailing cultural attitudes, customs, and laws. But, as Dennis Altman points out in the first article in this section, this gay and lesbian movement was a particularly modern phenomenon, grounded mostly in the urban areas of wealthy, industrialized nations of the north. He warns that within the context of globalization, the emergence of modern gay and lesbian identities in the Southern Hemisphere's poorer nations could be as much a sign of new forms of neocolonial control as it is a sign of sexual liberation. Next, Michael Messner draws partly on autobiography to reflect on the social processes involved in a young male's construction of himself as "100% heterosexual." The next two articles reveal the nuanced ways in which immigrant women and girls are challenging and reinventing sexual identities. Yen Le Espiritu's study illustrates the ways that Filipina immigrant girls in the United States often define themselves in opposition to their conception of white women as sexually "immoral." Espiritu's analysis reveals the complex interweavings of identities that are constructed in contexts of unequal power by race, gender, sexuality and national origin. Finally, in the last article in this section, Gloria Gonzalez-Lopez shows how Mexican immigrant women and men experience shifting sexual relations in the context of Los Angeles, urban poverty and demanding work schedules. New sexual opportunities arise along with new sexual risks and dangers.

15

Getting Off and Getting Intimate

How Normative Institutional Arrangements Structure Black and White Fraternity Men's Approaches Toward Women

RASHAWN RAY

JASON A. ROSOW

Despite the proliferation of research on collegiate gender and sexual relations (Martin and Hummer 1989; Boswell and Spade 1996; Armstrong, Hamilton, and Sweeney 2006), we know little about one of the key groups within this institutional arrangement—fraternity men. Meanwhile, we know even less about differences and similarities in Black and White high-status men's relations with women (Brandes 2007; Peralta 2007; Flood 2008). Because fraternity men typically are situated on top of the peer culture hierarchy, a comprehensive understanding of the organization of collegiate social life must take into account how these specific enclaves of men understand and perceive gender relations and sexuality, and whether these understandings and perceptions vary by race.

Scholars have offered three competing explanations regarding racial differences in men's approaches toward women: (a) Black and White men objectify women similarly; (b) Black men objectify women more than White men; (c) White men objectify women more than Black men. The first possibility contends that most men, irregardless of status or race, sexually objectify women in the same manner. Thus, Black and White men's performances in masculinities are expected to be similar. In patriarchal societies, men control sexual and romantic environments by promoting sexually aggressive behavior among men (Clark and Hatfield 1989; Hatfield et al. 1998; Flood 2008). Through the emphasis of the importance of sexual prowess, cultural mandates concerning gender encourage men to "sexually objectify" women and appear "sexual." However, such mandates encourage women to stress relationship viability and appear "romantic" (Hatfield et al. 1998). Hence, men are often authorized to express themselves sexually, while women who act this way are shunned. This possibility suggests that gender trumps race and status concerning men's interactions with women.

A second possibility is that Black men exhibit more sexually objectifying approaches toward women than do White men. This explanation is most in line with scholarship on Black men's relations with women. More specifically, cultural motifs like the "cool pose" (Majors and Billson 1992) portray Black men as culprits of sexual violence (Majors and Billson 1992; Anderson 1999). However, this perspective, which is echoed with public discourses and much scholarly research, gives the impression that all Black men are part of the same cultural spaces, thereby neglecting the fact that Black men may be part of different sociocultural[1] spaces that yield distinctly different structural consequences for their treatment of women. It should also be noted that the stereotypical nature of Black men as the Mandingo—overly aggressive, sexually promiscuous, physically superior yet intellectually inferior—has long been purported in mainstream discourses (Hunter and Davis 1992; Collins 2004). Race scholars assert this is a problematized, dramatized, and monolithic perception of Black men that is often exacerbated in the media (Staples 1982; Hoberman 1997).

Finally, the third possibility asserts that White men are more sexually objectifying than Black men. By virtue of their presumed greater status and esteem, White men are more likely to control social environments and accept, and even normalize, sexual objectifications of women (Connell 1987; Kimmel and Messner 1989; Kimmel 2006). This perspective echoes the sentiments of women who claim sexual harassment in high-status institutions such as law, academia, and corporate America where White men are typically the controllers of social environments (Kanter 1977). In contrast to the aforementioned "cool pose," some extant literature finds that Black men's gender attitudes, compared to their White counterparts, are more supportive of gender equality because of a shared oppression and subordination with women (Millham and Smith 1986; Konrad and Harris 2002).

In this article, we assess these three predictions by analyzing 30 in-depth, individual interviews and surveys and two focus group interviews with Black and White high-status fraternity men. We find evidence that White men are more sexually objectifying than their Black counterparts, in support of the third prediction. However, we also find that the reasons behind this pattern go beyond the explanations typically asserted by this prediction and the first two predictions. Collectively, the three explanations noted above neglect the extent to which cultural and social norms are embedded within and shaped by the structure of institutions, and in turn, how structure shapes men's approaches toward women and the performances of masculinities. Accordingly, we contend that "normative institutional arrangements" are one of the key factors that underlie racial differences regarding how men interact with women romantically and sexually on college campuses.

NORMATIVE INSTITUTIONAL ARRANGEMENTS IN HIGHER EDUCATION

Normative institutional arrangements are boundaries that shape social interactions and establish control over social environments (Gerson and Peiss 1985; Hays 1994; Britton 2003), and one structural mechanism that should be of importance to scholars interested in intersectionality research. Normative institutional arrangements identify social contexts (e.g., social environments in fraternity houses), whereby certain behaviors are more or less acceptable and certain structures hold individuals more or less accountable for their treatment of others. Such arrangements represent taken-for-granted assumptions that are external and exist outside of individuals, "social, durable, and layered" (Hays 1994), and constraining and enabling. Normative institutional arrangements focus on the accepted arrangement of relationships within social institutions. In this article, normative institutional arrangements draw attention to the ways in which performances of masculinities are legitimized across different sociocultural categories of men, and the role structure plays in men's approaches toward women. Here, we showcase the implications of the intersecting forces of race and status by examining two normative institutional arrangements that are common themes in Black and White men's understandings and perceptions of gender and sexual relations: (a) small Black student and Greek communities; (b) living arrangements including a lack of on-campus fraternity houses.

The Black student community at most Predominately White Institutions (PWIs) is small and insular. There is also a limited amount of social interaction between Black and White fraternities and between Black and White students overall (Allen 1992; Massey et al. 2003). Similar to patterns at the societal level, interracial dating is infrequent (Joyner and Kao 2005). As a result, even high-status Black fraternity men are mostly invisible in White social arenas.

In contrast, the relatively small number of Black students and limited interactions with Whites indicate that Black fraternity men are much more visible in the Black community. In fact, this group of Black men aligns with the ideals of what DuBois (1903, 1939) conceptualized as the "Talented Tenth." Such members of the Black elite are expected to sacrifice personal interests and endeavors to provide leadership and guidance to the Black community (Battle and Wright II 2002). However, being part of the Talented Tenth signifies the monitoring of this group's behavior, particularly actions that are inconsistent with a greater good for the Black community. This monitoring by others on Black fraternity men is intensified in a structural setting with a small community size, and in turn, increases the likelihood that their treatment of women will be publicized and scrutinized by members of their own social community and the broader college and off-campus communities. Although White fraternity men may also be visible, the sheer number of White students leads to them being held less accountable, and consequently, able to perform masculinity in a manner that Black fraternity men cannot.

Not only is the Black community relatively small but Black Greeks have very different on-campus living arrangements than White Greeks. There is a historical legacy of racial discrimination, both within and external to the university, that has traditionally precluded Black fraternities and sororities from gaining equal access to economic resources such as Greek houses and large alumni endowments (Kimbrough and Hutcheson 1998). To date, most Black Greek Letter Organizations

(BGLOs) do not have fraternity or sorority houses on university property (Harper, Byars, and Jelke 2005). If they do, these houses normally are not the same size or stature of those of their White counterparts. To the extent that the structure of living arrangements facilitates a certain treatment of women, racial differences in access to housing on-campus may have implications in potential racial differences in approaches toward women.

In sum, the claims by masculinities, sexualities, and race scholars suggest that culture provides a portal whereby men view women as physical objects. However, research in this area suffers from three important shortcomings. First, the structural mechanisms by which normative institutional arrangements promote women's subordination have been underemphasized. Most recently, scholars have called for a resurgence of such research and have pointed to the exploration of contextual and structural factors to uncover these mechanisms (Reskin 2003; Epstein 2007). Second, the perspectives of high-status men remain absent in the literature. Hence, this study seeks to understand how elite men decipher their worlds and how privileged statuses influence the processes underlying gender dynamics. Third, research largely has not explored the potential for racial differences in men's gender relations. Consequently, gender and sexuality research has portrayed men as homogenous proponents of gender inequality, irregardless of race and/or social context.

Our work offers an opportunity to address these gaps in the literature by reporting on interviews with Black and White high-status men. Some high-status Black men (e.g., Black fraternity men) may have attitudes and beliefs that are similar to their White male counterparts. However, due in part to a hyper level of visibility and accountability, Black men may be unable to perform hegemonic masculinity similar to their White male counterparts.[2] Actually, because of a relative lack of accountability and visibility afforded to high-status White fraternity men in this structural setting,[3] it is White men's performances of masculinities that may be closer to that of the "cool pose." Therefore, we hypothesize that Black men will exhibit less sexually objectifying approaches toward women than their White counterparts.

Accordingly, we pose two essential questions: (a) Regarding high-status fraternity men's relations with women, are there racial differences in romantic versus sexually objectifying approaches? (b) How do "normative institutional arrangements" structure men's approaches toward women? Because there has been limited empirical research on elite men, we privilege their accounts and voices to gain an insider's perspective into the intersections of masculinities, status, sexuality, and race.

SETTING AND METHOD

We conducted 30 in-depth individual interviews and surveys, along with two focus group interviews, from 15 Black and 15 White fraternity men at a PWI that we call Greek University (GU). Enrolling approximately 30,000 undergraduates, GU is ideal for this study because of its strong academic reputation, vibrant social life, and party scene. GU's emphasis on Greek life facilitates the examination of gender relations among high-status men. About 20% of GU undergraduates are members of Greek letter organizations, which is larger than similar universities.[4] For members, the Greek system normally offers a home away from home, friendships, and social and philanthropic activities. There are approximately 25 White fraternities with memberships around 100, some with on-campus and some with off-campus status, and five Black fraternities with memberships around 10 and all hold off-campus status.[5] Although approximately 25% of White students are members of Greek organizations, less than 10% of Black students are members of Greek organizations.[6] Black and White fraternities are operated by two different governing bodies, the National Pan-Hellenic Council (NPHC)[7] and the Interfraternity Council (IFC), respectively. Although none of these fraternities appear to explicitly discriminate on the basis of race, there is virtually no overlap in race among members of these organizations.

Data Collection

To select our sample, we used a reputational approach (Boswell and Spade 1996) to identify high-status fraternities. Relying on rankings of fraternities by members of sororities and fraternities,

students in sociology classes, informants in Greek Affairs, and the Assistant Dean of Students that rank fraternities based on popularity, academic and philanthropic events, and athletic prowess, three White fraternities consistently ranked high on all lists. We include all three in our study. Because only five historically Black fraternities are recognized by the NPHC, membership in any of these fraternities normally conveys a certain high-status, particularly at GU because the Black population is only about 4% (1,524). We interviewed members from four of the five Black fraternities. We attempted to interview all five and gained entry to four. The sampling strategy enables us to check for commonalities and differences within and between race. Participants were recruited by emailing the fraternity presidents to see if the investigators could attend a chapter meeting to make an announcement about the study, invite members to participate, and leave detailed study flyers.

As a Black and White team of male researchers, we note that gender may elicit certain responses with participants de-emphasizing romanticism. We also conducted interviews with the authors matched with participants by race to elicit candid responses about the other racial group. Based on the data presented throughout this article, we are confident that we limited methodological biases. For example, one White respondent states, "Blacks will fuck anything." Another says, "Yeah, my friends at home are Black. They like to put it in girls' asses." Based on our experiences interacting with these respondents, we believe they would not have made these comments if they were being interviewed by a Black interviewer. (See The Fraternity House section for a Black quotation about Whites.) These quotations show that respondents did not hesitate to make derogatory statements about the other group.

All the men in our study report being family-oriented and having lofty career goals. Most participants are active on campus and have higher GPAs than non-Greeks. However, a substantial class difference exists between Blacks and Whites. The Black men's self-reported family household income is lower middle class, whereas the White men's self-reported family household income is upper-middle class. Many of the Black fraternity men have schol-

Table 1 Descriptive Statistics of Sample by Race

Variable	Range	Variable Description	White = 15	Black = 15	Total = 30
Age	18–24	Years	20.11	21.27	20.69
Classification	1–4	1 = Freshman, 2 = Sophomore, 3 = Junior, 4 = Senior	2.22	3.73	2.98
GPA	0–4	Cumulative Grade Point Average	3.31	2.92	3.12
Living Situation	0–1	0 = Lives off-campus, 1 = Lives in a Fraternity House	0.87	0.00	0.45
Years in Fraternity	1–5	Years respondent has been a fraternity member	1.94	2.00	1.97
Religiosity	1–4	1 = Not at all, 2 = Slightly, 3 = Moderately, 4 = Very	2.00	3.07	2.54
Family's Social Class	1–6	1 = Poor, 2 = Working, 3 = Lower-middle, 4 = Middle, 5 = Upper-middle, 6 = Upper	4.56	3.87	4.22
Relationship Status	0–1	0 = Single or daring, 1 = Committed relationship	0.33	0.67	0.50

arships, student loans, and/or jobs to pay for tuition and housing costs, whereas most of the White fraternity men have scholarships and/or their parents pay a substantial portion of their tuition and living expenses. All respondents self-identify as heterosexual (see Table 1).

Interview Procedure

Most of the data presented come from the individual interviews. In-depth interviews are useful for developing a broad understanding of students' experiences in various aspects of college life and for exploring the meanings students attach to these experiences (Denzin and Lincoln 1994). Similar to Armstrong, Hamilton, and Sweeney (2006), we used an 8-page, semi-structured interview guide to ask participants about many topics including the Greek system, race relations, partying, hooking-up, dating, sexual attitudes and experiences, and their goals for the future. With interviews averaging 2 hours, we aimed to obtain a holistic perspective of these men's collegiate lives. All interviews were digitally recorded and transcribed using pseudonyms to ensure personal and organizational anonymity. Following the interviews, we recorded ethnographic field notes to capture aspects of the interview interactions that might not be evident in the transcripts (Emerson, Fretz, and Shaw 1995). At

the end of each interview, we asked respondents to complete a paper-and-pencil survey. Data from this survey on sociodemographics, family background, sexual attitudes and experiences, and relationship history provide contextual information about each respondent.

The focus groups were conducted after the individual interviews were completed to support the individual interviews. Most focus group respondents were part of the 30 individual interviews. The focus groups were used to triangulate the data and focused on themes that evolved from the individual interviews. They also allowed us to interrogate emerging propositions. Because shared discourses are documented to occur in peer groups, the unique environment generated in focus groups was well suited to this project (Morgan 1997; Hollander 2004). Although focus groups have been criticized for their lack of ability to elicit truthful views about gender and sexuality from young men, the interviewers had preexisting knowledge of the men and could question specific accounts and perspectives.

Analytical Strategy

We use deductive and inductive reasoning as analytic approaches to "double fit" the data with emergent theory and literature (Ragin 1994). We initially allowed analytical categories to emerge as we searched for similarities and differences in how Black and White fraternity men interact with women. Guided by these themes and patterns, we then used deductive reasoning to look for evidence and theories to make sense of the data. We used ATLAS.ti, a qualitative data analysis software package, to connect memos, notes, and transcriptions. After establishing patterns in the coding, we searched the interviews thoroughly again looking for examples that both confirmed and contradicted emerging patterns. Our emerging propositions were then refined or eliminated to explain these negative cases (Rizzo, Corsaro, and Bates 1992).

RACIALIZING GENDER RELATIONS ON CAMPUS

The interviews suggest that Black fraternity men exhibit more romantic approaches than White fraternity men. Although both groups sexually objectify women, Black men emphasize romanticism more than their White counterparts. They indicate that women are physical objects of enjoyment but should also be respected. White fraternity men make few romantic references and primarily view women as sexual objects.

The following quotations exemplify sexually objectifying approaches. This participant suggests that romance is unnecessary in the quest for gratification.

> Pretty much you do not need to do all that wine and dine them and all that. You can skip all that and just bring them back to the house and do what's important to you. (White)

In two different parts of the interview, a participant explains which factors affect how far he will go with a woman.

R: If they [women] were decent or just okay, I'll just mess around with them . . . Get head.

I: When she gives you head, do you go down on her?

R: Honestly, I don't like that . . . I do it every once in a while. Honestly depends how hot the girl is. If I'm drunk and into the girl, I probably would. But other girls, I just make out with them for a little bit.

R: We were talking for about a week and we started messing around. She starts giving me head, and when I took her shirt off, I put my hand on her stomach and this girl had abs. I think that's the most disgusting thing. Like, girls with abs, its like . . . too masculine. So that like turned me off and I couldn't get off and I never called her again. (White)

Nine of the 15 White participants report engaging in sexual behavior that they do not prefer including performing oral sex because of a woman's desirable physical characteristics. They also rarely describe "hot girls" in terms of social competence and popularity. Reports from Black men also contain sexually objectifying approaches. While describing what he desires in a woman, a participant compares women to cars as he explains why his standards for sexual encounters are lower than for relationships.

I: Are your standards lower for a hookup than a committed relationship?

R: I use this analogy. Some people say it's corny, but whatever. When you have the title of a car, you want it to be nice, but you'll jump in your friend's car. You'll ride, you'll ride anything because it's not your title. But if I'm going to have the title to you, you've got to be nice because you represent me! But now I'll ride in a pinto, but I just won't buy one. (Black)

Although both groups exhibit sexually objectifying approaches, romantic approaches in quality and content are far more prevalent among Black men. They respond when asked to "describe ways you or your friends respect women on campus."

> I definitely think my fraternity brothers do a lot of stuff that make them [women] feel appreciated like getting them flowers; whether write them a poem, whether it's just tell them they look beautiful. (Black)

> I think you have to treat women with respect. I think because of how society is I think a lot of males have been misshapen to be like the world leader; the dominant figure in the relationship. They wear the pants in the relationship. I feel like I would treat a woman the way that I would want to be treated. (Black)

Conversely, many White men describe a very different notion of respecting women.

> We respect women. We won't take advantage of them if they're wasted. If she's puking in our bathroom, one of the pledges will get her a ride bome. (White)

> One way that I respect women? A lot of ways. I'll never ask if she needs a ride home after we hookup. I'll let her bring it up or let her spend the night. You respect a girl more if you let her stay. (White)

Black and White differences are also evident in responses to "what do you consider a serious relationship?" White men understand a serious relationship primarily in terms of physical monogamy, whereas Black men define serious relationships in terms of socioemotional exchanges.

> R: If you're in a serious relationship, you shouldn't be making out . . . that's wrong.

> I: So serious relationships are when you don't cheat on a girl.

> R: No. You shouldn't be making out in front of people. If you have a girlfriend you can't be like all over girls at parties. (White)

> Serious relationship is pretty much a basic understanding that two people are together. You have somebody to talk to; somebody who is going to be there on the other end of the phone call. When you leave that message they're calling back. Maybe at night you got somebody to cuddle with. Somebody that could possibly cook for you. Somebody that might be taking you out, picking you up. Somebody that is worrying about what you're doing. (Black)

Twelve of the 15 Black fraternity men explain that having someone to "share" and do "special" things with is the best thing about being in a serious relationship.

> I'd say you get the companionship, the love. You've got somebody there in daytime hours, not just in nighttime hours. The nine to five hours they're going to be there to go out with you. They might send you out with some stuff, take you out to eat, go see a movie, and like it's that constant companionship. (Black)

Comparatively, only 7 of the 15 White fraternity men mention that this is a benefit of a committed relationship. Instead, 12 of them explain that having a "regular hookup" is the best thing about being in a relationship.

> Lots of sex. You can have it everyday without having to go out and get it. It's a lot easier, but you do have to put up with shit occasionally. (White)

> The best thing is you don't have to use a condom. It feels better and you can go right to it. And you got someone to call that you know what they want and knows what you like. (White)

In contrast, only 3 of the 15 Black men mention sexual convenience as a benefit of being in a committed relationship.

Perhaps most revealing are the responses to "describe a romantic evening." Black men volunteer specific details without hesitation and reveal intimate knowledge of their partners, thoughtful planning, and intricate execution.

> I try to do romantic things on occasion, not just on occasions. On her birthday I surprised her. I told her we were going out to dinner. There is a whole day of events. I left a dozen roses in front of her door. I have a key to her apartment just because she likes to have that kind of security just in case I need to go over there and do something for her. When she came home I had prepared a dinner for her. I cooked her favorite dinner which was spaghetti and she was really surprised. It was a candlelight dinner, lights were off, food all served, salad, and spaghetti. She really liked that and I gave her some more gifts, but the last thing I got her was a ring that she loves. (Black)

Of course, "romantic" does not necessarily imply equitable gender relations. "Romantic" can also have negative connotations for gender relations (e.g., women need to be taken care of, pampered, put on a pedestal). Comparatively, most White men's narratives imply less thought and planning. Only three of them could describe a romantic evening, two of which were descriptions encompassing "dinner and a movie," preferably an "expensive establishment."

I clean up, shave, put on a nice shirt with a nice pair of pants, you come out of the car, you wait for her, open the door for her. Nice expensive restaurant; something with a good reputation. Maybe somewhere someone's parents would take them, because that lets them know you're dropping some cheddar, you know, you're dropping some money. Have some easy conversation, then come back have a few more drinks, and then, you know, {laughs}. (White)

Another White participant says, "Well, on her birthday I got her an iPod. She loved it. I took her out to dinner, an expensive dinner."

Finally, the language used by White fraternity men to describe women in gender interactions suggests sexually objectifying approaches, whereas the language exhibited most frequently by Black fraternity men implies more romantic approaches. White men commonly refer to women as "chicks," "girls," and other belittling terms. Conversely, Black men generally use more "respectful" terms like "women," "ladies," and "females" or refer to individuals by name.[8] As seen in many quotations throughout the article, the examples below illustrate the role of language regarding gender relations.

> I know this one time I was real drunk, a little too flirtatious with a female who was actually a friend of mine. I did—I was not trying to hook up with her. Actually, she was trying to hook up with me. And when the alcohol mixed with the flirtatious lady, mixing with me not driving having to be at her house that night. I did regret it when I woke up the next morning {laughs}. (Black)

> When the booze settles in you can make mistakes and you'll screw up with a "frat rat" or something. (White)

Collectively, Black excerpts normally acknowledge women's agency, whereas the White accounts typically display the use of the passive voice, whereby a woman is always acted on and never acting. Black men emphasize more romanticism in their accounts regarding experiences with and attitudes about women. However, these differences are not solely related to race.

NORMATIVE INSTITUTIONAL ARRANGEMENTS STRUCTURE APPROACHES TOWARD WOMEN

We find that differences in men's approaches toward women are structured by normative institutional arrangements centering on community size and living arrangements. Participant accounts suggest that the size of their respective racial communities on campus and the presence or absence of a fraternity house underlie racial differences in romantic versus sexually objectifying approaches toward women.

Greek and Racially Based Communities

Fraternity men are concerned about their individual and group reputations when making gender relation choices. Thus, they aim to steer clear of certain social scenes to preserve their status as elite men. In the following accounts, participants indicate that to maintain their reputations they normally will not "hookup" with low-status women. We asked, "Are there any women you wouldn't hook up with?"

> Fat girls. I stay away from them. Sluts too. They're disgusting. I don't need to hookup with that, that's not *our* [his fraternity] style. (White)

> Everyone has the one, two, or three girls that they're like what the hell was I doing? But you don't want to have too many. I mean its good to hookup, but you don't want to do it with a girl that's easy. If it's a girl that every guy wants and you bring her back its like, "Wow! You hooked up with that girl? That's impressive!" It feels good. If you hookup with an ugly girl, you're friends will give you shit for it. (White)

> Yes. They're not attractive, [laughs] That might sound mean, but that's what they are. Not attractive girls. I don't think there's no woman here that's higher than what we think we can reach. And then lower, yes there is a group of people that you should just not touch. I hear a lot of guys in other fraternities say, "Man I wish I could get a girl like that." Instead, we just get the girl like that. (Black)

White fraternity men indicate that the "word" gets around easily within the Greek community regarding gender interactions. They normally engage in a variety of unspoken rules to preserve their reputations. The following White participant describes the "card" rule.

R: You got one card to play. You can hookup with two girls in the same house [sorority organization] and you might be alright. As long as you don't piss off the first one. If you do, you're done. You won't have a chance with any other girls in that house. But you can't play the card unless some time has passed.

I: How much time do you need?

R: It can't be the same weekend for sure. Probably after a week or so you should be okay. (White)

The Greek community seems to hold White fraternity men accountable to sorority women. As the quotation above alludes, it is only for reasons of saving face that will allow them access to other women in the same sorority. Another White participant describes how cheating could result in a bad reputation if he got caught.

I: What would happen if you got caught cheating?

R: The way I could see it [cheating] affecting something is if it's a sorority girl you fuck over.

I: You can't screw with a sorority sister?

R: You could, but you could get the name, you're an asshole, you're a player, or something like that. I mean it might. It could spread around the [her sorority] house. Then you're Blacklisted. (White)

Although repercussions exist with sorority women, there are an abundance of non-Greek women with no reputational constraints. The large number and high percentage of White students give White fraternity men an ample pool of women not connected to the Greek community. When relating with non-Greek women or GDIs.[9] White fraternity men do not have to worry about "the word" getting around. Moreover, White fraternity men can disassociate from the fraternity, blend into the crowd, and interact as they please.

R: GDIs come here and it's like sensory overload. They are like in awe. If you're in awe, it's like so easy. {laughs} You can say anything to a GDI. Adam makes girls cry.

I: He wouldn't do that to a sorority girl?

R: You make a sorority girl cry she's going to tell all her friends. "I was at XYZ [fraternity] and this guy made me cry and he's such an asshole." If you say it to a GDI, she's going home and you're probably never going to see her again and she's not going to tell all of XYZ [sorority] that you said this and you're not going to have a whole sorority that hates you. (White)

Black fraternity men face a different organizational structure. These men feel that they cannot "do things like other guys."

Because there's only seven [Black Greek] organizations on campus, we have a huge impact on the Black race here. Where there's like 750 different [White] organizations, their impact is not as severe. It's not as deep, especially cause they have more people than our race. (Black)

It's kind a like being on the basketball team or being on a football team. You know what I'm saying? Its kinda like "Eta" [his fraternity name] puts you on the next level. Like you're Black Greek but you are like the . . . you are supposed to be representing the Black Greek. It's kinda hard to get that out, but when we do something we are suppose to be setting the bar for everybody else. It's like a known thing that we suppose to be setting a bar. You know what I mean? (Black)

Black fraternity men, and many Black students, cannot overcome the reputational constraints of the small Black population. Black men report being very conscious of their behavior when interacting with women. Although White fraternity men can generally be anonymous and "get off" safely, Black fraternity men perceive themselves to be constantly visible and therefore continuously held accountable for their treatment of women.

The Fraternity House

The organizational structure of "the house" facilitates sex, discourages intimacy, and is used as a resource, which affords White fraternity men control of sexual environments. For instance, these men report that women normally engage in relationships to be associated with a particular fraternity and to have access to fraternity functions and/or alcohol.

I know I'm Jack "B" ["B" represents his fraternity's name], and there's probably a Jack "C," but I don't care. I know she just wants to come to our parties and know someone there. (White)

College-aged women younger than 21 years old seem to rely on fraternities for basic ingredients of the mainstream version of the college experience—big parties and alcohol. In fact, an interview with a White participant was interrupted twice because of orders for alcohol placed by an ex-girlfriend and another woman from the dorm.

"The house" also facilitates a convenient means of engaging sexual behavior. A participant discusses the difference between living in "the house" and living off-campus.

You meet a lot more girls in the house. The frat [house] is easier, a lot easier too in that sense cause coming back from the bars, it's not necessarily like "let's go back to my place." Instead it's like, "Let's go back to the frat [house] and have a couple more drinks." It's like you don't sound like you're trying to hook up with them. "Let's go back to my house and just . . . get it on" . . . [laughs] . . . It's easier. (White)

"The house" also constrains men's gender relations. Although the fraternity houses at GU are impressive mansion-like structures, they are chaotic, nonprivate spaces that promote nonromantic activities. Most White fraternities require a "live-in" period. In the first year, members sleep in cold dorms, which are rooms composed of dozens of bunk beds.

It's like fifty of us sleep together. But you put your beds together and have all these sheets and stuff. It's like a bungalow. But sometimes you can hear other people having sex. (White)

If members earn enough "house points" for representing the fraternity well through activities like philanthropy or sports, they then typically live with three roommates in a tiny bunk-style room.

White fraternity men indicate that they could never "get away" with having romantic time. A White participant says, "There's so many people running around that house, someone's bound to see or hear something." The public nature of fraternity living arrangements is also confirmed in our field notes. While entering a fraternity room to do an interview, the interviewee and interviewer interrupted a roommate who was masturbating. The interviewer reported surprise that the masturbator seemed only slightly uncomfortable with the interruption. This suggests that interruptions like these are commonplace.

Although privacy would intuitively be linked to more sexually objectifying approaches, in the context of Greek social life, a lack of privacy facilitates these approaches by preventing intimacy. While having other people as witnesses should reduce the degree of exploitation, Greek social life is a normative institutional arrangement structured by hegemonic masculinity with sexual prowess as one of its essential ideals. Thus, men who engage in public displays of sexual objectification are applauded. A participant describes one evening in the cold dorm.

Lunch on Fridays are the best. It's like all the stories from Thursday night. It's pretty funny. It's a good time. For instance, Tom came into the cold dorm and he was with his girlfriend and they were really drunk. And he's like, "We're having sex." I was like, "You should have heard him. He punished her."[10] (White)

Romantic displays, because they are not in concert with hegemonic ideals, are sanctioned. For example, participants indicate that men who make romantic displays like saying "I love you" or opting for alone time with a woman over "hanging with the guys" will quickly be referred to as "pussy-whipped."

You don't want to be known as pussy-whipped. Guys that are pussy-whipped are wimps. They just let their girl tell them what to do. You can't count on them. They'll tell you one thing, but if the girl says something different, they're doing what she says. (White)

Another White participant characterizes how public displays of romanticism are considered to be uncool by the general Greek community.

> I don't know how romantic it gets. Am I like going to set up a table in my frat room and light a candle? It'd be cool, if I had the balls to do it. (White)

When asked directly "why don't you and your friends have romantic evenings," a White participant explains.

> Frat houses aren't the place for that [romantic behavior]. Have you looked around? The place is filthy and you have no privacy. None. I shower with five guys; people always coming in and out. You're never alone. I used to feel weird about it [sex], but now I don't. Like I used to try to be quiet, but I'm having sex less than four feet from where my roommate, whose having sex with his girlfriend. You're going to hear something. So you don't worry about it. (White)

Conversely, Black fraternity men's off-campus status offers private space for romantic relations. Most members are scattered across two- to four-person apartments and rental houses. Interviews conducted in bedrooms at Black residencies were devoid of interruptions, whereas interviews with Whites had three to four interruptions, on average. Field notes document that Black men's rooms are frequently decorated with expressions of personal achievement and style, whereas White men's rooms are often decorated with mainstream posters and sexually objectifying appeals. Consider the following field notes.

> We conducted the interview in E3's room. He had mafia posters around his room from the movies *Godfather* and *Scarface*. He also had a Dr. Seuss book and a pimp poster in his room as well. E3 is a martial arts champion and has several of his large trophies in his room and around the house. (Black)

> The room was filthy. It felt dirty like it hadn't been disinfected in a while. There were many posters and artifacts on the walls of beer or liquor companies and one wall decoration was of some Dr. Dre records. The coffee table had three Playboy magazines laid out in a

fan-like shape and the windows had two suction cup Playboy Bunnies hanging off of them. (White)

A Black participant comments on his interactions with the decoration styles of White men.

> I go through some of these [White] male's rooms and that's all they got—they got posters. I mean I just can't have no posters of naked women just *all* around my room. Like when you walk in you see nothing but nude! (Black)

In sum, normative institutional arrangements—the presence or absence of a fraternity "house" and the size of the Greek and racially based community in the larger student population—afford Blacks and Whites different opportunity structures for romantic and sexual relations. The small, highly visible and insular Black communities normally force Black fraternity men to be conscious about their positions as leaders and role models, thus affecting their experiences with and treatment of women. This consciousness often leads Black fraternity men to conveying more romantic approaches toward women. Because of the size of the White student population, White fraternity men often find relief from reputational constraints. "The house" facilitates White fraternity men's relations with women by putting them in control of sexual environments. At the same time, however, the "public" nature of fraternity houses constrains gender relations by providing only nonprivate and unromantic spaces, thereby promoting more sexually objectifying approaches.

Culture Mediating Normative Institutional Arrangements

Although we have emphasized the importance of structure in approaches toward women, some may assert that maturation or relationship status may be factors. Black fraternity men are one year older and further along in college. Because of different recruitment practices between Black and White fraternities, most Blacks do not become members until their sophomore or junior years, whereas Whites primarily "rush" during their freshman year. Hence, the number of years Blacks and Whites have been fraternity members is roughly the same. So this 1 year age difference should not be overstressed. More importantly, we compared the responses of older White fraternity men with those of their younger counterparts. We find their approaches toward women to be similar. Because Black men tend to be in more committed relationships, it could be argued that higher relationship rates result in more romantic approaches. Our data do not offer much support for this argument. White men in committed relationships still report more sexually objectifying approaches than Black men. Comparatively, Black men who are not in committed relationships report similar romantic approaches to Black men in committed relationships.

Religiosity, however, seems to play a factor in approaches toward women, albeit mediating normative institutional arrangements. A White participant explains why he is still a virgin. He says, "Well, because I'm a Christian. I'm waiting to share that with my wife. It's a faith thing." While explaining how he manages to be a virgin, he explains that "they [women] just have to understand. I don't do that [intercourse]. It's been tough because girls say 'are you serious?'" He continues to explain his frustrations with the Greek community's emphasis on sexuality.

> I'm sure you're not going to find too many twenty-two year old virgins around. It's kind of funny too, because it is almost frowned upon around here. It's almost like you're the Black sheep of the crew, because it's socially acceptable to have sex and stuff like that. You see me, nobody ever believes it. But it's almost like a stigma that you're kind of labeled with people that know. Always when people find out it's a surprise to them. (White)

Another participant explains why he does not hookup as often as his fraternity brothers.

> Not as much as some of the guys in this house. I'm not that way. It's a conscious decision. I need to really like the girl and feel comfortable. My parents have been together forever. You don't just do that kind of stuff with just anybody. (White)

Although the two negative cases highlighted above demonstrate the significance of cultural values, they also stress the importance of normative institutional arrangements for approaches toward women. These men feel uncomfortable and are frequently ridiculed and scrutinized by their fraternity brothers and women for not adhering to the hegemonic ideals reinforced by the normative institutional arrangements of Greek social life. Moreover, they are the exceptions that prove the rule.

As an added point of emphasis, focus group and ethnographic field note excerpts highlight participants own awareness of the importance of normative institutional arrangements. When Black men were asked in a focus group if things would be different if GU was not a PWI, and instead a Historically Black College or University (HBCU), they unanimously responded, "Yes." If Black men had a house, they think their behavior would be similar to their White counterparts. They perceive "the house" as a place to socialize in large groups that is free from police contact and potentially hostile strangers. If they were the "majority," they perceive being free from the incessant scrutiny of the general campus community. Black men explain how "nice it would be" to not have to represent "every Black man on the planet." An ethnographic field note is fitting here.

> While attending Etas step practice, the members began discussing their Spring Break plans. They planned to go "road tripping" to Panama City Beach. I asked why Panama City? They replied that it was cheap and a place where they could go and meet new women who do not go to GU. I asked why this was so important. They replied because the new women cannot come back to school and tell everyone else what they did and who they were with. One member replied, "We can just wild out!" (Black)

When White men were asked in a focus group to imagine life without "the house," they replied, "It would be like being a GDI." They further explained that "the house" is "like a face" which enables them to "meet girls." White men also mirror issues of safety indicated by Black men. For instance, they are concerned that if they lose "the house," they would have to go to bars, small house-parties, or third-party vendors and would then have to worry about drinking and driving, public intoxication, and police breaking up parties. In other words, White fraternity men perceive that losing "the house" would make them "just like everybody else."

DISCUSSION AND CONCLUSION

We have explored whether there are racial differences in men's approaches toward women. By characterizing elite Black and White fraternity men's understandings of their sexual and romantic relationships, this research fills three critical empirical gaps. First, we explore the perspectives and insights of a group that is often implicated in mainstream discourses in romantic and sexual relations on college campuses—high-status fraternity men. Second, we explicitly compare Black and White men. Third, we examine how the normative institutional arrangements of institutions shape the performances of masculinities.

Our findings suggest that both Black and White fraternity men sexually objectify women; however, Black fraternity men exhibit more romantic approaches in their perceptions of their relations with women. Black college social scenes, particularly Black Greek scenes, are often more gender egalitarian. Although the small size of the Black community and the organizational structure of the Black Greek system generally force Black men to be more conscious about their treatment of women, the organizational structure of the White Greek community facilitates sexually objectifying approaches toward women. White fraternity men also have a larger pool of non-Greek women to engage; therefore, they are held less accountable for their relations with women because of a hyper level of anonymity. Although the presence of a fraternity house enables White fraternity men to be in control of sexual environments, it also constrains gender relations by offering nonprivate and nonintimate spaces.

Unlike the lower class men in studies by Majors and Billson (1992) and Anderson (1999), Black men in this study are more affiliated with DuBois (1903, 1939) Talented Tenth and double-consciousness concepts.[11] For Black men who identify as or with this elite group, the racialization of high-status institutions holds them more accountable for their treatment of women and constrains their approaches. As a result, some may assert these Black men's attitudes and values about the treatment of women are different from other Black men and their White fraternity male counterparts. Although there is support for this perspective, particularly because Black fraternity men stress more holistic qualities of women and tend to perceive more aspects of romanticism to be masculine, we argue the influential effects normative institutional arrangements have on shaping racial and status differences in men's gender scripts surfaces in the behavior or at the performance level of these men. To save face and status, Black fraternity men have to be more concerned about how their interactions with women are perceived by others. This leads to a unique set of reputational boundaries and constraints for Black fraternity men not exhibited by White fraternity men.

Our emphasis on normative institutional arrangements does not deny the presence of other factors that may be implicated in racial differences. For example, Black men in this study report being more religious than White men. Therefore, we would still expect for them to have cultural values that buffer sexually objectifying approaches. Less religious Black men, however, still exhibit more romantic approaches than the White men in the sample. Thus, we contend these patterns are an artifact of the racialized level of accountability and visibility within the normative institutional arrangements of campus social life. Our research confirms that when normative institutional arrangements are in concert with mainstream hegemonic ideals, sexual objectifications are more likely to occur.

Our findings offer an interesting parallel to Armstrong, Hamilton, and Sweeney's (2006) ethnographic examination of women who reside on a women's floor in a "party dorm." They find that female college students, especially those in their first year and under the legal drinking age, rely on fraternities for parties and alcohol, and consequently, relinquish power and control of social and sexual environments to these men. They conclude that individual, organizational, and institutional practices (e.g., prohibiting alcohol in dormitories) contribute to higher levels of sexual assault.

Our research further argues that structural settings shape how actors perceive others (e.g., as sexual, romantic, and/or holistic others) and reflect the racial and gender dynamics of college campuses including racial segregation and skewed gender ratios. Along these lines, hegemonic masculinity is about much more than gender beliefs and masculine performances. Hegemonic masculinity is also about normative accountability structures and the preservation of normative personal, social, and institutional resources. Privileges across gender, race, and status divides afford White fraternity men less accountability when performing a hegemonic masculine self during interactions with women. As shown here, under certain institutional arrangements, racial disadvantage, as with Black fraternity men, can decrease gender inequality and reduce a traditional hegemonic style of engagement toward women. However, race and/or class advantage, as with White fraternity men, and disadvantage, as with the Black men in Majors and Billson's (1992) and Anderson's (1999) studies, can increase gender inequality and propel a hegemonic presentation of self such as the "cool pose."

Now that we have a greater understanding of the importance of not just being a racial/ethnic minority but also being a numerical minority or majority and how these normative institutional arrangements structure the gender relations of high-status men on campus, future research should investigate how common these patterns are among individuals across a range of institutional settings. Specifically, our research has implications for masculinities and its relationships with White men at small colleges, or where they are the minority group, and men of other racial/ethnic groups in institutional settings where they are the majority group. Although these propositions cannot be sufficiently answered in this study, it does provide a blueprint for how scholars should approach research in this area.

Particularly useful in extrapolating the findings presented here is DeLamater's (1987) recreational-centered approach,[12] whereby approaches toward others are facilitated by contextual and structural factors. Applied here, the recreational approach assumes that actors can exhibit both romantic and sexually objectifying approaches based on the dynamics of the structural setting. Men and women do not fit into monolithic groups. Although the literature has traditionally established a gender dichotomy whereby men exhibit sexual prowess and women cling to romantic ideals, we find men exhibit both sexually objectifying and romantic approaches. By integrating the recreational approach into the discourse on romantic and sexual relations, scholars will be better equipped to extrapolate the interconnections between masculinities, sexualities, gender inequality, and race.

Taken together, our findings suggest that efforts to increase gender equality on college campuses should center on increasing the perceived accountability of men by offering social spaces that enable communicative and intimate gender relations. For example, Boswell and Spade (1996) find that fraternity houses and commercial bars that are low-risk for sexual assault encourage men and women to get acquainted. Although the data implicate the presence of a fraternity house in unequal gender relations, they do not necessarily suggest that the elimination of fraternity houses is required to accomplish gender equality. Many sorority houses do not seem to have these problems because they have strict guidelines regarding gender ratios, parties, alcohol, and overnight guests (Armstrong, Hamilton, and Sweeney 2006). Thus, the normative institutional arrangements that afford men—in this context White fraternity men—a lack of accountability to exploit hegemonic prowess must be restructured to alter the level of accountability that encourages gender inequality. Our study concludes with an optimistic suggestion: by promoting normative institutional arrangements that facilitate accountability structures and romantic and equitable approaches, improvements toward gender equality are possible.

NOTES

1. Allport (1954) uses "sociocultural" to refer to the intersection between class (status) and caste (race).

2. Previous research has suggested that Black men's performances of masculinities are constrained by their marginalized status within the racial paradigm (Connell 1987, 1995; Kimmel 1987, 2006; Kimmel and Messner 1989; Hearn 2004). We advance this thesis by focusing on the intersections of race and status within a specific institutional structure (e.g., fraternity house).

3. Edwards (2008) states, "White structural advantage is Whites' disproportionate control or influence over nearly every social institution in this country. This affords Whites the ability to structure social life so that it privileges them. White normativity is the normalization of Whites' cultural practices . . . their dominant social location over other racial groups as accepted as just how things are. White normativity also privileges Whites because they, unlike nonwhites, do not need to justify their way of being."

4. The statistics concerning GU come from Student Activities and Greek Affairs.

5. On-campus status means the fraternity has a fraternity house on university property, whereas off-campus status means the fraternity does not.

6. Since the founding of Phi Beta Kappa (now an honor society), Greek organizations have been an integral part of colleges and universities for more than 200 years (Brown, Parks, and Phillips 2005). Fraternities are national organizations composed of college students that are men, usually designated by Greek letters. Most fraternities were founded on principles such as scholarship, community service, sound learning, and leadership and are distinguished by highly symbolic and secretive rituals. Greek fraternities and sororities are normally high-status organizations on collegiate campuses. Members of Greek fraternities and sororities are often members of student government and honor societies, are frequently some of the most recognizable student leaders on campus, and have higher grades and graduation rates than other students (Kimbrough and Hutcheson 1998).

7. Some of the most influential and celebrated African American leaders—Martin Luther King, W. E. B. DuBois, Thurgood Marshall, and Maya Angelou—became members or nationally recognized African American fraternities and sororities. Having such a distinguished lineage of past members often makes members of African American fraternities and sororities feel that they must uphold an esteemed legacy (Kimbrough and Hutcheson 1998).

8. Throughout the duration of the project, women were categorized as many sexually objectifying and derogatory terms by Black and White fraternity men including "bitch," "hoe" (whore), "skank," "freak," and "tramp." Most of these names are given to fraternity groupies or women who are perceived to be sexually promiscuous.

9. "GDI" is an acronym for "God Damn Independent," which is a derogatory term used to describe non-Greeks.

10. In this context, the statement "punish her" implies that "Tom" was making his girlfriend moan and that the bed was rocking because of sexual movements.

11. The comparison between this study and the ones by Majors and Billson (1992) and Anderson (1999) should not be overstated. Although the men in all three studies are Black men, they are embedded within different normative institutional arrangements. As asserted in the literature review, minority men exhibit intragroup differences in the performances of masculinities and should be evaluated outside the tradition monolithic box they are often placed within.

12. Although DeLamater (1987) at times interchanges the sexual objectifying approach (which he calls body-centered) with the recreational-centered approach, we choose to distinguish these two approaches. As we have discussed throughout the article, normative institutional arrangements propel more or less sexual objectification and romanticism. The recreational approach allows the researcher the ability to assess complex decisions actors make based on structural settings.

REFERENCES

Allen, Walter R. 1992. The color of success: African-American college student outcomes at predominantly white and historically black public colleges and universities. *Harvard Educational Review* 62:26–44.

Allport, Gordon W. 1954. *The Nature of Prejudice*. Reading, MA: Addison-Wesley.

Anderson, Elijah. 1999. *Code of the street: Decency, violence, and the moral life of the inner city*. New York, NY: W. W. Norton & Company.

Armstrong, Elizabeth, Laura Hamilton, and Brian Sweeney. 2006. Sexual assault on campus: A multilevel explanation of party rape. *Social Problems* 53:483–99.

Battle, Juan, and Earl Wright II. 2002. W.E.B. DuBois's talented tenth: A quantitative assessment. *Journal of Black Studies* 32:654–72.

Boswell, A. A., and J. Z. Spade. 1996. Fraternities and collegiate rape culture: Why are some fraternities more dangerous places for women? *Gender & Society* 10:133–47.

Brandes, Holger. 2007. Hegemonic Masculinities in East and West Germany (German Democratic Republic and Federal Republic of Germany). *Men and Masculinities* 10: 178–196.

Britton, Dana. M. 2003. *At work in the iron cage: The prison as gendered organization*. New York, NY: New York University Press.

Brown, T. L, G. L. Parks, and C. M. Phillips, eds. 2005. *African American fraternities and sororities: The history and the vision*. Lexington, KY: University Press of Kentucky.

Clark, R. D., and E. Hatfield. 1989. Gender differences in receptivity to sexual offers. *Journal of Psychology and Human Sexuality* 2:39–55.

Collins, Patricia Hill. 2004. *Black sexual politics: African Americans, gender, and the new racism*. New York, NY: Routledge.

Connell, R. W. 1987. *Gender and power*. Stanford, CA: Stanford University Press.

———. 1995. *Masculinities*. Second Ed. Berkeley: University of California Press.

DeLamaler, J. 1987. Gender differences in sexual scenarios. In *Females, males, and sexuality: Theories and research*, ed. K. Kelley. Albany, NY: SUNY Press.

Denzin, Norman K., and Yvonna S. Lincoln, eds. 1994. *Handbook of qualitative research*. Thousand Oaks, CA: Sage.

DuBois, W. E. B. 1903. *The souls of black folk*. New York, NY: Dover.

———. 1939. *Black folk, then and now: An essay in the history and sociology of the Negro race.* New York: Henry Holt.

Edwards, Korie. 2008. Bringing race to the center: The importance of race in racially diverse religious organizations. *Journal for the Scientific Study of Religion* 47:5–9.

Emerson, Richard, Rachel Fretz, and Linda Shaw. 1995. *Writing ethnographic fieldnotes.* Chicago, IL: University of Chicago Press.

Epstein, Cynthia Fuchs. 2007. Women's subordination in global context. *American Sociological Review* 72:1–2.

Flood, Michael. 2008. How bonds between men shape their sexual relations with women. *Men and Masculinities* 10:339–59.

Gerson, Judith M., and Kathy Peiss. 1985. Boundaries, negotiation, consciousness: Reconceptualizing gender relations. *Social Problems* 32:317–31.

Harper, Shaun R., Byars, L. F., and Jelke, T. B. 2005. How Black Greek-Letter Organization Membership Affects Adjustment and Undergraduate Outcomes. In *African American fraternities and sororities: The legacy and the vision,* ed. T. L. Brown, G. S. Parks, and C. M. Phillips, 393–416. Lexington, KY: University Press of Kentucky.

Hatfield, E., S. Sprecher, J. T. Pillemer, D. Greenberger, and P. Wexler. 1998. Gender differences in what is desired in the sexual relationship. *Journal of Psychology and Human Sexuality* 1:39–52.

Hays, Sharon. 1994. Structure and agency and the sticky problem of culture. *Sociological Theory* 12:57–72.

Hearn, Jeff. 2004. From hegemonic masculinity to the hegemony of men. *Feminist Theory* 5:49–72.

Hoberman, John. 1997. *Darwin's athletes.* New York, NY: Houghton.

Hollander, Jocelyn A. 2004. The social contexts of focus groups. *Journal of Contemporary Ethnography* 33:605–37.

Hunter, Andrea G., and James E. Davis. 1992. Constructing gender: An exploration of Afro-American men's conceptualization of manhood. *Gender and Society* 6:464–79.

Joyner, Kara, and Grace Kao. 2005. Interracial relationships and the transition to adulthood. *American Sociological Review* 70:563–81.

Kanter, Rosenbath Moss. 1977. Some effects of proportions of group life: Skewed sex ratios and responses to token women. *American Journal of Sociology* 5:965–90.

Kimbrough, Walter M., and Philo A. Hutcheson. 1998. The impact of membership in black Greek-letter organizations on black students' involvement in collegiate activities and their development of leadership skills. *The Journal of Negro Education* 67:96–105.

Kimmel, Michael S., ed. 1987. *Changing men: New directions in research on men and masculinity.* Newbury Park, CA. Sage.

———. 2006. Racism as adolescent male rite of passage: Ex-nazis in Scandinavia. *Journal of Contemporary Ethnography* 36:202–18.

Kimmel Michael S., and Michael A. Messner, eds. 1989. *Men's lives.* New York, NY: Macmillan.

Konrad, A. M., and C. Harris. 2002. Desirability of the Bern sex-role inventory items for women and men: A comparison between African-Americans and European Americans. *Sex Roles* 47:259–72.

Majors, Richard G., and Janet Billson. 1992. *Cool pose: The dilemmas of black manhood in America.* New York, NY: Lexington Books.

Martin, P. Yancey, and R. A. Hummer. 1989. Fraternities and rape on campus. *Gender and Society* 3:457–73.

Massey, Douglas S., Camille Z. Charles, Garvey F. Lundy, and Mary L. Fischer. 2003. *The source of the river; The social origins of freshman at America's selective colleges and universities.* Princeton, NJ: Princeton University Press.

Millham, J., and L. E. Smith. 1986. Sex Role Differential among Black and White Americans: A Comparative Study. *The Journal of Black Psychology* 7:77–50.

Morgan, David L. 1997. *Focus groups and qualitative research.* Thousand Oaks, CA: Sage.

Peralta, Robert L. 2007. College Alcohol Use and the Embodiment of Hegemonic Masculinity among European American Men. *Sex Roles* 56:741–56.

Ragin, Charles C. 1994. Constructing social research: The unity and diversity of method. Thousand Oaks, CA: Sage.

Reskin, Barbara F. 2003. Including mechanisms in our models of ascriptive inequality: 2002 presidential address. *American Sociological Review* 68:1–21.

Rizzo, Thomas A., William A. Corsaro, and John E. Bates. 1992. Ethnographic methods and interpretive analysis: Expanding the methodological options of psychologists. *Developmental Review* 12:101–23.

Staples, R. 1982. *Black masculinity: The black males' role in American society.* San Francisco, CA: Black Scholar.

16

Because She Looks like a Child

KEVIN BALES

When Siri wakes it is about noon.[1] In the instant of waking she knows exactly who and what she has become. As she explained to me, the soreness in her genitals reminds her of the fifteen men she had sex with the night before. Siri is fifteen years old. Sold by her parents a year ago, she finds that her resistance and her desire to escape the brothel are breaking down and acceptance and resignation are taking their place.

In the provincial city of Ubon Ratchathani, in northeastern Thailand, Siri works and lives in a brothel. About ten brothels and bars, dilapidated and dusty buildings, line the side street just around the corner from a new Western-style shopping mall. Food and noodle vendors are scattered between the brothels. The woman behind the noodle stall outside the brothel where Siri works is also a spy, warder, watchdog, procurer, and dinner lady to Siri and the other twenty-four girls and women in the brothel.

The brothel is surrounded by a wall, with iron gates that meet the street. Within the wall is a dusty yard, a concrete picnic table, and the ubiquitous spirit house, a small shrine that stands outside all Thai buildings. A low door leads into a windowless concrete room that is thick with the smell of cigarettes, stale beer, vomit, and sweat. This is the "selection" room (*hong du*). On one side of the room are stained and collapsing tables and booths; on the other side is a narrow elevated platform with a bench that runs the length of the room. Spotlights pick out this bench, and at night the girls and women sit here under the glare while the men at the tables drink and choose the one they want.

Passing through another door, at the far end of the bench, the man follows the girl past a window, where a bookkeeper takes his money and records which girl he has selected. From there he is led to the girl's room. Behind its concrete front room, the brothel degenerates even further, into a haphazard shanty warren of tiny cubicles where the girls live and work. A makeshift ladder leads up to what may have once been a barn. The upper level is now lined with doors about five feet apart, which open into rooms of about five by seven feet that hold a bed and little else.

Scraps of wood and cardboard separate one room from the next, and Siri has plastered her walls with pictures of teenage pop stars cut from magazines. Over her bed, as in most rooms, there also hangs a framed portrait of the king of Thailand; a single bare lightbulb dangles from the ceiling. Next to the bed a large tin can holds water; there is a hook nearby for rags and towels. At the foot of the bed, next to the door, some clothes are folded on a ledge. The walls are very thin, and everything can be heard from the surrounding rooms;

Kevin Bales, "Because She Looks like a Child," from Barbara Ehrenreich & Arlie Russell Hochschild, eds., *Global Women: Nannies, Maids, and Sex Workers in the New Economy.* Copyright © 2003 Henry Holt and Company.

a shout from the bookkeeper echoes through all of them, whether their doors are open or closed.

After rising at midday, Siri washes herself in cold water from the single concrete trough that serves the brothel's twenty-five women. Then, dressed in a T-shirt and skirt, she goes to the noodle stand for the hot soup that is a Thai breakfast. Through the afternoon, if she does not have any clients, she chats with the other girls and women as they drink beer and play cards or make decorative handicrafts together. If the pimp is away the girls will joke around, but if not they must be constantly deferential and aware of his presence, for he can harm them or use them as he pleases. Few men visit in the afternoon, but those who do tend to have more money and can buy a girl for several hours if they like. Some will even make appointments a few days in advance.

At about five, Siri and the other girls are told to dress, put on their makeup, and prepare for the night's work. By seven the men will be coming in, purchasing drinks, and choosing girls; Siri will be chosen by the first of the ten to eighteen men who will buy her that night. Many men choose Siri because she looks much younger than her fifteen years. Slight and round faced, dressed to accentuate her youth, she could pass for eleven or twelve. Because she looks like a child, she can be sold as a "new" girl at a higher price, about $15, which is more than twice that charged for the other girls.

Siri is very frightened that she will get AIDS. Long before she understood prostitution she knew about HIV, as many girls from her village returned home to die from AIDS after being sold into the brothels. Every day she prays to Buddha, trying to earn the merit that will preserve her from the disease. She also tries to insist that her clients use condoms, and in most cases she is successful, because the pimp backs her up. But when policemen use her, or the pimp himself, they will do as they please; if she tries to insist, she will be beaten and raped. She also fears pregnancy, but like the other girls she receives injections of the contraceptive drug Depo-Provera. Once a month she has an HIV test. So far it has been negative. She knows that if she tests positive she will be thrown out to starve.

Though she is only fifteen, Siri is now resigned to being a prostitute. The work is not what she had thought it would be. Her first client hurt her, and at the first opportunity she ran away. She was quickly caught, dragged back, beaten, and raped. That night she was forced to take on a chain of clients until the early morning. The beatings and the work continued night after night, until her will was broken. Now she is sure that she is a very bad person to have deserved what has happened to her. When I comment on how pretty she looks in a photograph, how like a pop star, she replies, "I'm no star; I'm just a whore, that's all." She copes as best she can. She takes a dark pride in her higher price and the large number of men who choose her. It is the adjustment of the concentration camp, an effort to make sense of horror.

In Thailand prostitution is illegal, yet girls like Siri are sold into sex slavery by the thousands. The brothels that hold these girls are but a small part of a much wider sex industry. How can this wholesale trade in girls continue? What keeps it working? The answer is more complicated than we might think. Thailand's economic boom and its social acceptance of prostitution contribute to the pressures that enslave girls like Siri. . . .

ONE GIRL EQUALS ONE TELEVISION

The small number of children sold into slavery in the past has become a flood today. This increase reflects the enormous changes in Thailand over the past fifty years as the country has gone through the great transformation of industrialization—the same process that tore Europe apart over a century ago. If we are to understand slavery in Thailand, we must understand these changes as well, for like so many other parts of the world, Thailand has always had slavery, but never before on this scale.

The economic boom of 1977 to 1997 had a dramatic impact on the northern villages. While the center of the country, around Bangkok, rapidly industrialized, the north was left behind. Prices of food, land, and tools all increased as the economy grew, but the returns for rice and other agriculture were stagnant, held down by government policies guaranteeing cheap food for factory workers in Bangkok. Yet visible everywhere in the north is a flood of consumer goods—refrigerators, televisions, cars and trucks, rice cookers, air conditioners—all of which are extremely tempting. Demand for these goods is high as families try to join the ranks of the prosperous. As it happens, the cost of participating in this consumer boom can be met from an old source that has become much more profitable: the sale of children.

In the past, daughters were sold in response to serious family financial crises. Under threat of losing its mortgaged rice fields and facing destitution, a family might sell a daughter to redeem its debt, but for the most part daughters were worth about as much at home as workers as they would realize when sold. Modernization and economic growth have changed all that. Now parents feel a great pressure to buy consumer goods that were unknown even twenty years ago; the sale of a daughter might easily finance a new television set. A recent survey in the northern provinces found that of the families who sold their daughters, two-thirds could afford not to do so but "instead preferred to buy color televisions and video equipment."[2] And from the perspective of parents who are willing to sell their children, there has never been a better market.

The brothels' demand for prostitutes is rapidly increasing. The same economic boom that feeds consumer demand in the northern villages lines the pockets of laborers and workers in the central plain. Poor economic migrants from the rice fields now work on building sites or in new factories, earning many times what they did on the land. Possibly for the first time in their lives, these laborers can do what more well-off Thai men have always done: go to a brothel. The purchasing power of this increasing number of brothel users strengthens the call for northern girls and supports a growing business in their procurement and trafficking.

Siri's story was typical. A broker, a woman herself from a northern village, approached the families in Siri's village with assurances of well-paid work for their daughters. Siri's parents probably understood that the work would be as a prostitute, since they knew that other girls from their village had gone south to brothels. After some negotiation they were paid 50,000 baht (US$2,000) for Siri, a very significant sum for this family of rice farmers.[3] This exchange began the process of debt bondage that is used to enslave the girls. The contractual arrangement between the broker and the parents requires that this money be paid by the daughter's labor before she is free to leave or is allowed to send money home. Sometimes the money is treated as a loan to the parents, the girls being both the collateral and the means of repayment. In such cases the exorbitant interest charged on the loan means there is little chance that a girl's sexual slavery will ever repay the debt.

Siri's debt of 50,000 baht rapidly escalated. Taken south by the broker, Siri was sold for 100,000 baht to the brothel where she now works. After her rape and beating Siri was informed that the debt she must repay to the brothel equaled 200,000 baht. In addition, Siri learned of the other payments she would be required to make, including rent for her room, at 30,000 baht per month, as well as charges for food and drink, fees for medicine, and fines if she did not work hard enough or displeased a customer.

The total debt is virtually impossible to repay, even at Siri's higher rate of 400 baht. About 100 baht from each client is supposed to be credited to Siri to reduce her debt and pay her rent and other expenses; 200 goes to the pimp and the remaining 100 to the brothel. By this reckoning, Siri must have sex with three hundred men a month just to pay her rent, and what is left over after other expenses barely reduces her original debt. For girls who can charge only 100 to 200 baht per client, the debt grows even faster. This debt bondage keeps the girls under complete control as long as the brothel owner and the pimp believe they are worth having. Violence reinforces the control, and any resistance earns a beating as well as an increase in the debt. Over time, if the girl becomes a good and cooperative prostitute, the pimp may tell her she has paid off the debt and allow her to send small sums home. This "paying off" of the debt usually has nothing to do with an actual accounting of earnings but is declared at the discretion of the pimp, as a means to extend the brothel's profits by making the girl more pliable. Together with rare visits home, money sent back to the family operates to keep her at her job.

Most girls are purchased from their parents, as Siri was, but for others the enslavement is much more direct. Throughout Thailand agents travel to villages, offering work in factories or as domestics. Sometimes they bribe local officials to vouch for them, or they befriend the monks at the local temple to gain introductions. Lured by the promise of good jobs and the money that the daughters will send back to the village, the deceived families dispatch their girls with the agent, often paying for the privilege. Once they arrive in a city, the girls are sold to a brothel, where they are raped, beaten, and locked in. Still other girls are simply kidnapped. This is especially true of women and children who have come to visit relatives in Thailand from Burma or Laos. At bus and train stations, gangs watch for women and children who can be snatched or drugged for shipment to brothels.

Direct enslavement by trickery or kidnapping is not really in the economic interest of the brothel owners. The steadily growing market for prostitutes, the loss of girls to HIV infection, and the especially strong demand for younger and younger girls make it necessary for brokers and brothel owners to cultivate village families so that they can buy more daughters as they come of age. In Siri's case this means letting her maintain ties with her family and ensuring that after a year or so she send a monthly postal order for 10,000 baht to her parents. The monthly payment is a good investment, since it encourages Siri's parents to place their other daughters in the brothel as well. Moreover, the young girls themselves become willing to go when their older sisters and relatives returning for holidays bring stories of the rich life to be lived in the cities of the central plain. Village girls lead a sheltered life, and the appearance of women only a little older than themselves with money and nice clothes is tremendously appealing. They admire the results of this thing called prostitution with only the vaguest notion of what it is. Recent research found that young girls knew that their sisters and neighbors had become prostitutes, but when asked what it means to be a prostitute their most common answer was "wearing Western clothes in a restaurant."[4] Drawn by this glamorous life, they put up little opposition to being sent away with the brokers to swell an already booming sex industry.

By my own conservative estimate there are perhaps thirty-five thousand girls like Siri enslaved in Thailand. Remarkably, this is only a small proportion of the country's prostitutes. In the mid-1990s the government stated that there were 81,384 prostitutes in Thailand—but that official number is calculated from the number of registered (though still illegal) brothels, massage parlors, and sex establishments. One Thai researcher estimated the total number of prostitutes in 1997 to be around 200,000.[5] Every brothel, bar, and massage parlor we visited in Thailand was unregistered, and no one working with prostitutes believes the government figures. At the other end of the spectrum are the estimates put forward by activist organizations such as the Center for the Protection of Children's Rights. These groups assert that there are more than 2 million prostitutes. I suspect that this number is too high in a national population of 60 million. My own reckoning, based on information gathered by AIDS workers in different cities, is that there are between half a million and 1 million prostitutes.

Of this number, only about one in twenty is enslaved. Most become prostitutes voluntarily, though some start out in debt bondage. Sex is sold everywhere in Thailand: barbershops, massage parlors, coffee shops and cafés, bars and restaurants, nightclubs and karaoke bars, brothels, hotels, and even temples traffic in sex. Prostitutes range from the high-earning "professional" women who work with some autonomy, through the women working by choice as call girls or in massage parlors, to the enslaved rural girls like Siri. Many women work semi-independently in bars, restaurants, and nightclubs—paying a fee to the owner, working when they choose, and having the power to decide whom to take as a customer. Most bars and clubs cannot use an enslaved prostitute like Siri, as the women are often sent out on call and their clients expect a certain amount of cooperation and friendliness. Enslaved girls serve the lowest end of the market: the laborers, students, and workers who can afford only the 100 baht per half hour. It is low-cost sex in volume, and the demand is always there. For a Thai man, buying a woman is much like buying a round of drinks. But the reasons why such large numbers of Thai men use prostitutes are much more complicated and grow out of their culture, their history, and a rapidly changing economy.

"I DON'T WANT TO WASTE IT, SO I TAKE HER"

Until it was officially disbanded in 1910, the king of Thailand maintained a harem of hundreds of concubines, a few of whom might be elevated to the rank of "royal mother" or "minor wife." This form of polygamy was closely imitated by status-hungry nobles and emerging rich merchants of the nineteenth century. Virtually all men of any substance kept at least a mistress or a minor wife. For those with fewer resources, prostitution was a perfectly acceptable option, as renting took the place of out-and-out ownership.

Even today everyone in Thailand knows his or her place within a very elaborate and precise status system. Mistresses and minor wives continue to enhance any man's social standing, but the consumption of commercial sex has increased dramatically.[6] If an economic boom is a tide that raises all boats, then vast numbers of Thai men have now been raised to a financial position from which they can regularly buy sex. Nothing like the economic growth in Thailand was ever experienced in the West, but a few facts show its scale: in a country the size of Britain, one-tenth of the workforce moved from the land to industry in just the three years from 1993 to 1995; the number of factory workers doubled from less than 2 million to more than 4 million in the eight years from 1988 to 1995; and urban wages doubled from 1986 to 1996. Thailand is now the world's largest importer of motorcycles and the second-largest importer of pickup tricks, after the United States. Until the economic downturn of late 1997, money flooded Thailand, transforming poor rice farmers into wage laborers and fueling consumer demand.

With this newfound wealth, Thai men go to brothels in increasing numbers. Several recent studies show that between 80 and 87 percent of Thai men have had sex with a prostitute. Most report that their first sexual experience was with a prostitute. Somewhere between 10 and 40 percent of married men have paid for commercial sex within the past twelve months, as have up to 50 percent of single men. Though it is difficult to measure, these reports suggest something like 3 to 5 million regular customers for commercial sex. But it would be wrong to imagine millions of Thai men sneaking furtively on their own along dark streets lined with brothels; commercial sex is a social event, part of a good night out with friends. Ninety-five percent of men going to a brothel do so with their friends, usually at the end of a night spent drinking. Groups go out for recreation and entertainment, and especially to get

drunk together. That is a strictly male pursuit, as Thai women usually abstain from alcohol. All-male groups out for a night on the town are considered normal in any Thai city, and whole neighborhoods are devoted to serving them. One man interviewed in a recent study explained, "When we arrive at the brothel, my friends take one and pay for me to take another. It costs them money; I don't want to waste it, so I take her."[7] Having one's prostitute paid for also brings an informal obligation to repay in kind at a later date. Most Thais, men and women, feel that commercial sex is an acceptable part of an ordinary outing for single men, and about two-thirds of men and one-third of women feel the same about married men.[8] . . .

MILLIONAIRE TIGERS AND BILLIONAIRE GEESE

Who are these modern slaveholders? The answer is anyone and everyone—anyone, that is, with a little capital to invest. The people who *appear* to own the enslaved prostitutes—the pimps, madams, and brothel keepers—are usually just employees. As hired muscle, pimps and their helpers provide the brutality that controls women and makes possible their commercial exploitation. Although they are just employees, the pimps do rather well for themselves. Often living in the brothel, they receive a salary and add to that income by a number of scams; for example, food and drinks are sold to customers at inflated prices, and the pimps pocket the difference. Much more lucrative is their control of the price of sex. While each woman has a basic price, the pimps size up each customer and pitch the fee accordingly. In this way a client may pay two or three times more than the normal rate, and all of the surplus goes to the pimp. In league with the bookkeeper, the pimp systematically cheats the prostitutes of the little that is supposed to be credited against their debt. If they manage the sex slaves well and play all of the angles, pimps can easily make ten times their basic wage—a great income for an ex-peasant whose main skills are violence and intimidation, but nothing compared to the riches to be made by the brokers and the real slaveholders.

The brokers and agents who buy girls in the villages and sell them to brothels are only short-term slaveholders. Their business is part recruiting agency, part shipping company, part public relations, and part kidnapping gang. They aim to buy low and sell high while maintaining a good flow of girls from the villages. Brokers are equally likely to be men or women, and they usually come from the regions in which they recruit. Some are local people dealing in girls in addition to their jobs as police officers, government bureaucrats, or even schoolteachers. Positions of public trust are excellent starting points for buying young girls. In spite of the character of their work, they are well respected. Seen as job providers and sources of large cash payments to parents, they are well known in their communities. Many of the women brokers were once sold themselves; some spent years as prostitutes and now, in their middle age, make their living by supplying girls to the brothels. These women are walking advertisements for sexual slavery. Their lifestyle and income, their Western clothes and glamorous, sophisticated ways promise a rosy economic future for the girls they buy. That they have physically survived their years in the brothel may be the exception—many more young women come back to the village to die of AIDS—but the parents tend to be optimistic.

Whether these dealers are local people or traveling agents, they combine the business of procuring with other economic pursuits. A returned prostitute may live with her family, look after her parents, own a rice field or two, and buy and sell girls on the side. Like the pimps, they are in a good business, doubling their money on each girl within two or three weeks; but also like the pimps, their profits are small compared to those of the long-term slaveholders.

The real slaveholders tend to be middle-aged businessmen. They fit seamlessly into the community, and they suffer no social discrimination for what they do. If anything, they are admired as successful, diversified capitalists. Brothel ownership is normally only one of many business interests for the slaveholder. To be sure, a brothel owner may have some ties to organized crime, but in Thailand organized crime includes the police and much of the government. Indeed, the work of the modern slaveholder is best seen not as aberrant criminality but as a perfect example of disinterested capitalism. Owning the brothel that holds young girls in bondage is simply a business matter. The investors

would say that they are creating jobs and wealth. There is no hypocrisy in their actions, for they obey an important social norm: earning a lot of money is good enough reason for anything.

The slaveholder may in fact be a partnership, company, or corporation. In the 1980s, Japanese investment poured into Thailand, in an enormous migration of capital that was called "Flying Geese."[9] The strong yen led to buying and building across the country, and while electronics firms built television factories, other investors found that there was much, much more to be made in the sex industry. Following the Japanese came investment from the so-called Four Tigers (South Korea, Hong Kong, Taiwan, and Singapore), which also found marvelous opportunities in commercial sex. (All five of these countries further proved to be strong import markets for enslaved Thai girls, as discussed below.) The Geese and the Tigers had the resources to buy the local criminals, police, administrators, and property needed to set up commercial sex businesses. Indigenous Thais also invested in brothels as the sex industry boomed; with less capital, they were more likely to open poorer, working-class outlets.

Whether they are individual Thais, partnerships, or foreign investors, the slaveholders share many characteristics. There is little or no racial or ethnic difference between them and the slaves they own (with the exception of the Japanese investors). They feel no need to rationalize their slaveholding on racial grounds. Nor are they linked in any sort of hereditary ownership of slaves or of the children of their slaves. They are not really interested in their slaves at all, just in the bottom line on their investment.

To understand the business of slavery today we have to know something about the economy in which it operates. Thailand's economic boom included a sharp increase in sex tourism tacitly backed by the government. International tourist arrivals jumped from 2 million in 1981 to 4 million in 1988 to over 7 million in 1996.[10] Two-thirds of tourists were unaccompanied men; in other words, nearly 5 million unaccompanied men visited Thailand in 1996. A significant proportion of these were sex tourists.

The recent downturn in both tourism and the economy may have slowed, but not dramatically altered, sex tourism. In 1997 the annual illegal income generated by sex workers in Thailand was roughly $10 billion, which is more than drug trafficking is estimated to generate.[11] According to ECPAT, an organization working against child prostitution, the economic crisis in Southeast Asia may have increased the exploitation of young people in sex tourism:

> According to Professor Lae Dilokvidhayarat from Chulalongkorn University, there has been a 10 percent decrease in the school enrollment at primary school level in Thailand since 1996. Due to increased unemployment, children cannot find work in the formal sector, but instead are forced to "disappear" into the informal sector. This makes them especially vulnerable to sexual exploitation. Also, a great number of children are known to travel to tourist areas and to big cities hoping to find work.
>
> We cannot overlook the impact of the economic crisis on sex tourism, either. Even though travelling costs to Asian countries are approximately the same as before mid 1997, when the crisis began, the rates for sexual services in many places are lower due to increased competition in the business. Furthermore, since there are more children trying to earn money, there may also be more so called situational child sex tourists, i.e. those who do not necessarily prefer children as sexual partners, but who may well choose a child if the situation occurs and the price is low.[12]

In spite of the economic boom, the average Thai's income is very low by Western standards. Within an industrializing country, millions still live in rural poverty. If a rural family owns its house and has a rice field, it might survive on as little as 500 baht ($20) per month. Such absolute poverty means a diet of rice supplemented with insects (crickets, grubs, and maggots are widely eaten), wild plants, and what fish the family can catch. If a family's standard of living drops below this level, which can be sustained only in the countryside, it faces hunger and the loss of its house or land. For most Thais, an income of 2,500 to 4,000 baht per month ($100 to $180) is normal. Government figures from December 1996 put two-thirds of the population at this level. There is no system of welfare or health care, and pinched budgets allow no space for saving. In these families, the 20,000 to 50,000 baht ($800 to $2,000) brought by selling a daughter provides a year's income. Such a vast sum is a powerful

inducement that often blinds parents to the realities of sexual slavery. . . .

BURMESE PROSTITUTES

The same economic boom that has increased the demand for prostitutes may, in time, bring an end to Thai sex slavery. Industrial growth has also led to an increase in jobs for women. Education and training are expanding rapidly across Thailand, and women and girls are very much taking part. The ignorance and deprivation on which the enslavement of girls depends are on the wane, and better-educated girls are much less likely to fall for the promises made by brokers. The traditional duties to family, including the debt of obligation to parents, are also becoming less compelling. As the front line of industrialization sweeps over northern Thailand, it is bringing fundamental changes. Programs on the television bought with the money from selling one daughter may carry warning messages to her younger sisters. As they learn more about new jobs, about HIV/AIDS, and about the fate of those sent to the brothels, northern Thai girls refuse to follow their sisters south. Slavery functions best when alternatives are few, and education and the media are opening the eyes of Thai girls to a world of choice.

For the slaveholders this presents a serious problem. They are faced with an increase in demand for prostitutes and a diminishing supply. Already the price of young Thai girls is spiraling upward. The slaveholders' only recourse is to look elsewhere, to areas where poverty and ignorance still hold sway. Nothing, in fact, could be easier: there remain large, oppressed, and isolated populations desperate enough to believe the promises of the brokers. From Burma to the west and Laos to the east come thousands of economic and political refugees searching for work; they are defenseless in a country where they are illegal aliens. The techniques that worked so well in bringing Thai girls to brothels are again deployed, but now across borders. . . .

Once in the brothels they are in an even worse situation than the enslaved Thai girls: because they do not speak Thai their isolation is increased, and as illegal aliens they are open to even more abuse. The pimps tell them repeatedly that if they set foot outside the brothel, they will be arrested. And when they are arrested, Burmese and Lao girls and women are afforded no legal rights. They are often held for long periods at the mercy of the police, without charge or trial. A strong traditional antipathy between Thais and Burmese increases the chances that Burmese sex slaves will face discrimination and arbitrary treatment. . . .

TO JAPAN, SWITZERLAND, GERMANY, THE UNITED STATES

Women and girls flow in both directions over Thailand's borders.[13] The export of enslaved prostitutes is a robust business, supplying brothels in Japan, Europe, and America. Thailand's Ministry of Foreign Affairs estimated in 1994 that as many as 50,000 Thai women were living illegally in Japan and working in prostitution. Their situation in these countries parallels that of Burmese women held in Thailand. The enticement of Thai women follows a familiar pattern. Promised work as cleaners, domestics, dishwashers, or cooks, Thai girls and women pay large fees to employment agents to secure jobs in rich, developed countries. When they arrive, they are brutalized and enslaved. Their debt bonds are significantly larger than those of enslaved prostitutes in Thailand, since they include airfares, bribes to immigration officials, the costs of false passports, and sometimes the fees paid to foreign men to marry them and ease their entry.

Variations on sex slavery occur in different countries. In Switzerland girls are brought in on "artist" visas as exotic dancers. There, in addition to being prostitutes, they must work as striptease dancers in order to meet the carefully checked terms of their employment. The brochures of the European companies that have leaped into the sex-tourism business leave the customer no doubt about what is being sold:

Slim, sunburnt, and sweet, they love the white man in an erotic and devoted way. They are masters of the art of making love by nature, an art that we Europeans do not know. (Life Travel, Switzerland) [M]any girls from the sex world come from the poor north-eastern region of the country and from the slums of Bangkok.

It has become a custom that one of the nice looking daughters goes into the business in order to earn money for the poor family . . . [Y]ou can get the feeling that taking a girl here is as easy as buying a package of cigarettes . . . little slaves who give real Thai warmth. (Kanita Kamha Travel, the Netherlands)[14]

In Germany they are usually bar girls, and they are sold to men by the bartender or bouncer. Some are simply placed in brothels or apartments controlled by pimps. After Japanese sex tours to Thailand began in the 1980s, Japan rapidly became the largest importer of Thai women. The fear of HIV in Japan has also increased the demand for virgins. Because of their large disposable incomes, Japanese men are able to pay considerable sums for young rural girls from Thailand. Japanese organized crime is involved throughout the importation process, sometimes shipping women via Malaysia or the Philippines. In the cities, the Japanese mob maintains bars and brothels that trade in Thai women. Bought and sold between brothels, these women are controlled with extreme violence. Resistance can bring murder. Because the girls are illegal aliens and often enter the country under false passports, Japanese gangs rarely hesitate to kill them if they have ceased to be profitable or if they have angered their slaveholders. Thai women deported from Japan also report that the gangs will addict girls to drugs in order to manage them more easily.

Criminal gangs, usually Chinese or Vietnamese, also control brothels in the United States that enslave Thai women. Police raids in New York, Seattle, San Diego, and Los Angeles have freed more than a hundred girls and women.[15] In New York, thirty Thai women were locked into the upper floors of a building used as a brothel. Iron bars sealed the windows and a series of buzzer-operated armored gates blocked exit to the street. During police raids, the women were herded into a secret basement room. At her trial, the brothel owner testified that she'd bought the women outright, paying between $6,000 and $15,000 for each. The women were charged $300 per week for room and board; they worked from 11:00 A.M. until 4:00 A.M. and were sold by the hour to clients. Chinese and Vietnamese gangsters were also involved in the brothel, collecting protection money and hunting down es-caped prostitutes. The gangs owned chains of brothels and massage parlors, through which they rotated the Thai women in order to defeat law enforcement ef-forts. After being freed from the New York brothel, some of the women disappeared—only to turn up weeks later in similar circumstances three thousand miles away, in Seattle. One of the rescued Thai women, who had been promised restaurant work and then enslaved, testified that the brothel owners "bought something and wanted to use it to the full extent, and they didn't think those people were human beings."[16]

OFFICIAL INDIFFERENCE AND A GROWTH ECONOMY

In many ways, Thailand closely resembles another country, one that was going through rapid industrial-ization and economic boom one hundred years ago. Rapidly shifting its labor force off the farm, experi-encing unprecedented economic growth, flooded with economic migrants, and run by corrupt politicians and a greedy and criminal police force, the United States then faced many of the problems confronting Thailand today. In the 1890s, political machines that brought to-gether organized crime with politicians and police ran the prostitution and protection rackets, drug sales, and extortion in American cities. Opposing them were a weak and disorganized reform movement and a muck-raking press. I make this comparison because it is im-portant to explore why Thailand's government is so in-effective when faced with the enslavement of its own citizens, and also to remember that conditions *can* change over time. Discussions with Thais about the horrific nature of sex slavery often end with their as-sertion that "nothing will ever change this . . . the problem is just too big . . . and those with power will never allow change." Yet the social and economic underpinnings of slavery in Thailand are always changing, sometimes for the worse and sometimes for the better. No society can remain static, particularly one undergoing such upheavals as Thailand.

As the country takes on a new Western-style mate-rialist morality, the ubiquitous sale of sex sends a clear message: women can be enslaved and exploited for

profit. Sex tourism helped set the stage for the expan-sion of sexual slavery.

Sex tourism also generates some of the income that Thai men use to fund their own visits to brothels. No one knows how much money it pours into the Thai economy, but if we assume that just one-quarter of sex workers serve sex tourists and that their customers pay about the same as they would pay to use Siri, then 656 billion baht ($26.2 billion) a year would be about right. This is thirteen times more than the amount Thailand earns by building and exporting computers, one of the country's major industries, and it is money that floods into the country without any concomitant need to build factories or improve infrastructure. It is part of the boom raising the standard of living generally and al-lowing an even greater number of working-class men to purchase commercial sex.

Joining the world economy has done wonders for Thailand's income and terrible things to its society. According to Pasuk Phongpaichit and Chris Baker, economists who have analyzed Thailand's economic boom,

> Government has let the businessmen ransack the na-tion's human and natural resources to achieve growth. It has not forced them to put much back. In many re-spects, the last generation of economic growth has been a disaster. The forests have been obliterated. The urban environment has deteriorated. Little has been done to combat the growth in industrial pollution and hazardous wastes. For many people whose labour has created the boom, the conditions of work, health, and safety are grim.
>
> Neither law nor conscience has been very effective in limiting the social costs of growth. Business has reveled in the atmosphere of free-for-all. The machin-ery for social protection has proved very pliable. The legal framework is defective. The judiciary is suspect. The police are unreliable. The authorities have consis-tently tried to block popular organizations to defend popular rights.[17]

The situation in Thailand today is similar to that of the United States in the 1850s; with a significant part of the economy dependent on slavery, religious and cultural leaders are ready to explain why this is all for the best. But there is also an important difference: this is the new slavery, and the impermanence of modern slavery and the dedication of human-rights workers offer some hope.

NOTES

1. Siri is, of course, a pseudonym; the names of all respondents have been changed for their protection. I spoke with them in December 1996.

2. "Caught in Modern Slavery: Tourism and Child Prostitution in Thailand," Country Report Summary prepared by Sudarat Sereewat-Srisang for the Ecumenical Consultation held in Chiang Mai in May 1990.

3. Foreign exchange rates are in constant flux. Unless otherwise noted, dollar equivalences for all currencies reflect the rate at the time of the research.

4. From interviews done by Human Rights Watch with freed child prostitutes in shelters in Thailand, reported in Jasmine Caye, *Preliminary Survey on Regional Child Trafficking for Prostitution in Thailand* (Bangkok: Center for the Protection of Children's Rights, 1996), p. 25.

5. Kulachada Chaipipat, "New Law Targets Human Trafficking," Bangkok *Nation,* November 30, 1997.

6. Thais told me that it would be very surprising if a well-off man or a politician did not have at least one mistress. When I was last in Thailand there was much public mirth over the clash of wife and mistress outside the hospital room of a high government official who had suffered a heart attack, as each in turn barricaded the door.

7. Quoted in Mark Van Landingham, Chanpen Saengtienchai, John Knodel, and Anthony Pramualratana, *Friends, Wives, and Extramarital Sex in Thailand* (Bangkok: Institute of Population Studies, Chulalongkorn University, 1995), p. 18.

8. Van Landingham et al., 1995, pp. 9–25.

9. Pasuk Phongpaichit and Chris Baker, *Thailand's Boom* (Chiang Mai: Silkworm Books, 1996), pp. 51–54.

10. Center for the Protection of Children's Rights, *Case Study Report on Commercial Sexual Exploitation of Children in Thailand* (Bangkok, October 1996), p. 37.

11. David Kyle and John Dale, "Smuggling the State Back In: Agents of Human Smuggling Reconsidered," in *Global Human Smuggling: Comparative Perspectives,* ed. David Kyle and Rey Koslowski (Baltimore: Johns Hopkins University Press, 2001).

12. "Impact of the Asian Economic Crisis on Child Prostitution," *ECPAT International Newsletter* 27 (May 1, 1999), found at http://www.ecpat.net/eng/Ecpat.inter/IRC/articles.asp?articleID=143&NewsID=21.

13. *International Report on Trafficking in Women (Asia-Pacific Region)* (Bangkok Global Alliance Against Traffic in Women, 1996); Sudarat Sereewat, *Prostitution: Thai-European Connection* (Geneva: Commission on the Churches' participation in Development, World Council of Churches, n.d.). Women's rights and anti-trafficking organizations in Thailand have also published a number of personal accounts of women enslaved as prostitutes and sold overseas. These pamphlets are disseminated widely in the hope of making young women more aware of the threat of enslavement. Good examples are Siriporn Skrobanek *The Diary of Prang* (Bangkok: Foundation for Women, 1994); and White Ink (pseud.), *Our Lives, Our Stories* (Bangkok: Foundation for Women, 1995). They follow the lives of women "exported," the first to Germany and the second to Japan.

14. The brochures are quoted in Truong, *Sex, Money, and Morality: Prostitution and Tourism in Southeast Asia* (London: Zed Books, 1990), p. 178.

15. Carey Goldberg, "Sex Slavery, Thailand to New York," *New York Times* (September 11, 1995), p. 81.

16. Quoted in Goldberg.

17. Phongpaichit and Baker, 1996, p. 237.

17

The Sex Tourist, the Expatriate, His Ex-Wife, and Her "Other"

The Politics of Loss, Difference, and Desire

JULIA O'CONNELL DAVIDSON

The English word "desire" comes from the Latin *desiderare*, literally, to be away from the stars, whence to cease to see, regret the absence of, to seek.
—*(Bishop and Robinson, 1998: 114)*

[W]e go to the exotic other to lose everything, including ourselves—everything that is but the privilege which enabled us to go in the first place.
—*(Dollimore, 1991: 342)*

In Western discourses on "racial" Otherness, the notion of "civilization" as the apex of an evolutionary process of social development has often been read as implying a radical separation from and/or a corruption of "nature," and thus involving a kind of loss, even as it confers intellectual supremacy upon the "civilized races." A number of authors have drawn attention to the relationship between this sense of loss and sexual desire for the Other (Bhatacharyya, 1997; Dollimore, 1991; Mercer, 1995; Said, 1978), and it is also highlighted in Bishop and Robinson's (1998) compelling analysis of the sex tourist industry in Thailand. Bishop and Robinson (1998) explore sex tourism in relation to discursive traditions which have constructed "Other cultures as qualitatively and quantitatively different with regard to sexual practices and mores" (1998: 114). One of the things their analysis of 18th-, 19th- and 20th-century western texts that eroticize Other cultures illuminates is the tension surrounding the idea of "civilization." Paying particular attention to the writings of Denis Diderot and, to a lesser extent Jean-Jacques Rousseau, Bishop and Robinson interrogate a discursive tradition wherein a vision of Other cultures as closer to "the state of nature" serves as a foil against which to critique certain aspects of European morality and social development. They show very clearly how contemporary accounts of sex tourism to Thailand (provided by sex tourists themselves as well as other commentators) resonate with these 18th-century representations of Other cultures' sexuality as in tune with "nature" and "untainted by European morality" (p. 114).

Whether and how these accounts of sex tourism resonate with post-Enlightenment representations of European and North American "civilization" is less explicitly addressed in Bishop and Robinson's work, and these questions provide the starting point for this article. Drawing on an ethnographic study of sex tourism in the Dominican Republic,[1] this article explores the worldview of a group of white European and North American male heterosexual tourists and expatriates whose sexual desires are immediately and transparently linked to a set of political discontents with contemporary "civilization." Their desire for the Other does not express a wish to lose everything, so much as a wish to reclaim what they feel they have already lost. These are sexually hostile men, and my aim is not to suggest that they are somehow representative of *all* European and North American heterosexual men or even necessarily of *all* male sex tourists. What I do want to argue, however, is that the model of human sociality they use to make sense of their experience is informed by a mainstream political tradition within liberalism. The sense of loss which lies behind their desire is not extraordinary or unique to them as individuals, and an interrogation of that desire therefore sheds light on European/North American constructions of Self as well as of Other. Above all, the moral philosophy of these men reveals something of the whiteness, maleness and heterosexuality of classical liberalism's sovereign self and the tensions generated by its partial and exclusive universalism.

SEX TOURISM AND THE DOMINICAN REPUBLIC

The Dominican Republic, which occupies the eastern two-thirds of the island of Hispaniola, has a population of almost 8 million. Historically, the country's economy has been weakened by colonial neglect, Trujillo's 32-year dictatorship, foreign intervention and, above all in recent decades, by international debt. In the early 1980s, debt crisis and negotiations with the International Monetary Fund (IMF) led to the adoption of structural adjustment measures. These measures did little to improve the lot of the ordinary people (according to World Bank estimates in 1992, 60% of Domini-

cans were living in poverty, Howard, 1999: 33), but they did stimulate the expansion of tourism, a sector which the Dominican government had been promoting since the 1970s. The country now hosts around 1.8 million tourists annually, most of whom are North American or European (WTO, 1997).

Many, perhaps the majority, of these visitors are "ordinary" tourists seeking a cheap holiday or honeymoon in the Caribbean, but the country does also attract "sex tourists." Defined as those tourists who enter into some form of sexual-economic exchange with women, men or children resident in the host destination, sex tourists are a heterogeneous group. They vary in terms of nationality, gender, age, ethnicity and racialized identity, sexual orientation and socioeconomic background, as well as in terms of their sexual practices whilst abroad and the subjective meanings they attach to their sexual encounters (Clift and Carter, 2000; Kruhse-MountBurton, 1995; O'Connell Davidson, 1995; Pruitt and LaFont, 1995; Sanchez Taylor, 2000). They also differ as regards how central sex is to their travel experience.

For those to whom I shall refer to as "hardcore" sex tourists, however, the desire for particular kinds of sexual experience (generally those which are expensive, scarce or risky at home, such as sex with multiples of prostitute women or men, and/or with children, or transsexuals and/or with racialized Others) is a conscious and explicit part of the motivation to travel. Some hardcore sex tourists find the pleasures associated with a particular destination so great that they eventually decide to migrate and settle permanently in their chosen "sexual paradise." Such expatriates (or "sexpatriates") often play an active role in promoting sex tourism and organizing tourist-related prostitution in a given destination (see Ireland, 1993; O'Connell Davidson and Sanchez Taylor, 1996; Seabrook, 1996; Truong, 1990), and this is certainly the case in the Dominican Republic.

Many of the hotels, restaurants and bars that facilitate prostitute-use by tourists in Boca Chica, Puerto Plata and in Sosua (the country's three main sex tourist destinations) are owned or managed by North American or European expatriates. The more entrepreneurial amongst them have discovered that the internet offers excellent marketing opportunities, and their hotels and bars now feature on several websites that promote sex tourism. For instance, a number of American sexpatriates living in Boca Chica have established strong links with an American-based travel club, Travel and the Single Male (TSM), through which their businesses are advertised. The club, which is one of several similar organizations run by and for male sex tourists, boasts some 5000 members, most of whom are white Americans. TSM publishes a guidebook (Cassirer, 1992) and sells club membership for US$50 per annum. Members receive a quarterly newsletter, discounts in some hotels and brothels, and most importantly, are provided access to the TSM internet site. This provides information on travel and prostitution in various countries around the world, access to softcore pornographic photographs of female sex workers from those countries two message boards and a chat room for members to swap "sexperiences," views, news and handy travel tips.

As well as drawing on interviews with 31 sexpatriates and 30 hardcore sex tourists in the Dominican Republic, five of whom were members of TSM, this article makes fairly extensive use of materials published by TSM. The worldview of its members typifies that of hardcore male heterosexual sex tourists more generally (O'Connell Davidson, 1995, 1996, 1998), and their attitudes towards gender, "race" and sexuality are consistent with those expressed in other guidebooks and internet sites which promote this form of sex tourism (for instance, "Travel Philippines," "Brothels, Bordellos and Sinbins of the World)," and the "World Sex Guide," (see Bishop and Robinson, 1998; Hughes, 1998/9). The following extract from a posting on TSM's message board captures these attitudes well:

> Boca is a place of [European/North American] men's dreams and [European/North American] women's nightmares. It finds the heart of desire within all of us. Boca . . . is a place where sexual fantasies become commonplace. A place where you can go into your room with a pack of multi-colored girls and no one will blink twice. A place where an older man can convince himself that the young girl rotating on his lap cares for him and understands his needs more than the women from his homeland. It's a place where men come for lust and sometimes end up confusing it for love. It's where a man can be a star in his own adult videos. It's a place where a young pretty girl once offered me sex for a [plate of] lasagna. It's where

every woman you see whether whore or maid or waitress, young or old, can be bought for a few hundred pesos. It's a place where you can have a girl, her sisters and her cousins. (TSM, posted 19 March 1998)

Though its organizers and members would not describe it as a political organization, the ethos of TSM is aggressively heterosexist, deeply misogynist and profoundly racist, and the club thus expresses and promotes a particular worldview, as well as a particular form of travel. Indeed, it implicitly, and sometimes explicitly, presents travel to "Third World" countries as a means of release from the restraints that are supposedly placed on the white male's self-sovereignty in the "First World." This form of sex tourism reflects a particular political vision of the West, then, as well as of the so-called "Third World." The following section considers this vision in relation to a mainstream discursive tradition of liberal political theory.

"NATURAL RIGHTS" AND SOCIAL CONTRACT

Classical political theory starts from the proposition that human beings are naturally competitive and self-interested and for this reason need safeguarding from each other. Hobbes (1968), for instance, holds that in a state of nature, each man would use all means available to him to possess, use and enjoy all that he would, or could, get. By agreeing (on condition that all men do the same) to a social contract that creates a political society or state, and by transferring rights of law-making and enforcement to that state, individuals can, it is argued, simultaneously retain powers of sovereignty over themselves, and be restrained from invading and destroying others. The legitimacy of the liberal democratic state hinges upon its role as enactor of laws that preserve and protect the "natural rights" of its citizens, "rights" which include possessing property, disposing of their own labour, exercising sovereignty over themselves, their own minds and bodies.

Carole Pateman (1988) has observed that missing from this story that social contract theorists tell about the origins of the liberal democratic state is the tale of the sexual contract. She argues that the pact through which powers of law-making and enforcement are transferred to the state is a pact between men, and is:

> a sexual as well as a social contract: it is sexual in the sense of patriarchal—that is, the contract establishes men's political right over women—and also sexual in the sense of establishing orderly access by men to women's bodies. (Pateman, 1988: 2)

Pateman's thesis thus suggests that the legitimacy of the liberal state actually rests on its role as enactor of laws which preserve and protect the "natural rights" of its *male* citizens, "rights" which are understood to include a right of access to women's bodies. Viewed in this way, it is possible to see how the extent and nature of such rights of access to female bodies, alongside the details of other "natural rights," can become the focus of political dispute. In other words, while in principle happy to enter into a pact with other men as regards access to women's bodies and other social arrangements, men might feel that the particular restraints imposed on male sexuality by a given state conflict with, rather than protect, the "natural rights" of its citizens. This was precisely the nature of Diderot's dispute with European moral and legal regulation of sexuality in the 18th century (for his criticisms of monogamy and the private ownership of women through the institution of marriage, see Bishop and Robinson, 1998: 120).

A similar case can be made in relation to "race," for as Mills (1998) and Puwar (1999) argue, the social contract is "raced" as well as gendered. In the sense that the myth of the original pact is a story about white men agreeing to transfer rights of law-making and enforcement to a political body, we can say that the legitimacy of the liberal democratic state is based upon and reinforces a particular racialized hierarchy. Again, the extent and precise details of white male rights over Others may be subject to dispute, even amongst those who are, in principle, reconciled to the liberal model of political contract.[2]

Here I want to suggest that hardcore sex tourists' political vision is informed by a classical liberal model of self, community and contract, within which naturally brutish men living in a "state of nature" are simultaneously free to conquer and at risk of invasion. They are "suspended between a fantasy of conquest

and a dread of engulfment, between rape and emasculation" (McClintock, 1995: 27). The social contract of "civilization" is imagined as a release from this paranoiac paralysis, but only so long as it guarantees each man his "natural rights." If the "civilized" state comes to invade and deny individual men's "natural rights" over themselves, and over women and "racialized" Others, it loses legitimacy. This, I will argue, helps to explain the attraction that sites perceived as closer to "the state of nature" hold for hardcore male heterosexual sex tourists.

Rejecting the Authority of the "Civilized" State

In the course of interview work in the Dominican Republic, we have found that European and North American male sexpatriates and hardcore sex tourists are more than willing to hold forth on what is wrong with European/North American societies. The developments that trouble them most are those which they perceive to undermine a "natural" hierarchy that is classed, gendered and "faced." They rail against taxes, and most especially against tax-payers' money being spent on social welfare programmes for the undeserving poor (and more or less anyone who is poor in the West is deemed to be undeserving); they remonstrate against affirmative action programmes and/or equal opportunities legislation, as well as against divorce laws which empower women in relation to men, against women's entitlement to child support payments, and so on. Without prompting, they also bemoan the state's increasing incursion into spheres of life which they believe should be a matter of individual (white male) conscience, so that, for example, they take great exception to laws which compel them to wear seatbelts in cars and which prohibit drink-driving.

For all of the sexpatriates we have interviewed, the decision to migrate to the Dominican Republic was at least partially informed by their unwillingness to accept the authority of their home state, and in several cases, their move was urgently precipitated by their active refusal of this authority. Sometimes migration represented an attempt to escape prosecution for drugs or other offences, but more commonly sexpatriates are tax exiles from their own country (indeed, there is a

British-based organization called Scope, which provides members with information about tax avoidance schemes and tax havens as well as "sex havens"). A French-Canadian expatriate interviewed in Boca Chica is fairly typical of such men, if perhaps more unashamed than most about his desire to exercise white male privilege.

"Richard" worked as a real estate notary in Montreal until he pulled off a major deal in 1994. The Canadian government presented him with a tax bill for $200,000, so he put his money in a Swiss bank, bought a luxury yacht and left Canada for good. After cruising around the Caribbean for a couple of months, he ended up in the Dominican Republic, where he bought a bar. The bar he says, does not make money, "but I don't need money. It's just for fun." Richard loves the Dominican Republic:

Here, the white man is king, everyone treats you like a king. You see, no one has forgotten Trujillo. It was a reign of terror, and everyone here, well, everyone over 60, they still tremble when a white man talks to them. . . . In Canada, we don't have so many blacks, but the Indians own the place. The whites are the second-class citizens in their own country because the Indians have all the rights now. Things are much better here, much better. This is really a racist country, everyone knows their place.

In his mid-50s, Richard is on his eighth wife, a Dominican woman in her 20s. This marriage will last he believes, because "In the Dominican Republic, women are slaves." They have to keep their husbands happy, or the men will beat them. So Richard is married, but free: "I can do what I want, and she can't say a thing. She doesn't have the right." Richard uses prostitutes and facilitates tourist-related prostitution by encouraging women and teenagers to solicit from his bar. He boasts that he is immune from prosecution by the Dominican authorities because he knows how to "do business" here:

You have to understand it's corrupt from the top to the bottom. So you have to be in with the Dominicans, get a Dominican wife, make contacts, make some friends in the police and the military. You have to make your own security.

Richard's male bar staff are, he says, "fully armed," and this further adds to the impression that he views his bar as his own private fiefdom.

In interviews, hardcore male heterosexual sex tourists as well as sexpatriates emphasize contrasts between the burdens carried by the white male in "civilized" countries and the freedoms he enjoys in the Dominican Republic. A rather lengthy extract from an interview with an American sexpatriate and two of his sex-tourist friends (one of whom was a New Jersey police officer) shows how deeply disturbed such men are by legal and social changes which undermine what they see as their 'natural rights' in relation to women and racialized minority groups:

SEXPATRIATE: I'm 53 years old. Up in New York I've gotta screw 50-year-old women. Down here, 15 to 20 year olds, gorgeous women. . . . A friend of mine, he just threw out a 13-year-old girlfriend . . . [in the States] they've got laws. . . . I pay $1100 child support a month [to his American ex-wife] . . . 17 percent of your gross income for one child she gets, 25 percent for two, 33 percent for three. I've no idea what happens to men who have four kids. . . . Women's lib in America in the United States has killed marriage in America for any man who has brains. I wouldn't even marry a rich woman. . . . [Here] they're raised different. Women's lib hasn't hit here. . . .

SEX TOURIST A: In the States, [women] hire folks with cameras. They go to bed with cameras. If they wake up with a bruise, they take a picture of it. Call it abuse. Possible abuse.

SEXPATRIATE: In the United States, if you grab your wife like that, and you yell at her, put a little black blue mark, just a little one, she'll. . . .

SEX TOURIST A: When you've got a goddamn female announcing the NBA basketball game. These females go into the men's locker rooms, but the males cannot go into the ladies locker rooms. Most of these girls are dykes anyways. . . .

SEXPATRIATE: Oh yeah. She can call the police and say "He hit me. Didn't leave a bruise, but he hit me." And he never even punched her and he goes to jail. She can take a knife to him, and nothing.

SEX TOURIST B: Yeah, no marks, nothing. . . .

O'CD: Is it here like it was 40 years ago in the States?

SEX TOURIST A: 50 years ago. The worst thing that ever ever happened in the States was they gave women the right to vote.

SEXPATRIATE: The right to vote and the right to drive. . . .

O'CD: Is this what people mean when they talk about political correctness in America?

SEXPATRIATE: You can't use the N word, nigger. Always when I was raised up, the only thing was the F word, you can't use the F word. Now you can't say cunt, you can't say nigger. . . . There's just so many words I could use against women in the United States. I don't like white women. . . .

O'CD: What about black women in the States?

SEXPATRIATE: They're Americanized. They've all got their lawyer's number tattooed on their wrist just like the white women.

Read as a commentary on the social contract between the state and its citizens, this interview extract, as well as earlier quotes from Richard, suggest that hardcore sex tourists and sexpatriates are only really able to reconcile themselves to the authority of a state which is overtly patriarchal and white supremacist. Legal measures which accord even basic rights of self-sovereignty to women or non-whites are perceived as attacks upon the white male citizen's "natural rights," upon his selfhood, bodily integrity and honour. This response is clearly paranoid, but I do not think it can be dismissed as merely *individual* paranoia. Rather, I would argue that it has its basis in the contradictions of the liberal political theory that informs their world-view.

Bodies, "Natural Rights" and the "State of Nature"

Wellman (1997: 321) has commented on the increasing visibility of whiteness and maleness in the contemporary USA:

Until recently, the categories "white" and "male" were taken for granted. . . . The taken for granted world of white male Americans, then, was their normalcy, not their whiteness or gender. As a result, the privileges that came with whiteness and masculinity were experienced as "normal," not advantages. But

that is no longer possible. The normal has been made problematic by people of color and women, who have, through their visibility, challenged assumptions once taken for granted.

Similar developments are occurring in European societies, and are, at one level, a logical result of liberalism's rhetoric of universalism. Yet these developments also draw attention to the tension between that rhetoric of universal rights and liberalism's basis in a social contract that is gendered, classed and "raced." For many white European/North American men, the extension of universal rights to persons of colour and women is experienced as a loss of male sovereignty and selfhood. The sex tourists and sexpatriates under consideration here are certainly not alone in their disquiet, but they are distinguished by the fact that they attach such an immediate *erotic* significance to this sense of loss. This perhaps reflects their unusually intense anxiety about/fascination with matters corporeal (such as the ageing process, sexual functions and organs, phenotypical characteristics), something which may well be explained as a function of individual psychology and personal history.

At the same time, however, this anxiety/fascination resonates with the post-Enlightenment discourses about "nature" and "civilization" that perpetuated a Cartesian and Christian tradition which views the body as part of the physical world that must be controlled (see Seidler, 1987: 94). Where men are imagined as victims of biologically given heterosexual drives, control over male and female bodies can easily come to seem like a zero-sum game. Men can only control their own bodies if they can command control over women's bodies and access to women's bodies is thus one of the "natural" rights that the liberal state must guarantee men.

Equally, where a "racial" hierarchy is assumed to exist in nature, self-control over the white body entails dominance over Other bodies. The political and social order must ensure that Others pay white men their "natural" dues, not just by suffering themselves to be called "nigger," for example, but also by physically trembling when the white man speaks. Ferber (1999: 40) notes that under the Jim Crow system, it was commonly assumed that "a white boy doesn't become a man until he has had sexual relations with a black girl," and it seems to me that this too can be read as the physical exaction of a "natural" due. It is telling, therefore that the sexpatriate quoted above conjured with an image of equal rights as inscriptions on the body when he stated that black American women have "their lawyer's number tattooed on their wrist just like the white women."[3] Fantasies about the "Third World" as closer to a "state of nature" have to be understood in the context of these anxieties and discontents about the political order in the West. It is not a generalized nostalgia for a mythical past that informs these men's desires, but a wish to reclaim very specific powers. Hardcore sex tourists and sexpatriates see the Dominican Republic as a lawless and corrupt place ("There is no law here," they say), but it is simultaneously described as a place where "natural laws" operate. Thus, white men are feared, revered and obeyed by their "racial" and gender subordinates, while "naturally" promiscuous Dominican women and girls are available to meet the white man's "needs" uninhibited by European/ North American codes of sexual morality, Here, then, white men can shed the burdens of First World "civilization," even as they retain all its economic and political privileges and collect their "natural" dues as "civilized" white men.

This leaves them in a position to make almost unlimited choices, and so to exercise quite extraordinary powers of sovereignty (their description of themselves as "kings" is, in this respect, not so very far-fetched). They are relieved of the burdens of civic responsibility beyond those that they choose for themselves. It is down to them to decide whether or not they provide economic support for the children they father, whether or not to beat their wives, or to leave bruises on women they sleep with, whether or not to mete out racist abuse, whether to pay prostitutes for the "services" they have "consumed" or to simply offer them a plate of lasagne, even whether or not to sexually abuse children. It is, in short, down to them to choose whether to harm or help their "natural" subordinates (Brace and O'Connell Davidson, 1996).

For these men, the exercise of power over "natural" subordinates does not appear to be simply an end in itself, however. As the following section will show, they are as concerned to establish and maintain "proper" re-lations among themselves as they are to reinstate traditional hierarchies of gender and "race." Again it will be argued that their preoccupations are perfectly consistent with traditional liberal discourses about selfhood and sovereignty.

SEX TOURISM AND THE "COMMUNITY"

In Sosua, Puerto Plata and Boca Chica, there are networks of European and North American heterosexual sexpatriates and sex tourists who visit regularly and/or for lengthy periods, whose ties to each other are both economic and social. They variously provide each other with custom, business, employment and/or services and enjoy a hard-drinking social life together. They "hang out" in bars, they gossip, they complain about the petty hardships they encounter in the Dominican Republic, give each other advice, reminisce together and generally enjoy a sense of collective inclusion in what would otherwise be an alien environment. These networks can loosely be termed "communities," and sexuality is pivotal to sex tourists' and sexpatriates' sense of collective inclusion. Rey Chow's (1999) discussion of community formation and the politics of admittance can be usefully applied here:

> As the etymological associations of the word 'community' indicate, community is linked to the articulation of commonality and consensus; a community is always based on a kind of collective inclusion. . . . At the same time, however, there is no community formation without the implicit understanding of who is and is not to be admitted. As the principle that regulates community formations, admittance operates in several crucial senses. There is first, admittance in the most physical sense of letting enter . . . to "let enter" is . . . closely connected with recognition and acknowledgement, which is the second major connotation of admittance. . . . Third, there is admittance in the sense of a confession—such as the admittance of a crime. Insofar as confession is an act of repentance, a surrender of oneself in reconciliation with the rules of society, it is also related to community. (1999: 35)

In the Dominican Republic, it is sexual contact with local women and teenagers which admits the male expatriate or tourist into the sex tourist "community" in the first two senses of admittance which Chow identifies. Take "Biggles," for example, a 52-year-old white Canadian sexpatriate living in Sosua. He first visited the country for a one-week holiday with a friend in 1990. At this point, he was not a habitual prostitute-user back home in Canada, nor did he travel to the Dominican Republic with the intention of sexually exploiting local women or children. Indeed, he had no particular desire to sexually experience the Other:

> I came down here . . . for a week and I stayed for a month. I came down with this guy, and as soon as we get down to the beach, he's got these two black girls, and I mean black. They weren't Dominican, they were Haitian. The blackest girls on the beach. And I said "no." I wasn't interested, I said I would never do that. . . . I'm not a bigot or anything but I just, I just don't, whatever, whatever. But hell, within the next couple of days I went with this girl and it was fantastic. . . . It was something I'd never done before. I don't know, I just thought, "Give it a try."

Biggles penetrated the "black girl" and entered the sex tourist "scene." So pleasing did he find the subculture of hardcore sex tourism that, over the next six years, he made repeated and regular visits to Sosua, always engaging in prostitute-use. In 1996, he decided to retire there, and his life now revolves entirely around this subculture.

Dominican women and girl's bodies are also often transacted between sexpatriates who own bar-brothels, or who make a living by procuring prostitutes for male tourists, and these exchanges also serve to establish and cement relationships between sexpatriates and sex tourists. Thus, for example, a 63-year-old white American expatriate who owns a beachside bar in Boca Chica explains that he gets "a lot of steady customers, a lot of guys that come here three, four, six, seven times a year." His bar, and photographs of its female bar staff, feature in the information on the Dominican Republic on TSM's website, and the owner is frequently referred to in the "chat" between members. He estimates that between 15 to 20 TSM members arrive at his bar each month and other American sexpatriates and sex tourists interviewed in Boca Chica described him as "the biggest pimp in town." In facilitating

tourists' "entry" into Dominican women and teen-agers, he simultaneously admits them to the sex tourist "community." They become "one of the guys."

Sexual contact with Dominican women and girls is also central to admittance in the sense that it provides the basis for recognition and acknowledgement between men. As one TSM member explains in a message board posting, he spent a great deal of time in his hotel bar in Boca Chica "bullshitting with guys" and "making friends":

> We are all there for the same carnal reason—[the] hotel is probably 95% single men—and a typical opening conversation would be—pointing at one of the girls—"have you been blown by her yet?"—"no, but I hear from so and so that she gives a great one." It makes for great comradery (TSM, posted 26 September 1997).

Another posting reads:

> Day 2. . . . I must comment on the fantastic cama-raderie that was nurtured between Worm, Omega, Voodoo Chile and yours truly. It was just a whole lot of fun the whole time. And later we ran into Ronnie, Bogey, Pat, Newt, Jann, Digger, Woolf, JD and probably a couple more TSMers I can't remember. A quick breakfast . . . then down to . . . the beach . . . for a day in Paradise. Before I knew it, a large-breasted black woman in tight attire was grinning at me and massaging my back . . . At one point, I headed into the bathroom and before I knew it she was standing behind me at the toilet, trying to grab my dick. She wanted to suckee suckee me right then and there. (TSM, posted 11 January 1999)

And another:

> [The taxi] took me to the now infamous Ronnie's, upon entering I met some of the TSM crew. Omega (also known as Obi-wan, for his willingness to provide his invaluable wisdom to TSM newbies such as myself) . . . and of course Ronnie. After speaking to them for perhaps 5 minutes, I notice a cute girl enter the bar. She locked her gaze on me and promptly began to suck a bottle in a way not usually seen. Needless to say she had my undivided attention. I . . . inquire about her and whether Omega had any

advice . . . I proceeded to throw her over my shoulder and carry her out of the bar, [back] to the hotel, and . . . the fun was underway. (TSM, posted 10 January 1999)

In these and other similar postings, Boca Chica is constructed as a sexual playground for European/North American men, and Dominican women and girls as play-objects shared amongst them. The hardcore sex tourist's play-*mates,* that is, the subjects who give recognition and acknowledgement, are other European/North American men.

It is also worth noting that because admittance is predicated upon a common European/North American masculine identity and consensus about sexuality, it tends to nullify differences between sex tourists and sexpatriates in terms of age and class identity. Men in their 70s bond with men in their 20s and 30s; wealthier sexpatriates who own businesses socialize with the relatively poor sexpatriates who work for them; sex tourists who are police officers or scaffolders back home "have a whole lot of fun" with those who are senior accountants or company directors. The sense of group belonging comes from sharing the "natural" privileges of masculinity and whiteness, and sex tourists/sexpatriates enjoy the idea that they have secured a competitive advantage not just over local men, but also over the European/North American men who remain at home. As a 71-year-old American sex tourist told us:

We all like to look like heroes. . . . Would I rather have a 70-year-old woman or an 18-year-old or a 25-year-old? Please. . . . You'll find very few men . . . that has done what I've done in the last 50 years. Right now they're all sitting in Hyde Park, feeding the pigeons.

This man is reliant on his sex tourist and sexpatriate friends to affirm this pleasing image. What good is heroically fucking 18-year-olds while your contemporaries feed pigeons in a park if nobody of equal worth recognises this mark of your distinction?

Finally, I would argue that the hardcore sex tourist's impulse to divulge the details of his sexual experience (in conversations with other sex tourists/sexpatriates and in postings on internet sites) can be read as an attempt at group formation through admittance in Chow's third sense, that of confession:

Little Ingris. . . . She isn't totally pro yet. I had her 3 times—my limit on a girl. . . . She is so tight that I broke 5 condoms on her and she was crying out something I've never heard before "*Tu Lance, ai ai*" over and over. . . . [Another] girl, broke 2 condoms on her. . . . After several screws I got her to do a posing session and used some of my toys with her, thank god 4 KY jelly. . . . I have some good poses of her for TSM.

I do not think such passages can be interpreted as acts of repentance, but they could be read as attempts at reconciliation with the rules of a subculture that bases membership and identity upon a shared willingness to reduce women and girls to sexual objects and to flout what are seen as repressive social strictures on heterosexual male sexuality (hardcore sex tourists fondly describe themselves as "bad boys"). In repeatedly confessing to his sexual transgressions, the sex tourist demonstrates himself to be "one of the guys." Homosexual acts cannot be confessed, of course, and male homosexuals are not admitted to the heterosexual male sex tourist "community." As one interviewee in Boca Chica put it, "Gays do come down here, but we don't have nothing to do with them."[4]

Thus far, I have been emphasizing the fact that "racially" Other female bodies serve as vehicles for relationships between European/North American male heterosexual sex tourists and sexpatriates in the Dominican Republic. Female bodies are exchanged, sometimes for money (as in the case of sexpatriates who organize prostitution), sometimes as free gifts (as in cases where sex tourists or sexpatriates "recommend" or share a woman/girl), and, as Rubin has observed, where "it is women who are being transacted, then it is the men who give and take them who are linked, the woman being a conduit of a relationship rather than a partner to it" (1975: 174).

It should also be clear that a hardcore sex tourist's worldview is nothing if not contradictory. They buy into overtly denigrating racisms, but women of colour are their chosen sexual objects. They say that women are the weaker sex, but berate them for the power they supposedly exercise over men. They are virulent ho-

mophobes, but are endlessly fascinated by the sex of
other men. Let me now examine their urge to forge relationships with each other in relation to these contradictions and those implicit in the model of human sociality they accept.

DIFFERENCE AND INVASION

Late-19th-century and early-20th-century scientific
discourses on race, gender and sexuality informed and
buttressed one another (Somerville, 1997), and their
legacy is conspicuous in overtly racist politics, which
are invariably also sexist and homophobic politics. To
the extent that biologically essentialist models of difference naturalize social and political inequalities
based on gender and sexual orientation as well as
"race," they can perhaps be said to inform an internally
consistent worldview. But this *menage à trois* does not
always appear to be a happy one. Indeed, essentialist
understandings of gender and sexual difference seemingly pose huge problems for those whose imaginary
communities are premised on notions of "race" sameness, problems which can become particularly acute
during periods of social upheaval or change.[5]

The contradiction between men's perceived dependency upon women as mothers of "the race" and
their dread of women's physical difference may be
most visible in "racial" supremacist politics, but similar problems dog any model of community formation
within which men establish links with each other
through the exchange of women (see Chow, 1999).
Wherever the traditional masculinist view that equates
women with sex is accepted, women's relation to "the
community" is necessarily difficult and ambiguous.
Female sexuality and sexual difference is the key to
maintaining the boundaries of community, not simply
in the sense that women biologically reproduce its
members, but also in the sense that, as objects of exchange between men, women serve to reproduce social
links between the male members of the community.
The ultimate taboo is thus the taboo against the sameness of men and women, for women's difference is
vital to community formation (Chow, 1999; Freud,
1985; Rubin, 1975).

At the same time, however, female sexuality poses
a profound threat to the boundaries of community.
Since women are not actually objects, but only treated
as such, their potential sexual agency is extremely dangerous. They could refuse:

> . . . their traditional position as "gifts," as the con-
> duits and vehicles that facilitate social relations and
> enable group identity, [and] actually *give themselves*.
> By giving themselves, such women enter social rela-
> tionships as active partners in the production of mean-
> ings rather than simply as the bearers of those mean-
> ings. (Chow, 1999:47–8)

If women break the taboo against the sameness of men
and women by assuming sexual agency, they "no
longer represent reliable conduits for men's relationships with each other and there is further a risk of
boundary loss through acts of miscegenation" (Chow,
1999: 49). These anxieties are central to the worldview
of hardcore male heterosexual sex tourists and sexpatriates. For these men, the legal construction of women
as men's equals, combined with shifts to the traditional
gendered division of labour, has broken this ultimate
taboo. European/North American women claim male
territory (they announce the NBA basketball game,
they go into the men's locker rooms) and male rights
(they call the police when beaten, they demand child
support payments from absent fathers). They can no
longer simply be treated as objects of exchange, and
this has ramifications not just for European/North
American men's relationships with European/North
American women, but also for European/North American men's relationships with each other.

Without the certainty of sexual difference, all the
laws and bonds of community that were based upon it
are in jeopardy. As active agents in the production of
community, women cannot be relied upon to reproduce a political order that these men are willing to
contract into, indeed, they are likely to push for laws
and law enforcement that conflict with, rather than
protect, men's "natural rights." For hardcore sex
tourists and sexpatriates, European/North American
women's transgression of the fundamental taboo
against the sameness of men and women also raises the
spectre of another disastrous boundary loss, that be-

tween heterosexuality and homosexuality. Bishop and Robinson quote from a novel written by a Canadian expatriate who lives in Bangkok—"fucking a white woman is a step away from homosexuality" (Moore, 1993:107, cited in Bishop and Robinson, 1998: 167), and the same sentiment is reproduced in TSM postings on the subject of white women.

This draws attention to the relationship between taboos against the sameness of men and women and against homosexuality, and traditional liberal discourses about selfhood and sovereignty. Brace's (1997) discussion of Hobbes' vision of the "territorial" self is particularly useful here. Hobbes was preoccupied by the idea of a self that is vulnerable to invasion, a self "bounded by a hostile world it must seek to conquer and restrain":

> Hobbes encloses the self, the "rational inside" within a fortress, buttressed by our own sense of esteem and relating to others as outsiders or as absentees. Each person becomes a potential invader and a potential resistance fighter. We understand and experience our selfhood as enclosed, in need of protection against intrusion and invasion. . . . Each person may be a bounded sphere, but the boundary may prove fragile. Hobbes exhorts us to look at fully grown men "and consider how brittle the frame of our humane body is" . . . Hobbes's emphasis on the brittleness, the fragility of the human body is . . . central to male anxiety about boundary loss (1997: 143–4)

Brace goes on to note that the Hobbesian self, like McClintock's (1995) colonial self, is characterized by "dread of catastrophic boundary *loss* (implosion), associated with fears of impotence and infantalization and attended by an *excess* of boundary order and fantasies of unlimited power" (McClintock, 1995: 26). Imagining the self as territory and relations between selves in terms of invasion or conquest must, in sexual terms, translate into a fear of rape. If sex tourists imagine the Dominican Republic as close to a "state of nature," a space where fragile-bodied men are not constrained by any law, then their fantasies of conquest would simultaneously invoke the spectre of invasion and engulfment by other, stronger-bodied men. As well as shedding light on their obsessive fascination with each other as sexual beings, this, I believe, helps

us to understand hardcore sex tourist/sexpatriates' impulse to forge links with each other in the Dominican Republic and other sites of sex tourism. The sexual objectification and exchange of women not only facilitates social relations and group identity, but also diffuses fears about homosexual invasion.

CONCLUSION

The subculture of male heterosexual sex tourism that has been considered in this article has grave consequences for the safety, health and well being of local women and girl children in the countries it targets. It also reveals something of the extent and chilling human consequences of global inequalities. Individual sexual agency is mediated through institutions of power, and the hardcore sex tourist's capacity to reclaim a particular vision of the European/North American Self through the sexual objectification of Others is predicated upon the existence of an equally particular economic, legal and political world order. And in terms of our understandings of the politics of "race," gender and sexuality in the West, the phenomenon of hardcore male heterosexual sex tourism sounds a warning bell, for the sense of loss which lies behind these sex tourists and sexpatriates' desires is not so very extraordinary. The same regrets, the same sense of being "away from the stars" can be found in speeches by right-wing politicians in North America and Europe and in the works of right-wing "think-tanks," newspaper editors and columnists and academics (for instance, Herrnstein and Murray, 1994; Murray, 1990), as well as in the publications of organizations like the UK Men's Movement (UKMM, 1999).

The men considered in this article are not differentiated from their more conventional right-wing compatriots by their preoccupation with European/North American notions of "civilization" and "nature," whiteness and blackness, maleness and femaleness, heterosexuality and homosexuality, merely by the fact that they seek to diffuse those tensions and reconcile contradictions through very specific sexual practices. Concluding her study of white supremacism in the USA, Ferber observes that "White supremacist discourse rearticulates dominant discourses on race and gender: therefore, any effective political response to the white supremacist movement must also attack these mainstream narratives" (1999: 156). The same point holds good in relation to the subculture of hardcore male heterosexual sex tourism.

NOTES

1. The interview data presented in this article was collected by Jacqueline Sanchez Taylor and the author in the course of ESRC funded research on tourist-related prostitution in the Caribbean.

2. See, for example, Hall's (1992) discussion of the debate between Thomas Carlyle and John Stuart Mill on Governor Eyre's reprisals against black Jamaicans following the 1865 Morant Bay riot, also Parekh (1995).

3. See Elizabeth Grosz's discussion of Nietzsche and "body inscription as the cultural condition for establishing social order and obedience" (1994: 129).

4. Men who seek sexual contact with boy children are the focus of particularly intense hostility from hardcore male heterosexual tourists, but the boundary between "regular guys" and "paedophiles" is less clear cut in relation to girl children.

5. See Theweleit's (1989) analysis of the writings of members of the German *Freikorps* in the 1920s, and Ferber's (1999) discussion of white supremacists in the contemporary USA.

REFERENCES

Bhattacharyya, G. (1997) "The Fabulous Adventures of the Mahogany Princesses," in H. Mirza (ed.) *Black British Feminism*. London: Routledge.

Bishop, R. and Robinson, L. (1998) *Night Market: Sexual Cultures and the Thai Economic Miracle*. London: Routledge.

Brace, L. (1997) "Imagining the Boundaries of a Sovereign Self," in L. Brace and J. Hoffman (eds) *Reclaiming Sovereignty*, pp. 137–54. London: Cassell.

Brace, L. and O'Connell Davidson, J. (1996) "Desperate Debtors and Counterfeit Love: The Hobbesian World of the Sex Tourist," *Contemporary Politics* 2(3): 55–78.

Cassirer, B. (1992) *Travel & the Single Male*. Channel Island, CA: TSM.

Chow, R. (1999) "The Politics of Admittance: Female Sexual Agency, Miscegenation, and the Formation of Community in Frantz Fanon," in A. Alessandrini (ed.) *Frantz Fanon: Critical Perspectives*, pp. 34–56. London: Routledge.

Clift, S. and Carter, S., eds (2000) *Tourism and Sex: Culture, Commerce and Coercion*. London: Pinter.

Dollimore, J. (1991) *Sexual Dissidence: Augustine to Wilde, Freud to Foucault*. Oxford: Clarendon Press.

Ferber, A. (1999) *White Man Falling: Race, Gender and White Supremacy*. New York: Rowman and Littlefield.

Freud, S. (1985 [1913]) "Totem and Taboo," in Sigmund Freud *The Origins of Religion*, vol 13, pp. 43–224. Harmondsworth: Penguin.

Grosz, E. (1994) *Volatile Bodies: Toward a Corporeal Feminism*. Bloomington and Indianapolis: Indiana University Press.

Hall, C. (1992) *White, Male and Middle Class*. Cambridge: Polity.

Herrnstein, R. and Murray, C. (1994) *The Bell Curve: Intelligence and Class Structure in American Life*. New York: The Free Press.

Hobbes, T. (1968) *Leviathan*. Harmondsworth: Penguin.

Howard, D. (1999) *Dominican Republic*. London: Latin America Bureau.

Hughes, D. (1998/9) "men@exploitation.com," *Trouble & Strife* 38: 21–27.

Ireland, K. (1993) *Wish You Weren't Here*. London: Save the Children.

Kruhse-MountBurton, S. (1995) "Sex Tourism and Traditional Australian Male Identity," in M. Lanfant, J. Allcock and E. Bruner (eds) *International Tourism: Identity and Change*. London: Sage.

McClintock, A. (1995) *Imperial Leather: Race, Gender and Sexuality in the Colonial Contest*. London: Routledge.

Mercer, K. (1995) "Busy in the Ruins of Wretched Phantasia," in R. Farr (ed.) *Mirage: Enigmas of Race, Difference and Desire*. London: ICA/Institute of International Visual Arts.

Mills, C. (1998) *The Racial Contract*. Ithaca: Cornell University Press.

Moore, C. (1993) *A Haunting Smile*. Bangkok: White Lotus Press.

Murray, C. (1990) *The Emerging British Underclass*. London: The IEA Health and Welfare Unit.

O'Connell Davidson, J. (1995) "British Sex Tourists in Thailand," in M. Maynard and J. Purvis (eds), *(Hetero)sexual Politics*, pp. 42–64. London: Taylor & Francis.

O'Connell Davidson, J. (1996) "Sex Tourism in Cuba," *Race & Class* 37(3): 39–48.

O'Connell Davidson, J. (1998) *Prostitution, Power and Freedom*. Cambridge: Polity.

O'Connell Davidson, J. and Sanchez Taylor, J. (1996) "Child Prostitution and Sex Tourism," research papers 1–7. Bangkok: ECPAT.

Parekh, B. (1995) "Liberalism and Colonialism: A Critique of Locke and Mill," in J. Nederveen and B. Parekh (eds) *The Decolonisation of Imagination: Culture, Knowledge and Power,* pp. 81–98. London: Zed.

Pateman, C. (1988) *The Sexual Contract.* Cambridge: Polity.

Pruitt, D. and LaFont, S. (1995) "For Love and Money: Romance Tourism in Jamaica," *Annals of Tourism Research* 22(2): 422–40.

Puwar, N. (1999) "Embodying the Body Politic: Race and Gender in the British State Elite," PhD thesis, University of Essex.

Rubin, G. (1975) "The Traffic in Women: Notes on the "Political Economy" of Sex," in R. Reiter (ed) *Toward an Anthropology of Women.* New York: Monthly Review Press.

Said, E. (1978) *Orientalism: Western Conceptions of the Orient.* Harmondsworth: Penguin.

Sanchez Taylor, J. (2000) "Tourism and 'Embodied' Commodities: Sex Tourism in the Caribbean," in S. Clift and S. Carter (eds) *Tourism and Sex: Culture, Commerce and Coercion,* pp. 41–53. London: Pinter.

Seabrook, J. (1996) *Travels in the Skin Trade: Tourism and the Sex Industry.* London: Pluto Press.

Seidler, V. (1987) "Reason, Desire and Male Sexuality," in P. Caplan (ed) *The Cultural Construction of Sexuality,* pp. 82–112. London: Routledge.

Somerville, S. (1997) "Scientific Racism and the Invention of the Homosexual Body," in R. Lancaster and M. di Leonardo (eds) *The Gender/Sexuality Reader,* pp. 37–52. London: Routledge.

Theweleit, K. (1987) *Male Fantasies, Volume 1.* Cambridge: Polity.

Truong, T. (1990) *Sex, Money and Morality: Prostitution and Tourism in Southeast Asia.* London: Zed Books.

UKMM (1999) *UK Men's Movement Mission Statement* http://www.ukmm.org.net

Wellman, D. (1997) "Minstrel Shows, Affirmative Action Talk, and Angry White Men: Marking Racial Otherness in the 1990s," in R. Frankenberg (ed) *Displacing Whiteness,* pp. 311–31. London: Duke University Press.

WTO (World Tourism Organization) (1997) "International Arrivals in the Americas 1996," cited in *Travel Weekly,* November 6.

18

The Globalization of Sexual Identities

DENNIS ALTMAN

Most of the literature about globalization and identity is concerned with the rebirth of nationalist, ethnic, and religious fundamentalism, or the decline of the labor movement.[1] (I am using "identity" to suggest a socially constructed myth about shared characteristics, culture, and history which comes to have real meaning for those who espouse it.)[2] Here I concentrate on the identity politics born of sexuality and gender, and the new social movements which arise from these. These new identities are closely related to the larger changes of globalization: consider the globalization of "youth," and the role of international capitalism in creating a teenage identity in almost every country, with specific music, language, fashion, and mores.[3] In recent years this is expressed in terms of "boy" and "girl" cultures, as in references to "boy bands" or "a booming girl culture worldwide,"[4] which suggests the invention of an intermediate generational identity between "children" and "youth."

Over the past decade I've been researching and thinking about the diffusion of certain sorts of "gay/lesbian" identities, trying to trace the connections between globalization and the preconditions for certain sexual subjectivities.[5] My examples are drawn predominantly from Southeast Asia because this is the part of the "developing" world I know best, but they could even more easily be drawn from Latin America, which has a particularly rich literature exploring these questions.[6] The question is not whether homosexuality exists—it does in almost every society of which we know—but how people incorporate homosexual behavior into their sense of self. Globalization has helped create an international gay/lesbian identity, which is by no means confined to the western world: there are many signs of what we think of as "modern" homosexuality in countries such as Brazil, Costa Rica, Poland, and Taiwan. Indeed the gay world—less obviously the lesbian, largely due to marked differences in women's social and economic status—is a key example of emerging global "subcultures," where members of particular groups have more in common across national and continental boundaries than they do with others in their own geographically defined societies.

It is worth noting that even within the "first world" there is a range of attitudes toward the assertion of gay/lesbian identities. While they have flourished in the English-speaking countries and in parts of northern Europe, there is more resistance to the idea in Italy and France, where ideas of communal rights—expressed through the language of multiculturalism in Australia and Canada, and through a somewhat different tradition of religious pluralism in the Netherlands and Switzerland—seem to run counter to a universalist rhetoric of rights, which are not equated with the recognition of separate group identities.[7] The United States shares both traditions, so that its gay and lesbian movement argues for recognition of "civil rights" on the basis of being just like everyone else, and in some cases deserving of special protection along the lines developed around racial and gender discrimination.

At the same time the United States has gone farthest in the development of geographically based gay and lesbian communities, with defined areas of its large cities—the Castro in San Francisco, West Hollywood, Halsted in Chicago, the West Village in New York— becoming urban "ghettos," often providing a base to develop the political clout of the community. (In almost all large American cities politicians now recognize the importance of the gay vote.) This model has been replicated in a number of western countries, whether it is the Marais in Paris or Darlinghurst in Sydney. There is some irony in the fact that, while homosexual rights have progressed much further in the countries of northern Europe, the United States remains the dominant cultural model for the rest of the world.

This dominance was symbolized in accounts in Europe of "gay pride" events in the summer of 1999, which often ignored national histories and attributed the origins of gay political activism to the Stonewall riots of 1969, ignoring the existence of earlier groups in countries such as Germany, the Netherlands, Switzerland, and France, and the radical gay groups which grew out of the 1968 student movements in both France and Italy. (Stonewall was a gay bar in New York City which was raided by the police, leading to riots by angry homosexuals and the birth of the New York Gay Liberation Front.) In cities as diverse as Paris, Hamburg, and Warsaw the anniversary of Stonewall was celebrated with Christopher Street Day, and the dominance of American culture is summed up by the press release from the Lisbon Gay, Lesbian, Bisexual, and Transgender Pride committee boasting of the performances of a "renowned DJ from New York City" and "Celeda—the Diva Queen from Chicago."

Thinking and writing about these questions, it became clear to me that observers, indigenous and foreign alike, bring strong personal investments to how they understand what is going on, in particular whether (in words suggested to me by Michael Tan) we are speaking of "ruptures" or "continuities." For some there is a strong desire to trace a continuity between precolonial forms of homosexual desire and its contemporary emergence, even where the latter might draw on the language of (West) Hollywood rather than indigenous culture. Such views are argued strenuously by those who cling to an identity based on traditional assumptions about the links between gender performance and sexuality, and deny the relevance of an imported "gay" or "lesbian" identity for themselves. Thus the effeminate *bakkla* in the Philippines or the *kathoey* in Thailand might see those who call themselves "gay" as hypocrites, in part because they insist on their right to behave as men, and to desire others like them.[8] For others there is a perception that contemporary middle-class self-proclaimed gay men and lesbians in, say, New Delhi, Lima, or Jakarta have less in common with "traditional" homosexuality than they do with their counterparts in western countries. As Sri Lankan author Shaym Selvadurai said of his novel *Funny Boy,* which is in part about "coming out" as gay: "The people in the novel are in a place that has been colonized by Western powers for 400 years. A lot of Western ideas—bourgeois respectability, Victorian morality—have become incorporated into the society, and are very much part of the Sri Lankan society."[9]

"Modern" ways of being homosexual threaten not only the custodians of "traditional" morality, they also threaten the position of "traditional" forms of homosexuality, those which are centered around gender nonconformity and transvestism. The title of the Indonesian gay/lesbian journal *Gaya Nusantara,* which literally means "Indonesian style," captures this ambivalence nicely with its echoes of both "traditional" and "modern" concepts of nation and sexuality, but at the same time it is clearly aimed at "modern" homosexuals rather than the "traditional" transvestite *waria*.[10]

It is often assumed that homosexuals are defined in most "traditional" societies as a third sex, but that too is too schematic to be universally useful. As Peter Jackson points out, the same terms in Thailand can be gender *and* sexual categories. Here, again, we are confronted by considerable confusion, where similar phenomena can be viewed as either culturally specific or as universal. Insofar as there is a confusion between sexuality and gender in the "traditional" view that the "real" homosexual is the man who behaves like a woman (or, more rarely, vice versa) this is consistent with the dominant understanding of homosexuality in western countries during the hundred years or so before the birth of the contemporary gay movement. The idea of a "third sex" was adopted by people like Ulrichs and Krafft-Ebing as part of an apologia for homosexuality (giving rise to Carpenter's "intermediate sex").[11] In the 1918 novel *Despised and Rejected* the hero laments: "What had nature been about, in giving him the soul of a woman in the body of a man?"[12] Similar views can be found in Radclyffe Hall's novel *The Well of Loneliness* (1928), whose female hero calls herself Stephen. Today many people who experience homosexual desires in societies which do not allow space for them will see themselves as "men trapped in women's bodies" or vice versa.

In popular perceptions something of this confusion remains today—and persists in much popular humor, such as the remarkably successful play/film *La cage aux folles* (*The Birdcage*) or the film *Priscilla, Queen of the Desert*. George Chauncey argues that the very idea of a homosexual/heterosexual divide became dominant in the United States only in the mid-twentieth century: "The most striking difference between the dominant sexual culture of the early twentieth century and that of our own era is the degree to which the earlier culture permitted men to engage in sexual relations with other men, often on a regular basis, without requiring them to regard themselves—or be regarded by others—as gay. . . . Many men . . . neither understood nor organised their sexual practices along a hetero-homosexual axis."[13] John Rechy's landmark novel *City of Night* (1963) captures the transition to

"modern" concepts: his world is full of "hustlers," "queens," "masculine" or "butch" homosexuals, whom he sometimes calls "gay."[14]

If one reads or views contemporary accounts of homosexual life in, say, Central America, Thailand, and Côte d'Ivoire,[15] one is immediately struck by the parallels. It is of course possible that the observers, all of whom are trained in particular ethnographic and sociological methods, even where, as in the case of Schifter they are indigenous to the country of study, are bringing similar—and one assumes unconscious—preconceptions with them. Even so, it is unlikely that this itself would explain the degree of similarity they identify. In the same way, the Dutch anthropologist Saskia Wieringa has pointed to the similarities of butch-femme role-playing in Jakarta and Lima, and how they echo that of preliberation western lesbian worlds.[16] In many "traditional" societies there were complex variations across gender and sex lines, with "transgender" people (Indonesian *waria*, Thai *kathoey*, Moroccan *hassas*, Turkish *kocek*, Filipino *bayot*, Luban *kitesha* in parts of Congo) characterized by both transvestite and homosexual behavior. These terms are usually—not always—applied to men, but there are other terms sometimes used of women, such as *mati* in Suriname, which also disrupt simplistic assumptions about sex and gender.[17] As Gilbert Herdt says: "Sexual orientation and identity are not the keys to conceptualizing a third sex and gender across time and space."[18] In many societies there is confusion around the terms—for example the *hijras* of India, who were literally castrated, are sometimes considered equivalent to homosexuals even though the reality is more complex.[19]

Different people use terms such as *bayot* or *waria* in different ways, depending on whether the emphasis is on gender—these are men who wish in some way to be women—or on sexuality—these are men attracted to other men. Anthropology teaches us the need to be cautious about any sort of binary system of sex/gender; Niko Besnier uses the term "gender liminality" to avoid this trap[20] and it should also alert us against the sort of romanticized assumptions that some Americans have brought to understanding the Native American *bedarche*.[21] Besnier also stresses that such "liminality" is not the same as homosexuality. "Sexual relations with men are seen as an optional consequence of gender liminality, rather than its determiner, prerequisite or primary attribute."[22] The other side of this distinction is that there are strong pressures to define *fa'afine* (the Samoan term) or other such groups in Pacific countries as asexual, thus leading to a particular denial in which both Samoans and outsiders are complicit.[23]

Certainly most of the literature about Latin America stresses that a homosexual *identity* (as distinct from homosexual practices) is related to rejection of dominant gender expectations, so that "a real man" can have sex with other men and not risk his heterosexual identity. As Roger Lancaster put it: "Whatever else a *cochon* might or might not do, he is tacitly understood as one who assumes the receptive role in anal intercourse. His partner, defined as 'active' in the terms of their engagement, is not stigmatized, nor does he acquire a special identity of any sort."[24] Thus the *nature* rather than the *object* of the sexual act becomes the key factor. However, there is also evidence that this is changing, and a more western concept of homosexual identity is establishing itself, especially among the middle classes.

Sexuality becomes an important arena for the production of modernity, with "gay" and "lesbian" identities acting as markers for modernity.[25] There is an ironic echo of this in the Singapore government's bulldozing of Bugis Street, once the center of transvestite prostitution in the city—and its replacement by a Disneyland-like simulacrum where a few years ago I was taken to see a rather sanitized drag show presented to a distinctly yuppie audience.[26] There is an equal irony in seeing the decline of a homosexuality defined by gender nonconformity as a "modern" trend just when transsexuals and some theorists in western countries are increasingly attracted by concepts of the malleability of gender.[27] From one perspective the fashionable replica of the stylized "lipstick lesbian" or "macho" gay man is less "post-modern" than the *waria* or the Tongan *fakaleiti*.[28]

Perhaps the reality is that androgyny is postmodern when it is understood as performance, not when it represents the only available way of acting out certain deep-seated beliefs about one's sexual and gender identity. Even so, I remain unsure just why "drag," and its female equivalents, remains a strong part of the contemporary homosexual world, even where there is increasing space for open homosexuality and a range of acceptable ways of "being" male or female. Indeed there is evidence that in some places there is a simultaneous increase in both gay/lesbian identities *and* in transgender performance, as in recent developments in Taiwan where drag shows have become very fashionable, and some of the performers, known as "third sex public relations officers," insist that they are not homosexual even when their behavior would seem to contradict this.[29] Similar comments could probably be made about *onnabe,* Japanese women who dress as men and act as the equivalent of geishas for apparently heterosexual women, and Jennifer Robertson describes the incorporation of androgyny into the "'libidinal' economy of the capitalist market" as "gender-bending" performers are turned into marketable commodities.[30] In the west it has become increasingly fashionable to depict transvestism in unmistakably heterosexual terms; what was daring (and possibly ambiguous) in the 1959 film *Some Like It Hot* becomes farce in the 1993 film *Mrs. Doubtfire.*[31] But at the same time there is, particularly in the United States, the emergence of a somewhat new form of transgender politics, in which the concern of an older generation to be accepted as the woman or man they "really" are is replaced by an assertion of a transgender identity and the malleability of gender.[32] (Western writers tend to be reasonably careful to distinguish between *transsexual* and *transvestite.* However, this distinction is often not made in parts of Asia and, I assume, other parts of the world.)

Speaking openly of homosexuality and transvestism, which is often the consequence of western influence, can unsettle what is accepted but not acknowledged. Indeed there is some evidence in a number of societies that those who proclaim themselves "gay" or "lesbian," that is, seek a public identity based on their sexuality, encounter a hostility which may not have been previously apparent. But there is a great deal of mythology around the acceptance of gender/sexual nonconformity outside the west, a mythology to which for different reasons both westerners and nonwesterners contribute. Romanticized views about homoeroticism in many nonwestern cultures, often based on travel experiences, disguise the reality of persecution, discrimination, and violence, sometimes in unfamiliar forms. Firsthand accounts make it clear that homosexuality is far from being universally accepted—or even tolerated—in such apparent "paradises" as Morocco, the Philippines, Thailand, or Brazil: "Lurking behind the Brazilians' pride of their flamboyant drag queens, their recent adulation of a transvestite chosen as a model of Brazilian beauty, their acceptance of gays and lesbians as leaders of the country's most widely practised religion and the constitutional protection of homosexuality, lies a different truth. Gay men, lesbians and transvestites face widespread discrimination, oppression and extreme violence."[33]

Just as the most interesting postmodern architecture is found in cities like Shanghai or Bangkok, so too the emphasis of postmodern theory on pastiche, parody, hybridity, and so forth is played out in a real way by women and men who move, often with considerable comfort, from apparent obedience to official norms to their own sense of gay community. The dutiful Confucian or Islamic Malaysian son one weekend might appear in drag at Blueboy, Kuala Lumpur's gay bar, the next—and who is to say which is "the real" person? Just as many Malaysians can move easily from one language to another, so most urban homosexuals can move from one style to another, from camping it up with full awareness of the latest fashion trends from Castro Street to playing the dutiful son at a family celebration.

To western gay liberationists these strategies might seem hypocritical, even cowardly (and some westerners expressed surprise at the apparent silence from Malaysian gay men after the arrest of Anwar on sodomy charges). But even the most politically aware Malaysians may insist that there is no need to "come out" to their family, while explaining that in any case their lover is accepted as one of the family—though not so identified. (The Malaysian situation is further complicated by the fact that Muslims are subject to both civil and *sharia* laws, and the latter have been used quite severely, against transvestites in particular.) Some people have suggested that everything is possible *as long as it is not stated,* but it is probably more complex than that. For many men I have met in Southeast Asia being gay does mean a sense of communal identity, and even a sense of "gay pride," but this is not necessarily experienced in the vocabulary of the west.

Middle-class English-speaking homosexuals in places like Mexico City, Istanbul, and Mumbai will speak of themselves as part of a gay (sometimes "gay and lesbian") community, but the institutions of such a community will vary considerably depending on both economic resources and political space. Thus in Kuala Lumpur, one of the richer cities of the "developing" world, there are no gay or lesbian bookstores, restaurants, newspapers, or businesses—at least not in the open way we would expect them in comparable American or European cities. There is, however, a strong sense of gay identity around the AIDS organization Pink Triangle—its name is emblematic—and sufficient networks for a gay sauna to open and attract customers. Yet when a couple of years ago I gave some copies of the Australian gay magazine *Outrage* to the manager of the Kuala Lumpur sauna, I was told firmly there could be no display of something as overtly homosexual as these magazines—which are routinely sold by most Australian newsagents. In the same way there is also a strong lesbian network in the city, and many women use office faxes and email to arrange meetings and parties.

At that same sauna I met one man who told me he had heard of the place through a friend now living in Sydney. In conversations I have had with middle-class gay men in Southeast Asia there are frequent references to bars in Paris and San Francisco, to Sydney's Gay and Lesbian Mardi Gras, to American gay writers. Those who take on gay identities often aspire to be part of global culture in all its forms, as suggested by this quote from a Filipino anthology of gay writing: "I met someone in a bar last Saturday . . . He's a bank executive. He's mestizo (your type) and . . . loves Barbra Streisand, Gabriel Garcia Marquez, Dame Margot Fonteyn, Pat Conroy, Isabel Allende, John Williams, Meryl Streep, Armistead Maupin, k. d. lang, Jim Chappell, Margaret Atwood and Luciano Pavarotti."[34]

Similarly magazines like *G & L* in Taiwan—a "lifestyle" magazine launched in 1996—mix local news and features with stories on international, largely American, gay and lesbian icons. As mobility increases, more and more people are traveling abroad and meeting foreigners at home. It is as impossible to prevent new identities and categories traveling as it is to prevent pornography traveling across the Internet.

As part of the economic growth of south and east Asia the possibilities of computer-based communications have been grasped with enormous enthusiasm, and have created a new set of possibilities for the diffusion of information and the creation of (virtual) communities. Whereas the gay movements of the 1970s in the west depended heavily on the creation of a gay/lesbian press, in countries such as Malaysia, Thailand, and Japan the Internet offers the same possibilities, with the added attraction of anonymity and instant contact with overseas, thus fostering the links with the diaspora already discussed. Work by Chris Berry and Fran Martin suggests that the Internet has become a crucial way for young homosexuals to meet each other in Taiwan and Korea—and in the process to develop a certain, if privatized, form of community.[35] In Japan the Internet has become a central aid to homosexual cruising.

It is precisely this constant dissemination of images and ways of being, moving disproportionately from north to south, which leads some to savagely criticize the spread of sexual identities as a new step in neocolonialism: "The very constitution of a subject entitled to rights involves the violent capture of the disenfranchised by an institutional discourse which inseparably weaves them into the textile of global capitalism."[36] This position is argued with splendid hyperbole by Pedro Bustos-Aguilar, who attacks both "the gay ethnographer . . . [who] kills a native with the charm of his camera" and "the union of the New World Order and Transnational Feminism" which asserts neocolonialism and western hegemony in the name of supposed universalisms.[37]

Bustos-Aguilar's argument is supported by the universalist rhetoric which surrounded the celebration of the twenty-fifth anniversary of Stonewall, but he could have had great fun with a 1993 brochure from San Francisco which offered "your chance to make history . . . [at] the first ever gay & lesbian film festival in India & parallel queer tour"—and even more with the reporter from the Washington Blade who wrote of Anwar's "ostensibly being gay."[38] It finds a troubling echo in the story of an American, Tim Wright, who founded a gay movement in Bolivia, and after four years was found badly beaten and amnesiac: "And things have gone back to being what they were."[39]

A more measured critique comes from Ann Ferguson, who has warned that the very concept of an international lesbian *culture* is politically problematic, because it would almost certainly be based upon western assumptions, even though she is somewhat more optimistic about the creation of an international *movement*, which would allow for self-determination of local lesbian communities.[40] While western influences were clearly present, it is as true to see the emergence of groups in much of Latin America, in Southeast Asia, and among South African blacks as driven primarily by local forces.

It is certainly true that the assertion of gay/lesbian identity can have neocolonial implications, but given that many anti/postcolonial movements and governments deny existing homosexual traditions it becomes difficult to know exactly whose values are being imposed on whom. Both the western outsider and the local custodians of national culture are likely to ignore existing realities in the interest of ideological certainty. Those outside the west tend to be more aware of the difference between traditional homosexualities and contemporary gay identity politics, a distinction sometimes lost by the international gay/lesbian movement in its eagerness to claim universality.[41] New sexual identities mean a loss of certain traditional cultural comforts while offering new possibilities to those who adopt them, and activists in nonwestern countries will consciously draw on both traditions. In this they may be inconsistent, but no more than western gay activists who simultaneously deploy the language of universal rights and special group status.

In practice most people hold contradictory opinions at the same time, reminding us of Freud's dictum that "it is only in logic that contradictions cannot exist." There are large numbers of men and fewer women in nonwestern countries who will describe themselves as "gay" or "lesbian" in certain circumstances, while sometimes claiming these labels are inappropriate to their situation. It is hardly surprising that people want both to identify with and to distinguish themselves from a particular western form of homosexuality, or that they will call upon their own historical traditions to do so. This ambivalence is caught in this account by a Chinese-Australian: "[Chinese] gays were determined to advance their cause but in an evolutionary rather than revolutionary way. They seized on issues such as gayness, gay culture, gay lifestyle, equal rights for gays and so on. In romantic poems the gay dreams of our ancestors were represented by two boys sharing a peach and the emperor who cut his sleeves of his gown rather than disturb his lover sleeping in his arms. To revive this dream, and enable millions of Chinese-born gays to choose their lifestyle, is a huge task. But it has happened in Taiwan, as it did in Hong Kong, and so it will in China."[42]

There are of course examples of Asian gay groups engaging in political activity of the sort associated with their counterparts in the west. Indonesia has a number of gay and lesbian groups, which have now held three national meetings. The best-known openly gay figure in Indonesia, Dede Oetomo, was a candidate of the fledg-ling Democratic People's Party in the 1999 elections, which followed the overthrow of Suharto. There have been several small radical gay political groups estab-lished in the Philippines in recent years, and gay demonstrations have taken place in Manila. ProGay (the Progressive Organization of Gays in the Philip-pines), as its name suggests, is concerned to draw links between specifically gay issues and larger questions of social justice.[43] The first lesbian conference was held in Japan in 1985,[44] and there have been lesbian organiza-tions in Taiwan since 1990 and the Philippines since 1992.[45] The international lesbigay press carried reports of a national conference of lesbians in Beijing in late 1998 and in Sri Lanka the following year. There have been several *tongzhi* gatherings in Hong Kong (a term adopted to cover "lesbians, bisexuals, gays and trans-gendered people"), and a manifesto adopted by the 1996 meeting argued that "[c]ertain characteristics of confrontational politics, such as through coming out and mass protests and parades may not be the best way of achieving *tongzhi* liberation in the family-centred, community-oriented Chinese societies which stress the importance of social harmony."[46] (An odd myth, given the revolutionary upheavals in twentieth-century China.) None of these groups have the history or the reach of gay/lesbian movements in Latin America, where Brazil, Argentina, Chile, and Mexico all have significant histories of a politicized homosexuality.

In many cases homosexual identities are asserted without an apparent gay/lesbian movement. In 1998 there was a move by bar owners in Kuala Lumpur to organize a gay-pride party which was canceled after a protest by the Malaysian Youth Council. The best ex-ample of a nonpolitical gay world can probably be found in Thailand, where there is a growing middle-class gay world, based neither on prostitution nor on traditional forms of gender nonconformity (as in the person of the *kathoey*), but only a small lesbian group, Anjaree, and no gay male groups at all since the col-lapse of a couple of attempts to organize around HIV in the late 1980s.[47] In late 1996 controversy erupted in Thailand after the governing body of the country's teacher-training colleges decreed that "sexual de-viants" would be barred from entering the colleges. While there was considerable opposition to the ban (subsequently dropped), other than Anjaree most of this came from nongay sources. In the ensuing public debate one could see contradictory outside influences at work—both an imported fear of homosexuals and a more modern emphasis on how such a ban infringed human rights. As Peter Jackson concluded: "A dy-namic gay scene has emerged . . . in the complete absence of a gay rights movement."[48]

Indeed it may be that a political movement is the least likely part of western concepts of homosexual identity to be adopted in many parts of the world, even as some activists enthusiastically embrace the mores and imagery of western queerdom. The particular form of identity politics which allowed for the mobilization of a gay/lesbian electoral pressure in countries like the United States, the Netherlands, and even France may not be appropriate elsewhere, even if western-style lib-eral democracy triumphs. The need of western les-bian/gays to engage in identity politics as a means of enhancing self-esteem may not be felt in other soci-eties. Even so, one should read Jackson's comment about Thailand with some caution. Already when he wrote it there was an embryonic group in Bangkok around an American-owned and -run gay bookstore. At the end of 1999 one of the country's gay papers organ-ized a gay festival and twilight parade in the heart of Bangkok, announcing it as "the first and biggest gay parade in Asia where Asian gay men have a basic human right to be who they want to be and love who they want to love."[49] Similarly, accounts of homosex-ual life in Japan alternate between assuming a high degree of acceptance—and therefore no reason for a political movement—and severe restrictions on the space to assert homosexual identity, though the gay group OCCUR has recently gained a certain degree of visibility.

The western gay/lesbian movement emerged in conditions of affluence and liberal democracy, where despite other large social issues it was possible to develop a politics around sexuality, which is more difficult in countries where the basic structures of political life are constantly contested.[50] Writing of contemporary South Africa Mark Gevisser notes: "Race-identification overpowers everything else—class, gender and sexuality."[51] In the same way basic questions of political economy and democratization will impact the future development of gay/lesbian movements in much of Asia and Africa. Yet in Latin America and eastern Europe gay/lesbian movements have grown considerably in the past decade, and there are signs of their emergence in some parts of Africa, for example in Botswana and in Zimbabwe, where President Mugabe has consistently attacked homosexuality as the product of colonialism.[52] Similar rhetoric has come from the leaders of Kenya,[53] Namibia, and Uganda, whose President Museveni has denounced homosexuality as "western"—using the rhetoric of the Christian right to do so.[54] Anglican bishops from Africa—though not South Africa—were crucial in defeating moves to change the Church of England's attitudes toward homosexuality at the 1998 decennial Lambeth Conference. South Africa is a crucial exception, perhaps because apartheid's denunciation of homosexuality made it easier for the African National Congress to develop a policy of acceptance as part of their general support for "a rainbow nation." Even so, some elements of the ANC are strongly homophobic, revealed in the rhetoric of many of Winnie Mandela's supporters.[55]

While many African officials and clergy maintain that homosexuality is not part of precolonial African culture, the evidence for its existence—and the slow acknowledgment of its role in African life—is emerging across the continent. One might speculate that the strong hostility from some African political and religious leaders toward homosexuality as a "western import" is an example of psychoanalytic displacement, whereby anxieties about sexuality are redirected to

continuing resentment against colonialism and the subordinate position of Africa within the global economy. Western-derived identities can easily become markers of those aspects of globalization which are feared and opposed. Similarly, a 1994 conference for gay/MSMs (men who have sex with men) in Bombay was opposed by the National Federation of Indian Women, an affiliate of the Communist party of India, as "an invasion of India by decadent western cultures and a direct fall-out of our signing the GATT agreement."[56] Whether the federation was aware of how close its rhetoric was to right-wing Americans such as Patrick Buchanan is unknown.

Part of the appearance of modernity is the use of western languages. Rodney Jones has noted the importance of English as part of the cultural capital of Hong Kong homosexuals,[57] and when I attended an AIDS conference in Morocco in 1996 participants complained that despite an attempt to ensure equal use of Arabic it was "easier" to talk about sexuality in French. A similar emphasis on English is noted by James Farrar in presumably heterosexual discos in Shanghai, where ironically the Village People song "YMCA" has now become "a globalized dance ritual in which the dancers are encouraged to use their hands to make shapes of the English letters, identifying themselves momentarily with a boundless global ecumene of sexy happy youth 'at the YMCA.' "[58] One assumes the Shanghai dancers are unaware of the clearly gay overtones to both the song and the group. I admit to particular pleasure in reading this piece; an early proposal for my book *The Homosexualization of America* was rejected by an editor who complained (this was in 1982) that in a year no one would remember the Village People, the image with which I began that book.

A common language is essential for networking, and the past twenty years have seen a rapid expansion of networks among lesbian and gay groups across the world. In 1978 the International Lesbian and Gay Association (ILGA) was formed at a conference in Coventry, England.[59] While ILGA has largely been driven by northern Europeans, it now has member groups in more than seventy countries and has organized international meetings in several southern cities. Other networks, often linked to feminist and AIDS organizing, have been created in the past two decades, and emerging lesbian and gay movements are increasingly likely to be in constant contact with groups across the world. The inspiration from meeting with other lesbians at international women's conferences has been a powerful factor in the creation of lesbian groups in a number of countries. Thus the Asian Lesbian Network, which now includes women from twelve or thirteen countries, began at an International Lesbian Information Service conference in Geneva in 1986.[60]

In recent years there has been some attempt to promote international networking among transgendered people—or, as Americans now call them, transfolk—with both the British-based International Gender Transient Affinity and the U.S.-based Gender Freedom International lobbying to protect transgendered people across the world from what seems to be routine harassment and persecution. The paradox of globalization is played out in constructions of sex/gender which combine the premodern with the modern, so that people identifying with "traditional" forms of transgender identity will employ modern techniques of surgery and hormone therapy to alter their bodies.

The two largest international gay/lesbian institutions are probably those based around the Metropolitan Community Church and the Gay Games. The MCC is a Protestant sect founded by the Reverend Troy Perry in Los Angeles in 1968, whose congregations and ministers are largely homosexual, with an estimated congregation of more than 40,000 in some sixteen countries. Similar gay churches have emerged somewhat independently in several other societies such as South Africa and Mexico.[61] The Gay Games, modeled on the Olympics, which refused the use of its name, were first held in San Francisco in 1982, and have since become a major international event every four years, for which cities contend very bitterly. They also generate considerable international publicity, much of it of a somewhat voyeuristic nature.[62] Both of these "networks," it is worth stressing, originated in the United States.

Homosexuality becomes a particularly obvious measure of globalization, for the transformation of local regimes of sexuality and gender is often most apparent in the emergence of new sorts of apparently "gay" and "lesbian," even "queer," identities. Yet we must beware reading too much into these scripts. What is happening in Bangkok, Rio, and Nairobi is the creation of new forms of understanding and regulating the sexual self, but it is unlikely that they will merely repeat those forms which were developed in the Atlantic world. Walking through the "gay" area of Tokyo's Shinjuku you will see large numbers of young men in sneakers and baseball caps (or whatever happens to be the current "gay" look) but this does not mean they will behave or view themselves in the same way as equivalent young men in North America or northern Europe. . . .

NOTES

1. E.g., Frances Fox Piven, "Globalizing Capitalism and the Rise of Identity Politics," In L. Panitch, ed., *Socialist Register* (London: Merlin, 1995), 102–16; Leslie Sklair, "Social Movements and Global Capitalism," in F. Jameson and M. Miyoshi, eds., *The Cultures of Globalization* (Durham: Duke University Press, 1998), 291–311.

2. For a clear exposition of this view of social constructionism see Jeffrey Weeks, *Sexuality and Its Discontents* (London: Routledge & Kegan Paul, 1985).

3. E.g., Beverley Hooper, "Chinese Youth: The Nineties Generation," *Current History* 90:557 (1991):264–69.

4. See Sherrie Inness, ed., *Millennium Girls* (Lanham, MD: Rowman & Littlefield, 1999); Marion Leonard, "Paper Planes: Travelling the New Grrrl Geographies," in T. Skelton and G. Valentine, eds., *Cool Places: Geographies of Youth Cultures* (London: Routledge, 1998), 101–18.

5. Much of this section draws on work originally published in the mid-1990s. See especially Dennis Altman, "Rupture or Continuity? The Internationalization of Gay Identities," *Social Text* 14:3 (1996): 77–94; Altman, "On Global Queering," *Australian Humanities Review*, no. 2, July 1996 (electronic journal, www.lib.latrobe.edu.au); Altman, "Global Gaze/Global Gays." *GLQ* 3 (1997): 417–36.

6. The chapters on Brazil and Argentina in B. Adam, J. W. Duyvendak, and A. Krouwel, eds., *The Global Emergence of Gay and Lesbian Politics* (Philadelphia: Temple University Press, 1999): 259–77 and the special issue of *Culture, Health, and Society* (1:3 [1999]) on "alternative sexualities and changing identities among Latin American men," edited by Richard Parker and Carlos Carceres.

7. On the Netherlands see Judith Schuyf and Andre Krouwel, "The Dutch Lesbian and Gay Movement: The Politics of Accommodation," in Adam, Duyvendak, and Krouwel, *Global Emergence of Gay and Lesbian Politics*, 158–83. On Australia see Dennis

Altman, "Multiculturalism and the Emergence of Lesbian/Gay Worlds," in R. Nile, ed., *Australian Civilisation* (Melbourne: Oxford University Press, 1994), 110–24.

8. I owe thanks to a long list of people who over the years have discussed these issues with me, including Ben Anderson, Eufracio Abaya, Hisham Hussein, Lawrence Leong, Shivananda Khan, Peter Jackson, Julian Jayaseelan, Ted Nierras, Dede Oetomo, and Michael Tan.

9. Jim Marks, "The Personal Is Political: An Interview with Shaym Selvadurai," *Lambda Book Report* (Washington) 5:2 (1996): 7.

10. The original Indonesian term was *banci*. The term *waria* was coined in the late 1970s by combining the words for "woman" and "man." See Dede Oetomo, "Masculinity in Indonesia," in R. Parker, R. Barbosa, and P. Aggleton, eds., *Framing the Sexual Subject* (Berkeley: University of California Press, 2000), 58–59 n. 2.

11. See Jeffrey Weeks, *Coming Out* (London: Quartet, 1977); John Lauritsen and David Thorstad, *The Early Homosexual Rights Movement* (New York: Times Change Press, 1974).

12. A. T. Fitzroy, *Despised and Rejected* (London: Gay Men's Press, 1988; originally published 1918), 223.

13. George Chauncey, *Gay New York* (New York: Basic Books, 1994), 65.

14. John Rechy, *City of Night* (New York: Grove, 1963).

15. E.g., Annick Prieur, *Mema's House, Mexico City* (Chicago: University of Chicago Press, 1998); Jacobo Schifter, *From Toads to Queens* (New York: Haworth, 1999); Peter Jackson and Gerard Sullivan, eds., *Lady Boys, Tom Boys, Rent Boys* (New York Haworth, 1999); *Woubi Cheri*, (1998), directed by Philip Brooks and Laurent Bocahul.

16. Saakia Wieringa, "Desiring Bodies or Defiant Cultures: Butch-Femme Lesbians in Jakarta and Lima," in E. Blackwood and S. Wieringa, eds., *Female Desires: Same-Sex Relations and Transgender Practices across Cultures* (New York: Columbia University Press, 1999), 206–29.

17. Gloria Wekker, "What's Identity Got to Do with It? Rethinking Identity in Light of the Mati Work in Suriname," in Blackwood and Wieringa, *Female Desires,* 119–38. Compare the very complex typologies of "same-sex" groups in Murray and Roscoe, *Boy-Wives and Female Husbands,* 279–82, and the chapter by Rudolph Gaudio on "male lesbians and other queer notions in Hausa," 115–28.

18. Herdt, *Third Sex, Third Gender,* 47.

19. See Serena Nanda, "The Hijras of India: Cultural and Individual Dimensions of an Institutionalized. Third Gender Role," in E. Blackwood, ed., *The Many Faces of Homosexuality* (New York: Harrington Park Press, 1986), 35–54.

20. See Niko Besnier, "Polynesian Gender Liminality through Time and Space," in Herdt, *Third Sex, Third Gender,* 285–328. Note that the subtitle of Herdt's book is "Beyond Sexual Dimorphism in Culture and History."

21. See Ramon Gutierrez, "Must We Deracinate Indians to Find Gay Roots?" *Outlook* (San Francisco), winter 1989, 61–67.

22. Besnier, "Polynesian Gender Liminality," 300.

23. See Lee Wallace, "*Fa'afafine: Queens of Samoa* and the Elision of Homosexuality," *GLQ* 5:1 (1999): 25–39.

24. Roger Lancaster, "'That We Should All Turn Queer?' Homosexual Stigma in the Making of Manhood and the Breaking of Revolution in Nicaragua," in Parker and Gagnon, *Conceiving Sexuality,* 150.

25. See Henning Bech, *When Men Meet: Homosexuality and Modernity* (Chicago: University of Chicago Press, 1997); Kenneth Plummer, *The Making of the Modern Homosexual* (London: Hutchinson, 1981); Seidman, *Difference Troubles.*

26. See Laurence Wai-teng Leong, "Singapore," in West and Green, *Sociolegal Control of Homosexuality,* 134: and the remarkable Singapore film *Bugis Street* (1995), directed by Yon Fan—remarkable for having been made at all.

27. E.g., Sandy Stone, "The Empire Strikes Back: A Posttranssexual Manifesto," in P. Treichler, L. Cartwright, and C. Penley, eds., *The Visible Woman* (New York: New York University Press, 1998), 285–309.

28. See Niko Besnier, "Sluts and Superwomen: The Politics of Gender Liminality in Urban Tonga," *Ethnos* 62:1–2 (1997): 5 31.

29. Thanks to Arthur Chen of the AIDS Prevention and Research Center, Taipei, for this information.

30. Jennifer Robertson, *Takaraznka: Sexual Politics and Popular Culture in Modern Japan* (Berkeley: University of California Press, 1998), 207.

31. For some of the complications in reading cinematic versions of cross-dressing see Marjorie Garber, *Vested Interests* (New York: Routledge, 1992).

32. See Leslie Feinberg, *Transgender Warriors* (Boston: Beacon, 1996); Kate Bornstein, *Gender Outlaw* (New York: Routledge, 1993).

33. Sereine Steakley, "Brazil Can Be Tough and Deadly for Gays," *Bay Windows* (Boston), June 16, 1994.

34. Jerry Z. Torres, "Coming Out," in N. Garcia and D. Remoto, eds., *Ladlad: An Anthology of Philippine Gay Writing* (Manila: Anvil, 1994), 128.

35. Chris Berry and Fran Martin, "Queer'n'Asian on the Net: Syncretic Sexualities in Taiwan and Korean Cyberspaces," *Inqueeries* (Melbourne), June 1998, 67–93.

36. Pheng Cheah, "Posit(ion)ing Human Rights in the Current Global Conjuncture," *Public Culture* 9 (1997): 261.

37. Pedro Bustos-Aguilar, "Mister Don't Touch the Banana," *Critique of Anthropology* 15:2 (1995): 149–70.

38. Kai Wright, "Industrializing Nations Confront Budding Movement," *Washington Blade,* October 23, 1998.

39. Pedro Albornoz, "Landlocked State," *Harvard Gay and Lesbian Review* 6:1 (1999): 17.

40. Ann Ferguson, "Is There a Lesbian Culture?" in J. Allen, ed., *Lesbian Philosophies and Cultures* (Albany: State University of New York Press, 1990), 63–88.

41. See, e.g., the interview by William Hoffman with Mumbai activist Ashok Row Kavi, *Poz,* July 1998, which proclaims him "the Larry Kramer of India."

42. Bing Yu, "Tide of Freedom," *Capital Gay* (Sydney), May 1, 1998.

43. In July 1999 the paper ManilaOUT listed over twenty gay, lesbian, and "gay and lesbian-friendly" organizations in Manila.

44. Naeko, "Lesbian = Woman," in B. Summerhawk et al., eds., *Queer Japan* (Norwich, VT: New Victoria Publishers, 1998), 184–87.

45. Malu Marin, "Going beyond the Personal." *Women in Action* (ISIS International Manila) 1 (1996): 58–62.

46. Manifesto of Chinese Tongzhi Conference, Hong Kong, December 1996. Thanks to Graham Smith for providing this source.

47. See Andrew Matzner, "Paradise Not," *Harvard Gay and Lesbian Review* 6:1 (winter 1999): 42–44.

48. Peter Jackson, "Beyond Bars and Boys: Life in Gay Bangkok," *Outrage* (Melbourne), July 1997, 61–63.

49. Statement from *Male* magazine, quoted in *Brother/Sister* (Melbourne), September 16, 1999, 51.

50. There is a similar argument in Barry Adam, Jan Willem Duyvendak, and Andre Krouwel, "Gay and Lesbian Movements beyond Borders?" in Adam, Duyvendak, and Krouwel, *Global Emergence of Gay and Lesbian Politics,* 344–71.

51. Mark Gevisser, "Gay Life in South Africa," in Drucker, *Different Rainbows:* 116.

52. Dean Murphy, "Zimbabwe's Gays Go 'Out' at Great Risk," *Los Angeles Times,* July 27, 1998.

53. For one view of the situation in Kenya see Wanjira Kiama, "Men Who Have Sex with Men in Kenya," in Foreman, *AIDS and Men,* 115–26.

54. Chris McGreal, "Gays Are Main Evil, Say African Leaders." *Guardian Weekly,* October 7–13, 1999, 4.

55. See Carl Stychin, *A Nation by Rights* (Philadelphia: Temple University Press, 1998), chap. 3.

56. *Times of India.* November 9, 1994, quoted by Sherry Joseph and Pawan Dhall, "No Silence Please, We're Indians!" in Drucker, *Different Rainbows:* 164.

57. Rodney Jones, "'Potato Seeking Rice': Language, Culture, and Identity in Gay Personal Ads in Hong Kong," *International Journal of the Sociology of Language* 143 (2000): 31–59.

58. James Farrar, "Disco 'Super-Culture': Consuming Foreign Sex in the Chinese Disco," *Sexualities* 2:2 (1999): 156.

59. John Clark, "The Global Lesbian and Gay Movement," in A. Hendriks, R. Tielman, and E. van der Veen, eds., *The Third Pink Book* (Buffalo: Prometheus Books, 1993), 54–61.

60. "The Asian Lesbian Network," *Breakout* (newsletter of Can't Live in the Closet, Manila) 4:3–4 (1998): 13.

61. On South Africa see Graeme Reid, "'Going Back to God, Just as We Are': Contesting Identities in the Hope and Unity Metropolitan Community Church," *Development Update* (Johannesburg) 2:2 (1998): 57–65. For a discussion of a gay church in Azcapotzalco, on the outskirts of Mexico City, see "Living la Vida Local." *Economist,* December 18, 1999, 85–87.

62. Coverage of the 1994 games in New York by the Brazilian press is discussed in Charles Klein, "'The Ghetto Is Over, Darling': Emerging Gay Communities and Gender and Sexual Politics in Contemporary Brazil," *Culture, Health, and Society* 1:3 (1999): 239–41.

19

Becoming 100% Straight

MICHAEL A. MESSNER

In 1995, as part of my job as the President of the North American Society for the Sociology of Sport, I needed to prepare a one-hour long Presidential Address for the annual meeting of some 200 people. This presented a challenge to me: how might I say something to my colleagues that was challenging, at least somewhat original, and above all, not boring. Students may think that their professors are especially boring in the classroom, but believe me, we are usually much worse at professional meetings. For some reason, many of us who are able to speak to our students in the classroom in a relaxed manner, and using relatively jargon-free language, seem at these meetings to become robots, dryly reading our papers—packed with impressively unclear jargon—to our yawning colleagues.

Since I desperately wanted to avoid putting 200 sport studies scholars to sleep, I decided to deliver a talk which I entitled "studying up on sex." The title, which certainly did get my colleagues' attention, was intended as a play on words—a double entendre. "Studying up" has one, generally recognizable colloquial meaning, but in sociology, it has another. It refers to studying "up" in the power structure. Sociologists have perhaps most often studied "down"— studied the poor, the blue- or pink-collar workers, the "nuts, sluts and perverts," the incarcerated. The idea of "studying

up" rarely occurs to sociologists unless and until we are living in a time when those who are "down" have organized movements that challenge the institutional privileges of elites. So, for instance, in the wake of labor movements, some sociologists like C. Wright Mills studied up on corporate elites. And recently, in the wake of racial/ethnic civil rights movements, some scholars like Ruth Frankenberg have begun to study the social meanings of "whiteness." Much of my research, inspired by feminism, has involved a studying up on the social construction of masculinity in sport. Studying up, in these cases, has raised some fascinating new and important questions about the workings of power in society.

However, I realized, when it comes to understanding the social and interpersonal dynamics of sexual orientation in sport, we have barely begun to scratch the surface of a very complex issue. Although sport studies has benefited from the work of scholars like Helen Lenskyj, Brian Pronger and others who have delineated the experiences of lesbians and gay men in sports, there has been very little extension of these scholars' insights into a consideration of the social construction of heterosexuality in sport. In sport, just as in the larger society, we seem obsessed with asking "how do people become gay?" Imbedded in this question is the assumption that people who identify as heterosexual, or "straight," require no explanation, since they are simply acting out the "natural" or "normal" sexual orientation. It's the "sexual deviants" who require explanation, we seem to be saying, while the experience of heterosexuals, because we are considered normal, seems to require no critical examination or explanation. But I knew that a closer look at the development of sexual orientation or sexual identity reveals an extremely complex process. I decided to challenge myself and my colleagues by arguing that although we have begun to "study up" on corporate elites in sport, on whiteness, on masculinity, it is now time to extend that by studying up on heterosexuality.

But in the absence of systematic research on this topic, where could I start? How could I explore, raise questions about, and begin to illuminate the social construction of heterosexuality for my colleagues? Fortunately, I had for the previous two years been working with a group of five men (three of whom identified as heterosexual, two as gay) who were mutually exploring our own biographies in terms of our earlier bodily experiences that helped to shape our gender and sexual identities. We modeled our project after that of a German group of feminist women, led by Frigga Haug, who created a research method which they call "memory work." In short, the women would mutually choose a body part, such as "hair," and each of them would then write a short story, based on a particularly salient childhood memory that related to their hair (for example, being forced by parents to cut your hair, deciding to straighten one's curly hair, in order to look more like other girls, etc.). Then, the group would read all of the stories and discuss them one-by-one, with the hope of gaining some more general understanding of, and raising new questions about, the social construction of "femininity." What resulted from this project was a fascinating book called *Female Sexualization,* which my men's group used as an inspiration for our project.

As a research method, memory work is anything but conventional. Many sociologists would argue that this is not really a "research method" at all, because the information that emerges from the project can't be used very confidently as a generalizable "truth," and especially because in this sort of project, the researcher is simultaneously part of what is being studied. How, my

more scientifically oriented colleagues might ask, is the researcher to maintain his or her objectivity in this project? My answer is that in this kind of research, objectivity is not the point. In fact, the strength of this sort of research is the depth of understanding that might be gained through a systematic group analysis of one's experience, one's *subjective* orientation to social processes. A clear understanding of the subjective aspect of social life—one's bodily feelings, emotions, and reactions to others—is an invaluable window that allows us to see and ask new sociological questions about group interaction and social structure. In short, group memory work can provide an important, productive, and fascinating insight into aspects of social reality, though not a complete (or completely reliable) picture.

So, as I pondered the lack of existing research on the social construction of heterosexuality in sport, I decided to draw on one of my own stories from my memory work men's group. Some of my most salient memories of embodiment are sports memories. I grew up the son of a high school coach, and I eventually played point guard on my dad's team. In what follows, I juxtapose one of my stories with that of a gay former Olympic athlete, Tom Waddell, whom I had interviewed several years earlier for a book that I wrote on the lives of male athletes.

TWO SEXUAL STORIES

Many years ago I read some psychological studies that argued that even for self-identified heterosexuals, it is a natural part of their development to have gone through "bisexual" or even "homosexual" stages of life. When I read this, it seemed theoretically reasonable, but it did not ring true in my experience. I have always been, I told myself, 100% heterosexual! The group process of analyzing my own autobiographical stories challenged this conception I had developed of myself, and also shed light on the way that the institutional context of sport provided a context for the development of my definition of myself as "100% straight." Here is one of the stories.

When I was in the 9th grade, I played on a "D" basketball team, set up especially for the smallest of high school boys. Indeed, though I was pudgy with baby fat, I was a short 5′2″, still pre-pubescent with no facial hair and a high voice that I artificially tried to lower. The first day of practice, I was immediately attracted to a boy I'll call Timmy, because he looked like the boy who played in the Lassie TV show. Timmy was short, with a high voice, like me. And like me, he had no facial hair yet. Unlike me, he was very skinny. I liked Timmy right away, and soon we were together a lot. I noticed things about him that I didn't notice about other boys: he said some words a certain way, and it gave me pleasure to try to talk like him. I remember liking the way the light hit his boyish, nearly hairless body. I thought about him when we weren't together. He was in the school band, and at the football games, I'd squint to see where he was in the mass of uniforms. In short, though I wasn't conscious of it at the time, I was infatuated with Timmy—I had a crush on him. Later that basketball season, I decided—for no reason that I could really articulate then—that I hated Timmy. I aggressively rejected him, began to make fun of him around other boys. He was, we all agreed, a geek. He was a faggot.

Three years later, Timmy and I were both on the varsity basketball team, but had hardly spoken a word to each other since we were freshmen. Both of us now had lower voices, had grown to around 6 feet tall, and we both shaved, at least a bit. But Timmy was a skinny, somewhat stigmatized reserve on the team, while I was the team captain and starting point guard. But I wasn't so happy or secure about this. I'd always dreamed of dominating games, of being the hero. Halfway through my senior season, however, it became clear that I was not a star, and I figured I knew why. I was not aggressive enough.

I had always liked the beauty of the fast break, the perfectly executed pick and roll play between two players, and especially the long twenty-foot shot that touched nothing but the bottom of the net. But I hated and feared the sometimes brutal contact under the basket. In fact, I stayed away from the rough fights for rebounds and was mostly a perimeter player, relying on my long shots or my passes to more aggressive teammates under the basket. But now it became apparent to me that time was running out in my quest for greatness: I needed to change my game, and fast. I decided one day before practice that I was gonna get aggressive. While practicing one of our standard plays, I passed the ball to a teammate, and then ran to the spot at which I was to set a pick on a defender. I knew that

one could sometimes get away with setting a face-up screen on a player, and then as he makes contact with you, roll your back to him and plant your elbow hard in his stomach. The beauty of this move is that your own body "roll" makes the elbow look like an accident. So I decided to try this move. I approached the defensive player, Timmy, rolled, and planted my elbow deeply into his solar plexus. Air exploded audibly from Timmy's mouth, and he crumbled to the floor momentarily.

Play went on as though nothing had happened, but I felt bad about it. Rather than making me feel better, it made me feel guilty and weak. I had to admit to myself why I'd chosen Timmy as the target against whom to test out my new aggression. He was the skinniest and weakest player on the team.

At the time, I hardly thought about these incidents, other than to try to brush them off as incidents that made me feel extremely uncomfortable. Years later, I can now interrogate this as a *sexual* story, and as a *gender* story unfolding within the context of the heterosexualized and masculinized institution of sport. Examining my story in light of research conducted by Alfred Kinsey a half-century ago, I can recognize in myself what Kinsey saw as a very common **fluidity and changeability of sexual desire over the lifecourse.** Put simply, Kinsey found that large numbers of adult, "heterosexual" men had previously, as adolescents and young adults, experienced sexual desire for males. A surprisingly large number of these men had experienced sexual contact to the point of orgasm with other males during adolescences or early adulthood. Similarly, my story invited me to consider what is commonly called the **"Freudian theory of bisexuality."** Sigmund Freud shocked the post-Victorian world by suggesting that all people go through a stage, early in life, when they are attracted to people of the same sex. Adult experiences, Freud argued, eventually led most people to shift their sexual desire to what Freud called an appropriate "love object"—a person of the opposite sex. I also considered my experience in light of what lesbian feminist author Adrienne Rich called **institution of compulsory heterosexuality.** Perhaps the extremely high levels of homophobia that are often endemic in boys' and men's organized sports led me to deny and repress my own homoerotic desire through a direct and overt rejection of Timmy, through homophobic banter with male peers, and through the resultant stigmatization of the feminized Timmy. And eventually, I considered my experience in light of what the radical theorist Herbert Marcuse called the **sublimation of homoerotic desire** into an aggressive, violent act as serving to construct a clear line of demarcation between selfn and other. Sublimation, according to Marcuse, involves the driving underground, into the unconscious, of sexual desires that might appear dangerous due to their socially stigmatized status. But sublimation involves more than simple repression into the unconscious—it involves a transformation of sexual desire into something else—often into aggressive and violent acting out toward others, acts that clarify boundaries between one's self and others and therefore lessen any anxieties that might be attached to the repressed homoerotic desire.

Importantly, in our analysis of my story, my memory group went beyond simply discussing the events in psychological terms. My story did suggest some deep psychological processes at work, perhaps, but it also revealed the importance of social context—in this case, the context of the athletic team. In short, my rejection of Timmy and the joining with teammates to stigmatize him in ninth grade stands as an example of what sociologist R. W. Connell calls a **moment of engagement with hegemonic masculinity,** where I actively took up the male group's task of constructing heterosexual/masculine identities in the context of sport. The elbow in Timmy's gut three years later can be seen as a punctuation mark that occurred precisely because of my fears that I might be failing at this goal.

It is helpful, I think, to compare my story with gay and lesbian "coming out" stories in sport. Though we have a few lesbian and bisexual coming out stories among women athletes, there are very few gay male coming out stories. Tom Waddell, who as a closeted gay man finished sixth in the decathlon in the 1968 Olympics, later came out and started the Gay Games, an athletic and cultural festival that draws tens of thousands of people every four years. When I interviewed Tom Waddell over a decade ago about his sexual identity and athletic career, he made it quite clear that for many years sports *was* his closet. Tom told me,

When I was a kid, I was tall for my age, and was very thin and very strong. And I was usually faster than most other people. But I discovered rather early that I liked gymnastics and I liked dance. I was very interested in being a ballet dance . . . [but] something became obvious to me right away—that male ballet dancers were effeminate, that they were what most people would call faggots. And I thought I just couldn't handle that . . . I was totally closeted and very concerned about being male. This was the fifties, a terrible time to live, and everything was stacked against me. Anyway, I realized that I had to do something to protect my image of myself as a male—because at that time homosexuals were thought of primarily as men who wanted to be women. And so I threw myself into athletics—I played football, gymnastics, track and field. . . . I was a jock—that's how I was viewed, and I was comfortable with that.

Tom Waddell was fully conscious of entering sports and constructing a masculine/heterosexual athletic identity precisely because he feared being revealed as gay. It was clear to him, in the context of the 1950s, that being revealed as gay would undercut his claims to the status of manhood. Thus, though he described the athletic closet as "hot and stifling," he remained in the closet until several years after his athletic retirement. He even knowingly played along with locker room discussions about sex and women, knowing that this was part of his "cover":

I wanted to be viewed as male, otherwise I would be a dancer today. I wanted the male, macho image of an athlete. So I was protected by a very hard shell. I was clearly aware of what I was doing . . . I often felt compelled to go along with a lot of locker room garbage because I wanted that image—and I know a lot of others who did too.

Like my story, Waddell's story points to the importance of the athletic institution as a context in which peers mutually construct and re-construct narrow definitions of masculinity—and heterosexuality is considered to be a rock-solid foundation of this conception of masculinity. But unlike my story, Waddell's story may invoke what sociologist Erving Goffman called a "dramaturgical analysis": Waddell seemed to be consciously "acting" to control and regulate others' perceptions of him by constructing a public "front stage" persona that differed radically from what he believed to be his "true" inner self. My story, in contrast, suggests a deeper, less consciously strategic repression of my homoerotic attraction. Most likely, I was aware on some level of the dangers of such feelings, and was escaping the dangers, disgrace, and rejection that would likely result from being different. For Waddell, the decision to construct his identity largely within sport was a decision to step into a fiercely heterosexual/masculine closet that would hide what he saw to be his "true" identity. In contrast, I was not so much stepping into a "closet" that would hide my identify—rather, I was stepping out into an entire world of heterosexual privilege. My story also suggests how a *threat* to the promised privileges of hegemonic masculinity—my failure as an athlete—might trigger a momentary sexual panic that could lay bare the constructedness, indeed, the *instability* of the heterosexual/masculine identity.

In either case—Waddell's or mine—we can see how, as young male athletes, heterosexuality and masculinity were not something we "were," but something we were *doing*. It is very significant, I think, that as each of us was "doing heterosexuality," neither of us was actually "having sex" with women (though one of us desperately wanted to!). This underscores a point made by some recent theorists, that heterosexuality should not be thought of simply as sexual acts between women and men; rather, **heterosexuality is a constructed identity, a performance, and an institution** that is not necessarily linked to sexual acts. Though for one of us it was more conscious than for the other, we were both "doing heterosexuality" as an ongoing practice through which we sought (a) to avoid stigma, embarrassment, ostracism, or perhaps worse if we were even suspected of being gay; and (b) to link ourselves into systems of power, status, and privilege that appear to be the birthright of "real men" (i.e., males who are able to successfully compete with other males in sport, work, and sexual relations with women). In other words, each of us actively scripted our own sexual/gender performances, but these scripts were constructed within the constraints of a socially organized (institutionalized) system of power and pleasure.

QUESTIONS FOR FUTURE RESEARCH

As I prepared to tell my above sexual story publicly to my colleagues at the sport studies conference, I felt extremely nervous. Part of the nervousness was due to the fact that I knew some of my colleagues would object to my claim that telling personal stories can be a source of sociological insights. But a larger part of the reason for my nervousness was due to the fact that I was revealing something very personal about my sexuality in such a public way. Most of us aren't used to doing this, especially in the context of a professonal conference. But I had learned long ago, especially from feminist women scholars, and from gay and lesbian scholars, that biography is linked to history, and that part of "normal" academic discourse has been to hide "the personal" (including the fact that the researcher is himself or herself a person, with values, feelings, and, yes, biases) behind a carefully constructed facade of "objectivity." Rather than trying to hide—or be ashamed of—one's subjective experience of the world, I was challenging myself to draw on my experience of the world as a resource. Not that I should trust my experience as the final word on "reality"—white, heterosexual males like myself have made the mistake for centuries of calling their own experience "objectivity," and then punishing anyone who does not share their world view as "deviant." Instead, I hope to use my experience as an example of how those of us who are in dominant sexual/racial/gender/class categories can get a new perspective on the "constructedness" of our identities by juxtaposing our subjective experiences against the recently emerging world views of gay men and lesbians, women, and people of color.

Finally, I want to stress that, juxtaposed, my and Tom Waddell's stories do not shed much light on the question of why some individuals "become" gay while others "become" heterosexual or bisexual. Instead, I'd like to suggest that this is a dead-end question, and that there are far more important and interesting questions to be asked:

• How has heterosexuality, as an institution and as an enforced group practice, constrained and limited all of us—gay, straight, and bi?

- How has the institution of sport been an especially salient institution for the social construction of heterosexual masculinity?
- Why is it that when men play sports they are almost always automatically granted masculine status, and thus assumed to be heterosexual, while when women play sports, questions are raised about their "femininity" and their sexual orientation?

These kinds of questions aim us toward an analysis of the workings of power within institutions—including the ways that these workings of power shape and constrain our identities and relationships—and point us toward imagining alternative social arrangements that are less constraining for everyone.

REFERENCES

Haug, Frigga. 1987. *Female Sexualization: A Collective Work of Memory.* London: Verso.

Katz, Jonathan Ned. 1995. *The Invention of Heterosexuality.* New York: Dutton.

Messner, Michael A. 1992. *Power at Play: Sports and the Problem of Masculinity.* Boston: Beacon Press.

———. 1994. "Gay Athletes and the Gay Games: An interview with Tom Waddell," in M. A. Messner & D. F. Sabo (Eds.), *Sex, Violence and Power in Sports: Rethinking Masculinity* (pp. 113–119). Freedom, CA: The Crossing Press.

Pronger, Brian. 1990. *The Arena of Masculinity: Sports, Homosexuality, and the Meaning of Sex.* New York: St. Martin's Press.

20

"Americans Have a Different Attitude"

Family, Sexuality, and Gender in Filipina American Lives

YEN LE ESPIRITU

I want my daughters to be Filipino especially on sex. I always emphasize to them that they should not participate in sex if they are not married. We are also Catholic. We are raised so that we don't engage in going out with men while we are not married. And I don't like it to happen to my daughters as if they have no values. I don't like them to grow up that way, like the American girls.

—*Filipina immigrant mother*

I found that a lot of the Asian American friends of mine, we don't date like White girls date. We don't sleep around like White girls do. Everyone is really mellow at dating because your parents were constraining and restrictive.

—*Second generation Filipina daughter*

Drawing from my research on Filipino American families in San Diego, California, this paper explores the ways in which racialized immigrants claim through gender the power denied them through racism. Gender shapes immigrant identity and allows racialized immigrants to assert cultural superiority over the dominant group. For Filipino immigrants who come from a homeland that was once a U.S. colony, cultural reconstruction has been a way to counter the cultural Amer-icanization of the Philippines, to resist the assimilative and alienating demands of U.S. society, and to reaffirm to themselves their self-worth in the face of colonial, racial, and gendered subordination.

The opening narratives above, made by a Filipina immigrant mother and a second generation Filipina daughter, suggest that the virtuous Filipina daughter is partially constructed on the conceptualization of white women as sexually immoral. They also reveal the ways in which women's sexuality—and their enforced "morality"—is fundamental to the structuring of social inequalities. Historically, the sexuality of racialized women has been systematically demonized and denigrated by dominant or oppressor groups to justify and bolster nationalist movements, colonialism, and/or racism. But as the above narratives indicate, racialized groups also castigate the morality of white women as a strategy of resistance—a means to assert a morally superior public face to the dominant society. But this strategy is not without costs. The elevation of Filipina chastity (particularly that of young women) has the effect of reinforcing masculinist and patriarchal power in the name of a greater ideal of national/ethnic self-respect. Because the control of women is one of the principal means of asserting moral superiority, young women in immigrant families face numerous restrictions on their autonomy, mobility, and personal decision making.

STUDYING FILIPINOS IN SAN DIEGO

The information on which this article is based come mostly from original research: in-depth interviews that I conducted with about one hundred Filipinos in San Diego. As in other Filipino communities along the Pacific Coast, the San Diego community grew dramatically in the twenty-five years following passage of the 1965 Immigration Act. In 1990, there were close to 96,000 Filipinos in San Diego County. Although they comprised only 4 percent of the county's general population, they constituted close to 50 percent of the Asian American population (Espiritu 1995). Many post-1965 Filipinos have come to San Diego as professionals—most conspicuously as health care workers. A 1992 analysis of the socio-economic characteristics of recent Filipino immigrants in San Diego indicated that they were predominantly middle class, college-educated, and English-speaking professionals who were much more likely to own rather than rent their homes (Rumbaut 1994).

Using the "snowball" sampling technique, I started by interviewing Filipino Americans whom I knew and then asking them to refer me to others who might be willing to be interviewed. In other words, I chose participants not randomly but rather through a network of Filipino American contacts whom the first group of respondents trusted. To capture as much as possible the diversity within the Filipino American community, I sought and selected respondents of different backgrounds and with diverse viewpoints. The interviews, tape-recorded in English, ranged from three to ten hours each and took place in offices, coffee shops, and homes. My questions were open-ended and covered three general areas: family and immigration history, ethnic identity and practices, and community development among San Diego's Filipinos. The interviewing process varied widely: some respondents needed to be prompted with specific questions, while others spoke at great length on their own. Some chose to cover the span of their lives; others focused on specific events that were particularly important to them.

CONSTRUCTING THE DOMINANT GROUP: THE MORAL FLAWS OF WHITE AMERICANS

In this section, I argue that female morality—defined as women's dedication to their families and sexual restraints—is one of the few sites where economically and politically dominated groups can construct the dominant group as "other" and themselves as superior. Because womanhood is idealized as the repository of tradition, the norms which regulate women's behaviors become a means of determining and defining group status and boundaries. As a consequence, the burdens and complexities of cultural (re)presentation fall most heavily on immigrant women and their daughters. Below, I show that Filipino immigrants claim moral distinctiveness for their community by (re)presenting "Americans" as morally flawed and themselves as family-oriented model minorities and their wives and daughters as paragons of morality.

Family-Oriented Model Minorities: "White Women Will Leave You . . ."

Many of my respondents constructed their "ethnic" culture as principled and the "American" culture as deviant. Most often, this morality narrative revolves around family life and family relations. When asked what set Filipinos apart from other Americans, my respondents—of all ages and class backgrounds—repeatedly contrasted the close-knit Filipino families to what they perceived to be the more impersonal quality of U.S. family relations. In the following narratives, "Americans" are characterized as lacking in strong family ties and collective identity, less willing to do the work of family and cultural maintenance, and less willing to abide by patriarchal norms in husband/wife relations:

> Our [Filipino] culture is different. We are more close-knit. We tend to help one another. Americans, ya know, they are all right, but they don't help each other that much. As a matter of fact, if the parents are old, they take them to a convalescent home and let them rot there. We would never do that in our culture. We would nurse them; we would help them until the very end (Filipino immigrant, 60 years old).

Our (Filipino) culture is very communal. You know that your family will always be there, that you don't have to work when you turn 18, you don't have to pay rent when you are 18, which is the American way of thinking. You also know that if things don't work out in the outside world, you can always come home and mommy and daddy will always take you and your children in (second generation Filipina, 33 years old).

Asian parents take care of their children. Americans have a different attitude. They leave their children to their own resources. They get baby sitters to take care of their children or leave them in day care. That's why when they get old, their children don't even care about them (Filipina immigrant, 46 years old).

Implicit in the negative depiction of U.S. families—as uncaring, selfish, and distant—is the allegation that White women are not as dedicated to their families as Filipina women. Several Filipino men who married White women recalled being warned by their parents and relatives that "White women will leave you." As one man related, "My mother said to me, 'Well, you know, don't marry a White person because they would take everything that you own and leave you.'" For some Filipino men, perceived differences in attitudes about women's roles between Filipina and non-Filipina women influenced their marital choice. A Filipino American navy man explained why he went back to the Philippines to look for a wife:

My goal was to marry a Filipina. I requested to be stationed in the Philippines to get married to a Filipina. I'd seen the women here and basically they are spoiled. They have a tendency of not going along together with their husband. They behave differently. They chase the male, instead of the male, the normal way of the traditional way is for the male to go after the female. They have sex without marrying. They want to do their own things. So my idea was to go back home and marry somebody who has never been here. I tell my son the same thing: if he does what I did and finds himself a good lady there, he will be in good hands.

Another man who had dated mostly White women in high school recounted that when it came time for him to marry, he "looked for the kind of women that I'd met in the Philippines."

It is important to note the gender implications of these claims. That is, while both men and women identify the family system as a tremendous source of cultural pride, it is women—through their unpaid housework and kin work—who shoulder the primary responsibility for maintaining family closeness. Because the moral status of the community rests on women's labor, women, as wives and daughters, are not only applauded for but are expected to dedicate themselves to the family. Writing on the constructed image of ethnic family and gender, di Leonardo (1984) reminds us that "a large part of stressing ethnic identity amounts to burdening women with increased responsibilities for preparing special foods, planning rituals, and enforcing 'ethnic' socialization of children" (p. 222). A twenty-three-year-old Filipina spoke about the reproductive work that her mother performed and expected her to learn:

In my family, I was the only girl, so my mom expected a lot from me. She wanted me to help her to take care of the household. I felt like there was a lot of pressure on me. It's very important to my mom to have the house in order: to wash the dishes, to keep the kitchen in order, vacuuming, and dusting and things like that. She wants me to be a perfect housewife. It's difficult. I have been married now for about four months and my mother asks me every now and then what have I cooked for my husband. My mom is also very strict about families getting together on holidays and I would always help her to organize that. Each holiday, I would try to decorate the house for her, to make it more special.

The burden of unpaid reproductive and kin work is particularly stressful for women who work outside the home. In the following narrative, a Filipina wife and mother described the pulls of family and work that she experienced when she went back to school to pursue a doctoral degree in nursing:

The Filipinos, we are very collective, very connected. Going through the doctoral program, sometimes I think it is better just to forget about my relatives and just concentrate on school. All that connectedness, it steals parts of myself because all of my energies are devoted to my family. And that is the reason why I think Americans are successful. The majority of the

American people they can do what they want. They don't feel guilty because they only have a few people to relate to. For us Filipinos, it's like roots under the tree, you have all these connections. The Americans are more like the trunk. I am still trying to go up to the trunk of the tree but it is too hard. I want to be more independent, more like the Americans.

It is important to note that this Filipina interprets her exclusion and added responsibilities as only racial when they are largely gendered. For example, when she says, "the American people they can do what they want," she ignores the differences in the lives of white men and white women—the fact that most white women experience similar pulls of family, education, and work.

Racialized Sexuality and (Im)morality: "In America . . . Sex Is Nothing"

Sexuality, as a core aspect of social identity, is fundamental to the structuring of gender inequality (Millett 1970). Sexuality is also a salient marker of Otherness and has figured prominently in racist and imperialist ideologies (Gilman 1985; Stoler 1991). Filipinas—both in the Philippines and in the United States—have been marked as desirable but dangerous "prostitutes" and/or submissive "mail order brides" (Halualani 1995; Egan 1996). These stereotypes emerged out of the colonial process, especially the extensive U.S. military presence in the Philippines. Until the early 1990s, the Philippines housed—at times unwillingly—some of the United States' largest overseas airforce and naval bases (Espiritu 1995, 14). Many Filipino nationalists have charged that "the prostitution problem" in the Philippines stemmed from U.S. and Philippine government policies that promoted a sex industry— brothels, bars, massage parlors—for servicemen stationed or on leave in the Philippines (Coronel and Rosca 1993; Warren 1993). In this context, *all* Filipinas were racialized to be sexual commodities, usable and expendable. The sexualized racialization of Filipina women is captured in Marianne Villanueva's short story "Opportunity" (1991). As the protagonist Nina, a "mail order bride" from the Philippines, enters the lobby to meet her American fiancé, the bellboys

snicker and whisper *puta,* whore: a reminder that U.S. economic and cultural colonization of the Philippines always forms a backdrop to any relations between Filipinos and Americans (Wong 1993, 53).

In an effort to counter the pervasive hypersexualization of Filipina women, many of my respondents constructed American society—and White American women in particular—to be much more sexually promiscuous than Filipino. In the following narrative, a mother who came to the United States in her thirties contrasted the controlled sexuality of Filipinas in the Philippines with the perceived promiscuity of White women in the United States:

In the Philippines, we always have chaperons when we go out. When we go to dances, we have our uncle, our grandfather, and auntie all behind us to make sure that we behave in the dance hall. Nobody goes necking outside. You don't even let a man put his hand on your shoulders. When you were brought up in a conservative country, it is hard to come here and see that it is all freedom of speech and freedom of action. Sex was never mentioned in our generation. I was thirty already when I learned about sex. But to the young generation in America, sex is nothing.

Similarly, another immigrant woman criticized the way young American women are raised, "Americans are so liberated. They allow their children, their girls, to go out even when they are still so young." In contrast, she stated that "the Filipino way, it is very important, the value of the woman, that she is a virgin when she gets married."

In this section on the "moral flaws of White Americans," I have suggested that the ideal "Filipina" is partially constructed on the community's conceptualization of White women. The former was everything which the latter was not: the one was sexually modest and dedicated to her family; the other sexually promiscuous and uncaring. Embodying the moral integrity of the idealized ethnic community, immigrant women, particularly young daughters, are expected to comply with male-defined criteria of what constitutes "ideal" feminine virtues. While the sexual behavior of adult women is confined to a monogamous and heterosexual context, that of young women is denied completely (c.f. Dasgupta and DasGupta 1996, 229–231). In the next section, I detail the ways in which Filipino immigrant parents, under the rubric of "cultural preservation," police their daughters' behaviors in order to safeguard their sexual innocence and virginity.

THE CONSTRUCTION(S) OF THE "IDEAL" FILIPINA: "BOYS ARE BOYS AND GIRLS ARE DIFFERENT . . ."

As the designated "keepers of the culture" (Billson 1995), the behaviors of immigrant women come under intensive scrutiny from both women and men of their own groups and from U.S.-born Americans (Gabbacia 1994, xi). In a study of the Italian Harlem community, 1880–1950, Robert Anthony Orsi (1985, 135) reports that "all the community's fears for the reputation and integrity of the domus came to focus on the behavior of young women." Because women's moral and sexual loyalties were deemed central to the maintenance of group status, changes in female behavior, especially of growing daughters, were interpreted as signs of moral decay and ethnic suicide, and were carefully monitored and sanctioned (Gabbacia 1994, 113).

Although immigrant families have always been preoccupied with passing on culture, language, and traditions to both male and female children, it is daughters who have the unequal burden of protecting and preserving the family name. Because sons do not have to conform to the image of an "ideal" ethnic subject as daughters do, they often receive special day-to-day privileges denied to daughters (Waters 1996, 75–76; Haddad and Smith 1996, 22–24). This is not to say that immigrant parents do not place undue expectations on their sons; it is rather that these expectations do not pivot around the sons' sexuality or dating choices. In contrast, parental control over the movement and action of daughters begins the moment she is perceived as a young adult and sexually vulnerable. It regularly consists of monitoring her whereabouts and rejecting dating (Wolf 1997). For example, the immigrant parents I interviewed seldom allowed their daughters to date, to stay out late, to spend the night at a friend's house, or to take an out-of-town trip.

Many of the second generation women I spoke to complained bitterly about these parental restrictions.

They particularly resent what they see as gender inequity in their families: the fact that their parents place far more restrictions on their activities and movements than on their brothers. Some decried the fact that even their *younger* brothers had more freedom than they did. "It was really hard growing up because my parents would let my younger brothers do what they wanted but I didn't get to do what I wanted even though I was the oldest. I had a curfew and my brothers didn't. I had to ask if I could go places and they didn't. My parents never even asked my brothers when they were coming home."

When questioned about this "double standard," parents responded by pointing to the fact that "girls are different:"

> I have that Filipino mentality that boys are boys and girls are different. Girls are supposed to be protected, to be clean. In the early years, my daughters have to have chaperons and curfews. And they know that they have to be virgins until they get married. The girls always say that is not fair. What is the difference between their brothers and them? And my answer always is, "In the Philippines, you know, we don't do that. The girls stay home. The boys go out." It was the way that I was raised. I still want to have part of that culture instilled in my children. And I want them to have that to pass on to their children.

Even among self-described western-educated and "tolerant" parents, many continue to ascribe to "the Filipino way" when it comes to raising daughters. As one college-educated father explains:

> Because of my Western education, I don't raise my children the way my parents raised me. I tended to be a little more tolerant. But at times, especially in certain issues like dating, I find myself more towards the Filipino way in the sense that I have only one daughter so I tended to be a little bit stricter. So the double standard kind of operates: it's alright for the boys to explore the field but I tended to be overly protective of my daughter. My wife feels the same way because the boys will not lose anything, but the daughter will lose something, their virginity, and it can be also a question of losing face, that kind of thing.

Although many parents generally discourage dating or forbid their daughters to date, they still fully expect these young women to fulfill their traditional roles as women: to get married and have children. A young Filipina recounted the mixed messages she received from her parents:

This is the way it is supposed to work. Okay, you go to school. You go to college. You graduate. You find a job. Then you find your husband, and you have children. That's the whole time line. But my question is, if you are not allowed to date, how are you supposed to find your husband? They say "no" to the whole dating scene because that is secondary to your education, secondary to your family. They do push marriage, but at a later date. So basically my parents are telling me that I should get married and I should have children but that I should not date.

The restrictions on girls' movement sometimes spill over to the realms of academics. Dasgupta and Das-Gupta (1996, 230) recount that in the Indian American community, while young men were expected to attend faraway competitive colleges, many of their female peers were encouraged by their parents to go to the local colleges so that they could live at or close to home. Similarly, Wolf (1997, 467) reports that some Filipino parents pursued contradictory tactics with their children's, particularly their daughters', education by pushing them to achieve academic excellence in high school, but then "pulling the emergency brake" when they contemplated college by expecting them to stay at home, even if it means going to a less competitive college, if at all.

The above narratives suggest that the process of parenting is gendered in that immigrant parents tend to restrict the autonomy, mobility, and personal decision making of their daughters more so than of their sons. I argue that these parental restrictions are attempts to construct a model of Filipina womanhood that is chaste, modest, nurturing, and family-oriented. This is not to say that parent-daughter conflicts exist in all Filipino immigrant families. Certainly, Filipino parents do not respond in a uniform way to the challenges of being racial-ethnic minorities. I met parents who have had to change some of their ideas and practices in response to their inability to control their children's movements and choices:

I have three girls and one boy. I used to think that I wouldn't allow my daughters to go dating and things like that, but there is no way I could do that. I can't stop it. It's the way of life here in America. Sometimes you kind of question yourself, if you are doing what is right. It is hard to accept but you got to accept it. That's the way they are here.

My children are born and raised here, so they do pretty much what they want. They think they know everything. I can only do so much as a parent. . . . When I try to teach my kids things, they tell me that I sound like an old record. They even talk back to me sometimes. . . .

These narratives, made by a professional Filipino immigrant father and a working-class Filipino immigrant mother, respectively, call attention to the shifts in the generational power caused by the migration process and to the possible gap between what parents say they want for their children and their ability to control the young. On the other hand, the interview data do suggest that intergenerational conflicts are socially recognized occurrences in the Filipino community(ies). Even when respondents themselves had not experienced intergenerational tensions, they could always recall a cousin, a girlfriend, or a friend's daughter who had.

SANCTIONS AND REACTIONS: "THAT IS NOT WHAT A DECENT FILIPINO GIRL SHOULD DO . . ."

I do not wish to suggest that immigrant communities are the only ones who regulate their daughters mobility and sexuality. Feminist scholars have long documented the construction, containment, and exploitation of women's sexuality in various societies (Maglin and Perry 1996). We also know that the cultural anxiety over unbounded female sexuality is most apparent with regard to adolescent girls (Tolman and Higgins 1996, 206). The difference, I believe, is in the ways that immigrant and non-immigrant families sanction girls' sexuality. Non-immigrant parents rely on the gender-based good girl/bad girl dichotomy to control sexually assertive girls (Tolman and Higgins 1996,

206). In the dominant cultural accounts of women's sexuality, "good girls" are passive, threatened sexual objects while "bad girls" are active, desiring sexual agents (Tolman and Higgins 1996). As Dasgupta and DasGupta write (1996, 236), "the two most pervasive images of women across cultures are the goddess and whore, the good and bad women." This good girl/bad girl cultural story conflates femininity with sexuality, increases women's vulnerability to sexual coercion, and justifies women's containment in the domestic sphere.

Immigrant families, on the other hand, have an extra disciplining mechanism: they can discipline their daughters as racial/national subjects as well as gendered ones. That is, as self-appointed guardians of "authentic" cultural memory, immigrant parents can opt to regulate their daughters' independent choices by linking them to cultural ignorance or betrayal. As both parents and children recounted, young women who disobeyed parental strictures were often branded "non-ethnic," "untraditional," "radical," "selfish," and not "caring about the family." Parents were also quick to warn their daughters about "bad" Filipinas who had gotten pregnant outside of marriage. Filipina Americans who veered from acceptable behaviors were deemed "Americanized"—women who have adopted the sexual mores and practices of White women. As one Filipino immigrant father described the "Americanized" Filipinas: "They are spoiled because they have seen the American way. They go out at night. Late at night. They go out on dates. Smoking. They have sex without marrying."

From the perspective of the second generation daughters, these charges are stinging. Largely unacquainted with the "home" country, U.S.-born children depend on their parents' tutelage to craft and affirm their ethnic self and thus are particularly vulnerable to charges of cultural ignorance or betrayal (Espiritu 1994). The young women I interviewed were visibly pained—with many breaking down and crying—when they recounted their parents' charges. This deep pain—stemming in part from their desire to be validated as Filipina—existed even among the more "rebellious" daughters. As a 24-year-old daughter explained:

My mom is very traditional. She wants to follow the Filipino customs, just really adhere to them, like what is proper for a girl, what she can and can't do, and what other people are going to think of her if she doesn't follow that way. When I pushed these restrictions, when I rebelled and stayed out later than allowed, my mom would always say, "That is not what a decent Filipino girl should do. You should come home at a decent hour. What are people going to think of you?" And that would get me really upset, you know, because I think that my character is very much the way it should be for a Filipina. I wear my hair long, I wear decent make-up. I dress properly, conservative. I am family oriented. It hurts me that she doesn't see that I am decent, that I am proper and that I am not going to bring shame to the family or anything like that.

This narrative suggests that even when parents are unable to control the behaviors of their children, their (dis)approval remained strong and powerful in shaping the emotional lives of their daughters (see Wolf 1997). Although better-off parents can and do exert greater controls over their children's behaviors than poorer parents (Wolf 1992; Kibria 1993), I would argue that *all* immigrant parents—regardless of class backgrounds—possess this emotional hold on their children. Therein lies the source of their power.

These emotional pains withstanding, many young Filipinas I interviewed contest and negotiate parental restrictions in their daily lives. Faced with parental restrictions on their mobility, young Filipinas struggle to gain some control over their own social lives, particularly over dating. In many cases, daughters simply misinform their parents of their whereabouts or date without their parents' knowledge. They also rebel by vowing to create more egalitarian relationships with their own husbands and children. A thirty-year-old Filipina who is married to a White American explained why she chose to marry outside her culture:

In high school, I dated mostly Mexican and Filipino. It never occurred to me to date a white or black guy. I was not attracted to them. But as I kept growing up and my father and I were having all these conflicts, I knew that if I married a Mexican or a Filipino, they would be exactly like my father. And so I tried to date anyone that would not remind me of my dad. A lot of my Filipina friends that I grew up with had similar experiences. So I knew that it wasn't only me. I was determined to marry a white person because he would treat me as an individual.

Another Filipina who was labeled "radical" by her parents indicated that she would be more open-minded in raising her own children: "I see myself as very traditional in upbringing but I don't see myself as constricting on my children one day and I wouldn't put the gender roles on them. I wouldn't lock them into any particular way of behaving." It is important to note that even as these Filipinas desired new gender norms and practices for their own families, the majority hoped that their children would remain connected to the Filipino culture. My respondents also reported more serious reactions to parental restrictions, recalling incidents of someone they knew who had run away, joined gangs, or attempted suicide.

CONCLUSION

In this paper, I have shown that many Filipino immigrants use the largely gendered discourse of morality as one strategy to decenter Whiteness and to locate themselves above the dominant group, demonizing it in the process. Like other immigrant groups, Filipinos praise the United States as a land of significant economic opportunity but simultaneously denounce it as a country inhabited by corrupted and individualistic people of questionable morals. In particular, they criticize American family life, American individualism, and American women (cf. Gabbacia, 1994, 113). Enforced by distorting powers of memory and nostalgia, this rhetoric of moral superiority often leads to patriarchal calls for cultural "authenticity" which locates family honor and national integrity in its female members. Because the policing of women's bodies is one of the main means of asserting moral superiority, young women face numerous restrictions on their autonomy, mobility, and personal decision making. This practice of cultural (re)construction reveals how deeply the conduct of private life can be tied to larger social structures.

The construction of White Americans as the "other" and American culture as deviant serves a dual purpose:

It allows immigrant communities to reinforce patriarchy through the sanctioning of women's (mis)behavior *and* to present an unblemished, if not morally superior, public face to the dominant society. Strong in family values, heterosexual morality, and a hierarchical family structure, this public face erases the Filipina "bad girl" and ignores competing (im)moral practices in the Filipino communities. Through the oppression of Filipina women and the castigation of White women's morality, the immigrant community attempts to exert its moral superiority over the dominant Western culture and to reaffirm to itself its self-worth in the face of economic, social, political, and legal subordination. In other words, the immigrant community uses restrictions on women's lives as one form of resistance to racism. Though significant, this form of cultural resistance severely restricts women's lives, particularly those of the second generation, and casts the family as a site of potentially the most intense conflict and oppressive demands in immigrant lives.

REFERENCES

Billson, Janet Mancini. 1995. *Keepers of the Culture: The Power of Tradition in Women's Lives.* New York: Lexington Books.

Coronel, Sheila and Ninotchka Rosca. 1993. "For the Boys: Filipinas Expose Years of Sexual Slavery by the U.S. and Japan." *Ms.,* November/December p. 11+.

Dasgupta, Shamita Das and DasGupta, Sayantani. 1996. "Public Face, Private Face: Asian Indian Women and Sexuality." Pp. 226–243 in *Women, Sex, and Power in the Nineties,* edited by Nan Bauer Maglin and Donna Perry. New Brunswick, NJ: Rutgers University Press.

Di Leonardo, Micaela. 1984. *The Varieties of Ethnic Experience: Kinship, Class, and Gender among California Italian-Americans.* Ithaca and London: Cornell University Press.

Eastmond, Marita. 1993. "Reconstructing Life: Chilean Refugee Women and the Dilemmas of Exile." Pp. 35–53 in *Migrant Women: Crossing Boundaries and Changing Identities,* edited by Gina Buijs. Oxford: Berg.

Egan, Timothy. 1996. "Mail-Order Marriage, Immigrant Dreams and Death." *New York Times,* 26 May, p. 12+.

Espiritu, Yen Le. 1994. "The Intersection of Race, Ethnicity, and Class: The Multiple Identities of Second Generation Filipinos." *Identities* 1(2–3):249–273.

————. 1995. *Filipino American Lives.* Philadelphia: Temple University Press.

Gabbacia, Donna. 1994. *From the Other Side: Women, Gender, and Immigrant Life in the U.S., 1820–1990.* Bloomington and Indianapolis: Indiana University Press.

Gilman, Sander L. 1985. *Difference and Pathology: Stereotypes of Sexuality, Race, and Madness.* Ithaca: Cornell University Press.

Haddad Yvonne Y. and Jane I. Smith. 1996. "Islamic Values among American Muslims." Pp. 19–40 in *Family and Gender among American Muslims: Issues Facing Middle Eastern Immigrants and Their Descendants,* edited by Barbara C. Aswad and Barbara Bilge. Philadelphia: Temple University Press.

Halualani, Rona Tamiko. 1995. "The Intersecting Hegemonic Discourses of an Asian Mail-Order Bride Catalog: Philipina 'Oriental Butterfly' Dolls for Sale." *Women's Studies in Communication* 18(1):45–64.

Kibria, Nazli. 1993. *Family Tightrope: The Changing Lives of Vietnamese Immigrant Community.* Princeton, NJ: Princeton University Press.

Maglin, Nan Bauer and Donna Perry. 1996. "Introduction." Pp. xiii–xxvi in *"Bad Girls/Good Girls": Women, Sex, and Power in the Nineties,* edited by Nan Bauer Maglin and Donna Perry.

Millet, Kate. 1970. *Sexual Politics.* Garden City, NY: Doubleday.

Rumbaut, Ruben. 1994. "The Crucible Within: Ethnic Identity, Self-Esteem, and Segmented Assimilation Among Children of Immigrants." *International Migration Review,* 28(4):748–794.

Stoler, Ann Laura. 1991. "Carnal Knowledge and Imperial Power: Gender, Race, and Morality in Colonial Asia." Pp. 51–101 in *Gender at the Crossroads of Knowledge: Feminist Anthropology in the Postmodern Era,* edited by Micaela di Leonardo. Berkeley: University of California Press.

Tolman, Deborah L. and Tracy E. Higgins. 1996. "How Being a Good Girl Can Be Bad for Girls." Pp. 205–225 in *"Bad Girls/Good Girls": Women, Sex, and Power in the Nineties,* edited by Nan Bauer Maglin and Donna Perry. New Brunswick, NJ: Rutgers University Press.

Villanueva, Marianne. 1991. *Ginseng and Other Tales from Manila.* Corvallis, OR: Calyx.

Warren, Jenifer. 1993. "Suit Asks Navy to Aid Children Left in Philippines." *Los Angeles Times,* 5 March, p. A3+.

Waters, Mary C. 1996. "The Intersection of Gender, Race, and Ethnicity in Identity Development of Caribbean American Teens." Pp. 65–81 in *Urban Girls: Resisting Stereotypes, Creating Identities,* edited by Bonnie J. Ross Leadbeater and Niobe Way. New York and London: New York University Press.

Wolf, Diane L. 1992. *Factory Daughters: Gender, Household Dynamics, and Rural Industrialization in Java.* Berkeley: University of California Press.

————. 1997. "Family Secrets: Transnational Struggles among Children of Filipino Immigrants." *Sociological Perspectives* 40(3):457–482.

Wong, Sau-ling. 1993. *Reading Asian American Literature: From Necessity to Extravagance.* Princeton, NJ: Princeton.

21

Sex and the Immigrant Communities

Risky Opportunities, Opportune Risks

GLORIA GONZALEZ-LOPEZ

"This whole thing about *el país de las oportutnidades* [the land of opportunities] . . . I will change the name, I will change the version. I will call it *el país de las enfermedades* [the land of diseases] because you get sick for any reason at all." Eugenio, a forty-three-year-old from Mexico City, spoke in a melodic Spanish rhythm as he described the various health problems he has suffered in the United States, including relapse and recovery from alcoholism and a pattern of addiction that sometimes made him behave in sexually risky ways.

Diamantina, a thirty-one-year-old, also from Mexico City, complained: "I already told my husband that if he continues working here [in the United States], I better go back to Mexico, because I am just like a piece of furniture here." Diamantina explained that her husband's strenuous schedule made her feel emotionally devalued, and that the emotional and sexual intimacy of their marriage had deteriorated. Returning to Mexico would be one way to deal with her personal circumstances, but the fear of economic hardship if she went back made her tolerate her current dissatisfaction.

For Eugenio and Diamantina, their incorporation into the labor force of an advanced industrialized economy has provided them with the opportunity to survive and improve their financial situation. However, for them and for many of the study's informants, becoming part of a highly urbanized capitalist society had also presented them with contradictions and challenges to their everyday survival, and these situations ultimately affected their sex lives. This chapter examines how after migrating and establishing a permanent life in Los Angeles, poverty, segregation, and incorporation into the labor market, among other forces, exposed these immigrants to hazards that would reshape their sex lives. These risks, along with the capitalist society and the fast-paced life found in the United States, would exacerbate an already existing culture of sexual fear, which would take new forms in Los Angeles.

AMERICAN DREAMS, MEXICAN REALITIES

Olga, a thirty-two-year-old woman from Mexico City, explained: "I do not know about Mexico, but here, life is screwed up. That is the truth, and more with children, the whole thing about rape of girls, and that kind of thing. And AIDS, as well. And also the whole thing about boys who hang out in gangs." Olga's words reflect the disenchantment and vulnerability that surrounds the migration experience of the overwhelming majority of the informants in this study. They also echo immigration studies that have described the inadequate health care Latino immigrants receive in the United States (Brown and Yu 2002; Freire 2002; Hayes-Bautista 2002; E. Díaz et al. 2001) and the deterioration in mental and physical health they experience as they are assimilated into North American society (Portes and Rumbaut 1996; Scribner 1996; Rumbaut 1997). For the immigrants in this study, becoming part of American society did not necessarily improve their health and general lifestyle, and certainly not their sex lives.

Most informants reported that living in the United States was more dangerous than living in Mexico. Some have witnessed shootings in their neighborhoods or felt threatened by gang activity, fights, police arrests of neighbors involved in drug trafficking, INS apprehensions, and drug dealing on the streets. They have witnessed or personally experimented with drugs and have faced language difficulties, xenophobic laws and racism, emotional isolation and loneliness, a lack of paid employment, crowded housing, homelessness, and prostitution. All of these conditions make them vulnerable, but informants also identified some as specifically influencing their sex lives. These included the additional risks associated with sexual violence against young girls, alcohol and drug use, gang activity, and sexually transmitted diseases (AIDS in particular). And these risks are not experienced in a social vacuum. Gender issues and the socioeconomics of their communities, both in Mexico and the United States, also shape the ways in which immigrants interpret, negotiate, and cope with their new lives.

SEXUAL ABUSE OF CHILDREN

The sexual abuse of children was of special concern for all of the women in this study. Regardless of their place of origin, women were more likely than men to be concerned that their children were more vulnerable to sexual abuse in the United States compared to Mexico. This is not to say that fathers did not express their love and concern for their children's welfare;

many of them openly did. However, a mother's direct responsibility for her children's education seemed to be the reason why the women worried about their children being raised in the United States.

The women's perceptions of the sexual abuse of children shape their views of sexuality. How? Mainly through the sex education they gave to their children, especially daughters. Some of the women worried about how permissive they should be with their adolescent daughters. They also were concerned about the "when" and "how" of talking to their children about sex and coercive sex, as well as the need to be protective and vigilant regarding their children's sexual behavior. These mothers were keenly aware of sexual violence. Said Norma:

> I would have liked to stay in my country precisely because many things happen at a very early age over here, and in Mexico it is not that way. That is the concern I am experiencing here, and I know that my daughters are taking a higher risk over here than if I went back to live in Mexico. That is the only reason why I would like to go back to Mexico, so they have more safety because of the malice that we have over here. Had I stayed in Mexico, sex education [for my daughters] would not have been the same because I learned many things over here, and I learned about the malevolence that exists in the U.S., which I didn't know about.

Women like Norma do not deny that sexual abuse also happens in Mexico (some of them reported incidents of abuse in their own childhood or adolescence). However, discussions about the kidnapping of children on television talk shows and in the print media, plus the women's own isolation, poverty, marginality, and language barriers all contributed to making the women feel that they and their children were more susceptible, vulnerable, and at greater risk in the United States.

Jimena stated her concern for her adolescent daughter this way: "Sometimes they [potential rapists] give young women something in their drinks so they fall asleep and then two or three men abuse them. That is what I tell my daughter 'See?' Because we don't give our daughter permission to go anywhere." Based on the stories she had heard since migrating, Felicia said: "I have changed because of

the violence we have these days. You find all these ma-
niac characters who rape children and girls. So I tell
them to be very careful. I tell them what they may find
out in the streets. Because these days there is a lot of
drugs, lots of gang violence, and sex. 'A drug addict
can rape you, even kill you and leave you half dead in
the middle of the street.'"

Such fears and anxieties about the potential for
sexual violence were emphasized more by mothers
who had a personal and family history of sexual mo-
lestation. In my essay "De madres a hijas" (2003) I explain how an immigrant mother's personal history of
sexual violence shapes her views on women and sexuality, sexism, and the sex education she wants to give
to a daughter with regard to virginity. For example,
Candelaria, who tearfully spoke about her fears that
her daughter would be a victim of sexual violence,
cited the statistics on sexual violence in the United
States to justify her overprotective attitude. And
Deyanira also expressed fears for her youngest daughter, based on an event that had happened within her
family. "I feel like I changed here. My sister had a
daughter and she was raped. She was about five; it
happened here."

Mothers said that they used their best parenting
skills to cope with these threats, and they also turned to
networking with other Latina/o immigrants, workshops on sexuality at community-based agencies, and
the Spanish-language media. For example, Romelia
explained how she uses talk shows to teach her children about these dangers. She relayed the message she
gave her two adolescent daughters as all of them
watched a talk show in Spanish: "Look, you see all
these young girls who are talking about the same thing
you are talking about? "I know how to take care of myself, I know how to do this and how to do that. And
look at what is happening!' I tell them so they can take
care of themselves out in the streets."

The mothers' keen awareness of the greater dangers their daughters may face in the United States
compared to Mexico seems to be accurate. Even
though sexual and domestic violence is a harsh reality
for women living in Mexico, a study showed that
"U.S.-born Mexicans were three times more likely
than Mexico-born Mexicans to have been sexually
assaulted."

ALCOHOL, DRUGS, GANGS, AND SEX

The men in this study primarily reflected on their
vulnerability to drug and alcohol use after migration;
none of the women reported this pattern. As mainly
working-class immigrants, the men's socioeconomic
marginalities and migration- and settlement-related
psychological stressors make them susceptible to alcohol use (Portes and Rumbaut 1996). They match other
Mexicanos (Brandes 2002) and men from developed
nations in their vulnerabilities to alcohol when compared with women (Connell 2000, 180). These risks
did not happen in isolation. Men with a previous history of substance abuse became more vulnerable after
immigration, due to such contributing factors as emotional distress, geographic dislocation, economic hardship, racism, uncertain legal status, language limitations, isolation, peer pressure, and crowded housing.
But immigrant men are also exposed to social and economic forces that may offer potential coping mechanisms.

The parallel lives of Eugenio and Fermín exemplify
the experiences of some immigrant men. Both began to
use alcohol and drugs while they lived in Mexico City.
In the United States, a sense of anomie and peer pressure made it hard for both men to stay sober. When I
asked Fermín if he knew why he started to use alcohol,
marijuana, and cocaine in Los Angeles, he replied,
"Well, I think it's because when you come over here,
you don't end up living with a family. In my case, I
came by myself, and wherever I ended up living, I had
to take it." Fermín had struggled to cope with peer
pressure where drug use was part of everyday life, as
he tried to fit into a new environment.

Poverty and a lack of medical insurance or access to
professionals who might help them overcome their addictions coincided in the lives of both men. However,
they both found a way to cope with their addictions in
the United States through the Catholic faith they had
previously practiced before migrating. Both men said
they found that swearing a *juramento*—an oath made to
God or the Virgin of Guadalupe—had been the best way
to remain sober. The *juramento* as a strategy to cope with
addictions is a common practice among many Mexicans
raised in the Catholic faith (Brandes 2002). Said Eugenio: "From July 1993 to this day, I have not drunk any

alcohol. In other words, I have tried to keep my *juramento* that I made to the Virgin of Guadalupe, and I already have seven years without drinking." Said Fermín: "Religion is the best thing that ever happened to me." He used, and periodically renews, his oath to God as a way to stop drinking and using drugs in Los Angeles.

For both men, practicing their faith did more than reshape their addictive behaviors. Sobriety made them aware of the sexual dangers existing within their communities (i.e., HIV/AIDS) and led to changes in their sexual behavior. Eugenio described his sex lifestyle after becoming sober:

> I have not had sex for five years. Then, when I go out to the streets, I do not have the desire to have sexual relations. I go out to the street and if I see a woman, and she smiles with me, I look at her appearance, and I ask her questions, and I see what she does for a living. If I see that she is a prostitute or she uses drugs, I do not get involved with her.

For a married man like Fermín, becoming sober through his *juramento* not only meant developing a keen awareness of potential dangers but also revisiting some values with regard to marital life and sexual behavior.

> These days to have sex with another woman would be very, very, very difficult for me. To betray my wife would be . . . ah . . . first, I would not do it because . . . first, there's AIDS, right? So, having sex with a woman these days is like flipping a coin and telling yourself, "She has AIDS or she does not have AIDS," right? You don't know anymore who is infected at this moment. Many women are having sex with many men, and men are having sex with so many women that who knows with whom they are getting involved. So that is what worries me. And religion is the other thing that does not allow me to do it; it's adultery.

Eugenio and Fermín's stories illustrate how men coping with addiction may make use of cultural expressions of religiosity within the immigrant community to achieve not only sobriety but to develop a safer sex lifestyle. The other end of the spectrum is represented by the risky sexual behaviors that emerge out of the combined effects of drug and alcohol use, gang ac-

tivity, and the social lifestyles of some groups of immigrant men.

A twenty-six-year-old man from Mexico City, Mauricio talked about his many experiences as a gang member before and after migrating. When I asked him if some of my questions had been controversial or difficult for him, a stimulating dialogue on the intersection between gang activity, sex, and drug abuse ensued. He began by recalling his early experiences with drug use as one part of his gang activities. "When I had just arrived in this country, my friends were more liberal, my friends were more crazy [laughs]. Because if a woman wants to belong to a gang, the woman has to have sex with all the men." He had participated in gang-related activities in Mexico, but he had not witnessed coercive sex as an initiation ritual for *las pandilleras,* his female gang counterparts. Since migrating, he explained, he had participated in these collective sexual rituals on at least three occasions. He recalled being part of groups of ten or twelve men who would take turns having intercourse with a girl whom the women members of the gang had previously beaten up. I attempted to get a clear picture of the initiation ritual, which many times involved drug use.

AUTHOR: When you talk about the girls and their gangs, and the fact that the woman has to have sex with all the men, are the other men looking while she is having sex with one of the guys?

MAURICIO: Yes, yes, in fact, you are touching her. One is on top, and the other guys are there, kissing her, touching her.

AUTHOR: How does she react when all this is happening?

MAURICIO: Sometimes they enjoy it, sometimes they cry. For example, the first guy did it already, and then the woman does not want to do it anymore, she may leave but the same women tell her, "Do not be stupid, if you put up with one, put up with the rest." But at times, they cry and leave.

AUTHOR: And what do the men do if she cries?

MAURICIO: They swear, they curse, they call her names, they force her. At times, they tell her that if she tells the police, her family is going to pay the price. They threaten her.

Mauricio seemed remorseful and reserved as he remembered these events. I asked him what other issues he found hard to discuss during the interview. "The one on sex with men," he said. As I probed, he explained the surprise he felt after learning that some attractive women he had met at bars in Los Angeles were actually "homosexuals dressed up like women": "By the time you realize, you already kissed them and did everything." Of his sexual involvement with other immigrant men, he said:

My friends had homosexual friends, but they had them only so they could give them oral sex, not to have sexual relations. I have had oral sex with homosexuals, when I had just arrived to this country. But not relationships in which they penetrate.

Mauricio's ideas about sexual relations stemmed from pre-migration social and cultural constructions of masculine identities and sexuality. In Mexican society, self-identified heterosexual men who have sex with men (MSM) do not identify themselves as homosexual when they play the active role during anal penetration (Carrier 1976, 1977, 1985; Almaguer 1993; Alonso and Koreck 1993; Flaskerud et al. 1996; Díaz 1998; Szasz 1998), or when they receive oral sex (Bronfman and López Moreno 1996). In addition, for self-identified heterosexual MSM who play the insertive role, penetration may become an expression of honor, power, and masculinity (Alonso and Koreck 1993; Bronfman and López Moreno 1996, 59; Prieur 1998). This "split" between the sexual and the emotional (Rubin 1983, 113) may facilitate the men's sexual involvement with other men. Even though penetrating another man does not compromise a man's sense of masculinity, being penetrated by the other man may. This pattern became evident when Mauricio insisted that he had not been penetrated by homosexual men in the United States. Prieur's (1998) ethnographic work on Mexican homosexual identities illustrates how men like Mauricio and his self-identified heterosexual friends actively participate in the gay subculture in a Mexico City working-class suburb. Prieur's informants might call Mauricio and his immigrant friends *mayates,* meaning "men who have sex with other men without being feminine and without seeing themselves as homosexual" (179).

Eugenio, Fermín, and Mauricio's narratives confirm that gender and sexual identity are socially and culturally constructed. The social aspect of sexuality is also reproduced in reciprocal interactions between an individual's emotions and their subjective interpretations and meanings (Chodorow 1995). Gender and sexuality are social but also personal and emotional. I asked Mauricio, "As a man, how do you feel after having sex with a person of your same sex?" He replied, "I feel bad. If I am with my buddies, I am talking with my friends, I will never tell them *'Me eché a un maricón'* [I screwed a queer] because they would tease me. They would give me a hard time." Besides fear of peer pressure, social stigma, ridicule, and homophobia, other emotions shaped Mauricio's subjective experience of masculinity and sexuality. Though male bisexual practices are frequent in Mexican society (Liguori 1995), bisexuality is not necessarily accepted (Prieur 1998). I also asked Mauricio if he liked men or if he felt sexually attracted to them. He reacted emphatically, "No, no! And that is what I think about. And I ask myself, Why? In other words, when I am drunk, I do it. But then, after I do it, I do not like myself. But then I say, what if later on I begin to feel attracted to men?"

Mauricio has kept his sexual practices from his circle of close friends, but he is open about them with casual acquaintances and roommates. His voluntary and involuntary sexual contact with other immigrant men when he felt peer pressure or was under the influence of alcohol and drugs had provoked a roller-coaster ride of mixed feelings in him. When I asked him if he remembered on how many occasions he had received oral sex from other men in Los Angeles, he said,

About twenty times or more. Yes, and with different men because they would arrive at our apartment and when you get drunk or drugged, and I did not know, by the time they told me, they had already got me undressed, but I was not aware of it when they did it. I did not like it.

Mauricio was not alone in his sexual experimentation with other men. He reported that some of his self-identified heterosexual migrant friends had had similar experiences. In Mauricio's case, he had begun experiencing same-sex activities as a young adolescent in Mexico City, when he was seduced by a friend he identified as homosexual. He explained that he had felt obliged to have sex with his friend on three or four occasions: the man had helped Mauricio get a job and had offered him a room to live when he was younger. However, there was one common denominator in all of Mauricio's sexual experiences, both pre- and post-migration. For Mauricio, being under the influence of drugs or alcohol always accompanied and facilitated his sexual activity with other men.

Mauricio has struggled to stay sober. Fear of being arrested by the police, as well as concerns about the safety of his two daughters and maintaining a relatively stable relationship with his wife were some of the reasons he gave for having withdrawn from both his gang activities and from sexual activity with other men. In addition, he described his growing awareness of sexually transmitted diseases (i.e., AIDS). Indeed, alcoholism and drug use are the primary risk factors that propel Latino men like Mauricio into unprotected sex with its accompanying high risk of becoming infected with HIV/AIDS (Marín, Gómez, and Hearst 1993; Hines and Caetano 1998; Marín et al. 1998).

Other informants also mentioned the combined effects of drug and alcohol use, peer pressure, and isolation on their sexual behavior and on the behavior of male friends. Alfredo and Alejandro, who are from Mexico City and who both said they are now sober, talked about what they had observed among their immigrant friends. Sounding defensive, Alfredo described an incident at a bar:

> When they drink, it's like homosexuality takes over, because they say, "I like you, I love you," that kind of words. It's okay for them to say to a person, "I am fond of you, I love you, I like you as a friend," within what's normal. But when they get drunk, they get closer and they want to hold you and that makes you think . . . [They have told me,] "I even feel like giving you a kiss." [And I say,] "Hey! Get away from here!"

With a similarly guarded attitude, Alejandro made sure I understood he did not hang out with immigrants who had homosexual desires, although he knew some:

> Men do it out of loneliness. A friend of mine, well, he is not my friend like that, right? He told me that he used drugs and also alcohol and then he started to have

an inclination toward men. So it was loneliness. He found out that he was alone and perhaps his friends pushed him to do other kinds of sex acts.

Researchers have noted the link between alcohol use and eroticism between men. De la Vega (1990) examined how some self-identified heterosexual Latino men who live in the United States engage in sex acts with other men when they are under the influence of alcohol and other substances. Bronfman and López Moreno (1996) studied a group of rural immigrant men living in Watsonville, California. The authors note that the men explained that sex that took place "under the influence of alcohol did not count. . . . Alcohol consumption constituted another effective mechanism to protect masculinity and reinforced the separation of roles" (59). In his research with Mexican men, Gutmann identifies alcohol as a trigger for homosexual desire in "even the most macho" (1996, 126). Carrillo has argued that *hombres normales* (normal men) who have sex with both women and men may engage in sex with the latter if they are exposed to the "right kind of encouragement, sometimes through alcohol consumption" (2002, 90). And Brandes has shown how, for a group of working-class men in Alcoholics Anonymous in Mexico who are now in primary loving relationships with women, "homosexual wishes and encounters are part of their dark alcoholic past" (2002, 127). Interestingly, this pattern seems to indicate that "becoming straight" is part of an alcoholic man's recovery, as heterosexuality becomes the ideal of sobriety.

In addition to the influence of alcohol and drug use, similar behaviors emerge from emotional isolation, socioeconomic segregation, and overcrowded housing conditions. Of his difficult years after arriving in the United States, Raúl said:

> I lived with these buddies, and they were about fifteen men living in one apartment. They lived like sardines inside the apartment. Suddenly, *el albur* [sexual wordplay] made them start touching each other on their buttocks because they did not have anyone to socialize or even go out with.

El albur refers to the very popular, nuanced games that use words with sexual connotations and double meanings. Such games are widely played by Mexicans in a variety of social contexts and circumstances. They may even predate the late colonial period (Stern 1995).

Raúl's story confirms research in Mexico that describes the variety of sexual exchanges—including collective sex, body-touching, and joking and bragging about sex—that take place among working-class men in such all-male settings as neighborhood streets and soccer fields (Szasz 1998). In a similar vein, Alfredo reported: "I lived with these five men in an apartment, who were also immigrants, and every week they rented pornographic movies. And I did not like to join them, because you see that movie with a group, and then what? In fifteen minutes your sexuality changes, you end up doing things you shouldn't. That is when some men reveal their homosexuality."

Alfonso went on: "I have seen men who have sex with men because they cannot find women, because if you want to have a woman over here, you need to have money." Though that had not been his experience, he had been deceived while dancing at a bar with "a pretty transvestite." Other informants talked about same-sex eroticism before and after migrating. Sebastián described the avowals of romantic love he had received from a male friend. Diego recalled the sexual advances of a man he had met at work in Los Angeles. Fermín explained that as a naive adolescent he had accepted an invitation from an older man to have coffee with him. He had allowed the man to touch him, but when he started to perform oral sex on him, Fermín had thrown up and run away. Emiliano had had a similar experience when he was fourteen when a man in his early fifties had seduced him. Like Fermín, he resisted and ran away. Fidel recalled a story about "the mayates from Guadalajara" that he had met as an adolescent. Joaquín explained that since "homosexuals prefer ugly, strong men," he was not surprised to have received so many proposals from *"maricones"* Marcos recalled incidents of men flirting with him when he had used public transportation in Los Angeles. Felipe talked about *"los hormsexuales del pueblo"* and of how he had successfully avoided their advances. Even though he had "just observed," Ernesto graphically described the group sex among men that he had witnessed on at least one occasion. And Nicolás said he had frequently been chased by homosexuals but always rejected them with respect and honesty. Other

men recalled being similarly chased, seduced, or harassed by transvestites; or of being either attracted to them "by mistake," or of sexually teasing them, either in their adolescent years or, at times, after migrating.

The men's reports, of their own and others' same-sex desires, erotic innuendo, and actual sexual practices among immigrants who self-identify as heterosexuals differs remarkably from Gutmann's (1996) findings for a Mexico City neighborhood. Like Prieur (1998, 190), I am also struck by the fact that only one of Gutmann's informants revealed having experienced sex with other men (1966, 125). However, knowing that I am a psychotherapist might have made it easier for my informants to disclose these experiences. Unlike the men in my study, the women rarely reported same-sex experiences.

Besides reflecting on the influence of drugs and alcohol on the sexual behavior they observed among groups of men, some of my male informants discussed the impact of their drug and alcohol use on their sexuality and on the quality of their heterosexual relationships. Alejandro, who was proud of his current sobriety, revealed that he had experimented with marijuana, LSD, peyote, mushrooms, inhalants, and other substances while still living in Mexico. In college, Alejandro had become a passionate reader of sociology and psychology texts, which, he claimed, had helped him decide to stop "these habits," a decision he was proud of. He was critical of some of the couples he had met in Los Angeles who were involved with drugs and alcohol, and particularly concerned about the effects of their use on women. "Risks are more for women. The woman is affected a lot, because let's say the man, when he arrives in this country, becomes an alcoholic or a drug addict, right? If they are in a relationship, many problems arise, such as economic, sexual, and at times, domestic violence."

Joaquín, a forty-four-year-old from Guadalajara, reflected on his sobriety while expressing concern about the drinking habits of his roommates, who had lived in Los Angeles for five years. "Many come with the desire to work, and I have met many people who send money to their wives. But then, many of them, 60 or 40 percent of them start using drugs, wine. I have lived with people who are that way." He associated his friends' alcohol and drug use with the deterioration he had noticed in the quality of the men's long-distance marital relationships. He noted that many men were involved in non-monogamous relationships on both sides of the border. I asked, "How often have you seen men who are involved with other women in the United States while still having their wives over there?" He replied:

> Out of twenty friends, ten have done it. It's like now, I live with two friends, and one of them drinks beer every day and the other one uses drugs. Both are married. I am not a saint, but I stopped doing all that. I have told them: "Many men use drugs within their groups of friends, they are drinking, but then your sex appetite goes down, yon are killing yourself that way, you are locking yourself up inside a circle and you are not going to get out of it."

In one of my longest interviews, Joaquín talked about the many individual and group conversations he had had with his friends about sexuality and of how he has shared with them his own journey of psychological evolution after migrating. As I will discuss in the next chapter, for Joaquín, and for many women and men in this study, networking became a way to discuss and examine their concerns about sexuality.

The variety of backgrounds and immigrant experiences of the men is also reflected in the complex similarities and differences among them. Like Alejandro and Joaquín, Emiliano, Fidel, Jacobo, and Daniel also talked about drug or alcohol experimentation that they had overcome before migrating. Others, like Vinicio, said they had been pleased to discover and attend Alcoholics Anonymous meetings shortly after migrating. But regardless of their personal coping mechanisms or their past histories, most men associated substance abuse in the United States with their immigration and settlement experiences. Even though not all rural men had difficulties in adjusting to urban Los Angeles, men who had migrated from urban areas in Mexico were more likely to report that they had already been exposed to similar risks in the home country. For example, Jacobo explained:

> I am from a barrio in Guadalajara where we had all sorts of stuff. We had drugs of all calibers, alcohol, prostitution, everything. Right there in the barrio, there was a part of the neighborhood where many prostitutes lived. They worked in San Juan de Dios. So, I was exposed to all that, and had invitations to do everything. I just did not want to take it.

Eugenio, who clings to his *juramento* to help him cope with alcoholism in Los Angeles, explained how he confronted his friends: "Look, you know what? I come from Mexico City, I come from a very poor barrio, I know all this stuff from A through Z, I can even give you a lecture on it."

Some men used their previous experience of growing up in an urban center in Mexico as a coping strategy to avoid the use of alcohol. But others used liquor as a strategy for solving the problems of legal uncertainty, emotional isolation, and sexual urges. Sebastián told of a popular bar where his immigrant friends would go to drink and dance at night. "Out of curiosity, I went once to know what the hell was going on at that place. I said to myself, this can't be real!" He described what he observed:

> A lot of old women go there, or fat women, the kind of women who would not be able to get a man in a different way. And young men go over there to get their papers, their legal documents, or they go to get a woman so she can buy a car for them. I know someone who caught this woman at this place, I think she has houses in Tijuana. Anyway, he has a truck, and he does not work, and he has money and everything.

The use of alcohol and drugs are post-migration risks that can affect men's sex lives and their heterosexual relationships. Men are vulnerable because of the social, economic, legal, and emotional stresses they face as part of the immigrant experience although a man's vulnerability is mediated by the quality and the intensity of his immigration experience, as well as by his personal history. Emotional isolation, peer pressure, and gang activity may evoke experiences of a painful past and enhance danger. But desperately looking for an alternative or renewed faith within the community may offer a chance to some.

EL SIDA

Gender selectively shapes the risks faced by women and men, but both women and men identified a ghost that haunts their lives after migration and settlement: el SIDA—AIDS.

Both women and men reported being fearful and concerned about their own health and the health of their children when the topic of AIDS was discussed. This was especially true for those who knew or were related to AIDS victims, or whose partners had or were having extramarital relationships. A few, mainly those from rural towns, reported not having any information about the disease. Those who were more informed said that their main source of information was the Spanish-language media—radio, magazines, brochures—and workshops, or *pláticas,* they attended at clinics and schools, as well as other community-sponsored programs.

As I analyzed my data, I found that gender strongly shaped women's and men's reactions to the risk of HIV/AIDS. And often, gender was shaped by socioeconomic background.

As a group, women expressed feelings of concern about the potential negative consequences of infection on their marital relationships and the possible consequences for their children (i.e., the death of one or both parents). Regardless of their place of origin, about half of the informants reported that the AIDS epidemic had helped them to open up conversations with their partners about sexuality-related issues. However, when I asked them if the AIDS epidemic had affected their sex lives, women from rural Jalisco were more likely than urban women to report that they had not experienced changes in their actual sexual behavior. Rural women less frequently reported fear of AIDS when compared to either their urban counterparts or to men from all locations. Rural women were also more likely to use the phrase *"Le tengo confianza a mi esposo"* (I trust my husband) to explain why they did not worry about AIDS/HIV infection. Women from Mexico City were more likely to report the use of condoms as a protection against AIDS. This was especially the case for women whose husbands had had extramarital affairs, or who knew people infected with the virus. Women who had engaged in their own past extramarital affairs or temptations were more likely to be from urban areas, and were also more likely to express feelings of apprehension and regret regarding the epidemic.

The socioeconomic contexts in which the women were educated often shaped their views and behavior with regard to AIDS. In particular, the social prescriptions they learned for gender relations defined these women's ways of caring for their own bodies and health. The social acceptance by rural women of a husband's extramarital affairs offers an example. Beatriz, who is from a small town, reported what she recommended to her husband:

> I am careful, and he is the same way. We have to take care of each other because you never know what may happen, at least with men. I tell him, "If you are going to go out with another woman, you have to be careful." So, in that way, we take care of each other. That has helped me a lot.

Gabriela, a woman who is aware of gender inequality, articulated her rationale differently. "Many men are macho, I know, and they do not protect themselves," she said. "Therefore, I talk with my husband a lot and I tell him to take care of himself."

Thus, as long as it is perceived to be safe, an extramarital affair and sex with a secondary partner may not lead to a change in the quality of a marital relationship. However, for some women, a husband's potential extramarital adventure not only represents a health risk. A woman may also use an affair as a strategy in preventing both the risk of infection and a deterioration in the relationship. Deyanira explained how this might be the case for some rural women:

> I would not like my husband to cheat on me, but I tell him, "The day you want to have sex with another woman, you better wear *el gorrito* [the "little hat"]. If you are going to have sexual relations with someone else, I do not want to have sex with you. It would be better if we treat each other like siblings."

Compared to the women, the men's answers offered some consistent patterns and also some differences. The overwhelming majority of the men said that AIDS had shaped their opinions about sexuality. Their views of sex were infused by feelings of fear, terror, concern, risk, and curiosity about learning more about protection. Fear of infection as a result of casual, extramarital, or commercial sex lay at the core of the vast majority of the men's testimony. However, as they discussed changes in their actual sexual behavior, some patterns emerged. Like the women, the men from Jalisco reported more changes in their opinions about sex due to AIDS, but not in their sexual behavior. Men from Mexico City were more likely to report changes in both attitudes and sex behavior. A broader exposure to a variety of sexual discourses, earlier and easier access to health-related information, and education and employment opportunities may have helped women and men educated in urban areas to develop a greater concern about their bodies and their sexual health.

Regardless of their places of origin, many of the men identified different strategies to protect themselves from infection, including a decrease in the frequency of casual or commercial sex and in extramarital relationships. But only a minority reported they had become monogamous or totally abstinent because of the AIDS epidemic. Even though embracing these strategies was a challenge for many, knowing someone who was living with the HIV virus made it easier. As illustrated in the next chapter, some immigrants experienced changes in their view of sexuality after they had interacted socially with other individuals living in their immigrant communities. Emiliano, who was fearful of HIV infection and identified himself as completely monogamous at the time of our interview, told about four friends he had met at various stages in his migration who had died of AIDS. Similarly, Marcos described the ways in which he had learned to discipline his body out of fear of infection while recalling the experience of one his friends. His friend had told him, "¡Híjole mano! [Gee whiz, man!]. Now to know who the hell was the one who infected me! I have taken many women to bed and which one is the one who infected me?" Marcos, who did not report any alcohol or drug use problems, explained that he had developed "la disciplina del cuerpo" (discipline of the body), a value emphasized by his Catholic faith and which he used to practice abstinence and to protect himself from sexually transmitted diseases.

Even though a link between religion and the lack of risky sexual behavior was present in the lives of only a few men, their cases are relevant because they show the contrasting ways in which some immigrant men cope with the risk of infection. For Eugenio and Fermín, who are single and married, respectively, a religious oath offered a way to remain sober and also led to a concern for their sexual health. Eugenio reported that he had been sexually abstinent during the previous five years. Fermín said he had never experienced casual sex while single, nor had he had an extramarital

relationship. In contrast, some men took risks even though they knew they might become infected. However, these men may protect themselves by assessing their risk of infection in distinctive ways. Alejandro used the term "mujer limpia" (clean woman) to explain that he had learned to protect himself from infection by exploring the personal history of a potential partner through in-depth conversations. Likewise, Raúl said he had always known that his ex-wife was a "mujer limpia" and so he had not worn a condom when they engaged in premarital sex.

About half of the men from both rural and urban areas said they did not use condoms due to physical discomfort and die anticlimactic effect on die sexual experience. Regardless of their places of origin, the remainder said they were amenable to wearing a condom if their wife or a sexual partner demanded it. In this group were some of the urban men, including Mauricio, Diego, and Emiliano, who had reported extramarital affairs or secondary partners. But some of the men who reported discomfort with wearing a condom had an additional reason to avoid using one: the possibility that its use would provoke conflict in the relationship. I asked Joaquín what he would do if he went back to visit his wife in Mexico and she asked him to use a condom. He imagined the dialogue that might take place between them:

> I think that she would make me think, "Why do you want me to wear a condom?" That is what I would say, kind of defensively. "Why do you want me to put it on?" "Because I don't know in what condition you come from." "Ay! You don't trust me!" And then we would go: "Yes." "No." "Yes." "No." So, I would not put it on.

A second man, Alfonso, gave a similar answer.

> Well, I would feel lack of trust toward her. Why, after all these years, is she asking me to do this? If I ever had to wear a condom, it would be because she is sick or I am sick, and that's it.

During our interviews, Joaquín and Alfonso talked about the unprotected sexual contact they had at times engaged in within extramarital relationships. Avoiding the kinds of struggles over trust and power they described in their interviews might be one of the reasons why, upon returning to Mexico, such men, who may not know they are HIV-positive, are very likely to engage in unprotected sex with a compliant primary partner (i.e., wife) who perceives sex as a marital obligation (Salgado de Snyder et al. 2000). Even though Joaquín and Alfonso are from Guadalajara and Mexico City, respectively, their behavior might be associated with the following migration-related patterns related to HIV/AIDS in Mexico:

1. Migrants who have lived in the United States represent twenty-five percent of rural Mexican men infected with HIV (Magis-Rodríguez et al. 1995).
2. Heterosexual transmission is the primary cause of HIV infection in rural Mexican communities that send farm workers to the United States (Del Río Zolezzi et al. 1995).
3. Mexicans make between 800,000 and 1,000,000 round-trips between Mexico and the United States every year; most of these travelers are young men between twelve and thirty-four years old (U.S.–Mexico Migration Panel 2001).
4. In general, heterosexual sex is the leading cause of women contracting HIV in Mexico (Chávez 1999). (The attitudes and behaviors reported by both rural women and men in this study—for example, that rural women do not change their sexual behavior even after being educated about the risks of AIDS, that they are less in control of their sexualized bodies, and that they are influenced by more rigid moralities—may exacerbate this problem.)

The men and women in this study who reported having a satisfying marital relationship identified monogamy and lack of condom use as an expression of mutual love, respect, trust, and intimacy. This finding echoes that of another study whose respondents associated "unprotected sex as the most intimate kind of sex" (Hirsch et al. 2002, 1230). Two of my male respondents, Sebastián and Fidel, boasted about being faithful to their wives and felt that this behavior was reciprocated. They used the expression "I trust my wife," as they expressed their preference for unprotected sex. Fear of infection, however, was at the core of these decisions.

SEBASTIÁN: Because of the diseases you find here, because of the promiscuity that you find over here, that is the only reason, that is the reason why I have refrained from having another relationship. I do not understand how people can take those risks. But it happens and we are seeing it.

FIDEL: I am afraid because of all the diseases, these days. I have been married for twelve years, and I have a very stable family life. I could blow it or make a mistake, right? But I have tried to avoid it. I am afraid of having extramarital relationships, especially because of AIDS.

Some of the women and men reported that migration had made them more concerned about the cruel reality of AIDS. Others characterized the disease as an international problem, one they had also witnessed in their places of origin. For instance, Cecilia said that her cousin, who was living with AIDS in Mexico, had asked her to buy a special treatment for him that was not available in Mexico City. Similarly, Idalia talked about an AIDS case that had become controversial in her small town.

In sum, my informants' perceptions and interpretations of the dangers of sexual violation of children, alcohol and drug use, gang activity, same-sex eroticism, and the AIDS epidemic arose as part of their settlement and immigration experiences. These fears influenced in many ways their sexual health, as well as the quality of their sex lives and their heterosexual relationships in the United States. For some of them, the use of alcohol and drugs, and participation in gang activity, had brought erotic pleasure and emotional comfort, but always in the shadow of serious threats and potential harm.

But why are immigrants exposed to these dangerous situations that selectively shape their sex lives? They are responding to a "political economy of risk," a concept introduced by Rayna Rapp (1999) in her investigation of women of diverse racial or edinic, class, religious, and national backgrounds and their decisions about using or refusing new reproductive technology. Inspired by Rapp's work, Castañeda and Zavella (2003) have utilized this paradigm to study immigrant Mexicana farm workers in north-central California. The farm workers face dangers to their sex lives within the context of economic, political, and social forces. Similar forces also threaten the sex lives of Mexicans migrating to and settling in Los Angeles, but they are played out in distinctive ways.

Los Angeles has become the main destination of undocumented immigrants coming to the United States (Valenzuela 2002). Mexicans represent over 95 percent of those who have been apprehended during the last two decades (Portes and Rumbaut 1996, 10). Many immigrants arrive in L.A. financially needy, legally vulnerable, and looking for work. They first settle in segregated yet resourceful communities that provide them with kin, a familiar language, and a familiar culture (Valenzuela and Gonzalez 2000), along with places to exchange goods and services (Sassen-Koob 1984). These vibrant communities witnessed an increase of more than 300 percent in the Latino workforce from 1970 to 1990 (Grant 2000). However, in 1990, two-thirds of the foreign-born, lacking a high school diploma, were hired for jobs at the bottom of the occupational hierarchy, and they had the highest poverty rate. Immigrants concentrate in specific occupations in part because those who are already established help the recently arrived to get jobs. "By 1990, 72 percent of Mexican immigrants worked in occupations that could be classified as Mexican immigrant niches" (Ortiz 1996, 257). Businesses that depend on economic migrants use these social networks to fill vacancies that are low-paying and frequently boring, dirty, hazardous, and without prospects for advancement (Cornelius 1998; Waldinger and Lichter 2003). This low-wage labor force is described by employers as reliable and diligent and willing to work hard and for less pay (Portes and Rumbaut 1996; Waldinger and Lichter 2003).

As a "global city" (Sassen-Koob 1984), Los Angeles depends on immigrant labor, which has become part of an international division of labor indispensable in the United States, a country with a widely uneven distribution of wealth and a widening gap between rich and poor (Valle and Torres 2000). These forces include the process *of segmented assimilation* (Portes 1995; Portes and Rumbaut 1996, 255–56), which drove many of the immigrants I interviewed into the inner city and other neglected areas of Los Angeles. There, insecurity, segregation, and poor-quality housing exist

hand-in-hand with devalued real estate and low rents (Vigil 2002), Some Mexican immigrants jokingly refer to these urban settlements as "Hell A" and "Lost Angeles."

The culture of sexual fear that shaped the lives of the women and men I interviewed as they grew up in Mexico takes different forms in the United States. Old fears around sexual matters are transformed in a different society as people get older and become parents. The social forces that affect their fears and their coping mechanisms include some paradoxes: socioeconomic segregation versus job opportunities, xenophobia versus avenues for social change, new social connections versus anonymity and isolation, and the Spanish-language media and immigrant communities versus language barriers. Some informants, for instance, said that fears of sexual danger are in part promoted by Spanish-language talk shows, where deviance is paraded and terrible stories are discussed by panelists.

In Mexico, fears often revolved around premarital sex. In the United States, parents share those fears, but they are also fearful of sexual abuse and rape, gang violence, drug use, and AIDS. During periods of social and political turbulence, sexual fears can merge into a more general culture of fear. Cyclical waves of xenophobia, illustrated by the anti-immigrant Proposition 187 in California, and, more recently, by racial profiling at airports after the September 11 terrorist attacks, affect the hierarchy of immigrants' concerns. Such fears never completely paralyze these women and men, however. My respondents cope with their fears (and with a wide variety of sex-related concerns) through the social networks they construct within their communities. In addition, everyday survival in a large metropolis can create distinct interpretations of what they perceive as dangerous.

The words "risk" and "danger" might be synonymous; both possess a similar linguistic meaning. Socially speaking, however, class, ethnicity, gender, and legal status may give an additional semantic twist to these words. As immigrants, these women and men identified additional paradoxes surrounding their personal lives. When I told Alfredo that some of the women that I had previously interviewed had stated that HIV/AIDS, alcohol and drug abuse, violence, and crime were risks many immigrants faced, he exclaimed, "What risks? Not having a job, that's what I call a risk! The rest of the stuff isn't a risk. My risk, for me, my preoccupation is not to have a job." Similarly, but paradoxically, when I presented Felipe with the same statement, he replied, "Well, a risk? What I call a risk is that practically all you do in this country is to work."

Even though men like Alfredo and Felipe may give contrasting interpretations to their employment experiences, attaining a paid job in a capitalistic society may be linked to an immigrant's sex life in a particular way: sex is vulnerable to the pressures of time. At times, sex improves, at times, it degenerates. It all depends on how sex is organized by the demands of busy schedules and efforts to survive in a contemporary society that craves mote and more time.

WITH THE CLOCK BY THE BED: THE TAYLORIZATION OF SEX

"My beau and I travel a lot for work and have a zillion social and professional commitments," says Fergusson, a self-employed marketing consultant and triathlete whose name has been changed for this article. "I am totally organized and anal retentive. My life is planned in 15-minute increments. So we schedule time for sex. Quite frankly, I would be surprised if most people don't."

— *"Making Time for Sex Makes a Difference,"*
San Francisco Chronicle, 2001

Work, time, and sex were intimately connected in the lives of the immigrants in this study. Diamantina is a married, full-time housewife who lives with her husband and their two daughters. She said her husband's busy schedule has hurt the quality of her sex life. "I think my sexuality is fading in this country," she said intensely, "because *en este país puro trabajo, puro trabajo!*" [in this country, it's just work, work, work!]. The deteriorating nature of Diamantina's intimate life is part of her immigration experience, but it has parallels in the personal lives of the white, middle-class people Arlie Hochschild discusses in her book *The Time Bind: When Work Becomes Home and Home Becomes Work* (1997).

Hochschild examined how the personal and family lives of working women and men were damaged by busy routines, the demands of work, financial needs, fears of losing one's jobs, and a sophisticated culture of the workplace that exists at every level in the workplace, even among companies that claim to promote "family-friendly" policies. Interestingly, Hochschild did not look at her subjects' sex lives.

Diamantina started to notice a deterioration in her sex life with her husband after migrating to the United States:

¡Puro trabajo! ¡puro trabajo! The man works day and night, so his sexuality fades away. When he comes home, he is so tired he just goes to sleep and that's it! He doesn't even pay attention to the girls, or to me, either.

Unable to earn enough in his former day job, Diamantina's husband now works around the clock for the transportation company that hired him as a trailer driver some time ago. His busy schedule has created an emotional and sexual distance and tension between them, and Diamantina worries about the future:

I feel bad because then you get older and then you cannot do anything, and then I believe the menopause will come. And then, what if I do not want to do it and then he wants to? What is going to happen? He is going to look for someone else. But I am a woman, so I would not dare to do something like that.

From a feminist perspective, Diamantina's fears have important implications. They reflect a central mechanism of sexual power: a woman's sexual potency deteriorates with age and therefore she becomes devalued. A woman is more likely than a man to be abandoned if she does not satisfy her partner's sexual needs; and, unlike a sexually dissatisfied married man, a sexually dissatisfied married woman is inherently constrained from looking for another sexual partner. At one point, Diamantina blushed and admitted that her frustration had led her to think about having a lover.

What would happen if a woman like Diamantina pursued her sexual fantasies of looking for a lover? How would that be interpreted by an immigrant man? When I interviewed Emiliano, he said he had been lucky enough not to be personally affected in his sexual life by the pressures of survival in the United States. However, he asserted that Mexican women change sexually when they come to the United States. "They become more liberal," he said, "because the man does not dedicate enough time to them." Emiliano had reached that conclusion because of the story an immigrant friend, who worked a strenuous schedule in order to support his family, had confided to him.

> A friend of mine works a lot. He is a baker, so he has to start working, I don't know, about 3 or 4 A.M., and he gets off from work around noon or 1 P.M. And then, he still goes somewhere else to bake more cakes, and to work at I don't know how many places. And I saw it, when his wife was cheating on him, and then he realized that she was being unfaithful to film.

For men like Emiliano, a busy routine of survival in Los Angeles may trigger the fear that a man will be abandoned and betrayed if he does not find enough time to satisfy his wife's sexual needs. In light of the view of masculine identity as being that of the bread-winner and also maintaining the quality of the marriage, how did the men in this study sexually react to the demands of their busy schedules? What do men like Diamantina's husband have to say about the effects of the fast pace of a highly industrialized capitalist society on their sex lives?

When I interviewed the men, I asked them if the fast pace of their daily routine in the United States had influenced their sex lives. Most nodded, while noting that they didn't have much choice: hard work was their only legal avenue for survival in Los Angeles. A few explained in detail how their daily survival routines had reshaped their sex lives. Diego observed, angrily:

> Los Angeles, California, is an urban plantation. It is a large factory. Here, you work in the morning, you work in the afternoon, and you work at night . . . and in your spare time, you also work! It absorbs your life, the pace of work in this city is overwhelming, it does not allow you to do anything. The city has one thousand hours to work in it, and one thousand distractions to spend your earnings. You are tied to the city, you live in a chain, there is no social life in the city, there is no social bonding.

Diego used the expression "*Mi tiempo es sagrado*" (My time is sacred) to explain why he had deliberately chosen to survive on a series of part-time jobs in order to have a modest but enjoyable routine. He proudly explained how his flexible schedule allowed him to have a close relationship with his children, whom he periodically visits; a romantic partner with whom he claims a satisfying intimate and emotional life; and an active social life with his friends.

Though Diego says he is careful not to allow his schedule to invade the privacy of his bedroom, he is aware of the negative consequences of a busy life on the sex lives of immigrants he has known in Los Angeles.

> The woman gets off from work and the man gets off from work, they invested eight hours at their work places, and two hours of overtime, and after that . . . do you think she is going to be willing to flirt with or to' be teased by her husband? Or to wear intimate and beautiful underwear? Or to allow her man to be romantic with her? Or to have a glass of wine before going to bed? By 8 or 9 P.M., they are fried. All they want to do is to lie down and go to sleep. The little time left after a meal is dedicated to the children, or to watch the news at Channel 34, 52, or 22, which are always fighting against each other to show you who killed more people in the city. And then, they go to sleep. The man falls down on the bed, just like the woman does, anesthetized. And then, sexual relations? Well, I have become aware—which is not my case—that they are not that frequent, once a week, or once a month, as something extraordinary, something I am against. . . . So there is more mental and physical exhaustion in this city. In Mexico, there is more chance to relax.

Diego's criticisms of how daily survival routines structure the family and marital lives of many immigrants were echoed by other men, especially those from small towns. Said Vinicio, who is from rural Jalisco: "That is the punishment you have to pay at times. People tell you this is the land of opportunities, the country where you can get everything, but you have to pay a price." He added, "Do you want to live earning the greenback? Well, you have to deprive yourself of many things." Vinicio then outlined how his post-migration routine had shaped both the quality of his family life and his marital relationship with his wife, who works full time as a clerk:

In my ranch, we used to have breakfast at 8, lunch at 2, and supper at 8. That way, you have die opportunity to be with your family. But not here. Here, you start working at 6 A.M. because you have to work for the rich, right? Then, you miss breakfast with your family. Then, you also miss lunch, because you don't get off from work until 3 P.M., or not until dinner.

Vinicio also said that his work schedule cut into the intimate times he had to be with his partner:

It happens to me because my wife many times has to start working at 5. Then, she wants to go to sleep at 8 so she can get up at 4 to get dressed and ready for work, and I want to be more relaxed watching TV up until 11 at night, and I cannot wake her up, I have to respect her sleep. Even when she is off, the days when she does not work, I have to work. So, it affects me as well.

Fidel, also from a small town, explained the strategies he and his wife (a full-time housewife) follow, as he works forty hours a week, plus five or six hours of weekly overtime periodically. I asked him if his work schedule had influenced his intimate life with his wife. Sensitively, he said:

I think it does, but you have to overcome that in order to have a sex life with your partner. At times, my wife gives me the chance to sleep, but then about midnight I wake up to have sexual relations with her. Or at times she sleeps and I go and wake her up. The fact that she is at home all day is not a honeymoon for her because I know it is really difficult to put up with the kids. They can be terrible!

Even men whose sex lives were not hurt by their work worried about that happening in the future. Jacobo, from Guadalajara, talked about the radical decisions he might face:

Well, that is not my case at this moment, but I would consider it as very important because when I remarried, I remarry with the idea of having a very good relationship, one we could share, and I do not see how we could share a relationship if we have different schedules. So, if I am going to start working at 8 a.m. and she starts working also at 8 A.M., but if she starts working at 6 P.M., definitely, we are not going to have

time to share. So, I think, that would affect me. I would not like to be in that kind of situation. But if I had to live that way, and that is what I say, I better get a divorce and look for another woman with whom I can really share a relationship.

Fermín had similar concerns. He was recovering from an accident that had placed him on disability for nearly a year, and had been taking care of his daughters while his wife worked full-time. As the day for him to resume working got closer, he began to think about the potential changes. in the quality of his marital relationship. He used the word *"distanciamiento"* to explain that he was afraid of emotional distancing in their marital relationship:

I would not like it, but what else can I do? She will have to work in the morning and in the afternoon. Then, we are not going to see each other that much because of the girls. I have to take them to school in the morning, and she has to take her classes in the afternoon. We cannot stop working until the girls grow up. So, I see it coming. When I get back to work, it may create some problems for us.

For women like Diamantina, their sexuality and sex lives were defined by their husbands' busy schedules, which seemed out of anyone's control due to the limitations and realities of their lives as immigrants. In addition, Diamantina explained the reasons for her overwhelming routine—all a part of her immigration experience: her full-time obligations as a housewife; the many doctor's visits she made on foot to various free clinics in order to take care of the health of her two daughters; her commitments at her Protestant church; and her daily struggle to find a paid job. As we have seen, Diamantina is not alone in her capitalist predicament.

Unlike the white, middle-class employees and professionals Hochschild interviewed, these women needed to survive in a new country. But both groups shared the experience of having their intimate lives redefined by the world of work in a highly industrialized capitalistic society.

Diamantina's expression, *"En este país puro trabajo, puro trabajo!"* and Diego's complaint, "Here, you work in the morning, you work in the afternoon, and you work at night . . . and in your spare time, you also work!" may have the same linguistic equivalent in English. However, in sociological language, they may have more than one meaning. "Time, work-discipline, and industrial capitalism" is also an accurate translation of these statements. The line is the title of a chapter in E. P. Thompson's book *Customs in Common* (1991), in which he analyzes time management as a crucial transitional component between pre-industrial and industrial societies. Thompson examines how industrial societies implemented time regulation and measurement as the ideal way to control and manage labor and work. He explains how the task-oriented system utilized in pre-industrial societies (i.e., the family economy of a small farmer in the nineteenth century) as a way to manage and control labor was replaced by a system of time measurement resulting from the multiple mechanisms that emerged in industrial societies, such as employment of labor, division of labor, discipline between employer and employee, production needs, and so on. The concept of time—its efficient management and its place in the history of capitalism and industrial development—is also central in Hochschild's book *The Time Bind* (1997). She cites Frederick Taylor (the engineering genius who studied and established the principles of time management and efficiency in factories almost one hundred years ago) to argue that "family life gets Taylorized" as work invades family life. That is, family life comes to be designed and lived based on principles of time efficiency learned at the workplace. The cult of time management and efficiency that her informants worship at work is carried home. Hochschild describes how some of these dedicated employees learn to cover all their family needs on time and in a very efficient manner. This experience is not an easy process and requires a great deal of investment of emotional energy (and needless to say, it also requires more "time").

In my study, Diamantina, Diego's and Emiliano's friends, Vinicio, and Fidel were already paying a "sexual cost," and Jacobo and Fermín were keenly aware of the possible high price to their sex lives. Their sex lives were clearly deteriorating as a result of the demands of survival and the pressures of time and work in an industrial society. A few of my informants, in contrast, had experienced "Taylorization" of their sex lives, which, interestingly enough, had had a positive effect.

"Yes, it is nicer! It is terrific to do it once a week or once every other week!" exclaimed Rosalía. She added, "It is nicer than having sex every day because everyday sex gets kind of boring." Being responsible for six children and working full time had made Rosalía redefine her sex life in a "timely efficient manner" by establishing a sexual agreement with her husband of less than a year. With great excitement, she talked about how working full-time had created the need for them to establish a schedule for their sexual encounters. Interestingly, waiting for the appropriate day to have sex had created an atmosphere of sexual excitement in her marital life and a "sexual gain" as part of her life in the United States. Coordinating work within a busy schedule has turned out to be an aphrodisiac, she said.

> Sometimes when I do it once every eight days, or once every fifteen days, we are happy because it is like doing it everyday. Because when we make it once a week or once every two weeks, I give myself more. It's like . . . you do not give yourself the same way when you do it every day.

Rosalía reminded me of the highly attuned ways in which other informants—beyond the context of work and time—had perceived different expressions of prohibition as sexually exciting. For them, forbiddance had increased sexual yearning and passion. Felipe, for example, told me he still remembers the rainy season in his small town with special pleasure. Back then, a rainy day was a golden opportunity for him and his friends. "When it rained, we would watch carefully to see when women would raise their long skirts," he said with a giggle. "Now, with miniskirts, well, it's not the same."

Immigrant women like Diamantina and Rosalía may not be aware of the changing rhythms in the history of industrialization and capitalism. However, the important transitions in their sex lives do allow them to measure the contrasts of time management and economy between a developing nation, like Mexico, and the United States—the mecca of capitalism, modernity, and industrialization, and the place where they have to survive as immigrants.

As part of my own personal experience in the United States, I have observed that North Americans use the expression "Thank you for your time" to express their gratitude after someone has spent "time" helping them with a particular issue. In my years living in Mexico, I never heard anyone use its equivalent in Spanish, *"Gracias por su tiemp."* In general, in Mexico, people would use the expression *"Gracias por ayudarme"* (Thank you for helping me). Socially speaking, in capitalistic societies "time" seems to have a higher value than "help." Time means capital, time means money.

Diamantina and Rosalía's stories bear on discussions of employment, personal empowerment, and sex. An immigrant woman may develop a sense of sexual autonomy as a consequence of obtaining paid full-time employment outside the home, earning a salary, and becoming financially independent. As a full-time housewife who is financially dependent on her husband's income, a woman like Diamantina may not have much power in negotiations with him. In fact, she may be in a devalued and disempowered position and therefore lack control over negotiations involving her sex life. Therefore, she is more likely to experience negative changes in sexuality. By contrast, Rosalía—a full-time employee in a paid position outside her home who shares household expenses equally with her husband—may have the opportunity to experience a positive transition in her sex life.

Unlike women, men reported more elaborate and sophisticated responses with regard to the negative influence of a busy and fast-paced routine, on their sex lives as well as on their marriages and their families. This pattern is important given the sample size, forty female versus twenty male informants. Some explanations may include the following;

All the men had full-time paid employment, whereas 60 percent of the women had part-time or full-time paid employment. Men's sex lives seem to be more directly negatively affected by survival when they are the breadwinners in an economy of time. In addition, men more frequently complained about the intrusion of work and schedule on their family lives. Whereas a full-time housewife with no paid employment may develop a closer bond with her children and home, the demands of economic survival may increase a man's feelings of isolation and disconnection from his family and marital life.

As a group, women appeared to be socially trained to be more tolerant of sexual frustration and more re-

served with regard to their sexual needs and desires when compared to men. It is significant that the only two women who clearly noted "sexual costs" (Diamantina) or "sexual gains" (Rosalía) as a consequence of their busy schedules in the United States were from Mexico City. As a consequence of more education and employment opportunities in urban centers, women living in industrialized areas may feel they have more social and cultural permission to identify and express their sexual needs, desires, and frustrations when compared to their rural counterparts. Amuchástegui observed in her sex research in Mexico: "There seems to be a greater awareness and acceptance of sexual desire among women participants who have had more contact with urban culture and formal education" (2001, 291). This is consistent with research that concludes that urban women are less disadvantaged with regard to negotiating preventive sexual practices when compared to their rural counterparts (Del Río Zolezzi et al. 1995). Diamantina's and Rosalía's testimony, as well as the testimony of Amuchástegui and Del Río Zolezzi's informants, seem to have a connection with recent reports by the Instituto Mexicano de Sexología which indicate that women from urban Mexico are twice as likely as rural women to report that they have experienced an orgasm (Gómez Mena 2001). This finding also coincides with research on rural women from Michoacán who complained of lacking sexual desire because they were sexually dissatisfied or had never experienced an orgasm in their heterosexual encounters (Bronfman and López Moreno 1996, 64); and on rural women from Jalisco who reported a lack of negotiating power in their heterosexual encounters and perceived intercourse not as a voluntary act but as an apparent marital obligation (Salgado de Snyder et al. 2000).

Women who have learned to perceive sexual intercourse as a marital obligation may experience a sense of relief from not having to be sexually available to an absent or physically exhausted husband who is too busy working. Thus, within a traditional family arrangement, a busy economy may hurt an immigrant man's sex life, but it may give a break to a woman who doesn't enjoy sex.

The women and men in this study revealed the sexual vulnerabilities and paradoxes for immigrants settling in the ultra-industrialized city mecca of die capitalist system that is Los Angeles. As shown, these challenges unfold through specific social mechanisms. Even though many of the immigrants shared their awareness of their susceptibility to crime, violence, and drugs, among other things, they identified only some of them as having prompted changes in their views of sexuality or their actual sexual behaviors and attitudes. The discourses and realities of child sexual abuse, alcohol and drug use, gang activity, and sexually transmitted diseases (especially AIDS) unfolded through the socioeconomic segregation, peer pressure, emotional isolation and uncertain legal status, among other factors, that shape Mexican immigrants' sex lives. In addition, the world of work may also have affected their sex lives, by virtue of the invasive nature of a fast-paced capitalist society. Even though many of the women and men in this study may have felt (and at times reported) that they had no control over the hazardous situations and circumstances affecting their sex lives, some of them exhibited coping mechanisms and strategies to protect the quality of their marital and family relationships, and their sex lives. As some of them eloquently told their stories, it became clear that many of these immigrant women and men had not been passive social actors; they had actively sought out the best coping mechanisms available.

For many women and men who migrate to and establish permanent lives in the United States, internal and external sexual boundaries are socially defined, created, and recreated. Beyond the hazards of socioeconomic segregation and the contradictions of the world of work, these immigrants dynamically reconstruct their sex lives as they deal with the predicaments and the rich sexual redefinitions that take place within their immigrant communities.

REFERENCES

Almaguer, Tomás. 1993. Chicano Men: A Cartography of Homosexual Identity and Behavior. In *The Lesbian and Gay Studies Reader,* edited by Henry Abelove, Michele A. Barale, and David M. Halperin, 255–73. New York: Routledge.

Alonso, Ana María, and María Teresa Koreck. 1993. Silences: "Hispanics," AIDS, and Sexual Practices. In *The Lesbian and Gay Studies Reader,* edited by Henry

Abelove, Michele A. Barale, and David M. Halperin, 110–26. Now York: Routledge.

Amuchástegui, *Ana.* 2001. *Virginidad e iniciacíon sexual on México: Experiancias y significados.* Mexico City: EDAMEX and Population Council.

Basnayake, Sriani. 1990. The Virginity Test—A Bridal Nightmare. *Journal of Family Welfare* 36, no. 2: 50–59.

Brandes, Stanley. 2002. *Staying Sober in Mexico City.* Austin: University of Texas Press.

Bronfman, Mario, and Sergio López Moreno. 1996. Perspectives on HIV/AIDS Prevention among Immigrants on the U.S.–Mexico Border. In *AIDS Crossing Borders,* edited by Shiraz I. Mishra, Ross F. Conner, and J. Raúl Magaña, 49–76. Boulder, Colo.: Westview Press.

Brown, E. Richard, and Hongjian Yu. 2002. Latinos' Access to Employment-based Health Insurance. In *Latinos: Remaking America,* edited by Marcelo M. Suárez-Orozco and Mariela M. Páez, 236–53. Berkeley: University of California Press.

Carrier, Joseph M. 1976. Cultural Factors Affecting Urban Mexican Male Homosexual Behavior. *Archives of Sexual Behavior* 5, no. 2: 103–24.

———. 1977. "Sex-Role Preference" as an Explanatory Variable in Homosexual Behavior. *Archives of Sexual Behavior* 6, no. 1: 53–65.

———. 1985. Mexican Male Bisexuality. In *Bisexualities: Theory and Research,* edited by Fritz Klein and Timothy J. Wolf, 75–85. New York: Haworth Press.

Carrillo, Héctor. 2002. *The Night is Young: Sexuality in Mexico in the Time of AIDS.* Chicago: University of Chicago Press.

Castañeda, Xóchtl, and Patricia Zavella. 2003. Changing Constructions of Sexuality and Risk: Migrant Mexican Women Farmworkers in California. *Journal of Latin American Anthropology* 8, no. 2: 126–51.

Chávez, Eda. 1999. Domestic Violence and HIV/AIDS in Mexico. In *AIDS and Men: Taking Risks or Taking Responsibility?* edited by Martin Foreman, 51–63. London: Panos Institute and Zed Books.

Chodorow, Nancy J. 1978. *The Reproduction of Mothering: Psychoanalysis and the Sociology of Gender.* Berkeley: University of California Press.

———. 1995. Gender as a Personal and Cultural Construction. *Signs* 20, no. 3: 516–44.

Connell, R. W. 1987. *Gender and Power: Society, the Person, and Sexual Politics.* Stanford, Calif.: Stanford University Press.

———. 2000. *The Men and the Boys.* Berkeley: University of California Press.

Cornelius, Wayne A. 1998. The Structural Embeddedness of Demand for Mexican Immigrant Labor: New Evidence from California. In *Crossings: Mexican Immigration in Interdisciplinary Perspectives,* edited by Marcelo M. Suárez-Orozco, 113–44. Cambridge, Mass.: Harvard University, David Rockefeller Center for Latin American Studies.

De la Vega, Ernesto. 1990. Considerations for Reaching the Latino Population with Sexuality and HIV/AIDS Information and Education. *SIECUS Report* 18, no. 3.

Del Río Zolezzi, Aurora, Ana Luisa Liguori, Carlos Magis-Rodríguez, José Luis Valdespino-Gómez, María de Lourdes García-García, and Jaime Sepúlveda Amor. 1995. La epidemia de VIH/SIDA y la mujer en México. *Salud Pública de México* 37, no. 6: 581–91.

Diaz, Esperanza, Holly Prigerson, Rani Desai, and Robert Rosenbeck. 2001. Perceived Needs and Service Use of Spanish Speaking Monolingual Patients Followed at a Hispanic Clinic. *Community Mental Health Journal* 37, no. 4: 335–46.

Díaz, Rafael M. 1998. *Latino Gay Men and HIV: Culture, Sexuality, and Risk Behavior.* New York: Routledge.

Flaskerud, Jacquelyn H., Gwen Uman, Rosa Lara, Lillian Romero, and Karen Taka. 1996. Sexual Practices, Attitudes, and Knowledge Related to HIV Transmission in Low Income Los Angeles Hispanic Women. *Journal of Sex Research* 33, no. 4: 343–53.

Freire, Gloria M. 2002. Hispanics and the Politics of Health Care. *Journal of Health and Social Policy* 14, no. 4: 21–35.

Gómez Mena, Carolina. 2001. Califican como "bastante pobre" la calidad erótica del mexicano. *La Jornada,* March 26, 2001. http://www.jornada.unam.mx.

Gonzalez-López, Gloria. 2003. De madres a hijas: Gendered Lessons on Virginity across Generations of Mexican Immigrant Women. In *Gender and U.S. Migration: Contemporary Trends,* edited by Pierrette Hondagneu-Sotelo, 217–40. Berkeley: University of California Press.

Grant, David M. 2000. A Demographic Portrait of Los Angeles County, 1970 to 1990. In *Prismatic Metropolis: Inequality in Los Angeles,* edited by Lawrence D. Bobo, Melvin L. Oliver, James H. Johnson Jr., and Abel Valenzuela Jr., 51–80. New York: Russell Sage Foundation.

Gutmann, Matthew C. 1996. *The Meanings of Macho: Being a Man in Mexico City.* Berkeley: University of California Press.

———. 2003. Machismo (macho). In *Men and Masculinities: A Social, Cultural, and Historical Encyclopedia,* edited by Michael Kimmel and Amy Aronson. Santa Barbara: ABC-CLIO.

Hayes-Bautista, David E. 2002. The Latino Health Research Agenda for the Twenty-first Century. In *Latinos: Remaking America,* edited by Marcelo M. Suárez-Orozco and Mariela M. Páez, 215–35. Berkeley: University of California Press; Cambridge, Mass.: Harvard University, David Rockefeller Center for Latin American Studies.

Hines, Alice M., and Raúl Caetano. 1995. Alcohol and AIDS-related Sexual Behavior among Hispanics: Acculturation and Gender Differences. *AIDS Education and Prevention* 10, no. 6: 533–47.

Hirsch, Jennifer S., Jennifer Higgins, Margaret E. Bentley, and Constance A. Nathanson. 2002. The Social Constructions of Sexuality: Marital Infidelity and Sexually Transmitted Disease—HIV Risk in a Mexican Migrant Community. *American Journal of Public Health* 92, no. 8: 1227–37.

Hochschild, Arlie R. 1997. *The Time Bind: When Work Becomes Home and Home Becomes Work.* New York: Metropolitan Books.

Liguori, Ana Luisa. 1995. Las investigaciones sobre bisexualidad en México. *Debate Feminista* 6, no. 11: 132–56.

Magis-Rodríguez, Carlos, Aurora Del Río Zolezzi, José Luis Valdespino-Gómez, and María de Lourdes García-García. 1995. Casos de sida en el área rural de México. *Salud Pública de México* 37, no. 6: 615–23.

Marín, Barbara Van Oss, Cynthia A. Gómez, and Norman Hearst. 1993. Multiple Heterosexual Partners and Condom Use among Hispanics and Non-Hispanic Whites. *Family Planning Perspectives* 25, no. 4: 170–74.

Marín, Barbara V, Jeanne M. Tschann, Cynthia A. Gómez, and Steve Gregorich. 1998. Self-Efficacy to Use Condoms in Unmarried Latino Adults. *American Journal of Community Psychology* 26, no. 1: 53–71.

Ortiz, Vilma. 1996. The Mexican-Origin Population: Permanent Working Class or Emerging Middle Class? In *Ethnic Los Angeles,* edited by Roger Waldinger and Mehdi Bozorgmehr, 247–77. New York: Russell Sage Foundation.

Portes, Alejandro. 1995. Children of Immigrants: Segmented Assimilation and Its Determinants. In *The Economic Sociology of Immigration: Essays on Neworks, Ethnicity, and Entrepreneurship,* edited by Alejandro Portes, 248–79. New York: Russell Sage Foundation.

Portes, Alejandro, and Rubén G. Rumbaut. 1996. *Immigrant America.* Berkeley: University of California Press.

Prieto, Yolanda. 1992. Cuban Women in New Jersey: Gender Relations and Change. In *Seeking Common Ground: Multidisciplinary Studies of Immigrant Women in the United States,* edited by Donna Gabaccia, 185–201. Westport, Conn.: Greenwood Press.

Prieur, Annick. 1998. *Mema's House, Mexico City: On Transvestites, Queens, and Machos.* Chicago: University of Chicago Press.

Rapp, Rayna. 1999. *Testing Women, Testing the Fetus: The Social Impact of Amniocentesis in America.* New York: Routledge.

Rubin, Lillian B. 1979. *Women of a Certain Age: The Midlife Search for Self.* New York: Harper and Row.

———. 1983. *Intimate Strangers: Men and Women Together.* New York: Harper and Row.

Rumbaut, Rubén G. 1997. Assimilation and Irs Discontents: Between Rhetoric and Reality. *International Migration Review* 31, no. 4: 923–60.

Salgado de Snyder, V. Nelly, Andrea Acevedo, María de Jesús Díaz-Pérez, and Alicia Saldívar-Garduño. 2000. Understanding the Sexuality of Mexican-born Women and Their Risk for HIV/AIDS. *Psychology of Women Quarterly* 24, no. 1: 100–109.

Sassen-Koob, Saskia. 1984. The New Labor Demand in Global Cities. In *Cities in Transformation: Class, Capital and the State,* edited by Michael Peter Smith, 139–71. Beverly Hills, Calif.: Sage.

Scribner, Richard. 1996. Paradox as Paradigm: The Health Outcomes of Mexican Americans (editorial). *American Journal of Public Health* 86, no. 3: 303–5.

Stern, Steve J. 1995. *The Secret History of Gender: Women, Men, and Power in Late Colonial Mexico.* Chapel Hill: University of North Carolina Press.

Szasz, Ivonne. 1997. Género y valores sexuales: Un estudio de caso entre un grupo de mujeres mexicanas. *Estudios Demográficos y Urbanos* 12, no. 1–2: 155–75.

———. 1998. Masculine Identity and Meanings of Sexuality: A Review of Research in Mexico. *Reproductive Health Matters* 6, no. 12: 97–104.

Thompson, E.P. 1991. *Customs in Common* New York: New press.

U.S.–Mexico Migration Panel. 2001. *Mexico–U.S. Migration: A Shared Responsibility.* Report of the Panel, convened by the Carnegie Endowment for International Peace (International Migration Policy Program) and the Instituto Tecnológico Aurónomo de México (Faculty of International Relations). Washington, D.C.: Carnegie Endowment for International Peace. http://www.migrationpolicy.org/pubs/2001.php.

Valenzuela, Abel, Jr. 1999. Day Laborers in Southern California: Preliminary Findings from the Day Labor Survey. Working Paper, no. 99–04. Center for the Study of Urban Poverty, Institute for Social Science Research, University of California, Los Angeles.

———. 2002. Working on the Margins in Metropolitan Los Angeles: Immigrants in Day Labor Work. *Migraciones Internacionales* 1, no. 2: 5–28.

———. 2003. Day Labor Work. *Annual Review of Sociology* 29, no. 1: 307–33.

Valenzuela, Abel, Jr., and Elizabeth Gonzalez. 2000. Latino Earnings Inequality: Immigrant and Native-Born Differences. In *Prismatic Metropolis: Inequality in Los Angeles,* edited by Lawrence D. Bobo, Melvin L. Oliver, James H. Johnson Jr., and Abel Valenzuela Jr., 249–78. New York: Russell Sage Foundation.

Valle, Victor M., and Rodolfo D. Torres. 2000. *Latino Metropolis.* Minneapolis: University of Minnesota Press.

Vigil, Diego. 2002. Community Dynamics and the Rise of Street Gangs. In *Latinos: Remaking America,* edited by Marcelo M. Suárez-Orozco and Mariela M. Páez, 97–109. Berkeley: University of California Press; Cambridge, Mass.: Harvard University, David Rockefeller Center for Latin American Studies.

Waldinger, Roger, and Michael I. Lichter. 2003. *How the Other Half Works: Immigration and the Social Organization of Labor.* Berkeley: University of California Press.

PART IV

IDENTITIES

Our sense of who we are as women and men is not likely to remain the same over the span of our lives, but how are our identities formed and contested? How do our gendered identities change as they feed into our identities as members of religious groups, nations, or social movements? There is nothing automatic about identities. Identities are fluid rather than primordial, socially constructed rather than inherited, and they shift with changing social contexts. As the world grows more complex and interconnected, our identities, or self-definitions, respond to diverse and sometimes competing pulls and tugs.

Identities are both intensely private and vociferously public. Identities are also fundamentally about power and alliances. Racial-ethnic, religious, national, and sexual identities are at the core of many of today's social movements and political conflicts. Intertwined with these emergent and contested identities are strong ideas—stated or implicit—of what it is to be feminine and masculine. Most of the articles in this section rely on strong, first-person narratives as a vehicle to reflect how gender interacts with the creation and contestation of multifaceted identities. Together, the authors suggest some of the ways that identities are actively shaped and defined in contradistinction to other identities, and the ways in which identities are sometimes imposed from above or resisted. In this view, identities involve a process of simultaneously defining and erasing difference, and of claiming and constructing spheres of autonomy.

This section opens with the classic article by Peggy McIntosh on white privilege. As McIntosh suggests, privileged identities—white, male, heterosexual, middle or upper class—are often invisible *as* identities. This is a key way in which power operates, by rendering invisible the very mechanisms that create and perpetuate group-based inequities. The second article is also a classic. Here the poet and lesbian activist Audre Lorde draws on her own experience to argue that age, race, class, and sex are all simultaneous aspects of one's identity that cannot be easily separated out. Lorde argues that embracing these intertwined differences can offer opportunities for personal and collective growth and can point the way toward peaceful and just changes in the world. In the following article, Karen Pyke and Denise Johnson examine the lives of young Korean and Vietnamese immigrant women in the United States. They show the ways that these young women shape unique femininities, as they negotiate the tensions between dominant forms of femininity in "mainstream White America," with their experience of gender in their more gender-dichotomous immigrant families and communities. In the next chapter, Jen'Nan Ghazal Read and John Bartkowski take up similar themes, but they examine a different group, Muslim women, largely middle-class and well-educated, in Austin, Texas.

Relying on in-depth interviews, they examine what veiling means to these women, exploring how agency and identity are negotiated within systems of gender, religion and culture. In the final chapter in this section, Hernan Ramirez and Edward Flores move away from old stereo-types of Latino men as homogeneously "macho" and instead they offer us a view of the multi-plicity of Latino masculinities. Contrasting the lived experiences of Mexican immigrant gar-deners and Chicano gang members in Los Angeles, they show how culture, discrimination and structural constraints shape the ability of Latino men to live up to dominant masculine ideals.

22

White Privilege

Unpacking the Invisible Knapsack

PEGGY MCINTOSH

Through work to bring materials from Women's Studies into the rest of the curriculum, I have often noticed men's unwillingness to grant that they are over-privileged, even though they may grant that women are disadvantaged. They may say they will work to improve women's status, in the society, the university, or the curriculum, but they can't or won't support the idea of lessening men's. Denials which amount to taboos surround the subject of advantages which men gain from women's disadvantages. These denials protect male privilege from being fully acknowledged, lessened or ended.

Thinking through unacknowledged male privilege as a phenomenon, I realized that since hierarchies in our society are interlocking, there was most likely a phenomenon of White privilege which was similarly denied and protected. As a White person, I realized I had been taught about racism as something which puts others at a disadvantage, but had been taught not to see one of its corollary aspects, White privilege, which puts me at an advantage.

I think Whites are carefully taught not to recognize White privilege, as males are taught not to recognize male privilege. So I have begun in an untutored way to ask what it is like to have White privilege. I have come to see White privilege as an invisible package of unearned assets which I can count on cashing in each day, but about which I was "meant" to remain oblivious. White privilege is like an invisible weightless knapsack of special provisions, maps, passports, code-books, visas, clothes, tools and blank checks.

Describing White privilege makes one newly accountable. As we in Women's Studies work to reveal male privilege and ask men to give up some of their power, so one who writes about having White privilege must ask, "Having described it, what will I do to lessen or end it?"

After I realized the extent to which men work from a base of unacknowledged privilege, I understood that much of their oppressiveness was unconscious. Then I remembered the frequent charges from women of color that White women whom they encounter are oppressive. I began to understand why we are justly seen as oppressive, even when we don't see ourselves that way. I began to count the ways in which I enjoy unearned skin privilege and have been conditioned into oblivion about its existence.

My schooling gave me no training in seeing myself as an oppressor, as an unfairly advantaged person, or as a participant in a damaged culture. I was taught to see myself as an individual whose moral state depended on her individual moral will. My schooling followed the pattern my colleague Elizabeth Minnich has pointed out: Whites are taught to think of their lives as morally neutral, normative, and average, and also ideal, so that when we work to benefit others, this is seen as work which will allow "them" to be more like "us."

I decided to try to work on myself at least by identifying some of the daily effects of White privilege in my life. I have chosen those conditions which I think in my case *attach somewhat more to skin-color privilege* than to class, religion, ethnic status, or geographical location, though of course all these other factors are intricately intertwined. As far as I can see, my African American co-workers, friends and acquaintances with whom I come into daily or frequent contact in this particular time, place, and line of work cannot count on most of these conditions.

1. I can if I wish arrange to be in the company of people of my race most of the time.
2. If I should need to move, I can be pretty sure of renting or purchasing housing in an area which I can afford and in which I would want to live.
3. I can be pretty sure that my neighbors in such a location will be neutral or pleasant to me.
4. I can go shopping alone most of the time, pretty well assured that I will not be followed or harassed.
5. I can turn on the television or open to the front page of the paper and see people of my race widely represented.
6. When I am told about our national heritage or about "civilization," I am shown that people of my color made it what it is.
7. I can be sure that my children will be given curricular materials that testify to the existence of their race.
8. If I want to, I can be pretty sure of finding a publisher for this piece on White privilege.
9. I can go into a music shop and count on finding the music of my race represented, into a supermarket and find the staple foods which fit with my cultural traditions, into a hairdresser's shop and find someone who can cut my hair.
10. Whether I use checks, credit cards, or cash, I can count on my skin color not to work against the appearance of financial reliability.
11. I can arrange to protect my children most of the time from people who might not like them.
12. I can swear, or dress in second hand clothes, or not answer letters, without having people attribute these choices to the bad morals, the poverty, or the illiteracy of my race.
13. I can speak in public to a powerful male group without putting my race on trial.
14. I can do well in a challenging situation without being called a credit to my race.
15. I am never asked to speak for all the people of my racial group.
16. I can remain oblivious of the language and customs of persons of color who constitute the world's majority without feeling in my culture any penalty for such oblivion.
17. I can criticize our government and talk about how much I fear its policies and behavior without being seen as a cultural outsider.
18. I can be pretty sure that if I ask to talk to "the person in charge," I will be facing a person of my race.
19. If a traffic cop pulls me over or if the IRS audits my tax return, I can be sure I haven't been singled out because of my race.
20. I can easily buy posters, postcards, picture books, greeting cards, dolls, toys, and children's magazines featuring people of my race.
21. I can go home from most meetings of organizations I belong to feeling somewhat tied in, rather than isolated, out-of-place, outnumbered, unheard, held at a distance, or feared.
22. I can take a job with an affirmative action employer without having co-workers on the job suspect that I got it because of race.
23. I can choose public accommodation without fearing that people of my race cannot get in or will be mistreated in the places I have chosen.
24. I can be sure that if I need legal or medical help, my race will not work against me.

25. If my day, week, or year is going badly, I need not ask of each negative episode or situation whether it has racial overtones.

26. I can choose blemish cover or bandages in "flesh" color and have them more or less match my skin.

I repeatedly forgot each of the realizations on this list until I wrote it down. For me White privilege has turned out to be an elusive and fugitive subject. The pressure to avoid it is great, for in facing it I must give up the myth of meritocracy. If these things are true, this is not such a free country; one's life is not what one makes it; many doors open for certain people through no virtues of their own.

In unpacking this invisible knapsack of White privilege, I have listed conditions of daily experience which I once took for granted. Nor did I think of any of these perquisites as bad for the holder. I now think that we need a more finely differentiated taxonomy of privilege, for some of these varieties are only what one would want for everyone in a just society, and others give licence to be ignorant, oblivious, arrogant and destructive.

I see a pattern running through the matrix of White privilege, a pattern of assumptions which were passed on to me as a White person. There was one main piece of cultural turf; it was my own turf, and I was among those who could control the turf. *My skin color was an asset for any move I was educated to want to make.* I could think of myself as belonging in major ways, and of making social systems work for me. I could freely disparage, fear, neglect, or be oblivious to anything outside of the dominant cultural forms. Being of the main culture, I could also criticize it fairly freely.

In proportion as my racial group was being made confident, comfortable, and oblivious, other groups were likely being made inconfident, uncomfortable, and alienated. Whiteness protected me from many kinds of hostility, distress, and violence, which I was being subtly trained to visit in turn upon people of color.

For this reason, the word "privilege" now seems to me misleading. We usually think of privilege as being a favored state, whether earned or conferred by birth or luck. Yet some of the conditions I have described here work to systematically overempower certain groups. Such privilege simply *confers dominance* because of one's race or sex.

I want, then, to distinguish between earned strength and unearned power conferred systemically. Power from unearned privilege can look like strength when it is in fact permission to escape or to dominate. But not all of the privileges on my list are inevitably damaging. Some, like the expectation that neighbors will be decent to you, or that your race will not count against you in court, should be the norm in a just society. Others, like the privilege to ignore less powerful people, distort the humanity of the holders as well as the ignored groups.

We might at least start by distinguishing between positive advantages which we can work to spread, and negative types of advantages which unless rejected will always reinforce our present hierarchies. For example, the feeling that one belongs within the human circle, as Native Americans say, should not be seen as privilege for a few. Ideally it is an *unearned entitlement*. At present, since only a few have it, it is an *unearned advantage* for them. This paper results from a process of coming to see that some of the power which I originally saw as attendant on being a human being in the U.S. consisted in *unearned advantage* and *conferred dominance*.

I have met very few men who are truly distressed about systemic, unearned male advantage and conferred dominance. And so one question for me and others like me is whether we will be like them, or whether we will get truly distressed, even outraged, about unearned race advantage and conferred dominance and if so, what we will do to lessen them. In any case, we need to do more work in identifying how they actually affect our daily lives. Many, perhaps most, of our White students in the U.S. think that racism doesn't affect them because they are not people of color; they do not see "whiteness" as a racial identity. In addition, since race and sex are not the only advantaging systems at work, we need similarly to examine the daily experience of having age advantage, or ethnic advantage, or physical ability, or advantage related to nationality, religion, or sexual orientation.

Difficulties and dangers surrounding the task of finding parallels are many. Since racism, sexism, and heterosexism are not the same, the advantaging associated with them should not be seen as the same. In addition, it is hard to disentangle aspects of unearned advantage which rest more on social class, economic class, race, religion, sex and ethnic identity than on other factors. Still, all of the oppressions are interlocking, as the Combahee River Collective Statement of 1977 continues to remind us eloquently.

One factor seems clear about all of the interlocking oppressions. They take both active forms which we can see and embedded forms which as a member of the dominant group one is taught not to see. In my class and place, I did not see myself as a racist because I was taught to recognize racism only in individual acts of meanness by members of my group, never in invisible systems conferring unsought racial dominance on my group from birth.

Disapproving of the systems won't be enough to change them. I was taught to think that racism could end if White individuals changed their attitudes. (But) a "white" skin in the United States opens many doors for Whites whether or not we approve of the way dominance has been conferred on us. Individual acts can palliate, but cannot end, these problems.

To redesign social systems we need first to acknowledge their colossal unseen dimensions. The silences and denials surrounding privilege are the key political tool here. They keep the thinking about equality or equity incomplete, protecting unearned advantage and conferred dominance by making these taboo subjects. Most talk by Whites about equal opportunity seems to me now to be about equal opportunity to try to get into a position of dominance while denying that *systems* of dominance exist.

It seems to me that obliviousness about White advantage, like obliviousness about male advantage, is kept strongly inculturated in the United States so as to maintain the myth of meritocracy, the myth that democratic choice is equally available to all. Keeping most people unaware that freedom of confident action is there for just a small number of people props up those in power, and serves to keep power in the hands of the same groups that have most of it already.

Though systemic change takes many decades, there are pressing questions for me and I imagine for some others like me if we raise our daily consciousness on the perquisites of being light-skinned. What will we do with such knowledge? As we know from watching men, it is an open question whether we will choose to use unearned advantage to weaken hidden systems of advantage, and whether we will use any of our arbitrarily awarded power to try to reconstruct power systems on a broader base.

23

Age, Race, Class, and Sex

Women Redefining Difference

AUDRE LORDE

Much of western European history conditions us to see human differences in simplistic opposition to each other: dominant/subordinate, good/bad, up/down, superior/inferior. In a society where the good is defined in terms of profit rather than in terms of human need, there must always be some group of people who, through systematized oppression, can be made to feel surplus, to occupy the place of the dehumanized inferior. Within this society, that group is made up of Black and Third World people, working-class people, older people, and women.

As a forty-nine-year-old Black lesbian feminist socialist mother of two, including one boy, and a member of an interracial couple, I usually find myself a part of some group defined as other, deviant, inferior, or just plain wrong. Traditionally, in American society, it is the members of oppressed, objectified groups who are expected to stretch out and bridge the gap between the actualities of our lives and the consciousness of our oppressor. For in order to survive, those of us for whom oppression is as American as apple pie have always had to be watchers, to become familiar with the language and manners of the oppressor, even sometimes adopting them for some illusion of protection.

Whenever the need for some pretense of communication arises, those who profit from our oppression call upon us to share our knowledge with them. In other words, it is the responsibility of the oppressed to teach the oppressors their mistakes. I am responsible for educating teachers who dismiss my children's culture in school. Black and Third World people are expected to educate White people as to our humanity. Women are expected to educate men. Lesbians and gay men are expected to educate the heterosexual world. The oppressors maintain their position and evade responsibility for their own actions. There is a constant drain of energy which might be better used in redefining ourselves and devising realistic scenarios for altering the present and constructing the future.

Institutionalized rejection of difference is an absolute necessity in a profit economy which needs outsiders as surplus people. As members of such an economy, we have all been programmed to respond to the human differences between us with fear and loathing and to handle that difference in one of three ways: ignore it, and if that is not possible, copy it if we think it is dominant, or destroy it if we think it is subordinate. But we have no patterns for relating across our human differences as equals. As a result, those differences have been misnamed and misused in the service of separation and confusion.

Certainly there are very real differences between us of race, age, and sex. But it is not those differences between us that are separating us. It is rather our refusal to recognize those differences, and to examine the distortions which result from our misnaming them and their effects upon human behavior and expectation.

Racism, the belief in the inherent superiority of one race over all others and thereby the right to dominance. Sexism, the belief in the inherent superiority of one sex over the other and thereby the right to dominance. Ageism. Heterosexism. Elitism. Classism.

It is a lifetime pursuit for each one of us to extract these distortions from our living at the same time as we recognize, reclaim, and define those differences upon which they are imposed. For we have all been raised in a society where those distortions were endemic within our living. Too often, we pour the energy needed for recognizing and exploring difference into pretending those differences are insurmountable barriers, or that they do not exist at all. This results in a voluntary isolation, or false and treacherous connections. Either way, we do not develop tools for using human difference as a springboard for creative change within our lives. We speak not of human difference, but of human deviance.

Somewhere, on the edge of consciousness, there is what I call a *mythical norm*, which each one of us within our hearts knows "that is not me." In America, this norm is usually defined as White, thin, male, young, heterosexual, Christian, and financially secure. It is with this mythical norm that the trappings of power reside within this society. Those of us who stand outside that power often identify one way in which we are different, and we assume that to be the primary cause of all oppression, forgetting other distortions around difference, some of which we ourselves may be practicing. By and large within the women's movement today, White women focus upon their oppression as women and ignore differences of race, sexual preference, class, and age. There is a pretense to a homogeneity of experience covered by the word *sisterhood* that does not in fact exist.

Unacknowledged class differences rob women of each others' energy and creative insight. Recently a women's magazine collective made the decision for one issue to print only prose, saying poetry was a less "rigorous" or "serious" art form. Yet even the form our creativity takes is often a class issue. Of all the art forms, poetry is the most economical. It is the one which is the most secret, which requires the least physical labor, the least material, and the one which can be done between shifts, in the hospital pantry, on the subway, and on scraps of surplus paper. Over the last few years, writing a novel on tight finances, I came to appreciate the enormous differences in the material demands between poetry and prose. As we reclaim our literature, poetry has been the major voice of poor, working-class, and Colored women. A room of one's own may be a necessity for writing prose, but so are reams of paper, a typewriter, and plenty of time. The actual requirements to produce the visual arts also help determine, along class lines, whose art is whose. In this day of inflated prices for material, who are our sculptors, our painters, our photographers? When we speak of a broadly based women's culture, we need to be aware of the effect of class and economic differences on the supplies available for producing art.

As we move toward creating a society within which we can each flourish, ageism is another distortion of relationship which interferes without vision. By ignoring the past, we are encouraged to repeat its mistakes. The "generation gap" is an important social tool for any repressive society. If the younger members of a community view the older members as contemptible or suspect or excess, they will never be able to join hands and examine the living memories of the community, nor ask the all important question, "Why?" This gives rise to a historical amnesia that keeps us working to invent the wheel every time we have to go to the store for bread.

We find ourselves having to repeat and relearn the same old lessons over and over that our mothers did because we do not pass on what we have learned, or because we are unable to listen. For instance, how many times has this all been said before? For another, who would have believed that once again our daughters are allowing their bodies to be hampered and purgatoried by girdles and high heels and hobble skirts?

Ignoring the differences of race between women and the implications of those differences presents the most serious threat to the mobilization of women's joint power.

As White women ignore their built-in privilege of Whiteness and define *woman* in terms of their own experience alone, then women of Color become "other," the outsider whose experience and tradition is too "alien" to comprehend. An example of this is the signal absence of the experience of women of Color as a resource for women's studies courses. The literature of women of Color is seldom included in women's literature courses and almost never in other literature courses, nor in women's studies as a whole. All too often, the excuse given is that the literatures of women of Color can only be taught by Colored women, or that they are too difficult to understand, or that classes cannot "get into" them because they come out of experiences that are "too different." I have heard this argument presented by White women of otherwise quite clear intelligence, women who seem to have no trouble at all teaching and reviewing work that comes out of the vastly different experiences of Shakespeare, Molière, Dostoyefsky, and Aristophanes. Surely there must be some other explanation.

This is a very complex question, but I believe one of the reasons White women have such difficulty reading Black women's work is because of their reluctance to see Black women as women and different from themselves. To examine Black women's literature effectively requires that we be seen as whole people in our actual complexities—as individuals, as women, as human—rather than as one of those problematic but familiar stereotypes provided in this society in place of genuine images of Black women. And I believe this holds true for the literatures of other women of Color who are not Black.

The literatures of all women of Color recreate the textures of our lives, and many White women are heavily invested in ignoring the real differences. For as long as any difference between us means one of us must be inferior, then the recognition of any difference must be fraught with guilt. To allow women of Color to step out of stereotypes is too guilt provoking, for it threatens the complacency of those women who view oppression only in terms of sex.

Refusing to recognize difference makes it impossible to see the different problems and pitfalls facing us as women.

Thus, in a patriarchal power system where White-skin privilege is a major prop, the entrapments used to neutralize Black women and White women are not the same. For example, it is easy for Black women to be used by the power structure against Black men, not because they are men, but because they are Black. Therefore, for Black women, it is necessary at all times to separate the needs of the oppressor from our own legitimate conflicts within our communities. This same problem does not exist for White women. Black women and men have shared racist oppression and still share it, although in different ways. Out of that shared oppression we have developed joint defenses and joint vulnerabilities to each other that are not duplicated in the White community, with the exception of the relationship between Jewish women and Jewish men.

On the other hand, White women face the pitfall of being seduced into joining the oppressor under the pretense of sharing power. This possibility does not exist in the same way for women of Color. The tokenism that is sometimes extended to us is not an invitation to join power; our racial "otherness" is a visible reality that makes that quite clear. For White women there is a wider range of pretended choices and rewards for identifying with patriarchal power and its tools.

Today, with the defeat of ERA, the tightening economy, and increased conservatism, it is easier once again for White women to believe the dangerous fantasy that if you are good enough, pretty enough, sweet enough, quiet enough, teach the children to behave, hate the right people, and marry the right men, then you will be allowed to co-exist with patriarchy in relative peace, at least until a man needs your job or the neighborhood rapist happens along. And true, unless one lives and loves in the trenches it is difficult to remember that the war against dehumanization is ceaseless.

But Black women and our children know the fabric of our lives is stitched with violence and with hatred, that there is no rest. We do not deal with it only on the picket lines, or in dark midnight alleys, or in the places where we dare to verbalize our resistance. For us, increasingly, violence weaves through the daily tissues of our living—in the supermarket, in the classroom, in the elevator, in the clinic and the schoolyard, from the plumber, the baker, the saleswoman, the bus driver, the bank teller, the waitress who does not serve us.

Some problems we share as women, some we do not. You fear your children will grow up to join the patriarchy and testify against you, we fear our children will be dragged from a car and shot down in the street, and you will turn your backs upon the reasons they are dying.

The threat of difference has been no less blinding to people of Color. Those of us who are Black must see that the reality of our lives and our struggle does not make us immune to the errors of ignoring and mis-naming difference. Within Black communities where racism is a living reality, differences among us often seem dangerous and suspect. The need for unity is often misnamed as a need for homogeneity, and a Black feminist vision mistaken for betrayal of our common interests as a people. Because of the continu-ous battle against racial erasure that Black women and Black men share, some Black women still refuse to recognize that we are also oppressed as women, and that sexual hostility against Black women is practiced not only by the White racist society, but implemented within our Black communities as well. It is a disease striking the heart of Black nationhood, and silence will not make it disappear. Exacerbated by racism and the pressures of powerlessness, violence against Black women and children often becomes a standard within our communities, one by which manliness can be mea-sured. But these woman-hating acts are rarely dis-cussed as crimes against Black women.

As a group, women of Color are the lowest paid wage earners in America. We are the primary targets of abortion and sterilization abuse, here and abroad. In certain parts of Africa, small girls are still being sewed shut between their legs to keep them docile and for men's pleasure. This is known as female circumcision, and it is not a cultural affair as the late Jomo Kenyatta insisted, it is a crime against Black women.

Black women's literature is full of the pain of frequent assault, not only by a racist patriarchy, but also by Black men. Yet the necessity for and history of shared battle have made us, Black women, par-ticularly vulnerable to the false accusation that anti-sexist is anti-Black. Meanwhile, womanhating as a recourse of the powerless is sapping strength from Black communities, and our very lives. Rape is on the increase, reported and unreported, and rape is not aggressive sexuality, it is sexualized aggression. As Kalamu ya Salaam, a Black male writer points out,

"As long as male domination exists, rape will exist. Only women revolting and men made conscious of their responsibility to fight sexism can collectively stop rape."[1]

Differences between ourselves as Black women are also being misnamed and used to separate us from one another. As a Black lesbian feminist comfortable with the many different ingredients of my identity, and a woman committed to racial and sexual freedom from oppression, I find I am constantly being encouraged to pluck out some one aspect of myself and present this as the meaningful whole, eclipsing or denying the other parts of self. But this is a destructive and frag-menting way to live. My fullest concentration of en-ergy is available to me only when I integrate all the parts of who I am, openly, allowing power from par-ticular sources of my living to flow back and forth freely through all my different selves, without the re-strictions of externally imposed definition. Only then can I bring myself and my energies as a whole to the service of those struggles which I embrace as part of my living.

A fear of lesbians, or of being accused of being a lesbian, has led many Black women into testifying against themselves. It has led some of us into destruc-tive alliances, and others into despair and isolation. In the White women's communities, heterosexism is sometimes a result of identifying with the White patri-archy, a rejection of that interdependence between women-identified women which allows the self to be, rather than to be used in the service of men. Sometimes it reflects a die-hard belief in the protective coloration of heterosexual relationships, sometimes a self-hate which all women have to fight against, taught us from birth.

Although elements of these attitudes exist for all women, there are particular resonances of heterosex-ism and homophobia among Black women. Despite the fact that woman-bonding has a long and honorable history in the African and African-American commu-nities, and despite the knowledge and accomplish-ments of many strong and creative women-identified Black women in the political, social and cultural fields, heterosexual Black women often tend to ignore or dis-count the existence and work of Black lesbians. Part of this attitude has come from an understandable terror of

Black male attack within the close confines of Black society, where the punishment for any female self-assertion is still to be accused of being a lesbian and therefore unworthy of the attention or support of the scarce Black male. But part of this need to misname and ignore Black lesbians comes from a very real fear that openly women-identified Black women who are no longer dependent upon men for their self-definition may well reorder our whole concept of social relationships.

Black women who once insisted that lesbianism was a White woman's problem now insist that Black lesbians are a threat to Black nationhood, are consorting with the enemy, are basically un-Black. These accusations, coming from the very women to whom we look for deep and real understanding, have served to keep many Black lesbians in hiding, caught between the racism of White women and the homophobia of their sisters. Often, their work has been ignored, trivialized, or misnamed, as with the work of Angelina Grimke, Alice Dunbar-Nelson, and Lorraine Hansberry. Yet women-bonded women have always been some part of the power of Black communities, from our unmarried aunts to the amazons of Dahomey.

And it is certainly not Black lesbians who are assaulting women and raping children and grandmothers on the streets of our communities.

Across this country, as in Boston during the spring of 1979 following the unsolved murders of twelve Black women, Black lesbians are spear-heading movements against violence against Black women.

What are the particular details within each of our lives that can be scrutinized and altered to help bring about change? How do we redefine difference for all women? It is not our differences which separate women, but our reluctance to recognize those differences and to deal effectively with the distortions which have resulted from the ignoring and misnaming of those differences.

As a tool of social control, women have been encouraged to recognize only one area of human difference as legitimate, those differences which exist between women and men. And we have learned to deal across those differences with the urgency of all oppressed subordinates. All of us have had to learn to live or work or coexist with men, from our fathers on. We have recognized and negotiated these differences, even when this recognition only continued the old dominant/subordinate mode of human relationship, where the oppressed must recognize the masters' difference in order to survive.

But our future survival is predicated upon our ability to relate within equality. As women, we must root out internalized patterns of oppression within ourselves if we are to move beyond the most superficial aspects of social change. Now we must recognize differences among women who are our equals, neither inferior nor superior, and devise ways to use each others' difference to enrich our visions and our joint struggles.

The future of our earth may depend upon the ability of all women to identify and develop new definitions of power and new patterns of relating across difference. The old definitions have not served us, nor the earth that supports us. The old patterns, no matter how cleverly rearranged to imitate progress, still condemn us to cosmetically altered repetitions of the same old exchanges, the same old guilt, hatred, recrimination, lamentation, and suspicion.

For we have, built into all of us, old blueprints of expectation and response, old structures of oppression, and these must be altered at the same time as we alter the living conditions which are a result of those structures. For the master's tools will never dismantle the master's house.

As Paulo Freire shows so well in *The Pedagogy of the Oppressed*,[2] the true focus of revolutionary change is never merely the oppressive situations which we seek to escape, but that piece of the oppressor which is planted deep within each of us, and which knows only the oppressors' tactics, the oppressors' relationships.

Change means growth, and growth can be painful. But we sharpen self-definition by exposing the self in work and struggle together with those whom we define as different from ourselves although sharing the same goals. For Black and White, old and young, lesbian and heterosexual women alike, this can mean new paths to our survival.

We have chosen each other
and the edge of each others battles
the war is the same

if we lose
someday women's blood will congeal
upon a dead planet
if we win
there is no telling
we seek beyond history
for a new and more possible meeting.[3]

NOTES

1. From "Rape: A Radical Analysis, An African-American Perspective" by Kalamu ya Salaam in *Black Books Bulletin,* vol. 6, no. 4 (1980).

2. Seabury Press, New York, 1970.

3. From "Outlines," unpublished poem.

24

To Veil or Not To Veil?

A Case Study of Identity Negotiation Among
Muslim Women in Austin, Texas

JEN'NAN GHAZAL READ

JOHN P. BARTKOWSKI

In light of expanded social opportunities for women in Western industrialized countries, scholars have turned their attention to the status of women in other parts of the world. This burgeoning research literature has given rise to a debate concerning the social standing of Muslim women in the Middle East. On one hand, some scholars contend that Muslim women occupy a subordinate status within many Middle Eastern countries. Some empirical evidence lends support to this view, as many researchers have highlighted the traditional and gendered customs prescribed by Islam—most notably, the veiling and shrouding of Muslim women (Afshar 1985; Fox 1977; Odeh 1993; Papanek 1973; see Dragadze 1994 for review).

On the other hand, a growing number of scholars now argue that claims about the oppression and subjugation of veiled Muslim women may, in many regards, be overstated (Brenner 1996; El-Guindi 1981, 1983; El-Solh and Mabro 1994; Fernea 1993, 1998; Gocek and Balaghi 1994; Hessini 1994; Kadioglu 1994; Kandiyoti

1991, 1992; Webster 1984). Scholars who have generated insider portraits[1] of Islamic gender relations have revealed that Muslim women's motivations for veiling can vary dramatically. Some Muslim women veil to express their strongly held convictions about gender difference, others are motivated to do so more as a means of critiquing Western colonialism in the Middle East. It is this complexity surrounding the veil that leads Elizabeth Fernea (1993, 122) to conclude that the veil (or *hijab*) "means different things to different people within [Muslim] society, and it means different things to Westerners than it does to Middle Easterners" (see also Abu-Lughod 1986; Walbridge 1997).

Our study takes as its point of departure the conflicting meanings of the veil among both Muslim religious elites and rank-and-file Islamic women currently living in the United States. In undertaking this investigation, we supplement the lone study (published in Arabic) that compares the gender attitudes of veiled and unveiled women (see L. Ahmed 1992 for review). That study,

Jen'nan Ghazal Read and John P. Bartkowski, "To Veil or Not to Veil? A Case Study of Identity Negotiation Among Muslim Women in Austin, Texas," from *Gender & Society,* Volume 14/2000, p. 395–417. Copyright © 2000. Sage Publications, Inc. Reprinted by permission.

based largely on survey data collected from university women living in the Middle East, demonstrates that while veiled women evince somewhat conservative gender attitudes, the vast majority of them support women's rights in public life and a substantial proportion subscribe to marital equality. We seek to extend these suggestive findings by using in-depth, personal interviews, because data from such interviews are more able to capture the negotiation of cultural meanings by veiled and unveiled respondents, as well as the nuances of these women's gender identities (Mishler 1986). . . .

THE LANDSCAPE OF ISLAM

. . . The most germane aspects of Muslim theology for this study concern two sets of Islamic sacred texts, the Qur'an and the hadiths (e.g., Munson 1988). The Qur'an is held in high esteem by virtually all Muslims. Not unlike the "high view" of the Bible embraced by various conservative Christian groups, many contemporary Muslims believe that the Qur'an is the actual Word of God that was ably recorded by Muhammad during the early portion of the seventh century. In addition to the Qur'an, many Muslims also look to the hadiths for moral and spiritual guidance in their daily lives. The hadiths, second-hand reports of Muhammad's personal traditions and lifestyle, began to be collected shortly after his death because of the difficulty associated with applying the dictates of the Qur'an to changing historical circumstances. The full collection of these hadiths has come to be known as the *sunna*. Along with the Qur'an, the hadiths constitute the source of law that has shaped the ethics and values of many Muslims.

Within Islam, the all-male Islamic clergy (variously called *faghihs, imams, muftis, mullahs,* or *ulumas*) often act as interpretive authorities who are formally charged with distilling insights from the Qur'an or hadiths and with disseminating these scriptural interpretations to the Muslim laity (Munson 1988). Given that such positions of structural privilege are set aside for Muslim men, Islam is a patriarchal religious institution. Yet, patriarchal institutions do not necessarily produce homogeneous gender ideologies, a fact underscored by the discursive fissures that divide Muslim religious authorities and elite commentators concerning the veil.

COMPETING DISCOURSES OF THE VEIL IN CONTEMPORARY ISLAM

Many Muslim clergy and Islamic elites currently prescribe veiling as a custom in which "good" Muslim women should engage (Afshar 1985; Al-Swailem 1995; Philips and Jones 1985; Siddiqi 1983). Proponents of veiling often begin their defense of this cultural practice by arguing that men are particularly vulnerable to corruption through unregulated sexual contact with women (Al-Swailem 1995, 27–29; Philips and Jones 1985, 39–46; Siddiqi 1983). These experts contend that the purpose of the hijab or veil is the regulation of such contact:

> The society that Islam wants to establish is not a sensate, sex-ridden society. . . . The Islamic system of *Hijab* is a wide-ranging system which protects the family and closes those avenues that lead toward illicit sex relations or even indiscriminate contact between the sexes in society. . . . To protect her virtue and to safeguard her chastity from lustful eyes and covetous hands, Islam has provided for purdah which sets norms of dress, social get-together . . . and going out of the four walls of one's house in hours of need. (Siddiqi 1983, vii–viii)

Many expositors of the pro-veiling discourse call attention to the uniquely masculine penchant for untamed sexual activity and construe the veil as a God-ordained solution to the apparent disparities in men's and women's sexual appetites. Women are therefore deemed responsible for the management of men's sexuality (Al-Swailem 1995, 29). Some contend that the Muslim woman who veils should be sure that the hijab covers her whole body (including the palms of her hands), should be monotone in color ("so as not to be attractive to draw the attentions to"), and should be opaque and loose so as not to reveal "the woman's shape or what she is wearing underneath" (Al-Swailem 1995, 24–25).

Pro-veiling Muslim luminaries also defend veiling on a number of nonsexual grounds. The veil, according to these commentators, serves as (1) a demonstration of the Muslim woman's unwavering obedience to the tenets of Islam; (2) a clear indication of the essential differences distinguishing men from women; (3) a reminder to women that their proper place is in the home rather than in pursuing public-sphere activities; and (4) a sign of the devout Muslim woman's disdain for the profane, immodest, and consumerist cultural customs of the West (e.g., Al-Swailem 1995, 27–29; Siddiqi 1983, 140, 156). In this last regard, veiling is legitimated as an anti-imperialist statement of ethnic and cultural distinctiveness.

Nevertheless, the most prominent justifications for veiling entail, quite simply, the idea that veiling is prescribed in the Qur'an (see Arat 1994; Dragadze 1994; Hessini 1994; Sherif 1987; Shirazi-Mahajan 1995 for reviews). Several Muslim clergy place a strong interpretive emphasis on a Qur'anic passage (S. 24:31) that urges women "not [to] display their beauty and adornments" but rather to "draw their head cover over their bosoms and not display their ornament." Many of these same defenders of the veil marshal other Qur'anic passages that bolster their pro-veiling stance: "And when you ask them [the Prophet's wives] for anything you want ask them from before a screen (hijab); that makes for greater purity for your hearts and for them" (S. 33:53); "O Prophet! Tell your wives and daughters and the believing women that they should cast their outer garments over themselves, that is more convenient that they should be known and not molested" (S. 33:59).

In addition to these Qur'anic references, pro-veiling Muslim clergy highlight hadiths intended to support the practice of veiling (see Sherif 1987 for review). Many pro-veiling Muslim clergy maintain that the veil verse was revealed to Muhammad at a wedding five years before the Prophet's death. As the story goes, three tactless guests overstayed their welcome after the wedding and continued to chat despite the Prophet's desire to be alone with his new wife. To encourage their departure, Muhammad drew a curtain between the nuptial chamber and one of his inconsiderate companions while ostensibly uttering "the verse of the hijab" (S. 33:53, cited above). A second set of hadiths claim that the verse of hijab was prompted when one of the Prophet's companions accidentally touched the hand of one of Muhammad's wives while eating dinner. Yet a third set of hadiths suggests that the verse's objective was to stop the visits of an unidentified man who tarried with the wives of the Prophet, promising them marriage after Muhammad's death.

In stark contrast to the pro-veiling apologias discussed above, an oppositional discourse against veiling has emerged within Islamic circles in recent years. Most prominent among these opponents of veiling are Islamic feminists (Al-Marayati 1995; Mernissi 1991; Shaheed 1994, 1995; see contributions in Al-Hibri 1982; Gocek and Balaghi 1994; see AbuKhalil 1993; An-Na'im 1987; Anees 1989; Arat 1994; Badran 1991; Fernea 1998 for treatments of Islamic feminism and related issues). Although Islamic feminists are marginalized from many of the institutional apparatuses available to the all-male Muslim clergy, they nevertheless exercise considerable influence via the dissemination of dissident publications targeted at Islamic women and through grassroots social movements (Fernea 1998; Shaheed 1994). Fatima Mernissi (1987, 1991), arguably the most prominent Muslim feminist, is highly critical of dominant gender conceptualizations that construe veiling as the ultimate standard by which the spiritual welfare and religious devoutness of Muslim women should be judged. In *The Veil and the Male Elite: A Feminist Interpretation of Women's Rights in Islam*, Mernissi (1991, 194) queries her readers:

> What a strange fate for Muslim memory, to be called upon in order to censure and punish [Islamic women]! What a strange memory, where even dead men and women do not escape attempts at assassination, if by chance they threaten to raise the *hijab* [veil] that covers the mediocrity and servility that is presented to us [Muslim women] as tradition. How did the tradition succeed in transforming the Muslim woman into that submissive, marginal creature who buries herself and only goes out into the world timidly and huddled in her veils? Why does the Muslim man need such a mutilated companion?

Mernissi and other Muslim commentators who oppose veiling do so on a number of grounds. First, Mernissi seeks to reverse the sacralization of the veil by linking the hijab with oppressive social hierarchies and male domination. She argues that the veil represents a tradition of "mediocrity and servility" rather than a sacred standard against which to judge Muslim women's devotion to Allah. Second, antiveiling Muslim commentators are quick to highlight the historical fact that veiling is a cultural practice that originated from outside of Islamic circles (see Schmidt 1989).

Although commonly assumed to be of Muslim origin, historical evidence reveals that veiling was actually practiced in the ancient Near East and Arabia long before the rise of Islam (Esposito 1995; Sherif 1987; Webster 1984). Using this historical evidence to bolster their antiveiling stance, some Muslim feminists conclude that because the veil is not a Muslim invention, it cannot be held up as the standard against which Muslim women's religiosity is to be gauged.

Finally, Islamic feminists such as Mernissi (1991, chap. 5) point to the highly questionable scriptural interpretations on which Muslim clergy often base their pro-veiling edicts (see Hessini 1994; Shirazi-Mahajan 1995). Dissident Islamic commentators call attention to the fact that the Qur'an refers cryptically to a "curtain" and never directly instructs women to wear a veil. Although proponents of veiling interpret Qur'anic edicts as Allah's directive to all Muslim women for all time, Islamic critics of veiling counter this interpretive strategy by placing relatively greater weight on the "occasions of revelation" (*asbab nuzul al-Qur'an*)— that is, the specific social circumstances under which key Qur'anic passages were revealed (Mernissi 1991, 87–88, 92–93; see Sherif 1987). It is with this interpretive posture that many Islamic feminists believe the veil verse (S. 33:53) to be intended solely for the wives of Muhammad (Mernissi 1991, 92; see Sherif 1987). Muslim critics of veiling further counter many of the pro-veiling hadith citations by arguing that they are interpretations of extrascriptural texts whose authenticity is highly questionable (Mernissi 1991, 42–48; see Sherif 1987; Shirazi-Mahajan 1995). Finally, critics of hijab point to select verses in the Qur'an that invoke images of gender egalitarianism, including one passage that refers to the "vast reward" Allah has prepared for both "men who guard their modesty and women who guard their modesty" (S. 33:35).

THE VEIL AND GENDER IDENTITY NEGOTIATION AMONG MUSLIM WOMEN IN AUSTIN

To this point, we have drawn comparisons between pro-veiling edicts that link devout, desexualized Muslim womanhood to the practice of veiling and antiveiling discourses that reject this conflation of hijab and

women's religious devotion. We now attempt to gauge the impact of these debates on the gender identities of a sample of 24 Muslim women—12 of whom veil, 12 of whom do not. All women in our sample define themselves as devout Muslims (i.e., devoted followers of Muhammad who actively practice their faith). These women were recruited through a combination of snowball and purposive sampling. Taken together, the respondents identify with a range of different nationalities (e.g., Iranian, Pakistani, Kuwaiti) and Muslim sects (e.g., Sunni, Shi'i, Ahmadia). Nineteen women have lived 10 or more years in the United States, while five women in our sample have immigrated in the past 5 years. Their ages range from 21 to 55 years old, and they occupy a range of social roles (e.g., college students, professional women, homemakers). Consistent with the demographic characteristics of U.S. Muslim immigrants at large (Haddad 1991b), our sample is composed of middle-class women with some postsecondary education (either a college degree or currently attending college). Class homogeneity among the respondents is also partly a product of the locale from which the sample was drawn, namely, a university town. Consequently, this study extends cross-cultural scholarship on the intersection of veiling, ethnicity, and nationality for middle-class Muslim women living in Western and largely modernized societies (e.g., Bloul 1997; Brenner 1996; Hatem 1994). . . .

Interview data collected from these women, identified below by pseudonyms, are designed to address several interrelated issues: What does the veil itself and the practice of veiling mean to these women? Among the women who veil, why do they do so? Among the women who do not veil, how have they arrived at the decision to remain unveiled? Finally, how does each group of our respondents feel about women who engage in the "opposite" cultural practice?

VEILED CONTRADICTIONS: PERCEPTIONS OF HIJAB AND GENDER PRACTICES AMONG VEILED MUSLIM WOMEN

Religious Edicts and Social Bonds

In several respects, the veiled respondents' accounts of wearing hijab conform to the pro-veiling gender discourse explicated above. Many of the veiled women invoke various sorts of religious imagery and theological edicts when asked about their motivations for veiling. One respondent in her early twenties, Huneeya, states flatly: "I wear the hijab because the Qur'an says it's better [for women to be veiled]." Yet another veiled woman, Najette, indicates that hijab "makes [her] more special" because it symbolizes her commitment to Islam. Mona says outright: "The veil represents submission to God," and Masouda construes the veil as a "symbol of worship" on the part of devout Muslim women to Allah and the teachings of the Prophet Muhammad. Not surprisingly, many veiled women contend that veiling is commanded in the Qur'an.

Of course, this abundance of theological rationales is not the only set of motivations that the veiled women use to justify this cultural practice. For many of the veiled respondents, the scriptural edicts and the religious symbolism surrounding the veil are given palpable force through their everyday gender practices and the close-knit social networks that grow out of this distinctive cultural practice. Indeed, narratives about some women's deliberate choice to begin veiling at a particular point in their lives underscore how religious edicts stand in tension with the women's strategic motivations. Several women recount that they began to veil because they had friends who did so or because they felt more closely connected to significant others through this cultural practice. Aisha, for example, longed to wear the veil while she attended high school in the Middle East approximately three decades ago. Reminiscent of issues faced by her teen counterparts in the United States, Aisha's account suggests that high school was a crucial time for identity formation and the cultivation of peer group relationships. The veil served Aisha as a valuable resource in resolving many of the dilemmas she faced 30 years ago as a maturing high school student. She decided to begin veiling at that time after hearing several prominent Muslim speakers at her school "talk[ing] about how good veiling is." The veil helped Aisha not only to form meaningful peer relationships at that pivotal time in her life (i.e., adolescence) but also continues to facilitate for her a feeling of connectedness with a broader religious community of other veiled Muslim women. During her recent trip to Egypt during the summer, Aisha says that the veil helped her "to fit in" there in a way that she would not have if she were unveiled.

Several other respondents also underscore the significance of Islamic women's friendship networks that form around the veil, which are particularly indispensable because they live in a non-Muslim country (i.e., the United States). In recounting these friendship circles that are cultivated around hijab in a "foreign" land, our veiled respondents point to an important overlay between their gender identities (i.e., good Muslim women veil) and their ethnic identities (i.e., as Middle Easterners). The common foundation on which these twin identities are negotiated is distinctively religious in nature. Hannan touts the personal benefits of veiling both as a *woman*—"the veil serves as an identity for [Islamic] women"—and as a *Muslim:* "[Because I veil,] Muslim people know I am Muslim, and they greet me in Arabic." This interface between gender and ethnicity is also given voice by Aisha, whose initial experiences with the veil were noted above. Aisha maintains, "The veil differentiates Muslim women from other women. When you see a woman in hijab, you know she's a Muslim." Much like the leading Muslim commentators who encourage Islamic women to "wear" their religious convictions (literally, via the veil) for all to see, these veiled respondents find comfort in the cultural and ethnic distinctiveness that the veil affords them. In this way, hijab is closely connected with their overlapping religious-gender-ethnic identities and links them to the broader community (*ummah*) of Islamic believers and Muslim women.

Gender Difference and Women's "Emancipation"

In addition to providing religious rationales for wearing the veil, many of the women who wear hijab also invoke the discourse of masculine-feminine difference to defend the merits of veiling. For several women, the idea of masculine hyper-sexuality and feminine vulnerability to the male sex drive is crucial to this essentialist rationale for veiling. Despite the fact that veiled women were rather guarded in their references to sex, their nods in that direction are difficult to interpret in any other fashion. In describing the veil's role in Islam and in the lives of Muslim men and women (such as herself), Sharadda states, "Islam is natural and men need some things naturally. If we abide by these needs [and veil accordingly], we will all be happy." She continues, "If the veil did not exist, many evil things would happen. Boys would mix with girls, which will result in evil things."

Similarly, Hannan describes what she perceives to be women's distinctive attributes and their connection to the veil: "Women are like diamonds; they are so precious. They should not be revealed to everyone—just to their husbands and close kin." Like Qur'anic references to women's "ornaments," Hannan is contrasting the "precious" diamond-like feminine character to the ostensibly less refined, less distinctive masculine persona. Interestingly, it is by likening women to diamonds that Hannan rhetorically inverts traditional gender hierarchies that privilege "masculine" traits over their "feminine" counterparts. In the face of those who would denigrate feminine qualities, Hannan reinterprets the distinctiveness of womanhood as more "precious" (i.e., more rare and valuable) than masculine qualities. Women's inherent difference from men, then, is perceived to be a source of esteem rather than denigration.

It is important to recognize, however, that the respondents who invoke this rhetoric of gender difference are not simply reproducing the pro-veiling discourse advanced by Muslim elites. Despite their essentialist convictions, many of the veiled respondents argue that the practice of wearing hijab actually liberates them from men's untamed, potentially explosive sexuality and makes possible for them various sorts of public-sphere pursuits. So, whereas pro-veiling Islamic elites often reason that women's sexual vulnerability (and, literally, their fragile bodily "ornaments") should restrict them to the domestic sphere, many of the veiled women in this study simply do not support this view of domesticized femininity. To the contrary, these women—many of whom are themselves involved in occupational or educational pursuits—argue that the veil is a great equalizer that enables women to work alongside of men. In the eyes of Hannan, women's "preciousness" should not be used to cajole them to remain in the home: "Women who wear the hijab are not excluded from society. They are freer to move around in society because of it."

Rabbab, who attends to various public-sphere pursuits, offers a similar appraisal. She argues that the face veil (hijab) is an invaluable aid for Muslim women who engage in extradomestic pursuits. In advancing this claim, Rabbab uses women who veil their whole bodies (such body garments are called *abaya*) as a counterpoint of excessive traditionalism. When asked what the veil means to her personally, as well as to Muslim women and Islamic culture at large, she says,

It depends on the extent of the hijab [that is worn]. . . . Women who wear face veils and cover their whole bodies [with abaya] are limited to the home. They are too dependent on their husbands. How can they interact when they are so secluded? . . . [However,] taking away the hijab [i.e., face veil] would make women have to fight to be taken seriously [in public settings]. . . . With hijab, men take us more seriously.

This hijab-as-liberator rationale for veiling was repeated by many of the veiled women who pursued educational degrees in schools and on college campuses where young predatorial men ostensibly rove in abundance. Aisha, a 41-year-old former student, recounts how the veil emancipated her from the male gaze during her school years:

There was a boy who attended my university. He was very rude to all of the girls, always whistling and staring at them. One day, I found myself alone in the hallway with him. I was very nervous because I had to walk by him. But because I was wearing the hijab, he looked down when I walked past. He did not show that respect to the unveiled girls.

Drawing on experiences such as these, Aisha concludes succinctly: "The veil gives women advantages. . . . They can go to coeducational schools and feel safe." A current student, Najette, says that the veil helps her to "feel secure" in going about her daily activities. Finally, the account of a young female student who is 22 years of age sheds further light on the hijab's perceived benefits in the face of men's apparent propensity to objectify women: "If you're in hijab, then someone sees you and treats you accordingly. I feel more free.

Especially men, they don't look at your appearance—they appreciate your intellectual abilities. They respect you." For many of the veiled women in this study, the respect and protection afforded them by the hijab enables them to engage in extradomestic pursuits that would ironically generate sharp criticism from many pro-veiling Muslim elites.

The Discontents of Hijab and Tolerance for the Unveiled

While the foregoing statements provide clear evidence of these women's favorable feelings about hijab, many of the veiled women also express mixed feelings about this controversial cultural symbol. It was not uncommon for the veiled respondents to recount personal difficulties that they have faced because of their decision to wear hijab. Some dilemmas associated with the veil emanate from the fact that these women live in a secular society inhabited predominantly by Christians rather than Muslims. Najette, the same respondent who argued that veiling makes her feel "special," was quick to recognize that this esteem is purchased at the price of being considered "weird" by some Americans who do not understand her motivations for veiling. For women like her, engaging in a dissident cultural practice underscores Najette's cultural distinctiveness in a way that some people find refreshing and others find threatening.

Such points of tension surrounding the veil are evident not only in cross-cultural encounters such as that mentioned above. Even within Muslim circles, the practice of veiling has generated enough controversy to produce rifts among relatives and friends when some of the veiled respondents appear publicly in hijab. Huneeya, a student who veils because she wishes to follow Qur'anic edicts and enjoys being treated as an intellectual equal by her male peers, highlighted just this point of friction with her family members, all of whom except her are "against hijab. [My family members] think it is against modernity."

For some women, the tensions produced within intimate relationships by the veil move beyond the realm of intermittent family squabbles. One veiled respondent, Asma, revealed that extended family difficulties surrounding the veil have caused her to alter the prac-

tice of veiling itself, if only temporarily. Her recent experiences underscore the complex machinations of power involved in the contested arenas of family relations and friendships where veiling is concerned. Asma moved to the United States with her husband only two years ago. Asma was quite conscientious about veiling. She relished the sense of uniqueness and cultural distinctiveness afforded to her by the hijab while living in a non-Muslim country. Yet, recent summer-long visits from her mother-in-law presented her with a dilemma. Asma's mother-in-law had arranged the marriage between her son and daughter-in-law. At the time, the mother-in-law greatly appreciated the conservative religious values embraced by her future daughter-in-law, evidenced in Asma's attentiveness to wearing the veil. Yet, since that time, Asma's mother-in-law had undergone a conversion of sorts concerning the practice of veiling. Quite recently, Asma's mother-in-law stopped wearing the veil and wanted her daughter-in-law to follow suit by discarding the veil as well. Indeed, this mother-in-law felt that Asma was trying to upstage her by using the veil to appear more religiously devout than her elder. Asma's short-term solution to this dilemma is to submit to the wishes of her mother-in-law during her summer visits to the United States. Consequently, for two months each summer, Asma discards her veil. Yet, this solution is hardly satisfactory to her and does not placate Asma's veiled friends who think less of her for unveiling:

> I feel very uncomfortable without the veil. The veil keeps us [Muslim women] from getting mixed up in American culture. But I don't want to make my mother-in-law feel inferior, so I take it off while she is here. I know my friends think I am a hypocrite.

Although Asma is sanctioned by her friends for unveiling temporarily during her mother-in-law's visit, our interview data suggest that the preponderance of veiled women in this study harbor no ill will toward their Muslim sisters who choose not to veil. Despite these veiled women's enthusiastic defenses of hijab, they are willing to define what it means to be a good Muslim broadly enough to include Islamic women who do not veil. When asked, for instance, what she thought being a good Muslim entails, one of our veiled respondents (Najette) states simply: "You must be a good person and always be honest." Echoing these sentiments, Masouda suggests, "Your attitude towards God is most important for being a good Muslim—your personality. You must be patient, honest, giving." Even when asked point-blank if veiling makes a woman a good Muslim, another veiled respondent answers, "Hijab is not so important for being a good Muslim. Other things are more important, like having a good character and being honest." One respondent even took on a decidedly ecumenical tone in detaching veiling from Islamic devotion: "Being a good Muslim is the same as being a good Christian or a good Jew—treat others with respect and dignity. Be considerate and open-minded." In the end, then, these women in hijab are able to distinguish between what veiling means to them at a personal level (i.e., a sign of religious devotion) versus what the veil says about Muslim women in general (i.e., a voluntary cultural practice bereft of devotional significance). These veiled women's heterogeneous lived experiences with the hijab—both comforting and uncomfortable, affirming and tension producing, positive and negative—seem to provide them with a sensitivity to cultural differences that often seems lacking in the vitriolic debates about veiling currently waged by leading Muslims.

ISLAMIC FEMINISM MODIFIED: PERCEPTIONS OF HIJAB AND GENDER PRACTICES AMONG THE UNVEILED

Patriarchal Oppression and Religious Fanaticism

Just as veiled women draw on the pro-veiling discourse to defend the wearing of hijab, the unveiled women in this study often justify their abstention from this cultural practice by invoking themes from the antiveiling discourse. Several of these unveiled women argue quite straightforwardly that the veil reinforces gender distinctions that work to Muslim women's collective disadvantage. According to many of the unveiled women, the veil was imposed on Muslim women because of Middle Eastern men's unwillingness to tame their sexual caprice and because of their desire to dominate

women. Rabeeya, for example, contends that Muslim women are expected to veil because "Middle Eastern men get caught up in beauty. The veil helps men control themselves." Offering a strikingly similar response, Najwa argues that "men can't control themselves, so they make women veil." Using the same critical terminology—that is, control—to make her point, Fozia has an even less sanguine view of the veil's role in Islam. When asked about the significance of the veil in Muslim societies, she states flatly: "The veil is used to control women." In short, many of the unveiled respondents view hijab in much the same way as elite Islamic feminists; that is, as a mechanism of patriarchal control.

Comments such as these suggest points of congruence between the veiled and unveiled respondents' understandings of hijab. Both groups of women seem to agree that hijab is closely related to men's sexuality. Recall that some of the veiled women contrast masculine hypersexuality to a desexualized view of femininity. Such women conclude that the veil is the God-ordained corrective for men's inability to control their own sexual impulses. Likewise, as evidenced in several statements from unveiled women, they link the veil to men's apparent inability (or, better, unwillingness) to contain their sexual desires. However, whereas several of the veiled women see masculine hypersexuality as natural and view the veil as a divine remedy for such sexual differences, many of the unveiled women reject these views. The unveiled respondents seem less willing to accept the notion that categorical gender differences should translate into a cultural practice that (literally and figuratively) falls on the shoulders of women. In a key point of departure from their sisters who wear hijab, the unveiled women in this study trace the origin of the veil not to God but rather to men's difficulties in managing their sexuality (again, "men can't control themselves, so they make women veil"). In men's attempt to manage their sexual impulses, so the account goes, they have foisted the veil on women. Very much in keeping with feminist discourses that take issue with such gendered double standards, the unveiled women conclude that it is unfair to charge women with taming men's sexuality.

Apart from these issues of social control and sexuality, several of the unveiled respondents also invoke themes of religious devotion and ethnic identity when discussing the significance of the veil for Muslims in general and for themselves (as unveiled Islamic women) in particular. Recall that leading Muslims who support veiling often highlight the religious and ethnic distinctiveness of hijab; however, prominent Muslim feminists counter that veiling did not originate with Islam and should not be understood as central to women's religious devoutness or ethnic identities (as non-Westerners). Echoing these Muslim feminist themes, several of the unveiled respondents seek to sever the veil from its religious and ethnic moorings. Fozia says that Muslim "women are made to believe that the veil is religious. In reality, it's all political," while Fatima asserts, "The veil is definitely political. It is used by men as a weapon to differentiate us from Westerners." Yet another respondent, Mah'ha, argues that it is only "fanatical" and "strict" Muslims who use the veil to draw sharp distinctions between Middle Easterners and Westerners. These remarks and others like them are designed to problematize the conflation of religious devotion, ethnic distinctiveness, and hijab evidenced in the pro-veiling discourse. Whereas the dominant discourse of veiling measures women's devotion to Islamic culture against hijab, many of the unveiled respondents imply—again, via strategic terms such as *political, fanatical,* and *strict*—that religious devotion and ethnic identification are good only in proper measure.

This rhetorical strategy allows these unveiled women to claim more moderate (and modern) convictions over and against those whose devotion to Allah has in their view been transmogrified into political dogmatism, religious extremism, and racial separatism. The unveiled women in our study do not eschew religious commitment altogether, nor are they in any way ashamed of their ethnic heritage. To the contrary, the unveiled respondents champion religious commitment (again, in good measure) and are proud to count themselves among the followers of Muhammad. Yet, they are quick to illustrate that their devotion to Allah and their appreciation of their cultural heritage are manifested through means that do not include the practice of veiling. Amna, for example, says, "Religious education makes me feel like a more pious Muslim. I read the Qur'an weekly and attend Friday prayer sermons," while Rabeeya states, "Being a good Mus-

lim means believing in one God; no idolatry; following the five pillars of Islam; and believing in Muhammad." Concerning the issue of ethnoreligious identity, the basic message articulated by many of the unveiled women can be stated quite succinctly: A Muslim women can be true to her cultural and religious heritage without the veil. Samiya, a 38-year-old unveiled woman, says as much: "Muslim society doesn't exist on the veil. Without the veil, you would still be Muslim." Therefore, many of the unveiled women believe that the veil is of human (actually, male) origin rather than of divine making. And it is this very belief about the veil's this-worldly origins that enables many of the unveiled women to characterize themselves as devout followers of Muhammad who honor their cultural heritage even though they have opted not to veil.

Standing on Common Ground: Tolerance for the Other Among Unveiled Women

Finally, we turn our attention to the subjective contradictions that belie the prima facie critical reactions of our unveiled respondents toward the veil. Interestingly, just as the veiled women are reluctant to judge harshly their unveiled counterparts, these unveiled women who eschew hijab at a personal level nevertheless express understanding and empathy toward their Middle Eastern sisters who veil. At several points during interview encounters, the unveiled respondents escape the polemical hold of the antiveiling discourse by building bridges to their sisters who engage in a cultural practice that they themselves eschew.

First, several respondents imply that it would be wrong to criticize veiled women for wearing hijab when it is men—specifically, male Muslim elites—who are to blame for the existence and pervasiveness of the veil in Islamic culture. Amna, who does not veil, takes on a conciliatory tone toward women who do so by conceding that "the veil helps women in societies where they want to be judged solely on their character and not on their appearances." How is it that such statements, which sound so similar to the justifications for wearing hijab invoked by veiled women, emanate from the unveiled respondents? The strongly antipatriarchal sentiments of the unveiled women (described in the preceding section) seem to exonerate veiled women from charges of gender traitorism. Recall that many of the unveiled respondents, in fact, locate the origin of the veil in *men*'s sexual indiscretion and in *men*'s desire to control women: "Middle Eastern *men* get caught up in beauty. The veil helps *men* control *themselves*" (Rabeeya); "*Men* can't control *themselves*, so *they* make women veil" (Najwa); "The veil is *used to control women*. The women are *made to believe* that the veil is religious" (Fozia) (emphasis added). Ironically, it is the very antipatriarchal character of these statements that simultaneously enables the unveiled women to express their stinging criticism of the veil itself while proclaiming tolerance and respect for Islamic women who wear the veil. Indeed, since many of the unveiled respondents construe hijab to be a product of *patriarchal* oppression and assorted *masculine* hang-ups (e.g., struggles with sexuality, a preoccupation with domination and control), veiled women cannot legitimately be impugned for wearing hijab.

Second, many of the unveiled respondents are willing to concede that despite their own critical views of the veil, hijab serves an important cultural marker for Islamic women other than themselves. When asked about the role of the veil among Muslim women she knows in the United States, Rabeeya recognizes that many of her veiled Islamic sisters who currently live in America remain "very, very tied to their culture. Or they are trying to be. They [veil because they] want to feel tied to their culture even when they are far away from home." Because she herself is a devout Islamic woman living in a religiously pluralistic and publicly secularized society, Rabeeya is able to empathize with other Muslim women residing in the United States who veil in order to shore up their cultural identity. Similarly, Sonya draws noteworthy distinctions between her personal antipathy toward veiling and veiled women's attraction to hijab: "Some Muslim women need the veil to identify themselves with the Muslim culture. I don't feel that way."

Finally, several of the unveiled women in our study seem to express tolerance and empathy for their sisters in hijab because, at one time or another in the past, they themselves have donned the veil. Two of the unveiled respondents, for example, are native Iranians who are currently living in the United States. When these women return to Iran, they temporarily don the veil. Najwa, one of these women, explains, "As soon as we cross the Iranian border, I go to the bathroom on the airplane and put on the hijab." The experiences of our other native-born Iranian woman, Fatima, speak even more directly to the practical nuances that undergird unveiled women's tolerance for their veiled counterparts. On one hand, Fatima is highly critical of the veil, which has been the legally required dress for women in Iran during the past two decades. Referring to this fact, she impugns the veil as a "political . . . weapon" used by religious elites to reinforce invidious distinctions between Westerners and Middle Easterners. Yet, on the other hand, her personal experiences with hijab lead her to reject the stereotype that women who veil are "backward": "Progress has nothing to do with veiling. Countries without veiling can be very backwards . . . I have nothing against veiling. I feel very modern [in not veiling], but I respect those who veil." Like so many of her unveiled sisters, then, Rabeeya is critical of the veil as a religious icon but is unwilling to look down on Islamic women who wear hijab.

CONCLUSION AND DISCUSSION

This study has examined how a sample of Muslim women living in Austin, Texas, negotiate their gender identities in light of ongoing Islamic disputes about the propriety of veiling. Interview data with 12 veiled and 12 unveiled women reveal that many of them draw upon the pro-veiling and antiveiling discourses of Muslim elites, respectively, to justify their decisions about the veil. At the same time, the women highlight various subjective contradictions manifested in many of their accounts of veiling. Women who veil are not typically disdainful toward their unveiled Muslim sisters, and unveiled women in our sample seem similarly reluctant to impugn their veiled counterparts. Such findings were unanticipated in light of elite Muslim debates about the propriety of veiling.

What are we to make of the fact that the acrimony manifested between elite Muslim proponents and opponents of veiling is largely absent from these women's accounts of the veil? Several possible answers to this question emerge from our investigation. First, both the veiled and unveiled women in our study clearly exercise agency in crafting their gender identities. Drawing on themes of individualism and tolerance for diversity, the women are able to counterpose their own "choice" to veil or to remain unveiled on one hand with the personal inclinations of their sisters who might choose a path that diverges from their own. In this way, the respondents fashion gender identities that are malleable and inclusive enough to navigate through the controversy surrounding the veil. Second, the social context within which the women are situated seems to provide them with resources that facilitate these gender innovations. As noted above, our sample is composed of middle-class, well-educated Muslim women. We suspect that the progressive, multicultural climate of Austin and the human capital enjoyed by the women foster greater empathy between the veiled respondents and their unveiled counterparts. This degree of tolerance between veiled and unveiled Muslim women evinced in our study may be decidedly different for Islamic women living in other parts of the United States, other Western nations, or particular countries in the Middle East where the veil is a more publicly contested symbol.

Consequently, this study lends further credence to the insight that culture is not simply produced from "above" through the rhetoric of elites to be consumed untransformed by social actors who are little more than judgmental dopes. While the pro-veiling and antiveiling discourses have carved out distinctive positions for veiled Muslim women and their unveiled counterparts within the late twentieth century, the respondents in our study are unique and indispensable contributors to contemporary Islamic culture. It is these women, rather than the often combative elite voices within Islamic circles, who creatively build bridges across the contested cultural terrain of veiling; who forge ties of tolerance with their sisters, veiled and unveiled; and who help foster the sense of community (*ummah*) that is so esteemed by Muslims around the world. Convictions about Islamic culture and community take on new meaning as they are tested in the crucible of Muslim women's everyday experiences. . . .

NOTE

1. The merits of this insider or "emic" perspective are also clearly evidenced by a growing body of research that highlights the heterogeneous and contested character of gender relations among conservative Protestants (e.g., Bartkowski 1997a, 1997b, 1998, 1999, 2000; Gallagher and Smith 1999; Griffith 1997; Stacey 1990) and Orthodox Jews (Davidman 1993), an issue to which we return in the final section of this article.

REFERENCES

AbuKhalil, As'ad. 1993. Toward the study of women and politics in the Arab world: The debate and the reality. *Feminist Issues* 13:3–23.

Abu-Lughod, Lila. 1986. *Veiled sentiments.* Berkeley: University of California Press.

Acker, Joan. 1990. Hierarchies, jobs, bodies: A theory of gendered organizations. *Gender & Society* 4:139–58.

Afshar, Haleh. 1985. The legal, social and political position of women in Iran. *International Journal of the Sociology of Law* 13:47–60.

Ahmed, Gutbi Mahdi. 1991. Muslim organizations in the United States. In *The Muslims of America,* edited by Y. Y. Haddad. Oxford, UK: Oxford University Press.

Ahmed, Leila. 1992. *Women and gender in Islam: Historical roots of a modern debate.* New Haven, CT: Yale University Press.

Al-Hibri, Azizah, ed. 1982. *Women and Islam.* Oxford, UK: Pergamon.

Al-Marayati, Laila. 1995. Voices of women unsilenced—Beijing 1995 focus on women's health and issues of concern for Muslim women. *UCLA Women's Law Journal* 6:167.

Al-Swailem, Sheikh Abdullah Ahmed. 1995. Introduction. In *A comparison between veiling and unveiling,* by Halah bint Abdullah. Riyadh, Saudi Arabia: Dar-us-Salam.

Anees, Munawar Ahmad. 1989. Study of Muslim women and family: A bibliography. *Journal of Comparative Family Studies* 20:263–74.

An-Na'im, Abdullahi. 1987. The rights of women and international law in the Muslim context. *Whittier Law Review* 9:491.

Arat, Yesim. 1994. Women's movement of the 1980s in Turkey: Radical outcome of liberal Kemalism? In *Reconstructing gender in the Middle East: Tradition, identity, and power,* edited by F. M. Gocek and S. Balaghi. New York: Columbia University Press.

Badran, Margot. 1991. Competing agendas: Feminists, Islam and the state in 19th and 20th century Egypt. In *Women, Islam & the state,* edited by D. Kandiyoti. Philadelphia: Temple University Press.

Bartkowski, John P. 1997a. Debating patriarchy: Discursive disputes over spousal authority among evangelical family commentators. *Journal for the Scientific Study of Religion* 36:393–410.

———. 1997b. Gender reinvented, gender reproduced: The discourse and negotiation of spousal relations within contemporary Evangelicalism. Ph.D. diss., University of Texas, Austin.

———. 1998. Changing of the gods: The gender and family discourse of American Evangelicalism in historical perspective. *The History of the Family* 3:97–117.

———. 1999. One step forward, one step back: "Progressive traditionalism" and the negotiation of domestic labor within Evangelical families. *Gender Issues* 17:40–64.

———. 2000. Breaking walls, raising fences: Masculinity, intimacy, and accountability among the promise keepers. *Sociology of Religion* 61:33–53.

Bloul, Rachel A. 1997. Victims or offenders? "Other" women French sexual politics. In *Embodied practices: Feminist perspectives on the body,* edited by K. Davis. Thousand Oaks, CA: Sage.

Bozorgmehr, Mehdi, Claudia Der-Martirosian, and Georges Sabagh. 1996. Middle Easterners: A new kind of immigrant. In *Ethnic Los Angeles,* edited by R. Waldinger and M. Bozorgmehr. New York: Russell Sage Foundation.

Brasher, Brenda E. 1998. *Godly women: Fundamentalism and female power.* New Brunswick, NJ: Rutgers University Press.

Brenner, Suzanne. 1996. Reconstructing self and society: Javanese Muslim women and the veil. *American Ethnologist* 23:673–97.

Britton, Dana M. 1997. Gendered organizational logic: Policy and practice in men's and women's prisons. *Gender & Society* 11:796–818.

Currie, Dawn H. 1997. Decoding femininity: Advertisements and their teenage readers. *Gender & Society* 11:453–57.

Davidman, Lynn. 1993. *Tradition in a rootless world: Women turn to Orthodox Judaism.* Berkeley: University of California Press.

Davis, Kathy, ed. 1997. *Embodied practices: Feminist perspectives on the body.* Thousand Oaks, CA: Sage.

Dellinger, Kirsten, and Christine L. Williams. 1997. Makeup at work: Negotiating appearance rules in the workplace. *Gender & Society* 11:151–77.

Dragadze, Tamara. 1994. Islam in Azerbaijan: The position of women. In *Muslim women's choices: Religious belief and social reality,* edited by C. F. El-Solh and J. Mabro. New York: Berg.

El-Guindi, Fadwa. 1981. Veiling Infitah with Muslim ethic: Egypt's contemporary Islamic movement. *Social Problems* 28:465–85.

———. 1983. Veiled activism: Egyptian women in the contemporary Islamic movement. *Mediterranean Peoples* 22/23:79–89.

El-Solh, Camillia Fawzi, and Judy Mabro, eds. 1994. *Muslim women's choices: Religious belief and social reality.* New York: Berg.

Esposito, John L., ed. 1995. *The Oxford encyclopedia of the modern Islamic world.* New York: Oxford University Press.

———. 1998. Women in Islam and Muslim societies. In *Islam, gender, and social change,* edited by Y. Y. Haddad and J. L. Esposito. New York: Oxford University Press.

Fernea, Elizabeth W. 1993. The veiled revolution. In *Everyday life in the Muslim Middle East,* edited by D. L. Bowen and E. A. Early. Bloomington: Indiana University Press.

———. 1998. *In search of Islamic feminism: One woman's journey.* New York: Doubleday.

Fox, Greer L. 1977. "Nice girl": Social control of women through a value construct. *Signs: Journal of Women in Culture and Society* 2:805–17.

Gallagher, Sally K., and Christian Smith. 1999. Symbolic traditionalism and pragmatic egalitarianism: Contemporary Evangelicals, families, and gender. *Gender & Society* 13:211–233.

Gerami, Shahin. 1996. *Women and fundamentalism: Islam and Christianity.* New York: Garland.

Ghanea Bassiri, Kambiz. 1997. *Competing visions of Islam in the United States: A study of Los Angeles.* London: Greenwood.

Gocek, Fatma M., and Shiva Balaghi, eds. 1994. *Reconstructing gender in the Middle East: Tradition, identity, and power.* New York: Columbia University Press.

Griffith, R. Marie. 1997. *God's daughters: Evangelical women and the power of submission.* Berkeley: University of California Press.

Haddad, Yvonne Yazbeck. 1991a. American foreign policy in the Middle East and its impact on the identity of Arab Muslims in the United States. In *The Muslims of America,* edited by Y. Y. Haddad. Oxford, UK: Oxford University Press.

———. 1991b. Introduction. In *The Muslims of America,* edited by Y. Y. Haddad. Oxford, UK: Oxford University Press.

Hatem, Mervat F. 1994. Egyptian discourses on gender and political liberalization: Do secularist and Islamist views really differ? *Middle East Journal* 48:661–76.

Hermansen, Marcia K. 1991. Two-way acculturation: Muslim women in America between individual choice (liminality) and community affiliation (communitas). In *The Muslims of America,* edited by Y. Y. Haddad. Oxford, UK: Oxford University Press.

Hessini, Leila. 1994. Wearing the hijab in contemporary Morocco: Choice and identity. In *Reconstructing gender in the Middle East: Tradition, identity, and power,* edited by F. M. Gocek and S. Balaghi. New York: Columbia University Press.

Hollway, Wendy. 1995. Feminist discourses and women's heterosexual desire. In *Feminism and discourse,* edited by S. Wilkinson and C. Kitzinger. London: Sage.

Hunter, James Davison. 1994. *Before the shooting begins: Searching for democracy in America's culture war.* New York: Free Press.

Johnson, Steven A. 1991. Political activity of Muslims in America. In *The Muslims of America,* edited by Y. Y. Haddad. Oxford, UK: Oxford University Press.

Kadioglu, Ayse. 1994. Women's subordination in Turkey: Is Islam really the villain? *Middle East Journal* 48:645–60.

Kandiyoti, Deniz. 1988. Bargaining with patriarchy. *Gender & Society* 2:274–90.

———. ed. 1991. *Women, Islam & the state.* Philadelphia: Temple University Press.

———. 1992. Islam and patriarchy: A comparative perspective. In *Women in Middle Eastern history: Shifting boundaries in sex and gender,* edited by N. R. Keddie and B. Baron. New Haven, CT: Yale University Press.

Mahoney, Maureen A., and Barbara Yngvesson. 1992. The construction of subjectivity and the paradox of resistance: Reintegrating feminist anthropology and psychology. *Signs: Journal of Women in Culture and Society* 18:44–73.

Mann, Susan A., and Lori R. Kelley. 1997. Standing at the crossroads of modernist thought: Collins, Smith, and the new feminist epistemologies. *Gender & Society* 11:391–408.

Manning, Cristel. 1999. *God gave us the right: Conservative Catholic, Evangelical Protestant, and Orthodox Jewish women grapple with feminism.* New Brunswick, NJ: Rutgers University Press.

Mernissi, Fatima. 1987. *Beyond the veil.* Rev. ed. Bloomington: Indiana University Press.

———. 1991. *The veil and the male elite: A feminist interpretation of women's rights in Islam.* Translated by Mary Jo Lakeland. New York: Addison-Wesley.

Mishler, Elliot G. 1986. *Research interviewing: Context and narrative.* Cambridge, MA: Harvard University Press.

Munson, Henry Jr. 1988. *Islam and revolution in the Middle East.* New Haven, CT: Yale University Press.

Odeh, Lama Abu. 1993. Post-colonial feminism and the veil: Thinking the difference. *Feminist Review* 43:26–37.

Papanek, Hanna. 1973. Purdah: Separate worlds and symbolic shelter. *Comparative Studies in Society and History* 15:289–325.

Philips, Abu Ameenah Bilal, and Jameelah Jones. 1985. *Polygamy in Islam.* Riyadh, Saudi Arabia: International Islamic Publishing House.

Schmidt, Alvin J. 1989. *Veiled and silenced: How culture shaped sexist theology.* Macon, GA: Mercer University Press.

Shaheed, Farida. 1994. Controlled or autonomous: Identity and the experience of the network, women living under Muslim laws. *Signs: Journal of Women in Culture and Society* 19:997–1019.

———. 1995. Networking for change: The role of women's groups in initiating dialogue on women's issues. In *Faith and freedom: Women's human rights in the Muslim world,* edited by M. Afkhami. New York: Syracuse University Press.

Sherif, Mostafa H. 1987. What is hijab? *The Muslim World* 77:151–63.

Shirazi-Mahajan, Faegheh. 1995. A dramaturgical approach to hijab in post-revolutionary Iran. *Journal of Critical Studies of the Middle East* 7 (fall): 35–51.

Siddiqi, Muhammad Iqbal. 1983. *Islam forbids free mixing of men and women.* Lahore, Pakistan: Kazi.

Smith, Dorothy E. 1987. *The everyday world as problematic: A feminist sociology.* Boston: Northeastern University Press.

Stacey, Judith, 1990. *Brave new families.* New York: Basic Books.

Stombler, Mindy, and Irene Padavic. 1997. Sister acts: Resisting men's domination in Black and white fraternity little sister programs. *Social Problems* 44:257–75.

Stone, Carol L. 1991. Estimate of Muslims living in America. In *The Muslims of America,* edited by Y. Y. Haddad. Oxford, UK: Oxford University Press.

Todd, Alexandra Dundas, and Sue Fisher, eds. 1988. *Gender and discourse: The power of talk.* Norwood, NJ: Ablex.

Walbridge, Linda S. 1997. *Without forgetting the imam: Lebanese Shi'ism in an American community.* Detroit, MI: Wayne State University Press.

Webster, Sheila K. 1984. Harim and hijab: Seclusive and exclusive aspects of traditional Muslim dwelling and dress. *Women's Studies International Forum* 7:251–57.

West, Candace, and Sarah Fenstermaker. 1995. Doing difference. *Gender & Society* 9:8–37.

Wodak, Ruth, ed. 1997. *Discourse and gender.* Thousand Oaks, CA: Sage.

25

Latino Masculinities in the Post-9/11 Era

EDWARD FLORES

American television, movies and magazines depict Latino[1] men in contradictory ways, as dangerous gun-toting hardened criminals and as family-oriented, low-wage laborers. The subordinate, "sleepy Mexican" still circulates in satirical form, as we saw in the 2009 film *Brüno*, which featured a talk show where Mexican gardeners kneel on all fours, substituting as chairs for the guests. Meanwhile, the image of Latino men as foreign, dangerous, and subversive appears more frequently in news reports of drug traffickers and gang members. The *Los Angeles Times* recently reported on military-style gang sweeps involving over one thousand law enforcement officials, assault rifles, and tanks. Readers posted racist comments online, such as, "They don't get deported and we taxpayers have to support them."

These two popular images of Latino men—as violently subversive foreign threats, or as docile low-wage workers—reflect sociologist Alfredo Mirande's (1997) analysis of Latino masculinity as rooted in dualistic cultural expressions of honor and dishonor. Over time, these dualistic images have had tremendous staying power. The mid-twentieth century movie image of Joaquin Murrieta's Mexican bandits marauding on horseback, killing lawmen, and stealing gold has morphed today into stereotypical portrayals of the violent urban Latino gang. The past image of the sleepy Mexican in a poncho and a sombrero has today

become that of the docile Latino gardener. Mirande would argue that together, these two images have their origins in Mexican men's compensatory reactions to colonial subordination. The cultural meanings of "macho," Mirande emphasizes, are best understood not as an attempt by Latino men to dominate women, but rather, as Latino men's multifaceted attempts to forge a respected and honored position in a context of cultural subordination.

Alternatively, gender scholars have located Latino masculinities within shifting political-economic relations in the United States. Maxine Baca Zinn (1982) argues that "manhood takes on greater importance for those who do not have access to socially valued roles," and that "to be 'hombre' . . . may take on greater significance when other roles and sources of masculine identity are structurally blocked." This view emphasizes that Latino men's masculine expressions are a result of contemporary structural conditions. Blocked economic mobility, poor schools, and dangerous urban neighborhoods compromise Latinos' and Blacks' access to conventional masculine expressions (i.e., Smith 2006, Lopez 2003, Bourgois 1995, Anderson 1990, Ferguson 2000).

In this article we report on our in-depth ethnographic research with Latino men behind these two images, the gardener and the gangster. Hernan Ramirez's research highlights Mexican immigrant gardeners' experience with low-wage labor and economic mobility, and the masculinities that organize, and are organized by, such a precarious social position. Edward Flores's research focuses on recovering gang members' experiences with rehabilitation, and the way in which masculinity organizes such rehabilitation. Our research is based in Los Angeles, and highlights how nativist backlash and persisting structural obstacles shape Latino men's masculine expressions.

We begin by considering the larger political and economic conditions in which the masculinity of Latino gang members and gardeners is embedded and expressed. By understanding some of the structural conditions that funnel Chicano men into gang activity and Mexican immigrant men into suburban maintenance gardening, respectively, we can enlarge our inquiry into contemporary Latino men and masculinities beyond the cultural stereotype of machismo.

CONTEXT

In the 1970s and 1980s, the effects of economic restructuring and deindustrialization were evident in major cities throughout the United States, as stable, relatively well-paid manufacturing jobs disappeared while low-wage service sector jobs grew (Kasarda 1995). In global cities (Sassen 1991) such as New York and Los Angeles, this decline in manufacturing was accompanied by an expanding high-income professional and managerial class. Problems endemic to America's inner cities—including gangs, drugs, unemployment, and violent crime—were linked to the disappearance of blue-collar jobs in the wake of deindustrialization (Wilson 1987, 1996). Moreover, with changes to U.S. immigration law in 1965, large numbers of immigrants from Asia and Latin America began entering the United States. By the 1990s, these new immigrants were increasingly present in retail and service employment (Lamphere, Stepick, and Grenier 1994), as exploited workers in hotels and restaurants, and in other jobs where wages are low and career ladders are short (Bobo et al. 2000). These structural transformations, coupled with years of disinvestment in our nation's public school systems, have left many young, urban Latino men at a marked economic disad-

vantage. Today, Mexican immigrant and Chicano men often find themselves on insecure economic ground, relying on casual work and a growing informal economy (i.e., one largely outside of formal regulations, union contracts, and guaranteed benefits) for their livelihoods.

Against this backdrop of swirling economic changes, the political climate faced by post-1965 Mexican immigrants has been ambivalent at best, and outright xenophobic at worst. For example, a 2001 *Time* magazine cover featured the word "Amexica," with colors from the national Mexican and American flags, and a statement about the vanishing border. Anthropologist Leo Chavez (2008) argues that by juxtaposing foreign images onto familiar American icons, media representations of Latinos suggest that post-1965 immigrants are unlike those of previous generations and will soon alter the nation's landscape. Similarly, the *Los Angeles Times* article on the gang sweep was presented in ways that meshed racist/sexist constructions of Latino males as foreigners and subversive.

The image of Latino men as foreign invaders has grown in the post-9/11 era. The USA PATRIOT Act of 2001 enhanced the discretion of law enforcement and immigration authorities in detaining and deporting immigrants suspected of terrorism-related acts, and it also added a looser definition of "domestic terrorism," now vague enough to apply not just to anti-American militia groups but urban gang members (Brotherton and Kretsedemas 2008). Although the FBI found no established link between gang members and international terrorism, these fears of urban gang members as foreign and subversive coalesced when the FBI investigated suspicions that Jose Padilla, an arrested Al-Qaeda operative, had gang ties in the United States (Brotherton and Kretsedemas 2008).

At the same time that this debate has unfolded, there has been an upswing in the number of right-wing pundits and politicians who characterize Latino immigrant men as a threat. Espousing a fear of immigrants as potential "terrorist" intruders, criminals, and threats to national security, radio and television hosts such as Lou Dobbs, Rush Limbaugh, and Glenn Beck rally support for restrictive immigration policies, increased federal funding for Border Patrol/ICE activities, and the building of a fence along the U.S.–Mexico border.

The degree of virulent, xenophobic rhetoric leveled against Mexican immigrant men can be explained as an outgrowth of the post-9/11 fear of brown-skinned "outsiders" as well as a continuation of decades-old patterns of anti-Latino immigrant hysteria and discrimination. Since 9/11, cities across the United States have formulated anti-day laborer ordinances that have had the indirect—but intended—effect of excluding undocumented immigrants from their jurisdictions (Varsanyi 2008). One extreme right-wing nativist website claims that "some of the most violent murderers, rapists, and child molesters are illegal aliens who work as day laborers" (daylaborers.org), even though the social scientific literature indicates that most day laborers attend church regularly, and that nearly two-thirds of them have children (Valenzuela et al. 2006). These are certainly not characteristics one would expect to find among a population of men purportedly out to prey upon America's women and children.

In reality, the large concentrations of Latino immigrant men who work in the construction and home improvement trades, including roofers, painters, and drywall installers, as well as landscapers and gardeners, have become integral pistons in America's economic engine. Remarkably, one out of every eight Mexican immigrants in the United States currently works in the construction industry (Siniavskaia 2005). In New Orleans, post–Hurricane Katrina reconstruction efforts were spearheaded by thousands of immigrant men from Mexico and Central America (Quiñones 2006). This reliance on Mexican immigrant men to fill the nation's labor needs has historical precedence, as evidenced by the Bracero Program of the mid-twentieth century. Nevertheless, the link between images of Latino men, immigration, and crime has crystallized in the post-9/11 era. This has spurred a heightened fear of Latinos and has renewed interest in militarization of the border and the deportation of undocumented immigrants.

The political and economic transformations outlined have placed Chicano and Mexican immigrant men in a precarious situation vis-à-vis access to jobs and resources. Moreover, they have been subjected to discriminatory treatment and vilified as dangerous "outsiders" and potential criminal threats in the wake of 9/11. We can now take a closer look at a specific group of Latino men, *jardineros*—or Mexican immigrant gardeners—and think about how their masculinity is a response to structural inequality, exclusion, and discrimination.

LATINO MASCULINITY AT WORK: *JARDINERO* MASCULINITY

Gendered divisions of labor are well established and found throughout the economy. In fact, scholars of gender and work have long been concerned with understanding the ways in which gender itself is constructed on the job. While our knowledge of masculinity in blue-collar work settings has been growing (Ouellet 1994, Paap 2006, Desmond 2007), less is known about Latino immigrant men's work and how predominantly Latino immigrant workplaces serve as an arena for the construction and negotiation of Latino working-class masculinities. Although it was historically associated with the labor of Japanese American men in Pacific Coast cities (Tsuchida 1984; Tsukashima 1991), suburban maintenance gardening is today institutionalized as a Mexican man's job. Particularly large concentrations of Mexican immigrant men can be found working in the sunny climes of Los Angeles and Southern California more generally, mowing lawns, pruning trees, and maintaining the lush, leafy landscapes with which the region is so often associated.

As Smith (2003) notes, much of the literature on immigration is too quick to treat men as thoughtlessly embracing a traditional "ranchero" masculinity they may have been raised on in their rural villages of origin, one which legitimizes men's dominant and women's subordinate position. In reality, some migrant men pragmatically adapt to their new environment and engage in an ongoing critique of traditional masculinity (Smith 2006). Most *jardineros* come from ranches or rural villages in central-western Mexico, yet their displays of masculinity are influenced and shaped by their immigration experiences and by their structural position as low-wage laborers in the U.S. informal economy.

Jardinero masculinity refers to the distinctly working-class form of masculinity that Mexican immigrant men construct through their daily work activities in residential maintenance gardening, a male-dominated occupational niche, and in their daily on-the-job interactions with their fellow workers. This particular version of masculinity is unique in that it unfolds in the specific, working-class occupational and regional context of Southern Californian maintenance gardening and is deployed against a backdrop of racialized nativism and citizenship hierarchy in the United States. It finds its expression on the ground level, *as jardineros* engage in hard, dirty work on a daily basis to provide sustenance for their family members; as they engage in on-the-job conversations with their co-workers that can range from measured talk to friendly verbal banter; and as they put their bodies to the test in the course of their daily work routines.

Understanding *jardinero* masculinity requires sensitivity both to culture and to social structure. Moving beyond a sort of reiteration of a one-dimensional, cultural concept of "machismo," one culturally grounded in Mexico and simply re-articulated in the United States, *jardinero* masculinity stresses a more nuanced structural understanding of Mexican immigrant men's masculinity and how it is intertwined with their daily performance of masculinized "dirty" work in private residences. Yes, *jardineros* sometimes engage in on-the-job drinking and catcalling, traditionally "machista" modes of behavior. But the better part of these men's days is not spent in those activities, but rather with back-breaking, dangerous, physically hard manual work.

Like most men, *jardineros* derive their status primarily from their control of subsistence, through which they fulfill their primary cultural obligation, the economic support of their wives and children (Stone and McKee 2002: 129). The ideal man, one who is truly "manly," will provide for all of his family's needs. In practice, though, this ideal of male behavior may be very difficult for Mexican immigrant *jardineros* to achieve in the public world. This is especially true for *ayudantes*, young, apprentice gardeners who—unlike more experienced, self-employed owners of gardening routes—tend to be recently arrived, undocumented immigrants. *Ayudantes* typically share crowded apartments with other undocumented *paisanos* who are in a similar situation. They must work long hours while making low wages and evading the gaze of the authorities. *Ayudantes* present us with one type of *jardinero* masculinity, in which men's ability to fulfill socially valued breadwinner roles is severely limited by an important structural barrier: undocumented status.

Mexican immigrant gardeners express their masculinity in subtle ways, through their words and actions. While on the job, they often use humor as a "male bonding" mechanism, playfully teasing each in order to alleviate the tedium of working together for long hours under the sun. Their workplace is where the *jardineros* develop the strong bodies and weathered hands that are a hallmark of their masculinity. Although they are readily available, *jardineros* often prefer to work without protective gloves. This can be explained in part by one *jardinero*'s observation that it is better to develop a pair of rough and callused hands because they are "manos de hombre," or "man hands," an outward symbol of their working-class masculinity.

Through their hard work cleaning and maintaining other people's properties, Mexican immigrant gardeners are able to provide for their families, but they are also able to gain the respect and esteem of their co-workers, projecting a masculinity that is honored by their fellow working-class men. For instance, as Carlos, a very young, recently arrived *ayudante,* proclaimed that he had entered the United States in order "to work hard, not to be lazy" ("a trabajar duro, no a estar de huevon"), his older co-workers nodded in approval.

The difficulties faced by undocumented *jardineros* who hope to better provide for their loved ones by becoming self-employed route owners are described by Jose, a *veteran jardinero* with more than 20 years of experience:

> Well, there are obstacles that make things more difficult, really, because if a guy doesn't have a driver's license nowadays, how can he start his business? Without "papeles" (legal papers), you can't get a license. What do you do? Nobody knows you. How do you charge your clients? They give you a check, where do you cash it? It's tough, it's really tough without a license, because how are you going to go ahead and invest money in a truck and in equipment and everything, if later they're going to take everything away? The police will catch you driving without a license and will take everything away from you. That's what happened to a guy that I know.

Once again we are reminded of the importance of understanding the structural constraints faced by Mexican immigrant men and how these impinge on their masculinity. Nationwide, many states have banned the issuance of driver's licenses to undocumented immigrants (Vock 2007; Seif 2003). This has had a deleterious effect on the livelihoods of undocumented Mexican immigrant men who work in gardening and landscaping, as well as in other jobs that require driving from jobsite to jobsite on a daily basis.

Many people believe that since Mexican immigrant gardeners wear dirty clothes, do dirty jobs, and have little formal education, they are necessarily drains on social services and the economy. Yet things are not as they appear to outsiders, as the maintenance gardening sector has allowed some *veteran jardineros* to achieve financial success and upward mobility (Ramirez and Hondagneu-Sotelo 2009). Most self-employed, independent owners of gardening routes entered the United States as undocumented immigrants some 20 or 30 years ago, speaking little or no English, but have since gone on to become legal residents or U.S. citizens, purchasing homes in the United States and even putting their children through college. Such men are *worker-entrepreneurs* who have worked hard day in and day out alongside their *ayudantes,* but who have done quite well for themselves by building and looking after gardening routes that can generate six-figure incomes. These financially solvent, self-employed owners of gardening routes (or "rutas") present us with a second type of *jardinero* masculinity: as *worker-entrepreneurs*, gardening route owners enjoy a great deal of autonomy and are able to fulfill the masculine ideal of providing for their families.

While *ayudantes* might fit the public's conception of Mexican immigrant men as "docile" low-wage workers, gardening route owners are essentially small entrepreneurs who display a remarkable degree of business acumen. However, behind the potential for economic success and mobility that comes with running one's own business there lay some hidden costs. Gardening route owners typically work very long hours, six days a week. Consequently, the amount of "quality time" they are able to spend with their spouses and children is very limited. Miguel, a gardening route owner, poignantly describes his situation:

I would want the best for my kids. That they wouldn't . . . well, that they wouldn't have to work like I've had to work. I'd want them to have a better life. Better for them. Less backbreaking. I also get home late. I get home late from work, tired. Sometimes, I can't describe what I feel—[My kids] even tell me, "You don't want to play with us, papi. I tell them, "No, son, it's because I get back home really tired. You want me to start playing with you, to play, to run, to play basketball . . . Son, don't you know how tired I am when I return home from work? And you still want to keep playing . . . [laughs]. I tell them, "No, it's because I can't."

Gardening route owners must thus grapple with work-family conflicts that can diminish their ability to be as present in the lives of their children and spouses as they would like to be. Unlike *ayudantes*, who are low-wage workers, gardening route owners are a hybrid form of worker and entrepreneur; as such, they must spend long days toiling under the sun while constantly strategizing and thinking about ways of keeping their businesses afloat, even if it detracts from the amount—and quality—of time they spend with their family members. The work takes a physical toll on them, but it also takes a toll on their ability to fulfill their masculine roles as husbands and fathers.

Having considered the case of masculinity among Mexican immigrant gardeners, encompassing the experiences of young *ayudantes* and veteran gardening route owners, let us turn now to an examination of masculinity among another group of Latino men in Los Angeles: recovering gang members.

LATINO MASCULINITY IN RECOVERY: REFORMED BARRIO MASCULINITY

In contrast to immigrant Latino men employed in the densely concentrated maintenance gardening sector, men who have spent the majority of their life in the United States express different types of masculinities. Male Latinos are exposed to a particular type of masculine socialization in the barrio that makes them vulnerable to join gangs (Vigil 1988, Moore 1991, Yablonski 1997, Smith 2006). Three activities form the core of male Latino gang life, or *deviant barrio masculinity*: substance abuse, gang violence, and extramarital affairs. These three activities are embodied in a gang member's clothes, speech, and swagger. As one man said, "My role model was a gang member, all tattoos, coming out of prison, being buff, having all kinds of women, that's what I wanted to grow up to be" (Flores 2009).

Nevertheless, some Chicano gang members do want to exit from gang lifestyle, and do so by reconstructing notions of what it means to be a man. Gang members in recovery have conventional aspirations, such as getting married and having children, working in the formal labor market, and owning a home (Flores 2009). The young man quoted above said he had converted to Christianity the night he attended a play in which a Pentecostal church performed a drama with ex-gang members, "So I seen all that in the play, I see nothing but homeys with big ole' whips, tattoos, in the play talking about God, and that they're not using drugs, and they're not in prison no more, and I say, 'ey, cool.'"

Masculinity is central to faith-based rehabilitation, as leaders facilitate the process of recovery by transforming gang members' gendered expressions from deviant barrio masculinity to *reformed barrio masculinity* (Brusco 1995). Pastors frequently chastise members for abusing substances, not holding down a job, or engaging in extramarital affairs. Recovering gang members, instead of desiring to be like the leaders of the gang hierarchy, desire to become more like the leaders in the organization facilitating rehabilitation. Yablonski (1997) corroborates this and finds that ex-gang members often find meaning by becoming counselors in a therapeutic community. In such communities men are instructed to make social and economic contributions to their household and to abstain from substance abuse, gang violence, and extramarital affairs.

At sites such as Victory Outreach, a highly spiritual Pentecostal church, and Homeboy Industries, a nondenominational nonprofit, leaders and members contest the notion that urban gang members are unable to change. The Latino men at these organizations approach this process in different ways. Spiritual worship plays an important role in the process of gendered recovery. At Homeboy Industries, Latino ex-gang members make use of Native American spiritual practices, such as sweat lodges, or Eastern spiritual practices, such as meditation and yoga, to symbolically expel cravings for drugs or violence. They get involved in 12-step programs, such as Alcoholics Anonymous, Substance Abuse, or Criminals and Gang Members Anonymous. The class moderators use the clinical language of therapeutic rehabilitation to encourage respect and honesty among class participants. They also juxtapose social critiques of the United States as an unequal society, such as the heightened sentencing handed out to gang members, with personal narratives that ask for redemption and seek personal change.

At Victory Outreach, a Latino pastor makes an altar call at the end of each sermon, proclaiming the opportunity for persons who are "serious" about "changing" or "rededicating" their life to God. Often, many members of the congregation gather in front of the pastor, worshipping in a tightly congested space, placing hands on each other, and speaking stream-of-thought prayers. During the regular sermon, a band plays loud, fast-paced Christian music that members clap and move to, and this alternates with soft music and prayer for roughly 45 minutes. A Victory Outreach pastor then allows men in recovery to "take the pulpit" and give announcements, recaps of important events, share testimonies, or even give a guest sermon. They also juxtapose biblical references of helping persons in need, such as that found in the Book of Mark, with their personal narratives of redemption and change. In these spiritually-based social interactions, men repeatedly frame the meaning of "being a man."

The patriarchal characteristics of reformed barrio masculinity motivate many Latino men to continue with recovery. Members at Victory Outreach often voice their ambition to be a "man of God," to one day get "launched out," or to "take a city" as the pastor of a new church.

Members aspire not only to recover from gang life, but to fulfill the ideals of the patriarchal American dream: to get married, hold a good job, and own a home. Several claim to have faith in God and to want to follow in the footsteps of their leaders because God "blessed" their pastor with a wife and children and a home. Members at Homeboy Industries talk about wanting to experience rehabilitation in order to provide for their mothers, partners, and children.

Members that experienced close relationships with Father Greg, during the early years of a much smaller Homeboy Industries, say they aspire to be like Father Greg.

Unfortunately, the process of recovery is not a straight-line trajectory; many Latino gang members oscillate between recovery and sometimes the elements of gang lifestyle, such as smoking marijuana, drinking, or socializing with old acquaintances in the gang's neighborhood, that can spur a complete relapse. Several men became weary of placing themselves in situations that could escalate to a full relapse. Chris, a member of Victory Outreach who has been in recovery for four years, expressed a fear that he could easily engage in the same types of destructive social interactions by simply being around old gang members. As he put it, "I was really afraid to run into my old homies, because I know they were a big influence on me . . . it would just take a couple of hours for me to start drinking, or start getting high . . . you never know what could happen. You could get into a fight, you could get shot. [I]t doesn't take very long for you to go all the way back into your whole lifestyle." In order to prevent from engaging in gang behavior, Chris must now make his therapeutic community (Victory Outreach) his primary sphere of socialization. He hopes to become a leader, possibly even a pastor, within the Victory Outreach hierarchy.

Some men also admitted to relapsing into gang activity. Matthew, a 20-year-old member of Homeboy Industries, asked if I knew of any vocational programs that could lead to stable employment. He said he had recently called a well-known vocational school but that they were reluctant to answer his questions after they found out he had two felonies on his record. A week later, I read in the *Los Angeles Times* that Matthew was picked up in a major gang sweep. I scanned through the photos of the military-style operation and read that a police officer alleged he had been selling drugs; the evidence—FBI wiretaps linking Matthew's involvement to his gang—however was four to five years old, predating his entry into rehabilitation. For carrying a gun during drug deals several years ago, Matthew is now facing a third felony. Under California law, this carries a mandatory sentence of life in prison without the possibility of parole.

CONCLUSION

The true diversity and complexity of Latino masculinities in the post-9/11 era goes well beyond the images that circulate in American television, movies, and magazines. Two dominant media images of Latino men, that of the docile low-wage worker and the hyper-masculine, criminal gang member, reiterate Mirande's (1997) views of machismo: It is a strictly cultural response to colonization and European domination, wherein the docile worker is colonized and the gangster remains defiant. Our ethnographic research with the real men behind these two images reveals an array of masculinities that, taken together, highlight the deficiencies of thinking about Latino men strictly in terms of traditional machismo, or a rigid cult of masculinity. Instead, our approach follows the lead of Baca Zinn (1982), who calls on students of Latino masculinity to view it as a response to structural inequality, exclusion, and discrimination. Culture plays a role, but structural constraints that keep men from living up to dominant masculine ideals must also be taken into consideration. As we saw, recent political and economic transformations have placed Chicano and Mexican immigrant men in an especially difficult situation vis-à-vis access to jobs and resources. Moreover, they have been vilified as brown-skinned "outsiders" and potential criminal threats in the wake of the terrorist attacks of 9/11.

Against this structural context, *jardinero masculinity* has developed as a distinctly working-class form of masculinity that Mexican immigrant men construct through their daily work activities in residential maintenance gardening, a male occupational niche. Its very expression is linked to their daily performance of hard, dirty, manual labor. In addition, while young apprentice gardeners, or *ayudantes*, find their ability to fulfill traditional masculine roles blocked by their undocumented status, upwardly mobile owners of gardening routes face unique constraints on their ability to balance work and family life. With *jardineros* as with gang members, looks can be deceiving. Just as it may be difficult to tell an *ayudante* from a successful gardening route owner based strictly on their appearance, it may also be difficult to tell an active gang member from a recovering one. But by looking closely at recovering gang members in two faith-based out-reach organizations, Homeboy Industries and Victory Outreach, we can see men leaving behind a life of sub-stance abuse and gang violence, and actively embrac-ing a *reformed barrio masculinity,* characterized by more conventional aspirations, such as getting married and starting a family. In the post-9/11 era, it is impera-tive that we continue to explore the structural condi-tions that are linked to multiplicities of Latino mas-culinities.

NOTE

1. Although this article is concerned with both native and for-eign-born Latino men living in the United States, its primary em-phasis is on first-generation Mexican immigrant men and Chicano, or Mexican American, men in the Los Angeles area.

REFERENCES

Anderson, Elijah. 1990. *Streetwise: Race, Class, and Change in an Urban Community.* Chicago: University of Chicago Press.

Baca Zinn, Maxine. 1982. "Chicano Men and Masculinity." *Journal of Ethnic Studies* 10(2):29–144.

Bobo, Lawrence D., Melvin L. Oliver, James H. Johnson, Jr., and Abel Valenzuela, Jr. 2000. "Analyzing Inequality in Los Angeles." Pp. 3–50 in *Prismatic Metropolis: Inequality in Los Angeles.* New York: Russell Sage Foundation.

Bourgois, Philippe. 1995. *In Search of Respect: Selling Crack in El Barrio.* Cambridge: Cambridge University Press.

Brotherton, David C., and Philip Kretsedemas (eds.). 2008. *Keeping Out the Other: A Critical Introduction to Immigration Enforcement Today.* New York: Columbia University Press.

Brusco, Elizabeth. 1995. *The Reformation of Machismo: Evangelical Conversion and Gender in Colombia.* Austin: University of Texas Press.

Chavez, Leo R. 2008. *The Latino Threat: Constructing Immigrants, Citizens, and the Nation.* Stanford, CA: Stanford University Press.

Desmond, Matthew. 2007. *On the Fireline: Living and Dying with Wildland Firefighters.* Chicago: University of Chicago Press.

Ferguson, Ann Arnett. 2000. *Bad Boys: Public Schools in the Making of Black Masculinity.* Ann Arbor: University of Michigan Press.

Flores, Edward. 2009. "I Am Somebody: Barrio Pentecostalism and Gendered Acculturation among Chicano Ex-Gang Members." *Ethnic and Racial Studies* 32:6.

Kasarda, John. 1995. "Industrial Restructuring and the Changing Location of Jobs." Pp. 215–267 in *State of the Union: America in the 1990s,* edited by Reynolds Farley. New York: Russell Sage Foundation.

Lamphere, Louise, Alex Stepick, and Guillermo Grenier. 1994. *Newcomers in the Workplace: Immigrants and the Restructuring of the U.S. Economy.* Philadelphia: Temple University Press.

Lopez, Nancy. 2003. *Hopeful Girls, Troubled Boys: Race and Gender Disparity in Urban Education.* New York: Routledge.

Mirande, Alfredo. 1997. *Hombres y Machos: Masculinity and Latino Culture.* Boulder: Westview Press.

Moore, Joan. 1991. *Going Down to the Barrio: Homeboys and Homegirls in Change.* Philadelphia: Temple University Press.

Ouellet, Lawrence J. 1994. *Pedal to the Metal: The Work Lives of Truckers.* Philadelphia: Temple University Press.

Paap, Kris. 2006. *Working Construction: Why White Working-Class Men Put Themselves—and the Labor Movement—in Harm's Way.* Ithaca, NY: Cornell University Press.

Quiñones, Sam. 2006. "Migrants Find a Gold Rush in New Orleans." *Los Angeles Times,* April 4.

Ramirez, Hernan, and Pierrette Hondagneu-Sotelo. 2009. "Mexican Immigrant Gardeners: Entrepreneurs or Exploited Workers?" *Social Problems* 56(1):70–88.

Sassen, Saskia. 1991. *The Global City: New York, London, Tokyo.* Princeton: Princeton University Press.

Seif, Hinda. 2003. " 'Estado de Oro' o 'Jaula de Oro'? Undocumented Mexican Immigrant Workers, the Driver's License, and Subnational legalization in California." UC San Diego, Working Papers, The Center for Comparative Immigration Studies.

Siniavksaia, Natalia. 2005. "Immigrant Workers in Construction." National Association of Home Builders. Available at: http://www.nahb.org/generic.aspx?genericContentID=49216) (accessed October 2009).

Smith, Robert C. 2006. *Mexican New York: Transnational Lives of New Immigrants.* Berkeley: University of California Press.

———. 2003. "Gender Strategies, Settlement and Transnational Life." Paper presented at the 2003 Meetings of the American Sociological Association. Atlanta, GA.

Stone, Linda, and Nancy P. McKee. 2002. *Gender and Culture in America.* 2nd edition. Upper Saddle River, NJ: Prentice Hall.

Tsuchida, Nobuya. 1984. "Japanese Gardeners in Southern California, 1900–1941." Pp. 435–469 in *Labor Immigration Under Capitalism: Asian Workers in the United States Before World War II,* edited by Lucie Cheng and Edna Bonacich. Berkeley: University of California Press.

Tsukashima, Ronald Tadao. 1991. "Cultural Endowment, Disadvantaged Status and Economic Niche: The Development of an Ethnic Trade." *International Migration Review* 25(2):333–354.

Valenzuela, Abel, Nik Theodore, Edwin Melendez, and Ana Luz Gonzalez. 2006. "On the Corner: Day Labor in the United States." UCLA Center for the Study of Urban Poverty.

Varsanyi, Monica W. 2008. "Immigration Policing through the Backdoor: City Ordinances, the 'Right to the City,' and the Exclusion of Undocumented Day Laborers." *Urban Geography* 29(1):29–52.

Vigil, James Diego. 1988. *Barrio Gangs: Street Life and Identity in Southern California.* Austin: University of Texas Press.

Vock, Daniel C. 2007. "Tighter License Rules Hit Illegal Immigrants." *Stateline.* August 24. Available at: http://www.stateline.org/live/details/story?contentId=234828 (accessed October 2009).

Wilson, William Julius. 1996. *When Work Disappears: The World of the New Urban Poor.* New York: Vintage Books.

———. 1987. *The Truly Disadvantaged.* Chicago: University of Chicago Press.

Yablonski, Lewis. 1997. *Gangsters: Fifty Years of Madness, Drugs, and Death on the Streets of America.* New York: New York University Press.

PART V

FAMILIES

In the late twentieth and early twenty-first centuries, major transformations in world economic and cultural systems have affected all families and households and given rise to new patterns of family living. Despite these changes, family life remains shrouded in myth. No matter how much families change, they remain idealized as natural or biological units based on the timeless functions of love, motherhood, and childbearing. "Family" evokes ideas of warmth, caring, and unconditional love in a refuge set apart from the public world. In this image, family and society are separate. Relations *inside* the family are idealized as nurturant, and those *outside* the family are seen as competitive. This ideal assumes a gendered division of labor: a husband/father associated with the public world and a wife/mother defined as the heart of the family. Although this image bears little resemblance to the majority of family situations, it is still recognizable in cultural ideals and public policies.

In the past four decades, feminist thought has been in the forefront of efforts to demythologize the family. Feminist thinkers have demonstrated that family forms are socially and historically constructed, not monolithic universals that exist across all times and all places or the inevitable result of unambiguous differences between women and men. Feminist thinkers have drawn attention to myths that romanticize "traditional" families in deference to male privilege and to the contradictions between idealized and real patterns of family life. They have directed attention to the close connections between families and other institutions in society. Early feminist critiques of the family characterized it as a primary site of women's oppression and argued in support of women's increased participation in the labor force as a means of attaining greater autonomy. But this analysis did not apply well to women of color or working-class women generally, because it falsely universalized the experiences of white middle-class women.

More recently, feminist thought has begun to create a more complex understanding of the relationship between family and work by examining differences among women and taking men's experiences into account. The first four articles in this part of the book explore the symbolic meanings and lived realities of motherhood and fatherhood. They uncover experiences that are not simply gendered, but shaped by other lines of difference as well. First Patricia Hill Collins takes race, class, and history into account as she investigates mother–daughter relations among African Americans. In contrast to Eurocentric views of motherhood, she describes patterns of communal and collective mothering relations. Collins's concept of "other mothers" is adopted in the reading by Lisa J. Udel as she explains why Native American women are loyal to cultural traditions that puzzle white U.S. feminists.

A growing U.S. market for domestic and child care workers is redefining motherhood for many Latinas. In their article, Pierrette Hondagneu-Sotelo and Ernestine Avila reveal a family arrangement in which immigrant mothers work in the United States while their children remain in Mexico or Central America. Calling this adaptation "transnational mothering," their study shows how global patterns of family dispersal produce variations in the meanings and priorities of motherhood. Like motherhood, current scholarship on fatherhood opens the gender field to new kinds of questions. In Sweden, government policies and reforms support new gender ideals of caretaking fathers. Although Swedish men in general have positive attitudes toward parental leave, they don't use it as their attitudes would suggest. What explains the discrepancy between what Swedish men *say* and what they *do* regarding paternity leave? Thomas Johannsen and Roger Klinth examine Swedish men's views of fatherhood and paternity leave. Their study finds that factors such as age, class, occupation, and religion strongly influence how different groups of men think and relate to new visions of gender equal fatherhood.

The second section takes up questions about and family linkages and changing gender relations. Women's and men's new employment trends are transforming family realms. Yet the worldwide entrance of women into public sphere employment has not resulted in gender equality not freed women from demands of labor in the private sphere. The reading by Pamela Stone illustrates the connections between work experience and family matters by looking at the experiences of stay-at-home mothers to understand gender in the workplace. Media stories often feature contemporary women who are "opting out" of the workplace in favor of domesticity. But Stone's study offers a very different explanation as she reveals multiple conditions that force women out of high-powered careers and back to traditional family and gender arrangements.

Gendered divisions of labor in families and workplaces often extend to other domains of society as Michael A. Messner and Suzel Bozada-Deas show in the next reading, a study of youth sports organizations in which most men volunteers become coaches and most women volunteers become team moms. Their findings challenge commonsense ideas about "natural" gender divisions. Although participants say the division of labor between men and women volunteers results from individual choices, Messner and Bozada-Deas uncover informal patterns of socially structured gender disparities that reproduce the work/family divide in youth sports organizations.

By now, it is a truism that the movement of women into the workforce everywhere affects families. But work and family opportunities vary greatly because they are linked within a larger society that is structured by class, race, and gender. The next two readings address the shaping power of larger economic forces on women's family roles. The reading by Elizabeth Higginbotham and Lynn Weber examines the role of the family in the achievements of Black and white professional women. Their intersectional approach offers new understandings about race, class, and the upward mobility of women and men. Finally, Kathryn Edin addresses the connections between economic marginality and marriage in the lives of low-income single mothers. Although the mothers in this study aspire to marriage, they think it is more risky than rewarding. Their stories provide an understanding of the retreat from marriage as it is conditioned by men's employment and women's desire for marriage with a measure of trust, respectability, and control.

26

The Meaning of Motherhood in Black Culture and Black Mother–Daughter Relationships

PATRICIA HILL COLLINS

"What did your mother teach you about men?" is a question I often ask students in my courses on African-American women. "Go to school first and get a good education—don't get too serious too young," "Make sure you look around and that you can take care of yourself before you settle down," and "Don't trust them, want more for yourself than just a man," are typical responses from Black women. My students share stories of how their mothers encouraged them to cultivate satisfying relationships with Black men while anticipating disappointments, to desire marriage while planning viable alternatives, to become mothers only when fully prepared to do so. But, above all, they stress their mothers' insistence on being self-reliant and resourceful.

These daughters, of various ages and from diverse social class backgrounds, family structures and geographic regions, had somehow received strikingly similar messages about Black womanhood. Even though their mothers employed diverse teaching strategies, these Black daughters had all been exposed to common themes about the meaning of womanhood in Black culture.[1]

This essay explores the relationship between the meaning of motherhood in African-American culture and Black mother–daughter relationships by addressing three primary questions. First, how have competing perspectives about motherhood intersected to produce a distinctly Afrocentric ideology of motherhood? Second, what are the enduring themes that characterize this Afrocentric ideology of motherhood? Finally, what effect might this Afrocentric ideology of motherhood have on Black mother–daughter relationships?

COMPETING PERSPECTIVES ON MOTHERHOOD

The Dominant Perspective: Eurocentric Views of White Motherhood

The cult of true womanhood, with its emphasis on motherhood as woman's highest calling, has long held a special place in the gender symbolism of White Americans. From this perspective, women's activities should be confined to the care of children, the nurturing of a husband, and the maintenance of the household. By managing this separate domestic sphere, women gain social influence through their roles as mothers, transmitters of culture, and parents for the next generations.[2]

While substantial numbers of White women have benefited from the protections of White patriarchy provided by the dominant ideology, White women themselves have recently challenged its tenets. On one pole lies a cluster of women, the traditionalists, who aim to retain the centrality of motherhood in women's lives. For traditionalists, differentiating between the experience of motherhood, which for them has been quite satisfying, and motherhood as an institution central in reproducing gender inequality, has proved difficult. The other pole is occupied by women who advocate dismantling motherhood as an institution. They suggest that compulsory motherhood be outlawed and that the experience of motherhood can only be satisfying if women can also choose not to be mothers. Arrayed between these dichotomous positions are women who argue for an expanded, but not necessarily different, role for women—women can be mothers as long as they are not *just* mothers.[3]

Three themes implicit in White perspectives on motherhood are particularly problematic for Black women and others outside of this debate. First, the assumption that mothering occurs within the confines of a private, nuclear family household where the mother has almost total responsibility for child-rearing is less applicable to Black families. While the ideal of the cult of true womanhood has been held up to Black women for emulation, racial oppression has denied Black families sufficient resources to support private, nuclear family households. Second, strict sex-role segregation,

with separate male and female spheres of influence within the family, has been less commonly found in African-American families than in White middle-class ones. Finally, the assumption that motherhood and economic dependency on men are linked and that to be a "good" mother one must stay at home, making motherhood a full-time "occupation," is similarly uncharacteristic of African-American families.[4]

Even though selected groups of White women are challenging the cult of true womanhood and its accompanying definition of motherhood, the dominant ideology remains powerful. As long as these approaches remain prominent in scholarly and popular discourse, Eurocentric views of White motherhood will continue to affect Black women's lives.

Eurocentric Views of Black Motherhood

Eurocentric perspectives on Black motherhood revolve around two interdependent images that together define Black women's roles in White and in African-American families. The first image is that of the Mammy, the faithful, devoted domestic servant. Like one of the family, Mammy conscientiously "mothers" her White children, caring for them and loving them as if they were her own. Mammy is the ideal Black mother for she recognizes her place. She is paid next to nothing and yet cheerfully accepts her inferior status. But when she enters her own home, this same Mammy is transformed into the second image, the too-strong matriarch who raises weak sons and "unnaturally superior" daughters.[5] When she protests, she is labeled aggressive and unfeminine, yet if she remains silent, she is rendered invisible.

The task of debunking Mammy by analyzing Black women's roles as exploited domestic workers and challenging the matriarchy thesis by demonstrating that Black women do not wield disproportionate power in African-American families has long preoccupied African-American scholars.[6] But an equally telling critique concerns uncovering the functions of these images and their role in explaining Black women's subordination in systems of race, class, and gender oppression. As Mae King points out, White definitions of Black motherhood foster the dominant group's exploitation of Black women by blaming Black women for their characteristic reactions to their own subordination.[7] For example, while the stay-at-home mother has been held up to all women as the ideal, African-American women have been compelled to work outside the home, typically in a very narrow range of occupations. Even though Black women were forced to become domestic servants and be strong figures in Black households, labeling them Mammies and matriarchs denigrates Black women. Without a countervailing Afrocentric ideology of motherhood, White perspectives on both White and African-American motherhood place Black women in a no-win situation. Adhering to these standards brings the danger of the lowered self-esteem of internalized oppression, one that, if passed on from mother to daughter, provides a powerful mechanism for controlling African-American communities.

African Perspectives on Motherhood

One concept that has been constant throughout the history of African societies is the centrality of motherhood in religions, philosophies, and social institutions. As Barbara Christian points out, "There is no doubt that motherhood is for most African people symbolic of creativity and continuity."[8]

Cross-cultural research on motherhood in African societies appears to support Christian's claim.[9] West African sociologist Christine Oppong suggests that the Western notion of equating household with family be abandoned because it obscures women's family roles in African cultures.[10] While the archetypal White, middle-class nuclear family conceptualizes family life as being divided into two oppositional spheres—the "male" sphere of economic providing and the "female" sphere of affective nurturing—this type of rigid sex-role segregation was not part of the West African tradition. Mothering was not a privatized nurturing "occupation" reserved for biological mothers, and the economic support of children was not the exclusive responsibility of men. Instead, for African women, emotional care for children and providing for their physical survival were interwoven as interdependent, complementary dimensions of motherhood.

In spite of variations among societies, a strong case has been made that West African women occupy influential roles in African family networks.[11] First, since they are not dependent on males for economic support and provide much of their own and their children's economic support, women are structurally central to families.[12] Second, the image of the mother is one that is culturally elaborated and valued across diverse West African societies. Continuing the lineage is essential in West African philosophies, and motherhood is similarly valued.[13] Finally, while the biological mother-child bond is valued, child care was a collective responsibility, a situation fostering cooperative, age-stratified, woman-centered "mothering" networks.

Recent research by Africanists suggests that much more of this African heritage was retained among African-Americans than had previously been thought. The retention of West African culture as a culture of resistance offered enslaved Africans and exploited African-Americans alternative ideologies to those advanced by dominant groups. Central to these reinterpretations of African-American institutions and culture is a re-conceptualization of Black family life and the role of women in Black family networks.[14] West African perspectives may have been combined with the changing political and economic situations framing African-American communities to produce certain enduring themes characterizing an Afrocentric ideology of motherhood.

ENDURING THEMES OF AN AFROCENTRIC IDEOLOGY OF MOTHERHOOD

An Afrocentric ideology of motherhood must reconcile the competing worldviews of these three conflicting perspectives of motherhood. An ongoing tension exists between efforts to mold the institution of Black motherhood for the benefit of the dominant group and efforts by Black women to define and value their own experiences with motherhood. This tension leads to a continuum of responses. For those women who either aspire to the cult of true womanhood without having the resources to support such a lifestyle, or who believe the stereotypical analyses of themselves as dominating matriarchs, motherhood can be oppressive. But the experience of motherhood can provide Black women with a base of self-actualization, status in the Black community, and a reason for social activism. These alleged contradictions can exist side by side in African-American communities, families, and even within individual women.

Embedded in these changing relationships are four enduring themes that I contend characterize an Afrocentric ideology of motherhood. Just as the issues facing enslaved African mothers were quite different from those currently facing poor Black women in inner cities, for any given historical moment the actual institutional forms that these themes take depend on the severity of oppression and Black women's resources for resistance.

Bloodmothers, Othermothers, and Women-Centered Networks

In African-American communities, the boundaries distinguishing biological mothers of children from other women who care for children are often fluid and changing. Biological mothers, or bloodmothers, are expected to care for their children. But African and African-American communities have also recognized that vesting one person with full responsibility for mothering a child may not be wise or possible. As a result, "othermothers," women who assist bloodmothers by sharing mothering responsibilities, traditionally have been central to the institution of Black motherhood.[15]

The centrality of women in African-American extended families is well known.[16] Organized, resilient, women-centered networks of bloodmothers and othermothers are key to this centrality. Grandmothers, sisters, aunts, or cousins acted as othermothers by taking on child care responsibilities for each other's children. When needed, temporary child care arrangements turned into long-term care or informal adoption.[17]

In African-American communities, these women-centered networks of community-based child care often extend beyond the boundaries of biologically related extended families to support "fictive kin."[18] Civil rights activist Ella Baker describes how informal adoption by othermothers functioned in the Southern, rural community of her childhood:

My aunt who had thirteen children of her own raised three more. She had become a midwife, and a child was born who was covered with sores. Nobody was particularly wanting the child, so she took the child and raised him . . . and another mother decided she didn't want to be bothered with two children. So my aunt took one and raised him . . . they were part of the family.[19]

Even when relationships were not between kin or fictive kin, African-American community norms were such that neighbors cared for each other's children. In the following passage, Sara Brooks, a Southern domestic worker, describes the importance of the community-based child care that a neighbor offered her daughter. In doing so, she also shows how the African-American cultural value placed on cooperative child care found institutional support in the adverse conditions under which so many Black women mothered:

She kept Vivian and she didn't charge me nothin either. You see, people used to look after each other, but now it's not that way. I reckon it's because we all was poor, and I guess they put theirself in the place of the person that they was helpin.[20]

Othermothers were key not only in supporting children but also in supporting bloodmothers who, for whatever reason, were ill-prepared or had little desire to care for their children. Given the pressures from the larger political economy, the emphasis placed on community-based child care and the respect given to othermothers who assume the responsibilities of child care have served a critical function in African-American communities. Children orphaned by sale or death of their parents under slavery, children conceived through rape, children of young mothers, children born into extreme poverty, or children who for other reasons have been rejected by their bloodmothers have all been supported by othermothers who, like Ella Baker's aunt, took in additional children, even when they had enough of their own.

Providing as Part of Mothering

The work done by African-American women in providing the economic resources essential to Black family well-being affects motherhood in a contradictory fashion. On the one hand, African-American women have long integrated their activities as economic providers into their mothering relationships. In contrast to the cult of true womanhood, in which work is defined as being in opposition to and incompatible with motherhood, work for Black women has been an important and valued dimension of Afrocentric definitions of Black motherhood. On the other hand, African-American women's experiences as mothers under oppression were such that the type and purpose of work Black women were forced to do had a great impact on the type of mothering relationships bloodmothers and othermothers had with Black children.

While slavery both disrupted West African family patterns and exposed enslaved Africans to the gender ideologies and practices of slaveowners, it simultaneously made it impossible, had they wanted to do so for enslaved Africans to implement slaveowners' ideologies. Thus, the separate spheres of providing as a male domain and affective nurturing as a female domain did not develop within African-American families.[21] Providing for Black children's physical survival and attending to their affective, emotional needs continued as interdependent dimensions of an Afrocentric ideology of motherhood. However, by changing the conditions under which Black women worked and the purpose of the work itself, slavery introduced the problem of how best to continue traditional Afrocentric values under oppressive conditions. Institutions of community-based child care, informal adoption, greater reliance on othermothers, all emerge as adaptations to the exigencies of combining exploitative work with nurturing children.

In spite of the change in political status brought on by emancipation, the majority of African-American women remained exploited agricultural workers. However, their placement in Southern political economics allowed them to combine child care with field labor. Sara Brooks describes how strong the links between providing and caring for others were for her:

> When I was about nine I was nursin my sister Sally— I'm about seven or eight years older than Sally. And when I would put her to sleep, instead of me goin somewhere and sit down and play, I'd get my little old hoe and get out there and work right in the field around the house.[22]

Black women's shift from Southern agriculture to domestic work in Southern and Northern towns and cities represented a change in the type of work done, but not in the meaning of work to women and their families. Whether they wanted to or not, the majority of African-American women had to work and could not afford the luxury of motherhood as a noneconomically productive, female "occupation."

Community Othermothers and Social Activism

Black women's experiences as othermothers have provided a foundation for Black women's social activism. Black women's feelings of responsibility for nurturing the children in their own extended family networks have stimulated a more generalized ethic of care where Black women feel accountable to all the Black community's children.

This notion of Black women as community othermothers for all Black children traditionally allowed Black women to treat biologically unrelated children as if they were members of their own families. For example, sociologist Karen Fields describes how her grandmother, Mamie Garvin Fields, draws on her power as a community othermother when dealing with unfamiliar children.

> She will say to a child on the street who looks up to no good, picking out a name at random, "Aren't you Miz Pinckney's boy?" in that same reproving tone. If the reply is, "No, ma'am, my mother is Miz Gadsden," whatever threat there was dissipates.[23]

The use of family language in referring to members of the Black community also illustrates this dimension of Black motherhood. For example, Mamie Garvin Fields describes how she became active in surveying the poor housing conditions of Black people in Charleston.

> I was one of the volunteers they got to make a survey of the places where we were paying extortious rents for indescribable property. I said "we," although it wasn't Bob and me. We had our own home, and so did many of the Federated Women. Yet we still fell like it really was "we" living in those terrible places, and it was up to us to do something about them.[24]

To take another example, while describing her increasingly successful efforts to teach a boy who had given other teachers problems, my daughter's kindergarten teacher stated, "You know how it can be—the majority of children in the learning disabled classes are *our children.* I know he didn't belong there, so I volunteered to take him." In these statements, both women invoke the language of family to describe the ties that bind them as Black women to their responsibilities to other members of the Black community as family.

Sociologist Cheryl Gilkes suggests that community othermother relationships are sometimes behind Black women's decisions to become community activists.[25] Gilkes notes that many of the Black women community activists in her study became involved in community organizing in response to the needs of their own children and of those in their communities. The following comment is typical of how many of the Black women in Gilkes' study relate to Black children: "There were a lot of summer programs springing up for kids, but they were exclusive . . . and I found that most of *our kids* (emphasis mine) were excluded."[26] For many women, what began as the daily expression of their obligations as community othermothers, as was the case for the kindergarten teacher, developed into full-fledged roles as community leaders.

Motherhood as a Symbol of Power

Motherhood, whether bloodmother, othermother, or community othermother, can be invoked by Black women as a symbol of power. A substantial portion of Black women's status in African-American communities stems not only from their roles as mothers in their own families but from their contributions as community othermothers to Black community development as well.

The specific contributions Black women make in nurturing Black community development form the basis of community-based power. Community othermothers work on behalf of the Black community by trying, in the words of late nineteenth-century Black feminists, to "uplift the race," so that vulnerable members of the community would be able to attain the self-reliance and independence so desperately needed for Black community development under oppressive conditions. This is the type of power many African-Americans have in mind when they describe the "strong, Black women" they see around them in traditional African-American communities.

When older Black women invoke this community othermother status, its results can be quite striking. Karen Fields recounts an incident described to her by her grandmother illustrating how women can exert power as community othermothers:

> One night . . . as Grandmother sat crocheting alone at about two in the morning, a young man walked into the living room carrying the portable TV from upstairs. She said, "Who are you looking for this time of night?" As Grandmother [described] the incident to me over the phone, I could hear a tone of voice that I know well. It said, "Nice boys don't do that." So I imagine the burglar heard his own mother or grandmother at that moment. He joined in the familial game just created: "Well, he told me that I could borrow it." "Who told you?" "John." "Um um, no John lives here. You got the wrong house."[27]

After this dialogue, the teenager turned around, went back upstairs and returned the television.

In local Black communities, specific Black women are widely recognized as powerful figures, primarily because of their contributions to the community's well-being through their roles as community othermothers. Sociologist Charles Johnson describes the behavior of an elderly Black woman at a church service in rural Alabama of the 1930s. Even though she was not on the program, the woman stood up to speak. The master of ceremonies rang for her to sit down but she refused to do so claiming, "I am the mother of this church, and I will say what I please." The master of ceremonies later explained to the congregation—"Brothers, I know you all honor Sister Moore. Course our time is short but she has acted as a mother to me. . . . Any time old folks get up I give way to them."[28]

IMPLICATIONS FOR BLACK MOTHER–DAUGHTER RELATIONSHIPS

In her discussion of the sex-role socialization of Black girls, Pamela Reid identifies two complementary approaches in understanding Black mother–daughter relationships.[29] The first, psychoanalytic theory, examines the role of parents in the establishment of personality and social behavior. This theory argues that the development of feminine behavior results from the girls' identification with adult female role models. This approach emphasizes how an Afrocentric ideology of motherhood is actualized through Black mothers' activities as role models.

The second approach, social learning theory, suggests that the rewards and punishments attached to girls' childhood experiences are central in shaping women's sex-role behavior. The kinds of behaviors that Black mothers reward and punish in their daughters are seen as key in the socialization process. This approach examines specific experiences that Black girls have while growing up that encourage them to absorb an Afrocentric ideology of motherhood.

African-American Mothers as Role Models

Feminist psychoanalytic theorists suggest that the sex-role socialization process is different for boys and girls. While boys learn maleness by rejecting femaleness via separating themselves from their mothers, girls establish feminine identities by embracing the femaleness of their mothers. Girls identify with their mothers, a sense of connection that is incorporated into the female personality. However, this mother-identification is problematic because, under patriarchy, men are more highly valued than women. Thus, while daughters identify with their mothers, they also reject them, since in patriarchal families, identifying with adult women as mothers means identifying with persons deemed inferior.[30]

While Black girls learn by identifying with their mothers, the specific female role with which Black girls identify may be quite different than that modeled by middle-class White mothers. The presence of working mothers, extended family othermothers, and powerful community othermothers offers a range of role models that challenge the tenets of the cult of true womanhood.

Moreover, since Black mothers have a distinctive relationship to White patriarchy, they may be less likely to socialize their daughters into their proscribed role as subordinates. Rather, a key part of Black girls' socialization involves incorporating the critical posture that allows Black women to cope with contradictions. For example, Black girls have long had to learn how to do domestic work while rejecting definitions of themselves as Mammies. At the same time they've had to take on strong roles in Black extended families without internalizing images of themselves as matriarchs.

In raising their daughters, Black mothers face a troubling dilemma. To ensure their daughters' physical survival, they must teach their daughters to fit into systems of oppression. For example, as a young girl in Mississippi, Black activist Ann Moody questioned why she was paid so little for the domestic work she began at age nine, why Black women domestics were sexually harassed by their White male employers, and why Whites had so much more than Blacks. But her mother refused to answer her questions and actually became angry whenever Ann Moody stepped out of her "place."[31] Black daughters are raised to expect to work, to strive for an education so that they can support themselves, and to anticipate carrying heavy responsibilities in their families and communities because these skills are essential for their own survival as well as for the survival of those for whom they will eventually be responsible.[32] And yet mothers know that if daughters fit too well into the limited opportunities offered Black women, they become willing participants in their own subordination. Mothers may have ensured their daughters' physical survival at the high cost of their emotional destruction.

On the other hand, Black daughters who offer serious challenges to oppressive situations may not physically survive. When Ann Moody became involved in civil rights activities, her mother first begged her not to participate and then told her not to come home because she feared the Whites in Moody's hometown would kill her. In spite of the dangers, many Black mothers routinely encourage their daughters to develop skills to confront oppressive conditions. Thus, learning that they will work, that education is a vehicle for advancement, can also be seen as ways of preparing Black girls to resist oppression through a variety of mothering roles. The issue is to build emotional strength, but not at the cost of physical survival.

This delicate balance between conformity and resistance is described by historian Elsa Barkley Brown as the "need to socialize me one way and at the same time to give me all the tools I needed to be something else."[33] Black daughters must learn how to survive in interlocking structures of race, class, and gender oppression while rejecting and transcending those very same structures. To develop these skills in their daughters, mothers demonstrate varying combinations of behaviors devoted to ensuring their daughters' survival—such as providing them with basic necessities and ensuring their protection in dangerous environments to helping their daughters go farther than mothers themselves were allowed to go.

The presence of othermothers in Black extended families and the modeling symbolized by community othermothers offer powerful support for the task of teaching girls to resist White perceptions of Black womanhood while appearing to conform to them. In contrast to the isolation of middle-class White mother/daughter dyads, Black women-centered extended family networks foster an early identification with a much wider range of models of Black womanhood, which can lead to a greater sense of empowerment in young Black girls.

Social Learning Theory and Black Mothering Behavior

Understanding this goal of balancing the needs of ensuring their daughters' physical survival with the vision of encouraging them to transcend the boundaries confronting them sheds some light on some of the apparent contradictions in Black mother–daughter relationships. Black mothers are often described as strong disciplinarians and overly protective parents; yet these same women manage to raise daughters who are self-reliant and assertive.[34] Professor Gloria Wade-Gayles offers an explanation for this apparent contradiction by suggesting that Black mothers "do not socialize their daughters to be passive or irrational. Quite the contrary, they socialize their daughters to be independent, strong and self-confident. Black mothers are suffocatingly protective and domineering precisely because they are determined to mold their daughters into whole

and self-actualizing persons in a society that devalues Black women."[35]

Black mothers emphasize protection either by trying to shield their daughters as long as possible from the penalties attached to their race, class, and gender or by teaching them how to protect themselves in such situations. Black women's autobiographies and fiction can be read as texts revealing the multiple strategies Black mothers employ in preparing their daughters for the demands of being Black women in oppressive conditions. For example, in discussing the mother–daughter relationship in Paule Marshall's *Brown Girl, Brownstones*, Rosalie Troester catalogues some of these strategies and the impact they may have on relationships themselves:

> Black mothers, particularly those with strong ties to their community, sometimes build high banks around their young daughters, isolating them from the dangers of the larger world until they are old and strong enough to function as autonomous women. Often these dikes are religious, but sometimes they are built with education, family, or the restrictions of a close-knit and homogeneous community . . . this isolation causes the currents between Black mothers and daughters to run deep and the relationship to be fraught with an emotional intensity often missing from the lives of women with more freedom.[36]

Black women's efforts to provide for their children also may affect the emotional intensity of Black mother–daughter relationships. As Gloria Wade-Gayles points out, "Mothers in Black women's fiction are strong and devoted . . . but . . . they are rarely affectionate."[37] For far too many Black mothers, the demands of providing for children are so demanding that affection often must wait until the basic needs of physical survival are satisfied.

Black daughters raised by mothers grappling with hostile environments have to confront their feelings about the difference between the idealized versions of maternal love extant in popular culture and the strict, assertive mothers so central to their lives.[38] For daughters, growing up means developing a better understanding that offering physical care and protection is an act of maternal love. Ann Moody describes her growing awareness of the personal cost her mother paid as a single mother of three children employed as a domestic worker. Watching her mother sleep after the birth of another child, Moody remembers:

> For a long time I stood there looking at her. I didn't want to wake her up. I wanted to enjoy and preserve that calm, peaceful look on her face, I wanted to think she would always be that happy . . . Adline and Junior were too young to feel the things I felt and know the things I knew about Mama. They couldn't remember when she and Daddy separated. They had never heard her cry at night as I had or worked and helped as I had done when we were starving.[39]

Renita Weems's account of coming to grips with maternal desertion provides another example of a daughter's efforts to understand her mother's behavior. In the following passage, Weems struggles with the difference between the stereotypical image of the super strong Black mother and her own alcoholic mother, who decided to leave her children:

> My mother loved us. I must believe that. She worked all day in a department store bakery to buy shoes and school tablets, came home to curse out neighbors who wrongly accused her children of any impropriety (which in an apartment complex usually meant stealing), and kept her house cleaner than most sober women.[40]

Weems concludes that her mother loved her because she provided for her to the best of her ability.

Othermothers often play central roles in defusing the emotional intensity of relationships between bloodmothers and their daughters and in helping daughters understand the Afrocentric ideology of motherhood. Weems describes the women teachers, neighbors, friends, and othermothers that she turned to for help in negotiating a difficult mother/daughter relationship. These women, she notes, "did not have the onus of providing for me, and so had the luxury of talking to me."[41]

June Jordan offers one of the most eloquent analyses of a daughter's realization of the high personal cost Black women have paid as blood-mothers and othermothers in working to provide an economic and emotional foundation for Black children. In the

following passage, Jordan captures the feelings that my Black women students struggled to put into words:

> As a child I noticed the sadness of my mother as she sat alone in the kitchen at night. . . . Her woman's work never won permanent victories of any kind. It never enlarged the universe of her imagination or her power to influence what happened beyond the front door of our house. Her woman's work never tickled her to laugh or shout or dance. But she did raise me to respect her way of offering love and to believe that hard work is often the irreducible factor for survival, not something to avoid. Her woman's work produced a reliable home base where I could pursue the privileges of books and music. Her woman's work invented the potential for a completely different kind of work for us, the next generation of Black women: huge, rewarding hard work demanded by the huge, new ambitions that her perfect confidence in us engendered.[42]

Jordan's words not only capture the essence of the Afrocentric ideology of motherhood so central to the well-being of countless numbers of Black women. They simultaneously point the way into the future, one where Black women face the challenge of continuing the mothering traditions painstakingly nurtured by prior generations of African-American women.

NOTES

1. The definition of culture used in this essay is taken from Leith Mullings, "Anthropological Perspectives on the Afro-American Family," *American Journal of Social Psychiatry* 6 (1986): 11–16. According to Mullings, culture is composed of "the symbols and values that create the ideological frame of reference through which people attempt to deal with the circumstances in which they find themselves" (13).

2. For analyses of the relationship of the cult of true womanhood to Black women, see Leith Mullings, "Uneven Development: Class, Race and Gender in the United States Before 1900," in *Women's Work, Development and the Division of Labor by Gender,* ed. Eleanor Leacock and Helen Safa (South Hadley, MA: Bergin & Garvey, 1986), pp. 41–57; Bonnie Thornton Dill, "Our Mothers' Grief: Racial Ethnic Women and the Maintenance of Families," Research Paper 4, Center for Research on Women (Memphis, TN: Memphis State University, 1986); and Hazel Carby, *Reconstructing*

Womanhood: The Emergence of the Afro-American Woman Novelist (New York: Oxford University Press, 1987), esp. chapter 2.

3. Contrast, for example, the traditionalist analysis of Selma Fraiberg, *Every Child's Birthright: In Defense of Mothering* (New York: Basic Books, 1977) to that of Jeffner Allen, "Motherhood: The Annihilation of Women," in *Mothering, Essays in Feminist Theory,* ed. Joyce Trebilcot (Totawa, NJ: Rowan & Allanheld, 1983). See also Adrienne Rich, *Of Woman Born: Motherhood as Experience and Institution* (New York: Norton, 1976). For an overview of how traditionalists and feminists have shaped the public policy debate on abortion, see Kristin Luker, *Abortion and the Politics of Motherhood* (Berkeley, CA: University of California, 1984).

4. Mullings, "Uneven Development"; Dill, "Our Mother's Grief"; and Carby, *Reconstructing Womanhood.* Feminist scholarship is also challenging Western notions of the family. See Barrie Thorne and Marilyn Yalom, eds., *Rethinking the Family* (New York: Longman, 1982).

5. Since Black women are no longer heavily concentrated in private domestic service, the Mammy image may be fading. In contrast, the matriarch image, popularized in Daniel Patrick Moynihan's, *The Negro Family: The Case for National Action* (Washington, D.C.: U.S. Government Printing Office, 1965), is reemerging in public debates about the feminization of poverty and the urban underclass. See Maxine Baca Zinn, "Minority Families in Crisis: The Public Discussion," Research Paper 6, Center for Research on Women (Memphis, TN: Memphis State University, 1987).

6. For an alternative analysis of the Mammy image, see Judith Rollins, *Between Women: Domestics and Their Employers* (Philadelphia: Temple University, 1985). Classic responses to the matriarchy thesis include Robert Hill, *The Strengths of Black Families* (New York: Urban League, 1972); Andrew Billingsley, *Black Families in White America* (Englewood Cliffs, NJ: Prentice-Hall, 1968); and Joyce Ladner, *Tomorrow's Tomorrow* (Garden City, NY: Doubleday, 1971). For a recent analysis, see Linda Burnham, "Has Poverty Been Feminized in Black America?" *Black Scholar* 16 (1985):15–24.

7. Mae King, "The Politics of Sexual Stereotypes," *Black Scholar* 4 (1973):12–23.

8. Barbara Christian, "An Angle of Seeing: Motherhood in Buchi Emecheta's *Joys of Motherhood* and Alice Walker's *Meridian,*" in *Black Feminist Criticism,* ed. Barbara Christian (New York: Pergamon, 1985), p. 214.

9. See Christine Oppong, ed., *Female and Male in West Africa* (London: Allen & Unwin, 1983); Niara Sudarkasa, "Female Employment and Family Organization in West Africa," in *The Black Woman Cross-Culturally,* ed. Filomina Chiamo Steady (Cambridge, MA: Schenkman, 1981), pp. 49–64; and Nancy Tanner, "Matrifocality in Indonesia and Africa and Among Black Americans," in *Woman, Culture, and Society,* ed. Michelle Rosaldo and Louise Lamphere (Stanford, CA: Stanford University Press, 1974), pp. 129–56.

10. Christine Oppong, "Family Structure and Women's Reproductive and Productive Roles: Some Conceptual and Methodological Issues," in *Women's Roles and Population Trends in the*

Third World, ed. Richard Anker, Myra Buvinic, and Nadia Youssef (London: Croom Heim, 1982), pp. 133–50.

11. The key distinction here is that, unlike the matriarchy thesis, women play central roles in families and this centrality is seen as legitimate. In spite of this centrality, it is important not to idealize African women's family roles. For an analysis by a Black African feminist, see Awa Thiam, *Black Sisters, Speak Out: Feminism and Oppression in Black Africa* (London: Pluto, 1978).

12. Sudarkasa, "Female Employment."

13. John Mbiti, *African Religions and Philosophies* (New York: Anchor, 1969).

14. Niara Sudarkasa, "Interpreting the African Heritage in Afro-American Family Organization," in *Black Families,* ed. Harriette Pipes McAdoo (Beverly Hills, CA: Sage, 1981), pp. 37–53; and Deborah Gray White, *Ar'n't I a Woman? Female Slaves in the Plantation South* (New York: W. W. Norton, 1985).

15. The terms used in this section appear in Rosalie Riegle Troester's "Turbulence and Tenderness: Mothers, Daughters, and 'Othermothers' in Paule Marshall's *Brown Girl, Brownstones,*" *SAGE: A Scholarly Journal on Black Women* 1 (Fall 1984):13–16.

16. See Tanner, "Matrifocality"; see also Carrie Allen McCray, "The Black Woman and Family Roles," in *The Black Woman,* ed. LaFrances Rogers-Rose (Beverly Hills, CA: Sage, 1980), pp. 67–78; Elmer Martin and Joanne Mitchell Martin, *The Black Extended Family* (Chicago: University of Chicago Press, 1978); Joyce Aschenbrenner, *Lifelines, Black Families in Chicago* (Prospect Heights, IL: Waveland, 1975); and Carol B. Stack, *All Our Kin* (New York: Harper & Row, 1974).

17. Martin and Martin, *The Black Extended Family;* Stack, *All Our Kin;* and Virginia Young, "Family and Childhood in a Southern Negro Community," *American Anthropologist* 72 (1970):269–88.

18. Stack, *All Our Kin.*

19. Ellen Cantarow, *Moving the Mountain: Women Working for Social Change* (Old Westbury, NY: Feminist Press, 1980), p. 59.

20. Thordis Simonsen, ed., *You May Plow Here, The Narrative of Sara Brooks* (New York: Touchstone, 1986), p. 181.

21. White, *Ar'n't I a Woman?;* Dill, "Our Mothers' Grief"; Mullings, "Uneven Development."

22. Simonsen, *You May Plow Here,* p. 86.

23. Mamie Garvin Fields and Karen Fields, *Lemon Swamp and Other Places, A Carolina Memoir* (New York: Free Press, 1983), p. xvii.

24. Ibid, p. 195.

25. Cheryl Gilkes, "'Holding Back the Ocean with a Broom,' Black Women and Community Work," in *The Black Woman,* ed. Rogers-Rose, 1980, pp. 217–31, and "Going Up for the Oppressed: The Career Mobility of Black Women Community Workers," *Journal of Social Issues* 39 (1983):115–39.

26. Gilkes, "'Holding Back the Ocean,'" p. 219.

27. Fields and Fields, *Lemon Swamp,* p. xvi.

28. Charles Johnson, *Shadow of the Plantation* (Chicago: University of Chicago Press, 1934, 1979), p. 173.

29. Pamela Reid, "Socialization of Black Female Children," in *Women: A Developmental Perspective,* ed. Phyllis Berman and Estelle Ramey (Washington, DC: National Institutes of Health, 1983).

30. For works in the feminist psychoanalytic tradition, see Nancy Chodorow, "Family Structure and Feminine Personality," in *Woman, Culture, and Society,* ed. Rosaldo and Lamphere, 1974; Nancy Chodorow, *The Reproduction of Mothering* (Berkeley, CA: University of California, 1978); and Jane Flax, "The Conflict Between Nurturance and Autonomy in Mother–Daughter Relationships and Within Feminism," *Feminist Studies* 4 (1978):171–89.

31. Ann Moody, *Coming of Age in Mississippi* (New York: Dell, 1968).

32. Ladner, *Tomorrow's Tomorrow;* Gloria Joseph, "Black Mothers and Daughters: Their Roles and Functions in American Society," in *Common Differences,* ed. Gloria Joseph and Jill Lewis (Garden City, NY: Anchor, 1981), pp. 75–126; Lena Wright Myers, *Black Women, Do They Cope Better?* (Englewood Cliffs, NJ: Prentice-Hall, 1980).

33. Elsa Barkley Brown, "Hearing Our Mothers' Lives," paper presented at fifteenth anniversary of African-American and African Studies at Emory College, Atlanta, 1986. This essay appeared in the Black Women's Studies issue of *SAGE: A Scholarly Journal on Black Women,* vol. 6, no. 1:4–11.

34. Joseph, "Black Mothers and Daughters"; Myers, 1980.

35. Gloria Wade-Gayles, "The Truths of Our Mothers' Lives: Mother–Daughter Relationships in Black Women's Fiction," *SAGE: A Scholarly Journal on Black Women* 1 (Fall 1984):12.

36. Troester, "Turbulence and Tenderness," p. 13.

37. Wade-Gayles, "The Truths," p. 10.

38. Joseph, "Black Mothers and Daughters."

39. Moody, *Coming of Age,* p. 57.

40. Renita Weems, " 'Hush. Mama's Gotta Go Bye Bye': A Personal Narrative," *SAGE: A Scholarly Journal on Black Women* 1 (Fall 1984):26.

41. Ibid, p. 27.

42. June Jordan, *On Call, Political Essays* (Boston: South End Press, 1985), p. 145.

27

Revision and Resistance

The Politics of Native Women's Motherwork

LISA J. UDEL

Contemporary Native women of the United States and Canada, politically active in Indigenous rights movements for the past thirty years, variously articulate a reluctance to affiliate with white feminist movements of North America. Despite differences in tribal affiliation, regional location, urban or reservation background, academic or community setting, and pro- or anti-feminist ideology, many Native women academics and grassroots activists alike invoke models of preconquest, egalitarian societies to theorize contemporary social and political praxes. Such academics as Paula Gunn Allen, Rayna Green, and Patricia Monture-Angus, as well as Native activists Wilma Mankiller, Mary Brave Bird, and Yet Si Blue (Janet McCloud) have problematized the reformative role white feminism can play for Indigenous groups, arguing that non-Native women's participation in various forms of Western imperialism have often made them complicit in the oppression of Native peoples.[1] More important, Native women contend that their agendas for reform differ from those they identify with mainstream white feminist movements. The majority of contemporary Native American women featured in recent collections by Ronnie Farley, Jane Katz, and Steve Wall, for example, are careful to stress the value of traditional, pre-contact female and male role models in their culture.[2] One aspect of traditional culture that Native women cite as crucial to their endeavor is what Patricia Hill Collins calls "motherwork."[3] Many Native women valorize their ability to procreate and nurture their children, communities, and the earth as aspects of motherwork. "Women are sacred because we bring life into this world," states Monture-Angus. "First Nations women are respected as the centre of the nation for [this] reason."[4] Native women argue that they have devised alternate reform strategies to those advanced by Western feminism. Native women's motherwork, in its range and variety, is one form of this activism, an approach that emphasizes Native traditions of "responsibilities" as distinguished from Western feminism's notions of "rights."

Writing for an ethnically diverse feminist audience in the journal *Callaloo,* Clara Sue Kidwell (Choctaw/Chippewa) warns: "Although feminists might deny this equation of anatomy and destiny, the fact is that the female reproductive function is a crucial factor in determining a woman's social role in tribal societies. Women bear children who carry on the culture of the group."[5] Mary Gopher (Ojibway) explains the analogy of woman/Earth inherent in philosophies of many tribes: "In our religion, we look at this planet as a woman. She is the most important female to us because she keeps us alive. We are nursing off of her."[6] Carrie Dann (Western Shoshone) adds: "Indigenous women, they're supposed to look at themselves as the Earth. That is the way we were brought up. This is what I try to tell the young people, especially the young girls."[7] Gopher and Dann invest motherwork with religious and cultural authority that they, as elders, must transmit to younger women in their communities. Many contemporary Native women argue that they must also educate white women in their traditional roles as women in order to safeguard the Earth, so that they will survive. Calling upon traditions of female leadership, Blue (Tulalip) contends:

> It is going to be the job of Native women to begin teaching other women what their roles are. Women have to turn life around, because if they don't, all of future life is threatened and endangered. I don't care what kind of women they are, they are going to have to worry more about the changes that are taking place on this Mother Earth that will affect us all.[8]

Blue, like many Native women activists, links women's authority as procreators with their larger responsibilities to a personified, feminized Earth.

Several Native women condemn Western feminism for what they perceive as a devaluation of motherhood and refutation of women's traditional responsibilities.[9] Paula Gunn Allen attributes the pronatalist stance articulated by so many Native women to the high incidence of coerced sterilization in Indian Health Service (IHS) facilities. An overpowering awareness of the government's abduction of Indian children, the nonconsensual sterilization of Native women, along with the nation's highest infant mortality rates, pervades the work of Native writers and activists.[10] American Indian Movement (AIM) veteran and celebrated author Mary Brave Bird, for instance, discusses the sterilization of her mother and sister, performed without their consent.[11] Many women told Jane Katz stories of the forced abduction of their children by social welfare agencies and mission schools that were published in *Messengers of the Wind*.[12] In her autobiography *Halfbreed*, Maria Campbell (métis) tells a similar story of

the Canadian government placing her siblings in foster care when her mother died, despite the fact that her father—the children's parent and legal guardian—was still alive.[13]

Native women argue that in their marital contracts with Euramerican men they lost power, autonomy, sexual freedom, and maternity and inheritance rights, which precluded their ability to accomplish motherwork. Green observes, for example, that an eighteenth-century Native woman allied to a fur trader relinquished control over her life and the lives of the children she bore from her white partner. This lack of control was compounded by the fact that Native women married to white men gave birth to more children than those partnered with Native men. Furthermore, a Native woman lost the freedom to divorce of her own free will, and the "goods and dwelling that might have been her own property in Indian society became the possession of her white husband."[14] In contrast, within many Native traditions, notes Green:

> The children belonged entirely to women, as did the property and distribution of resources. Indian men abided by the rules of society. If a couple separated, the man would leave with only that which had belonged to him when he entered the relationship; if a woman formed an alliance with a European by choice, she had every reason to imagine that her society's rules would be followed. For Indians, a white man who married an Indian was expected to acknowledge the importance and status of women. . . . In some tribes, adult women were free to seek out sexual alliances with whomever they chose.[15]

In order to do motherwork well, Native women argue, women must have power.

Euramericans held different ideas about female sexuality and inheritance. Many white men married Indian women who owned land in order to acquire their inheritance. When conflict over property rights inevitably arose, European laws dominated, Native women lost ownership rights to their land and suffered diminished economic autonomy and political status. Examples of this phenomenon occurred in the early twentieth century when oil was discovered in Oklahoma; white men married into wealthy female-centered Osage families and inherited the family's property. "Under Osage practice, the oil revenues would have been reserved for the woman's family and controlled by her. Common property laws established by white men gave the husband control," explains Green. "In a number of notorious instances in Oklahoma, women were murdered so that their husbands could inherit their wealth."[16] Certainly the concept that Indian women suffer through sexual contact with non-Native men is evident in the works of Beth Brant, Green, and Mankiller, as well as in the story of the women of Tobique, who lost their Indian status once they married white men.

Native women also experienced the loss of economic and political power through diminished reproductive freedom. Christian ideology recast women's sexuality, emphasizing procreation, virtue, and modesty. Early records show missionaries' agitation over the sexual autonomy of most unmarried Native women. As Christian-based roles were asserted, Native traditions of birth control and population control were forgotten. For example, Cherokee women traditionally held the right to limit population through infanticide. Similarly, Seneca women were able to limit their families, starting childbearing early and ending it early. Seneca society also did not mandate marriage for legitimate childbearing.[17]

The involuntary sterilization of Native women (as well as Mexican American and African American women) is common knowledge among those communities affected but remains largely unknown to those outside the communities. A federal government investigation in 1976 discovered that in the four-year period between 1973 and 1976 more than three thousand Native women were involuntarily sterilized. Of the 3,406 women sterilized, 3,001 were between the ages of fifteen and forty-four.[18] A 1979 report revealed that six out of ten hospitals routinely sterilized women under the age of twenty-one, a clear violation of the 1974 Department of Health, Education, and Welfare (DHEW) guidelines prohibiting involuntary sterilization of minors.[19] According to Bertha Medicine Bull, a leader on the Montana Lame Deer Reservation, two local fifteen-year-old girls were sterilized when they had appendectomies, without their knowledge or consent.[20] Only four out of twelve IHS facilities were investi-

gated; therefore, the estimated number of women sterilized either coercively (often through the illegal threat of withholding government aid or the removal of existing children), or without their knowledge, during this period is estimated at twelve thousand.[21]

Green writes that because of "sterilization and experimentation abuse on Native American women and men in Indian Health Service facilities, Native American people have been warier than ever of contraceptive technologies."[22] Many Native women, responding to the involuntary sterilization cases they have encountered directly and indirectly, blame the U.S. government for genocidal policies toward Native populations. Connie Uri (Choctaw), for example, observed in 1978: "We are not like other minorities. We have no gene pool in Africa or Asia. When we are gone, that's it."[23] Activist Barbara Moore (the sister Mary Brave Bird describes) links sterilization with genocide much more explicitly: "There are plans to get rid of Indians. They actually plan different kinds of genocide. One way to do that is through alcohol, another way is birth control, and one of the most cruel ways is to sterilize Indian women by force."[24] Moore recounts the story of her child's birth, delivered by Cesarean section and reported as a stillbirth, although the autopsy she demanded determined the cause of death as inconclusive. Moore states: "My child was born healthy. Besides this, they told me that I could not have any more children because they have had to sterilize me. I was sterilized during the operation without my knowledge and without my agreement."[25]

Native women thus value and argue for reproductive autonomy, which they link with empowered motherwork; but, they approach this autonomy from a perspective that they feel differs from mainstream feminism. Given the history of the IHS campaign to curtail Native women's reproductive capacity and thus Native populations, Native women emphasize women's ability, sometimes "privilege," to bear children. Within this paradigm, they argue, Native women's procreative capability becomes a powerful tool to combat Western genocide. Motherhood recovered, along with the tribal responsibility to nurture their children in a traditional manner and without non-Indigenous interference, assumes a powerful political meaning when viewed this way.[26]

WHITE FEMINISM AND
REPRODUCTIVE AUTONOMY

The role of white feminism in the campaign for reproductive autonomy has been a sore point among many Native women who link the American eugenics movement with American birth control movements of the early twentieth century. Both movements, which involved the participation of white feminists of their time, began as an effort to grant women control over their fertility, and thus gain some measure of economic and political autonomy, but eventually gave way to eugenic and population control forces. The focus moved from "self determination" to the "social control" of immigrant and working classes by "the elite." As historian Linda Gordon explains, eugenics became a dominant aspect of the movement to legalize contraception and sterilization, and, eventually, "Birth controllers from the socialist-feminist revolution . . . made accommodations with eugenists."[27]

White-dominated feminism's historic failure to combat racist and classist ideologies, compounded by promotion of ideologies to gain suffrage in the past, has perpetuated the link between white mainstream feminism to eugenics. The resulting conflation of birth control movements with eugenics and population control has had a negative impact both on disadvantaged people vulnerable to external social control and also on the feminist movement. Gordon argues that feminist birth control advocates accepted racist attitudes of the eugenicists and population controllers, even sharing anti–working-class, anti-immigrant sentiment.[28] The population control and eugenics movements dominated early and mid-twentieth-century white feminism, obfuscating the latter's agenda and efficacy. This history continues to influence theories of birth control today. According to Gordon, "Planned Parenthood's use of small-family ideology and its international emphasis on sterilization rather than safe and controllable contraception have far overshadowed its feminist program for women's self-determination."[29]

The public does not distinguish between birth control "as a program of individual rights" and population control as social policy that strips the individual of those very rights. It is this blurred distinction that Na-

tive women criticize. Brave Bird, for instance, points out the irrelevance of abortion rights to Indian women who see tribal repopulation as one of their primary goals. A self-identified Indian feminist, Brave Bird recognizes the value of reproductive rights for women whose bodies have been controlled by others; however, she objects to white feminists who would dictate an Indian feminist agenda to her.[30] In 1977 the Hyde Amendment withdrew federal funding for abortions but left free-on-demand surgical sterilizations funded by the DHEW; consequently some poor women were forced to choose infertility as their method of birth control because pregnancy prevention was also not funded.

Native women employ motherist rhetoric in their critiques of Western feminism as a response to their history of enforced sterilization and also as a defensive strategy crucial to marking women's dignity and contributions to Native cultures. Speaking to a predominantly white audience of feminists at the National Women's Studies Association meeting in 1988, Green explained that "models of kinship [mother, sister, grandmother, aunt] are used by Indian women to measure their capacity for leadership and to measure the success of their leadership."[31] Such kinship models of evaluation, however, are not to be read literally. These roles are *not* biologically determined, Green emphasized; they are symbolic:

> Women like me are going to blow it in the role of mother if left to the narrow, biological role. But in Indian country, that role was never understood necessarily only as a biological role; grandma was never understood as a biological role; sister and aunt were never understood in the narrow confines of genetic kinship.[32]

As leaders, Native women must oversee the survival of Native peoples, notes Green. While Green, like Blue and Carrie Dann, sees Native people as the primary redeemers of America, she emphatically refutes the appropriation of Native traditions to "heal" mainstream American culture. "We cannot do that," she explains.

> There has been so much abuse of this role that it's frightening. . . . *All* Indigenous people have that power, because we speak from the earth. . . . But

we cannot heal you; only you can heal yourselves.
. . . If we have any model to give, it is an aesthetic
model, a cultural model, that works for us.

Green warns that Western appropriation of Indigenous
traditions, rituals, and philosophies (made popular in
the New Age Movement, for example) will not provide
a "quick fix" for the problems of Western culture.
Green's position is an attempt to clarify the role of Native traditions in the reformative enterprise. Native activists will not perform the service-work of healing
Western cultures. Green points out that such expectations are embedded in colonial histories; they keep the
"sick" Western subject at the center to be tended by the
Native "other."[33]

Native women's strategic use of a motherist stance
is a conscious act of separation from traditional feminists.[34] The women locate their activism not in feminist struggle, but in cultural survival, identifying themselves, as Anne Snitow explains, "not as feminists but
as militant mothers, fighting together for [the] survival
[of their children]." Women become motherists, Snitow writes, when "men are forced to be absent (because they are migrant workers or soldiers) or in times
of crisis, when the role of nurturance assigned to
women has been rendered difficult or impossible."[35] A
motherist position would apply to Native women living on and off reservations where employment opportunities are scarce for men, as well as for women who
lose their mothering capacity to sterilization or their
living children to boarding schools. The motherists
Snitow describes intuitively relied upon the presence
of their female community because "crisis made the
idea of a separate, private identity beyond the daily
struggle for survival unimportant."[36]

White feminists and Native motherists endorsed divergent strategies, notes Snitow. Her model perfectly
characterizes dichotomies between Native women's
collective identifications—including their loyalties to
traditions that puzzle white women—and non-Native
feminists' individuating theories. "Collectivist movements are powerful, but they usually don't raise questions about women's work," she explains. "Feminism
has raised the questions, and claimed an individual
destiny for each woman, but remains ambivalent toward older traditions of female solidarity."[37] For ex-

ample, traditional dichotomies of public and private
domains, characteristic of much feminist writing of the
1970s and 1980s, does not work for women of color
for whom "those domains are not separate or at least
not separate in the same ways as for white women."[38]
This is especially true with Native cultures, which are
structured along collective rather than individual dynamics characteristic of Western cultures.[39] The separation of public and private spheres, along with "the
primacy of gender conflict as a feature of the family,
and the gender-based assignment of reproductive
labor," constitute three concepts of traditional white
feminist theory that ignore the interaction of race and
gender and thus fail to account for Native women's experience of motherwork.[40]

Evelyn Nakano Glenn observes that for racial ethnic women, the concept of the "domestic" extends beyond the nuclear family to include broadly defined relations of kin and community. Often living in
situations of economic insecurity and assault on their
culture, racially ethnic women have not been able to
rely solely on the nuclear family because it is not self-
sufficient, but have relied upon and contributed to an
extended network of family and community. Thus,
work conducted in the domestic, hence "private,"
sphere includes contributions to the extended "public"
network, where women care for each other's children,
exchange supplies, and help nurse the sick. Racial ethnic women's work has simultaneously moved into the
public sphere of the ethnic community, in support of
the church, political organizing, and other activities on
behalf of their collective. Glenn writes that racial ethnic women are "often the core of community organizations, and their involvement is often spurred by a desire to defend their children, their families, and their
ways of life."[41]

Certainly Glenn's point is relevant to contemporary
Native women living on and off the reservation. Focused on strengthening Native economies and traditions, contemporary Native women may engage in traditional skills of beadwork or quilting, for example, in
order to earn money and prestige to benefit, feed, and
educate their children. Women may engage in activities historically associated with men in order to revise
and strengthen tribal culture. Such women drum at
local powwows, or are political activists, such as Mary

Brave Bird of AIM and, more recently, Winona LaDuke (White Earth Ojibwa), founder of the White Earth Land Recovery Project, cochair of the Indigenous Women's Network, and vice presidential candidate for the Green Party in the last two elections. Patricia Hill Collins notes that work and family do not function as separate, dichotomous spheres for women of color, but are, in fact, often overlapping. By linking individual and collective welfare, Collins neatly articulates the philosophy underlying most Native cultures. While individual achievement is sought and recognized, it is always within the context of the collective that such endeavors are valued. It follows that Wilma Mankiller became Principal Chief of the Cherokee to benefit the Cherokee.[42]

For women of color, then, motherwork involves working for the physical survival of children and community, confronting what Collins calls the "dialectical nature of power and powerlessness in structuring mothering patterns, and the significance of self-definition in constructing individual and collective racial identity." This type of motherwork, while ensuring individual and community survival, can result in the loss of individual autonomy "or the submersion of individual growth for the benefit of the group."[43] The deemphasis on individual autonomy proves troubling to white feminists who have sought to extricate the individual woman's identity from the debilitating influences of social expectation in order to articulate and celebrate her emergence into what has generally been viewed as a more liberated individual. Once again we experience the fallout of conflicting ideas between Western liberalism and Native collectivism.

When feminist theory posits "the family" as "the locus of gender conflict," focusing on the economic dependence of women and the inequitable division of labor, it inevitably draws upon models of the white, middle-class, nuclear family. Viewed thus, marriage within the white, middle-class, nuclear family oppresses women. In order to gain liberation, white feminists have argued, women must be free from the unequal balance of power marriage has conferred. In contrast, Glenn points out, women of color often experience their families as a "source of resistance to oppression from outside institutions." Within Glenn's construct, we see that women of color engage in activ-ities to keep their families unified and teach children survival skills. This work is viewed as a method of resistance to oppression rather than gender exploitation. Unified in struggle against colonial oppression, family members focus on individual survival, maintenance of family authority, and the transmission of cultural traditions. Economically, Glenn notes, women of color remain less dependent upon men than white women because they must earn an income to support the family. Both incomes are necessary for a family's survival. Glenn writes that because the earning gap between women and men of color is narrower than that of whites, "men and women [of color have been] mutually dependent; dependence rarely ran in one direction." Such families may be sustained by members whose relationships are characterized by interdependence and gender complementarity.[44]

Glenn's paradigm of the family can be applied in a broader context in order to consider aspects of contemporary reservation and urban life. For example, Christine Conte's study of western Navajo women examines how they employ kin ties and cooperative networks to perform tasks, obtain resources, and acquire wealth. Such cooperation typically includes the exchange of labor, commodities, subsistence goods, information, cash, and transportation.[45] Similarly, women featured in Steve Wall's collection of interviews with tribal elders describe themselves as family leaders, intent on transmitting cultural traditions to the generation that follows them.[46] AIM schools of the 1970s, typically run by women, provide one example of offering Native children an alternative value system to the mission and boarding schools that many of their parents (such as Mary Brave Bird) experienced.

Like Glenn and Collins, Patricia Monture-Angus points to the differing roles that the family plays for Native women and non-Native women. Citing Marlee Kline, Monture-Angus notes that, while women of color and white women can both experience violence in the family, women of color look to their family as a system of support against violent racism from outside the family. Thus, while the Native family may "provide a site of cultural and political resistance to White supremacy,"[47] Native women can also experience contradictory relationships within their families, requiring that they also revise their families as they go along.

Drawing upon networks of kin for support, survival, and pleasure, Native women also combat trends in domestic violence and prescribed gender roles that threaten and constrain them.[48]

Collins identifies three main themes that comprise ethnic women's struggles for maternal empowerment: 1) reproductive autonomy; 2) parental privileges; and 3) the threat of cultural eradication by the dominant culture.[49] Many women of color have not known the experience of determining their own fertility. For Native women sterilized without their consent, choosing to become a mother takes on political meaning, an act that challenges, as Angela Davis has said, "institutional policies that encourage white middle-class women to reproduce and discourage low-income racial ethnic women from doing so, even penalizing them."[50] Once a woman of color becomes a parent, she is threatened with the physical and/or psychological separation from her children "designed to disempower racial ethnic individuals and undermine their communities."[51] The Indian boarding and mission schools of the nineteenth and twentieth centuries serve as an example of this disempowerment, coupled, as they were, with "the pervasive efforts by the dominant group to control their children's minds" by forbidding any use of Native languages and the denigration of "the power of mothers to raise their children as they see fit."[52] For women of color, motherwork entails the difficult tasks of "trying to foster a meaningful racial identity in children within a society that denigrates people of color" and sustaining a form of resistance.[53]

For many Native women, motherwork is linked with the authority of leadership.[54] Discussing Western imperialism's degenerative effect on female leadership, Chief Wilma Mankiller contends:

> Europeans brought with them the view that men were the absolute heads of households, and women were to be submissive to them. It was then that the role of women in Cherokee society began to decline. One of the new values Europeans brought to the Cherokees was a lack of balance and harmony between men and women. It was what we today call sexism. This was not a Cherokee concept. Sexism was borrowed from Europeans.[55]

Mankiller characterizes the resistance she encountered to her campaign for the position of Principal Chief of the Cherokee as evidence of the erosion of traditional Native political structures under the onslaught of Western influence. Although traditionally matrilineal, the Cherokee adopted Western configurations of gender that favor patriarchal structures, notes Mankiller. Among recent Cherokee accomplishments, such as addressing issues of poverty and education reform, and the revitalization of cultural traditions, Mankiller includes revised gender roles and the reclamation of women's power.

The current status of Native women—both on and off the reservations involved in tribal political, cultural, and religious revitalization—drives many contemporary writers to emphasize the richness of traditional Native women's lives as models for reform. Just as Green insists on traditions that cultivate women's leadership, Lakota anthropologist Beatrice Medicine emphasizes the importance women play in Lakota ceremonial and artistic life, along with the status their work garners. Medicine contends that "the traditional woman was greatly respected and revered," that she hosted feasts and participated in sacred ceremonies, and that women's societies held competitions in the arts of sewing, beading, and other crafts that proved economically lucrative in trade and were thus prestigious for the winner. Contemporary life on the reservations is very different, Medicine notes. Lakota women suffer diminished prestige, and they are threatened by poor economic conditions, government usurpation of the functions traditionally provided by the family (such as welfare and education), and the loss of traditional values that unify kinship roles and obligations. Where Sioux women formerly used their artistic talents to make a respectable marriage and to earn prestige and wealth, they now continue their artistic work but with diminished economic return. At one time a woman might have earned one horse in exchange for a "skillfully decorated robe"; now she will earn approximately sixty cents an hour for a quilt.[56]

Many Native women agree with Allen, who contends, "The tradition of strong, autonomous, self-defining women comes from Indians. They [Euroamericans] sure didn't get it in sixteenth-century Europe."[57] Monture-Angus explains that the term "traditional" privileges neither "static" nor regressive perspectives, but embraces holistic approaches to reform. Monture-Angus points out that "traditional perspectives include the view that the past and all its experiences inform the present reality."[58] She advocates an interpretation of traditions that is fluid and adaptive, one that will enable Native societies to confront situations of contemporary life such as domestic violence, substance addiction, and youth suicide. Because many precontact cultures did not condone abuse of women, Monture-Angus argues, a literal interpretation of traditions will fail to provide a contemporary model of social reform. "What we can reclaim is the values [sic] that created a system where the abuses did not occur. We can recover our own system of law, law that has at its centre the family and our kinship relations. . . . We must be patient with each other as we learn to live in a decolonized way."[59] Monture-Angus articulates a belief in the beauty and efficacy of Native traditions shared by many Native women writing about strategies for battling colonialism and supporting tribal survival.

Part of the reclamation of cultural traditions involves the recognition of "responsibilities," a term many Native theorists distinguish from Western notions of "rights." Native women thus articulate their responsibilities in terms of their roles as mothers and leaders, positing those roles as a form of motherwork. "Responsibility focuses attention not on what is mine, but on the relationships between people and creation (that is, both the individual and the collective)," writes Monture-Angus.[60] Native activists argue that rights-based theories predispose Western cultures to abuse the earth and to oppress other societies that value their relationship to the earth. Renee Senogles (Red Lake Chippewa) notes: "The difference between Native American women and white feminists is that the feminists talk about their rights and we talk about our responsibilities. There is a profound difference. Our responsibility is to take care of our natural place in the world."[61] Osennontion and Skonaganleh:rá concur, clarifying the emphasis of Haudenosaunee law on responsibilities within political and social realms, which include the observance of clan structure and communal ties, and a personal code of honor, integrity, compassion, and strength, linked to the maintenance of a relationship with the natural world.[62]

One primary goal of Native activists involves restructuring and reinforcing Indian families. This includes their reevaluation of both women's and men's roles. If Native women are to fulfill traditions of female leadership, they argue, Native men must reclaim their responsibilities so that the enterprise supporting Indigenous survival and prosperity can move forward. Native women repeatedly fault white feminists for the devaluation of men in their revisionary tactics. Part of a man's responsibility is to protect and provide for his family, as well as to expedite political and social duties. If a man fails in his responsibilities, it falls upon the society's women to instruct, reeducate, and remind him of his obligations. Native activists fault Western hegemony and capitalism as systems responsible for alienating so many Native men from their traditional responsibilities.

In the face of coerced agrarianism and the attending devaluation of hunting, and the consequences of forced removal and relocation, Native men have suffered a loss of status and traditional self-sufficiency even more extensive than their female counterparts, argue many Native women.[63] Women's traditional roles as procreator, parent, domestic leader, and even artisan have, to some extent, remained intact. For example, Clara Sue Kidwell observes that during early contact, women's "functions as childbearers and contributors to subsistence were not threatening to white society and were less affected than those of Indian men."[64] In situations of contact, Kidwell points out, women often became the custodians of traditional cultural values, engaging in reproductive labor and motherwork. In contrast, men suffer from an inability to fulfill traditional roles. On the Pine Ridge reservation of the Lakota, employment opportunities for Lakota men are practically nonexistent. Federal agencies, such as the BIA and IHS provide the majority of the employment available. Very few businesses are owned by the Lakota, and, because of the land allotment, less than 10 percent of reservation land is actually owned by Native Americans. Jobs available to men, such as construction, are project-oriented and thus sporadic, whereas job opportunities for women, such as nursing, teaching, clerical, and domestic work, are more consistently available.[65] Ramona Ford observes that contemporary Native women hold down more jobs than do Native men, although they earn inadequate wages.[66] It is evident that such cash-based, gender-delimited jobs keep the majority of Native people living below the poverty line in both the United States and Canada.[67]

Part of their responsibilities then, contend many Native women, is the restoration of traditional male roles, along with the selection and training of appropriate male leaders. Once installed in leadership roles, Osennontion and Skonaganleh:rá write, the men are responsible to the women who have empowered them, and the women ensure that their leaders remain "good men," mindful of the reciprocal relationship between leader and subject.[68] The definition of their responsibilities—their attendance to clan and communal structure through an investment in male esteem—coincides with the taxonomy I discuss in reproductive labor and motherwork.

While some Western feminists might recoil from such an investment in the restoration of male psyche, seeing it as a refined form of female abjection, it is important to remember that the majority of Native women writing and speaking today—who are political activists, feminist scholars, anthropologists, law professors, and grassroots organizers—all emphasize the importance of men to the revitalization of Native communities. Obviously then, these Native women do not prescribe female subjugation, but rather the solidification of a communal, extended network of support that acts as the family. This family takes many forms and rarely resembles the Western model of the nuclear, patriarch-led unit. For example, the two collections *Women of the Native Struggle* and *Wisdom's Daughters* feature vastly extended, matrilineal and matrilocal families, often with single, pregnant women as their members and leaders.[69] Such families seek to reintegrate men into communal life, but not within Western patriarchal paradigms. Osennontion and Skonaganleh:rá argue for the necessity of women's participation on the Band Council, the governing body for many East Coast Canadian tribes, including the Haudenosaunee: "Women have a responsibility to make sure that we don't lose any more, that we don't do any more damage, while we work on getting our original government system back in good working order."[70] As Monture-Angus notes, an emphasis on Native traditions does not preclude the integration of old and new. While recognizing the value of traditional culture and practice, Native activists and feminists do not blindly embrace behavior simply because it may be called "traditional," especially if it is oppressive to women. Just who determines what is to be called "traditional" and therefore valuable is also under scrutiny.

Indigenous women activists cite the difficulties that inform their theories and praxes of activism: the widespread violence committed against Native women; the common occurrence of rape; the murder of family members (Brave Bird, Campbell, and Lee Maracle, for instance, all recount such experiences); the murder and mutilation of leaders and friends (such as activist Annie Mae Aquash); the government's abduction of Indian children; and sterilization of Native women. It is vital that Native communities retrieve lost traditions of gender complementarity, they argue. The majority of Native American women involved in women's rights point to their own brand of feminism that calls on obscured traditions of women's autonomy and power. Such efforts, which are generally grassroots, reflect Native traditions of community-based activism comparable to the paradigm Snitow outlines.

In any discussion of possible coalition between contemporary Indigenous groups and white feminist groups, Native women insist that their prospective partners recognize Indigenous traditions of female autonomy and prestige, traditions that can provide models of social reform in white, as well as Native, America. This proposed coalition suggests a move beyond idealized appropriation, to a shared vision of political and cultural reform. In their eagerness to coalesce, white feminists have been rightly accused of ignoring or eliding differences between and among women. Native women resist reductionist impulses inherent in Western feminism, insisting that we examine the varying historical contingencies of each group that continue to shape feminist discourses into the next century.

NOTES

1. Examples include Paula Gunn Allen, *Off the Reservation: Reflections on Boundary-Busting, Border-Crossing, Loose Canons* (Boston: Beacon Press, 1998), *The Sacred Hoop: Recovering the Feminine in American Indian Traditions* (Boston: Beacon Press, 1986), and *Spider Woman's Granddaughters: Traditional Tales and*

Contemporary Writing by Native American Women (Boston: Beacon Press, 1989); Jane Caputi, "Interview with Paula Gunn Allen," *Trivia* 16 (1990): 50–67, and "Interview" in *Backtalk: Women Writers Speak Out,* ed. Donna Perry (New Brunswick, N.J.: Rutgers University Press, 1993); Rayna Green, "American Indian Women: Diverse Leadership for Social Change," in *Bridges of Power: Women's Multicultural Alliances,* ed. Lisa Albrecht and Rose M. Brewer (Philadelphia: New Society Publishers, 1990), "Review Essay: Native American Women," *Signs: Journal of Women in Culture and Society* 6:2 (1980): 248–67, and *Women in American Indian Society* (New York: Chelsea House Publishers, 1992); Patricia A. Monture-Angus, *Thunder in My Soul: A Mohawk Woman Speaks* (Halifax: Fernwood Publishing, 1995); Patricia A. Monture, "I Know My Name: A First Nations Woman Speaks," in *Limited Edition: Voices of Women, Voices of Feminism,* ed. Geraldine Finn (Halifax: Fernwood Publishing, 1993); Wilma Mankiller and Michael Wallis, *Mankiller: A Chief and Her People* (New York: St. Martin's Press, 1993); Mary Brave Bird and Richard Erdoes, *Ohitika Woman* (New York: Harper Collins, 1993); Mary Crow Dog and Richard Erdoes, *Lakota Woman* (New York: Harper Collins, 1991); and Janet McCloud, in *Women of the Native Struggle: Portraits and Testimony of Native American Women,* ed. Ronnie Farley (New York: Orion Books, 1993).

2. Farley, *Women of the Native Struggle,* Jane Katz, ed., *Messengers of the Wind: Native American Women Tell Their Life Stories* (New York: Ballantine Books, 1995); and Steve Wall, ed., *Wisdom's Daughters: Conversations with Women Elders of Native America* (New York: Harper Perennial, 1993).

3. Patricia Hill Collins applies the term "motherwork" to the tasks engaged in by women/mothers of color. Collins contends that women of color recognize the embattled nature of their families and identify the most destructive forces as coming from outside their families rather than from within. Part of women's work, or motherwork, consists of maintaining "family integrity." The kind of motherwork Collins outlines, and many Native women describe, reflects the belief that "individual survival, empowerment, and identity require group survival, empowerment, and identity" ("Shifting the Center: Race, Class, and Feminist Theorizing About Motherhood," in *Representations of Motherhood,* ed. Donna Bassin, Margaret Honey, and Meryle Mahrer Kaplan [New Haven: Yale University Press, 1994], 59).

4. Monture-Angus, *Thunder in My Soul,* 49.

5. Clara Sue Kidwell, "What Would Pocahontas Think Now? Women and Cultural Persistence," *Callaloo* 17:1 (1994): 149.

6. Mary Gopher, in Farley, *Women of the Native Struggle,* 77.

7. Carrie Dann in Farley, *Women of the Native Struggle,* 77.

8. Yet Si Blue in Farley, *Women of the Native Struggle,* 83.

9. Monture-Angus, *Thunder in My Soul,* 210; Paula Gunn Allen, quoted in Caputi, "Interview," 8; and Ingrid Washinawatok-El Issa in Farley, *Women of the Native Struggle,* 48.

10. Allen, "Interview," in Perry, *Backtalk,* 17.

11. Mary Crow Dog and Richard Erdoes, *Lakota Woman* (New York: Harper-Perennial, 1991) 78–79.

12. Jane Katz, ed., *Messangers of the Wind: Native American Women Tell Their Life Stories* (New York: Ballantine Books, 1995), 35–37, 60, 80–81.

13. Maria Campbell, *Halfbreed* (Lincoln: University of Nebraska Press, 1973), 103–7.

14. Green, *Women in American Indian Society,* 37.

15. Green, *Women in American Indian Society,* 37–38.

16. Green, *Women in American Indian Society,* 38. Linda Hogan's *Mean Spirit* (New York: Ivy Books, 1990) is a fictionalized account of this gynocidal episode in Native-Euramerican history.

17. Ramona Ford, "Native American Women: Changing Statuses, Changing Interpretations," in *Writing the Range: Race, Class, and Culture in the Women's West,* ed. Elizabeth Jameson and Susan Armitage (Norman: University of Oklahoma Press, 1997), 58; and Nancy Shoemaker, "The Rise Or Fall of Iroquois Women," *Journal of Women's History* 2:3 (1991): 39–57, 51. For further discussion of gender in precontact cultures, see Evelyn Blackwood's "Sexuality and Gender in Certain Native American Tribes," *Signs: Journal of Women in Culture and Society* 10:1 (1984): 27–42.

18. Janet Karsten Larson, "And Then There Were None: Is Federal Policy Endangering the American Indian Species?" *Christian Century* 94, January 26, 1977, 61–63; and Mark Miller, "Native American Peoples on the Trail of Tears Once More: Indian Health Service and Coerced Sterilization," *America* 139 (1978): 422–25.

19. R. Bogue and D. W. Segelman, "Survey Finds Seven in 10 Hospitals Violate DHEW Guidelines on Informed Consent for Sterilization," *Family Planning Perspectives* 11:6 (1979): 366–67.

20. Miller, "Native American Peoples on the Trail of Tears," 424.

21. Charles R. England, "A Look at the Indian Health Service Policy of Sterilization, 1972–1976," *Native American Homepage,* October 10, 1997, 6. For a fuller discussion of this topic, see Myla F. Thyrza Carpio, "Lost Generation: The Involuntary Sterilization of American Indian Women" (master's thesis, Johns Hopkins, 1991).

22. Green, "Review Essay," 261.

23. Connie Uri, quoted in Miller, "Native American Peoples on the Trail of Tears," 423.

24. Barbara Moore quoted in Fee Podarski, "An Interview with Barbara Moore on Sterilization," *Akwesasne Notes* 11:2 (1979): 11–12.

25. Barbara Moore, quoted in Podarski, "An Interview with Barbara Moore," 11.

26. Indian status is another aspect of the eradication of Native populations. Both in Canada and the United States, entire tribes have lost their status as "Indian" or "Native" and are identified instead as "colored." For an example in early-twentieth-century Virginia see J. David Smith, *The Eugenic Assault on America: Scenes in Red, White, and Black* (Fairfax, Va.: George Mason University Press, 1993); and for a more recent example pertaining to the Tobique in Canada, see Tobique Women's Group, *Enough is Enough: Aboriginal Women Speak Out,* as told to Janet Silman, (Toronto: The Women's Press, 1987).

27. Linda Gordon, "Why Nineteenth-Century Feminists Did Not Support 'Birth Control' and Twentieth-Century Feminists Do: Feminism, Reproduction, and the Family," in *Rethinking the Family: Some Feminist Questions,* ed. Barrie Thorne and Marilyn Yalom (Boston: Northeastern University Press, 1992), 149.

28. Linda Gordon, *Woman's Body, Woman's Right: A Social History of Birth Control in America* (New York: Grossman Publishers, 1976), 281.

29. Gordon, "Why Nineteenth-Century Feminists Did Not Support 'Birth Control,'" 150.

30. Mary Brave Bird and Richard Erdoes, *Ohitika Woman* (New York: Harper-Perennial, 1993), 58.

31. Green, "American Indian Women," 65.

32. Green, "American Indian Women," 66.

33. Green, "American Indian Women," 63, 64, 71.

34. Ironically, early feminists and advocates of "voluntary motherhood" proposed an agenda similar to Native women's. Both saw voluntary motherhood as part of a movement to empower women (Gordon, "Why Nineteenth-Century Feminists Did Not Support 'Birth Control,'" 145). Suffragists' desire to exalt motherhood was a way of creating a dignified, powerful position for women in contrast to popular notions of womanhood that connoted fragility and virtue. By evoking a powerful model, women responded to their sexual subjugation to men and created an alternate arena where they had authority (Gordon, *Woman's Body,* 133–34).

35. Ann Snitow, "A Gender Diary," in *Conflicts in Feminism,* ed. Mariann Hirsch and Evelyn Fox Keller (New York: Routledge, 1990), 20.

36. Snitow, "A Gender Diary," 20.

37. Snitow, "A Gender Diary," 22.

38. Quotation from in Bassin, Honey, and Kaplan, *Representations of Motherhood,* 5. See, for example, Jessica Benjamin, "Authority and the Family Revisted: Or, A World Without Fathers," *New German Critique* 4:3 (1978): 35–57; Nancy Chodorow, "Family Structure and Feminine Personality," in *Women, Culture, and Society,* ed. Michelle Zimbalist Rosaldo and Louise Lamphere (Stanford: Stanford University Press, 1974), 43–66; and Jean Bethke Elshtain, *Public Man, Private Woman: Women in Social and Political Thought* (Princeton: Princeton University Press, 1981).

39. For more detailed critiques of the limitations of dualistic separation of private and public sectors for gender analysis generally, see Susan Himmelweit, "The Real Dualism of Sex and Class," *Review of Radical Political Economics* 16:1 (1984): 167–83. For Native women more particularly, see Patricia Albers, "Sioux Women in Transition: A Study of Their Changing Status in a Domestic and Capitalist Sector of Production," in *The Hidden Half: Studies of Plains Indian Women,* ed. Patricia Albers and Beatrice Medicine (Latham, Md. University Press of America, 1983), and Albers, "Autonomy and Dependency in the Lives of Dakota Women: A Study in Historical Change," *Review of Radical Political Economics* 17:3 (1985): 109–34.

40. Evelyn Nakano Glenn, "Racial Ethnic Women's Labor: The Intersection of Race, Gender and Class Oppression," *Review of Radical Political Economics* 17:3 (1985): 101; Patricia Hill Collins, "Shifting the Center"; and Bonnie Thornton Dill, "Our Mothers' Grief: Racial Ethnic Women and the Maintenance of Families," *Journal of Family History* 13:4 (1988): 415–31, use the term "reproductive labor" to refer to all of the work of women in the home. Dill describes reproductive labor to include "the buying and preparation of food and clothing, provision of emotional support and nurturance for all family members, bearing children, and planning, organizing, and carrying out a wide variety of tasks associated with the socialization" ("Our Mothers' Grief," 430).

I adopt Patricia Hill Collins's use of the term "motherwork," which she employs to "soften the dichotomies in feminist theorizing about motherhood that posit rigid distinctions between private and public, family and work, the individual and the collective, identity as individual autonomy and identity growing from the collective self-determination of one's group. Racial ethnic women's mothering and work experiences occur at the boundaries demarking these dualities" ("Shifting the Center," 59).

41. Glenn, "Racial Ethnic Women's Labor," 102, 103. Several recent studies of modern Native household units find that women often head extended families and kinship networks that resist capitalist models that marginalize them. See Albers, "Autonomy and Dependency in the Lives of Dakota Women," "From Illusion to Illumination: Anthropological Studies of American Indian Women," in *Gender and Anthropology. Critical Reviews for Research and Teaching,* ed. Sandra Morgan (Washington, D.C. American Anthropological Association, 1989), and "Sioux Women in Transition"; Martha C. Knack, *Life is With People: Household Organization of the Contemporary Southern Paiute Indians* (Socorro, N. Mex.: Ballena Press, 1980); and Loraine Littlefield, "Gender, Class and Community: The History of Sne-Nay-Muxw Women's Employment" (Ph.D. diss., University of British Columbia, 1995).

42. Collins, "Shifting the Center," 58. Obviously, personal ambition is usually seen as selfish and suspect for women generally. Women have typically couched descriptions of their ambitions in terms of altruism and collective responsibility. My point here, however, is that leadership within Native paradigms embraces collective more than individual identity.

43. Collins, "Shifting the Center," 61, 62.

44. Glenn, "Racial Ethnic Women's Labor," 103–4. The high rate of single, female-headed households undermines Glenn conclusions somewhat. As seen in Wall's *Wisdom's Daughters,* for example, contemporary Native women may not "require" the income of Native men to survive at the subsistence level; however, they argue that women require men's economic contribution to live well, or above subsistence/poverty level. More important, Native women argue, they require men's social and cultural participation in tribal life in order to ensure survival of specific collective experiences and to perpetuate their traditions.

45. Christine Conte, "Ladies, Livestock, and Land and Lucre: Women's Networks and Social Status on the Western Navajo Reservation," *American Indian Quarterly* 6:1/2 (1982): 105, 116.

46. For example, Wall, *Wisdom's Daughters,* 169–70, 224–26.

47. Marlee Kline, cited in Monture-Angus, *Thunder in My Soul,* 42.

48. Not all Native women experience capitalism equally. Conte's study shows that while most Navajo women have been adversely affected by the forces of a market economy, several are able to manipulate elements of capitalism to benefit themselves and their households, while others experience diminished wealth ("Ladies, Livestock, and Land and Lucre," 120). Albers draws similar conclusions from her research on the Devil's Lake Sioux, particularly in "Autonomy and Dependency in the Lives of Dakota Women," 124–28.

49. Collins, "Shifting the Center," 65.

50. Angela Davis, quoted by Collins in "Shifting the Center," 65.

51. Collins, "Shifting the Center," 65.

52. Collins, "Shifting the Center," 66.

53. Collins, "Shifting the Center," 68.

54. See the proceedings from the United Nations Fourth World Conference on Women, Mothers of Our Nations, *Indigenous Women Address the World: Our Future—Our Responsibility* (Rapid City, S.Dak., 1995).

55. Mankiller and Wallis, *Mankiller,* 20.

56. Beatrice Medicine, "The Hidden Half Lives," in *Cante Ohitika Win (Brave-Hearted Women): Images of Lakota Women From the Pine Ridge Reservation South Dakota,* ed. Caroline Reyer (Vermillion: University of South Dakota Press, 1991), 5; and Albers and Medicine, *The Hidden Half,* 134–35. Nonetheless, Albers and Medicine contend that in contemporary life, star quilts remain one of the most prestigious items in the Sioux give-away system. Quilts are displayed or given at honoring ceremonies and when "Sioux return home from military service or college," at community events of importance such as memorial feasts and naming ceremonies, and during "donations of powwow officials" (Patricia Albers and Beatrice Medicine, "The Role of Sioux Women in the Production of Ceremonial Objects: The Case of the Star Quilt").

57. Allen, "Interview," in Perry, *Backtalk,* 10.

58. Monture-Angus, *Thunder in My Soul,* 244.

59. Monture-Angus, *Thunder in My Soul,* 258.

60. Monture-Angus, *Thunder in My Soul,* 28.

61. Renee Senogles, quoted in Farley, *Women of the Native Struggle,* 69.

62. Osennontion (Marlyn Kane) and Skonaganleh:rá (Sylvia Maracle), "Our World: According to Osennontion and Skonaganleh:rá," *Canadian Woman Studies/Les Cahiers de la Femme* 10:2/3 (1989): 7–19, 11.

63. Medicine, "Hidden Half Lives," 5; and Lindy Trueblood, "Interview," in Reyer, *Cante Ohitika Win,* 50.

64. Kidwell, "What Would Pocahontas Think Now?" 150.

65. Trueblood, "Interview," in Reyer, *Cante Ohitika Win,* 50.

66. Ford, "Native American Women," 59.

67. In Canada the 1986 average income for Aboriginal people was $12,899 compared to $18,188 earned by the average non-Native Canadian. The 1990 U.S. census reported the median household income of Indians living on a reservation was $19,865, compared with the U.S. median of $30,056. Thirty-five percent of U.S. Natives live below the federal poverty level (Jo Ann Kauffman and Yvette K. Joseph-Fox, "American Indian and Alaska Native Women," in *Race, Gender, and Health,* ed. Marcia Bayne-Smith [Thousand Oaks, Calif.: Sage Publications, 1996], 71).

68. Osennontion and Skonaganleh:rá, "Our World," 14.

69. Katz, *Messengers of the Wind;* and Wall, *Wisdom's Daughters.*

70. Osennontion and Skonaganleh:rá, "Our World," 14.

28

"I'm Here, but I'm There"

The Meanings of Latina Transnational Motherhood

PIERRETTE HONDAGNEU-SOTELO

ERNESTINE AVILA

While mothering is generally understood as a practice that involves the preservation, nurturance, and training of children for adult life (Ruddick 1989), there are many contemporary variants distinguished by race, class, and culture (Collins 1994; Dill 1988, 1994; Glenn 1994). Latina immigrant women who work and reside in the United States while their children remain in their countries of origin constitute one variation in the organizational arrangements, meanings, and priorities of motherhood. We call this arrangement "transnational motherhood," and we explore how the meanings of motherhood are rearranged to accommodate these spatial and temporal separations. In the United States, there is a long legacy of Caribbean women and African American women from the South, leaving their children "back home" to seek work in the North. Since the early 1980s, thousands of Central American women, and increasing numbers of Mexican women, have migrated to the United States in search of jobs, many of them leaving their children behind with grandmothers, with other female kin, with the children's fathers, and sometimes with paid caregivers. In some cases, the separations of time and distance are substantial; 10 years may elapse before women are reunited with their children. In this article we confine our analysis to Latina transnational mothers currently employed in Los Angeles in paid domestic work, one of the most gendered and racialized occupations.[1] We examine how their meanings of motherhood shift in relation to the structures of late-20th-century global capitalism.

Motherhood is not biologically predetermined in any fixed way but is historically and socially constructed. Many factors set the stage for transnational motherhood. These factors include labor demand for Latina immigrant women in the United States, particularly in paid domestic work; civil war, national economic crises, and particular development strategies, along with tenuous and scarce job opportunities for women and men in

Mexico and Central America; and the subsequent in-creasing numbers of female-headed households (al-though many transnational mothers are married). More interesting to us than the macro determinants of transna-tional motherhood, however, is the forging of new arrangements and meanings of motherhood.

Central American and Mexican women who leave their young children "back home" and come to the United States in search of employment are in the process of actively, if not voluntarily, building alter-native constructions of motherhood. Transnational motherhood contradicts both dominant U.S., White, middle-class models of motherhood, and most Latina ideological notions of motherhood. On the cusp of the millennium, transnational mothers and their families are blazing new terrain, spanning national borders, and improvising strategies for mothering. It is a brave odyssey, but one with deep costs. . . .

RETHINKING MOTHERHOOD

Feminist scholarship has long challenged monolithic notions of family and motherhood that relegate women to the domestic arena of private/public dichotomies and that rely on the ideological conflation of family, woman, reproduction, and nurturance (Collier and Yanagisako 1987, 36).[2] "Rethinking the family" prompts the rethinking of motherhood (Glenn 1994; Thorne and Yalom 1992), allowing us to see that the glorification and exaltation of isolationist, privatized mothering is historically and culturally specific.

The "cult of domesticity" is a cultural variant of motherhood, one made possible by the industrial revo-lution, by breadwinner husbands who have access to employers who pay a "family wage," and by particular configurations of global and national socioeconomic and racial inequalities. Working-class women of color in the United States have rarely had access to the eco-nomic security that permits a biological mother to be the only one exclusively involved with mothering dur-ing the children's early years (Collins 1994; Dill 1988, 1994; Glenn 1994). As Evelyn Nakano Glenn puts it, "Mothering is not just gendered, but also racialized" (1994, 7) and differentiated by class. Both historically and in the contemporary period, women lacking the

resources that allow for exclusive, full-time, round-the-clock mothering rely on various arrangements to care for children. Sharing mothering responsibilities with female kin and friends as "other mothers" (Collins 1991), by "kin-scription" (Stack and Burton 1994), or by hiring child care (Uttal 1996) are widely used alternatives.

Women of color have always worked. Yet, many working women—including Latina women—hold the cultural prescription of solo mothering in the home as an ideal. We believe this ideal is disseminated through cul-tural institutions of industrialization and urbanization, as well as from preindustrial, rural peasant arrangements that allow for women to work while tending to their chil-dren. It is not only White, middle-class ideology but also strong Latina/o traditions, cultural practices, and ideals—Catholicism, and the Virgin Madonna figure—that cast employment as oppositional to mothering. Cul-tural symbols that model maternal femininity, such as *La Virgen de Guadalupe,* and negative femininity, such as *La Llorona* and *La Malinche,* serve to control Mexican and Chicana women's conduct by prescribing idealized visions of motherhood.[3]

Culture, however, does not deterministically dictate what people do.[4] Many Latina women must work for pay, and many Latinas innovate income-earning strate-gies that allow them to simultaneously earn money and care for their children. They sew garments on indus-trial sewing machines at home (Fernández Kelly and Garcia 1990) and incorporate their children into infor-mal vending to friends and neighbors, at swap meets, or on the sidewalks (Chinchilla and Hamilton 1996). They may perform agricultural work alongside their children or engage in seasonal work (Zavella 1987); or they may clean houses when their children are at school or alternatively, incorporate their daughters into paid house cleaning (Romero 1992, 1997). Engage-ment in "invisible employment" allows for urgently needed income and the maintenance of the ideal of pri-vatized mothering. The middle-class model of mother-ing is predicated on mother-child isolation in the home, while women of color have often worked with their children in close proximity (Collins 1994), as in some of the examples listed above. In both cases, how-ever, mothers are with their children. The long dis-tances of time and space that separate transnational mothers from their children contrast sharply to both mother-child isolation in the home or mother-child integration in the workplace.

Performing domestic work for pay, especially in a live-in job, is often incompatible with providing primary care for one's own family and home (Glenn 1986; Rollins 1985; Romero 1992, 1997).[5] Transnational mothering, however, is neither exclusive to live-in domestic workers nor to single mothers. Many women continue with transnational mothering after they move into live-out paid domestic work, or into other jobs. Women with income-earning husbands may also become transnational mothers.[6] The women we interviewed do not necessarily divert their mothering to the children and homes of their employers but instead reformulate their own mothering to accommodate spatial and temporal gulfs.

Like other immigrant workers, most transnational mothers came to the United States with the intention to stay for a finite period of time. But as time passes and economic need remains, prolonged stays evolve. Marxist-informed theory maintains that the separation of work life and family life constitutes the separation of labor maintenance costs from the labor reproduction costs (Burawoy 1976; Glenn 1986). According to this framework, Latina transnational mothers work to maintain themselves in the United States and to support their children—and reproduce the next generation of workers—in Mexico or Central America. One precursor to these arrangements is the mid-20th-century Bracero Program, which in effect legislatively mandated Mexican "absentee fathers" who came to work as contracted agricultural laborers in the United States. Other precursors, going back further in history, include the 18th- and 19th-centuries' coercive systems of labor, whereby African American slaves and Chinese sojourner laborers were denied the right to form residentially intact families (Dill 1988, 1994).

Transnational mothering is different from some of these other arrangements in that now women with young children are recruited for U.S. jobs that pay far less than a "family wage." When men come north and leave their families in Mexico—as they did during the Bracero Program and as many continue to do today— they are fulfilling familial obligations defined as breadwinning for the family. When women do so, they are embarking not only on an immigration journey but on a more radical gender-transformative odyssey. They are initiating separations of space and time from their communities of origin, homes, children, and—sometimes—husbands. In doing so, they must cope with stigma, guilt, and criticism from others. A second difference is that these women work primarily not in production of agricultural products or manufacturing but in reproductive labor, in paid domestic work, and/or vending. Performing paid reproductive work for pay— especially caring for other people's children—is not always compatible with taking daily care of one's own family. All of this raises questions about the meanings and variations of motherhood in the late 20th century.

TRANSNATIONAL MOTHERHOOD AND PAID DOMESTIC WORK

Just how widespread are transnational motherhood arrangements in paid domestic work? Of the 153 domestic workers surveyed, 75 percent had children. Contrary to the images of Latina immigrant women as breeders with large families—a dominant image used in the campaign to pass California's Proposition 187— about half (47 percent) of these women have only one or two children. More significant for our purposes is this finding: Forty percent of the women with children have at least one of their children "back home" in their country of origin.

Transnational motherhood arrangements are not exclusive to paid domestic work, but there are particular features about the way domestic work is organized that encourage temporal and spatial separations of a mother-employee and her children. Historically and in the contemporary period, paid domestic workers have had to limit or forfeit primary care of their families and homes to earn income by providing primary care to the families and homes of employers, who are privileged by race and class (Glenn 1986; Rollins 1985; Romero 1992). Paid domestic work is organized in various ways, and there is a clear relationship between the type of job arrangement women have and the likelihood of experiencing transnational family arrangements with their children. To understand the variations, it is necessary to explain how the employment is organized. Although there are variations within categories, we find it useful to employ a tripartite taxonomy of paid domestic work arrangements. This includes live-in and live-out nanny-housekeeper jobs and weekly housecleaning jobs.

Weekly house cleaners clean different houses on different days according to what Romero (1992) calls modernized "job work" arrangements. These contractual-like employee-employer relations often resemble those between customer and vendor, and they allow employees a degree of autonomy and scheduling flexibility. Weekly employees are generally paid a flat fee, and they work shorter hours and earn considerably higher hourly rates than do live-in or live-out domestic workers. By contrast, live-in domestic workers work and live in isolation from their own families and communities, sometimes in arrangements with feudal remnants (Glenn 1986). There are often no hourly parameters to their jobs, and as our survey results show, most live-in workers in Los Angeles earn below minimum wage. Live-out domestic workers also usually work as combination nanny-housekeepers, generally working for one household, but contrary to live-ins, they enter daily and return to their own home in the evening. Because of this, live-out workers better resemble industrial wage workers (Glenn 1986).

Live-in jobs are the least compatible with conventional mothering responsibilities. Only about half (16 out of 30) of live-ins surveyed have children, while 83 percent (53 out of 64) of live-outs and 77 percent (45 out of 59) of house cleaners do. As Table 1 shows, 82 percent of live-ins with children have at least one of their children in their country of origin. It is very difficult to work a live-in job when your children are in the United States. Employers who hire live-in workers do so because they generally want employees for jobs that may require round-the-clock service. As one owner of a domestic employment agency put it,

> They (employers) want a live-in to have somebody at their beck and call. They want the hours that are most difficult for them covered, which is like six thirty in the morning 'till eight when the kids go to school, and four to seven when the kids are home, and it's homework, bath, and dinner.

According to our survey, live-ins work an average of 64 hours per week. The best live-in worker, from an employer's perspective, is one without daily family obligations of her own. The workweek may consist of six very long workdays. These may span from dawn to midnight and may include overnight responsibilities with sleepless or sick children, making it virtually impossible for live-in workers to sustain daily contact with their own families. Although some employers do allow for their employees' children to live in as well (Romero 1996), this is rare. When it does occur, it is often fraught with special problems, and we discuss these in a subsequent section of this article. In fact, minimal family and mothering obligations are an informal job placement criterion for live-in workers. Many of the agencies specializing in the placement of live-in nanny-housekeepers will not even refer a woman who has children in Los Angeles to interviews for live-in jobs. As one agency owner explained, "As a policy here, we will not knowingly place a nanny in a live-in job if she has young kids here." A job seeker in an employment agency waiting room acknowledged that she understood this job criterion more broadly, "You can't have a family, you can't have anyone (if you want a live-in job)."

Table 1 Domestic Workers: Wages, Hours Worked and Children's Country of Residence

	Live-ins (n = 30)	Live-outs (n = 64)	House cleaners (n = 59)
Mean hourly wage	$3.79	$5.90	$9.40
Mean hours worked per week	64	35	23
Domestic workers with children	(n = 16)	(n = 53)	(n = 45)
All children in the United States (%)	18	58	76
At least one child "back home"	82	42	24

The subminimum pay and the long hours for live-in workers also make it very difficult for these workers to have their children in the United States. Some live-in workers who have children in the same city as their place of employment hire their own nanny-housekeeper—often a much younger, female relative—to provide daily care for their children, as did Patricia, one of the interview respondents whom we discuss later in this article. Most live-ins, however, cannot afford this alternative; ninety-three percent of the live-ins surveyed earn below minimum wage (then $4.25 per hour). Many live-in workers cannot afford to bring their children to Los Angeles, but once their children are in the same city, most women try to leave live-in work to live with their children.

At the other end of the spectrum are the house cleaners that we surveyed, who earn substantially higher wages than live-ins (averaging $9.46 per hour as opposed to $3.79) and who work fewer hours per week than live-ins (23 as opposed to 64). We suspect that many house cleaners in Los Angeles make even higher earnings and work more hours per week, because we know that the survey undersampled women who drive their own cars to work and who speak English. The survey suggests that house cleaners appear to be the least likely to experience transnational spatial and temporal separations from their children.

Financial resources and job terms enhance house cleaners' abilities to bring their children to the United States. Weekly housecleaning is not a bottom-of-the-barrel job but rather an achievement. Breaking into housecleaning work is difficult because an employee needs to locate and secure several different employers. For this reason, relatively well-established women with more years of experience in the United States, who speak some English, who have a car, and who have job references predominate in weekly housecleaning. Women who are better established in the United States are also more likely to have their children here. The terms of weekly housecleaning employment—particularly the relatively fewer hours worked per week, scheduling flexibility, and relatively higher wages—allow them to live with, and care for, their children. So, it is not surprising that 76 percent of house cleaners who are mothers have their children in the United States.

Compared with live-ins and weekly cleaners, live-out nanny-housekeepers are at an intermediate level with respect to the likelihood of transnational motherhood. Forty-two percent of the live-out nanny-housekeepers who are mothers reported having at least one of their children in their country of origin. Live-out domestic workers, according to the survey, earn $5.90 per hour and work an average workweek of 35 hours. Their lower earnings, more regimented schedules, and longer workweeks than house cleaners, but higher earnings, shorter hours, and more scheduling flexibility than live-ins explain their intermediate incidence of transnational motherhood.

The Meanings of Transnational Motherhood

How do women transform the meaning of motherhood to fit immigration and employment? Being a transnational mother means more than being the mother to children raised in another country. It means forsaking deeply felt beliefs that biological mothers should raise their own children, and replacing that belief with new definitions of motherhood. The ideal of biological mothers raising their own children is widely held but is also widely broken at both ends of the class spectrum. Wealthy elites have always relied on others—nannies, governesses, and boarding schools—to raise their children (Wrigley 1995), while poor, urban families often rely on kin and "other mothers" (Collins 1991).

In Latin America, in large, peasant families, the eldest daughters are often in charge of the daily care of the younger children, and in situations of extreme poverty, children as young as five or six may be loaned or hired out to well-to-do families as "child-servants," sometimes called *criadas* (Gill 1994).[7] A middle-aged Mexican woman that we interviewed, now a weekly house cleaner, homeowner, and mother of five children, recalled her own experience as a child-servant in Mexico: "I started working in a house when I was 8 . . . they hardly let me eat any food. . . . It was terrible, but I had to work to help my mother with the rent." This recollection of her childhood experiences reminds us how our contemporary notions of motherhood are historically and socially circumscribed, and also correspond to the meanings we assign to childhood (Zelizer 1994).

This example also underlines how the expectation on the child to help financially support her mother required daily spatial and temporal separations of mother and child. There are, in fact, many transgressions of the mother-child symbiosis in practice—large families where older daughters care for younger siblings, child-servants who at an early age leave their mothers, children raised by paid nannies and other caregivers, and mothers who leave young children to seek employment—but these are fluid enough to sustain ideological adherence to the prescription that children should be raised exclusively by biological mothers. Long-term physical and temporal separation disrupts this notion. Transnational mothering radically rearranges mother-child interactions and requires a concomitant radical reshaping of the meanings and definitions of appropriate mothering.

Transnational mothers distinguish their version of motherhood from estrangement, child abandonment, or disowning. A youthful Salvadoran woman at the domestic employment waiting room reported that she had not seen her two eldest boys, now ages 14 and 15 and under the care of her own mother in El Salvador, since they were toddlers. Yet, she made it clear that this was different from putting a child up for adoption, a practice that she viewed negatively, as a form of child abandonment. Although she had been physically separated from her boys for more than a decade, she maintained her mothering ties and financial obligations to them by regularly sending home money. The exchange of letters, photos, and phone calls also helped to sustain the connection. Her physical absence did not signify emotional absence from her children. Another woman who remains intimately involved in the lives of her two daughters, now ages 17 and 21 in El Salvador, succinctly summed up this stance when she said, "I'm here, but I'm there." Over the phone, and through letters, she regularly reminds her daughters to take their vitamins, to never go to bed or to school on an empty stomach, and to use protection from pregnancy and sexually transmitted diseases if they engage in sexual relations with their boyfriends.

Transnational mothers fully understand and explain the conditions that prompt their situations. In particular, many Central American women recognize that the gendered employment demand in Los Angeles has produced transnational motherhood arrangements. These new mothering arrangements, they acknowledge, take shape despite strong beliefs that biological mothers should care for their own children. Emelia, a 49-year-old woman who left her five children in Guatemala nine years ago to join her husband in Los Angeles explained this changing relationship between family arrangements, migration, and job demand:

> One supposes that the mother must care for the children. A mother cannot so easily throw her children aside. So, in all families, the decision is that the man comes (to the U.S.) first. But now, since the man cannot find work here so easily, the woman comes first. Recently, women have been coming and the men staying.

A steady demand for live-in housekeepers means that Central American women may arrive in Los Angeles on a Friday and begin working Monday at a live-in job that provides at least some minimal accommodations. Meanwhile, her male counter-part may spend weeks or months before securing even casual day laborer jobs. While Emelia, formerly a homemaker who previously earned income in Guatemala by baking cakes and pastries in her home, expressed pain and sadness at not being with her children as they grew, she was also proud of her accomplishments. "My children," she stated, "recognize what I have been able to do for them."

Most transnational mothers, like many other immigrant workers, come to the United States with the intention to stay for a finite period of time, until they can pay off bills or raise the money for an investment in a house, their children's education, or a small business. Some of these women return to their countries of origin, but many stay. As time passes, and as their stays grow longer, some of the women eventually bring some or all of their children. Other women who stay at their U.S. jobs are adamant that they do not wish for their children to traverse the multiple hazards of adolescence in U.S. cities or to repeat the job experiences they themselves have had in the United States. One Salvadoran woman in the waiting room at the domestic employment agency—whose children had been raised on earnings predicated on her separation from them—put it this way:

I've been here 19 years, I've got my legal papers and everything. But I'd have to be crazy to bring my children here. All of them have studied for a career, so why would I bring them here? To bus tables and earn minimum wage? So they won't have enough money for bus fare or food?

Who Is Taking Care of the Nanny's Children?

Transnational Central American and Mexican mothers may rely on various people to care for their children's daily, round-the-clock needs, but they prefer a close relative. The "other mothers" on which Latinas rely include their own mothers, *comadres* (co-godmothers) and other female kin, the children's fathers, and paid caregivers. Reliance on grandmothers and *comadres* for shared mothering is well established in Latina culture, and it is a practice that signifies a more collectivist, shared approach to mothering in contrast to a more individualistic, Anglo-American approach (Griswold del Castillo 1984; Segura and Pierce 1993). Perhaps this cultural legacy facilitates the emergence of transnational motherhood.

Transnational mothers express a strong preference for their own biological mother to serve as the primary caregiver. Here, the violation of the cultural preference for the biological mother is rehabilitated by reliance on the biological grandmother or by reliance on the ceremonially bound *comadres*. Clemencia, for example, left her three young children behind in Mexico, each with their respective *madrina,* or godmother.

Emelia left her five children, then ranging in ages from 6 to 16, under the care of her mother and sister in Guatemala. As she spoke of the hardships faced by transnational mothers, she counted herself among the fortunate ones who did not need to leave the children alone with paid caregivers:

One's mother is the only one who can really and truly care for your children. No one else can. . . . Women who aren't able to leave their children with their mother or with someone very special, they'll wire money to Guatemala and the people (caregivers) don't feed the children well. They don't buy the children clothes the mother would want. They take the money and the children suffer a lot.

Both Central American and Mexican woman stated preferences for grandmothers as the ideal caregivers in situations that mandated the absence of the children's biological mother. These preferences seem to grow out of strategic availability, but these preferences assume cultural mandates. Velia, a Mexicana who hailed from the border town of Mexicali, improvised an employment strategy whereby she annually sent her three elementary school-age children to her mother in Mexicali for the summer vacation months. This allowed Velia, a single mother, to intensify her housecleaning jobs and save money on day care. But she also insisted that "if my children were with the woman next door (who babysits), I'd worry if they were eating well, or about men (coming to harass the girls). Having them with my mother allows me to work in peace." Another woman specified more narrowly, insisting that only maternal grandmothers could provide adequate caregiving. In a conversation in a park, a Salvadoran woman offered that a biological mother's mother was the one best suited to truly love and care for a child in the biological mother's absence. According to her, not even the paternal grandmother could be trusted to provide proper nurturance and care. Another Salvadoran woman, Maria, left her two daughters, then 14 and 17, at their paternal grandmother's home, but before departing for the United States, she trained her daughters to become self-sufficient in cooking, marketing, and budgeting money. Although she believes the paternal grandmother loves the girls, she did not trust the paternal grandmother enough to cook or administer the money that she would send her daughters.

Another variation in the preference for a biological relative as a caregiver is captured by the arrangement of Patricia, a 30-year-old Mexicana who came to the United States as a child and was working as a live-in, caring for an infant in one of southern California's affluent coastal residential areas. Her arrangement was different, as her daughters were all born, raised, and residing in the United States, but she lived apart from them during weekdays because of her live-in job. Her three daughters, ages 1 1/2, 6, and 11, stayed at their apartment near downtown Los Angeles under the care of their father and a paid nanny-housekeeper, Patricia's teenage cousin. Her paid caregiver was not an especially close relative, but she rationalized this arrangement by emphasizing that her husband, the girls' father, and therefore a biological relative, was with them during the week.

> Whenever I've worked like this, I've always had a person in charge of them also working as a live-in. She sleeps here the five days, but when my husband arrives he takes responsibility for them . . . When my husband arrives (from work) she (cousin/paid caregiver) goes to English class and he takes charge of the girls.

And another woman who did not have children of her own but who had worked as a nanny for her aunt stated that "as Hispanas, we don't believe bringing someone else in to care for our children." Again, the biological ties help sanction the shared child care arrangement.

New family fissures emerge for the transnational mother as she negotiates various aspects of the arrangement with her children, and with the "other mother" who provides daily care and supervision for the children. Any impulse to romanticize transnational motherhood is tempered by the sadness with which the women related their experiences and by the problems they sometimes encounter with their children and caregivers. A primary worry among transnational mothers is that their children are being neglected or abused in their absence. While there is a long legacy of child-servants being mistreated and physically beaten in Latin America, transnational mothers also worry that their own paid caregivers will harm or neglect their children. They worry that their children may not receive proper nourishment, schooling and educational support, and moral guidance. They may remain unsure as to whether their children are receiving the full financial support they send home. In some cases, their concerns are intensified by the eldest child or a nearby relative who is able to monitor and report the caregiver's transgression to the transnational mother.

Transnational mothers engage in emotion work and financial compensation to maintain a smoothly functioning relationship with the children's daily caregiver. Their efforts are not always successful, and when problems arise, they may return to visit if they can afford to do so. After not seeing her four children for seven years, Carolina abruptly quit her nanny job and returned to Guatemala in the spring of 1996 because she was concerned about one adolescent daughter's rebelliousness and about her mother-in-law's failing health. Carolina's husband remained in Los Angeles, and she was expected to return. Emelia, whose children were cared for by her mother and sister with the assistance of paid caregivers, regularly responded to her sister's reminders to send gifts, clothing, and small amounts of money to the paid caregivers. "If they are taking care of my children," she explained, "then I have to show my gratitude."

Some of these actions are instrumental. Transnational mothers know that they may increase the likelihood of their children receiving adequate care if they appropriately remunerate the caregivers and treat them with the consideration their work requires. In fact, they often express astonishment that their own Anglo employers fail to recognize this in relation to the nanny-housekeeper work that they perform. Some of the expressions of gratitude and gifts that they send to their children's caregivers appear to be genuinely disinterested and enhanced by the transnational mothers' empathy arising out of their own similar job circumstances. A Honduran woman, a former biology teacher, who had left her four sons with a paid caregiver, maintained that the treatment of nannies and housekeepers was much better in Honduras than in the United States, in part, because of different approaches to mothering:

> We're very different back there . . . We treat them (domestic workers) with a lot of affection and respect, and when they are taking care of our kids, even more so. The Americana, she is very egotistical. When the nanny loves her children, she gets jealous. Not us. We are appreciative when someone loves our children, and bathes, dresses, and feeds them as though they were their own.

These comments are clearly informed by the respondent's prior class status, as well as her simultaneous position as the employer of a paid nanny-housekeeper in Honduras and as a temporarily unemployed nanny-housekeeper in the United States. (She had been fired from her nanny-housekeeper job for not showing up on Memorial Day, which she erroneously believed was a work holiday.) Still, her comments underline the importance of showing appreciation and gratitude to the caregiver, in part, for the sake of the children's well-being.

Transnational mothers also worry about whether their children will get into trouble during adolescence or if they will transfer their allegiance and affection to the "other mother." In general, transnational mothers, like African American mothers who leave their children in the South to work up North (Stack and Burton 1994), believe that the person who cares for the children has the right to discipline. But when adolescent youths are paired with elderly grandmothers, or ineffective disciplinary figures, the mothers may need to intervene. Preadolescent and adolescent children who show signs of rebelliousness may be brought north because they are deemed unmanageable by their grandmothers or paid caregivers. Alternatively, teens who are in California may be sent back in hope that it will straighten them out, a practice that has resulted in the migration of Los Angeles–based delinquent youth gangs to Mexican and Central American towns. Another danger is that the child who has grown up without the transnational mother's presence may no longer respond to her authority. One woman at the domestic employment agency, who had recently brought her adolescent son to join her in California, reported that she had seen him at a bus stop, headed for the beach. When she demanded to know where he was going, he said something to the effect of "and who are you to tell me what to do?" After a verbal confrontation at the bus kiosk, she handed him $10. Perhaps the mother hoped that money will be a way to show caring and to advance a claim to parental authority.

Motherhood and Breadwinning

Milk, shoes, and schooling—these are the currency of transnational motherhood. Providing for children's sustenance, protecting their current well-being, and preparing them for the future are widely shared concerns of motherhood. Central American and Mexican women involved in transnational mothering attempt to ensure the present and future well-being of their children through U.S. wage earning, and as we have seen, this requires long-term physical separation from their children.

For these women, the meanings of motherhood do not appear to be in a liminal stage. That is, they do not appear to be making a linear progression from a way of motherhood that involves daily, face-to-face caregiving toward one that is defined primarily through breadwinning. Rather than replacing caregiving with breadwinning definitions of motherhood, they appear to be expanding their definitions of motherhood to encompass breadwinning that may require long-term physical separations. For these women, a core belief is that they can best fulfill traditional caregiving responsibilities through income earning in the United States while their children remain "back home."

Transnational mothers continue to state that caregiving is a defining feature of their mothering experiences. They wish to provide their children with better nutrition, clothing, and schooling, and most of them are able to purchase these items with dollars earned in the United States. They recognize, however, that their transnational relationships incur painful costs. Transnational mothers worry about some of the negative effects on their children, but they also experience the absence of domestic family life as a deeply personal loss. Transnational mothers who primarily identified as homemakers before coming to the United States identified the loss of daily contact with family as a sacrifice ventured to financially support the children. As Emelia, who had previously earned some income by baking pastries and doing catering from her home in Guatemala, reflected,

> The money (earned in the U.S.) is worth five times more in Guatemala. My oldest daughter was then 16, and my youngest was 6 (when I left). Ay, it's terrible, terrible, but that's what happens to most women (transnational mothers) who are here. You sacrifice your family life (for labor migration).

Similarly, Carolina used the word *sacrifice* when discussing her family arrangement, claiming that her children "tell me that they appreciate us (parents), and the sacrifice that their papa and mama make for them. That is what they say."

The daily indignities of paid domestic work—low pay, subtle humiliations, not enough food to eat, invisibility (Glenn 1986; Rollins 1985; Romero 1992)—

means that transnational mothers are not only stretching their U.S.-earned dollars further by sending the money back home but also by leaving the children behind, they are providing special protection from the discrimination the children might receive in the United States. Gladys, who had four of her five children in El Salvador, acknowledged that her U.S. dollars went further in El Salvador. Although she missed seeing those four children grow up, she felt that in some ways, she had spared them the indignities to which she had exposed her youngest daughter, whom she brought to the United States at age 4 in 1988. Although her live-in employer had allowed the four-year-old to join the family residence, Gladys tearfully recalled how that employer had initially quarantined her daughter, insisting on seeing vaccination papers before allowing the girl to play with the employer's children. "I had to battle, really struggle," she recalled, "just to get enough food for her (to eat)." For Gladys, being together with her youngest daughter in the employer's home had entailed new emotional costs.

Patricia, the mother who was apart from her children only during the weekdays when she lived in with her employer, put forth an elastic definition of motherhood, one that included both meeting financial obligations and spending time with the children. Although her job involves different scheduling than most employed mothers, she shares views similar to those held by many working mothers:

> It's something you have to do, because you can't just stay seated at home because the bills accumulate and you have to find a way . . . I applied at many different places for work, like hospitals, as a receptionist—due to the experience I've had with computers working in shipping and receiving, things like that, but they never called me . . . One person can't pay all the bills.

Patricia emphasized that she believes motherhood also involves making an effort to spend time with the children. According to this criterion, she explained, most employers were deficient, while she was compliant. During the middle of the week, she explained, "I invent something, some excuse for her (the employer) to let me come home, even if I have to bring the (employer's) baby here with me . . . just to spend time with my kids."

Transnational mothers echoed these sentiments. Maria Elena, for example, whose 13-year-old son resided with his father in Mexico after she lost a custody battle, insisted that motherhood did not consist of only breadwinning: "You can't give love through money." According to Maria Elena, motherhood required an emotional presence and communication with a child. Like other transnational mothers, she explained how she maintained this connection despite the long-term geographic distance: "I came here, but we're not apart. We talk (by telephone) . . . I know (through telephone conversations) when my son is fine. I can tell when he is sad by the way he speaks." Like employed mothers everywhere, she insisted on a definition of motherhood that emphasized quality rather than quantity of time spent with the child: "I don't think that a good mother is one who is with her children at all times . . . It's the quality of time spent with the child." She spoke these words tearfully, reflecting the trauma of losing a custody battle with her ex-husband. Gladys also stated that being a mother involves both breadwinning and providing direction and guidance. "It's not just feeding them, or buying clothes for them. It's also educating them, preparing them to make good choices so they'll have a better future."

Transnational mothers seek to mesh caregiving and guidance with breadwinning. While breadwinning may require their long-term and long-distance separations from their children, they attempt to sustain family connections by showing emotional ties through letters, phone calls, and money sent home. If at all financially and logistically possible, they try to travel home to visit their children. They maintain their mothering responsibilities not only by earning money for their children's livelihood but also by communicating and advising across national borders, and across the boundaries that separate their children's place of residence from their own places of employment and residence.

Bonding with the Employers' Kids and Critiques of "Americana" Mothers

Some nanny-housekeepers develop very strong ties of affection with the children they care for during long workweeks. It is not unusual for nanny-housekeepers to be alone with these children during the workweek, with no one else with whom to talk or interact. The nannies, however, develop close emotional ties selectively, with some children, but not with others. For nanny-housekeepers who are transnational mothers, the loving daily caregiving that they cannot express for their own children is sometimes transferred to their employers' children. Carolina, a Guatemalan woman with four children between the ages of 10 and 14 back home, maintained that she tried to treat the employers' children with the same affection that she had for her own children "because if you do not feel affection for children, you are not able to care for them well." When interviewed, however, she was caring for two-year-old triplets—for whom she expressed very little affection—but she recalled very longingly her fond feelings for a child at her last job, a child who vividly reminded her of her daughter, who was about the same age:

> When I saw that the young girl was lacking in affection, I began to get close to her and I saw that she appreciated that I would touch her, give her a kiss on the cheek . . . And then I felt consoled too, because I had someone to give love to. But, I would imagine that she was my daughter, ah? And then I would give pure love to her, and that brought her closer to me.

Another nanny-housekeeper recalled a little girl for whom she had developed strong bonds of affection, laughingly imitating how the preschooler, who could not pronounce the "f" sound, would say "you hurt my peelings, but I don't want to pight."

Other nanny-housekeepers reflected that painful experiences with abrupt job terminations had taught them not to transfer mother love to the children of their employers. Some of these women reported that they now remained very measured and guarded in their emotional closeness with the employers' children, so that they could protect themselves for the moment when that relationship might be abruptly severed.

> I love these children, but now I stop myself from becoming too close. Before, when my own children weren't here (in the United States), I gave all my love to the children I cared for (then toddler twins). That was my recompensation (for not being with my chil-

dren). When the job ended, I hurt so much. I can't let that happen again.

> I love them, but not like they were my own children because they are not! They are not my kids! Because if I get to love them, and then I go, then I'm going to suffer like I did the last time. I don't want that.

Not all nanny-housekeepers bond tightly with the employers' children, but most of them are critical of what they perceive as the employers' neglectful parenting and mothering. Typically, they blame biological mothers (their employers) for substandard parenting. Carolina recalled advising the mother of the above-mentioned little girl, who reminded her of her own child, that the girl needed to receive more affection from her mother, whom she perceived as self-absorbed with physical fitness regimes. Carolina had also advised other employers on disciplining their children. Patricia also spoke adamantly on this topic, and she recalled with satisfaction that when she had advised her current employer to spend more than 15 minutes a day with the baby, the employer had been reduced to tears. By comparison to her employer's mothering, Patricia cited her own perseverance in going out of her way to visit her children during the week:

> If you really love your kids, you look for the time, you make time to spend with your kids . . . I work all week and for some reason I make excuses for her (employer) to let me come (home) . . . just to spend time with my kids.

Her rhetoric of comparative mothering is also inspired by the critique that many nanny-housekeepers have of female employers who may be out of the labor force but who employ nannies and hence do not spend time with their children.

> I love my kids, they don't. It's just like, excuse the word, shitting kids . . . What they prefer is to go to the salon, get their nails done, you know, go shopping, things like that. Even if they're home all day, they don't want to spend time with the kids because they're paying somebody to do that for them.

Curiously, she spoke as though her female employer is a wealthy woman of leisure, but in fact, both her current and past female employers are wealthy business executives who work long hours. Perhaps at this distance on the class spectrum, all class and racially privileged mothers look alike. "I work my butt off to get what I have," she observed, "and they don't have to work that much."

In some ways, transnational mothers who work as nanny-housekeepers cling to a more sentimentalized view of the employers' children than of their own. This strategy allows them to critique their employers, especially homemakers of privilege who are occupied with neither employment nor daily caregiving for their children. The Latina nannies appear to endorse motherhood as a full-time vocation in contexts of sufficient financial resources, but in contexts of financial hardship such as their own, they advocate more elastic definitions of motherhood, including forms that may include long spatial and temporal separations of mother and children.

As observers of late-20th-century U.S. families (Skolnick 1991; Stacey 1996) have noted, we live in an era wherein no one normative family arrangement predominates. Just as no one type of mothering unequivocally prevails in the White middle class, no singular mothering arrangement prevails among Latina immigrant women. In fact, the exigencies of contemporary immigration seem to multiply the variety of mothering arrangements. Through our research with Latina immigrant women who work as nannies, housekeepers, and house cleaners, we have encountered a broad range of mothering arrangements. Some Latinas migrate to the United States without their children to establish employment, and after some stability has been achieved, they may send for their children or they may work for a while to save money, and then return to their countries of origin. Other Latinas migrate and may postpone having children until they are financially established. Still others arrive with their children and may search for employment that allows them to live together with their children, and other Latinas may have sufficient financial support—from their husbands or kin—to stay home full-time with their children.

In the absence of a universal or at least widely shared mothering arrangement, there is tremendous uncertainty about what constitutes "good mothering,"

and transnational mothers must work hard to defend their choices. Some Latina nannies who have their children with them in the United States condemn transnational mothers as "bad women." One interview respondent, who was able to take her young daughter to work with her, claimed that she could never leave her daughter. For this woman, transnational mothers were not only bad mothers but also nannies who could not be trusted to adequately care for other people's children. As she said of an acquaintance, "This woman left her children (in Honduras) . . . she was taking care (of other people's children), and I said, 'Lord, who are they (the employers) leaving their children with if she did that with her own children!'"

Given the uncertainty of what is "good mothering," and to defend their integrity as mothers when others may criticize them, transnational mothers construct new scales for gauging the quality of mothering. By favorably comparing themselves with the negative models of mothering that they see in others—especially those that they are able to closely scrutinize in their employers' homes—transnational mothers create new definitions of good-mothering standards. At the same time, selectively developing motherlike ties with other people's children allows them to enjoy affectionate, face-to-face interactions that they cannot experience on a daily basis with their own children.

DISCUSSION: TRANSNATIONAL MOTHERHOOD

In California, with few exceptions, paid domestic work has become a Latina immigrant women's job. One observer has referred to these Latinas as "the new employable mothers" (Chang 1994), but taking on these wage labor duties often requires Latina workers to expand the frontiers of motherhood by leaving their own children for several years. While today there is a greater openness to accepting a plurality of mothering arrangements—single mothers, employed mothers, stay-at-home mothers, lesbian mothers, surrogate mothers, to name a few—even feminist discussions generally assume that mothers, by definition, will reside with their children.

Transnational mothering situations disrupt the notion of family in one place and break distinctively with what some commentators have referred to as the "epoxy glue" view of motherhood (Blum and Deussen 1996; Scheper-Hughes 1992). Latina transnational mothers are improvising new mothering arrangements that are borne out of women's financial struggles, played out in a new global arena, to provide the best future for themselves and their children. Like many other women of color and employed mothers, transnational mothers rely on an expanded and sometimes fluid number of family members and paid caregivers. Their caring circuits, however, span stretches of geography and time that are much wider than typical joint custody or "other mother" arrangements that are more closely bound, both spatially and temporally.

. . . Although not addressed directly in this article, the experiences of these mothers resonate with current major political issues. For example, transnational mothering resembles precisely what immigration restrictionists have advocated through California's Proposition 187 (Hondagneu-Sotelo 1995).[8] While proponents of Proposition 187 have never questioned California's reliance on low-waged Latino immigrant workers, this restrictionist policy calls for fully dehumanized immigrant workers, not workers with families and family needs (such as education and health services for children). In this respect, transnational mothering's externalization of the cost of labor reproduction to Mexico and Central America is a dream come true for the proponents of Proposition 187.

Contemporary transnational motherhood continues a long historical legacy of people of color being incorporated into the United States through coercive systems of labor that do not recognize family rights. As Bonnie Thornton Dill (1988), Evelyn Nakano Glenn (1986), and others have pointed out, slavery and contract labor systems were organized to maximize economic productivity and offered few supports to sustain family life. The job characteristics of paid domestic work, especially live-in work, virtually impose transnational motherhood for many Mexican and Central American women who have children of their own.

The ties of transnational motherhood suggest simultaneously the relative permeability of borders, as witnessed by the maintenance of family ties and the new meanings of motherhood, and the impermeability of nation-state borders. Ironically, just at the moment when free trade proponents and pundits celebrate globalization and transnationalism, and when "borderlands" and "border crossings" have become the metaphors of preference for describing a mind-boggling range of conditions, nation-state borders prove to be very real obstacles for many Mexican and Central American women who work in the United States and who, given the appropriate circumstances, wish to be with their children. While demanding the right for women workers to live with their children may provoke critiques of sentimentality, essentialism, and the glorification of motherhood, demanding the right for women workers to choose their own motherhood arrangements would be the beginning of truly just family and work policies, policies that address not only inequalities of gender but also inequalities of race, class, and citizenship status.

NOTES

1. No one knows the precise figures on the prevalence of transnational motherhood just as no one knows the myriad consequences for both mothers and their children. However, one indicator that hints at both the complex outcomes and the frequencies of these arrangements is that teachers and social workers in Los Angeles are becoming increasingly concerned about some of the deleterious effects of these mother-child separations and reunions. Many Central American women who made their way to Los Angeles in the early 1980s, fleeing civil wars and economic upheaval, pioneered transnational mothering, and some of them are now financially able to bring the children whom they left behind. These children, now in their early teen years, are confronting the triple trauma of simultaneously entering adolescence—with its own psychological upheavals; a new society—often in an inner-city environment that requires learning to navigate a new language, place and culture; and they are also entering families that do not look like the ones they knew before their mothers' departure, families with new siblings born in the United States, and new step-fathers or mothers' boyfriends.

2. Acknowledgment of the varieties of family and mothering has been fueled, in part, by research on the growing numbers of women-headed families, involving families of all races and socioeconomic levels—including Latina families in the United States and elsewhere (Baca Zinn 1989; Fernández Kelly and Garcia 1990), and

by recognition that biological ties do not necessarily constitute family (Weston 1991).

3. *La Virgen de Guadalupe,* the indigenous virgin who appeared in 1531 to a young Indian boy and for whom a major basilica is built, provides the exemplary maternal model, *la mujer abnegada* (the self-effacing woman), who sacrifices all for her children and religious faith. *La Malinche,* the Aztec woman that served Cortes as a translator, a diplomat, and a mistress, and *La Llorona* (the weeping one), a legendary solitary, ghostlike figure reputed either to have been violently murdered by a jealous husband or to have herself murdered her children by drowning them, are the negative and despised models of femininity. Both are failed women because they have failed at motherhood. *La Malinche* is stigmatized as a traitor and a whore who collaborated with the Spanish conquerors, and *La Llorona* is the archetypal evil woman condemned to eternally suffer and weep for violating her role as a wife and a mother (Soto 1986).

4. A study comparing Mexicanas and Chicanas found that the latter are more favorably disposed to homemaker ideals than are Mexican-born women. This difference is explained by Chicanas' greater exposure to U.S. ideology that promotes the opposition of mothering and employment and to Mexicanas' integration of household and economy in Mexico (Segura 1994). While this dynamic may be partially responsible for this pattern, we suspect that Mexicanas may have higher rates of labor force participation because they are also a self-selected group of Latinas; by and large, they come to the United States to work.

5. See Romero (1997) for a study focusing on the perspective of domestic workers' children. Although most respondents in this particular study were children of day workers, and none appear to have been children of transnational mothers, they still recall significant costs stemming from their mothers' occupation.

6. This seems to be more common among Central American women than Mexican women. Central American women may be more likely than are Mexican women to have their children in their country of origin, even if their husbands are living with them in the United States because of the multiple dangers and costs associated with undocumented travel from Central America to the United States. The civil wars of the 1980s, continuing violence and economic uncertainty, greater difficulties and costs associated with crossing multiple national borders, and stronger cultural legacies of socially sanctioned consensual unions may also contribute to this pattern for Central Americans.

7. According to interviews conducted with domestic workers in La Paz, Bolivia, in the late 1980s, 41 percent got their first job between the ages of 11 and 15, and one-third got their first job between the ages of 6 and 8. Some parents received half of the child-servant's salary (Gill 1994, 64). Similar arrangements prevailed in preindustrial, rural areas of the United States and Europe.

8. In November 1994, California voters passed Proposition 187, which legislates the denial of public school education, health care, and other public benefits to undocumented immigrants and their children. Although currently held up in the courts, the facility with which Proposition 187 passed in the California ballots rejuvenated anti-immigrant politics at a national level. It opened the door to new legislative measures in 1997 to deny public assistance to legal immigrants.

REFERENCES

Blum, Linda, and Theresa Deussen. 1996. Negotiating independent motherhood: Working-class African American women talk about marriage and motherhood. *Gender & Society* 10:199–211.

Burawoy, Michael. 1976. The functions and reproduction of migrant labor: Comparative material from Southern Africa and the United States. *American Journal of Sociology* 81:1050–87.

Chang, Grace. 1994. Undocumented Latinas: Welfare burdens or beasts of burden? *Socialist Review* 23:151–85.

Chinchilla, Norma Stoltz, and Nora Hamilton. 1996. Negotiating urban space: Latina workers in domestic work and street vending in Los Angeles. *Humbolt Journal of Social Relations* 22:25–35.

Collier, Jane Fishburne, and Sylvia Junko Yanagisako. 1987. *Gender and kinship: Essays toward a unified analysis.* Stanford, CA: Stanford University Press.

Collins, Patricia Hill. 1991. *Black feminist thought. Knowledge, consciousness, and the politics of empowerment.* New York: Routledge.

———. 1994. Shifting the center: Race, class, and feminist theorizing about motherhood. In *Mothering: Ideology, experience, and agency,* edited by Evelyn Nakano Glenn, Grace Chang, and Linda Rennie Forcey. New York: Routledge.

Dill, Bonnie Thornton. 1988. Our mothers' grief. Racial-ethnic women and the maintenance of families. *Journal of Family History* 13:415–31.

———. 1994. Fictive kin, paper sons and compadrazgo: Women of color and the struggle for family survival. In *Women of color in U.S. society,* edited by Maxine Baca Zinn and Bonnie Thornton Dill. Philadelphia: Temple University Press.

Fernández Kelly, M. Patricia, and Anna Garcia. 1990. Power surrendered, power restored: The politics of work and family among Hispanic garment workers in California and Florida. In *Women, politics & change,* edited by Louise A. Tilly and Patricia Gurin. New York: Russell Sage.

Gill, Lesley. 1994. *Precarious dependencies: Gender-class and domestic service in Bolivia.* New York: Columbia University Press.

Glenn, Evelyn Nakano. 1986. *Issei, Nisei, warbride: Three generations of Japanese American women in domestic service.* Philadelphia: Temple University Press.

———. 1994. Social constructions of mothering: A thematic overview. In *Mothering: Ideology, experience, and agency,* edited by Evelyn Nakano Glenn, Grace Chang, and Linda Rennie Forcey. New York: Routledge.

Griswold del Castillo, Richard. 1984. *La Familia: Chicano families in the urban Southwest, 1848 to the present.* Notre Dame, IN: University of Notre Dame Press.

Hondagneu-Sotelo, Pierrette. 1995. Women and children first: New directions in anti-immigrant politics. *Socialist Review* 25:169–90.

Rollins, Judith. 1985. *Between women: Domestics and their employers.* Philadelphia: Temple University Press.

Romero, Mary. 1992. *Maid in the U.S.A.* New York: Routledge.

———. 1996. Life as the maid's daughter: An exploration of the everyday boundaries of race, class and gender. In *Feminisms in the academy: Rethinking the disciplines,* edited by Abigail J. Steward and Donna Stanon. Ann Arbor: University of Michigan Press.

———. 1997. Who takes care of the maid's children? Exploring the costs of domestic service. In *Feminism and families,* edited by Hilde L. Nelson. New York: Routledge.

Ruddick, Sara. 1989. *Maternal thinking: Toward a politics of peace.* Boston: Beacon.

Scheper-Hughes, Nancy. 1992. *Death without weeping: The violence of everyday life in Brazil.* Berkeley: University of California Press.

Segura, Denise A. 1994. Working at motherhood: Chicana and Mexican immigrant mothers and employment. In *Mothering: Ideology, experience, and agency,* edited by Evelyn Nakano Glenn, Grace Chang, and Linda Rennie Forcey. New York: Routledge.

Segura, Denise A., and Jennifer L. Pierce. 1993. Chicana/o family structure and gender personality: Chodorow, familism, and psychoanalytic sociology revisited. *Signs: Journal of Women in Culture and Society* 19:62–79.

Skolnick, Arlene S. 1991. *Embattled paradise: The American family in an age of uncertainty.* New York: Basic Books.

Soto, Shirlene. 1986. Tres modelos culturales: La Virgin de Guadalupe, la Malinche, y la Llorona. *Fem* (Mexico City), no. 48:13–16.

Stacey, Judith. 1996. *In the name of the family: Retaining family values in the postmodern age.* Boston: Beacon.

Stack, Carol B., and Linda M. Burton. 1994. Kinscripts: Reflections on family, generation, and culture. In *Mothering: Ideology, experience, and agency,* edited by Evelyn Nakano Glenn, Grace Chang, and Linda Rennie Forcey. New York: Routledge.

Thorne, Barrie, and Marilyn Yalom. 1992. *Rethinking the family: Some feminist questions.* Boston: Northeastern University Press.

Uttal, Lynet. 1996. Custodial care, surrogate care, and coordinated care: Employed mothers and the meaning of child care. *Gender & Society* 10:291–311.

Weston, Kath. 1991. *Families we choose: Lesbians, gays, kinship.* New York: Columbia University Press.

Wrigley. 1995. *Other people's children.* New York: Basic Books.

Zavella, Patricia. 1987. *Women's work and Chicano families: Cannery workers of the Santa Clara Valley.* Ithaca, NY: Cornell University Press.

Zelizer, Viviana. 1994. *Pricing the priceless child: The social value of children.* Princeton, NJ: Princeton University Press.

Zinn, Maxine Baca. 1989. Family, race and poverty in the eighties. *Signs: Journal of Women in Culture and Society* 14:856–69.

29

Caring Fathers

The Ideology of Gender Equality and Masculine Positions

THOMAS JOHANSSON

ROGER KLINTH

The image of a muscular man holding an infant in his arms has forever engraved itself in the collective Swedish memory as the symbol of paternity leave. With his tousled red hair, his bulging biceps, and his blue and yellow shirt—the color of the Swedish flag— weightlifter Leif "Hoa Hoa" Dahlgren integrates conceptions of masculinity, caring, and national iden- tity—he's a family-oriented version of a Swedish wel- fare-state Viking. The message is crystal clear: There are no conflicts between parental leave and masculin- ity. A real man takes paternity leave!

This now classic picture was part of the first pater- nity leave campaign carried out by the national social insurance office. It began in 1976 and was launched under the heading "Daddy on Paternity Leave." The campaign has had a number of successors. From the 1970s to the present, the Swedish Government Offices, other national authorities, trade unions, and special in- terest organizations have used advertisements, films, brochures, TV spots, photo exhibits, radio jingles, and personal letters in an attempt to convince men of the value of paternity leave. This material is a rich source of information for understanding paternity leave as a political project in Sweden. Present in the campaigns are normative images of how men should feel, think, and act—normative images to which men must relate in some way.

Attitude surveys conducted since the beginning of the 1980s have shown that Swedish men have positive attitudes toward parental leave. However, the statistics on the use of parental leave tell another story. At the beginning of the 1980s, men's proportion of the total leave taken had risen to a modest 5 percent. This figure has gradually increased, and in 2004, men took 18.7 percent of the total leave time (Statens Offentliga Utredningar 2005, 73).

The discrepancy between what men say and what they do raises a number of questions. How do men un- derstand and relate to the various messages concerning paternity leave? Do attempts to shape public opinion have their intended effects, or do they miss the mark? These and similar questions have been addressed in research and other types of inquiries, but in this article, we go a step further by bringing together the normative images of these campaigns and the men they were intended to influence. In a number of focus group

Thomas Johansson & Roger Klinth, *Men and Masculinities 11*, pp. 42–62. Copyright © 2008 Sage Publications. Reprinted by permission of Sage Publications.

interviews, we have asked groups of men to discuss several campaign images taken from the paternity leave campaigns of the past thirty years or so. Our overall interest is in how men construct fatherhood in the field of tension between societal visions and their own lived reality.[1]

THE NEW MAN: HISTORICAL AND POLITICAL BACKGROUND

The various paternity leave campaigns should be understood in relation to the wider societal and political context. In Sweden, as in many other countries, the questioning of traditional gender relations has its roots in the 1960s. In 1968, the Swedish government backed the following declaration of principles:

> A policy which attempts lo give women an equal place with men in economic life while at the same time confirming woman's traditional responsibility for the care of home and children has no prospect of fulfilling me first of these aims. This can be realised only if the man is also educated and encouraged to take an active part in parenthood and is given the same rights and duties as the woman in his parental capacity (Sandlund 1968, 4).

The idea content was largely taken from the gender equality debate of the 1960s and its questioning of women's as well as men's social roles. The concept of the new man came to epitomize the vision of a new care-oriented masculinity (Beckman 1965; Klinth 2003). This new man concept was discussed in terms of liberation, but acquired a strong moral charge through its ties to conceptions of modernity, enlightenment, democracy, and health (Klinth 2002). Already in 1970, then Prime Minister Olof Palme gave words to the political charge that had been established with regard to this issue. He stressed that if any of today's politicians were to declare that women should have a role different from the man's "and that it is natural that she devotes more time to the children, he would be regarded to be of the Stone Age" (Palme 1972, 242–43).

The political vision formulated at the end of the 1960s may be described as a struggle on two fronts. One was intended to strengthen women's position in working life and society, while the other was intended to increase men's responsibility and involvement in child care and housework (Nyberg 2004). In the mid-1970s, one young, liberal member of the Riksdag (the Parliament of Sweden) summarized the motto of Swedish gender equality politics in the following way: Our policies should "get jobs for moms and get dads pregnant" (Klinth 2002, 243).

Thus, the ambition to get dads pregnant was principally expressed politically in the new parental leave insurance policy that took effect in 1974. The policy gave men the right to paid parental leave. This reform was historical as well as unique in an international comparison. Men had never before been offered such an opportunity. In contrast to the taxation system as well as the systems for health insurance and social security insurance, parental leave insurance was designed to be a collective right. The parents themselves were to determine which of them would use the leave.

The question of paternity leave has been shown to contain a number of political complications. It has often been the cause of hot debate both within and between political parties. It has not, in any simple or clear way, constituted an issue in bloc politics. Instead, the initiative has shifted between the nonsocialist and socialist parlies. It is primarily the issue of compulsory division, imposition of quotas, and individualization with regard to parental leave insurance that has given rise to contention. Already in 1975, a government report challenged the collective idea on which parental leave insurance rested by proposing an "earmarked" month for fathers (Klinth 2002; Karlsson 1996). It took an additional twenty years, however, before such a proposal was met with political sympathy. The "daddy month" was first introduced into parental leave insurance in 1995.[2]

The question of imposing quotas is interesting in many ways. The political management of this question in particular has helped to make visible a number of fundamental principles in the thinking about family politics—principles that have formed the latent conditions for work with political reform. As long as reform work has been in line with these principles, they have remained invisible, but when demands for basic change have been formulated, they have become apparent. From a gender perspective, these principles may be understood as forming the inner core of the gender order—its discursive foundation. Compromises and reinterpretations have only been possible as long as they have not fundamentally threatened the leading principles of the gender order.

One example of such a principle is that concerning the family's freedom of choice. Those wishing to bring about a sharpening of men's individual responsibility have been forced to question or radically redefine this principle. This has not been possible as a rule (Klinth 2004, 2005). Moreover, most public opinion surveys have shown broad support for the family's right to choose (Statens Offentliga Utredningar 2005, 73).

Another important principle has been that concerning men's scope of action. In contrast to the freedom of choice principle, this principle has not been expressed explicitly. Instead, it has been discernable as an implicit condition of political action. The principle of men's scope of action has strongly marked the information and public opinion building carried out to persuade men to take more parental leave. This shaping of public opinion has been generally characterized by a "rhetoric of the gift" as opposed to an emphasis on shared responsibility. The fact that men have used their right to parental leave only to a limited extent has been defined as a problem of attitudes rather than one of power. Based on such logic, the problem is located in men's brains, and the role of the state thus becomes to set men straight, to inform them of the social, psychological, and labor-market-related gains they can make through active fatherhood (Klinth 2005). What this rhetoric of the gift has concealed, however, is the risk entailed in men not choosing to accept the gift, namely diminished chances for women to have influence in society, to have a career, and to achieve wage equality (Statens Offentliga Utredningar 2005, 73; Åström 1992; Widerberg 1993).

It is difficult to determine the extent to which opinion-building campaigns of the kind discussed above have led to the desired result. There are some indications that local campaigns, in certain cases, have actively helped to increase men's propensity to use their right to parental leave. On the national level, however, it is difficult to attribute statistical changes to particular efforts to shape public opinion (Bekkengen 1996, 2002, 2003; Statens Offentliga Utredningar 2005, 73; Klinth 2005).

Although it has taken more than thirty years for Swedish men to reach a level of utilization of about 20 percent of the total parental leave allowance, it is clear that the new, gender-equal man lives on as an idea and moral guiding principle. The government-initiated campaigns to promote paternity leave have been one of the most important producers of the image of this man and of what he should look like, what he should think, and how he should act. Through constant repetition, the discourse on gender equality and its implications for masculinity and fatherhood have been embodied and become a central part of social and professional practices of various kinds.

According to Marie Nordberg (2005), the discourse on gender equality often exists "as a "third presence" that individuals measure themselves in relation to and present themselves through and are careful to articulate in their politically correct self-presentations" (p. 80). The discourse on the new man has attained a hegemonic status. In most situations, it is nearly impossible to avoid relating to it or to openly criticize it. This is not to say, however, that it has not been or is not threatened or that it is similarly interpreted in all contexts (Magnusson 2001). As we established above, there are clear differences in the attitudes and values men express and in how they then choose to act.

There are a number of qualitative studies of how individual men who have taken longer periods of parental leave relate to their own fatherhood, to the family, and to the reactions of others (Lupton and Barclay 1997; Dienhart 1998; Deutch 1999; Chronholm 2004). Most studies deal with middle-class men who have positive attitudes about taking care of their infant children. These studies focus on a carefully selected group of men who are united by their interest in standing out as gender equal and modern. We know little, however, about what men in different social and cultural groups think and how they relate to these questions.

What are men's opinions on sharing parental leave? What resistance to the idea might exist? What factors could have a negative impact on men's readiness to stay home with their children? Based on Connell's (1995) model of multiple masculine positions, it is conceivable that there are a number of different viewpoints on these issues and thereby also different ways of constructing the gender-equal man.

METHOD

This study is based on the material from four focus groups, each with its own constellation of men. This is the first of several similar studies in which other groups will be contacted. Selection of participants in the present study has been based on our desire to include the following; (1) men who are directly involved in issues of justice and who run various types of men's projects and (2) men who, in contrast, may conceivably have given somewhat less thought to these issues. Thus, we have chosen to try to identify four relatively dissimilar masculine positions. These groups are briefly described as follows:

1. Men's crisis center (three men). All men in this group work actively with men in crisis. They meet with men for both therapeutic and guidance talks of varying duration.
2. Male network (six men). This is an association working with different types of men's issues. For example, members participate in campaigns against violence toward women and arrange lectures and informational evenings.
3. The Equal Project (seven men). This particular group works to create social security in poor neighborhoods in Gothenburg. Most of them are immigrants from Iran, Kurdistan, and Chile. These men have different educational backgrounds, but they all live in a rather poor suburb in Gothenburg.
4. Christian men (three men). These men are members of congregations belonging to the evangelical free churches, which embrace a pietistic tradition, including, among other things, an emphasis on personal conversion, emotional experiences, and the importance of the Bible. The Baptist church and the Pentecostal movement are other representatives of this tradition.

The four focus groups represent different parts of the Swedish middle class with the exception of the third group. These men have different educational backgrounds, but they all live and work in the same suburb. In many ways, they are quite representative of a broader Swedish population of refugees and immigrants. These groups are characterized by various degrees of cultural capital and education, but what they often have in common is a low degree of economic capital.

The use of focus groups has been shown to be a successful method for studying how different groups relate to well-delimited questions (Krueger 1994; Hylander 1998; Morgan and Krueger 1998; Wibeck 2000). We are not primarily interested in what individual men have to say, but instead we view the group as our object of study. Our ambition was to allow the men to consider the campaign material we had collected and to react to the various ways in which the state and other important actors in society have tried to encourage men to become more gender equal. The groups were shown a selection of pictures that reflected the spirit of the times as well as various strategies to encourage men to take more daddy leave. By allowing them to think about and discuss the material, we hoped to capture some of the attitudes and conceptions that may be associated with a given social position or a certain involvement in these issues. In this way, the historical and contemporary sociological parts of our study meet in the same situation.

In the analysis, we have chosen not to use and comment on exactly the same pictures. For this reason, the order in which we presented the pictures varies, and in the analysis we have even chosen to use different examples and pictures in the different groups. Our aim has not been to compare the same pictures point for point to see how the groups react to the same stimuli but instead to let each group emerge in terms of its own distinctive character. The pictures have been used more to capture certain central arguments, mechanisms, and the dynamics characterizing the group.

The pictures were taken from nine different daddy leave campaigns carried out during the period from 1976 to 2005. Eight of these were developed by the Swedish Social Insurance Administration (central or local offices). One of the campaigns, "The Men's Trap," was directed by the Swedish Ministry of Health and Social Affairs. Two pictures were provided with some type of brief caption.

In most cases, we began with the picture from the 1970s and moved gradually forward in time. But this order was varied in some cases, mostly considering the specific experiences and structures of the groups. The pictures used are briefly described below. Given the space limitation, we describe only the pictures specifically mentioned in the article.

Picture 1 was taken from the Swedish Social Insurance Administration's campaign "Daddy on Paternity Leave" from the end of the 1970s. It shows three fathers, each pushing a baby carriage. Their gaze is directed toward a child in one of the carriages, and they seem to be engaged in a cheerful conversation. Two of the fathers are well known in the media: weightlifter Leif "Hoa Hoa" Dahlgren and actor Janne "Loffe" Carlsson. The third father is unknown to us. They are dressed simply (jean jackets, red-checkered work shirts), suggesting working-class or lower-middle-class affiliation.

Pictures 2 and 3 were taken from the Swedish Ministry of Health and Social Affairs' campaign "The Men's Trap" (early 1990s). Picture 2 shows a naked man standing with his arms and legs outstretched on a large cogwheel. The man is in his thirties and remarkably well muscled. The picture is reminiscent of the famous drawing by Leonardo da Vinci, *Vitruvian Man* (a naked man in a circle). Picture 3 shows the same man. Here he is naked from the waist up. The only item of clothing he has on is a tie wrapped around his neck and up over his eyes—the tie is blindfolding him. Both pictures are dramatic and artistic in nature.

Pictures 4 and 5 come from the Swedish Social Insurance Administration's campaign, "Both Is Best." This campaign was carried out at the beginning of this century. Picture 4 is captioned "No repeats of childhood." A two- to three-year-old girl is pushing a baby carriage and looking with a smile at the observer. It is a black and white picture. Picture 5 shows a child (of indeterminable sex) with a muddy face and wearing muddy rainwear. The child is laughing and holding up an earthworm. The caption states, "An investment with immediate dividends." This picture is also in black and white.

CASE 1: THERAPEUTIC INTERVENTIONS INTO FATHERHOOD

The first group consisted of men who had long worked with men in crisis—men who have lost custody of their children, who have alcohol problems, or who have dif-

ficulty handling their own aggression. The three men we interviewed have undergraduate degrees in social work or psychology as well as training as therapists. This background characterized many of their reactions to the campaign pictures presented. The interviewed men considered primarily how the men they encounter would react and respond to the pictures' messages. Thus, they interpreted the pictures from a therapeutic perspective and with a therapeutic gaze. This led to thoughts about emotional reactions to the messages and the difficulties entailed in going forward too quickly with this type of campaign and message. Here, thoughts were based on theories of maturity, development, and psychological gender. We wish to highlight a few examples to illustrate the principles guiding how this group reacted and reflected on fatherhood.

The second picture (picture 2) presented shows a man suspended on a cogwheel. The idea is to illustrate how men tend to become prisoners of the fast pace of working life, thereby losing contact with their children. The message concerns the importance of breaking loose from the treadmill of working life and instead spending more time with one's children. This picture evoked a number of reactions. The following are excerpts from discussions in this focus group:

M1: This is so typical of the times, Guillou's Hamilton books, his male ideal. The closest you can get to the male genitals. You've used your sex, and now we're gonna nail you up. It contains a lot of aggression toward men. It's a stereotype that a man is his role and that he hides in it; deep-going prejudices, a narrow register.

M3: . . . an identification thing too. How many wear a tie to work? How many are hunters? . . . Not very pleasant, a target, darts.

M1: It's much more fun to joke about men. Should have been one with smaller biceps, a little snuff under his lip and unshaven and so on.

This group of men was marked by their work situation and their basic ambition to improve conditions for men—to make it easier for men to talk about their feelings and live a better life. It is natural, then, that they tended to perceive as stereotypical pictures and messages that play on a certain male image. Here we see associations to notions that the man is burdened by guilt, that he is vulnerable and a victim of prejudices. Moreover, the group members took exception to the fact that it is a seemingly physically fit man of high status who is portrayed. They thought that this draws attention away from "the regular man" and helps to strengthen the notion that men should work out at the gym and attain a high position in society. Instead, they wished to work toward creating a more nuanced image of masculinity that stresses complexity, depth, and the multifaceted nature of fatherhood.

This focus group constantly stressed the importance of trusting men and of understanding how they reason about things and of not disparaging them. They looked critically on the type of feminist thought that solely emphasizes men's complete superordination and women's subordination. Reality is more complex. One of the men stated that the Swedish government would like to paint Swedish men either black or white. Another considered that there seems to be a political aim in presenting men in such a superficial manner.

In general, this group thought there is too much focus on structures and societal views and that such a focus tends to lose sight of the individual. Instead of constantly presenting men as either black or white or taking the perspective that men do not want to take paternity leave, we should trust men and assume that they actually wish to participate in family life and spend a great deal of time with their children. Such positive treatment would also help to strengthen men in their role as fathers.

The therapists took exception to the state always trying to control and influence families. They focused more on the individual and the subjective level. Their interpretations of the material seem to have been guided by their therapeutic perspective. The reasoning here is not so much at the political level. Instead, the issues thought to be important were more likely to concern men's experiences, reactions, and subjective resistance.

M2: It's important to get people thinking, like in therapy. To get them thinking, processing, taking a stand. When the state uses regulations, lecturing, overexplicitness, then it's putting itself at another level, seeing this person as someone who can be told what to do. The greatest benefits come when people think. . . . I don't believe in the model of standing there and telling people what to think, like a superego, but when the superego disappears, you need to be able to think. I wish the state would step back and give more room to the inner life, go in for change, so people can think and ponder. This isn't such a society unfortunately.

The campaign pictures presented were experienced as either guilt imposing or as if they minimize men's experiences and active will to bring about change. The picture considered to be most positive is the one from the 1970s, showing three middle-age men, each in front of a baby carriage (picture 1). The reason for this is that it is apparent that the men are being portrayed in a positive manner. The picture is a manifestation of the fact that something has happened, that men now take their share of the responsibility. Another factor judged to be important is that it is possible to identify with the men in the picture; they are of middle age, have a normal appearance, and do not connote the upper middle class. The following excerpts concern one of the most successful Swedish campaigns to date, which included a picture of a Swedish weightlifter, dressed in a short-sleeved T-shirt and holding a naked infant in his muscular arms.

M3: . . . Hoa Hoa helped us men strengthen our inner musculature. That's why I think it was powerful. A message that speaks to me as an individual who can develop causes a discussion to happen inside me. Men talk about developing their caring side. Most men have experienced being cared for, but maybe don't believe they own produce that side in relation to their own children.

Toward the end of the focus group interview, the men talked about the risks associated with the state, feminists, and researchers wishing to hurry development, perhaps too quickly. They thought that if development was too rapid, men would not be able to catch up, which would only result in a backlash. One participant told about a father he had seen who had considerable trouble controlling his child. He gave this as an example of how parents can lose control. Thus, this is primarily a question of maturity and of a process that must come from within and be well grounded in the individual (cf. Seidler 1994a, 1994b). According to these men, all attempts to force development through political or social measures are doomed to failure. So altogether, this is a quite individualistically oriented group, and the power perspective is more or less absent.

CASE 2: THE MALE NETWORK

Male networks consist of men who work actively to counteract unequal relations between men and women and to attain a more gender-equal society. Thus, these men are greatly involved, in different ways, in issues concerning a changing masculinity. The group we met consisted of five men of different ages and backgrounds. Most of them, however, were in their thirties and had children of preschool age. All members of the group expressed rather radical ideas about gender issues. Here, we do not find similarly negative reactions to campaign material from the 1990s and to the pictures the previous group thought created feelings of guilt and shame in men. These men worked either as teachers, as social workers, or in other types of middle-class occupations. Rather than reacting solely to the most explicit content of the pictures, they tried to bring together the message, text, and picture. Several of the men in this group expressed their appreciation for the aesthetic content and design of the campaigns. In contrast to the previous group, which largely discussed the level of the individual, this discussion moved to a political or aesthetic level. At the same time, there was constant criticism of hegemonic masculinity (Connell 1995; Johansson 2000).

This group consisted of men of different ages; thus, in some cases, there arose a clear generational difference in how they perceived the pictures and messages. The first pictures we showed were captioned "No repeats of childhood" and "An investment with immediate dividends" (pictures 4 and 5). The pictures stress the importance of fathers taking their paternity leave, because this is their only chance to spend time with their young children. If they don't, they may regret it later on in life. There is only one chance. This focus group expressed both positive and negative opinions in relation to these pictures.

M1: I think the caption is good—an investment. That's pretty much how we try to talk about becoming a father—right away when you've done your part. If you miss several years in the beginning, you can never make them up; that time never returns. . . . No repeats of childhood.

M2: At the same time though, throwing in words like *investment, repeats, no repeats.* It's nothing you sell off cheap or so. You check the situation and see, yeah, now's a good time for kids or staying at home. It's not like you plan when the mother will take her maternity leave; instead she takes hers and then we plan ours in so it suits us during the year . . . there are good possibilities to plan your paternity leave in a flexible way. It sounds like they're trying to sell insurance or something. The language is very masculine.

These participants' reactions to the expression *investment* were unusually strong. They reacted primarily not to how the men were presented, but to the fact that there are many men who think this rationally and who use this type of language. Thus, this is not only a question of defending masculinity but of criticizing the actual situation at the same time as they took exception to this type of masculinity. The men in the focus group joked a bit about men who plan their parental leave, write the days in their calendars, and check off every changed diaper or house cleaning. Everything should simply work, and the will should simply be there. The basic outlook here is that gender equality is something natural and that men want to stay at home with their children. Most men in this group did not think they required this kind of pressure or campaign, but they thought many men did need to be exposed to such messages and pressures. Their attitudes toward the campaigns and the political pressure were basically positive. In relation to picture 2, the man on the cogwheel, the participants had the following comments:

M1: You're stuck in the machinery, crushed by the cogwheel. Daddy leave isn't so much fun if it's like that.

M5: I think it's better. . . . It could be due to interfering bosses, colleagues; everything's consistent in a way. It brings up the usual problems, work, many have problems, good to discuss them. . . .

M3: The men's trap. Great! Don't focus directly on the individual but on larger structures; that's how I feel. You understand the picture better when you've read the text.

Although these men thought such campaigns are necessary, they also thought that many men today do not need to be pushed to spend time with their children. Reactions to the picture from the 1970s (picture 1) were somewhat different in this group. Even though the oldest participant liked the picture, the others' reactions were marked by a more joking tone. They related that at that time, it was new and bold for a man to push a baby carriage and that it raised your status a bit and, in that way, you became more of a man. It marked the very onset of attempts to elaborate a new male image: the gender-equal and successful man. The hegemonic conceptual world was displaced and changed, and gradually emerging are new images of masculinity. The image of our age is divided. On one hand, the men thought there was a need for campaigns and measures by the state, but they also saw risks for negative reactions on the part of men who already understood. The following excerpt deals with this:

M3: I think things have progressed pretty far now so when you talk to people who've had a baby there's never any discussion; the guys stay home a lot, maybe not half the time but not just the first two weeks; longer. No discussion. The mother stays home first; then it's my turn. . . .

M5: That's the basic attitude from the start. I'm not sure I even thought about it; it was clear I'd stay home. I don't like it when they play on masculinity. It's not ridiculing but limiting. They can stop it.

The point of departure for this discussion is that masculinity as a category should be uninteresting in this context. Responsible and involved parenting should be a matter of course for men as well as women. In accordance with this, the group expressed positive attitudes toward imposing quotas on parental leave, that is, carrying through compulsory division of paid leave between the two parents. While the participants saw the possibilities and development toward a more gender-equal society, their discussion also dealt with the obstacles that exist and that can lead to problems for men in realizing a gender-equal family situation. One such problem is the private economy—the fact that men earn more—though this was viewed not as an absolute but as a possible obstacle. The question of how women think and relate to this also came up. Several in the group thought that women sometimes create obstacles to men's presence and that they help to create weak self-esteem in men by criticizing men for changing diapers incorrectly, for bathing the child too seldom, or for other deficiencies.

This group provided a partially different picture of fatherhood and men's way of looking at gender equality. These men have a basically positive attitude toward feminism and to the state's trying to encourage men to stay home with their children (cf. Kimmel and Messner 1995; Dienhart 1998). Most of them were in their thirties and working toward gender equality and justice in society. Thus, they read the campaign pictures in a slightly different manner. They did not see themselves as the intended recipients of the messages; that is, they talked primarily about "other men" and thought that pressure must be put on them. At the same time, they thought that many men today embrace the idea of equality in the family in a natural way. Here, we see hopefulness. They saw the obstacles and identified them in a rather neutral way, but they also saw great possibilities in their work with men and for gender equality. Although these men discussed different obstacles, such as economy and other material conditions, they tended quite strongly to put forward motivational and psychological factors. If men really want to, they also can contribute to change and a more gender-equal society.

CASE 3: IMMIGRANT MEN

This group consisted of seven men with quite varied backgrounds. Two were ethnic Swedes, and the others came from a number of different countries. All except one spoke Swedish well. The idea behind including a group of men who live in poor neighborhoods in Gothenburg was to see how nationality and the specific life conditions created in multiethnic neighborhoods may affect views on fatherhood and on the issues we are interested in. The men who participated were all, in one way or another, active and involved in trying to influence their own life situations and in creating better living conditions and improving safety in their neighborhoods. The men selected were all involved, and some were politically active refugees.

In this group, we began with the picture from the 1970s showing the men with their baby carriages (picture 1). One of the men, a Kurdish refugee from Iran, reacted as follows:

M1: This picture—when was it?

ROGER KLINTH: The 1970s.

M1: The 1970s . . . it wasn't normal in my country in Asia. But after the 1990s or so . . . when I came to Sweden and sent a picture to my parents in Iran of their grandchildren . . . yeah completely normal. They didn't say anything. . . . They say we've seen our grandchildren and you with the baby carriage and . . . I go out with my children; is that strange? No totally normal, but society doesn't accept this. It depends on the situation. But who has the power in Iran, the mullahs [Islamic clerics]!

It is apparent that this group was dominated by political refugees. They had all worked to bring about justice in their homelands and then had to flee to Sweden. They expressed clearly their desire that men and women should live under conditions of gender equality. In this group, those who were more doubtful concerning this goal were the Swedish men, who were either openly doubtful about parents sharing household responsibilities or who had a more somber picture of the actual situation in society.

One Chilean man held long expositions on a just society, the importance of creating better economic conditions, and of fathers staying home with their young children. Most of the others agreed. Participants in this group had a clear political interest and a will to influence society. Reactions in this group were more mixed in many ways, and it also became clear how closely inter-

woven gender issues are with issues of economy and class. We began to understand this when we presented picture 4 (little girl pushing a baby carriage).

M4: It's about putting the blame on fathers.

M7: In my case, I've been at home with my son, but in recent years I've had work and worked a lot day and night. . . . But now that he's a teenager I spend more time with him.

ROGER KLINTH: No repeats of childhood!

M7: Guilt! In many cases when men work, but I'm the only one working in our family, my wife has arthritis and can't work. I have to work.

THOMAS JOHANSSON: Are dads still not very good at this?

M7: No, I don't think so, but I think it's difficult among immigrants, less common [that men take care of babies].

The subtext here deals largely with the notion that one must earn a living and that this often overrides all other issues. The neighborhoods these men live in are marked by clear patterns of poverty: high unemployment, public assistance, and a high degree of social exclusion. Many families find themselves outside the labor market. Thus, in many cases, the issue is more about surviving and creating a tolerable existence. The question of sharing or not sharing parental leave is not considered, since it may be the case that both parents are unemployed and at home.

We approached these issues when we asked the men about how they perceived the pictures, pointing out that the only men portrayed in the campaigns are ethnic Swedes.

ROGER KLINTH: The pictures we've seen so far are dominated by ethnic Swedes. Are other role models missing?

M7: I've never thought so, but then I came to Sweden when I was little.

M5: If you look at the statistics then many immigrant men are unemployed. Then there is no daddy leave, that's important.

M1: Immigrant women get jobs sooner and the men are unemployed . . . immigrant fathers and some mothers never enter Swedish society. In 1987, when we came to Sweden, we got a book on Sweden written in different languages. We learned a lot about this society. Now, in the 1990s, all that information is gone, difficult for immigrant parents, especially fathers to adjust to this society.

ROGER KLINTH: Should there be campaigns aimed at immigrant men?

M5: We have good relations with other immigrants in the area, the biggest family problem is unemployment, dads and moms are sitting at home. They look at each other and conflicts develop, they can't control their teenagers. All this parental leave doesn't mean a thing if you don't have a job!

This group is markedly different from the others in one way. Here, the focus is on how economic and social conditions impact the whole issue of shared parenting. It's not about who earns the most or if the family will lose money if, for example, the father stays home more than two months, but instead it's about what happens in poor families when they are placed outside society. Just as in the other groups, these men have basically positive attitudes toward the image of the gender-equal man, but their work toward gender equality is made difficult by the social exclusion created in multiethnic neighborhoods (Sernhede 2002).

CASE 4: EVANGELICAL MEN

This group consisted of three middle-age men who were active members of an evangelical church. Two had middle-class occupations, one as a computer consultant and the other as a company president. The third worked as a bus driver. Each was married and had three children. The men in this group had as their starting point the conceptions that exist about men in Christian movements, that they are conservative and not particularly interested in gender equality. This group presented a picture that is different in many ways. They took clear exception to the stereotypical image of the conservative Christian man. They spoke warmly about dividing parental leave and considered that spending time with one's children is of the utmost importance.

The first picture presented deals with childhood and how important it is that fathers take advantage of this time (picture 5, child with earthworm).

ROGER KLINTH: An investment with immediate dividends. What do you think?

M1: I react to the part about investment, that I should do this for my own sake.

ROGER KLINTH: What ate your thoughts, then?

M1: Well, it just reflects what society, the buttons you have to push to get people to do something, of course I've taken paternity leave and I want to be with my children and take that time. It's not just for my sake. I react to the method, that they have to prompt men and play on their own interests.

M2: It's almost like you feel it becomes a burden instead. I've lost the opportunity to make contact with my children. . . . There's more you need to think about in your role as a parent. This leads to guilt feelings.

ROGER KLINTH: Isn't it guilt feelings they're trying to arouse?

M1: To me it feels more like an offer, take the chance in order to get the dividend.

This picture gave rise to various reactions. One man thought it created guilt feelings and caused fathers to feel uneasy. The most negative reaction, however, concerned the appeals made to men's own interests. Taking care of children should not be about self-fulfillment and the individual, but more about the will to create a positive family life. On the whole, it is just this line of thought that recurred in this group. The greatest emphasis is placed on creating a balance in life, being able to work and support the family, but at the same time safeguarding it. This is not primarily a question of gender equality as a political value but of another, deeper value base, in which the family and unity are valued most highly.

In this group, the general attitude toward the gender-equal family was positive, but some statements did concern weighing paternity leave against other things. What seemed to be most important was maintaining certain fundamental values and cultivating a certain lifestyle. A parental presence guarantees that children will develop the same values as their parents. What is prioritized is family life and its continuity; work is always secondary. We might say at this point that these men, as compared to those in the previous group, had relatively stable and perhaps even well-paid jobs.

M2: It's about other things. Sometimes the focus is on the first months when the child is an infant and you should share it, and then I don't understand how that's supposed to work when you work full time. We've never done that, we have young children now so we're at home, but even at other times we haven't both worked full time. There has to be time for other activities you're involved in. Life is more than being on daddy leave.

M3: There's too much emphasis on the first year . . . it's important to talk about their entire period of growing up. . . .

M2: It's a matter of reflecting on things, how you conduct your life. . . .

Much of the discussion concerned how one could develop working life conditions that are fit for human beings and that take into account the whole person. One of the men talked extensively about his workplace. He worked as a consultant, and when he began his job, he was informed that the company's policy was that employees should not work overtime too often but instead have time left over for family and free time. The philosophy of this company was to promote a comprehensive vision of life. What's more, this company lived up to its principles. In relation to picture 2, the man on the cogwheel, the men had the following comments:

M1: I haven't seen this either, but there's something here I agree with, because I feel pretty alone in being home so much with my kids.

ROGER KLINTH: How long?

M1: . . . About half a year. I don't understand why this should be so controlled, that mothers should be home as much as fathers, I think it's natural that the family deals with this. I've worked for a company that supports fathers who're at home, no problem,

perfectly natural. No obstacles and I've been very willing to take the chance. There are so many opportunities in Sweden and so I don't understand why there aren't more men who want to. . . .

M3: It's nice when employers have a clearly positive attitude toward creating good opportunities for families. . . . Much easier to make a good plan for the family if your employer is with you.

These men's attitudes toward fatherhood, family life, and parenthood were in good accord with the ideal of gender equality found in Swedish society (Plantin 2001, 2003). They also related that some evangelical churches try to keep up with societal ideals in many respects. They did not see any direct conflict between how they view the family and the general values in society. What primarily differentiates this group from the other focus groups is perhaps their strong emphasis on the family and on the importance of passing on their values and creating continuity across the generations.

CONCLUSIONS

Ever since the 1970s, a great deal of effort has gone into constructing the gender-equal man and father. At first, this dealt with getting men to take their share of the responsibility for children and the household, but the focus has shifted and today's discussions concern the possibility of dividing parental leave equally between the parents. The model has also changed from one that encourages men to support the mother in caring for the children to one that stresses the importance of shared responsibility. Both parents should have equal opportunities to work and care for their children. The state has also carried through a large number of campaigns aimed at achieving and constructing this new type of father. In spite of these efforts, we see from statistical and sociological studies that women still have primary responsibility for the children and the home. Men do take a greater proportion of parental leave today but not at all as great a proportion as one might have expected following the various campaigns.

The aim of the present study has been to analyze how men with different social and cultural backgrounds relate to these daddy campaigns as well as to the issue of men's increased presence in the home and increased involvement in their children's lives. The four groups we chose to study showed variation regarding a number of factors, including, among others, the importance of class, religion, nationality, living conditions, involvement in men's issues, and occupational position. We will comment on some of our results here.

It is striking how all the focus groups clearly related to the ideal of gender equality (Nordberg 2005). Today, the notion that fathers should get involved with their children, stay at home, and help care foe infants seems to be met with complete acceptance and is almost the predominant figure of thought. Regardless of what one thinks about it, it is necessary to relate to the notion of a gender-equal fatherhood. Most of the men we interviewed also had a positive view and showed relatively great involvement in these issues. Thus, the hegemonic structure is changing. To qualify for hegemonic masculinity, it is no longer enough to be rational, goal-means oriented, career oriented, and disciplined. Today, men must also show their readiness to engage in child care, their child orientation, and their willingness to live up to the ideal of gender equality (Johansson and Kuosmanen 2003).

Even if the men in the different focus groups were consensual as to the importance of fathers taking care of their children, there was variation in the meanings, language, and thoughts revealed in relation to these issues. Several of these differences concern how social position or convictions affect how men speak about fatherhood. Other differences concern what is in focus in the discussion. We will discuss below some of the analytical shifts that are observable in our interview material.

The Individual or Society?   When we discuss questions concerning fatherhood, the focus is either on the individual or at a more political level. This becomes clear when we touch on how the various campaigns affect men. For example, the issue of blame was predominant in certain groups. The therapists thought men could react negatively to all the campaigns, and that men could become stressed and feel inadequate. These participants used psychological terms and considered that men are perhaps not ready to accept every-

thing but instead need time to reflect if they are to change. Several of the other groups dealt with issues at a more political level, talking about the importance of making an impact and gelling men to take responsibility. Here, the state is not viewed as the enemy or as intrusive but as a helper. The men's views on the state were also highly variable, from those who thought that men and families react negatively to state intrusion into the private sphere to those who thought the state creates possibilities for a better family life.

Fathers, Children, or the Family?   It is noticeable, in some cases, that we have concentrated particularly on men's issues. This is clearest in the group of therapists but also in other groups; for example, the male network and the predominantly immigrant group spoke primarily about the situation for men and the importance of getting men involved in these issues. In this regard, the Christian group constituted a sharp contrast. Here, the concern was with the family and values connected to the family as a unit. The discussion on fatherhood was never detached from the family. These men thought that fatherhood and family should always be treated in unison and with a focus on common values. Child issues, on the other hand, seemed to fall into the background in all the groups.

Possibilities or Limitations?   Another factor differentiating the groups involves how the present situation was viewed. In several groups, for example, the male network and the Christians, participants expressed a realistic but still hopeful outlook on change and men's ability to change. This is in sharp contrast to men in the predominantly immigrant group, who embraced the same basic goal of creating the gender-equal father but who also saw many obstacles. They primarily mentioned material obstacles but also social exclusion. When families find themselves outside society, there are no chances and no reasons to consider who should stay home with the children. Most of the men interviewed were aware that there are a number of obstacles to gender equality but that these are manifested in different ways.

All in all, we can see that there is a great deal uniting the focus groups. At the same time, however, we see a number of interesting dividing lines. For example, the men's analyses shifted between the individual and the societal level, and in one group—the Christian men—the focus was placed on the family. The obstacles to change were also varyingly marked and clear in the predominantly immigrant group, where the discussion not only dealt with which decision the family can make or wants to make but also with the family's overall situation in society.

Recent studies of how Scandinavian men relate to family and parenthood have shown a strong family orientation. The demands of being the breadwinner were toned down, and work was not as highly valued as previously. At the same time, a number of investigations have indicated the emergence of a partially new fatherhood (Holter and Aarseth 1993; Hagström 1998; Plantin 2001). Statistics, on the other hand, gave a somewhat different picture. Fathers earned two-thirds of the family's income. Moreover, men were more likely than women to work full time.

What is the situation today? Researchers agree that the greatest obstacle to development of gender equality and more present fathers may be found in the organization of working life (Johansson and Kuosmanen 2003). Many parents are forced to choose between work and family life. In their study of the family strategies of Swedish businesses, Hwang, Haas, and Rissell (2000) show that only 3 percent of businesses had developed active approaches and support to families with children. A Norwegian study by Brandth and Kvande (2003) shows that even if fathers wish to become involved and take responsibility, this ambition is often limited by what is sanctioned by employers.

Today, Scandinavian men participate more and more in housework. But it is still women who take primary responsibility for the children and the home (Plantin 2001, 2003). There is a tendency for men to participate in the "fun" aspects of parenthood, while women are in charge of the rest. The division of labor is still such that men are responsible for play, sports, and outdoor activities, while women's area of responsibility is the home. A political ambition to change this division of labor entails encouraging new parental identities.

Bekkengen (2002, 2003) differentiates between child-oriented masculinity and gender-equal men.

According to her, what we see today is a strong tendency toward men wanting to be at home with their children and that men have developed a more caring attitude, but this does not necessarily mean men are more gender equal. Bekkengen considers that these phenomena must be held apart. Men's child orientation is more a question of their "picking out the good bits" than of a radical transformation of masculinity.

Maybe men's possibility to pick and choose a suitable parental role is the most significant expression of their power position. Today men are expected to be good and present fathers, but there are still clear and important gender differences in the construction of parenthood. Even though the Swedish debate has been under heavy impact of political ideals and "the gender equality paradigm," the conception of "good enough parenthood" is still gendered and polarized. It is more legitimate and normal for a man to use economic or career arguments in discussions concerning parenthood. Men's power positions are to a great extent formed around their abilities and possibilities to choose—and to form their parenthood in any way they wish. As we have already pointed out, this scenario has a great impact on the political discussion about parental leave insurance. The distinction made by Bekkengen between child-oriented and gender-equal masculinity contributes to making this visible, but it is also important to emphasize and put forward the potential to change in the child-oriented masculinity. Perhaps we should see men's increased interest in caring for their children as an important step on the way toward a changed and more gender-equal parenthood (Plantin 2003).

NOTES

1. The study reported on in this article is part of a larger research project aimed at studying how the gender-equal and caring man is constructed in the meeting between a political macro-perspective on gender equality and men's own reflections and everyday experiences of gender equality. The project is funded by the Swedish Council for Working Life and Social Research.

2. Today, parental leave insurance consists of a total of 480 days. Formally, half of these belong to the father, but all days except the two earmarked "daddy months" (an additional month was introduced in 2002) may be transferred to the mother.

REFERENCES

Åström. G. 1992. Fasta förbindelser. Om välfärdsreformer och kvinnors välfärd. I *Kontrakt i kris: Om kvinnors plats i välfärdsstaten* [Welfare reforms and women's welfare. In Women's roles in the Swedish welfare model], edited by Gertrud Åström and Yvonne Hirdman. Stockholm: Carlssons.

Beckman, B. 1965. Mannens andra roll. I *Könsroller: Debatt om jämställdhet* [Men's second rote. In Gender roles: Discussions on equality], edited by Ingrid Fredriksson. Uppsala/Stockholm: Studentföreningen Verdandi/Bokförlaget Prisma.

Bekkengen, L. 1996. Mäns föräldraledighet—en kunskapsöversikt [Men on parental leave—a knowledge report]. Working report 96:12, Karlstad, Sweden: Högskolan i Karlstad.

———. 2002. *Man får välja—om föräldraskap och föräldraledighet i arbetsliv och sumhälle.* [Men can choose—parenthood and parental leave in Swedish society]. Malmö, Sweden: Liber.

———. 2003. Föräldralediga män och barnorienterad maskulinitet. I *Manlighetens många ansikten—fäder, feminister, frisörer och andra män* [Men on parental leave and child-oriented masculinity. In The many faces of masculinity—fathers, feminists, hair-dressers and other men], edited by T. Johansson and J. Kuosmanen, 181–203. Malmö, Sweden: Liber.

Brandth, B., and E. Kvande. 2003. *Fleksible fedre* [Flexible fathers]. Oslo: Universitetsforlaget.

Chronholm, A. 2004. *Föräldraledig pappa: Mäns erfarenheter av delad föräldraledighet* [Fathers on parental leave: Men's experiences of shared parenting]. Gothenburg, Sweden: University of Göteborg, Department of Sociology.

Connell, R. W. 1995. *Masculinities.* Cambridge: Polity.

Deutch, F. M. 1999. *Having it all: How equally shared parenting works.* Cambridge, MA: Harvard University Press.

Dienhart, A. 1998. *Reshaping fatherhood: The social construction of shared parenting.* Thousands Oaks, CA: Sage.

Hagström, C. 1998. *Man är inte far man blir far* [One is not a father, one becomes a father]. Lund, Sweden: Akademilitteratur.

Holter, Ø, and H. Aarseth. 1993. *Mäns livssammanhang* [Men's lives]. Stockholm: Bonniers.

Hwang, P., L. Haas, and G. Rissell. 2000. *Organizational change and gender equity: International perspectives on fathers and mothers at the workplace.* London: Sage.

Hylander, I. 1998. *Fokusgrupper som kvalitativ datainsamlingsmetod* [Focus groups as a qualitative method]. FOG Report, No. 42.

Johansson, T. 2000. *Det första könet? Mansforskning soin reflexiv praktik* [The primary gender? Research on men as a reflexive practice]. Lund, Sweden: Studentlitttteratur.

Johansson, T., and J. Kuosmanen, eds. 2003. *Manlighetens många ansikten* [The many faces of masculinity]. Lund, Sweden: Liber.

Karlsson, G. 1996. Från broderekap till systerskap: Det socialdemokratiska kvinnoförbundets kamp för makt och inflytande. I Socialdemokratiska arbetarpartiet. [From brothers to sisters: The social democratic struggle for the liberation of women. In Socialdemokratiska arbetarpartiet]. Lund, Sweden: Arkiv.

Kimmel, M., and M. A. Messner. 1995. *Men's lives,* 3rd ed. Boston: Allyn & Bacon.

Klinth. R. 2002. *Göra pappa med barn—den svenska pappapolitiken 1960–95* [Making dad pregnant—the Swedish political agenda on fatherhood 1960–95). Umeå, Sweden: Borea förlag.

———. 2003. Män gör jämställdhet—eller kan en man vara feminist? 1 *Manlighetens många ansikten—fäder, feminister. frisörer och andra män* [Men doing equality—or can a man become a feminist? In The many faces of masculinity], edited by T. Johansson and J. Kuosmanen, 30–45. Malmö, Sweden: Liber.

———. 2004. Att kvotera eller inte. I *Vems valfrihet? Debattbok om en delad föräldraförsäkring* [In To share or not? Who's choice? In *A Debate Book on Shared Parental Leave*], edited by Ulrika Lorentzi, 55–75. Stockholm: Agora och HTF.

———. 2005. Pappaledighet som jämställdhetsprojekt—om den svenska pappaledighetens politiska hisloria [Parental leave as an equality project—the history of Swedish parental leave), in *Statens offentliga utredningar.* edited by Gertrud Åström, 66. Stockholm: Fritzes.

Krueger, R. A. 1994. *Focus groups: A practical guide for applied research.* London: Sage.

Lupton, D., and L. Barclay. 1997. *Constructing fatherhood: Discourses and experiences.* London: Sage.

Magnusson, E. 2001. *Gender equality in many different versions: Patterns in political gender equality rhetoric in the Swedish 1990s.* Oslo: Nordiska Rådet.

Morgan, D., and R. Krueger. 1998. *The focus group kit.* Thousands Oaks, CA: Sage.

Nordberg, M. 2005. *Jämställdhetens spjutspets? Manliga arbetstagare i kvinnoyrken. jämställdhet, maskulinitet, femininitet och heteronormativitet.* [The avant-garde of gender equality? Male employers in female occupations, equality, femininity and heteronormativity]. Götebotg, Sweden: Arkipelag.

Nyberg. A. 2004. Framsieg och fallgrop, In *Vems valfrihet? Debattbok om en delad föräldraförsäkring* [Progress or Pitfall? In Who's Freedom or Choice? In *A Debate Book on Shared Parental Leave*], edited by Ulrika Lorentzi, 210–35. Stockholm: Agora och HTF.

Palme. O. 1972. The emancipation of man. *Journal of Social Issues* 28 (2): 237–46.

Plantin. L. 2001. *Män, familjeliv och föräldraskap* [Men. family life and parenthood]. Umeå. Sweden: Boréa.

———. 2003. "Del nya faderskapet"—ett faderskap för alla? Om kön. klass och faderskap. I *Manlighetens många ansikten* [The new fatherhood—a fatherhood for all men? Gender, class and fatherhood. In The many faces of masculinity], edited by T. Johansson and J. Kuosinanen, 164–80. Lund, Sweden: Liber.

Stalens Offentliga Utredningar. 2005. Reformerad föräldraförsäkring—Kärlek, omvårdnad, trygghet [Reformed parental insurance—Love, care and security], 73. Stockholm: Fritzes.

Sandlund. M. B. 1968. *The status of women in Sweden: Report to the United Nations 1968.* Stockholm: Sweden Today.

Seidler, V. 1994a. *Unreasonable men: Masculinity and social theory.* London: Routledge

———. 1994b. *Recovering the self: Morality and social theory.* London: Routledge.

Sernhede, O. (2002) *Alienation is my nation.* Stockholm: Ordfront.

Wibeck, V. 2000, *Fokusgrupper: Om fokuserade gruppintervjuer som undersökningsmetod* [Focus groups: Focused group interviews as a method of investigation]. Lund, Sweden: Studentlitteratur.

Widerberg, K. 1993. Kvinnoperspektiv på rätten: Den svenska föräldraförsäkringen som ett exempel. I *Jämställdhetsforskning: Sökljus på Sverige som jämställdhetens förlovade land.* [Feminist perspectives on justice: The example of the Swedish parental insurance. In *Research on equal Status Policy: Searchlight on Sweden as the Promised Land of Equality*]. edited by Liselott Jakobsen and Jan Karlsson. Forskningsrapport 93:5. Karlstad, Sweden: Högskolan i Karlstad.

30

Getting to Equal

Progress, Pitfalls, and Policy Solutions on the Road to Gender Parity in the Workplace

PAMELA STONE

Kate Hadley aspired to do it all—pursue a successful career and raise a family. With a BA and MBA from Ivy League schools, Kate was a poster girl for the feminist movement, having easily cracked the boys' club of the corporate suite. She was committed to her job, experienced (with more than 10 years as an international marketing executive), and—when I interviewed her—at home full time with her kids. Part of the so-called "opt-out revolution" popularized by the media, Kate epitomizes high-achieving women who are said to be throwing over careers for family, their decision to be home a choice and part of a larger social movement, not simply a retro echo. Stay-at-home moms like Kate might not be the first group of women you'd think to study if you wanted to learn more about inequality in the workplace, but in fact their experiences are central to understanding recent trends. These women offer a unique lens for viewing the processes underlying women's progress—and lack thereof—in achieving gender parity in employment.

TRENDS IN THE GENDER REVOLUTION

Since the 1970s, women have made great and, by historical standards, rapid gains in the workplace. They have closed the college education gap, and their graduation rate now eclipses men's. While their labor force participation rate is still lower than men's (60 percent versus 75 percent in 2008 for those aged 16 and over), it has risen rapidly over a period that saw men's begin to dip. Importantly, over this same period, women (particularly white and middle-class women) began eschewing the pattern of dropping out of the labor force after becoming mothers, instead working continuously throughout the years of peak family formation (as less-privileged women have always done). Fully two-thirds of mothers of preschoolers are in the labor force today. And fulfilling the basis for those old "You've come a long way, baby" ads, many women have entered formerly male-dominated, high-prestige, lucrative, and powerful professions once all but closed to them.

With respect to advancing in the workplace, women have been doing everything right for close to four decades now getting educated, working more and more continuously, and moving out of dead-end, low-paying "pink-collar" jobs. That's the good news. The bad news is that despite women's best and sustained efforts, progress toward gender equality is uneven and appears to be stalling.

Let's start by looking at one of the bright spots: the mobility of women out of low-paying historically "female" jobs such as child care providers and secretaries. One such measure of this movement is the index of dissimilarity, which expresses the extent of sex segregation in terms of the proportion of workers who would have to change jobs in order to create a fully integrated workplace. A fully integrated workplace is defined as one in which women's representation in any occupation would be equal to their representation in the labor force as a whole. In 1970, this index stood at 0.57; today, it is around 047. Progress, yes, but there's a long way to go when you consider that about half of all workers would still have to switch jobs for the workplace to be completely integrated.

Another sobering observation is that most of the gains in this index resulted from dramatic declines in segregation in the distant 1970s. Recent decades have shown virtually no change. Nor has women's progress in integrating jobs occurred across the board. Rather, integration has been experienced almost entirely by middle-class, college-educated, predominately white women who were able to respond quickly to opportunities afforded by the late 20th-century shift to a postindustrial economy and the attendant growth of professional and managerial jobs. Less well-educated women did not enjoy similar opportunities and remain mired in low-wage jobs. Finally, even in professional fields where women are well- and long-represented, they are often concentrated in less prestigious and less lucrative niches, and do not appear to be making it to the very top. Law, one of the first fields to open up to women, is a notable case in point. Women received about half of all law degrees conferred in 2001, when they made up 30 percent of the profession. At the same time, however, they accounted for only 15 percent of federal judges, 15 percent of law firm partners (only 5 percent of managing partners), 10 percent of law school deans, and 10 percent of general counsels.

The most widely used bottom-line indicator of gender inequality is the wage gap, computed as the ratio of women's to men's median earnings. Since the 1970s, when women earned roughly 59 cents to every dollar earned by a man, the gap has narrowed considerably, and now stands at 78 cents to every dollar. This progress is largely a function of women's entry into higher-paying fields, but also of declines in men's earnings. Trends in the gender wage gap show rapid and sizeable improvement, starting in the 1980s (see Figure 1). This improvement, however, was followed by a subsequent slowdown.

For today's twenty somethings, the wage gap narrows to near parity, as would be expected for these beneficiaries of the gender revolution. By the time they reach their thirties, however, women have become parents. And despite the fact that these women have become more experienced workers, the wage gap widens, approaching overall levels. The wage gap is

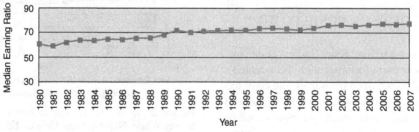

Figure 1. Trends in Women's Earnings (Relative to men): 1980–2007
Source: Institute for Women's Policy Research, *Fact Sheet on the Gender Wage Gap: 2007,* August 2008, based on compilation of data from Current Population Surery.

also wider for women of color (African American women earn 63 cents and Latinas 53 cents to every dollar earned by a white man). Even in the professional and managerial ranks, where formal credentials are critical (and meritocratic principles govern recruitment, promotion, and pay), sizeable gender gaps remain. In 2000, these gaps were 65 cents to the dollar for financial managers, 72 cents for physicians, 73 cents for lawyers, and 81 cents for editors and reporters, to name but a few fields in which women have made considerable inroads.

What explains the overall gender wage gap? Between 1983 and 2000, according to a 3003 report by the U.S. Government Accountability Office, just over half of the gap is due to "legitimate" or "valid" sources, including differences in human capital (such as education and training), hours worked, industrial and occupational positions, and unionization levels. The remaining 45 percent is unexplained, which most analysts attribute to differences in tastes or preferences and/or outright discrimination, although some suggest that it is attributable lo very fine-grained occupational segregation.

Not only are major sources of the gap unknown, so too are prospects for future progress. Leading experts on gender inequality, such as sociologist Reeve Vanneman and his colleagues, have raised the worrying question: "Are we seeing the end of the gender revolution?" Others, such as psychologist Virginia Valian, ask impatiently "Why so slow?" The decade-long slowdown in integrating jobs and closing the wage gap—at a virtual standstill in the new millennium—is a red flag lo scholars, activists, and policymakers alike that something is seriously amiss on the road to gender equality.

OPTING OUT? OR PUSHED OUT?

This is where women like Kate Hadley come in. I talked with Kate as part of a larger study I conducted of women who had transitioned from lives that combined professional careers with family—a contemporary, feminist model—to lives in which careers were left behind and taking care of children and family became their major focus—typically understood as a neo-traditional, counter-feminist lifestyle. Kate and women like

her in their thirties and forties were responsible for much of the improvement registered in the aggregate indicators described above. If these women are retreating from professional success, or "opting out" as media pundits claim, this might explain some of the slowdown in women's progress, or even portend a greater stall. I wanted to learn two things: (1) What was happening to this cohort of fast-track women? Were they turning away from combining careers with motherhood and, if so, how widespread was this phenomenon? (2) Among women who have "opted out," what led them to do so? In particular, what role did those hard-to-measure, unexplained "choices," tastes, and preferences (said to be evolving to reflect traditional gender roles) play? Likewise, what role did discrimination play?

In answer to the first questions, Figure 2 shows trends in full-time family caregiving and employment among the demographic said to be heading home (white, married, college-educated mothers). The overall trend in caregiving is downward, but not straightforward: In 1981, 25.2 percent of women stayed home, which declined to an all-time low in 1993 of 16.5 percent, rising again in 2005 to 21.3 percent. The uptick in staying home in the mid-1990s was attributable primarily to unemployment levels, rising husbands' earnings, and deferred childbearing. Furthermore, among

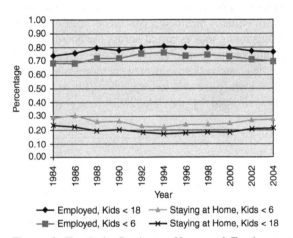

Figure 2. Trends in Staying at Home and Employment among White, Non-Hispanic College-Educated Mothers
Source: Tabulation of March Curent Population Survey microdata, 1984-2004, by Cordelia Reimers, Department of Economics, Hunter College and Graduate Center, CUNY

mothers, college-educated women exhibit the highest rates of labor force participation, and more recent cohorts of professional women are combining careers with motherhood in greater proportions than ever before: 77 percent in 2004. Overall, these trends show little sign of women reverting to 1950s stereotypes. Whether looking at staying at home or employment, however, we see a plateau or slowdown after an initial burst of rapid change. And, as with trends in job desegregation and the wage gap, this leveling off is not fully understood, though the parallels strongly suggest that the trends are interrelated.

To understand more about the decision-making underlying these trends, I interviewed dozens of at-home moms across the country who had worked in a variety of high-status professional and managerial jobs (more than half of whom had advanced degrees). What I found is that working moms are not "opting out" of the workplace because of family. They're being shut out. Their decisions did not reflect a change in favor of domesticity nor even a newfound appreciation of mothering (that came after they quit). Women spoke much more about work than about family in discussing why and how they'd come to quit. Nor did outright old-fashioned sex discrimination play a role (these women were surprisingly resilient, recounting overtly sexist experiences with tough matter-of-factness, almost gusto).

Instead, the combination of rising hours, travel, and 24/7 accountability demanded in today's workplaces, coupled with insufficient and inadequate part-time and flexible options, put these working moms in a classic time bind. As I talked with them, I heard the same thing over and over: that their jobs were "all-or-nothing," forcing these high-achieving women into decisions to reluctantly interrupt, and sometimes terminate, their once-flourishing careers. Married to men with comparable credentials and work histories—until they became parents—women found themselves "home alone" and primarily responsible for child care, their husbands' inability to help out a function of their own high-demand jobs.

One of the paradoxes of my findings is that these at-home moms, seemingly the most traditional of women, were actually highly work-committed. Despite being married to equally successful men who could support them at home, most women, after becoming mothers, stuck it out, trying to make work work. Some were denied flexibility outright, but more quit because their efforts to fashion flexible careers—films that should have been applauded—were instead penalized. Indicative of the mommy-tracking and stigma these innovators experienced, one woman invoked *Scarlet Letter*–like imagery as she explained to me "When you job share, you have 'MOMMY' stamped in huge letters on your head." Once women shifted away from a full-time-plus schedule, their formerly high-flying careers nosedived, undermining their attachment to their careers in a classic scenario of negative reinforcement.

My results highlight the way in which time demands and professional occupations' inflexibility create a de facto "motherhood bar." This bar operates in tandem with the secondary influence of intensive parenting to cause women to quit their careers. Ostensibly meritocratic and unbiased time demands, coupled with ideal worker standards of commitment, appear to be replacing essentialist stereotypes in preventing women's full integration in professional fields. More women than ever are professionals and managers (over a third of all employed women), and the hours of these jobs have ratcheted up, such that the United States now enjoys the dubious distinction of having the world's longest workweek. That's not to say that essentialist stereotypes have disappeared. Indeed, they are at the heart of the double bind of work-family conflict. But stereotypes now operate in less overt ways, under the cover of time norms and related job imperatives. And because women facing untenable work conditions voluntarily "quit," unequal outcomes become their "choice" rather than a reflection of employers' (often discriminatory) practices.

Most women, of course, cannot quit, and instead persevere in the face of inflexible schedules, mommy-tracking, and low pay. Less-educated and less-advantaged women accommodate their caregiving needs by cycling in and out of the labor force through a series of low-wage jobs, often fired when they take time off or show up late because they have to attend to family needs. These different strategies to accommodate family responsibilities share the same result: considerable costs not just to women in the form of lost earnings, but also to firms and the economy in the form of underused skills and talent. The motherhood penalty has now been well-documented. Incidentally, men—

perceived as primary breadwinners—enjoy a 'father-hood premium" that further exacerbates the gender gap. The deep-seated and entrenched nature of moth-erhood bias means that it is more difficult to discern, more taken for granted as the norm, than is outright old-style sexism. Witness the easy acceptance of the notion that women like the ones I studied, who've spent a lifetime devoted to the pursuit of professional success, happily throw it all over in a (baby's) heart-beat.

REMEMBERING THE LADIES: POLICIES FOR GENDER EQUALITY

The motherhood penalty reminds us that workplace in-equality is deeply rooted in the division of labor at home. The gendered nature of care, coupled with the absence of public supports in the United States for caregiving, redound to women's detriment and remain a lingering basis of labor market inequality. Women must trade time in paid employment for time devoted to unpaid caregiving, a trade-off that looms ever larger as we face a widely acknowledged care crisis occa-sioned by an aging society, changes in family and household structure, and gaps in the social safety net. An effective policy response requires that we confront both sides of the work-family equation to neutralize the penalty to caregiving and break the link between gender and care. To accomplish this, we must provide supports for more gender-equitable caring *and* earn-ing. In devising policy initiatives, we do not need to start from scratch, but can instead look to Europe's ex-perience to draw both positive and negative lessons. While work-family policies and supports are more widespread and well-established there, somewhat surprisingly these countries exhibit less gender equal-ity than the United States. This outcome alerts us to steer clear of policies that unintentionally cement women's secondary labor market position as part-time workers in highly segregated female ghettoes. Such policies include the long unpaid leave in Germany that reinforces a traditional division of labor and women's lesser labor force attachment. A better approach would be to err in favor of more egalitarian approaches like those in Sweden and Norway, which provide generous wage-replacement policies and family leave provi-sions to promote men's caregiving.

Current economic circumstances, coupled with a new administration led by President Barack Obama, create a moment of crisis and opportunity. Congress and the Obama administration are off to a good start, putting more teeth into existing equal pay laws with the swift passage and signing into law of the Lilly Ledbet-ter Fair Pay Act. As the Ledbetter case demonstrated, garden variety sexism is alive and well. Ledbetter, an experienced plant manager for the Goodyear Tire & Rubber Company, filed suit when she learned that she was earning less than her male counterparts, a case that made its way to the Supreme Court. The court did not deny that Ledbetter had suffered pay discrimination, but ruled that she had failed to file her claim in time. The Ledbetter bill closes that loophole, effectively ex-tending the deadline under which plaintiffs can bring suit under existing equal pay laws. Several pending fair pay bills go even further, requiring proactive oversight and enforcement of anti-discrimination laws. The new stimulus package also contains provisions to strengthen and re-energize the Equal Employment Opportunity Commission (EEOC). Together, these laws send a pow-erful signal that puts employers on notice and empow-ers women workers who are experiencing sex discrim-ination. Under the Bush administration, the EEOC was already paying increased attention to family caregiving discrimination (FCD). Currently the fastest-growing area of employment discrimination litigation, FCD at-tacks the motherhood penalty directly, and these cases must be vigorously pursued.

The recently passed stimulus package, insofar as it contains numerous tax and spending policies related to employment and earnings, can also be used to advance gender equity and parity—a true win-win—and must be evaluated and implemented with this goal in mind. A guiding principle should be to maintain and hasten the progress women have made, largely at the top, while increasing opportunities for those at the bottom who have not enjoyed the same gains and suffer the triple penalty of gender, race, and class. Thus, we need a two-pronged approach to move closer to gender equality, one that raises the ceiling and lifts the floor.

Women's jobs appear to be a little more recession-proof than men's in the current downturn, but women's groups have called on the new administration to "remember the ladies" to create more public-sector jobs in fields such as education, health care, and social services. While the stimulus package does so, it appears to be weighted somewhat more heavily toward creating male-dominated infrastructure jobs. The enormous scale of new job creation offers a rare chance to challenge existing stereotypes about what constitutes "women's" and "men's" work. By coupling job creation with new training and recruitment efforts, the employment-stimulus package can bring more women into high-paying "male" jobs, while at the same time encouraging men to enter lower-paying, but seemingly reliable "female" jobs, thereby reducing unemployment *and* shrinking the wage gap.

The kind of job creation entailed in the stimulus package would especially benefit women at the true middle and bottom of the income spectrum. The problem for women at the very bottom is that work doesn't pay enough to offset its associated costs, especially child care. In addition to creating more employment opportunities, we need to make work worth it for these women, and the enhanced earned income tax credits in the stimulus package are a good beginning. Nearly one-third of women in the labor force work in low-wage jobs compared with one-fifth of male workers. To really move women out of poverty and to economic self-sufficiency and parity with men, we need more aggressive policies that address low pay directly, such as raising the minimum wage or implementing more comprehensive policies like living wage and pay equity reforms. All of these, but especially pay equity, which expands the reach of equal pay laws to level earnings for comparable jobs with similar requirements and responsibilities, will go far to increase women's earnings and narrow the gender gap by addressing the sizeable pay disparities associated with job segregation.

Policies that facilitate mothers' labor force attachment by nullifying the trade-off between unpaid care work and employment are also needed. In this regard, extension of the Family and Medical Leave Act to provide *paid* family leave with fewer restrictions in coverage is the obvious answer, and already a reality in a number of states, notably California and New Jersey. Providing child care, either directly or in the form of

subsidies, as well as universal early childhood education, will make it possible for women to hold on to jobs and accrue valuable experience while simultaneously affording their children well-documented educational benefits. Finally, universal health insurance, insofar as it promotes health and wellness, reduces the need for women to take costly absences and interruptions from work to care for sick children and other family members.

Last, we need to find ways to undermine the long-hour work culture that effectively bars women's progress in elite jobs and robs all parents, fathers and mothers, of time with their families. One way to reduce hours is to extend overtime provisions to the professional and managerial jobs that are now exempt from them, requiring employers to pay workers for those 40-hour-plus workweeks. A good place to start would be to overturn Bush-era policies that broadened exempt coverage. Absent this, we need to look to the private sector to come up with meaningful, non-stigmatized, and gender-neutral ways of working flexibly, including better-paying and more equitable part-time jobs with prorated benefits (health care reform will advance this goal by making part-time positions less costly to employers). Many American companies already have innovative and successful work-life and work-family policies and practices in place that can serve as a model. While some argue that curtailed hours and family-friendly flexibility are no longer feasible in an era of economic insecurity, news reports make dear that both are being used in innovative ways to avoid layoffs in the current deep recession. Similar strategies of shortening the workweek and encouraging flexibility have a long track record in dealing with unemployment in Europe. As an added attraction, research demonstrates that flexibility and family-friendly innovations enhance employee morale, productivity, and retention.

Current policies and work arrangements short-change women's employment and earnings, but they also shortchange men's participation in parenting and family life. We'll know we have achieved true gender parity when men and women participate equally and fully in market-based work and the unpaid work of the family, when women are not only just as likely as men to be CEOs, but men are just as likely as women to stay at home.

31

Separating the Men from the Moms

The Making of Adult Gender Segregation in Youth Sports

Michael A. Messner

Suzel Bozada-Deas

In volunteer work, just as in many families and workplaces, gender divisions are pervasive and persistent. Women are often expected to do the work of caring for others' emotions and daily needs. Women's volunteer labor is routinely devalued in much the same ways that housework and childcare are devalued in the home and women's clerical and other support work is devalued in the professions (Hook 2004). Similarly, men tend to do the instrumental work of public leadership, just as they do in the family and the workplace, and their informal work is valued accordingly.

This article examines the social construction of adult gender divisions of labor in a community volunteer activity, youth sports. A few scholars have examined women's invisible labor in sports (Boyle & McKay 1995). In her study of a Little League Baseball league, Grasmuck (2005) estimates that the 111 league administrators, head coaches, and assistant coaches (mostly men) contribute a total of 33,330 hours of volunteer labor in a season—an average of about 300 hours per person. Much of the work women do in youth sports is behind-the-scenes support that is less visible than coaching (Thompson 1999). In a study of Little League Baseball in Texas, Chafetz and Kotarba (1999, 48–49) observed that "team mothers" in this "upper middle class, 'Yuppie' Texas community" do gender in ways that result in "the re-creation and strengthening of the community's collective identity as a place where, among other things, women are primarily mothers to their sons." As yet, no study has focused on how this gender divide among adults in youth sports happens. How do most men become coaches, while most women become "team moms"? How do adult gender divisions of labor in youth sports connect with commonsense notions about divisions between women and men in families and workplaces? This is important: Millions of children play community-based youth sports every year, and these athletic activities are a key part of the daily lives of many families. It is also important for scholars of gender—studying segregation in this context can reveal much about how gender divisions are created and sustained in the course of everyday life.

COACHES AND "TEAM MOMS"

In 1995, when we (the first author, Mike, and his family) arrived at our six-year-old son's first soccer practice, we were delighted to learn that his coach was a woman. Coach Karen, a mother in her mid-30s, had grown up playing lots of sports. She was tall, confident, and athletic, and the kids responded well to her leadership. It seemed to be a new and different world than the one we grew up in. But during the next decade, as our two sons played a few more seasons of soccer, two years of youth basketball, and more than decade of baseball, they never had another woman head coach. It is not that women were not contributing to the kids' teams. All of the "team parents" (often called "team moms")—parent volunteers who did the behind-the-scenes work of phone-calling, organizing weekly snack schedules and team parties, collecting money for gifts for the coaches, and so on—were women. And occasionally, a team had a woman assistant coach. But women head coaches were few and far between.

In 1999, we started keeping track of the numbers of women and men head coaches in Roseville's[1] annual American Youth Soccer Organization (AYSO) and Little League Baseball/Softball (LLB/S) yearbooks we received at the end of each season. The yearbooks revealed that from 1999 to 2007, only 13.4 percent of 1,490 AYSO teams had women head coaches. The numbers were even lower for Little League Baseball and Softball; only 5.9 percent of 538 teams were managed by women. In both AYSO and LLB/S, women coaches were clustered in the younger kids' teams (ages five to eight) and in coaching girls. Boys—and especially boys older than age 10—almost never had women coaches. These low numbers are surprising for several reasons. First, unlike during the 1950s and 1960s, when there were almost no opportunities for girls to play sports, today, millions of girls participate in organized soccer, baseball, softball, basketball, and other sports. With this demographic shift in youth sports, we expected that the gender division of labor among parents would have shifted as well. Second, today's mothers in the United States came of age during and after the 1972 institution of Title IX and are part of the generation that ignited the booming growth

of female athletic participation. We wondered how it happened that these women did not make a neat transition from their own active sports participation into coaching their own kids. Third, women in Roseville outnumber men significantly in every volunteer activity having to do with kids, such as the Parent and Teacher Association (PTA), Scouts, and school special events. Coaching youth sports is the great exception to this rule. Sport has changed over the past 30 years, from a world set up almost exclusively by and for boys and men to one that is moving substantially (although incompletely) toward gender equity (Messner 2002). Yet, men dominate the very public on-field volunteer leadership positions in community youth sports.

This article is part of a larger study of gender in adult volunteering in two youth sports programs in a small independent suburb of Los Angeles that we call Roseville. Both of the sports leagues are local affiliates of massive national and international organizations. LLB/S and AYSO offer an interesting contrast in youth sports organizations, especially with respect to gender. Little League Baseball began in 1938 and for its first 36 years was an organization set up exclusively for boys. When forced against its will by a court decision in 1974 to include girls, Little League responded by creating a separate softball league into which girls continue to be tracked. Today, LLB/S is an organization that boasts 2.7 million child participants worldwide, 2.1 million of them in the United States. There are 176,786 teams in the program, 153,422 of them in baseball and 23,364 in softball. Little League stays afloat through the labor of approximately 1 million volunteers.

When AYSO started in 1964, it was exclusively for boys, but by 1971, girls' teams had been introduced, Thus, over the years, the vast majority of people who have participated in AYSO have experienced it as an organization set up for boys *and* girls. AYSO remains today mostly a U.S. organization, with more than 650,000 players on more than 50,000 teams. The national AYSO office employs 50 paid staff members, but like LLB/S, AYSO is an organization largely driven by the labor of volunteers, with roughly 250,000 volunteer coaches, team parents, and referees.

The differently gendered history of these two organizations offers hints as to the origins of the differences we see; there are more women head coaches in soccer than in baseball. Connell (1987) argues that every social institution—including the economy, the military, schools, families, or sport—has a "gender regime," which is defined as the current state of play of gender relations in the institution. We can begin to understand an institution's gender regime by measuring and analyzing the gender divisions of labor and power in the organization (i.e., what kinds of jobs are done by women and men, who has the authority, etc.). The idea that a gender regime is characterized by a "state of play" is a way to get beyond static measurements that result from a quick snapshot of an organizational pyramid and understanding instead that organizations are always being created by people's actions and discourse (Britton 2000). These actions often result in an organizational inertia that reproduces gender divisions and hierarchies; however, organizations are also subject to gradual—or occasionally even rapids—change.

Institutional gender regimes are connected with other gender regimes. Put another way, people in their daily lives routinely move in, out, and across different gender regimes—families, workplaces, schools, places of worship, and community activities such as youth sports. Their actions within a particular gender regime—for instance, the choice to volunteer to coach a youth soccer team—and the meanings they construct around these actions are constrained and enabled by their positions, responsibilities, and experiences in other institutional contexts. We will show how individual decisions to coach or to serve as team parents occur largely through nonreflexive, patterned interactions that are infused with an ascendant gender ideology that we call "soft essentialism." These interactions occur at the nexus of the three gender regimes of community youth sports, families, and workplaces.

RESEARCH METHODS

The low numbers of women coaches in Roseville AYSO and LLB/S and the fact that nearly all of the team parents are women gave us a statistical picture of persistent gender segregation. But simply trotting out these numbers couldn't tell us *how* this picture is drawn. We wanted to under stand the current state of play of the adult gender regime of youth sports, so we developed a study based on the following question: What are the social processes that sustain this gender segregation? And by extension, we wanted to explore another question: What is happening that might serve to destabilize and possibly change this gender segregation? In other words, are there ways to see and understand the internal mechanisms—the face-to-face interactions as well as the meaning-making processes—that constitute the "state of play" of the gender regime of community youth sports?

Questions about social processes—how people, in their routine daily interactions, reproduce (and occasionally challenge) patterned social relations—are best addressed using a combination of qualitative methods. Between 2003 and 2007, we systematically explored the gender dynamics of volunteer coaches in Roseville by deploying several methods of data collection. First, we conducted a content analysis of nine years (1999–2007) of Roseville's AYSO and LLB/S yearbooks (magazine-length documents compiled annually by the leagues, containing team photos as well as names and photos of coaches and managers). The yearbook data on the numbers and placement of women and men coaches provides the statistical backdrop for our study of the social processes of gender and coaching that we summarized above.

Second, we conducted field observations of numerous girls' and boys' soccer, baseball, and softball practices and games. We participated in clinics that were set up to train soccer and baseball coaches and a clinic to train soccer referees. We observed annual baseball and softball tryouts, a managers' baseball "draft," and several annual opening ceremonies for AYSO and LLB/S.

Third, Mike conducted several seasons of participant observation—as a volunteer assistant coach or as scorekeeper—of his son's Little League Baseball teams, ranging from six- and seven-year old co-ed T-ball teams to 13- and 14-year-old boys' baseball teams. These positions gave him observational vantage points near the coaches from which he could jot down short notes that he would later develop into longer field notes. Mike's "insider" role as a community member and a father of kids in these sports leagues allowed him easy access. He always informed the coaches of his sons' teams that he was doing a study, but like many who conduct participant observation, it seemed that his role as researcher was frequently "forgotten" by others and that he was most often seen as a father, an assistant coach, or a scorekeeper.

Fourth, we conducted 50 in-depth interviews with women and men volunteers—mostly head soccer coaches and baseball or softball managers of both boys' and girls' teams but also a small number of assistant coaches and team parents. The interviewees were selected through a snowball sampling method. All but three of those interviewed were parents of children playing in the Roseville soccer, baseball, or softball leagues. Although there were far more men coaches than women coaches from whom to choose, we purposely interviewed roughly equal numbers of women (24) and men (26) coaches. Two of the women coaches were single with no children, one was a divorced single mother, one was a mother living with her female partner, and the rest were mothers living with a male spouse. One of the men coaches was single with no children, two were divorced fathers, and the rest were fathers living with a female spouse. Most of the men interviewed were in their 40s, with an average age of 45. The women were, on average, 39 years old. Nearly all of the interviewees were college educated, living in professional-class families. They self-identified ethnically as 68 percent white, 18 percent Hispanic, 4 percent Asian American, and 10 percent biracial or other. This ethnic breakdown of our interviewees reflects roughly the apparent ethnic composition of coaches in the annual yearbooks. However, since whites are only 44 percent and Asian Americans are 27 percent of the population of Roseville, it is apparent that whites are overrepresented as coaches and Asian Americans are underrepresented (Roseville is 16 percent Hispanic).

We conducted the first three interviews together. Suzel then conducted 38 of the subsequent interviews, while Mike did nine. Mike used his insider status as a member of the community and as a parent of kids who had played in the local youth sports leagues to establish trust and rapport with interviewees. No doubt his status as a white male college professor with a deep background in sports also gave him instant credibility with some interviewees. Suzel, by contrast, was an outsider in most ways. She was a Latina graduate student, not a resident of Roseville, and her own two daughters did not play local youth sports. Moreover, she had almost no sports background. Suzel closed the social distance with her interviewees by enrolling in a coaching clinic and a refereeing clinic and by observing several practices and games to better understand the role that coaches play with the kids. In the interviews, Suzel judiciously used her knowledge from these clinics and her observations of practices and games to ask knowledgeable questions and sharp follow-up probes. This strategy created rapport and it also allowed Suzel to demonstrate knowledge of sports and coaching, thus bridging what might otherwise have been a credibility gap between her and some of those with deep athletic experience and knowledge. At times, Suzel used her outsider status as a benefit, asking naïve questions about the particularities of Roseville that might have sounded disingenuous coming from an insider.

THE COACHES' STORIES

When we asked a longtime Little League Softball manager why he thinks most head coaches are men while nearly all team parents are women, he said with a shrug, 'They give opportunities to everybody to manage or coach and it just so happens that no women volunteer, you know?" This man's statement was typical of head coaches and league officials who generally offered up explanations grounded in individual choice: Faced with equal opportunities to volunteer, men just *choose* to be coaches, while women *choose* to be team parents.

But our research shows that the gendered division of labor among men and women volunteers in youth coaching results not simply from an accumulation of individual choices; rather, it is produced through a profoundly *social* process. We will first draw from our interviews with head coaches to illustrate how gender divisions of labor among adult volunteers in youth sports are shaped by gendered language and belief systems and are seen by many coaches as natural extensions of gendered divisions of labor in families and workplaces. We next draw observations from our field notes to illustrate how everyday interactions within the gendered organizational context of youth sports shapes peoples' choices about men's and women's roles as coaches or team parents. Our main focus here will be on reproductive agency—the patterns of action that reproduce the gender division of labor. But we will also discuss moments of resistance and disruption that create possibilities for change.

Gendered Pipelines

When we asked coaches to describe how they had decided to become coaches, most spoke of having first served as assistant coaches—sometimes for just one season, sometimes for several seasons—before moving into head coaching positions. Drawing from language used by those who study gender in occupations, we can describe the assistant coach position as an essential part of the "pipeline" to the head coach position (England 2006). One of the reasons for this is obvious: many parents—women and men—believe that as a head coach, they will be under tremendous critical scrutiny by other parents in the community. Without previous youth coaching experience, many lack the confidence that they feel they need to take on such a public leadership task. A year or two of assistant coaching affords one the experience and builds the confidence that can lead to the conclusion that "I can do that" and the decision to take on the responsibility of a head coaching position.

But the pipeline from assistant coaches to head coaches does not operate in a purely individual voluntarist manner. A male longtime Little League manager and a member of the league's governing board gave us a glimpse of how the pipeline works when there is a shortage of volunteers:

> One time we had 10 teams and only like six or seven applicants that wanted to be strictly manager. So you kinda eyeball the yearbook from the year before, maybe a couple or years [before], and see if the same dad is still listed as a[n assistant] coach, and maybe now it's time he wants his own team. So you make a lot of phone calls. You might make 20 phone calls and hopefully you are going to get two or three guys that say, "Yes, I'll be a manager."

The assistant coach position is a key part of the pipeline to head coaching positions both because it makes people more confident about volunteering to be a head coach and, as the quote above illustrates, because it gives them visibility in ways that make them more likely to be actively recruited by the league to be a head coach. To understand how it is that most head coaches are men, we need to understand how the pipeline operates—how it is that, at the entry level, women's and men's choices to become assistant coaches and/or team parents are constrained or enabled by the social context.

Recruiting Dads and Moms to Help

There is a lot of work involved in organizing a successful youth soccer, baseball, or softball season. A head coach needs help from two, three, even four other parents who will serve as assistant coaches during practices and games. Parents also have to take responsibility for numerous support tasks like organizing snacks, making team banners, working in the snack bar during games, collecting donations for year-end gifts for the coaches, and organizing team events and year-end parties. In AYSO, parents also serve as volunteer referees. When we asked head coaches how they determined who would help them with these assistant coaching and other support tasks, a very common storyline developed: the coach would call a beginning-of-the-season team meeting, sometimes preceded by a letter or e-mail to parents, and ask for volunteers. Nearly always, they ended up with dads volunteering to help as assistant coaches and moms volunteering to be team parents. A woman soccer coach told a typical story:

> At the beginning of the season I sent a little introductory letter [that said] I really badly need an assistant coach and referee and a "team mom." You know anyone that is keen on that, let's talk about it at the First practice. And this year one guy picked up the phone and said. "Please, can I be your assistant coach?" And I spoke to another one of the mums who I happen to know through school and she said, "Oh, I can do the team mum if you find someone to help me." And by the first practice, they'd already discussed it and it was up and running.

We can see from this coach's statement how the assistant coach and team parent positions are sometimes informally set up even before the first team meeting and how a coach's assumption that the team parent will be a "team *mom*" might make it more likely that women end up in these positions. But even coaches—such as the woman soccer coach quoted below—who try to emphasize that team parent is not necessarily a woman's job find that only women end up volunteering:

> Before the season started, we had a team meeting and I let the parents know that I would need a team parent and I strongly stressed *parent,* because I don't think it should always be a mother. But we did end up with the mom doing it and she assigns snacks and stuff like that.

None of the head coaches we interviewed said that they currently had a man as the team parent. Four coaches recalled that they had once had a man as a team parent (although one of these four coaches said, "Now that I think about it, that guy actually volunteered his wife do it"). When we asked if they had ever had a team parent who was a man, nearly all of the coaches said never. Many of them laughed at the very thought. A woman soccer coach exclaimed with a chuckle, "I just can't imagine! I wonder if they've *ever* had a 'team mom' who's a dad. I don't know [laughs]." A man soccer coach stammered his way through his response, punctuating his words with sarcastic laughter: "Ha! In fact, that whole concept—I don't think I've ever *heard* of a team dad [laughs]. Uh—there *is* no team dad, I've never heard of a team dad. But I don't know why that would be." A few coaches, such as the following woman softball coach, resorted to family metaphors to explain why they think there are few if any men volunteering to be team parents: "Oh, it's always a mom [laughs]. 'Team mom.' That's why it's called 'team *mom.*' You know, the coach is a male. And the mom—I mean, that's the *housekeeping—you* know: Assign the snack."

There are gendered assumptions in the language commonly linked to certain professions, so much so that often, when the person holding the position is in the statistical minority, people attach a modifier, such as *male* nurse, *male* secretary, *woman* judge, *woman* doctor. Or *woman* head coach. Over and over, in interviews with coaches, during team meetings, and in interactions during games, practices, and team parties, we noticed this gendered language. Most obvious was the frequent slippage from official term *team parent* to commonly used term *"team mom."* But we also noticed that a man coach was normally just called a coach, while a woman coach was often gender marked as a woman coach. As feminist linguists have shown, language is a powerful element of social life—it not only reflects social realities such as gender divisions of labor, it also helps to construct our notions of what is normal and what is an aberration (Thorne, Kramarae, and Henley 1983). One statement from a woman soccer coach, "I wonder if they've *ever* had a 'team mom' who's a dad," illustrates how gendered language makes the idea of a man team parent seem incongruous, even laughable. In youth sports, this gendered language supports the notion that a team is structured very much like a "traditional" heterosexual family: The head coach—nearly always a man—is the leader and the public face of the team; the team parent—nearly always a woman—is working behind the scenes, doing support work; assistant coaches—mostly men, but including the occasional woman—help the coach on the field during practices and games.

Teams are even talked about sometimes as "families," and while we never heard a head coach referred to as a team's "dad," we did often and consistently hear the team parent referred to as the "team mom." This gendered language, drawn from family relations, gives us some good initial hints as to how coach and team parent roles remain so gender segregated. In their study of self-managing teams, which was intended to break down gender divisions in workplaces, Ollilainen and Calasanti (2007) show how team members' use of family metaphors serves to maintain the salience of gender, and thus, helps to reproduce a gendered division of labor. Similarly, in youth sports contexts, gendered language structures people's conversations in ways that shape and constrain their actions. Is a man who volunteers to be a team parent now a "team mom"?

Gender Ideology and Work/Family Analogies

When we asked the coaches to consider why it is nearly always women who volunteer to be the team parent, many seemed never to have considered this question before. Some of the men coaches seemed especially befuddled and appeared to assume that women's team-parenting work is a result of an almost "natural" decision on the part of the woman. Some men, such as the following soccer coach, made sense of this volunteer division of labor by referring to the ways that it reflected divisions of labor in men's own families and in their community: "In this area we have a lot of stay-at-home moms, so it seems to kind of fall to them to take over those roles." Similarly, a man baseball coach whose wife served as the team parent explained, "I think it's because they probably do it at home. You know, I mean my wife—even though she can't really commit the time to coach, I don't think she would *want* to coach—uh, she's very good with that [team parent] stuff." A man soccer coach explained the gender divisions on youth sports teams in terms of people's comfort with a nostalgic notion of a "traditional family":

> That's sort of the classical family, you know, it's like the Donna Reed family is AYSO, right? . . . They have these assigned gender roles . . . and people in Roseville, probably all over the United Slates, they're fairly comfortable with them, right? It's, uh, maybe insidious, maybe not, [but] framed in the sort of traditional family role of dad, mom, kids. . . . people are going to be comfortable with that.

Another man baseball coach broadened the explanation, drawing connections to divisions of labor in his workplace:

> It's kinda like in business. I work in real estate, and most of your deal makers that are out there on the front lines, so to speak, making the deals, doing the shuckin' and jivin', doing the selling, are men. It's avery Good Ol' Boys network on the real estate brokerage side. There are a ton a females who are on the property management side, because it's *housekeeping*, it's *managing*, it's like running the *household*, it's behind the scenes, it's like cooking in the kitchen—[laughs]— I mean, I hate to say that, but it's that kind of role that's secondary. Coach is out in the front leading the squad, mom sitting behind making sure that the snacks are in order and all that. You know—just the way it is.

Having a male coach and a "team mom" just seemed normal to this man, "You know, just the way it is," because it seemed to flow naturally from divisions of labor in his household and in his workplace—gendered

divisions of labor that have the "the Good Ol' Boys" operating publicly as the leaders "on the front lines . . . shuckin' and jivin'," while the women are offering support "behind the scenes . . . like cooking in the kitchen." Echoing this view, a man soccer coach said, "I hate to use the analogy, but it's like a secretary: You got a boss and you've got a secretary, and I think that's where most of the opportunities for women to be active in the sports is, as the secretary."

When explaining why it is that team parents are almost exclusively women, a small number of women coaches also seemed to see it in essentialist terms—like most of the men coaches saw it.

Many women coaches, however, saw the gendering of the team parent position as a problem and made sense of its persistence, as did many of the men, by referring to the ways that it reflects family- and work-related divisions of labor. But several of the women coaches added an additional dimension to their explanations by focusing on why they think the men don't or won't consider doing team parent work. A woman soccer coach said, "I think it's because the dads want to be involved with the action. And they are not interested in doing paperwork and collecting money for photos or whatever it is. They are not interested in doing that sort of stuff." Another woman soccer coach extended this point: "I think it's probably, well, identity, which is probably why not many men do it. You know, they think that is a woman's job, like secretary or nurse or, you know." In short, many of the women coaches were cognizant of the ways that the team parent job was viewed by men, like all "women's work," as nonmasculine and thus undesirable. A woman Little League coach found it ironically funny that her husband, in fact, does most of the cooking and housework at home but will not take on the role of team parent for his daughter's team. When asked if changing the name to "team dad" might get more men to volunteer, she replied with a sigh,

> I don't know. I wish my husband would be a team dad because he's just very much more domesticated than I am [laughs]. You know, "Bring all the snacks, honey, hook us up," you know. I think there's a lot of men out there, but they don't want to be perceived as being domesticated.

This coach's comment illustrates how—even for a man who does a substantial amount of the family labor at home—publicly taking on a job that is defined as "feminine" threatens to saddle him with a "domesticated" public image that would be embarrassing or even humiliating. In sum, most coaches—both women and men—believe that men become coaches and women become team parents largely because these public roles fit with their domestic proclivities and skills. But the women add an important dimension to this explanation: women do the team parent work because it has to be done . . . and because they know that the men will not do it.

Finding a "Team Mom"

The interview data give us a window into how people make sense of decisions that they have made as youth sports volunteers and provide insights into how gendered language and beliefs about men's and women's work and family roles help to shape these decisions. Yet, asking people to explain how (and especially why) things such as gendered divisions of labor persist is not by itself the most reliable basis for building an explanation. Rather, watching *how* things happen gives us a deeper understanding of the social construction of gender (Thorne 1993). Our observations from team meetings and early season practices reveal deeper social processes at work—processes that shaped people's apparently individual decisions to volunteer for assistant coach or team parent positions. This excerpt from field notes from the first team meeting of a boys' baseball team illustrates how men's apparent resistance to even consider taking on the team parent position ultimately leaves the job in the hands of a woman (who might also have been reluctant to do it):

Coach Bill stands facing the parents, as we sit in the grandstands. He doesn't ask for volunteers for assistant coaches; instead, he announces that he has "invited" two of the fathers "who probably know more about baseball than I do" to serve as his assistants. He then asks for someone to volunteer as the "team mom." He adds, "Now, 'team mom' is not a gendered job: it can be done by a mom or a dad. But we really need a 'team mom.'" Nobody volunteers immediately.

One mom sitting near me mutters to another mom, "I've done this two years in a row, and I'm not gonna do it this year." Coach Bill goes on to ask for a volunteer for scorekeeper. Meanwhile, two other moms have been whispering, and one of them suddenly bursts out with "Okay! She's volunteered to be 'team mom!'" People applaud. The volunteer seems a bit sheepish; her body-language suggests someone who has just reluctantly agreed to do something. But she affirms that, yes, she'll do it.

This first practice of the year is often the moment at which the division of labor—who will be the assistant coaches, who will be the team parent—is publicly solidified. In this case, the men assistant coaches had been selected before the meeting by the head coach, but it apparently took some cajoling from a mother during the team meeting to convince another mother to volunteer to be the "team mom." We observed two occasions when a woman who did not volunteer was drafted by the head coach to be the "team mom." one case, the reluctant volunteer was clearly more oriented toward assistant coaching, as the following composite story from field notes from the beginning of the season of a seven-year-old boys' baseball team illustrates:

At the first practice, Coach George takes charge, asks for volunteers. I tell him that I am happy to help out at practice and games and that he should just let me know what he 'd like me to do. He appoints me Assistant Coach. This happens with another dad, too. We get team hats. Elena, a mother, offers to help out in any way she can. She's appointed "co-team mom" (the coach's wife is the other 'team mom'). She shrugs and says okay, fine. Unlike most 'team moms,' Elena continues to attend all practices. At the fifth practice. Coach George is pitching batting practice lo the kids; I'm assigned to first base, the other dad is working with the catcher. Elena (the 'team mom') is standing alone on the sidelines, idly tossing a ball up in the air to herself. Coach George's son suddenly has to pee, so as George hustles the boy off to the bathroom, Elena jumps in and starts pitching. She's good, it turns out, and can groove the pitch right where the kids want it. (By contrast, George has recently been plunking the kids with wild pitches.) Things move along well. At one point, when Coach George has returned from the bathroom, with Elena still pitching to the kids, a boy picks up a ball near second base and doesn't know what to do with it. Coach George yells at the kid: "Throw it! Throw it to the 'team mom!'" The kid, confused, says, "Where is she?" I say, "The pitcher, throw it to the pitcher." Coach George says, "Yeah, the 'team mom.'"

A couple of years later, we interviewed Elena and asked her how it was that she became a team parent and continued in that capacity for five straight years. Her response illuminated the informal constraints that channel many women away from coaching and toward being team parents:

> The first year, when [my son] was in kindergarten, he was on a T-ball team, and I volunteered lo be manager, and of course the league didn't choose me, but they did allow me to be assistant coach. And I was so excited, and [laughs] of course I showed up in heels for the first practice, because it was right after work, and the coach looked at me, and I informed him that "I'm your new assistant." And he looked at me—and I don't know if *distraught* is the correct word, but he seemed slightly *disappointed,* and he went out of his way to ask the parents who were there watching their children if there was anyone who wanted to volunteer, even though I was there. So there was this male who did kind of rise to the occasion, and so that was the end. He demoted me without informing me of his decision [laughs]—I was *really* enthused, because [my son] was in kindergarten, so I *really* wanted to be coach—or assistant coach at least—and it didn't happen. So after that I didn't feel comfortable to volunteer to coach. I just thought, okay, then I can do "team mom."

As this story illustrates, women who have the background, skills, and desire to work as on-field assistant coaches are sometimes assigned by head coaches to be "team mom." Some baseball teams even have a niche for such moms: a "dugout coach" (or "dugout mom") is usually a mom who may help out with on-field instruction during practices, but on game days, she is assigned the "indoors" space of the dugout, where it is her responsibility to keep track of the line-up and to be sure that the boy who is on-deck (next up to bat) is ready with his batting gloves and helmet on. The dugout coach also—especially with younger kids'

teams—might be assigned to keep kids focused on the game, to keep equipment orderly, to help with occasional first aid, and to help see that the dugout is cleaned of empty water bottles and snack containers after the game is over. In short, the baseball, softball, and soccer fields on which the children play are gendered spaces (Dworkin 2001; Montez de Oca 2005). The playing field is the public space where the (usually male) coach exerts his authority and command. The dugout is like the home—a place of domestic safety from which one emerges to do one's job. Work happens in the indoor space of the dugout, but it is like family labor, behind-the-scenes, supporting the "real" work of leadership that is done on the field.

CHALLENGES AND RESISTANCE

The head coach's common assumption that fathers will volunteer to be assistant coaches and mothers to be "team moms" creates a context that powerfully channels men and women in these directions. Backed by these commonsense understandings of gendered divisions of labor, most men and women just "go with the flow" of this channeling process. Their choices and actions help to reproduce the existing gendered patterns of the organization. But some do not; some choose to swim against the tide. A mother who had several seasons of experience as a head soccer coach described the first team meeting for her youngest child's team:

> At our first team meeting, the coach announced, "I'm looking for a couple of you to help me out as assistant coaches," and he looked directly at the men, and *only* at the men. None of them volunteered. And it was really amazing because he didn't even *look* at me or at any of the other women. So after the meeting, I went up to him and said, "Hey, I've coached soccer for like 10 seasons; I can help you out, okay?" And he agreed, so I'm the assistant coach for him.

This first team meeting is an example of a normal gendered interaction that, if it had gone unchallenged, would have reproduced the usual gender divisions of labor on the team. It is likely that many women in these situations notice the ways that men are, to adopt Martin's

(2001) term, informally (and probably unconsciously) "mobilizing masculinities" in ways that reproduce men's positions of centrality. But this woman's 10 years of coaching experience gave her the confidence and the athletic "capital" that allowed her not only to see and understand but also to challenge the very gendered selection process that was taking place at this meeting. Most mothers do not have this background, and when faced with this sort of moment, they go with the flow.

On another occasion, as the following composite story from field notes describes, Mike observed a highly athletic and coaching-inclined woman assertively use her abilities in a way that initially *seemed* to transcend the gender segregation process, only to be relegated symbolically at season's end to the position of "team mom":

A new baseball season, the first team meeting of the year; a slew of dads volunteer to be assistant coaches. Coach George combs the women for a "team mom" and gets some resistance; at first, nobody will do it, but then he finds a volunteer. At the first few practices, few assistant coaches actually show up. Isabel, a mom, clearly is into baseball, very knowledgeable and athletic, and takes the field. She pitches to the kids, gives them good advice. On the day when George is passing out forms for assistant coaches to sign, he hands her one loo. She accepts it, in a matter-of-fact way. Isabel continues to attend practices, working with the kids on the field.

Though few dads show up for many of the practices, there never seems to be a shortage of dads to serve as assistant coaches at the games. At one game, Coach George invites Isabel to coach third base, but beyond that, she is never included in an on-field coaching role during a game.

End of season, team party. Coach George hands out awards to all the kids. He hands out gift certificates to all the assistant coaches but does not include Isabel. Then he hands out gift certificates to the "team moms," and includes Isabel, even though I don't recall her doing any team parent tasks. She had clearly been acting as an assistant coach all season long.

This story illustrates how, on one hand, a woman volunteer can informally circumvent the sorting process that pushes her toward the "team mom" role by persistently showing up to practices and assertively

doing the work of a coach. As Thorne (1993, 133) points out, individual incidences of gender crossing are often handled informally in ways that affirm, rather than challenge, gender boundaries: An individual girl who joins the boys' game gets defined "as a token, a kind of 'fictive boy,' not unlike many women tokens in predominantly men settings, whose presence does little to challenge the existing arrangements." Similarly, Isabel's successful "crossing" led to her becoming accepted as an assistant coach during practices but rarely recognized as a "real" coach during games. She was a kind of "token" or "fictive" coach whose gender transgression was probably unknown to the many adults who never attended practices. So, in the final moment of the season, when adults and children alike were being publicly recognized for their contributions to the team, she was labeled and rewarded for being a "team mom," reaffirming gender boundaries.

A few coaches whom we interviewed consciously attempted to resist or change this gendered sorting system. Some of the women coaches, especially, saw it as a problem that the team parent job was always done by a woman. A woman softball coach was concerned that the "team mom" amounted to negative role-modeling for kids and fed into the disrespect that women coaches experienced:

The kids think that the moms should just be "team moms." Which means that they don't take the mothers seriously, and I think that's a bad thing. I mean it's a *bad thing*. I think that's a lack of respect to women, to mothers.

Another woman Little League coach said that most team parents are women because too many people assume

that's all the women are good for. I think that's what the mentality is. I made it very clear to our parents that it did not have to be a mother, that it could be a father and that I encourage any dad out there that had time to do what team parents are supposed to do, to sign up and do it. But it didn't happen.

Such coaches find that simply degendering the language by calling this role *team parent* and even stressing that this is not a gendered job is unlikely to yield men volunteers. So what some women coaches do is simply refuse to have a team parent. A woman soccer coach said, "I do it all. I don't have a team parent." Another said, "I think in general, compared to the men who coach, I do more of that [team parent work]." This resistance by women coaches is understandable, especially from those who see the phenomenon of "team mom" as contributing to a climate of disrespect for women coaches. However, this form of resistance ends up creating extra work for women coaches—work that most men coaches relegate to a "team mom."

The very few occasions when a father does volunteer—or is recruited by the coach—to be the team parent are moments of gender "crossing" that hold the potential to disrupt the normal operation of the gender-category sorting process. But ironically, a team parent who is a man can also reinforce gender stereotypes. One man soccer coach told me that the previous season a father had volunteered to be the team parent, but that

he was a disaster [laughs]. He didn't do *anything,* you know, and what little he did it was late; it was ineffective assistance. He didn't come, he didn't make phone calls, I mean he was just like a black hole. And so that—that was an unfortunate disaster. This year it's a woman again.

The idea that a man volunteered—and then failed miserably to do the learn parent job—may serve ultimately to reinforce the taken-for-granted assumption that women are naturally better suited to do this kind of work.

THE DEVALUATION OF WOMEN'S INVISIBLE LABOR

The Roseville "team moms" we observed were similar to those studied by Chafetz and Kotarba (1999) in terms of their education, professional-class status, and family structure. The Texasville and Roseville "team moms" are doing the same kinds of activities, simultaneously contributing to the "concerted cultivation" of their own children (Lareau 2003) while helping to en-

hance the social cohesion of the team, the league, and the community.

Despite the importance of the work team parents are doing, it is not often recognized as equivalent to the work done by coaches. Of course, the team parent typically puts in far fewer hours of labor than does the head coach. However, in some cases, the team parents put in more time than some assistant coaches (dads, for instance, whose work schedules don't allow them to get to many practices but who can be seen on the field during a Saturday game, coaching third base). Yet, the team parent's work remains largely invisible, and coaches sometimes talk about team parents' contributions as trivial or unimportant. Several coaches, when asked about the team parent job, disparaged it as "not very hard to do," "an easy job." But our interviews suggest that the women team parents are often doing this job as one of many community volunteer jobs, while most of the men who coach are engaged in this and only this volunteer activity. A field note from a boys' baseball game illustrates this:

It is the second to last game of the season. During the first inning, Dora, the "team mom," shows up and immediately starts circulating among the parents in the stands, talking and handing out a flier. Tile flier announces the "year end party," to be held in a couple of weeks. She announces that she will supply ice cream and other makings for sundaes. Everyone else can just bring some drinks. She also announces (and it's on the flier) that she's collecting $20 from each family to pay for a "thank you gift . . . for all their hard work" for the head coach and for each of the three assistant coaches (all men). People start shelling out money, and Dora starts a list of who has donated. By the start of the next inning, she announces that she's got to go saying "I have a Webelos [Cub Scouts] parents meeting." She's obviously multitasking as a parent volunteer. By the fourth inning, near the end of the game, she is back, collecting more money, and informing parents on details concerning the party and the upcoming playoffs. Finally, during the last inning, she sits and watches the end of the game with the rest of us.

Dora, like other "team moms," doing work before, during, and after the game—making fliers, communicating with parents, collecting money, keeping lists and records, organizing parties, making sure everyone knows the schedule of upcoming events. And she is sandwiching this work around other volunteer activities with another youth organization. This kind of labor keeps organizations running, and it helps to create and sustain the kind of vibrant community "for the kids" that people imagine when they move to a town like Roseville (Daniels 1985).

SORTING AND SOFT ESSENTIALISM

In this article, we have revealed the workings of a gender-category sorting process that reflects the interactional "doing" of gender discussed by West and Zimmerman (1987). Through this sorting process, the vast majority of women volunteers are channeled into a team parent position, and the vast majority of men volunteers become coaches. To say that people are "sorted" is not to deny their active agency in this process. Rather, it is to underline that organizations are characterized by self-perpetuating "inequality regimes" (Acker 2006). What people often think of as "free individual choices" are actually choices that are shaped by social contexts. We have shown how women's choices to become team parents are constrained by the fact that few, if any, men will volunteer to do this less visible and less honored job. Women's choices are enabled by their being actively recruited—"volunteered"—by head coaches or by other parents to become the "team mom." Moreover, men's choices to volunteer as assistant coaches and not as team parents are shaped by the gendered assumptions of head coaches, enacted through active recruiting and informal interactions at the initial team meeting.

This gender-category sorting system is at the heart of the current state of play of the gender regime of adult volunteer work in youth sports in Roseville. There are several ways we can see the sorting system at work. First, our research points to the role of gendered language and meanings in this process. The term *coach* and the term *"team mom"* are saturated with gendered assumptions that are consistent with most people's universe of meanings. These gendered meanings mesh with—and mutually reinforce—the conventional gendered divisions of labor and power in the organization in ways that make decisions to "go with the flow" appear natural. Second, we have shown how having women do the background support work while men do the visible leadership work on the team is also made to appear natural to the extent that it reiterates the gender divisions of labor that many parents experience in their families and in their workplaces. Roseville is a diverse community that is dominated culturally by white, professional-class families, who—partly through the language and practice of youth sports—create a culturally hegemonic (though not a numerical majority) family form in which educated mothers have "opted out" of professional careers to engage in community volunteer work and "intensive mothering," of their own children (Hays 1996; Stone 2007).

The women we interviewed who had opted out of professional careers narrated their decisions to do so in language of personal choice, rather than constraint. The husbands of these women say that they support their wives' choices. This language of (women's) personal choice also saturates coaches' discussions of why women become "team moms." By contrast, when people talk about men, they are far less likely to do so using a language of choice. Men seem to end up in public careers or as youth sports coaches as a matter of destiny. Grounded in the strains and tensions of contemporary professional-class work–family life, this discourse on gender recasts feminist beliefs in a woman's "right to choose" as her responsibility to straddle work and family life, while the man continues "naturally" to be viewed as the main family breadwinner. We call this ascendant gender ideology "soft essentialism."

Youth sports is a powerful institution into which children are initiated into a gender-segregated world with its attendant ideology of soft essentialism (Messner forthcoming).

In the past, sport tended to construct a categorical "hard" essentialism—boys and men, it was believed, were naturally suited to the aggressive, competitive world of sport, while girls and women were not, Today, with girls' and women's massive influx into sport, these kinds of categorical assumptions of natural difference can no longer stand up to even the most cursory examination. Soft essentialism, as an ascendant professional-class gender ideology, frames sport as a realm in which girls are empowered to exercise individual choice (rehearsing choices they will later face in straddling the demands of careers and family labor), while continuing to view boys as naturally "hard wired" to play sports (and ultimately, to have public careers). Girls are viewed as flexibly facing a future of choices; boys as inflexible, facing a linear path toward public careers. Soft essentialism, in short, initiates kids into an adult world that has been only partially transformed by feminism, where many of the burdens of bridging and balancing work and family strains are still primarily on women's shoulders. Men coaches and "team moms" symbolize and exemplify these tensions.

Time after time, we heard leaders of leagues and some women coaches say that the league leadership works hard to recruit more women coaches but just cannot get them to volunteer. The *formal agency* here is to "recruit more women coaches." But what Martin (2001) calls the *informal practicing of gender* (revealed most clearly in our field-note vignettes) amounts to a collective and (mostly) nonreflexive sorting system that, at the entry level, puts most women and men on separate paths. Martin's work has been foundational in showing how gender works in organizations in informal, nonreflexive ways that rely on peoples' "tacit knowledge" about gender. In particular, she points out "how and why well-intentioned, 'good people' practise gender in ways that do harm" (Martin 2006, 255).

Our study shows a similar lack of "bad guys" engaged in overt acts of sexism and discrimination. Instead, we see a systemic reproduction of gender categorization, created nonreflexively by "well intentioned, good people." The mechanisms of this nonreflexive informal practicing of gender are made to seem normal through their congruence with the "tacit knowledge" of soft essentialism that is itself embedded in hegemonic professional-class family and workplace gender divisions of labor. The fact that soft essentialism emerges from the intersections of these different social contexts means that any attempt to move toward greater equality for women and men in youth sports presupposes simultaneous movements toward equality in workplaces and families.

NOTE

1. Roseville is a pseudonym for the town we studied, and all names or people interviewed or observed for this study are also pseudonyms.

REFERENCES

Acker, Joan. 2006. Inequality regimes: Gender, class and race in organizations. *Gender & Society* 20:441–64.

Boyle, Maree, and Jim McKay. 1995. You leave your troubles at the gate: A case study of the exploitation of older women's labor and "leisure" in sport. *Gender & Society* 9:556–76.

Britton, Dana. 2000. The epistemology of the gendered organization. *Gender & Society* 14:418–34.

Chafetz, Janet Saltzman, and Joseph A. Kotarba. 1999. Little League mothers and the reproduction of gender. In *Inside sports,* edited by Jay Coakley and Peter Donnelly. London and New York: Routledge.

Connell, R. W. 1987. *Gender and power.* Stanford, CA: Stanford University Press.

Daniels, Arlene Kaplan. 1985. Invisible work. *Social Problems* 34:363–74.

Dworkin, Shari L. 2001. Holding back: Negotiating a glass ceiling on women's muscular strength. *Sociological Perspectives* 44:333–50.

England, Paula. 2006. Toward gender equality: Progress and bottlenecks. In *The declining significance of gender?* edited by Francine D. Blau, Mary C. Brinlon, and David B. Grusky. New York: Russell Sage.

Grasmuck, Sherri. 2005. *Protecting home: Class, race, and masculinity in boys' baseball.* Piscataway, NJ: Rutgers University Press.

Hays, Sharon. 1996. *The cultural contradictions of motherhood.* New Haven, CT: Yale University Press.

Hook, Jennifer L. 2004. Reconsidering the division of household labor: Incorporating volunteer work and informal support. *Journal of Marriage and Family* 66:101–17.

Lareau, Annette. 2003. *Unequal childhoods: Class, race, and family life.* Berkeley: University of California Press.

Martin, Patricia Yancy. 2001. Mobilizing masculinities: Women's experiences of men al work. *Organization* 8:587–618.

———. 2006. Practicing gender at work: Further thoughts on reflexivity. *Gender, Work and Organization* 13:254–76.

Messner, Michael A. 2002. *Taking the field: Women, men, and sports.* Minneapolis: University of Minnesota Press.

————. Forthcoming. *It's all for the kids: Gender, families and youth sports.* Berkeley: University of California Press.

Montez de Oca, Jeffrey. 2005. As our muscles get softer, our missile race becomes harder: Cultural citizenship and the "muscle gap." *Journal of Historical Sociology* 18:145–71.

Ollilainen, Marjukka, and Toni Calasanti. 2007. Metaphors al work: Maintaining the salience of gender in self-managing teams. *Gender & Society* 21:5–27.

Stone, Pamela. 2007. *Opting out: Why women really quit careers and head home.* Berkeley: University of California Press.

Thompson, Shona. 1999. The game begins at home: Women's labor in the service of sport. In *Inside sports,* edited by Jay Coakley and Peter Donnelly. London and New York: Routledge.

Thorne, Barrie. 1993. *Gender play: Girls and boys in school.* New Brunswick, NJ: Rutgers University Press.

Thorne, Barrie, Cheris Kramarae, and Nancy Henley. 1983. *Language, gender and society.* Rowley, MA: Newbury House.

West, Candace, and Don Zimmerman. 1987. Doing gender. *Gender & Society* 1:125–51.

32

Moving Up with Kin and Community

Upward Social Mobility for Black and White Women

ELIZABETH HIGGINBOTHAM

LYNN WEBER

. . . When women and people of color experience upward mobility in America, they scale steep structural as well as psychological barriers. The long process of moving from a working-class family of origin to the professional-managerial class is full of twists and turns: choices made with varying degrees of information and varying options; critical junctures faced with support and encouragement or disinterest, rejection, or active discouragement; and interpersonal relationships in which basic understandings are continuously negotiated and renegotiated. It is a fascinating process that profoundly shapes the lives of those who experience it, as well as the lives of those around them. Social mobility is also a process engulfed in myth. One need only pick up any newspaper or turn on the television to see that the myth of upward mobility remains firmly entrenched in American culture: With hard work, talent, determination, and some luck, just about anyone can "make it." . . .

The image of the isolated and detached experience of mobility that we have inherited from past scholarship is problematic for anyone seeking to understand the process for women or people of color. Twenty

years of scholarship in the study of both race and gender has taught us the importance of interpersonal attachments to the lives of women and a commitment to racial uplift among people of color . . .

. . . Lacking wealth, the greatest gift a Black family has been able to give to its children has been the motivation and skills to succeed in school. Aspirations for college attendance and professional positions are stressed as *family* goals, and the entire family may make sacrifices and provide support . . . Black women have long seen the activist potential of education and have sought it as a cornerstone of community development—a means of uplifting the race. When women of color or White women are put at the center of the analysis of upward mobility, it is clear that different questions will be raised about social mobility and different descriptions of the process will ensue. . . .

RESEARCH DESIGN

These data are from a study of full-time employed middle-class women in the Memphis metropolitan

Elizabeth Higginbotham and Lynn Weber, "Moving Up with Kin and Community: Upward Social Mobility for Black and White Women," from *Gender & Society,* Volume 6/1992, p. 416–440. Copyright © 1992. Reprinted by permission.

area. This research is designed to explore the processes of upward social mobility for Black and White women by examining differences between women professionals, managers, and administrators who are from working- and middle-class backgrounds—that is, upwardly mobile and middle-class stable women. In this way, we isolate subjective processes shared among women who have been upwardly mobile from those common to women who have reproduced their family's professional-managerial class standing. Likewise, we identify common experiences in the attainment process that are shared by women of the same race, be they upwardly mobile or stable middle class. Finally, we specify some ways in which the attainment process is unique for each race-class group . . .

. . . We rely on a model of social class basically derived from the work of Poulantzas (1974), Braverman (1974), Ehrenreich and Ehrenreich (1979), and elaborated in Vanneman and Cannon (1987). These works explicate a basic distinction between social class and social status. Classes represent bounded categories of the population, groups set in a relation of opposition to one another by their roles in the capitalist system. The middle class, or professional-managerial class, is set off from the working class by the power and control it exerts over workers in three realms: economic (power through ownership), political (power through direct supervisory authority), and ideological (power to plan and organize work; Poulantzas 1974; Vanneman and Cannon 1987).

In contrast, education, prestige, and income represent social statuses—hierarchically structured relative rankings along a ladder of economic success and social prestige. Positions along these dimensions are not established by social relations of dominance and subordination but, rather, as rankings on scales representing resources and desirability. In some respects, they represent both the justification for power differentials vested in classes and the rewards for the role that the middle class plays in controlling labor.

Our interest is in the process of upward social class mobility, moving from a working-class family of origin to a middle-class destination—from a position of working-class subordination to a position of control over the working class. Lacking inherited wealth or other resources, those working-class people who attain

middle-class standing do so primarily by obtaining a college education and entering a professional, managerial, or administrative occupation. Thus we examine carefully the process of educational attainment not as evidence of middle-class standing but as a necessary part of the mobility process for most working-class people.

Likewise, occupation alone does not define the middle class, but professional, managerial, and administrative occupations capture many of the supervisory and ideologically based positions whose function is to control workers' lives. Consequently, we defined subjects as *middle class* by virtue of their employment in either a professional, managerial, or administrative occupation. . . . Classification of subjects as either professional or managerial-administrative was made on the basis of the designation of occupations in the U.S. Bureau of the Census's (1983) "Detailed Population Characteristics: Tennessee." Managerial occupations were defined as those in the census categories of managers and administrators; professionals were defined as those occupations in the professional category, excluding technicians, whom Braverman (1974) contends are working class.

Upwardly mobile women were defined as those women raised in families where neither parent was employed as a professional, manager, or administrator. Typical occupations for working-class fathers were postal clerk, craftsman, semiskilled manufacturing worker, janitor, and laborer. Some working-class mothers had clerical and sales positions, but many of the Black mothers also worked as private household workers. *Middle-class stable* women were defined as those women raised in families where *either* parent was employed as a professional, manager, or administrator. Typical occupations of middle-class parents were social worker, teacher, and school administrator as well as high-status professionals such as attorneys, physicians, and dentists. . . .

FAMILY EXPECTATIONS FOR EDUCATIONAL ATTAINMENT

Four questions assess the expectations and support among family members for the educational attainment of the subjects. First, "Do you recall your father or mother stressing that you attain an education?" Yes was the response of 190 of the 200 women. Each of the women in this study had obtained a college degree, and many have graduate degrees. It is clear that for Black and White women, education was an important concern in their families. . . .

The comments of Laura Lee,[1] a 39-year-old Black woman who was raised middle class, were typical:

Going to school, that was never a discussable issue. Just like you were born to live and die, you were going to go to school. You were going to prepare yourself to do something.

It should be noted, however, that only 86 percent of the White working-class women answered yes, compared to 98 percent of all other groups. Although this difference is small, it foreshadows a pattern where White women raised in working-class families received the least support and encouragement for educational and career attainment.

"When you were growing up, how far did your father expect you to go in school?" While most fathers expected college attendance from their daughters, differences also exist by class of origin. Only 70 percent of the working-class fathers, both Black and White, expected their daughters to attend college. In contrast, 94 percent of the Black middle-class and 88 percent of the White middle-class women's fathers had college expectations for their daughters.

When asked the same question about mother's expectations, 88 percent to 92 percent of each group's mothers expected their daughters to get a college education, except the White working-class women, for whom only 66 percent of mothers held such expectations. In short, only among the White working-class women did a fairly substantial proportion (about one-third) of both mothers and fathers expect less than a college education from their daughters. About 30 percent of Black working-class fathers held lower expectations for their daughters, but not the mothers; virtually all middle-class parents expected a college education for their daughters.

Sara Marx is a White, 33-year-old director of counseling raised in a rural working-class family. She is among those whose parents did not expect a college education for her. She was vague about the roots of attending college:

It seems like we had a guest speaker who talked to us. Maybe before our exams somebody talked to us. I really can't put my finger on anything. I don't know where the information came from exactly.

"Who provided emotional support for you to make the transition from high school to college?" While 86 percent of the Black middle-class women indicated that family provided that support, 70 percent of the White middle-class, 64 percent of the Black working class, and only 56 percent of the White working class received emotional support from family.

"Who paid your college tuition and fees?" Beyond emotional support, financial support is critical to college attendance. There are clear class differences in financial support for college. Roughly 90 percent of the middle-class respondents and only 56 percent and 62 percent of the Black and White working-class women, respectively, were financially supported by their families. These data also suggest that working-class parents were less able to give emotional or financial support for college than they were to hold out the expectation that their daughters should attend.

FAMILY EXPECTATIONS FOR OCCUPATION OR CAREER

When asked, "Do you recall your father or mother stressing that you should have an occupation to succeed in life?" racial differences appear: Ninety-four percent of all Black respondents said yes. In the words of Julie Bird, a Black woman raised-middle-class junior high school teacher.

My father would always say, "You see how good I'm doing? Each generation should do more than the generation before." He expects me to accomplish more than he has.

Ann Right, a 36-year-old Black attorney whose father was a janitor, said:

They wanted me to have a better life than they had. For all of us. And that's why they emphasized education and emphasized working relationships and how you get along with people and that kind of thing.

Ruby James, a Black teacher from a working-class family, said:

They expected me to have a good-paying job and to have a family and be married. Go to work every day. Buy a home. That's about it. Be happy.

In contrast, only 70 percent of the White middle-class and 56 percent of the White working-class women indicated that their parents stressed that an occupation was needed for success. Nina Pentel, a 26-year-old white medical social worker, expressed a common response: "They said 'You're going to get married but get a degree, you never know what's going to happen to you.' They were pretty laid back about goals."

When the question focuses on a career rather than an occupation, the family encouragement is lower and differences were not significant, but similar patterns emerged. We asked respondents, "Who, if anyone, encouraged you to think about a career?" Among Black respondents, 60 percent of the middle-class and 56 percent of the working-class women answered that family encouraged them. Only 40 percent of the White working-class women indicated that their family encouraged them in their thinking about a career, while 52 percent of the White middle-class women did so. . . .

When working-class White women seek to be mobile through their own attainments, they face conflicts. Their parents encourage educational attainment, but when young women develop professional career goals, these same parents sometimes become ambivalent. This was the case with Elizabeth Marlow, who is currently a public interest attorney—a position her parents never intended her to hold. She described her parents' traditional expectations and their reluctance to support her career goals fully.

My parents assumed that I would go college and meet some nice man and finish, but not necessarily work after. I would be a good mother for my children. I don't think that they ever thought I would go to law school. Their attitude about my interest in law school was, "You can do it if you want to, but we don't think it is a particularly practical thing for a woman to do."

Elizabeth is married and has three children, but she is not the traditional housewife of her parents' dreams. She received more support outside the family for her chosen lifestyle.

Although Black families are indeed more likely than White families to encourage their daughters to prepare for careers, like White families, they frequently steer them toward highly visible traditionally female occupations, such as teacher, nurse, and social worker. Thus many mobile Black women are directed toward the same gender-segregated occupations as White women. . . .

MARRIAGE

Although working-class families may encourage daughters to marry, they recognize the need for working-class women to contribute to family income or to support themselves economically. To achieve these aims, many working-class girls are encouraged to pursue an education as preparation for work in gender-segregated occupations. Work in these fields presumably allows women to keep marriage, family, and child rearing as life goals while contributing to the family income and to have "something to fall back on" if the marriage does not work out. This interplay among marriage, education, financial need, and class mobility is complex (Joslin 1979).

We asked, "Do you recall your mother or father emphasizing that marriage should be your primary life goal?" While the majority of all respondents did not get the message that marriage was the *primary* life goal, Black and White women's parents clearly saw this differently. Virtually no Black parents stressed marriage as the primary life goal (6 percent of the working class and 4 percent of the middle class), but significantly more White parents did (22 percent of the working class and 18 percent of the middle class).

Some White women said their families expressed active opposition to marriage, such as Clare Baron, a raised-working-class nursing supervisor, who said, "My mother always said, 'Don't get married and don't have children!' "

More common responses recognized the fragility of marriage and the need to support oneself. For example, Alice Page, a 31-year-old White raised-middle-class librarian, put it this way:

> I feel like I am really part of a generation that for the first time is thinking, "I don't want to have to depend on somebody to take care of me because what if they say they are going to take care of me and then they are not there? They die, or they leave me or whatever." I feel very much that I've got to be able to support myself and I don't know that single women in other eras have had to deal with that to the same degree.

While White working-class women are often raised to prepare for work roles so that they can contribute to family income and, if necessary, support themselves, Black women face a different reality. Unlike White women, Black women are typically socialized to view marriage separately from economic security, because it is not expected that marriage will ever remove them from the labor market. As a result, Black families socialize all their children—girls and boys—for self-sufficiency (Clark 1986; Higginbotham and Cannon 1988). . . .

. . . Fairly substantial numbers of each group had never married by the time of the interview, ranging from 20 percent of the White working-class to 34 percent of the Black working-class and White middle-class respondents. Some of the women were pleased with their singlehood, like Alice Page, who said:

> I am single by choice. That is how I see myself. I have purposely avoided getting into any kind of romantic situation with men. I have enjoyed going out but never wanted to get serious. If anyone wants to get serious, I quit going out with him.

Other women expressed disappointment and some shock that they were not yet married. When asked about her feeling about being single, Sally Ford, a 32-year-old White manager, said:

> That's what I always wanted to do: to be married and have children. To me, that is the ideal. I want a happy, good marriage with children. I do not like being single at all. It is very, very lonesome. I don't see any advantages to being single. None!

SUBJECTIVE SENSE OF DEBT TO KIN AND FRIENDS

McAdoo (1978) reports that upwardly mobile Black Americans receive more requests to share resources from their working-class kin than do middle-class Black Americans. Many mobile Black Americans feel a "social debt" because their families aided them in the mobility process and provided emotional support. When we asked the White women in the study the following question: "Generally, do you feel you owe a lot for the help given to you by your family and relatives?" many were perplexed and asked what the question meant. In contrast, both the working- and middle-class Black women tended to respond immediately that they felt a sense of obligation to family and friends in return for the support they had received. Black women, from both the working class and the middle class, expressed the strongest sense of debt to family, with 86 percent and 74 percent, respectively, so indicating. White working-class women were least likely to feel that they owed family (46 percent), while 68 percent of white middle-class women so indicated. In short, upwardly mobile Black women were almost twice as likely as upwardly mobile White women to express a sense of debt to family.

Linda Brown, an upwardly mobile Black women, gave a typical response, "Yes, they are there when you need them." Similar were the words of Jean Marsh, "Yes, because they have been supportive. They're dependable. If I need them I can depend upon them."

One of the most significant ways in which Black working-class families aided their daughters and left them with a sense of debt related to care for their children. Dawn March expressed it thus:

They have been there more so during my adult years than a lot of other families that I know about. My mother kept all of my children until they were old enough to go to day care. And she not only kept them, she'd give them a bath for me during the daytime and feed them before I got home from work. Very, very supportive people. So, I really would say I owe them for that.

Carole Washington, an upwardly mobile Black woman occupational therapist, also felt she owed her family. She reported:

I know the struggle that my parents have had to get me where I am. I know the energy they no longer have to put into the rest of the family even though they want to put it there and they're willing. I feel it is my responsibility to give back some of that energy they have given to me. It's self-directed, not required.

White working-class women, in contrast, were unlikely to feel a sense of debt and expressed their feelings in similar ways. Irma Cox, part owner of a computer business, said, "I am appreciative of the values my parents instilled in me. But I for the most part feel like I have done it on my own." Carey Mink, a 35-year-old psychiatric social worker, said, "No, they pointed me in a direction and they were supportive, but I've done a lot of the work myself." Debra Beck, a judge, responded, "No, I feel that I've gotten most places on my own." . . .

COMMITMENT TO COMMUNITY

The mainstream "model of community stresses the rights of individuals to make decisions in their own self interest, regardless of the impact on the larger society" (Collins 1990, 52). This model may explain relations to community of origin for mobile White males but cannot be generalized to other racial and gender groups. In the context of well-recognized structures of racial oppression, America's racial-ethnic communities develop collective survival strategies that contrast with the individualism of the dominant culture but ensure the community's survival (Collins 1990; McAdoo 1978; Stack 1974; Valentine 1978). McAdoo (1978)

argues that Black people have *only* been able to advance in education and attain higher status and higher paying jobs with the support of the wider Black community, teachers in segregated schools, extended family networks, and Black mentors already in those positions. This widespread community involvement enables mobile people of color to confront and challenge racist obstacles in credentialing institutions, and it distinguishes the mobility process in racial-ethnic communities from mobility in the dominant culture. For example, Lou Nelson, now a librarian, described the support she felt in her southern segregated inner-city school. She said:

There was a closeness between people and that had a lot to do with neighborhood schools. I went to Tubman High School with people that lived in the Tubman area. I think that there was a bond, a bond between parents, the PTA . . . I think that it was just that everybody felt that everybody knew everybody. And that was special.

Family and community involvement and support in the mobility process means that many Black professionals and managers continue to feel linked to their communities of origin. Lillian King, a high-ranking city official who was raised working class, discussed her current commitment to the Black community. She said:

Because I have more opportunities, I've got an obligation to give more back and to set a positive example for Black people and especially for Black women. I think we've got to do a tremendous job in building self-esteem and giving people the desire to achieve.

Judith Moore is a 34-year-old single parent employed as a health investigator. She has been able to maintain her connection with her community, and that is a source of pride.

I'm proud that I still have a sense of who I am in terms of Black people. That's very important to me. No matter how much education or professional status I get, I do not want to lose touch with where I've come from. I think that you need to look back and that kind of pushes you forward. I think the degree and other things can make you lose sight of that, especially us Black folks, but I'm glad that I haven't and I try to teach that [commitment] to my son.

For some Black women, their mobility has enabled them to give to an even broader community. This is the case with Sammi Lewis, a raised-working-class woman who is a director of a social service agency. She said, "I owe a responsibility to the entire community, and not to any particular group." . . .

CROSSING THE COLOR LINE

Mobility for people of color is complex because in addition to crossing class lines, mobility often means crossing racial and cultural ones as well. Since the 1960s, people of color have increasingly attended either integrated or predominantly White schools. Only mobile White ethnics have a comparable experience of simultaneously crossing class and cultural barriers, yet even this experience is qualitatively different from that of Black and other people of color. White ethnicity can be practically invisible to White middle-class school peers and co-workers, but people of color are more visible and are subjected to harsher treatment. Our research indicates that no matter when people of color first encounter integrated or predominantly White settings, it is always a shock. The experience of racial exclusion cannot prepare people of color to deal with the racism in daily face-to-face encounters with White people.

For example, Lynn Johnson was in the first cohort of Black students at Regional College, a small private college in Memphis. The self-confidence and stamina Lynn developed in her supportive segregated high school helped her withstand the racism she faced as the first female and the first Black to graduate in economics at Regional College. Lynn described her treatment:

I would come into class and Dr. Simpson (the Economics professor) would alphabetically call the roll. When he came to my name, he would just jump over it. He would not ask me any questions, he would not do anything. I stayed in that class. I struggled through. When it was my turn, I'd start talking. He would say, "Johnson, I wasn't talking to you" [because he never said Miss Johnson]. I'd say, "That's all right, Dr. Simpson, it was my turn. I figured you just overlooked

me. I'm just the littlest person in here. Wasn't that the right answer?" He would say, "Yes, that was the right answer." I drove him mad, I really did. He finally got used to me and started to help me.

In southern cities, where previous interaction between Black and White people followed a rigid code, adjustments were necessary on both sides. It was clear to Lynn Johnson and others that college faculty and students had to adapt to her small Black cohort at Regional College.

Wendy Jones attended a formerly predominantly White state university that had just merged with a formerly predominantly Black college. This new institution meant many adjustments for faculty and students. As a working-class person majoring in engineering, she had a rough transition. She recalled:

I had never gone to school with White kids. I'd always gone to all Black schools all my life and the Black kids there [at the university] were snooty. Only one friend from high school went there and she flunked out. The courses were harder and all my teachers were men and White. Most of the kids were White. I was in classes where I'd be the only Black and woman. There were no similarities to grasp for. I had to adjust to being in that situation. In about a year I was comfortable where I could walk up to people in my class and have conversations.

For some Black people, their first significant interaction with White people did not come until graduate school. Janice Freeman described her experiences:

I went to a Black high school, a Black college and then worked for a Black man who was a former teacher. Everything was comfortable until I had to go to State University for graduate school. I felt very insecure. I was thrown into an environment that was very different—during the 1960s and 1970s there was so much unrest anyway—so it was extremely difficult for me.

It was not in graduate school but on her first job as a social worker that Janice had to learn to work *with* White people. She said, "After I realized that I could hang in school, working at the social work agency allowed me to learn how to work *with* White people. I had never done that before and now I do it better than anybody."

Learning to live in a White world was an additional hurdle for all Black women in this age cohort. Previous generations of Black people were more likely to be educated in segregated colleges and to work within the confines of the established Black community. They taught in segregated schools, provided dental and medical care to the Black communities, and provided social services and other comforts to members of their own communities. They also lived in the Black community and worshiped on Sunday with many of the people they saw in different settings. As the comments of our respondents reveal, both Black and White people had to adjust to integrated settings, but it was more stressful for the newcomers.

SUMMARY AND CONCLUSIONS

Our major aim in this research was to reopen the study of the subjective experience of upward social mobility and to begin to incorporate race and gender into our vision of the process. In this exploratory work, we hope to raise issues and questions that will cast a new light on taken-for-granted assumptions about the process and the people who engage in it. The experiences of these women have certainly painted a different picture from the one we were left some twenty years ago. First and foremost, these women are not detached, isolated, or driven solely by career goals. Relationships with family of origin, partners, children, friends, and the wider community loom large in the way they envision and accomplish mobility and the way they sustain themselves as professional and managerial women.

Several of our findings suggest ways that race and gender shape the mobility process for baby boom Black and White women. Education was stressed as important in virtually all of the families of these women; however, they differed in how it was viewed and how much was desired. The upwardly mobile women, both Black and White, shared some obstacles to attainment. More mobile women had parents who never expected them to achieve a college education. They also received less emotional and financial support for college attendance from their families than the women in middle-class families received. Black

women also faced the unique problem of crossing racial barriers simultaneously with class barriers.

There were fairly dramatic race differences in the messages that the Black and White women received from family about what their lives should be like as adults. Black women clearly received the message that they needed an occupation to succeed in life and that marriage was a secondary concern. Many Black women also expressed a sense that their mobility was connected to an entire racial uplift process, not merely an individual journey.

White upwardly mobile women received less clear messages. Only one-half of these women said that their parents stressed the need for an occupation to succeed, and 20 percent said that marriage was stressed as the primary life goal. The most common message seemed to suggest that an occupation was necessary, because marriage could not be counted on to provide economic survival. Having a career, on the other hand, could even be seen as detrimental to adult happiness.

Upward mobility is a process that requires sustained effort and emotional and cognitive, as well as financial, support. The legacy of the image of mobility that was built on the White male experience focuses on credentialing institutions, especially the schools, as the primary place where talent is recognized and support is given to ensure that the talented among the working class are mobile. Family and friends are virtually invisible in this portrayal of the mobility process.

Although there is a good deal of variation in the roles that family and friends play for these women, they are certainly not invisible in the process. Especially among many of the Black women, there is a sense that they owe a great debt to their families for the help they have received. Black upwardly mobile women were also much more likely to feel that they give more than they receive from kin. Once they have achieved professional managerial employment, the sense of debt combines with their greater access to resources to put them in the position of being asked to give and of giving more to both family and friends. Carrington (1980) identifies some potential mental health hazards of such a sense of debt in upwardly mobile Black women's lives.

White upwardly mobile women are less likely to feel indebted to kin and to feel that they have accomplished alone. Yet even among this group, connections to spouses and children played significant roles in defining how women were mobile, their goals, and their sense of satisfaction with their life in the middle class.

These data are suggestive of a mobility process that is motivated by a desire for personal, but also collective, gain and that is shaped by interpersonal commitments to family, partners and children, community, and the race. Social mobility involves competition, but also cooperation, community support, and personal obligations. Further research is needed to explore fully this new image of mobility and to examine the relevance of these issues for White male mobility as well.

NOTE

1. This and all the names used in this article are pseudonyms.

REFERENCES

Braverman, Harry. 1974. *Labor and monopoly capital.* New York: Monthly Review Press.

Carrington, Christine. 1980. Depression in Black women: A theoretical appraisal. In *The Black women,* edited by La Frances Rodgers Rose. Beverly Hills, CA: Sage.

Clark, Reginald. 1986. *Family life and school achievement.* Chicago: University of Chicago Press.

Collins, Patricia Hill. 1990. *Black feminist thought: knowledge, consciousness, and the politics of empowerment.* Boston: Routledge.

Ehrenreich, Barbara, and John Ehrenreich. 1979. The professional-managerial class. In *Between labor and capital,* edited by Pat Walker. Boston: South End Press.

Higginbotham, Elizabeth, and Lynn Weber Cannon. 1988. *Rethinking mobility: Towards a race and gender inclusive theory.* Research Paper no. 8. Center for Research on Women, Memphis State University.

Joslin, Daphne. 1979. Working-class daughters, middle-class wives: Social identity and self-esteem among women upwardly mobile through marriage. Ph.D. diss., New York University, New York.

McAdoo, Harriette Pipes. 1978. Factors related to stability in upwardly mobile Black families. *Journal of Marriage and the Family* 40:761–76.

Poulantzas, Nicos. 1974. *Classes in contemporary capitalism.* London: New Left Books.

U.S. Bureau of the Census. 1983. Detailed population characteristics: Tennessee. Census of the Population, 1980. Washington, DC: GPO.

Vanneman, Reeve, and Lynn Weber Cannon. 1987. *The American perception of class.* Philadelphia: Temple University Press.

33

What Do Low-Income Single Mothers
Say about Marriage?

KATHRYN EDIN

When marriage rates among the poor plunged during the 1970s and 1980s, the American public began to blame welfare. During that time, an unmarried mother who had little or no income or assets could claim welfare until her youngest child aged out of the program (this was the case until 1996, when welfare became time-limited). If she were to marry, her access to welfare would be restricted. Up until the late 1980s, only about half of the states offered any benefits to married couples. By 1990, all states were required to offer welfare benefits to married couples with children who met certain income and eligibility criteria. Yet these benefits were hard to claim because the husband's income and assets were counted in determining the family's ongoing eligibility for the program (all of his income if he was the children's father, and a portion of his income if he was not), and the couple had to prove the principal wage earner had a recent history of work. One study indicates that few welfare recipients understood these complex rules regarding marriage; they generally assumed that marrying would mean the loss of welfare, food stamp, and Medicaid benefits (Edin and Lein 1997).

Not surprisingly, the public viewed the program as one that discouraged the poor from marrying. The Per-

sonal Responsibility and Work Opportunity Reconciliation Act of 1996 (PRWORA) has many aims, but one is to increase the costs of non-marriage by decreasing the resources an unmarried mother can claim from the state (see Corbett 1998). To accomplish this goal, PRWORA mandates states to ensure that recipients comply with certain requirements and offers them new flexibility to go beyond these mandates and impose further requirements. At minimum, PRWORA requires that states limit cash benefit receipt to no more than five years in an adult recipient's lifetime. A second minimum requirement is that states must impose a 20-hour work requirement after two years of receipt. States can opt for other requirements such as school attendance for minor children and participation in "work-related activities" like job search or short-term training. Violations of these requirements can result in a full cut-off or a partial reduction of benefits (these are referred to as "sanctions"). These new time limits and participation requirements sharply limit (or make more costly) the resources that single mothers can claim from the state. Meanwhile, the welfare rolls have fallen to nearly half their early 1990s levels. Though some of the decline is a response to improving economic conditions, the decline is much greater than the improvement in the economy would lead us to expect. Some scholars have claimed that the remainder is due to the "signaling effect" of welfare reform (e.g., that PRWORA has signaled to current and prospective clients that the rules have changed and that welfare is no longer an acceptable or feasible way of life), though there is little clear evidence in this regard.

. . . Yet despite this new world of welfare that confronts low-income adults, an analysis of ethnographic data from two cities suggests that the large majority of welfare recipients who are experiencing the changes with regard to welfare reform, are not planning on marrying in the near future. Furthermore, these recipients report that welfare reform has not changed their views on marriage. This is the case even though recipients said they believed welfare reform was "real" and would indeed be implemented (Edin, Scott, London, and Mazelis 1999).

. . . I utilize data drawn from in-depth, repeated ethnographic interviews with 292 low-income African American and white single mothers in three U.S. cities, to add qualitative grounding to our understanding of these trends. I seek to explicate the social role that marriage plays in the lives of low-income single mothers more fully. Drawing from these data, I show that though most low-income single mothers aspire to marriage, they believe that, in the short term, marriage usually entails more risks than potential rewards. Mothers say these risks may be worth taking if they can find the "right" man—and they define "rightness" in both economic and non-economic terms. They say they are willing, and even eager, to marry if the marriage represents an increase in their class standing and if, over a substantial period of time, their prospective husband's behavior indicates he won't beat them, abuse their children, refuse to share in household tasks, insist on making all the decisions, be sexually unfaithful, or abuse alcohol or drugs. However, many women also believe they can mitigate against these risks if they forgo marriage until the tasks of early child rearing are completed and they can concentrate more fully on labor market activities (e.g., holding a stable job). These women believe that by forgoing marriage until they can make regular and substantial contributions to the household economy, they can purchase the right to share more equally in economic and household deci-

sion-making within marriage. Additionally, an income of their own insures them against destitution if the marriage should fail. Mothers often say that they are hesitant to enter into marriage unless they have enough resources to legitimately threaten to leave the marriage if the previously mentioned behavioral criteria are violated. In this way, they believe they will have more control over a prospective husband's behavior and insurance against financial disaster should the marriage ultimately fail.

LITERATURE REVIEW

The median age at a first marriage is the highest it has been since the United States began keeping reliable statistics: twenty-four for women and twenty-six for men (U.S. Bureau of the Census 1991b). The propensity to remarry has also declined (Cherlin 1992). Furthermore, more women and men are choosing not to marry during the prime family-building years, and thus, more children are living with a single parent. Both non-marriage and single parenthood are particularly common among the poorest segments of American society (U.S. Bureau of the Census 1991a; Schoen and Owens 1992:116). . . .

Both rates of entry into first marriage and remarriage are far lower for poor women than for their more advantaged counterparts (Bumpass and Sweet 1989). Once a woman has children, her chances of marrying are also lower than a childless woman's (Bennett, Bloom, and Craig 1991). There are also large differences by race (Bennett, Bloom and Craig 1990, 1989; Staples 1988). Yet it is poor women with children, a disproportionate share of whom are African Americans, on whom social welfare policy has focused.

Current theories that attempt to explain the decline in marriage have generally focused on four areas: women's economic independence; the inability of men (particularly minority men) to obtain stable family-wage employment; the role that welfare has played in creating marriage disincentives among the poor; and on what might be called cultural factors, such as the stalled revolution in gender roles (see Luker 1996:158–160).

Many scholars argue that women's prospects for economic independence through work make it possible for them to raise their children apart from fathers who are wife beaters, child abusers, or otherwise difficult to live with (Becker 1981; South and Trent 1988; Teachman, Polonko, and Leìgh 1987; Trent and South 1989). In the classic version of this argument (Becker 1981), women who specialize in child rearing and household management, while their spouses specialize in market work, will find marriage very attractive. Women who combine such tasks with work will be less dependent on men to fulfill the bread-winning role. As wages rise, women's employment also rises, and the attractiveness of marriage declines. . . .

A second argument is that there is a shortage of marriageable men among some groups. Most work in this area has focused on African Americans, since it is among blacks that marriage rates are lowest. Some have addressed the question of whether this is due to an insufficient supply of marriageable black men, either because of rising unemployment and incarceration (Wilson 1996, 1987), declining earnings (Oppenheimer 1993), or sex-ratio imbalances (South and Lloyd 1992; Tucker and Mitchell-Kernan 1996). Most analyses show there is some evidence to support each of these variations on the male marriageable pool hypothesis, but the proportion of families headed by a single mother is simply much greater than this approach would predict (Fossett and Kielcolt 1993; Lichter, LeClere and McLaughlin 1991; South and Lloyd 1992).

Third, some have argued that the government may keep poor parents apart by making it more rewarding for the mother to collect welfare benefits than to marry a father with a menial job (Becker 1991; Murray 1984). According to this theory, welfare, rather than work, provides the economic independence that makes it possible, and even profitable, for mothers to eschew marriage. There is little evidence that out-of-wedlock birth rates are affected by either state variations in welfare levels or by changes in state benefits over time, though there is a modest negative effect for remarriage (Bane and Ellwood 1994; Hoffman 1997; Moffitt 1995).

Finally, some scholars argue that marriage decisions are influenced by what are generally termed "cultural" factors, even though these factors can sometimes be traced back to material realities. One argument points to the stalled revolution in sex roles. Although many men are earning less money than previously, and although wives are much more likely to work, few men truly share the household labor and childcare tasks (Hochschild 1989). Kristen Luker argues that when "men are increasingly less able to contribute financially to the household and when they show little willingness to do more work around the house, women will inevitably revise their thinking about marriage, work, and the raising of children" (1996:132). The gender gap in sex-role expectations has grown in recent decades. Scanzoni (1970:148) found that the divergence between husbands and wives over what constitutes legitimate male authority is widest at the lowest class levels. He also found that low status husbands exercised more power in conflict resolution than higher status husbands (1970:156). White women's views tend to be more egalitarian than white men's, both in terms of work and household duties. Black men and women both hold egalitarian views in terms of women's work, but black men lag behind their female counterparts (and white males) in their view of gender roles (Blee and Tickameyer 1995; Collins 1987). No study I know of estimates the strength of the relationship between the gender gap in sex-role expectations and marriage rates. . . .

METHOD

I chose to study the social role of marriage among low-income single mothers for three reasons. First, they are the targets of recent legislation that attempts to encourage marriage. Second, the majority of low-income adult women, for whom the costs of non-marriage and child bearing are presumably the highest, are neither childless nor married (either because they never married or they divorced), and this trend appears to be growing stronger over time (U.S. Bureau of the Census 1993). . . . Third, it is most appropriate for the method I employ. Qualitative research designs typically focus on a single group or "case" and involve an in-depth investigation of the rich interplay of factors involved in some aspect of that group's shared experience (Becker 1992:209–210). . . .

These data consist of transcripts and field notes from in-depth, repeated, qualitative interviews with

292 low-income single mothers in three U.S. cities. In each city, my collaborators and I interviewed roughly 100 low-income single mothers: 87 in Charleston, South Carolina, 105 in Chicago, and 100 in Camden, New Jersey/Philadelphia, Pennsylvania. In Chicago and Charleston, the sample was evenly divided between African Americans and whites. Interviews were conducted between 1989 and 1992. In Camden/Philadelphia, the sample is also predominately African American and white. These interviews were conducted between 1996 and 1999. About half of the respondents in each city and racial group relied on welfare, and about half worked at low-wage jobs (they earned less than $7.50 per hour).

The cities vary in a number of interesting ways. Chicago offered average welfare benefits ($376 for a three-person family) and had an average labor market in the early 1990s, when we did most of our interviewing there. Charleston, South Carolina had very modest welfare benefits ($205 for a family of three) and a tight labor market. Camden, New Jersey is an industrial suburb of Philadelphia, Pennsylvania. In both states, residents received better-than-average welfare benefits in the mid-1990s (roughly $420 for three persons) but the labor market in the Philadelphia region was quite slack. . . .

In all three cities, we scheduled conversations with each respondent at least twice to ensure that there was sufficient time to develop adequate rapport. Within the context of these conversations, we addressed a predetermined set of topics, as well as additional topics brought up by the respondents. The order and precise wording of the questions regarding each topic was not prescribed, but followed the natural flow of conversation.

The primary goal of this analysis is to show what a relatively large, heterogeneous group of low-income single mothers say about the declining propensity of poor mothers and fathers to marry. The analysis is not meant to prove or disprove existing theories of family formation among the poor, but rather to give an in-depth account of the social role marriage plays in the lives of a relatively heterogeneous (in terms of city and race) groups of mothers within a single social category. The analysis will show that much of what poor mothers say supports existing theory, though mothers' accounts show a greater degree of complexity than these theories recognize. The reader will also see that poor mothers' accounts reveal motivations that existing approaches generally neglect. The result is a complex set of personal accounts that can lend crucial qualitative grounding to other representative studies of the retreat from marriage among the poor.

RESULTS

Analysis of the Chicago and Charleston low-income single mothers' accounts reveals five primary reasons why poor parents do not form or reform a legal union with a man (see Table 1). The first line of Table 1 shows the percentage of mothers whose transcripts re-

Table 1 Percent of Low-Income Single Mothers with Positive Views Regarding Marriage, Plans to Marry, and the Percent who Discussed the Importance of Various Factors on Marriage Attitudes by City and Race

	Chicago African American	Chicago White	Charleston African American	Charleston White	Sig. of F Race	Sig. of F City
Positive Orientation toward Marriage	46	60	41	62	*	
Affordability	79	66	55	39	*	***
Respectability	62	50	69	52	*	
Control	79	54	55	36	*	
Trust	66	94	44	60	**	***
Domestic violence	21	54	16	48	***	

Notes: *p < .10 **p < .05 ***p < .001

vealed positive views toward marriage and hoped to marry in the future. As is true in nationally representative surveys (South 1993), whites are somewhat more positively oriented toward marriage than are African Americans, particularly in our Southern site. There are no differences by city. Lines two through six show the five motivations the Chicago and Charleston women most often discussed when they talked about these views in depth. Since we asked all of the Camden/ Philadelphia mothers about each of these motivations, all talked about them, and nearly all felt they were relevant in mothers' decisions regarding marriage (even if they were not relevant to them personally).

Affordability

Men's income is an issue that matters enormously in poor parents' willingness and ability to stay together. Though the *total* earnings a father can generate is clearly the most important dimension for mothers, so is the *regularity* of those earnings, the *effort* men expend finding and keeping work, and the *source* of his income.

One African American mother in Chicago summed her views about contemporary marriage this way: "Men simply don't earn enough to support a family. This leads to couples breaking up." When we asked mothers specifically about their criteria for marriage, nearly every one told us the father would have to have a "good job." One reason was their recognition that the couple would probably not be able to sustain an independent household unless the father made a "decent" living. One African American Camden respondent told us:

> You can't get married and go on living with your mother. That's just like playing house. She expects your husband to be able to provide for you and if he can't, what is he doing marrying you in the first place! She's not going to put up with having him under her roof.

When mothers judge the merits of marriage, they worry a lot about the stability of men's earnings simply because they have to. At the bottom of the income distribution, single mothers who must choose between welfare or low-wage employment to pay their bills face a constant budget shortfall and thus, must continually find ways of getting extra money to pay their bills (Edin and Lein 1997). To generate extra cash, mothers must either find a side job or another adult who can provide regular and substantial economic support. Meanwhile, any given father or boyfriend is likely to have limited skills and a troubled employment history. In sum, while mothers have constant income needs, the men who father their children often cannot consistently meet these needs.

Mothers said their men often complained that women did not understand how difficult it was for men to find steady work. Yet, even mothers who were inclined to sympathize with men's employment difficulties were in a bind: they simply could not afford to keep an economically unproductive man around the house. Because of this, almost all of the low-income single mothers we interviewed told us that rather than marry the father of their children, they preferred to live separately or to cohabit. In cohabiting situations, mothers nearly always said they enforced a "pay and stay" rule. If a father quit his job or lost his job and did not (in the mother's view) try very hard to find another one, or drank or smoked up his paycheck, he lost his right to co-reside in the household. Since her name, not his, was generally on the lease, she had the power to evict him. A black mother from the Philadelphia area explained her practices in this regard:

> We were [thinking about marriage] for a while, but he was real irresponsible. I didn't want to be mean or anything, [but when he didn't work] I didn't let him eat my food. I would tell him, "If you can't put any food here, you can't eat here. These are your kids, and you should want to help your kids, so if you come here, you can't eat their food." Finally, I told him he couldn't stay here either. Right now, I think I would never [get tied to] a[nother] man who is irresponsible and without a job.

Keeping an unemployed man in the house puts a strain on a mother's, already overstrained, budget. It also precludes a woman's ability to offer co-residence to an alternative man who is employed. One African American mother from Charleston told us:

I've been with my baby's father for almost 10 years, since high school graduation. He's talking marriage, but what I'm trying to do now is get away from him. He just lost his job [at the Naval base]. He worked there for 18 years. [Now] he's in work, out of work, then in work again. Right now he's just working part-time at McDonalds. I can do bad by myself, I don't need no one helping me [do bad]. I want somebody better, somebody [who can bring home] a regular paycheck. [So] I'm trying to get away from him right now.

If they are not married, she has the flexibility to lower her household costs by getting rid of him, and the possibility of replacing him with another more economically productive man (or at least one who is working at the time).

Women whose male partners couldn't, or wouldn't, find work, often lost respect for them and "just couldn't stand" to keep them around. A white Chicago divorcee told us:

I couldn't get him to stay working. [T]he kids would be hungry and I'd throw a fit and he'd have a nerve to tell me, "Who cares? You're always over [at your mother's], why can't you ask her for some food?" Talk about a way [to lose someone's respect]. It's hard to love somebody if you lose respect. . . . [Finally, I couldn't take it and I made him leave].

As one can well imagine, men in this situation knew they were purchasing their place in the household and, to some extent, their hold on the woman's affections. The women we interviewed said this made men feel that their girlfriends "only want me for my money." They told us their children's fathers resented their girlfriends' "materialistic" attitudes. Holding fathers to these standards was often emotionally wrenching for mothers. One African American Camden mother expressed her emotional dilemma as follows:

It was like there was a struggle going on inside of me. I mean, he lost his job at the auto body shop when they went [bankrupt] and closed down. Then he couldn't find another one. But it was months and months. I was trying to live on my welfare check and it just wasn't enough. Finally, I couldn't do it any more [because] it was just too much pressure on me [even though] he is

the love of my life. I told him he had to leave, even though I knew it wasn't really his fault that [he wasn't working]. But I had nothing in the house to feed the kids, no money to pay the bills. Nothing. And he was just sitting there, not working. I couldn't take it, so I made him leave.

An African American mother from Charleston emphasized the fact that women not only value earnings, but respect a man who is making his best effort to support his family. She said, "Am I gonna marry him? Of course! If he didn't have a steady job? No, no. [But] If he's helping out the best he can, yeah, I would. He drives a truck [right now]." According to these mothers, a man who could not find work in the formal sector had two choices: he could stay home and wait for the children's mother to kick him out, or he could try to maintain his place in the family by finding work in the underground economy. Sometimes this technique worked, but more often, it backfired. Work in criminal trades was generally easier to get, but mothers said that fathers who engaged in crime for any length of time, generally lost their place in the family as well. When a father began to earn his living by selling drugs, a mother feared that he would bring danger into the household. Mothers worried that fathers' criminal companions might "come for them" at the house, or that fathers might store drugs, drug proceeds, or weapons in the house. Even worse, mothers feared that a father might start "using his product." Mothers also felt that a drug-dealing father would be a very poor role model for their children. Thus, mothers did not generally consider earnings from crime as legitimate earnings (they said they wouldn't marry such a man no matter how much he earned from crime).

Chicago respondents were more likely to discuss economic factors than Charleston mothers were. This difference could be due to the fact that, when the interviews took place, Chicago's unemployment rate was higher than Charleston's, or possibly due to more traditional values among Southerners regarding marriage. Blacks also discussed economic factors more often than whites. This is presumably because black men's earnings are lower than those of whites with similar skill levels.

Respectability

Even within very poor communities, residents make class-based distinctions among themselves. Most of our mothers' eventual goal was to become "respectable," and they believed that respectability was greatly enhanced by a marriage tie to a routinely employed partner earning wages significantly above the legal minimum. However, mothers said that they could not achieve respectability by marrying someone who was frequently out of work, otherwise underemployed, supplemented his income through criminal activity, and had little chance of improving his situation over time. Mothers believed that marriage to such a man would diminish their respectability, rather than enhance it.

Mothers seldom romanticized a father's economic prospects when it came to marriage (though they sometimes did so when conceiving the man's child [see Kefalas and Edin 2000]). They generally knew that if they entered into marriage with a lower-class man, the marriage was unlikely to last because the economic pressures on the relationship would simply be too great. Even if they had contemplated marriage to their children's father "for love" or "romantic feelings," their family members and friends generally convinced poor parents that such a marriage would collapse under economic strain (see also Stack 1974). For these mothers, marriage meant tying oneself to the class position of one's partner "for life." Even if a woman could afford to marry a man whose economic prospects were bleak, her decision would have signaled to her kin and neighbors that he was the best she could do. Mothers expected that marriage should pull them up the class ladder. Community notions of respectability help to explain sentiments like the one revealed by this African American mother in Charleston:

> I want to get married. I've always wanted to get married and have a family. [My baby's father,] he is doing pretty good, but I am not going to marry him until . . . we get some land. [We'll] start off with a trailer, live in that for about 10 years, and then build a dream house. But I am not going to get married and pay rent to someone else. When we save up enough money to [buy] an acre of land and [can finance] a trailer, then we'll marry.

Many mothers told us that their children's fathers also said that they planned to marry them, but wanted to "wait 'till we can afford a church wedding, not just a justice of the peace thing." Marriage made a statement to the larger community about each partner's current and prospective class standing. Thus, marriage could either confer respectability or deny it. If a low-income woman had a child with an erratically employed and unskilled man to whom she was not married, she had not tied herself in any permanent way to him or his class position. Most mothers weren't willing to sign an apartment lease with the man they were with, much less a marriage license. Mothers who remained unmarried were able to maintain their dream of upward mobility. "Marrying up" guaranteed the woman the respect of her community, while marrying at her own class level only made her look foolish in the eyes of her family and neighbors. When we asked mothers whether they would marry the erratic or low earners that had fathered their children, the most common response was "I can do bad by myself."

In addition to the importance women placed on respectability, they also had strong moral (and oftentimes religious) objections to marrying men whose economic situation would, in their view, practically guarantee eventual marital dissolution. Mothers often talked about the "sacred" nature of marriage, and believed that no "respectable" woman would marry under these circumstances (some spoke of such a marriage as a "sacrilege"). In interview after interview, mothers stressed the seriousness of the marriage commitment and their belief that "it should last forever." Thus, it is not that mothers held marriage in low esteem, but rather the fact that they held it in such high esteem that convinced them to forgo marriage, at least until their prospective marriage partner could prove himself worthy economically or they could find another partner who could. To these mothers, marriage was a powerful symbol of respectability, and should not be diluted by foolish unions.

Respectability was equally important for respondents in Chicago and Charleston, though it was somewhat more important for African Americans than for whites (and probably for the same reasons that affordability concerns were). Respondents' discourse in regard to respectability, however, varied quite dramatically by race (Bulcroft and Bulcroft 1993). Many African American respondents who claimed they wanted to marry "up or not at all" knew that holding to such standards might well mean not marrying at all. Whites had less of these anxieties. White respondents typically had sisters, other kin, and friends who had married men who earned a "decent" wage, and were somewhat more sanguine about their own chances of finding such a man than were blacks. A handful of white respondents even told us they planned to "marry out of poverty" so they could become housewives. Only one black respondent reported such plans.

Control and the Stalled Sex Role Revolution at Home

In a non-marital relationship, women often felt they had more control than they would have had if they married. Even if the couple cohabited, they nearly always lived with her mother or in an apartment with her name on the lease. Thus, mothers had the power to evict fathers if they interfered with child rearing, or tried to take control over financial decision-making. Mothers said that fathers who knew they were "on trial" could do little about this state of affairs, especially since they needed a place to live and could not generally afford one on their own. One African American Philadelphia-area respondent's partner quipped, "her attitude is like, 'it's either my way or the highway.'"

Why was control, not power, such an important issue for these women? Most mothers said they thought their children's fathers had very traditional notions of sex roles—notions that clashed with their more egalitarian views. One white cohabiting mother from Charleston said, "If we were to marry, I don't think it would be so ideal. [Husbands] want to be in charge, and I can't deal with that." Regardless of whether or not the prospective wife worked, mothers feared that prospective husbands would expect to be "head of the house," and make the "final" decisions about child rearing, finances, and other matters. Women, on the other hand, felt that since they had held the primary responsibility for both raising and supporting their children, they should have an equal say.

When we asked single mothers what they liked best about being a single parent, their most frequent re-

sponse was "I am in charge," or "I am in control." Mothers seemed willing to take on the responsibilities of child rearing if they were also able to make and enforce the rules. In most mothers' views, the presence of fathers often interfered with their parental control, particularly if the couple married. Most women also felt that the presence of a husband might impede their efforts to discipline and spend time with their children. Mothers criticized men for being "too demanding" of their time and attention. A white Chicago mother answered the question, "What is it like being a single mother?" as follows: "It's great in terms of being independent. I'm just thrilled being away from my ex-husband. The joy of that hasn't worn off. I feel more freedom to be a parent how I want [to be]. We did not agree on parenting at all." A white Charleston respondent said, "[Marriage isn't an option] right now. I don't want any man thinking that he has any claim on my kids or on how I raise them."

Mothers were also concerned about losing control of the family's financial situation. One African American Chicago mother told us, "[I won't marry because] the men take over the money. I'm too afraid to lose control of my money again." Still another said, "I'm the head of the household right now, and I make the [financial] decisions. I [don't want to give that up]."

Finally, mothers often expressed the view that if they married, their men would expect them to do all of the household chores, plus "cook and clean" and otherwise "take care of" them. Some described their relationships with their ex-partners as "like having one more kid to take care of." We asked another divorced white Charleston mother whether she would ever consider marriage again. She answered,

I don't know, I can't think that far ahead. I can't see it. This guy I'm with right now, I don't know. I like being by myself. The thought of having to cook and clean for somebody else? I'm like, "No." I'm looking for somebody who is going to cook and clean for me!

Concerns over control did not, however, mean that most women had abandoned their plans to marry. But they felt their own situations had to be such as to maximize their chances of exerting control in the marriage relationship. The primary way mothers who wanted to marry thought they could maintain power in a marriage relationship was by working and contributing to the family budget. One African American mother living in Charleston told me,

One thing my mom did teach me is that you must work some and bring some money into the household so you can have a say in what happens. If you completely live off a man, you are helpless. That is why I don't want to get married until I get my own [career] and get off of welfare.

Mothers also wanted to get established economically prior to marriage because men had failed them in the past. This is why they often told us that if they did get married, they would make sure "the car is in my name, the house is in my name" and so on. They wanted to "get myself established first, and then get married" so if the marriage broke up, they wouldn't be "left with nothing." One African American Camden mother commented, "[I will consider marriage] one day when I get myself together. When I have my own everything, so I won't be left depending on a man."

The experience of breakup or divorce and the resulting financial hardship and emotional pain fundamentally transformed these women's relational views. I heard dozens of stories of women who had held traditional views regarding sex roles while they were younger and still in a relationship with their children's fathers. When the men for whom they sacrificed so much gave them nothing but pain and anguish, they felt they had been "duped." Their childhood fantasy of marriage was gone, as was their willingness to be dependent on or subservient to men.

Because of these painful experiences, formerly married white mothers generally placed as high priority on increasing their labor market skills and experience as their black never-married counterparts. They felt that a hasty remarriage might distract them from this goal (possibly because their husbands' income would make them too comfortable and tempt them to quit school or work). Like the African American mothers who had seldom been married, whites also said that once they remarried, they would keep working no matter what. The "little money of my own" both African American and white mothers spoke of was valued, not

only for its contribution to the household economy, per se, but for the power it purchased them within the relationship, as well as its insurance value against destitution if the marriage should fail.

Mothers told us that the more established they became economically, the more bargaining power they believed they would have in a marital relationship. The mothers they knew who were economically dependent on men had to "put up with all kinds of behavior" because they could not legitimately threaten to leave without serious financial repercussions (due to the fact that they could not translate their homemaking skills into wages). Mothers felt that if they became more economically independent (had the car in their name, the house in their name, no common debts, etc.), they could legitimately threaten to leave their husbands if certain conditions (i.e., sexual fidelity) weren't met. These threats would, in turn they believed, keep a husband on his best behavior.

Taking on these attitudes of self-reliance and independence wasn't always easy. Some formerly married women whose partner failed them had never lived alone before, having gone straight from their parents' household to their husband's. In addition, some hadn't held a job in years, had no marketable skills, and had no idea about how to make their way in the world of employed women. One white Chicago resident was a full-time homemaker until her divorce. After getting no child support from her ex-husband for several months, this mother decided she had better get a job, but the best job she could find paid only minimum wage at the time. Her journey from her first job to her current position (which paid $7 an hour) was a painful one. Giving up this hard-won self-sufficiency for dependence on a man was simply too great a risk for her to take. She said, "I don't want to depend on nobody. It's too scary."

The often difficult life experiences of these mothers had convinced them of competencies they might not have known they had before single motherhood. Because of these experiences, their roles expanded to encompass more traditionally male responsibilities than before. The men, in their view, weren't respectful of these competencies. Instead, they expected them to revert to more traditional female roles. When we asked a white Chicago mother whether there were any advantages to being apart from the father of her children, she replied:

> You're the one in control. The good thing is that I feel good about myself. I feel more independent. Whereas when I was with Brian, I didn't. I had never been out on my own, but I took that step to move out and, since I did, I feel much better about myself as a person, that I can do it.

While it was true that some women were poorer financially than before their relationships ended, the increased pride they felt in being able to provide for themselves and their children partially compensated for economic hardship. Another white Chicago mother said "You know, I feel better [being alone] because I am the provider, I'm getting the things that I want and I'm getting them for myself, little by little."

Concerns about power might explain why childbearing and marriage have become separated from one another, particularly among the low-income population. Though we did not ask our Chicago and Charleston mothers questions about the ideal time to bear children and to marry, we did ask our Camden/Philadelphia mothers these questions. Most felt childbearing should ideally occur in a woman's early 20s, but that marriage should ideally occur in a woman's late 20s or early 30s. These answers are somewhat suspect because respondents might simply have been rationalizing past behavior (most hadn't been married when they had had their children, and half had never married). Even more confusing is the fact that these same respondents generally said that one should be married before having children. When interviewers probed deeper, respondents revealed that, though the goal of getting married first and having children second was indeed their ideal, it was hardly a practical choice given their economic situations and those of their partners.

Respondents' explanations of their views also revealed that many felt that childbearing required at least a temporary or partial withdrawal from the labor market. Childbearing within marriage and the labor market withdrawal it required, made women "dependent" and "vulnerable" and weakened their control. When mothers told us they wanted to wait to marry or re-

marry until their late 20s or early 30s, most assumed that, at this point, their youngest child would be in school. Thus, they would be free to more fully pursue labor market activities and, in this way, enhance their potential bargaining and decision-making role in any subsequent marital relationship. One African American Camden mother said.

> One guy was like, "marry me, I want a baby." I don't want to have to depend on anybody. No way. I [would rather] work. [If I married him and had his baby], I'd [have to quit work and] be dependent again. It's too scary.

There was no significant difference between cities in the salience of sex roles and power. Blacks were more concerned about these issues than whites, yet the differences are probably smaller than other studies of racial differences in sex-role attitudes would suggest. Many of the white women we interviewed had been married in the past and most of them reported that they had begun their marriages thinking that they would stay at home or work part-time (at least while their children were young). Their husbands, they assumed, would be the primary breadwinners, while they specialized in household management and parenting. After the breakup of these relationships, white mothers were often shocked by how vulnerable their withdrawal from the labor market had made them. It was after learning these hard lessons that most white mothers developed the conviction that it was foolish to marry unless they had "established themselves" first.

Trust

For some mothers, the reaction of their partner to an unplanned pregnancy became their first hard lesson in "the way men are." Mothers said that fathers' responses ran the gamut from strong negative responses to strong positive ones, but some men were clearly panicked by the prospect of being responsible for a child—particularly those who feared a child support order. Some fathers denied paternity even when they had encouraged the mother to get pregnant and/or carry the child to term. In these situations, fathers often claimed that the child was not theirs because the mother was "a whore." One partner of a pregnant Camden mother told the interviewer (in the mother's presence), "how do I know the baby's mine? Who knows if she hasn't been stepping out on me with some other man and now she wants me to support another man's child!"

Subsequent hard lessons were learned when mothers' boyfriends or husbands proved unfaithful. This experience was so common among respondents that many simply did not believe men "could be faithful to only one woman." This "men will be men" belief did not mean that women were willing to simply accept infidelity as part of the natural course of a marriage. Most said they would rather never marry than to "let him make a fool out of me." One black Chicago resident just couldn't conceive of finding a marriageable man.

> All those reliable guys, they are gone, they are gone. They're either thinking about one of three things: another woman, another man, or dope. . . . [M]y motto is "there is not a man on this planet that is faithful." It's a man thing. I don't care, you can love your wife 'til she turns three shades of avocado green. A man is gonna be a man and it's not a point of a woman getting upset about it. It's a point of a woman accepting it. 'Cause a man's gonna do what a man's gonna do. . . . [Other] black women, they say "once you find a man that's gonna be faithful, you go ahead and get married to him." [They] got it all wrong. Then they gonna [be surprised when they find out] he ain't faithful. And the wife gonna end up in a nut house. It's better not to get married, so you don't get your expectations up.

A white mother from Charleston said, "I was married for three years before I threw him out after discovering that he had another woman. I loved my husband, but I don't [want another one]. This is a wicked world we are living in." A black Charlestonian said,

> I would like to find a nice man to marry, but I know that men cannot be trusted. That's why I treat them the way I do—like the dogs they are. I think that all men will cheat on their wives regardless of how much he loves her. And you don't ever want to be in that position.

Mother after mother told us cautionary tales of married couples they knew where either the man or the woman was "stepping out" on their spouse. They viewed the wounded spouse as either hopelessly naive (if they did not know) or without self-respect (if they did know). They did not want to place themselves in a similar position. Demands for sexual fidelity within marriage had a practical, as well as an emotional dimension. Women often gave examples of married men they knew who "spen[t] all his money on the little woman he [had] on the side." Mothers often feared that men would promise them and their children "the world" and then abandon them. One African American Camden mother summed up her views as follows: "Either they leave or they die. The first thing is, don't get close to them, 'cause they ain't no good from the beginning. When that man ain't doing right for me, I learn to dump [him]." A white mother from Chicago said: "I've been a single parent since the day my husband walked out on me. He tried to come back, but I am not one to let someone hurt me and my children twice. I am living on welfare [rather than living with him]."

Even the most mistrustful of our respondents generally held out some hope that they would find a man who could be trusted and who would stay around. One white Chicago mother said, "I want to meet a man who will love me and my son and want us to grow together. I just don't know if he exists." An African American mother living in Chicago said,

> Maybe I'll find a good person to get married to, someone to be a stepfather to my son. They're not all the same; they're not all bad. There are three things in my life: my school, my work, and my son. Not men. At first they love you, they think you're beautiful, and then they leave. When I got pregnant, he just left. My father is like that. He has kids by several different women. I hate him for it. I say, "I hate you. Why do you do that? Why?"

A white divorcee from Chicago explained her views of the differences between the sexes in this regard as follows:

> Men can say. "Well honey, I'm going out for the night." And then they disappear for two months.

Whereas, the mother has a deeper commitment, conscience, or compassion. . . . If [women] acted like men, our kids would be in the park, left. We'd say "Oh, somebody else is going to take care of it." Everybody would be orphaned.

An African American mother from the Philadelphia area told us,

I'm frustrated with men, period. They bring drugs and guns into the house, you take care of their kids, feed them, and then they steal your rent money out of your purse. They screw you if you put your self out for them. So now, I don't put myself out there any more.

Because their own experiences and the experiences of their friends, relatives, and neighbors has been so overwhelmingly negative, many women reduced the expressive value they placed on their relationships over time. Some instrumentalized their relationships with men to the point that they didn't "give it away anymore," meaning they no longer had sex without expecting something, generally something material, in return. A white Chicago mother put it this way: "Love is blind. You fall in love with the wrong one sometimes. It's easy to do. [Now] I am so mean . . . [when] I sleep with a guy I am like, 'Give me the money and leave me alone.'" Nonetheless, many of *these same women* often held out hope of finding a man who was "different," one who could be trusted.

Chicago mothers were significantly more likely to voice trust issues than their Charleston counterparts. This difference may reflect regional differences (Southerners may be more trusting than Northerners). It may also be true that trust issues are least salient in a tight labor market where jobs for unskilled men are more plentiful. Whites talked about the issue more than African Americans and could reflect differences in spontaneous self-reports of domestic abuse (discussed below).

Domestic Violence

In Chicago and Charleston, we did not ask directly about domestic abuse, yet, a surprisingly high number spontaneously spoke of some history of domestic violence in their childhood or adult lives. In Table 1, we include only those mothers for which the abuse had some bearing on marriage attitudes. We see no important differences across cities, but rather startling differences by race. One white mother living in Chicago decided to have her child with the assumption that she would marry the father, but after a series of physically abusive episodes triggered by arguments about his drinking and drug use, she changed her mind.

The person I was with wasn't quite what I thought he was. We were going to get married, [but] I don't believe in making two mistakes. [There were about] four [big] blowouts before I finally actually [ended it]. The last one was probably the worst. We went to a friend's house [and] he started drinking, [doing] drugs, and stuff. I said, "please take me home now." So [we got in the car] and we started arguing about why he had to hang around people like that [who do] drugs and all that sort of stuff. One thing led to another and he kind of tossed me right out of the car.

Many women reported physical abuse during pregnancy. Several mothers reported having miscarriages because of such abuse. For others, the physical abuse began after the child was born. It was not uncommon for women to report injuries serious enough to warrant trips to the hospital emergency room. Two African American women from Charleston ended up in the emergency room following beatings from their boyfriends. One recounted:

My daughter's father, we used to fight. I got to where nobody be punching on me because love is not that serious. And I figure somebody is beating on you and the only thing they love is watching you go the emergency room. That's what they love. A lot of these chicks, they think "he [hitting] me because [he loves me and] he don't want me looking at nobody [else]." Honey, he need help, and you need a little more help than he do because you stand there [and take it].

The other interjected: "Just leave him [if he abuses you], you get over [him]. You will be over [him eventually]."

The fact that women tended to experience repeated abuse from their children's fathers before they decided to leave attests to their strong desire to make things work with their children's fathers. Many women finally left when they saw the abuse beginning to affect their children's well-being. One white Charleston mother explained:

> . . . it was an abusive situation. It was physical. . . . [My daughter] saw us fighting a lot. The minute she would see us fighting, she would go into hysterics. It would turn into an all-out brawl. She was terrified. And this was what that did to her and I thought. "I've got to get out of here."

But the economic pressures associated with leaving sometimes propelled mothers into another harmful relationship. One white Chicago mother explained:

> I married [my first husband] a month after I had [our son]. And I married him because I couldn't afford [to live alone]. Boy, was that stupid. And I left him [two years after that] when our daughter was five months old. I got scared. I was afraid because my kids were starting to get in the middle. [My son] still to this day, when he thinks someone is hurting me, he'll start screaming and crying and beating on him. He had seen his father [beat me up]. I didn't want him to see that. I remarried six months later because I couldn't make it [financially]. And I got into another abusive marriage. And we got separated before the year was even up. He would burn me [with cigarettes]. He was an alcoholic. He was a physical abuser, mental [too]. I think he would have killed me [if I had stayed].

Another white Chicagoan said, "after being abused, physically abused, by him the whole time we were married, I was ready to [kill him]. He put me in the hospital three times. I was carrying our child four and a half months, he beat me and I miscarried." A white Charlestonian said, "I was terrified to leave because I knew it would mean going on welfare. . . . But that is okay. I can handle that. The thing I couldn't deal with is being beat up." When we asked one black Charleston woman if there were any advantages to being a single mom, she replied, "not living with someone there to abuse you. I'm not scared anymore. I'm scared of my bills and I'm scared of I get sick, what's going to happen to my kids, but I'm not afraid for my life."

We are not sure why there is so much domestic violence among poor parents, but our interviews with mothers give us a few clues. First, mothers sometimes linked episodes of violence to fathers' fears about their ability to provide, especially in light of increased state efforts toward child support enforcement. This explanation was most often invoked in reference to the beatings women received when they were pregnant. Second, some mothers living in crime-ridden, inner-city neighborhoods talked about family violence as a carry-over from street violence. The Camden/Philadelphia mothers talked at length about the effect this exposure had had on their children's fathers' lives (and their own), and some even described the emotional aftermath of this exposure as "Post-Traumatic Stress Syndrome."

DISCUSSION

Since the 1970s, a sharply declining proportion of unskilled men have been able to earn enough to support a family (U.S. House of Representatives 1997). These trends clearly have had a profound influence on marriage among low-income men and women. But even when a marriage might be affordable, mothers might judge the risks marriage entails as too great for other reasons, some of which reflect changes in the economy, but are not economic *per se*.

In these mothers' view, wives still borrow their class standing from their husbands. Since a respectable marriage is one that lasts "forever," mothers who marry low-skilled males must themselves give up their dreams of upward mobility. In the interim, single motherhood holds a somewhat higher status than a "foolish" marriage to a low-status man. . . .

Beyond affordability and respectability concerns, these interviews offer powerful evidence that there has been a dramatic revolution in sex-role expectations among women at the low end of the income distribution, and that the gap between low-income men's and women's expectations in regard to gender roles is wide. Women who have proven their competencies through the hard lessons of single parenthood aren't generally willing to enter subservient roles—they want to have substantial control and bargaining power in subsequent relationships. Some mothers learned the dangers of economic dependence upon men through the pain and financial devastation that accompanied a separation and divorce. Others were schooled by their profound disappointment at their baby's father's reaction to the pregnancy and his failure to live up to the economic and emotional commitments of fatherhood. Both groups of mothers equate marital power with economic power, and believe that the emotional and financial risk that marriage entails is only sustainable when they themselves have reached some level of economic self-sufficiency.

The data also show that, though a small number of women want to marry and become housewives, the overwhelming majority want to continue working during any subsequent marriage. Since these mothers generally believe that childbearing and rearing young children necessitate a temporary withdrawal from the labor market, many place the ideal age at which to marry in the late 20s (when their youngest child is school age) and the ideal age to bear children in the early 20s—the age they say is the "normal" time for women to have children. Delaying marriage until they can concentrate more fully on labor market activity maximizes their chances of having a marriage where they can have equal bargaining power. The income from work also allows them to legitimately threaten to leave the husband if certain behavioral standards are not met and many women believe that such threats will serve to keep husbands in line. These data suggest that the bargaining perspective, which many studies of housework currently employ, may be useful in understanding marriage attitudes and non-marital relational dynamics, as well.

Mothers believe that marital power is crucial, at least partially, because of their low trust of men. I know of no data that demonstrate that gender mistrust has grown over time, but certainly the risk of divorce, and the economic destitution for women that so often accompanies it, has grown. Trust issues are exacerbated by the experience of domestic violence. Many mothers told interviewers that it was these experiences that taught them "not to have any feeling for men." National-level data show that violence is more frequent among those with less income (Ptacek 1998). Presumably, such violence, along with the substance abuse that frequently accompanies it, is a way of "doing gender" for men who cannot adequately fulfil the bread-

winner role. Though women's accounts did not always allow me to establish the sequence of events leading up to episodes of violence, many of those that did showed that violence followed job loss or revelation of a pregnancy. Both are sources of economic stress.

These data also reveal some interesting differences by city and by race, though the sample size is small. Charleston mothers worried less about affordability and trust issues than Chicago mothers. The first difference could result from the differences in local labor markets (tight versus somewhat slack) which disproportionately affect the employment of unskilled and minority men (Jencks 1992), or regional differences (Southerners might be more traditional than Northerners). The second difference is harder to explain, though regional differences and economic differences between the cities may also play a role. If men behave in an untrustworthy manner (i.e., "unfaithful") in order to compensate for their inability to fulfil the provider role, we would expect that women in tight labor markets might find it easier to trust male partners than women in slack labor markets. The impact of labor market conditions and regional variations on the marriage attitudes and rates for low-skilled men and women would be fruitful topics for further study across a wider range of labor markets and regions.

The analysis also revealed some interesting race difference. In both Charleston and Chicago, African Americans were more likely to name affordability, respectability, and control concerns, while whites mentioned trust and domestic violence more often. Affordability and respectability might be more salient for blacks because their chances of finding a marriage partner with sufficient economic resources to satisfy such concerns are lower than for whites. The salience of trust for whites might reflect higher rates of domestic violence, though these figures reflect spontaneous comments and probably underestimate the actual rate of violence for women in the sample. They may also reflect the fact that whites who elaborated on these experiences generally stayed with the violent partner (to whom they were often married) longer than African Americans. Whites' living arrangements might also have afforded less protection from violent men than blacks' in that whites were more likely to cohabit with their partner, while blacks were more likely to live in an extended-kin household. Nationally representative data also show that low-income whites cohabit significantly more often than comparable African Americans (Harris and Edin 1996).

In relation to theories of the retreat from marriage, there is no doubt that economic factors are necessary, though not sufficient, criteria for marriage among most low-income women interviewed. Theories that posit the importance of the stalled revolution of sex roles and Wilson's argument that non-marriage among blacks results from very low levels of trust, were both strongly supported, though our analysis revealed that trust was even more important for whites. Drake and Cayton and Rainwater's notions of instrumentality in male-female relationships also received support. I will say more about the economic independence and welfare disincentives arguments below.

In sum, the mothers we spoke to were quite forthcoming about the fact that the men who had fathered their children often weren't "worth a lifetime commitment" given their general lack of trustworthiness, the traditional nature of their sex-role views, the potential loss of control over parental and household decisions, and their risky and sometimes violent behavior. While mothers maintained hopes of eventual marriage, they viewed such hopes with some level of skepticism. Thus, they devoted most of their time and energy toward raising their children and "getting it together financially" rather than "waiting on a man." Those that planned on marrying, generally assumed they would put off marriage until their children were in school and they were able to be fully engaged in labor market activity. By waiting to marry until the tasks associated with early child rearing and the required temporary withdrawal from the labor market were completed, mothers felt they could enhance their bargaining power within marriage.

This complex set of motivations to delay marriage or remarriage (or less frequently, to avoid them altogether) has interesting implications for welfare reform. The authors of PRWORA explicitly sought to encourage marriage among the poor by increasing the cost of non-marriage (e.g., reducing the amount of resources an unmarried mother can claim from the state). Put in the language of the welfare disincentives argument, PRWORA decreases the disincentives to marry, or, ac-

cording to the economic independence theory, limits one source of financial independence for women who forgo marriage. If single mothers have fewer resources from the state, it is reasonable to argue that they might become more dependent on men and men's income. This may seem particularly likely given the fact that unskilled and semiskilled ex-welfare recipients will probably not be able to make enough money in the low-wage sector to meet their monthly expenses (Edin and Lein 1997) and that the gap between their income and expenses is likely to grow as they move from welfare to work (at least after the increased earned-income disregards some states offer elapse at the five year point or sooner). To make matters worse, unless the labor market remains extremely tight, low-skilled mothers' wages are not likely to increase over time because of a lack of premium on experience in the low-wage sector (Blank 1995; Burtless 1995; Harris and Edin 1996).

If PRWORA is fully implemented, these new financial realities might well encourage some couples to marry. However, if men's employment opportunities and wages do not increase dramatically, these data suggest that mothers might continue to opt for boyfriends (cohabiting or not), who can be replaced if they do not contribute, rather than husbands who cannot be so easily traded for a more economically productive man. Even if mothers believed that they would be no worse off, or even slightly better off, by marrying than by remaining single, these data show that marriage is far more complicated than a simple economic cost-benefit assessment. The women's movement has clearly influenced what behaviors (i.e., infidelity) women are willing to accept within a marital relationship, and the level of power they expect to be able to exert within the relationship. Given the low level of trust these mothers have of men—often times rooted in the experience of domestic violence—and given their view that husbands want more control than the women are willing to give them, women recognize that any marriage that is also economically precarious, might well be conflict-ridden and short lived. Interestingly, mothers say they reject entering into economically risky marital unions out of respect for the institution of marriage, rather than because of a rejection of the marriage norm.

In the light of PRWORA and the new set of financial incentives and disincentives it provides, it is likely that cohabitation will increase, given the fact that cohabitation nearly always allowed the mothers interviewed to make a substantial claim on the male cohabiter's income. However, increased cohabitation might put women and children at greater risk if their partner is violent. In these situations, a separate residence may be a protective factor, as the race differences in the experience of domestic abuse I report here may indicate.

CONCLUSIONS

In short, the mothers interviewed here believe that marriage will probably make their lives more difficult than they are currently. They do not, by and large, perceive any special stigma to remaining single, so they are not motivated to marry for that reason. If they are to marry, they want to get something out of it. If they cannot enjoy economic stability and gain upward mobility from marriage, they see little reason to risk the loss of control and other costs they fear marriage might exact from them. Unless low-skilled men's economic situations improve and they begin to change their behaviors toward women, it is quite likely that most low-income women will continue to resist marriage even in the context of welfare reform. Substantially enhanced labor market opportunities for low-skilled men would address both the affordability and respectability concerns of the mothers interviewed. But other factors, such as the stalled sex-role revolution at home (control), the pervasive mistrust of men, and the high probability of domestic abuse, probably mean that marriage rates are unlikely to increase dramatically.

REFERENCES

Bane, Mary Jo, and David T. Ellwood. 1994. *Welfare Realities.* Cambridge, MA: Harvard University Press.

Becker, Gary S. 1981. *A Treatise on the Family.* Cambridge, MA: Harvard University Press.

Becker, Howard S. 1992. "Cases, causes, conjectures, stories, and imagery." In *What is a case?*, eds. Charles C.

Ragin and Howard S. Becker, 205–216. New York: Cambridge University Press.

Bennett, N. C., D. E. Bloom, and P. H. Craig. 1990. "American marriage patterns in transition." Paper presented at the Conference on Demographic Perspective on the American Family, April, Albany, New York.

Blank, Rebecca M. 1995. "Outlook for the U.S. labor market and prospects for low-wage entry jobs." In *The Work Alternative,* eds. Demetra Smith Nightingale and Robert H. Haveman. Washington, DC: The Urban Institute Press; Cambridge, MA: Harvard University Press.

Blee, Kathleen M., and Ann R. Tickameyer. 1995. "Racial differences in men's attitudes about women's gender roles." *Journal of Marriage and the Family* 57:21–30.

Bulcroft, Richard A., and Kris A. Bulcroft. 1993. "Race differences in attitudinal and motivational factors in the decision to marry." *Journal of Marriage and the Family* 55:338–355.

Bumpass, Larry, and James A. Sweet. 1989. "Children's experience in single parent families: Implications of cohabitation and marital transitions." *Family Planning Perspectives* 61(6):256–260.

Burtless, Gary. 1995. "Employment prospects of welfare recipients." In *The Work Alternative,* eds Demetra Smith Nightingale and Robert H. Haveman. Washington, DC: The Urban Institute Press; Cambridge, MA: Harvard University Press.

Cherlin, Andrew. 1992. *Marriage, Divorce, Remarriage.* Cambridge, MA: Harvard University Press.

Collins, Patricia H. 1987 "The meaning of motherhood in black culture and black mother/daughter relationships." *Signs* 4:3–10.

Corbett, Thomas. 1998. "Reallocation, redirection, and reinvention: Assessing welfare reform in an era of discontinuity." Unpublished manuscript.

Edin, Kathryn, and Laura Lein. 1997. *Making Ends Meet: How Single Mothers Survive Welfare and Low Wage Work.* New York: Russell Sage Foundation.

Fossett, Mark A., and K. Jill Kielcolt. 1993. "Mate availability and family structure among African Americans in U.S. metropolitan areas." *Journal of Marriage and the Family* 55:302–331.

Harris, Kathleen Mullan, and Kathryn Edin. 1996. "From welfare to work and back again." Unpublished manuscript.

Hochschild, Arlie. 1989. *The Second Shift.* New York: Viking.

Hoffman, Saul. 1997. "Could it be true after all? AFDC benefits and non-marital births to young women." *Poverty Research News.* Chicago: Joint Center for Poverty Research, 1(2):1–3.

Hoffman, Saul D., and Greg Duncan. 1994. "The role of incomes, wages, and AFDC benefits on marital disruption." *The Journal of Human Resources* 30(10):19–41.

Jencks, Christopher. 1992. *Rethinking Social Policy.* Cambridge, MA: Harvard University Press, 120–142.

Kefalas, Maria, and Kathryn Edin. 2000. "The meaning of motherhood." Unpublished manuscript.

Lichter, Daniel T., F. B. LeClere, and Diane K. McLaughlin. 1991. "Local marriage market conditions and the marital behavior of black and white women." *American Journal of Sociology* 96:843–867.

Luker, Kristin. 1996. *Dubious Conceptions: The Politics of Teenage Pregnancy.* Cambridge. MA: Harvard University Press.

Moffitt, Robert A. 1995. "The effect of the welfare system on non-marital childbearing." *Report to Congress on Out of Wedlock Childbearing.* Department of Health and Human Services. Washington, DC: U.S. Government Printing Office, 167–173.

Murray, Charles. 1984. *Losing Ground.* New York: Basic Books.

Nelson, Timothy, Kathryn Edin, and Susan Clampet-Lundquist. 1999. "Doing the best I can: How low-income non-custodial fathers talk about their families." Unpublished manuscript.

Oppenheimer, Valerie K. 1993. "Women's rising employment and the future of the family in industrial societies." *Population and Development Review* 20(2): 293–342.

Ptacek, James. 1988. "Why do men batter wives." In *Feminist Perspectives on Wife Abuse,* eds. K. Yllo and M. Bograd. Thousand Oaks: Sage Publications.

Raphael, Jody, and Richard D. Tolman. 1997. *Trapped by Poverty, Trapped by Abuse.* Chicago, IL: The Taylor Institute.

Scanzoni, John H. 1970. *Opportunity and the Family.* New York: Free Press.

Schoen, Robert, and Dawn Owens. 1992. "A further look at first unions and fist marriages," In *In The Changing American Family,* eds. Scott J. South and Steward E. Tolnay. Boulder, CO: Westview Press.

South, Scott J. 1992. "For love or money? Sociodemographic determinants of the expected benefits from marriage." In *The Changing American Family: Sociological and Demographic Perspectives,* eds. S. J. South and S. E. Tolnay, 171–194. Boulder, CO: Westview.

———. 1993. "Racial and ethnic differences in the desire to marry." *Journal of Marriage and the Family* 55:357–370.

South, Scott J., and Kim M. Lloyd. 1992. "Marriage opportunities and family formation: Further implications of imbalanced sex ratios." *Journal of Marriage and the Family* 54:440–451.

Stack, Carol B. 1974. *All Our Kin.* New York: Harper and Row.

Staples, Robert. 1988. "An overview of race and marital status." In *Black Families,* ed. H. P. McAdoo, 187–189. Newbury Park, CA: Sage.

Teachman, Jay D., Karen A. Polonko, and Geoffrey K. Leigh. 1987. "Marital timing: Race and sex comparisons." *Social Forces* 66:239–268.

Trent, Katherine, and Scott J. South. 1989. "Structural determinants of the divorce rate: A cross-societal comparison." *Journal of Marriage and the Family* 51:391–404.

Tucker, Belinda B., and Claudia Mitchell-Kernan. 1996. *The Decline in Marriage Among African Americans: Causes, Consequences, and Policy Implications.* New York: Russell Sage Foundation.

U.S. Bureau of the Census. 1993. *Poverty in the United States: 1992. Current Population Reports,* Series P60, No. 185, Washington, DC: U.S. Government Printing Office.

———. 1991a. "Marital status and living arrangements, 1990." *Current Population Reports,* Series P-20, No. 450:1, Table A. Washington DC: U.S. Government Printing Office.

———. 1991b. "Marital status and living arrangements, 1990." *Current Population Reports,* Series P-20, No. 461. Washington DC: U.S. Government Printing Office.

U.S. House of Representatives, Committee on Ways and Means. 1997. *Overview of Entitlement Programs (Greenbook).* Washington DC: U.S. Government Printing Office.

Wilson, William J. 1996. *When Work Disappears.* New York: Alfred A. Knopf.

———. 1987. *The Truly Disadvantaged.* Chicago: University of Chicago Press.

PART VI

CONSTRUCTING GENDER
IN THE WORKPLACE

How much does gender influence one's status at work? Does the feminization of paid labor around the world place women on a more equal footing with men? Or is paid labor another arena that intensifies women's disadvantages? Is it an arena that intensifies *some* women's disadvantages more than others? *Why* is gender inequality such a pervasive feature of work? Is it built into the workplace, or is it the outcome of differences in women and men themselves, their socialization, their behaviors, and their interactions? The readings in this part rely on studies of women and men in different work settings to address these questions. They show how the societal patterns of gender, race, class, sexuality, and immigrant status shape the work experiences of different groups.

Paid workers are increasingly diverse. Today's average worker in the global economy may be either a man or a woman and of any age, race, class, sexual orientation, or nationality. The average worker in the global economy may labor virtually unseen inside the home or may work in a public workplace as an assembler, teacher, secretary, or restaurant worker. Yet whatever the average worker does for a living, she or he is very likely to work at a job assigned on the basis of gender. Everywhere, gender organizes workplaces. Even five-year-olds can readily identify what is a "man's job" and what is a "woman's job." Women's jobs and men's jobs are structured with different characteristics and different rewards. Seldom do women and men do the same jobs in the same place for the same pay. In every society we find a familiar pattern: women earn less than men, even when they work in similar occupations and have the same level of education. But exactly *how* does work become so dramatically divided? How is workplace inequality maintained? Can gender boundaries be dismantled? All of the readings in this section speak these questions.

The experience of workers is further complicated by the interplay of gender and other power systems. Women and men of different races, national origins, and immigrant groups become clustered in certain kinds of work. Job opportunities are shaped by *who* people are—by their being women or men, educated or uneducated, of a certain race, sexual orientation, and residents of specific geopolitical settings—rather than their skills or talents.

For example, many men who work in women's professions experience a glass escalator effect that facilitates their mobility within these fields. But we know little about minority men's encounters within these fields. In her study of how racial dynamics shape men's experiences in the field of nursing, Adia Harvey Wingfield finds that upward mobility is not uniformly available to all men who do women's work. She provides new insights on the glass escalator as a concept that is both racialized and gendered. Kristin Schilt furthers the intersectional analysis of the gendered workplace by looking at the experiences of female-to-male transsexuals. Their transition to men gives them a unique angle of vision on many hard-to-observe practices that reproduce gender inequality. Once they become "one of the guys," they receive more respect and benefits in the workplace. But like the previous study, Schilt's research finds that men are not a monolithic group. Despite the gender advantages of transitioning, cross-cutting power systems create differences in just *which* men gain authority. Cross-cutting hierarchies also define what constitutes acceptable behavior on the job. In their study of restaurant workers, Pattie A. Giuffre and Christine A. Williams discover that the definition of sexual harassment depends on *who* the victim is. Double standard of race, class, and sexual orientation mask a good deal of sexual discrimination in workplaces.

The last reading considers some of the complex matters related to the effects of globalization on women's work in the rapidly expanding sex industry. In a study of the strip club boom, Sheila Jeffries takes up questions about women's oppression and women's empowerment. Whereas some gender scholars have argued that stripping can represent a unique form of equality for women, Jeffries puts the discussion in a different light. She offers an analysis of the context that shapes stripping in a globalized world. Her study reveals how profits are made, the involvement of organized crime, the trafficking of women and girls into the clubs, and the exploitation that structures the strip club industry.

34

Racializing the Glass Escalator

Reconsidering Men's Experiences with Women's Work

Adia Harvey Wingfield

Sociologists who study work have long noted that jobs are sex segregated and that this segregation creates different occupational experiences for men and women (Charles and Grusky 2004). Jobs predominantly filled by women often require "feminine" traits such as nurturing, caring, and empathy, a fact that means men confront perceptions that they are unsuited for the requirements of these jobs. Rather than having an adverse effect on their occupational experiences, however, these assumptions facilitate men's entry into better paying, higher status positions, creating what Williams (1995) labels a "glass escalator" effect.

The glass escalator model has been an influential paradigm in understanding the experiences of men who do women's work. Researchers have identified this process among men nurses, social workers, paralegals, and librarians and have cited its pervasiveness as evidence of men's consistent advantage in the workplace, such that even in jobs where men are numerical minorities they are likely to enjoy higher wages and faster promotions (Floge and Merrill 1986; Heikes 1991; Pierce 1995; Williams 1989, 1995). Most of these studies implicitly assume a racial homogenization of men workers in women's profes-sions, but this supposition is problematic for several reasons. For one, minority men are not only present but are actually overrepresented in certain areas of reproductive work that have historically been domi-nated by white women (Duffy 2007). Thus, research that focuses primarily on white men in women's pro-fessions ignores a key segment of men who perform this type of labor. Second, and perhaps more impor-tant, conclusions based on the experiences of white men tend to overlook the ways that intersections of race and gender create different experiences for different men. While extensive work has documented the fact that white men in women's professions encounter a glass escalator effect that aids their occu-pational mobility (for an exception, see Snyder and Green 2008), few studies, if any, have considered how this effect is a function not only of gendered advan-tage but of racial privilege as well.

In this article, I examine the implications of race–gender intersections for minority men employed in a female-dominated, feminized occupation, specifically focusing on Black men in nursing. Their experiences doing "women's work" demonstrate that the glass esca-lator is a racialized as well as gendered concept.

Adia Harvey Wingfield, *Gender & Society 23*, pp. 5–25. Copyright © 2009 Sage Publications. Reprinted by permission of Sage Publications.

THEORETICAL FRAMEWORK

In her classic study *Men and Women of the Corporation,* Kanter (1977) offers a groundbreaking analysis of group interactions. Focusing on high-ranking women executives who work mostly with men, Kanter argues that those in the extreme numerical minority are tokens who are socially isolated, highly visible, and adversely stereotyped. Tokens have difficulty forming relationships with colleagues and often are excluded from social networks that provide mobility. Because of their low numbers, they are also highly visible as people who are different from the majority, even though they often feel invisible when they are ignored or overlooked in social settings. Tokens are also stereotyped by those in the majority group and frequently face pressure to behave in ways that challenge and undermine these stereotypes. Ultimately, Kanter argues that it is harder for them to blend into the organization and to work effectively and productively, and that they face serious barriers to upward mobility.

Kanter's (1977) arguments have been analyzed and retested in various settings and among many populations. Many studies, particularly of women in male-dominated corporate settings, have supported her findings. Other work has reversed these conclusions, examining the extent to which her conclusions hold when men were the tokens and women the majority group. These studies fundamentally challenged the gender neutrality of the token, finding that men in the minority fare much better than do similarly situated women. In particular, this research suggests that factors such as heightened visibility and polarization do not necessarily disadvantage men who are in the minority. While women tokens find that their visibility hinders their ability to blend in and work productively, men tokens find that their conspicuousness can lead to greater opportunities for leadership and choice assignments (Floge and Merrill 1986; Heikes 1991). Studies in this vein are important because they emphasize organizations—and occupations—as gendered institutions that subsequently create dissimilar experiences for men and women tokens (see Acker 1990).

In her groundbreaking study of men employed in various women's professions, Williams (1995) further develops this analysis of how power relationships shape the ways men tokens experience work in women's professions. Specifically, she introduces the concept of the glass escalator to explain men's experiences as tokens in these areas. Like Floge and Merrill (1986) and Heikes (1991), Williams finds that men tokens do not experience the isolation, visibility, blocked access to social networks, and stereotypes in the same ways that women tokens do. In contrast, Williams argues that even though they are in the minority, processes are in place that actually facilitate their opportunity and advancement. Even in culturally feminized occupations, then, men's advantage is built into the very structure and everyday interactions of these jobs so that men find themselves actually struggling to remain in place. For these men, "despite their intentions, they face invisible pressures to move up in their professions. Like being on a moving escalator, they have to work to stay in place" (Williams 1995, 87).

The glass escalator term thus refers to the "subtle mechanisms in place that enhance [men's] positions in [women's] professions" (Williams 1995, 108). These mechanisms include certain behaviors, attitudes, and beliefs men bring to these professions as well as the types of interactions that often occur between these men and their colleagues, supervisors, and customers. Consequently, even in occupations composed mostly of women, gendered perceptions about men's roles, abilities, and skills privilege them and facilitate their advancement. The glass escalator serves as a conduit that channels men in women's professions into the uppermost levels of the occupational hierarchy. Ultimately, the glass escalator effect suggests that men retain consistent occupational advantages over women, even when women are numerically in the majority (Budig 2002; Williams 1995).

Though this process has now been fairly well established in the literature, there are reasons to question its generalizability to all men. In an early critique of the supposed general neutrality of the token, Zimmer (1988) notes that much research on race comes to precisely the opposite of Kanter's conclusions, finding that as the numbers of minority group members increase (e.g., as they become less likely to be "tokens"), so too do tensions between the majority and minority groups. For instance, as minorities move into predominantly white neighborhoods, increasing numbers do not create the likelihood of greater acceptance and better treatment. In contrast, whites are likely to relocate when neighborhoods become "too" integrated, citing concerns about property values and racialized ideas about declining neighborhood quality (Shapiro 2004). Reinforcing, while at the same time tempering, the findings of research on men in female-dominated occupations, Zimmer (1988, 71) argues that relationships between tokens and the majority depend on understanding the underlying power relationships between these groups and "the status and power differentials between them." Hence, just as men who are tokens fare better than women, it also follows that the experiences of Blacks and whites as tokens should differ in ways that reflect their positions in hierarchies of status and power.

The concept of the glass escalator provides an important and useful framework for addressing men's experiences in women's occupations, but so far research in this vein has neglected to examine whether the glass escalator is experienced among all men in an identical manner. Are the processes that facilitate a ride on the glass escalator available to minority men? Or does race intersect with gender to affect the extent to which the glass escalator offers men opportunities in women's professions? In the next section, I examine whether and how the mechanisms that facilitate a ride on the glass escalator might be unavailable to Black men in nursing.[1]

RELATIONSHIPS WITH COLLEAGUES AND SUPERVISORS

One key aspect of riding the glass escalator involves the warm, collegial welcome men workers often receive from their women colleagues. Often, this reaction is a response to the fact that professions dominated by women are frequently low in salary and status and that greater numbers of men help improve prestige and pay (Heikes 1991). Though some women workers resent the apparent ease with which men enter and advance in women's professions, the generally warm welcome men receive stands in stark contrast to the cold reception, difficulties with mentorship, and blocked access to social networks that women often

encounter when they do men's work (Roth 2006; Williams 1992). In addition, unlike women in men's professions, men who do women's work frequently have supervisors of the same sex. Men workers can thus enjoy a gendered bond with their supervisor in the context of a collegial work environment. These factors often converge, facilitating men's access to higher-status positions and producing the glass escalator effect.

The congenial relationship with colleagues and gendered bonds with supervisors are crucial to riding the glass escalator. Women colleagues often take a primary role in casting these men into leadership or supervisory positions. In their study of men and women tokens in a hospital setting, Floge and Merrill (1986) cite cases where women nurses promoted men colleagues to the position of charge nurse, even when the job had already been assigned to a woman. In addition to these close ties with women colleagues, men are also able to capitalize on gendered bonds with (mostly men) supervisors in ways that engender upward mobility. Many men supervisors informally socialize with men workers in women's jobs and are thus able to trade on their personal friendships for upward mobility. Williams (1995) describes a case where a nurse with mediocre performance reviews received a promotion to a more prestigious specialty area because of his friendship with the (male) doctor in charge. According to the literature, building strong relationships with colleagues and supervisors often happens relatively easily for men in women's professions and pays off in their occupational advancement.

For Black men in nursing, however, gendered racism may limit the extent to which they establish bonds with their colleagues and supervisors. The concept of gendered racism suggests that racial stereotypes, images, and beliefs are grounded in gendered ideals (Collins 1990, 2004; Espiritu 2000; Essed 1991; Harvey Wingfield 2007). Gendered racist stereotypes of Black men in particular emphasize the dangerous, threatening attributes associated with Black men and Black masculinity, framing Black men as threats to white women, prone to criminal behavior, and especially violent. Collins (2004) argues that these stereotypes serve to legitimize Black men's treatment in the criminal justice system through methods such as racial profiling and incarceration, but they may also hinder

Black men's attempts to enter and advance in various occupational fields.

For Black men nurses, gendered racist images may have particular consequences for their relationships with women colleagues, who may view Black men nurses through the lens of controlling images and gendered racist stereotypes that emphasize the danger they pose to women. This may take on a heightened significance for white women nurses, given stereotypes that suggest that Black men are especially predisposed to raping white women. Rather than experiencing the congenial bonds with colleagues that white men nurses describe, Black men nurses may find themselves facing a much cooler reception from their women coworkers.

Gendered racism may also play into the encounters Black men nurses have with supervisors. In cases where supervisors are white men, Black men nurses may still find that higher-ups treat them in ways that reflect prevailing stereotypes about threatening Black masculinity. Supervisors may feel uneasy about forming close relationships with Black men or may encourage their separation from white women nurses. In addition, broader, less gender-specific racial stereotypes could also shape the experiences Black men nurses have with white men bosses. Whites often perceive Blacks, regardless of gender, as less intelligent, hardworking, ethical, and moral than other racial groups (Feagin 2006). Black men nurses may find that in addition to being influenced by gendered racist stereotypes, supervisors also view them as less capable and qualified for promotion, thus negating or minimizing the glass escalator effect.

Suitability for Nursing and Higher-Status Work

The perception that men are not really suited to do women's work also contributes to the glass escalator effect. In encounters with patients, doctors, and other staff, men nurses frequently confront others who do not expect to see them doing "a woman's job." Sometimes this perception means that patients mistake men nurses for doctors; ultimately, the sense that men do not really belong in nursing contributes to a push *"out* of the most feminine-identified areas and *up* to those regarded as more legitimate for men" (Williams 1995,

104). The sense that men are better suited for more masculine jobs means that men workers are often assumed to be more able and skilled than their women counterparts. As Williams writes (1995, 106), "Masculinity is often associated with competence and mastery," and this implicit definition stays with men even when they work in feminized fields. Thus, part of the perception that men do not belong in these jobs is rooted in the sense that, as men, they are more capable and accomplished than women and thus belong in jobs that reflect this. Consequently, men nurses are mistaken for doctors and are granted more authority and responsibility than their women counterparts, reflecting the idea that, as men, they are inherently more competent (Heikes 1991; Williams 1995).

Black men nurses, however, may not face the presumptions of expertise or the resulting assumption that they belong in higher-status jobs. Black professionals, both men and women, are often assumed to be less capable and less qualified than their white counterparts. In some cases, these negative stereotypes hold even when Black workers outperform white colleagues (Feagin and Sikes 1994). The belief that Blacks are inherently less competent than whites means that, despite advanced education, training, and skill, Black professionals often confront the lingering perception that they are better suited for lower-level service work (Feagin and Sikes 1994). Black men in fact often fare better than white women in blue-collar jobs such as policing and corrections work (Britton 1995), and this may be, in part, because they are viewed as more appropriately suited for these types of positions.

For Black men nurses, then, the issue of perception may play out in different ways than it does for white men nurses. While white men nurses enjoy the automatic assumption that they are qualified, capable, and suited for "better" work, the experiences of Black professionals suggest that Black men nurses may not encounter these reactions. They may, like their white counterparts, face the perception that they do not belong in nursing. Unlike their white counterparts, Black men nurses may be seen as inherently less capable and therefore better suited for low-wage labor than a professional, feminized occupation such as nursing. This perception of being less qualified means that they also may not be immediately assumed to be better suited for the higher-level, more masculinized jobs within the medical field.

As minority women address issues of both race and gender to negotiate a sense of belonging in masculine settings (Ong 2005), minority men may also face a comparable challenge in feminized fields. They may have to address the unspoken racialization implicit in the assumption that masculinity equals competence. Simultaneously, they may find that the racial stereotype that Blackness equals lower qualifications, standards, and competence clouds the sense that men are inherently more capable and adept in any field, including the feminized ones.

Establishing Distance from Femininity

An additional mechanism of the glass escalator involves establishing distance from women and the femininity associated with their occupations. Because men nurses are employed in a culturally feminized occupation, they develop strategies to disassociate themselves from the femininity associated with their work and retain some of the privilege associated with masculinity. Thus, when men nurses gravitate toward hospital emergency wards rather than obstetrics or pediatrics, or emphasize that they are only in nursing to get into hospital administration, they distance themselves from the femininity of their profession and thereby preserve their status as men despite the fact that they do "women's work." Perhaps more important, these strategies also place men in a prime position to experience the glass escalator effect, as they situate themselves to move upward into higher-status areas in the field.

Creating distance from femininity also helps these men achieve aspects of hegemonic masculinity, which Connell (1989) describes as the predominant and most valued form of masculinity at a given time. Contemporary hegemonic masculine ideals emphasize toughness, strength, aggressiveness, heterosexuality, and, perhaps most important, a clear sense of femininity as different from and subordinate to masculinity (Kimmel 2001; Williams 1995). Thus, when men distance themselves from the feminized aspects of their jobs, they uphold the idea that masculinity and femininity are distinct, separate, and mutually exclusive. When

these men seek masculinity by aiming for the better paying or most technological fields, they not only position themselves to move upward into the more acceptable arenas but also reinforce the greater social value placed on masculinity. Establishing distance from femininity therefore allows men to retain the privileges and status of masculinity while simultaneously enabling them to ride the glass escalator.

For Black men, the desire to reject femininity may be compounded by racial inequality. Theorists have argued that as institutional racism blocks access to traditional markers of masculinity such as occupational status and economic stability, Black men may repudiate femininity as a way of accessing the masculinity— and its attendant status—that is denied through other routes (hooks 2004; Neal 2005). Rejecting femininity is a key strategy men use to assert masculinity, and it remains available to Black men even when other means of achieving masculinity are unattainable. Black men nurses may be more likely to distance themselves from their women colleagues and to reject the femininity associated with nursing, particularly if they feel that they experience racial discrimination that renders occupational advancement inaccessible. Yet if they encounter strained relationships with women colleagues and men supervisors because of gendered racism or racialized stereotypes, the efforts to distance themselves from femininity still may not result in the glass escalator effect.

On the other hand, some theorists suggest that minority men may challenge racism by rejecting hegemonic masculine ideals. Chen (1999) argues that Chinese American men may engage in a strategy of repudiation, where they reject hegemonic masculinity because its implicit assumptions of whiteness exclude Asian American men. As these men realize that racial stereotypes and assumptions preclude them from achieving the hegemonic masculine ideal, they reject it and dispute its racialized underpinnings. Similarly, Lamont (2000, 47) notes that working-class Black men in the United States and France develop a "caring self in which they emphasize values such as "morality, solidarity, and generosity." As a consequence of these men's ongoing experiences with racism, they develop a caring self that highlights work on behalf of others as an important tool in fighting oppression. Although caring is associated with femininity, these men culti-vate a caring self because it allows them to challenge racial inequality. The results of these studies suggest that Black men nurses may embrace the femininity associated with nursing if it offers a way to combat racism. In these cases, Black men nurses may turn to pediatrics as a way of demonstrating sensitivity and therefore combating stereotypes of Black masculinity, or they may proudly identify as nurses to challenge perceptions that Black men are unsuited for profes-sional, white-collar positions.

Taken together, all of this research suggests that Black men may not enjoy the advantages experienced by their white men colleagues, who ride a glass esca-lator to success. In this article, I focus on the experi-ences of Black men nurses to argue that the glass esca-lator is a racialized as well as a gendered concept that does not offer Black men the same privileges as their white men counterparts.

DATA COLLECTION AND METHOD

I collected data through semistructured interviews with 17 men nurses who identified as Black or African American. Nurses ranged in age from 30 to 51 and lived in the southeastern United States. Six worked in suburban hospitals adjacent to major cities, six were located in major metropolitan urban care centers, and the remaining five worked in rural hospitals or clinics. All were registered nurses or licensed practical nurses. Six identified their specialty as oncology, four were bedside nurses, two were in intensive care, one managed an acute dialysis program, one was an ortho-pedic nurse, one was in ambulatory care, one was in emergency, and one was in surgery. The least experi-enced nurse had worked in the field for five years; the most experienced had been a nurse for 26 years. I initially recruited participants by soliciting attendees at the 2007 National Black Nurses Association annual meetings and then used a snowball sample to create the remainder of the data set. All names and identifying details have been changed to ensure confidentiality (see Table 1).

I conducted interviews during the fall of 2007. They generally took place in either my campus office or a coffee shop located near the respondent's home or workplace. The average interview lasted about an hour. Interviews were tape-recorded and transcribed. Interview questions primarily focused on how race and gender shaped the men's experiences as nurses. Questions addressed respondents' work history and current experiences in the field, how race and gender shaped their experiences as nurses, and their future career goals. The men discussed their reasons for going into nursing, the reactions from others on enter-ing this field, and the particular challenges, difficul-ties, and obstacles Black men nurses faced. Respon-dents also described their work history in nursing, their current jobs, and their future plans. Finally, they talked about stereotypes of nurses in general and of Black men nurses in particular and their thoughts about and responses to these stereotypes. I coded the data according to key themes that emerged: relation-ships with white patients versus minority patients, personal bonds with colleagues versus lack of bonds, opportunities for advancement versus obstacles to advancement.

The researcher's gender and race shape interviews, and the fact that I am an African American woman undoubtedly shaped my rapport and the interactions

Table 1 Respondents

Name	Age	Specialization	Years of Experience	Years at Current Job
Chris	51	Oncology	26	16
Clayton	31	Emergency	6	6
Cyril	40	Dialysis	17	7
Dennis	30	Bedside	7	7 (months)
Evan	42	Surgery	25	20
Greg	39	Oncology	10	3
Kenny	47	Orthopedics	23	18 (months)
Leo	50	Bedside	20	18
Ray	36	Oncology	10	5
Ryan	37	Intensive care	17	11
Sean	46	Oncology	9	9
Simon	36	Oncology	5	5
Stuart	44	Bedside	6	4
Terrence	32	Bedside	10	6
Tim	39	Intensive care	20	15 (months)
Tobias	44	Oncology	25	7
Vern	50	Ambulatory care	7	7

with interview respondents. Social desirability bias may compel men to phrase responses that might sound harsh in ways that will not be offensive or problematic to the woman interviewer. However, one of the benefits of the interview method is that it allows respondents to clarify comments diplomatically while still giving honest answers. In this case, some respondents may have carefully framed certain comments about working mostly with women. However, the semistructured interview format nonetheless enabled them to discuss in detail their experiences in nursing and how these experiences are shaped by race and gender. Furthermore, I expect that shared racial status also facilitated a level of comfort, particularly as respondents frequently discussed issues of racial bias and mistreatment that shaped their experiences at work.

FINDINGS

The results of this study indicate that not all men experience the glass escalator in the same ways. For Black men nurses, intersections of race and gender create a different experience with the mechanisms that facilitate white men's advancement in women's professions. Awkward or unfriendly interactions with colleagues, poor relationships with supervisors, perceptions that they are not suited for nursing, and an unwillingness to disassociate from "feminized" aspects of nursing constitute what I term *glass barriers* to riding the glass escalator.

Reception from Colleagues and Supervisors

When women welcome men into "their" professions, they often push men into leadership roles that ease their advancement into upper-level positions. Thus, a positive reaction from colleagues is critical to riding the glass escalator. Unlike white men nurses, however, Black men do not describe encountering a warm reception from women colleagues (Heikes 1991). Instead, the men I interviewed find that they often have unpleasant interactions with women coworkers who treat them rather coldly and attempt to keep them at bay. Chris is a 51-year-old oncology nurse who describes one white nurse's attempt to isolate him

from other white women nurses as he attempted to get his instructions for that day's shift:

> She turned and ushered me to the door, and said for me to wait out here, a nurse will come out and give you your report. I stared at her hand on my arm, and then at her, and said, "Why? Where do you go to get your reports?" She said, "I get them in there." I said, "Right. Unhand me." I went right back in there, sat down, and started writing down my reports.

Kenny, a 47-year-old nurse with 23 years of nursing experience, describes a similarly and particularly painful experience he had in a previous job where he was the only Black person on staff:

> [The staff] had nothing to do with me, and they didn't even want me to sit at the same area where they were charting in to take a break. They wanted me to sit somewhere else. . . . They wouldn't even sit at a table with me! When I came and sat down, everybody got up and left.

These experiences with colleagues are starkly different from those described by white men in professions dominated by women (see Pierce 1995; Williams 1989). Though the men in these studies sometimes chose to segregate themselves, women never systematically excluded them. Though I have no way of knowing why the women nurses in Chris's and Kenny's workplaces physically segregated themselves, the pervasiveness of gendered racist images that emphasize white women's vulnerability to dangerous Black men may play an important role. For these nurses, their masculinity is not a guarantee that they will be welcomed, much less pushed into leadership roles. As Ryan, a 37-year-old intensive care nurse says, "[Black men] have to go further to prove ourselves. This involves proving our capabilities, *proving to colleagues that you can lead,* be on the forefront" (emphasis added). The warm welcome and subsequent opportunities for leadership cannot be taken for granted. In contrast, these men describe great challenges in forming congenial relationships with coworkers who, they believe, do not truly want them there.

In addition, these men often describe tense, if not blatantly discriminatory, relationships with supervisors. While Williams (1995) suggests that men supervisors can be allies for men in women's professions by facilitating promotions and upward mobility, Black men nurses describe incidents of being overlooked by supervisors when it comes time for promotions. Ryan, who has worked at his current job for 11 years, believes that these barriers block upward mobility within the profession:

> The hardest part is dealing with people who don't understand minority nurses. People with their biases, who don't identify you as ripe for promotion. I know the policy and procedure, I'm familiar with past history. So you can't tell me I can't move forward if others did. [How did you deal with this?] By knowing the chain of command, who my supervisors were. Things were subtle. I just had to be better. I got this mostly from other nurses and supervisors. I was paid to deal with patients, so I could deal with [racism] from them. I'm not paid to deal with this from colleagues.

Kenny offers a similar example. Employed as an orthopedic nurse in a predominantly white environment, he describes great difficulty getting promoted, which he primarily attributes to racial biases:

> It's almost like you have to, um, take your ideas and give them to somebody else and then let them present them for you and you get no credit for it. I've applied for several promotions there and, you know, I didn't get them. . . . When you look around to the, um, the percentage of African Americans who are actually in executive leadership is almost zero percent. Because it's less than one percent of the total population of people that are in leadership, and it's almost like they'll go outside of the system just to try to find a Caucasian to fill a position. Not that I'm not qualified, because I've been master's prepared for 12 years and I'm working on my doctorate.

According to Ryan and Kenny, supervisors' racial biases mean limited opportunities for promotion and upward mobility. This interpretation is consistent with research that suggests that even with stellar performance and solid work histories, Black workers may receive mediocre evaluations from white supervisors that limit their advancement (Feagin 2006; Feagin and Sikes 1994). For Black men nurses, their race may

signal to supervisors that they are unworthy of promotion and thus create a different experience with the glass escalator.

Strong relationships with colleagues and supervisors are a key mechanism of the glass escalator effect. For Black men nurses, however, these relationships are experienced differently from those described by their white men colleagues. Black men nurses do not speak of warm and congenial relationships with women nurses or see these relationships as facilitating a move into leadership roles. Nor do they suggest that they share gendered bonds with men supervisors that serve to ease their mobility into higher-status administrative jobs. In contrast, they sense that racial bias makes it difficult to develop ties with coworkers and makes superiors unwilling to promote them. Black men nurses thus experience this aspect of the glass escalator differently from their white men colleagues. They find that relationships with colleagues and supervisors stifle, rather than facilitate, their upward mobility.

Perceptions of Suitability

Like their white counterparts, Black men nurses also experience challenges from clients who are unaccustomed to seeing men in fields typically dominated by women. As with white men nurses, Black men encounter this in surprised or quizzical reactions from patients who seem to expect to be treated by white women nurses. Ray, a 36-year-old oncology nurse with 10 years of experience, states,

> Nursing, historically, has been a white female's job [so] being a Black male it's a weird position to be in. . . . I've, several times, gone into a room and a male patient, a white male patient has, you know, they'll say, "Where's the pretty nurse? Where's the pretty nurse? Where's the blonde nurse?" . . . "You don't have one. I'm the nurse."

Yet while patients rarely expect to be treated by men nurses of any race, white men encounter statements and behaviors that suggest patients expect them to be doctors, supervisors, or other higher-status, more masculine positions (Williams 1989, 1995). In part, this expectation accelerates their ride on the glass escalator, helping to push them into the positions for which they are seen as more appropriately suited.

(White) men, by virtue of their masculinity, are assumed to be more competent and capable and thus better situated in (nonfeminized) jobs that are perceived to require greater skill and proficiency. Black men, in contrast, rarely encounter patients (or colleagues and supervisors) who immediately expect that they are doctors or administrators. Instead, many respondents find that even after displaying their credentials, sharing their nursing experience, and, in one case, dispensing care, they are still mistaken for janitors or service workers. Ray's experience is typical:

> I've even given patients their medicines, explained their care to them, and then they'll say to me, "Well, can you send the nurse in?"

Chris describes a somewhat similar encounter of being misidentified by a white woman patient:

> I come [to work] in my white uniform, that's what I wear—being a Black man, I know they won't look at me the same, so I dress the part— I said good evening, my name's Chris, and I'm going to be your nurse. She says to me, "Are you from housekeeping?" . . . I've had other cases. I've walked in and had a lady look at me and ask if I'm the janitor.

Chris recognizes that this patient is evoking racial stereotypes that Blacks are there to perform menial service work. He attempts to circumvent this very perception through careful self-presentation, wearing the white uniform to indicate his position as a nurse. His efforts, however, are nonetheless met with a racial stereotype that as a Black man he should be there to clean up rather than to provide medical care.

Black men in nursing encounter challenges from customers that reinforce the idea that men are not suited for a "feminized" profession such as nursing. However, these assumptions are racialized as well as gendered. Unlike white men nurses who are assumed to be doctors (see Williams 1992), Black men in nursing are quickly taken for janitors or housekeeping staff. These men do not simply describe a gendered process where perceptions and stereotypes about men serve to aid their mobility into higher-status jobs. More specifically, they describe interactions that are simultaneously raced *and* gendered in ways that reproduce stereotypes of Black men as best suited for certain blue-collar, unskilled labor.

These negative stereotypes can affect Black men nurses' efforts to treat patients as well. The men I interviewed find that masculinity does not automatically endow them with an aura of competency. In fact, they often describe interactions with white women patients that suggest that their race minimizes whatever assumptions of capability might accompany being men. They describe several cases in which white women patients completely refused treatment. Ray says,

> With older white women, it's tricky sometimes because they will come right out and tell you they don't want you to treat them, or can they see someone else.

Ray frames this as an issue specifically with older white women, though other nurses in the sample described similar issues with white women of all ages. Cyril, a 40-year-old nurse with 17 years of nursing experience, describes a slightly different twist on this story:

> I had a white lady that I had to give a shot, and she was fine with it and I was fine with it. But her husband, when she told him, he said to me, I don't have any problem with you as a Black man, but I don't want you giving her a shot.

While white men nurses report some apprehension about treating women patients, in all likelihood this experience is compounded for Black men (Williams 1989). Historically, interactions between Black men and white women have been fraught with complexity and tension, as Black men have been represented in the cultural imagination as potential rapists and threats to white women's security and safety—and, implicitly, as a threat to white patriarchal stability (Davis 1981; Giddings 1984). In Cyril's case, it may be particularly significant that the Black man is charged with giving a shot and therefore literally penetrating the white wife's body, a fact that may heighten the husband's desire to shield his wife from this interaction. White men nurses may describe hesitation or awkwardness that accompanies treating women patients, but their experiences are not shaped by a pervasive racial imagery that suggests that they are potential threats to their women patients' safety.

This dynamic, described primarily among white women patients and their families, presents a picture of how Black men's interactions with clients are shaped in specifically raced and gendered ways that suggest they are less rather than more capable. These interactions do not send the message that Black men, because they are men, are too competent for nursing and really belong in higher-status jobs. Instead, these men face patients who mistake them for lower-status service workers and encounter white women patients (and their husbands) who simply refuse treatment or are visibly uncomfortable with the prospect. These interactions do not situate Black men nurses in a prime position for upward mobility. Rather, they suggest that the experience of Black men nurses with this particular mechanism of the glass escalator is the manifestation of the expectation that they should be in lower-status positions more appropriate to their race and gender.

Refusal to Reject Femininity

Finally, Black men nurses have a different experience with establishing distance from women and the feminized aspects of their work. Most research shows that as men nurses employ strategies that distance them from femininity (e.g., by emphasizing nursing as a route to higher-status, more masculine jobs), they place themselves in a position for upward mobility and the glass escalator effect (Williams 1992). For Black men nurses, however, this process looks different. Instead of distancing themselves from the femininity associated with nursing, Black men actually embrace some of the more feminized attributes linked to nursing. In particular, they emphasize how much they value and enjoy the way their jobs allow them to be caring and nurturing. Rather than conceptualizing caring as anathema or feminine (and therefore undesirable), Black men nurses speak openly of caring as something positive and enjoyable.

This is consistent with the context of nursing that defines caring as integral to the profession. As nurses, Black men in this line of work experience professional socialization that emphasizes and values caring, and

this is reflected in their statements about their work. Significantly, however, rather than repudiating this feminized component of their jobs, they embrace it. Tobias, a 44-year-old oncology nurse with 25 years of experience, asserts,

> The best part about nursing is helping other people, the flexibility of work hours, and the commitment to vulnerable populations, people who are ill.

Simon, a 36-year-old oncology nurse, also talks about the joy he gets from caring for others. He contrasts his experiences to those of white men nurses he knows who prefer specialties that involve less patient care:

> They were going to work with the insurance industries, they were going to work in the ER where it's a touch and go, you're a number literally. I don't get to know your name, I don't get to know that you have four grandkids, I don't get to know that you really want to get out of the hospital by next week because the following week is your birthday, your 80th birthday and it's so important for you. I don't get to know that your cat's name is Sprinkles, and you're concerned about who's feeding the cat now, and if they remembered to turn the TV on during the day so that the cat can watch *The Price is Right*. They don't get into all that kind of stuff. OK, I actually need to remember the name of your cat so that tomorrow morning when I come, I can ask you about Sprinkles and that will make a world of difference. I'll see light coming to your eyes and the medicines will actually work because your perspective is different.

Like Tobias, Simon speaks with a marked lack of self-consciousness about the joys of adding a personal touch and connecting that personal care to a patient's improvement. For him, caring is important, necessary, and valued, even though others might consider it a feminine trait.

For many of these nurses, willingness to embrace caring is also shaped by issues of race and racism. In their position as nurses, concern for others is connected to fighting the effects of racial inequality. Specifically, caring motivates them to use their role as nurses to address racial health disparities, especially those that disproportionately affect Black men. Chris describes his efforts to minimize health issues among Black men:

With Black male patients, I have their history, and if they're 50 or over I ask about the prostate exam and a colonoscopy. Prostate and colorectal death is so high that that's my personal crusade.

Ryan also speaks to the importance of using his position to address racial imbalances:

I really take advantage of the opportunities to give back to communities, especially to change the disparities in the African American community. I'm more than just a nurse. As a faculty member at a major university, I have to do community hours, services. Doing health fairs, in-services on research, this makes an impact in some disparities in the African American community. [People in the community] may not have the opportunity to do this otherwise.

As Lamont (2000) indicates in her discussion of the "caring self" concern for others helps Chris and Ryan to use their knowledge and position as nurses to combat racial inequalities in health. Though caring is generally considered a "feminine" attribute, in this context it is connected to challenging racial health disparities. Unlike their white men colleagues, these nurses accept and even embrace certain aspects of femininity rather than rejecting them. They thus reveal yet another aspect of the glass escalator process that differs for Black men. As Black men nurses embrace this "feminine" trait and the avenues it provides for challenging racial inequalities, they may become more comfortable in nursing and embrace the opportunities it offers.

CONCLUSIONS

Existing research on the glass escalator cannot explain these men's experiences. As men who do women's work, they should be channeled into positions as charge nurses or nursing administrators and should find themselves virtually pushed into the upper ranks of the nursing profession. But without exception, this is not the experience these Black men nurses describe. Instead of benefiting from the basic mechanisms of the glass escalator, they face tense relationships with colleagues, supervisors' biases in achieving promotion, patient stereotypes that inhibit caregiving, and a sense

of comfort with some of the feminized aspects of their jobs. These "glass barriers" suggest that the glass escalator is a racialized concept as well as a gendered one. The main contribution of this study is the finding that race and gender intersect to determine which men will ride the glass escalator. The proposition that men who do women's work encounter undue opportunities and advantages appears to be unequivocally true only if the men in question are white.

This raises interesting questions and a number of new directions for future research. Researchers might consider the extent to which the glass escalator is not only raced and gendered but sexualized as well. Williams (1995) notes that straight men are often treated better by supervisors than are gay men and that straight men frequently do masculinity by strongly asserting their heterosexuality to combat the belief that men who do women's work are gay. The men in this study (with the exception of one nurse I interviewed) rarely discussed sexuality except to say that they were straight and were not bothered by "the gay stereotype." This is consistent with Williams's findings. Gay men, however, may also find that they do not experience a glass escalator effect that facilitates their upward mobility. Tim, the only man I interviewed who identified as gay, suggests that gender, race, and sexuality come together to shape the experiences of men in nursing. He notes,

I've been called awful things—you faggot this, you faggot that. I tell people there are three *F*s in life, and if you're not doing one of them it doesn't matter what you think of me. They say, "Three *F*s?" and I say yes. If you aren't feeding me, financing me, or fucking me, then it's none of your business what my faggot ass is up to.

Tim's experience suggests that gay men—and specifically gay Black men—in nursing may encounter particular difficulties establishing close ties with straight men supervisors or may not automatically be viewed by their women colleagues as natural leaders. While race is, in many cases, more obviously visible than sexuality, the glass escalator effect may be a complicated amalgam of racial, gendered, and sexual expectations and stereotypes.

It is also especially interesting to consider how men describe the role of women in facilitating—or denying—access to the glass escalator. Research on white men nurses includes accounts of ways white women welcome them and facilitate their advancement by pushing them toward leadership positions (Floge and Merrill 1986; Heikes 1991; Williams 1992, 1995). In contrast, Black men nurses in this study discuss white women who do not seem eager to work with them, much less aid their upward mobility. These different responses indicate that shared racial status is important in determining who rides the glass escalator. If that is the case, then future research should consider whether Black men nurses who work in predominantly Black settings are more likely to encounter the glass escalator effect. In these settings, Black men nurses' experiences might more closely resemble those of white men nurses.

Future research should also explore other racial minority men's experiences in women's professions to determine whether and how they encounter the processes that facilitate a ride on the glass escalator. With Black men nurses, specific race or gender stereotypes impede their access to the glass escalator; however, other racial minority men are subjected to different race or gender stereotypes that could create other experiences. For instance, Asian American men may encounter racially specific gender stereotypes of themselves as computer nerds, sexless sidekicks, or model minorities and thus may encounter the processes of the glass escalator differently than do Black or white men (Espiritu 2000). More focus on the diverse experiences of racial minority men is necessary to know for certain.

Finally, it is important to consider how these men's experiences have implications for the ways the glass escalator phenomenon reproduces racial and gendered advantages. Williams (1995) argues that men's desire to differentiate themselves from women and disassociate from the femininity of their work is a key process that facilitates their ride on the glass escalator. She ultimately suggests that if men reconstruct masculinity to include traits such as caring, the distinctions between masculinity and femininity could blur and men "would not have to define masculinity as the negation of femi-

ninity" (Williams 1995, 188). This in turn could create a more equitable balance between men and women in women's professions. However, the experiences of Black men in nursing, especially their embrace of caring, suggest that accepting the feminine aspects of work is not enough to dismantle the glass escalator and produce more gender equality in women's professions. The fact that Black men nurses accept and even enjoy caring does not minimize the processes that enable *white* men to ride the glass escalator. This suggests that undoing the glass escalator requires not only blurring the lines between masculinity and femininity but also challenging the processes of racial inequality that marginalize minority men.

NOTE

1. I could not locate any data that indicate the percentage of Black men in nursing. According to 2006 census data, African Americans compose 11 percent of nurses, and men are 8 percent of nurses (http://www.census.gov/compendia/statab/tables/08s0598.pdf). These data do not show the breakdown of nurses by race and sex.

REFERENCES

Acker, Joan. 1990. Hierarchies, jobs, bodies: A theory of gendered organizations. *Gender & Society* 4:139–58.

Britton, Dana. 1995. *At work in the iron cage.* New York: New York University Press.

Budig, Michelle. 2002. Male advantage and the gender composition of jobs: Who rides the glass escalator? *Social Forces* 49 (2): 258–77.

Charles, Maria, and David Grusky. 2004. *Occupational ghettos: The worldwide segregation of women and men.* Palo Alto, CA: Stanford University Press.

Chen, Anthony. 1999. Lives at the center of the periphery, lives at the periphery of the center: Chinese American masculinities and bargaining with hegemony. *Gender & Society* 13:584–607.

Collins, Patricia Hill. 1990. *Black feminist thought.* New York: Routledge.

———. 2004. *Black sexual politics.* New York: Routledge.

Connell, R. W. 1989. *Gender and power.* Sydney, Australia: Allen and Unwin.

Davis, Angela. 1981. *Women, race, and class.* New York: Vintage.

Duffy, Mignon. 2007. Doing the dirty work: Gender, race, and reproductive labor in historical perspective. *Gender & Society* 21:313–36.

Espiritu, Yen Le. 2000. *Asian American women and men: Labor, laws, and love.* Walnut Creek, CA: AltaMira.

Essed, Philomena. 1991. *Understanding everyday racism.* New York: Russell Sage.

Feagin, Joe. 2006. *Systemic racism.* New York: Routledge.

Feagin, Joe, and Melvin Sikes. 1994. *Living with racism.* Boston: Beacon Hill Press.

Floge, Liliane, and Deborah M. Merrill. 1986. Tokenism reconsidered: Male nurses and female physicians in a hospital setting. *Social Forces* 64:925–47.

Giddings, Paula. 1984. *When and where I enter: The impact of Black women on race and sex in America.* New York: HarperCollins.

Harvey Wingfield, Adia. 2007. The modern mammy and the angry Black man: African American professionals' experiences with gendered racism in the workplace. *Race, Gender, and Class* 14 (2): 196–212.

Heikes, E. Joel. 1991. When men are the minority: The case of men in nursing. *Sociological Quarterly* 32:389–401.

hooks, bell. 2004. *We real cool.* New York: Routledge.

Kanter, Rosabeth Moss. 1977. *Men and women of the corporation.* New York: Basic Books.

Kimmel, Michael. 2001. Masculinity as homophobia. In *Men and masculinity,* edited by Theodore F. Cohen. Belmont, CA: Wadsworth.

Lamont, Michelle. 2000. *The dignity of working men.* New York: Russell Sage.

Neal, Mark Anthony. 2005. *New Black man.* New York: Routledge.

Ong, Maria. 2005. Body projects of young women of color in physics: Intersections of race, gender, and science. *Social Problems* 52 (4): 593–617.

Pierce, Jennifer. 1995. *Gender trials: Emotional lives in contemporary law firms.* Berkeley: University of California Press.

Roth, Louise. 2006. *Selling women short: Gender and money on Wall Street.* Princeton, NJ: Princeton University Press.

Shapiro, Thomas. 2004. *Hidden costs of being African American: How wealth perpetuates inequality.* New York: Oxford University Press.

Snyder, Karrie Ann, and Adam Isaiah Green. 2008. Revisiting the glass escalator: The case of gender segregation in a female dominated occupation. *Social Problems* 55 (2): 271–99.

Williams, Christine. 1989. *Gender differences at work: Women and men in non-traditional occupations.* Berkeley: University of California Press.

———. 1992. The glass escalator: Hidden advantages for men in the "female" professions. *Social Problems* 39 (3): 253–67.

———. 1995. *Still a man's world: Men who do women's work.* Berkeley: University of California Press.

Zimmer, Lynn. 1988. Tokenism and women in the workplace: The limits of gender neutral theory. *Social Problems* 35 (1): 64–77.

35

JUST ONE OF THE GUYS?

How Transmen Make Gender Visible at Work

KRISTEN SCHILT

Theories of gendered organizations argue that cultural beliefs about gender difference embedded in workplace structures and interactions create and reproduce workplace disparities that disadvantage women and advantage men (Acker 1990; Martin 2003; Williams 1995), As Martin (2003) argues, however, the practices that reproduce gender difference and gender inequality at work are hard to observe. As these gendered practices are citations of established gender norms, men and women in the workplace repeatedly and unreflectively engage in "doing gender" and therefore "doing inequality" (Martin 2003; West and Zimmerman 1987). This repetition of well-worn gender ideologies naturalizes workplace gender inequality, making gendered disparities in achievements appear to be offshoots of "natural" differences between men and women, rather than the products of dynamic gendering and gendered practices (Martin 2003). As the active reproduction of gendered workplace disparities is rendered invisible, gender inequality at work becomes difficult to document empirically and therefore remains resistant to change (Acker 1990; Martin 2003; Williams 1995).

The workplace experiences of female-to-male transsexuals (FTMs), or trans-men, offer an opportunity to examine these disparities between men and women at work from a new perspective. Many FTMs enter the workforce as women and, after transition, begin working as men.[1] As men, they have the same skills, education, and abilities they had as women; however, how this "human capital" is perceived often varies drastically once they become men at work. This shift in gender attribution gives them the potential to develop an "outsider-within" perspective (Collins 1986) on men's advantages in the workplace. FTMs can find themselves benefiting from the "patriarchal dividend" (Connell 1995, 79)—the advantages men in general gain from the subordination of women—after they transition. However, not being "born into it" gives them the potential to be cognizant of being awarded respect, authority, and prestige they did not have working as women. In addition, the experiences of transmen who fall outside of the hegemonic construction of masculinity, such as FTMs of color, short FTMs, and young FTMs, illuminate how the interplay of gender, race, age, and bodily characteristics can constrain access to gendered workplace advantages for some men (Connell 1995).

In this article, I document the workplace experiences of two groups of FTMs, those who openly transition and remain in the same jobs (open FTMs) and those who find new jobs posttransition as "just men" (stealth FTMs).[2] I argue that the positive and negative changes they experience when they become men can illuminate how gender discrimination and gender advantage are created and maintained through workplace interactions. These experiences also illustrate that masculinity is not a fixed character type that automatically commands privilege but rather that the relationships between competing hegemonic and marginalized masculinities give men differing abilities to access gendered workplace advantages (Connell 1995).

THEORIES OF WORKPLACE GENDER DISCRIMINATION

Sociological research on the workplace reveals a complex relationship between the gender of an employee and that employee's opportunities for advancement in both authority and pay. While white-collar men and women with equal qualifications can begin their careers in similar positions in the workplace, men tend to advance faster, creating a gendered promotion gap (Padavic and Reskin 2002; Valian 1999). When women are able to advance, they often find themselves barred from attaining access to the highest echelons of the company by the invisible barrier of the "glass ceiling" (Valian 1999). Even in the so-called women's professions, such as nursing and teaching, men outpace women in advancement to positions of authority (Williams 1995). Similar patterns exist among blue-collar professions, as women often are denied sufficient training for advancement in manual trades, passed over for promotion, or subjected to extreme forms of sexual, racial, and gender harassment that result in women's attrition (Byrd 1999; Miller 1997; Yoder and Aniakudo 1997). These studies are part of the large body of scholarly research on gender and work finding that white- and blue-collar workplaces are characterized by gender segregation, with women concentrated in lower-paying jobs with little room for advancement.

Among the theories proposed to account for these workplace disparities between men and women are human capital theory and gender role socialization.

Human capital theory posits that labor markets are neutral environments that reward workers for their skills, experience, and productivity. As women workers are more likely to take time off from work for child rearing and family obligations, they end up with less education and work experience than men. Following this logic, gender segregation in the workplace stems from these discrepancies in skills and experience between men and women, not from gender discrimination. However, while these differences can explain some of the disparities in salaries and rank between women and men, they fail to explain why women and men with comparable prestigious degrees and work experience still end up in different places, with women trailing behind men in advancement (Valian 1999; Williams 1995).

A second theory, gender socialization theory, looks at the process by which individuals come to learn, through the family, peers, schools, and the media, what behavior is appropriate and inappropriate for their gender. From this standpoint, women seek out jobs that reinforce "feminine" traits such as caring and nurturing. This would explain the predominance of women in helping professions such as nursing and teaching. As women are socialized to put family obligations first, women workers would also be expected to be concentrated in part-time jobs that allow more flexibility for family schedules but bring in less money. Men, on the other hand, would be expected to seek higher-paying jobs with more authority to reinforce their sense of masculinity. While gender socialization theory may explain some aspects of gender segregation at work, however, it leaves out important structural aspects of the workplace that support segregation, such as the lack of workplace child care services, as well as employers' own gendered stereotypes about which workers are best suited for which types of jobs (Padavic and Reskin 2002; Valian 1999; Williams 1995).

A third theory, gendered organization theory, argues that what is missing from both human capital theory and gender socialization theory is the way in which men's advantages in the workplace are maintained and reproduced in gender expectations that are embedded in organizations and in interactions between employers, employees, and coworkers (Acker 1990; Martin 2003; Williams 1995). However, it is difficult to study this process of reproduction empirically for several reasons. First, while men and women with similar education and workplace backgrounds can be compared to demonstrate the disparities in where they end up in their careers, it could be argued that differences in achievement between them can be attributed to personal characteristics of the workers rather than to systematic gender discrimination. Second, gendered expectations about which types of jobs women and men are suited for are strengthened by existing occupational segregation; the fact that there are more women nurses and more men doctors comes to be seen as proof that women are better suited for helping professions and men for rational professions. The normalization of these disparities as natural differences obscures the actual operation of men's advantages and therefore makes it hard to document them empirically. Finally, men's advantages in the workplace are not a function of simply one process but rather a complex interplay between many factors, such as gender differences in workplace performance evaluation, gendered beliefs about men's and women's skills and abilities, and differences between family and child care obligations of men and women workers.

The cultural reproduction of these interactional practices that create and maintain gendered workplace disparities often can be rendered more visible, and therefore more able to be challenged, when examined through the perspective of marginalized others (Collins 1986; Martin 1994, 2003; Yoder and Aniakudo 1997). As Yoder and Aniakudo note, "marginalized others offer a unique perspective on the events occurring within a setting because they perceive activities from the vantages of both nearness (being within) and detachment (being outsiders)" (1997, 325–26). This importance of drawing on the experiences of marginalized others derives from Patricia Hill Collins's theoretical development of the "outsider-within" (1986, 1990). Looking historically at the experience of Black women, Collins (1986) argues that they often have become insiders to white society by virtue of being forced, first by slavery and later by racially bounded labor markets, into domestic work for white families. The insider status that results from being immersed in the daily lives of white families carries

the ability to demystify power relations by making evident how white society relies on racism and sexism, rather than superior ability or intellect, to gain advantage; however, Black women are not able to become total insiders due to being visibly marked as different. Being a marginalized insider creates a unique perspective, what Collins calls "the outsider-within," that allows them to see "the contradictions between the dominant group's actions and ideologies" (Collins 1990, 12), thus giving a new angle on how the processes of oppression operate. Applying this perspective to the workplace, scholars have documented the production and reproduction of gendered and racialized workplace disparities through the "outsider-within" perspective of Black women police officers (Martin 1994) and Black women firefighters (Yoder and Aniakudo 1997).

In this article, I posit that FTMs' change in gender attribution, from women to men, can provide them with an outsider-within perspective on gendered workplace disparities. Unlike the Black women discussed by Collins, FTMs usually are not visibly marked by their outsider status, as continued use of testosterone typically allows for the development of a masculine social identity indistinguishable from "bio men."[3] However, while both stealth and open FTMs can become social insiders at work, their experience working as women prior to transition means they maintain an internalized sense of being outsiders to the gender schemas that advantage men. This internalized insider/outsider position allows some transmen to see clearly the advantages associated with being men at work while still maintaining a critical view to how this advantage operates and is reproduced and how it disadvantages women. I demonstrate that many of the respondents find themselves receiving more authority, respect, and reward when they gain social identities as men, even though their human capital does not change. This shift in treatment suggests that gender inequality in the workplace is not continually reproduced only because women make different education and workplace choices than men but rather because coworkers and employers often rely on gender stereotypes to evaluate men's and women's achievements and skills.

METHOD

I conducted in-depth interviews with 29 FTMs in the Southern California area from 2003 to 2005. My criteria for selection were that respondents were assigned female at birth and were currently living and working as men or open transmen. These selection criteria did exclude female-bodied individuals who identified as men but had had not publicly come out as men at work and FTMs who had not held any jobs as men since their transition, as they would not be able to comment about changes in their social interactions that were specific to the workplace. My sample is made up of 18 open FTMs and 11 stealth FTMs.

At the onset of my research, I was unaware of how I would be received as a non-transgender person doing research on transgender workplace experiences, as well as a woman interviewing men. I went into the study being extremely open about my research agenda and my political affiliations with feminist and transgender politics. I carried my openness about my intentions into my interviews, making clear at the beginning that I was happy to answer questions about my research intentions, the ultimate goal of my research, and personal questions about myself. Through this openness, and the acknowledgment that I was there to learn rather than to be an academic "expert," I feel that I gained a rapport with my respondents that bridged the "outsider/insider" divide (Merton 1972).

Generating a random sample of FTMs is not possible as there is not an even dispersal of FTMs throughout Southern California, nor are there transgender-specific neighborhoods from which to sample. I recruited interviewees from transgender activist groups, transgender listservers, and FTM support groups. In addition, I participated for two years in Southern California transgender community events, such as conferences and support group meetings. Attending these community events gave me an opportunity not only to demonstrate long-term political commitment to the transgender community but also to recruit respondents who might not be affiliated with FTM activist groups. All the interviews were conducted in the respondents' offices, in their homes, or at a local café or restaurant. The interviews ranged from one and a half to four

hours. All interviews were audio recorded, transcribed, and coded.

Drawing on sociological research that reports long-standing gender differences between men and women in the workplace (Reskin and Hartmann 1986; Reskin and Roos 1990; Valian 1999; Williams 1995), I constructed my interview schedule to focus on possible differences between working as women and working as men. I first gathered a general employment history and then explored the decision to openly transition or to go stealth. At the end of the interviews, I posed the question, "Do you see any differences between working as a woman and working as a man?" All but a few of the respondents immediately answered yes and began to provide examples of both positive and negative differences. About half of the respondents also, at this time, introduced the idea of male privilege, addressing whether they felt they received a gender advantage from transitioning. If the concept of gender advantage was not brought up by respondents, I later introduced the concept of male privilege and then posed the question, saying, "Do you feel that you have received any male privilege at work?" The resulting answers from these two questions are the framework for this article.

In reporting the demographics of my respondents, I have opted to use pseudonyms and general categories of industry to avoid identifying my respondents. Respondents ranged in age from 20 to 48. Rather than attempting to identify when they began their gender transition, a start date often hard to pinpoint as many FTMs feel they have been personally transitioning since childhood or adolescence, I recorded how many years they had been working as men (meaning they were either hired as men or had openly transitioned from female to male and remained in the same job). The average time of working as a man was seven years. Regarding race and ethnicity, the sample was predominantly white (17), with 3 Asians, 1 African American, 3 Latinos, 3 mixed-race individuals, 1 Armenian American, and 1 Italian American. Responses about sexual identity fell into four main categories, heterosexual (9), bisexual (8), queer (6), and gay (3). The remaining 3 respondents identified their sexual identity as celibate/asexual, "dating women," and pansexual. Finally, in terms of region, the sample included a

Table 1 Sample Characteristics

Pseudonym	Age	Race/ Ethnicity	Sexual Identity	Approximate Number of Years Working as Male	Industry	Status at Work
Aaron	28	Black/White	Queer	5	Semi-Professional	Open
Brian	42	White	Bisexual	14	Semi-Professional	Stealth
Carl	34	White	Heterosexual	16	Higher Professional	Stealth
Christopher	25	Asian	Pansexual	3	Semi-professional	Open
Colin	31	White	Queer	1	Lower Professional	Open
Crispin	42	White	Heterosexual	2	Blue-Collar	Stealth
David	30	White	Bisexual	2	Higher Professional	Open
Douglas	38	White	Gay	5	Semi-Professional	Open
Elliott	20	White	Bisexual	1	Retail/Customer Service	Open
Henry	32	White	Gay	5	Lower Professional	Open
Jack	30	Latino	Queer	1	Semi-Professional	Open
Jake	45	White	Queer	9	Higher Professional	Open
Jason	48	White/Italian	Celibate	20	Retail/Customer Service	Stealth
Keith	42	Black	Heterosexual	1	Blue-Collar	Open
Kelly	24	White	Bisexual	2	Semi-Professional	Open
Ken	26	Asian/White	Queer	6 months	Semi-Professional	Open
Paul	44	White	Heterosexual	2	Semi-Professional	Open
Peter	24	White/Armenian	Heterosexual	4	Lower Professional	Stealth
Preston	39	White	Bisexual	2	Blue-Collar	Open
Riley	37	White	Dates women	1	Lower Professional	Open
Robert	23	Asian	Heterosexual	2	Retail/Customer Service	Stealth
Roger	45	White	Bisexual	22	Lower Professional	Stealth
Sam	33	Latino	Heterosexual	15	Blue-Collar	Stealth
Simon	42	White	Bisexual	2	Semi-Professional	Open
Stephen	35	White	Heterosexual	1	Retail/Customer Service	Stealth
Thomas	42	Latino	Queer	13	Higher Professional	Open
Trevor	35	White	Gay/Queer	6	Semi-Professional	Open
Wayne	44	White/Latino	Bisexual	22	Higher Professional	Stealth
Winston	40	White	Heterosexual	14	Higher Professional	Stealth

mixture of FTMs living in urban and suburban areas. (See Table 1 for sample characteristics.)

The experience of my respondents represents a part of the Southern California FTM community from 2003 to 2005. As Rubin (2003) has demonstrated, however, FTM communities vary greatly from city to city, meaning these findings may not be representative of the experiences of transmen in Austin, San Francisco, or Atlanta. In addition, California passed statewide gender identity protection for employees in 2003, meaning that the men in my study live in an environment in which they cannot legally be fired for being transgender (although most of my respondents said

they would not wish to be a test case for this new law). This legal protection means that California transmen might have very different workplace experiences than men in states without gender identity protection. Finally, anecdotal evidence suggests that there are a large number of transgender individuals who transition and then sever all ties with the transgender community, something known as being "deep stealth." This lack of connection to the transgender community means they are excluded from research on transmen but that their experiences with the workplace may be very different than those of men who are still connected, even slightly, to the FTM community.

TRANSMEN AS OUTSIDERS WITHIN AT WORK

In undergoing a physical gender transition, transmen move from being socially gendered as women to being socially gendered as men (Dozier 2005). This shift in gender attribution gives them the potential to develop an "outsider-within" perspective (Collins 1986) on the sources of men's advantages in the workplace. In other words, while they may find themselves, as men, benefiting from the "patriarchal dividend" (Connell 1995, 79), not being "born into it" can make visible how gendered workplace disparities are created and maintained through interactions. Many of the respondents note that they can see clearly, once they become "just one of the guys," that men succeed in the workplace at higher rates than women because of gender stereotypes that privilege masculinity, not because they have greater skill or ability. For transmen who do see how these cultural beliefs about gender create gendered workplace disparities, there is an accompanying sense that these experiences are visible to them only because of the unique perspective they gain from undergoing a change in gender attribution. Exemplifying this, Preston reports about his views on gender differences at work posttransition: "I swear they let the guys get away with so much stuff"! Lazy ass bastards get away with so much stuff and the women who are working hard, they just get ignored. . . . I am really aware of it. And that is one of the reasons that I feel like I have become much more of a feminist since transition. I am just so aware of the difference that my experience has shown me." Carl makes a similar point, discussing his awareness of blatant gender discrimination at a hardware/home construction store where he worked immediately after his transition: "Girls couldn't get their forklift license or it would take them forever. They wouldn't make as much money. It was so pathetic. I would have never seen it if I was a regular guy. I would have just not seen it. . . . I can see things differently because of my perspective. So in some ways I am a lot like a guy because I transitioned younger but still, you can't take away how I was raised for 18 years." These comments illustrate how the outsider-within perspective of many FTMs can translate into a critical perspective on men's advantages at work. The idea that a

"regular guy," here meaning a bio man, would not be able to see how women were passed over in favor of men makes clear that for some FTMs, there is an ability to see how gender stereotypes can advantage men at work.

However, just as being a Black woman does not guarantee the development of a Black feminist perspective (Collins 1986), having this critical perspective on gender discrimination in the workplace is not inherent to the FTM experience. Respondents who had held no jobs prior to transition, who were highly gender ambiguous prior to transition, or who worked in short-term, high-turnover retail jobs, such as food service, found it harder to identify gender differences at work. FTMs who transitioned in their late teens often felt that they did not have enough experience working as women to comment on any possible differences between men and women at work. For example, Sam and Robert felt they could not comment on gender differences in the workplace because they had begun living as men at the age of 15 and, therefore, never had been employed as women. In addition, FTMs who reported being very "in-between" in their gender appearance, such as Wayne and Peter, found it hard to comment on gender differences at work, as even when they were hired as women, they were not always sure how customers and coworkers perceived them. They felt unable to speak about the experience of working as a woman because they were perceived either as androgynous or as men.

The kinds of occupations FTMs held prior to transition also play a role in whether they develop this outsider-within perspective at work. Transmen working in blue-collar jobs—jobs that are predominantly staffed by men—felt their experiences working in these jobs as females varied greatly from their experiences working as men. This held true even for those transmen who worked as females in blue-collar jobs in their early teens, showing that age of transition does not always determine the ability to see gender discrimination at work. FTMs working in the "women's professions" also saw a great shift in their treatment once they began working as men. FTMs who transitioned in their late teens and worked in marginal "teenage" jobs, such as fast food, however, often reported little sense of change posttransition, as they felt that most employees were doing the same jobs regardless of gender. As a gendered division of labor often does exist in fast food jobs (Leidner 1993), it may be that these respondents worked in atypical settings, or that they were assigned "men's jobs" because of their masculine appearance.

Transmen in higher professional jobs, too, reported less change in their experiences posttransition, as many of them felt that their workplaces guarded against gender-biased treatment as part of an ethic of professionalism. The experience of these professional respondents obviously runs counter to the large body of scholarly research that documents gender inequality in fields such as academia (Valian 1999), law firms (Pierce 1995), and corporations (Martin 1992). Not having an outsider-within perspective, then, may be unique to these particular transmen, not the result of working in a professional occupation.

Thus, transitioning from female to male can provide individuals with an outsider-within perspective on gender discrimination in the workplace. However, this perspective can be limited by the age of transition, appearance, and type of occupation. In addition, as I will discuss at the end of this article, even when the advantages of the patriarchal dividend are seen clearly, many transmen do not benefit from them. In the next section, I will explore in what ways FTMs who expressed having this outsider-within perspective saw their skills and abilities perceived more positively as men. Then, I will explore why not all of my respondents received a gender advantage from transitioning.

TRANSITION AND WORKPLACE GENDER ADVANTAGES[4]

A large body of evidence shows that the performance of workers is evaluated differently depending on gender. Men, particularly white men, are viewed as more competent than women workers (Olian, Schwab, and Haberfeld 1988; Valian 1999). When men succeed, their success is seen as stemming from their abilities while women's success often is attributed to luck (Valian 1999). Men are rewarded more than women for offering ideas and opinions and for taking on leadership roles in group settings (Butler and Geis 1990; Valian 1999). Based on these findings, it would be expected

that stealth transmen would see a positive difference in their workplace experience once they have made the transition from female to male, as they enter new jobs as just one of the guys. Open FTMs, on the other hand, might find themselves denied access to these privileges, as they remain in the same jobs in which they were hired as women. Challenging these expectations, two-thirds of my respondents, both open and stealth, report receiving some type of posttransition advantage at work. These advantages fell into four main categories: gaining competency and authority, gaining respect and recognition for hard work, gaining "body privilege," and gaining economic opportunities and status.

Authority and Competency

Illustrating the authority gap that exists between men and women workers (Elliott and Smith 2004; Padavic and Reskin 2002), several of my interviewees reported receiving more respect for their thoughts and opinions posttransition. For example, Henry, who is stealth in a professional workplace, says of his experiences, "I'm right a lot more now. . . . Even with folks I am out to [as a transsexual], there is a sense that I know what I am talking about." Roger, who openly transitioned in a retail environment in the 1980s, discussed customers' assumptions that as a man, he knew more than his boss, who was a woman: "People would come in and they would go straight to me. They would pass her and go straight to me because obviously, as a male, I knew [sarcasm]. And so we would play mind games with them. . . . They would come up and ask me a question, and then I would go over to her and ask her the same question, she would tell me the answer, and I would go back to the customer and tell the customer the answer." Revealing how entrenched these stereotypes about masculinity and authority are, Roger added that none of the customers ever recognized the sarcasm behind his actions. Demonstrating how white men's opinions are seen to carry more authority, Trevor discusses how, posttransition, his ideas are now taken more seriously in group situations—often to the detriment of his women coworkers: "In a professional workshop or a conference kind of setting, a woman would make a comment or an observation and be overlooked and be dissed essentially. I would raise my hand and make the same point in a way that I am trying to reinforce her and it would be like [directed at me], That's an excellent point!' I saw this shit in undergrad. So it is not like this was a surprise to me. But it was disconcerting to have happen to me." These last two quotes exemplify the outsider-within experience: Both men are aware of having more authority simply because of being men, an authority that happens at the expense of women coworkers.

Looking at the issue of authority in the women's professions, Paul, who openly transitioned in the field of secondary education, reports a sense of having increased authority as one of the few men in his work environment:

> I did notice [at] some of the meetings I'm required to attend, like school district or parent involvement [meetings], you have lots of women there. And now I feel like there are [many times], mysteriously enough, when I'm picked [to speak]. . . . I think, well, why me, when nobody else has to go to the microphone and talk about their stuff? That I did notice and that [had] never happened before. I mean there was this meeting . . . a little while ago about domestic violence where I appeared to be the only male person between these 30, 40 women and, of course, then everybody wants to hear from me.

Rather than being alienated by his gender tokenism, as women often are in predominantly male workplaces (Byrd 1999), he is asked to express his opinions and is valued for being the "male" voice at the meetings, a common situation for men in "women's professions" (Williams 1995). The lack of interest paid to him as a woman in the same job demonstrates how women in predominantly female workspaces can encourage their coworkers who are men to take more authority and space in these careers, a situation that can lead to the promotion of men in women's professions (Williams 1995).

Transmen also report a positive change in the evaluation of their abilities and competencies after transition. Thomas, an attorney, relates an episode in which an attorney who worked for an associated law firm commended his boss for firing Susan, here a pseudonym for his female name, because she was incompetent—padding that the "new guy" [i.e., Thomas]

was "just delightful." The attorney did not realize that Susan and "the new guy" were the same person with the same abilities, education, and experience. This anecdote is a glaring example of how men are evaluated as more competent than women even when they do the same job in careers that are stereotyped requiring "masculine" skills such as rationality (Pierce 1995; Valian 1999). Stephen, who is stealth in a predominantly male customer-service job, reports, "For some reason just because [the men I work with] assume I have a dick, [they assume] I am going to get the job done right, where, you know, they have to second guess that when you're a woman. They look at [women] like well, you can't handle this because you know, you don't have the same mentality that we [men] do, so there's this sense of panic . . . and if you are a guy, it's just like, oh, you can handle it." Keith, who openly transitioned in a male-dominated blue-collar job, reports no longer having to "cuddle after sex," meaning that he has been able to drop the emotional labor of niceness women often have to employ to when giving orders at work. Showing how perceptions of behavior can change with transition, Trevor reports, "I think my ideas are taken more seriously [as a man]. I had good leadership skills leaving college and um . . . I think that those work well for me now. . . . Because I'm male, they work better for me. I was 'assertive' before. Now I'm 'take charge.'" Again, while his behavior has not changed, his shift in gender attribution translates into a different kind of evaluation. As a man, being assertive is consistent with gendered expectations for men, meaning his same leadership skills have more worth in the workplace because of his transition. His experience underscores how women who take on leadership roles are evaluated negatively, particularly if their leadership style is perceived as assertive, while men are rewarded for being aggressive leaders (Butler and Geis 1990; Valian 1999).[5]

This change in authority is noticeable only because FTMs often have experienced the reverse: being thought, on the basis of gender alone, to be less competent workers who receive less authority from employers and coworkers. This sense of a shift in authority and perceived competence was particularly marked for FTMs who had worked in blue-collar occupations as women. These transmen report that the stereotype of women's incompetence often translated into difficulty in finding and maintaining employment. For example, Crispin, who had worked as a female construction worker, reports being written up by supervisors for every small infraction, a practice Yoder and Aniakudo (1997, 330) refer to as "pencil whipping." Crispin recounts, "One time I had a field supervisor confront me about simple things, like not dotting i's and using the wrong color ink. . . . Anything he could do, he was just constantly on me. . . . I ended up just leaving." Paul, who was a female truck driver, recounts, "Like they would tell [me], 'Well we never had a female driver. I don't know if this works out.' Blatantly telling you this. And then [I had] to go, 'Well let's see. Let's give it a chance, give it a try. I'll do this three days for free and you see and if it's not working out, well then that's fine and if it works out, maybe you want to reconsider [not hiring me].'" To prove her competency, she ended up working for free, hoping that she would eventually be hired.

Stephen, who was a female forklift operator, described the resistance women operators faced from men when it came to safety precautions for loading pallets:

> [The men] would spot each other, which meant that they would have two guys that would close down the aisle . . . so that no one could go on that aisle while you know you were up there [with your forklift and load] . . . and they wouldn't spot you if you were a female. If you were a guy . . . they got the red vests and the safety cones out and it's like you know—the only thing they didn't have were those little flashlights for the jets. It would be like God or somebody responding. I would actually have to go around and gather all the dykes from receiving to come out and help and spot me. And I can't tell you how many times I nearly ran over a kid. It was maddening and it was always because [of] gender.

Thus, respondents described situations of being ignored, passed over, purposefully put in harm's way, and assumed to be incompetent when they were working as women. However, these same individuals, as men, find themselves with more authority and with their ideas, abilities, and attributes evaluated more positively in the workforce.

Respect and Recognition

Related to authority and competency is the issue of how much reward workers get for their workplace contributions. According to the transmen I interviewed, an increase in recognition for hard work was one of the positive changes associated with working as a man. Looking at these stories of gaining reward and respect, Preston, who transitioned openly and remained at his blue-collar job, reports that as a female crew supervisor, she was frequently short staffed and unable to access necessary resources yet expected to still carry out the job competently. However, after his transition, he suddenly found himself receiving all the support and materials he required:

> I was not asked to do anything different [after transition]. But the work I did do was made easier for me. [Before transition] there [were] periods of time when I would be told, "Well, I don't have anyone to send over there with you." We were one or two people short of a crew or the trucks weren't available. Or they would send me people who weren't trained. And it got to the point where it was like, why do I have to fight about this? If you don't want your freight, you don't get your freight. And, I swear it was like from one day to the next of me transitioning [to male], I need this, this is what I want and [snaps his fingers]. I have not had to fight about anything.

He adds about his experience, "The last three [performance] reviews that I have had have been the absolute highest that I have ever had. New management team. Me not doing anything different than I ever had. I even went part-time." This comment shows that even though he openly transitioned and remained in the same job, he ultimately finds himself rewarded for doing less work and having to fight less for getting what he needs to effectively do his job. In addition, as a man, he received more positive reviews for his work, demonstrating how men and women can be evaluated differently when doing the same work.

As with authority and competence, this sense of gaining recognition for hard work was particularly noticeable for transmen who had worked as women in blue-collar occupations in which they were the gender minority. This finding is not unexpected, as women are also more likely to be judged negatively when they are in the minority in the workplace, as their statistical minority status seems to suggest that women are unsuited for the job (Valian 1999). For example, Preston, who had spent time in the ROTC as a female cadet, reported feeling that no matter how hard she worked, her achievements were passed over by her men superiors: "On everything that I did, I was the highest. I was the highest-ranking female during the time I was there. . . . I was the most decorated person in ROTC. I had more ribbons, I had more medals, in ROTC and in school. I didn't get anything for that. There was an award every year called Superior Cadet, and guys got it during the time I was there who didn't do nearly what I did. It was those kinds of things [that got to me]." She entered a blue-collar occupation after ROTC and also felt that her workplace contributions, like designing training programs for the staff, were invisible and went unrewarded.

Talking about gender discrimination he faced as a female construction worker, Crispin reports,

> I worked really hard. . . . I had to find myself not sitting ever and taking breaks or lunches because I felt like I had to work more to show my worth. And though I did do that and I produced typically more than three males put together—and that is really a statistic—what it would come down to a lot of times was, "You're single. You don't have a family." That is what they told me. "I've got guys here who have families." . . . And even though my production quality [was high], and the customer was extremely happy with my work . . . I was passed over lots of times. They said it was because I was single and I didn't have a family and they felt bad because they didn't want Joe Blow to lose his job because he had three kids at home. And because I was intelligent and my qualities were very vast, they said, "You can just go get a job anywhere." Which wasn't always the case. A lot of people were— it was still a boy's world and some people were just like, uh-uh, there aren't going to be any women on my job site. And it would be months . . . before I would find gainful employment again.

While she reports eventually winning over many men who did not want women on the worksite, being female excluded her from workplace social interac-

tions, such as camping trips, designed to strengthen male bonding.

These quotes illustrate the hardships that women working in blue-collar jobs often face at work: being passed over for hiring and promotions in favor of less productive male coworkers, having their hard work go unrecognized, and not being completely accepted.[6] Having this experience of being women in an occupation or industry composed mostly of men can create, then, a heightened appreciation of gaining reward and recognition for job performance as men.

Another form of reward that some transmen report receiving posttransition is a type of bodily respect in the form of being freed from unwanted sexual advances or inquiries about sexuality. As Brian recounts about his experience of working as a waitress, that customer service involved "having my boobs grabbed, being called 'honey' and 'babe.' " He noted that as a man, he no longer has to worry about these types of experiences. Jason reported being constantly harassed by men bosses for sexual favors in the past. He added, "When I transitioned . . . it was like a relief! [laughs] . . . I swear to God! I am not saying I was beautiful or sexy but I was always attracting something." He felt that becoming a man meant more personal space and less sexual harassment. Finally, Stephen and Henry reported being "obvious dykes," here meaning visibly masculine women, and added that in blue-collar jobs, they encountered sexualized comments, as well as invasive personal questions about sexuality, from men uncomfortable with their gender presentation, experiences they no longer face posttransition. Transitioning for stealth FTMs can bring with it physical autonomy and respect, as men workers, in general, encounter less touching, groping, and sexualized comments at work than women. Open FTMs, however, are not as able to access this type of privilege, as coworkers often ask invasive questions about their genitals and sexual practices.

Economic Gains

As the last two sections have shown, FTMs can find themselves gaining in authority, respect, and reward in the workplace posttransition. Several FTMs who are stealth also reported a sense that transition had brought with it economic opportunities that would not have been available to them as women, particularly as masculine women.

Carl, who owns his own company, asserts that he could not have followed the same career trajectory if he had not transitioned:

> I have this company that I built, and I have people following me; they trust me, they believe in me, they respect me. There is no way I could have done that as a woman. And I will tell you that as just a fact. That when it comes to business and work, higher levels of management, it is different being a man. I have been on both sides [as a man and a woman], younger obviously, but I will tell you, man, I could have never done what I did [as a female]. You can take the same personality and it wouldn't have happened. I would have never made it.

While he acknowledges that women can be and are business entrepreneurs, he has a sense that his business partners would not have taken his business venture idea seriously if he were a woman or that he might not have had access to the type of social networks that made his business venture possible. Henry feels that he would not have reached the same level in his professional job if he were a woman because he had a nonnormative gender appearance:

> If I was a gender normative woman, probably. But no, as an obvious dyke, I don't think so . . . which is weird to say but I think it's true. It is interesting because I am really aware of having this job that I would not have had if I hadn't transitioned. And [gender expression] was always an issue for me. I wanted to go to law school but I couldn't do it. I couldn't wear the skirts and things females have to wear to practice law. I wouldn't dress in that drag. And so it was very clear that there was a limit to where I was going to go professionally because I was not willing to dress that part. Now I can dress the part and it's not an issue. It's not putting on drag; it's not an issue. I don't love putting on a tie, but I can do it. So this world is open to me that would not have been before just because of clothes. But very little has changed in some ways. I look very different but I still have all the same skills and all the same general thought processes. That is intense for me to consider.

As this response shows, Henry is aware that as an "obvious dyke," meaning here a masculine-appearing woman, he would have the same skills and education level he currently has, but those skills would be devalued due to his nonnormative appearance. Thus, he avoided professional careers that would require a traditionally feminine appearance. As a man, however, he is able to wear clothes similar to those he wore as an "obvious dyke," but they are now considered gender appropriate. Thus, through transitioning, he gains the right to wear men's clothes, which helps him in accessing a professional job.

Wayne also recounts negative workplace experiences in the years prior to his transition due to being extremely ambiguous or "gender blending" (Devor 1987) in his appearance. Working at a restaurant in his early teens, he had the following experience:

> The woman who hired me said, "I will hire you only on the condition that you don't ever come in the front because you make the people uncomfortable." 'Cause we had to wear like these uniforms or something and when I would put the uniform on, she would say, "That makes you look like a guy." But she knew I was not a guy because of my name that she had on the application. She said, "You make the customers uncomfortable." And a couple of times it got really busy, and I would have to come in the front or whatever, and I remember one time she found out about it and she said, "I don't care how busy it gets, you don't get to come up front." She said I'd make people lose their appetite.

Once he began hormones and gained a social identity as a man, he found that his work and school experiences became much more positive. He went on to earn a doctoral degree and become a successful professional, an economic opportunity he did not think would be available had he remained highly gender ambiguous.

In my sample, the transmen who openly transitioned faced a different situation in terms of economic gains. While there is an "urban legend" that FTMs immediately are awarded some kind of "male privilege" posttransition (Dozier 2005), I did not find that in my interviews. Reflecting this common belief, however, Trevor and Jake both recount that women colleagues told them, when learning of their transition plans, that they would probably be promoted because they were becoming white men. While both men discounted these comments, both were promoted relatively soon after their transitions. Rather than seeing this as evidence of male privilege, both respondents felt that their promotions were related to their job performance, which, to make clear, is not a point I am questioning. Yet these promotions show that while these two men are not benefiting undeservedly from transition, they also are not disadvantaged.[7] Thus, among the men I interviewed, it is common for both stealth and open FTMs to find their abilities and skills more valued posttransition, showing that human capital can be valued differently depending on the gender of the employee.

Is It Privilege or Something Else?

While these reported increases in competency and authority make visible the "gender schemas" (Valian 1999) that often underlie the evaluation of workers, it is possible that the increases in authority might have a spurious connection to gender transitions. Some transmen enter a different work field after transition, so the observed change might be in the type of occupation they enter rather than a gender-based change. In addition, many transmen seek graduate or postgraduate degrees posttransition, and higher education degrees afford more authority in the workplace. As Table 2 shows, of the transmen I interviewed, many had higher degrees working as men than they did when they worked as women. For some, this is due to transitioning while in college and thus attaining their bachelor's degrees as men. For others, gender transitions seem to

be accompanied by a desire to return to school for a higher degree, as evidenced by the increase in master's degrees in the table.

A change in educational attainment does contribute to getting better jobs with increased authority, as men benefit more from increased human capital in the form of educational attainment (Valian 1999). But again, this is an additive effect, as higher education results in greater advantages for men than for women. In addition, gender advantage alone also is apparent in these experiences of increased authority, as transmen report seeing an increase in others' perceptions of their competency outside of the workplace where their education level is unknown. For example, Henry, who found he was "right a lot more" at work, also notes that in daily, nonworkplace interactions, he is assumed, as a man, to know what he is talking about and does not have to provide evidence to support his opinions. Demonstrating a similar experience, Crispin, who had many years of experience working in construction as a woman, relates the following story:

> I used to jump into [situations as a woman]. Like at Home Depot, I would hear . . . [men] be so confused, and I would just step over there and say, "Sir, I work in construction and if you don't mind me helping you." And they would be like, "Yeah, yeah, yeah" [i.e., dismissive]. But now I go [as a man] and I've got men and women asking me things and saying, "Thank you so much," like now I have a brain in my head! And I like that a lot because it was just kind of like, "Yeah, whatever." It's really nice.

Table 2 Highest Level of Eduction Attained

Highest Degree Level	Stealth FTMs		Open FTMs	
	As Male	As Male	As Female	As Male
High school/GED	7	2	3	2
Associate's degree	2	3	3	3
Bachelor's degree	2	4	7	4
Master's degree	0	1	2	4
Ph.D.	0	1	1	2
J.D.	0	0	1	2
Other	0	0	1	1
Total	11	11	18	18

NOTE: FTMs = female-to-male transsexuals.

His experience at Home Depot shows that as a man, he is rewarded for displaying the same knowledge about construction—knowledge gendered as masculine—that he was sanctioned for offering when he was perceived as a woman. As a further example of this increased authority outside of the workplace, several FTMs report a difference in their treatment at the auto shop, as they are not assumed to be easy targets for unnecessary services (though this comes with an added expectation that they will know a great deal about cars). While some transmen report that their "feminine knowledge," such as how to size baby clothes in stores, is discounted when they gain social identities as men, this new recognition of "masculine knowledge" seems to command more social authority than prior feminine knowledge in many cases. These stories show that some transmen gain authority both in and out of the workplace. These findings lend credence to the argument that men can gain a gender advantage, in the form of authority, reward, and respect.

BARRIERS TO WORKPLACE GENDER ADVANTAGES

Having examined the accounts of transmen who feel that they received increased authority, reward, and recognition from becoming men at work, I will now discuss some of the limitations to accessing workplace gender advantages. About one-third of my sample felt that they did not receive any gender advantage from transition. FTMs who had only recently begun transition or who had transitioned without using hormones ("no ho") all reported seeing little change in their workplace treatment. This group of respondents felt that they were still seen as women by most of their coworkers, evidenced by continual slippage into feminine pronouns, and thus were not treated in accordance with other men in the workplace. Other transmen in this group felt they lacked authority because they were young or looked extremely young after transition. This youthful appearance often is an effect of the beginning stages of transition. FTMs usually begin to pass as men before they start taking testosterone. Successful passing is done via appearance cues, such as hairstyles,

clothes, and mannerisms. However, without facial hair or visible stubble, FTMs often are taken to be young boys, a mistake that intensifies with the onset of hormone therapy and the development of peach fuzz that marks the beginning of facial hair growth. Reflecting on how this youthful appearance, which can last several years depending on the effects of hormone therapy, affected his work experience immediately after transition, Thomas reports, "I went from looking 30 to looking 13. People thought I was a new lawyer so I would get treated like I didn't know what was going on." Other FTMs recount being asked if they were interns, or if they were visiting a parent at their workplace, all comments that underscore a lack of authority. This lack of authority associated with looking youthful, however, is a time-bounded effect, as most FTMs on hormones eventually "age into" their male appearance, suggesting that many of these transmen may have the ability to access some gender advantages at some point in their careers.

Body structure was another characteristic some FTMs felt limited their access to increased authority and prestige at work. While testosterone creates an appearance indistinguishable from bio men for many transmen, it does not increase height. Being more than 6 feet tall is part of the cultural construction for successful, hegemonic masculinity. However, several men I interviewed were between 5' 1" and 5' 5", something they felt put them at a disadvantage in relation to other men in their workplaces. Winston, who managed a professional work staff who knew him only as a man, felt that his authority was harder to establish at work because he was short. Being smaller than all of his male employees meant that he was always being looked down on, even when giving orders. Kelly, who worked in special education, felt his height affected the jobs he was assigned: "Some of the boys, especially if they are really aggressive, they do much better with males that are bigger than they are. So I work with the little kids because I am short. I don't get as good of results if I work with [older kids]; a lot of times they are taller than I am." Being a short man, he felt it was harder to establish authority with older boys. These experiences demonstrate the importance of bringing the body back into discussions of masculinity and gender advantage, as being short can constrain men's benefits from the "patriarchal dividend" (Connell 1995).

In addition to height, race/ethnicity can negatively affect FTMs' workplace experiences posttransition. My data suggest that the experiences of FTMs of color is markedly different than that of their white counterparts, as they are becoming not just men but Black men, Latino men, or Asian men, categories that carry their own stereotypes. Christopher felt that he was denied any gender advantage at work not only because he was shorter than all of his men colleagues but also because he was viewed as passive, a stereotype of Asian men (Espiritu 1997). "To the wide world of America, I look like a passive Asian guy. That is what they think when they see me. Oh Asian? Oh passive. . . . People have this impression that Asian guys aren't macho and therefore they aren't really male. Or they are not as male as [a white guy]." Keith articulated how his social interactions changed with his change in gender attribution in this way: "I went from being an obnoxious Black woman to a scary Black man." He felt that he has to be careful expressing anger and frustration at work (and outside of work) because now that he is a Black man, his anger is viewed as more threatening by whites. Reflecting stereotypes that conflate African Americans with criminals, he also notes that in his law enforcement classes, he was continually asked to play the suspect in training exercises. Aaron, one of the only racial minorities at his workplace, also felt that looking like a Black man negatively affected his workplace interactions. He told stories about supervisors repeatedly telling him he was threatening. When he expressed frustration during a staff meeting about a new policy, he was written up for rolling his eyes in an "aggressive" manner. The choice of words such as "threatening" and "aggressive," words often used to describe Black men (Ferguson 2000), suggests that racial identity and stereotypes about Black men were playing a role in his workplace treatment. Examining how race/ethnicity and appearance intersect with gender, then, illustrates that masculinity is not a fixed construct that automatically generated privilege (Connell 1995), but that white, tall men often see greater returns from the patriarchal dividend than short men, young men and men of color.

CONCLUSION

Sociological studies have documented that the workplace is not a gender-neutral site that equitably rewards workers based on their individual merits (Acker 1990; Martin 2003; Valian 1999; Williams 1995); rather "it is a central site for the creation and reproduction of gender differences and gender inequality" (Williams 1995, 15). Men receive greater workplace advantages than women because of cultural beliefs that associate masculinity with authority, prestige, and instrumentality (Martin 2003; Padavic and Reskin 2002; Rhode 1997; Williams 1995)—characteristics often used to describe ideal "leaders" and "managers" (Valian 1999). Stereotypes about femininity as expressive and emotional, on the other hand, disadvantage women, as they are assumed to be less capable and less likely to succeed than men with equal (or often lesser) qualifications (Valian 1999). These cultural beliefs about gender difference are embedded in workplace structures and interactions, as workers and employers bring gender stereotypes with them to the workplace and, in turn, use these stereotypes to make decisions about hiring, promotions, and rewards (Acker 1990; Martin 2003; Williams 1995). This cultural reproduction of gendered workplace disparities is difficult to disrupt, however, as it operates on the level of ideology and thus is rendered invisible (Martin 2003; Valian 1999; Williams 1995).

In this article, I have suggested that the "outsider-within" (Collins 1986) perspective of many FTMs can offer a more complex understanding of these invisible interactional processes that help maintain gendered workplace disparities. Transmen are in the unique position of having been socially gendered as both women and men (Dozier 2005). Their workplace experiences, then, can make the underpinnings of gender discrimination visible, as well as illuminate the sources of men's workplace advantages. When FTMs undergo a change in gender attribution, their workplace treatment often varies greatly—even when they continue to interact with coworkers who knew them previously as women. Some posttransition FTMs, both stealth and open, find that their coworkers, employers, and customers attribute more authority, respect, and prestige to them. Their experiences make glaringly visible the process through which gender inequality is actively created in informal workplace interactions. These informal workplace interactions, in turn, produce and reproduce structural disadvantages for women, such as the glass ceiling (Valian 1999), and structural advantages for men, such as the glass escalator (Williams 1995).

However, as I have suggested, not all of my respondents gain authority and prestige with transition. FTMs who are white and tall received far more benefits posttransition than short FTMs or FTMs of color. This demonstrates that while hegemonic masculinity is defined against femininity, it is also measured against subordinated forms of masculinity (Connell 1995; Messner 1997). These findings demonstrate the need for using an intersectional approach that takes into consideration the ways in which there are crosscutting relations of power (Calasanti and Slevin 2001; Collins 1990; Crenshaw 1989), as advantage in the workplace is not equally accessible for all men. Further research on FTMs of color can help develop a clearer understanding of the role race plays in the distribution of gendered workplace rewards and advantages.[8]

The experiences of this small group of transmen offer a challenge to rationalizations of workplace inequality. The study provides counterevidence for human capital theories: FTMs who find themselves receiving the benefits associated with being men at work have the same skills and abilities they had as women workers. These skills and abilities, however, are suddenly viewed more positively due to this change in gender attribution. FTMs who may have been labeled "bossy" as women become "go-getting" men who seem more qualified for managerial positions. While FTMs may not benefit at equal levels to bio men, many of them do find themselves receiving an advantage to women in the workplace they did not have prior to transition. This study also challenges gender socialization theories that account for inequality in the workplace. Although all of my respondents were subjected to gender socialization as girls, this background did not impede their success as men. Instead, by undergoing a change in gender attribution, transmen can find that the same behavior, attitudes,

or abilities they had as females bring them more reward as men. This shift in treatment suggests that gender inequality in the workplace is not continually reproduced only because women make different education and workplace choices than men but rather because coworkers and employers often rely on gender stereotypes to evaluate men and women's achievements and skills.

It could be argued that because FTMs must overcome so many barriers and obstacles to finally gain a male social identity, they might be likely to overreport positive experiences as a way to shore up their right to be a man. However, I have reasons to doubt that my respondents exaggerated the benefits of being men. Transmen who did find themselves receiving a workplace advantage posttransition were aware that this new conceptualization of their skills and abilities was an arbitrary result of a shift in their gender attribution. This knowledge often undermined their sense of themselves as good workers, making them continually second-guess the motivations behind any rewards they receive. In addition, many transmen I interviewed expressed anger and resentment that their increases in authority, respect, and recognition came at the expense of women colleagues. It is important to keep in mind, then, that while many FTMs can identify privileges associated with being men, they often retain a critical eye to how changes in their treatment as men can disadvantage women.

This critical eye, or "outsider-within" (Collins 1986) perspective, has implications for social change in the workplace. For gender equity at work to be achieved, men must take an active role in challenging the subordination of women (Acker 1990; Martin 2003; Rhode 1997; Valian 1999; Williams 1995). However, bio men often cannot see how women are disadvantaged due to their structural privilege (Rhode 1997; Valian 1999). Even when they are aware that men as a group benefit from assumptions about masculinity, men typically still "credit their successes to their competence" (Valian 1999, 284) rather than to gender stereotypes. For many transmen, seeing how they stand to benefit at work to the detriment of women workers creates a sense of increased responsibility to challenge the gender discrimination they can see so clearly. This challenge can take many different forms.

For some, it is speaking out when men make derogatory comments about women. For others, it means speaking out about gender discrimination at work or challenging supervisors to promote women who are equally qualified as men. These challenges demonstrate that some transmen are able, at times, to translate their position as social insiders into an educational role, thus working to give women more reward and recognition at these specific work sites. The success of these strategies illustrates that men have the power to challenge workplace gender discrimination and suggests that bio men can learn gender equity strategies from the outsider-within at work.

NOTES

1. Throughout this article, I endeavor to use the terms "women" and "men" rather than "male" and "female" to avoid reifying biological categories. It is important to note, though, that while my respondents were all born with female bodies, many of them never identified as women but rather thought of themselves as always men, or as "not women." During their time as female workers, however, they did have social identities as women, as coworkers and employers often were unaware of their personal gender identities. It is this social identity that I am refereneing when I refer to them as "working as women," as I am discussing their social interactions in the workplace. In referring to their specific work experiences, however, I use "female" to demonstrate their understanding of their work history. I also do continue to use "female to male" when describing the physical transition process, as this is the most common term employed in the transgender community.

2. I use "stealth," a transgender community term, if the respondent's previous life as female was not known at work. It is important to note that this term is not analogous with "being in the closet," because stealth female-to-male transsexuals (FTMs) do not have "secret" lives as women outside of working as men. It is used to describe two different workplace choices, not offer a value judgment about these choices.

3. "Bio" man is a term used by my respondents lo mean individuals who are biologically male and live socially as men throughout their lives. It is juxtaposed with "transman" or "FTM."

4. A note on pronoun usage: This article draws from my respondents' experiences working as both women and men. While they now live as men, I use feminine pronouns to refer to their female work histories.

5. This change in how behavior is evaluated can also be negative. Some transmen felt that assertive communication styles they actively fostered to empower themselves as lesbians and feminists had to be unlearned after transition. Because they were suddenly given more space to speak as men, they felt they had to censor themselves or they would be seen as "bossy white men" who talked over women and people of color. These findings are similar to those reported by Dozier (2005).

6. It is important to note that not all FTMs who worked blue-collar jobs as women had this type of experience. One respondent felt that he was able to fit in, as a butch, as "just one of the guys." However, he also did not feel he had an outsider-within perspective because of this experience.

7. Open transitions are not without problems, however. Crispin, a construction worker, found his contract mysteriously not renewed after his announcement. However, he acknowledged that he had many problems with his employers prior to his announcement and had also recently filed a discrimination suit. Aaron, who announced his transition at a small, medical site, left after a few months as he felt that his employer was trying to force him out. He found another job in which he was out as a transman. Crispin unsuccessfully attempted to find work in construction as an out transman. He was later hired, stealth, at a construction job.

8. Sexual identity also is an important aspect of an intersectional analysis. In my study, however, queer and gay transmen worked either in lesbian, gay, bisexual, transgender work sites, or were not out at work. Therefore, it was not possible to examine how being gay or queer affected their workplace experiences.

REFERENCES

Acker, Joan. 1990. Hierarchies, jobs, bodies: A theory of gendered organizations. *Gender & Society* 4:139–58.

Butler, D., and F. L. Geis. 1990. Nonverbal affect responses to male and female leaders: Implications for leadership evaluation. *Journal of Personality and Social Psychology* 58:48–59.

Byrd, Barbara. 1999. Women in carpentry apprenticeship: A case study. *Labor Studies Journal* 24 (3): 3–22.

Calasanti, Toni M., and Kathleen F. Slevin. 2001. *Gender, social inequalities, and aging.* Walnut Creek, CA: Alta Mira Press.

Collins, Patricia Hill. 1986. Learning from the outsider within: The sociological significance of Black feminist thought. *Social Problems* 33 (6): S14–S31.

———. 1990. *Black feminist thought.* New York: Routledge.

Connell, Robert. 1995. *Masculinities.* Berkeley: University of California Press.

Crenshaw, Kimberle. 1989. Demarginalizing the intersection of race and sex: A Black feminist critique of antidiscrimination doctrine, feminist theory, and antiracist politics. *University of Chicago Legal Forum* 1989:139–67.

Devor, Holly. 1987. Gender blending females: Women and sometimes men. *American Behavioral Scientist* 31 (1): 12–40.

Dozier, Raine. 2005. Beards, breasts, and bodies: Doing sex in a gendered world. *Gender & Society* 19:297–316.

Elliott, James R., and Ryan A. Smith. 2004. Race, gender, and workplace power. *American Sociological Review* 69:365–86.

Espiritu, Yen. 1997. *Asian American women and men.* Thousand Oaks, CA: Sage.

Ferguson, Ann Arnett. 2000. *Bad boys: Public schools in the making of Black masculinity.* Ann Arbor: University of Michigan Press.

Leidner, Robin. 1993. *Fast food, fast talk: Service work and the routinization of everyday life.* Berkeley: University of California Press.

Martin, Patricia Yancy. 1992. Gender, interaction, and inequality in organizations. In *Gender, interaction, and inequality,* edited by Cecelia L. Ridgeway. New York: Springer-Verlag.

———. 2003. "Said and done" versus "saying and doing": Gendering practices, practicing gender at work. *Gender & Society* 17:342–66.

Martin, Susan. 1994. "Outsiders-within" the station house: The impact of race and gender on Black women police officers. *Social Problems* 41:383–400.

Merton, Robert, 1972. Insiders and outsiders: A chapter in the sociology of knowledge. *American Journal of Sociology* 78 (1): 9–47.

Messner, Michael. 1997. *The politics of masculinities: Men in movements.* Thousand Oaks, CA: Sage.

Miller, Laura. 1997. Not just weapons of the weak: Gender harassment as a form of protest for army men. *Social Psychology Quarterly* 60 (1): 32–51.

Olian, J. D., D. P. Schwab, and Y. Haberfeld. 1988. The impact of applicant gender compared to qualifications on hiring recommendations: A meta-analysis of experimental studies. *Organizational Behavior and Human Decision Processes* 41:180–95.

Padavic, Irene, and Barbara Reskin. 2002. *Women and men at work.* 2d ed, Thousand Oaks, CA: Pine Forge Press.

Pierce, Jennifer. 1995. *Gender trials: Emotional lives in contemporary law firms.* Berkeley: University of California Press.

Reskin, Barbara, and Heidi Hartmann, 1986. *Women's work, men's work: Sex segregation on the job.* Washington, DC: National Academic Press.

Reskin, Barbara, and Patricia Roos. 1990. *Job queues, gender queues.* Philadelphia: Temple University Press.

Rhode, Deborah L. 1997. *Speaking of sex: The denial of gender inequality.* Cambridge, MA: Harvard University Press.

Rubin, Henry. 2003. *Self-made men: Identity and embodiment among transsexual men.* Nashville, TN: Vanderbilt University Press.

Valian, Virginia. 1999. *Why so slow? The advancement of women.* Cambridge, MA: MIT Press.

West, Candace, and Don Zimmerman. 1987. Doing gender. *Gender & Society* 1:13–37.

Williams, Christine. 1995. *Still a man's world: Men who do "women's" work.* Berkeley: University of California Press.

Yoder, Janice, and Patricia Aniakudo. 1997. Outsider within the firehouse: Subordination and difference in the social interactions of African American women firefighters. *Gender & Society* 11:324–41.

36

Boundary Lines

Labeling Sexual Harassment in Restaurants

PATTI A. GIUFFRE

CHRISTINE L. WILLIAMS

Sexual harassment occurs when submission to or rejection of sexual advances is a term of employment, is used as a basis for making employment decisions, or if the advances create a hostile or offensive work environment (Konrad and Gutek 1986). Sexual harassment can cover a range of behaviors, from leering to rape (Ellis, Barak, and Pinto 1991; Pryor 1987; Reilly et al. 1992; Schneider 1982). Researchers estimate that as many as 70 percent of employed women have experienced behaviors that may legally constitute sexual harassment (MacKinnon 1979; Powell 1986); however, a far lower percentage of women claim to have experienced sexual harassment. Paludi and Barickman write that "the great majority of women who are abused by behavior that fits legal definitions of sexual harassment—and who are traumatized by the experience—do not label what has happened to them 'sexual harassment'" (1991, 68).

Why do most women fail to label their experiences as sexual harassment? Part of the problem is that many still do not recognize that sexual harassment is an actionable offense. Sexual harassment was first described in 1976 (MacKinnon 1979), but it was not until 1986 that the U.S. Supreme Court included sexual harassment in the category of gender discrimination, thereby making it illegal (Paludi and Barickman 1991); consequently, women may not yet identify their experiences as sexual harassment because a substantial degree of awareness about its illegality has yet to be developed.

Many victims of sexual harassment may also be reluctant to come forward with complaints, fearing that they will not be believed, or that their charges will not be taken seriously (Jensen and Gutek 1982). As the Anita Hill–Clarence Thomas hearings demonstrated, women who are victims of sexual harassment often become the accused when they bring charges against their assailant.

There is another issue at stake in explaining the gap between experiencing and labeling behaviors "sexual harassment": many men and women experience some sexual behaviors in the workplace as pleasurable. Research on sexual harassment suggests that men are more likely than women to enjoy sexual interactions at work (Gutek 1985; Konrad and Gutek 1986; Reilly et al. 1992), but even some women experience sexual overtures at work as pleasurable (Pringle 1988). This attitude may be especially strong in organizations that use and exploit the bodies and sexuality of the workers (Cockburn 1991). Workers in many jobs are hired on the basis of their attractiveness and solicitousness—including not only sex industry workers, but also service sector workers such as receptionists, airline attendants, and servers in trendy restaurants. According to Cockburn (1991), this sexual exploitation is not completely forced: many people find this dimension of their jobs appealing and reinforcing to their own sense of identity and pleasure; consequently, some men and women resist efforts to expunge all sexuality from their places of work.

This is not to claim that all sexual behavior in the workplace is acceptable, even to some people. The point is that it is difficult to label behavior as sexual harassment because it forces people to draw a line between illicit and "legitimate" forms of sexuality at work—a process fraught with ambiguity. Whether a particular interaction is identified as harassment will depend on the intention of the harasser and the interpretation of the interchange by the victim, and both of these perspectives will be highly influenced by workplace culture and the social context of the specific event.

This article examines how one group of employees—restaurant workers—distinguishes between sexual harassment and other forms of sexual interaction in the workplace. We conducted an in-depth interview study of waitpeople and found that complex double standards are often used in labeling behavior as sexual harassment: identical behaviors are labeled sexual harassment in some contexts and not others. Many respondents claimed that they enjoyed sexual interactions involving coworkers of the same race/ethnicity, sexual orientation, and class/status backgrounds. Those who were offended by such interactions nevertheless dismissed them as natural or inevitable parts of restaurant culture.[1] When the same behavior occurred in contexts that upset these hegemonic heterosexual norms—in particular, when the episode involved interactions between gay and heterosexual men, or men and women of different racial/ethnic backgrounds—people seemed willing to apply the label sexual harassment.

We argue that identifying behaviors that occur only in counterhegemonic contexts as sexual harassment can potentially obscure and legitimate more insidious forms of domination and exploitation. As Pringle points out, "Men control women through direct use of power, but also through definitions of pleasure— which is less likely to provoke resistance" (1988, 95). Most women, she writes, actively seek out what Rich (1980) termed "compulsory heterosexuality" and find pleasure in it. The fact that men and women may enjoy certain sexual interactions in the workplace does not mean they take place outside of oppressive social relationships, nor does it imply that these routine interactions have no negative consequences for women. We argue that the practice of labeling as "sexual harassment" only those behaviors that challenge the dominant definition of acceptable sexual activity maintains and supports men's institutionalized right of sexual access and power over women.

METHODS

The occupation of waiting tables was selected to study the social definition of sexual harassment because many restaurants have a blatantly sexualized workplace culture (Cobble 1991; Paules 1991). According to a report published in a magazine that caters to restaurant owners, "Restaurants . . . are about as informal a workplace as there is, so much so as to actually encourage—or at the very least tolerate—sexual banter" (Anders 1993, 48). Unremitting sexual banter and innuendo, as well as physical jostling, create an environment of "compulsory jocularity" in many restaurants (Pringle 1988, 93). Sexual attractiveness and flirtation are often institutionalized parts of a waitperson's job description; consequently, individual employees are often forced to draw the line for themselves to distinguish legitimate and illegitimate expressions of sexuality, making this occupation an excellent context for examining how people determine what constitutes sexual harassment. In contrast, many more sexual behaviors may be labeled sexual harassment in less highly sexualized work environments.[2]

Eighteen in-depth interviews were conducted with male and female waitstaff who work in restaurants in Austin, Texas. Respondents were selected from restaurants that employ equal proportions of men and women on their waitstaffs. Overall, restaurant work is highly sex segregated: women make up about 82 percent of all waitpeople (U.S. Department of Labor 1989), and it is common for restaurants to be staffed only by either waitresses or waiters, with men predominating in the higher-priced restaurants (Cobble 1991; Hall 1993; Paules 1991). We decided to focus only on waitpeople who work in mixed-sex groups for two reasons. First, focusing on waitpeople working on integrated staffs enables us to examine sexual harassment between co-workers who occupy the same position in an organizational hierarchy. Co-worker sexual harassment is perhaps the most common form of sexual harassment (Pryor 1987; Schneider 1982); yet most case studies of sexual harassment have examined either unequal hierarchical relationships (e.g., boss-secretary harassment) or harassment in highly skewed gender groupings (e.g., women who work in nontraditional occupations) (Benson and Thomson 1982; Carothers and Crull 1984; Gruber and Bjorn 1982). This study is designed to investigate sexual harassment in unequal hierarchical relationships, as well as harassment between organizationally equal co-workers.

Second, equal proportions of men and women in an occupation implies a high degree of male-female interaction (Gutek 1985). Waitpeople are in constant contact with each other, help each other when the restaurant is busy, and informally socialize during slack periods. In contrast, men and women have much more limited interactions in highly sex-segregated restaurants and indeed, in most work environments. The high degree of interaction among the waitstaff provides ample opportunity for sexual harassment between men and women to occur and, concomitantly, less opportunity for same-sex sexual harassment to occur.

The sample was generated using "snowball" techniques and by going to area restaurants and asking waitpeople to volunteer for the study. The sample includes eight men and ten women. Four respondents are Latina/o, two African American, and twelve White. Four respondents are gay or lesbian; one is bisexual; thirteen are heterosexual. (The gay men and lesbians in the sample are all "out" at their respective restaurants.) Fourteen respondents are single; three are married; one is divorced. Respondents' ages range from 22 to 37.

Interviews lasted approximately one hour, and they were tape-recorded and transcribed for this analysis. All interviews were conducted by the first author, who has over eight years' experience waiting tables. Respondents were asked about their experiences working in restaurants; relationships with managers, customers, and other co-workers; and their personal experiences of sexual harassment. Because interviews were conducted in the fall of 1991, when the issue was prominent in the media because of the Hill-Thomas hearings, most respondents had thought a lot about this topic.

FINDINGS

Respondents agreed that sexual banter is very common in the restaurant: staff members talk and joke about sex constantly. With only one exception, respondents described their restaurants as highly sexualized. This means that 17 of the 18 respondents said that sexual joking, touching, and fondling were common, everyday occurrences in their restaurants. For example, when asked if he and other waitpeople ever joke about sex, one waiter replied, "about 90 percent of [the jokes] are about sex." According to a waitress, "at work . . . [we're] used to patting and touching and hugging." Another waiter said, "I do not go through a shift without someone . . . pinching my nipples or poking me in the butt or grabbing my crotch. . . . It's just what we do at work."

These informal behaviors are tantamount to "doing heterosexuality," a process analogous to "doing gender" (West and Zimmerman 1987).[3] By engaging in these public flirtations and open discussions of sex, men and women reproduce the dominant cultural norms of heterosexuality and lend an air of legitimacy—if not inevitability—to heterosexual relationships. In other words, heterosexuality is normalized and naturalized through its ritualistic public display. Indeed, although most respondents described their workplaces as highly sexualized, several dismissed the constant sexual innuendo and behaviors as "just joking," and nothing to get upset about. Several respondents claimed that this is simply "the way it is in the restaurant business," or "just the way men are."

With only one exception, the men and women interviewed maintained that they enjoyed this aspect of their work. Heterosexuality may be normative, and in these contexts, even compulsory, yet many men and women find pleasure in its expression. Many women—as well as men—actively reproduce hegemonic sexuality and apparently enjoy its ritual expression; however, in a few instances, sexual conduct was labeled as sexual harassment. Seven women and three men said they had experienced sexual harassment in restaurant work. Of these, two women and one man described two different experiences of sexual harassment, and two women described three experiences. Table 1 describes the characteristics of each of the respondents and their experiences of sexual harassment.

We analyzed these 17 accounts of sexual harassment to find out what, if anything, these experiences shared in common. With the exception of two episodes (discussed later), the experiences that were labeled "sexual harassment" were not distinguished by any specific words or behaviors, nor were they distinguished by their degree of severity. Identical behaviors were considered acceptable if they were perpetrated by some people, but considered offensive if perpetrated by others. In other words, sexual behavior in the workplace was interpreted differently depending on the context of the interaction. In general, respondents labeled their experiences sexual harassment only if the offending behavior occurred in one of three social contexts: (1) if perpetrated by someone in a more powerful position, such as a manager; (2) if by someone of a different race/ethnicity; or (3) if perpetrated by someone of a different sexual orientation.

Our findings do not imply that sexual harassment did not occur outside of these three contexts. Instead, they simply indicate that our respondents *labeled* behavior as "sexual harassment" when it occurred in these particular social contexts. We will discuss each of these contexts and speculate on the reasons why they were singled out by our respondents.

Table 1 Description of Respondents and Their Reported Experiences of Sexual Harassment at Work

Pseudonym	Age	Race[a]	SO[b]	MS[c]	Years in Restaurant[d]	Sexualized Environment[e]	Sexually Harassed[f]
Kate	23	W	H	S	1	yes	yes (1)
Beth	26	W	H	S	5	yes	yes (1)
Ann	29	W	H	S	1*	yes	yes (2)
Cathy	29	W	H	S	8 mos.*	yes	yes (3)
Carla	22	W	H	M	5 mos.*	yes	yes (3)
Diana	32	L	H	M	6	no	no
Maxine	30	L	H	M	4	yes	no
Laura	27	W	B	S	2*	yes	yes (1)
Brenda	23	W	L	S	3	yes	yes (2)
Lynn	37	B	L	D	5*	yes	no
Jake	22	W	H	S	1	yes	yes (1)
Al	23	W	H	S	3	yes	no
Frank	29	W	H	S	8	yes	yes (1)
John	31	W	H	S	2	yes	no
Trent	23	W	G	S	1*	yes	no
Rick	24	B	H	S	1.5	yes	yes (2)
David	25	L	H	S	5	yes	no
Don	24	L	G	S	1*	yes	no

a. Race: B = Black, L = Latina/o, W = White.

b. SO = sexual orientation: B = bisexual, G = gay, H = heterosexual, L = lesbian.

c. MS = marital status: D = divorced, M = married, S = single.

d. Years in restaurant refers to length of time employed in current restaurant. An asterisk indicates that respondent has worked in other restaurants.

e. Whether or not the respondent claimed sexual banter and touching were common occurrences in their restaurant.

f. Responded yes or no to the question: "Have you ever been sexually harassed in the restaurant?" Number in parentheses refers to number of incidents described in the interview.

Powerful Position

In the restaurant, managers and owners are the highest in the hierarchy of workers. Generally, they are the only ones who can hire or fire waitpeople. Three of the women and one of the men interviewed said they had been sexually harassed by their restaurants' managers or owners. In addition, several others who did not personally experience harassment said they had witnessed managers or owners sexually harassing other waitpeople. This finding is consistent with other research indicating people are more likely to think that sexual harassment has occurred when the perpetrator is in a more powerful position (e.g., Ellis et al. 1991).

Carla describes being sexually harassed by her manager:

> One evening, [my manager] grabbed my body, not in a private place, just grabbed my body, period. He gave me like a bear hug from behind a total of four times in one night. By the end of the night I was livid. I was trying to avoid him. Then when he'd do it, I'd just ignore the conversation or the joke or whatever and walk away.

She claimed that her co-workers often give each other massages and joke about sex, but she did not label any of their behaviors sexual harassment. In fact, all four individuals who experienced sexual harassment from their managers described very similar types of behavior from their co-workers, which they did not define as sexual harassment. For example, Cathy said that she and the other waitpeople talk and joke about sex constantly: "Everybody stands around and talks about sex a lot. . . . Isn't that weird? You know, it's something about working in restaurants and, yeah, so we'll all sit around and talk about sex." She said that talking with her co-workers about sex does not constitute sexual harassment because it is "only joking." She does, however, view her male manager as a sexual harasser:

> My employer is very sexist. I would call that sexual harassment. Very much of a male chauvinist pig. He kind of started [saying] stuff like, "You can't really wear those shorts because they're not flattering to your figure. . . . But I like the way you wear those jeans. They look real good. They're right." It's like, you know [I want to say to him], "You're the owner,

you're in power. That's evident. You know, you need to find a better way to tell me these things." We've gotten to a point now where we'll joke around now, but it's never ever sexual ever. I won't allow that with him.

Cathy acknowledges that her manager may legitimately dictate her appearance at work, but only if he does so in professional—and not personal—terms. She wants him "to find a better way to tell me these things," implying that he is not completely out-of-line in suggesting that she wear tight pants. He "crosses the line" when he personalizes his directive, by saying to Cathy "*I like* the way you wear those jeans." This is offensive to Cathy because it is framed as the manager's personal prerogative, not the institutional requirements of the job.

Ann described a similar experience of sexual harassment from a restaurant owner:

> Yeah, there's been a couple of times when a manager has made me feel real uncomfortable and I just removed myself from the situation. . . . Like if there's something I really want him to hear or something I think is really important there's no touching. Like, "Don't touch me while I'm talking to you." You know, because I take that as very patronizing. I actually blew up at one of the owners once because I was having a rough day and he came up behind me and he was rubbing my back, like up and down my back and saying, you know, "Oh, is Ann having a bad day?" or something like that and I shook him off of me and I said, "You do not need to touch me to talk to me."

Ann distinguishes between legitimate and illegitimate touching: if the issue being discussed is "really important"—that is, involving her job status—she insists there be no touching. In these specific situations, a back rub is interpreted as patronizing and offensive because the manager is using his powerful position for his *personal* sexual enjoyment.

One of the men in the sample, Frank, also experienced sexual harassment from a manager:

> I was in the bathroom and [the manager] came up next to me and my tennis shoes were spray-painted silver so he knew it was me in there and he said something

about, "Oh, what do you have in your hand there?" I was on the other side of a wall and he said, "Mind if I hold it for a while?" or something like that, you know. I just pretended like I didn't hear it.

Frank also described various sexual behaviors among the waitstaff, including fondling, "joking about bodily functions," and "making bikinis out of tortillas." He said, "I mean, it's like, what we do at work. . . . There's no holds barred. I don't find it offensive. I'm used to it by now. I'm guilty of it myself." Evidently, he defines sexual behaviors as "sexual harassment" only when perpetrated by someone in a position of power over him.[4]

Two of the women in the sample also described sexual harassment from customers. We place these experiences in the category of "powerful position" because customers do have limited economic power over the waitperson insofar as they control the tip (Crull 1987). Cathy said that male customers often ask her to "sit on my lap" and provide them with other sexual favors. Brenda, a lesbian, described a similar experience of sexual harassment from women customers:

One time I had this table of lesbians and they were being real vulgar towards me. Real sexual. This woman kind of tripped me as I was walking by and said, "Hurry back." I mean, gay people can tell when other people are gay. I felt harassed.

In these examples of harassment by customers, the line is drawn using a similar logic as in the examples of harassment by managers. These customers acted as though the waitresses were providing table service to satisfy the customers' private desires, instead of working to fulfill their job descriptions. In other words, the customers' demands were couched in personal—and not professional—terms, making the waitresses feel sexually harassed.

It is not difficult to understand why waitpeople singled out sexual behaviors from managers, owners, and customers as sexual harassment. Subjection to sexual advances by someone with economic power comes closest to the quid pro quo form of sexual harassment, wherein employees are given the option to either "put out or get out." Studies have found that this type of sexual harassment is viewed as the most threatening and

unambiguous sort (Ellis et al. 1991; Fitzgerald 1990; Gruber and Bjorn 1982).

But even in this context, lines are drawn between legitimate and illegitimate sexual behavior in the workplace. As Cathy's comments make clear, some people accept the employers' prerogative to exploit the workers' sexuality, by dictating appropriate "sexy" dress, for example. Like airline attendants, waitresses are expected to be friendly, helpful, and sexually available to the male customers (Cobble 1991). Because this expectation is embedded in restaurant culture, it becomes difficult for workers to separate sexual harassment from the more or less accepted forms of sexual exploitation that are routine features of their jobs. Consequently, some women are reluctant to label blatantly offensive behaviors as sexual harassment. For example, Maxine, who claims that she has never experienced sexual harassment, said that customers often "talk dirty" to her:

I remember one day, about four or five years ago when I was working as a cocktail waitress, this guy asked me for a "Slow Comfortable Screw" [the name of a drink]. I didn't know what it was. I didn't know if he was making a move or something. I just looked at him. He said, "You know what it is, right?" I said, "I bet the bartender knows!" (laughs). . . . There's another one, "Sex on the Beach." And there's another one called a "Screaming Orgasm." Do you believe that?

Maxine is subject to a sexualized work environment that she finds offensive; hence her experience could fit the legal definition of sexual harassment. But because sexy drink names are an institutionalized part of restaurant culture, Maxine neither complains about it nor labels it sexual harassment: Once it becomes clear that a "Slow Comfortable Screw" is a legitimate and recognized restaurant demand, she accepts it (albeit reluctantly) as part of her job description. In other words, the fact that the offensive behavior is institutionalized seems to make it beyond reproach in her eyes. This finding is consistent with others' findings that those who work in highly sexualized environments may be less likely to label offensive behavior "sexual harassment" (Gutek 1985; Konrad and Gutek 1986).

Only in specific contexts do workers appear to define offensive words and acts of a sexual nature as sexual harassment—even when initiated by someone in a more powerful position. The interviews suggest that workers use this label to describe their experiences only when their bosses or their customers couch their requests for sexual attentions in explicitly personal terms. This way of defining sexual harassment may obscure and legitimize more institutionalized—and hence more insidious—forms of sexual exploitation at work.

Race/Ethnicity

The restaurants in our sample, like most restaurants in the United States, have racially segregated staffs (Howe 1977). In the restaurants where our respondents are employed, men of color are concentrated in two positions: the kitchen cooks and bus personnel (formerly called busboys). Five of the White women in the sample reported experiencing sexual harassment from Latino men who worked in these positions. For example, when asked if she had ever experienced sexual harassment, Beth said:

> Yes, but it was not with the people . . . it was not, you know, the people that I work with in the front of the house. It was with the kitchen. There are boundaries or lines that I draw with the people I work with. In the kitchen, the lines are quite different. Plus, it's a Mexican staff. It's a very different attitude. They tend to want to touch you more and, at times, I can put up with a little bit of it but . . . because I will give them a hard time too but I won't touch them. I won't touch their butt or anything like that.

> [Interviewer: So sometimes they cross the line?]

> It's only happened to me a couple of times. One guy, like, patted me on the butt and I went off. I lost my shit. I went off on him. I said, "No. Bad. Wrong. I can't speak Spanish to you but, you know, this is it." I told the kitchen manager who is a guy and he's not . . . the head kitchen manager is not Hispanic. . . . I've had to do that over the years only a couple of times with those guys.

Beth reported that the waitpeople joke about sex and touch each other constantly, but she does not consider their behavior sexual harassment. Like many of the other men and women in the sample, Beth said she

feels comfortable engaging in this sexual banter and play with the other waitpeople (who were predominantly White), but not with the Mexican men in the kitchen.

Part of the reason for singling out the behaviors of the cooks as sexual harassment may involve status differences between waitpeople and cooks. Studies have suggested that people may label behaviors as sexual harassment when they are perpetrated by people in lower status organizational positions (Grauerholz 1989; McKinney 1990); however, it is difficult to generalize about the relative status of cooks and waitpeople because of the varied and often complex organizational hierarchies of restaurants (Paules 1991, 107–10). If the cook is a chef, as in higher-priced restaurants, he or she may actually have more status than waitpeople, and indeed may have the formal power to hire and fire the waitstaff. In the restaurants where our respondents worked, the kitchen cooks did not wield this sort of formal control, but they could exert some informal power over the waitstaff by slowing down food orders or making the orders look and/or taste bad. Because bad food can decrease the waitperson's tip, the cooks can thereby control the waitperson's income; hence servers are forced to negotiate and to some extent placate the wishes and desires of cooks to perform their jobs. The willingness of several respondents to label the cooks' behavior as sexual harassment may reflect their perception that the cooks' informal demands had become unreasonable. In such cases, subjection to the offensive behaviors is a term of employment, which is quid pro quo sexual harassment. As mentioned previously, this type of sexual harassment is the most likely to be so labeled and identified.

Because each recounted case of sexual harassment occurring between individuals of different occupational statuses involved a minority man sexually harassing a White woman, the racial context seems equally important. For example, Ann also said that she and the other waiters and waitresses joke about sex and touch each other "on the butt" all the time, and when asked if she had ever experienced sexual harassment, she said,

> I had some problems at [a previous restaurant] but it was a communication problem. A lot of the guys in the

kitchen did not speak English. They would see the waiters hugging on us, kissing us and pinching our rears and stuff. They would try to do it and I couldn't tell them, "No. You don't understand this. It's like we do it because we have a mutual understanding but I'm not comfortable with you doing it." So that was really hard and a lot of times what I'd have to do is just sucker punch them in the chest and just use a lot of cuss words and they knew that I was serious. And there again, I felt real weird about that because they're just doing what they see go on everyday.

Kate, Carla, and Brenda described very similar racial double standards. Kate complained about a Mexican busser who constantly touched her:

This is not somebody that I talk to on a friendly basis. We don't sit there and laugh and joke and stuff. So, when he touches me, all I know is he is just touching me and there is no context about it. With other people, if they said something or they touched me, it would be funny or . . . we have a relationship. This person and I and all the other people do not. So that is sexual harassment.

And according to Brenda:

The kitchen can be kind of sexist. They really make me angry. They're not as bad as they used to be because they got warned. They're mostly Mexican, not even Mexican-American. Most of them, they're just starting to learn English.

[Interviewer: What do they do to you?]

Well, I speak Spanish, so I know. They're not as sexual to me because I think they know I don't like it. Some of the other girls will come through and they will touch them like here [points to the lower part of her waist]. . . . I've had some pretty bad arguments with the kitchen.

[Interviewer: Would you call that sexual harassment?]

Yes, I think some of the girls just don't know better to say something. I think it happens a lot with the kitchen guys. Like sometimes, they will take a relleno in their hands like it's a penis. Sick!

Each of these women identified the sexual advances of the minority men in their restaurants as sexual harass-

ment, but not the identical behaviors of their White male co-workers; moreover, they all recognize that they draw boundary lines differently for Anglo men and Mexican men: each of them willingly participates in "doing heterosexuality" only in racially homogamous contexts. These women called the behavior of the Mexican cooks "sexual harassment" in part because they did not "have a relationship" with these men, nor was it conceivable to them that they *could* have a relationship with them, given cultural and language barriers—and, probably, racist attitudes as well. The White men, on the other hand, can "hug, kiss, and pinch rears" of the White women because they have a "mutual understanding"—implying reciprocity and the possibility of intimacy.

The importance of this perception of relationship potential in the assessment of sexual harassment is especially clear in the cases of the two married women in the sample, Diana and Maxine. Both of these women said that they had never experienced sexual harassment. Diana, who works in a family-owned and -operated restaurant, claimed that her restaurant is not a sexualized work environment. Although people occasionally make double entendre jokes relating to sex, according to Diana, "there's no contact whatsoever like someone pinching your butt or something." She said that she has never experienced sexual harassment:

Everybody here knows I'm married so they're not going to get fresh with me because they know that it's not going to go anywhere, you know so . . . and vice versa. You know, we know the guys' wives. They come in here to eat. It's respect all the way. I don't think they could handle it if they saw us going around hugging them. You know what I mean? It's not right.

Similarly, Maxine, who is Colombian, said she avoids the problem of sexual harassment in her workplace because she is married:

The cooks don't offend me because they know I speak Spanish and they know how to talk with me because I set my boundaries and they know that. . . . I just don't joke with them more than I should. They all know that I'm married, first of all, so that's a no-no for all of them. My brother used to be a manager in that restaurant so he probably took care of everything. I never had any problems anyway in any other jobs because, like I said, I set my boundaries. I don't let them get too close to me.

[Interviewer, You mean physically?]

Not physically only. Just talking. If they want to talk about, "Do you go dancing? Where do you go dancing?" Like I just change the subject because it's none of their business and I don't really care to talk about that with them . . . not because I consider them to be on the lower levels than me or something but just because if you start talking with them that way then you are just giving them hope or something. I think that's true for most of the guys here, not just talking about the cooks. . . . I do get offended and they know that so sometimes they apologize.

Both Maxine and Diana said that they are protected from sexual harassment because they are married. In effect, they use their marital status to negotiate their interactions with their co-workers and to ward off unwanted sexual advances. Furthermore, because they do not view their co-workers as potential relationship "interests," they conscientiously refuse to participate in any sexual banter in the restaurant.

The fact that both women speak Spanish fluently may mean that they can communicate their boundaries unambiguously to those who only speak Spanish (unlike the female respondents in the sample who only speak English). For these two women, sexual harassment from co-workers is not an issue. Diana, who is Latina, talks about "respect all around" in her restaurant; Maxine claims the cooks (who are Mexican) aren't the ones who offend her. Their comments seem to reflect more mutual respect and humanity toward their Latino co-workers than the comments of the white waitresses. On the other hand, at least from Maxine's vantage point, racial harassment is a bigger problem in her workplace than is sexual harassment. When asked if she ever felt excluded from any groups at work, she said:

Yeah, sometimes. How can I explain this? Sometimes, I mean, I don't know if they do it on purpose or they don't but they joke around you about being Spanish . . . Sometimes it hurts. Like they say, "What are you doing here? Why don't you go back home?"

Racial harassment—like sexual harassment—is a means used by a dominant group to maintain its dominance over a subordinated group. Maxine feels that, because she is married, she is protected from sexual harassment (although, as we have seen, she is subject to a sexualized workplace that is offensive to her); however, she does experience racial harassment where she works, and she feels vulnerable to this because she is one of very few non-Whites working at her restaurant.

One of the waiters in the sample claimed that he had experienced sexual harassment from female co-workers, and race may have also been a factor in this situation. When Rick (who is African American) was asked if he had ever been sexually harassed, he recounted his experiences with some White waitresses:

Yes. There are a couple of girls there, waitpeople, who will pinch my rear.

[Interviewer: Do you find it offensive?]

No (laughs) because I'm male. . . . But it is a form of sexual harassment.

[Interviewer: Do you ever tell them to stop?]

If I'm really busy, if I'm in the weeds, and they want to touch me, I'll get mad. I'll tell them to stop. There's a certain time and place for everything.

Rick is reluctant about labeling this interaction "sexual harassment" because "it doesn't bother me unless I'm, like, busy or something like that." In those cases where he is busy, he feels that his female co-workers are subverting his work by pinching him. Because of the race difference, he may experience their behaviors as an expression of racial dominance, which probably influences his willingness to label the behavior as sexual harassment.

In sum, the interviews suggest that the perception and labeling of interactions as "sexual harassment" may be influenced by the racial context of the interaction. If the victim perceives the harasser as expressing a potentially reciprocal relationship interest they may be less likely to label their experience sexual harassment. In cases where the harasser and victim have a different race/ethnicity and class background, the possibility of a relationship may be precluded because of racism, making these cases more likely to be labeled "sexual harassment."

This finding suggests that the practices associated with "doing heterosexuality" are profoundly racist. The White women in the sample showed a great reluctance to label unwanted sexual behavior sexual harassment when it was perpetrated by a potential (or real) relationship interest—that is, a White male co-worker. In contrast, minority men are socially constructed as potential harassers of White women: any expression of sexual interest may be more readily perceived as nonreciprocal and unwanted. The assumption of racial homogamy in heterosexual relationships thus may protect White men from charges of sexual harassment of White women. This would help to explain why so many White women in the sample labeled behaviors perpetrated by Mexican men as sexual harassment, but not the identical behaviors perpetrated by White men.

SEXUAL ORIENTATION

There has been very little research on sexual harassment that addresses the sexual orientation of the harasser and victim (exceptions include Reilly et al. 1992; Schneider 1982, 1984). Surveys of sexual harassment typically include questions about marital status but not about sexual orientation (e.g., Fain and Anderton 1987; Gruber and Bjorn 1982; Powell 1986). In this study, sexual orientation was an important part of heterosexual men's perceptions of sexual harassment. Of the four episodes of sexual harassment reported by the men in the study, three involved openly gay men sexually harassing straight men. One case involved a male manager harassing a male waiter (Frank's experience, described earlier). The other two cases involved co-workers. Jake said that he had been sexually harassed by a waiter:

> Someone has come on to me that I didn't want to come on to me. . . . He was another waiter [male]. It was laughs and jokes the whole way until things got a little too much and it was like, "Hey, this is how it is. Back off. Keep your hands off my ass." . . . Once it reached the point where I felt kind of threatened and bothered by it.

Rick described being sexually harassed by a gay baker in his restaurant:

> There was a baker that we had who was really, really gay. . . . He was very straightforward and blunt. He would tell you, in detail, his sexual experiences and tell you that he wanted to do them with you. . . . I knew he was kidding but he was serious. I mean, if he had a chance he would do these things.

In each of these cases, the men expressed some confusion about the intentions of their harassers—"I knew he was kidding but he was serious." Their inability to read the intentions of the gay men provoked them to label these episodes sexual harassment. Each man did not perceive the sexual interchange as reciprocal, nor did he view the harasser as a potential relationship interest. Interestingly, however, all three of the men who described harassment from gay men claimed that sexual banter and play with other *straight* men did not trouble them. Jake, for example, said that "when men get together, they talk sex," regardless of whether there are women around. He acceded, "people find me offensive, as a matter of fact," because he gets "pretty raunchy" talking and joking about sex. Only when this talk was initiated by a gay man did Jake label it as sexual harassment.

Johnson (1988) argues that talking and joking about sex is a common means of establishing intimacy among heterosexual men and maintaining a masculine identity. Homosexuality is perceived as a direct challenge and threat to the achievement of masculinity and consequently, "the male homosexual is derided by other males because he is not a real man, and in male logic if one is not a real man, one is a woman" (p. 124). In Johnson's view, this dynamic not only sustains masculine identity, it also shores up male dominance over women; thus, for some straight men, talking about sex with other straight men is a form of reasserting masculinity and male dominance, whereas talking about sex with gay men threatens the very basis for their masculine privilege. For this reason they may interpret the sex talk and conduct of gay men as a form of sexual harassment.

In certain restaurants, gay men may in fact intentionally hassle straight men as an explicit strategy to undermine their privileged position in society. For example, Trent (who is openly gay) realizes that heterosexual men are uncomfortable with his sexuality, and he intentionally draws attention to his sexuality in order to bother them:

[Interviewer: Homosexuality gets on whose nerves?]

The straight people's nerves. . . . I know also that we consciously push it just because, we know, "Okay. We know this is hard for you to get used to but tough luck. I've had my whole life trying to live in this straight world and if you don't like this, tough shit." I don't mean like we're shitty to them on purpose but it's like, "I've had to worry about being accepted by straight people all my life. The shoe's on the other foot now. If you don't like it, sorry."

[Interviewer: Do you get along well with most of the waitpeople?]

I think I get along with straight women. I get along with gay men. I get along with gay women usually. If there's ever going to be a problem between me and somebody it will be between me and a straight man.

Trent's efforts to "push" his sexuality could easily be experienced as sexual harassment by straight men who have limited experience negotiating unwanted sexual advances. The three men who reported being sexually harassed by gay men seemed genuinely confused about the intentions of their harassers, and threatened by the possibility that they would actually be subjected to and harmed by unwanted sexual advances. But it is important to point out that Trent works in a restaurant owned by lesbians, which empowers him to confront his straight male co-workers. Not all restaurants provide the sort of atmosphere that makes this type of engagement possible; indeed, some restaurants have policies explicitly banning the hiring of gays and lesbians. Clearly, not all gay men would be able to push their sexuality without suffering severe retaliation (e.g., loss of job, physical attacks).

In contrast to the reports of the straight men in this study, none of the women interviewed reported sexual harassment from their gay or lesbian co-workers. Although Maxine was worried when she found out that one of her co-workers was lesbian, she claims that this fact no longer troubles her:

Six months ago I found out that there was a lesbian girl working there. It kind of freaked me out for a while. I was kind of aware of everything that she did towards me. I was conscious if she walked by me and accidently brushed up against me. She's cool. She doesn't bother me. She never touches my butt or anything like that. The gay guys do that to the [straight] guys but they know they're just kidding around. The [straight] guys do that to the [straight] girls, but they don't care. They know that they're not supposed to do that with me. If they do it, I stop and look at them and they apologize and they don't do it anymore. So they stay out of my way because I'm a meanie (laughs).

Some heterosexual women claimed they feel *more* comfortable working with gay men and lesbians. For example, Kate prefers working with gay men rather than heterosexual men or women. She claims that she often jokes about sex with her gay co-workers, yet she does not view them as potential harassers. Instead, she feels that her working conditions are more comfortable and more fun because she works with gay men. Similarly, Cathy prefers working with gay men over straight men because "gay men are a lot like women in that they're very sensitive to other people's space." Cathy also works with lesbians, and she claims that she has never felt sexually harassed by them.

The gays and lesbians in the study did not report any sexual harassment from their gay and lesbian co-workers. Laura, who is bisexual, said she preferred to work with gays and lesbians instead of heterosexuals because they are "more relaxed" about sex. Brenda said she feels comfortable working around all of her male and female colleagues—regardless of their sexual orientation:

The guys I work with [don't threaten me]. We always run by each other and pat each other on the butt. It's no big deal. Like with my girlfriend [who works at the same restaurant], all the cocktailers and hostesses love us. They don't care that we're gay. We're not a threat. We all kind of flirt but it's not sexual. A lesbian is not going to sexually harass another woman unless they're pretty gross anyway. It has nothing to do with their sexuality; it has to do with the person. You can't generalize and say that gays and lesbians are the best to work with or anything because it depends on the person.

Brenda enjoys flirtatious interactions with both men and women at her restaurant, but distinguishes these behaviors from sexual harassment. Likewise, Lynn, who is a lesbian, enjoys the relaxed sexual atmosphere at her workplace. When asked if she ever joked about sex in her workplace, she said:

> Yes! (laughs) All the time! All the time—everybody has something that they want to talk about on sex and it's got to be funny. We have gays. We have lesbians. We have straights. We have people who are real Christian-oriented. But we all jump in there and we all talk about it. It gets real funny at times. . . . I've patted a few butts . . . and I've been patted back by men, and by the women, too! (laughs)

Don and Trent, who are both gay, also said that they had never been sexually harassed in their restaurants, even though both described their restaurants as highly sexualized.

In sum, our interviews suggest that sexual orientation is an important factor in understanding each individual's experience of sexual harassment and his or her willingness to label interactions as sexual harassment. In particular, straight men may perceive gay men as potential harassers. Three of our straight male respondents claimed to enjoy the sexual banter that commonly occurs among straight men, and between heterosexual men and women, but singled out the sexual advances of gay men as sexual harassment. Their contacts with gay men may be the only context where they feel vulnerable to unwanted sexual encounters. Their sense of not being in control of the situation may make them more willing to label these episodes sexual harassment.

Our findings about sexual orientation are less suggestive regarding women. None of the women (straight, lesbian, or bisexual) reported sexual harassment from other female co-workers or from gay men. In fact, all but one of the women's reported cases of sexual harassment involved a heterosexual man. One of the two lesbians in the sample (Brenda) did experience sexual harassment from a group of lesbian customers (described earlier), but she claimed that sexual orientation is not key to her defining the situation as harassment. Other studies have shown that lesbian and bisexual women are routinely subjected to sexual harassment in the workplace (Schneider 1982, 1984);

however, more research is needed to elaborate the social contexts and the specific definitions of harassment among lesbians.

The Exceptions

Two cases of sexual harassment were related by respondents that do not fit in the categories we have thus far described. These were the only incidents of sexual harassment reported between co-workers of the same race: in both cases, the sexual harasser is a White man, and the victim, a White woman. Laura—who is bisexual—was sexually harassed at a previous restaurant by a cook:

> This guy was just constantly badgering me about going out with him. He like grabbed me and took me in the walk-in one time. It was a real big deal. He got fired over it too. . . . I was in the back doing something and he said, "I need to talk to you," and I said. "We have nothing to talk about." He like took me and threw me against the wall in the back. . . . I ran out and told the manager, "Oh my God. He just hit me," and he saw the expression on my face. The manager went back there . . . and then he got fired.

This episode of sexual harassment involved violence, unlike the other reported cases. The threat of violence was also present in the other exception, a case described by Carla. When asked if she had ever been sexually harassed, she said,

> I experienced two men, in wait jobs, that were vulgar or offensive and one was a cook and I think he was a rapist. He had the kind of attitude where he would rape a woman. I mean, that's the kind of attitude he had. He would say totally, totally inappropriate [sexual] things.

These were the only two recounted episodes of sexual harassment between "equal" co-workers that involved White men and women, and both involved violence or the threat of violence.[5]

Schneider (1982, 1991) found the greatest degree of consensus about labeling behavior sexual harassment when that behavior involves violence. A victim of sexual harassment may be more likely to be believed when there is evidence of assault (a situation that is analogous to acquaintance rape). The assumption of reciprocity among homogamous couples may protect assailants with similar characteristics to their victims (e.g., class background, sexual orientation, race/ethnicity, age)—*unless* there is clear evidence of physical abuse. Defining only those incidents that involve violence as sexual harassment obscures—and perhaps even legitimatizes—the more common occurrences that do not involve violence, making it all the more difficult to eradicate sexual harassment from the workplace.

DISCUSSION AND CONCLUSION

We have argued that sexual harassment is hard to identify, and thus difficult to eradicate from the workplace, in part because our hegemonic definition of sexuality defines certain contexts of sexual interaction as legitimate. The interviews with waitpeople in Austin, Texas, indicate that how people currently identify sexual harassment singles out only a narrow range of interactions, thus disguising and ignoring a good deal of sexual domination and exploitation that take place at work.

Most of the respondents in this study work in highly sexualized atmospheres where sexual banter and touching frequently occur. There are institutionalized policies and practices in the workplace that encourage—or at the very least tolerate—a continual display and performance of heterosexuality. Many people apparently accept this ritual display as being a normal or natural feature of their work; some even enjoy this behavior. In the in-depth interviews, respondents labeled such experiences as sexual harassment in only three contexts: when perpetrated by someone who took advantage of their powerful position for personal sexual gain; when the perpetrator was of a different race/ethnicity than the victim—typically a minority man harassing a white woman; and when the perpetrator was of a different sexual orientation than the victim—typically a gay man harassing a straight man. In only two cases did respondents label experiences involving co-workers of the same race and sexual orientation as sexual harassment—and both episodes involved violence or the threat of violence.

These findings are based on a very small sample in a unique working environment, and hence it is not clear whether they are generalizable to other work settings. In less sexualized working environments, individuals may be more likely to label all offensive sexual advances as sexual harassment, whereas in more highly sexualized environments (such as topless clubs or striptease bars), fewer sexual advances may be labeled sexual harassment. Our findings do suggest that researchers should pay closer attention to the interaction context of sexual harassment taking into account not only gender but also the race, occupational status, and sexual orientation of the assailant and the victim.

Of course, it should not matter who is perpetrating the sexually harassing behavior: sexual harassment should not be tolerated under any circumstances. But if members of oppressed groups (racial/ethnic minority men and gay men) are selectively charged with sexual harassment, whereas members of the most privileged groups are exonerated and excused (except in cases where institutionalized power or violence are used), then the patriarchal order is left intact. This is very similar to the problem of rape prosecution: minority men are the most likely assailants to be arrested and prosecuted, particularly when they attack White women (LaFree 1989). Straight White men who sexually assault women (in the context of marriage, dating, or even work) may escape prosecution because of hegemonic definitions of "acceptable" or "legitimate" sexual expression. Likewise, as we have witnessed in the current debate on gays in the military, straight men's fears of sexual harassment justify the exclusion of gay men and lesbians, whereas sexual harassment perpetrated by straight men against both straight and lesbian women is tolerated and even endorsed by the military establishment, as in the Tailhook investigation (Britton and Williams, forthcoming). By singling out these contexts for the label "sexual harassment," only marginalized men will be prosecuted, and the existing power structure that guarantees privileged men's sexual access to women will remain intact.

Sexual interactions involving men and women of the same race and sexual orientation have a hegemonic status in our society, making sexual harassment difficult to identify and eradicate. Our interviews suggest that many men and women are active participants in the sexualized culture of the workplace, even though ample evidence indicates that women who work in these environments suffer negative repercussions to their careers because of it (Jaschik and Fretz 1991; Paludi and Barickman 1991; Reilly et al. 1992; Schneider 1982). This is how cultural hegemony works—by getting under our skins and defining what is and is not pleasurable to us, despite our material or emotional interests.

Our findings raise difficult issues about women's complicity with oppressive sexual relationships. Some women obviously experience pleasure and enjoyment from public forms of sexual engagement with men; clearly, many would resist any attempt to eradicate all sexuality from work—an impossible goal at any rate. Yet it is also clear that the sexual "pleasure" many women seek out and enjoy at work is structured by patriarchal, racist, and heterosexist norms. Heterosexual, racially homogamous relationships are privileged in our society: they are institutionalized in organizational policies and job descriptions, embedded in ritualistic workplace practices, and accepted as legitimate normal, or inevitable elements of workplace culture. This study suggests that only those sexual interactions that violate these policies, practices, and beliefs are resisted and condemned with the label "sexual harassment."

We have argued that this dominant social construction of pleasure protects the most privileged groups in society from charges of sexual harassment and may be used to oppress and exclude the least powerful groups. Currently, people seem to consider the gender, race, status, and sexual orientation of the assailant when deciding to label behaviors as sexual harassment. Unless we acknowledge the complex double standards people use in "drawing the line," then sexual domination and exploitation will undoubtedly remain the normative experience of women in the workforce.

NOTES

1. It could be the case that those who find this behavior extremely offensive are likely to leave restaurant work. In other words, the sample is clearly biased in that it includes only those who are currently employed in a restaurant and presumably feel more comfortable with the level of sexualized behavior than those who have left restaurant work.

2. It is difficult, if not impossible, to specify which occupations are less highly sexualized than waiting tables. Most occupations probably are sexualized in one way or another; however, specific workplaces may be more or less sexualized in terms of institutionalized job descriptions and employee tolerance of sexual banter. For example, Pringle (1988) describes some offices as coolly professional—with minimal sexual joking and play—whereas others are characterized by "compulsory jocularity." Likewise, some restaurants may de-emphasize sexual flirtation between waitpeople and customers, and restrain informal interactions among the staff (one respondent in our sample worked at such a restaurant).

3. We thank Margaret Andersen for drawing our attention to this fruitful analogy.

4. It is also probably significant that this episode of harassment involved a gay man and a heterosexual man. This context of sexual harassment is discussed later in this article.

5. It is true that both cases involved cooks sexually harassing waitresses. We could have placed these cases in the "powerful position" category, but did not because in these particular instances, the cooks did not possess institutionalized power over the waitpeople. In other words, in these particular cases, the cook and waitress had equal organizational status in the restaurant.

REFERENCES

Anders, K. T. 1993. Bad sex: Who's harassing whom in restaurants? *Restaurant Business,* 20 January, pp. 46–54.

Benson, Donna J., and Gregg E. Thomson. 1982. Sexual harassment on a university campus: The confluence of authority relations, sexual interest and gender stratification. *Social Problems* 29:236–51.

Britton, Dana M., and Christine L. Williams. Forthcoming. Don't ask, don't tell, don't pursue: Military policy and the construction of heterosexual masculinity. *Journal of Homosexuality.*

Carothers, Suzanne C., and Peggy Crull. 1984. Contrasting sexual harassment in female- and male-dominated occupations. In *My troubles are going to have trouble with me: Everyday trials and triumphs of women workers,* edited by K. B. Sacks and D. Remy. New Brunswick, NJ: Rutgers University Press.

Cobble, Dorothy Sue. 1991. *Dishing it out: Waitresses and their unions in the twentieth century.* Urbana: University of Illinois Press.

Cockburn. Cynthia. 1991. *In the way of women.* Ithaca, NY: I.L.R. Press.

Crull, Peggy. 1987. Searching for the causes of sexual harassment: An examination of two prototypes. In *Hidden aspects of women's work,* edited by Christine Bose,

Roslyn Feldberg, and Natalie Sokoloff. New York: Praeger.

Ellis, Shmuel, Azy Barak, and Adaya Pinto. 1991. Moderating effects of personal cognitions on experienced and perceived sexual harassment of women at the workplace. *Journal of Applied Social Psychology* 21: 1320–37.

Fain, Terri C., and Douglas L. Anderton. 1987. Sexual harassment: Organizational context and diffuse status. *Sex Roles* 17:291–311.

Fitzgerald, Louise F. 1990. Sexual harassment: The definition and measurement of a construct. In *Ivory power: Sexual harassment on campus,* edited by Michele M. Paludi. Albany: State University of New York Press.

Grauerholz, Elizabeth. 1989. Sexual harassment of women professors by students: Exploring the dynamics of power, authority, and gender in a university setting. *Sex Roles* 21:789–801.

Gruber, James E., and Lars Bjorn. 1982. Blue-collar blues: The sexual harassment of women auto workers. *Work and Occupations* 9:271–98.

Gutek, B. A. 1985. *Sex and the workplace.* San Francisco: Jossey-Bass.

Hall, Elaine J. 1993. Waitering/waitressing: Engendering the work of table servers. *Gender & Society* 7:329–46.

Howe, Louise Kapp. 1977. *Pink collar workers: Inside the world of women's work.* New York: Avon.

Jaschik, Mollie L., and Bruce R. Fretz. 1991. Women's perceptions and labeling of sexual harassment. *Sex Roles* 25:19–23.

Jensen, Inger W., and Barbara A. Gutek. 1982. Attributions and assignment of responsibility in sexual harassment. *Journal of Social Issues* 38: 122–36.

Johnson, Miriam. 1988. *Strong mothers, weak wives.* Berkeley: University of California Press.

Konrad, Alison M. and Barbara A. Gutek. 1986. "Impact of work experiences on attitudes toward sexual harassment. *Administrative Science Quarterly* 31:422–438.

———. 1996. Impact of work experiences on attitudes toward sexual harassment. *Administrative Science Quarterly* 31:422–38.

LaFree, Gary D. 1989. *Rape and criminal justice: The social construction of sexual assault.* Belmont, CA: Wadsworth.

MacKinnon, Catherine A. 1979. *Sexual harassment of working women: A case of sex discrimination.* New Haven, CT: Yale University Press.

McKinney, Kathleen. 1990. Sexual harassment of university faculty by colleagues and students. *Sex Roles* 23: 421–38.

Paludi, Michele, and Richard B. Barickman. 1991. *Academic and workplace sexual harassment.* Albany: State University of New York Press.

Paules, Greta Foff. 1991. *Dishing it out: Power and resistance among waitresses in a New Jersey restaurant.* Philadelphia: Temple University Press.

Powell, Gary N. 1986. Effects of sex role identity and sex on definitions of sexual harassment. *Sex Roles* 14:9–19.

Pringle, Rosemary. 1988. *Secretaries talk: Sexuality, power and work.* London: Verso.

Pryor, John B. 1987. Sexual harassment proclivities in men. *Sex Roles* 17:269–90.

Reilly, Mary Ellen, Bernice Lott, Donna Caldwell, and Luisa DeLuca. 1992. Tolerance for sexual harassment related to self-reported sexual victimization. *Gender & Society* 6:122–38.

Rich, Adrienne, 1980. Compulsory heterosexuality and lesbian existence. *Signs* 5:631–60.

Schneider, Beth E. 1982. Consciousness about sexual harassment among heterosexual and lesbian women workers. *Journal of Social Issues* 38:75–98.

———. 1984. The office affair. Myth and reality for heterosexual and lesbian women workers. *Sociological Perspectives* 27:443–64.

———. 1991. Put up and shut up: Workplace sexual assaults. *Gender & Society* 5:533–48.

U.S. Department of Labor, Bureau of Labor Statistics. 1989, January. *Employment and earnings.* Washington, DC: Government Printing Office.

West, Candace, and Don H. Zimmerman. 1987. Doing gender. *Gender & Society* 1:125–51.

37

Keeping Women Down and Out

The Strip Club Boom and the Reinforcement of Male Dominance

SHEILA JEFFREYS

In the Western world in the past decade there has been a rapid expansion of the strip club industry, particularly in the form of lap-dancing clubs: the industry is currently estimated to be worth US$75 billion worldwide (Montgomery 2005). Some writers in the field of gender studies have defended the practice of stripping, arguing that stripping should be understood as socially transgressive, an exercise of women's agency, or a form of empowerment for women.[1] These arguments exemplify the decontextualized individualism that is common to many defenses of the sex industry. However, the tradition of women dancing to sexually excite men (usually followed by the men's commercial sexual use of the women) is a historical practice of many cultures, as seen, for instance, in the *auletrides* of classical Greece (Murray and Wilson 2004) and the dancing girls of Lahore, who are prostituted by their families from adolescence on (Saeed 2001). This practice does not signify women's equality. The harmful Western practice of stripping (see Jeffreys 2004), too, I will argue here, signifies sexual inequality. This article will examine the context in which stripping takes place, looking at who owns and controls the industry and who benefits most from it, in order to expose some weaknesses in the argument that stripping can be a positive career for women. It will look at the evidence that suggests that both national and international crime gangs run the most profitable sectors of the industry, and it will show how, as the industry both expands and becomes more exploitative to create greater profits, the trafficking of women and girls into debt bondage has become a staple way of sourcing strippers in Europe and North America. Rather than empowering women, the strip club boom, as this article will contend, helps to compensate men for lost privileges.

THE STRIP CLUB BOOM

Striptease is not a new phenomenon in the West. However, during the twentieth century, the practice was gradually decensored, becoming increasingly explicit in the amount of nudity and touching permitted, from tableaux vivants, in which women were not permitted to move and were made to wear skin-colored coverings, to the lap dancing of the present day. In lap dancing, women are usually naked and use their geni-

Sheila Jeffreys, *Signs: Journal of Women in Culture and Society 34*, pp. 151–173. Copyright © 2008 University of Chicago Press. Reprinted by permission.

tals to massage the penises of clothed men while seated on their laps in private booths. Customers in this recently expanding industry are likely to have been trained and encouraged in the commercial sexual use of women through the decensorship of the pornography industry from the 1960s onward. The pornography industry in the 1960s and 1970s experienced huge growth and became strong enough, through large profits, to fight legal cases and make its product more accessible (Lane 2001). Many of the strip clubs and chains that opened during this boom are owned by men who got rich through pornography, such as the Hustler chain of Larry Flynt.

In the 1980s, striptease moved into a new phase, beginning in the United States. Prior to that time, it was traditional for clubs to pay women to dance: Dawn Passar, a former stripper who now organizes the Exotic Dancers' Alliance, explains that when she first danced in San Francisco, at the well-known Mitchell Brothers O'Farrell Theatre, "the girls would make minimum wage an hour and tips" (Passar, n.d.). However, in the mid-1980s the Market Street Cinema in the same city introduced "stage fees—dancers were required to pay management in order to dance in the club, making a living through tips from private dances. This arrangement spread to the other venues, creating a profound change that enabled the venue owners to increase their profits considerably. Managers were now charging the dancers instead of paying them. From this point on, the amount of the stage fee rose very quickly, reaching the point at which women sometimes could dance all evening with no net profit for themselves or could even take a loss. This new principle that workers should pay to work, and the consequent new level of profitability for owners, stimulated the strip club boom. One media report estimated the U.S. industry to be worth much more than baseball: "$4 billion a year is spent by men on baseball, the national pastime. Compare that to $15 billion a year spent by men at strip clubs" (Sawyer and Weir 2006).

THE FEMINIST DEBATE

In response to this boom in strip clubs, it might be expected that there would be a lively feminist discus-

sion of the issue, but this is not so. Feminist critiques of stripping are thin on the ground; instead, there are many articles and books influenced by poststructuralism and queer theory that represent stripping as an exemplification of Judith Butler's ideas on the transgression of gender through the performance of femininity and masculinity. Katherine Liepe-Levinson, for instance, uses Butler's work in her own book, from the Routledge series Gender in Performance, in which she argues that strip shows involve "social transgressiveness" because female dancers "play desired sex-object roles as they openly defy the expectations of the double standard" (Liepe-Levinson 2002, 4).

Dahlia Schweitzer also argues that stripping is transgressive. Striptease, in her view, enables women to reverse roles and have power over men: "With men the suckers, and women pocketing the cash, the striptease becomes a reversal of society's conventional male/female roles. Striptease is, at its core, a form of role removal" in which women are "clearly in charge" (Schweitzer 2000, 71). In arguing that "by removing her clothes, the stripper disrupts years of patriarchal hegemony" (72), Schweitzer gives the impression that a pro-stripping line is the correct feminist position. Anthropologist Judith Lynne Hanna, however, takes the approach of pure American liberal individualism. She both researches and writes in the field of dance studies and now serves as an expert witness on behalf of the strip club industry in cases in which local authorities seek to exercise control over the clubs. She argues that attempts to limit strip clubs and activities in the United States violate First Amendment rights to freedom of communication, concluding that "it is time to cease stripping the First Amendment, corsetting the exotic dancer and patron, and tying up the community and to promote equality of opportunity for everyone" (1998, 21).

Interestingly, however, Katherine Frank, who worked as a stripper to get funding for graduate school and to research her PhD dissertation on strip clubs and their patrons, is critical of the notion that stripping is transgressive. She seeks to create a "feminist politics of stripping" and writes of how she performs femininity through the practice but also argues that the male buyers are not aware of the performance and "hold very normative views about gender roles." She is forced to ask whether the transgression works, wondering "what is the effect of my double-agent approach to womanhood on the men who gaze up at me? The hard truth is that I cannot predict or prescribe how my performances will be interpreted" (Frank 2002b, 200).

This form of literature on strip clubs, much of it written by women who have experience in the industry, tends to stress the agency that women who strip are able to exercise. Frank, now an academic, says that she had increased feelings of self-efficacy when dancing, although she acknowledges in her writing that the feet that she was known to be a graduate student and had other work options is likely to have made her personal experience atypical, Frank is well aware that there are constraints on the exercise of agency; she speaks, for example, of stripping being "deeply intertwined with gendered and sexual positionings and power relations" (Frank 2002a, 4). But she is quite positive about what stripping offers to women. Frank speaks, for instance, of the "potential economic and personal rewards" and the "radical political potential of mixing money, sexuality, and the public sphere" so that "sex work cannot be dismissed as a possible form of feminist resistance or an exercise in female agency" (16). Of strippers, she writes that "we open spaces of resistance within the heteronormative culture of the strip club and elsewhere" (2002b, 206). The constraints themselves—such as the structural dimensions of the industry; the exploitative and abusive practices of strip club owners, managers, and clients; and restrictions on how much money is made by women who strip and what precisely they have to do to get it—are scarcely mentioned.

Although there is now a considerable feminist literature looking at the psychological and physical effects that women experience from being prostituted (Jeffreys 1997, 2004; Farley et al. 2003), this has not been the case for stripping, where there is little analysis of its harms.[2] Scholarship has only just begun to discuss the effects of the strip club boom on women who aren't strippers, such as those residing in the neighborhoods where the clubs are located and those seeking equality in the business world, where in some sectors the majority of deals are made in strip clubs that exclude female patrons (Morgan and Martin 2006). A literature is just beginning to develop on the gains that the male buyers make from their involvement in the strip club

industry (Erickson and Tewksbury 2000; Frank 2003). Most significantly, there has been a conspicuous gap in the literature in relation to the context in which the stripping takes place. Structural factors, such as who is in control and who makes the profits, have been central to much research on other aspects of the sex industry, such as prostitution, trafficking, and pornography (Barry 1995; Taylor and Jamieson 1999). The sex industry is now being considered, for example, as an important aspect of globalization (Jeffreys 1999; Poulin 2005). Stripping, however, has not been approached from a political economy viewpoint. The feminist literature does not discuss who is developing this industry and who benefits from it.

This article presents an examination, mainly from media reports, of the context of stripping, looking at who owns the industry, the involvement of organized crime in it, and the trafficking of women that supplies it. It looks, farther, at the harms suffered by the women who strip within this exploitative context and uses a combination of the little research that does exist and material from strip club industry magazines and sex work organizations. The impact of strip clubs on equality between the sexes is then surveyed through the experiences both of the male buyers and of the women in the world of business who are confronting a new glass ceiling created by their male colleagues' use of strip clubs. This article will consider only strip clubs catering to heterosexual men, the predominant form of the industry.

THE CONTEXT OF THE STRIP CLUB INDUSTRY

Strippers do not work independently. The practice of striptease generally takes place in strip clubs, which are often part of national or international business chains. Because of the high profit levels in the business, the strip club industry is expanding. In the United States in 2005 there were an estimated three thousand clubs employing three hundred thousand women (Stossel 2005). In 2002 there were two hundred lap-dancing clubs in the United Kingdom (Jones, Shears, and Hillier 2003). A 2003 media report estimates the annual turnover of UK lap-dancing clubs at £300 million, commenting that "they are one of the fastest growing elements in the UK's leisure services industry" (Jones, Shears, and Hillier 2003, 215). The strip club industry is estimated to be worth £22.1 million yearly to the Scottish economy alone (Currie 2006, 11). The industry in the United States is estimated to be worth $15 billion, constituting about one-fifth of the US$75 billion world market (Montgomery 2005, C1).

Spearmint Rhino, the American strip club chain owned by John Gray, now also has clubs in the United Kingdom, Russia (Moscow), and Australia. British investigative journalist Adrian Gatton reports that the club on Tottenham Court Road in London makes profits of more than £3 per minute. In 2001, a year after it opened, this club made a "tax profit of more than £1.75 million from sales of £7.8 million, equivalent to takings of £150,000 a week" (Gatton 2003). During the Christmas holiday season, the revenues were £300,000 each week. Gatton points out that a busy city pub would normally take in around £20,000 in a good week, which explains why many pubs in the United Kingdom have been converted to strip clubs in recent years. Spearmint Rhino clubs in the United Kingdom operate in the common style of lap-dancing clubs, with dancers paying £80 per night to work and the club taking 35 percent of the dancers' earnings from customers (Gatton 2003).

According to the work of investigative journalists in the United Kingdom and the United States, strip clubs are likely to have criminal connections, with media reports suggesting that some strip club owners and managers are associated with organized crime (Blackhurst and Gatton 2002; Gatton 2003). The owners of strip clubs are careful to represent themselves as upstanding members of the community in their sponsorship of football teams, donations to charity, and so on. The owners of upmarket clubs promote them as elegant destinations for socially elite men. However, there are indications, despite all attempts to maintain the veneer of respectability, that strip club owners have disreputable associations. One indication is the number of unexplained deaths and injuries sustained by the owners, managers, and associates of these clubs. The manager of Spearmint Rhino UK was viciously attacked while walking from the Tottenham Court Road club to its parking lot in 2002: "Two men came up behind, struck him on the head with a machete and knocked Mr. Cadwell to the ground. He somehow fought back but was stabbed at least twice, one blow puncturing a lung." No one was charged, and the police "suspect this was no ordinary street robbery, that Mr. Cadwell was targeted by associates of a notorious north London crime family in a feud with his company" (Blackhurst and Gatton 2002, 20). Another unexplained death occurred in California in September 1990, when a twenty-one-year-old woman who had been riding with Cadwell in his helicopter was killed. She was the girlfriend of Cadwell's close friend David Amos, and the incident was described by Blackhurst and Gatton as follows: "She stepped out of the helicopter as it stood on the tarmac at Long Beach Airport to greet Mr. Amos, who was waiting for her, and walked into the still turning tail rotor blades" (20). The police investigation concluded that the death was an accident. In 2001 Amos was convicted of the 1989 machine-gun killing of a strip club boss in Los Angeles. He was close to a member of the Bonnano Mafia family in New York and had paid a hit man to shoot Horace McKenna at his home (20). An attack similar to that on Cadwell took place in Edinburgh in 2005. The manager of one of Scorland's biggest lap-dancing bars "was stabbed as he locked up for night" (Hamilton 2005, 37). *Sunday Mail* reporter Jane Hamilton also notes that "police believe he may have been caught up in a feud between the capital's gangsters" (37).

John Gray's Spearmint Rhino is the most successful international strip club chain. These clubs go to particular lengths to establish themselves as upmarket venues popular with business executives for entertaining clients and not just as strip joints. Gray, however, is a controversial figure. He has been convicted six times in the United States, for offenses ranging from carrying a concealed weapon to writing bad checks, for which he received a suspended sentence, sixty-eight months' probation, and periods in jail (Blackhurst and Gatton 2002, 20). According to an *Evening Standard* (London) investigation, although "born John Leldon Gray . . . he has used the names, John Luciano, John Luciano Gianni and Johnny Win" (20). The *Evening Standard* article makes the interesting point that "oddly, there is also a John L. Gray, born in February 1957 and linked to two Spearmint Rhino addresses and one of Mr. Gray's home addresses, who is registered in the United States as 'deceased'" (20). Journalists in different countries are clearly interested in the connections between organized crime and the strip club industry but have to be careful about what they say in case of libel claims.

There are also clear connections between organized crime and the strip club industry in Queensland, Australia (Whittaker and Callinan 1999, 5). Crime figures are able to dominate ownership of the lap-dancing clubs in the state without their own names officially appearing anywhere. The apparent owners of the clubs are "often 'cleanskins' put up by the faceless men in the background" (5). According to a report in the *Courier Mail* on Queensland strip clubs, former bankrupts, loan sharks, and convicted drug dealers run the industry through secret stakes in clubs that are officially operated by nephews, for instance, who do not have convictions to their names. Thus one convicted criminal, who figured in an inquiry into police corruption conducted in the state, is described in the same newspaper report as the "godfather" of the industry, but his name is not listed in company records (5). In Sydney, the Hells Angels motorcycle gang was connected to so many shootings in or outside the strip clubs that a special police strike force has been set up to investigate the violence (Kennedy 2006, 5).

Arguments about women gaining agency and empowerment through stripping need to be considered in the context of organized crime's extensive involvement in the industry. Employers and managers involved in organized crime are men who bully, threaten, and kill to gain their profits. This needs to be factored in as a powerful form of inequality between the sex entrepreneurs and the women they exploit. It is interesting to note that one of the arguments made for legalizing the prostitution industry in many countries where brothels are still illegal is that legalization will drive out organized crime, which presumably thrives only because the industry, being illegal, is driven underground. But strip clubs are legal everywhere, and men connected with organized crime are running them and collecting the considerable profits.

An approach of decontextualized individualism is inappropriate for analysis of stripping because, unlike the women who strip, the club owners and entrepreneurs are very organized nationally and internationally. They are not operating simply as individuals. Many are involved in networks of organized crime. But even those for whom there is no evidence of such involvement organize with one another to influence—and, in many cases, bribe—politicians and to engage lawyers and experts who can devise means of avoiding regulation and defeating community activism against their enterprises. These legal networks are linked through membership associations and online resources such as the U.S. newsletter of the Association of Club Executives, *Strip-magazine* in Europe, and the Eros Foundation in Australia. As a result of their careful efforts to achieve respectability—through sex exhibitions, stripping competitions, support for charities, and the cultivation of positive coverage in the media—strip clubs have experienced a remarkable normalization. Prominent figures of the UK establishment, including Margaret Thatcher, Prince Harry, and Tony Blair's son Euan, have all been recorded as patronizing the clubs in 2005 and 2006. Thatcher, for example, was a guest at a Tory Party fund-raiser in Peter Stringfellow's London club in April 2005 (Tyke 2005). Euan Blair was observed "spending the evening in the Hustler club late in November while on work experience in Paris" in 2005 (Tyke 2006). In April 2006, Prince Harry was observed at a lap-dancing club: "He (Harry) and a group of mates arrived at Spearmint Rhino at Colnbrook near Slough, Berkshire, at 3 am. . . . Harry grabbed a seat near the topless dancers—and stripper Mariella Butkute sat on his lap" (Rousewell 2006). Meanwhile, the industry is promoted in the business pages of newspapers, in how-to books, and, presendy, in some academic disciplines such as business studies (Jones, Shears, and Hillier 2003) and leisure studies. In one leisure studies collection, for example, visiting a strip club is described positively as "a satisfying leisure experience" and "passive recreation" (Suren and Stiefvater 1998, 114).

TRAFFICKING

One aspect of organized crime involvement in the strip club industry is trafficking, which has become a common way of supplying clubs with dancers. All over Europe and North America, women and girls are brought into the clubs by deception, by force, or, initially, by consent (Anderson and O'Connell David-son 2003; Dickson 2004; Monzini 2005). In such cases, they are kept in debt bondage, are deprived of their travel documents (which are confiscated by the traffickers), and are controlled by threats to themselves or their families—all traditional aspects of this modern form of slavery. Governments can be seen as complicit in the trafficking of women to strip clubs through the issuing of visas for women who will work in debt bondage in strip clubs. In Canada, for instance, the importation of women was institutionalized through exotic dancer visas issued by the state since visas for particular skilled occupations that could not be staffed by local citizens were a formal part of the government's immigration program. Until 2004, the Canadian government issued four hundred to five hundred visas a year for Eastern European women to work as exotic dancers. In order to gain visas, women had to supply proof that they were strippers, which was accomplished by their provision of soft-porn pictures to immigration authorities (*Agence France-Presse* 2004). Audrey Macklin argues in the *International Migration Review* that local strippers could not be found because the conditions of work in strip clubs had deteriorated drastically with the advent of lap dancing and private booths (Macklin 2003): Canadian citizens were not prepared to experience the extreme degradation involved. Macklin makes the fascinating argument that the strippers from Eastern Europe should therefore be seen as the spoils of war. She explains: "If the fall of the Berlin Wall symbolizes the defeat of communism and the triumph of capitalism, then perhaps commodified East European women, exported to serve Western men, are the spoils of the Cold War served up by the global market to the victors" (2003, 471). The soldiers of liberty from the West, in the form of strip club habitues in North America and Western Europe, can claim and use the bodies of women of the defeated Communist regime. These strip club patrons exercise the colonizing power of rich males within a globalized economy.

Strip club owners have such power and influence within national economies that they are frequently able to get governments to act as procurers for their industry. Mendel Green, a lawyer for the Canadian clubs, asserted that the state owed a duty to the private sector to provide labor inputs where market incentives failed (Macklin 2003). Indeed, he is quoted in a newspaper at the time reducing women to items of merchandise, saying "They're a critical sort of product in the entertainment industry that is not readily available in Canada" (*Guelph Mercury* 2004, A6). Interestingly, Green argued that foreign women were needed because "Canadian-born dancers were controlled by biker gangs" (*Guelph Mercury* 2004, A6), an admission by an industry representative of the involvement of organized crime. Canadian government officials became sufficiently embarrassed by having acted so clearly as pimps for the local strip club owners that the exotic dancer visas were discontinued in 2004.

The trafficking of women from Eastern Europe into strip clubs has also caused considerable concern in Ireland. Until 2002, the Irish state, like Canada, issued work permits for lap dancers under the category of "entertainment," thus making the trafficking effortless (Haughey 2003, 4). Justice Minister Michael McDowell told the Parliament in 2002 that "there was clear evidence that human traffickers from Eastern Europe used lap dancing clubs as a front for the sex trade" (Wheeler 2003, 7). In June 2003, the gardai (police) in Ireland "blocked a bid by Eastern European organised crime gangs to take control of the money-spinning lap dancing industry" (Brady 2003). These gangs were thought to have links to paramilitaries and criminals in Ireland. The *Irish Times* commented that the industry is plagued by reports that prostitution occurs in the clubs: in Dublin, one club was closed by a court order after illegal sex acts were found to have been taking place (Haughey 2003, 4). The Dublin-based feminist antiviolence organization Ruhama argues that the clubs groom women for prostitution while "in every other country in the world they are just a cover for prostitution" (Haughey 2003, 4). There is trafficking of women into the clubs in the United States, too. In once such instance from 2005, "Russian entertainment promoter Lev Trakhtenberg of Brooklyn, N.Y., got five years in prison after admitting he and his wife . . . helped more than 25 women to come illegally from Russia to the United States to perform nude lap dances at strip clubs" (Parry 2006).

EXPLOITATION OF AND VIOLENCE TOWARD STRIPPERS

It is in the context of huge profits to club owners, of organized crime and trafficking, that women strip in the clubs. The profits would not be so large if women were being fairly remunerated for stripping. In fact, the vast majority of the profits go to the club owners and not to the dancers, who may find it hard to earn enough just to pay the stage fees. In San Diego, dancers "can make several hundred dollars on a weekend night, but most struggle to make $100 a night, many of them earning only what they can make in tips. . . . Another dancer at Minx Showgirls . . . said she averages closer to $45 a night" (Washburn and Davies 2004, A1). "Tyke," a strip club habitue of twenty-five years who writes for the industry journal *Strip-magazine*, explains that the idea that UK dancers can make £2,000 a night is a myth. This myth is in feet a story repeated frequently by club owners, who would find it hard to attract dancers if they told the truth. Tyke explains, "To make £2,000 in 1 night would involve 100 table dances ie around 15 an hour for a typical 7 hour shift, I just don't think that happens" (2003). He flirdier explains that strippers might in exceptional circumstances find a merchant banker who will spend his "Christmas bonus" on them, a scenario that can help to create the idea of large earnings.

The profit levels in the industry are enhanced by the fact that strippers do not get the benefits—such as sick leave or superannuation—that other club workers receive, because the club owners treat strippers as individual agents who simply rent space in the club. As Kelly Holsopple points out in her research on stripping, although the club owners argue that they are not employers and that the strippers are independent agents, the owners control hours and schedules, fees and tips, and even set the price of table dances and private dances. They pressure dancers to completely shave their pubic hair, to acquire year-long tans, and to undergo surgical breast augmentation. They regulate when women can use the bathroom, mix with other women, and smoke. Rules are enforced, with fines charged for being late, calling in sick, talking back to customers or staff, and many other, often invented, infringements that can deplete strippers' earnings. On top of this, strippers have to tip those who are employed by the club on regular wages: managers enforce "a mandatory tip out to bouncers and disc jockeys" (Holsopple 1998, 3). Furthering this point, Liepe-Levinson also writes of fines for minor transgressions and harsh work schedules (2002).

As the clubs seek to maximize profits, they work greater numbers of dancers, which creates greater competition among the strippers, forces down earnings, and pressures strippers to engage in practices they would rather avoid, such as lap dancing or prostitution. Retired stripper Amber Cooke explained in a 1980s collection on sex work that strippers are forced to compete because there are too many dancers and not enough male buyers, and are encouraged to provide "hands-on entertainment rather than dance, in order to make their money" (Cooke 1987, 98). She points out that this is dangerous, particularly because bouncers are not an effective protection: they cannot watch all the tables—let alone the private booths—and may be reluctant to defend a stripper against a group of aggressive male customers. The advent of lap dancing in strip clubs has therefore been seen by stripper advocacy groups and individual dancers as creating severe harm. Private booths, because of their nature, enable male buyers to sexually assault women and to engage in forms of intimate contact that the women find intolerable. For example, in a Melbourne court case a man was jailed in July 2006 for raping a stripper in a private booth: "During the dance, she took off her G'string and was naked. Her breasts were about 30 cm from Nguyen's face. . . . [He] lunged at the woman, digitally raping her" and "pinned the woman to a couch" (Associated Press 2006, 9).

Canadian strippers formed an organization to oppose the practice of lap dancing, arguing that it is harmful to the dancers, and those interviewed in one study particularly objected to having to come into contact with "customers' ejaculate," which could occur "when ejaculate penetrated the men's clothing during lap dances" (Lewis 2000, 210). One interviewee explained to researcher Jacqueline Lewis, "So halfway through the song, like no warning, you're sitting on their lap, and all of a sudden you're wet." Another concern was "dancers' genital contact with other dancers' vaginal secretions, left on customers[2] clothing" (210). These opponents of lap dancing also talked about the harm they experienced both from being pressured by owners, managers, and customers to engage in lap dancing and from being threatened with job loss if they did not comply. Such practices made them feel "disempowered and victimized." Two dancers told Lewis they were "crying their eyes out" after their first night of lap dancing and were distressed by, for instance, "these strangers' fingers all over you—it was really nasty" (210). Nonetheless, Lewis herself opposes the ban on lap dancing that many of her interviewees saw as necessary for their survival in the industry. She contends that the solution to the problems strippers face is to treat stripping as just like any other form of work. However, there are no other forms of work, apart from those in the sex industry, in which women have to battle to keep their naked bodies away from men's fingers and ejaculate.

There has been very little research on the physical and psychological harms that strippers face in clubs. Information on the harms of stripping may be difficult for some researchers to elicit. Thus R. Danielle Egan, who writes about stripping from what she calls a "sex radical perspective" and who rejects radical feminist analyses that focus on harm, comments that the women she worked with as a stripper and interviewed for her book avoided elaborating on their "experiences with bad nights" (2006, 83). Egan interprets "bad nights" as those during which women made very little money and were made to feel bad or "like whores"; she understands "good nights" as those on which they made money and felt good (83). She does not enlarge on the women's experiences of being touched by men or having to touch them, nor how they felt about such practices. This more detailed analysis is quite scarce. However, a useful study by Holsopple (1998) provides information about such harms. She worked as a stripper in the United States for thirteen years and researched the effects of the industry on the dancers by conducting forty-one interviews and eighteen face-to-face surveys followed by discussions. She argues that the "common underlying element in strip clubs is that male customers, managers, staff, and owners use diverse methods of harassment, manipulation, exploitation, and abuse to control female strippers" (1998, 1).

Holsopple's interviewees did not report the empowerment or expression of agency that some gender stud-

ies scholars have attributed to stripping (e.g., Egan 2006). Women had to engage in activities they found repugnant if they were to make a living from their work in the clubs, because their income was "entirely dependent on compliance with customer demands in order to earn tips" (Holsopple 1998, 3). Holsopple concluded from her interviews that "customers spit on women, spray beer, and flick cigarettes at them" and that the strippers are "pelted with ice, coins, trash, condoms, room keys, pornography, and golf balls" (8). Missiles from the audience have included a live guinea pig, a dead squirrel, and cans and bottles. Male buyers also "pull women's hair, yank them by the arm or ankle, rip their costumes, and try to pull their costumes off." Women are commonly "bitten, licked, slapped, punched, and pinched" (8). The male buyers attempt to penetrate women vaginally and anally with "fingers, dollar bills, and bottles" (8). Successful vaginal and anal penetration was common.

Holsopple's study shows that women suffered particular harm from the conditions in which they were required to dance. They had to dance on elevated runways so narrow that they could not get away from men on either side touching them. In the private dances in booths, men would openly masturbate and "stick their fingers inside women." Wall dancing, for example, "requires a stripper to carry alcohol swabs to wash the customer's fingers before he inserts them into her vagina. His back is stationary against the wall and she is pressed against him with one leg lifted" (Holsopple 1998, 6). Holsopple's interviewees describe clearly the forms of pressure and sexual harassment that they experienced from the male buyers in private dances: "I don't want him to touch me, but 1 am afraid he will say something violent if I tell him 'no' "; "I could only think about how bad these guys smell and try to hold my breath"; and "I spent the dance hyper vigilant to avoiding their hands, mouths, and crotches" (6). Every one of the eighteen women in her survey reported being both physically and sexually abused in the clubs and being verbally harassed, often multiple times. Most had been stalked—from one to seven times each—by someone associated with the club. Holsopple states that regulations prohibiting customers from touching dancers are "consistently violated" and that "stripping usually involves prostitution" (4). Liepe-

Levinson reports that the strippers she interviewed experienced pressure to provide sexual favors to club bosses and employees (2002).

The advice offered to strippers from within the industry and from statefunded sex work agencies on how to avoid violence illuminates just how significant a threat this violence is. On the *Strip-magazine* Web site, for instance, Ram Mani offers advice to strippers on how to be constantly alert to all the possibilities of men's violence (Mani 2004). Women are advised not to leave the clubs alone. Once outside the club, they should get straight into their cars and lock the doors, moving off immediately. They should not take a direct route home and should keep an eye on the car's mirror to check that they are not being followed. They should park neither so far from the club that they have a dangerously long walk to their cars nor so close that a man may be able to note their car's license number. When they register their cars, they should not use their home address. They are warned that "the odds of being stalked, mugged and attached [*sic*] are on increase and you must always keep your guard up" (2004). The advice offered to strippers by the sex work advocacy Web site STAR (Sex Trade Advocacy and Research) in Toronto includes tips for combating sexual assault: "Watch for roaming hands. Clients have an easier time touching you when you dance on a box, especially when you're bending over" (STAR 2004, 3). Dancers are told to "watch out for unruly or aggressive customers" and to "use the mirrors to keep track of your back." There is specific advice for private dances, since "there's a greater possibility of assault. . . . If a customer is trying to manhandle you, try holding his hands in a sexy way to control him. But be aware that touching violates some municipal bylaws. . . . If you're being assaulted, scream" (3).

REINFORCING GENDER INEQUALITY: THE GLASS CEILING FOR WOMEN IN BUSINESS

It is not just the women who strip who experience the harms of strip clubs. All women living in a society in which strip clubs flourish are likely to be affected by them in a variety of ways. Women whose husbands, partners, sons, male friends, and male workmates visit strip clubs will feel some effects. Wives and partners of pornophiles, for instance, report in interviews that they lose self-esteem as men compare them with the women in pornography, that they are asked to perform poses and practices that come from pornography to satisfy their male partners, and that they have lost needed family income to men's obsession with pornography (Paul 2005). Frank's research found that men reported visiting strip clubs in order to take revenge on their wives if they had an argument and were well aware of the distress that their behavior would cause if their wives knew of it, and did cause to wives who suspected it (2002a). When areas of cities are commandeered for men's sexual commodification of women, women who are not in the sex industry are likely to feel excluded from these spaces. While men may take for granted their right to access public space freely, women have always suffered a reduction in this right because of male violence and its threat.

Strip clubs are not separate from society but influence on many levels the way men relate to women. One type of harm relates to the obstacles that strip clubs place in the way of equality for women in the business world, an issue now gaining attention legally and in research. A fascinating 2006 study by Laurie Morgan and Karin Martin shows how women professionals are blocked from engaging in the vital social networking that secures business clients and contracts. Morgan and Martin explain that many women professionals "traverse other settings beyond that of the office" in the course of their work, "including conferences, airplanes, hotel rooms and lobbies, restaurants, shop floors, golf courses, tennis courts, sporting events, bars, cars, and trade shows" (2006, 109). They state that "employer-sponsored out-of-the-office socializing with colleagues, customers and suppliers is institutionalized," for it is through these socializations that day-to-day work is done, as is the "relationship building" that "embeds the foundation for reciprocity and long-lasting organizational ties in personal ones" (109). Thus, this out-of-office socializing has important purposes, which are completely necessary to a woman's work and career, and is not optional at all. Morgan and Martin explain that in many industries the "entertainment" of male clients at strip clubs is an ordinary part of the work of the sales representatives they were researching. They write that "accounts from industry trade magazines suggest that almost half of salesmen, but only 5 percent of saleswomen, had entertained clients in topless bars" (116). Saleswomen, they point out, are thereby excluded from "industry contacts and denied access to professional information exchange" (116). The interview information Morgan and Martin examined showed that while some of the women professionals were disgusted by the visits to strip clubs, others were just angry that they were excluded from these meetings by being sent to their hotel rooms while their male coworkers went on to the clubs. The entertainment receipts showed the clubs as restaurants so that the accountants did not have to know where the events had taken place.

There is plenty of evidence to suggest that when men enter strip clubs in groups the atmosphere becomes even more exaggeratedly masculine (Erickson and Tewksbury 2000; Frank 2003). As Morgan and Martin put it, "Patrons tend to be louder and more raucous. The male-bonding bravado permeates the entire audience to some degree. The level of objectification of the dancers also appears to increase as a result of this phenomenon" (2006, 118). Women are not able to join in this bonding, which is expressly constructed between men through their objectification of naked women: "Saleswomen said that at these events they undermined the 'cavorting' and 'fun' and ultimately the 'bonding' that the events were intended to promote" (118). One woman described trying to attend a strip club with a customer and two company managers. During the visit to the club, she ended up speaking, and perhaps bonding, with the strippers rather than with her male companions, stating in an interview, "And I'm like, 'Okay where do 1 look?' I'm talking to the strippers" (118). Her interaction with the strippers would be likely to humanize them and provide an impediment to the men's enjoyment of objectification.

The practice of taking clients to strip clubs seems to be particularly common in the finance industry. An estimated 80 percent of city finance workers (presumably male) visit strip clubs in London as a part of their work. This statistic came out in a court case about the poaching of clients between two London finance firms in 2006. Matthew Lynn, reporting on this interesting

piece of information, comments helpfully, "In effect, just as their fathers might have taken clients to one of the gendemen's clubs of Pall Mall, so brokers today take their business associates to see lap dancers. The old gendemen's clubs banned women—some still do—whereas the lap-dancing establishments merely intimidate them" (2006). He explains that if one bank would not let its workers take clients to lap-dancing clubs, then its rivals certainly would. In the United States this form of exclusion of women from equal opportunities has resulted in women employees' filing some high-profile actions for sex discrimination against top finance houses. Morgan Stanley, for instance, agreed in 2004 to pay $54 million to settle Equal Employment Opportunity Commission charges that it had "discriminated against women in pay and promotions, and tolerated crude comments about sex and men-only outings to strip clubs with clients" (Lublin 2006, 33).

So integral and accepted have strip clubs become within corporate culture that their importance to business is now being used as an argument as to why town councils should encourage their development (Valler 2005). When the issue of granting a lap-dancing club license was before the council in Coventry, England, in 2005, a "leading businessman" argued that "a lap-dancing club would boost Coventry's reputation as a major centre of commerce. . . . When businessmen travel to a major city where they stay overnight, they almost expect to find a lap-dancing club. If Coventry has aspirations to be a major business area, then it has to have a quality adult entertainment area, and that would include a lap-dancing club" (8). Strip clubs are but one aspect of the international sex industry that is integral to the way that men do business now. The effect is to reinforce the glass ceiling for women in business and the professions.

REINFORCING GENDER INEQUALITY: A MASCULINIZING PRACTICE

Concomitant with the losses women in general experience from the existence of strip clubs, there appears to be a direct enhancement of men's self-esteem, their feelings of masculinity, and their bonding with other men.

Although there is little evidence from research on strip club practices to suggest that the strippers experience a reversal of gender roles and an increased sense of empowerment, there is, however, some very interesting research on what the male buyers experience in terms of personal power in relation to women from visiting the clubs. Frank used her status as a stripper to gain access to male customers and interview them, and her work is most revealing about the motivations of buyers (Frank 2003). She studied men in traditional strip clubs that did not provide lap dancing. She reports that none of the men she interviewed said they went to the clubs for "sexual release" (2003, 64). They had other motives, of which the most common were the "desire to relax" and to visit a place where they could "be a man" (64). Frank explains that the clubs "provide an environment where men, singularly or in groups, can engage in traditionally 'masculine' activities and forms of consumption frowned upon in other spheres, such as drinking, smoking cigars, and . . . being 'rowdy,' vulgar or aggressive" (65). Strip clubs re-create the gendered spaces for men that were challenged by second-wave feminism. In the 1970s and 1980s, some major equal rights' campaigns were directed at eliminating the male privilege of men-only spaces, places in which men could socialize and do business but in which women were not allowed. These campaigns included demands for and achievement of women's entry to public houses, sporting clubs, and other places of entertainment on an equal basis with men. The boom in strip clubs can be seen as a counter-attack, in which men have reasserted their "right" to network through male dominance, without the irritating presence of women, unless those women are naked and servicing their pleasures.

Frank found that an important reason why men visit the clubs is that the clubs provide a compensation for the decline in power that men have experienced as their wives, partners, and women workmates have shed their own subordination, begun to compete with them, and demanded equality. The strip clubs provide an antidote to the erosion of male dominance by reinstitutionalizing the traditional hierarchy of gender relations. The men reported finding everyday relationships with women "a source of pressure and expectations" and "described relations between women and men in general as being 'strained,' 'confused,' or 'tense.' " One buyer "referred to the 'war between the sexes' " (Frank 2003, 65). They sought respite from the problems of having to treat women as equals in the workplace too. One of Frank's respondents, Philip, said that visiting the clubs "let frustration out" and that because of "this sexual harassment stuff going around these days, men need somewhere to go where they can say and act like they want" (66). Some buyers, Frank found, "desire to interact with women who were not 'feminist,' and who still wanted . . . to interact with men in 'more traditional' ways." One of these traditional ways, it seems, is women's unconditional servicing of male sexual demands. Other buyers told her that outside the sex industry "men had to continually 'be on guard' against offending women" (66). Frank points out that "several of the [men's] comments could be analysed as part of a backlash against feminism" but that she prefers to see them as resting "within a framework of confusion and frustration rather than one of privilege or domination" (66), a result of anxieties caused by feminism and the women's movement toward equality. She does say, however, that the rapid increase in strip clubs in the United States in the 1980s "was concurrent with a massive increase of women into the workforce and an upsurge of attention to issues of sexual harassment, date rape, and the condemnation of the sex industry" (66). Many of the men she spoke with said they were confused about what women expected of them in relationships, particularly when their wives worked, had their own incomes, and wanted to be included in decision making.

Frank believes that what takes place in the clubs does more than compensate men for these changes. The visits to strip clubs can be understood as "masculinizing practices" in their own right (Frank 2003, 74). In the clubs, otherwise unattainable women could be subjected to men's control, exercised through men's ability to refuse payment and to determine the length of their conversations with the women, what would be discussed, and whether and when the woman had to strip. Men reported that they got an "ego boost" (70), because there was no fear of rejection or of competition with other men. Frank concludes that strip clubs help to reinforce male power through maintaining "imbalanced power dynamics in [men's] personal relationships with women, especially when visits are used to shame or anger wives or partners" (74). However, she remains determined not to place too strong an emphasis on this. She remarks that, despite the evidence she presents, "this is not to say that commodified sexual exchanges are inherently about the preservation and reproduction of male power" (74–75).

Another study of strip club patrons by two male researchers supports Frank's findings about the role the clubs play in upholding male dominance. This study analyzes how the "ultra-masculine context of the setting affects and illuminates patrons' motives for frequenting strip clubs" (Erickson and Tewksbury 2000, 272). It also points out that the men in the club are in control, as the women are bound to "reciprocate most of the attention paid to them by the customer," unable to reject male attention as they can in the world outside (273). The customer "may dictate the nature, and often the course, of the interactions because the dancer is both obligated and financially motivated to cooperate with the direction of the customer in defining the interactions" (273). These claims affirm Frank's argument that the clubs are male-only environments that confirm masculinity: "It is almost exclusively a 'man thing' to go to strip clubs. It is one of the very few places where men have the opportunity to openly exhibit their latent sexual desires and to perform their 'male privilege' " (Erickson and Tewksbury 2000, 289). The context of the strip club serves to affirm masculinity because it is "pervaded by images and norms that openly objectify women, [that] is ultra-masculine" (289). David John Erickson and Richard Tewksbury conclude, however, in a way that seems to challenge their earlier findings, saying that their study contradicts the notion that strippers are exploited, because the dancers "control the sequencing and content of their interactions with patrons and, in doing so, . . . generate a substantial income for themselves and provide men with access to important social commodities" (292). In these researchers' view, this is a fair exchange. Yet Erickson and Tewksbury explicitly state earlier in their article that the men in the clubs are in charge of the interactions, unlike in the world outside the clubs, where women can decline to service them, and their article provides no evidence of the good earnings of the dancers. Their research thus seems to represent a male buyer's perspective.

Unlike the traditional gentlemen's clubs of London's Pall Mall, the strip clubs offer men the opportunity to debase women, not just to bond and do business in their absence. These new "gentiemen's clubs" require women to be present—but only when they are naked and available to be bought. Men can drink with their friends while staring into a woman's genitals or shoving their fingers into her anus or vagina. The context in which the male buyers are delivered this bounty is created for them by masculine networks of club owners and franchisees.

CONCLUSION

Feminist scholars and activists should pay serious attention to the strip club boom. The research on stripping that has taken place has been influenced by poststructuralist and queer tiieory, which concentrate on individual agency and transgression rather than on economics and power dynamics. An examination of the context of the strip club boom, of the way that profits are made, of the involvement of organized crime, of the trafficking of women and girls into the clubs, and of the violence and exploitation that take place in them makes the arguments of some researchers—that dancers are empowered by stripping, exercise agency, and transgress gender relations—look thin. Such arguments represent a decontextualized individualism that takes little account of existing inequality between men and women and of the way strip clubs derive from and serve to reinforce this inequality. I suggest, rather, that the strip club boom represents both a rebalancing of the power relations of male dominance and a compensation to men for what has been gained through feminist movements and as a result of the social and economic changes of the last quarter century. Strip clubs have achieved this readjustment through their role in the growth of international capitalism and organized crime, the masculinizing effects of club patronage on male buyers, the subordination of hundreds of thousands of women in the clubs, and the exclusion of women from equal opportunities in national and international professional and business networks, which continue to be the special preserve of men. More research is needed on all aspects of the burgeoning international sex industry to enable us to understand how it operates and how it affects the power dynamics of male dominance.

NOTES

1. See Hanna 1998; Schweitzer 2000; Liepe-Levinson 2002; Egan 2006.

2. A notable exception is Kelly Holsopple's *Strip Club Testimony* (1998).

REFERENCES

Agenee France-Presse. 2004. "Canada Denies Foreign Strippers Must Bare All to Get Visas." *Agence France-Presse*, July 28.

Anderson, Bridget, and Julia O'Connell Davidson. 2003. "Is Trafficking in Human Beings Demand Driven? A Multi-country Pilot Study." IOM Migration Research Series, no. 15. International Organization for Migration, Geneva.

Associated Press. 2006. "Jail for Rape of Stripper." *Weekend Australian*, July 8.

Barry, Kathleen. 1995. *The Prostitution of Sexuality.* New York: New York University Press.

Blackhurst, Chris, and Adrian Gatton. 2002. "A Gangland Killing: Lap Dancers Who Are Said to Sell Sev and the Criminal Past of the Man behind the Spearmint Rhino Empire." *Evening Standard*, September 16, 20.

Brady, Tom. 2003. "Crime Czars Targeted in Swoop on Lap Dance Clubs." *Irish Independent*, June 7. http://www.independent.ie/national-news/crime-czars-targeted-in-swoop-on-lap-dance-clubs-216173.html.

Cooke, Amber. 1987. "Stripping: Who Calls the Tune?" In *Good Girls, Bad Girls*: Sex *Trade Workers and Feminists Face to Face*, ed. Laurie Bell, 92–99. Toronto: Women's Press.

Currie, Brian. 2006. "Lap Dancing Boosts City by GBP 6 M a Year." *Evening Times*, April 26, 11.

Dickson, Sandra. 2004. *Sex in the City: Mapping Commercial Sex across London.* London: The Poppy Project.

Egan, R. Danielle. 2006. *Dancing for Dollars and Paying for Love: The Relationships bctiveen Exotic Dancers and Their Regulars.* New York: Palgrave Macmillan.

Erickson, David John, and Richard Tewksbury. 2000. "The 'Gentlemen' in the Club: A Typology of Strip Club Patrons." *Deviant Behavior* 21(3):271–93.

Farley, Melissa, Ann Cotton, Jacqueline Lynne, Sybille Zumbeck, Frida Spiwak, Maria E. Reyes, Dinorah Alvarez, and Ufuk Sezgin. 2003. "Prostitution and Trafficking in Nine Countries: An Update on Violence and Posttraumatic Stress Disorder." In *Prostitution, Trafficking, and Traumatic Stress*, ed. Melissa Farley, 33–74. Binghamton, NY: Haworth Maltreatment and Trauma Press.

Frank, Katherine. 2002a. *G-Strings and Sympathy: Strip Club Regulars and Male Desire.* Durham, NC: Duke University Press.

———. 2002b. "Stripping, Starving, and the Politics of Ambiguous Pleasure." In *Jane Sexes It Up: True Confessions of Feminist Desire*, ed. Merri Lisa Johnson, 171–206. New York: Four Walls Eight Windows.

———. 2003. "'Just Trying to Relax': Masculinity, Masculinizing Practices, and Strip Club Regulars." *Journal of Sex Research* 40(1):61–75.

Gatton, Adrian. 2003. "Spearmint Rhino Makes £1.75m." *Evening Standard,* March 14.

Guelph Mercury. 2004. "Stripper Shortage Reflects Industry Demands for More Demeaning Acts, Professor Says." *Guelph Mercury*, November 26, A6.

Hamilton, Jane. 2005. "Lap-Dance King Stabbed at Club: Cops Link Knife Attack to Gangland Feud for Control of Capital's Sex lndusty." *Sunday Mail*, April 17, 37.

Hanna, Judith Lynne. 1998. "Undressing the First Amendment and Corsetting the Striptease Dancer." *Drama Review* 42(2): 38–69.

Haughey, Nuala. 2003. "Lap-Dancing Cannot Shed Seedy Side." *Irish Times*, June 7, 4.

Holsopple, Kelly. 1998. *Strip Club Testimony.* Minneapolis: Freedom and Justice Center for Prostitution Resources. http://www.ccv.org/downloads/pdf/Strip_club_study.pdf.

Jeffreys, Sheila. 1997. *The Idea of Prostitution.* Melbourne: Spinifex.

———. 1999. "Globalizing Sexual Exploitation: Sex Tourism and the Traffic in Women." *Leisure Studies* 18(3):179–96.

———. 2004. "Prostitution as a Harmful Cultural Practice." In *Not for Sale: Feminists Resisting Prostitution and Pornography*, ed. Christine Stark and Rebecca Whisnant, 386–99. Melbourne: Spinifex.

Jones, Peter, Peter Shears, and David Hillier. 2003. "Retailing and the Regulatory State: A Case Study of Lap Dancing Clubs in the UK." *International Journal of Retail and Distribution Management* 31(4):214–19.

Kennedy, Les. 2006. "Bikies Face Court after Raid on Alleged Firearm Stash." *Sydney Morning Herald*, May 4, 5.

Lane, Frederick S., III. 2001. *Obscene Profits: The Entrepreneurs of Pornography in the Cyber Age.* New York: Routledge.

Lewis, Jacqueline. 2000. "Controlling Lap Dancing: Law, Morality, and Sex Work." In *Sex for Sale: Prostitution, Pornography, and the Sex Industry,* ed. Ronald Weitzer, 203–16. New York: Routledge.

Liepe-Levinson, Katherine. 2002. *Strip Show: Performances of Gender and Desire.* New York: Routledge.

Lublin, Joann S. 2006. "Harassment Issue Roils Firms: Foreigners Find Laws in U.S. Are Stricter than Other Countries." *Wall Steet Journal*, May 15, 33.

Lynn, Matthew. 2006. "Morgan Stanley Can't Declare War on Lap Dancers." *Bloomberg.com*, January 11.

Macklin, Audrey. 2003. "Dancing across Borders: 'Exotic Dancers,' Trafficking, and Canadian Immigration Policy." *International Migration Review* 37(2): 464–500.

Mani, Ram. 2004. "Risk Management for Dancers, Part 2." *Strip-magazine.com*, August 31. http://www.strip-magazine.com/mmagazine/new_welcome.php?subaction=showfull&id=109398367&archive=&start_from=&ucat=3&category=3.

Montgomery, Dave. 2005. "Industry Trying to Take Its Image Upscale." *Fort Worth Star-Telegram*, October 3. http://www.accessmylibrary.com/coms2/summary_0286-9666939_ITM.

Monzini, Paola. 2005. *Sex Traffic: Prostitution, Crime, and Exploitation*. Trans. Patrick Camiller. London: Zed.

Morgan, Laurie A., and Karin A. Martin. 2006. "Taking Women Professionals Out of the Office: The Case of Women in Sales." *Gender and Society* 20(1): 108–28.

Murray, Penelope, and Peter Wilson, eds. 2004. *Music and the Muses: The Culture of Mousikê in the Classical Athenian City*. Oxford: Oxford University Press.

Parry, Wayne. 2006. "Traffickers Exploit Foreign Women at NJ Bars and Brothels." *Associated Press Newswires*, May 3.

Passar, Dawn. n.d. "Exotic Dancers," interview by Siobhan Brooks. *Shaping San Francisco*, http://www.shapingsf.org/ezine/womens/dancers/main.html.

Paul, Pamela. 2005. *Pornified: How Pornography Is Transforming Our Lives, Our Relationships, and Our Families*. New York: Times Books.

Poulin, Richard. 2005. *La mondialisation des industries du sexe: Prostitution, pornographic, traite des fammies et des enfants* [The globalization of the sex industry: Prostitution, pornography, the trafficking of women and children]. Paris: Imago.

Rousewell, Dean. 2006. "Chel Shocked Exclusive: Charles and Camilla's Anniversary Joy as Prince Faces Showdown with Lover after Lap-Dance Antics Chelsy Fury at Harry's Shame. Now He Fears It's Over." *The People*, April 9. http://www.people.co.uk/news/tm_objectid=16921837%26method=full%26siteid=93463%26headline=chel%2dshocked-name_page.html.

Saeed, Fouzia. 2001. *Taboo! The Hidden Culture of a Red Light Area*. Karachi: Oxford University Press.

Sawyer, Diane, and Bill Weir. 2006. "Undercover Stripper: Tyra Banks Spies on Different World." *Good Morning America*, March 1, ABC News Transcripts.

Schweitzer, Dahlia. 2000. "Striptease: The Art of Spectacle and Transgression." *Journal of Popular Culture* 34(1):65–75.

STAR. 2004. "Dancing Matters." STAR (Sex Trade Advocacy and Research). http://web2.uwindsor.ca/courses/sociology/maticka/star/pdfs/dancing_matters_prnt.pdf.

Stossel, John. 2005. "Women Who Dance: A Look at the Lives of Strippers." *ABC News*, April 15, ABC News Transcripts.

Suren, Asunción, and Robert Stiefvater. 1998. "Topless Dancing: A Case for Recreational Identity." In *Sex Tourism and Prostitution: Aspects of Leisure, Recreation, and Work*, ed. Martin Oppermann, 107–15. New York: Cognizant Communication Corporation.

Taylor, Ian, and Ruth Jamieson. 1999. "Sex Trafficking and the Mainstream of Market Culture: Challenges to Organized Crime Analysis." *Crime, Law and Social Change* 32(3):257–78.

Tyke. 2003. "Advice for Would Be Strippers/Pole/Lap Dancers." *Strip-magazine.com*, April 6. hrtp://www.strip-magazine.com/mmagazine/new_welcome.php?subaction=showfull&id=1090341882&ucat=3.

———. 2005. "Get the May Gossip from the Strip, Lap, and Exotic Dancers Scene in UK!" *Strip-magazine.com*, May 4. http://www.strip-magazine.com/mmagazine/new_welcome.php?subaction=showfull&id=1115239580&ucat=7.

———. 2006. "London's Lap Dancing Scene Gossip for the New Year! London Strip Scene Gossip" *Strip-magazine.com*, January. http://www.strip-magazine.com/mmagazine/new_welcome.php?subaction=showfull&id=1135201134&ucat=7.

Valler, Dean. 2005. "Business Visitors Expect This on Agenda." *Coventry Evening Telegraph*, November 9, 8.

Washburn, David, and Jennifer Davies. 2004. "Shifting Fortunes: Long Targeted by Tough Zoning and Conduct Laws, S.D. Strip Club Industry Is Less Lucrative Today." *San Diego Union-Tribune*, October 19, A1.

Wheeler, Caroline. 2003, "Forger Being a Prostitute, Have a New Career in . . . Lap Dancing: Union's Amazing Offer to Retrain Hookers." *Sunday Mercury*, December 14, 7.

Whittaker, Paul, and Rory Callinan. 1999. "Pole Position." *Courier Mail*, July 24, 5.

PART VII

EDUCATION AND SCHOOLS

In the United States, education is heralded as the great leveler of class, racial, and gender inequalities, promising social mobility to working-class and nonwhite youth, and to women and girls. The reality often falls short, as social inequalities are often reproduced within schools. But while holding out the promise of upward social mobility, what do schools teach about gender? As all of the articles in the section attest, schools teach far more than the standard curriculum.

What do schools teach children about themselves? Popular culture and educational institutions are imbued with gendered images of "nice girls" and "naughty boys." Boys in our culture are thought of as naughty and rambunctious, but innocent. When they commit minor transgressions, they are frequently let off the hook by the idea that "boys will be boys," and that their natural development entails mischievous tumbles with "snakes and snails and puppy dog tails." This, afterall, is seen as preparation for manhood. But as Ann Ferguson's research, based on a detailed ethnographic study in Oakland schools and neighborhoods shows, boys' special dispensation for transgressive behavior comes packaged with white racial privilege. When inner-city African American boys misbehave, they do not receive the protections of childhood. African American elementary school boys are routinely perceived to be hyper-dangerous and plain old bad, and this has serious repercussions in many arenas, including education.

In the next chapter, Carla O'Conner and her colleagues consider how the culture of Black femininity shapes successful educational outcomes for black women. Based on interviews with black women who are first-generation college graduates, they find that a culture and family socialization of black femininity—which values girls' self-sufficiency, independence and assertiveness—positively supports black women's educational achievement. In the following chapter, the focus remains on girls, but here the subjects are high achieving white and Mexican American working class high school students. Based on ethnographic and interview research, Julie Bettie shows that these teens must not only show their mastery of classroom work, but they must carefully navigate relations with the other "prep" students, and here negotiating class and racial differences is paramount. In some cases, a bicultural class identity becomes a necessary resource. The final article in this section is also based on ethnographic research at a high school, and here, C.J. Pascoe examines the intersecting relations between homophobia, race, and adolescent masculinity. Being called a "faggot" or a "fag" remains an enduringly popular insult among high school boys, and in some cases, it is also a racialized epithet.

38

Naughty by Nature

ANN ARNETT FERGUSON

Two representations of black masculinity are widespread in society and school today. They are the images of the African American male as a criminal and as an endangered species. These images are routinely used as resources to interpret and explain behavior by teachers at Rosa Parks School when they make punishment decisions. An ensemble of historical meanings and their social effects is contained within these images.

The image of the black male criminal is more familiar because of its prevalence in the print and electronic media as well as in scholarly work. The headlines of newspaper articles and magazines sound the alarm dramatically as the presence of black males in public space has come to signify danger and a threat to personal safety. But this is not just media hype. Bleak statistics give substance to the figure of the criminal. Black males are disproportionately in jails: they make up 6 percent of the population of the United States, but 45 percent of the inmates in state and federal prisons; they are imprisoned at six times the rate of whites.[1] In the state of California, one-third of African American men in their twenties are in prison, on parole, or on probation, in contrast to 5 percent of white males in the same age group. This is nearly five times the number who attend four-year colleges in the state.[2] The mor-

tality rate for African American boys fourteen years of age and under is approximately 50 percent higher than for the comparable group of white male youth, with the leading cause of death being homicide.[3]

The second image, that of the black male as an endangered species, is one which has largely emanated from African American social scientists and journalists who are deeply concerned about the criminalization and high mortality rate among African American youth.[4] It represents him as being marginalized to the point of oblivion. While this discourse emanates from a sympathetic perspective, in the final analysis the focus is all too often on individual maladaptive behavior and black mothering practices as the problem rather than on the social structure in which this endangerment occurs.

These two cultural representations are rooted in actual material conditions and reflect existing social conditions and relations that they appear to sum up for us. They are lodged in theories, in commonsense understandings of self in relation to others in the world as well as in popular culture and the media. But they are condensations, extrapolations, that emphasize certain elements and gloss over others. They represent a narrow selection from the multiplicity, the heterogeneity of actual relations in society.

Since both of these images come to be used for identifying, classification, and decision making by teachers at Rosa Parks School, it is necessary to analyze the manner in which these images, or cultural representations of difference, are produced through a racial discursive formation. Then we can explain how they are utilized by teachers in the exercise of school rules to produce a context in which African American boys become more visible, more culpable as "rule-breakers."

A central element of a racist discursive formation is the production of subjects as essentially different by virtue of their "race." Historically, the circulation of images that represent this difference has been a powerful technique in this production.[5] Specifically, blacks have been represented as essentially different from whites, as the constitutive Other that regulates and confirms "whiteness." Images of Africans as savage, animalistic, subhuman without history or culture—the diametric opposite of that of Europeans—rationalized and perpetuated a system of slavery. After slavery was abolished, images of people of African descent as hypersexual, shiftless, lazy, and of inferior intellect, legitimated a system that continued to deny right of citizenship to blacks on the basis of race difference. This regime of truth about race was articulated through scientific experiments and "discoveries," law, social custom, popular culture, folklore, and common sense. And for three hundred years, from the seventeenth century to the middle of the twentieth century, this racial distinction was policed through open and unrestrained physical violence. The enforcement of race difference was conscious, overt, and institutionalized.

In the contemporary period, the production of a racial Other and the constitution and regulation of racial difference has worked increasingly through mass-produced images that are omnipresent in our lives. At this moment in time it is through culture—or culturalism[6]—that difference is primarily asserted. This modern-day form for producing racism specifically operates through symbolic violence and representations of Blackness that circulate through the mass media, cinematic images and popular music, rather than through the legal forms of the past. The representational becomes a potent vehicle for the transmission of racial meanings that reproduce relations of differ-

ence, of division, and of power. These "controlling images" make "racism, sexism, and poverty appear to be natural, normal, and an inevitable part of everyday life."[7]

CULTURAL REPRESENTATIONS OF "DIFFERENCE"

The behavior of African American boys in school is perceived by adults at Rosa Parks School through a filter of overlapping representations of three socially invented categories of "difference": age, gender, and race. These are grounded in the commonsense, taken-for-granted notion that existing social divisions reflect biological and natural dispositional differences among humans: so children are essentially different from adults, males from females, blacks from whites.[8] At the intersection of this complex of subject positions are African American boys who are doubly displaced: as black children, they are not seen as childlike but adultified; as black males, they are denied the masculine dispensation constituting white males as being "naturally naughty" and are discerned as willfully bad. Let us look more closely at this displacement.

The dominant cultural representation of childhood is as closer to nature, as less social, less human. Childhood is assumed to be a stage of development: culture, morality, sociability is written on children in an unfolding process by adults (who are seen as fully "developed," made by culture not nature) in institutions like family and school. On the one hand, children are assumed to be dissembling, devious, because they are more egocentric. On the other hand, there is an attribution of innocence to their wrongdoing. In both cases, this is understood to be a temporary condition, a stage prior to maturity. So they must be socialized to fully understand the meaning of their acts.

The language used to describe "children in general" by educators illustrates this paradox. At one districtwide workshop for adult school volunteers that I attended, children were described by the classroom teacher running the workshop as being "like little plants, they need attention, they gobble it up." Later in the session, the same presenter invoked the other dominant representation of children as devious, manipulative, and powerful. "They'll run a number on you. They're little lawyers, con artists, manipulators—and they usually win. They're good at it. Their strategy is to get you off task. They pull you into their whirlwind."

These two versions of childhood express the contradictory qualities that adults map onto their interactions with children in general. The first description of children as "little plants," childhood as identical with nature, is embedded in the ideology of childhood. The second version that presents children as powerful, as self-centered, with an agenda and purpose of their own, arises out of the experience adults have exercising authority over children. In actual relations of power, in a twist, as children become the objects of control, they become devious "con artists" and adults become innocent, pristine in relation to them. In both instances, childhood has been constructed as different in essence from adulthood, as a phase of biological, psychological, and social development with predictable attributes.

Even though we treat it this way, the category "child" does not describe and contain a homogeneous and naturally occurring group of individuals at a certain stage of human development. The social meaning of childhood has changed profoundly over time.[9] What it means to be a child varies dramatically by virtue of location in cross-cutting categories of class, gender, and race.[10]

Historically, the existence of African American children has been constituted differently through economic practices, the law, social policy, and visual imagery. This difference has been projected in an ensemble of images of black youth as not childlike. In the early decades of this century, representations of black children as pickaninnies depicted them as verminlike, voracious, dirty, grinning, animal-like savages. They were also depicted as the laugh-provoking butt of aggressive, predatory behavior; natural victims, therefore victimizable. An example of this was their depiction in popular lore as "alligator bait." Objects such as postcards, souvenir spoons, letter-openers and cigar-box labels were decorated with figures of half-naked black children vainly attempting to escape the open toothy jaws of hungry alligators.[11]

Today's representations of black children still bear traces of these earlier depictions. The media demo-

nization of very young black boys who are charged with committing serious crimes is one example. In these cases there is rarely the collective soul-searching for answers to the question of how "kids like this" could have committed these acts that occurs when white kids are involved. Rather, the answer to the question seems to be inherent in the disposition of the kids themselves.[12] The image of the young black male as an endangered species revitalizes the animalistic trope. Positioned as part of nature, his essence is described through language otherwise reserved for wildlife that has been decimated to the point of extinction. Characterized as a "species," they are cut off from other members of family and community and isolated as a form of prey.

There is continuity, but there is a significant new twist to the images. The endangered species and the criminal are mirror images. Either as criminal perpetrator or as endangered victim, contemporary imagery proclaims black males to be responsible for their fate. The discourse of individual choice and responsibility elides the social and economic context and locates predation as coming from within. It is their own maladaptive and inappropriate behavior that causes African Americans to self-destruct. As an endangered species, they are stuck in an obsolete stage of social evolution, unable to adapt to the present. As criminals, they are a threat to themselves, to each other, as well as to society in general.

As black children's behavior is refracted through the lens of these two cultural images, it is "adultified." By this I mean their transgressions are made to take on a sinister, intentional, fully conscious tone that is stripped of any element of childish naïveté. The discourse of childhood as an unfolding developmental stage in the life cycle is displaced in this mode of framing school trouble. Adultification is visible in the way African American elementary school pupils are talked about by school adults.

One of the teachers, a white woman who prided herself on the multicultural emphasis in her classroom, invoked the image of African American children as "looters" in lamenting the disappearance of books from the class library. This characterization is especially meaningful because her statement, which was made at the end of the school year that had included the riots in Los Angeles, invoked that event as a framework for making children's behavior intelligible.

> I've lost so many library books this term. There are quite a few kids who don't have any books at home, so I let them borrow them. I didn't sign them out because I thought I could trust the kids. I sent a letter home to parents asking them to look for them and turn them in. But none have come in. I just don't feel the same. *It's just like the looting in Los Angeles.*

By identifying those who don't have books at home as "looters," the teacher has excluded the white children in the class, who all come from more middle-class backgrounds so, it is assumed, "have books at home." In the case of the African American kids, what might be interpreted as the careless behavior of children is displaced by images of adult acts of theft that conjure up violence and mayhem. The African American children in this teacher's classroom and their families are seen not in relation to images of childhood, but in relation to the television images of crowds rampaging through South Central Los Angeles in the aftermath of the verdict of the police officers who beat Rodney King. Through this frame, the children embody a willful, destructive, and irrational disregard for property rather than simple carelessness. Racial difference is mediated through culturalism: blacks are understood as a group undifferentiated by age or status with the proclivity and values to disregard the rights and welfare of others.

Adultification is a central mechanism in the interpretive framing of gender roles. African American girls are constituted as different through this process. A notion of sexual passivity and innocence that prevails for white female children is displaced by the image of African American females as sexual beings: as immanent mothers, girlfriends, and sexual partners of the boys in the room.[13] Though these girls may be strong, assertive, or troublesome, teachers evaluate their potential in ways that attribute to them an inevitable, potent sexuality that flares up early and that, according to one teacher, lets them permit men to run all over them, to take advantage of them. An incident in the Punishing Room that I recorded in my field notes made visible the way that adult perceptions of youthful behavior were filtered through racial representa-

tions. African American boys and girls who misbehaved were not just breaking a rule out of high spirits and needing to be chastised for the act, but were adultified, gendered figures whose futures were already inscribed and foreclosed within a racial order:

> Two girls, Adila and a friend, burst into the room followed by Miss Benton a black sixth-grade teacher and a group of five African American boys from her class. Miss Benton is yelling at the girls because they have been jumping in the hallway and one has knocked down part of a display on the bulletin board which she and her class put up the day before. She is yelling at the two girls about how they're wasting time. This is what she says: "You're doing exactly what they want you to do. You're playing into their hands. Look at me! Next going to be tracking you."
>
> One of the girls asks her rather sullenly who "they" is.
>
> Miss Benton is furious. "Society, that's who. You should be leading the class, not fooling around jumping around in the hallway. Someone has to give pride to the community. All the black men are on drugs, or in jail, or killing each other. Someone has got to hold it together. And the women have to do it. And you're jumping up and down in the hallway."
>
> I wonder what the black boys who have followed in the wake of the drama make of this assessment of their future, seemingly already etched in stone. The teacher's words to the girls are supposed to inspire them to leadership. The message for the boys is a dispiriting one.

Tracks have already been laid down for sixth-grade girls toward a specifically feminized responsibility (and, what is more prevalent, blame) for the welfare of the community, while males are bound for jail as a consequence of their own socially and self-destructive acts.

There is a second displacement from the norm in the representation of black males. The hegemonic, cultural image of the essential "nature" of males is that they are different from females in the meaning of their acts. Boys will be boys: they are mischievous, they get into trouble, they can stand up for themselves. This vision of masculinity is rooted in the notion of an essential sex difference based on biology, hormones, uncontrollable urges, true personalities. Boys are naturally more physical, more active. Boys are naughty by *nature*. There is something suspect about the boy who is "too docile," "like a girl." As a result, rule breaking on the part of boys is looked at as something-they-can't-help, a natural expression of masculinity in a civilizing process.

This incitement of boys to be "boylike" is deeply inscribed in our mainstream culture, winning hearts and stirring imaginations in the way that the pale counterpart, the obedient boy, does not. . . .

African American boys are not accorded the masculine dispensation of being "naturally" naughty. Instead the school reads their expression and display of masculine naughtiness as a sign of an inherent vicious, insubordinate nature that as a threat to order must be controlled. Consequently, school adults view any display of masculine mettle on the part of these boys through body language or verbal rejoinders as a sign of insubordination. In confrontation with adults, what is required from them is a performance of absolute docility that goes against the grain of masculinity. Black boys are expected to internalize a ritual obeisance in such exchanges so that the performance of docility appears to come naturally. According to the vice principal, "These children have to learn not to talk back. They must know that if the adult says you're wrong, then you're wrong. They must not resist, must go along with it, and take their punishment," he says.

This is not a lesson that all children are required to learn, however. The disciplining of the body within school rules has specific race and gender overtones. For black boys, the enactment of docility is a preparation for adult racialized survival rituals of which the African American adults in the school are especially cognizant. For African American boys bodily forms of expressiveness have repercussions in the world outside the chain-link fence of the school. The body must be taught to endure humiliation in preparation for future enactments of submission. The vice principal articulated the racialized texture of decorum when he deplored one of the Troublemakers', Lamar's, propensity to talk back and argue with teachers.

Lamar had been late getting into line at the end of recess, and the teacher had taken away his football. Lamar argued and so the teacher gave him detention. Mr. Russell spelled out what an African American male needed to learn about confrontations with power.

Look, I've told him before about getting into these show-down situations—where he either has to show off to save face, then if he doesn't get his way then he goes wild. He won't get away with it in this school. Not with me, not with Mr. Harmon. But I know he's going to try it somewhere outside and it's going to get him in *real* trouble. He has to learn to ignore, to walk away, not to get into power struggles.

Mr. Russell's objective is to hammer into Lamar's head what he believes is the essential lesson for young black males to learn if they are to get anywhere in life: to act out obeisance is to survive. The specter of the Rodney King beating by the Los Angeles Police Department provided the backdrop for this conversation, as the trial of the police officers had just begun. The defense lawyer for the LAPD was arguing that Rodney King could have stopped the beating at any time if he had chosen.

This apprehension of black boys as inherently different both in terms of character and of their place in the social order is a crucial factor in teacher disciplinary practices. . . .

Let us examine now more closely some widespread modes of categorizing African American boys, the normalizing judgments that they circulate, and the consequences these have on disciplinary intervention and punishment.

BEING "AT-RISK": IDENTIFYING PRACTICE

The range of normalizing judgments for African American males is bounded by the image of the ideal pupil at one end of the spectrum and the unsalvageable student who is criminally inclined at the other end. The ideal type of student is characterized here by a white sixth-grade teacher:

Well, it consists of, first of all, to be able to follow directions. Any direction that I give. Whether it's get this out, whether it's put this away, whether it's turn to this page or whatever, they follow it, and they come in and they're ready to work. It doesn't matter high skill or low skill, they're ready to work and they know that's what they're here for. Behaviorally, they're appropriate all day long. When it's time for them to listen, they listen. The way I see it, by sixth grade, the ideal student is one that can sit and listen and learn from me—work with their peers, and take responsibility on themselves and understand what is next, what is expected of them.

This teacher, however, drew on the image of the Good Bad Boy when she described the qualities of her "ideal" male student, a white boy in her class. Here the docility of the generic ideal student becomes the essentially naughty-by-nature male:

> He's not really Goody Two-shoes, you know. He's not quiet and perfect. He'll take risks. He'll say the wrong answer. He'll fool around and have to be reprimanded in class. There's a nice balance to him.

The modal category for African American boys is "at-risk" of failure. The concept of "at-riskness" is central to a discourse about the contemporary crisis in urban schools in America that explains children's failure as largely the consequence of their attitudes and behaviors as well as those of their families. In early stages of schooling they are identified as "at-risk" of failing, as "at-risk" of being school drop-outs. The category has been invested with enormous power to identify, explain, and predict futures. For example, a white fifth-grade teacher told me with sincere concern that as she looked around at her class, she could feel certain that about only four out of the twenty-one students would eventually graduate from high school. Each year, she said, it seemed to get worse.

Images of family play a strong role in teacher assessments and decisions about at-risk children. These enter into the evaluative process to confirm an original judgment. Families of at-risk children are said to lack parental skills; they do not give their children the kind of support that would build "self-esteem" necessary for school achievement. But this knowledge of family is superficial, inflamed by cultural representations and distorted through a rumor mill.

The children themselves are supposed to betray the lack of love and attention at home through their own "needy" behavior in the classroom. According to the teachers, these are pupils who are always demanding attention and will work well only in one-to-one or small-group situations because of this neglect at home. They take up more than their share of time and space. Donel, one of the African American boys who has been identified as at-risk by the school, is described by his teacher:

> He's a boy with a lot of energy and usually uncontrolled energy. He's very loud in the classroom, very inappropriate in the class. He has a great sense of humor, but again its inappropriate. I would say most of the time that his mouth is open, it's inappropriate, it's too loud, it's disrupting. But other than that [dry laugh] he's a great kid. You know if I didn't have to teach him, if it was a recreational setting, it would be fine.

So Donel is marked as "inappropriate" through the very configuration of self that school rules regulate: bodies, language, presentation of self. The stringent exercise of what is deemed appropriate as an instrument of assessment of at-riskness governs how the behavior of a child is understood. The notion of appropriate behavior in describing the ideal pupil earlier, and here as a way of characterizing a Troublemaker, reveals the broad latitude for interpretation and cultural framing of events. For one boy, "fooling around" behavior provides the balance between being a "real" boy and being a "goody-goody," while for the other, the conduct is seen through a different lens as "inappropriate," "loud," "disruptive."

Once a child is labeled "at-risk," he becomes more visible within the classroom, more likely to be singled out and punished for rule-breaking activity. An outburst by an African American boy already labeled as "at-risk" was the occasion for him to be singled out and made an example of the consequences of bad behavior before an audience of his peers; this was an occasion for a teacher to (re)mark the identity of a boy as disruptive. . . .

. . . Once a reputation has been established, the boy's behavior is usually refigured within a framework that is no longer about childish misdemeanors but comes to be an ominous portent of things to come. They are tagged with futures: "He's on the fast track to San Quentin Prison," and "That one has a jail-cell with his name on it." For several reasons, these boys are more likely to be singled out and punished than other children. They are more closely watched. They are more likely to be seen as intentionally doing wrong than a boy who is considered to be a Good Bad Boy. Teachers are more likely to use the "moral principle" in determining whether to call attention to misdemeanors because "at-risk" children need discipline, but also as an example to the group, especially to other African American boys who are "endangered." The possibility of contagion must be eliminated. Those with reputations must be isolated, kept away from the others. Kids are told to stay away from them: "You know what will happen if you go over there." In the case of boys with reputations, minor infractions are more likely to escalate into major punishments.

UNSALVAGEABLE STUDENTS

In the range of normalizing judgments, there is a group of African American boys identified by school personnel as, in the words of a teacher, "insalvageable." This term and the condition it speaks to is specifically about masculinity. School personnel argue over whether these unsalvageable boys should be given access even to the special programs designed for those who are failing in school. Should resources, defined as scarce, be wasted on these boys for whom there is no hope? Should energy and money be put instead into children who can be saved? I have heard teachers argue on both sides of the question. These "boys for whom there is no hope" get caught up in the school's punishment system: surveillance, isolation, detention, and ever more severe punishment.

These are children who are not children. These are boys who are already men. So a discourse that positions masculinity as "naturally" naughty is reframed for African American boys around racialized representations of gendered subjects. They come to stand as if already adult, bearers of adult fates inscribed within a racial order.

NOTES

1. *New York Times,* September 13, 1994, 1.

2. *Los Angeles Times,* November 2, 1990, 3.

3. G. Jaynes and R. Williams Jr., eds., *A Common Destiny: Blacks in American Society* (Washington, D.C.: National Academic Press, 1989), 405, 498.

4. See, for example, Jewelle Taylor Gibbs, "Young Black Males in America: Endangered, Embittered, and Embattled," in Jewelle Taylor Gibbs et al., *Young, Black, and Male in America: An Endangered Species* (New York: Auburn House, 1988); Richard Majors and Janer Mancini Billson, *Cool Pose: The Dilemmas of Black Manhood in America* (New York: Lexington Press, 1992); Jawanza Kunjufu, *Countering the Conspiracy to Destroy Black Boys,* 2 vols. (Chicago: African American Images, 1985).

5. See, for example, W. E. B. Du Bois, *Souls of Black Folk* (1903); reprint, New York: Bantam, 1989): Frantz Fanon, *Black Skins, White Masks,* trans. Charles Lam Markmann (New York: Grove Press, 1967); Stuart Hall, "The Rediscovery of 'Ideology': Return of the Repressed in Media Studies." in *Culture, Society, and the Media,* ed. Michael Gurevitch et al. (New York: Methuen, 1982); Leith Mullings, "Images, Ideology, and Women of Color," in *Women of Color in U.S. Society,* ed. Maxine Baca Zinn and Bonnie Thornton Dill (Philadelphia: Temple University Press, 1994); Edward Said, *Orientalism* (New York: Vintage, 1978).

6. Gilroy, *Small Acts,* 24, argues that "the culturalism of the new racism has gone hand in hand with a definition of race as a matter of difference rather than a question of hierarchy."

7. Collins, *Black Feminist Thought,* 68.

8. While many of the staff at Rosa Parks School would agree at an abstract level that social divisions of gender and race are culturally and historical produced, their actual talk about these social distinctions as well as their everyday expectations, perceptions, and interactions affirm the notion that these categories reflect intrinsic, *real* differences.

9. See, for example, Phillipe Ariès, *Centuries of Childhood: A Social History of Family Life* (New York: Vintage, 1962).

10. Thorne, *Gender Play;* and Valerie Polakow, *Lives on the Edge: Single Mothers and Their Children in the Other America* (Chicago: University of Chicago Press, 1993).

11. Patricia Turner, *Ceramic Uncles and Celluloid Mammies: Black Images and Their Influence on Culture* (New York: Anchor, 1994), 36.

12. A particularly racist and pernicious example of this was the statement by the administrator of the Alcohol, Drug Abuse, and Mental Health Administration. Dr. Frederick K. Goodwin, who stated without any qualms: "If you look, for example, at male monkeys, especially in the wild, roughly half of them survive to adulthood. The other half die by violence. That is the natural way of it for males, to knock each other off and, in fact, there are some interesting evolutionary implications. . . . The same hyper aggressive monkeys who kill each other are also hyper sexual, so they copulate more and therefore they reproduce more to offset the fact that half of them are dying." He then drew an analogy with the "high impact [of] inner city areas with the loss of some of the civilizing evolutionary things that we have built up. . . . Maybe it isn't just the careless

use of the word when people call certain areas of certain cities, jungles." Quoted in Jerome G. Miller, *Search and Destroy: African American Males in the Criminal Justice System* (New York: Cambridge University Press, 1996), 212–13.

13. The consensus among teachers in the school about educational inequity focuses on sexism. Many of the teachers speak seriously and openly about their concern that girls are being treated differently than boys in school: girls are neglected in the curriculum, overlooked in classrooms, underencouraged academically, and harassed by boys. A number of recent studies support the concern that even the well-intentioned teacher tends to spend less classroom time with girls because boys demand so much of their attention. These studies generally gloss over racial difference as well as make the assumption that *quantity* rather than *quality* of attention is the key factor in fostering positive sense of self in academic setting. See, for example, Myra Sadker and David Sadker, *Failing at Fairness: How America's Schools Cheat Girls* (New York: C. Scribner's Sons, 1994). Linda Grant looks at both race and gender as she examines the roles that first- and second-grade African American girls play in desegregated classrooms. She finds that African American girls and white girls are positioned quite differently vis-à-vis teachers. In the classrooms she observed, white girls were called upon to play an academic role in comparison with African American girls, who were cast in the role of teacher's helpers, in monitoring and controlling other kids in the room, and as intermediaries between peers. She concluded that black girls were encouraged in stereotypical female adult roles that stress service and nurture, while white girls were encouraged to press toward high academic achievement. Most important for this study, Grant mentions in passing that black boys in the room receive the most consistent negative attention and were assessed as having a lower academic ability than any other group by teachers. See Linda Grant, "Helpers, Enforcers, and Go-Betweens: Black Females in Elementary School Classrooms, " in *Women of Color in U.S. Society*, ed. Maxine Baca Zinn and Bonnie Thornton Dill (Philadelphia: University of Pennsylvania Press, 1994).

39

The Culture of Black Femininity and School Success

Carla O'Connor

R. L'Heureux Lewis

Jennifer Mueller

Now my grandfather was a provider for his family, and he taught his sons to be providers. But they [grandmother and grandfather] also taught their girls to stand up. So there was never any question that I was going to work, or that I was waiting for someone to rescue me. That was not part of my upbringing. People didn't get rescued. You did what you had to do in order to do what you had to do.

—*Theresa Renier, 46 years old, December, 1997*

She was out there finger popping and trying to get through this world. And the world was trying to pull her down and tear her apart. And they didn't know what they were up against. She just kept on coming back for more. And smashing hands and "Here I am, still. Skin a cat another way. Get that skin off that cat."

—*Sidney Ellwood, 60 years old, speaking about herself, December, 1997*

SIDNEY ELLWOOD AND THERESA RENIER, like the other 17 women featured in this chapter, are black women of lower social class origins who became first-generation college graduates. Like the other women, Ellwood and Renier vividly recalled how being black,

being female, and being poor or working class had circumscribed their educational opportunity and threatened their chances of going to and completing college. But Ellwood, Renier, and the other women also discussed how living life on the margins also facilitated their ability to succeed in school. It was from these margins that they were often provided the impetus, orientations, and dispositions necessary for persevering through school. It was also there that they cultivated strategies necessary for negotiating or confronting those barriers that promised to limit their educational attainment and subsequent life chances.

Herein, we show how living life at the intersections of race and gender developed these women's sensibilities that they would not be "rescued." Rather, they would have to do what they had to do to smash those hands that promised to pull them down, tear them apart, and circumscribe their educational outcomes. We reveal how black womanhood or, more precisely, cultural conventions of black femininity, enabled these women to "keep coming back" academically to eventually become the first (or among the first) in their families to receive a college and, in many cases, a graduate school degree.

In this chapter, cultural conventions of femininity signify culturally inscribed presumptions about how women should look, how they should behave, and for what roles they should assume or hope. In the case of the women featured in this text, we specifically focus on how gender socialization and sex role expectations were articulated within the black community to affect the actions and imaginations of these women in ways that had a positive impact on their experience with school.

THE CULTURE OF BLACK FEMININITY AND SCHOOL EXPERIENCES

Researchers who study conventions of black femininity repeatedly document the finding that black people raise their girls to be assertive and independent (Lewis, 1975; Slevin & Wingrove, 1998). Additionally, black families socialize their girls not only to take the roles of wife and mother, but to assume the role of worker. The heightened attention to developing voice, independence, and the worker identity has been linked to black men's historic marginalization in the workforce relative to white men. Black families necessarily had to raise their daughters in ways that would facilitate their girls' ability to assume partial, if not full, responsibility for the financial survival of their families upon becoming women (Lewis, 1975; Ward, 1996).

On the one hand, researchers have argued that this orientation toward voice and independence is a positive adaptation. Unlike white women—particularly upper-middle-class, white women—black women are not necessarily expected to silence their experiences, thoughts, and desires in relations with others. Researchers have subsequently suggested that these differential expectations might explain why black girls generally have higher self-esteem than their white and Latina counterparts and why they are able to maintain this esteem throughout adolescence (AAUW, 1991). Fordham (1993) also showed how this orientation toward voice enables the "loud black girl" to "retrieve a safe cultural space" for herself in school—one in which she is not rendered invisible. Instead, she can creatively subvert the expectations that she be female (rather than male) in a black (and not a white) sense.

Finally, Holland and Eisenhart (1990) showed that as a consequence of how black femininity is articulated, black *women*, compared to their white counterparts, were less preoccupied with romance and were less likely to be manipulated by men. Researchers, however, associate these same expressions of black women's agency with negative educational outcomes.

The same voice and power that are said to protect women against the loss of esteem and the loss of a culturally specific gendered self are also said to place them at academic risk when they produce psychological isolation and are realized in conflict with school officials (Fordham, 1993; Taylor, Gilligan, & Sullivan, 1995). In the case of Fordham's (1993) work, she identified a high-achieving African American female who used her voice to affirm her existence. This expression of voice "propel[led] this young woman to the margins of good behavior'" but never "actually forc[ed] her into the realm of 'bad behavior.'" Fordham, however, maintained that most "loud black girls" are not as strategic in their use of voice, and such "loudness" eventually "mutilates the academic achievement of large numbers of female African American students" (p. 5). Researchers also find that it is often the most assertive low-income and minority girls who leave or are pushed out of school (Fine, 1991; Fine & Zane, 1991). Those more likely to stay in school mute their own voices and express high conformity and limited political awareness.

In a similarly contradictory fashion, Holland and Eisenhart (1990) showed that black women focused less of their attention on men and were less manipulated by them. However, this independence did not translate into strong and consistent efforts in school. Having determined that grades of "C" would be sufficient for completing college, the black women were more likely than the white women to accept this grade. Holland and Eisenhart attributed this less than competitive performance to the black women's recognition that blacks were not equitably rewarded for their efforts in school. In the case of this text, there was nothing about the culture of black femininity that mitigated the negative effects associated with the perception of a limited opportunity structure. The culture of black femininity may have been cast in agentic terms, but such agency did not translate into competitive academic performance.

In sum, when reporting on cultures of femininity, researchers have most often emphasized the reproductive rather than the liberatory nature of these cultures. Having identified the liberatory "potential" of these cultures, this work rarely demonstrated how this potential was articulated in the lives of women to facilitate rather than impede their life chances. What work has been done on the liberatory possibilities and practices of black womanhood has been generally conducted outside of the field of education. This work emphasizes how the culture of black femininity informs the general resilience of black women—especially their ability to maintain their mental health, affirm their identities, and nurture their families (e.g., Collins, 2000; hooks, 1992). Little work examines how this culture is specifically articulated in school to generate academic success. We are therefore left with little indication that there is anything in black women's cultural tool kit that makes them able to work against those aforementioned race- and school-based phenomena that promise to constrain their educational and subsequent life chances. In light of this gap in the literature, this chapter focuses on how particular elements of the culture of black femininity informs black women's educational success rather than their academic vulnerability.

In reporting on the liberatory potential and practices associated with the culture of black femininity, this chapter recognizes that conventions of femininity are not static phenomena. Rather, these conventions change over time in response to shifting social and economic opportunities. Importantly, then, our 19 women are distributed across 3 age cohorts that will be elaborated upon below. This cohort distribution affords us the opportunity to show how cultural conventions of black femininity were differently articulated across time to affect the women's experience with school success. In total then, this chapter will not only discuss the liberatory potential and practices of the culture of black femininity in relation to how well and how far these women went in school but also will show that elements of this culture were differentially reflected over time and thus differentially taken up (or not) by the women to facilitate their educational success. Before discussing the findings of this investigation, we will briefly report on how we documented the voices and experiences of the women in this study.

DOCUMENTING THE WOMEN'S VOICES AND EXPERIENCES

The data for this chapter derive from a larger investigation of the life histories of 19 black women who were first-generation college graduates and grew up in low-income and working-class households. The women were born and then first attended a postsecondary institution within the following age cohorts. Cohort I (the precivil rights era cohort) includes those women who were born between 1926 and 1931 and first attended a postsecondary school before the 1950s. Cohort II (the postcivil rights era cohort) includes those women who were born between 1946 and 1955 and first attended a postsecondary school during the mid-1960s to mid-1970s. Cohort III (the post-Reagan era cohort) represents those women who were born between 1966 and 1970 and first attended a postsecondary school after 1984. All of the respondents were first-generation college graduates, and in all but two cases they were the first in their families to receive a baccalaureate degree. In every case, they were the first females in their immediate families to earn this degree. All of the respondents also attended what I will refer to as "Midwest University" (MU).

We captured the women's life stories via in-depth individual interviews that were audiotaped and transcribed verbatim. For the purposes of this chapter, data analysis was directed toward answering the following questions: (1) What gender-related narratives were communicated in these women's life stories? (2) How did these gender-related narratives reveal constraints to and/or opportunities for educational achievement and mobility? (3) What were the processes by which the women developed, maintained, and exercised commitment to school to attain high levels of education given the representation of gender-based constraints and opportunities that were particular to their space and time? More specifically, we focused on how the women articulated the ways that gender (including how it may have intersected with race and/or social class) operated in their "everyday," as well as within the greater social context in which they grew up. Some of this data was generated in response to questions like the following:

- Did anyone ever talk to you about what it was like to be a woman in general and a black woman in particular?
- Have you experienced or felt any hostility from others because you were female?
- Were there times when you may have benefited from being a woman?
- What were the most significant events affecting the lives of women when you were growing up? How do you think these events affected your life in particular?
- When did you begin dating?
- What messages did you receive about dating or about boys?

The women also volunteered information about how their physical appearance; their experiences as daughters, mothers, and wives; and their being female in school or work affected their life chances and trajectories. Often they would introduce gender-related issues in light of talking about how they experienced other social identities (i.e., racial and social class).

Beginning with within-case analyses, we analyzed each case to identify any data that was relevant to gender. We identified interview excerpts in which the respondents (1) answered a question that either imposed gender as a social category or introduced gender-related issues (e.g., dating), or (2) volunteered information about how their own gender or that of others factored into the experiences they had, were privy to, or about which they were informed. We also attended to the sex of the actors in the respondents' narratives in order to assess whether males and females operated differently in the women's lived experiences and, therefore, provided the women with implicit messages about gender roles, expectations, and experiences. We also examined the women's life stories in an effort to determine whether aspects of the women's narratives appeared consistent with or contradictory to previous research findings about the culture of femininity in general and black femininity in particular. Across-case analyses were subsequently conducted within and then across the three age cohorts in order to interpret any shifts in the content or representation of these gender-based narratives across the age cohorts.

FROM WHENCE THEY CAME

Before reporting on how these 19 women lived and responded to their experiences with how black women should look, the characteristics women should possess, and the roles women should assume, we will offer some basic background information about them. At the time in which the women shared their life stories, they were employed in or retired from a wide variety of professions that signaled their evident upward mobility in light of their lower social class origins. In our efforts to document those origins, we learned that for the most part these women grew up in homes that were solidly working class. With few exceptions, they grew up in two-parent households. And with only one breadwinner in the home, their families in most cases (even when extremely large) generated the financial resources necessary to avoid public or even charitable assistance. Most of the women additionally reported that for much of their childhood their family owned their home (though for the oldest cohort the homes were in most cases built rather than bought by their parents or guardians). In the majority of the cases, such homeownership coincided with the upward mobility of the family. That is, more than half of the women indicated that over time (particularly in relation to buying a first or a larger house) their families moved to "better," safer, and more economically stable communities.

Most of the women also grew up with fairly well educated caretakers. Although none of their primary caretakers was a graduate of a four-year college, seven of the women had at least one parent or guardian who had received some postsecondary school training, and thirteen had at Least one caretaker who had graduated from high school.

Growing up in a financially stable household with two parents who are more, rather than less, educated has long been interpreted as protecting youth against failure in school (see Masten, 1994 for a review). Life in economically viable communities is also positively correlated with higher educational achievements and attainment (e.g., Crane, 1991; Benard, 1991). Consequently, with regards to socioeconomic indices, this sample of women, when taken as a whole, experienced advantages (if only relative) when it came to doing well in school. These socioeconomic advantages did not, however, protect these women against those risks that were specifically tied to them being women, and black women in particular. The women's life stories, among other things, revealed how racism and cultural conventions (both dominant and culturally specific) surrounding how (black) women should look, how they should act, and the roles they should assume and hope for circumscribed their "everyday" experiences and threatened their life chances. But their life stories also revealed that they often drew strength specifically from the culture of black femininity. This culture not only developed their voice and independence but also extended their imaginations regarding life's possibilities. We show how through the coupling of this power and imagination the women came to resist those race- and gender-based expectations and barriers that constrained their access to, progression through, and equitable treatment in school.

THE CULTURE OF BLACK FEMININITY: DEVELOPING VOICE, INDEPENDENCE, AND POSSIBILITY

Across the age cohorts the women discussed the messages they received within the community with regards to how black women should look, how they should behave, and for what roles they should assume or hope. In many instances, these messages seemed orientated toward circumscribing these women's bodies and, to a lesser degree, their life chances. And as might be expected, Cohort I was most apt to discuss how these conventions were directed toward such circumscription. Only in this cohort did women report that it was not only schooling agents but also their own family members who sought to suppress their educational ambitions precisely because they were women. The first, Sidney Ellwood, explained that her father had "slapped [her] face" when he learned that she had applied and had been admitted to Midwest University. Given his own sexism that was articulated via religious dogma, he had determined that women should not go to college because it would make them "worldly" and would cultivate rather than suppress their "evil power." The second, Dee Hawk, remembered that her own mother did not see any point in her pursuing higher ed-

ucation, as she imagined that Hawk would only end up getting married.

Across the age cohorts, the women's stories also revealed that physical indices of femininity required women to be light in complexion, have fine and long hair, and be "thick" (neither fat nor skinny) in body. However, these physical requirements of femininity were more salient in the experiences of Cohort I. Although darker women, skinny women, women who were more round than thick, and women with short hair revealed that they received less if not negative attention from men and were less welcomed into popular or middle-class circles, the oldest cohort (Cohort I) most often referenced how these physical "requirements" impacted their social interactions. The youngest cohort (Cohort III) made the least reference to the influence of these requirements. While these findings are consistent with other accounts of how skin color and hair length, in particular, operated in the black community over time (e.g., Russell, 1992), these women's life stories suggest that these physical requirements of beauty had important educational effects. This was particularly revealed in the case of Cohort I members who, in the absence of school-sanctioned support for their educational ambitions, had to rely heavily on informal social networks to access information and encouragement for their college attendance. Their stories revealed that their physical appearance determined whether they would be welcomed into more elite social circles that had accordant access to knowledge and resources upon which they could draw to facilitate their educational mobility.

With regards to how the women's lives were otherwise circumscribed, they reported (without evident distinctions between the cohorts) that while growing up, restrictions were placed upon their bodies. Sometimes these restrictions were articulated via their inability to move as freely about public space as compared to their brothers and other male counterparts. For example, Leona Holmes recounted that she would often question why her brother experienced a degree of freedom that was not accorded her. She would ask her mother, "And how come he does that?" Her mother would respond, "He's the oldest." Leona further explained, "But, you know, he was the boy. The oldest but a boy again, you know. He's out in the street running wild with my uncle, cause they were like a couple of years apart. No street running for me." Later she added, "He was older than me—yes—but I never reached an age where I could do what he did."

At other times, the women found that these bodily restrictions were a function of how "etiquette" prescribed how, where, when, and with whom they could or could not use or move their bodies. Sometimes indices of etiquette referred to dating etiquette or if and when they could begin dating and in accordance with what rules. The women indicated that compared to the males in their family, they encountered severe or at least more severe dating rules and regulations. Otherwise, etiquette lessons focused on defining the women's physical comportment. For example, when Tia Richardson was asked whether anyone had spoken with her about what it was like to be a woman, in general, and a black woman, in particular, she responded:

> I know definitely etiquette-wise, for lack of a better word, you know. And that came from my mother, my grandparents, extended family. You know, ladies don't do that. How you sit. How you dressed. How you talked. I mean, the whole kind of etiquette side.

In the case of Cohorts II and III as well as for most members of Cohort I, these restrictions on the body did not coincide with familial efforts consciously directed at restricting the women's imaginations of life's possibilities. Thus, in the same breath that Richardson (above) reports on the restrictions she received about being a woman "etiquette-wise," she stressed that no such restrictions were imposed upon her ambitions. In the absence of our prompting and without her skipping a beat, Richardson continued, "Career-wise I was never told that women can't do anything. I was never told that. Never, you know. What do you want to do? [was how I was approached] I was *never* discouraged" (original emphasis).

Repeatedly, the women conveyed that they received communications that they should not be constrained in their ambitions *became* they were women. Sometimes these communications were conveyed in light of what was not said, as when Tia reported that she was "never told that women can't do anything." Other times, these

communications were modeled on the bodies of other women. Sometimes this modeling was reflected in the actions of seemingly ordinary women pursuing more routine activities. For example, when we asked Desiree Strong whether anyone had ever taught her what it meant to be a woman, in general, or a black woman, in particular, she responded:

> Well, first of all, my mother . . . taught me in her own way that *you could do anything*. My mother didn't start driving till I think she was in her 40s.... Got tired of waiting on my father to teach her how to drive. Saved her little change, bought her own car, took driving lessons, was driving. (Original emphasis)

The actions of Desiree s mother conveyed how women could define their power independent of men through more mundane efforts. In other instances, the participants of this study referenced black women who had accomplished seemingly extraordinary acts and were mavericks of a place or a time. For example, when Doreen Kingsley was asked to discuss persons who stood out in her life, she discussed three of the extraordinary women she knew and how each of them provided a model of black womanhood that was distinct from the one afforded by her mother. She spoke of Mrs. Blaine who was "so active out in the community . . . and . . . was always very politically involved [when her own] mother wasn't." She "remember[ed] [her] good friend's mother . . . who became Supreme Basmith for [a black sorority]. She also recalled a good friend of her mother, Dr. Rachel Jefferson, who helped "build the women's clubhouse ... on the corner of Forest and Bradford . . . [and who] met with presidents . . . and with governors." Kingsley explained that she saw these three women "as women . . . that had done good things." Additionally, they were "models"—"get out and do kind of models."

While Kingsley's recollections spoke to those mavericks whose lives had extended the notion of what black women could do, other mavericks conveyed that in the pursuit of these extraordinary acts, there were things that black women did not *have* to do. Candace Weber-Smith recalled the aunt who she "modeled [herself] after." She explained that at the same time that her aunt was the only woman she knew who had financial power, she had acquired this power in the midst of bucking conventions of feminine beauty:

> I remember my aunt was overweight. . . . [And] I remember other aunts commenting negatively. [Among other things, they would say] she needs to wear more jewelry. My aunt didn't care anything about that. She just was who she was and did not need an external confirmation, affirmation, validation. And I just watched her in awe, move things. And so, for some people, they found her abrasive. I saw her, of course, as no-nonsense and powerful. But I know others had difficulty with her authority and her power. . . . I watched her. I knew there was a correlation between money and power. And I saw so few females who could, if they wanted to, do something, reach in their pocket and pull out their own money. . . . But I watched my aunt, and there was no other female I knew who had financial power.

Sometimes the women reported that they came to understand the voice and power of black women outside of those women who were personally known to them. This was especially the case for the members of Cohort II, five of whom discussed how Angela Davis, in particular, signaled what they were capable of as black women. An exchange with Renee Kirkland illustrates how publicly available maverick figures were able to extend the imaginations of some of the participants.

In Kirkland's effort to explain the significant events that affected her life, she began by discussing "the life of Martin Luther King, the death of Martin Luther King, the life of Malcolm X, the death of Malcolm X, Rosa Parks, the whole civil rights movement . . . all the people that were very active in that." She continued to explain that these persons and events made her "aware of the challenges, that faced [her] as an African American . . . made [her] more aware of the past . . . where [she] c[a]me from . . . what situation [she] was in at that point and time." Additionally, she became aware of "the different roads that led . . . into the future [and] also, the many choices that [she] faced [and] the different roles [she] could have taken. Having followed up by asking her whether there were any figures who made her especially aware of the roles she could have taken, she responded:

> For me, I would have to say Angela Davis, cause she was a *strooong* black woman and ... I am aware of the fact that the civil rights movement was mostly a male-dominated movement and . . . although not to . . . take anything away from it but . . . there was not a real strong role that African American women played in that. Martin Luther King's wife, she was kind of . . . docile, you know, in the background. But Angela Davis, I think, made an impact on me about strong black women. . . . The potential that we . . . have, and I think . . . I got a lot of my strength from . . . just watching . . . and learning more about Angela Davis—knowing that women can be strong, *just* as strong, too. (Original emphasis)

The stories recounted above demonstrate the multiple ways in which women in this study came to know and/or emulate the voice and power of black women. Candace's aunt taught her, if only indirectly, that black women not only can wield financial power but also can move things and benefit from a no-nonsense stance. Desiree's mother showed her that women need not wait on a man but can act efficaciously in their "everyday" efforts to pursue their own interests. Angela Davis and the extraordinary women in Kingsley's life provided evidence of black women's political will and agency. These different representations of black women's voice and power were weaved throughout the participants' life stories. Importantly, when the women further reported on their familiarity with black women's voice and power and the processes by which they became acculturated to these expressions of womanhood, they often discussed how family members often established an explicit link between these expressions and the receipt of higher education. For example, Leona Holmes' mother told her, "Honey, get your degree so that you don't have to be tied down to no Negro. . . . You can always take care of yourself." Tia Richardson explained that her parents wanted her sister and her "to be able to go to college so that we could, you know, provide for ourselves and, you know, be self-sufficient so where we would have to necessarily rely on someone else to provide . . . for us." Nora Bentley explained that her father provided her with the most "predominate" message regarding dating or the role that romantic relationships should play in her life. His message was, "Get a degree. Don't depend upon any man."

Nearly to a person, the members of Cohort III indicated that they received explicit exhortations that they needed to get an education so that they could enact their agency by being independent of men. In contrast, most of the women in Cohort I did not recall their family members encouraging them to pursue an education in order to ensure their power in relationships with men. In two instances, in fact, members of Cohort I found that family members sought to constrain their educational ambitions. The life stories that Cohort I members told indicated that they were, nevertheless, able to develop a sense of black feminine agency via maverick female figures who were intimately involved in their lives. These figures were grandmothers, aunts, family friends, mothers, and neighbors who transcended traditional notions of womanhood because they were financially independent, highly educated, physically strong, unusually courageous, or sexually powerful. In the case of Cohort II, their life stories indicated that they came to understand the social, political, and/or economic efficacy they could and should wield as black women in light of publicly available maverick figures such as Angela Davis, as well as their intimate ties with black women who had demonstrated their agency in sometimes routine and otherwise extraordinary acts. Many of the Cohort II members, like the members of Cohort III, also experienced the same verbal exhortation to go far in school in order to ensure their domestic efficacy and independence.

COPING WITH CONSTRAINTS

Having been socialized toward voice and power as a consequence of explicit exhortation, as well as via intimate and publicly available models of black women's individual, economic, social, and political agency, it is not surprising to learn that the women in this study described themselves as "pushy," "strong," "loud," "aggressive," "assertive," "demanding," "determined." Having asked one participant, L'Nette Farnsworth, why she used one of the adjectives above to describe herself (in her case, she was explaining why she would describe herself as strong), we were not surprised to receive the following response:

I feel that I can take a stand even though I am female. . . . I don't have to succumb to certain issues because, you know, men are supposed to be the superior sex and, you know, wear the pants in the family. . . . I'm not afraid to speak up for what I believe, and . . . if I feel that someone is stepping on my toes or because I am a woman or whatever, . . . I'm not afraid to challenge someone as it relates to being a woman.

While some have suggested that such voice and power are likely to put black women at academic risk (e.g., Taylor, Gilligan, & Sullivan, 1995; Orenstein, 1994; Fine &c Zane, 1991), Cohort III members (along with some members of Cohort II) explained that it was this very socialization that explained, in part, their pursuit of and persistence in higher education. Members of Cohort III indicated that much of their motivation to go far in school was fostered in light of the explicit exhortation that they achieve high levels of education in order to wield their power in relationship with or independent of men. Sometimes they would hold onto these exhortations when they encountered educational obstacles. Cyrillene James remembers feeling out of place at Midwest University. She recalled sometimes feeling overwhelmed by the academic demands and the inhospitable racial climate. She, however, indicated that when "the thought of quitting crossed [her] mind, [her] mother's voice would ring in [her] ears—Baby you don't want to *have to* depend on a man" (original emphasis).

In contrast to Cohort III, Cohorts I and II specifically indicated how they actually employed their voice and power in their effort to have others respond to, support, or not hinder their own school-related pursuits. Thus, when Ellwood's father slapped her face for applying to and being admitted to Midwest University, she stated that she "drew strength" from her grandmother whom she "quietly emulated." She explained:

[I did] not [emulate] my pious grandmother but my worldly grandmother. I just didn't tell anybody, you know. . . . 'Cause she wouldn't take any stuff from anybody . . . She was raunchy. She was downright nasty. . . . 'Cause she would have a wicked little grin and laugh at men. . . . And she told us about puntang. I always cracked up . . . because that was do it and do it right, you know. So grandma was a worldly lady.

She worked. . . . I'm not sure what she did. But she was like the beginning of women's lib. She became what she wanted to, and if she got tired of the man, she said, "Get out!" And she said, "I didn't marry 'em. And I divorced them meant, 'I divorce you, turn and go out the door.'"

In a follow-up interview, Ellwood explained, "I looked to her [her worldly grandmother], and I knew I could and would defy my father." Most of the women in the study did not, however, find that it was their family members who sought to constrain their educational ambitions. In most instances, they discussed how schooling agents, teachers, and professors sought to circumscribe their educational experiences and outcomes. In these instances, they again drew upon their socialization toward voice and power. Sometimes they invoked these orientations to claim a space for themselves and to protest the discrimination they experienced in white-dominated schools. For example, Karen Washington recalled that there was only one high school in her community, and the blacks had to "cross the tracks to go there." She continued:

I wanted to get out there and jump around like the rest of those people—with all the whites. And my grandmother said, "Well go ahead and try." So I tried . . . and they allowed me to [become a cheerleader]. But when we would go into places like Pelham, which is a suburb, it's like an enclave—white folks for sure enough serious—like Klan territory, they would not allow me to cheer. . . . Now I rode with them on the bus, but they made me sit on the bench. But, you know, I went. I never said I'm not going because I can't cheer. *I went and sat there as a symbol of what you all don't want.* [There had not been a black] on the debating . . . I got on the debating team, I'd shoot, girl. I was smart. I could talk. There was no reason why I couldn't get on there. *Anything I wanted to do, my grandmother never told me I could not do it Even at that time, I pushed.* (Authors' emphasis)

In this excerpt, Washington revealed that her grandmother did not bind her imagination regarding what she could do as a black woman. So she would push. She pushed her way into school spaces that had been previously all white. In these spaces, she then used her voice to her advantage (i.e., on the debate team) and expressed her strength via silent and symbolic protest against evident inequities (being denied the opportunity to cheer at those away games that were played in racially hostile communities).

In other instances the women reported that their very willingness to express their voice and power in conflict with teachers or professors sometimes reaped them better academic outcomes. For example, Weber-Smith first discussed how she successfully challenged a high school teacher who graded her down on a writing assignment because she found the content unacceptable:

I had a writing class where a teacher gave me a B, and I argued, for lack of a better word, with her, and she changed my grade to an A. The reason why I argued . . . it was a creative writing thing, and I had written that I was the inside of a bullet . . . in a black revolutionary's gun pointed at the head of a white person. . . . I had no shame, I didn't care, I was radical. I did not care. . . . She bad enough to teach on the east side of [Mid City]. But anyway so I write this paper, and I remember describing the smell of gunpowder because I'm inside the bullet. She wrote back and said that . . . the paper was good, but I should have used a term [that reflected the] accurate smell of gunpowder. . . . And I told her I didn't know what that word meant. I never heard it before. . . . We went back and forth. She changed it to an A. . . . [She was] an excellent teacher, but she didn't like the content . . . the nerve, to mark me down for that. . . . I knew that she could get me on sentence structure, or I hadn't developed my point, something, but not on one word—Oh no! I don't think so, uh uh, uh uh! So that was it.

Weber-Smith subsequently explained that she sometimes had to get "a bit feisty" with her professors in college "so that they too would give [her her] due."

Leona Holmes similarly reported on how she too became "bold" with her college instructors in her effort to receive better, if not equitable, academic treatment. In her effort to account for her boldness, Holmes began by reporting that her professors "arbitrarily would give you a grade, and then they wouldn't write anything on your paper." She added that they were subsequently hostile to her inquiries about the grade she received. In her words, "And then you would go and question them and then that's when they would just like . . . cut you down, Are you questioning me?' 'Yes.' 'No, you don't question me. You have no right to question me. It's a C. It's not worth anything more. . . . It's not even worth the paper.'" Having experienced such treatment "one time after another," Holmes initially began saying, "God, I'm not meant to be here." "But then [she] took a look at . . . the mess [her white peers] were turning in, and they got B+, A." It was then that "she realized the professors were just out [t]here to do a number on [her]." She; therefore, became "really bold" and would

> BAM BAM BAM . . . knock on that door, "Excuse me professor, can 1 talk to you?" *[both laugh]* . . . I just got really bold with it 'cause I realized, hey, I'm going to flunk out or they just going to put me out, or they going to flunk me out anyway 'cause they could. . . . So I figured, hey, let's go out with a bang. So I just became very . . . what do they say? Brazen or whatever.

It is evident from her inclusion in this study that Holmes never flunked out of Midwest University. Additionally, she reported that her brazen efforts to have teachers account for their evaluations of her work sometimes led to her receiving a more favorable assessment of her performance on a given assignment.

Sometimes the women reported that they waged conflict not only to receive more favorable educational outcomes but also to affirm nondominant perspectives that had been marginalized in their schools. These perspectives, in some instances, affirmed the humanity and experience of African Americans. For example, Renee Kirkland reported on her conflict with one of her teachers in Midwest's nursing program. She explained:

> [I was] supposed to write like a little thesis for [a nursing] classy—something to deal with cultural differences, and my paper was on African Americans and how Midwest University does not adequately address the cultural differences of the patients that they serve, and that's not meeting their needs. . . . I focused on . . . [how] they don't teach about differences in hair. They don't teach about their skin, dotta, dotta, da. I remember her giving me a "D." And that was a good paper. Sol remember meeting with her, and she just

went off on me. You people, you know, you have to learn to do what the Jewish people did. You have to learn to assimilate into society. And I . . . said, "Look, you have blue eyes. You have white skin, you can assimilate." I said, "How the hell am I going to assimilate?" And I said, "Besides what does that have to do with my paper?" But basically she felt that African Americans—we were just making trouble. That the Jews, they had their troubles, but they're okay now and they're doing well, and we're not. And we need to take a lesson from them. So she was just gonna pound on me. So . . . she wanted me to redo my paper. I went and talked to . . . one of the deans and, you know, she gave me a passing grade, but it was . . . begrudgingly.

In short, it was Kirkland's willingness to make "trouble" that allowed her to receive a higher grade (if not the grade she deserved) while forwarding black cultural frames and experiences that had been silenced in the academy. Like Weber-Smith and Holmes, Kirkland's assertive stance with her teachers proved to be an asset rather than a liability.

SUMMARY AND CONCLUSION

These women's stories require us to reassess previous research, which suggests that black women's socialization toward voice and power is likely to put them at risk for school failure. Though little research has been conducted on this topic, what work is available suggests that when black girls express their voice and power in school, they are placed at an academic disadvantage. They experience psychological isolation, find themselves in conflict with school officials, and are more likely to be "pushed" out of school. The findings of this study, however, require us to generate a more complicated picture regarding how the culture of black femininity can shape the educational experiences and outcomes of black girls. More precisely, the findings reported herein reveal how the culture of black femininity can be productive in relation to schooling.

The life stories featured in this chapter show how the culture of black femininity impacted black women's ability to imagine that black women in general, and they in particular, could act efficaciously despite gender-based barriers that operate in the "everyday" and in society at large. Just as important, these stories convey how this culture (articulated via exhortation or feminine models) informed the cognitive and behavioral processes by which the women actually resisted those constraints that threatened their academic success and persistence. Researchers have otherwise provided evidence that success within and outside of school is in part a function of how individuals begin to imagine and then act upon life's possibilities despite constraint (O'Connor, 1997; Etter-Lewis, 1993; Young, 1999).

The women in Cohorts II and III indicated that, in part, their positive valuation of education, their college aspirations, and their persistence through school were fostered by their family members' efforts in socializing them to become self-sufficient (i.e., independent of men). Additionally, the women were able to invoke their voice and power in ways that enabled them to resist those efforts, cultures, and practices directed at circumscribing their educational experiences and outcomes. In most instances, these women experienced such circumscription in academic settings and at the hands of schooling agents. However, they would draw on black feminine agency to protest inequitable treatment and to claim school spaces that had been previously denied to blacks. Often the women's protests and their willingness to be in conflict with school officials produced (more) positive educational outcomes. Conflict in these instances was productive. In the absence of engaging in conflict, these women would have been further marginalized in academic settings. Additionally, they would have resigned themselves to inequitable grading practices and lower grades.

Although these findings reveal the productive character of the women's socialization towards black feminine agency, we must be mindful of evidence that the voice and power of black women is at best suppressed and often negatively sanctioned in schools. What is at stake when schools and educators seek to suppress, sanction, or push out those traits that are central to cultivation of worldviews and strategies that can expand black people's life chances? If we have any chance of working toward a more just society, schools and educators must take up the challenge to explore how they might build upon, rather than work against, the socially productive nature of black femininity.

REFERENCES

American Association of University Women & Greenberg Lake the Analysis Group. (1991). *Shortchanging girls, shortchanging America. A nationwide poll to assess self esteem, educational experiences, interest in math and science, and career aspirations of girls and boys ages 9–15*, Washington, D.C.: American Association of University Women.

Benard, B. (1991). *Fostering resiliency in kids: Protective factors in the family, school, and community*. Portland, OR: Northwest Regional Educational Laboratory.

Collins, P. H. (2000). *Black feminist thought: Knowledge, consciousness, and the policies of empowerment*. New York: Routledge.

Crane, J. (1991). Effects of neighborhoods on dropping out of school and teenage childbearing. In C. Jencks & P. E. Peterson (Eds.), *The urban underclass* (pp. 299–320). Washington, DC: Brookings Institution.

Etter-Lewis, G. (1993). *My soul is my own: Oral narratives of African American woman in the professions*. New York: Routledge.

Fine, M. (1991). *Framing dropouts: Notes on the politics of an urban public high school*. Albany, NY: State University of New York Press.

Fine, M. & Zane, N. (1991). Bein' wrapped too tight: When low-income women drop out of high school. *Women's Studies Quarterly, 1 & 2*, 77–99.!

Fordham, S. (1996). *Blacked out: Dilemmas of race, identity, and success at Capital High*. Chicago, IL: University of Chicago Press.

Holland, D. C. & Eisenhart, M. A. (1990). *Educated in romance; Women, achievement, and college culture*. Chicago, IL: University of Chicago Press.

Hooks, b. (1992). *Black looks*. Boston, MA: South End.

Lewis, D. K. (1975). The black family: Socialization and sex roles. *Phylon, 36*, 221–238.

O'Connor, C. (1997). Dispositions toward (collective) struggle and educational resilience in the inner city: A case analysis of six African American high school students. *American Educational Research Journal, 34*(4), 593–629.

Orenstein, P. (1994). *Schoolgirls: Young women, self-esteem, and the confidence gap*. New York: Anchor Books.

Russell, K. (1992). *The color complex: The politics of skin color among African Americans.* New York: Harcourt Brace Jovanovich.

Slevin, K. F., & Wingrove, C. R. (1998). *From stumbling blocks to stepping stones: The life experiences of fifty professional African American women.* New York: New York University Press.

Taylor, J. M. Gilligan, C., & Sullivan, A. M. (1995). *Between voice and silence: Women and girls, race and relationship.* Cambridge, MA: Harvard University Press.

Ward, J. V. (1996). Raising resisters: The role of truth telling in the psychological development of African American girls. In B. J. Ross Leadbeater and N. Way (Eds.), *Urban girls: Resisting stereotypes, creating identities.* New York: New York University Press.

Young, A. (1999, July 17). The (non) accumulation of capital: Explicating the relationship of structure and agency in the lives of poor black men. *Sociological Theory, 2,* 201–227.

40

Girls, Race, and Identity

Border Work Between Classes

JULIE BETTIE

Many school ethnographies are comparative studies of students across class categories and make generalizations about the experiences of middle-class students and of working-class students. In order to speak about these class categories as if they are two clearly distinct peer groupings, one must ignore many students who are exceptions to the rule that class origin equates to class future. While the correlation is strong between parents' socioeconomic status and a student's membership in a middle- or working-class peer group, tracking experience, academic achievement, and consequent class future, it is imperfect, and there are always at least a handful of working-class students who are college-prep and upwardly mobile and a handful of middle-class students who are on the vocational track and downwardly mobile. Nonetheless, because research generally tends to highlight patterns, such cases are typically ignored, precisely because they are exceptions to the rule. . . .

In this chapter I want to focus on those few girls, both white and Mexican-American, who were from working-class origins but who were upwardly mobile middle-class performers in high school, en route to achieving a university education, and to ask what we might learn from their exceptionalism. Foregrounding

these exceptions to the rule, I explore what their experience might reveal about the way in which race ethnicity and gender, as autonomous axes of social inequality, intersect with class. . . .

The . . . question is *how* they do it. How do they negotiate the disparity between the working-class identity acquired from home and the performance of a middle-class identity at school, the disparity between t heir family lives and the family lives of their middle-class peers? What is the subjective experience of class passing, of "choosing" upward mobility and all that comes with it? . . .

WHITE GIRLS: CONTINGENT ROUTES TO MOBILITY

I met Staci during a slow day in the yearbook class. Most of the students were working on various aspects of pulling that year's annual together, but Staci felt she needed to put her energy elsewhere on this day and was headed to the library to look up some information for a history paper due at the end of the week. Staci's membership in the prep crowd was unusual, given her

---

parents' economic and cultural capital. Her father worked "doing maintenance" at a retirement community. But the fact that her mother worked for a time in the kitchen at the private elementary school in town enabled Staci to receive a subsidized private school education, and she ran with the most academically elite crowd of girls at the school.

Like Staci, Heather had also attended private school but not with a subsidy, and it was difficult to understand how her parents could have afforded it. Her father worked as a mechanic and her mother as a nurse's aide. Between them they were nearing middle-income, but most Waretown families in this category were not sending their kids to private schools. As I pushed for a clearer explanation, she indicated that her parents experienced great financial sacrifice in order to send her to school, even borrowing money from relatives, but they felt it was worth it. According to her, her parents wanted to segregate her from "bad influences." This turned out to be a euphemism for Mexican-American students.

Likewise, Jennifer told me that while her parents had been able to afford to send her to private elementary school, they could not afford to send her brother too. Instead, they arranged for him to attend school in a neighboring town, and, once again, the reason was to avoid "bad influences." . . .

Mandy was also college-prep, although her membership among these girls was even more difficult to explain. She had not attended private elementary school yet did reasonably well academically in junior high and managed to get in with the prep crowd by high school. . . .

At times, . . . an individual girls academic motivation seemed to come from defining herself in opposition to older brothers who were labeled delinquent and who, as the girls had witnessed, caused their parent(s) angst. It seemed that feminine norms sometimes allowed girls to forgo the delinquent paths their brothers might have felt compelled to follow as working-class boys, the need to engage in rituals of proving masculinity. I heard this story frequently enough, among both white and Mexican-American girls, that I began to suspect that working-class girls might experience a certain advantage over their male counterparts as a consequence of being girls. The social pressure for girls to conform and follow rules as part of the defini-

tion of femininity makes it a possibility that they might do better in school than working-class boys, for whom defining manhood includes more pressure to engage in risk-taking behavior and overt resistance to control. Girls may not only be less likely to engage in such activities but are relatively less likely to be labeled and punished as delinquents if they do (although this was somewhat less true for Mexican-American girls). That working-class girls might actually do better academically than working-class boys is a possibility easily missed by those taking an additive analytical approach to race, class, and gender as social forces. Such an approach would simply presume that girls' educational experiences and opportunities are in all cases "worse" than boys', rather than exploring the unique set of challenges girls face. . . .

Liz articulated yet another route to mobility. When I asked how it was that she came to be a part of her college-prep friendship circle, she explained that early on she discovered that she was good at basketball, and it was through this sport that she met and began to spend time with girls who were far more privileged than she was. Through association with high achievers, she was exposed to information that helped her get ahead. Overhearing conversations about college requirements and college-prep courses made her aware of the existence of two tracks of schooling and what she was missing out on. She clung to a middle-class girl, Amber, her best friend, hoping, it seemed, that she might "catch" the middle-classness Amber took for granted. Unable to name her desire as class envy, she simply said, "I'd like to be in a situation like that." . . .

WHITE GIRLS: BECOMING UPWARDLY MOBILE

Common among those girls whose families were much more working-class than the families of their closest friends was their nascent awareness of the difference between these class cultures. Class is a relational identity; awareness of class difference is dependent upon the class and race geography of the environment in which one lives and moves. While the community of one's formative years and schooling experiences, in particular, may be key shapers of one's perceptions of class difference, awareness of one's location in a class hierarchy is an ongoing and context-specific process. Beverley Skeggs (1997), in her semi-autobiographical book, explains that because her childhood was spent in a class-segregated community, "My first real recognition that I could be categorized by others as working-class happened when I went to university. . . . For the first time in my life I started to feel insecure. All the prior cultural knowledge [capital] in which I had taken pride lost its value, and I entered a world where I knew little and felt I could communicate even less." The working-class, upwardly mobile girls I met, by virtue of their location in mixed-class peer groups, had an earlier awareness of class distinctions, although they did not often name those differences as such.

In other words, upward mobility might occur at various points in life. As they acquire cultural and economic capital at different ages, upwardly mobiles begin passing in middle-class contexts at different times. Where Skeggs only began passing upon entry into college, some of the girls I knew began in junior high, and those with private school educations, in elementary school. Given that Staci has been part of a middle-class peer group since her private elementary school education, even though she is from a working-class family, her experience of college will likely be far different than the one Skeggs describes for herself. . . .

Geographic variability shapes the likelihood of class mobility. Being working-class and attending a well-funded school with a middle-class clientele where a curriculum of knowledge that is highly valued by society is made available is a far different experience than attending school in an isolated working-class community where the mere exposure to a college-prep curriculum is limited. Upwardly mobile girls from Waretown will likely develop an even greater awareness of class difference when they leave this agricultural community behind.

Due to their location in a college-prep rather than a vocational curriculum, these upwardly mobile working-class girls at times showed a clearer understanding of the fact of class differences than did their vocational counterparts. Liz was one of very few students I met who actually named herself as "working-class."

JULIE: You said you were "working-class" earlier. Where did you get that term, what does it mean?

LIZ: I learned it in a social science class or maybe in history. Working-class is like the serfs you know, the working-class are the majority, blue-collar versus the college-educated. . . .

Unlike working-class girls who were segregated in vocational tracks and so were rarely in mixed-class settings or peer groups, those working-class girls who were middle-class performers were not *as* mystified by the success of preps. By virtue of crossing, they could see the advantages and privileges their middle-class friends experienced. They were more acutely aware of the cultural differences based on class, as they found themselves exposed to the children of middle-class professionals in the college-prep curriculum, on the basketball court, in student government, and in middle-class homes. They could see the reasons why they had to work harder, and they were less likely to attribute friends' success to some innate difference between them. . . .

These girls also perceived that they had to work exceptionally hard to earn their high school diploma and to get into college relative to their middle-class friends. As Staci said,

They've always been kind of handed everything, that they've never really had to think about their future, and I was always, like, I don't want my future to be like my parents. And, I mean, that was like a big influence on me, I mean, my goal is I don't ever want to have to worry about money, like we have all my life. My friends never had to deal with that or anything and, it's just like everything has always been handed to them, and they, I mean, they never knew anything else.

I want to go to college and get a good education so I can have a better life, and they have always had a good life. I work my butt off, but it just seems easier for them. It's just always everything has always kinda been there for them. . . .

Moreover, these girls were aware of the fact that they exceeded their parents' educational level early on, and they perceived the fact that their parents were unable to help them with school as a handicap. As Mandy explained,

> Ever since I've been in honors classes, I've always been around these people, you know, their parents have advanced degrees and everything else. My parents were never able to help me out with math. Once I entered algebra, that was it, that was as far as they could help me. I remember one time in this one class we had this project, we had to build something. One girl's father was an architect, and her father designed and basically built the entire project for her. We all had these dinky little things, and she's got this palace!

Later, however, she attempted to define her parents' lack of education as an asset.

> I mean, I was never mad at my parents because they couldn't help me. I was actually happy, because once we get to college, you're not gonna call your parents up and say "Hey, Dad, can you design this for me?" You're on your own then. And so I've always had to work on my own with my schoolwork, it was always on my own, whereas other students, they always had their parents standing right there, you know?...

These middle-class-performing working-class girls were . . . readily able to see the differences between their own parents and those of their friends. They were painfully aware of the fact that their friends' parents viewed their own parents with indifference at best, disdain at worst.

. . . I sat next to Heather at a girls' basketball game one evening. She was sitting on the bleachers with the rest of her prep friends, front and center, cheering on the team, many of whom were part of their peer group. She kept glancing at the corner of the gym where several adults were standing, people who had come after halftime (when admission was free) to watch for a few minutes but weren't committed enough to staying to take a spot on the bleachers. I asked her if she was expecting someone, and she whispered, "My dad said he might stop by and check the score. I hope he doesn't.". . .

Where I first thought the idea of her father attending the game represented the standard embarrassment teens experience in relationship to having their parents near them at social events, I recognized later that its

meaning went beyond this for her. In the middle-class milieu of the school, some parents are more embarrassing than others.

MEXICAN-AMERICAN GIRLS: CONTINGENT ROUTES TO MOBILITY

There was a small group of Mexican-American girls, mostly second generation but also including two girls who had immigrated, who were from poor and working-class families and who were exceptional in that they did not identify with the [vocational students] but rather were middle-class performers on the college-prep track. . . .

As with the white girls, it is difficult to account for upwardly mobile Mexican-American girls' exceptional status, but there are a variety of enabling conditions for each of these individual girls' mobility. Although the experience of exceptionalism that these girls articulated in some ways paralleled white working-class girls' accounts, in other ways the two groups' experiences diverged, revealing the racial/ethnic specificity of their early mobility experiences.

Like Liz, Adriana's location in the college-prep curriculum seemed in part to be linked to organized sports. She showed a talent for soccer early on and received much support for it from home, because her father was a big fan. ("Soccer is always on our TV," she said. "He gets cable just for the soccer.") Adriana's friendship group in junior high thus included many of the college-prep girls who tend to dominate organized sports. Like Liz, through association with preps, she experienced the benefit of the privileged treatment by teachers and counselors that is often reserved for college-prep students. But while she was friendly with these girls in the classroom and on the playing field, she primarily located herself in a peer group of other working-class Mexican-American girls who were middle-class performers.

Like the white working-class girls, these girls at times told stories of defining self in opposition to delinquent brothers. . . .

But more often they told stories of older siblings as the source of help and inspiration to go to college. Usually, but not always, these older siblings were sisters, generally an older sister who had finally managed, through a long and circuitous route that included junior college and many part-time and full-time jobs, to attend a four-year school. The older sisters sought to help their younger siblings manage more easily by advising them on the importance of getting the courses required for state university or UC admission done in high school (rather than in junior college), on taking SAT tests, and on filling out applications for financial aid and admissions on time. Luisa had two older sisters attending state schools, and she had been accepted to three university campuses. . . .

When I asked her if she had understood the differences between attending a junior college versus a state university or UC school, she said,

> Yeah, just from my sister. She always taught me what, you know, she's the one who told me what the differences were, and she helped me figure out that I wanted to go to UC, because I didn't want to go spend two yews at a JC and [then] like go for four more years, because I thought that was like a waste of two years."

Although Angela did not have older siblings guiding her, she clearly saw it as her job to help her five younger siblings. When I asked her about her social life, she said,

> Well, I don't spend time like I used to, with friends so much. My family, my little brothers and sister are more important than friends. They need to get ahead. And I don't want them to get behind or something. I want to help them do well.

Because she had so many younger siblings to help, who took energy away from her own schooling and who would need to use the family's economic resources, I had doubts that Angela's college dream would be realized, but it seemed likely that her siblings would benefit from her sacrifices. Indeed, this was a factor for Victoria, whose mobility was fostered by having older siblings—much older, in fact, since her mother was forty-two when Victoria was born. Not only were these older siblings able to advise her, but by the time she was ready to go to college many of them were established and could help her financially.

In short, older siblings who were the first in the family to go to college turned out to be important sources of insider information already known to students whose parents were college-educated, providing cultural and social capital not available from parents, and at times economic capital as well.

Two of the girls in this middle-class performing group were immigrants, and explaining their exceptionalism requires other considerations. These two girls were fluent enough in English to be able to complete college-prep courses. The remainder of immigrant girls in the senior class were on the vocational track. Many authors have noted the greater educational success of immigrant students compared to their second- and third-generation counterparts. It was Waretown school counselors' subjective impression that immigrant students "do better" in school. . . .

One explanation for the achievement of these two immigrant girls is that their parents had some other benefits and resources that enabled them to be more mobile than their vocational track counterparts. In her work on the educational mobility of low-income Chicana/os, Patricia Gándara (1995) asks not why low-income Chicana/os fail, but why those who experience class mobility succeed. She suggests that "family stories" can work as a kind of cultural capital for these students. The people in her study told stories of coming from families that were well-to-do or had achieved high levels of education in Mexico, or of families that had lost their fortunes—and so their status and financial well-being—in fleeing Mexico because they were on the losing side in the Mexican revolution.

When I asked Lupita, who had immigrated at thirteen, had quickly learned English, was an academic star at the school, and had been admitted to several University of California campuses, why she was different from the other students in her neighborhood, she explained that while their families had immigrated from rural areas of Mexico, her family had come from an urban environment where there was greater access to education. In fact, she had an older sibling who had received a college degree in Mexico. . . .

The girls I studied were fully aware of the fact that the status of Mexican-Americans was not on a linear progression upward and that their lives might not be any easier, even given the Mexican-American civil rights movement. In just the past five years, they had witnessed the passage of three ballot measures in California that put clear brakes on the possibility of mobility for Mexican Americans. Proposition 187, passed in 1994, took social services such as public health care and public school education away from undocumented immigrants. Proposition 209, passed in 1996, eliminated affirmative action and thus encouraged other states to do the same. Proposition 227, passed in 1998, formally ended bilingual education in the state of California, re-igniting an English-only movement that spread throughout the country.

I began to identify an "immigrant orientation" (Ogbu and Matute-Bianchi 1986) that existed among some girls, regardless of whether they were immigrants or not, meaning they employed as a mobility strategy the belief in the classical immigrant story of using education as a route to the American dream of upward mobility. . . . This group of working-class college-prep students engaged this strategy, holding out hope for education as their route to mobility, more than did vocational students . . . , who were far more cynical about their ability to achieve success via education. However, these college-prep girls were not blind to the barriers that exist or to new ones that were currently being created by the state legislature. They were in fact, neither duped by achievement ideology or blindly assimilated, but rather were able to hold both hope and a practical cynicism in their minds simultaneously.

If . . . working-class students of color at times have higher aspirations than white working-class students, this does not mean that those higher aspirations result in higher achievement; a variety of structural barriers remain in place that inhibit their mobility. In the cases of Lupita and Angela, while family benefits, whether real or imagined, shape student aspirations, they do not dictate outcomes. Lupita did appear to come from an educated extended family in Mexico, and her college-educated sibling provided her with cultural capital that would possibly benefit her. But with five younger siblings, no health care, and a sick mother, Angela remains less likely to reap the benefits of her higher aspirations. Even though she was admitted to a UC campus, she was hoping to attend a nearby junior college:

That's the only place I can go, because I can't afford to go away.

And when I asked Lupita about her family's income, she explained,

Oh, you know how Mexican families are, a little bit from here, a little bit from there. My dad pays the rent, mom buys the food, my little brother pays the phone bill, and I'm responsible for the gas bill. My uncles fill in whatever else is needed.

Adriana cannot afford not to live at home, and her family cannot spare her economic contribution to the household.

MEXICAN-AMERICAN GIRLS: BECOMING UPWARDLY MOBILE

As with white working-class upwardly mobiles, these Mexican-American middle-class performers could see the differences between themselves and middle-class preps (mostly white) somewhat more clearly than their vocational counterparts could. But where whites articulated their difference from preps in veiled class term, Mexican-American girls articulated their difference clearly in terms of race. For example, Luisa commented:

I think it is harder for Mexican-American students, because I think most white people have, like, money, like their parents, they went to college, and they have money. They have an education. But, you know, I'm not saying, well, you know, it's my mom's fault that she didn't go to college. She could have, you know, but I don't know, it's just, like, that's just what it is, kind of. The white students don't understand because, you know, their parents got to go to college, you know, had an education, they all have jobs.

Like white girls, Mexican-American girls wanted to point to the importance of mobility, yet did not want this to mean that their parents' lives were without value. They thus expressed a certain amount of ambivalence toward mobility and/or the acquisition of the middle-class cultural forms that accompany mobility. . . .

Mobility experiences can never be understood out-side of their racial/ethnic specificity. Like white work-ing-class girls, these girls were well aware of having exceeded their parents' abilities. But for them the ac-quisition of middle-class cultural forms also meant be-coming bilingual, while their parents remained prima-rily Spanish speakers.

Where white working-class girls would say gener-ally that they didn't want to struggle for money the way their parents did, Mexican-American girls were cognizant of the correlation between being Mexican-American and being poor and were more likely to name the specific occupations that the poorest people in their community worked and identified their motivation to escape these kinds of work. Angela declared:

I don't want to be like everyone else, I want to, I want something better. I hate working in the fields, that's not for me, and I don't want to do that. It is minimum wage and I don't want to work for that. . . .

Unlike third-generation girls of middle-class ori-gin who struggled hard in this particular context with being at once Mexican-American and middle-class and who tended at times to buy into the idea that to be authentically Mexican one must adopt working-class cultural forms, the college-prep working-class girls discussed here refused to interpret mobility as assim-ilation to whiteness and were not apologetic about their mobility; they did not feel any "less Mexican" for being college bound. John Ogbu and Maria Euge-nia Matute-Bianchi (1986) suggest there is a differ-ence between students who adopt an immigrant ori-entation toward schooling and those who adopt a caste-like orientation. A caste-like orientation equates schooling with a loss of racial/ethnic identity (i.e., "acting white") and leads to an adaptive strategy of resistance (often resulting in school failure). . . . The exact reason why some students of color equate educational mobility with acting white while others do not and instead formulate a bicultural identity is unclear. . . .

This handful of working-class college-prep girls enacted a different strategy than students who experi-enced or feared school success as assimilation. The former saw themselves as disproving white stereo-types about Mexican-Americans through their hard work and success, and they took pleasure from that. They adopted a strategy of "accommodation without assimilation," meaning that in the face of racial conflict and inequality, they made accommodations "for the purpose of reducing conflict," yet at the same time allowed their "separate group [identity and cul-ture] to be maintained" (Gibson 1988, 24–25). In this formulation it is indeed possible to do well in school and not objectively be assimilated or "acting white " In short, they found ways to reject assimilation without resisting educational mobility. . . .

The correlation of race and poverty promotes the common-sense belief that middle- class and whiteness are one and the same; as a result Mexican-American students must negotiate educational mobility with the broader social perception that this mobility represents assimilation to whiteness. This assimilation is resisted and gets played out as intraethnic tension, as voca-tional Mexican-American students accuse college-preps of "acting white." These working-class up-wardly mobiles did occasionally receive such accusations from their working- class peers, but they interpreted this as a joke, which though painful at times, was not taken as a real challenge, and their racial/ethnic identity remained unthreatened by their college-prep status . . . .

The fact that upwardly mobile students grew up working-class meant that their identity as Mexican-American was consistent with the common under-standing of race and class as correlated. Their Mexican identity appeared less challenged (both internally and externally) than was the case for some middle-class Mexican-American girls, whose middle-class status made them appear to themselves and to others as ac-culturated. This, even though they were not so far re-moved from Mexican-American cultural forms. Some of their grandparents, with whom they had much con-tact, were immigrants; their parents were fluent in Spanish; and parents' work (as an ethnic studies professor, a labor lawyer, and a university administra-tor of minority programs, for example) promoted or at least made available a cultural and political racial/eth-nic identity. Perhaps they were not "actually" or "re-ally" more acculturated, but they were more middle-class, and this affected their view of themselves and others' view of them. . . .

RACE MATTERS

While all of these girls, across race/ethnicity, have not articulated their early mobility as particularly painful, it is likely to become more so as they (if they) proceed into college, which will take them much further away culturally from family and community than mere high school mobility could. Many have written of the pain that working-class upwardly mobile people experience when leaving their community behind and/or the difficulty of finding ways to reconcile the discord between class background and present status due to mobility. This experience differs, of course, for whites and people of color, as racial/ethnic groups of color are more consciously aware of themselves as a community of people because of a common history of colonization and oppression that results from being historically defined as a racial group. Alternatively, an aspect of whiteness is that whites often do not immediately experience themselves as members of the racial/ethnic category "white," but as individuals, and, without a cultural discourse of class identity, they do not readily experience themselves as members of a class community either. Evidence of this can be seen in the way white working-class college-prep girls expressed their experience of and concern over how education was distancing themselves from their parents. They did not articulate this as a distancing from their working-class *community*; their pain was more often articulated in relationship to an *individual* family, not a people. In short, these white working-class girls were not routinely accused of acting "too bourgeois" the way that middle-class performing Mexican-American girls were accused of acting "too white," because such clear language for class difference was unavailable. Their mobility appears less complicated because they are not made to feel that they are giving up racial/ethnic belonging in the process. . . . In a way, the lack of class discourse may be either a hindrance or a help for white working-class students. On the one hand, because class is unarticulated, they have only individual characteristics to blame for their class lo-

cation: their status is a consequence of the fact that they and/or their parents are just "losers." On the other hand, their mobility may be made easier since they did not experience the same intra-ethnic tension or antagonism within their community over the link between mobility and assimilation that Mexican-American girls did.

As we have seen, being brown or black tends to signify working-class in the United States, given the high correlation between race and class. Consequently, for white working-class upwardly mobiles, the class referent is escapable precisely because of their whiteness. For whites, class does not as easily appear encoded onto the body (although it certainly can be and often is). White working-class upwardly mobiles can pass as middle-class more readily. At school, where no one necessarily knew where working-class white students lived or what their parents looked like, their classed identities could be invisible if they worked at it and learned how to pass, as many do. The possibility of, and perhaps ease of, upward mobility favor white working-class students may also be greater, given that Mexican-American girls were more likely to experience tracking as a consequence of counselors' perceptions and stereotypes. The correlation between race/ethnicity and class means that counselors are likely to assume that brown students are from low-income families (even when they are not) and therefore to make assumptions about what educational resources they need and can handle. White working-class students can escape tracking more easily because their color does not stand in for or signify lowness. . . .

The experiences of these girls reveal that, in order not to be vulnerable to tracking, a Mexican-American student has to be phenomenally good academically, perform a school-sanctioned femininity that signifies middle-classness to school personnel, and have no transgressions or slip-ups along the way. . . .

REFERENCES

Gándara, Patricia, 1995. *Over the Ivy Walls: The Educational Mobility of Low-Income Chicanos.* Albany: State University of New York Press.

Gibson, Margaret A. 1988. *Accommodation without Assimilation: Sikh Immigrants in an American High School.* Ithaca, N.Y.: Cornell University Press.

Ogbu, John V. and Maria Eugenia Matute-Bianchi, 1986. "Understanding Sociocultural Factors: Knowledge Identity and School Adjustment." In *Beyond Language: Social and Cultural Factors in Schooling Language Minority Students*, developed by the Bilingual Education Office, California State Department of Education, 73–142. Los Angeles: Evaluation Dissemination and Assessment Center, California State University, Los Angeles.

Skeggs, Beverley. 1997. *Formations of Class and Gender: Becoming Respectable.* London: Sage.

41

"Dude, You're a Fag"

Adolescent Masculinity and the Fag Discourse

C. J. Pascoe

'There's a faggot over there! There's a faggot over there! Come look!' yelled Brian, a senior at River High School, to a group of 10-year-old boys. Following Brian, the 10 year olds dashed down a hallway. At the end of the hallway Brian's friend, Dan, pursed his lips and began sashaying towards the 10-year-olds. He minced towards them, swinging his hips exaggeratedly and wildly waving his arms. To the boys Brian yelled, 'Look at the faggot! Watch out! He'll get you!' In response the 10-year-olds raced back down the hallway screaming in terror.

—(From author's fieldnotes)

The relationship between adolescent masculinity and sexuality is embedded in the specter of the faggot. Faggots represent a penetrated masculinity in which "to be penetrated is to abdicate power" (Bersani, 1987: 212). Penetrated men symbolize a masculinity devoid of power, which, in its contradiction, threatens both psychic and social chaos. It is precisely this specter of penetrated masculinity that functions as a regulatory mechanism of gender for contemporary American adolescent boys.

Feminist scholars of masculinity have documented the centrality of homophobic insults to masculinity (Lehne, 1998; Kimmel, 2001) especially in school settings (Wood, 1984; Smith, 1998; Burn, 2000; Plummer, 2001; Kimmel, 2003). They argue that homophobic teasing often characterizes masculinity in adolescence and early adulthood, and that anti-gay slurs tend to primarily be directed at other gay boys.

This article both expands on and challenges these accounts of relationships between homophobia and masculinity. Homophobia is indeed a central mechanism in the making of contemporary American adolescent masculinity. This article both critiques and builds on this finding by (1) pointing to the limits of an argument that focuses centrally on homophobia, (2) demonstrating that the fag is not only an identity linked to homosexual boys[1] but an identity that can temporarily adhere to heterosexual boys as well and (3) highlighting the racialized nature of the fag as a disciplinary mechanism.

"Homophobia" is too facile a term with which to describe the deployment of "fag" as an epithet. By calling the use of the word "fag" homophobia—and letting the argument stop with that point—previous research obscures the gendered nature of sexualized insults (Plummer, 2001). Invoking homophobia to describe the ways in which boys aggressively tease each other overlooks the powerful relationship between masculinity and this sort of insult. Instead, it seems incidental in this conventional line of argument that girls do not harass each other and are not harassed in this same manner.[2] This framing naturalizes the relationship between masculinity and homophobia, thus obscuring the centrality of such harassment in the formation of a gendered identity for boys in a way that it is not for girls.

"Fag" is not necessarily a static identity attached to a particular (homosexual) boy. Fag talk and fag imitations serve as a discourse with which boys discipline themselves and each other through joking relationships.[3] Any boy can temporarily become a fag in a given social space or interaction. This does not mean that those boys who identify as or are perceived to be homosexual are not subject to intense harassment. But becoming a fag has as much to do with failing at the masculine tasks of competence, heterosexual prowess and strength or an anyway revealing weakness or femininity, as it does with a sexual identity. This fluidity of the fag identity is what makes the specter of the fag such a powerful disciplinary mechanism. It is fluid enough that boys police most of their behaviors out of fear of having the fag identity permanently adhere and definitive enough so that boys recognize a fag behavior and strive to avoid it.

The fag discourse is racialized. It is invoked differently by and in relation to white boys' bodies than it is by and in relation to African-American boys' bodies. While certain behaviors put all boys at risk for becoming temporarily a fag, some behaviors can be enacted by African-American boys without putting them at risk of receiving the label. The racialized meanings of the fag discourse suggest that something more than simple homophobia is involved in these sorts of interactions. An analysis of boys' deployments of the specter of the fag should also extend to the ways in which gendered power works through racialized selves. It is not that this gendered homophobia does not exist in African-American communities. Indeed, making fun of "Negro faggotry seems to be a rite of passage among contemporary black male rappers and filmmakers" (Riggs, 1991: 253). However, the fact that "white women and men, gay and straight, have more or less colonized cultural debates about sexual representation" (Julien and Mercer, 1991: 167) obscures varied systems of sexual-

ized meanings among different racialized ethnic groups (Almaguer, 1991; King, 2004).

THEORETICAL FRAMING

The sociology of masculinity entails a "critical study of men, their behaviors, practices, values and perspectives" (Whitehead and Barrett, 2001: 14). Recent studies of men emphasize the multiplicity of masculinity (Connell, 1995) detailing the ways in which different configurations of gender practice are promoted, challenged, or reinforced in given social situations. This research on how men do masculinities has explored gendered practices in a wide range of social institutions, such as families (Coltrane, 2001) schools (Skelton, 1996; Parker, 1996; Mac an Ghaill, 1996; Francis and Skelton, 2001), workplaces (Cooper, 2000), media (Craig, 1992), and sports (Messner, 1989; Edly and Wetherel, 1997; Curry, 2004). Many of these studies have developed specific typologies of masculinities: gay, Black, Chicano, working class, middle class, Asian, gay Black, gay Chicano, white working class, militarized, transnational business, New Man, negotiated, versatile, healthy, toxic, counter, and cool masculinities, to name a few (Messner, 2004). In this sort of model the fag could be (and often has been) framed as a type of subordinated masculinity attached to homosexual adolescent boys' bodies.

Heeding Timothy Carrigan's admonition that an "analysis of masculinity needs to be related as well to other currents in feminism" (Carrigan et al., 1987: 64), in this article I integrate queer theory's insights about the relationships between gender, sexuality, identities, and power with the attention to men found in the literature on masculinities. Like the sociology of gender, queer theory destabilizes the assumed naturalness of the social order (Lemert, 1996). Queer theory is a "conceptualization which sees sexual power as embedded in different levels of social life" and interrogates areas of the social world not usually seen as sexuality (Stein and Plummer, 1994). In this sense queer theory calls for sexuality to be looked at not only as a discrete arena of sexual practices and identities, but also as a constitutive element of social life (Warner, 1993; Epstein, 1996).

While the masculinities' literature rightly high-lights very real inequalities between gay and straight men (see for instance Connell, 1995), this emphasis on sexuality as inhered in static identities attached to male bodies, rather than major organizing principles of social life (Sedgwick, 1990), limits scholars' ability to analyze the myriad ways in which sexuality, in part, constitutes gender. This article does not seek to establish that there are homosexual boys and heterosexual boys and the homosexual ones are marginalized. Rather this article explores what happens to theories of gender if we look at a *discourse* of sexualized identities in addition to focusing on seemingly static identity categories inhabited by men. This is not to say that gender is reduced only to sexuality, indeed feminist scholars have demonstrated that gender is embedded in and constitutive of a multitude of social structures—the economy, places of work, families, and schools. In the tradition of post-structural feminist theorists of race and gender who look at "border cases" that explode taken-for-granted binaries of race and gender (Smith, 1994), queer theory is another tool which enables an integrated analysis of sexuality, gender, and race.

As scholars of gender have demonstrated, gender is accomplished through day-to-day interactions (Fine, 1987; Hochschild, 1989; West and Zimmerman, 1991; Thorne, 1993). In this sense gender is the "activity of managing situated conduct in light of normative conceptions of attitudes and activities appropriate for one's sex category" (West and Zimmerman, 1991: 127). Similarly, queer theorist Judith Butler argues that gender is accomplished interactionally through "a set of repeated acts within a highly rigid regulatory frame that congeal over time to produce the appearance of substance, of a natural sort of being" (Butler, 1999: 43). Specifically she argues that gendered beings are created through processes of citation and repudiation of a "constitutive outside" (Butler, 1993: 3) in which is contained all that is cast out of a socially recognizable gender category. The "constitutive outside" is inhabited by abject identities, unrecognizably and unacceptably gendered selves. The interactional accomplishment of gender in a Butlerian model consists, in part, of the continual iteration and repudiation of this abject identity. Gender, in this sense, is "constituted through

the force of exclusion and abjection, on which produces a constitutive outside to the subject, an abjected outside, which is, after all, 'inside' the subject as its own founding repudiation" (Butler, 1993: 3). This repudiation creates and reaffirms a "threatening specter" (Butler, 1993: 3) of failed, unrecognizable gender, the existence of which must be continually repudiated through interactional processes.

I argue that the "fag" position is an "abject" position and, as such, is a "threatening specter" constituting contemporary American adolescent masculinity. The fag discourse is the interactional process through which boys name and repudiate this abjected identity. Rather than analyzing the fag as an identity for homosexual boys, I examine uses of the discourse that imply that any boy can become a fag, regardless of his actual desire or self-perceived sexual orientation. The threat of the abject position infuses the faggot with regulatory power. This article provides empirical data to illustrate Butler's approach to gender and indicates that it might be a useful addition to the sociological literature on masculinities through highlighting one of the ways in which a masculine gender identity is accomplished through interaction.

METHOD

Research Site

I conducted fieldwork at a suburban high school in north-central California which I call River High.[4] River High is a working class, suburban 50-year-old high school located in a town called Riverton. With the exception of the median household income and racial diversity (both of which are elevated due to Riverton's location in California), the town mirrors national averages in the percentages of white collar workers, rates of college attendance, and marriages, and age composition (according to the 2000 census). It is a politically moderate to conservative, religious community. Most of the students' parents commute to surrounding cities for work.

On average Riverton is a middle class community. However, students at River are likely to refer to the town as two communities: "Old Riverton" and "New

Riverton." A busy highway and railroad tracks bisect the town into these two sections. River High is literally on the "wrong side of the tracks," in Old Riverton. Exiting the freeway, heading north to Old Riverton, one sees a mix of 1950s-era ranch-style homes, some with neatly trimmed lawns and tidy gardens, others with yards strewn with various car parts, lawn chairs, and appliances. Old Riverton is visually bounded by smoke-puffing factories. On the other side of the freeway New Riverton is characterized by wide sidewalk-lined streets and new walled-in home developments. Instead of smokestacks, a forested mountain, home to a state park, rises majestically in the background. The teens from these homes attend Hillside High, River's rival.

River High is attended by 2000 students. River High's racial/ethnic breakdown roughly represents California at large: 50 percent white, 9 percent African-American, 28 percent Latino, and 6 percent Asian (as compared to California's 46, 6, 32, and 11 percent, respectively, according to census data and school records). The students at River High are primarily working class.

Research

I gathered data using the qualitative method of ethnographic research. I spent a year and a half conducting observations, formally interviewing 49 students at River High (36 boys and 13 girls), one male student from Hillside High, and conducting countless informal interviews with students, faculty, and administrators. I concentrated on one school because I explore the richness rather than the breadth of data (for other examples of this method see Willis, 1981; MacLeod, 1987; Eder et al., 1995; Ferguson, 2000).

I recruited students for interviews by conducting presentations in a range of classes and hanging around at lunch, before school, after school, and at various events talking to different groups of students about my research, which I presented as "writing a book about guys." The interviews usually took place at school, unless the student had a car, in which case he or she met me at one of the local fast food restaurants where I treated them to a meal. Interviews lasted anywhere from half an hour to two hours.

The initial interviews I conducted helped me to map a gendered and sexualized geography of the school, from which I chose my observation sites. I observed a "neutral" site—a senior government classroom, where sexualized meanings were subdued. I observed three sites that students marked as "fag" sites—two drama classes and the Gay/Straight Alliance. I also observed two normatively "masculine" sites—auto-shop and weightlifting.[5] I took daily field notes focusing on how students, faculty, and administrators negotiated, regulated, and resisted particular meanings of gender and sexuality. I attended major school rituals such as Winter Ball, school rallies, plays, dances, and lunches. I would also occasionally "ride along" with Mr. Johnson (Mr. J.), the school's security guard, on his battery-powered golf cart to watch which, how, and when students were disciplined. Observational data provided me with more insight to the interactional processes of masculinity than simple interviews yielded. If I had relied only on interview data I would have missed the interactional processes of masculinity which are central to the fag discourse.

Given the importance of appearance in high school, I gave some thought as to how I would present myself, deciding to both blend in and set myself apart from the students. In order to blend in I wore my standard graduate student gear—comfortable, baggy cargo pants, a black t-shirt or sweater, and tennis shoes. To set myself apart I carried a messenger bag instead of a back-pack, didn't wear makeup, and spoke slightly differently than the students by using some slang, but refraining from uttering the ubiquitous "hecka" and "hella."

The boys were fascinated by the fact that a 30-something white "girl" (their words) was interested in studying them. While at first many would make sexualized comments asking me about my dating life or saying that they were going to "hit on" me, it seemed eventually they began to forget about me as a potential sexual/romantic partner. Part of this, I think, was related to my knowledge about "guy" things. For instance, I lift weights on a regular basis and as a result the weightlifting coach introduced me as a "weightlifter from U.C. Berkeley" telling the students they should ask me for weight-lifting advice. Additionally, my taste in movies and television shows often coincided with theirs. I am an avid fan of the movies

"Jackass" and "Fight Club," both of which contain high levels of violence and "bathroom" humor. Finally, I garnered a lot of points among boys because I live off a dangerous street in a nearby city famous for drug deals, gang fights, and frequent gun shots.

WHAT IS A FAG?

"Since you were little boys you've been told, 'hey, don't be a little faggot,'" explained Darnell, an African-American football player, as we sat on a bench next to the athletic field. Indeed, both the boys and girls I interviewed told me that "fag" was the worst epithet one guy could direct at another. Jeff, a slight white sophomore, explained to me that boys call each other fag because "gay people aren't really liked over here and stuff." Jeremy, a Latino Junior told me that this insult literally reduced a boy to nothing, "To call someone gay or fag is like the lowest thing you can call someone. Because that's like saying that you're nothing."

Most guys explained their or other's dislike of fags by claiming that homophobia is just part of what it means to be a guy. For instance Keith, a white soccer-playing senior, explained, "I think guys are just homophobic." However, it is not just homophobia, it is a *gendered* homophobia. Several students told me that these homophobic insults only applied to boys and not girls. For example, while Jake, a handsome white senior, told me that he didn't like gay people, he quickly added, "Lesbians, okay that's *good*." Similarly Cathy, a popular white cheerleader, told me "Being a lesbian is accepted because guys think 'oh that's cool.'" Darnell, after telling me that boys were told not to be faggots, said of lesbians, "They're [guys are] fine with girls. I think it's the guy part that they're like ewwww!" In this sense it is not strictly homophobia, but a gendered homophobia that constitutes adolescent masculinity in the culture of this school. However, it is clear, according to these comments, that lesbians are "good" because of their place in heterosexual male fantasy not necessarily because of some enlightened approach to same-sex relationships. It does however, indicate that using only the term homophobia to describe boys' repeated use of the word "fag" might be a bit simplistic and misleading.

Additionally, girls at River High rarely deployed the word "fag" and were never called "fags." I recorded girls uttering "fag" only three times during my research. In one instance, Angela, a Latina cheerleader, teased Jeremy, a well-liked white senior involved in student government, for not ditching school with her, "You wouldn't 'cause you're a faggot." However, girls did not use this word as part of their regular lexicon. The sort of gendered homophobia that constitutes adolescent masculinity does not constitute adolescent femininity. Girls were not called dykes or lesbians in any sort of regular or systematic way. Students did tell me that "slut" was the worst thing a girl could be called. However, my field notes indicate that the word "slut" (or its synonym "ho") appears one time for every eight times the word "fag" appears. Even when it does occur, "slut" is rarely deployed as a direct insult against another girl.

Highlighting the difference between the deployment of "gay" and "fag" as insults brings the gendered nature of this homophobia into focus. For boys and girls at River High "gay" is a fairly common synonym for "stupid." While this word shares the sexual origins of "fag," it does not *consistently* have the skew of gender-loaded meaning. Girls and boys often used "gay" as an adjective referring to inanimate objects and male or female people, whereas they used "fag" as a noun that denotes only un-masculine males. Students used "gay" to describe anything from someone's clothes to a new school rule that the students did not like, as in the following encounter:

> In auto-shop Arnie pulled out a large older version black laptop computer and placed it on his desk. Behind him Nick said "That's a gay laptop! It's five inches thick!"

A laptop can be gay, a movie can be gay, or a group of people can be gay. Boys used "gay" and "fag" interchangeably when they refer to other boys, but "fag" does not have the non-gendered attributes that "gay" sometimes invokes.

While its meanings are not the same as "gay," "fag" does have multiple meanings which do not necessarily replace its connotations as a homophobic slur, but rather exist alongside. Some boys took pains to say that "fag" is not about sexuality. Darnell told me "It doesn't even have anything to do with being gay." J.L., a white sophomore at Hillside High (River High's cross-town rival) asserted "Fag, seriously, it has nothing to do with sexual preference at all. You could just be calling somebody an idiot you know?" I asked Ben, a quiet, white sophomore who wore heavy metal t-shirts to auto-shop each day, "What kind of things do guys get called a fag for?" Ben answered "Anything . . . literally, anything. Like you were trying to turn a wrench the wrong way, 'dude, you're a fag.' Even if a piece of meat drops out of your sandwich, 'you fag!'" Each time Ben said "you fag" his voice deepened as if he were imitating a more masculine boy. While Ben might rightly *feel* like a guy could be called a fag for "anything . . . literally, anything," there are actually specific behaviors which, when enacted by most boys, can render him more vulnerable to a fag epithet. In this instance Ben's comment highlights the use of "fag" as a generic insult for incompetence, which in the world of River High, is central to a masculine identity. A boy could get called a fag for exhibiting any sort of behavior defined as non-masculine (although not necessarily behaviors aligned with femininity) in the world of River High: being stupid, incompetent, dancing, caring too much about clothing, being too emotional or expressing interest (sexual or platonic) in other guys. However, given the extent of its deployment and the laundry list of behaviors that could get a boy in trouble it is no wonder that Ben felt like a boy could be called "fag" for "anything."

One-third (13) of the boys I interviewed told me that, while they may liberally insult each other with the term, they would not actually direct it at a homosexual peer. Jabes, a Filipino senior, told me

> I actually say it [fag] quite a lot, except for when I'm in the company of an actual homosexual person. Then I try not to say it at all. But when I'm just hanging out with my friends I'll be like, "shut up, I don't want you hear you any more, you stupid fag."

Similarly J.L. compared homosexuality to a disability, saying there is "no way" he'd call an actually gay guy a fag because

> There's people who are the retarded people who nobody wants to associate with. I'll be so nice to those guys and I hate it when people make fun of them. It's like, "bro do you realize that they can't help that?" And then there's gay people. They were born that way.

According to this group of boys, gay is a legitimate, if marginalized, social identity. If a man is gay, there may be a chance he could be considered masculine by other men (Connell, 1995). David, a handsome white senior dressed smartly in khaki pants and a white button-down shirt said, "Being gay is just a lifestyle. It's someone you choose to sleep with. You can still throw around a football and be gay." In other words there is a possibility, however slight, that a boy can be gay and masculine. To be a fag is, by definition, the opposite of masculine, whether or not the word is deployed with sexualized or non-sexualized meanings. In explaining this to me, Jamaal, an African-American junior, cited the explanation of popular rap artist, Eminem,

> Although I don't like Eminem, he had a good definition of it. It's like taking away your title. In an interview they were like, "you're always capping on gays, but then you sing with Elton John." He was like "I don't mean gay as in gay."

This is what Riki Wilchins calls the "Eminem Exception. Eminem explains that he doesn't call people 'faggot' because of their sexual orientation but because they're weak and unmanly" (Wilchins, 2003). This is precisely the way in which this group of boys at River High uses the term "faggot." While it is not necessarily acceptable to be gay, at least a man who is gay can do other things that render him acceptably masculine. A fag, by the very definition of the word, indicated by students' usages at River High, cannot be masculine. This distinction between "fag" as an un-masculine and problematic identity and "gay" as a possibly masculine, although marginalized, sexual identity is not limited to a teenage lexicon, but is reflected in both psychological discourses (Sedgwick, 1995) and gay and lesbian activism.

BECOMING A FAG

"The ubiquity of the word faggot speaks to the reach of its discrediting capacity" (Corbett, 2001: 4). It is almost as if boys cannot help but shout it out on a regular basis—in the hallway, in class, across campus as a greeting, or as a joke. In my fieldwork I was amazed by the way in which the word seemed to pop uncontrollably out of boys' mouths in all kinds of situations. To quote just one of many instances from my fieldnotes:

> Two boys walked out of the P.E. locker room and one yelled "fucking faggot!" at no one in particular.

This spontaneous yelling out of a variation of fag seemingly apropos of nothing happened repeatedly among boys throughout the school.

The fag discourse is central to boys' joking relationships. Joking cements relationships between boys (Kehily and Nayak, 1997; Lyman, 1998) and helps to manage anxiety and discomfort (Freud, 1905). Boys invoked the specter of the fag in two ways: through humorous imitation and through lobbing the epithet at one another. Boys at River High imitated the fag by acting out an exaggerated "femininity," and/or by pretending to sexually desire other boys. As indicated by the introductory vignette in which a predatory "fag" threatens the little boys, boys at River High link these performative scenarios with a fag identity. They lobbed the fag epithet at each other in a verbal game of hot potato, each careful to deflect the insult quickly by hurling it toward someone else. These games and imitations make up a fag discourse which highlights the fag not as a static but rather as a fluid identity which boys constantly struggle to avoid.

In imitative performances the fag discourse functions as a constant reiteration of the fag's existence, affirming that the fag is out there; at any moment a boy can become a fag. At the same time these performances demonstrate that the boy who is invoking the fag is *not* a fag. By invoking it so often, boys remind themselves and each other that at any point they can become fags if they are not sufficiently masculine.

Mr. McNally, disturbed by the noise outside of the classroom, turned to the open door saying "We'll shut this unless anyone really wants to watch sweaty boys playing basketball." Emir, a tall skinny boy, lisped "I wanna watch the boys play!" The rest of the class cracked up at his imitation.

Through imitating a fag, boys assure others that they are not a fag by immediately becoming masculine again after the performance. They mock their own performed femininity and/or same-sex desire, assuring themselves and others that such an identity is one deserving of derisive laughter. The fag identity in this instance is fluid, detached from Emir's body. He can move in and out of this "abject domain" while simultaneously affirming his position as a subject.

Boys also consistently tried to put another in the fag position by lobbing the fag epithet at one another.

> Going through the junk-filled car in the auto-shop parking lot, Jay poked his head out and asked "Where are Craig and Brian?" Neil, responded with "I think they're over there," pointing, then thrusting his hips and pulling his arms back and forth to indicate that Craig and Brian might be having sex. The boys in auto-shop laughed.

This sort of joke temporarily labels both Craig and Brian as faggots. Because the fag discourse is so familiar, the other boys immediately understand that Neil is indicating that Craig and Brian are having sex. However these are not necessarily identities that stick. Nobody actually thinks Craig and Brian are homosexuals. Rather the fag identity is a fluid one, certainly an identity that no boy wants, but one that a boy can escape, usually by engaging in some sort of discursive contest to turn another boy into a fag. However, fag becomes a hot potato that no boy wants to be left holding. In the following example, which occurred soon after the "sex" joke, Brian lobs the fag epithet at someone else, deflecting it from himself:

> Brian initiated a round of a favorite game in auto-shop, the "cock game." Brian quietly, looking at Josh, said, "Josh loves the cock," then slightly louder, "Josh loves the cock." He continued saying this until he was

yelling "JOSH LOVES THE COCK!" The rest of the boys laughed hysterically as Josh slinked away saying "I have a bigger dick than all you mother fuckers!"

These two instances show how the fag can be mapped, momentarily, on to one boy's body and how he, in turn, can attach it to another boy, thus deflecting it from himself. In the first instance Neil makes fun of Craig and Brian for simply hanging out together. In the second instance Brian goes from being a fag to making Josh into a fag, through the "cock game." The "fag" is transferable. Boys move in and out of it by discursively creating another as a fag through joking interactions. They, somewhat ironically, can move in and out of the fag position by transforming themselves, temporarily, into a fag, but this has the effect of reaffirming their masculinity when they return to a heterosexual position after imitating the fag.

These examples demonstrate boys invoking the trope of the fag in a discursive struggle in which the boys indicate that they know what a fag is—and that they are not fags. This joking cements bonds between boys as they assure themselves and each other of their masculinity through repeated repudiations of a non-masculine position of the abject.

RACING THE FAG

The fag trope is not deployed consistently or identically across social groups at River High. Differences between white boys' and African-American boys' meaning making around clothes and dancing reveal ways in which the fag as the abject position is racialized.

Clean, oversized, carefully put together clothing is central to a hip-hop identity for African-American boys who identify with hip-hop culture.[6] Richard Majors calls this presentation of self a "cool pose" consisting of "unique, expressive and conspicuous styles of demeanor, speech, gesture, clothing, hairstyle, walk, stance and handshake," developed by African-American men as a symbolic response to institutionalized racism (Majors, 2001: 211). Pants are usually several sizes too big, hanging low on a boy's waist, usually revealing a pair of boxers beneath. Shirts and sweaters are similarly oversized, often hanging down to a boy's knees. Tags are frequently left on baseball hats worn slightly askew and sit perched high on the head. Meticulously clean, unlaced athletic shoes with rolled up socks under the tongue complete a typical hip-hop outfit.

This amount of attention and care given to clothing for white boys not identified with hip-hop culture (that is, most of the white boys at River High) would certainly cast them into an abject, fag position. White boys are not supposed to appear to care about their clothes or appearance, because only fags care about how they look. Ben illustrates this:

Ben walked in to the auto-shop classroom from the parking lot where he had been working on a particularly oily engine. Grease stains covered his jeans. He looked down at them, made a face and walked toward me with limp wrists, laughing and lisping in a in a high pitch sing-song voice "I got my good panths all dirty!"

Ben draws on indicators of a fag identity, such as limp wrists, as do the boys in the introductory vignette to illustrate that a masculine person certainly would not care about having dirty clothes. In this sense, masculinity, for white boys, becomes the carefully crafted appearance of not caring about appearance, especially in terms of cleanliness.

However, African-American boys involved in hip-hop culture talk frequently about whether or not their clothes, specifically their shoes, are dirty:

In drama class both Darnell and Marc compared their white Adidas basketball shoes. Darnell mocked Marc because black scuff marks covered his shoes, asking incredulously "Yours are a week old and they're dirty—I've had mine for a month and they're not dirty!" Both laughed.

Monte, River High's star football player echoed this concern about dirty shoes when looking at the fancy red shoes he had lent to his cousin the week before, told me he was frustrated because after his cousin used them, the "shoes are hella scuffed up." Clothing, for these boys, does not indicate a fag position, but rather defines membership in a certain cultural and racial group (Perry, 2002).

Dancing is another arena that carries distinctly fag associated meanings for white boys and masculine meanings for African-American boys who participate in hip-hop culture. White boys often associate dancing with "fags." J.L. told me that guys think "'nSync's gay" because they can dance. 'nSync is an all white male singing group known for their dance moves. At dances white boys frequently held their female dates tightly, locking their hips together. The boys never danced with one another, unless engaged in a round of "hot potato." White boys often jokingly danced together in order to embarrass each other by making someone else into a fag:

> Lindy danced behind her date, Chris. Chris's friend, Matt, walked up and nudged Lindy aside, imitating her dance moves behind Chris. As Matt rubbed his hands up and down Chris's back, Chris turned around and jumped back startled to see Matt there instead of Lindy. Matt cracked up as Chris turned red.

However dancing does not carry this sort of sexualized gender meaning for all boys at River High. For African-American boys dancing demonstrates membership in a cultural community (Best, 2000). African-American boys frequently danced together in single sex groups, teaching each other the latest dance moves, showing off a particularly difficult move or making each other laugh with humorous dance moves. Students recognized K.J. as the most talented dancer at the school. K.J. is a sophomore of African-American and Filipino descent who participated in the hip-hop culture of River High. He continually wore the latest hip-hop fashions. K.J. was extremely popular. Girls hollered his name as they walked down the hall and thrust urgently written love notes folded in complicated designs into his hands as he sauntered to class. For the past two years K.J. won first place in the talent show for dancing. When he danced at assemblies the room reverberated with screamed chants of "Go K.J.! Go K.J.! Go K.J.!" Because dancing for African-American boys places them within a tradition of masculinity, they are not at risk of becoming a fag for this particular gendered practice. Nobody called K.J. a fag. In

fact in several of my interviews boys of multiple racial/ethnic backgrounds spoke admiringly of KJ.'s dancing abilities.

IMPLICATIONS

These findings confirm previous studies of masculinity and sexuality that position homophobia as central to contemporary definitions of adolescent masculinity. These data extend previous research by unpacking multi-layered meanings that boys deploy through their uses of homophobic language and joking rituals. By attending to these meanings I reframe the discussion as one of a fag discourse, rather than simply labeling this sort of behavior as homophobia. The fag is an "abject" position, a position outside of masculinity that actually constitutes masculinity. Thus, masculinity, in part becomes the daily interactional work of repudiating the "threatening specter" of the fag.

The fag extends beyond a static sexual identity attached to a gay boy. Few boys are permanently identified as fags; most move in and out of fag positions. Looking at "fag" as a discourse rather than a static identity reveals that the term can be invested with different meanings in different social spaces. "Fag" may be used as a weapon with which to temporarily assert one's masculinity by denying it to others. Thus "fag" becomes a symbol around which contests of masculinity take place.

The fag epithet, when hurled at other boys, may or may not have explicit sexual meanings, but it always has gendered meanings. When a boy calls another boy a fag, it means he is not a man, not necessarily that he is a homosexual. The boys in this study know that they are not supposed to call homosexual boys "fags" because that is mean. This, then has been the limited success of the mainstream gay rights movement. The message absorbed by some of these teenage boys is that "gay men can be masculine, just like you." Instead of challenging gender inequality, this particular discourse of gay rights has reinscribed it. Thus we need to begin to think about how gay men may be in a unique position to challenge gendered as well as sexual norms.

This study indicates that researchers who look at the intersection of sexuality and masculinity need to attend to the ways in which racialized identities may affect how "fag" is deployed and what it means in various social situations. While researchers have addressed the ways in which masculine identities are racialized (Connell, 1995; Ross, 1998; Bucholtz, 1999; Davis, 1999; Price, 1999; Ferguson, 2000; Majors, 2001) they have not paid equal attention to the ways in which "fag" might be a racialized epithet. It is important to look at when, where, and with what meaning "the fag" is deployed in order to get at how masculinity is defined, contested, and invested in among adolescent boys.

Research shows that sexualized teasing often leads to deadly results, as evidenced by the spate of school shootings in the 1990s (Kimmel, 2003). Clearly the fag discourse affects not just homosexual teens, but all boys, gay and straight. Further research could investigate these processes in a variety of contexts: varied geographic locations, sexualized groups, classed groups, religious groups and age groups.

NOTES

1. While the term "homosexual" is laden with medicalized and normalizing meanings, I use it instead of "gay" because "gay" in the world of River High has multiple meanings apart from sexual practices or identities.

2. Girls do insult one another based on sexualized meanings. But in my own research I found that girls and boys did not harass girls in this manner with the same frequency that boys harassed each other through engaging in joking about the fag.

3. I use discourse in the Foucauldian sense, to describe truth producing practices, not just text or speech (Foucault, 1978).

4. The names of places and respondents have been changed.

5. Auto-shop was a class in which students learned how to build and repair cars. Many of the students in this course were looking into careers as mechanics.

6. While there are several white and Latino boys at River High who identify with hip-hop culture, hip-hop is identified by the majority of students as an African-American cultural style.

REFERENCES

Almaguer, Tomas (1991) "Chicano Men: A Cartography of Homosexual Identity and Behavior," *Differences* 3: 75–100.

Bersani, Leo (1987) "Is the Rectum a Grave?" *October* 43: 197–222.

Best, Amy (2000) *Prom Night: Youth, Schools and Popular Culture.* New York: Routledge.

Bucholtz, Mary (1999) " 'You Da Man': Narrating the Racial Other in the Production of White Masculinity," *Journal of Sociolinguistics* 3/4: 443–60.

Burn, Shawn M. (2000) "Heterosexuals' Use of 'Fag' and 'Queer' to Deride One Another: A Contributor to Heterosexism and Stigma," *Journal of Homosexuality* 40: 1–11.

Butler, Judith (1993) *Bodies that Matter.* Routledge: New York.

Butler, Judith (1999) *Gender Trouble.* New York: Routledge.

Carrigan, Tim, Connell, Bob and Lee, John (1987) "Toward a New Sociology of Masculinity," in Harry Brod (ed.) *The Making of Masculinities: The New Men's Studies,* pp. 188–202. Boston, MA: Allen & Unwin.

Coltrane, Scott (2001) "Selling the Indispensable Father," paper presented at *Pushing the Boundaries Conference: New Conceptualizations of Childhood and Motherhood,* Philadelphia.

Connell, R.W. (1995) *Masculinities.* Berkeley: University of California Press.

Cooper, Marianne (2000) "Being the 'Go-To Guy': Fatherhood, Masculinity and the Organization of Work in Silicon Valley," *Qualitative Sociology* 23: 379–405.

Corbett, Ken (2001) "Faggot = Loser," *Studies in Gender and Sexuality* 2: 3–28.

Craig, Steve (1992) *Men, Masculinity and the Media.* Newbury Park: Sage.

Curry, Timothy J. (2004) "Fraternal Bonding in the Locker Room: A Profeminist Analysis of Talk about Competition and Women," in Mchael Messner and Michael Kimmel (eds.) *Men's Lives.* Boston, MA: Pearson.

Davis, James E. (1999) "Forbidden Fruit, Black Males' Constructions of Transgressive Sexualities in Middle School," in William J. Letts IV and James T. Sears (eds.) *Queering Elementary Education: Advancing the Dialogue about Sexualities and Schooling,* pp. 49 ff. Lanham, MD: Rowan & Littlefield.

Eder, Donna, Evans, Catherine and Parker, Stephen (1995) *School Talk: Gender and Adolescent Culture.* New Brunswick, NJ: Rutgers University Press.

Edly, Nigel and Wetherell, Margaret (1997) "Jockeying for Position: The Construction of Masculine Identities," *Discourse and Society* 8: 203–17.

Epstein, Steven (1996) "A Queer Encounter," in Steven Seidman (ed.) *Queer Theory/Sociology,* pp. 188–202. Cambridge, MA: Blackwell.

Ferguson, Ann (2000) *Bad Boys: Public Schools in the Making of Black Masculinity*. Ann Arbor: University of Michigan Press.

Fine, Gary (1987) *With the Boys: Little League Baseball and Preadolescent Culture*. Chicago, IL: University of Chicago Press.

Foucault, Michel (1978) *The History of Sexuality, Volume I*. New York: Vintage Books.

Francis, Becky and Skelton, Christine (2001) "Men Teachers and the Construction of Heterosexual Masculinity in the Classroom," *Sex Education* 1: 9–21.

Freud, Sigmund (1905) *The Basic Writings of Sigmund Freud* (translated and edited by A.A. Brill). New York: The Modern Library.

Hochschild, Arlie (1989) *The Second Shift*. New York: Avon.

Julien, Isaac and Mercer, Kobena (1991) "True Confessions: A Discourse on Images of Black Male Sexuality," in Essex Hemphill (ed.) *Brother to Brother: New Writings by Black Gay Men*, pp. 167–73. Boston, MA: Alyson Publications.

Kehily, Mary Jane and Nayak, Anoop (1997) "Lads and Laughter: Humour and the Production of Heterosexual Masculinities," *Gender and Education* 9: 69–87.

Kimmel, Michael (2001) "Masculinity as Homophobia: Fear, Shame, and Silence in the Construction of Gender Identity," in Stephen Whitehead and Frank Barrett (eds.) *The Masculinities Reader*, pp. 266–187. Cambridge: Polity.

Kimmel, Michael (2003) "Adolescent Masculinity, Homophobia, and Violence: Random School Shootings, 1982–2001," *American Behavioral Scientist* 46: 1439–58.

King, D. L. (2004) *Double Lives on the Down Low*. New York: Broadway Books.

Lehne, Gregory (1998) "Homophobia among Men: Supporting and Defining the Male Role," in Michael Kimmel and Michael Messner (eds.) *Men's Lives*, pp. 237–149. Boston, MA: Allyn and Bacon.

Lemert, Charles (1996) "Series Editor's Preface," in Steven Seidman (ed.) *Queer Theory/Sociology*. Cambridge, MA: Blackwell.

Lyman, Peter (1998) "The Fraternal Bond as a Joking Relationship: A Case Study of the Role of Sexist Jokes in Male Group Bonding," in Michael Kimmel and Michael Messner (eds.) *Men's Lives*, pp. 171–93. Boston, MA: Allyn and Bacon.

Mac an Ghaill, Martain (1996) "What about the Boys—School, Class and Crisis Masculinity," *Sociological Review* 44: 381–97.

MacLeod, Jay (1987) *Ain't No Makin It: Aspirations and Attainment in a Low Income Neighborhood*. Boulder, CO: Westview Press.

Majors, Richard (2001) "Cool Pose: Black Masculinity and Sports," in Stephen Whitehead and Frank Barrett (eds.) *The Masculinities Reader*, pp. 208–17. Cambridge: Polity.

Messner, Michael (1989) "Sports and the Politics of Inequality," in Mchael Kimmel and Michael Messner (eds.) *Men's Lives*. Boston, MA: Allyn and Bacon.

Messner, Michael (2004) "On Patriarchs and Losers: Rethinking Men's Interests," paper presented at Berkeley *Journal of Sociology* Conference, Berkeley.

Parker, Andrew (1996) "The Construction of Masculinity within Boys' Physical Education," *Gender and Education* 8: 141–57.

Perry, Pamela (2002) *Shades of White: White Kids and Racial Identities in High School*. Durham, NC: Duke University Press.

Plummer, David C. (2001) "The Quest for Modern Manhood: Masculine Stereotypes, Peer Culture and the Social Significance of Homophobia," *Journal of Adolescence* 24: 15–23.

Price, Jeremy (1999) "Schooling and Racialized Masculinities: The Diploma, Teachers and Peers in the Lives of Young, African-American Men," *Youth and Society* 31: 224–63.

Riggs, Marlon (1991) "Black Macho Revisited: Reflections of a SNAP! Queen," in Essex Hemphill (ed.) *Brother to Brother: New Writings by Black Gay Men*, pp. 153–260. Boston, MA: Alyson Publications.

Ross, Marlon B. (1998) "In Search of Black Men's Masculinities," *Feminist Studies* 24: 599–626.

Sedgwick, Eve K. (1990) *Epistemology of the Closet*. Berkeley: University of California Press.

Sedgwick, Eve K. (1995) "Gosh, Boy George, You Must be Awfully Secure in Your Masculinity!" in Maurice Berger, Brian Wallis, and Simon Watson (eds.) *Constructing Masculinity*, pp. 11–20. New York: Routledge.

Skelton, Christine (1996) "Learning to be Tough: The Fostering of Maleness in One Primary School," *Gender and Education* 8: 185–97.

Smith, George W. (1998) "The Ideology of 'Fag': The School Experience of Gay Students," *The Sociological Quarterly* 39: 309–35.

Smith, Valerie (1994) "Split Affinities: The Case of Interracial Rape," in Anne Herrmann and Abigail Stewart (eds.) *Theorizing Feminism*, pp. 155–70. Boulder, CO: Westview Press.

Stein, Arlene and Plummer, Ken (1994) " 'I Can't Even Think Straight': 'Queer' Theory and the Missing Sexual Revolution in Sociology," *Sociological Theory* 12: 178 ff.

Thorne, Barrie (1993) *Gender Play: Boys and Girls in School.* New Brunswick, NJ: Rutgers University Press.

Warner, Michael (1993) "Introduction," in Michael Warner (ed.) *Fear of a Queer Planet: Queer Politics and Social Theory,* pp. vi–xxxi. Minneapolis: University of Minnesota Press.

West, Candace and Zimmerman, Don (1991) "Doing Gender," in Judith Lorber (ed.) *The Social Construction of Gender,* pp. 102–21. Newbury Park: Sage.

Whitehead, Stephen and Barrett, Frank (2001) "The Sociology of Masculinity," in Stephen Whitehead and Frank Barrett (eds.) *The Masculinities Reader,* pp. 472–6. Cambridge: Polity.

Wilchins, Riki (2003) "Do You Believe in Fairies?" *The Advocate,* 4 February.

Willis, Paul (1981) *Learning to Labor: How Working Class Kids Get Working Class Jobs.* New York: Columbia University Press.

Wood, Julian (1984) "Groping Toward Sexism: Boy's Sex Talk," in Angela McRobbie and Mica Nava (eds.) *Gender and Generation.* London: Macmillan Publishers.

PART VIII

POPULAR CULTURE

Most of the chapters in this book have examined gender and other relations of inequality primarily in terms of people's lived experiences within social institutions such as families, workplaces, and schools. However, the arena of beliefs, symbols, and values is also of crucial importance. Take, for example, the recent debates about sexual violence in the media, about sex education in schools, about "family values," and about gay and lesbian marriage. To be sure, the results of these debates will have a real impact on people's lives within social institutions. But the terrain of these debates is largely the arena of ideas, values, and symbols. And one of the most dynamics places in which people learn, contest, and forget values and beliefs is in the vast arena of popular culture. In this part, the articles reflect on who the magazines we read, the music we listen to, and the internet sites and Facebook pages that we frequent are cultural creations through which dominant values are often imposed on people. But they may also become arenas in which these values are contested and new values forged.

Dominant cultural beliefs about media images of subordinated groups—be they women, racialized or colonized "others," working-class people, or sexual minorities—tend to obscure, and thus legitimize, the privileges of dominant groups. In the first article in this section, Susan Jane Gilman draws on her own childhood memories of playing ambivalently with Barbie dolls to level a stinging critique on the ways these dolls "quickly become the defining criteria" for beauty and for little girls' sense of status and worth. Gilman notes that the pain that accompanies this realization can be more acute for "other" girls like she and her friends—urban, Jewish, black, Asian, and Latina girls. But she notes that many girls develop their own modes of playing with Barbie—including decapitation! She ends with a humorous list of Barbie dolls that she would like to see—dolls that speak to a spectrum of girls' body types, sexualities, ethnicities, and religions. Emily Rutherford next examines the implications of Facebook's website design, which requires users to choose identities as "male" or "female." While the internet is sometimes construed as a new site of gender freedom, here we see how one of the popular mediums reproduces gender binaries. LBGT groups are starting to protest these Facebook constraints, but so far Facebook has not addressed these concerns. The next article focuses on the popular television show, now in reruns and also a popular movie, Sex in the City. Here, Rebecca Brasfield notes that while the four main characters of the show are ostensibly intended to express different views on love, sex, and career, they are all homogenously white, middle-class and heterosexual. Differences of sexual orientation, age, race and class are erased in the show, and instead, one dominant form of femininity is projected.

42

Klaus Barbie, and Other Dolls I'd Like to See

SUSAN JANE GILMAN

For decades, Barbie has remained torpedo-titted, open-mouthed, tippy-toed and vagina-less in her cellophane coffin—and, ever since I was little, she has threatened me.

Most women I know are nostalgic for Barbie. "Oh," they coo wistfully, "I used to *loooove* my Barbies. My girlfriends would come over, and we'd play for hours . . ."

Not me. As a child, I disliked the doll on impulse; as an adult, my feelings have actually fermented into a heady, full-blown hatred.

My friends and I never owned Barbies. When I was young, little girls in my New York City neighborhood collected "Dawns." Only seven inches high, Dawns were, in retrospect, the underdog of fashion dolls. There were four in the collection: Dawn, dirty-blond and appropriately smug; Angie, whose name and black hair allowed her to pass for Italian or Hispanic; Gloria, a redhead with bangs and green eyes (Irish, perhaps, or a Russian, Jew?); and Dale, a black doll with a real afro.

Oh, they had their share of glitzy frocks—the tiny wedding dress, the gold lamé ball gown that shredded at the hem. And they had holes punctured in the bottoms of their feet so you could impale them on the model's stand of the "Dawn Fashion Stage" (sold separately), press a button and watch them revolve jerkily around the catwalk. But they also had "mod" clothes like white go-go boots and a multicolored dashiki outfit called "Sock It to Me" with rose-colored sunglasses. Their hair came in different lengths and—although probably only a six-year-old doll fanatic could discern this—their facial expressions and features were indeed different. They were as diverse as fashion dolls could be in 1972, and in this way, I realize now, they were slightly subversive.

Of course, at that age, my friends and I couldn't spell subversive, let alone wrap our minds around the concept. But we sensed intuitively that Dawns were more democratic than Barbies. With their different colors and equal sizes, they were closer to what we looked like. We did not find this consoling—for we hadn't yet learned that our looks were something that required consolation. Rather, our love of Dawns was an offshoot of our own healthy egocentrism. We were still at that stage in our childhood when little girls want to be everything special, glamorous and wonderful—and believe they can be.

As a six-year-old, I remember gushing, "I want to be a ballerina, and a bride, and a movie star, and a model, and a queen. . . ." To be sure, I was a disgustingly girly girl. I twirled. I skipped. I actually wore a tutu to school. (I am not kidding.) For a year, I refused to wear blue. Whenever the opportunity presented itself, I dressed up in my grandmother's pink chiffon nightgowns and rhinestone necklaces and paraded around the apartment like the princess of the universe. I dressed like my Dawn dolls—and dressed my Dawn dolls like me. It was a silly, fabulous narcissism—but one that sprang from a crucial self-love. These dolls were part of my fantasy life and an extension of my ambitions. Tellingly, my favorite doll was Angie, who had dark brown hair, like mine.

But at some point, most of us prima ballerinas experienced a terrible turning point. I know I did. I have an achingly clear memory of myself, standing before a mirror in all my finery and jewels, feeling suddenly ridiculous and miserable. *Look at yourself,* I remember thinking acidly. *Nobody will ever like you.* I could not have been older than eight. And then later, another memory: my friend Allison confiding in me, "The kids at my school, they all hate my red hair." Somewhere, somehow, a message seeped into our consciousness telling us that we weren't good enough to be a bride or a model or a queen or anything because we weren't pretty enough. And this translated into not smart enough or likable enough, either.

Looks, girls learn early, collapse into a metaphor for everything else. They quickly become the defining criteria for our status and our worth. And somewhere along the line, we stop believing in our own beauty and its dominion. Subsequently, we also stop believing in the power of our minds and our bodies.

Barbie takes over.

Barbie dolls had been around long before I was born, but it was precisely around the time my friends and I began being evaluated on our "looks" that we became aware of the role Barbie played in our culture.

Initially, my friends and I regarded Barbies with a sort of vague disdain. With their white-blond hair, burnt orange "Malibu" skin, unblinking turquoise eyes and hot-pink convertibles, Barbie dolls represented a world utterly alien to us. They struck us as clumsy, stupid, overly obvious. They were clearly somebody else's idea of a doll—and a doll meant for vapid girls in the suburbs. Dawns, my friend Julie and I once agreed during a sleepover, were far more hip.

But eventually, the message of Barbie sunk in. Literally and metaphorically, Barbies were bigger than Dawns. They were a foot high. They merited more plastic! More height! More visibility! And unlike Dawns, which were pulled off the market in the mid-'70s, Barbies were ubiquitous and perpetual bestsellers.

We urban, Jewish, black, Asian and Latina girls began to realize slowly and painfully that if you didn't look like Barbie, you didn't fit in. Your status was diminished. You were less beautiful, less valuable, less worthy. *If you didn't look like Barbie, companies would discontinue you.* You simply couldn't compete.

I'd like to think that, two decades later, my anger about this would have cooled off—not heated up. (I mean, it's a *doll* for chrissake. Get over it.) The problem, however, is that despite all the flag-waving about multiculturalism and girls' self-esteem these days, I see a new generation of little girls receiving the same message I did twenty-five years ago, courtesy of Mattel. I'm currently a "big sister" to a little girl who recently moved here from Mexico. When I first began spending time with her, she drew pictures of herself as she is: a beautiful seven-year-old with café au lait skin and short black hair. Then she began playing with Barbies. Now she draws pictures of both herself and her mother with long, blond hair. "I want long hair," she sighs, looking woefully at her drawing.

A coincidence? Maybe, but Barbie is the only toy in the Western world that human beings actively try to mimic. Barbie is not just a children's doll; it's an adult cult and an aesthetic obsession. We've all seen the evidence. During Barbie's thirty-fifth anniversary, a fashion magazine ran a "tribute to Barbie," using live models posing as dolls. A New York museum held a "Barbie retrospective," enshrining Barbie as a pop artifact—at a time when most human female pop artists continue to work in obscurity. Then there's Pamela Lee. The Barbie Halls of Fame. The websites, the newsletters, the collectors clubs. The woman whose goal is to transform herself, via plastic surgery, into a real Barbie. Is it any wonder then that little girls have been longing for generations to "look like Barbie"—and that the irony of this goes unchallenged?

For this reason, I've started calling Barbie dolls "Klaus Barbie dolls" after the infamous Gestapo commander. For I now clearly recognize what I only sensed as a child. This "pop artifact" is an icon of Aryanism. Introduced after the second world war, in the conservatism of the Eisenhower era (and rumored to be modeled after a German prostitute by a man who designed nuclear warheads), Barbies, in their "innocent," "apolitical" cuteness, propagate the ideals of the Third Reich. They ultimately succeed where Hitler failed: They instill in legions of little girls a preference for whiteness, for blond hair, blue eyes and delicate features, for an impossible *über*figure, perched eternally and submissively in high heels. In the Cult of the Blond, Barbies are a cornerstone. They reach the young, and they reach them quickly. *Barbie, Barbie!* The Aqua song throbs. *I'm a Barbie girl!*

It's true that, in the past few years, Mattel has made an effort to create a few slightly more p.c. versions of its best-selling blond. Walk down the aisle at Toys-R-Us (and they wonder why kids today can't spell), and you can see a few boxes of American Indian Barbie, Jamaican Barbie, Cowgirl Barbie. Their skin tone is darker and their outfits ethnicized, but they have the same Aryan features and the same "tell-me-anything-and-I'll-believe-it" expressions on their plastic faces. Ultimately, their packaging reinforces their status as "Other." These are "special" and "limited" edition Barbies, the labels announce: clearly *not* the standard.

And, Barbie's head still pops off with ease. Granted, this makes life a little sweeter for the sadists on the playground (there's always one girl who gets more pleasure out of destroying Barbie than dressing her), but the real purpose is to make it easier to swap your Barbies' Lilliputian ball gowns. Look at the literal message of this: Hey, girls, a head is simply a neck plug, easily disposed of in the name of fashion. Lest anyone think I'm nit-picking here, a few years ago, a "new, improved" Talking Barbie hit the shelves and created a brouhaha because one of the phrases it parroted was *Math is hard.* Once again, the cerebrum took a backseat to "style." Similarly, the latest "new, improved" Barbie simply trades in one impossible aesthetic for another: The bombshell has now become the waif. Why? According to a Mattel spokesperson, a Kate Moss figure is better suited for today's fashions. Ah, such an improvement.

Now, I am not, as a rule, anti-doll. Remember, I once wore a tutu and collected the entire Dawn family myself. I know better than to claim that dolls are nothing but sexist gender propaganda. Dolls can be a lightning rod for the imagination, for companionship, for learning. And they're *fun*—something that must never be undervalued.

But dolls often give children their first lessons in what a society considers valuable—and beautiful. And so I'd like to see dolls that teach little girls something more than fashion-consciousness and self-consciousness. I'd like to see dolls that expand girls' ideas about what is beautiful instead of constricting them. And how about a few role models instead of runway models as playmates? If you can make a Talking Barbie, surely you can make a Working Barbie. If you can have a Barbie Townhouse, surely you can have a Barbie business. And if you can construct an entire Barbie world out of pink and purple plastic, surely you can construct some "regular" Barbies that are more than white and blond. And remember, Barbie's only a doll! So give it a little more inspired goofiness, some real *pizzazz!*

Along with Barbies of all shapes and colors, here are some Barbies I'd personally like to see:

Dinner Roll Barbie. A Barbie with multiple love handles, double chin, a real, curvy belly, generous tits and ass and voluminous thighs to show girls that voluptuousness is also beautiful. Comes with miniature basket of dinner rolls, bucket o' fried chicken, tiny Entenmann's walnut ring, a brick of Sealtest ice cream, three packs of potato chips, a T-shirt reading "Only the Weak Don't Eat" and, of course, an appetite.

Birkenstock Barbie. Finally, a doll made with horizontal feet and comfortable sandals. Made from recycled materials.

Bisexual Barbie. Comes in a package with Skipper and Ken.

Butch Barbie. Comes with short hair, leather jacket, "Silence=Death" T-shirt, pink triangle buttons, Doc Martens, pool cue and dental dams. Packaged in cardboard closet with doors flung wide open. Barbie Carpentry Business sold separately.

Our Barbies, Ourselves. Anatomically correct Barbie, both inside and out, comes with spreadable legs, her own speculum, magnifying glass and detailed diagrams of female anatomy so that little girls can learn about their bodies in a friendly, nonthreatening way. Also included: tiny Kotex, booklets on sexual responsibility. Accessories such as contraceptives, sex toys, expanding uterus with fetus at various stages of development and breast pump are all optional, underscoring that each young women has the right to choose what she does with her own Barbie.

Harley Barbie. Equipped with motorcycle, helmet, shades. Tattoos are non-toxic and can be removed with baby oil.

Body Piercings Barbie. Why should Earring Ken have all the fun? Body Piercings Barbie comes with changeable multiple earrings, nose ring, nipple rings, lip ring, navel ring and tiny piercing gun. Enables girls to rebel, express alienation and gross out elders without actually having to puncture themselves.

Blue Collar Barbie. Comes with overalls, protective goggles, lunch pail, UAW membership, pamphlet on union organizing and pay scales for women as compared to men. Waitressing outfits and cashier's register may be purchased separately for Barbies who are holding down second jobs to make ends meet.

Rebbe Barbie. So why not? Women rabbis are on the cutting edge in Judaism. Rebbe Barbie comes with tiny satin *yarmulke,* prayer shawl, *tefillin,* silver *kaddish* cup, Torah scrolls. Optional: tiny *mezuzah* for doorway of Barbie Dreamhouse.

B-Girl Barbie. Truly fly Barbie in midriff-baring shirt and baggy jeans. Comes with skateboard, hip hop accessories and plenty of attitude. Pull her cord, and she says things like, "I don't *think* so," "Dang, get outta my face" and "You go, girl." Teaches girls not to take shit from men and condescending white people.

The Barbie Dream Team. Featuring Quadratic Equation Barbie (a Nobel Prize—winning mathematician with her own tiny books and calculator), Microbiologist Barbie (comes with petri dishes, computer and Barbie Laboratory) and Bite-the-Bullet Barbie, an anthropologist with pith helmet, camera, detachable limbs, fake blood and kit for performing surgery on herself in the outback.

Transgender Barbie. Formerly known as G.I. Joe.

43

Choose One

EMILY RUTHERFORD

Miles Wilcox, a sophomore at Bard College at Simon's Rock, is an avid Facebook user, but he's disgruntled with the website's design. "I have serious issues with how Facebook is so heterosexist," he says. Wilcox, who identifies as a queer transman, objects to the very first field in the Facebook profile: a drop-down box asking users to select a sex from the options "male" and "female." He continues, "Facebook needs to get a grip on reality and acknowledge that not everyone feels comfortable with explicitly identifying as one gender or the other . . . I see no need for Facebook to know what is in my pants, but that's what they ask everyone that signs up."

When the Facebook's creators and designers decided how to structure the website's profile, they placed strict limits on users' choices. Users must rank sex and relationship status above political and religious views, and those above favorite books and movies due to the design of Facebook's profile page. Furthermore, Facebook rigidly reinforces a gender binary, offering only "male" and "female" as options in the "sex" drop-down box, and only allowing users to check "men" and "women" under "interested in." The world around us is increasingly accepting of a spectrum of sexual orientations and gender identities, but Facebook is still sticking to outdated, problematic paradigms.

In July 2008, Facebook took the rigidity beyond the male/female binary in the "sex" information box, citing issues with translating the website into other languages. The company asked users to select a gender-specific pronoun, "he" or "she," so that the News Feed would know which pronoun to use instead of the ungrammatical single "they"—as in, "John added *The Great Gatsby* to **his** favorite books" or "Jane updated **her** political views" (emphasis added). All this is distinctly marginalizing for transgender or gender-nonconforming people like Wilcox who are less able to shelve themselves or the recipients of their interest into one of only two categories.

Ironically, groups that object to Facebook's practices are protesting and raising awareness using Facebook itself. For example, Moriya Vanderhoef, a student at University of Wisconsin-Milwaukee, created a group called "Expand Gender Options on Facebook Petition," which currently has 2,326 members. Vanderhoef, who studies LGBT history, says that she started the group "because there are far more genders and sexes in the world than just 'male' and 'female'. . . I do not appreciate Facebook giving me the option to name my religious [affiliations], but restricting my gender and sexuality to the ultra narrow 'male' or 'female.'" However, the petition has not achieved its goal of bringing this problem to Facebook's attention: Vanderhoef

Figure 1. Facebook still excludes those that don't accept gender binaries. (Illustration: Brett Marler)

has "never once heard from anyone in power about [the] group or the possibility of changing this problem."

Rebecca Bettencourt is another Facebook user who was frustrated by the company's lack of response to user concerns about the "sex" field, believing that "Facebook's limited set of options is not only problematic but grossly misrepresentative and insulting to thousands—maybe even millions—of people." She tried addressing the problem in a different way: when Facebook first allowed users to design their own applications, Bettencourt says, "I immediately knew what my mission was. If Facebook wasn't going to fix this error, I was going to have to take matters into my own hands. As soon as the Facebook API was available, I created the SGO application."

SGO, which stands for "sex/gender/orientation," provides more options than Facebook's own, including fill-in fields so that users can describe their gender and sexuality however they wish. SGO has had a modest amount of success among Facebook's LGBT population, but users cannot accord its content the same level of importance as the official Facebook fields.

Bettencourt would like to see a change. "I do believe that Facebook, as well as other websites, should standardize their gender and orientation options along the lines of my app," she says. "Not all the fields my app offers would be necessary, of course; I'd just like to see the fields for Gender Identity and Sexual Orientation that offered these additional options and/or a text field."

Wilcox, who uses the application, agrees: "The SGO app is a really awesome tool, but essentially what it is an addition to supplement where people feel Face-

book is lacking or failing them. Right now it's helping, but I do think that Facebook should identify these issues and try to fix them," he says.

However, Facebook has done little to address these concerns. The company attempted to mollify those who disagreed with its gender-specific pronouns decision with a June 27, blog post last summer: "We've received pushback in the past from groups that find the male/female distinction too limiting. We have a lot of respect for these communities, which is why it will still be possible to remove gender entirely from your account, including how we refer to you in Mini-Feed."

That is not an adequate solution, however, for those who actually want to display a gender option outside of the male-female binary. Bettencourt, who has followed the issue closely, observed, "This is the only peep ever heard from Facebook regarding this issue, and it only confirms my suspicions of transphobia among the people running Facebook." (Facebook did not respond to requests for further comment on the policy.)

Other efforts to organize on Facebook as a means of changing its available options have been successful in the past. A few years ago, a different group of concerned Facebook users was able to successfully expand the options available in the "political views" field beyond a spectrum from "very liberal" to "very conservative." In 2007 and early 2008, as Facebook became increasingly popular in countries outside of the United States, a series of groups and petitions with titles like "By 'Libertarian' I mean Anarchist" generated a fair amount of attention from the Facebook user base. In contrast to the company's unresponsiveness on the gender issue, Facebook seemed to have taken notice of this campaign. As of March 2008, users are now allowed a fill-in-the-blank political views field.

Of course, the political views movement had numbers on its side. Demographically speaking, far more people desire to label themselves as "socialist" or "libertarian" than, say, "genderqueer" or "pansexual." The minority of gender-variant individuals who feel limited by Facebook's gender binary—unable to sustain a critical mass or to impress upon Facebook's staff the importance of their cause—has been unable to lobby successfully for the change it wants to see.

Some might argue that Facebook is not doing anything particularly shocking—after all, we are asked to choose from "male" or "female" just about every time we fill out a job application, complete a silly online quiz, or use a public restroom. But a policy is not the right choice simply because it is the status quo. Because of its ubiquity among our generation, Facebook plays as important a role in shaping cultural norms and expectations as it does in reflecting them. Facebook has done much to revolutionize the way we present ourselves and communicate with one another, but it could be even more revolutionary if it were to embrace the diversity of its user base.

44

Rereading Sex and the City

Exposing the Hegemonic Feminist Narrative

REBECCA BRASFIELD

. . . *Sex and the City* is an Emmy award–winning cable television program. The show originally aired on HBO for six seasons from 1998–2004. . . . Based in New York City, the show is about four single women in their thirties and forties, navigating the often complicated and chaotic dating scene. Carrie Bradshaw, the protagonist, narrates each episode as she seeks insight and answers to relationship dilemmas. Employed as a columnist, Carrie writes a weekly article titled "Sex and the City" for the New York Star (a fictional newspaper). She is known for her designer shoe obsession and unique and glamorous fashion statements. Carrie's on-again, off-again relationship with Mr. Big anchors *Sex and the City's* primary story line.

Although Carrie provides the major plotlines, *Sex and the City* also follows the stories of her three friends: Miranda Hobbs, Samantha Jones, and Charlotte York. Miranda is a career-oriented Harvard Law School graduate who eventually becomes partner at her law firm. Miranda is the first of her friends to have a baby and is a single mother for the first months of her child's life. Miranda's cynicism toward relationships is the essence of her character. She has a sarcastic sense of humor and usually counterbalances the views of her friends by providing what might be viewed as a voice of reason. The only character to don a short hairstyle (majority of seasons), Miranda appears to cut straight to the point in her analysis of dating. . . .

Often characterized by portraying a man's view on sex and relationships, Samantha is known for her numerous sexual encounters. Confident and secure with her sexuality, Samantha could be described as promiscuous. Her disinterest in conventional relationships separates her from the other women. Employed as a successful public relations executive, Samantha is in her forties, making her the oldest of the four women. . . .

Frequently offended by Samantha's lustful views on sex, Charlotte is, by far, the most sexually conservative of the group. Charlotte works as an art dealer until deciding to end her career to concentrate on raising a family. Charlotte's views on relationships are traditional, making her the voice of romantic love. . . .

Carrie, Miranda, Samantha, and Charlotte represent a continuum of women's views and dilemmas when it comes to sex, love, and dating. The range of perspectives may be one of the reasons why *Sex and the City* sparks so much interest, enthusiasm, and criticism. . . .

Rebecca Brasfield, *Journal of Popular Film and Television* (Vol. 34, No. 3), pp. 130–138. Copyright © 2006 Heldref Publications. Reprinted by permission of the publisher.

HEGEMONIC FEMINIST PRACTICES AND *SEX AND THE CITY*

... *Sex and the City* provides an excellent example of how hegemonic feminism looks, how it thinks, and what it does. . . .

Sex and the City, as a medium for social analysis, reflects almost exclusively the perspectives and values of white, middle-class, heterosexual women who define themselves primarily as oppressed victims of patriarchy. Carrie, Miranda, Samantha, and Charlotte are protagonists and subjects whose voices are heard. The telling of their stories centers their perspective. Their voices and narration dominate the discourse and as viewers we comprehend their experiences through their thoughts, feelings, and behaviors. Are the views presented by *Sex and the City* representative of a hegemonic discourse or do these views represent socially constructed, apolitical perspectives? White, middle-class, heterosexual women are centered subjects, and their values and attitudes comprise the program's underlying master narrative.

Sex and the City's master narrative is that the women's aim is to gain equal power to white, heterosexual, middle-class men within the existing hegemonic social structure. This reform narrative solely addresses the centered subjects. By developing the subjectivity of centered subjects, while simultaneously exploiting marginalized groups, *Sex and the City* sustains a hegemonic feminist discourse.

RACISM, ETHNOCENTRISM, AND *SEX AND THE CITY*

In her assessment of the contemporary women's movement, Audre Lorde points out that, "White women focus upon their oppression as women and ignore differences of race, sexual preference, class and age. There is a pretense to homogeneity of experience covered by the word sisterhood that does not in fact exist" (Lorde 289). Throughout six seasons of *Sex and the City*, viewers are introduced to tokenized racism and ethnocentrism dominant storylines. These episodes explore the women's experiences with nonwhite and non-American-born characters whose race or ethnicity serve as the focus of their interaction.

African American characters like, other marginalized groups, are mostly absent from the hit series. When they do appear, they are cast in unimaginative, stereotypical roles. In episode 35, titled "No Ifs, Ands or Butts," an African American brother and sister are featured. Samantha, known for her promiscuity, dates Chivon. Chivon's sister Adeena confronts Samantha by telling her that she does not want her brother dating a white woman. Carrie, Miranda, and Charlotte dance around the stereotypical Mandingo representations of black men, while Samantha rejects their overt racism in favor of the covert type. Samantha declares, "I don't see color, I see conquests." Conveniently adopting the color-blind standpoint, Samantha's character avoids appearing racist by erasing the racial dimension of his identity.

On one hand, Samantha is viewed as the liberal white woman who dates interracially because she has moved beyond superficial color politics, while on the other, Adeena reads as the angry black woman who hysterically sees color and practices separatism. The power struggle or conflict is located between the white woman (Samantha) and the black woman (Adeena). The women are friendly, until Chivon, the black man, is positioned between them. When Samantha cannot "conquer" Chivon, she emasculates him by calling him a "pussy." The passive black man and his angry sister could not be conquered, so they had to be dismissed and subjugated.

Sex and the City castrates an African American man who allies himself with an African American woman. That Adeena is Chivon's sister, rather than an attractive single black woman, is no mere accident and further demonstrates the show's allegiance to hegemonic feminism. It is too far-fetched to consider that a black man is more sexually attracted to a black woman than to a white woman. Family ties and the fear of a crazy black woman make more sense and are more believable to the viewer. *Sex and the City* is careful to employ plotlines promoting limited and racist depictions of persons of color. . . .

African Americans are not the only racial-ethnic group exploited by *Sex and the City*. When the woman giggles while taking Miranda's take-out order, Miranda misinterprets this stereotypical laughter for negative judgments ("Cock-a-Doodle-Doo," episode 48). The truth is, the Chinese restaurant employee simply giggles and smiles in response to any order. Miranda is relieved to learn that this Asian stereotype is actually a reality. Her self-esteem is restored through the recognition of this stereotype. Charlotte seeks out racial minorities to meet her needs when all else fails. She has a sexual affair with the tanned-skinned gardener after many unsuccessful attempts at intercourse with her husband Trey ("What Goes Around Comes Around," episode 47). Charlotte pursues overseas adoption for a Mandarin baby as her last resort in raising a family. In her second marriage, to Harry, Charlotte sees a Chinese fertility doctor, prior to becoming pregnant. Again and again, nonwhite characters are tokenized for stereotypical story line purposes. . . .

SEXISM, PATRIARCHY, AND *SEX AND THE CITY*

Gender and sex are important themes in rereading *Sex and the City*, because so much of the women's identities is determined by their views of masculinity and its dominance over their lives. Whether one of the women is being exploited by a man or has internalized patriarchal thinking, sex and gender issues are always present. . . .

Sex and the City's centered subjects are portrayed as biological women. It serves as no surprise that *Sex and the City* positions biological women higher in the social hierarchy than transgendered women. In a patriarchal society, men becoming women will assume an oppressed position to both biological men and biological women. Men and women, as gendered constructs can be viewed as relational or even relative identities. . . .

Male-to-female transitioning contributes to our understanding of sex and gender. Marcia Yudkin offers a critical perspective in "Transsexualism and Women." In her investigation of the concept of woman, she proposes three levels of identity: biological, social, and psychological. Framing the concept of woman with levels suggests there is a hierarchy of womanness or womanhood. The biological level refers to sex organs, the social level describes the sex roles enacted or sustained, and the psychological level is the subjective identification with a gender identity. Yudkin specifies that transsexuals identify with the "opposite sex role" (101), as opposed to the opposite sex. . . .

The trilevel framework for understanding sex and gender reflects feminist discourses rampant within *Sex and the City* story lines. Episode 48 of Sex and the City ("Cock-a-Doodle-Doo") features the "pre-op [operation] up my ass crew." The preoperative transsexual males to females work the streets as prostitutes. They are loud, dirty-talking "working girls" whose late night noise disrupts Samantha's sleep. All crew members are cast as persons of color. Following a series of back and forth battles of the divas, the transgendered prostitutes of color are eventually defeated by the embodiment of woman and assume their place in the hierarchy.

While there are intersections clearly visible within this hierarchy, it is *Sex and the City*'s view of sex and gender that is formative. Socially and psychologically, the pre-ops identify themselves as women. They demonstrate stereotypically feminine characteristics such as wearing long hairstyles, makeup, and women's clothing. Yet *Sex and the City* writers are careful to point out that these "women" are preoperative and have not yet become biological women. The pre-op "up my ass crew" are transsexuals whose sex transition is incomplete, thus making them merely transgendered instead of women.

Further characterizing this hierarchical view of "woman," is reflected by depicting preoperative transsexuals as prostitutes. Sex is situated as a commodity that can be bought and sold. Therefore, the centered subjects of *Sex and the City* are inherently privileged with female biological sex organs. The battle of Samantha versus the "pre-ops" is not only about the dominance of biological women over nonbiological women, but it can also be conceptualized as biological women's triumph over biological men. The absence of female biological sex organs, renders "The Pre-ops" mere female impersonators, performing gender. They are no match for "real women."

Confusion regarding sex and gender provide challenges for the *Sex and the City* women. "Evolution" (episode 23) tells the story of Stephen, an effeminate man who dates Charlotte. Stephen resides in Chelsea and is employed as a pastry chef. Charlotte is "so confused. Is he gay or is he straight?" Stephen is effeminate in mannerism and has an acute awareness of fashion and cooking. With this interest in women-associated domains, Stephen fits Charlotte's schema of a gay man. Even after a goodnight kiss and a second date, "Charlotte wanted to be open-minded, but Stephen seemed to be making it as hard as possible." Unable to resolve her inner conflict and inability to understand Stephen, Charlotte recruits a team of experts (Carrie and Stanford) to help her determine Stephen's sexual orientation.

The purpose of discussing this episode in regard to sex and gender issues is to explicate the master narrative of *Sex and the City*. While on the surface, gender and sexual orientation are clearly intersections within this story line, a deeper understanding of this presentation shows us that patriarchal thinking is internalized within these women. . . . Writers of this episode make clear that Charlotte's quest is to discern Stephen's sexual orientation in the face of questionable masculinity. We do not read the story as Charlotte's inability to accept that Stephen is heterosexual, or not gay. Viewers are also discouraged from interpreting "Evolution" as Charlotte's exploration of Stephen's gender identity, which is what seems to be the purpose of the story line.

Instead, *Sex and the City* opts for a mundane discussion of an evolutionary phenenomenon: "The gay straight man was a new string of heterosexuals spawned in Manhattan as a result of overexposure to fashion, exotic cuisine, musical theater and antique furniture." This episode is powerful in that it shows us how difficult it is to move beyond our narrow frameworks for understanding gender. In fact, Charlotte enjoys Stephen's company and a two-orgasm sexual encounter, but in the end cannot accept his feminine characteristics. "Her masculine side wasn't evolved enough for a man whose feminine side was as highly evolved as Stephen's." The *Sex and the City* women are not attracted to men who have evolved into homosexuals, and they reject notions that they can have romantic relationships with men who display their feminine sides. . . .

HETEROSEXISM, HOMOPHOBIA AND *SEX AND THE CITY*

Sexual orientation is a regular theme for *Sex and the City*. Stanford Blache is a white, gay character on the show. During season four, Samantha has a "lesbian relationship" with a Brazilian artist named Maria. *Sex and the City* exploits nonheterosexual orientations.

Bisexual, lesbian, and gay male characters are all presented in ways that marginalize their existence and reify the dominance of heterosexuality.

Bisexuality is a deeply misunderstood sexual orientation that receives little research attention. Currently, there is no specific model of bisexual identity development. . . . Furthermore, . . . many persons engaging in bisexual behavior do not label themselves as such. The lack of research, a clear definition of the term, and invisibility contributes to our society's adoption of myths. These misconceptions marginalize bisexuality and uphold binary systems of sexual orientation. . . .

[I]n *Sex and the City*'s "Boy, Girl, Boy, Girl" (episode 34). Carrie dates Sean, a younger man, who she casually learns has dated both men and women. Carrie becomes preoccupied by trying to figure out whom he is more attracted to, men or women. She wants to understand how bisexuality works. Eventually, the focus moves away from the development of their relationship to Carrie's persistent confusion as she tries to comprehend and fit in with Sean's bisexual lifestyle. Throughout the episode, viewers are treated to a review of the myths of bisexuality.

Joy Morgenstern outlines myths of bisexuality. One is that bisexuals are sexually promiscuous nymphomaniacs. Episode 34 ("Boy, Girl") ends with a gathering of Sean's bisexual friends. They are introduced to Carrie by detailing their previous romantic partnerships with each other. These bisexuals, you see, have all dated each other. A second myth of bisexuality is that bisexuals are gay people who are still in the closet. Bisexuality is then viewed as a transitional phase that will end in homosexuality or heterosexuality. . . . *Sex and the City* builds on this myth by casting Sean's character as younger than Carrie. Being in his twenties, Sean is still developing and transitioning. According to the myth, one day he will self-actualize and end his exploration.

And a third myth of bisexuality that we see in this *Sex and the City* episode is that bisexuals are indecisive neurotics who will never be sexually satisfied. Sean and his friends decide to play a game of spin the bottle at the party. Not only does this build on the characterization of bisexuality as a developmental phase, but it also lends itself to this indecisive myth. Just spin a bottle and have a sexual experience with whomever and whatever. Bisexuality is further marginalized by being cast as a game for which Carrie is "too old." Bisexuality is regarded as the problem, rather than Carrie's stereotypical and hegemonic views of it. As a centered subject, she chooses to relegate this sexual orientation to a status lower than that of her own. . . .

CLASS EXPLOITATION AND *SEX AND THE CITY*

. . . The women of *Sex and the City* enjoy economic privilege. As professional women, we learn that they are formally educated and able to independently support themselves. Yet their economic privilege does not exist within a vacuum. This class privilege is supported by a hierarchy that remains intact and a capitalist system that demands it. "The Caste System" (episode 22) reveals how the system—which has provided upward mobility for the *Sex and the City* women—continues to exploit working-class men and women.

Foreign domestic servants' labor provides the economically privileged increased freedom, at a low cost. In "The Caste System," Samantha separates herself from this contested feminist issue. While she, "didn't believe in having servants, she didn't mind dating a man who did." Samantha's abject stance on servitude reveals the unresolved nature of this debate within feminist discussions. Her statement reveals that she sees the value in having servants, but might experience discomfort in hiring servants for herself. The man she's dating, Harvey Turkell, is described as a real estate giant "who made a killing in the market, turning Chelsea sweatshops into condos for the upwardly trendy." Sum, his Asian domestic servant, initially appears servile and polite. However, when Harvey is absent, we learn that Sum is quite the opposite. Sum's English speaking improves and she is no longer restricted in her physical range of motion. Sum has been putting on an act to appear complicit with her boss's classist and racist views of her.

Samantha is abused by Sum and is falsely accused of assaulting her. While Sum cries to "Mr. Harvey," Samantha rolls her eyes in disgust. She did not have to feel discomfort about hiring servants after all. Sum was actually exploiting Mr. Harvey, not the other way around. Writing class exploitation in a way that subverts and distorts the reality of domestic servitude upholds the ruling class's ability to condone the power they maintain over manipulative domestics. . . .

Class exploitation is not only addressed among poor, immigrant women. *Sex and the City* also explores how class differences affect relationships between men and women.

When Miranda the lawyer dates Steve the bartender, class issues emerge sooner than later. At first, it seems that the issue is purely financial. How can a couple resolve the nontraditional dynamic of a woman earning and possessing more money than a man? "She was so crazy about him that she let him take her out to dinner, but only to the places he could afford." Miranda cares deeply for Steve and will not allow him to spend beyond his means. Later described as "yuppie guilt," Miranda seems to harbor conflicting feelings about her class privilege. She wants Steve to spend and live within his means, but she also wants the same for herself. She fails to acknowledge and accept what she truly feels, and this results in guilt. Miranda and her friends discuss the impact of class differences on her relationship:

MIRANDA: None of this matters to me. I just don't want it to matter to him. It's like when single men have a lot of money, it works to their advantage. But when a single woman has money, it's like a problem, you have to deal with. It's ridiculous. I wanna enjoy my success, not apologize for it.

SAMANTHA: Bravo, honey, bravo.

CHARLOTTE: But you're talking about more than a difference in income. You're talking about a difference in background and education. This guy is working class.

MIRANDA: Working class?

CARRIE: It's the millennium sweetie. We don't say things like "working class."

CHARLOTTE: But you're trying to pretend that we live in a classless society, and we don't. ("Old Dogs. New Dicks," episode 21)

In this instance, Charlotte is the voice of reason. Miranda wants to liberate herself from the discomfort she believes is the result of money mattering to Steve. In this instance, the problem has been misdiagnosed. Miranda has judged Steve negatively regarding his working-class background. In one scene, Miranda visits Steve's apartment for the first time. She is visibly constricted in her reaction. She scans the apartment and sees his corduroy suit. What remains unsaid is that Miranda thinks his apartment is trash and his suit is inappropriate for her upcoming company dinner party. Miranda believes that as is, Steve is inadequate, prompting her to take him shopping for a new suit.

Miranda offers to pay, but Steve will not let her. While up to this point, Miranda would not allow Steve to spend beyond his means, she has now decided that she "does not want to apologize for her success." Steve's credit card is denied, and he becomes upset with Miranda's attempts to pay for the suit. However, he does take the suit home by charging some on credit, writing a check, and paying in cash. Steve would later return the suit, explaining that he could not afford it. He ends the relationship with Miranda on the evening they were to attend the party. Miranda believes that Steve has ended the relationship because she's been punished for her success. When Miranda decided that Steve was not good enough and needed to be changed, it marked the beginning of the end.

Sex and the City tells us that Miranda and Steve's class difference is the cause of their break up. This is not true. Their relationship is going well until Miranda fails to admit to herself that she is ashamed of Steve and exploits his economic status in order to avoid feeling guilty and to further uphold her social position. Miranda and Steve eventually will resume their friendship, have a child together, and get married. This, of course, occurs after Steve gains class mobility by becoming a business owner.

Sex and the City, with its mass-based popularity and appeal, projects powerful images to audiences. When we fail to critically read and reread media presentations, we run the risk of internalizing and reproducing our own oppression.

WORKS CITED

"Boy, Girl, Boy, Girl." Episode 34. Writ. Jenny Bicks. Dir. Pam Thomas. *Sex and the City*. Home Box Office. 25 June 2000.

"The Caste System." Episode 22. Writ. Darren Star. Dir. Allison Anders. *Sex and the City*. Home Box Office. 8 Aug. 1999.

"Cock-a-Doodle-Doo." Episode 48. Writ. Michael Patrick King. Dir. Allen Coulter. *Sex and the City*. Home Box Office. 15 Oct. 2000.

"Evolution." Episode 23. Writ. Cindy Chupak. Dir. Pam Thomas. *Sex and the City*. Home Box Office. 15 Aug. 1999.

Labi, Nadya. "Girl Power" *Time*. (1998).

Lorde, Audre. (2000). "Age, Race, Class, and Sex: Women Redefining Women." *Feminist Theory: A Reader*. Ed. Wendy Kolmar and Frances Bartkowski. Mountain View: Mayfield, 2003. 288–93.

Maddox, Garry. "Is *Sex and the City* Gay?" *Sydney Morning Herald Online*. 9 Feb. 2004. 5 July 2006, www.smh.com.au/articles/2004/02/09/1076175068807.html?from=storyhrs.

Morgenstern, Joy. "Myths of Bisexuality." *Off Our Backs*. May–June (2004): 46–48.

"No Ifs, Ands, or Butts." Episode 35. Writ. Michael Patrick King. Dir. Nacole Holof-center. *Sex and the City*. Home Box Office. 9 July 2000.

"Old Dogs, New Dicks." Episode 21. Writ. Jenny Bicks. Dir. Alan Taylor. *Sex and the City*. Home Box Office. 1 Aug. 1999.

"What Goes Around Comes Around." Episode 47. Writ. Darren Starr. Dir. Allen Coulter. *Sex and the City*. Home Box Office. 8 Oct. 2000.

Yudkin, Marcia. "Transsexualism and Women: A Critical Perspective." Feminist Studies 4.3 (1978): 97–106.

PART IX

CHANGE AND POLITICS

Lesbians and gays flock to San Francisco to participate in marriage, an institution once denounced as a bastion of sexism by the early feminist and gay liberation movements. Young men in college "rush" to join gay fraternities, seemingly subverting homophobia by going straight into the heart of masculinist hegemony. Meanwhile, a multi-racial group of men from different nations gather to issue a declaration on gender rights. The chapters in this section examine how social change is emerging in the daily practices of individuals and communities, through social movement organizations and in renegotiated institutions and in the forward-looking visions of the future. Change is multifaceted and comes from unlikely candidates and in unlikely places.

College fraternity culture is widely recognized and portrayed in popular films such as *Animal House* as one of the stalwarts of homophobic masculinist culture. Yet no institution is immune to change, and as King-To Yeung and Mindy Strombler show, gay men on college campuses are embracing fraternities as their own, innovating Delta Lambda Phi as a gay fraternity. Becoming simultaneously gay and Greek does involves some tightrope tensions, and the men of Delta Lambda Phi negotiate these tensions, Yeung and Strombler observe, by desexualizing and defeminizing their fraternity activities and interactions. This strategy can be seen as either capitulation to conformity with gender norms, or as the assimilation of a heterosexual institution to homosexual culture. Social change, we learn from this article, is rarely uniformly simple or unidirectional; it is often contradictory and messy.

The next chapters examine several other spaces of social change. First, Thomas Rogers focuses our attention on the micro, specifically chromosomes and the reality that people are born neither fully female nor male. As he puts it, "everyone's a little bit of both," and this acknowledgement needs to be followed with social recognition of intersex persons. This is followed by a short but powerful declaration from a global symposium on men, boys and gender equality that occurred in Brazil in 2009. Here we hear the voices of a diverse group of men from eighty nations, mostly from the global South, speaking out against continued gender oppression of women and girls, and the violence and self-destruction that gendered systems of inequality pose for men and boys. The Rio Plan of Action calls for change from the bottom to the top. This includes changes in men's gender attitudes and practices, as well as programmatic efforts of community based organizations, employers, non-profit organizations, and state agencies to eradicate gender oppressions and inequalities. Can white women use their privileged positions and resources to promote social change for poor, incarcerated women of color? That is the topic of the next article, by Jodie Michelle Lawston. Based on a study of a white women's antiracist, anti-prison organization that works on behalf of incarcerated women, she finds that sisterhood across class and race can bridge differences and promote progressive social change. Along the way, complex negotiations of "sisterhood" and solidarity are forged, and the author argues that ultimately, white feminist organizations pursing social change cannot veil differences of race and class, but must be willing to recognize, name and understand those differences. The next article provides us with some retrospective reflections on Hillary Clinton's presidential campaign. As Kathyrn Kish Sklar compellingly shows, Hillary Clinton's campaign both challenged and echoed familiar American political patterns concerning race and gender. The author argues that Clinton deliberately projected a "masculine mystique" of competence, and she suggests that future women candidates will need to confront both gender and race issues more directly.

Is sexism a static, permanent and unyielding characteristic? Are men so committed to retaining patriarchal privileges that they are unable to change and support justice and equality in gender relations? The last chapter by Kevin Powell, suggests that the answer to this question is a resounding no. In his poignant and candid confession of the dilemmas he has faced as a recovering misogynist, Powell opens the door to a world based on new consciousness and newly negotiated relations of race and gender. Together, the authors in this final section of the book show us that embracing the prism of difference is a vital step toward building a more democratic future.

45

Gay and Greek

The Identity Paradox of Gay Fraternities

KING-TO YEUNG

MINDY STOMBLER

. . . Our research will examine the tensions faced by a group of self-identified gay men as they sought both to emulate and change the oppressive majority culture. We examine how the collective identity of a particular organization, a gay fraternity, emerged as members negotiated their precarious location with one foot placed in one of the most traditionally heterosexist cultures in straight society, the college fraternity culture (Martin and Hummer 1989; Moffatt 1989; Stombler 1994) and the other placed in an oppositional gay culture. Current gay identity research tends to focus on identity construction as an act of activism against mainstream culture. By concentrating research efforts on this subset of the gay population, sociologists learn more about oppositional strategies than "mainstreaming" strategies in gaining legitimization from the dominant culture. Given the heterosexist nature of the traditional fraternity, this research juxtaposes how assimilation into and subversion of the dominant order can co-exist in paradoxical ways.

The national gay fraternity, Delta Lambda Phi (DLP)—consisting of sixteen chapters across the United States—served as a social alternative for gay college men. DLP modeled itself after traditional fraternities and retained the traditional features of brotherhood, rituals, and group hierarchical structure.[1] Its members shared straight fraternity goals such as involvement in campus social life, enhanced prestige on campus, networking opportunities and alumni connections, and, although not explicitly stated, achieving power over women and other men[2] (cf. Martin and Hummer 1989; Sanday 1990; Stombler 1994; Stombler and Padavic 1997; Stombler and Martin 1994). Yet, based on our observations at the national convention and within the observed chapter and our interview and archival data, DLP rejected some traditional fraternity practices such as hazing, promoting single-race membership, encouraging sexual coercion, and enforcing individual conformity (Stombler, Wharton, and Yeung, 1997). We contend that DLP's choice to emulate the organizational structure of straight fraternities was not arbitrary, allowing DLP members to relate to both the gay and straight worlds. Using a fraternity model provided DLP members an opportunity to subvert the heterosexist fraternal

---

King-To Yeung and Mindy Stombler, "Gay and Greek: The Identity Paradox of Gay Fraternities," from *Social Problems,* Volume 47, Number 1, pp. 134–152. Copyright © 2000, by the Society for the Study of Social Problems. All rights reserved. Reprinted from *Social Problems.*

tradition and potentially achieve legitimacy within the college campus community. A fraternity model that stressed brotherhood also allowed members to embrace and criticize aspects of the gay culture that they found unfulfilling. In both ways, adopting the fraternity model was a unique vehicle for members to restate what it meant to be gay and Greek. In doing so, however, DLP was faced with dilemmas that demanded that members choose between incompatible group strategies and ideologies. We will discuss not only how members constructed a collective identity within the gay fraternity, but also how the gay fraternity's placement, straddling both the gay and straight worlds, affected this development, creating a paradox of identity.[3]

METHODS AND DATA

This paper is part of a larger research project on gay fraternities (Stombler, Wharton, and Yeung 1997). Data for the project came from 42 open-ended in-depth interviews, participant observation, official manuals, and archival data.

The project was divided into two phases. In the first phase Stombler conducted participant observation for a year in the mid-1990s in a DLP chapter-in-formation. She attended all fraternity chapter meetings, social events, rituals, and community service projects. In addition she conducted in-depth face-to-face interviews with fraternity members (all members volunteered to be interviewed). Stombler also attended the National Gay Fraternity (Diva Las Vegas) where she observed interaction among members across the nation, interviewed members who responded to her research project announcement, and solicited additional interview volunteers for in-depth phone interviews.

In the second phase Yeung and Wharton joined the project and interviewed the previously recruited members from various chapters by telephone.[4] They also contacted chapter presidents and asked them for a list of additional interview volunteers. We also used the deviant cases sampling technique that involves seeking out respondents who are atypical to a setting such as straight or bisexual men in the case of the gay fraternity. Interviews—which were tape recorded and transcribed—averaged two hours. When the emergent concepts be-

came "saturated" (Glaser and Strauss 1967), we ended the interview component of the project.[5] . . .

CONSTRUCTING A GAY IDENTITY

Gay organizations as communities of identity are self-reproducing (cf. Melucci 1989) in two ways. First, the organization depends on a membership that includes individuals who identify themselves as gays or lesbians. This individual identification makes it possible for the organization to exist. Second, by participating in a gay organization, members are able to authenticate their sexual identity and reproduce the gay identity collectively. Gay identity is a point of entry for both the individual members and the organization to place sexual identity in the foreground while relegating other social identities to the background. In this section, we illustrate the dynamics of personal and collective reproduction of the gay identity by examining the ways DLP helped members to come out of the closet, bringing them into the gay community, and draw a collective boundary that challenged the traditional straight fraternity institution.

Coming Out and Moving Into the Gay World

Coming out of the closet represents the experience that gay men and lesbians have when first acknowledging their sexual orientation, identifying themselves as gay, acting on their sexual desire, disclosing this desire to other, and publicly entering the gay community (Dank 1971; Herdt 1992; Rhoads 1994; Troiden 1988). Some members of the gay fraternity reported that joining DLP marked their first coming out experience. In the observed chapter, many men used the fraternity rush event as their first function in the gay community. For instance, one member said he was so nervous that he was shaking during the rush party. Too scared to dress for the party in his dorm for fear of repercussions, he left in workout clothes and went to the mall where he purchased an outfit for the formal event and then changed into it before going to rush. The rush events often turned out to be the first time isolated gay college men met other gay men as a group.

For many members of DLP, the gay fraternity was the first site where they experienced their sexual identity in a structured form. The fraternity activities such as parties, rituals, and community service provided opportunities for new gay members to share their experiences and realfirm their commonalities as members of the gay community:

> [During pledging] we have sort of a process where we go around and get signature from all the active brothers and you talk about whatever. I went and talked with everyone about their coming out experience. . . . I feel like what brings us together is the experience of the fear of coming out. . . . I was so amazed that I was suddenly able to make connections with people who I had never felt like I could make them with before. (B08)

DLP also used formal programming to explicitly bring forth the cultural aspect of gay sexual identity. For instance, one chapter held workshops on "how to do fabulous drag" and "how to deal with HIV-AIDS when it affects you or someone you love" (B07). Another chapter included the "essential gay history" in its coming out support program:

> There's a reason why [gay men] idolize Joan Crawford: there's a reason why they love Marilyn Monroe. . . . We teach gay history in the coming out group. Everybody is supposed to know the gay history [and id tested on it on fraternity pledge tests]. (B22)

Besides transmitting a stock of knowledge about gayness, DLP also used cultural resources regarding gayness to bind its members, constructing a microcosm of the larger gay sub-cultural community. On movie nights, for instance, members often chose gay-theme movies such as "Jeffrey," or watched movies popular within gay culture:

> Instead of watching a regular old hit movie, [they] would seek out campy movies like "Breakfast at Tiffany's," "Mommy Dearest," and anything with Bette Davis [a gay icon] . . . [then, we went to the park] to play croquet and [it was] really campy. I'm like, "oh my god, my god, this is so gay, I love it!". (B30)

In another event, members played a game called "Gay Monopoly," which included "having discos instead of railroads, as well as locations and resorts popular among the gay community" (Hahn 1995). Through these events, members learned and created the cultural meaning of being gay.

Ultimately, DLP worked to redefine the meaning of being gay and helped members to recover from the fear, shame, or guilt they had experienced. Since the organization structured itself with an emphasis on brotherhood and mutual support among its members as a main goal (see below), the autonomy to become "who you are" found a structural support within the organization:

> One of our fraternity brothers was still in the closet. He didn't want to tell his family, but Pete [another brother] helped him along. He said, "Don't be ashamed of who you are. If your parents don't approve of you, fine, this is who you are." He told him, "You take it easy. Tell your parents individually or together, but you take it slowly. We'll work with you." He come out just fine even though his parents didn't approve of it at first. [His parents] kicked him out, but we found him a place to live. (B27, observed chapter)

The secure environment that DLP fostered allowed members to identify, reaffirm, and celebrate their sexual identity as gay men, incorporating them into the larger gay community. These processes of identity formation were often grounded in group work and interaction within the organization. The processes of coming out as a group and as an individual were intertwined and reinforced one another:

> It's nice to belong to a group whose motto is "making your presence known" and to know that when you go out as a group, you are going out with the intention of letting people know you are there. You are not going to hide. It's very important to me when I came out to make people know. It was part of my battle to accept my sexuality and it is nice to be with a group of men. When go out, we wear our shirts and you know we are there. You can't miss us. (B32)

Group Boundaries in the Straight World

The extent to which members as individuals, and DLP as group, could openly be out in the public, nonetheless varied according to DLP chapters' external social environments. The group boundary DLP established within the straight world was a contentious one, challenging the traditional fraternity institution on two levels. On one hand, the gay fraternity was striving to gain recognition within one of the most heterosexist institutions in American college life—the fraternity. On the other hand, DLP actively modified the traditional model by prohibiting hazing and other practices that were deemed "homophobic." At either level, DLP reconfigured its relations with the traditional institution by drawing a collective boundary that framed gayness as it core.

As a gay group, DLP demanded the right to enter the fraternity institution: "We feel if straight men can have the 'traditional' Greek experience, gay men should be able to have it as well" (DLP Web site). DLP's existence as an openly gay fraternity had the potential to "shock" the traditionally homophobic fraternity institution that encourages a "macho image" (Martin and Hummer 1989). Since the word fraternity "and the word gay are not usually associated" (B36) within this system, establishing a gay fraternity was particularly meaningful for campuses located in conservative regions:

> I think by virtue of calling ourselves the gay fraternity was making a statement nationally, especially down here. In San Francisco or Washington, D.C. or New York, gay fraternities might not be such a huge statement, but in the Bible Belt, forming any kind of gay organization is making a statement. (B21)

By coming out as a group, DLP demanded recognition: "It is making a statement to colleges and campuses saying, 'Hey, you need to recognize that you do have gay students; you have large group of them.'" (B09)

DLP also challenged the traditional fraternity model by prohibiting hazing. In official statements and group interaction, gay members claimed that hazing was unacceptable. This rejection reflected DLP's acknowledgment of oppression as part of the collective gay identity: "We feel that gays have been hazed enough by society" (DLP Web site). Unlike straight fraternities that have similar policies but often fail to follow them in practice (Nuwer 1990), DLP strictly followed the no-hazing policy, even at the local level. . . .

. . . Men in straight fraternities tend to define masculinity narrowly, emphasizing sexual conquest, competition, ability to consume alcohol, and a devaluing of the feminine (Martin and Hummer 1989; Moffatt 1989). Members of DLP did not embrace this narrow definition of masculinity. For example, gay members did not stigmatize effeminate behaviors; indeed, DLP members encouraged expressions of femininity. One member explained that "one thing in the gay fraternity that you don't see in the straight fraternities is that we don't have to play out our masculinity. You know, like prove our masculinity in certain ways" (B03). Member desiring to dress up on drag found the fraternity a safe place to practice "femaling" (Ekins 1977) and to express their individuality.

Embracing this gender fluidity and resisting hegemonic masculinity have been major components of gay identity (see Norton 1996). DLP's organizational events frequently structured (both intentionally and unintentionally) an arena for members to transgress gender boundaries. One member described how, at an initiation party, the "butch" members who had never though of doing drag, attempted "border-crossing":

> The thing that sticks out the most from that evening is that we had what we call the Drag in the Bag Contest, which I think is unique to our chapter. . . . Without our knowledge, the little pledges got together all sorts of female and other paraphernalia . . . basically dress-up clothes, mostly female, but other things were in there also. You would see some of these really butch men dress up in drag and basically just have a good time with it. They were taking picture. (B23) . . .

THE PARADOX OF MAINSTREAMING

The group goals of DLP were inconsistent: although attempting to contest the traditional practices of straight fraternities, members also sought to construct a "normal," comparable fraternity image:

> We have a national [organization]; we have the same type of criteria that we all go through year after year. We're all men, and even though we are gay men, there's really not anything that really differentiates us

from other men down the block in the other [straight] fraternities. (B13)

Mainstreaming was thus a way for DLP to seek legitimacy in the straight world.[6] This process involved the fraternity seeking to build respectability and to emphasize sameness over difference vis-à-vis traditional fraternities. Downplaying differences to integrate into the mainstream was contradictory for an organization that was based on a gay membership. In order to reestablish what the fraternity thought was the appropriate image for gay men, primarily by defying sterotypes through desexualization and defeminization, DLP implicitly reaffirmed the negative stereotypes imposed by the straight world. We will discuss these strategies to illustrate how DLP sought to downplay the gay identity in paradoxical ways.

Desexualizing

The gay fraternity was well aware of the misconceptions that members of the Greek system and the campus community had about gay men, in general, and DLP, specifically. Members found it particularly disturbing that outsiders associated being gay exclusively with sexual behavior. One member complained: "Here at the university they think we are the biggest sex club in the world. People have that viewpoint because you see gay and you see sex and that is all they think. We are not like that" (B27, observed chapter).

One way DLP members promoted the desexualizing goal (and group solidarity in case of failed relationship) was to formally discourage casual sex and ingroup dating (especially between pledges and brothers whose relationships leaders defined as inherently unequal and therefore potentially exploitative). DLP was more tolerant of long-term monogamous relationships between brothers, especially considering that some brothers joined as couples. Even with a formal ban, some casual relationships and encounters did occur. We noted pledges interested in joining the fraternity to meet and date men, pledges dating brothers, brothers casually dating brothers, and rare incidences of open casual sex. Either way, intra-fraternity dating was more often a consequence of the men's proximity to one another than a characteristic of the fraternal form, and fraternity leaders explicitly discouraged it, promoting ideologies of familial relationships as opposed to sexual ones. Clearly by adopting the fraternal organization form with its pseudo-familial kinship network of "brothers," and stressing the ideal of brotherhood over romance, DLP leaders made a strong statement against an overtly sexualized gay identity.

While DLP members did not always succeed in their desexualizing goal, their levels of sensitivity and reflexivity were reflected in how they dealt with problematic situations regarding the sexual image of DLP. During one gay pride event, a DLP chapter sold snow cones with "gay theme flavors" such as "lesbian lime." When "Gilbert's grapes"—referring to male genitals—appeared as a flavor, it triggered serious criticism from some members of the chapter:

> I mean because children attend the event and some straight people attend the event, and to me, I am really quite tired of the sexual stereotype that straight people have of gays, and to me, I just thought that this strengthened the impression that other people have of us, and I think at a public event that there was no need to use that. . . . I don't want to belong to an organization that promotes or encourages sexual innuendo or the perception that straight people may have of us. (B02)

This member successfully brought the issue to a vote where brothers decided their behavior was inappropriate and should be avoided in the future, thus reaffirming the desexualizing goal.

Public presentation of a non-sexualized image of DLP was paradoxical. It was impossible for DLP to address its own existence as a fraternity without also addressing the sexuality of its members. While desexualizing strategies presented DLP members as "normal" in the straight world, this strategy also interfered with another major goal, the celebration of sexual diversity. At the very least, we observed destigmatization of homosexuality only occurring in the back-stage of fraternity interaction. For example, members welcomed private conversation and jokes packed with sexual innuendo (see Wharton 1998). Such a distinction between the public and private sphere reflected DLP's paradoxical efforts to establish both their identities as legitimized Greek members and as non-stigmatized gay males.

Defeminizing

Although some fraternity members enjoyed acting feminine within the private space of the fraternity, they were aware that, in order to gain acceptance on campus and in the general public, members could not act like "flaming queens." Feminine behavior was a concern for DLP and its public image, particularly in inter-fraternity functions:

> The queeny guys sometimes don't want to tone it down, you know? It becomes really uncomfortable . . . to the more butch guys. I guess it's because [the butch guys] don't mind, but they don't want to be stereotyped as queeny. So when we're in public, it becomes a problem when the queeny guys just go off: "Girl Friend! Oh he's got a nice ass." And the straight-acting guys are like: "Uh-oh . . . let's, let's tone it down there. We don't want to draw too much attention to ourselves. We just like to keep a low profile." (B18)

In this instance, the concern over feminine behavior appeared to be an issue only for the "butch" members who felt uncomfortable with the "queens." Butch members perceived that acting "queenly" reinforced the stereotypes the straight population had about gay people. Indeed, straight-acting brothers often won such public controversy. When asked to "tone down" their queeniness, the queeny brothers usually complied.

By defining feminine behavior as inappropriate in public, many members co-opted the conventional prejudice that defined femininity as negative. In one chapter, the fraternity designed a specific program to ascribe gender-appropriate behavior. While the fraternity promoted tolerance of "flaming" behavior, one member, nevertheless, admitted that tolerance of flaming behavior was bounded. "Flaming queens" were required to learn appropriate behavior from the chapter's "True Gentlemen Program," aimed at preparing members for the real world:

> [The program taught] what to do etiquette-wise when you are going out to dinner and when you are doing this or doing that. It is not appropriate in the business setting or in a meeting to turn around and snap your fingers and queen out. If we are in a social setting [i.e.,

within the chapter], you can do that all you want. It is just learning appropriateness. (B09)

Prescribing and proscribing behaviors through member interaction and organizational practice also contradicted the group ideology of celebrating individuality that emphasized "being who you are." One member complained about this inconsistency:

> I got very aggravated at the brothers who, in a large group, act all butch and put others down for being nelly.[7] Then, in private, or when they get drunk, they turn into the biggest queens this side of Branson, Missouri. (B10)

Concentrating on how straight people might reach toward gay people through self-sanctioning, DLP shifted their group orientation from gay-focused to straight-referencing. The gay fraternity achieved this shift by clearly distinguishing between private space and the public sphere, thus splitting the public self from the private self (cf. Goffman 1959) as described by the above brother. This split also resulted in different identity "markedness" (Brekhus 1996) according to the situation in which members were acting and interacting.

In the private fraternity space, the gay identity was salient both to the individual brothers and the fraternity as a collective. One brother explained that being feminine "was the standard pattern in the gay community, [such as] using feminine pronouns, and even by [calling one another] feminine names. It's very normal" (B19). Descried in the previous section, we also observed that the fraternity structured certain levels of gender fluidity, allowing members to pursue their individual preference of self-presentation.

In the public sphere, however, brothers often downplayed the stereotypical gay image, essentially reaffirming the negative connotation commonly attached to gay people.[8] Furthermore, by configuring a "normal" mainstream image, the gay fraternity restructured the gay identity at the collective level. Despite that essentially all of them were gay men, DLP used its group structure and group culture of brotherhood to reclaim their connection to the traditional fraternity institution in the hope of recognition. Rather than completely denying their gayness, members of DLP viewed main-streaming as a way to reconstruct a new, more palat-able gay image, if not a more realistic one, Yet DLP's decisions regarding how to operate in both the straight and gay worlds led to their public collective main-streaming goal contradicting their private organiza-tional goal of celebrating individuality, gay culture, and an uncompromised gay identity.

GAY BROTHERHOOD: CREATING AN ALTERNATIVE GAY SPACE

Just as mainstreaming strategies of the gay fraternity restated what it meant to be gay in the straight world, the formalization of a non-sexually defined brother-hood reshaped the meaning of membership in the larger gay community. Just as DLP utilized gay culture to challenge and modify the traditional fraternity model, it adopted the traditional fraternity ideal of brotherhood to create an alternative space in the gay community, attempting to improve a culture they found alienating and unfulfilling.

Despite their incorporation of aspects of the gay culture, many DLP members remained critical of as-pects of the larger gay community. The founders of DLP recognized that while the larger gay community supported a plethora of clubs, most were either prima-rily motivated toward political or service goals or in-volved in "deviant" activities (Chapter Handbook). Current members of DLP also viewed the gay culture as over-sexualized, filled with destructive behaviors, lacking depth, and too appearance-oriented. One member complained that:

> A big part of the gay culture is the culture of sex and all the rituals that surround it—from the bar scene to social things. . . . People are doing things that ostensi-bly are just fun and they are doing it because it is SO MUCH FUN. But if you think about it, there is really nothing all that fun about it; it is kind of self-destructive. (B05)

Members also felt that the gay culture, as a whole, em-phasized the "outside rather than the inside," because of its focus on appearance, youth, and power. Refer-ring to Los Angeles, known as a gay hub, one member described a "pervasive superficiality":

> There is this competition to look like a model, to have the best looking [penis], the perfect body with all these muscles, a perfect looking face, clothes and cars, and all this stuff." (B12)

The members also judged the gay culture to be lacking cohesion:

> Gay men are very alienated from each other. We go around; we walk around on the streets and see each other, but at the same time, there seems to be a lack of a real . . . there is just this lack of feeling that we are a community. . . . There is a substantial amount of re-jection of gay men toward each other. (B21)

Other members found that gay men were too opinion-ated, that they tended to judge each other critically, and that they lacked trust toward one another and "put each other down a lot."

Drawing on the traditional fraternity model, the gay fraternity promoted a bond among its members using mythical ideals of brotherhood (see Clawson 1989; Clemens 1996). Brothers used shared symbols and rit-uals to foster a collective identity, creating a semblance of close relationships and connectedness:

> We all go through the same ritual and education process. The common things that we all know are the same handshake; we all know the same signs; we know what letters stand for; we all wear the same let-ters. It is an opportunity to have something that links us and when we go out and see somebody and we talk about an event like the Night of Madness Party, every-body knows what a Night of Madness Party is. If they talk about the exam or learning the song or singing the song or doing the cheer, everybody knows it. (B04)

. . . Some members told how others who came from different backgrounds, had divergent political views, or had "extreme" personalities accepted each other and developed long-term friendships because, as one member put it, "in the end, brotherhood won out" (B24). The ideal of brotherhood was both a myth and an actual way for members to accomplish intimate re-lationships with one another.

Formalized rituals were particularly important for DLP members' expression of intimacy, especially for members who felt the need to get close to other gay men without the presence of any sexual connotations. Rituals such as the "warm fuzzy" helped achieve this goal:

> In our warm fuzzy exercise, we have a ball of yarn, or we have a warm, fuzzy pillow or something. And then one person starts and throws the pillow at somebody and gives that person a warm fuzzy. Like, "oh, thank you for helping me out, you're one of the nicest people I've seen." And that person has to throw it to somebody else in the fraternity. We did this like for two hours, until we're all like really comfortable and tired. Its all sappy, and then a box of Kleenex gets passed around. It's like, "boo hoo [weeping sound] you're so wonderful to me." You know, a big drama, but it's great; it really pulls us all together. (B18)

This organization practice produced "emotion work" (Hochschild 1985) through which DLP members realized the ideal of brotherhood. Emotion work facilitated solidarity and allowed this non-conventional group to "create and legitimize new emotion norms that include expectations about how members should feel about themselves" (Taylor and Whittier 1996: 177). By fostering intimacy and emotional expression among gay men, the gay fraternity broke the conventional norms that detach masculinity from emotional expression for men in general (Cancian 1987) and for gay men in the particular clone culture (Blachford 1981; Levine 1998).[9] Thus, the brotherhood that DLP cultivated was both a brotherhood for men and also uniquely "gay" in the sense that it was a direct response to the need of young, college, gay men who sought an alternative site for interaction and support. Using the traditional fraternity model, whose quasi-familial nature facilitated the desexualizing strategy that allowed DLP to both mainstream its image and redefine the meaning of gay male relationships in the gay world, helped DLP brothers address their dissatisfaction with the gay culture. Being gay and being brothers were two forms of collective identity that helped members of DLP connect themselves together in transcendental unity, downplaying all types of social differences. This collective identity also reflected the

placement of the fraternity in two worlds, as it simultaneously emulated and resisted the straight world and reproduced and criticized the gay world. . . .

CONCLUSION

. . . By emulating the organizational structure and drawing upon cultural resources such as the ideal of brotherhood from traditional fraternities, members of DLP were able to formalize intimate relations between gay men, thus addressing their dissatisfaction with a gay culture they considered too alienating and too sexual. At the same time, the gay fraternity drew upon cultural resources from the gay world, realized in policies that prohibited hazing, celebrated diversity, and supported in-group actions like performing gender fluidity, in order to resist the institutional oppression of the traditional fraternity system.

Gay fraternity group strategies included a mix of contradictory elements that frequently placed its collective identity in question. Mainstreaming strategies and downplaying gayness in public space created a paradoxical situation, similar to closeting, that contradicted DLP's goal of "making our presence known." This assimilation strategy was clearly limiting for a group that sought recognition in both the college and gay communities. In addition to the mainstream straight fraternity institution, the cultural configuration of the larger gay community shaped the way DLP organized its boundaries. Arguing for an alternative space that valued non-sexual intimacy, members' support of a men-only ideology based on the fraternity model also came into conflict with a gay culture that, to a great extent, advocates gender inclusivity. DLP thus operated in relative isolation compared to other gay organizations in the gay community and other fraternities in the collegiate Greek system. Consequently, DLP failed to become a full member of either world. . . .

NOTES

1. While DLP modeled itself after the traditional college fraternity, only one chapter had a fraternity house.

2. See Wharton and Stombler (1999) for a discussion of DLP's reproduction of hegemonic masculinity.

3. By "paradox" we mean something with seemingly contradictory qualities in reference both to being gay and to being involved in a fraternity (where masculinity has traditionally been defined hegemonically as not-gay and not-female) and to claiming simultaneous oppositional and mainstream identities.

4. The respondents either signed consent forms ensuring confidentiality or gave their verbal consent to participating. We use a number system in this paper to identity individual members (e.g., "B 23").

5. Saturation refers to the point in the process of data collection and analysis where incidents of a particular category becomes repetitive and additional data no longer elaborate upon the meaning of the category (Charmaz 1983).

6. DLP's group strategies were similar to the early Homophile movement in the pre-Stonewall era when activists engaged in mainstreaming to "normalize" the gay identity by establishing respectability in the public sphere (D'Emilio 1983). But unlike the early Homophiles, the post-Stonewall cultural and institutional configuration no longer provided DLP an environment in which the fraternity could seek normalization without also addressing itself as a transgressive "agent." The strategic use of public and private presentation, which we will discuss below, was a reflection of this dilemma.

7. According to DiLallo (1994), "nelly" refers to gay men being effeminate.

8. This public/private distinction was far from an intentional group goal for DLP. Downplaying the gay identity in public was a consequence and potentially a reconciliation of DLP's contradictory attempts at both legitimization and transgression.

9. According to Levine's (1998) ethnographic study, the gay clone culture, which emerged in the 1970s and gradually retreated in the mid-1980s, was a subset of the gay culture that parodied the presentational style of heterosexual working class men—a tough macho image—and favored anonymous sexual relations as a way of displaying "real" masculinity.

REFERENCES

Blachford, Gregg 1981 "Male dominance and the gay world." In *The Making of the Modern Homosexual,* ed. Kenneth Plummer, 184–210. Totowa, NJ: Barnes & Noble.

Brekhus, Wayne 1996 "Social marking and the mental coloring of identity: Sexual identity construction and maintenance in the United States." *Sociological Forum* 11(3):497–522.

Cancian, Francesca M. 1987 *Love in America: Gender and Self-Development.* Cambridge, UK: Cambridge University Press.

Chapter Handbook Delta Lambda Phi. (archival data).

Charmaz, Kathy 1983 "The grounded theory method: An explication and interpretation." In *Contemporary Field Research,* ed. R. Emerson, 109–126. Boston: Little Brown.

Clawson, Mary Ann 1989 *Constructing Brotherhood: Class, Gender, and Fraternalism.* Princeton, NJ: Princeton University Press.

Clemens, Elisabeth S. 1996 "Organizational form as framer Collective identity and political strategy in the American Labor Movement, 1880–1920." In *Comparative Perspectives on Social Movements: Political Opportunities, Mobilizing Structures, and Cultural Framings,* eds. Doug McAdam, John D. McCarthy and Mayer N. Zald, 205–226. Cambridge, MA: Cambridge University Press.

Dank, Barry M. 1971 "Coming out in the gay world." *Psychiatry* 34(2):180–197.

D'Emilio, John 1983 *Sexual Politics, Sexual Communities: The Making of a Homosexual Minority in the United States, 1940–1970.* Chicago: University of Chicago Press.

DiLallo, Kevin 1994 *The Unofficial Gay Manual: Living the Lifestyle (or at Least Appearing to).* New York: Doubleday.

DLP Web site http://members.aol.com/dlpalpha/faq.html (archival data).

Ehrhart, Julie D., and Bernice R. Sandler 1985 *Campus Gang Rape: Party Game?* Washington, DC: Association for American Colleges.

Ekins, Richard 1997 *Male Femaling: A Grounded Theory Approach to Cross-Dressing and Sex-Changing.* London: Routledge.

Epstein, Steven 1996 "A queer encounter: Sociology and the study of sexuality." In *Queer Theory/Sociology,* ed. Steven Seidman, 145–167. Cambridge, MA: Blackwell.

Garrett-Gooding, J., and Robert Senter, Jr. 1987 "Attitudes and acts of aggression on a university campus." *Sociological Inquiry* 57:348–372.

Glaser, Barney, and Anselm Strauss 1967 *The Discovery of Grounded Theory.* Chicago: Aldine.

Goffman, Erving 1959 *The Presentation of Self in Everyday Life.* Garden City, NY: Doubleday.

Hahn, Shannon 1995 "Gay frat first in U.S. to get house." *The Minnesota Daily,* October 24 (archival data).

Herdt, Gilbert 1992 "Coming out as a rite of passage: A Chicago study." In *Gay Culture in America: Essays from the Field,* ed. Gilbert Herdt, 29–67. Boston: Beacon Press.

Hochschild, Arlie Russell 1985 *The Managed Heart: Commercialization of Human Feeling.* Berkeley: University of California Press.

Levine, Martin P. 1998 *Gay Macho: The Life and Death of the Homosexual Clone.* New York: New York University Press.

———. 1986 "Grounded theory and organizational research." *Journal of Applied Behavioral Science* 22(2): 141–157.

Melucci, Alberto 1989 *Nomads of the Present: Social Movements and Individual Needs in Contemporary Society.* London: Century Hutchinson.

Moffatt, Michael 1989 *Coming of Age in New Jersey: College and American Culture.* New Brunswick: Rutgers University Press.

Norton, Rictor 1996 *The Myth of the Modern Homosexual: Queer History and the Search for Cultural Unity.* London: Cassell.

Nuwer, Hank 1990 *Broken Pledges: The Deadly Rite of Hazing.* Atlanta: Longstreet Press.

Rhoads, Robert A. 1994 *Coming Out in College: The Struggle for a Queer Identity.* Westport, CT: Bergin and Garvey.

Sanday, Peggy Reeves 1990 *Fraternity Gang Rape: Sex, Brotherhood, and Privilege on Campus.* New York: New York University Press.

Stombler, Mindy 1994 "'Buddies' or 'slutties': The collective sexual reputation of fraternity little sisters." *Gender and Society* 8(3):293–296.

Stombler, Mindy, and Patricia Yancey Martin 1994 "Bringing women in, keeping women down: Fraternity 'little sister' organizations." *Journal of Contemporary Ethnography* 23(2):150–184.

Stombler, Mindy, and Irene Padavic 1997 "Sister acts: Resisting men's domination in black and white fraternity little sister programs." *Social Problems* 44(2):257–275.

Taylor, Verta, and Nancy E. Whittier 1996 "Analytical approaches to social movement culture: The culture of the Women's Movement." In *Social Movements and Culture. Social Movements, Protest, and Contention,* Vol. 4, eds. Hank Johnston and Bert Klandermans, 163–187. Minneapolis, MN: University of Minnesota Press.

Troiden, Richard R. 1988 *Gay and Lesbian Identity: A Sociological Analysis.* Dix Hills, NY: General Hall.

Wharton, Renee 1998 *Hegemonic Masculinity in Gay Fraternities: Reproduction or Resistance?* Master's Thesis. Lubbock, TX: Texas Tech University.

Wharton, Renee, and Mindy Stombler 1999 "Making men in gay fraternities: Reproducing and resisting hegemonic masculinity." Unpublished manuscript. Texas Tech University.

46

We're All Intersex

Thomas Rogers

In the fall of 1998, Lisa May Stevens, a 32-year-old from Idaho, went on a camping trip. Stevens had been told for most of her life that she was a boy, but in her 20s had discovered the truth about her sex—that she had been born a hermaphrodite, and that doctors had conducted surgeries on her genitalia as an infant. After learning the news, she consulted her priest, who said that while God usually condemns suicides, for her he might make an exception. A decade later, on the third day of her camping trip, she put a pistol under her jaw and pulled the trigger.

Gerald N. Callahan, an associate professor in the microbiology, immunology and pathology department at Colorado State University, uses this heart-wrenching anecdote to open *Between XX and XY*, his new book about people who are born neither male nor female (at least in the traditional sense of those words). They are better known as "intersex," an umbrella term that includes people with a tremendous number of genetic conditions, from those born with an extra X chromosome to those with overdeveloped adrenal glands.

Stories about intersex people have had some cultural currency—from Jeffrey Eugenides' "Middlesex" to urban legends about Jamie Lee Curtis's hermaphroditism—but their experiences have yet to attain widespread recognition or become widely understood,

something that Callahan hopes to change. As he describes in the book, many children born with these conditions have been surgically (and often arbitrarily) assigned a gender shortly after their birth—but as his interviews with intersex people and doctors show, early surgical intervention has often had disastrous repercussions on patients' later lives. Many never fully fit into their assigned gender and don't learn about their reassignment until well into adulthood, with understandably traumatic results.

Between XX and XY combines the personal narratives of intersex people, semi-lyrical (and occasionally overdramatic) descriptions of the sexual development process, and examples from the natural world to argue for a less invasive approach to sexual reassignment for intersex children. More boldly, Callahan also attacks the "myth of the two sexes," arguing that most humans don't exist as purely "male" or "female," but somewhere in between.

Salon spoke with Callahan by phone about the diversity of the intersex world, what hyenas can teach us about gender, and why we shouldn't forget that sex ought to be fun.

S: Given that you work in the field of pathology, intersexuality isn't exactly your immediate area of expertise. How did you end up writing this book?

C: The area I'm most involved with within pathology is immunology, which on one level is the study of how we manage to distinguish ourselves from the rest of the universe. I was preparing for a course when I came across an article that mentioned that 65,000 children are born of indeterminate sex each year. I thought that was amazing—because that was a much higher number of individuals than those afflicted by many diseases I was very aware of—and I began to wonder why I hadn't heard about them.

S: Given that transgender issues have been getting so much more attention in the past few years, why haven't we heard about intersex people?

C: They haven't had movies like *Transamerica* to bring their issues to the fore. But I also think that intersex is something that makes people a little more uneasy [than gender dysphoria], because it makes us question these things we like to take more or less as God given, which is the sanctity and the gravity of sex.

S: Then you think that this polarized distinction—between men and women—isn't accurate?

C: There's no other place where we so quickly divide humans into two categories as sex. When I started doing research on the biology of sex development, one of the things that I realized is that the process is controlled by a series of enzymes and the reaction may be more or less complete. It's not just two poles where that whole process can end up. In between what we call the ideal biological male or ideal biological female, there's a whole range of other possibilities that don't differ from our basic preconceptions to the extent that we have names for them or call them a disorder. Just like with every other human trait, there are an infinite number of possibilities.

S: So in essence you'd like for people to think of sex in the same way that we think of hair color, or eye color, or other sorts of physiological traits.

C: Exactly. We might say two people have brown eyes but that doesn't mean that they're brown in exactly the same way, or what is seen through those eyes is the same.

S: Before reading the book, I was familiar with a few intersex conditions, like Turner Syndrome, in which people are missing an X chromosome, but I was honestly shocked by the sheer diversity of what you described.

C: The more I looked into it, the more I was amazed by the range of possibilities. My sampling of it is small at this point—otherwise my book would have been encyclopedic. There's XO, XY. There's non-disjunction during fetal development, so someone loses an X chromosome. Sometimes they get lost later on during cell division, so people can end up being mosaics, in which some of their cells have XO or XY or XX and their body can contain two or three different chromosomal cell types—and whether they appear physically as a man or a woman depends on which of those cells ends up in the developing gonads.

S: One of the people you speak with in the book claims that *Will & Grace* was good for intersex people, which I find interesting because I don't think many people think of them when they think of gay and lesbian culture, much less *Will & Grace*. Do you think the community should be lumped in with the gay and lesbian movement?

C: I don't claim to speak for intersex people, but I think no. I think that they have a different sense of their world than people who are gay or lesbian. Sexual preference is completely different in my mind from biological sex. Gay and lesbian people can fairly easily identify with the classic binary of male and female, and intersex people for the most part cannot. They have to me a much more complex and graduated series of events they need to deal with [than do gay and lesbian people]. I think that people have a tendency to group all of that together—sexual preference, gender dysphoria, transgender, intersex—and they're really in my mind very separate sorts of things.

S: In the book you argue that we need to think of sex as being fun—and not just for reproduction. What does that have to do with the intersex?

C: We have mutilated thousands of children a year [through genital surgery], and parents and physicians have felt the drive to do that because their

No. 1 goal is to maintain reproductive function. If we think the sole function of genitalia is reproduction, then nonreproductive genitalia is, in some sense, a bad thing and something needs to be done about it. If we think that genitals serve a lot of functions beyond reproduction, maybe we wouldn't feel like it was so necessary to try to make people look alike.

S: But don't these doctors also do these procedures to allow their patients to have a normal sex life?

C: I realize that on behalf of parents and physicians there's an enormous motivation to try to offer to this child as many opportunities as possible. But Dr. Alice Domurat Dreger [an associate professor at the Feinberg School of Medicine], whom I quote in the book, had interacted with an enormous number of intersex people, and she had met only one person who was pleased with the surgery—most thought they had lost, not gained, something.

S: So how do you think these decisions about surgery should be made?

C: This idea was introduced to me by Joel Frader [professor at Northwestern's Feinberg School of Medicine], but I think the best situation now is for the parents to be involved, for there to be a team of physicians—a surgeon, an endocrinologist, a psychiatrist—to be involved and for them to try to explain to the parents the most they can do in the most realistic way. In this world it may not be possible to raise a child without a gender, but that doesn't mean that surgery has to be performed. The ideal situation would be that, at a later date, the child could participate directly in the decision that might involve irreversible surgery.

S: You spoke with a number of intersex people in the book, most of whom have very moving stories. I imagine many of them were uncomfortable talking about their experience. How did you get them to open up to you?

C: It took me months to establish relationships where people finally acquired enough trust and were willing to share with me. I'm amazed in hindsight that it came together as well as it did, because my own stupidity at the outset alienated nearly everyone.

At first I put out an ad saying I was doing research for a book, without establishing my credentials, and I got several negative comments from people saying, "Here it goes again." A couple of people remained hostile to me after that—I think they'd just been burned. One of them had participated with an author before, and the author had ended up writing a book claiming, "Here's what intersex people think, and this is what it feels like to be intersex" based on a fairly small amount of information. Another person had been involved with someone who'd basically written something about how "weird" these people are.

S: You also go to great lengths describing how some other animals, like hyenas (whose females have penislike appendages) and fish (some of which can spontaneously change sex) reproduce in unconventional ways. It seemed like an arbitrary comparison to me, given that the natural world has such a diversity of reproductive strategies. Why do you think that it's helpful to look at other species' sexual reproduction?

C: Many species have evolved different ways of dealing with sex. It suggests the classic relationship of the male-female binary just doesn't fit very well with the real world. If that female-male division is true of humans, which as you know I don't believe it is, that would make us the biological exception rather than the rule.

S: But those adaptations you described have an evolutionary purpose, while most intersex conditions don't—at least to an immediate observer.

C: I didn't mean to suggest that intersex is a biological adaptation that will somehow further the species. The persistence of intersex reminds me that there's a continuum, that we isolate people in the middle and say they have a problem because they're reproductively incompetent or don't look right or whatever. None of us meet the criterion of being the perfect male or the perfect female. We are all intersex.

47

The Rio Declaration of Gender Independence

We come from eighty countries. We are men and women, young and old, working side by side with respect and shared goals. We are active in community organizations, religious and educational institutions; we are representatives of governments, NGOs and the United Nations.

We speak many languages. We look like the diverse peoples of the world and carry their diverse beliefs and religions, cultures, physical abilities, and sexual and gender identities. We are indigenous peoples, immigrants, and ones whose ancestors moved across the planet. We are fathers and mothers, daughters and sons, brothers and sisters, partners and lovers, husbands and wives.

What unites us is our strong outrage at the inequality that still plagues the lives of women and girls, and the self-destructive demands we put on boys and men. But even more so, what brings us together here is a powerful sense of hope, expectation, and possibility for we have seen the capacity of men and boys to change, to care, to cherish, to love passionately, and to work for justice for all.

We are outraged by the pandemic of violence women face at the hands of some men, by the relegation of women to second class status, and the continued domination by men of our economics, of our polities, of our social and cultural institutions, in far too many of our homes. We also know that among women there are those who fare even worse because of their social class, their religion, their language. Their physical differences, their ancestry, their sexual orientation, or simply where they live.

There are deep costs to boys and men from the ways our societies have defined men's power and raised boys to be men. Boys deny their humanity in search of an armor-plated masculinity. Young men and boys are sacrificed as cannon fodder in war for those men of political, economic, and religious power who demand conquest and domination at any cost. Many men cause terrible harm to themselves because they deny their own needs for physical and mental care or lack services when they are in need.

Too many men suffer because our male-dominated world is not only one of power of men over women, but of some groups of men over others. Too many men, like too many women, live in terrible poverty, in degradation, or are forced to do body- or soul-destroying work to put food on the table. Too many men carry the deep scars of trying to live up to the impossible demands of manhood and find terrible solace in risk-taking, violence, self-destruction, or the drink and drugs sold to make a profit for others. Too many men experience violence at the hands of other men. Too many men are stigmatized and punished for the simple fact that they love, desire, and have sex with other men.

We are here because we know that the time when women stood alone in speaking out against discrimination and violence—that this time is coming to an end. We also know this: This belief in the importance of engaging men and boys is no longer a remote hope. We see the emergence of organizations and campaigns that are directly involving hundreds of thousands, millions of men in almost every country on the planet. We hear men and boys speaking out against violence, practicing safer sex, and supporting women's and girls' reproductive rights. We see men caring, loving, and nurturing for other men and for women.

We see men who embrace the daily challenges of looking after babies and children, and delight in their capacity to be nurturers. We see many men caring for the planet and rejecting conquering nature just as men once conquered women. We are gathering not simply to celebrate our first successes, but, with all the strength we possess, to appeal to parents, teachers, and coaches, to the media and businesses; to our governments, NGOs, Religious institutions, and the United Nations; to mobilize the political will and economic resources required to increase the scale and impact of work with men and boys to promote gender equality. We know how critical it is that institutions traditionally controlled by men reshape their policies and priorities to support gender equality and the well-being of women, children, and men. And we know that a critical part of that is to reshape the world of men and boys, the beliefs of men and boys, and the lives of men and boys.

THE RIO PLAN OF ACTION: HIGHLIGHTS

- Change men's gender-related attitudes and practices. Effective programs and processes have led men and boys to stand up against violence and for gender equality in both their personal lives and their communities.
- Work with the women's movement for women's empowerment and rights in our commitment to contribute to the myriad efforts to achieve gender equality.
- Work against violence in all its forms: against women, against children, among men, and in armed conflict.
- Challenge economic and political policies and institutions that drive inequalities.

- Commit to strengthening the role of fathers and supporting men in positive fatherhood.
- Put in place strategies that shift gender norms and encourage men to share with women the joys and burdens of caring for others.
- Recognize and affirm sexual diversity among men and boys, and support the positive rights of men of all sexualities to sexual pleasure and well-being.
- Promote physical, mental, and emotional health among boys and young men and enable them to acquire health-seeking behaviors for themselves, as well as for their families.
- End sexual violence and exploitation through holistic strategies from the global to local level to engage men and boys in challenging attitudes that give men dominance, and to treat all human beings with dignity and respect.
- Work with men and boys to fully support and promote the sexual health and reproductive rights of women, girls, boys, and other men.
- Take urgent action to implement evidence-based prevention, treatment, care, and support strategies that address the gendered dimensions of HIV and AIDS, meet the needs of people living with HIV and AIDS, ensure access to treatment, challenge stigma and discrimination, and support men to reduce risk-taking behaviors and improve access to and use of HIV services.
- Create an environment where girls and boys are viewed as equals, enjoy dignified labor and easy access to quality education, mid live lives free from violence, including forced marriage.
- Urgently act to reverse the damage done to our environment and facilitate the process of healing.
- Celebrate diversity, including differences based on race, ethnicity, age, sexual and gender diversities, religion, physical ability, and class.
- Increase resources allocated to women's equality overall to achieve gender equality, including among men and boys.
- Continue to build the evidence base for gender-transformative programs through research and program evaluations to determine which strategies are most successful in different cultural contexts.

THE CALL TO ACTION

1. Individuals should take action within their communities and be agents of change to promote gender equality.

2. Community-based organizations should continue their groundbreaking work to challenge the status quo of gender and other inequalities and actively model social change.

3. Non-governmental organizations should develop and build on programs, interventions, and services that are based on the needs, rights, and aspirations of their communities that are accountable and reflect the principles in this document. They should develop synergies with other relevant social movements, and establish mechanisms for monitoring and reporting on government commitments.

4. Governments should repeal all discriminatory laws and act on their existing international and UN obligations and commitments, prioritize and allocate resources to gender-transformative interventions, and develop policies, frameworks, and concrete implementation plans that advance this agenda, including through working with other governments and adherence to the Paris Principles.

5. The private sector should promote workplaces that are gender equitable and free from violence and exploitation, and direct their corporate social responsibility towards inclusive social change.

6. Media and entertainment industries' role in maintaining and reinforcing traditional and unequal gender norms has to be addressed, confronted, and alternatives supported.

7. Donors should redirect their resources towards the promotion of inclusive-programming for gender equality and inclusive social justice, including changes to laws and policies, and develop synergies among donors.

8. The United Nations must show leadership in these areas, innovatively and proactively support member states to promote gender equitable and socially transformative law, policy, and practice, including through interagency coordination as articulated in the One UN approach. We must invest in men and boys to become engaged in changing their behavior and attitudes towards gender equality supported by communities, systems and national policies.

48

"We're All Sisters"

Bridging and Legitimacy in the Women's Antiprison Movement

JODIE MICHELLE LAWSTON

In both waves of the feminist movement, white middle-class feminists have drawn on notions of "sisterhood" to create and sustain solidarity. Their claims to sisterhood have largely been premised on women's experiences with gender oppression (Dill 1983; hooks 1984; Lorde 1984), ignoring differences among women, particularly in terms of race and class (Dill 1983; hooks 1984; Lorde 1984; Moraga and Anzaldua 1981; Romero 1988). Many white feminists insisted on the "universality and overriding importance of patriarchy," a claim that put womanhood above race and class (Dill 1983, 136). Critiques of the use of sisterhood and the corresponding failure of women's organizations to address multiple forms of oppression highlighted the failure to interrogate differences among women and led many researchers to dismiss sisterhood as a legitimate claim to solidarity. In dismissing this concept, however, scholarship has not fully examined the ways that sisterhood may continue to be utilized by feminist activists.

This article examines the complex functions of sisterhood in an ethnographic study of a white, middle-class, feminist, antiracist organization that uses the language of sisterhood in its work on behalf of incarcerated women, who are predominantly of color and poor. I find that sisterhood is rooted in women's experiences with oppression and in women's experiences with pride and pleasure and that sisterhood serves complex functions. Beyond creating and sustaining solidarity in feminist organizations that seek to work across difference, claims to sisterhood that are sensitive to differences influence an organization's stated intentions. I also offer insights into how structural inequality persists despite attention to difference.

SISTERHOOD

Prior research on the language of sisterhood has defined the concept (Dill 1983; hooks 1984), described who has used it and for what purposes (Dill 1983; Fox-Genovese 1979; Freedman 1981; hooks 1984; Shrom Dye 1975), and, especially, identified its shortcomings (Dill 1983; hooks 1984; Lorde 1984; Moraga and Anzaldua 1981; Romero 1988). Sisterhood has been defined as "a nurturant, supportive feeling of attachment and loyalty to other women" (Dill 1983, 132). It has been used in organizations—particularly those that were white and middle class—in an attempt to engender solidarity among women. Both Dill (1983) and Fox-Genovese (1979) point out that the promotion of solidarity has served two purposes: to maintain a separation between the public, political sphere of men and the private, domestic sphere of women and to inspire sociopolitical action based upon the shared needs and experiences of women (Dill 1983, 132).

For example, Freedman's (1981) research on the women's prison reform movement of the nineteenth century shows that the language of sisterhood was used to uphold separate spheres between men and women. Between 1840 and 1900, groups of white, middle-class, Quaker and other Protestant women located mostly in the Northeast began to visit and work with white, working-class, incarcerated women. Women were originally housed in men's prisons (Dodge 2006; Freedman 1981); however, women prison reformers ardently supported the division of labor and separate sexual spheres and believed that women were intrinsically nurturing and domestic. Reformers' belief in separate spheres propelled them to establish women's prisons—temed "reformatories"—where "fallen women" could be reformed into the nineteenth-century ideal: obedient wives and mothers relegated to the home (Dodge 2006; Freedman 1981). Interestingly, Rafter (1990) argues that the language of sisterhood meant that women prison reformers extended middle-class control over women who did not fit that ideal. In addition to class, what placed reformers in a dominant position relative to imprisoned women were institutional arrangements in which imprisoned women were required to be submissive to reformers in order to be released. Because those who were white and young were most likely to be sent to reformatories, women of color, especially Black women, remained in men's custodial institutions and were omitted from the sisterhood equation (Freedman 1981; Rafter 1990).

The use of sisterhood for the purpose of inspiring sociopolitical action is best exemplified by feminist activism in the 1960s and 1970s, during which time sisterhood was largely based on the contention that women are universally oppressed by virtue of their "secondary social and economic positions in all societies and in the family" (Dill 1983, 132). The women who used this language were largely white, heterosex-

ual, and middle class. It quickly became apparent that all women are not oppressed in the same ways, however. For example, because they had a history of being tied to childrearing and the home—and experienced this as oppressive—white, middle-class, heterosexual women conceptualized work *outside* of the home as liberation. In contrast, working-class women and women of color worked out of necessity in jobs that offered little autonomy and economic stability; as such, many conceptualized work outside of the home as a source of oppression (Nadasen 2002).

Critiques of sisterhood came from Black and Latina women in the late 1970s and 1980s, and from third-world feminists during the 1990s, who criticized white, middle-class, heterosexual feminists for, "organizing along the binary gender division male/female alone" (Sandoval 2000, 44.5; see also Dill 1983; hooks 1984; Lorde 1984; Moraga and Anzaldua 1981; Romero 1988). Critics argued that white feminists focused on analyzing women's experiences with patriarchal oppression and ignored inequalities based on race, class, and sexuality, hooks (1984, 46) argues that because this use of sisterhood focused on women's experiences as victims of oppression rather than their shared strengths and resources, white women were able to "abdicate responsibility for their role in the maintenance and perpetuation of sexism, racism, and classism, which they did by insisting that only men were the enemy."[1]

IMPLICATIONS FOR CURRENT RESEARCH

The language of sisterhood has historically assumed "homogeneity of experience" (Lorde 1984, 116) among women and has failed to consider the ways that race, class, and gender interact to produce inequality. Manifestations of this history can be seen in the contemporary women's prison movement, where some organizations adhere to the idea that women in prison and women on the outside of prison are united in a sisterhood of common gender experiences. While researchers have explored definitions and uses of sisterhood, the majority of this literature has critiqued this concept for not addressing differences among women and has not done enough to illustrate the complexities of a concept that continues to be fundamental to some organizations that are engaged in "on-the-ground" feminist work. Research has not pinpointed the varied functions that sisterhood may serve, beyond attempts at unity, maintenance of a distinction between the public and the private spheres, or inspiration of sociopolitical action.

Through an analysis of a white, middle-class, feminist, antiprison organization that uses the language of sisterhood in its work with incarcerated women—who are predominantly of color and poor—this article extends and complicates our understanding of this language. I ask the following questions: First, how is sisterhood conceptualized by white feminist activists? Second, beyond the uses enumerated thus far in the feminist literature and in light of the criticisms waged against it, what functions may sisterhood serve? In answering these questions, this article pushes the literature forward in four ways. First, it identifies the ways that contemporary white feminist activists define sisterhood. Building upon arguments that understand sisterhood as emerging from common experiences with oppression, I show that sisterhood is simultaneously predicated on oppression and women's experiences with pride and pleasure. Second, this article identifies the complex functions of a concept that has historic and continuing significance in feminist organizations. I find that sisterhood is used by white feminists in an attempt to bridge differences between women, particularly in regard to race, class, and life experiences, and that it functions to legitimate activists' work to one another.[2] Third, this article underscores the ways that sisterhood—through its functions of bridging and establishing legitimacy—influences an organization's stated intentions. Fourth, this article enumerates the ways that structural inequality persists in feminist organizations, despite attention to difference.

DATA AND METHODS

This study is based on an ethnographic research project that I conducted from 2002 to early 2005 on an organization that I refer to as Network for Prisoners (NP). NP is part of a women's prison movement that has emerged in the United States to contest the conditions of incarceration and, in some cases, the existence of prisons

themselves. This movement includes a variety of organizations, some of which include former prisoners, current prisoners, family members and friends of prisoners, lawyers, and academics.[3]

Description of the Organization

At the time of this study, NP was small, with fewer than twenty members, all of whom were women. The activists identified as white and middle class. They were highly educated, and none had been incarcerated. Like other segments of the contemporary prison movement (see McCorkel and Rodriquez 2009), activists realized that communities of color are targeted by the criminal justice system—therefore they believed NP should be led by the people most affected by the system. However, activists experienced difficulty in recruiting women of color and former prisoners. They explained that former prisoners wanted to put prison experiences behind them or were overwhelmed by difficulties in transitioning back into society, while communities of color that are connected in some way to the criminal justice system often struggle with the day-to-day of work, raising families, and visiting loved ones in prison, leaving little time for activism. While activists connected with other, more diverse prison groups in a spirit of support and collaboration, the organization's own racial and class privilege was of paramount importance for activists to analyze as they sought to work with incarcerated women.

During the study, activists met with fifteen prisoners to determine what issues are most important to them.[4] These fifteen women formed the core of the prisoners with whom activists were meeting; activists interacted with dozens of other prisoners on a less permanent basis. The prison restricted the number of prisoners with whom activists could meet during visits; one or two could meet with one prisoner for an hour or two at a time over a period of five hours; the more activists who could attend, the more prisoners they could see on a given afternoon. Prisoners explained that they initially heard about NP through "word of mouth" and contacted the group when they wanted to connect with activists on an issue, such as aid with parole. Activists met with prisoners with a range of sentences, from women serving a few months to those on death row.

One prisoner with whom activists worked was white, middle class, and educated; a second was white and working class. The remaining women had few resources; were African American, Latina, or First Nation; and were poor and undereducated: none had attended college, and few had finished high school. All but one of the prisoners reported experiencing physical and/or sexual violence before incarceration.

Interviews, Participant Observation, and Archival Research

This study draws from semistructured interviews, participant observation, and archival materials. I conducted fifteen semistructured interviews with activists. While I requested interviews with all members of the group, a few indicated reluctance to participate because of a perceived vulnerability to outsiders (Lofland and Lofland 1995). Questions on the interview guide covered activists' backgrounds and experiences with movement activities; identification in terms of race, class, and ideology; the ways gender did or did not connect them in a "sisterhood" to incarcerated women; and the ways that differences in race, class, and prison experience complicated this relationship. Interviews lasted from one and a half to two hours.

To interview women in prison, I was fortunate that NP invited me to join them on their prison visits. In total, I interviewed fifteen prisoners. Visits lasted five hours, during which time I conducted three to four interviews with prisoners and observed two to four discussions between activists and prisoners. The interview guide included questions about prisoners' lives, daily struggles in prison, and conceptions of NP. I spoke with prisoners about what the organization did for them and about their perceptions of the goals of the organization. To understand whether prisoners saw activists as "sisters," I asked them whether they felt that gender connected them to activists and how they felt about differences in race, class, and prison experience between themselves and members of the organization. Interviews lasted forty-five minutes to one hour.

Participant observation consisted of attending monthly meetings and events. During prison visits I was able to observe activist-prisoner interactions to further understand how the sisterhood frame was used. To cross-reference my data with organizational information, I examined the group's archival material, including Web site material and the mission statement. I used the program ATLAS/ti to code and analyze interview and archival material and field notes.

The Positionality of the Researcher   I am a white, middle-class woman, and I shared high levels of formal education, gender, and race with the NP activists. All of the activists I interviewed talked openly about the ways gender connects them to women in prison and how, simultaneously, differences in race, class, and prison experience impede their efforts to connect. I suspect that our shared race, gender, and class facilitated these conversations and provided activists with comfort during interviews.

With prisoners, I occupied an "insider" status insofar as I was raised in a working-class family that, like many prisoners' families, saw and continues to see drug and alcohol abuse, violence, and intervention by the police; my father also continues to be in and out of prison. Because I spoke openly about my life, these experiences helped me to relate to many of the imprisoned women. However, there still remained several differences between us—particularly my whiteness, my level of formal education, my current class status, and my having never been incarcerated—which contributed to my "outsider" position. While prisoners did not indicate that they *defined* me as an activist (I identified as a researcher during the project), I was like the activists in that I was a "free person" who was not subject to the same regulations and humiliating procedures (such as strip searches) to which prisoners are subject (see also McCorkel and Myers 2003). Because I could easily communicate with activists, prisoners may have feared that I would share their responses with the group. I report in this article the responses and observations that I received and made during the course of this project, while keeping in mind the influence that aspects of my identity had on the research process. I have changed the names of all respondents to respect their privacy and do not use any information that would identify the group.

THE EMERGENCE OF NP

NP can be situated in a rich tradition of women's prison activism, beginning with the women's prison reform movement of the nineteenth century and including women's prison activism of the 1970s. White, middle-class women reformers of the nineteenth century sought to "reform" imprisoned women to behave in ways that upheld a strict gender dichotomy (Dodge 2006; Freedman 1981). Prison reform in that era was initially more about upholding separate sexual spheres and reforming individual women rather than contesting the basis of imprisonment. While some women undoubtedly continued to visit and work with incarcerated women, organized efforts again emerged in the 1970.[5] These organizations did not seek to uphold gender norms or to reform individual women. Some were reformist in that they worked to alleviate harsh conditions in women's prisons, while other radical groups sought to abolish prisons as part of a commitment to transforming American institutions and values (Resources for Community Change 1975).

Prison activism for women again increased in the 1990s, when incarcerated women began to draw attention to prison conditions. Women complained about medical neglect and abusive treatment by correctional officers (Amnesty International 1999). Women on the outside of prison organized NP to support women inside and to educate the public about prison conditions. They banded together to become, as activists put it, "a voice and a presence" for incarcerated women, whom they referred to as their "sisters." Such phrasing was typical of activists during interviews, meetings, and in organizational publications.

Like prison reformers of the nineteenth century, activists were white and middle class. Unlike prison reformers of the nineteenth century, activists did not aim to uphold gender norms, blame women's incarceration on moral failing, or seek to reform prisoners. On the contrary—given that close to 70 percent of imprisoned women are Black, Latina, First Nation, or Asian and that most are poor or working class—activists maintained that the process of incarceration is "shaped by racial and economic status rather than by criminal or criminalized acts" (James 2005, xxxvi). Activists ar-

gued that prisons, which serve to maintain white supremacy and economic injustice, are sites where the poor and people of color are warehoused. They explained that prisons are a space in which racial and class oppression are intensely magnified.

Given their ideological base, NP activists identify as prison abolitionists. The abolition of the prison system "is a long-range goal that . . . requires an analysis of 'crime' that links it with social structures, as opposed to individual pathology, as well as 'anticrime' strategies that focus on the provision of social resources" (Davis and Rodriguez 2000, 215). Abolitionist activists argue that rather than relying on imprisonment, resources such as education, food, housing, jobs, health care, substance abuse treatment, and mental health services should be prioritized to create safe communities. NP members spent a considerable amount of time talking about abolition during meetings and with other activists.

At the same time, activists articulated that a critical role of their organization is to work on behalf of imprisoned women. As they explained, given the difficulty in access to prisoners—with prison administration determining when they can visit, for how long, what items can be sent to prisoners, and sometimes the substance of conversations during visits—the direct ideological work they can engage in with imprisoned women is limited. Hence, a significant portion of activists' sociopolitical action was support work rather than talks with prisoners about abolition. This included writing letters in support of parole and to demand health care for individual women, writing to the governor to demand improvements in the prison system, helping to find lawyers for incarcerated women, and providing resources to individual prisoners. This type of action is extremely important, as prisoners are constrained in the actions they can take on their own behalf. For instance, when incarcerated women file grievances, it is not unusual for the staff and administration to retaliate through write-ups, withholding of mail, or refusal of visitation. Activists could engage in support work from the outside of prison with limited threat of retaliation.[6] In practice, then, the organization's role was bifurcated. Activists engaged in support work on behalf of individual prisoners with whom they had direct contact. Largely outside prison, activists promoted their primary goal of abolition, which they saw as on behalf of all imprisoned people and communities disproportionately affected by the criminal justice system.

NP activists identify as feminist and antiracist. They believe women occupy a collective position of subordination in relation to men and that women must come together to fight for equality (Martin 1990). However, they are also ideologically "committed to challenging racism as systemic in institutions and everyday life" (Srivastava 2005, 36). NP activists are committed to fighting for a society in which race is no longer attached to differences in access to resources and power.

Despite activists' social change goals, they were faced with a quandary. Given glaring differences in race, class, and prison experience, on what basis could activists—as they hoped—authentically be "a voice and a presence" for incarcerated women?

MAKING SENSE OF DIFFERENCE

Activists knew that their differences from prisoners called into question their ability to adequately work on behalf of incarcerated women. Sandra explains,

> As a white middle-class woman I've benefited from a white supremacist society in many ways. Just being white means that I am not racially profiled and am not overrepresented m the prison system. My family benefited from programs that excluded people of color, like FHA loans, so I have more wealth, could go to college, and have access to good lawyers if I ever got arrested. It really brings into question whether we as white women can actually speak on behalf of prisoners.

Activists' lives have been shaped very differently through race and class than those of incarcerated women. Activists understand that gender is constructed by interlocking inequalities, or what Patricia Hill Collins (1990) has referred to as a "matrix of domination." White middle-class activists experience gender oppression differently than incarcerated women. While activists understand that differences in race,

class, and prison experience influence their work, they feel that race especially poses a barrier and repeatedly made reference to the fact that they do not know what it is like to experience racial discrimination.

The differences between activists and prisoners cast doubt on activists' claim that they are "a voice and a presence" for imprisoned women. Their awareness of the racial and class privileges afforded them by the system that oppresses prisoners created discomfort for activists because their capacity to help prisoners stems from their privileges. Activists made comments like, "I question whether I should do this work," suggesting that they doubt their legitimacy in engaging in antiprison work.

Despite these obstacles, activists did not abandon NP; they felt strongly that they had a responsibility to remain politically active on behalf of imprisoned women. Walking away, they maintained, would be a stronger indication of privilege as it would mean turning their back on structural inequality. How, then, did activists attempt to "bridge the gap" between themselves and prisoners, and legitimate their work? I use the term "bridge" to refer to the ways that activists connected to imprisoned women so that they had a working relationship and could more accurately represent their needs.

Activists drew on sisterhood as a collective action frame during prison visits. Collective action frames are "action oriented sets of beliefs that inspire meaning and legitimate social movement activities and campaigns" (Benford 1997, 416). Frames are used to produce and maintain meaning and provide a rationale for collective action. As I show, the sisterhood frame produced meaning for both activists and prisoners and was used by activists to bridge differences in racial, class, and prison experience and to legitimate their work.

CONCEPTUALIZING SISTERHOOD

During prison visits, activists employed a sisterhood frame to converse with incarcerated women. This frame focused on similar gender experiences under patriarchy, but unlike the women's prison reform movement of the nineteenth century, activists did not essentialize gender. Rather, they argued that in our current patriarchal system, women have experiences that have been socially constructed similarly. "Sisterhood" as used in NP is conceptualized as simultaneously rooted in oppression and in pride and pleasure and, as such, does not merely emerge from victimization (hooks 1984).

The sisterhood frame includes two components: a focus on gendered abuse, understood as oppressive; and a focus on women's experiences as caregivers, understood as both oppressive and pleasurable. Phrases like "we've all experienced abuse as women" and "we have a lot of similarities in that we have children" were used by activists to explain how they connect to women in prison despite differences in race, class, and prison experience, Statements such as "I can really relate to the abuse you suffered; I was abused" were used by activists during visits with prisoners to stress their connection to imprisoned women.

Abuse suffered at the hands of men was used most often as a common ground of discussion. This is a very salient component of sisterhood, and while feminists often identify experiences of gendered interpersonal violence as a shared experience among women (Dworkin 1997; MacKinnon 1988), prior research has not examined how white, middle-class activists deploy this shared experience in an attempt to bridge differences.

Half of the activists experienced abuse, witnessed domestic abuse in a family context, or knew women who had; and all but one of the incarcerated women had experienced physical or sexual abuse. Some research shows that 43 percent of women in the general population have reported physical or sexual abuse at some point in their lives (Walker et al. 1999), while between 57 percent (Bureau of Justice Statistics 1999) and 75 percent (Browne, Miller, and Maguin 1999) of women prisoners have histories of such violence. Abuse is therefore a gendered experience that cuts across race, class, and prison lines and was particularly salient for incarcerated women. The following is an excerpt from a conversation between Sandra and a prisoner named Barbara:

SANDRA: How are you dealing about the abuse you suffered?

BARBARA: The other day we were in group and I talked about it, and how terrified I was to leave him, and all the beatings. I cried for three days after that.

SANDRA: I know how you feel. Every time I talk about the abuse I went through I have meltdowns. It's something we as women have to constantly deal with.

Sandra relates with Barbara in terms of the domestic violence they both experienced but takes the connection a step further by stating, "It's something we *as women* have to constantly deal with." This suggests that experiences with abuse are a common point of reflection for women, cross race and class lines, and emerge from structural inequality between men and women.

Activists who did not experience abuse listened to incarcerated women and related to them by talking about larger trends of gender violence. The following excerpt comes from a conversation between an activist named Tanya and a prisoner named Jeni:

JENI: I continue to struggle with the abuse I went through, and not feeling like I could get out. I was talking to some other women and we all have the same problem of the violence coming back in our minds.

TANYA: Violence against women is common. It unites women because it's all around us. Either we experience it or see it in the media, or we have friends or family who have gone through it. It's enraging that women continue to be oppressed by it.

JENI: What helps is being able to talk to others about it—to talk to people who can understand, like you and the women in here who went through it.

Tanya connects Jeni's experiences to larger trends of violence against women. She alludes to a general experience of being controlled under a patriarchal system that oppresses women through violence or the threat of violence. What appears to be more important than Tanya's experiencing abuse herself is that she is able to understand Jeni's experiences.

Activists also established common ground with prisoners through discussions about their caregiving experiences. While some respondents defined caregiving broadly to include caring for other women, family, or friends, most activists and prisoners focused on caregiving experiences with children. Women have historically been the primary caretakers of children, and at least two-thirds of incarcerated women are mothers to children under age eighteen (Mumola 2000). Eight of the fifteen prisoners reported having children, whereas only four of the activists reported having children. This may help to explain why caretaking experiences were used less often to establish common ground between activists and prisoners. It was commonly activists with children who used caretaking experiences as part of a larger sisterhood frame. They spoke of the difficulty in rearing children and serving as primary caretakers (the "oppressive" aspect of caretaking) and also of the pride and pleasure that comes from it; activists who did not have children listened to prisoners as they spoke about their children. An activist named Linda and a prisoner named Mara discussed the accomplishments of their children:

LINDA: My daughter is graduating high school, I'm so proud of my baby.

MARA: That's wonderful news. They get big so fast, don't they? My kids have grown so fast, and I'm proud of them, especially given that I'm in here. They are the best things that happened to me.

LINDA: Kids can really change our lives for the better. They bring me so much happiness. We can feel like we have accomplished something through our kids.

While in some instances activists and prisoners focused on the difficulty in being the primary caretaker for children, conceptualizing mothering roles as oppressive through statements such as "men have it easy; we still end up doing most of the childrearing," in most cases they conceptualized childrearing as a source of satisfaction. Activists and prisoners related that caretaking has brought them pleasure and that they look at their children with pride and delight. The sisterhood frame therefore originates in experiences with both oppression in the form of abuse (and sometimes caretak-

ing) *and* shared pleasure that emerges from caretaking, and as such it cannot be reduced to only focusing on women's victimization. Sisterhood moves beyond victimization and begins to focus on the complexities of women's experiences as they relate to both subordination and joy.

Taking Direction from Prisoners

In addition to discussing abuse and caretaking, activists also asked prisoners to enumerate their needs. This process was important as activists recognized that prisoners had different needs, given their structural positions in relation to activists, from their own. The following is a discussion between Linda and a prisoner named Mara:

MARA: This place is sick. The food is awful, the guards don't give a shit about us. They refused to take a woman to the doctor the other day, she needs refills for her thyroid meds and they don't do a damn thing about it.

LINDA: What do you need from us? How can we support you?

MARA: You can start to send parole letters in for me. The more letters the better. If you can also send in a care package of food, I can. share it with the other women.

A fundamental part of prison visits and in establishing sisterhood is learning from incarcerated women about their needs. While activists did not have prolonged discussions with incarcerated women about their lack of prison experience, some activists made statements to prisoners such as, "You're the one experiencing this, you should tell us what you need." A key distinction between earlier and more contemporary uses of sisterhood, then, is that rather than basing their work on shared needs *and* experiences (Dill 1983), NP activists recognized the differing needs of women in varying racial and sociostructural positions. While rejecting the notion of shared needs, activists strategically deployed a rhetoric of shared experience. The difference between earlier and more contemporary uses of sisterhood is that NP activists abandoned assumptions of shared needs and engaged in ideological work to construct a basis for shared experience.

FUNCTIONS OF SISTERHOOD

Bridging

The sociopolitical action that prisoners can take on their own behalf is limited due to their confinement in a "total institution" (Goffman 1961) in which staff may retaliate against women. Activists can take actions on behalf of, but cannot easily organize large-scale actions together with, imprisoned women. Given the institutional difficulty and risk of organizing women in prison, coupled with differences in race, class, and prison experience between activists and incarcerated women, the sisterhood frame was used primarily to bridge activists to prisoners and, as I demonstrate, to legitimate activist work, rather than to promote sociopolitical action.

While frames are used to "inspire and legitimate" collective action, they are also used to recruit new members and to mobilize potential adherents and constituents (Snow et al. 1986). Efforts by social movement organizations to link their interests with those of prospective constituents are conceptualized as "frame alignment processes," which include the processes of frame bridging, frame amplification, frame extension, and frame transformation (Snow et al. 1986). Although these concepts have generally been used to understand how new recruits are added to movements, frame bridging is useful for understanding the ways that sisterhood functions to establish relationships with incarcerated women.

Frame bridging refers to the process of "linking two or more ideologically similar but unconnected frames regarding a specific issue or problem" (Snow et al. 1986, 467). It is used to induce groups or individuals with similar interests as one's own to join a movement and is achieved through organizational outreach (Snow et al. 1986). In NP, activists bridged to incarcerated women by using a sisterhood frame that is based on experiences with interpersonal violence and caretaking. Indeed, the frame that activists also received from prisoners was based on abuse and caretak-

ing. The two groups of women connected around experiences of violence and caretaking, and activists in turn provided resources and support (what prisoners identified as needs) to imprisoned women. This process does more than create and sustain solidarity. Sharing experiences with abuse and caretaking bridges activists to prisoners so that the two groups have a working relationship and so that activists can represent and fulfill prisoner needs.

That experiences with abuse and caretaking bridge activists to prisoners is a strong contention among activists. For example, Sandra states, "These experiences connect us to women inside; men could not relate in the same way." Activists contend that they understand many of incarcerated women's experiences because they too experience gender oppression and violence, and they too serve in caretaking roles that a patriarchal society has defined for them. Activists' experiential knowledge with gender replaces their lack of experiential knowledge with racial and class oppression and imprisonment.

Prisoners reported that the sisterhood frame resonates with them and provides them with the opportunity to share their own stories. Barbara states,

> As women I feel like we all have a lot in common. We have histories of abuse, for example, that women better understand because we have that direct experience with it, and then we can tell each other those stories. Men are less likely to be victims of domestic abuse so they wouldn't quite understand it the way a woman would.

Prisoners shared the belief with activists that women have particular experiences with gender oppression. The sisterhood frame worked to create a point of reciprocal identification for activists and prisoners. The exchanges between these groups of women provided an important opportunity for incarcerated women to overcome the prison system's silencing effects, as they were able to speak with individuals on the outside of prison walls who could understand their struggles as women.

However, prisoners' responses should be interpreted with caution. I have no doubt that prisoners felt connected with activists, as they had sustained relationships with them. But women prisoners are in a vulnerable position: they are silenced in the larger society, more often than not have few visitors, and are in need of resources. Prisoners' desire for outside contact and need for continued advocacy may have affected their responses.

In addition to understanding one another as connected by common gender experiences, another piece of the bridging puzzle relates to the question of agenda setting. Activists worked to build bridges across race, class, and prison experience, but who set the agenda for the group? While activists, like bridge leaders (Robnett 1997), worked to take direction from incarcerated women, their efforts were impeded by the prison system itself For example, incarcerated women repeatedly asked that activists exert pressure on their behalf to improve their health care. Activists found, however, that prison officials were unresponsive to their efforts to create large scale changes. The institution itself is resistant to change, which has resulted in *activists'* changing their focus to provide more manageable services to prisoners, such as writing letters for parole. The prison, to a large extent, defines the type of work that activists can successfully engage in on behalf of prisoners.

Legitimacy

Legitimacy is a crucial issue in any movement organization. Robnett (1997, 13) argues that "constituents must be convinced of the credibility and legitimacy of their participation." NP activists, as constituents of an organization that works on behalf of women in prison, must be convinced of the legitimacy of their work, especially given their feelings of doubt in their ability to work on behalf of imprisoned women.

Activists reported that their ability to bridge to incarcerated women based on gendered experiences with abuse and caretaking inspires feelings of legitimacy. Sandra states,

> I'm a woman and I have had some of the same experiences prisoners have. I may not be inside, hut I know what they have gone through. I don't think a man can relate in the same way. Our experiences as women connect us to women inside and therefore validate us and the work we are doing.

Activists feel more legitimate engaging in prison work because they have similar experiences as women. Activists never explicitly told prisoners that their work is legitimate because they are women—they implied it by talking with prisoners about the ways that they all connect based on abuse and caretaking. Activists did, however, speak in meetings of their gender experiences as legitimating their work. This suggests that activists are particularly concerned with negotiating their feelings of doubt amongst one another.

Incarcerated women—who are on the receiving end of the sisterhood framework—also conceptualized activists as credible because they are women. With the exception of one prisoner, who indicated that gender does not matter as long as someone helps her, prisoners explained that they feel more comfortable talking to women about their problems, as women "have keen insight into one another's needs" (Barbara). They explained that given the abuse they endured from male friends, acquaintances, or loved ones, and due to ongoing surveillance from male guards, they find it difficult to trust or relate to men.

All of the prisoners also reported that activists are credible because they have access to—and provide prisoners with—resources to which the prisoners do not have access. Stacy states,

> They have a lot of information that we don't have access to. These women know how everything works, so they can help us with what we need. I don't always know how the system works, how to get a lawyer, things like that.

Activists also reported feeling credible because of the information to which they have access. Sandra states, "We have information and resources that prisoners don't have access to, and I think this validates our work. We use our resources to give prisoners what they need." Interestingly, imprisoned women reported that receiving information and help from NP actually improved their status in the prison; they explained that if they did not have the information that NP gave them, other incarcerated women would ask, "Why should we listen to you, since you're still here?"

Prisoners acknowledged that activists have not experienced prison or racial discrimination and also differ in terms of class and educational backgrounds.

Even so, all of the prisoners I interviewed said that they have strong relationships with activists. One incarcerated woman, Ruby, states,

> I don't care what race they are, the women are important to me because they care about me, as a person . . . they help us with the things we need, and we can relate on many levels about our lives. They feel like sisters.

Sisterhood, here, is interestingly conceptualized as common gender experiences *and* activists' ability to provide prisoners with resources.

While a sisterhood connection between "giver" and "receiver" is not required for work with prisoners (NP could potentially do the same work it is doing without using a sisterhood frame), activists grounded their support work and resource provision in claims to sisterhood. Because activists want the relationship between them and prisoners to be egalitarian, it is important that they not view themselves as simply providing charity, as this would reproduce the hierarchal paradigm that they seek to eradicate. For activists, claims to sisterhood inscribe a sense of egalitarianism between them and prisoners as they engage in resource provision, which, to activists, legitimates their work.

It is important to analyze the arbiters of, and audiences for, legitimizing discourse. Legitimacy or credibility construction in framing theory is based on the ways that *constituents* legitimate their work. In this case, credibility depends greatly on activists' perceptions, so that the arbiters of and audience for discourses of legitimacy are activists themselves. The focus on how sisterhood legitimates activists—through statements such as "we can just understand women prisoner's experiences better than men, which validates our work"—occured during meetings and interviews, but not with prisoners and not with public audiences. This suggests that activists used the sisterhood frame as a legitimizing device *for themselves.* Sisterhood helps activists make sense of and justify why they are involved with NP despite difference vis-à-vis prisoners, which sustains their participation in the organization.

While activists are the primary audience for legitimizing discourse in that they determine whether their work on behalf of women prisoners is justified, prisoners are at the receiving end of the sisterhood frame and are also an audience for such language. Activists use language such as "we're all sisters" and "we can work to get you the resources you need." Prisoners construct activists as credible based on their gender *and* their ability to provide them with support. Some of NP's credibility, as understood by prisoners, is therefore received by virtue of its status as an outside organization and activists' positions of privilege relative to prisoners.

SISTERHOOD, NONDISCLOSURE OF ABOLITION, AND ORGANIZATIONAL INTENTIONS

While visits with prisoners are crucial, a significant portion of NP's organizational and ideological work is focused on abolition. Many of the discussions amongst activists centered on pathways to abolition, such as moving away from policing and instead using community-based models that hold people accountable for their actions. Activists also fought against prison expansion by contesting the construction of new prisons through methods such as letter-writing campaigns. But while activists identified prison abolition as a main goal of the organization, the language of abolition was absent from the sisterhood frame and activist-prisoner discussions. Activists explained this omission in three ways.

First, discussing abolition in a prison poses threats to activists and prisoners. Activists could potentially lose their access to prisoners as they may be construed as supporting nonconformity to institutional regulations that demand that prisoners be docile and compliant. Additionally, if such a discussion is broached and correctional officers overhear it, those officers may retaliate against prisoners for alleged malevolent intentions.

Second, activists have found that prisoners' goals differ from their own. Sandra states,

> As we got involved in this work and connected more and more to incarcerated women, we found that they have needs that must be addressed and are not necessarily focused on prison abolition. Admittedly, we have time to devote to abolition but prisoners are liv-

ing in this oppressive system and just need to survive. If we are to say we are representing prisoners' needs, we really need to represent those needs. That means taking direction from those women, not merely following our own agenda. This tends to get away from our goal of abolishing the prison system as women inside are more focused on service provision and really, reform keeps the prison going.

Sandra identifies a key class- and race-based tension found in many social movements, based on the fact that the beneficiaries of a movement often want their lives to be improved in the short term, while more privileged constituents often focus on Utopian notions of revolution. For example, in contemporary transnational movements such as those that have organized to prevent child labor in Bangladesh and to stop gender discrimination in the workplace in Mexico (Hertel 2006), beneficiaries "put forward alternative understandings of human rights norms" (Hertel 2006, 3) that addressed the issues they were most concerned about, not necessarily what constituents or outside observers would consider most important. In organizations within the anti–violence against women (Scott 2000) and reproductive justice movements (Nelson 2003), both white women and women of color worked to incorporate the needs and perspectives of women of color and poor women, with more privileged activists being challenged to reconceptualize their goals in the name of antiracism and social justice. In such movements, constituents ended up adapting, reformulating, and forgoing their own objectives to meet the needs and demands of beneficiaries. Similarly, NP activists adapted their agenda during visits with prisoners so that they could learn from and fulfill the needs of incarcerated women. In using the sisterhood frame to bridge to prisoners and legitimate their work, activists found that their organizational practices must focus on the urgent needs that weigh heavily on incarcerated women. Their intentions changed in light of the needs of prisoners.

Sandra interestingly explains that activists feel there is a tension between abolitionist and reformist work. Activists reported that their engagement in service-delivery work fails to challenge the basis of the prison system and only contests certain conditions within it. Since NP activists believe that the penal system is the chronotope that most poignantly embodies the material contradictions of U.S. capitalism, it is illogical to them to turn to a corrupt system to be the guarantor of civil rights when in fact the system is predicated upon maintaining inequality.

Finally, activists reported that they do not speak about abolition with prisoners because prisoners do not subscribe to such an ideology. Tanya states, "We don't talk about abolition. The language of punishment is internalized, so they believe they should be there." As a result, incarcerated women reported that NP is a service and resource organization. In explaining this discrepancy, activists made the case that prisoners are entrenched in a criminal justice system that repeatedly tells them they are "bad" or "pathological." This system denies the social patterns of racism and classism that channel certain groups of women into it. Activists argued that prisoners may not support abolition because they blame themselves for their imprisonment.

To be sure, prisoners explained their incarceration in terms of individual failings. Mara states, "I've made a lot of mistakes in my life, I take responsibility for my actions and it took prison to realize my mistakes." This statement exemplifies how prisoners use the language of individual responsibility." Prisoners must, if they go up for parole, express a *mea culpa* and prove to the parole board that they have been rehabilitated. Arguments for the structural reasons behind mass incarceration, from prisoners or their supporters, will not likely lead to parole. Moreover, the majority of the prisoners resisted the discourse of abolition, albeit indirectly. While one white, middle-class prisoner identified herself as an abolitionist, and one Black, working-class prisoner stated that abolition "would be wonderful but probably won't happen soon," the rest of the prisoners asserted that people who commit crimes need to be held responsible and incarcerated. Ruby states, "Most people deserve to be here, I would not want these people on the streets." Abolition, then, is not a realistic or immediate concern of the majority of prisoners. Still, the fact that activists chose not to disclose an integral organizational goal indicates a power relation: activists are in control of what information to divulge about themselves and their organization, which problematizes a sisterhood frame that implies both activists and prisoners are on equal footing.

DISCUSSION

NP activists have taken steps to address inequality in ways that some earlier feminist organizations have not, particularly in not assuming one overarching women's experience and in taking direction from marginalized women. This distinction is especially true when comparing contemporary prison activists to their predecessors of the nineteenth century. While nineteenth-century reformers sought to uphold patriarchal norms and prisons themselves, NP activists possess a radically different vision of a post-prison, egalitarian society. Nineteenth-century prison activists did not allow prisoners to define their needs and instead spoke for them. These reformers did not address the class privilege they held over incarcerated women or their failure to work with Black women (Rafter 1990). In contrast, contemporary activists take direction from and urge imprisoned women, both of color and poor, to define their needs. But while NP activists are sensitive to and have instated some strategies for addressing difference, inequality persists in this organization in four important ways.

First, the institutional barriers that the prison poses mean that NP activists have a freedom of movement to which prisoners are not privy. Activists are able to move in and out of the prison relatively easily, whereas prisoners are subject to rigid institutional rules that dictate their movement. The fact that prisoners are confined and cannot engage in day-to-day organizational work with activists means that they are omitted from important organizational work and decisions. Second, prisoners do not have the same access to resources as activists. This relationship makes prisoners continually dependent on activists, with the possibility that prisoners do not feel safe critiquing the group.

Third, activists control information, which complicates the sisterhood frame. Activists exercise the option to disclose or not disclose debates about differences in race, class, and prison experience, as well as abolitionism, which are intrinsic to the organization's work. This consolidates power for activists, as they possess information that is relevant to the relationship between the two groups. The fact that activists do not share their feelings about differences in race, class, and prison experience, which provoke discomfort for

them, forecloses prisoners' abilities to participate in and contribute to an important discussion, one that dictates the creation of the sisterhood frame. With its silence around race and class, the sisterhood frame fails to contest power hierarchies between activists and prisoners. Activists frame the terms of their relationships with incarcerated women.

Fourth, the sisterhood frame's function of legitimizing activists' work is complicated by the fact that its basis depends on prisoners' not contesting activist claims. If prisoners contest the sisterhood frame—as women of color and working-class women have done in other arenas—activists could not use this frame to legitimate their work *or* bridge to imprisoned women. Thus, the use of sisterhood depends largely on prisoners' silence around differences in race, class, and prison experience, which could be present because of a potential fear that in raising such issues—to me or activists—activists will stop visiting prisoners. While activists may be able to create some common ground, structures of race and class, combined with the institutional boundaries of prison, create hierarchies that are not easily overcome.

The relationship between bridging and legitimacy can also be looked at another way. Bridging can be understood as a conduit for flows in two directions: in one direction flows support, information, and resources for incarcerated women; in another, legitimacy. The bridge does little to contest the unequal relationship between activists and prisoners, which serves both sides, to an extent: prisoners receive support, while activists feel legitimate in their work. Inequality remains, limiting the effectiveness of the bridge in creating an egalitarian relationship between the two groups.

This article also has important implications for social movement theory. First, prison activism problematizes the idea of movement legitimacy, as beneficiary involvement is limited due to institutional constraints, difficulty in access to imprisoned women, and the dangers of incarcerated women's involvement in political activity. As McCarthy and Zald (1977) have noted, an organization's legitimacy may be compromised when it includes constituents—racially and economically privileged actors who do not stand to benefit from movement success—sans beneficiaries—marginalized groups and individuals who benefit directly from movement success—in its ranks. Second, frames are useful not only for producing and maintaining meaning but for bridging differences and legitimating an organization's collective action. Third, frames potentially affect an organization's stated intentions, especially when dominant and more marginalized groups work together. In NP, for privileged activists to use the sisterhood frame and work on behalf of imprisoned women meant that they had to foreground incarcerated women's experiences, needs, voices, and goals, which, for activists, overshadows their abolitionist work.

In thinking through the ways in which feminist organizations may better address difference, dialogue is necessary. As Lorde (1984) noted more than two decades ago, it is not differences between women that separate them, but the refusal to recognize those differences. In a society that continues to be predicated upon inequality, feminist activists must continue to find ways to productively discuss race and class, as well as sexuality, age, and other differences that may divide women. Feelings of illegitimacy or doubt, as experienced by many well-meaning activists, will not dissipate without productive dialogue amongst not just the women experiencing such feelings but also the women who experience the inequality that makes many white feminists doubt their organizational positions. Given structural inequality, white feminist organizations must identify the silence—*together with* women of color, working-class women, and women from all walks of life—that enshrouds differences (Lorde 1984).

NOTES

1. Feminists have responded to these criticisms by attempting to implement racially diverse organizations (Scott 1998) that meet the needs of women of color and working-class women. However, research shows that most feminist organizations have failed in this endeavor. This failure has been attributed to ongoing splits between white women and women of color over definitions of racism (Simonds 1996; Zajicek 2002); feelings of anger, fear, or betrayal that result from addressing racial difference in organizational contexts (Morgen 2002; Srivastava 2005); and the difficulty in bridging the stratified positions that women occupy in the social order (Poster 1995; Smith 1995).

2. While this article examines a white feminist group and its use of sisterhood, feminists of color, particularly Black feminists,

may use sisterhood in a different way. Black women, who have drawn on "sisterhood" and have called each other "sister" for some time, mark race and gender rather than erasing it.

3. Several antiprison organizations have emerged that are composed of women of color (see James 1999; Sudbury 2004). Organizing has also occurred by prisoners, especially those who are of color (see Cummins 1994; Diaz-Cotto 1996), and by the larger Black community (see McCorkel and Rodriquez 2009). NP should therefore be situated among a rich trajectory of activism in which women of color are also engaging.

4. Activists spoke of prisoners' "membership" in the group as complicated, given that prisoners could not engage in regular meetings and that access to them is strictly monitored by prison staff.

5. There was a radical men's prison movement that emerged, particularly in California, during the 1960s (see Cummins 1994).

6. There is always the chance that the prison could refuse activists visitation with prisoners, but at the time of study that had not occurred.

REFERENCES

Amnesty International. 1999. Not part of my sentence: Violations in the human rights of women in custody, www.amnestyusa.org/women/womeninprison.html (accessed April 5, 2008).

Benford, Robert. 1997. An insider's critique of the social movement framing perspective. *Sociological Inquiry* 67:409–30.

Browne, A., B. Miller, and E. Maguin. 1999. Prevalence and severity of lifetime physical and sexual victimization among incarcerated women. *International Journal of Law and Psychiatry* 22 (3–4): 301–22.

Bureau of Justice Statistics. 1999. *Women offenders.* Washington, DC: Government Printing Office.

Collins, Patricia Hill. 1990. *Black feminist thought: Knowledge, consciousness, and the politics of empowerment.* Boston: Unwin Hyman.

Cummins, Eric. 1994. *The rise and fall of California's radical prison movement.* Stanford, CA: Stanford University Press.

Davis, Angela, and Dylan Rodriguez. 2000. The challenge of prison abolition: A conversation. *Social Justice* 27 (3): 212–18.

Diaz-Cotto, Juanita. 1996. *Gender, ethnicity, and the state: Latino and Latina prison politics.* Albany: State University of New York Press.

Dill, Bonnie Thornton. 1983. Race, class and gender: Prospects for an all-inclusive sisterhood. *Feminist Studies* 9:131–50.

Dodge, L. Lara. 2006. *Whores and thieves of the worst kind: A study of women, crime, and prisons, 1835–2000.* DeKalb: Northern Illinois University Press.

Dworkin, Andrea. 1997. *Life and death.* New York: Free Press.

Fox-Genovese, Elizabeth. 1979. The personal is not political enough. *Marxist Perspectives* 8:94–113.

Freedman, Estelle B. 1981. *Their sister's keepers: Women's prison reform in America, 1830–1930.* Ann Arbor: University of Michigan Press.

Goffman, Erving. 1961. *Asylums: Essays on the social situation of mental patients and other inmates.* New York: Anchor.

Hertel, Shareen. 2006. *Unexpected power: Conflict and change among transnational activists.* Ithaca, NY: Cornell University Press.

hooks, bell. 1984. *Feminist theory: From margin to center.* Boston: South End.

James, Joy. 1999. Resting in gardens, battling in deserts: Black women's activism. *The Black Scholar* 29 (4): 2–7.

James, Joy. 2005. *The new abolitionists: (Neo) slave narratives and contemporary prison writings.* Albany: State University of New York Press.

Lofland, John, and Lyn Lofland. 1995. *Analyzing social settings: A guide to qualitative observation and analysis.* Belmont, CA: Wadsworth.

Lorde, Audre. 1984. *Sister outsider.* Trumansburg, NY: Crossing Press.

MacKinnon, Catherine. 1988. *Feminism unmodified: Discourses on life and law.* Boston: Harvard University Press.

Martin, Patricia Yancy. 1990. Rethinking feminist organizations. *Gender & Society* 4; 182–206.

McCarthy, John D., and Mayer Zald. 1977. Resource mobilization and social movements: A partial theory. *American Journal of Sociology* 82 (6): 1212–41.

McCorkel, Jill, and Kristen Myers. 2003. What difference does difference make? Position and privilege in the field. *Qualitative Sociology* 26 (2): 199–31.

McCorkel, Jill, and Jason Rodriquez. 2009. "Are you an African?" The politics of self construction in status-based social movement. *Social Problems* 56 (2): 357–84.

Moraga, Cherrie, and Gloria Anzaldua, eds. 1981. *This bridge called my back: Writings by radical women of color.* New York: Kitchen Table Women of Color Press.

Morgen, Sandra. 2002. *Into our own hands: The women's health movement in the United States, 1969–1990.* New Brunswick, NJ: Rutgers University Press.

Mumola, Christopher. 2000. *Incarcerated parents and their children.* Washington, DC: Bureau of Justice Statistics.

Nadasen, Premilla. 2002. Expanding the boundaries of the women's movement: Black feminism and the struggle for welfare rights. *Feminist Studies* 28 (2): 271–301.

Nelson, Jennifer. 2003. *Women of color and the reproductive rights movement.* New York: New York University Press.

Poster, Winifred. 1995. The challenges and promises of class and racial diversity in the women's movement: A study of two women's organizations. *Gender & Society* 9 (6): 659–79.

Rafter, Nicole H. 1990. *Partial justice: Women, prisons, and social control.* New Brunswick, NJ: Transaction Publishers.

Resources for Community Change. 1975. Women behind bars: An organizing tool. Barnard Center for Research on Women, http://www.barnard.edu/bcrw/archive/prison.htm (accessed April 2, 2009).

Robnett, Belinda. 1997. *How long? How long? African-American women in the struggle for civil rights.* New York: Oxford University Press.

Romero, Mary. 1988. Sisterhood and domestic service: Race, class, and gender in the mistress-maid relationship. *Humanity and Society* 12 (4): 318–46.

Sandoval, Chela. 2000. *Methodology of the oppressed.* Minneapolis: University of Minnesota Press.

Scott, Ellen. 1998. Creating partnerships for change: Alliances and betrayals in the racial politics in two feminist organizations. *Gender & Society* 12 (4): 400–23.

Scott, Ellen. 2000. Everyone against racism: Agency an the production of meaning in the anti-racism practices of two feminist organizations. *Theory and Society* 29:785–818.

Shrom Dye, Nancy. 1975. Creating a feminist alliance: Sisterhood and class conflict in the New York Women's Trade Union League, 1903–1914. *Feminist Studies* 2 (2–3): 24–38.

Simonds, Wendy. 1996. *Abortion at work: Ideology and practice in a feminist clinic.* Philadelphia: Temple University Press.

Smith, Barbara Ellen. 1995. Crossing the great divides: Race, class and gender in southern women's organizing, 1979–1991. *Gender & Society* 9:680–96.

Snow, David, E. Burke Rochford, Steven K. Worden, and Robert D. Benford. 1986. Frame alignment processes, micromobilization, and movement participation. *American Sociological Review* 51:464–81.

Srivastava, Sarita. 2005. You're calling me a racist? The moral and emotional regulation of anfiracism and feminism. *Signs: Journal of Women in Culture and Society* 31 (1): 29–62.

Sudbury, Julia. 2004. A world without prisons: Resisting militarism, globalized punishment, and empire. *Social Justice* 30 (3): 134–40.

Walker, E., J. Unutzer, C. Rutter, A. Gelfand, K. Saunders, M. VonKorff, M. Koss, and W Katon. 1999. Costs of heath care use by women HMO members with a history of childhood abuse and neglect. *Archive of General Psychiatry* 56:609–13.

Zajicek, Anna. 2002. Race discourses and antiracist practices in a local women's movement. *Gender & Society* 16 (2): 155–74.

49

A Women's History Report Card on Hillary Rodham Clinton's Presidential Primary Campaign, 2008

KATHRYN KISH SKLAR

HOW CAN WE BEST PLACE Hillary Clinton's primary campaign in historical perspective—what were its precedents and what might unfold from it?[1] Of course it's impossible to speak about her candidacy without also thinking about Barack Obama's—and once you start thinking about gender and race, can class be far behind?

Future historians might agree that her campaign revolved around three questions. First, on the "woman question," Clinton's candidacy built on the gradual change that took place over two generations since 1930; she consolidated those changes into a permanent base for women presidential candidates in the future. Second, on the "race question," Clinton's campaign reminds us of the historic precedent of 1869 in which white women competed with black men for the right to vote. Her example shows that future women candidates for president—black or white—need to seek an alternative precedent for white feminists' history on the race question. Third, Clinton's campaign prompts us to ask the "gender question" as well as the "woman question" and the "race question"—and ask questions about the relationship between gender and class. Why

has gender remained so prominent in American politics and class so submerged in the past half century? How might the gender question be answered differently in the future?

On the "woman question," I agree with Katha Pollitt who wrote in the *Nation* on June 6, "Thank you, Hillary, for opening the door for other women." Pollitt thought that "Because [Clinton] normalized the concept of a woman running for President, she made it easier for women to run for every office, including the White House. That is one reason women and men of every party and candidate preference, and every ethnicity too, owe Hillary Clinton a standing ovation, even if they can't stand her."[2]

The history of women presidential candidates has been helpfully summarized by Jo Freeman's recent book, *We Will Be Heard: Women's Struggles for Political Power in the United States.* She notes that although two women put themselves forward for the presidency in the nineteenth century (Victoria Woodhull and Belva Lockwood), none did so in the twentieth century before 1964, when Senator Margaret Chase Smith from Maine became a candidate. Then a profusion of women candi-

Kathryn Kish Sklar, "A Woman's History Report Card on Hillary Rodham Clinton's Presidential Primary Campaign," was originally published in *Feminist Studies*, Volume 34, Number 1/2 (Spring-Summer 2008): 315–322, by permission of the publisher, *Feminist Studies*, Inc.

dates appeared. Between 1964 and 2004 over fifty women were on at least one ballot as candidates for president, both as minor party candidates and as candidates in primaries for the nomination of the Republican or Democratic parties. But only a few of these were noticed by the national press, most notably Shirley Chisholm in 1972. One of the four founders of the National Women's Political Caucus in 1971, Chisholm often said of her twenty years in local politics in Brooklyn, "I . . . met far more discrimination because I am a woman than because I am black." Of all the women who ran for president in the twentieth century, Chisholm got the most votes. Four hundred thousand people voted for her in 14 Democratic primaries. On the first ballot at the Democratic convention, she got 152 delegate votes. No woman since has done as well. Freeman charted changes in public opinion polls from 1930 to 1990. In 1937 only a third of respondents were willing to vote for a woman for president. By 1945 that figure grew to 50 percent. In 1972 (elevated by the Second Wave) it grew to 70 percent. And in 1990 it reached 90 percent, where it has stayed.[3] So when Hillary Clinton's candidacy emerged in 2006, it built on 70 years of gradual change in public opinion with regard to women candidates for president.

But, of course, her candidacy was about more than "the woman question." Race too was deeply involved. And on this question Clinton failed to establish a path for future white women candidates. Her claim that more hard-working "white" Americans were voting for her exemplified her effort to use race to her advantage in ways that forever tarnished her reputation.[4]

What was she thinking?

Perhaps the historic precedent of 1869 was in her mind, or she had forgotten its lessons, or she never knew this history. That iconic moment shaped the woman suffrage movement for decades thereafter and has usually been interpreted as pitting the suffrage of white women against black men. But if we step back and look at the broader context of that moment, we see that its origins in 1837 offer a more useable past for future women presidential candidates.

In 1869 the woman suffrage movement tried to find a place in the politics of the post–Civil War era. After a bloody Civil War accomplished the abolition of slavery, the Fifteenth Amendment to the Constitution was debated. Adopted in 1870, it declared, "The right of citizens of the United States shall not be denied or abridged by the United States or by any State on account of race, color, or previous condition of servitude." Suffragists were divided over this revolutionary amendment, which for the first time created a "national" citizenship. One group, led by Elizabeth Cady Stanton and Susan B. Anthony decided not to support it because they wanted "sex" to be included in the protected categories. In 1869 they formed the National Woman Suffrage Association in New York and launched a periodical called *Revolution*. Feminist historians have generally seen them as radical in their insistence on women's rights. Another group, headed by Lucy Stone and Elizabeth Blackwell, supported the amendment and in 1869 formed the American Woman Suffrage Association in Boston. Feminist historians have generally seen them as more conservative.[5] Yet new views of these groups see them as quite similar, more mainstream than radical or conservative. If we measure radical change as the willingness to welcome the participation of black women, neither group qualifies. Famously, from 1869 forward, black women formed their own suffrage movement in local groups separate from these white national organizations.[6]

Yet these suffrage groups grew out of a moment of revolutionary change in 1837—when the women's rights movement first emerged to claim an equal place for women in American public life. A good way to measure their radical impulse is to notice that these 1837 white women condemned racism. Indeed they generated a social justice legacy that American feminists have drawn on ever since.

Why was 1837 a more innovative moment than 1869 for white women's political achievements related to racial justice? Gerda Lerner answered that question forty years ago. Angelina Grimké led women in the antislavery movement to claim equal participation in American public life—as public speakers and movement leaders. Raised in a wealthy South Carolina slave-holding family, Grimké moved north in 1829 and became a fabulously popular antislavery speaker, who, when attempts were made to silence her, insisted on her right to speak in public, declaring that "whatever is morally right for a man to do is morally right for a woman.[7] Grimké's revolutionary leadership came out

of a context in which antislavery women were courageous and well organized because they had to be. They
and their male colleagues were seen as threats to the
social order in the North as well as the South because
that order depended on the profits generated by slavery. Their lives were constantly at risk. William Lloyd
Garrison was dragged around Boston by a mob that
placed a noose around his neck in 1835.

But rather than be silenced by this context, antislavery women spoke out. They held three unprecedented
national conventions, beginning in 1837, when they asserted women's rights and condemned racism. Especially noteworthy is the way they drew on spiritual traditions to frame their revolution. They needed all the
help they could get and they drew on a higher law to assert women's rights and condemn racisms.[8] At the 1837
convention their women's rights resolution declared:
"the time has come for woman to move in that sphere
which Providence has assigned her and no longer remain satisfied in the circumscribed limits with which
corrupt custom and a perverted application of Scripture
has encircled her." Their anti-racism resolution declared: "this convention do firmly believe that the existence of an unnatural prejudice against our colored population . . . is crushing them to the earth in our
nominally Free States . . . and . . . we deem it a duty for
every woman to pray to be delivered from such an un-
holy feeling."[9] Thus in this anti-racist moment women
were challenging entire patterns of the social order—
the rule of white over black as well as the rule of men
over women—and they did so by asserting a higher law.

Women took the lead in this campaign against
racism. Antislavery men did not meet in multiracial
groups; it was too dangerous. In 1838, the second time
women met in a national convention that drew white
and black women together, a mob estimated at 10,000
men burned the hall where they were meeting to the
ground. They escaped with their lives by walking
through the mob, white women on each side of every
black woman.[10]

The suffrage movement grew out of these social
forces. The first women's rights convention, held in
Seneca Falls, New York, in 1848, was convened by
women who had met each other in the antislavery
movement. Yet the women's rights convention movement did not continue the campaign against racism that

had begun in the antislavery movement. We know it
did not because we have the printed proceedings of
about fifteen women's rights conventions held between 1848 and 1869. Amazingly enough, we do not
yet have an historical monograph focused on those
printed proceedings.[11] But you can find them online on
*Women and Social Movements in the United States,
1600 to 2000,* a quarterly journal to which many academic libraries subscribe, which also offers extensive
full-text sources, such as the proceedings of the
women's rights conventions.[12] The Web site's search
capabilities allow one to search those convention proceedings for the words "color," "Negro," and "race" to
find traces of the 1837 sentiment against northern
racism. Such a search reveals only a single example, a
resolution discussed at the women's rights convention
in Worcester, Massachusetts, in 1850, that supported
"Equality before the law, without distinction of sex or
color." No similar resolution appeared in any subsequent women's rights convention in the 1850s and
1860s, and the Worcester resolution unleashed a post-
convention debate in which one convention leader declared, "The convention was not called to discuss the
rights of color; and we think it was altogether irrelevant and unwise to introduce the question."[13]

Although former slave, Sojourner Truth, spoke at
some of these woman's rights conventions, nothing
like the 1837 resolution appeared after 1850. Why not?
The best answer, in my view, is that because the
women's rights conventions focused on secular, political issues, such as married women's properly rights,
rather than on the large moral issue of slavery, they did
not need to cultivate the spiritual strength that informed the antislavery women, and lacking that
strength, they took the easy route of not challenging
racism. Instead, they set their sights on non-utopian
goals.[14]

Nevertheless, other groups of women did draw on
the 1837 revolutionary legacy of challenging racism.
For example, Josephine Griffing led a group of women
in Washington, D.C., in the 1860s, who mobilized material support for recently freed slaves. She stood up to
male reformers who insisted she was creating dependency by providing clothes, schooling, employment,
and food.[15] And today, the legacy of 1837 is all around
us in the coalitions that feminists built across race.

That legacy offers a foundation for future presidential candidates and allows us to see coalitions that are not visible when we focus on 1869. Hillary Clinton's ignominious missteps on race might have been avoided if she had taken to heart the brave example of 1837.

Another broader historical perspective might help future women candidates navigate another minefield in American politics—the gender question and its relationship to class. If Clinton did superbly on the woman question, and poorly on the race question, how did she fare on the gender question? One doesn't have to be postmodern or Maureen Dowd to question Hillary's identity as a "woman." Many of her supporters within the political establishment view her as a surrogate for Bill. But since she self-identified as a "woman," and many of her grassroots supporters thought she represented "women," we can take her at her word and conclude that despite her imperfect record on women's issues, she demonstrated that a woman can stand the heat of our grueling political process and "perform" as well as any man.

In fact we can say that she "performed" especially well as a woman pretending to be a man. However, in that regard, her candidacy reminds us of the dominance of what we might call "the masculine mystique" in our political discourse. Since at least 1964, that mystique has been aggressively asserted by the Right wing of the Republican party as part of their effort to obscure their class agenda. The "masculine mystique" has been crucial to their success in shifting wealth upward and in privatizing and impoverishing our commons. Beginning with Barry Goldwater in 1964, and continuing more successfully with Ronald Reagan, Bush the father, and Bush the son, the masculine mystique has become a staple characteristic of American presidential campaigns. Michael Dukakis and John Kerry crucially failed masculinity tests—Dukakis with headgear in a tank, and Kerry windsurfing. Dukakis failed to appear fierce enough. And Kerry revealed his elite perspective on sports.

Hillary Clinton sustained the masculine mystique when she tried to discredit Obama as too feminine to be president. She campaigned as a woman, but she consistently made passing the masculinity test her top priority. When she entered the Senate in 2000, she sought a place on the Senate Armed Services Committee. When she supported the invasion of Iraq and refused to acknowledge the error of her judgment, she chose muscle-flexing over reality testing. And when her campaign emphasized her capacities as commander in chief who could answer the red telephone better than Obama and "obliterate" Iran, she proved her willingness to use muscle-flexing as a electoral tactic. Yet Clinton's embrace of "the masculine mystique" and militarist priorities left her behind the new curve that Obama created when he championed anti-war opinion. And her stance made many feminists realize that they couldn't support her just because she was a woman.

Clinton answered the woman question by showing that women can compete, but she failed the race question by choosing competition over coalition. And she failed the gender question by allowing the masculine mystique to distort her political agenda and obscure the class agendas of Right-wing Republicans. She couldn't make a "gender" speech equivalent to Obama's "race" speech because she was herself playing a game of gender deception.

Thus the challenge for the next woman candidate—especially one who campaigns as a progressive—will be to demonstrate more than endurance and competence. She will need to meet the race question by drawing on the legacy of cross-race coalitions that enrich the history of women of all races in the United States. And perhaps her greatest boost to progressive agendas will be to expose the "masculine mystique" as dysfunctional and show us how to champion priorities based on human rather than macho values.

NOTES

1. An earlier version of this essay was presented at "Two Historic Candidacies," Berkshire Conference in Women's History, Minneapolis, Minnesota, H June 2008.

2. Katha Pollitt, "Iron My Skirt,". *The Nation, 5* June 2008.

3. Jo Freeman, *We Will Be Heard: Women's Struggles for Political Power in the United States* (Lanharo, Md.: Rowman & Litdefield, 2008), 85–90, 92, 102–3.

4. Kate Phillips, "Clinton Touts White Support," New *York Times,* 8 May 2006.

5. See Gaylynn Welch, "Local and National Forces Shaping the American Woman Suffrage Movement, 1870–1890," (Ph.D. diss., Binghamton University, 2008).

6. Rosalyn Terborg-Penn, "Discontented Black Feminists: Prelude and Postscript to the Passage of the Nineteenth Amendment," *in Decades of Discontent: The Women's Movement, 1920–1940,* ed. Lois Scharf and Joan Jensen (Westport, Conn.: Greenwood Press, 1983).

7. Gerda Lerner, *The Grimké Sisters of South Carolina: Pioneers for Women's Rights and Abolition,* rev. ed. (Chapel Hill: University of North Carolina Press, 2004), 139.

8. Kathryn Kish Sklar, " 'The Throne of My Heart': Religion, Oratory, and Transatlantic Community in Angelina Grimké's Launching of Women's Rights, 1828–1838," in *Women's Rights and Transatlantic Antislavtry in the Era of Emancipation,* ed. Kathryn Kish Sklar and James Brewer Stewart (New Haven, Conn.: Yale University Press, 2007), 211–41.

9. *Proceedings of the Anti-Slavery Convention of American Women, Held in the City of New-York, May 9th, 10th, 11th, and 12th, 1837* (New York: William S. Dorr. 1837), xii, 9, 13.

10. Sklar, *Women's Rights Emerges within the Antislavery Movement, 1830–1870* (New York: Bedford/St. Martin's, 2000), 40–47, 153–56; Gerda Lerner, "The Grimké Sisters and the Struggle against Race Prejudice," *Journal of Negro History* 26 (October 1963): 277–91.

11. The closest analysis of these sources can be found in Nancy Isenberg, *Sex and Citizenship in Antebellum America* (Chapel Hill: University of North Carolina Press, 1998).

12. For more about *Women and Social Movements,* see http://chswg.binghamton.edu/wsm.htm.

13. *The Proceedings of the Woman's Rights Convention, Held at Worcester, October 23d and 24th, 1850* (Boston: Prentiss and Sawyer, 1851), 15; Jane Grey Swisshelm, "The Worcester Convention," *(Baltimore) Saturday Visiter* (2 Nov. 1850), 166. See also John McClymer, "How Do Contemporary Newspaper Accounts of the 1850 Worcester Woman's Rights Convention Enhance Our Understanding of the Issues Debated at That Meeting?" *Women and Social Movements, 1600–2000* 10, no. 1 (March 2006). The proceedings of women's rights conventions, 1848–1869, are available as full-text sources that can be searched on *Women and Social Movements.*

14. For more on the women's rights conventions of 1848–1869, see Sklar, *Women's Rights Emerges within the Antislavery Movement,* 170–204.

15. Carol Faulkner, *Women's Radical Reconstruction: The Freedmen's Aid Movement* (Philadelphia: University of Pennsylvania Press, 2004).

50

Confessions of a Recovering Misogynist

KEVIN POWELL

I Am a Sexist Male

I take no great pride in saying this. I am merely stating a fact. It is not that I was born this way; rather, I was born into this male-dominated society, and, consequently, from the very moment I began forming thoughts, they formed in a decidedly male-centered way. My "education" at home with my mother, at school, on my neighborhood playgrounds, and at church all placed males at the center of the universe. My digestion of 1970s American popular culture in the form of television, film, ads, and music only added to my training, so that by as early as age nine or ten I saw females, including my mother, as nothing more than the servants of males. Indeed, like the Fonz on that TV sitcom *Happy Days,* I thought I could snap my fingers and girls would come running.

My mother, working poor and a product of the conservative and patriarchal South, simply raised me as most women are taught to raise boys: The world was mine, there were no chores to speak of, and my aggressions were considered somewhat normal, something that we boys carry out as a rite of passage. Those "rites" included me routinely squeezing girls' butts on the playground. And at school boys were encouraged to do "boy" things: work and build with our hands,

fight each other, and participate in the most daring activities during our gym time. Meanwhile, the girls were relegated to home economics, drawing cute pictures, and singing in the school choir. Now that I think about it, school was the place that spearheaded the omission of women from my worldview. Save Betsy Ross (whom I remember chiefly for sewing a flag) and a stoic Rosa Parks (she was unfurled every year as an example of Black achievement), I recall virtually no women making appearances is my American history classes.

The church my mother and I attended, like most Black churches, was peopled mainly by Black women, most of them single parents, who dragged their children along for the ride. Not once did I see a preacher who was anything other than an articulate, emotionally charged, well-coiffed, impeccably suited Black man running this church and, truly, these women. And behind the pulpit of this Black man, where he convinced us we were doomed to hell if we did not get right with God, was the image of our savior, a male, always White, named Jesus Christ.

Not surprisingly the "savior" I wanted in my life was my father. Ten years her senior, my father met my mother, my father wooed my mother, my father impregnated my mother, and then my father—as per *his* socialization—moved on to the next mating call. Responsibility was about as real to him as a three-dollar bill. When I was eight, my father flatly told my mother, via a pay phone, that he felt she had lied, that I was not his child, and that he would never give her money for me again. The one remotely tangible image of maleness in my life was gone for good. Both my mother and I were devastated, albeit for different reasons. I longed for my father's affections. And my mother longed to be married. Silently I began to blame my mother for my father's disappearance. Reacting to my increasingly bad behavior, my mother turned resentful and her beatings became more frequent, more charged. I grew to hate her and all females, for I felt it was women who made men act as we do.

At the same time, my mother, a fiercely independent and outspoken women despite having only a grade-school education and being poor, planted within me the seeds of self-criticism, of shame for wrongful behavior—and, ultimately, of feminism. Clear that she alone would have to shape me, my mother spoke pointedly about my father for many years after that call, demanding that I not grow up to "be like him." And I noted the number of times my mother rejected low-life male suitors, particularly the ones who wanted to live with us free of charge. I can see now that my mother is a feminist, although she is not readily familiar with the term. Like many women before and since, she fell hard for my father, and only through enduring immense pain did she realize the power she had within herself.

I Once Hated Women, and I Take No Pride in this Confession

I entered Rutgers University in the mid-1980s, and my mama's-boy demeanor advanced to that of pimp. I learned quickly that most males in college are some variety of pimp. Today I lecture regularly, from campus to campus, all over the country, and I see that not much has changed. For college is simply a place where we men, irrespective of race or class, can—and do—act out the sexist attitudes entrenched since boyhood. Rape, infidelity, girlfriend beat-downs, and emotional

abuse are common, and pimpdom reigns supreme. There is the athlete pimp, the frat boy pimp, the independent pimp, and the college professor pimp. Buoyed by the antiapartheid movement and the presidential bids of Jesse Jackson, my social consciousness blossomed along racial lines, and behold—the student leader pimp was born.

Blessed with a gift for gab, a poet's sensibility, and an acute memory for historical facts, I baited women with my self-righteousness by quoting Malcolm X, Frantz Fanon, Machiavelli, and any other figure I was sure they had not studied. It was a polite form of sexism, for I was always certain to say "my sister" when I addressed women at Rutgers. But my politeness did not lend me tolerance for women's issues, nor did my affiliation with a variety of Black nationalist organizations, especially the Nation of Islam. Indeed, whenever women in our African Student Congress would question the behavior and attitudes of men, I would scream, "We don't have time for them damn lesbian issues!" My scream was violent, mean-spirited, made with the intention to wound. I don't think it is any coincidence that during my four years in college I did not have one relationship with a woman that lasted more than three or four months. For every friend or girlfriend who would dare question my deeds, there were literally hundreds of others who acquiesced to the ways of us men, making it easy for me to ignore the legitimate cries of the feminists. Besides, I had taken on the demanding role of pimp, of conqueror, of campus revolutionary—there was little time or room for real intimacy, and even less time for self-reflection.

Confessions Are Difficult Because They Force Me to Visit Ghettos in the Mind I Thought I Had Long Escaped

I was kicked out of college at the end of my fourth year because I drew a knife on a female student. We were both members of the African Student Congress, and she was one of the many "subversive" female leaders I had sought to purge from the organization. She *had* left but for some reason was in our office a few days after we had brought Louis Farrakhan to speak at Rutgers. Made tense by her presence, I ignored her and turned to a male student, asking him, as she stood there, to ask her to jet. As she was leaving, she turned and charge toward me. My instincts, nurtured by my inner-city upbringing and several months of receiving anonymous threats as the Farrakhan talk neared, caused me to reach into my pocket and pull out a knife I had been carrying.

My intent was to scare her into submission. The male student panicked and knocked the knife from my hand, believing I was going to stab this woman. I would like to believe that that was not the case. It did not matter. This woman pressed charges on and off campus, and my college career, the one I'd taken on for myself, my undereducated mother, and my illiterate grandparents, came to a screeching halt.

It Is Not Easy for Me to Admit I Have a Problem

Before I could be readmitted to school I had to see a therapist. I went, grudgingly, and agonized over my violent childhood, my hatred of my mother, my many problems with women, and the nauseating torment of poverty and instability. But then it was done. I did not bother to try to return to college, and I found myself again using women for money, for sex, for entertainment. When I moved to New York City in August 1990, my predator mentality was still in full effect. I met a woman, persuaded her to allow me to live with her, and then mentally abused her for nearly a year, cutting her off from some of her friends, shredding her peace of mind and her spirit. Eventually I pushed her into the bathroom door when she blew up my spot, challenging me and my manhood.

I do not want to recount the details of the incident here. What I will say is that I, like most Black men I know, have spent much of my life living in fear: fear of White racism, fear of the circumstances that gave birth to me, fear of walking out my door wondering what humiliation will be mine today. Fear of Black women—of their mouths, of their bodies, of their attitudes, of their hurts, of their fear of us Black men. I felt fragile, as fragile as a bird with clipped wings that day when my ex-girlfriend stepped up her game and spoke back to me. Nothing in my world, nothing in my self-definition prepared me for dealing with a woman as an equal. My world said women were inferior, that they must at all costs be put in their place, and my instant

reaction was to do that. When it was over, I found myself dripping with sweat, staring at her back as she ran barefoot out of the apartment.

Guilt consumed me after the incident. The women I knew through my circle of poet and writer friends begged me to talk through what I had done, to get counseling, to read the books of bell hooks, Pearl Cleage's tiny tome *Mad at Miles,* the poetry of Audre Lorde, the many meditations of Gloria Steinem. I resisted at first, but eventually I began to listen and read, feeling electric shocks running through my body when I realized that these women, in describing abusive, oppressive men, were talking about me. Me, who thought I was progressive. Me, who claimed to be a leader. Me, who still felt women were on the planet to take care of men.

During this time I did restart therapy sessions. I also spent a good deal of time talking with young feminist women—some friends, some not. Some were soothing and understanding, some berated me and all men. I also spent a great deal of time alone, replaying my life in my mind: my relationship with my mother, how my mother had responded to my father's actions, how I had responded to my mother's response to my father. I thought of my education, of the absence of women in it. How I'd managed to attend a major university affiliated with one of the oldest women's colleges in America, Douglas College, and visited that campus only in pursuit of sex. I thought of the older men I had encountered in my life—the ministers, the high school track coach, the street hustlers, the local businessmen, the college professors, the political and community leaders—and realized that many of the ways I learned to relate to women came from listening to and observing those men. Yeah, I grew up after women's studies classes had appeared in most of the colleges in America, but that doesn't mean feminism actually reached the people it really needed to reach: average, everyday American males.

The incident, and the remorse that followed, brought about something akin to a spiritual epiphany. I struggled mightily to rethink the context that had created my mother. And my aunts. And my grandmother. And all the women I had been intimate with, either physically or emotionally or both. I struggled to understand terms like *patriarchy, misogyny, gender oppression.* A year after the incident I penned a short essay for *Essence* magazine called, simply, "The Sexist in Me," because I wanted to be honest in the most public forum possible, and because I wanted to reach some men, some young Black men, who needed to hear from another male that sexism is as oppressive as racism. And at times worse.

I Am No Hero. I Am No Saint.
I Remain a Sexist Male

But one who is now conscious of it and who has been waging an internal war for several years. Some days I am incredibly progressive; other days I regress. It is very lonesome to swim against the stream of American male-centeredness, of Black male bravado and nut grabbing. It is how I was molded, it is what I know, and in rejecting it I often feel mad naked and isolated. For example, when I publicly opposed the blatantly sexist and patriarchal rhetoric and atmosphere of the Million Man March, I was attacked by Black men, some questioning my sanity, some accusing me of being a dupe for the White man, and some wondering if I was just "trying to get some pussy from Black women."

Likewise, I am a hip-hop head. Since adolescence I have been involved in this culture, this lifestyle, as a dancer, a graffiti writer, an activist, a concert organizer, and most prominently a hip-hop journalist. Indeed, as a reporter at *Vibe* magazine, I found myself interviewing rap icons like Dr. Dre, Snoop Dogg, and the late Tupac Shakur. And although I did ask Snoop and Tupac some pointed questions about *their* sexism, I still feel I dropped the ball. We Black men often feel so powerless, so sure the world—politically, economically, spiritually, and psychologically—is aligned against us. The last thing any of us wants if for another man to question how we treat women. Aren't we, Black men, the endangered species anyhow? This is how many of us think.

While I do not think hip-hop is any more sexist or misogynist than other forms of American culture, I do think it is the most explicit form of misogyny around today. It is also a form of sexism that gets more than its share of attention, because hip-hop—now a billion-dollar industry—is the sound track for young America, regardless of race, of class. What folks don't understand is that hip-hop was created on the heels of the Civil Rights era by impoverished Blacks and Latinos, who literally made something out of nothing. But in making that something out of nothing, many of us men of color have held tightly to White patriarchal notions of manhood—that is, the way to be a man is to have power. Within hip-hop culture, in our lyrics, in our videos, and on our tours, that power translates into material possessions, provocative and often foul language, flashes of violence, and blatant objectification of and disrespect for women. Patriarchy, as manifested in hip-hop, is where we can have our version of power within this very oppressive society. Who would want to even consider giving that up?

Well, I have, to a large extent, and these days I am a hip-hopper in exile. I dress, talk, and walk like a hip—hopper, yet I cannot listen to rap radio or digest music videos without commenting on the pervasive sexism. Moreover, I try to drop seeds, as we say, about sexism, whenever and wherever I can, be it at a community forum or on a college campus. Some men, young and old alike, simply cannot deal with it and walk out. Or there is the nervous shifting in seats, the uneasy comments during the question-and-answer sessions, generally in the form of "Why you gotta pick on the men, man?" I constantly "pick on the men" and myself because I truly wonder how many men actually listen to the concerns of women. Just as I feel it is Whites who need to be more vociferous about racism in their communities, I feel it is men who need to speak long and loud about sexism among ourselves.

I Am a Recovering Misogynist

I do not say this with pride. Like a recovering alcoholic or a crack fiend who has righted her or his ways, I am merely cognizant of the fact that I have had some serious problems in my life with and in regard to women. I am also aware of the fact that I can lapse at any time. My relationship with my mother is better than it has ever been, though there are days when speaking with her turns me back into that little boy cowering beneath the belt and tongue of a woman deeply wounded by my father, by poverty, by her childhood, by the sexism that has dominated her life. My relationships since the incident with my ex-girlfriend have been better, no doubt, but not the bomb.

But I am at least proud of the fact I have not reverted back to violence against women—and don't ever plan to, which is why I regularly go to therapy, why I listen to and absorb the stories of women, and why I talk about sexism with any men, young and old, who are down to rethink the definitions we've accepted so uncritically. Few of us men actually believe there is a problem, or we are quick to point fingers at women, instead of acknowledging that healing is a necessary and ongoing process, that women *and* men need to be a part of this process, and that we all must be willing to engage in this dialogue and work if sexism is to ever disappear.

So I fly solo, and have done so for some time. For sure, today I count among my friends, peers, and mentors older feminist women like bell hooks and Johnnetta B. Cole, and young feminists like Nikki Stewart, a girls' rights advocate in Washington, D.C., and Aishah Simmons, who is currently putting together a documentary on rape within the Black community. I do not always agree with these women, but I also know that if I do not struggle, hard and constantly, backsliding is likely. This is made worse by the fact that outside of a handful of male friends, there are no young men I know whom I can speak with regarding sexism as easily as I do with women.

The fact is, there was a blueprint handed to us in childhood telling us this is the way a man should behave, and we unwittingly followed the scrip verbatim. There was no blueprint handed to us about how to begin to wind ourselves out of sexism as an adult, but maybe there should have been. Every day I struggle within myself not to use the language of gender oppression, to see the sexism inherent in every aspect of America, to challenge all injustices, not just those that are convenient for me. I am ashamed of my ridiculously sexist life, of raising my hand to my girlfriend, and of two other ugly and hateful moments in college, one where I hit a female student in the head with a stapler during the course of an argument, and the other where I got into a punch-throwing exchange with a female student I had sexed then discarded like an old pair of shoes. I am also ashamed of all the lies and manipulations, the verbal abuse and reckless disregard for the views and lives of women. But with that shame has come a consciousness and, as the activists said during the Civil Rights Movement, this consciousness, this knowing, is a river of no return. I have finally learned how to swim. I have finally learned how to push forward. I may become tired, I may lose my breath, I may hit a rock from time to time and become cynical, but I am not going to drown this time around.